P9-DEC-939

International Directory of Acronyms
in Library, Information
and Computer Sciences

International Directory of Acronyms in Library, Information and Computer Sciences

Pauline M. Vaillancourt

R. R. Bowker Company

New York & London, 1980

To Rhea B. and Murielle T. Vaillancourt

Published by R. R. Bowker Company
1180 Avenue of the Americas, New York, NY 10036
Copyright © 1980 by Xerox Corporation
All rights reserved
Printed and bound in the United States of America

Library of Congress Cataloging in Publication Data

Vaillancourt, Pauline M.
  International directory of acronyms in library,
information, and computer sciences.

  Includes index.
  1. Library science—Acronyms. 2. Information
science—Acronyms. 3. Computers—Acronyms. I. Title.
Z1006.V33   020.28'54   80-18352
ISBN 0-8352-1152-5

Contents

Preface

"Knowing acronyms that someone else does not know immediately establishes you in the inner circle of the mystique." —Ralph R. Shaw

The fields of library, information and computer sciences have long used acronyms and initialisms for speed in communication. Within these closely related disciplines, the proliferation of acronyms has frequently resulted in the use of similar or identical acronyms to represent widely different terms and concepts. The *International Directory of Acronyms in Library, Information and Computer Sciences* was compiled not only to provide an integrated listing of the acronymic "vocabularies" of these fields, but also to supply additional information to aid the reader in accurately identifying the entities for which particular acronyms stand.

As used in this book the term acronym includes both "true" acronyms and initialisms. An acronym, strictly speaking, is a word formed from the initial letters or syllables of other words, as in MARC for MAchine Readable Cataloging. Initialisms, however, which are formed only by the initial letters of a series of words, frequently do not form pronounceable words, but may be recited by spelling out each letter separately, as in OCLC for Ohio College Library Center. In using the broad definition of an acronym to encompass both varieties, the policy here reflects current usage and enables the widest possible scope of entries.

Of the more than 5,500 acronyms listed in this directory, approximately 2,000 are international or foreign in origin or use. Nine categories of acronyms are represented: associations, societies and organizations in the library, information and computer sciences; commonly used terms from these fields; meetings, conferences and workshops of a continuing nature; publications, including books, journals and data tapes; libraries and information centers; information-related government agencies; commercial firms; consortia, networks and systems; and research or experimental projects and services. Acronyms from disciplines related to the library, information and computer sciences, such as communications and education, are selectively included, as are some historically important acronyms that are still referred to in current parlance.

The acronyms listed were found in the published literature of library, information and computer sciences by combing numerous journals, indexes, brochures, conference proceedings and monographs, as well as directories of libraries, associations, data bases, publications and other compilations of acronyms in broader fields. Dictionaries, encyclopedias and catalogs were also utilized. "Invented" acronyms are common in the literature, and to avoid the inclusion of temporary or little-used acronyms, only acronyms found in at least two sources are cited in this book. All sources consulted were published before 1980. In order to provide greater access to the material, a key word and key phrase index is provided.

Grateful acknowledgment of assistance and support during the process of compiling this directory is due to the School of Library and Information Science of the State University of New York at Albany. The school supplied a hospitable environment as well as the help of graduate assistants and typists. Because this was a long-term project, many individuals contributed to this work. Those who provided the most intensive and recent contributions are, alphabetically, Marlene S. Bobka, Lauri Chait, Barbara Feige, Mary Beth Gagnier, Patricia Peroni, Edward Wirth and Lorry Wynne. Typing of the manuscript was ably done with dispatch and goodwill by Barbara Feige and Joan A. Fiske.

How to Use This Book

Entries in this book are arranged alphabetically by acronym. When one acronym has more than one meaning (or full name), the entries for that acronym appear alphabetically by the words in the full name. For example, ALA (Arizona Library Association) is followed by ALA (Arkansas Library Association). Articles, conjunctions and prepositions are included in the alphabetization. Spacing, capitalization, punctuation and symbols, such as hyphens, are ignored in alphabetization, except for ampersands which are filed as if they were spelled "and."

Each entry contains three parts: acronym, full name of acronym, and a brief annotation providing further identifying information. The information given in an annotation varies according to the category of acronym. The following elements may be included in an entry: address or, for organizations that do not have permanent headquarters, contact information; relevant dates, such as the date an organization was established or changed its name, or the date a meeting was held; publication information; sponsoring organization or constituent societies; and alternative, former or succeeding acronyms, if any. For example:

Acronym)	**AECT**
Full Name)	Association for Educational Communications and Technology.
Annotation)	1126 16th St, NW, Washington, DC 20036. Established in 1923. Formerly (1970) DAVI. Publishes journals and a newsletter and maintains archives of materials and equipment.

If an entity's meaning or purpose is not implicit in the acronym or full name, or its relationship to the fields of library, information or computer sciences is not readily evident, a definition or explanatory statement is provided. Further, annotations for projects, consortia and international or foreign activities or organizations often include bibliographic citations to books or journal articles that provide additional information, as in the following sample entry.

> **CHIN** Community Health Information
> Network. c/o Mt. Auburn Hospital,
> 330 Mt. Auburn St, Cambridge, MA
> 02138. Six medical and public
> libraries cooperate to provide health-
> related and medical information to
> consumers and health professionals.
> *See* Ellen Gartenfeld. "The
> Community Health Information
> Network: A Model for Hospital and
> Public Library Cooperation." *Library
> Journal* 103 (Oct. 1, 1978): 1911–1914.

Bibliographic citations may also be recorded for proceedings of symposia or other meetings if they resulted in a published report.

Except for the geographic abbreviations for the United States and Canada, which are listed immediately following this section, any acronym that is mentioned within an annotation also appears as an independent entry. Thus the full name of an acronym is not supplied in an annotation under another term unless two or more entries appear in the book under the same acronym. In such cases, for clarity the full name is provided in parentheses following the acronym. For example, the acronym ALA (American Library Association) is always identified with its full name in parentheses to avoid confusion with other associations that also use the acronym ALA, as shown in the following entry:

> **RASD** Reference and Adult Services
> Division. 50 East Huron St, Chicago,
> IL 60611. A division of ALA
> (American Library Association)
> formed by the merger of ASD and
> RSD in 1972.

Because organizations and other entities often have more than one acronym, "see" references are frequently used to refer the reader to one main entry for such terms. For example, FID (Fédération Internationale de Documentation) is also referred to by the acronym IFD (International Federation for Documentation). Therefore, the entry under IFD contains a "see" reference to FID, the French-language acronym and main entry for this term. Similarly, the entry OE for Office of Education refers the reader to USOE for United States Office of Education. Readers are advised that because countries are not always indicated in the common names and acronyms of government agencies, all government agencies included in this book are those of the United States unless otherwise specified.

The key word and key phrase entries in the index to this volume are extracted from the full names of the acronyms. Both full names and acronyms are supplied as subentries under the appropriate key words or key phrases. Main index entries for foreign-language acronyms are extracted from the English-language translation of the name, if a translation has been provided.

Geographic Abbreviations

United States

AL	Alabama	MT	Montana
AK	Alaska	NE	Nebraska
AZ	Arizona	NV	Nevada
AR	Arkansas	NH	New Hampshire
CA	California	NJ	New Jersey
CZ	Canal Zone	NM	New Mexico
CO	Colorado	NY	New York
CT	Connecticut	NC	North Carolina
DE	Delaware	ND	North Dakota
DC	District of Columbia	OH	Ohio
FL	Florida	OK	Oklahoma
GA	Georgia	OR	Oregon
GU	Guam	PA	Pennsylvania
HI	Hawaii	PR	Puerto Rico
ID	Idaho	RI	Rhode Island
IL	Illinois	SC	South Carolina
IN	Indiana	SD	South Dakota
IA	Iowa	TN	Tennessee
KS	Kansas	TX	Texas
KY	Kentucky	UT	Utah
LA	Louisiana	VT	Vermont
ME	Maine	VI	Virgin Islands
MD	Maryland	VA	Virginia
MA	Massachusetts	WA	Washington
MI	Michigan	WV	West Virginia
MN	Minnesota	WI	Wisconsin
MS	Mississippi	WY	Wyoming
MO	Missouri		

Canada

AB	Alberta	ON	Ontario
BC	British Columbia	NT	Northwest Territories
LB	Labrador	PE	Prince Edward Island
MB	Manitoba	PQ	Quebec
NB	New Brunswick	SK	Saskatchewan
NF	Newfoundland	YT	Yukon Territory
NS	Nova Scotia		

Acronyms

AA Aluminum Association. 818 Connecticut Ave, NW, Washington, DC 20006. Publishes documents.

AAA American Accounting Association. 5717 Bessie Dr, Sarasota, FL 33581. Established in 1916. Publishes documents.

AAA American Anthropological Association. 1703 New Hampshire Ave, NW, Washington, DC 20009. Established in 1902. Publishes documents.

AAAA American Association of Advertising Agencies. 200 Park Ave, New York, NY 10017. Established in 1917.

AAAB American Association of Architectural Bibliographers. Campbell Hall, University of Virginia, Charlottesville, VA 22903. Established in 1954. Has issued mimeographed papers and published bibliographies on the work of individual architects.

AAAC Archival Association of Atlantic Canada. Contact president.

AAACE American Association of Agricultural College Editors. Name changed in 1978 to ACE (Agricultural Communicators in Education).

AAAE Alliance of Associations for the Advancement of Education. 3615 Wisconsin Ave, NW, Washington, DC 20016. Established in 1970. Acts as an information exchange for member associations. Publishes documents.

AAAH American Association for the Advancement of the Humanities. 918 16th St, NW, Washington, DC 20006. Established in 1979. Represents humanists as AAAS represents scientists. First annual meeting in 1980.

Publishes a monthly journal, *Humanities Report*.

AAAL American Academy of Arts and Letters. Merged with the National Institute of Arts and Letters in 1976 to form AAIL.

AAAS American Academy of Arts and Sciences. 165 Allendale St, Boston, MA 02130. National honor society established in 1780. Publishes documents, including the journal *Daedalus*.

AAAS American Association for the Advancement of Science. 1515 Massachusetts Ave, NW, Washington, DC 20005. Established in 1848. Publishes *Science* and other publications, including bibliographies. Sections include one concerned with information, computing and communications.

AABB/VABB Association des Archivistes et Bibliothécaires de Belgique/Vereniging van Archivarissen en Bibliothecarissen van België (Belgian Association of Archivists and Librarians). Bibliothèque Royale, Albert Ier, 4 blvd. de l'Empereur, B-1000, Brussels, Belgium. Established in 1907. Affiliated with IFLA and the International Council on Archives. Publishes documents.

AABevK Arbeitsgemeinschaft für das Archiv und Bibliothekswesen in der Evangelischen Kirche, Sektion Bibliothekswesen (Working Group for Archives and Libraries in the Lutheran Church, Library Section). Grindelallee 7, D-2000 Hamburg 13, Federal Republic of Germany. Established in 1960 to promote and represent the interests of church librarians.

AAC Association of American Colleges. 1818 R St, NW, Washington, DC 20009. Established in 1915. Publishes *Liberal Education*.

AACC American Association of Cereal Chemists, 3340 Pilot Knob Rd, St. Paul, MN 55121. Established in 1915. Publishes documents.

AACC American Association of Clinical Chemists. 1725 K St, NW, Washington, DC 20006. Established in 1948. Publishes documents.

AACC American Automatic Control Council. c/o Mr. M. A. Keyes, Bailey Meter Co, 29801 Euclid Ave, Wickliffe, OH 44092. Established in 1957. Federation of scientific and engineering societies in which one division is concerned with the development of computer-control engineering.

AACHIR Augusta Area Committee for Health Information Resources. Medical College of Georgia, 1459 Laney Walker Blvd, Augusta, GA 30902.

AACI American Association for Conservation Information. Contact president. Established in 1938.

AACJC American Association of Community and Junior Colleges. National Center for Higher Education, One Dupont Circle, NW, Washington, DC 20036. Established in 1920. Formerly AAJC. Maintains a library of college catalogs and other material. Publishes journal, directory and pamphlets.

AACOBS Australian Advisory Council on Bibliographical Services.

AACR *Anglo-American Cataloging Rules*. Originally established in 1949, the rules were revised and published in separate North American and British texts in 1967. Prepared by ALA (American Library Association), LC, LA and CLA (Canadian Library Association), *AACR* superseded the ALA cataloging rules for author and title entries and included a revision of the rules for descriptive cataloging in LC. The second edition of *AACR* appeared in 1978. *See* AACR 2.

AACR 2 *Anglo-American Cataloguing Rules*. Published in one text in 1978, the second edition of *AACR* was prepared by ALA (American Library Association), BL (The British Library), CCC (Canadian Committee on Cataloguing), LA and LC.

AACRAO American Association of Collegiate Registrars and Admissions Officers. One Dupont Circle, NW, Suite 330, Washington, DC 20036. Established in 1910. Publishes journal, newsletter and guides.

AACTE American Association of Colleges for Teacher Education. One Dupont Circle, Washington, DC 20036. Established in 1948. Publishes documents.

AADAC Alberta Alcoholism and Drug Abuse Commission. AADAC Library, Edmonton, AB T6G 2J4, Canada. Maintains library on alcoholism and drug abuse. *See* Charles H. Davis and Susan Dingle-Cliff. "Evidence of OCLC's Potential for Special Libraries and Technical Information Centers." *JASIS* 29 (Sept. 1978): 255–256.

AAEA American Agricultural Editors Association. 5520-G Touhy Ave, Skokie, IL 60077. Established in 1921.

AAEC Australian Atomic Energy Commission. Private Mail Bag, Sutherland, New South Wales, Australia.

AAF American Advertising Federation. 1225 Connecticut Ave, NW, Washington, DC 20036. Formerly AFA.

AAG Association of American Geographers. 1710 16th St, NW, Washington, DC 20009. Established in 1904. Publishes documents.

AAHE American Association for Higher Education. One Dupont Circle, Suite 780, Washington, DC 20036. Established in 1870. Publishes documents. Formerly AHE and Department of Higher Education, both of NEA (National Education Association).

AAHLA Albany Area Health Library Affiliates. c/o Schaffer Library of Health Sciences, 47 New Scotland Ave, Albany, NY 12208.

AAHPER American Alliance for Health, Physical Education and Recreation. 1201 16th St, NW, Washington, DC 20036. Publishes documents. Formerly (1974) American Association for Health, Physical Education and Recreation.

AAHPER American Association for Health, Physical Education and Recreation. Name changed in 1974 to American Alliance for Health, Physical Education and Recreation.

AAIE American Association of Industrial Editors. In 1970, merged with International Council of Industrial Editors and Corporate Communications Canada to form International Association of Business Communicators.

AAIL American Academy and Institute of Arts and Letters. 633 West 155 St, New York, NY 10032. Established in 1976 through the merger of AAAL and the National Institute of Arts and Sciences.

AAIM American Association of Industrial Management. 7425 Old York Rd, Philadelphia, PA 19126. Formerly NMTA. Publishes documents including *Consumer Price Index*.

AAIMS An Analytical Information Management System.

AAJC American Association of Junior Colleges. Name changed to AACJC.

AAL Association of Architectural Librarians. American Institute of Architects Library, 1735 New York Ave, NW, Washington, DC 20006.

AAL Association of Assistant Librarians. c/o J. S. Davey, 49 Halstead Gardens, Winchmore Hill, London N21, England. Established in 1895.

AALC Asian American Librarians Caucus. Western Languages, Harvard-Yen Ching Library, 2 Divinity Ave, Cambridge, MA 02138. Established in 1974.

AALL American Association of Law Libraries. 53 West Jackson Blvd, Chicago, IL 60604. Established in 1906. Publishes a journal, indexes and manuals.

AALO Association of Academic Librarians of Ontario. Contact president. A Canadian association.

AALS Association of American Library Schools. 471 Park La, State College, PA 16801. Established in 1915.

AALSED Association of Assistant Librarians, South East Division.

Contact chairperson or refer to current issue of *Assistant Librarian*.

AALT Alberta Association of Library Technicians. Contact president. A Canadian association.

AAMOA Afro-American Music Opportunities Association. 2801 Wayzata Blvd, Minneapolis, MN 55405. Established in 1969. Compiles *Resource Directory for Research in Black Music* irregularly.

AAMRL American Association of Medical Records Librarians. Name changed to AMRA in 1938.

A&HCI *Arts and Humanities Citation Index*. V. 1, 1977. Published by ISI (Institute for Scientific Information).

A&I Abstracting and Indexing. Also known as I&A.

AAP Affirmative Action Program. A plan required of all institutions receiving US federal funds in the form of grants or contracts.

AAP Association of American Publishers. One Park Ave, New York, NY 10016. Formed by the merger of ABPC (American Book Publishers' Council) and AEPI (American Educational Publishers Institute) in 1970.

AAP Australian Associated Press Proprietary Ltd. Melbourne, Australia.

AAPG American Association of Petroleum Geologists. Box 979, Tulsa, OK 74101. Established in 1917. Part of AGI. Publishes documents.

AAPIER American Association for Public Information, Education and Research. 1010 Vermont Ave, NW, Washington, DC 20005.

AAPT American Association of Physics Teachers. Graduate Physics Bldg, State University of New York, Stony Brook, NY 11794. Established in 1930. Member society of AIP (American Institute of Physics). Publishes documents.

AAPWC Affirmative Action Program for Women Committee. c/o University of California, Berkeley, University Library, Berkeley, CA 94720. Established in 1971 to prepare a written affirmative action plan detailing the goals of the university library with respect to achieving optimum employment and promotion opportunities for women.

AAQ Association des Archivistes du Québec (Association of Quebec Archivists). CP 159, Haute-Ville, PQ G1R 4P3, Canada.

AARL Advanced Automation Research Laboratory. Purdue University, School of Electrical Engineering, West Lafayette, IN 47907. Maintains a library.

AAS Academy of Applied Science. 65 India Wharf, Boston, MA 02110. Established in 1962. Publishes documents.

AAS American Antiquarian Society. 185 Salisbury, Worcester, MA 01609. Established in 1812. Publishes documents. Maintains research library, with emphasis on American history before 1876.

AAS American Astronautical Society. 6060 Duke St, Alexandria, VA 22304. Established in 1952. Publishes documents and supports research.

AAS American Astronomical Society. Physics Dept, University of Delaware, Sharp Laboratories, Newark, DE 19711. Established in 1899. A member society of AIP (American Institute of Physics).

AAS Asian and African Section. *See* ACRL/AAS.

AAS Association for Asian Studies. One Lane Hall, University of Michigan, Ann Arbor, MI 48109. Established in 1941. Publishes documents. Formerly (1957) Far Eastern Association.

AASA American Association of School Administrators. 1801 North Moore St, Arlington, VA 22209. ALA (American Library Association) related.

AASCU American Association of State Colleges and Universities. One Dupont Circle, Washington, DC 20036. Established in 1961. Publishes documents. Formerly Association of State Colleges and Universities.

AASDJ American Association of Schools and Departments of Journalism. School of Journalism and Mass Communications, University of Minnesota, Minneapolis, MN 55455. Established in 1917. Publishes *Journalism Quarterly*.

AASL American Association of School Librarians. 50 East Huron St, Chicago, IL 60611. A division of ALA (American Library Association) established in 1951. Publishes documents.

AASL American Association of State Libraries. Defunct. Merged with SLAD in 1957 to become ASLA (Association of State Library Agencies). In 1978 ASLA merged with HRLSD to form ASCLA.

AASL/EB AASL Encyclopaedia Britannica. A committee of AASL (American Association of School Librarians), which is a division of ALA (American Library Association). AASL/EB acts in an advisory capacity to Encyclopaedia Britannica, Inc, in the annual selection of an outstanding elementary school library media program to receive a cash award for excellence.

AASLH American Association for State and Local History. 1400 Eighth Ave South, Nashville, TN 37203. Established in 1940.

AASL/SS AASL Supervisors Section. Section of AASL (American Association of School Librarians), which is a division of ALA (American Library Association).

AATCC American Association of Textile Chemists and Colorists. Box 12215, Research Triangle Park, NC 27709. Established in 1921. Publishes documents.

AATSEEL American Association of Teachers of Slavic and East European Languages. Contact MLA (Modern Language Association).

AATT American Association for Textile Technology, Inc. 1040 Ave. of the Americas, New York, NY 10018. Established in 1933.

AAU Association of American Universities. One Dupont Circle, Suite 730, Washington, DC 20036. Established in 1900.

AAULC Association of Atlantic Universities Librarians Council. Contact chairperson. A Canadian association.

AAUP American Association of University Professors. One Dupont Circle, Washington, DC 20036. Established in 1915. In conjunction with AAC and

ACRL, AAUP drafted the "Statement on Faculty Status of College and University Librarians" in 1974.

AAUP Association of American University Presses. One Park Ave, New York, NY 10016.

AAUW American Association of University Women. 2401 Virginia Ave, NW, Washington, DC 20037. Established in 1882. Publishes documents. Maintains a library.

AAVRPHS American Association for Vital Records and Public Health Statistics. Bureau of Health Statistics, Box 2500, Salt Lake City, UT 84111. Established in 1933.

AAVSO American Association of Variable Star Observers. 187 Concord Ave, Cambridge, MA 02138. Established in 1911. Issues *AAVSO Abstracts*. Maintains a library and information center.

AAVT Association of Audiovisual Technicians. 2500 West Fourth Ave, Denver, CO 80219.

AB Automated Bibliography.

ABA American Bankers Association. 1120 Connecticut Ave, NW, Washington, DC 20036. Established in 1875. Publishes documents. Sponsors AIB.

ABA American Booksellers Association. 122 East 42 St, New York, NY 10017. Established 1900.

ABAA Antiquarian Booksellers Association of America. 50 Rockefeller Plaza, New York, NY 10020. Established in 1949.

ABACUS Australia, Britain, Canada, United States. Group of national libraries from the countries named. Organized to implement AACR 2.

ABADCAM Association des Bibliothécaires, Archivistes, Documentalistes et Muséographes du Cameroun (Association of Librarians, Archivists, Documentalists and Museum Curators of Cameroon). Bibliothèque Universitaire, BP 312, Yaounde, Federal Republic of Cameroon. Established in 1975.

ABAH Asociación de Bibliotecarios y Archiveros de Honduras (Association of Librarians and Archivists of Honduras).

3 Avenidas, 4 y 5 Calles, Numero 416 Comayagüela, D. C. Honduras. Established in 1951.

ABAK Asociation di Biblioteka i Archivo di Korsow (Association of Libraries and Archives). Contact president (Curaçao, Netherlands Antilles). Established in 1972. Affiliated with IFLA.

ABB Asociación Boliviana de Bibliotecarios (Association of Bolivian Librarians). Contact president. Established in 1951.

ABC American Book Center for War Devastated Libraries. Name changed in 1948 to USBE (United States Book Exchange) and in 1975 to USBE (Universal Serials and Book Exchange).

ABC American Bibliographical Center. *See* ABC-Clio.

ABC American Broadcasting Companies, Inc. ABC General Library, 7 West 66 St, New York, NY 10023. Library established in 1945. Specializes in current and background news, radio and television.

ABC Amigos Bibliographic Council. 11300 North Central Expressway, Suite 321, Dallas, TX 75243. Consortium of 140 libraries in AR, AZ, KS, LA, NM, OK and TX.

ABC Approach by Concept.

ABC Audit Bureau of Circulations. 123 North Wacker Dr, Chicago, IL 60606. Established in 1914. Issues standardized statements on the circulation of periodicals published by members.

ABC Australian Broadcasting Corporation.

ABC Automation of Bibliography through Computerization. *See* ABC-Clio.

ABCA American Business Communication Association. 3176 David Kinley Hall, University of Illinois, Urbana, IL 61801. Established in 1935. Formerly (1969) ABWA.

ABCA Association of British Columbia Archivists. Contact secretary.

ABC–Clio American Bibliographical Center-Clio Press. ABC-Clio, Inc, Riviera Campus, 2040 APS, Santa Barbara, CA 93103. Publisher of serial abstract publications and indexes in the humanities.

ABCL Association of British Columbia Librarians. This association was terminated in 1975.

ABCU Association of Burroughs Computer Users. Contact secretary.

ABD Association des Bibliothécaires-Documentalistes de l'Institut d'Études Sociales de l'État (Association of Librarians and Documentalists of the State Institute of Social Studies). 26 rue de l'Abbaye, B-1050 Brussels, Belgium. Established in 1971. Affiliated with IFLA.

ABD/BVD Association Belge de Documentation/Belgische Vereniging voor Documentatie (Belgian Documentation Association). 90 avenue des Armures, B-1190 Brussels, Belgium. Established in 1947.

ABE Adult Basic Education. Educational programs for disadvantaged adults. USOE funded two urban and two rural demonstration models at Morehead State University in Morehead, KY, between 1972 and 1975.

ABEBD Associação Brasileira de Escolas de Biblioteconomia e Documentação (Brazilian Association of Library Science and Documentation Schools). c/o Escola de Biblioteconomia e Documentação, Universidade Federal de Bahia, Campus Universitario do Canela, 40,000 Salvador, Bahia, Brazil. Established in 1967.

ABEF Association des Bibliothèques Ecclésiastiques de France (Association of French Theological Libraries). 6 rue du Regard, F-75006 Paris, France. Established in 1963.

ABELF Association Belge des Editeurs de Langue Française (Belgian Association of Publishers of French Language Books). Avenue du Parc 111, 1060 Brussels, Belgium. Association of publishers.

ABEND Abnormal End. Computer term for an abnormal job termination following an error condition.

ABES Asociación de Bibliotecarios de El Salvador (Association of El Salvador Librarians). Urbanización Gerardo Barrios Polígono, B Numero 5, San Salvador, El Salvador. Established in 1958.

ABES Association for Broadcast Engineering Standards, Inc. 1730 M St, NW, Suite 700, Washington, DC 20036. Formerly ABS (Association on Broadcasting Standards). Publishes documents.

ABF Association des Bibliothécaires Français (Association of French Librarians). 65 rue de Richelieu, 75002 Paris, France. Established in 1906.

ABGRA Asociación de Bibliotecarios Graduados de la República Argentina (Association of Graduate Librarians of Argentina). Talcahuane 1261, Dirección de Bibliotecas Públicas de la Municipalidad de Buenos Aires, Ciudad de Buenos Aires, Argentina. Established in 1953.

ABI Abstracted Business Information. Data Courier, Inc, Library and Information Center, 620 South Fifth St, Louisville, KY 40202. Library established in 1974. A special collection of unbound periodicals. Provides copying and search services on a contract basis.

ABI Association des Bibliothèques Internationales (Association of International Libraries). See AIL/ABI.

ABIESI Asociación de Bibliotecarios de Instituciones de Enseñanza Superior y de Investigación (Association of Librarians of Institutions of Higher Education and Research). Universidad Nacional Autónoma de México, Dirección General de Bibliotecas, Ciudad Universitaria, México 20, Mexico.

ABI/INFORM Abstracted Business Information/Information Needs. Coverage from 1971. Bibliographic data base covering business management and administration. Produced by DC (Data Courier, Inc.).

ABIISE Agrupación de Bibliotecas para la Integración de la Información Socio-Economica (Group of Special Libraries for the Integration of Socio-Economic Information). Apartado 2874, Lima 100, Peru. Established in 1969. The first group of special librarians in Peru. Publishes documents.

ABIPAR Asociación de Bibliotecarios de Paraguay (Paraguayan Librarians Association). Casilla de Correo 1505, Ascunción, Paraguay. Established in

1961 to promote the national bibliography.

ABIPC *Abstract Bulletin of the Institute of Paper Chemistry.* V. 1, 1930. Published by Institute of Paper Chemistry.

ABJA Association Belge des Journalistes Agricoles (Belgian Guild of Agricultural Journalists). *See* BVLJ/ABJA.

ABJPAA Association Belge des Journalistes Professionnels de l'Aéronautique et de l'Astronautique. Square de l'Arbalète 4, 1170 Brussels, Belgium. Established in 1961. Association of journalists. Publishes documents.

ABLE A Better Language Experiment.

ABLE Agricultural Biological Literature Exploitation. A systems study of NAL (National Agricultural Library).

ABLISS Association of British Library and Information Studies Schools. Dept. of Librarianship, Birmingham Polytechnic, Birmingham B42 2SU, England. Formerly ABLS.

ABLS Association of British Library Schools. Name changed to ABLISS.

ABO Association des Bibliotechniciens de l'Ontario (Ontario Association of Library Technicians). *See* OALT/ABO.

ABO Association des Bibliothèques d'Ottawa (Library Association of Ottawa). *See* LAO/ABO.

ABPC American Book Publishers Council. Merged with AEPI in 1970 to form AAP (Association of American Publishers).

ABPR *American Book Publishing Record.* New York: R. R. Bowker Co, 1960. A monthly publication (cumulated annually) listing titles published in the United States.

ABQ Association des Bibliothécaires de Québec (Quebec Library Association). *See* QLA/ABQ.

ABRACADABRA *Abbreviations and Related Acronyms Associated with Defense, Astronautics, Business and Radio-Electronics.* 2nd ed. Lexington, MA: Raytheon Co, 1969.

ABRC/CARL Association des Bibliothèques de Recherche du Canada/Canadian Association of Research Libraries. *See* CARL/ABRC.

ABS American Bureau of Shipping. 45 Broad St, New York, NY 10004. Established in 1862. Publishes documents.

ABS Association des Bibliothécaires Suisses (Association of Swiss Librarians). *See* VSB/ABS/ABS.

ABS Association on Broadcasting Standards. Name changed to ABES (Association for Broadcast Engineering Standards).

ABS Associazione dei Bibliotecari Suizzeri (Association of Swiss Librarians). *See* VSB/ABS/ABS.

ABSC/CHLA Association des Bibliothèques de la Santé du Canada/Canadian Health Libraries Association. *See* CHLA/ABSC.

ABSS Agricultural and Biological Sciences Section. *See* ACRL/ABSS.

ABSTI Advisory Board on Scientific and Technical Information. Contact NRC (National Research Council). An advisory group to the Canadian council.

ABSW Association of British Science Writers. c/o British Association for the Advancement of Science, 2 Sanctuary Bldgs, 20 Great Smith St, London SW1, England.

ABTAPL Association of British Theological and Philosophical Libraries. Contact chairperson. Established in 1956. Affiliated with LA.

ABTD *American Book Trade Directory.* New York: R. R. Bowker Co, 1915- . An annual publication.

ABTICS *Abstract and Book Title Index Card Service.* V. 1, 1960. An abstracting service on card format published by the Metals Society (England).

ABU Agrupación Bibliotecologica del Uruguay (Library Science Association of Uruguay). Cerro Largo 1666, Montevideo, Uruguay. Established in 1957.

ABUEN Asociación de Bibliotecas Universitarias y Especializadas de Nicaragua (Association of University and Special Libraries of Nicaragua). Biblioteca Central, Universidad Nacional Autonama de Nicaragua,

Apartado 68, León, Nicaragua. Established in 1969.

ABWA American Business Writing Association. Name changed in 1969 to ABCA (American Business Communication Association).

ABYDSA Asociación de Bibliotecarios y Documentalistas Sislenaticos Argentinos. Apartado 456, Lima, Peru.

AC Accumulator. *See* ACC (Accumulator).

ACA American Communications Association. 111 Broadway, New York, NY 10006. Established in 1934.

ACA American Composers Alliance. 170 West 74 St, New York, NY 10023. Established in 1937. Prints scores for publication, maintains a library of scores and serves as an information center for members.

ACA American Correctional Association. 4321 Hartwick Rd, College Park, MD 20740. Established in 1870. Suggests library standards for correctional institutions. Publishes a journal, newsletter, directory and books.

ACA American Crystallographic Association. Contact administrative secretary. Established in 1949 through the merger of CSA (Crystallographic Society of America) and ASXED. Maintains a publication office in Pittsburgh, PA.

ACA Association of Canadian Archivists. Public Archives of Canada, 395 Wellington St, Ottawa ON K1A ON3, Canada.

ACAC Colombian Association for the Advancement of Science. Air Mail Box 783, Bucaramanga, Colombia. Cooperates with the Universidad Industrial de Santander.

ACB Asociación Costarricense de Bibliotecarios (Association of Costa Rican Librarians). Apartado Postal 3308, San José, Costa Rica. Established in 1949.

ACB Association Canadienne des Bibliothèques. *See* CLA (Canadian Library Association).

ACBCU/CACUL Association Canadienne des Bibliothèques de Collège et

d'Université/Canadian Association of College and University Libraries. *See* CACUL/ACBCU.

ACBD/CALL Association Canadienne des Bibliothèques de Droit/Canadian Association of Law Libraries. *See* CALL/ACBD.

ACBF Association Canadienne des Bibliothécaires de Langue Française (Association of French Speaking Canadian Librarians). *See* ACBLF.

ACBLF Association Canadienne des Bibliothécaires de Langue Française (Association of French Speaking Canadian Librarians). Also known as ACBF. Name changed to ASTED in 1974.

ACBM/CAML Association Canadienne des Bibliothèques Musicales/Canadian Association of Music Libraries. *See* CAML/ACBM.

ACC Accumulator. A hardware register that stores the results of arithmetic, logical and I/O operations. Also known as AC.

ACC Amateur Computer Club. Contact secretary.

ACC Automatic Claiming and Canceling.

ACC/ACML Association des Cartothèques Canadiennes/Association of Canadian Map Libraries. *See* ACML/ACC.

ACC&CE Association of Consulting Chemists and Chemical Engineers. 50 East 41 St, Suite 92, New York, NY 10017. Established in 1928. Publishes documents.

ACCE/CERA Association Canadienne des Chercheurs en Éducation/Canadian Educational Researchers Association. *See* CERA/ACCE.

ACCESS *Applied Chemistry and Chemical Engineering Sections of Chemical Abstracts.* V. 1, 1963. Formerly *Chemical Abstracts–Applied Chemistry Sections.* Published by CAS (Chemical Abstracts Service).

ACCESS Automated Catalog of Computer Equipment and Software Systems. Used by USACSSEC. *See* Patricia Munson Malley. ''Development of a Technical Library to Support Computer Systems

Evaluation." *JOLA* 4 (Dec. 1971): 173–184.

ACCESS Automatic Computer-Controlled Electronics Scanning System.

ACCI American Council on Consumer Interests. 162 Stanley Hall, University of Missouri, Columbia, MO 62501. Formerly CCI. Publishes documents.

ACCK Associated Colleges of Central Kansas. 105 East Kansas, McPherson, KS 67460. A consortium of six church-related college libraries cooperating through union list of serials, joint reference services and educational programs.

ACCL Alberta Council of College Librarians. Box 5005, Red Deer AB T4N 5H5, Canada.

ACCO Associated Christian Colleges of Oregon. c/o Warner Pacific College, 2219 Southeast 68 Ave, Portland, OR 97215. Five libraries in an ILL network.

ACCOMP Academic Computer Group. Contact secretary.

ACDA Arms Control and Disarmament Agency. Communications and Information Center Library, Dept. of State Bldg, Rm. 5672, 21 St. & Virginia Ave, NW, Washington, DC 20451. Maintains a library.

ACDHE Alabama Consortium for the Development of Higher Education. Box 338, Demopolis, AL 36732.

ACDL Asynchronous Circuit Design Language. A computer language.

ACE Agricultural Communicators in Education. University of Missouri, 1-98 Agriculture Bldg, Columbia, MO 65211. Established in 1913. Formerly AAACE.

ACE American Council on Education. One Dupont Circle, Washington, DC 20036. Established in 1918. Publishes several journals.

ACEB/CALS Association Canadienne des Écoles de Bibliothécaires/Canadian Association of Library Schools. *See* CALS/ACEB.

ACEC American Consulting Engineers Council. Madison Bldg, 1155 15th St, NW, Washington, DC 20005. Established in 1973. Created from the 1973 merger of AICE and CEC

(Consulting Engineers Council). Maintains a library and publishes a bulletin, newsletter and directory.

ACEC Association Cattolica Esercenti Cinema. Via Filippo Corridoni 25, 00195 Rome, Italy. Association of film exhibitors.

ACEI Association for Childhood Education International. 3615 Wisconsin Ave, NW, Washington, DC 20016. Publishes *Guide to Children's Magazines, Newspapers, Reference Books* and other guides to children's literature.

ACEJ American Council on Education for Journalism. School of Journalism, University of Missouri, Columbia, MO 65201. Established in 1929. Federation of journalism education associations. Publishes documents.

ACELF Association Canadienne d'Éducation de Langue Française. 980 chemin Saint Louis, Sillery PQ G 1S1 C7, Canada. Library established in 1973.

ACER Australian Council for Educational Research. Frederick St, Hawthorn, Victoria 3122, Australia.

ACFAS Association Canadienne Française pour l'Avancement des Sciences. 2730 chemin de la Côte-Ste-Catherine, Montreal PQ, Canada.

ACHE Alabama Center for Higher Education. 2121 Eighth Ave. North, Suite 1520, Birmingham, AL 35203.

ACI American Concrete Institute. Box 19150, Redford Sta, Detroit, MI 48219. Established in 1905. Recognized by engineers as a source of standards, including standards for abbreviations and acronyms. Maintains a library.

ACI/CIPS Association Canadienne de l'Informatique/Canadian Information Processing Society. *See* CIPS/ACI.

ACIDA Atlantic Coast Independent Distributors Association. Contact secretary. A regional association of independent book distributors.

ACIR Advisory Commission on Intergovernment Relations. 1111 20th St, NW, Washington, DC 20575.

ACK Acknowledge Character. In data transmission, the character sent from a receiving terminal back to a sender terminal, confirming receipt of a message.

ACL Association for Computational Linguistics. Contact AFIPS. Established in 1962. Constituent society of AFIPS. Formerly (1968) AMTCL. Publishes a journal.

ACL Audit Command Language. A computer language.

ACLCP Area College Library Cooperative Program of Central Pennsylvania. Contact president. Seventeen public and academic libraries cooperate through ILL, union list of serials and borrowing privileges.

ACLO Association of Cooperative Library Organizations. Established in 1969. Merged into ASCLA in 1978.

ACLRTP Advisory Committee on Library Research and Training Projects. This committee has been terminated.

ACLS American Council of Learned Societies. 345 East 46 St, New York, NY 10017. Established in 1919. Federation of 42 national scholarly organizations in the humanities and social sciences. Prepares *DAB (Dictionary of American Biography)*.

ACM Associated Colleges of the Midwest. 18 South Michigan Ave, Chicago, IL 60603. Established in 1958. Includes 13 member colleges in CO, IA, IL, MN and WI. Maintains a periodical bank and coordinates joint programs.

ACM Association for Computing Machinery, Inc. 1133 Ave. of the Americas, New York, NY 10036. Established in 1947. Constituent society of AFIPS. Publishes numerous journals, including *JACM*, directories and reports.

ACMC/AFMC Association of Canadian Medical Colleges/Association des Facultés de Médecine du Canada. 151 Slater St, Ottawa ON K1A 0N3, Canada. Has an official Associate Committee on Medical School Libraries. Also known as AFMC/ACMC.

ACME Association of Consulting Management Engineers. 230 Park Ave, New York, NY 10017. Publishes documents. Maintains a library.

ACM/GAMM ACM German Association for Applied Mathematics and Mechanics. c/o Professor Bruno Brosowski, Fachbereich Mathematik der Johann Wolfgang Goethe Universität, 6000 Frankfurt/Main, Robert-Mayer-strasse 6-10, Federal Republic of Germany. Established in 1922 to promote scientific research and international collaboration in applied mathematics and mechanics. Aided in promotion of ALGOL. Affiliated with ACM (Association for Computing Machinery).

ACML/ACC Association of Canadian Map Libraries/Association des Cartothèques Canadiennes. National Map Collection, Public Archives of Canada, 395 Wellington St, Ottawa ON K1A 0N3, Canada. Also known as ACC/ACML.

ACM/SIGACT ACM Special Interest Group on Automata and Computability Theory. Contact ACM (Association for Computing Machinery).

ACM/SIGARCH ACM Special Interest Group on Architecture of Computer Systems. Contact ACM (Association for Computing Machinery).

ACM/SIGART ACM Special Interest Group on Artificial Intelligence. Contact ACM (Association for Computing Machinery).

ACM/SIGBDP ACM Special Interest Group on Business Data Processing. Contact ACM (Association for Computing Machinery).

ACM/SIGBIO ACM Special Interest Group on Biomedical Computing. Contact ACM (Association for Computing Machinery).

ACM/SIGCAI ACM Special Interest Group on Computer-Assisted Instruction. Contact ACM (Association for Computing Machinery).

ACM/SIGCAPH ACM Special Interest Group on Computers and the Physically Handicapped. Contact ACM (Association for Computing Machinery).

ACM/SIGCAS ACM Special Interest Group on Computers and Society. Contact ACM (Association for Computing Machinery).

ACM/SIGCOMM ACM Special Interest Group on Data Communications.

Contact ACM (Association for Computing Machinery).

ACM/SIGCOSIM ACM Special Interest Group on Computer Systems Installation Management. Contact ACM (Association for Computing Machinery).

ACM/SIGCPR ACM Special Interest Group on Computer Personnel Research. Contact ACM (Association for Computing Machinery).

ACM/SIGCSE ACM Special Interest Group on Computer Science Education. Contact ACM (Association for Computing Machinery).

ACM/SIGCUE ACM Special Interest Group on Computer Uses in Education. Contact ACM (Association for Computing Machinery).

ACM/SIGDA ACM Special Interest Group on Design Automation. Contact ACM (Association for Computing Machinery).

ACM/SIGGRAPH ACM Special Interest Group on Computer Graphics. Contact ACM (Association for Computing Machinery).

ACM/SIGIR ACM Special Interest Group on Information Retrieval. Contact ACM (Association for Computing Machinery).

ACM/SIGLASH ACM Special Interest Group on Language Analysis and Studies in the Humanities. Contact ACM (Association for Computing Machinery).

ACM/SIGMAP ACM Special Interest Group on Mathematical Programming. Contact ACM (Association for Computing Machinery).

ACM/SIGMETRICS ACM Special Interest Group on Measurement Evaluation. Contact ACM (Association for Computing Machinery).

ACM/SIGMICRO ACM Special Interest Group on Microprogramming. Contact ACM (Association for Computing Machinery).

ACM/SIGMINI ACM Special Interest Group on Minicomputers. Contact ACM (Association for Computing Machinery).

ACM/SIGMOD ACM Special Interest Group on Management of Data. Contact ACM (Association for Computing Machinery).

ACM/SIGNUM ACM Special Interest Group on Numerical Mathematics. Contact ACM (Association for Computing Machinery).

ACM/SIGOPS ACM Special Interest Group on Operating Systems. Contact ACM (Association for Computing Machinery).

ACM/SIGPLAN ACM Special Interest Group on Programming Languages. Contact ACM (Association for Computing Machinery).

ACM/SIGSIM ACM Special Interest Group on Simulation. Contact ACM (Association for Computing Machinery).

ACM/SIGSOC ACM Special Interest Group on Social and Behavioral Science Computing. Contact ACM (Association for Computing Machinery).

ACM/SIGUCC ACM Special Interest Group on University Computing Centers. Contact ACM (Association for Computing Machinery).

ACOMPLIS A Computerized London Information Service. Greater London Council, Dept. of Director General, County Hall, London SE1 7 PB, England.

ACORDD Advisory Committee for the Research and Development Department. An advisory committee to ASLIB and the Confederation of British Industries.

ACORN Associative Content Retrieval Network. *See* M. E. Stevens. "Automatic Indexing: A State-of-the-Art Report." National Bureau of Standards Monograph 91, 1965 (reissued 1970), p. 125.

ACP Associated Collegiate Press. 720 Washington Ave, SE, Suite 205, University of Minnesota, Minneapolis, MN 55414. Established in 1933. Publishes documents.

ACPA American College Personnel Association. 1605 New Hampshire Ave, NW, Washington, DC 20009.

ACPA Association of Computer Programmers and Analysts. Box 95, Kensington, MD 20795. Established in

1970. Publishes technical papers and other documents.

ACPE American Council of Pharmaceutical Education. One East Wacker Dr, Chicago, IL 60601. Established in 1932.

ACPU/CAUT Association Canadienne des Professeurs d'Université/Canadian Association of University Teachers. *See* CAUT/ACPU.

ACRE Automatic Checkout and Readiness Equipment. Numerous hardware-checking systems that constantly monitor the accuracy and readiness, or effective utilization capabilities, of a computer system.

ACRiLIS Australian Centre for Research in Library and Information Science. Riverina College of Advanced Education, Wagga Wagga, New South Wales, Australia.

ACRL Association of College and Research Libraries. 50 East Huron St, Chicago, IL 60611. Established in 1938. A division of ALA (American Library Association).

ACRL/AAS ACRL Asian and African Section. Contact ACRL. A section of ACRL, which is a division of ALA (American Library Association).

ACRL/ABSS ACRL Agricultural and Biological Sciences Section. Name changed to ACRL/STS.

ACRL/ANTS ACRL Anthropology Section. Contact ACRL. A section of ACRL, which is a division of ALA (American Library Association).

ACRL/ARTS ACRL Art Section. Contact ACRL. A section of ACRL, which is a division of ALA (American Library Association).

ACRL/BIS ACRL Bibliographic Section. Contact ACRL. A section of ACRL, which is a division of ALA (American Library Association).

ACRL/CJCLS ACRL Community and Junior College Libraries Section. Contact ACRL. A section of ACRL, which is a division of ALA (American Library Association). Formerly ACRL/JCLS.

ACRL/CLS ACRL College Libraries Section. Contact ACRL. A section of

ACRL, which is a division of ALA (American Library Association).

ACRL/EBSS ACRL Education and Behavioral Sciences Section. Contact ACRL. A section of ACRL, which is a division of ALA (American Library Association).

ACRL/JCLS ACRL Junior College Libraries Section. Name changed to ACRL/CJCLS.

ACRL/LPSS ACRL Law and Political Science Section. Contact ACRL. A section of ACRL, which is a division of ALA (American Library Association).

ACRL/RBMS ACRL Rare Books and Manuscripts Section. Contact ACRL. A section of ACRL, which is a division of ALA (American Library Association).

ACRL/SEES ACRL Slavic and East European Section. Contact ACRL. A section of ACRL, which is a division of ALA (American Library Association).

ACRL/STS ACRL Science and Technology Section. Contact ACRL. A section of ACRL, which is a division of ALA (American Library Association). Formerly ACRL/ABSS.

ACRL/ULS ACRL University Libraries Section. Contact ACRL. A section of ACRL, which is a division of ALA (American Library Association).

ACRL/WESS ACRL Western European Specialists Section. Contact ACRL. A section of ACRL, which is a division of ALA (American Library Association).

ACRODABA Acronym Data Base. A proposed directory of acronyms in the fields of library, information and computer science. *See* P. M. Vaillancourt and O. H. Buchanan. "Acronym Compilation by Computer (ACRODABA—ACROnym DAta BAse)." *Journal of Chemical Documentation* 12 (Aug. 1972): 178–180.

ACRPP Association pour la Conservation et la Reproduction Photographique de la Presse. France.

ACS American Chemical Society. 1155 16th St, NW, Washington, DC 20036. Established in 1876. Publishes *CA (Chemical Abstracts)* and *JACS (Journal of the American Chemical Society)*. Has several sections for the information and computer sciences and provides a variety of indexing and abstracting services through its CAS (Chemical Abstracts Service) division.

ACS American College of Surgeons. 55 East Erie St, Chicago, IL 60611. Established in 1913. Maintains a library of books and films. Publishes journals.

ACS Australian Computer Society, Inc. Contact president. Incorporated in 1969.

ACS/CLD ACS Chemical Literature Division. Contact ACS (American Chemical Society).

ACS/DCD ACS Division of Chemical Documentation. Name changed to ACS/DCI in 1975.

ACS/DCI ACS Division of Chemical Information. Contact ACS (American Chemical Society). Formerly ACS/DCD.

ACS/DCL ACS Division of Chemical Literature. Contact ACS (American Chemical Society).

ACSES Automated Computer Science Education System. University of Illinois, Urbana-Champaign, Dept. of Computer Science, Urbana, IL 61801. Project to automate introductory computer science courses.

ACSI/CAIS Association Canadienne des Sciences de l'Information/Canadian Association for Information Science. *See* CAIS/ACSI.

ACSIL Admiralty Centre for Scientific Information and Liaison. United Kingdom. Name changed to NSTIC.

ACSLV Associated Colleges of the Saint Lawrence Valley. Administration Building, SUNY–Potsdam, Potsdam, NY 13676. Four libraries cooperate through ILL, catalog card processing, reciprocal borrowing and sharing of OCLC terminals.

ACSM American Congress on Surveying and Mapping. 210 Little Falls St, Falls Church, VA 22046. Established in 1941. Formerly NCSM. One section is concerned with professional literature retrieval. Maintains a library. Publishes a journal and monographs. Affiliated with ICA (International Cartographic Association).

ACSP Advisory Council on Science Policy. 2 Richmond Terrace, Whitehall, London SW1, England.

ACSR Association Cinématographique Suisse Romande. 3 place Riponne, 1005 Lausanne, Switzerland. Established in 1928. Association of Swiss film exhibitors. Publishes documents.

ACSTI Advisory Committee for Scientific and Technical Information. c/o Dept. of Education and Science, Elizabeth House, York Rd, London SE1 7PH, England. Government committee established in April 1965. Reviewed policy and made recommendations regarding the continued development of information handling methods of OSTI.

ACT Action for Children's Television. 46 Austin St, Newtonville, MA 02160. National consumer group working through education, publications, research and legal action to improve child-oriented broadcasting practices. Maintains a resource library.

ACT Autocoder to COBOL Translator.

ACT Automatic Code Translator. A translator developed for the UNIVAC systems by Sperry Rand Corp.

ACT-I Algebraic Compiler and Translator I. A compiler developed for the LGB 30 computer by the Royal McBee Corp.

ACT-III Algebraic Compiler and Translator III. An extension of ACT-I developed by National Carbon Corp. for the LGB 30 computer.

ACTS Acquisitions, Cataloging, Technical Systems. Richard Alde & Co, Box 4245, Portland, OR 97208. A microfiche service.

ACTSU Association of Computer Time-Sharing Users (USA). Name changed to ATSU in 1975.

ACTT Association of Cinematograph, Television and Allied Technicians. 2 Soho Sq, London W1, England.

ACU Association of Commonwealth Universities. 36 Gordon Sq, London WC1, England.

ACU Automatic Calling Unit. A dialing device, supplied by a communications common carrier, which permits a business machine to dial calls automatically over communication networks.

ACUG Association of Computer User Groups. Contact president.

ACURIL Association of Caribbean University and Research Institute Libraries. Name changed to ACURL.

ACURL Association of Caribbean University and Research Libraries. 27 Tobago Ave, Kingston, Jamaica. Formerly ACURIL. Also known as Asociación de Bibliotecas Universitarias y de Investigación del Caribe.

ACUTE Accountants Computer Users Technical Exchange. 947 Old York Rd, Abington, PA 19001. Publishes documents.

ACYF Administration for Children, Youth, and Families. Office of Human Development Services, 200 Independence Ave, SW, Washington, DC 20201. A department of the Office of Human Development, which is an agency of DHEW.

AD *American Documentation.* (Journal). V. 1–20, 1950–1969. Name changed to *JASIS* in 1970.

ADA American Dental Association. 211 East Chicago Ave, Chicago, IL 60611. Established in 1859. Maintains a library and publishes documents. Formerly (1897–1922) National Dental Association.

ADABAS Adaptable Data Base System.

ADAL Action Data Automation Language.

ADAM Advanced Data Management. A software environment that a data center provides as a tool to analysts, administrators and programmers who are responsible for maintenance, query and analysis of a data base. *See* Thomas B. Connors. "ADAM: A Generalized Data Management System" in *AFIPS Conference Proceedings, Vol. 28; 1966 Spring Joint Computer Conference.* Washington, DC: Spartan Books, 1966, pp. 193–203.

ADAPSO Association of Data Processing Service Organizations, Inc. 1925 North Lynn St, Arlington, VA 22209. Established in 1960. Publishes an annual directory. Maintains a library.

ADAPT Adaptation of APT (Automatically Programmed Tools). A program for design calculations and preparation of control tapes for numerically controlled machine tools. ADAPT provides the ability to generate, relocate and alter copies of patterns of hole-and-cut sequences, through multilevel copy logic.

ADB Anlagendatenbank. Betriebsforschungsinstitut, VDEh-Institut für Angewandte Forschung GmbH (BFI), Verein Deutscher Eisenhuttenleute, Sohnstrasse 65, Düsseldorf D-4000, Federal Republic of Germany. Coverage from 1971. Nonbibliographic data base covering news and information on steel production.

ADBACI Association pour le Développement de la Documentation, des Bibliothèques et Archives de la Côte d'Ivoire (Association for the Development of Documentation, Libraries and Archives of the Ivory Coast). c/o Bibliothèque Nationale, BP V180 Abidjan, Ivory Coast.

ADBS Association Française des Documentalistes et des Bibliothécaires Spécialisés (French Association of Information Scientists and Special Librarians). 61 rue du Cardinal Lemoine, 75005 Paris, France. Established in 1963 to promote the profession. Also known as AFDBS.

ADC Aliquippa District Center Library. B. F. Jones Memorial Library, 663 Franklin Ave, Aliquippa, PA 15001. Consortium established in 1963. Affiliated with Beaver County Federated Library System.

ADC Analog to Digital Converter. A device that changes physical motion or electrical voltage into digital factors.

ADCIS Association for Development of Computer-based Instructional Systems. Computer Center, Western Washington State College, Bellingham, WA 98225. Established in 1968. Formerly (1973) ADIS (Association for Development of Instructional Systems). Publishes a newsletter and journal.

ADCON Address Constant. A value or expression used to calculate real or virtual storage addresses.

ADD *American Doctoral Dissertations*. Ann Arbor, MI: University Microfilms International, 1934– . An annual publication listing all doctoral dissertations accepted by American and Canadian universities. Includes degree statistics. Available on microfiche.

ADE Automatic Data Entry.

ADEPT Algebraic and Differential Equations Processor and Translator. A medium-scale, multiaccess system based on the IBM 360/50 and designed primarily for military data management. *See* C. Baum, ed. *Research and Technology Division Report for 1967*. Santa Monica, CA: System Development Corp, Jan. 1968.

ADES Association of Directors of Education in Scotland. 9 Drumsheugh Gardens, Edinburgh 3, Scotland.

ADES Automatic Digital Encoding System. A programming language used by the US Naval Ordnance Laboratory on the IBM 704 automatic data processing system.

ADES-II Automatic Digital Encoding System. A programming language used by the US Naval Ordnance Laboratory on the IBM 650 automatic data processing system.

ADI American Documentation Institute. Name changed to ASIS in 1968.

ADIA Automatic Documentation in Action. Meeting, held in 1959 in Frankfurt, West Germany, of the FID/MSR Subcommittee on Documentation of GdT, the Working Committee on Automation of Documentation of the German Society for Documentation, and the Gmelin Institute for Inorganic Chemistry of the Max-Planck Gesellschaft.

ADIS A Data Interchange System. A communication system developed by the Teletype Corp.

ADIS Association for the Development of Instructional Systems. Name changed to ADCIS in 1973.

ADIS Australasian Drug Information Services Pty. Limited. Box 33-274, Takapuna, Auckland 9, New Zealand.

ADIS Automatic Diffemic Identification of Speakers. Institute of Phonetics and Communications Research, Bonn University, Adenauer allee 98a, 53 Bonn, Federal Republic of Germany. Automatic discrimination of individual speakers based on text-dependent features.

ADM Archer Daniels Midland Company. Research Library, 4666 Faries Pkway, Decatur, IL 62526. Library established in 1969. Specializes in agricultural economics and statistics and food science.

ADMIG Australian Drug and Medical Information Group. Box 347, Lane Cove 2066, Australia.

ADMIRAL Automatic and Dynamic Monitor with Immediate Relocation, Allocation and Loading. *See* SPAR.

ADONIS Automatic Digital On-line Instrumentation System. Developed by Blackburn Electronics.

ADOPT Approach to Distributed Processing Transactions.

ADP Association of Data Producers. c/o Learned Information, Besselsleigh Rd, Abingdon, Oxford 0X13 6EF, England.

ADP Automated Data Processing.

ADP Automatic Data Processing.

ADPE Automatic Data Processing Equipment.

ADPE/S Automatic Data Processing Equipment and Software.

ADPESO Automatic Data Processing Equipment Selection Office. An office of the US Navy.

ADPS Automatic Data Processing System.

ADPSC Automatic Data Processing Service Center. Service of the US Military.

ADPSO Association of Data Processing Service Organizations. 1925 North Lynn St, Arlington, VA 22209. Established in 1960. Publishes newsletter, guides and directories.

ADRIS Association for the Development of Religious Information Systems. Dept. of Sociology and Anthropology, Marquette University, Milwaukee, WI 53233. Established in 1971. Members include bibliographical and indexing services related to religion and libraries.

ADRT Analog Data Recording Transcriber. Developed by Honeywell.

ADSTAR Automatic Document Storage and Retrieval. Refers to equipment and systems for storing and retrieving documents by an automatic device, specifically excluding digital computers. *See* Rodd S. Exelbert and Mitchell Badler. "Automatic Information Retrieval: A Report on the State of the Art." *Information and Records Management* 8 (Feb. 1974): 23–29.

ADSUP Automatic Data Systems Uniform Practices. A programming language.

ADTCB Association des Directeurs de Théâtres Cinématographiques de Belgique. Rue Royale 300, 1030 Brussels, Belgium. Member of the European Film Union.

ADTIC Arctic, Desert, Tropic Information Center. Aerospace Studies Institute, Maxwell Air Force Base, AL 36112.

ADU Automatic Dialing Unit. A device capable of automatically generating dialing digits.

ADV Arbeitsgemeinschaft für Datenverarbeitung. Billrothstrasse 14, 1190 Vienna, Austria.

ADX Automatic Data Exchange.

AEA American Education Association. 663 Fifth Ave, New York, NY 10022. Established in 1938. Conducts research on curriculum and textbooks.

AEB Asociación Ecuatoriana de Bibliotecarios (Ecuadorian Library Association). Casa de la Cultura Ecuatoriana, Casilla 87, Quito, Ecuador. Established in 1945. *See* Julian G. Bravo. "Ecuador, Libraries in" in *Encyclopedia of Library and Information Science*, ed. by Allen Kent et al. New York: Marcel Dekker, 1972, V. 7, pp. 387–396.

AEBIG ASLIB Economic and Business Information Group. Contact ASLIB.

AEBQ Association des Enseignants Bibliothécaires du Québec. Contact president.

AEC Atomic Energy Commission. Replaced by ERDA in 1974, which was consolidated into DOE in 1977.

AECDF Association des Exploitants de Cinéma et des Distributeurs de Films du Grand-Duché de Luxembourg. Case Postale 2558, Luxembourg. Established in 1954. Association of film exhibitors. Member of the European Film Union.

AECL Atomic Energy of Canada Limited. 275 Slater St, Ottawa ON K2G N8, Canada. Publishes documents.

AECT Association for Educational Communications and Technology. 1126 16th St, NW, Washington, DC 20036. Established in 1923. Formerly (1970) DAVI. Publishes journals and a newsletter and maintains archives of materials and equipment.

AED Atomkernenergie Dokumentation (Atomic Energy Documentation Center). *See* ZAED.

AED Automated Engineering Design System. An MIT (Massachusetts Institute of Technology) developed extension of ALGOL.

AEDS Association for Educational Data Systems. 1201 16th St, NW, Washington, DC 20036. Established in 1962. Constituent society of AFIPS. Publishes journals, handbooks and directories.

AEEP Association of European Engineering Periodicals. Contact secretary.

AEF Aerospace Education Foundation. 1750 Pennsylvania Ave, NW, Washington, DC 20036. Publishes documents. Formerly the Air Force Association Foundation, the Air Education Foundation and the Space Education Foundation.

AEG Association of Engineering Geologists. 8310 San Fernando Way, Dallas, TX 75218. Part of AGI. Publishes documents.

AEJ Association for Education in Journalism. 102 Reavis Hall, Northern Illinois University, De Kalb, IL 60115. Established in 1912. Conducts research and publishes journals, newsletters and monographs. Affiliated with AASDJ. Formerly the American Association of Teachers of Journalism.

AENSB Association de l'École Nationale Supérieure de Bibliothécaires (Association of the National School of

Librarianship). 17-21 boulevard du 11 Novembre 1918, 69621 Villeurbanne, France. Established in 1967.

AEPI American Educational Publishers Institute. Merged with ABPC in 1970 to form AAP (Association of American Publishers).

AEPS Alternative Education Programs Section. *See* PLA/AEPS.

AEPT Asociación Española de Prensa Tecnica. Balmes 200-2-7a, Barcelona 6, Spain. Established in 1925. Member of the International Federation of the Periodical Press. Publishes documents.

AERA American Educational Research Association. 1126 16th St, NW, Washington, DC 20036. Publishes *Review of Educational Research, Educational Researcher* and *American Educational Research Journal*, and numerous other journals and documents.

AERE Atomic Energy Research Establishment. Harwell, England. Publishes documents and conducts research.

AERT Association for Education by Radio-Television. This association has been terminated.

AES Aerospace Electrical Society. Box 24BB3, Village Sta, Los Angeles, CA 90025. Formerly Aircraft Electrical Society. Publishes documents.

AES Audio Engineering Society, Inc. 60 East 42 St, New York, NY 10017. Publishes documents.

AESE Association of Earth Science Editors. c/o American Geological Institute, 5205 Leesburg Pike, Falls Church, VA 22041. Established in 1967. Publishes a journal and a handbook series. Affiliated with NRC (National Research Council) of Canada.

AESL Associated Engineering Services, Limited. 10835 120th St, Edmonton AB T5H 3R1, Canada. Library established in 1960.

AESOP An Evolutionary System for On-line Processing. A direct access management information system. *See* J. Spiegel et al. *AESOP: A General Purpose Approach to Real-Time, Direct Access*

Management Systems. Bedford, MA: MITRE Corp, 1966.

AFA Advertising Federation of America. Name changed to AAF.

AFAC Arkansas Foundation of Associated Colleges. 309 Center St, Rm. 110, Little Rock, AR 72201. Consortium established in 1956. AFAC's Committee of Librarians cooperates through the joint purchase of materials.

AFACO Association Française des Amateurs Constructeurs l'Ordinateurs (French Association of Amateur Computer Builders). France.

AFAM Automatic Frequency Assignment Model.

AFCAL Association Française de Calcul (French Computing Association). Contact president.

AFCCE Association of Federal Communications Consulting Engineers. c/o Broome Associates, Inc, 525 Woodward Ave, Bloomfield Hills, MI 48013. Established in 1948.

AFCEA Armed Forces Communications and Electronics Association. 5205 Leesburg Pike, Falls Church, VA 22041. Established in 1946. Publishes documents.

AFCET Association Française pour la Cybernétique Économique et Technique. 156 boulevard Pereire, BP 571, 75826 Paris, Cedex 17, France. Established in 1968 to promote various scientific and technical activities concerned with the analysis, conduct and control of economic processes.

AFDBS L'Association Française des Documentalistes et Bibliothécaires Spécialisés. *See* ADBS.

AFEE Association Française pour l'Étude des Eaux. 23 rue de Madrid, 75008 Paris, France. Established in 1960 for the study of water supply, use and conservation.

AFESP Air Force English Syntax Project. Objective is to integrate the transformational analysis of English. Located at UCLA. *See* "TGT: Transformational Grammar Tester." *AFIPS Conference Proceedings* 32 (Spring 1968): 385–393.

AFFS American Federation of Film Societies. 3 Washington Sq. Village, New York, NY 10012. Established in 1955. Presently inactive.

AFGE American Federation of Government Employees. 1325 Massachusetts Ave, NW, Washington, DC 20005. Established in 1932. Publishes a newsletter.

AFI American Film Institute. John F. Kennedy Center for the Performing Arts, Washington, DC 20566. Established in 1967. Publishes documents, including the journal *American Film*.

AFIED Armed Forces Information and Education Division. The Pentagon, Washington, DC 20310.

AFIP American Federation for Information Processing. Name changed to AFIPS.

AFIPS American Federation of Information Processing Societies. 210 Summit Ave, Montvale, NJ 70645. Established in 1961. Formerly AFIP.

AFIRO Association Française d'Informatique et de Recherche Opérationnelle. Paris 16, France.

AFIRSS Automatic Fact Information Retrieval and Storage Systems. *See* A. A. Stogniy and V. N. Afanassiev. "Some Design Problems for Automatic Fact Information Retrieval and Storage Systems" in *Mechanized Information Storage, Retrieval & Disseminations*, ed. by Kjell Samuelson. New York: North Holland Publishing, 1968, p. 289.

AFJA Association Française des Journalistes Agricoles (French Association of Agricultural Journalists). 9 rue Papillon, 75009 Paris, France. Established in 1954. Publishes documents.

AFLA Asian Federation of Library Associations. Tokyo, Japan.

AFL-CIO American Federation of Labor and Congress of Industrial Organizations. 815 16th St, NW, Washington, DC 20006. Established in 1955. Publications include *AFL-CIO News, The American Federationist* and *Free Trade Union News*. Governs some library workers.

AFLS American Folklore Society. Dept. of Behavioral Science, College of Medicine, Milton S. Hershey Medical Center, Pennsylvania State University, Hershey, PA 17033. Established in 1888. Publishes a journal, a newsletter and several special series.

AFLS Armed Forces Librarians Section. *See* PLA/AFLS.

AFMC/ACMC Association de Facultés de Médecine du Canada/Association of Canadian Medical Colleges. *See* ACMC/AFMC.

AFNOR Association Française de Normalisation. Tour Europe—Cedex 7, 92080 Paris—la Défense, France. The French official body corresponding to ANSI. Issues the annual *Catalog des Normes Françaises*.

AFOS Automation of Field Operations and Services. A program of the National Weather Service.

AFOSR Air Force Office of Scientific Research. Bldg. 410, Bolling AFB, Washington, DC 20332.

AF-PDC Air Force Publications and Distribution Center. *See* PDC.

AFSARI Automation for Storage and Retrieval of Information. A computerized system at Bhabha Atomic Research Centre, Bombay, India. *See* Raju J. Srihari. "Library Automation Developments in India." *NETWORK* 1 (May 1974): 13–15.

AFSCME American Federation of State, County, and Municipal Employees. A union which negotiates for many libraries.

AFT An Foras Taluntais (Irish Agricultural Institute). The Agricultural Institute, Dublin, Ireland. An Irish agricultural research and development organization.

AFTOD Air Force Technical Objectives Documents Release Program. Of interest to librarians in the acquisition of federally produced information.

AFTRA American Federation of Television and Radio Artists. 1350 Ave. of the Americas, New York, NY 10019. A union of actors, announcers and other television and radio performers.

AGA American Gas Association, Inc. 1515 Wilson Blvd, Arlington, VA 22209. Established in 1918. Maintains a library and publishes newsletters and information bulletins.

AGAC American Guild of Authors and Composers. 40 West 57 St, New York, NY 10019. Established in 1931. Represents songwriters in matters relating to publication and copyright laws.

AGAPE Application de la Gestion aux Périodiques. Computerized catalog of periodicals at the University of Nice in France. *See* Michel Meinardi. "Premiers Résultats de la Gestion Automatisée des Périodiques à la Bibliothèque de l'Université de Nice." *Bulletin des Bibliothèques de France* 18 (Nov. 1973): 525.

AGARD Advisory Group for Aerospace Research and Development. 64 rue de Varenne, Paris 7, France.

AGE Aerospace Ground-Support Equipment. Developed by Laboratory for Electronics, Inc, for use with space studies, space vehicles and communications.

AGE Asian Information Center for Geotechnical Engineering. Asian Institute of Technology, Library and Information Center, Box 2754, Bangkok, Thailand. Maintains a library.

AGI American Geological Institute. 5205 Leesburg Pike, Falls Church, VA 22041. Sponsor of an information system for the geosciences.

AGILE Analytic Geometry Interpretive Language.

AGLC Alberta Government Libraries Council. Contact secretary. A Canadian association.

AGLINET Agricultural Libraries Information Network. A network of IAALD and FAO (Food and Agriculture Organization).

AGM Annual General Meeting. Annual meeting of the LAA (Library Association of Australia), which also holds biennial conferences.

AGN Archivos General de la Nación (National Archives). Tacuba 8-20 Piso, Apdo 1999, México 1, Districto Federal, Mexico.

AGO Art Gallery of Ontario. Grange Park, Toronto ON M5T 1G4, Canada. Established in 1913. Maintains a research library.

AG/PACK Agricultural Personal Alerting Card Kits. A weekly current awareness service developed by SDC (Scientific Documentation Centre).

AGREP Agricultural Research Projects in the European Community. Commission of the European Communities, Directorate General, Scientific and Technical Information and Information Management, 29 rue Aldringen, Luxembourg City, Luxembourg. Project to coordinate agricultural research by providing information about current projects.

AGRICOLA Agricultural On-Line Access. The NAL's (National Agricultural Library's) data base, which contains citations to all NAL holdings on agricultural and related sciences, including monographs, serials and government reports. Coverage since 1970. Formerly CAIN (Cataloging and Indexing Systems of NAL).

AGRINTER Sistema Interamericano de Informacion para las Ciencias Agricolas. An inter-American system of information for Latin American and Caribbean agricultural sciences. It became operational in January 1973. It is compatible with AGRIS.

AGRIS Agricultural Information System. An international information system for the agricultural sciences, emphasizing rapid notification to users and the provision of in-depth treatment for particular subject fields. *See* M. L. Wedderburn. "AGRIS AGRINTER: The Ministry of Agriculture Library's Participation in International Library Regional Cooperation for the Agricultural Sciences." *Jamaica Library Association Bulletin* (1976): 26–27.

AGROINFORM Agricultural Information. Mezogazdasági és Élelmezésügyi Minisztérium Információs Központja (Information Centre of the Ministry of Agriculture and Food), Attila ut. 93, Budapest I, Hungary.

AGU American Geophysical Union. 2000 Florida Ave, NW, Washington, DC 20009. Established in 1919. Publishes journals, monograph series and translations of USSR periodicals relating to geophysics.

AHA American Historical Association. 400 A St, SE, Washington, DC 20003. Established in 1884. Publishes documents.

AHA American Hospital Association. 840 North Lake Shore Dr, Chicago, IL 60611. Established in 1898. Publishes documents, has a reference library and is active in developing procedures for libraries in hospitals.

AHE Association for Higher Education. Name changed to AAHE.

AHEA American Home Economics Association. 2010 Massachusetts Ave, NW, Washington, DC 20036. Established in 1909. Publishes documents.

AHI Augmentation of Human Intellect. A phrase coined by the staff at Stanford Research Institute for innovative work in computer-based systems which aids the user in various tasks, including education.

AHIL Association of Hospital and Institution Libraries. Name changed in 1974 to HRLS (Health and Rehabilitative Library Services).

AHL America: History and Life. Coverage from 1964. Bibliographic data base covering American political and social history. Produced by ABC-Clio.

AHLC Areawide Hospital Library Consortium of Southwestern Illinois. c/o Saint Elizabeth's Hospital, 211 South Third St, Belleville, IL 62221. Nine health sciences libraries cooperate through ILL, acquisitions and information exchange.

AHMS Automated Health Multi-Phase Screening. A program that reads, processes and interprets past medical records; analyzes tests and provides a printed report to the family doctor.

AHPA American Health Planning Association. 1601 Connecticut Ave, Suite 700, Washington, DC 20009. Conducts research and provides information on health planning concepts. Publishes a weekly, an annual directory and numerous irregular bulletins.

AHSIC Alaskan Health Sciences Information Center. Contact PNRHSL. The Alaskan State Library, USPHS, University of Alaska and local medical and health-related organizations cooperate with PNRHSL for MEDLINE use. Located in Anchorage. *See* Gerard J. Oppenheimer. "The Regional Medical Libraries, Region X, PNRHSL." *NLM News* 30 (Dec. 1975): 3–4.

AIA *Abstracts in Anthropology.* V. 1, 1970. Published by Baywood Publishing Co.

AIA Aerospace Industries Association of America. 1725 DeSales St, NW, Washington, DC 20036. Established in 1919. Formerly Aircraft Industries Association. Publishes documents. Maintains a research center.

AIA American Institute of Architects. 1735 New York Ave, NW, Washington, DC 20006. Established in 1857. Maintains a library and publishes a journal and directory of architectural firms.

AIAA American Institute of Aeronautics and Astronautics. 1290 Ave. of the Americas, New York, NY 10019. Established in 1963. Constituent society of AFIPS. Has a Technical Specialty Group on Information Systems. *See also* AIAA-TIS. Publishes numerous journals, abstracts and technical reports.

AIAA-TIS American Institute of Aeronautics and Astronautics, Technical Information Services. 750 Third Ave, New York, NY 10017. *See* AIAA.

AIB American Institute of Banking. 1120 Connecticut Ave, NW, Washington, DC 20036. Sponsored by ABA (American Bankers Association). Conducts educational and training programs.

AIB Anthracite Information Bureau. This bureau has been terminated.

AIB Associazione Italiana Biblioteche (Italian Libraries Association). c/o Istituto di Patologia del Libro, Via Milano 76, 00184 Rome, Italy. Established in 1930. Affiliated with IFLA.

AIBA Agricultural Information Bank of Asia. Southeast Asian Regional Center for Graduate Study and Research in Agriculture, College, Laguna 3720, Philippines.

AIBDA Asociación Interamericana de Bibliotecarios y Documentalistas Agricolas (Inter-American Association of Agricultural Librarians and Documentalists). IICA-CIDIA, Turrialba, Costa Rica. Established in 1953.

AIBM/IAML/IVMB Association Internationale des Bibliothèques Musicales/International Association of Music Libraries/Internationale Vereinigung der Musikbibliotheken. Svenskt Musikhistoriskt Arkivm Strandvagen 82M S-115, 27 Stockholm, Sweden. Established in 1951.

AIBS American Institute of Biological Sciences. 1401 Wilson Blvd, Arlington, VA 22209. Established in 1947. Federation of 62 biological associations and industrial firms. Publishes a journal, a directory and numerous monographs.

AIC American Institute for Conservation of Historic and Artistic Works. 1522 K St, NW, Suite 804, Washington, DC 20005. Established in 1972. Publishes a journal and newsletter. Formerly IIC (International Institute for Conservation of Historic and Artistic Works)–American Group.

AIC American Institute of Chemists, Inc. 7315 Wisconsin Ave, Washington, DC 20014. Established in 1923. Publishes a journal and biennial directory.

AICA Association Internationale pour le Calcul Analogique (International Association for Mathematics and Computer Simulation). 496 Avenue Molière, B-1060 Brussels, Belgium. Also known as IMACS.

AICA Associazione Italiana per il Calco Automatico (Italian Association for Automatic Data Processing). Italy.

AICCE Augmented Individualized Courses in Continuing Education. Project of ACS (American Chemical Society).

AICCF Association Internationale du Congres des Chemins de Fer. Rue de Louvain 17-21, B-1000 Brussels, Belgium. Has an information center.

AICDT International Advisory Committee on Documentation and Terminology in Pure and Applied Science. 7 Place de Fontenoy, Paris 7, France.

AICE American Institute of Consulting Engineers. Established in 1910. Merged in 1973 with CEC (Consulting Engineers Council) to form ACEC (American Consulting Engineers Council).

AIChE American Institute of Chemical Engineers. 345 East 47 St, New York, NY 10017. Established in 1908. Publishes journals, symposium series and information pamphlets.

AICPA American Institute of Certified Public Accountants. 1211 Ave. of the Americas, New York, NY 10036. Established in 1887. Constituent society of AFIPS. Develops financial accounting standards. Maintains a library. Publishes a journal and numerous bulletins.

AID Agency for International Development. US State Dept, 320 21st St, NW, Washington, DC 20523. Formerly ICA (International Cooperation Administration).

AID Association Internationale des Documentalistes et Techniciens de l'Information (International Association of Documentalists and Information Officers). Contact secretary. Established in 1962. Also known as IAD.

AIDBA Association Internationale pour le Développement de la Documentation, des Bibliothèques et des Archives en Afrique (International Association for the Development of Documentation Libraries and Archives in Africa). Contact secretary. Established in 1957 as l'Association pour le Développement des Bibliothèques Publiques en Afrique. Present name assumed in 1968. Also known as IADLA. Affiliated with IFLA.

AIDBA–Section Mauritanienne AIDBA–Section Mauritanienne (AIDBA–Mauritanian Branch). c/o La Bibliothèque Nationale, BP 20, Nouakchott, Islamic Republic of Mauritania.

AIDBA–Section Togolaise AIDBA–Section Togolaise (AIDBA–Togo Branch). c/o Bibliothèque de l'Université du Bénin,

BP 1515, Lome, Republic of Togo. Established in 1959.

AIDC Association of Information and Dissemination Centers. Box 8105, Athens, GA 30603. Established in 1968. Formerly (1976) ASIDIC.

AIDI Associazione Italiana per la Documentazione e l'Informazione (Italian Association for Documentation and Information). National Institute for Productivity, Piazza Indipendenza, 11B Rome, Italy. Established in 1966.

AID-IFP Automatic Indexing of Documentation of IFP. *See* M. Moureau and J. M. Lasvergeres. "Automatic Indexing of IFP Scientific and Technical Reports" in *Mechanized Information Storage, Retrieval and Dissemination*, ed. by K. Samuelson. Amsterdam, the Netherlands: IFIP, 1968, p. 468.

AIDS Aerospace Intelligence Data System. Developed by IBM.

AIDS Automated Information Dissemination System. *See* R. D. Kerr-Waller. "Automated Information Dissemination System (AIDS) Data Processing Procedure" in *Mechanized Information Storage, Retrieval and Dissemination*, ed. by K. Samuelson. Amsterdam, the Netherlands: IFIP, 1968, p. 335.

AIDUS Automated Information Directory Update System.

AIDUS Automated Input and Document Update System.

AIE Associazione Italiana Editori (Italian Publishers Association). Via Pietro della Valle 13, 1-00193 Rome, Italy. Established in 1869. Publishes documents.

AIEE American Institute of Electrical Engineers. Merged with IRE to form IEEE in 1963. Sponsored Joint Computing Conferences with IRE from 1952 to 1961.

AIFE American Institute for Exploration. Main Library, 1809 Nichols Rd, Kalamazoo, MI 49007. Maintains three research libraries in AK, MI and OR. Sponsors expeditions worldwide.

AIGA American Institute of Graphic Arts. 1059 Third Ave, New York, NY 10021. Established in 1914. Maintains a library and slide archives and publishes a catalog and newsletter.

AIIE American Institute of Industrial Engineers. 25 Technology Pk./Atlanta, Norcross, GA 30092. Established in 1948. Publishes several journals, special studies and reports.

AIISUP Association Internationale d'Information Scolaire Universitaire et Professionelle (International Association for Education and Vocational Information). Contact secretary.

AIL/ABI Association of International Libraries/Association des Bibliothèques Internationales. Contact secretary. Established in 1963.

AIM *Abridged Index Medicus.* (Journal). V. 1, 1970. Published by NLM.

AIM Abstracts of Instructional Materials in Vocational and Technical Education. Published from 1967 to 1976. AIM merged with ARM (Abstracts of Research and Related Materials in Vocational and Technical Education) in 1974 to form AIM/ARM.

AIM American Institute of Management. 607 Boylston St, Boston, MA 02116. Established in 1948. Maintains library and publishes several periodicals.

AIM Associated Information Managers. 316 Pennsylvania Ave, SE, Suite 502, Washington, DC 20003. Established in 1978 as PRIM. Name changed to AIM in 1979. Affiliated with IIA (Information Industry Association). Publishes *AIM Network.*

AIM Association for Instructional Materials. 600 Madison Ave, New York, NY 10022.

AIM Association for Marine Research and Technology Information. Goethestrasse 27, D-3000 Hannover, Federal Republic of Germany. Developed a computerized information and documentation system.

AIM Automated Inventory Management.

AIMACO Air Materiel Command (US Air Force). A program compiling system developed for the Air Materiel Command, USAF, for use on the UNIVAC 1105 automatic data processing system.

AIM/ARM Abstracts of Instructional and Research Materials in Vocational and Technical Education. A historical data base of materials on vocational and technical education covering 1967 to 1976. Superseded by *RIVE* in 1977.

AIME American Institute of Mining, Metallurgical and Petroleum Engineers. 345 East 47 St, New York, NY 10017. Established in 1871. Publishes several periodicals. Formerly (1957) American Institute of Mining and Metallurgical Engineers. Constituent societies: SME, TMS and SPE. Also known as AIMMPE.

AIMLO Auto-Instructional Media for Library Orientation. Colorado State University Libraries, Fort Collins, CO 80523.

AIMMPE American Institute of Mining, Metallurgical and Petroleum Engineers. *See* AIME.

AIMS Auerbach Information Management System.

AIMS Author Index Manufacturing System. Computer-based system begun by CAS (Chemical Abstracts Service) in 1977. Aids in generation of bibliographic products and services.

AIMS Automated Instructional Materials Handling System of SDC (System Development Corporation). *See* Donald V. Black and Ann W. Luke. "A Comprehensive Automated Instructional Materials Handling System for School Districts." *Proceedings of ASIS* 8 (1971): 279–285.

AIM-TWX Abridged *Index Medicus*-Teletypewriter Exchange Service. On-line teletypewriter system developed for NLM by SDC (Systems Development Corporation). Intended to reach a wide audience of hospital libraries, the system includes an abridged version of *IM (Index Medicus)*, covering only clinical information.

AIMU American Institute of Marine Underwriters. 14 Wall St, New York, NY 10005. Established in 1898. Publishes reports on marine disasters and information about hulls and cargo.

AINA Arctic Institute of North America. University Library Tower, 2920 24th Ave, NW, Calgary AB T2N 1N4, Canada. US Office: 3426 North Washington Blvd, Arlington, VA 22207. Established in 1945. Publishes documents. Maintains a library and supports research and exploration in polar regions.

AINAI African Integrated Network of Administrative Information. African Training and Research Centre in Administration for Development, BP 310, Tangier, Morocco. A feasibility study done in 1975.

AINTD Association de l'Institut National des Techniques de la Documentation (Association of the National Institute for Information Sciences). 41 avenue de Charlebourg, 92250 La Garenne-Colombes, France. Established in 1953.

AIOPI Association of Information Officers in the Pharmaceutical Industry. c/o E. R. Squibbs and Sons, Ltd, Regal House, Twickenham TW1 3QT, England.

AIP American Institute of Physics. 335 East 45 St, New York, NY 10017. Established in 1931. Federation of national societies in the field of physics. Publishes numerous major journals and is active in information exchange studies.

AIP Automated Imagery Processing.

AIPR Association of International Publishers Representatives. This association has been terminated.

AIR American Institute for Research. Library, 1791 Arastradero Rd, Box 1113, Palo Alto, CA 94302. Library established in 1967.

AIRA Alberta Information Retrieval Association. c/o Research Council of Alberta, 11315 87th Ave, Edmonton AB T6G 2C2, Canada.

AIRHPER Alberta Information Retrieval for Health, Physical Education, and Recreation. University of Alberta, Edmonton, AB, Canada. A two-file system (linear and inverted) with a suitable thesaurus.

AIRS Appalachia Improved Reference Service. A federally funded project to serve business and industry.

AIRs Automatic Information Retrieval System. An IBM system using FAP (FORTRAN Assembly Program).

AIS Applicant Information Service. Institute of International Education, 809 United Nations Pl, New York, NY 10017.

AISC American Institute of Steel Construction. 1221 Ave. of the Americas, New York, NY 10020. Established in 1921. Publishes *AISC News, Engineering Journal* and *Modern Steel Construction*. Also publishes a manual, handbook, bibliographies, specifications and other literature.

AISC Association of Independent Software Companies. Absorbed in 1972 by ADAPSO as Software Section.

AISE Association of Iron and Steel Engineers. 3 Gateway Center, Suite 2350, Pittsburgh, PA 15222. Established in 1907. Publishes documents.

AISI American Iron and Steel Institute. 1000 16th St, NW, Washington, DC 20036. Established in 1908. Publishes documents. Conducts research in cooperation with universities.

AIST Automatic Information System.

AITC American Institute of Timber Construction. 333 West Hampden Ave, Englewood, CO 80110. Established in 1952. Recognized by engineers as a source of standards, including standards for abbreviations and acronyms. Maintains a library.

AJBD Arbeitsgemeinschaft für Juristisches Bibliotheks-und Dokumentationswesen (Association of Libraries for Law and Documentation). Contact IALL. Established in 1971. Affiliated with IALL. Publishes documents. *See* E. M. Mays. "German Law Librarians." *Law Librarian* 5 (Apr. 1973): 12.

AJC Association des Journalistes de la Consommation. 89 rue La Boétie, 75008 Paris, France. Established in 1971. Association of journalists.

AJEF Association des Journalistes Économiques et Financiers. 93 rue de Rivoli, 75001 Paris, France. Association of journalists.

AJL Association of Jewish Libraries. c/o Jewish Division, Rm. 84, The New York Public Library, Fifth Ave. & 42 St, New York, NY 10018. Formed in 1966 by merger of the Jewish Librarians Association and the Jewish Library Association. Publishes *AJL Bulletin* and other documents.

AKB Arbeitsgemeinschaft der Kunstbibliotheken (Working Group of Art Libraries). Bibliotheca Hertziana, Via Gregoriana 28, I-00187 Rome, Italy. Established in 1964. Coordinates activities of German art libraries and those in Berlin, Cologne, Florence, Munich, Nuremberg and Rome.

AKTHB Arbeitsgemeinschaft Katholisch-Theologischer Bibliotheken (Working Group of Catholic Theological Libraries). c/o Erzbischöfliche Akademische Bibliothek, Leostrasse 21, D-4790 Paderborn, Federal Republic of Germany. Established in 1947.

AKWIC Author and Keyword in Context. An index tested by *Applied Mechanics Review* which adds the author's name as an additional keyword. *See* S. Juhasz et al. "AKWIC," in *Applied Mechanics Review Report No. 53*. San Antonio, TX: 1969.

AL *American Libraries*. (Journal). V. 1, 1970. Published by ALA (American Library Association). Formerly *ALA Bulletin*.

ALA Afghan Library Association. University Library, Kabul, Afghanistan. Established in 1971.

ALA Alabama Library Association. Contact president or ALA (American Library Association).

ALA Alaska Library Association. Contact president or ALA (American Library Association).

ALA American Library Association. 50 East Huron St, Chicago, IL 60611. Established in 1876.

ALA Arizona Library Association. Contact president or ALA (American Library Association).

ALA Arkansas Library Association. Contact president or ALA (American Library Association).

ALADIN Automation of Agricultural Information and Documentation. Center for Agricultural Publishing and Documentation, Box 4, Wageningen, the Netherlands. A feasibility study of mechanized SDI search potential for agricultural research and development information.

ALAI Association Litteraire et Artistique Internationale. Hôtel du Cercle de la Libraire, 117 boulevard Saint-Germain, Paris 6, France.

ALAN Assembly on Literature for Adolescents. Dept. of Education, Technology, and Library Science, College of Education, Arizona State University, Tempe, AZ 85281.

ALAS Army Library Automated System. US Dept. of Army, Army Library, 1A518, The Pentagon, Washington, DC 20310. Ongoing project to mechanize functions of the Army Library in response to staff reductions and increased demands for services.

ALAS Automatic Literature Alerting Service.

ALBO Albo Dept Avvocati i Procuratori. Centro Elettronica di Documentazione-Italgiure, Corte Suprema di Cassaziono, Palazzo di Giustizia, Via Ulpiano 8, Rome 00193, Italy. Data base covering names of Italian attorneys.

ALCAPP Automatic List Classification and Profile Production.

ALCL Association of London Chief Librarians. Central Library, Oakfield Rd, Ilford, Essex, England.

ALCOM Algebraic Compiler. A mathematical program compiler for use on the Bendix G-20 automatic data processing system.

ALD *American Library Directory*. New York: R. R. Bowker Co, 1923– . An annual publication.

ALD Analog Line Driver. Power amplifier used on analog computer.

ALEBCI Asociación Latinoamericana de Escuelas de Bibliotecología y Ciencias de la Información (Latin American Library Schools Association). Contact president. Established in 1970. Affiliated with IFLA.

ALECS Automated Law Enforcement Communication System.

ALEJ Association Luxembourgeoise des Éditeurs de Journaux. 6 rue Jean Origer, Case Postale 1908, Luxembourg. Established in 1948. Member of the International Federation of Newspaper Publishers.

ALERB Asociación Latinoamericana de Redactores de Revistas Biológicas. Escuela de Ciencias Biológicas, Instituto Politecnico Nacional, Mexico, DF, Mexico.

ALERT Alternatives for Learning through Educational Research and Technology. West Laboratory for Educational Research and Development, Berkeley, CA. A project funded by USOE in 1970. Developed a model linkage system with educational information consultants. *See* Bela H. Banathy. "The Design, Development and Validation of an Instructional System for the Training of Educational Information Consultants." *Proceedings of ASIS* 8 (1971): 159–165.

ALERT Automated Linguistic Extraction and Retrieval Technique. A technique for indexing and retrieval of textual information developed for use on the Ramo Wooldridge 400 computer.

ALERTS Associated Library and Educational Research Team for Survival. Media Center T-1, Federal City College, 425 Second St, NW, Washington, DC 20001. A group formed by the inmates of the Lorton correctional complex in Washington, DC. The basic goal is to provide prisoners with materials which encourage their social, ethnic and political consciousness.

ALF Audiographic Learning Facility. A self-instruction system used at the School of Information and Computer Science of the Georgia Institute of Technology.

ALGOL Algorithmic Language (Algorithmic Oriented Language). Computer language developed by an international committee and widely used for programming mathematical problems.

ALHRT American Library History Round Table. Contact ALA (American Library Association).

ALI Associazione Librai Italiani (Italian Booksellers Association). Piazza G G Belli 2, 00153 Rome, Italy. Publishes documents.

ALIN *Agricultural Libraries Information Notes*. (Journal). V. 1, 1975. Name changed to *Agricultural Situation* in 1975. Published by the US Science and Education Administration, Technical Information Systems.

ALIS Arid Lands Information System. University of Arizona, 845 North Park Ave, Tucson, AZ 85721.

ALJ *Australian Library Journal.* V. 1, 1952. Published by LAA (Library Association of Australia).

ALLC Association of Literary and Linguistic Computing. Contact secretary.

ALLCeD Association of Library and Learning Center Directors. c/o Oklahoma Christian College, Rte. 1, Box 141, Oklahoma City, OK 73111. Eleven libraries cooperate to promote library and learning resource programs and to uphold high standards.

ALMA Association of Literary Magazines of America. 489 Second Ave, New York, NY 10016.

ALMIDS Army Logistics Management Integrated Data System. A data system used by the US Army.

ALP Academic Library Program. 1527 New Hampshire Ave, NW, Washington, DC 20036. A project of ARL Office of Management Studies designed to help academic libraries improve their effectiveness through self-study programs. Started in 1978.

ALP American Library in Paris. Paris, France.

ALPAC Automatic Language Processing Advisory Committee. A committee of the NAS's National Research Council. Published a report on machine translation in the US. *See* Automatic Language Advisory Committee. *Language and Machine: Computers in Translation and Linguistics.* Washington, DC: NAS–NRC, 1966.

ALPC Australian Library Promotion Council. State Library of Victoria, 324 Swanston St, Melbourne, Australia.

ALPHA Automated Literature Processing, Handling, and Analysis System. Redstone Scientific Information Center, US Army Missile Command, Redstone Arsenal, AL 35809. *See* Caryl McAllister. "On-line Library Housekeeping Systems." *Special Libraries* 62 (Nov. 1971): 457–468.

ALPS Advanced Linear Programming System. Operations research technique developed by Honeywell.

ALPS Automated Library Processing System. An SDC (System Development Corporation) library support system.

ALS American Library Society. This society has been terminated.

ALSA Area Library Service Authority. *See* ALSAs.

ALSAI Area Library Service Authorities of Indiana. *See* ALSAs.

ALSAs Area Library Service Authorities. Indiana State Library, Extension Division, 140 North Senate, Indianapolis, IN 46204. A network of cooperative Indiana libraries grouped within 10 service "areas," which correspond to the state's planning and development "regions."

ALSC Association for Library Service to Children. 50 East Huron St, Chicago, IL 60611. A division of ALA (American Library Association). Formerly CSD.

ALSEP Apollo Lunar Surface Experimental Package. Provides a mechanism for rapid retrieval of information. A NASA project.

ALSO Area Library Service Organizations of Ohio. Consortium of the Ohio Valley Libraries.

ALTA Alberta Library Trustees Association. Contact president. A Canadian association.

ALTA American Library Trustee Association. 50 East Huron St, Chicago, IL 60611. Established in 1961. Division of ALA (American Library Association).

ALTA Australian Library Technicians Association. GPO Box 313B, Melbourne, Victoria 3001, Australia.

ALTAC Algebraic Translator and Compiler. Programming language translator developed by the Philco Corp.

ALTRAN A language for symbolic algebraic manipulation in FORTRAN, developed by Bell Laboratories.

ALU Arithmetic and Logical Unit. The section of a computer which contains the circuits that perform arithmetic and similar operations.

AM *Abstracts of Mycology.* V. 1, 1967. Abstracts from *BA (Biological Abstracts)* and *BioResearch Index* pertaining to fungi, lichen and fungicides. Published by BioSciences Information Service.

AM Amplitude Modulation. A method of modulating the amplitude of a sine wave signal in order to make it carry information.

AMA American Management Associations. 135 West 50 St, New York, NY 10020. Established in 1923. Conducts conferences, maintains a library and publishes numerous journals and reports.

AMA American Medical Association. 535 North Dearborn St, Chicago, IL 60611. Established in 1847. Publishes documents.

AMACUS Automated Microfilm Aperture Card Update System. A system that permits a microfilm aperture card to become the primary unit of storage in an engineering drawing system.

AMBAC Asociación Mexicana de Bibliotecarios, A. C. (Mexican Association of Librarians). Apartado Postal 27-132, Mexico 7, DF, Mexico. Established in 1924 as Asociación de Bibliotecarios Mexicanos. Reactivated in 1954 under the present name.

AMBIT A programming language for algebraic symbol manipulation.

AMCOS Aldermaston Mechanized Cataloging and Ordering System. Atomic Energy Authority, Atomic Weapons Research Establishment, Aldermaston, Berkshire, England. Designed to implement a mechanized system for routine library procedures. The system produces MARC-style catalog records with punched cards that can be used for a number of purposes. Magnetic tape transfer was complete in 1970 and will eventually use an on-line computer system.

AMD Air Movement Data. Flight plan data used in reckoning aircraft movement.

AME Automatic Microfiche Editor.

AMEAS Asociación Mexicana de Educación Agricola Superior (Mexican Association for Agricultural Higher Education). Mariano Escobedo 375-1005, Mexico 5, DF, Mexico. Publishes directories.

AMERSERBI Agencia Metropolitanado Servicios Bibliotecarios. A plan

proposed in 1974 for the public libraries of Caracas, Venezuela.

AMETS American Meteorological Society. 45 Beacon St, Boston, MA 02108. Established in 1919. A member of NFAIS. Publishes journals, monographs and books.

AMF American Machine and Foundry, Inc. 689 Hope St, Stamford, CT 06907. Maintains a library and publishes documents.

AMFC Associated Mid-Florida Colleges. Stetson University, Library, Woodland Blvd, Deland, FL 32720. Library Affairs Section uses electronic data processing to facilitate cooperative exchange of materials.

AMFIS Automatic Microfilm Information System.

AMHS American Material Handling Society. Name changed to IMMS (International Material Management Society) in 1969.

AMIC Aerospace Materials Information Center. Rms. 47-48, Bldg 652, Area B, Wright-Patterson AFB, OH 45433. This library is part of the US Air Force Materials Laboratory. Formerly the University of Dayton Research Institute Air Force Materials Laboratory Information Center.

AMIDS Area Manpower Institutes for the Development of Staffs. Funded by DHEW to conduct training programs, particularly in the occupational/technical areas. Project was started in 1971 and terminated in 1973.

AMLAC Annual Medical Library Association Conference Committee. Contact MLA (Medical Library Association).

AMLI Americans for a Music Library in Israel. This association has been terminated.

AMLN Arizona Medical Library Network. University of Arizona College of Medicine, Tucson, AZ 85721. Project started 1970. Sponsored by the Arizona Regional Medical Program.

AMMINET Automated Mortgage Management Information Network.

AMMLA American Merchant Marine Library Association. One World Trade Center, Suite 2601, New York, NY 10048. Established in 1921. Provides free on-board library services to officers and crews of US vessels.

AMPA American Medical Publishers Association. Little, Brown and Co, 34 Beacon St, Boston, MA 02106. Established in 1961. Formerly Association of American Medical Book Publishers.

AMPL A Macro Programming Language.

AMPLO Administrators of Medium Public Libraries of Ontario. Contact chairperson. A Canadian association.

AMPP Advanced Microprogrammable Processor.

AMR Advanced Management Research. AMR International, Inc, 280 Park Ave, New York, NY 10017.

AMR Automatic Message Routing. Automatic directing of incoming messages to one or more outgoing circuits according to the content of the message.

AMRA American Medical Record Association. John Hancock Center, Suite 1850, 875 North Michigan Ave, Chicago, IL 60611. Established in 1928. Formerly (1938) AAMRL. Maintains a library and publishes a journal, newsletters and other materials.

AMS American Mathematical Society. Box 6248, Providence, RI 02904. Established in 1888. Publishes documents.

AMSAA Ambulance and Medical Services Association of America. Established in 1963. Name changed to American Ambulance Association.

AMTCL Association for Machine Translation and Computational Linguistics. Name changed to ACL (Association for Computational Linguistics) in 1968.

AMTRAN Automatic Mathematical Translation.

AMVER Atlantic Merchant Vessel Report. An IBM 305 Romoc in New York City; used to keep track of ships from 55 nations.

AMWA American Medical Writers Association. 5272 River Rd, Suite 290, Bethesda, MD 20016. Established in 1940.

AMWS *American Men and Women of Science*. 14th Edition. New York, NY: R. R. Bowker Co, 1979.

ANA Automated Naval Architecture.

ANABA Asociación Nacional de Bibliotecarios, Archiveros y Arqueólogos (National Association of Librarians, Archivists and Archeologists). Paseo Calvo Sotelo 22, Madrid 1, Spain. Established in 1949. Affiliated with IFLA.

ANAI Associazione Nazionale Archivistica Italiana (National Association of Italian Archivists). Viale Trastevere 215, 00153 Rome, Italy. Established in 1949.

ANB *Australian National Bibliography*. V. 1, 1961. Published by the National Library of Australia.

ANBADS Association Nationale des Bibliothécaires, Archivistes et Documentalistes Sénégalais (National Association of Librarians, Archivists and Documentalists of Senegal). École de Bibliothécaires, Archivistes et Documentalistes de Dakar (EBAD), Box 3252, Dakar, Senegal. Established in 1975.

ANBAI *Anuario de Bibliotecologia, Archivologia e Informatica*. Annual publication of the faculty of philosophy and letters of UNAM, Mexico City. Third series started in 1972.

ANBEF Association Nationale des Bibliothécaires d'Expression Française (National Association of French-Speaking Librarians). 56 rue de la Station, 5370 Havelange, Belgium. Established in 1964. Affiliated with IFLA.

ANC Academia Nacional de Ciencias. Apardo Postal 7798, Mexico.

ANCCAC Australian National Committee on Computation and Automatic Control. Part of ACS (Australian Computer Society).

ANCIRS Automated News Clipping, Indexing, and Retrieval System.

ANDBP Association Nationale pour le Développement des Bibliothèques

Publiques (National Association for the Development of Public Libraries). Secretariat, 107 rue Vercingétorix, F-75014 Paris, France. Established in 1971.

ANEC Associazione Nazionale Esercenti Cinema. Via di Villa Patrizi 10, 00161 Rome, Italy. Established in 1947. Association of film exhibitors.

ANEDA Association Nationale d'Études pour la Documentation Automatique (National Association of Automatic Documentation Studies). France.

ANFA Allied Non-theatrical Film Association. 303 Lexington Ave, New York, NY 10016.

ANICA Associazione Nazionale Industrie Cinematografiche ed Affini. Viale Regina Margherita 286, 00198 Rome, Italy. Publishes documents. Membership composed of organizations of film producers, film distributors and technical services.

ANIPLA Associazione Nazionale Italiana per l'Automazione. Piazza Belgioioso 1, 20121 Milan, Italy. Member of IFAC. Publishes documents.

ANIRC Annual National Information Retrieval Colloquium. Sponsored by several regional associations and library and information science schools through 1975, when it took the name Benjamin Franklin Colloquium on Information Science to reflect its local character. Held in Philadelphia. Also known as NIRC.

ANJIM Association Nationale des Journalistes d'Information Médicale. 23 boulevard de Latour-Maubourg, 75007 Paris, France. Established in 1970. Association of medical journalists. Publishes documents.

ANNA Automazione nella Nazionale di Firenze. A project of the Italian National Bibliography.

ANPA American Newspaper Publishers Association. 11600 Sunrise Valley Dr, Reston, VA 22091. Established in 1887. Maintains a research laboratory and library.

ANRT Association National de la Recherche Technique. One of the cosponsors of EURIM 3 (Munich, 1978).

ANS American Name Society. State University College, Potsdam, NY 13676.

ANS American National Standards. The standards adopted by ANSI.

ANS American Nuclear Society. 555 North Kensington Ave, LaGrange Park, IL 60525. Established in 1954. Forty-five local sections and 54 student branches. Publishes *Nuclear Science and Engineering, Nuclear News, Nuclear Applications* and other journals.

ANSA *Automatic New Structure Alert* (Journal). V. 1, 1972. Index published by ISI (Institute for Scientific Information).

ANSCR Alpha-Numerical System for Classification of Recordings.

ANSI American National Standards Institute. 1430 Broadway, New York, NY 10018. Publishes a catalog of standards, an annual and other serials. Formerly (1969) USASI and (1966) American Standards Association.

ANSI/SPARC ANSI Standards Planning and Requirements Committee. A committee of ANSI, established in 1972, which initiated an ad hoc Study Group on Data Base Management Systems referred to as ANSI/X3/SPARC/SGDBMS.

ANSI/X3/SPARC/SGDBMS. ANSI/SPARC Study Group on Data Base Management Systems. An ad hoc study group of ANSI/SPARC.

ANSI-Z39 American National Standards Institute–Standards Committee Z39. ANSI committee on library work, documentation and related publishing practices. Sponsored by CNLIA.

ANSLICS Aberdeen and North of Scotland Library and Information Cooperative Service.

ANSTEL Australian National Scientific and Technological Library. National Library of Australia, Canberra, Australia.

ANTS Anthropology Section. *See* ACRL/ANTS.

ANYLTS Association of New York Libraries for Technical Services. Established in 1967 by representatives of 22 public library systems utilizing data processing equipment for acquisitions, cataloging and processing operations. Terminated for lack of funds in 1972.

ANZAAS Australian and New Zealand Association for the Advancement of Science. Contact president.

AOA American Optometric Association. 243 North Lindbergh Blvd, Saint Louis, MO 63141. Publishes documents.

AOA American Ordnance Association. Became American Defense Preparedness Association in 1973.

AOAC Association of Official Agricultural Chemists. Name changed to AOAC (Association of Official Analytical Chemists).

AOAC Association of Official Analytical Chemists. 1111 North 19th St, Arlington, VA 22209. Established in 1884. Formerly AOAC (Association of Official Agricultural Chemists). Publishes a journal and numerous reference works.

AOCS American Oil Chemists Society. 508 South Sixth St, Champaign, IL 61820. Established in 1909. Publishes documents.

AOSP Automatic Operating and Scheduling Program. Automatically assigns memory locations, thus eliminating the need for the programmer to keep track of instruction or data locations.

AOTE Associated Organizations of Teachers of English. Contact president. Concerned with library-related continuing education.

AP Academic Press, Inc. 111 Fifth Ave, New York, NY 10003. Publishes scientific, technical, medical and scholarly books and journals.

AP Associated Press. An international news-gathering agency subscribed to by many newspapers.

AP Associative Processor.

APA American Pharmaceutical Association. 2215 Constitution Ave, NW, Washington, DC 20037. Established in 1852. Compiler of the *National Formulary*; involved in information activities in pharmaceutical sciences.

APA American Photoengravers Association. Merged with GEA to form APA (American Photoplatemakers Association) in 1969.

APA American Photoplatemakers Association. 105 West Adams St, Chicago, IL 60603. Formed by the merger of GEA and APA (American Photoengravers Association) in 1969. Publishes documents.

APA American Planning Association. 1313 East 60 St, Chicago, IL 60637. Established in 1978 through the merger of ASPO and the American Institute of Planners. Publishes documents.

APA American Psychological Association. 1200 17th St, NW, Washington, DC 20036. Established in 1892. Publishes documents and numerous journals, bulletins, newspapers and directories.

APADI Asosiasi Perpustakaan Arsip dan Dokumentasi Indonesia (Indonesian Library, Archive and Documentation Association). Established in 1962. Joined HPCI in 1973 to become IPI (Ikatan Pustakawan Indonesia).

APA-PSIP APA Project on Scientific Information in Psychology. This APA (American Psychological Association) project resulted in a series of publications and reports during the period 1961-1970.

APAR Automatic Programming and Recording. An automatic programming technique developed by Sandia Corp. Also a type of compiler.

APB Arbeitsgemeinschaft Pädagogischer Bibliotheken und Medienzentren (Working Group of Educational Libraries and Media Centers). Rheinlanddamm 199, 46 Dortmund, Federal Republic of Germany. Established in 1958. Publishes documents and sponsors conferences. Member of VDB.

APB Associação Paulista de Bibliotecários (São Paulo Library Association). Avenida Ipiranga 877, 9 andar, sala 93, Caixa Postal 343, CEP 01039 São Paulo, Brazil. Established in 1938. Member of FEBAB, FID and IFLA. Publishes documents; sponsors seminars, workshops, and Book Week; gives scholarships to students of library science; and holds joint conferences with related organizations.

APBEG Associação Profissional de Bibliotecários do Estado da Guanabara (Professional Association of Librarians in Guanabara). Contact president. Established in 1949. Affiliated with IFLA.

APBSM Association des Préposés aux Bibliothèques Scolaires de Montréal.

APCA Air Pollution Control Association. Box 2861, Pittsburgh, PA 15230. Established in 1907. Publishes numerous journals, manuals and books on air pollution. Maintains a library. Associate society of EJC.

APCS Associative Processor Computer System.

APDL Algorithmic Processor Description Language. A programming language.

APEL Associação Portuguesa dos Editores e Liveiros (Portuguese Association of Publishers and Booksellers). Largo de Andaluz 16-1, Lisbon 1, Portugal. Established in 1940. Publishes documents.

APER Association of Publishers Educational Representatives. 23 Lynton Gardens, Harrogate, Yorkshire, England.

APET Application Program Evaluator Tool.

APFAV/VSFAV Association des Producteurs Suisses de Films et de Production Audio-Visuelle (Association of Swiss Film and Audio-Visual Producers). *See* VSFAV/APFAV.

APFS *Asia/Pacific Forecasting Study*. New York: Business International Corp. Medium-term economic forecasts for 12 major countries of the area.

APG Association for Precision Graphics. Formerly Precision Plotter Users Association. This association has been terminated.

APGA American Public Gas Association. 2600 Virginia Ave, NW, Washington, DC 20037. Provides information service on federal developments affecting natural gas and conducts surveys of municipal systems. Publishes documents.

APH American Printing House for the Blind. 1839 Frankfort Ave, Box 6085, Louisville, KY 40206. Established in 1858. Oldest national agency for the visually handicapped in the United States.

APHA American Printing History Association. Box 4922, Grand Central Sta, New York, NY 10017.

APHA American Public Health Association. 1015 18th St, NW, Washington, DC 20036. Established in 1872. Official journal, *American Journal of Public Health*, reviews books and periodically publishes bibliographies.

API American Paper Institute. 260 Madison Ave, New York, NY 10016. Established in 1964. Gathers, compiles and disseminates information. Conducts research on scientific and technical problems. Publishes several periodicals on the pulp and paper industry. Supersedes (1964) APPA (American Pulp and Paper Association) and NPA (National Paperboard Association). Formerly (1966) PPPI (Pulp, Paper and Paperboard Institute).

API American Petroleum Institute. 2101 L St, NW, Washington, DC 20037. Established in 1919. Provides publications and information services and maintains a library.

APICS American Production and Inventory Control Society. Watergate Bldg, Suite 504, 2600 Virginia Ave, NW, Washington, DC 20037. Established in 1957. Publishes documents.

APILIT *API Abstracts/Literature*. American Petroleum Institute, 275 Madison Ave, New York, NY 10011. Coverage from 1964. Bibliographic data base covering petroleum refining and related sciences.

APIN Automatyzacja Przetwarzania Informacji Naukowej. Technical University of Wroclaw, Central Library and Scientific Information Center, Wybrzeze Wyspianskiego 27, 50-370 Wroclaw, Poland, Automation system for library and information processes based on MARC II.

APIPAT *API Abstracts/Patents*. American Petroleum Institute, 275 Madison Ave, New York, NY 10011. Coverage from 1964. Bibliographic data base covering patents in the field of petroleum refining.

APL A Programming Language. A general but unimplemented computer language.

APL Association for Programmed Learning. 27 Tarrington Sq, London WC1, England.

APLA American Patent Law Association. 2001 Jefferson Davis Hwy, Arlington, VA 22202. Established in 1897. Concerned with patents, trademarks and copyrights. Publishes journals and maintains a library.

APLA Arrowhead Professional Libraries Association. c/o Miller-Dwan Hospital and Medical Center, 502 East Second St, Duluth, MN 55805. Seventeen academic, medical and special libraries cooperate through ILL, reference help, photocopying, CE, collection development and acquisitions.

APLA Atlantic Provinces Library Association. c/o School of Library Service, Dalhousie University, Halifax NS B3H 4H8, Canada.

APLIC Association for Population/Family Planning Libraries and Information Centers. APLIC Secretary, 165 South Second Ave, Clarion, PA 16214. Established in 1968. Affiliated with ASIS and MLA (Medical Library Association).

APLIC Association of Parliamentary Librarians in Canada. Contact president.

APME Automated Processing of Medical English. *See* A. W. Pratt and M. G. Pasak. "Automated Processing of Medical English." *International Conference on Computational Linguistics*, Sept. 1–4, 1969, Stockholm, Sweden.

APP Advanced Placement Program. College Entrance Examination Board, 888 Seventh Ave, New York, NY 10019. Libraries often provide special services to aid those participating in this program.

APPA American Public Power Association. 2600 Virginia Ave, NW, Washington, DC 20037. Established in 1940. Publishes documents and maintains a library.

APPA American Pulp and Paper Association. Established in 1878. Superseded in 1964 by API (American Paper Institute).

APPCB Association Professionnelle de la Presse Cinématographique Belge. International Press Center, Maison de la Presse, Boulevard Charlemagne 1, 1040 Brussels, Belgium. Established in 1925. Association of journalists.

APPLE Associative Processor Programming Language.

APRO Aerial Phenomena Research Organization. 3910 East Kleindale Rd, Tucson, AZ 85712. Established in 1952. Maintains a library and publishes a bulletin.

APROC Adaptive Statistical Processor.

APS American Physical Society. 335 East 45 St, New York, NY 10017. Established in 1899. Publishes *Physical Review, Reviews of Modern Physics* and *Bulletin of the American Physical Society*.

APSE *Abstracts of Photographic Science and Engineering Literature*. V. 1–8, 1962–1969. Published by the Society of Photographic Scientists and Engineers, Washington, DC.

APT Automatic Picture Transmission.

APT Automatic Programmed Tool. A programming language developed by Sperry Rand and the Aerospace Industry of America to control the movement of machine tools.

APT Automatically Programmed Tools. Program used to cut straight lines as short as 1/1000th of an inch.

APT III Automatic Programmed Tool III. An extension of APT developed by Sperry Rand for use on the UNIVAC 1107 computer.

APTA American Public Transit Association. 1100 17th St, NW, Washington, DC 20036. Formed in 1974 by the merger of ATA (American Transit Association) and the Institute for Rapid Transit. Publishes documents.

APTIC Air Pollution Technical Information Center. Manpower and Technical Information Branch, EPA, NC Rte. 54 & Alexander Dr, Research Triangle Park, NC 27711. On-line bibliographic data base covering literature on all aspects of air pollution from 1966 to 1972.

AQL Acceptable Quality Level.

AR Arithmetic Register. A temporary storage location in a computer involved in all transfers of data and instructions in either direction between memory and the arithmetic and control registers.

ARAC Aerospace Research Applications Center. Indiana University, Poplars Research and Conference Center, 400 East Seventh St, Bloomington, IN 47401. Goal is to make existing scientific and technical knowledge more useful to industry.

ARBED Acieries Réunies de Burbach-Eich-Dudelange. Bibliothèque Technique de l'Administration Centrale de l'ARBED, 19 avenue de la Liberté, Luxembourg. Established in 1952.

ARBICA Arab Regional Branch of the International Council on Archives. Contact CIA/ICA.

ARC Action and Referral Center. Somerville Public Library, Highland Ave. & Walnut St, Somerville, MA 02143. Program to integrate community and library services.

ARCHON Archives On-line. Baltimore Region Institutional Studies Center, 847 North Howard St, Baltimore, MD 21201. An on-line information storage and retrieval system.

ARDIS Army Research and Development Information System. A system of the US Department of the Army.

ARE Association for Research and Enlightenment. Edgar Cayce Foundation Library, Box 595, Virginia Beach, VA 23451. Established in 1931. Maintains a library and publishes a journal.

AREA Association of Records Executives and Administrators. Merged with ARMA (American Records Management Association) in 1975 to form ARMA (Association of Records Managers and Administrators).

ARF Advertising Research Foundation. 3 East 54 St, New York, NY 10022. Established in 1936. Publishes documents. Maintains a library and conducts research.

ARGUS Automatic Routine Generating and Updating System. An integrated automatic programming system for Honeywell computers comprising automatic inclusion of library tapes and routines, file maintenance of a library of unchecked programs, a checkout system and a production scheduling and operating system.

ARI Agricultural Research Institute. Zirai Arastirma Enstitusu, Nicosia 115, Ministry of Agriculture and Natural Resources, Cyprus. Maintains an information center.

ARISE Adult Referral and Information Service in Education. 396 Smith St, Providence, RI 02908. Data base covering reports and surveys in adult education from 1966 to 1970.

ARIST *Annual Review of Information Science and Technology*. Carlos A. Cuadra, ed. White Plains, NY: Knowledge Industry Publications, 1966– . Published by KIP for ASIS.

ARJA Association Suisse Romande des Journalistes de l'Aéronautique et de l'Astronautique. c/o René Hug, Case Postale 52, 1211 Geneva 28, Switzerland. Established in 1971. Association of journalists.

ARL Association of Research Libraries. 1527 New Hampshire Ave, NW, Washington, DC 20036. Established in 1932. A consortium of 105 academic, public and special libraries in the US and Canada. Publishes documents.

ARLIS Art Libraries Society. Contact secretary or ARLIS/NA. Established in 1969. Publishes *ARLIS Newsletter. See* Clive Phillpot. "ARLIS—The Art Libraries' Society." *Library Association Record* 74 (Jan. 1972): 5-6.

ARLIS/ANZ ARLIS Australia New Zealand. Contact president or ARLIS/NA.

ARLIS/NA ARLIS North America. 7735 Old Georgetown Rd, Washington, DC 20014. Established in 1972. Publishes documents and bimonthly *ARLIS/NA Newsletter. See* "ARLIS/NA Conference: Growth, Gains Reported." *Library Journal* 99 (Apr. 15, 1974): 1088-1090.

ARLO Art Research Libraries of Ohio. Ohio State University, Fine Arts Library, 1813 North High St, Columbus, OH 43210.

ARM Abstracts of Research and Related Materials in Vocational and Technical Education. V. 1, 1967. ARM merged with AIM (Abstracts of Instructional Materials in Vocational and Technical Education) in 1974 to form AIM/ARM.

ARM Archival Records Management System. A stand-alone computer unit that manages and controls inactive records stored at off-site storage facilities. Designed by Index Systems and first installed in 1977 at Citibank, N.A., in New York City.

ARM Automated Route Manager. IBM computer program designed to control sales and production reports.

ARMA American Records Management Association. Merged with AREA in 1975 to form ARMA (Association of Records Managers and Administrators).

ARMA Association of Records Managers and Administrators. Box 281, Bradford, RI 02808. Formed in 1975 by the merger of AREA and ARMA (American Records Management Association). Publishes documents.

ARMIS Agricultural Research Management Information System.

ARPAC Agricultural Research Policy Advisory Committee. Symposium held in Washington, DC, Feb. 10–12, 1970, on ASIN. Established a task force to implement EDUCOM's "Agricultural Sciences Information Network Development Plan."

ARPL A Retrieval Process Language.

ARQ Automatic Request (for Correction). An automatic system which provides error correction by utilizing a constant ratio code and a closed loop to request retransmission of mutilated characters as indicated by receipt of nonconstant ratio characters.

ARRL American Radio Relay League. 225 Main St, Newington, CT 06111. Established in 1914. Publishes *QST* and *Radio Amateur's Handbook*.

ARS American Recorder Society. 141 West 20 St, New York, NY 10011. Established in 1939. Publishes documents.

ARS Automated Retrieval System.

ARSC Association for Recorded Sound Collections. Fine Arts Library, University of New Mexico, Albuquerque, NM 87131. Established in 1966. Aim is to communicate with libraries, recording archives and collectors and to act as a central information center.

ART ADMIRAL Run Tape. *See* SPAR.

ARTS Art Section. *See* ACRL/ARTS.

ARU Audio Response Unit. A computer-controlled device that can generate voice messages for telephone transmission. Each message is normally made up of a series of prerecorded units.

AS Acquisitions Section. *See* RTSD/AS.

AS [Aerospace Standards]. Prefix to Aerospace Standards issued by SAA (Standards Association of Australia).

AS Archives Section. *See* CLA/AS.

ASA Acoustical Society of America. 335 East 45 St, New York, NY 10017. Established in 1929. Publishes documents and standards. Affiliated with AIP (American Institute of Physics).

ASA American Standards Association. Name changed to ANSI (American National Standards Institute) in 1969.

ASA American Statistical Association. 806 15th St, NW, Washington, DC 20005. Established in 1839. Constituent society of AFIPS.

ASAE American Society of Association Executives. 1101 16th St, NW, Washington, DC 20036. Established in 1920. Maintains a library. Publishes documents. Formerly American Trade Association Executives.

ASAIHL Association of Southeast Asian Institutions of Higher Learning. Contact president.

AS&T *Applied Science and Technology Index*. V. 1, 1958. Published by H. W. Wilson Co.

ASC Advanced Science Computer.

ASC American Society for Cybernetics. College of Education, University of Maryland, College Park, MD 20742. Established in 1964. Publishes documents.

ASC American Society of Cartographers. Box 1493, Louisville, KY 40201. Established in 1965.

ASC American Society of Cinematographers. 1782 North Orange Dr, Hollywood, CA 90028. Established in 1919. Publishes documents.

ASC Association Suisse des Critiques de Cinéma (Swiss Association of Film Critics). *See* VSF/ASC/ASC.

ASC Associazione Svizzera dei Critici Cinematografici (Swiss Association of Film Critics). *See* VSF/ASC/ASC.

ASCA American School Counselors Association. Contact AASL (American Association of School Librarians). A joint committee with AASL, which is a division of ALA (American Library Association).

ASCA Automatic Subject Citation Alert. Institute for Scientific Information, 325 Chestnut St, Philadelphia, PA 19106. Bibliographic searches provided on computer tape or in print.

ASCAP American Society of Composers, Authors, and Publishers. One Lincoln Pl, New York, NY 10023. Established in 1914. Grants licenses and collects fees and royalties for the public performance of the copyrighted musical works of its members by broadcasting stations and other users.

ASCD Association for Supervision and Curriculum Development. 1701 K St, NW, Suite 1100, Washington, DC 20006. Established in 1921. Publishes documents. Formerly Department of Supervision and Curriculum Development of NEA (National Education Association).

ASCE American Society of Civil Engineers. 345 East 47 St, New York, NY 10017. Established in 1852. Maintains an Engineering Societies Library. Member society of EJC. Source of standards for acronyms and abbreviations.

ASCII American Standard Code for Information Interchange. *See* USASCII.

ASCLA Association of Specialized and Cooperative Library Agencies. 50 East Huron St, Chicago, IL 60611. A division of ALA (American Library Association). Formed September 1, 1978, by the merger of two ALA divisions—ASLA (Association of State Library Agencies) and HRLSD (Health and Rehabilitative Library Services)—and an affiliate organization, ACLO.

ASCLA/HCLS ASCLA Health Care Libraries Section. Contact ASCLA. A

section of ASCLA, which is a division of ALA (American Library Association).

ASCLA/LSBPHS ASCLA Library Service to the Blind and Physically Handicapped Section. Contact ASCLA. A section of ASCLA, which is a division of ALA (American Library Association).

ASCLA/LSDS ASCLA Library Service to the Deaf Section. Contact ASCLA. A section of ASCLA, which is a division of ALA (American Library Association).

ASCLA/LSIES ASCLA Library Services to the Impaired Elderly Section. Contact ASCLA. A section of ASCLA, which is a division of ALA (American Library Association).

ASCLA/LSPS ASCLA Library Services to Prisoners Section. Contact ASCLA. A section of ASCLA, which is a division of ALA (American Library Association).

ASCLA/MLCS ASCLA Multitype Library Cooperation Section. Contact ASCLA. A section of ASCLA, which is a division of ALA (American Library Association).

ASCLA/SLAS ASCLA State Library Agency Section. Contact ASCLA. A section of ASCLA, which is a division of ALA (American Library Association).

ASCOLBI Asociación Colombiana de Bibliotecarios (Colombian Library Association). Contact president. Established in 1956. Affiliated with IFLA.

ASCOM Analytico-Synthetic Classification of Medicine. Name changed to CASCUM.

ASCUFRO Association of State Colleges and Universities Forestry Research Organizations. Contact president.

ASD Adult Services Division. A division of ALA (American Library Association) that merged with RSD in 1972 to form RASD.

ASD Association Suisse de Documentation (Swiss Association of Documentation). *See* SVD/ASD.

ASDBAM Association Sénégalaise pour le Développement de la Documentation, des Bibliothèques, des Archives et des Musées (Senegal Association for the Development of Documentation,

Libraries, Archives and Museums). BP 375, Dakar, Senegal. Established in 1957.

ASDD Advanced Systems Development Division. IBM, Los Gatos, CA 95030. A division of IBM.

ASEAN Association of South East Asian Nations. c/o Indonesian Secretariat, 14 Merdeka Barat, Djakarta, Indonesia. Members are Indonesia, Malaysia, Philippines, Singapore and Thailand. Goal is to promote economic growth and social progress.

ASEE American Society for Engineering Education. One Dupont Circle, Suite 400, Washington, DC 20036. Established in 1893. Publishes documents.

ASEG Associazione Svizzera degli Editori di Giornali (Swiss Newspaper Publishers' Association). *See* SZV/ASEJ/ASEG.

ASEIB Asociación de Egresados de la Escuela Interamericana de Bibliotecología (Association of Graduates of the Interamerican Library School). In 1968, merged with CBC to become CCB (Colegio Colombiano de Bibliotecarios).

ASEJ Association Suisse des Éditeurs de Journaux (Swiss Newspaper Publishers' Association). *See* SZV/ASEJ/ASEG.

ASERL Association of Southeastern Research Libraries. c/o Louisiana State University Library, Baton Rouge, LA 70803. Twenty-nine member libraries promote cooperative activities.

ASFA American Science Film Association. 3624 Science Center, Philadelphia, PA 19104. Established in 1959. Publishes documents.

ASFA *Aquatic Sciences and Fisheries Abstracts*. V. 1, 1969. International venture with FAO. Published by Information Retrieval, Ltd. Abstracts from 1975 available on-line through Lockheed/DIALOG.

ASFP Association of Specialised Film Producers. 2 Brochier St, London W1, England.

ASGL Association of Saskatchewan Government Libraries. Box 754, Regina SK S4P 3A8, Canada.

ASHA American Social Health Association. 260 Sheridan Ave, Palo Alto, CA 94306. Established in 1912. Formerly American Social Hygiene Association. Publishes documents.

ASHP American Society of Hospital Pharmacists. 4630 Montgomery Ave, Washington, DC 20014. Developed and tested programs involving drug classification and coding and drug information and its dissemination.

ASI American Society of Indexers. Contact president. Established in 1968. Affiliated with the Society of Indexers.

ASI *American Statistics Index*. V. 1, 1973. Published by Congressional Information Service. Issued in two parts: Part 1, Index; Part 2, Abstracts.

ASICA Association Internationale pour le Calcul Analogique. 50 avenue Franklin D. Roosevelt, B-1050 Brussels, Belgium.

ASIDIC Association of Scientific Information Dissemination Centers. Name changed to AIDC in 1976.

ASIFA Association Internationale du Film d'Animation (International Animated Film Association). 21 rue de la Tour d'Auvergne, Paris 9, France.

ASIN Agricultural Sciences Information Network. National Agricultural Library, Beltsville, MD 20705. Started in 1970. Sponsored by NAL.

ASIRC Aquatic Sciences Information Retrieval Center. University of Rhode Island, Naragansett, RI 02882.

ASIS American Society for Information Science. 1010 16th St, NW, Washington, DC 20036. Established in 1937 as ADI. A constituent society of AFIPS and affiliated with ALA (American Library Association).

ASIS/SIG/AH ASIS Special Interest Group on Arts and Humanities. Contact ASIS.

ASIS/SIG/ALP ASIS Special Interest Group on Automated Language Processing. Contact ASIS.

ASIS/SIG/BC ASIS Special Interest Group on Biological and Chemical Information Systems. Contact ASIS.

ASIS/SIG/BSS ASIS Special Interest Group on the Behavioral and Social Sciences. Contact ASIS.

ASIS/SIG/CBE ASIS Special Interest Group on Costs Budgeting and Economics. Contact ASIS.

ASIS/SIG/CIS ASIS Special Interest Group on Community Information Services. Contact ASIS.

ASIS/SIG/CR ASIS Special Interest Group on Classification Research. Contact ASIS.

ASIS/SIG/CRS ASIS Special Interest Group on Computerized Retrieval Services. Contact ASIS.

ASIS/SIG/ED ASIS Special Interest Group on Education for Information Science. Contact ASIS.

ASIS/SIG/FIS ASIS Special Interest Group on Foundations of Information Science. Contact ASIS.

ASIS/SIG/IAC ASIS Special Interest Group on Information Analysis Centers. Contact ASIS.

ASIS/SIG/IP ASIS Special Interest Group on Information Publishing. Contact ASIS.

ASIS/SIG/ISE ASIS Special Interest Group on Information Services to Education. Contact ASIS.

ASIS/SIG/LAN ASIS Special Interest Group on Library Automation and Networks. Contact ASIS.

ASIS/SIG/LAW ASIS Special Interest Group on Law and Information Technology. Contact ASIS.

ASIS/SIG/MGT ASIS Special Interest Group on Management Information Activities. Contact ASIS.

ASIS/SIG/MR ASIS Special Interest Group on Medical Records. Contact ASIS.

ASIS/SIG/NDB ASIS Special Interest Group on Numerical Data Bases. Contact ASIS.

ASIS/SIG/NPM ASIS Special Interest Group on Non-Print Material. Contact ASIS.

ASIS/SIG/PPI ASIS Special Interest Group on Public-Private Interface. Contact ASIS.

ASIS/SIG/TIS ASIS Special Interest Group on Technology, Information, and Society. Contact ASIS.

ASIS/SIG/UOI ASIS Special Interest Group on User On-line Interaction. Contact ASIS.

ASIST Advanced Scientific Instruments Symbolic Translator. An assembly program developed by Advanced Scientific Instruments, Inc. Features assembly control, pseudo-operation and macrostatements.

ASIS/Wes-Can ASIS Western Canada Chapter. Contact ASIS.

ASJA Association Suisse des Journalistes Agricoles (Swiss Association of Agricultural Journalists). *See* SVAJ/ASJA.

ASJLP Association Suisse des Journalistes Libres Professionels (Swiss Association of Independent Professional Journalists). *See* SVFBJ/ASJLP.

ASK Aerospace Shared Knowledge. Aerospace Corp, Charles C. Lauritsen Library, Box 92957, Los Angeles, CA 90009. Goal is to develop an on-line, real-time, total library system using remote display consoles.

ASL Association for Symbolic Logic. Contact president or AMS. A part of AMS. Publishes documents.

ASLA Association of State Library Agencies. Merged into ASCLA in 1978.

ASLA Australian School Library Association. Box 118, Carlton 3053, Australia. Established in 1969. Publishes the quarterly *School Libraries in Australia* and other documents. *See* "The Australian School Library Association." *UNESCO Bulletin for Libraries* 24 (1970): 431–442.

ASLIB Association of Special Libraries and Information Bureaux. 3 Belgrave Sq, London SW1X 8PL, England. Established in 1924. Extensive publishing and research programs, including *LISA (Library and Information Science Abstracts)*. *See* "Aslib's Fiftieth Anniversary 1974." *UNESCO Bulletin for Libraries* 27 (July–Aug. 1974): 16–21. Also uses Aslib.

ASLP Association of Special Libraries of the Philippines. Box 4118, Manila, Republic of the Philippines. Established in 1954. Worked with PLA (Philippine Library Association) for professional certification of librarians.

ASLS Academic and Special Libraries Section. One of three sections of NLA (Nevada Library Association) established at the association's annual conference in 1972.

ASM American Society for Metals. Metals Park, OH 44073. Established in 1920. Publishes several journals, abstracts, etc., about metals and produces METALERT. Maintains a library.

ASM Association for Systems Management. 24587 Bagley Rd, Cleveland, OH 44138. Established in 1947. An international professional organization of administrative executives and specialists in management information systems work. Maintains a library. Formerly (1968) SPA (Systems and Procedures Association).

ASME American Society of Mechanical Engineers. 345 East 47 St, New York, NY 10017. Member society of EJC. Conducts research and maintains a library.

ASMI Associazione Stampa Medica Italiana. Via Aniello Falcone 428, 80127 Naples, Italy. Established in 1946. Association of journalists. ·

ASNE American Society of Naval Engineers. 1012 14th St, NW, Suite 807, Washington, DC 20005. Established in 1888. Publishes documents.

ASNIBI Asociación Nicaragüense de Bibliotecarios (Nicaraguan Library Association). Biblioteca Nacional, Ministerio de Educación Pública, Barrio "La Fuente," Managua, Republic of Nicaragua. Publishes a newsletter.

ASNT American Society for Nondestructive Testing. 3200 Riverside Dr, Columbus, OH 43221. Established in 1941. Maintains a library on radiography, magnetic testing, ultrasonics, etc. Publishes periodicals. Formerly (1947) American Industrial Radium and X-Ray Society, and (1969) SNT (Society for Nondestructive Testing).

ASODOBI Asociación Dominicana de Bibliotecarios (Dominican Association of Librarians). Biblioteca Nacional, Santo Domingo, Dominican Republic. Established in 1974. *See* Eugene W. Moushey. "Dominican Republic, Libraries in" in *Encyclopedia of Library and Information Science*, ed. by Allen Kent. New York: Marcel Dekker, 1972, V. 7, pp. 293–296.

ASP American Society for Photogrammetry. 105 North Virginia Ave, Falls Church, VA 22046. Established in 1934. Publishes documents. Provides technical information, maintains a library and offers a voluntary certification program.

ASP Archival Security Program. Box 8198, The Library, University of Illinois at Chicago Circle, Chicago, IL 60680. Established in 1975 by SAA (Society of American Archivists) for the prevention of theft through a register of stolen or missing manuscripts to alert dealers and librarians. Provides consultation and publications.

ASP Attached Support Processor. The utilization of multiple computers, usually two, connected via channel-to-channel adaptors, to increase the efficiency in processing many jobs of short duration.

ASpB Arbeitsgemeinschaft der Spezialbibliotheken (Association of Special Libraries in the Federal Republic of Germany). Senckenbergische Bibliothek, D-6 Frankfurt/Main, Federal Republic of Germany. Established in 1946.

ASPDA American Society of Professional Draftsmen and Artists. 415 Saint Paul Pl, Baltimore, MD 21202. Established in 1966. Publishes documents.

ASPEP Association of Scientists and Professional Engineering Personnel. 318 Cooper St, Camden, NJ 08102. Established in 1945. Publishes documents.

ASPER Assembly System for the Peripheral Processors. These CDC (Control Data Corporation) programs are separated by control cards which represent information to the loader for use at execute time, cause the system to assign a peripheral processor, and cause the ASPER routine to be loaded.

ASPIRE Access Service for Profitable Information Resource Exchanges. Emerald Valley Publishing Co, 2715 Terrace View Dr, Box 5537, Eugene, OR 97405. Established in 1977. Publishes *Encyclopedia of Information Marketing* and other documents.

ASPO American Society of Planning Officials. Established in 1934. Merged with the American Institute of Planners to form APA (American Planning Association) in 1978.

ASQC American Society for Quality Control. 161 West Wisconsin Ave, Milwaukee, WI 53203. Established in 1946. Publishes documents.

ASR Automatic Send-Receive Set. A combination teletypewriter, transmitter and receiver with transmission capability from either keyboard or paper tape. Most often used in half-duplex circuit.

ASRA Applied Science and Research Applications. Directorate for Applied Science and Research Applications, National Science Foundation, 1800 G St, NW, Washington, DC 20550. Identifies and supports research and related activities that may contribute to the understanding and resolution of significant national problems.

ASRT American Society of Radiologic Technologists. 500 North Michigan Ave, Chicago, IL 60611. Publishes documents.

ASSASSIN Agricultural System for Storage and Subsequent Selection of Information. Greater London Council, Dept. of Director General, County Hall, London SE1 7PB, England. A group of programs designed for batch processing.

ASSPA Association Suisse pour l'Automatique (Swiss Association for Automation). *See* SGA/ASSPA.

ASTAP Advanced Statistical Analysis Program. A computer program.

ASTD American Society for Training and Development. Box 5307, Madison, WI 53705. Established in 1944. Society of those who train business and government personnel. Publishes documents. Formerly American Society of Training Directors.

ASTED Association pour l'Avancement des Sciences et des Techniques de la Documentation (Association for the Advancement of the Science and Technology of Documentation). 360 rue Le Moyne, Montreal PQ H2Y 1Y3, Canada. Established in 1943. Formerly (1974) ACBLF. *See* G. A. Chartrand. "From ACBLF to ASTED." *Feliciter* 20 (Aug. 1974): 12–13.

ASTIA Armed Services Technical Information Agency. Formed in 1951 by the merger of CADO and LC's Navy Research Section. In March 1963, became DDC (Defense Documentation Center).

ASTM American Society for Testing and Materials. 1916 Race St, Philadelphia, PA 19103. Member society of EJC. Publishes documents.

ASTRA Automatic Scheduling and Time-dependent Resource Allocation.

ASTRID Association Scientifique et Technique pour la Recherche en Informatique Documentaire. Astrid House, Koningin Astridlaan, 9000 Ghent, Belgium.

ASXED American Society for X-Ray and Electron Diffraction. Merged with CSA (Crystallographic Society of America) to form ACA (American Crystallographic Association).

AT Audit Trail. A system that provides a means for tracing items of data through processing operations, particularly from a machine-produced report or other machine output, back to the original source data.

ATA Air Transport Association of America. 1709 New York Ave, NW, Washington, DC 20006. Publishes documents.

ATA American Transit Association. Merged in 1974 with the Institute for Rapid Transit to form APTA.

ATAA Advertising Typographers Association of America, Inc. 461 Eighth Ave, New York, NY 10001. Publishes documents. Involved in special printing.

ATAE Associated Telephone Answering Exchanges. Bankers' Sq, 100 Pitt St, Alexandria, VA 22314. Established in 1946. Aids member exchanges in negotiating with telephone companies. Publishes documents.

AT&T American Telephone and Telegraph Company. 195 Broadway, New York, NY 10007.

ATAS Association of Telephone Answering Services. 32 East 57 St, New York, NY 10022. Established in 1955. Membership concentrated in New York City.

ATAS/UCLA Academy of Television Arts and Sciences–University of California, Los Angeles–Television Archives. Theater Arts Dept, Melmitz Hall, Los Angeles, CA 90024. Library established in 1965.

ATCA Air Traffic Control Association. 525 School St, SW, Washington, DC 20024. Publishes documents.

ATD Aerospace Technology Division. A division of LC.

ATD Association Tunisienne des Documentalistes, Bibliothécaires et Archivistes (Tunisian Association of Documentalists, Librarians and Archivists). Institut Ali Bach Hawba, 2 rue de Champagne, Tunis, Tunisia. Established in 1965. Publishes documents. *See* "The Tunisian Library Association." *UNESCO Bulletin for Libraries* 19 (Jan. 1965): 54.

ATEMIS Automatic Traffic Engineering and Management Information System.

ATIC Associazione Tecnica Italiana per la Cinematografia. Viale Regina Margherita 286, 00198 Rome, Italy. Established in 1947 to promote the development of technical photographic equipment and professional training.

AT/L *Advanced Technology/Libraries*. (Journal). V. 1, 1971. Published by Knowledge Industry Publications.

ATLA American Theological Library Association, Inc. Lutheran Theological Seminary, 7301 Germantown Ave, Philadelphia, PA 19119. Established in 1947 and incorporated in 1973. Publishes *IRPL*. *See* Thomas E. Camp. "American Theological Library Association" in *Encyclopedia of Library and Information Science*, ed. by Allen Kent. New York: Marcel Dekker, 1968, V. 1, pp. 332–334.

ATLIS Army Technical Library Improvement Studies. Originally located at RSIC (Redstone Scientific Information Center). Became TISAP in 1968; terminated in 1974.

ATP Airline Tariff Publishers, Inc. Dulles International Airport, Chantilly, VA 22021. Publishes documents.

ATPI American Textbook Publishers Institute. *See* AEPI.

ATS Administrative Terminal System. A system developed by IBM to permit a typist to avoid the retyping of edited text by communicating with a computer in which the text is stored.

ATS American Technical Society. 848 East 58 St, Chicago, IL 60637. Publisher of educational texts and study guides.

ATS Application Technology Satellite. Used at NLM to communicate information.

ATS-1 Application Technology Satellite 1. National Library of Medicine, Lister Hill National Center for Biomedical Communications, 8600 Rockville Pike, Bethesda, MD 20209. Application Technology Satellite, a project implemented in cooperation with NASA, used voice communication to provide medical consultation in sparsely populated areas. *See also* ATS-6.

ATS-6 Application Technology Satellite 6. National Library of Medicine, Lister Hill National Center for Biomedical Communications, 8600 Rockville Pike, Bethesda, MD 20014. Application Technology Satellite 6 allows the addition of two-way video communication to the voice link established by ATS-1 to carry medical services to remote areas in Alaska.

ATSEEL American Association of Teachers of Slavic and East European Languages. *See* AATSEEL.

ATS-F Application Technology Satellite. An NLM experimental satellite launched in April 1974.

ATSU Association of Time-Sharing Users. 75 Manhattan Dr, Boulder, CO 80303. Established in 1974. Users and prospective users of computer time-sharing systems. Formerly (1975) ACTSU. Disseminates information about interactive services and products.

ATWE Association of Technical Writers and Editors. Established in 1953. Merged with STW to become STWE in 1960.

AUCC Association of Universities and Colleges of Canada/Association des Universités et Collèges du Canada. Contact president. Maintains a Library Committee.

AUDACIOUS Automatic Direct Access to Information with On-line UDC System. An interactive retrieval system employing UDC as the content-coding scheme. *See* R. R. Freeman and P. Atherton. "File Organization and Search Strategy Using UDC in Mechanized Information Storage, Retrieval, and Dissemination" in *Proceedings of the FID/IFIP Jt. Conf. (Rome, 1967)*, ed. by Kjell Samuelson. Amsterdam, the Netherlands: North Holland Publishing, 1968, pp. 122–152.

AULA Arab University Library Association. c/o Chief Librarian, Kuwait University, Kuwait.

AUPELF Association des Universités Partiellement ou Entierement de Langue Française (Association of Wholly or Partially French-language Universities). University of Montreal, BP 6128, Montreal PQ H3C 3J7, Canada. Established in 1961. Maintains a library and a Committee on Information and Documentation.

AUSINET Australian Information Network. National Library of Australia, Canberra 2600, Australia.

AUTOCLASS Automatic Classification. US National Cancer Institute, Rm. 10A35, Bldg. 31, Bethesda, MD 20014. System used by US National Cancer Institute for a hierarchical classification updating project.

AUTOCOM Automated Combustor Design Code.

AUTOCOMM AUTOCOMM Business System. Designed by CDC (Control Data Corporation) for commercial data processing problems. It is decimally oriented and uses powerful instructions to minimize programming time.

AUTOPIC Automatic Personal Identification Code. An IBM computer program.

AUTOPROMPT Automatic Programming of Machine Tools. A technique developed by IBM to direct the operations of machine tools with computer-executed programs.

AUTOPSY Automatic Operating System. Computer program and assembly system developed by Westinghouse Electric and IBM.

AUTRAN Automatic Translation.

AUUA American UNIVAC Users Association. Drawer S, Winston-Salem, NC 27108. Established in 1955. Membership held by corporations which have, or are contracting for, a computer system marketed by Sperry UNIVAC Division. Formerly (1976) UUA (UNIVAC Users Association). Sponsors conferences for exchange of technical information and publishes documents.

AV Audiovisual.

AVC Automatic Volume Control. Radio term.

AVDBAD Association Voltaique pour le Développement des Bibliothèques, des Archives et de la Documentation (Voltan Association for the Development of Libraries, Archives and Documentation). BP 1140, Ouagadougou, Republic of Upper Volta. Established in 1972. Affiliated with IFLA.

AVLA Audio-Visual Language Association. 7 Shelley Close, Langley, Buckinghamshire, England.

AVLINE Audiovisual Online. National Library of Medicine, 8600 Rockville Pike, Bethesda, MD 20209. Bibliographic data base containing citations to, and abstracts of, audiovisual teaching packages in the health sciences.

AVMP *Audiovisual Market Place.* New York: R. R. Bowker Co, 1969– . An annual publication.

AVS American Vacuum Society. 335 East 45 St, New York, NY 10017. Established in 1953. Publishes documents. Formerly CVT.

AVS Audio Visual Section. *See* LITA/AVS.

AVSL Association of Visual Science Librarians. Optometry Library, University of California, Berkeley, CA 94720. Established in 1968 by the American Academy of Optometry. Sets standards for optometric school libraries.

AWIS Arizona Water Information System. Sponsored by the University of Arizona, Office of Arid Land Studies. Monitors current information concerning Arizona water activities. Includes a computer data storage and retrieval system.

AWLNET Area Wide Library Network. 2420 Mariposa St, Fresno, CA 93721. Over 50 academic, school, research, medical and business libraries cooperate through ILL, photocopying, staff training and collection development.

AWP Air World Publications. 4210 Vanowen St, Burbank, CA 91504.

AWRA American Water Resources Association. Saint Anthony Falls Hydraulic Laboratory, Mississippi River at Third Ave, SE, Minneapolis, MN 55414. Established in 1964. Publishes documents relating to water resources science and technology.

AWRE Atomic Weapons Research Establishment. Aldermaston, Reading, Berkshire, England. Nuclear science and physics literature.

AWS American Welding Society. 2501 Northwest Seventh St, Miami, FL 33125. Established in 1919. Supports *EI (Engineering Index)*.

AZABDO Association Zairoise des Archivistes, Bibliothécaires et Documentalistes (Zairian Association of Archivists, Librarians and Documentalists). BP 805, Kinshasa XI, Zaire. Established in 1968. Affiliated with IFLA and FID.

BA *Biological Abstracts.* V. 1, 1927. Published semimonthly by BioSciences Information Service.

BA Booksellers Association of Great Britain and Ireland. 154 Buckingham Palace Rd, London SW1W 9TZ, England. Publishers as well as booksellers are members.

BA *Business Asia.* (Journal). V. 1, 1970. Published by Business International Corp. Weekly report.

BAA Bibliothèque d'Art et d'Archéologie. Fondation Jacques Doucet, Université de Paris, 3 rue Michelet, 75 Paris 6, France.

BACAIC Boeing Airplane Company Algebraic Interpretive Computing System.

BAD Associação Portuguesa de Bibliotecários, Arquivistas e Documentalistes (Portuguese Association of Librarians, Archivists and Documentalists). Rua Ocidental ao Campo Grande 83, Lisbon 5, Portugal. Established in 1973. Affiliated with IFLA and FID.

BADADUQ Banque de Données à Accès Direct de l'Université du Québec (Direct Access Data Bank of the University of Quebec). *See* Gilles Chaput. "BADADUQ Banque de Données à Accès Direct de l'Université du Québec." *Documentation et Bibliothèques* 20 (June 1974): 55-65.

BAG Buchhändler-Abrechnungs-Gesellschaft mbH. Established in Frankfurt, West Germany, to coordinate and centralize the book trade. Intended as an exchange between booksellers and publishers. *See* Jeanette M. Moehn. "The West German Book Trade: A Survey of Current Trends." *LRTS* 15 (Summer 1971): 329-344.

BAI *Biological and Agricultural Index.* V. 1, 1916. Published by H. W. Wilson Co.

BAIE British Association of Industrial Editors. 2a Elm Bank Gardens, London SW13 ONT, England. Purpose is to improve house journals. Publishes documents.

BAIT Bacterial Automated Identification Technique.

BAL Basic Assembly Language. A programming language.

BALLOTS Bibliographic Automation of Large Library Operations Using a Time-Sharing System. Name changed to RLIN in 1978. *See* "Project BALLOTS and the Stanford University Libraries." *JOLA* 8 (Mar. 1975): 31-50.

BAM Basic Access Method. An access method in which each input/output statement causes a corresponding machine input/output operation to be performed.

BAMIRAC Ballistic Missile Radiation Analysis Center. University of Michigan, Ann Arbor, MI 48109. Involved in R&D and analysis of information.

BAMP Basic Analysis and Mapping Program.

BANKPAC BANK Programming. A comprehensive group of generalized programs for banks, which automate demand deposit accounting, installment loan accounting, savings accounting, transit, and personal trust accounting functions.

BANSDOC Bangladesh National Scientific and Technical Documentation Center. Established in 1956.

BAP Basic Assembler Program.

BAPA British Amateur Press Association. 32 Waterloo Rd, Bedford, England. Established in 1890. Publishes *British Amateur Jorunalist.*

BARC Bay Area Reference Center. San Francisco Public Library, Civic Center, San Francisco, CA 94102. Provides reference referrals and workshops to 90 Northern California public libraries and many academic and research libraries in the Bay area.

BARDS Bucknell Automated Retrieval and Display System. Ellen Clark Bertrand Library, Information Systems Project, Lewisburg, PA 17837. An on-line retrieval system developed at Bucknell University.

BARON Business/Accounts Reporting Operating Network.

BARTS Bay Area Rapid Transit System. San Francisco's computer-controlled subway system.

BASF Badische Anilin und Soda-Fabrik AG. Ludwigshafen am Rhein, Federal Republic of Germany. Factory where E. Meye has conducted research on superimposed coding methods.

BASIC Battle Area Surveillance and Integrated Communications. The technique and programming language used for the detection, transmission, reception, transformation, processing and dissemination of information in a tactical situation.

BASIC Beginners All-purpose Symbolic Instruction Code. A programming language developed by Professors J. G. Kemeny and T. E. Kurtz of Dartmouth College.

BASIC *Biological Abstracts* Subjects in Context. A modified KWIC indexing approach. Involves computer-manipulated index of *BA (Biological Abstracts)* based on titles supplemented with keywords added by editors.

BASIL Barclays (Bank) Advanced Staff Information Language. A programming language used by Barclays Bank.

BA•SIS Bibliographic Author or Subject Interactive Search. Nexus Corporation, 3001 Red Hill Ave, Bldg. 3, Suite 201, Costa Mesa, CA 92626. A computerized social science bibliography service. *See* "Computerized Social Science Bibliography Service." *Information Part 1* 6 (Feb. 1974): 36.

BASIS *Bulletin of the American Society for Information Science.* V. 1, 1974. Published by the American Society for Information Science.

BASIS-E Bibliothekarisch-Analytisches System zur Informations-Speicherung-Erschliessung (Library Analytical System for Information Storage/Retrieval-Economics). A project based in the Federal Republic of Germany.

BASIS-L Bibliothekarisch-Analytisches System zur Informations-Speicherung-Leihverkehr (Library Analytical System for Information Storage/Retrieval-Loan). System for analyzing stored information about library loans. *See* Gertrud König and Bärbel Lischewsky. "ComputerUnterstützte Statistiken mit dem Ausleihsystem BASIS-L." *Buch und Bibliothek* 27 (May 1975): 449–456.

BASIS-70 Battelle Automated Search Information System for the Seventies. See *Battelle–Columbus BASIS-70: A User's Guide.* 3rd ed. Columbus, OH: Battelle, 1971.

BASR Bureau of Applied Social Research. Columbia University, 695 West 115 St, New York, NY 10025. A member of CRL, METRO, and RLG. Originally known as the Office of Radio Research, the bureau was established in 1937 at Princeton, and moved to Columbia University's graduate facilities for training and research in the social sciences.

BASS Basic Analog Simulation System.

BASS Belgian Archives for the Social Sciences. 2A, Van Everstraat, 3000 Louvain, Belgium. Produces data bases on demography and sociology.

BAT Battery. In telecommunications, a source of direct current but not necessarily a storage device.

BAT *Biological Abstracts* on Tape. BioSciences Information Service, 2100 Arch St, Philadelphia, PA 19103. Coverage from 1976. Bibliographic data base related to items from *BA (Biological Abstracts)* data base included in *BIOSIS Previews*.

BATAB Baker and Taylor Automated Buying. A computerized book-ordering system created for Baker and Taylor Co, Somerville, NJ.

BATMA Bookbinding and Allied Trades Management Association. 4 Jenton Ave, Bexley Heath, Kent DA7 4SP, England.

BATSC Bay Area Transportation Study Commission. *See* M. J. Kevany. *An Information System for Urban Transportation Planning: The BATSC Approach*. Santa Monica, CA: System Development Corp, 1968.

BB Bibliotheca Borgoriensis (Central Library for Natural Science). Djuanda 20, Bogor, Indonesia.

BBC Basic Bibliographic Citation.

BBC British Broadcasting Corporation. Maintains a Sound Archives. *See* Anthony Trebble. "BBC Sound Archives." *Audiovisual Librarian* 2 (Summer 1975): 65–69. Also produces a televised information magazine started in 1972. *See also* Liz Donnelly. "This Is CEEFAX." *Assistant Librarian* 69 (Jan. 1976): 2–4.

BBFC British Board of Film Censors. 3 Soho Sq, London W1, England.

BBIP *British Books in Print*. London: J. Whitaker, 1939–   (dist. in US and Mexico by R. R. Bowker Co.). A monthly publication, cumulated annually.

BBK Bibliotechno-Bibliograficheskaya Klassificatsiya (Library Bibliographical Classification). Term used in Slavic languages.

BBN Bolt, Beranek and Newman, Inc. 50 Moulton St, Cambridge, MA 02138. A research, development and consulting firm.

BC Bliss Classification. Classification scheme developed by Henry Evelyn Bliss. Uses 26 main classes, A–Z, with subdivision of a main class accomplished by the addition of letters.

BC *Business China*. (Journal). V.1, 1975. Published by Business International Corp.

BCA Bliss Classification Association. c/o Commonwealth Institute Library, Kensington High St, London W8 6NQ, England. Established in 1967. Seeks to promote use and development of Bliss Bibliographic Classification. Supersedes British Committee for Bliss Classification.

BCAB British Computer Association for the Blind. Box 950, London WC1V 6XX, England. Affiliated with BCS (British Computer Society).

BCC British Copyright Council. 29 Berners St, London W1P 3D3, England. Sponsored the Whitford Committee to change the 1956 Copyright Act to take into account the impact of technology. *See* Denis de Freitas. "Changing the Copyright Law." *The Author* 85 (Autumn 1974): 104–110.

BCD Binary Coded Decimal. A form of numeric representation in which binary numerals are used to represent the decimal digits of a decimal numeral. Synonymous with coded decimal.

BCIRA British Cast Iron Research Association. Alvechurch, Birmingham B48 7QB, England. Issued *BCIRA Abstracts of Foundry Literature* in 1969.

BCIT British Columbia Institute of Technology Information Resource Centre. 3700 Willingdon Ave, Burnaby V5G 342, Canada. Library established in 1964.

BCL *Books for College Libraries*. Second edition. Chicago, IL: American Library Association, 1975.

BCL Burroughs Common Language. A binary code representation of alphanumeric characters common to Burroughs equipment.

BCLA British Columbia Library Association. Box 46378, Sta. G, Vancouver BC V6R 4G6, Canada.

BCLTA British Columbia Library Trustees Association. Contact chairperson. A Canadian association.

BCM *British Catalogue of Music.* 7 Rathbone Pl, London W1P 2AL, England. Has its own classification published by British National Bibliography.

BCN Biomedical Communications Network. *See* SUNY-BCN.

BCO Binary Coded Octal. A form of numeric representation in which binary numerals are used to represent the octal digits of an octal number.

BCP Bibliothèques Centrals de Prêt. French term for mobile libraries used in France and Canada in small towns and rural areas.

BCPA British Copyright Protection Association, Ltd. 22-23 Little Portland St, London W1N 5AF, England. Established in 1973.

BCPL Baltimore County Public Library. Towson, MD 21204.

BCPL Basic Computer Programming Language.

BCR Bibliographical Center for Research. Rocky Mountain Region, Inc, 245 Columbine, Denver, CO 80206. All libraries in CO, KS, SD, UT, WY, North Dakota State University, Texas Tech University, the Nebraska Library Commission and the Boys Town Center for the Study of Youth Development cooperate through ILL, technical and on-line retrieval services.

BCR Bituminous Coal Research, Inc. 350 Hochberg Rd, Monroeville, PA 15146. Established in 1934. Publishes *Coal Research*, quarterly.

BCRA British Carbonization Research Association. Carbonization Research Center, Chesterfield, Derbys S42 6JS, England. Publishes documents. Formerly (1974) BCRA (British Coke Research Association).

BCRA British Ceramic Research Association. Queens Rd, Penkhull, Stoke-on-Trent ST4 7LQ, England. Publishes documents.

BCRA British Coke Research Association. Name changed to BCRA (British Carbonization Research Association) in 1974.

BCS British Cartographic Society. 11 Hope Terrace, Edinburgh EH9 2AP, Scotland.

Established in 1963. Maintains a library. Publishes *Cartographic Journal* and other documents.

BCS British Ceramic Society. Shelton House, Stoke Rd, Shelton, Stoke-on-Trent ST4 2DR, England. Publishes documents.

BCS British Computer Society. 22 Portland Pl, London W1N 4AP, England.

BCS Bureau of Ceylon Standards. 53 Dharmapala Mawatha, Columbia 3, Ceylon. Affiliated with ISO (International Standards Organization).

BCSAA British Computer Society ALGOL Association. 22 Portland Pl, London W1N 4AP, England.

BCSLA British Columbia School Librarians Association. British Columbia Teachers Federation, 105-2235 Burrard St, Vancouver BC V6J 3H9, Canada.

BCSO British Commonwealth Scientific Office. Washington, DC 20013.

BCTIC Biomedical Computing Technology Information Center. Oak Ridge National Laboratory, Box X, Oak Ridge, TN 37830. Provides computerized searches and document delivery in the biomedical sciences.

BCUA Business Computer Users Association. Contact president.

BDAM Basic Direct Access Method.

BDC Binary Decimal Counter.

BDC Book Development Council. c/o Publishers Association, 19 Bedford Sq, London WC1B 3HJ, England. Established in 1965. Amalgamated with the Publishers Association in 1960 but retained its name. Responsible for all cooperative export effort within the book industry.

BDC Bureau International de Documentation des Chemins de Fer. 27 rue de Londres, 75 Paris 9, France. Aim is to collect and place at the disposal of administrations belonging to UIC (Union Internationale des Chemins de Fer) all economic, legal, social and technical documentation concerning railways.

BDT Banques de Données Toxicologique. Équipe de Recherche sur les Banques de Données, Institut National de la Santé et de la Recherche Médicale, Hôpital de Bicêtre, 78 rue du General-Leclerc, Kremlin-Bicêtre 94270, France. Nonbibliographic data base covering the effects of toxic substances.

BDZV Bundesverband Deutscher Zeitungsverleger. Riemenschneider Strasse 10, 53 Bonn-Bad Gudesberg, Federal Republic of Germany. Established in 1954. Member of the International Federation of Newspaper Publishers.

BE *Business Europe.* Loose-leaf format. Published by Business International Corp.

BEAC Boeing Electronic Analog Computer.

BEACON Bibliographic Exchange and Communications Network. An unfunded proposal succeeded by CALBPC. *See* Lawrence E. Leonard. "Colorado Academic Libraries Book Processing Center: A Feasibility Study." *College and Research Libraries* 29 (Sept. 1968): 393–399.

BEC Bay Electric Company. 627 First St, Menominee, MI 49853. Makes film and book storage equipment.

BECAN *Bioengineering Current Awareness Bulletin.* Published by Project Fair, Clinical Research Centre, Bioengineering Division, Watford Rd, Harrow, Middlesex HA1 3UJ, England.

BEE Books for Equal Education. This association has been terminated.

BEE *Business Eastern Europe.* (Journal). V. 1, 1972. Published by Business International Corp. Formerly *Eastern Europe Report.*

BEEC Binary Error-Erasure Channel.

BEEF Business and Engineering Enriched FORTRAN. BEEF enhances FORTRAN's capabilities as a scientific processing language. Developed by Westinghouse Electric Corp.

BEL Bell Character. The member of a character set used to sound the bell on a terminal device.

BELC Black Employees of the Library of Congress. A group formed to negotiate promotional opportunities.

BELC Bureau pour l'Enseignement de la Langue et de la Civilisation Françaises à l'Étranger. Service à l'Information Linguistique, BELC, 6 rue Berthollet, Paris 5, France. In collaboration with CRLLB, issued *Language and Language Behavior Abstracts* in 1967.

BELLREL Bell Laboratories Library Real-Time Loan System. *See* R. A. Kennedy. "Bell Laboratories' Library Real-Time Loan System (BELLREL)." *JOLA* 1 (June 1968): 128–146.

BEMA Business Equipment Manufacturers Association. Formerly (1961) OEMI. Became CBEMA in 1972.

BES Building and Equipment Section. *See* LAMA/BES.

BEST Business EDP Systems Technique. A concept developed by NCR for programming business problem solutions on its computers.

BETA Business Equipment Trade Association. 109 Kingsway, London WC2, England.

BEX Broadband Exchange. Public switched communication system of Western Union featuring various widthband full duplex connections.

BF Bibliotekarforeningen (Association of Librarians). Hyskenstroede 4, 1207 Copenhagen, Denmark. Publishes documents.

BFI Betriebsforschungsinstitut, VDEh-Institut für Angewandte Forschung GmbH. Verein Deutscher Eisenhuttenleute, Sohnstrasse 65, Düsseldorf D-4000, Federal Republic of Germany. Established in 1922. Produces data bases and provides computerized searches and translations in industrial production.

BFI British Film Institute. 81 Dean St, London W1V 6AA, England. Established in 1933. Publishes a quarterly, *Sight and Sound*, and a monthly, *Film Bulletin.*

BGEA *Bibliographic Guide for Editors and Authors.* Washington, DC: American Chemical Society, 1974. Published in cooperation with BIOSIS. A single combined list of serials indexed by BIOSIS, CAS (Chemical Abstracts Service) and EI.

BGS Bangladesh Granthagar Samity (Library Association of Bangladesh).

Contact president. Established in 1956. Affiliated with IFLA.

BHME Bureau of Health Manpower Education. A division of NIH. Together with NLM, established OAED.

BHRA British Hydromechanics Research Association. Cranfield, Bedford MK43 OAJ, England. Established in 1947. Publishes documents.

BI Bibliografiska Institutet (Bibliographical Institute). Kungl. Biblioteket, Box 5039, S-102 41, Stockholm 5, Sweden.

BI *Business International*. (Journal). V. 1, 1954. Published by Business International Corp. Weekly report.

BIA Braille Institute of America, Inc. 741 North Vermont Ave, Los Angeles, CA 90029. Established in 1919. Maintains free circulation Braille library and publishes Braille documents. Formerly Universal Braille Press.

BIALL British and Irish Association of Law Librarians. Refer to latest issue of publication. Established in 1969. Publishes *Law Librarian*.

BIAM Banque d'Information Automatisée sur les Médicaments. Bureau d'Information BIAM, Division Hemey, Hôpital de la Salpetriere, 47 boulevard de l'Hôpital, 75634 Paris, Cedex 13, France. Data base covering properties of pharmaceutical products. Coverage from 1970.

BIBCENTER University of California Bibliographic Center. University of California, South Hall Annex, Berkeley, CA 94720. Provides technical bibliographic services.

BIBCON Bibliographic Records Control. A computer system operational at the University of California and the California State Library in Sacramento. *See* Liz Gibson. "BIBCON: A General Purpose Software System for MARC-based Book Catalog Production." *JOLA* 6 (Dec. 1973): 237–256.

BIBL Bibliografia. Centro Elettronico di Documentazione-Italgiure, Corte Suprema di Cassaziono, Palazzo di Giustizia, Via Ulpiano 8, Rome 00193, Italy. Bibliographic data base covering legal books.

BIBLIO Program BIBLIO. Systematic analysis of the structures and procedures in use at the National Central Library of Rome. *See* Angela Vinay. "Problems of Management and Automation in the National Central Library of Rome." *Network* 1 (Sept. 1974): 15–17.

BIBLIOS Book Inventory Building and Library Information Oriented System. Orange County Public Library, Orange, CA 92668. A modular system for library automation which began operation in March 1967. Comprised of six functionally discrete subsystems, each divided into recurring batch processing cycles. *See* J. C. Kountz and R. E. Norton. "BIBLIOS: A Modular System for Library Automation." *DATAMATION* 16 (Feb. 1970): 79–83.

BIBNET Bibliographic Network. A retrieval system used by OCLC in activities relating to technical services for ILL.

BIBPRO IV Bibliography Production. Informatics, Inc, 6000 Executive Blvd, Rockville, MD 20852. A library system used to develop a batch computer system utilizing MARC tapes and local cataloging.

BICEP GE language for process control procedures.

BID Bibliografia di Informatica e Diritto. Centro Elettronico di Documentazione-Italgiure, Corte Suprema di Cassaziono, Palazzo di Giustizia, Via Ulpiano 8, Rome 00193, Italy. Bibliographic data base covering the use of electronic information retrieval in law.

BIEP Business and Industry Extension Program. University of New Mexico, Technology Application Center, 2500 Central Ave, SE, Albuquerque, NM 87131. Aim is to provide scientific and technical knowledge that will aid in improving the New Mexican economy.

BIIT Bureau International d'Information sur les Télécommunications. 3 Saint Pierre, Lausanne, Switzerland. Established in 1975. Publishes documents and provides computerized searches in telecommunications and electronics.

BIM Beginning-of-Information Marker. A reflective spot on the back of a magnetic tape, ten feet from the physical beginning of the tape, indicating the point at which recording may begin.

BIM British Institute of Management. Management House, Parker St, London WC2B 5PT, England. Established in 1947. Publications include *Management Today, Management Review and Digest* and *Management Information*, a catalog of BIM publications.

BIMAG Bistable Magnetic Core. A magnetic core with the capability of adopting one of two states of magnetization.

BIMR *Business International Money Report*. (Journal). V. 1, 1975. Published by Business International Corp.

BINAC Binary Automatic Computer. Developed by Eckert-Maudely Computer Corp. in 1949; considered faster and more economical than the ENIAC. Used magnetic tape to store information.

BINET Bicentennial Information Network. Operated by the American Revolution Bicentennial Commission to provide computerized information on events and projects for the Bicentennial.

BIOETHICSLINE Bioethics Online. National Library of Medicine, 8600 Rockville Pike, Bethesda, MD 20014. Bibliographic data base covering bioethical topics.

BioI *BioResearch Index*. V. 1, 1967. Published monthly by BioSciences Information Service.

BIOR Business Input-Output Rerun. A compiling system developed for use on UNIVAC I and UNIVAC II computers.

BIOSIS BioSciences Information Service. BIOSIS, 2100 Arch St, Philadelphia, PA 19103. Publisher of *BA (Biological Abstracts), AM (Abstracts of Mycology)* and *BioI*.

BIOSIS Previews. BioSciences Information Service Previews. BIOSIS, 2100 Arch St, Philadelphia, PA 19103. Bibliographic data base covering citations from *BA (Biological Abstracts)* and *BioI*.

BIP *Books in Print*. New York: R. R. Bowker Co, 1948– . An annual publication and supplement.

BIPAD Bureau of Independent Publishers and Distributors. Name changed to MPMI.

BIPCO Built-in-Place Components. Developed by Burroughs Corp. for the construction of data processing equipment.

BIPS British Integrated Programme Suite.

BIREME Biblioteca Regional de Medicina. São Paulo, Brazil. Established in 1969 by PAHO (Pan American Health Organization) in cooperation with NLM and the Brazilian government. Serves as an interlibrary loan backstop and a MEDLINE linkage and development center for the countries of South America. *See* Amador Neghme. "Operations of the Biblioteca Regional de Medicina (BIREME)." *BMLA* 63 (Apr. 1975): 173–177.

BIRF Brewing Industry Research Foundation. Name changed to BRF.

BIRPI Bureaux Internationaux Réunis pour la Protection de la Propriété Intellectuelle (United International Bureaus for the Protection of Intellectual Property). 32 Chemin des Colombettes, 1211 Geneva 20, Switzerland.

BIRS Baptist Information Retrieval System. c/o Southern Baptist Convention Historical Commission, 127 Ninth Ave, Nashville, TN 37234.

BIRS British Institute of Recording Sounds. 29 Exhibition Rd, London SW7 2AS, England. An archival collection of recordings established in 1948.

BIS Bibliographic Section. *See* ACRL/BIS.

BIS Brain Information Service. UCLA Center for Health Sciences, University of California, Los Angeles, CA 90024. Indexes information for a retrieval system. Publishes documents.

BIS British Information Service. 845 Third Ave, New York, NY 10022.

BIS Business Information System. Sioux City Public Library, 705 Sixth St, Sioux City, IA 51105. Provides useful information to businesses in the area.

BISAC Book Industry Systems Advisory Committee. c/o Sandra Paul, Random House, 201 East 50 St, New York, NY

10022. Publicity and promotional committee for ISBN.

BI-SAL Bi-State Academic Libraries. c/o Marycrest College, Davenport, IA 52804. Eight libraries that cooperate through ILL, reciprocal borrowing and union list programs.

BISAM Basic Indexed Sequential Access Method. *See* F. T. Coyle. "The Hidden Speed of ISAM." *Datamation*, June 15, 1971, p. 48.

BISEC A GE process control language.

BISFA British Industrial and Scientific Film Association Ltd. 15 New Bridge St, London EC4V 6AU, England. Established in 1967. Promotes use of film and publishes guides.

BISG Book Industry Study Groups, Inc. Box 2062, Darien, CT 06820. Established in 1975. Composed of publishing companies and related industrial organizations.

BISITS British Iron and Steel Industry Translation Service. Sponsored by ISI (Iron and Steel Industry).

BITE Built-In Test Equipment.

BJA *Basic Journal Abstracts.* A magnetic tape service of CAS (Chemical Abstracts Service). Produced since 1968.

BKSTS British Kinematograph, Sound, and Television Society. 110 Victoria House, Vernon Pl, London WC1, England.

BL British Library. Reference Division: British Museum, Great Russell St, London WC1B 3DG, England; Lending Division: Boston Spa, Wetherby, Yorkshire LS23 7BQ, England; Bibliographic Services Division: Store St, London WC1E 7DG, England; Central Administration and the Research and Development Dept: Sheraton House, Great Chapel St, London W1V 4BH, England. Established in 1973, incorporating several existing national libraries.

BL *Business Latin America.* (Journal). V. 1, 1966. Published by Business International Corp. Weekly report.

BLADE Bell Laboratories Automatic Device.

BLADES Bell Laboratories Automatic Design System. A computer program.

BLAISE British Library Automated Information System. 7 Rathbone St, London W1P 2AL, England. System started in April 1977. Operates within the British Library's Bibliographic Services Division. Makes available to British libraries various data bases (BNB, MARC, MEDLARS and PRECIS) without need of a transatlantic link. *See* Brian Collinge. "BLAISE: The British Library Automated Information Service." *ASLIB Proceedings* 30 (Oct.–Nov. 1978): 394–402.

BLASA Bantu Library Association of South Africa. c/o Provincial Regional Library, Postal Bag 9393, Pietersburg, Republic of South Africa. Established in 1964.

BLATT *Bulletin of the Library Association of Trinidad and Tobago.* V. 1, 1961. Published by the Library Association of Trinidad and Tobago.

BLESSED Bell Little Electrodata Symbolic System for the Electrodata. A symbolic assembly program developed by Michigan Bell Telephone Co. and Arthur D. Little, Inc, for use on the Burroughs 220 computer.

BLET Bureau of Libraries and Educational Technology. Established in 1970. Name changed to BLLR in 1971.

BLIS Bell Laboratories Interpretive System. A computer program.

BLL British Lending Library, Boston Spa, Wetherly, Yorkshire, England.

BLLD British Library Lending Division. Boston Spa, Yorkshire LS23 7BQ, England. A division of BL (British Library). Incorporates the formerly independent libraries NCL and NLL.

BLLR Bureau of Libraries and Learning Resources. Formerly BLET. Name changed to DLP in 1974.

BLOC Booth Library On-Line Circulation. Booth Library, Eastern Illinois University, Charleston, IL 61920. *See* P. V. Rao and B. J. Szerenyi. "Booth Library On-Line Circulation System." *JOLA* 4 (June 1971): 86–102.

BLOCKSEARCH A utility computer program, available from NBS, which scans for the occurrence of certain strings of characters and lists the blocks in which they occur. *See also* EDPAC.

BLODI-G Block Diagram-Graphics.

BLOWS British Library of Wild Life Sounds. Tape and disc recordings of over 3,000 species, documented and indexed. *See* Patrick Sellar. "BLOWS: The First Five Years." *Recorded Sound* 54 (Apr. 1974): 273–275.

BLS Bureau of Labor Statistics. US Dept. of Labor, 200 Constitution Ave, NW, Washington, DC 20210. Collects data summaries and analyses of national, local and regional interest. Extensive information service provided at cost by central and regional offices.

BM British Museum. Great Russell St, London WC1B 3DG, England.

BMA British Medical Association. British Medical Association House, Tavistock Sq, London WC1H 9JP, England. Publishes documents.

BMD Biomedical Computer Programs. Originally used in biomedical applications. Now a series of general programs dealing with all kinds of statistical analyses.

BMES Biomedical Engineering Society. Box 2399, Culver City, CA 90230. Established in 1968. Publishes *Annals of Biomedical Engineering* and an annual directory.

BMI Book Manufacturers Institute. 111 Prospect, Stamford, CT 06901. Established in 1920. Formerly Employing Bookbinders of America. Members are manufacturers of books and suppliers of book materials. Publishes directory and newsletters.

BML British Museum Library. Now incorporated as a major part of the Reference Division of BL (British Library).

BMLA *Bulletin of the Medical Library Association.* V. 1, 1911. Published by MLA (Medical Library Association).

BN Bibliothèque Nationale. 58 rue de Richelieu, F-75002 Paris, France. The French national library.

BNA Blackwell/North America, Inc. 10300 Allen Blvd, SW, Beaverton, OR 97005. Provides technical and book services.

BNA Bureau of National Affairs. 1231 25th St, NW, Washington, DC 20037. Publishes reports in the fields of law and economics.

BNB *British National Bibliography.* V. 1, 1950. Published by the British National Bibliography, since 1974 a major part of the Bibliographic Services Division of BL (British Library), Store St, London WC1E 7DG, England. A weekly list of books printed in the UK with quarterly, semiannual, annual and five-year cumulations.

BNBC British National Book Centre. Formerly part of NCL. In 1974 incorporated as part of BLLD of BL (British Library) and name changed to the "Gift and Exchange Section." Functions as a center for British libraries wishing to dispose of publications.

BNCF Biblioteca Nazionale Centrale—Firenze (National Central Library of Florence). Piazza Cavalleggeri 1, Florence, Italy. Established in 1975.

BND British National Discography. A proposal for a national discography. *See* George H. Saddington. "Some Personal Thoughts on a British National Discography." *Audiovisual Librarian* 1 (Autumn 1973): 49–51.

BNF Backus-Naur Form. *See* BNF (Backus Normal Form).

BNF Backus Normal Form. A formal language structure for syntax phrasing used in the design of ALGOL-60. Also known as "Backus-Naur Form."

BNFC *British National Film Catalogue.* V. 1, 1963. Published by the British Film Institute.

BNIST Bureau National d'Information Scientifique et Technique (National Board for Scientific and Technical Information). 97 rue de Grenelle, 75007 Paris, France. In 1975 conducted a study of data banks maintained by automated documentation centers which store and retrieve true, or nonbibliographic, data. Formerly CND.

BNRJ Biblioteca Nacional do Rio de Janeiro (National Library of Rio de Janeiro). Avenida Rio Branco, 219/239, Rio de Janeiro, GB, Brasil.

BOADICEA British Overseas Airways Digital Information Computer for Electronic Automation.

BoB Bureau of the Budget. Name changed to OMB (Office of Management and Budget) in 1970.

BOCES Board of Cooperative Educational Services. NY State Education Dept, Albany, NY 12234. A regional educational services agency.

BOCS Board of Cooperative Services. 1750 30th St, Boulder, CO 80301. A regional educational services agency. *See also* PET and SID (Searches in Depth).

BOLD Bibliographic On-Line Display. A document storage and retrieval system. *See* H. Borko and H. P. Burnaugh. "Interactive Displays for Document Retrieval." *Information Display* 3 (Sept.–Oct. 1966): 47–90.

BOLT British Columbia Organization of Library Technicians. Contact president. A Canadian association.

BORAM Block-Oriented Random Access Memories.

BOS Basic Operating System. The smallest and simplest disk-resident operating system for the IBM 360 computer.

BOS Book Order and Selection. University of Massachusetts Library, Amherst, MA 01002. *See* C. McAllister. "On-Line Library Housekeeping Systems." *Special Libraries* 62 (Nov. 1971): 457–468.

BOSS Boeing Operational Supervisory System. A supervisory program developed by Boeing Aircraft Co. for use on the IBM 704 computer.

BOSS Business Oriented Software Systems. A Raytheon monitor and I/O control system that provides automatic control of the operations by a variety of "hands off" operations.

BP *British Pharmacopoeia.* London: Department of Health and Social Security, 1973.

BPI Bits Per Inch.

BPI *Bookman's Price Index.* Detroit, MI: Gale Research Co, 1964– .

BPI *Business Periodicals Index.* V. 1, 1958. Published by H. W. Wilson Co. Formerly *Industrial Arts Index.*

BPKT Basic Programming Knowledge Test.

BPL Boston Public Library. 666 Boylston St, Box 286, Boston, MA 02117.

BPM *BIOSIS Previews Memo.* Unnumbered newsletter sent to information centers leasing *BIOSIS Previews* tapes and to searchers.

BPMA British Photographic Manufacturers Association. 8 Saint Bride St, London EC4, England.

BPMA British Printing Machinery Association. 12 Clifford's Inn, London EC4, England.

BPR *(American) Book Publishing Record. See* ABPR.

BPRA Book Publishers Representatives Association. 144 Lennard Rd, Beckenham, Kent, England. Established in 1924.

BPS Basic Programming Support. The IBM 360 software system.

BPS Bits Per Second. Refers to the rate of speed with which bits are transmitted.

BPV Buitenlandse Persvereniging in Nederland (Foreign Press Association in the Netherlands). Tesselschadestraat 29, Amsterdam, the Netherlands. Established in 1925.

BQSI Brooklyn–Queens–Staten Island Health Sciences Group. Medical Research Library of Brooklyn, 450 Clarkson Ave, Brooklyn, NY 11203.

BRA British Records Association. The Charterhouse, Charterhouse Sq, London EC1, England.

BRAB Building Research Advisory Board. 2101 Constitution Ave, Washington, DC 20418. Established in 1949. Publishes documents. In 1969, absorbed BRI. Publishes a journal, a newsletter and technical reports.

BRASTACS Bradford Scientific, Technical and Commercial Service. Central Library, Prince's Way, Bradford 5, Yorkshire, England.

BRC Branch Conditional. An instruction which, if a specified condition or set of conditions is satisfied, is interpreted as an unconditional transfer. Synonymous with conditional jump and conditional transfer.

BRF Brewing Research Foundation. Lyttel Hall, Nutfield, Surrey RH1 4HY, Nutfield Ridge 2272, England. Established in 1948. Involved in the scientific investigation of the nature of the raw materials and processes involved in malting and brewing. Publishes *Bulletin of Current Literature.* Formerly BIRF.

BRI Building Research Institute. Established in 1952. Merged into BRAB in 1969.

BRIC Bureau de Recherche pour l'Innovation et la Convergence. 32 bis, rue Victor Hugo, 92800 Puteaux, France. Produces a machine-readable data base containing descriptions of inventions available for licensing.

BRICS Black Resources Information Coordinating Services, Inc. 614 Howard Ave, Tallahassee, FL 32304. Maintains a library and publishes guides to Afro-American publications.

BRIDGE A Honeywell liberator program that performs direct translation of machine languages of competitive systems to the machine languages of various Honeywell computers.

BRIMARC Brighton/MARC. Brighton Public Libraries, Church St, Brighton BN1 1UE, England. An experiment in the use of a machine-readable national data base and national center for producing a local book catalog.

BrMTL British Ministry of Technology. Harefield House, Harefield, Uxbridge, Middlesex, England. A government agency that funds research and publishes documents.

BROWSER Browsing On-Line with Selective Retrieval. A natural-language search system developed by IBM. *See* J. J. Williams. *BROWSER: An Automatic Indexing On-Line Text Retrieval System.* Gaithersburg, MD: IBM Federal Systems Div, 1969.

BRS Bibliographic Retrieval Services, Inc. Corporation Park, Scotia, NY 12302. Serves as an intermediary between data base suppliers and institutional users.

BRT *BioResearch Today.* A family of journals published by BioSciences Information Service in the field of biomedicine.

BRTA British Regional Television Association. 52 Mortimer St, London W1, England.

BS Backspace Character. A control character that causes backspacing to be performed.

BS Biochemical Society. 7 Warwick Court, Holborn, London WC1, England.

BSA Bibliographical Society of America. Box 397, Grand Central Sta, New York, NY 10017. Established in 1904. Publishes bibliographical material.

BSANZ Bibliographical Society of Australia and New Zealand. Dept. of English, Monash University, Clayton, Victoria 3168, Australia. Established in 1969.

BSCA Binary Synchronous Communicator Adapter.

BSCP Biological Science Communications Project. George Washington University Medical Center, 2001 S St, NW, Washington, DC 20009. Established in 1960. Dedicated to the bibliographic control of publications in the life sciences. Publishes documents. *See* Rebecca R. Wise. "Information Center Profile: Biological Sciences Communications Project." *Information, Part I: News/Sources/Profiles* 4 (Sept.–Oct. 1972): 299–301.

BSFA British Science Fiction Association. 77 College Rd, Blundellsands, Liverpool 23, England.

BSI British Standard Institution. Newton House, 101/103 Pentonville Rd, London N1, England. Affiliated with ISO (International Standards Organization).

BSIR *Bibliography of Scientific and Industrial Research.* Published by OTS from 1946 to 1953.

BSIRA British Scientific Instrument Research Association. *See* SIRA.

BSP Bibliographical Society of the Philippines. c/o National Archives, National Library Bldg, Teodoro M. Kalaw St, Ermita, Manila, Republic of the Philippines. Established in 1952.

BSP Bureau of Standards of the Philippines. Affiliated with ISO (International Standards Organization).

BSR Blip-Scan Ratio. Term pertaining to radar display systems.

BSRA British Sound Recording Association. 4 Fairfield Way, Ewell, Surrey, England.

BSRIA Buildings Services Research and Information Association. Old Bracknell Lane, Bracknell, Beeks RG 124AH, England. Established in 1959. Research in heating, ventilating and air conditioning. Formerly Heating and Ventilating Research Association. Name changed in 1975.

BSTL Bibliografické Středisko pro Techickou Literaturu (Bibliographical Center for Technical Literature). Klementinum 190, Prague I, Czechoslovakia.

BT Broader Term. Cross-reference in a thesaurus.

BTAM Basic Telecommunications Access Method. An access method in which, using telecommunications, each input/output statement results in a machine input/output operation.

BTAM Basic Terminal Access Method. Any access method in which an input/output statement results in a machine input/output operation.

BTI *British Technology Index*. V. 1, 1962. Published by the (British) Library Association. Computerized in Apr. 1968.

BTL Bell Telephone Laboratories. Murray Hill, NJ 07941.

BU Bibliothèques Universitaires. Contact ABF. Founded in 1885. An organization of French academic libraries.

BUCOP *British Union Catalog of Periodicals*. An international list of periodicals with holdings information for libraries in the UK. Published in four volumes from 1955 to 1958 and a fifth volume in 1962, the list is kept up to date by the Bibliographical Services Division of BL (British Library).

BUIC Back-Up Interceptor Control. A modular computing system developed by Burroughs Corp. for the D 825 military surveillance and warning systems for continental air defense.

BUP British United Press. 6 Bouverie St, London EC4, England.

BVD Belgische Vereniging voor Documentatie (Belgian Documentation Association). *See* ABD/BVD.

BVLJ/ABJA Belgische Vereniging van Landbouwjournalistes/Association Belge des Journalistes Agricoles (Belgian Guild of Agricultural Journalists). International Press Center, Maison de la Presse, boulevard Charlemagne 1, 1040 Brussels, Belgium. Established in 1957. Publishes documents.

BYGGDOK [Building Documentation]. Swedish Institute of Building Documentation, Halsingegatan 49, Stockholm S-113 31, Sweden. Coverage from 1975. Bibliographic data base covering architecture, civil engineering and urban planning.

BYGGREFERAT [Building References]. (Journal). V. 1, 1972. Published by the Swedish Institute of Building Documentation. Bibliographic references from the Nordic literature. *See also* BYGGDOK.

CA *Chemical Abstracts*. V. 1, 1907. Published by CAS (Chemical Abstracts Service).

CA Cuadra Associates, Inc. 1523 Sixth St, Santa Monica, CA 90401. Provides research, development and consulting in areas of on-line data base services and data base planning. Conducts educational seminars.

CAAA College Art Association of America. 16 East 52 St, New York, NY 10022. Established in 1912. Publishes documents. Sponsored by the International Conference on the Bibliography of Art History in Washington, DC, in Oct. 1971.

CAAS Canadian Association for Applied Spectroscopy. Name changed to Spectroscopy Society of Canada in 1967.

CAB Civil Aeronautics Board. 1825 Connecticut Ave, NW, Washington, DC 20428. Publishes documents. Maintains an Office of Information.

CAB Commonwealth Agricultural Bureaux. Farnham House, Farnham Royal, Near Slough, Buchs, England. Produces print and on-line abstracting and indexing services.

CABS Computer-Aided Batch Scheduling.

CABS Computer-Augmented Block System.

CABS Computerized Annotated Bibliography System.

CAC *Chemical Abstracts* Condensates. Bibliographic data base produced by CAS (Chemical Abstracts Service). Provides references to chemical literature and patents since 1968. Available on tape and on-line. Also known as CACon and CHEMCON.

CAC Committee on the Application of Computers in the Construction Industry. c/o Ministry of Public Building and Works, Lambeth Bridge House, Albert Embankment, London SE1, England. Established in 1966.

CAC *Current Abstracts of Chemistry.* Published by ISI (Institute for Scientific Information). Appeared as a separate publication only in 1977. Formerly and subsequently issued as *CAC&IC*. See also *IC (Index Chemicus).*

CAC&IC *Current Abstracts of Chemistry and Index Chemicus.* V. 1, 1970. Published by ISI (Institute for Scientific Information). Formerly *IC (Index Chemicus).*

CACL Canadian Association of Children's Librarians. c/o Canadian Library Association, 151 Sparks St, Ottawa ON K1P 5E3, Canada.

CACM *Communications of the Association for Computing Machinery.* No. 1, Jan. 1958.

CACon *Chemical Abstracts* Condensates. *See* CAC *(Chemical Abstracts* Condensates).

CACUL/ACBCU Canadian Association of College and University Libraries/Association Canadienne des Bibliothèques de Collège et d'Université. 151 Sparks St, Ottawa ON K1P 5E3, Canada. Established in 1963. Also known as ACBCU/CACUL.

CAD Computer-Aided Design.

CAD Computer-Aided Detection.

CADAP (Brazilian) Directory of Researchers. Instituto Brasileiro de Bibliografia e Documentação, Avenida General Justo 171, 20,000 Rio de Janeiro, GB, Brazil. Project to identify chemical and agricultural researchers in order to support SNICT and for policy making.

CADD Computer-Aided Design Drafting.

CADE Computer-Aided Design Engineering.

CADE Computer-Aided Design Evaluation.

CADET City Air Defense Evaluation Tool. A computer model used by the US Army.

CADFISS Computation and Data Flow Integrated Subsystems. Simulated flight tests for Mercury space flights.

CADIG Coventry and District Information Group. Reference and Technical Library, Trinity Churchyard, Coventry, Warwickshire, England.

CADO Central Air Documents Office. Consolidated with LC's Navy Research Section in 1951 to form ASTIA.

CADOCR Computer-Aided Design Optical Character Recognition.

CADPO Communication and Data Processing Operation.

CADPOS Communication and Data Processing Operation System.

CADRE Centre d'Animation, de Développement et de Recherche en Education. 1940 Est, boulevard Henri-Bourassa, Montreal PQ H5B 1S2, Canada. Library established in 1963.

CADRE Current Awareness and Document Retrieval for Engineers. A prototype of an automated information system, implemented as COMPENDEX.

CADS Computer-Aided Diagnosis System. University of Missouri Medical Center, Columbia, MO 65201. Developed at the University of Missouri Medical Center to calculate the probability of certain diseases, given particular symptom levels.

CADSS Combined Analog–Digital Systems Simulator.

CADSYS Computer-Aided Design System.

CAE Computer-Assisted Electro-cardiography.

CAFB Certificat d'Aptitude, Fonctions de Bibliothécaire. A recognition given for candidates in some French library schools who have library work experience. The recognition admits them to a different course of study than those who have never worked in a library. The certificate also qualifies holders to work as paraprofessionals.

CAFRAD Centre Africain de Formation et de Recherches Administratives pour le Développement. BP 310, Tangier, Morocco. Location of a developing network on administrative information and documentation.

CAHA Council of Academic Heads of Agriculture. A supporter of ASIN.

CAHSL Connecticut Association of Health Sciences Libraries. c/o Saint Francis Hospital and Medical Center, 114 Woodland St, Hartford, CT 06105. Forty-three hospital and academic medical libraries share in ILL, CE and standards programs.

CAHUMC Commission on Archives and History of the United Methodist Church. Box 488, Lake Junaluska, NC 28745. Established in 1968. Publishes documents. Maintains a library and museum.

CAI Computer-Aided Instruction. *See* CAI (Computer-Assisted Instruction).

CAI Computer-Assisted Instruction. Use of computers to teach. Also known as CAI (Computer-Aided Instruction) and CAI (Computer-Augmented Instruction).

CAI Computer-Assisted Instruction, Inc. 111 West Monroe St, Chicago, IL 60603.

CAI Computer-Assisted Instruction Regional Education Network. Lister Hill National Center for Biomedical Communication, Bethesda, MD 20014.

CAI Computer-Augmented Instruction. *See* CAI (Computer-Assisted Instruction).

CAIC Computer-Assisted Indexing and Categorizing. National Bureau of Standards, Administration Bldg, Washington, DC 20234. An automatic indexing system comprised of two programs: TESAT and IBSAT. *See* W. E. O'Toole and M. S. Keplinger. "An Experimental Program for Automatic Indexing at the National Bureau of Standards." *Proceedings of ASIS* 7 (1970): 301-303.

CAIFI Committee for Artistic and Intellectual Freedom in Iran. 853

Broadway, New York, NY 10003. Established in 1974. Conducts seminars and publishes a newsletter.

CAIM Computer-Assisted Instruction Management. Same as CMI (Computer-Managed Instructions) with emphasis on assistance to human manager of instruction rather than direct management by computer.

CAIM *Cumulated Abridged Index Medicus.* Washington, DC: Government Printing Office, 1970. Annual cumulation.

CAIN Cataloging and Indexing System of NAL. Coverage from 1970. A broad data base of agricultural and associated sciences information with five subsystems and a single keyboarding for inputs, editing, manipulation and merging of bibliographic data for many outputs. Now called AGRICOLA. *See* Vern J. Van Dyke and Nancy L. Ayer. "Multipurpose Cataloging and Indexing System (CAIN) at the National Agricultural Library." *JOLA* 5 (Mar. 1972): 21-29.

CAIN Cleveland Area Interloan Network. Name changed to CAMLS.

CAINT Computer-Assisted Interrogation. IBM Corp, Bethesda, MD. A system of computer programs for use in man-machine communications. Superficially resembles CAI (Computer-Assisted Instruction). *See* Charles T. Meadows and Douglas W. Waugh. "Computer Assisted Interrogation." *AFIPS Conference Proceedings* 29 (1966): 381-394.

CAIR Cost Analysis Information Report.

CAIRS Computer-Assisted Information Retrieval System.

CAIS Central Abstracting and Indexing Services.

CAIS/ACSI Canadian Association for Information Science/Association Canadienne des Sciences de l'Information. Box 158, Terminal A, Ottawa ON K1N 8V2, Canada. Established in 1970. Also known as ACSI/CAIS.

CAISM Computer-Assisted Industrial Simulation.

CAK Command Acknowledge. Recognition of the receipt of the signal to start, stop or continue computer or peripheral instruction.

CAL Center for Applied Linguistics. 1611 North Kent St, Arlington, VA 22209. Operates an information service for Americans going abroad for language training or for scholarly research in language fields.

CAL Central Association of Libraries. c/o Stockton–San Joaquin County Library, 605 Northeast Dorado, Stockton, CA 95202. Consortium of academic, public, school and special libraries of central California counties.

CAL Computer-Assisted Learning.

CAL Conversational Algebraic Language. A high-level language developed by the University of California for time-sharing purposes.

CALAS Computer-Assisted Language Analysis System.

CALB Computer-Aided Line Balancing.

CALBPC Colorado Academic Libraries Book Processing Center. Funded by NSF in August 1968. *See* Lawrence E. Leonard. "Colorado Academic Libraries Book Processing Center: A Feasibility Study." *C&RL* 29 (Sept. 1968): 393–399. *See also* Richard M. Daugherty and Joan M. Maies. *Centralized Processing for Academic Libraries*. Metuchen, NJ: Scarecrow Press, 1971.

CALC Chicago Academic Library Council. c/o Roosevelt University, Murray-Green Library, 430 South Michigan Ave, Chicago, IL 60605. Eight university libraries provide reciprocal borrowing privileges and cooperative systems of library service to students.

CALICO Columbus Area Library and Information Council of Ohio. 3359 Park St, Grove City, OH 43123.

CALINET California Library Network. 1237 Murphy Hall, University of California at Los Angeles, Los Angeles, CA 90024.

CALL *Current Awareness—Library Literature.* V. 1, 1972. Published by Goldstein Associates.

CALL/ACBD Canadian Association of Law Libraries/Association Canadienne des Bibliothèques de Droit. Box 220,

Adelaide St. Postal Sta, Toronto, ON M5C 2J1, Canada. Established in 1960. Official journal, *Canadian Association of Law Libraries Newsletter/Bulletin de l'Association Canadienne des Bibliothèques de Droit*, is published bimonthly. Also known as ACBD/CALL.

CALM Computer-Assisted Library Mechanization.

CALM Council of Academic Librarians of Manitoba. c/o Chief Librarian, University of Winnipeg Library, 515 Portage Ave, Winnipeg MB R3B 2E9, Canada.

CALOGSM Computer-Assisted Logistics Simulation.

CALROSA Committee on American Library Resources on South Asia. Name changed to CORMOSEA.

CALROSEA Committee on American Library Resources on Southeast Asia. Name changed to CORMOSEA.

CALS/ACEB Canadian Association of Library Schools/Association Canadienne des Écoles de Bibliothécaires. Contact president. Also known as ACEB/CALS.

CALUPL Council of Administrators of Large Urban Public Libraries. Contact secretary. A Canadian association.

CAM Communications Access Manager.

CAM Comprehensive Achievement Monitoring. Individualized instruction effort. Preceded TIES (Total Information for Educational Systems).

CAM Content-Addressed Memory.

CAMCOS Computer-Assisted Maintenance Planning and Control System.

CAMEL Computer-Aided Machine Loading.

CAMESA Canadian Military Electronics Standards Agency. Canadian Forces Headquarters, Dept. of National Defense, Ottawa 4, ON, Canada. Publishes documents and standards. Formerly JCNAAF.

CAM-I Computer-Aided Manufacturing International. 611 Ryan Plaza Dr, Suite 1107, Arlington, TX 76011. Established in 1972. Maintains a library, including a collection of software relating to computer-aided design and manufacturing.

CAML/ACBM Canadian Association of Music Libraries/Association Canadienne des Bibliothèques Musicales. c/o Music Division, National Library of Canada, 395 Wellington St, Ottawa ON K1A 0N4, Canada. Established in 1972. Also known as ACBM/CAML.

CAMLS Cleveland Area Metropolitan Library System. 11000 Euclid Ave, Cleveland, OH 44106. Twenty-one public, academic and special libraries cooperate through ILL and other services. Formerly CAIN (Cleveland Area Interloan Network).

CAMOL Computer-Assisted Management of Learning.

CAMP Computer-Assisted Mathematics Program. Glenview, IL: Scott, Foresman, 1968–1969. A series of books for junior and senior high school students on how to use the computer for the solution of mathematical problems and for the development of mathematical ideas.

CAMP Computer-Assisted Movie Production.

CAMP Cooperative Africana Microform Project. c/o Center for Research Libraries, 5721 Cottage Grove Ave, Chicago, IL 60637. Makes available microforms of scarce documents. Collection comprises newspapers, periodicals, archives, government documents and political ephemera, with an emphasis on Sub-Saharan Africa.

CANAC Catalogage National Centralisé. Centre de Traitement Informatique des Bibliothèques, Isle d'Abeau, France. A service that furnishes printed catalog cards recorded by BN.

CANCERLINE Cancer Online. A data base comprised of three segments: CANCERLIT, CANCERPROJ and CLINPROT. Available on-line through MEDLINE. Produced by ICRDB.

CANCERLIT Cancer Literature. Bibliographic data base on cancer. Coverage from 1963. A subset of CANCERLINE, available on-line

through MEDLINE. Produced by ICRDB.

CANCERNET Cancer Network. Institut Gustave Roussy, Service de Documentation Scientifique, 16 bis, avenue Paul Vaillant-Couturier, 94800 Villejuif, France. Bibliographic data base covering cancer research from 1968.

CANCERPROJ Cancer Projects. Data base describing international cancer research projects for the most recent three years. A subset of CANCERLINE. Available on-line through MEDLINE. Produced by CCRESPAC for ICRDB.

C&CA Cement and Concrete Association. 52 Grosvenor Gardens, London SW1, England. Maintains an information center.

CANDO Computer Analysis of Networks with Design Orientation.

C&RL *College and Research Libraries.* (Journal). V. 1, 1939. Published by the Association of College and Research Libraries.

CANFARM Canadian Farm Management Data System.

CAN/MARC Canadian MARC. Magnetic tapes holding records of Canadian monographs. Available by weekly subscription from MRDS. Also refers to the format into which cataloging information is put on CAN/MARC tapes.

CANMET Canada Centre for Mineral and Energy Technology. 555 Booth St, Ottawa ON K1A 0G1, Canada. Library was established in 1913.

CAN/OLE Canadian On-Line Enquiry. Canadian Institute for Scientific and Technical Information, National Research Council, Ottawa ON K1A 0S2, Canada. Provides 15 organizations with on-line access to the major scientific and technical data bases.

CAN/SDI Canadian Selective Dissemination of Information. A division of CISTI. *See* Jack E. Brown. "The CAN/SDI Project." *Special Libraries* 60 (Oct. 1969): 501–509. *See also* PIP.

CAN/TAP Canadian Technical Awareness Program. A program of CISTI.

CANTRAN Cancel Transmission. Indication to disregard a previous command to send data from one location to another.

CAOS Completely Automatic Operational System. Lockheed system for use on a UNIVAC computer.

CAP Configuration Analysis Program.

CAP Cooperative Acquisitions Program. Contact METRO. Publishes catalog of cooperative acquisitions of expensive materials to be shared by members of METRO.

CAPCON Capital Consortium Network. 1717 Massachusetts Ave, NW, Washington, DC 20036. Affiliated with OCLC.

CAPER Computer-Aided Perspective.

CAPERTSIM Computer-Assisted Program Evaluation Review Technique Simulation.

CAPESQ CADAP and CAIN. Instituto Brasileiro de Bibliografiae Documentação, Avenida General Justo 171, 20,000 Rio de Janeiro, GB, Brazil. Project to develop data bank serving as directory to ongoing scientific and technological agricultural research in Brazil linking CADAP and CAIN (Cataloging and Indexing System of NAL) into the Brazilian Data Bank Project.

CAPL Canadian Association of Public Libraries. c/o Canadian Library Association, 151 Sparks St, Ottawa ON K1P 5E3, Canada.

CAPM Computer-Aided Patient Management.

CAPPS Computer-Aided Project Planning System.

CAPS Cassette Programming System.

CAPS Computer-Aided Problem Solving.

CAPS Computer-Aided Project Study.

CAPSUL Computerized Access to Periodicals and Serials. Université Laval, Cité Universitaire, PQ G1K 7P4, Canada.

CAPTAIN Computer-Aided Processing and Terminal Access Information Network. Rutgers University, Alexander Library, New Brunswick, NJ 08903. System

established in 1973. Supports member libraries through centralized ordering, receiving, cataloging and reporting.

CARA Composition Automatic de Repertoires Analytiques. Centre de Documentation Bibliothèque, Université Laval, Cité Universitaire, PQ G1K 7P4, Canada.

CARBS Computer-Aided Rationalized Building System.

CARD Compact Automatic Retrieval Display.

CARDIAC Cardboard Illustrated Aid to Computation. Produced and distributed by Bell Telephone Co.

CARDOSEA Committee on Archives and Documents of Southeast Asia. Contact AAS (Association for Asian Studies).

CARDS Card-Automated Reproduction and Distribution System.

CARDS Computer-Aided Recording of Distribution Systems.

CARE Computer-Assisted Renewal Education. Pennsylvania State University, College of Education, University Park, PA 16802. A Computer-Assisted Instruction (CAI) course to help classroom teachers improve their ability to deal with handicapped children in regular classes.

CARES Central Advisory and Referral Service. An information referral service of METRO.

CARESS Career Retrieval Search System. Archive on Political Elites, Center for International Studies, G-7 Social Science Bldg, University of Pittsburgh, Pittsburgh, PA 15213.

CARIS Current Agricultural Research Information System. An information project of FAO (Food and Agriculture Organization).

CARL California Chapter of Academic and Research Libraries. Contact chairperson. Established in 1977.

CARL Canadian Academic Research Libraries. A division of CLA (Canadian Library Association).

CARL Comparative Animal Research Laboratory. 1299 Bethel Valley Rd, Oak Ridge, TN 37830. Maintains a library.

CARL/ABRC Canadian Association of Research Libraries/Association des Bibliothèques de Recherche du Canada. Contact secretary-treasurer. Established in 1976. Also known as ABRC/CARL.

CARML County and Regional Municipality Librarians. Contact secretary. Established in 1971. Replaces the County Library Institute. A Canadian association.

CARS Computer-Assisted Reliability Statistics.

CARS Computerized Automatic Reporting Service.

CART Computerized Automatic Rating Technique.

CAS Chemical Abstracts Service. Box 3012, Columbus, OH 43210. Major publishing division of ACS (American Chemical Society). Issues both machine-readable data bases and print products, including *CA (Chemical Abstracts)*, CAC *(Chemical Abstracts* Condensates), CASIA *(Chemical Abstracts* Subject Index Alert) and *CIN (Chemical Industry Notes)*.

CAS Computer Accounting System.

CAS Current Awareness Service.

CAS&ISR Center for African Studies and Institute for Social Research. University of Zambia, Box 900, Lusaka, Zambia. Formerly the Rhodes–Livingstone Institute, ISR became part of the university in 1966. CAS was founded in 1967. Library maintains microfiches of out-of-print Rhodes–Livingstone journals and papers.

CASC Computer-Assisted Cartography.

CASC Cooperative Acquisitions and Storage Center. METRO, 33 West 42 St, New York, NY 10036. *See* J. M. Cory. "The Network in a Major Metropolitan Center." *Library Quarterly* 39 (Jan. 1969): 90–98.

CASCUM Classification Analytico-Synthetica Cubana de Medicas. Formerly ASCOM. *See* Solomon M. Dorf Rudich et al. "ASCOM: Analytico-Synthetic Classification of Medicine." *Herald of Library Science* 12 (Oct. 1973): 299–312.

CASEA Center for the Advanced Study of Educational Administration. University of Oregon, 1472 Kincaid Ave, Eugene, OR 97403. Involved in information research.

CASH Computer-Aided Stock Holdings.

CASI Canadian Aeronautics and Space Institute. 77 Metcalfe St, Ottawa ON K1P 5L6, Canada. Publishes documents.

CASIA *Chemical Abstracts* Subject Index Alert. A biweekly computer-readable information service providing complete subject index entries for papers and patents abstracted in *CA (Chemical Abstracts)*. Produced by CAS (Chemical Abstracts Service).

CASIN Computer-Aided Subject Index. A machine indexing system used to process *Food Science and Technology Index* since 1975. *See* Klaus Schneider. *Computer Aided Subject Index System for the Life Sciences*. Frankfurt, Germany: ZMD, 1976.

CASLIS Canadian Association of Special Libraries and Information Services. Contact CLA (Canadian Library Association). Established in 1969. A division of CLA.

CASSI Chemical Abstracts Service Source Index. Available in both printed and machine-readable versions, CASSI provides bibliographic citations for all publications abstracted and indexed by CAS (Chemical Abstracts Service) and identifies libraries that hold these publications. Retrospective coverage since 1907.

CAST *Clearinghouse Announcements in Science and Technology*. V. 1, 1968. Published by CFSTI (Clearinghouse for Federal Scientific and Technical Information) until 1971.

CAST Computer-Assisted Scanning Techniques.

CASTOR College Applicant Status Report. A Honeywell system to compile information about college recruitment programs and college placement activities.

CAT Catalog of Computerized Subject Searches. Information Retrieval Center, Northern Colorado Educational BOCS,

1750 30th St, Suite 48, Boulder, CO 80301.

CATACEN Catalogoción Centralizada. A pilot project begun in 1973 for centralized cataloging based in Medellín, Colombia. Following MARC II format, the emphasis is on Latin American publications. Sponsored by OAS, UNESCO and others.

CATCH Computer Analysis of Thermo-Chemical Data Tables. School of Molecular Sciences, University of Sussex, Brighton BN1 9QH, Sussex, England. A project developed by Dr. J. B. Pedley.

CATED Centre d'Assistance Technique et de Documentation. Fédération Nationale du Bâtiment, 6-14 rue la Perouse, Cedex 16, 75784 Paris, France. Provides data base searches in the field of building construction.

CATLA Chicago Area Theological Library Association. c/o Western Theological Seminary, Beardslee Library, Holland, MI 49423. Fourteen libraries share resources and sponsor bibliographic projects.

CATLINE Cataloging On-Line. Data base including NLM monographic catalog entries from 1965, permitting retrieval of bibliographic information on-line. Available through MEDLINE.

CATSS Cataloguing Support System. Library Automation Systems Division, University of Toronto, 150 Saint George St, Toronto ON M5S 1A1, Canada.

CATV Cable Television.

CATV Community Antenna Television. The technology of CATV makes extensive use of coaxial cables and may be used by libraries. *See* Joseph Becker. "Telecommunications Primer." *JOLA* 2 (Sept. 1969): 148–156.

CAULPS Charlotte Area Union List of Periodicals and Serials. *See* J. F. Boykin. *North Carolina Libraries* 26 (Winter 1968): 21–23.

CAUT/ACPU Canadian Association of University Teachers/Association Canadienne des Professeurs d'Université. 66 Lisgar St, Ottawa ON K2P 0C1, Canada. Established in 1975. Has a Standing Committee of University Libraries that monitors conditions of employment of professional librarians and develops guidelines for the roles and functions of librarians within universities. Also known as ACPU/CAUT.

CAVAL Cooperative Action by Victorian Academic Libraries. Box 137, Parkville, Victoria 3052, Australia. An agency to further cooperation among Victorian libraries.

CAVE Catholic Audio-Visual Educators Association. Box 7195, Pittsburgh, PA 15213. Established in 1948. Publishes documents and sets standards for equipment used by members.

CAX Community Automatic Exchange. A small dial telephone office serving a community.

CB Conference Board. 845 Third Ave, New York, NY 10022. Established in 1916. Formerly NICB. Maintains a library. Conducts research and publishes studies.

C/B Cost-Benefit. A budgetary concept.

CBAC Chemical-Biological Activities. Bibliographic data base produced by CAS (Chemical Abstracts Service). Provides references to chemical/biological literature and patents since 1965. Available on tape and on-line.

CBC Canadian Broadcasting Corporation. CP 6000, Montreal PQ H3C 3A8, Canada. Has maintained a library since 1944.

CBC Children's Book Council. 67 Irving Pl, New York, NY 10003. Established in 1945. Maintains examination center for recently published children's books.

CBC Colegio de Bibliotecarios Colombianos (Association of Colombian Librarians). Merged with ASEIB to form CCB (Colegio Colombiano de Bibliotecarios) in 1968.

CBCT Customer Bank Communication Terminal.

CBD *Current Bibliographic Directory of the Arts and Sciences.* Philadelphia, PA: Institute for Scientific Information, 1979. Formerly *WIPIS*.

CBDA Comissão Brasileira de Documentação Agricola (Brazilian Commission for Agricultural Documentation). c/o Museu Paraense "Emilio Goeldi," Caixa Postal 399, Belém, Pará, Brazil. Established in 1967.

CBE Council of Biology Editors. Dept. of Anatomy-North Campus, School of Medicine, University of New Mexico, Albuquerque, NM 87131. Established in 1957. Investigates all aspects of biological communication, especially primary journals and retrieval in secondary media. Publications include *CBE Style Manual*.

CBEL *Cambridge Bibliography of English Literature*. Frederick Wilse Bateson, ed. Cambridge, England: The University Press, 1940-1957.

CBEM Computer-Based Educational Materials.

CBEMA Computer and Business Equipment Manufacturers Association. 1828 L St, NW, Washington, DC 20036. Formerly (1972) BEMA and (1961) OEMI.

CBHL Council on Botanical and Horticultural Libraries. c/o John Reed, Administrative Librarian, The New York Botanical Garden, Bronx, NY 10458. Established in 1970. One of its goals is to initiate and improve communication between persons and institutions in botany and horticulture.

CBI Confederation of British Industries. 21 Tothill St, London SW1, England. Includes computer and communication industries.

CBI *Cumulative Book Index*. New York: H. W. Wilson Co, 1898- . Cumulated annually since 1969.

CBIP *Children's Books in Print*. New York: R. R. Bowker Co, 1969- . Supersedes *CBSL*.

CBL Cercle Belge de la Libraire (Belgium Booksellers Association). Avenue du Parc 111, 1060 Brussels, Belgium. Established in 1883. Publishes documents. Does bibliographical research.

CBMS Conference Board of the Mathematical Sciences. 1500 Massachusetts Ave, NW, Washington,

DC 20005. Established in 1960. Publishes documents.

CBN Centre Bibliographique National. Established in 1977. One of several services divisions of the French national library set up under DICA.

CBPC Canadian Book Publishers Council. 45 Charles St. East, Toronto ON M4Y 1S2, Canada. Maintains a library.

CBPE-DDIP Centro Brasileiro de Pesquisas Educacionais-Divisão de Documentacão e Informacão Pedagógica (Brazilian Center of Educational Research-Department of Educational Documentation and Information). Rua Voluntários da Patria n 107, Botafogo, Rio de Janeiro, GB, Brazil.

CBPQ/CPLQ Corporation des Bibliothécaires Professionnels du Québec/Corporation of Professional Librarians of Quebec. *See* CPLQ/CBPQ.

CBR Centralna Biblioteka Rolnicza (Central Agricultural Library). Krakowskie Przedmiescie 66, Warsaw, Poland.

CBRA Copper and Brass Research Association. Name changed to CDA (Copper Development Association, Inc.).

CBS Central Bibliographic System. Developed by LC.

CBS Columbia Broadcasting System, Inc. CBS News Reference Library, 524 West 57 St, New York, NY 10019. Library established in 1940.

CBSL *Children's Books for Schools and Libraries*. New York: R. R. Bowker Co, 1966/67-1968/69. Superseded by *Children's Books in Print* in 1969.

CBST *Current Bibliography on Science and Technology*. Published by the Japan Information Center for Science and Technology. Eight current subject bibliographies in the fields of science and technology.

CC Collecióne de Consulta. Spanish term for reference collection.

CC Colon Classification. A faceted classification system developed by Ranganathan.

CC Current Contents. V. 1, 1961. Published by ISI (Institute for Scientific Information). A family of publications that reprint tables of contents of journals in many disciplines.

CC Cursor Control. A movable spot of light on the cathode ray tube of a visual display unit that indicates where the next character will be entered.

CCA *Computer and Control Abstracts.* V. 1, 1966. Published by the Institution of Electrical Engineers. Also called *Science Abstracts, Section C.*

CCA Computer Corporation of America. 575 Technology Sq, Cambridge, MA 02139.

CC/A&H *Current Contents/Arts and Humanities.* (Journal). V. 1, 1979. Published by ISI (Institute for Scientific Information).

CC/AB&ES *Current Contents/Agriculture, Biology and Environmental Sciences.* (Journal). V. 1, 1969. Published by ISI (Institute for Scientific Information). Formerly *CC/AFV.*

CC/AFV *Current Contents/Agricultural, Food and Veterinary Sciences.* (Journal). Name changed to *CC/AB&ES.*

CCB Colegio Colombiano de Bibliotecarios (Colombian Association of Librarians). Apartado Aereo 3272, Bogotá, Colombia. Established in 1968. Formed from the merger of ASEIB and CBC.

CC/BSE *Current Contents/Behavioral, Social and Educational Sciences.* (Journal). Name changed to *CC/S&BS.*

CCC Canadian Committee on Cataloguing/Comité Canadien de Catalogage. Secretariat, Office of Library Standards, Rm. 478, National Library of Canada, 395 Wellington St, Ottawa ON K1A 0N4, Canada.

CCC Catalog Card Corporation of America. 888 East 80 St, Minneapolis, MN 55420. Sells catalog cards.

CCC Copyright Clearance Center. Association of American Publishers, One Park Ave, New York, NY 10016. Operated by AAP (Association of American Publishers). Collects and distributes fees for copyrighted journal articles not covered by the "fair use" provisions of the US Copyright Law of 1976.

CC/CP *Current Contents/Clinical Practice.* (Journal). V. 1, 1973. Published by ISI (Institute for Scientific Information).

CC/CPML *Current Contents/Chemical, Pharmaco-Medical and Life Sciences.* (Journal). Name changed to *CC/LS.*

CCDA Commercial Chemical Development Association. In 1970 became CDA (Commercial Development Association).

CCDN Neutron Data Compilation Center. European Nuclear Energy Agency, B.P. 9, 91 Gif-Sur-Yvette, France.

CCEB/CCLS Conseil Canadien des Écoles de Bibliothécaires/Canadian Council of Library Schools. *See* CCLS/CCEB.

CCEI Colorado Committee for Environmental Information. Boulder, CO. Members are an action group of employees of the University of Colorado, private research laboratories and federal laboratories. Emphasis is on environmental problems within the state.

CCEP Commission Consultative des Études Postales (Consultative Commission for the Study of Postal Services). Box 15, Berne, Switzerland.

CC/ET&AS *Current Contents/Engineering, Technology and Applied Sciences.* (Journal). V. 1, 1970. Published by ISI (Institute for Scientific Information).

CCFMC Center for the Coordination of Foreign Manuscript Copying. Sponsored by LC from 1965 to 1970.

CCH Commerce Clearing House, Inc. 420 Lexington Ave, New York, NY 10017. Publishes loose-leaf services in the fields of business, law and economics.

CCI Council on Consumer Information. Name changed in 1969 to ACCJ.

CCIP/CCPE Conseil Canadien des Ingénieurs Professionels/Canadian Council of Professional Engineers. *See* CCPE/CCIP.

CCIR Center for Communication and Information Research. Graduate School of Librarianship, University of Denver, University Park, Denver, CO 80210.

CCIR Comité Consultatif International des Radiocommunications (International Radio Consultative Committee). Place des Nations, 1211 Geneva 20, Switzerland.

CCITT Consultative Committee on International Telegraph and Telephone (Comité Consultatif International Telegraphie et Telephonie). A committee of ITU and the international organization concerned with telecommunication standards and policies.

CCLC Cooperative College Library Center. 159 Forrest Ave, NE, Suite 602, Atlanta, GA 30303. Consortium of 34 college libraries in a 12-state area cooperate through aquisitions, processing and cataloging.

CCLIC Community College Library Consortium. c/o Shoreline Community College, 16101 Greenwood Ave. North, Seattle, WA 98133. Thirteen junior college libraries cooperate through ILL, union lists, depository and film libraries.

CCLM Coordinating Council of Literary Magazines. 80 Eighth Ave, Rm. 1302, New York, NY 10011. Established in 1967 through an NEA grant to provide grants and other services to noncommercial literary magazines. Maintains a library. Publishes a newsletter.

CCLN Council for Computerized Library Networks. 1225 Connecticut Ave, NW, Suite 201, Washington, DC 20036. Established in 1974.

CCLO Coordinating Council of Library Organizations. Millikan Library, 1-32, Caltech, Pasadena, CA 91109.

CC/LS *Current Contents/Life Sciences.* (Journal). V. 1, 1958. Published by ISI (Institute for Scientific Information). Formerly *CC/CPML.*

CCLS/CCEB Canadian Council of Library Schools/Conseil Canadien des Écoles de Bibliothécaires. Contact president. Established in 1971. Associate member of AUCC.

CCM Canadian Committee on MARC/Comité Canadien du MARC. Secretariat, Canadian MARC Office, Cataloging Branch, National Library of Canada, 395 Wellington St, Ottawa ON K1A 0N4, Canada. Canadian MARC advisory committee to the National Library.

CCOE Catalogue Collectif des Ouvrages Étrangers. Union catalog of non-French works in BU library collections.

CC/PC *Current Contents/Physical and Chemical Sciences.* (Journal). Name changed to *CC/PC&ES.*

CC/PC&ES *Current Contents/Physical, Chemical and Earth Sciences.* (Journal). V. 1, 1961. Published by ISI (Institute for Scientific Information). Formerly *CC/PC.*

CCPE/CCIP Canadian Council of Professional Engineers/Conseil Canadien des Ingénieurs Professionels. Suite 401, 116 Albert St, Ottawa ON K1P 5G3, Canada. Established in 1947. Publishes documents.

CCR *Current Chemical Reactions.* (Journal). V. 1, 1979. Published by ISI (Institute for Scientific Information). *CCR* is trademarked.

CCRESPAC Current Cancer Research Project Analysis Center. Operated by SSIE for the National Cancer Institute's ICRDB program. Produces CANCERPROJ and CLINPROT data bases and prepares technical bulletins and research project lists.

CCRG Canadian Classification Research Group/Groupe Canadien pour la Recherche en Classification. Contact coordinator. A regional group of FID.

CCRT Cataloging & Classification Roundtable. *See* CLA/CCRT.

CCRUR Consortium Canadien de Recherches Urbaines et Régionales. c/o URBARC Canada Library, 2500 Bates Rd, Montreal PQ H35 1A6, Canada.

CCS Canadian Ceramic Society. Contact secretary. Publishes documents.

CCS Cataloging and Classification Section. *See* RTSD/CCS.

CCS Council of Communication Societies. Box 1074, Silver Spring, MD 20910. Established in 1969. Publishes documents. Goal is to further research in communication methodologies.

CC/S&BS *Current Contents/Social and Behavioral Sciences.* (Journal). V. 1, 1969. Published by ISI (Institute for Scientific Information). Formerly *CC/BSE.*

CCSEM Computer-Controlled Scanning Electron Microscope.

CCTS Chicago Cluster of Theological Schools. 1100 East 55 St, Chicago, IL 60615. Consortium established in 1970. Nine libraries pursue complementary acquisitions policies and maintain a union catalog.

CCTV Closed-Circuit Television.

CCWI Collegiate Consortium of Western Indiana. c/o Cunningham Memorial Library, Indiana State University, Terre Haute, IN 47809. Six libraries provide reciprocal borrowing privileges to students.

CD Centro de Documentación. Spanish acronym for documentation center.

CDA Centrul de Documentare Agricolă (Agricultural Documentation Center). Boulevard Mărăsti 61, Bucharest 33, Rumania.

CDA Commercial Development Association. 999 Bedford St, Stamford, CT 06905. Established in 1943. Publishes documents. Formerly (1970) CCDA.

CDA Copper Development Association, Inc. 405 Lexington Ave, New York, NY 10017. Publishes documents. Formerly CBRA.

CDB Common Data Base. File used with the Substructure Search System used by *CA* (*Chemical Abstracts*) from 1970.

CDC Call-Directing Code. A code channeling contacts between two communications stations.

CDC Center for Disease Control. 1600 Clifton Rd, NE, Atlanta, GA 30333. Maintains a library and an information network. A unit of DHEW.

CDC Centro de Documentação Cientifica (Scientific Documentation Center). Biblioteca, Campo das Martires da Patria, Lisbon, Portugal. Established in 1937.

CDC Control Data Corporation. 8100 34th Ave. South, Minneapolis, MN 55440; 5272 River Rd, Washington, DC 20016.

CDC Cryogenic Data Center. US National Bureau of Standards–Cryogenics Division, Boulder, CO 80302.

CDCE Central Data Conversion Equipment. Centrally located equipment to change data from one form of representation to another or from one physical recording medium to another.

CDCR Center for Documentation and Communication Research. c/o Case Western Reserve University, 2040 Adelbert Rd, Cleveland, OH 44106.

CDDC Comisión de Documentación Científica (Scientific Documentation Center). Argentina.

CDDP Centro de Documentación y Divulgación Pedagógicas. Plaza de Cagancha 1175, Montevideo, Uruguay.

CDF Catalog Data File. A module of the BALLOTS System. Machine-readable catalog data for all roman alphabet material.

CDF Centrul de Documentare Technică Pentru Economia Forestieră (Documentation Center on Forestry). Soseana Pipera 46, Sector 2, Bucharest 30, Rumania.

CDI Comprehensive Dissertation Index. University Microfilms International, 300 North Zeeb Rd, Ann Arbor, MI 48106. Coverage from 1861. Bibliographic data base that indexes *DAI* (*Dissertations Abstracts International*).

CDICIP Centrul de Documentare al Industriei Chimice si Petroliere (Documentation Center of the Chemical and Oil Industry). Boulevard N.-Bălsescu 16, Sect. I, Bucharest, Rumania.

CDIF Centre de Documención e Información Educativa (Educational Documentation and Information Center). Presidente Mazarik 526, México, DF, Mexico.

CDIUPA Centre de Documentation International des Industries Utilisatrices de Produits Agricoles. Avenue des Olympiades, 91305 Massy, France. International documentation center for industries utilizing agricultural products.

CDL Citizens for Decency through Law. 450 Leader Bldg, Cleveland, OH 44114. Established in 1957. Publishes documents. Goal is to uphold existing laws against pornographic literature and its distribution.

CDL Citizens for Decent Literature. *See* CDL (Citizens for Decency through Law).

CDM Centrul de Documentare Medicală (Medical Documentation Center). Str. Polona 4, Bucharest 1, Rumania.

CDN Centre de Documentation Nationale (National Documentation Center). 2 rue d'Alger, Tunis, Tunisia.

CDPS Computing and Data Processing Society. Canada.

CDPT-MCF Centrul de Documentare si Publicatü Tehnice al Ministerulue Cailór Ferate (Technical Documentation and Publications Center of the Railway Ministry). Caléa Grivitei 193B, Bucharest 12, Rumania.

CDS Centrul de Documentare Stiitifică al Academiei Republicii Socialiste România (Scientific Documentation Center of the Academy of the Socialist Republic of Rumania). Str. Gutenberg 3 bis, Bucharest, Sect. VI, Rumania.

CDS Compatible Duplex System. A system in which a pair (of channels or of backup equipment) is compatible.

CDS Comprehensive Display System.

CE Continuing Education.

C/E Cost-Effectiveness.

CEA Canadian Education Association. 252 Bloor St. West, Toronto ON M5S 1V5, Canada.

CEA Cinematograph Exhibitors Association of Great Britain and Ireland. 22-25 Dean St, London W1, England.

CEA Commissariat à L'Energie Atomique (Atomic Energy Commission). 29-33 rue de la Fédération, 75 Paris 15, France.

CEA Cost-Effectiveness Analysis.

CEAL Committee on East Asian Libraries of the Association for Asian Studies. Contact AAS (Association for Asian Studies).

CEAS Cooperative Educational Abstracting Service. A service of UNESCO issued in 1968.

CEBFO Conseil des Enseignants— Bibliothécaires Franco-Ontariens. c/o Executive Assistant, l'Association des Enseignants Franco-Ontariens, 1427 Ogilvie Rd, Suite 202, Ottawa ON K1J 8M7, Canada. Established in 1975.

CEC Consulting Engineers Council. Established in 1956. Merged in 1973 with AICE to form ACEC (American Consulting Engineers Council).

CEC Council for Exceptional Children Information Services. 1920 Association Dr, Reston, VA 22091. Provides abstracts, bibliographies, computer searches, indexes, journals and other publications concerning exceptional (including handicapped) children. Produces ECER.

CECA Communauté Européenne du Carbon et de l'Acier. Documentation-Archives, 2 place de Metz, Luxemburg City, Luxembourg.

CED Centro de Esploroj Kaj Documentado (Research and Documentation Center). 77 Grasmere Ave, Wembley, Middlesex, England.

CEDAL Centro de Documentación Audiovisual para A.L. ILCE–UNESCO, Apardo Postal 15862, México, DF, Mexico.

CEDDA Center of Experiment Design and Data Analysis. Tries to control and standardize scientific data for reuse. *See* Elizabeth W. Stone and L. Christopher Wright. "Data and Information Services of the National Oceanic and Atmospheric Administration." *Special Libraries* 65 (Aug. 1974): 311-318.

CEDE Center for Studies in Economic Development. Calle 18-A, Carrera 1-E, Apartado Aereo 4976, Bogotá, Colombia. Produces data bases on demography and sociology.

CEDEL Centrale de Livraison de Valeurs Mobilieres. A system started in January 1971 to transfer bonds without physical delivery. Based in Luxembourg.

CEDIJ Centre d'Informatique Juridique. 5 rue Carnot, 78000 Versailles, France. Produces a data base for commercial, fiscal, municipal, urban and national defense legislation.

CEDO Center for Educational Development Overseas. The Studio, Nuffield Lodge, Regent's Park, London NW1, England. Formerly CETO.

CEDOBUL Centre de Documentation de la Biblothèque de l'Université Laval (Documentation Center of the Library of l'Université Laval). Cité Universitaire, Quebec PQ, Canada.

CEDOCA Centre de Documentation Africaine (African Documentation Center). Bibliothèque Royale Albert-Ier, 4 boulevard de l'Empereur, Brussels 1, Belgium.

CEDOCAR Centre de Documentation de l'Armament. 2 bis, boulevard Victor, 75015 Paris, France. Produces a data base and provides data base searches in the field of armaments.

CEDORES Centre de Documentation et de Recherche Sociales. Avenue Meurée 39, B-6001 Marcinelle, Belgium.

CEDPA California Educational Data Processing Association. Contact president.

CEE Comunità Economica Europea. See EEC (European Economic Community).

CEE Giurisprudenza Corte 2. Giurstizia delle CEE. Centro Elettronico di Documentazione-Italgiure, Corte Suprema di Cassaziono, Palazzo di Giustizia, Via Ulpiano 8, Rome 00193, Italy. Coverage from 1950. Full-text data base covering decisions of the EEC (European Economic Community) Court of Justice.

CEED Curricula for Ethnic Education Directory. University of Nevada, College of Education, Reno, NV 89507. A project, started in 1975, to develop a directory for elementary and secondary teachers.

CEEFAX A televised information magazine started by BBC (British Broadcasting Corporation) in 1972. See Liz Donnelly. "This Is CEEFAX." Assistant Librarian 69 (Jan. 1976): 2–4.

CEG Computer Education Group. Staffordshire College of Technology, Beaconside, Stafford, England.

CEI Committee for Environmental Information. 6267 Delmar Blvd, Saint Louis, MO 63130. Established in 1958. Local group of scientists and others involved in dissemination of environmental information. Maintains a library.

CEI Computer-Extended Instruction. An approach to teach high school students how to use a computer to handle complex problems within traditional disciplines. See William S. Dorn. "Computers in the High School: A Tool for Explorations." Datamation 13 (Feb. 1967): 34–38.

CEIR Corporation for Economics and Industrial Research. 5272 River Rd, Washington, DC 20016. A subsidiary of CDC (Control Data Corporation).

CEIS California Education Information System. See H. Adams. "CEIS in California Regional Centers." Journal of Educational Data Processing 6 (Summer 1969): 181–191.

CEIST Centro Europeo Informazioni Scientifiche e Tecniche. Via G. L. Squarcialupo 19 A, 00162 Rome, Italy. An information center providing reference services in the fields of hydrology, agriculture and environmental pollution.

CELPLO Chief Executives of Large Public Libraries. Contact chairperson. A Canadian organization.

CELS Continuing Education for Library Staffs in the Southwest. A project of SLA (Southwestern Library Association).

CELT Classified Entries in Lateral Transposition. Computer system generating a permuted index. Uses faceted classification schemes, rotating the classification code. See Helen M. Townley. "Computers and Indexes." The Indexer 6 (Spring 1969): 102–107.

CEMBA Collection and Evaluation of Materials on Black Americans. Alabama A&M University, Huntsville, AL 35762. Consortium established in 1969. Part of ACHE (Alabama Center for Higher Education). Developing archives emphasizing contributions of Blacks to American life.

CEMP Centre d'Étude des Matières Plastiques (Plastics Research Center). 21 rue Pinel, Paris 13, France.

CENDES Centro de Desarrollo Industrial (Center for Industrial Development). Casilla 2321, Quito, Ecuador.

CENID Centro Nacional de Información y Documentación (National Center for

Information and Documentation).
Bernarda Morin 560, Santiago, Chile.

CENTI Centre pour le Traitement de
l'Information (Information Processing
Center). 128 rue des Rennes, Paris 6,
France. Sponsors information seminars.

CENTRO Central New York Library
Resources Council. 763 Butternut St,
Syracuse, NY 13208. Thirty-four
academic, public, hospital and special
libraries cooperate through resource
sharing, NYSILL access point, teletype
network, workshops and union list of
serials.

CEP Council on Economic Priorities. 84
Fifth Ave, New York, NY 10011.
Established in 1969. A research and
information group. Publishes
documents.

CEPS Civil Engineering Problems. A
problem-oriented, modular language
with an expandable instruction
repertoire. Produced by CDC (Control
Data Corporation).

CEPT Conférence Européene des
Administrations des Postes et des
Télécommunications (European
Conference of Postal and
Telecommunication Administrations).
Bollwerk 25, 3000 Berne, Switzerland.

CERA/ACCE Canadian Educational
Researchers Association/Association
Canadienne des Chercheurs en
Éducation. Ontario Institute for Studies
in Education, 102 Bloor St, West,
Toronto 5, ON, Canada. Also known as
ACCE/CERA.

CERCHAR Centre d'Études et Recherches
des Charbonnages de France. 35 rue
Saint-Dominique, 75 Paris 7, France.

CERD Center for Environmental Research
and Development. University of New
Mexico, Technology Application
Center, 2500 Central Ave, SE,
Albuquerque, NM 87131. Maintains a
library.

CERI Center for Educational Research and
Innovation. Organization for Economic
Cooperation and Development, 2 rue
André Pascal, Paris 16, France. See
*Proceedings of the First IFIP World
Conference on Computer Education*,
Aug. 24–28, 1970. Amsterdam, the
Netherlands.

CERILH Centre d'Études et de Recherches
de l'Industrie des Liants Hydrauliques.
23 rue de Cronstadt, 75015 Paris,
France. Produces a data base on
concrete.

CERINDEX Céramique Index. Institut de
Céramique Française, 6 Grande Rue,
Sèvres 92310, France. Coverage from
1972. Bibliographic data base covering
ceramics.

CERLAL Centro Regional para el Fomento
del Libro en América Latina y el Caribe
(Regional Center for the Encouragement
of the Book in Latin America and the
Caribbean). Calle 70, Numéro 9-52,
Bogotá, Colombia. Publishes *Boletín
Bibliografico*.

CERN Centre Européene pour la Recherche
Nucléaire (European Center for Nuclear
Research). Now called Organisation
Européene pour la Recherche Nucléaire
(European Organization for Nuclear
Research), but still uses the acronym
CERN. Member countries include
Austria, Belgium, Denmark, France, the
Federal Republic of Germany, Greece,
Italy, the Netherlands, Norway,
Sweden, Switzerland and the UK.
Involved in information networks.

CESPO Centro d'Estudios Sociales y de
Población. Ciudad Universitaria
"Rodrigo Facio," Apartado 49, San
José, Costa Rica. Produces a data base
in sociology.

CESS Council of Engineering and Scientific
Society Secretaries. Formerly (1965)
Council of Engineering Society
Secretaries. Name changed to CESSE in
1970.

CESSE Council of Engineering and
Scientific Society Executives. United
Engineering Center, Rm. 306, 345 East
47 St, New York, NY 10017. Formerly
Council of Engineering Society
Secretaries; name changed to CESS in
1965 and to CESSE in 1970. Publishes
documents.

CET Centre Européene de Traduction
(European Translation Center).
Doelenstraat 101, Delft, the
Netherlands.

CET Council for Educational Technology.
160 Great Portland St, London W1N
5TB, England. Government agency
established in 1967 as NCET. Became

CET in 1973. Published *HELPIS*. Advises governmental bodies concerned with education, conducts research and publishes reports.

CETIB Centre de Traitement Informatique des Bibliothèques. Isle d'Abeau, France. Location of CANAC.

CETIS Centre de Traitement de l'Information Scientifique (European Scientific Information Processing Center). European Atomic Energy Community, Ispra Library, Varese, Italy. Developing a new version of the SLC (Simulated Linguistic Computer) system for automatic language translation; also worked with CNR of Italy on the ILS used in the EURATOM Ispra Library.

CETO Centre for Educational Television Overseas. Name changed to CEDO.

CEU Continuing Education Unit. Ten hours of participation in an organized continuing education class under responsible sponsorship and qualified instruction. Accepted as a standard by many professions.

CEUCORS European Center for the Coordination of Research and Documentation in the Social Sciences. Franz-Josephs Kai 3-4, Vienna 1, Austria.

CF Control Footing. A summary or total at the end of a control group or multiple control groups.

CFB Conselho Federal de Biblioteconomia (National Council of Librarianship). Edifício Marcia Sala 211, SCSul, Brasília, DF, Brazil. Established in 1962.

CFC Cinematographic Films Council. Board of Trade, One Victoria St, London SW1, England.

CFF Children's Film Foundation Ltd. 8 Great Portland St, London W1, England.

CFL Central Film Library. Government Bldg, Bromyard Ave, London W3, England.

CFM Cubic Feet per Minute.

CFP Canadian Forces Publications. Prefix to numbered series of Canadian Forces Publications issued by the Department of Defense of Canada.

CFRI Central Fuel Research Institute. PO Fri, District Dhanbad, Bihar, India.

CFS Combined File Search. An IBM program, the format of which consists of a searchable segment of all index terms and their qualifiers, and a display segment of titles and full citations.

CFSS Combined File Search System. CFSS selects a subset of a full file by matching the descriptors of a query with an inverted file without regard to logical restrictions. It then examines the selected subset in the linear file to determine which items in the subset meet the logical restrictions of the query statement.

CFSTI Clearinghouse for Federal Scientific and Technical Information. Established in 1965. Formerly OTS (Office of Technical Services). Name changed to NTIS in 1971.

CGE Canadian General Electric Company, Ltd. Corporate Library, Box 417, Commerce Court Postal Sta, Toronto ON M5L 1J2, Canada. Maintains libraries in four locations on different aspects of company interest.

CH Control Heading. A title or short definition of a control group of records which appears in front of each such group.

CHA Catholic Hospital Association. 1438 South Grand Blvd, Saint Louis, MO 63104. Established in 1915. Publishes *Hospital Progress* and *Guidebook of Catholic Health Care Facilities*. Maintains a library.

CHAIN Channeled Arizona Information Network. Dept. of Library, Archives and Public Records, Library Extension Service, 2219 South 48 St, Suite D, Tempe, AZ 85282. Provides ILL for all Arizona libraries.

CHARGE Consortium of Hospital and Rehabilitative Geriatric Enterprises. A plan to provide audiovisual materials to nursing homes in New Jersey.

CHARIBIDIS Chalk River Bibliographic Data Information System. Atomic Energy of Canada, Ltd, Chalk River Nuclear Laboratories, Chalk River ON K0J 1J0, Canada. Long-term project to automate major library services involving professional librarians.

CHDL Computer Hardware Description Language.

CHEMCON *Chemical Abstracts* Condensates. *See* CAC (*Chemical Abstracts* Condensates).

Chemico Chemical Construction Corporation. Library, One Penn Pl, New York, NY 10001. Library established in 1955.

CHEMLINE Chemical Dictionary On-Line. Toxicology Information Program, National Library of Medicine, 8600 Rockville Pike, Bethesda, MD 20014. Nonbibliographic data base covering chemical substance names, formulas and synonyms.

CHEMNAME *Chemical Abstracts* Chemical Name Dictionary. Data base listing chemical substances. Produced by CAS (Chemical Abstracts Service).

CHEN Council for Higher Education in Newark. 53 Washington St, Newark, NJ 07102. Six libraries cooperate for reciprocal borrowing, circulation and reference personnel meetings.

CHEOPS Chemical Information Systems Operators. Name changed to EUSIDIC.

CHERS Consortium for Higher Education Religion Studies. CHERS, Inc, 1810 Harvard Blvd, Dayton, OH 45406. Network for libraries involved in religious education.

CHF Canadian Hunger Foundation. 75 Parks St, Ottawa ON K1P 5A5, Canada. Library service available in both French and English. Also known as Fondation Canadienne Contre la Faim.

CHIEF Controlled Handling of Internal Executive Functions. A UNIVAC computer program.

CHIN Community Health Information Network. c/o Mt. Auburn Hospital, 330 Mt. Auburn St, Cambridge, MA 02138. Six medical and public libraries cooperate to provide health-related and medical information to consumers and health professionals. *See* Ellen Gartenfeld. "The Community Health Information Network: A Model for Hospital and Public Library Cooperation." *Library Journal* 103 (Oct. 1, 1978): 1911–1914.

CHIPS Calculator Help in Processing Signals.

CHIPS Consumer Health Information Program and Service. Carson Regional Library, 150 East 216 St, Carson City, CA 90745. *See* Eleanor Goodchild. "CHIPS: Consumer Health Information Programs and Services in Los Angeles." *California Librarian* 39 (Jan. 1978): 19–24.

CHIPS Cooperative High School Independent Press Syndicate. 2007 Washtenaw Ave, Ann Arbor, MI 48104. A membership organization of high school newspapers.

CHLA/ABSC Canadian Health Libraries Association/Association des Bibliothèques de la Santé du Canada. 380 Olivier Ave, Westmount PQ H3Z 2C9, Canada. Established in 1976. Also known as ABSC/CHLA.

CHOICE Clearinghouse for Options in Children's Education. Summer School Bldg, 17 & M Sts, NW, Washington, DC 20036. Maintains a library and publishes a newsletter. Formerly Washington Area Free School Clearinghouse.

CHORD—S Computer Handling of Reactor Data—Safety. Oak Ridge National Laboratory, Oak Ridge, TN 37830. An on-line system for direct retrieval of technical data relating to nuclear power plant design. *See* D. W. Cardwell. "Interactive Telecommunications Access by Computer to Design Characteristics of the Nation's Nuclear Power Stations." *AFIPS Conference Proceedings* 33 (1968): 243–253.

CHSL Cleveland Health Sciences Library. 2119 Abington Rd, Cleveland, OH 44106.

CHUM *Computers and the Humanities.* V. 1, 1966. Published by CHUM, Queens College, CUNY. Text in English, French and German. Also a machine-readable data base.

CI Centro de Información. Spanish acronym for information center.

CIA Central Intelligence Agency. Washington, DC 20505.

CIADES Centro Interamericano de Documentación Económia y Social (Interamerican Center for Economic and Social Documentation). Box 179D, Santiago, Chile.

CIA/ICA Conseil International des Archives/International Council on

Archives. 60 rue des Francs-Bourgeois, 75003 Paris, France. Established in 1950. Affiliated with FID and IFLA.

CIATO Centre International d'Alcoologie/Taxicomanies. 3 Clochetons, CH-1004 Lausanne, Switzerland. The Documentation Division collects printed, mimeographed and typewritten theses on drug addiction and alcoholism from Jan. 1966 to date.

CIBC Council on Interracial Books for Children. 1841 Broadway, New York, NY 10023. Established in 1965.

CIC Chemical Institute of Canada. 151 Slater St, Ottawa 4 ON, Canada.

CIC Committee on Institutional Cooperation. 820 Davis St, Suite 130, Evanston, IL 60201. Established in 1958. Consortium of 11 Midwestern universities for cooperative ventures through shared resources.

CIC Committee on Intersociety Cooperation. Contact ASIS.

CIC Commonwealth Information Centre. Marlborough House, Pall Mall, London SW1, England.

CIC Conseil International des Compositeurs. 72 Courtfield Gardens, London SW 5, England.

CICAE Confédération Internationale des Cinémas d'Art et d'Essai (International Experimental and Art Film Theatres Confederation). Bureau 22; 92 Champs Elysées, Paris 8, France.

CICAR Cooperative Investigations of the Caribbean and Adjacent Regions. A program supported by NODC (National Oceanographic Data Center).

CICAS Computer-Integrated Command and Attack Systems.

CICH Centro de Información Científica y Humanística (Center for Scientific and Humanistic Information). Established in 1971. A department of UNAM (Mexico).

CICIN Conference on Interlibrary Communications and Information Networks. Sept. 28–Oct. 2, 1970. Airlie House. See R. B. Lane. "The Conference on Interlibrary Communications and Information Networks." Special Libraries 61 (1970): 523–526.

CICIREPATO Committee for International Cooperation in Information Retrieval among Examining Patent Officers. See ICIREPAT.

CICRIS Cooperative Industrial and Commercial Reference and Information Service. Acton Central Public Library, High St, London W3, England. A consortium of West London libraries cooperate through coordinated purchasing and ILL.

CICS Customer Information Control System. Produced by IBM.

CID Center for Information and Documentation. European Atomic Energy Community, Rue de la Loi 200, 1040 Brussels, Belgium. Established in 1961. EURATOM's computerized information center has its own thesaurus. Includes documents from 1947. See Loll N. Rolling. "A Computer-Aided Information Service for Nuclear Science and Technology." Journal of Documentation 22 (June 1966): 93–115.

CID Centro de Información y Documentación del Patronato de Investigación Científica y Técnica Juan de la Cierva (Information and Documentation Center of the Juan de la Cierva Patronage). Joaquin Costa 22, Madrid-6, Spain. Established in 1952. Maintains a library and does reference work and abstracting.

CIDA Cancer Information Dissemination and Analysis. National Cancer Institute, Rm. 10A35, Bldg. 31, 9000 Rockville Pike, Bethesda, MD 20014. Segment of ICRDB program of the National Cancer Institute. Planned and developed CANCERLINE from 1972 to use free text search strategy. Also known as CIDAC.

CIDA Centre d'Informatique et Documentation Automatique. One rue Guy de la Brosse, 75005 Paris, France. Produces a data base covering chemical compounds.

CIDAC Cancer Information Dissemination and Analysis Center. See CIDA (Cancer Information Dissemination and Analysis).

CIDB Centre d'Information et de Documentation du Bâtiment. 100 rue du Cherche-Midi, F-75008 Paris, France. Established in 1946.

CIDEM Consejo Interamericano de Musica (Inter-American Music Council). Technical Unit of Music, Organization of American States Bldg, Washington, DC 20006. Established in 1956.

CIDES Centre de Documentation Économique et Sociale. 6 rue de l'Industrie, Brussels 4, Belgium.

CIDIA Centro Interamericano de Documentación e Información Agrícola (Interamerican Center for Agricultural Documentation and Information). Instituto Interamericano de Ciencias Agrícolas, Apartado 74, Turrialba, Costa Rica. A subgroup of IICA.

CIDNET Consortium for International Development Information Network. University of California, Riverside, US Agency for International Development, Moisture Utilization in Semi-Arid Tropics Information Center, Riverside, CA 92501.

CIDOC Centro Interamericano de Documentación. Apardo Postal 479, Cuernavaca, Mexico.

CIDS Chemical Information and Data System. US Army, Edgewood Arsenal, MD 21010.

CIDST Committee for Information and Documentation on Science and Technology. A committee of the European Communities.

CIES Council for International Exchange of Scholars. 11 Dupont Circle, Washington, DC 20036. Assists in the administration of Fulbright-Hays Scholarships, some of which are in the field of library science.

CIFE Conseil International pour les Films d'Éducation (International Council for Educational Films). 29 rue d'Ulm, Paris 5, France. Also known as ICEF.

CII Compagnie Internationale pour l'Informatique. A French computer manufacturer incorporated in 1966 with financial backing from the French government.

CIIA Commission Internationale des Industries Agricoles et Alimentaires. 18 avenue Villars, Paris 7, France. Maintains a library.

CIINTE Centralny Instytut Informacji Naukowo Technicznej i Ekonomicznej (Central Institute for Scientific, Technical and Economic Information). Poland.

CIITC Confédération Internationale des Industries Techniques du Cinéma (International Confederation of the Cinema Industry). 92 Champs Elysées, Paris 8, France.

CIJE *Current Index to Journals in Education.* V.1, 1969. Monthly index to educational journal literature, published by Macmillan Information Division in cooperation with ERIC.

C/I/L *Computer Information Library Patent Abstracts.* (Journal). V. 1, 1969. Published by Science Associates International.

CILA Centro Interamericano de Libros Académicos (Inter-American Scholarly Book Center). Sullivan 31-Bis, México 4, DF, Mexico. *See* John S. Clouston. *CILA: A New Approach to Problems in the Acquisition of Latin American Library Materials.* University of Illinois, School of Library Science, Publication #113 [1974].

CIM Centro de Información Metalúrgica (Center for Metallurgic Information). Liebnitz 1, 80 piso, México 5, DF, Mexico.

CIM Computer Input Microfilm.

CIM Continuous Image Microfilm (or Microfilming).

CIMS Computer-Integrated Manufacturing System.

CIN *Chemical Industry Notes.* (Journal). V. 1, 1971. Published by CAS (Chemical Abstracts Service).

CIN Cooperative Information Network. c/o Green Library, Stanford University Libraries, Stanford, CA 94305. Three hundred libraries in five California counties cooperate through ILL, staff development, interlibrary reference and transferal of information.

CINCH Computerized Information Network for Community Health. Dept. of Community Medicine, Mount Sinai School of Medicine, City University of New York, New York, NY 10036.

CINDAS Center for Information and Numerical Data Analysis and Synthesis.

Purdue University, Electronic Properties Information Center, 2595 Yeager Rd, West Lafayette, IN 47906. Library established in 1960.

CINFAC Counterinsurgency Information Analysis Center. American University, 5010 Wisconsin Ave, NW, Washington, DC 20016.

CININ Centro de Información Industrial (Industrial Information Center). San Luis Potosi 211, México, DF, Mexico.

CINL *Cumulative Index to Nursing Literature.* V. 1–17, 1961–1977. Retitled *Cumulative Index to Nursing and Allied Health Literature.*

CIOA Center for Information on America. Washington, CT 06793. Established in 1951. Publishes documents.

CIOCS Communications Input/Output Control System.

CIOMS Council for International Organizations on Medical Sciences. c/o World Health Organization, Avenue Appia, CH-1211 Geneva 27, Switzerland. Established in 1949. Publishes *International Nomenclature of Diseases.*

CIOS Community Input/Output Control System. A system that directs the input and output of information transfer.

CIP Canadian International Paper Company. CIP Research, Ltd, Hawkesbury ON K6A 2H4, Canada. Has maintained a library since 1926.

CIP Cataloging in Publication. Formerly CIS (Cataloging in Source). A cooperative effort between LC and publishers to provide cataloging information within books. Revived in 1970.

CIP Centro de Información Pecuaria. Kilometer 15½ Carr México–Toluca, (Palo Alto) México, DF, Mexico.

CIPC Centro de Información de Politica Cientifica y Tecnológica (Center for Information in Political Science and Technology). Barranca del Muerto 210-3er piso, México 20, DF, Mexico.

CIPCE Centre d'Information et de Publicité des Chemins de Fer Européens (Information and Publicity Center of European Railways). Chemin de Fer Néerlandais, SA, Moreelsepark 1, Utrecht, the Netherlands.

CIPP Context, Input, Process Product Model. A planning and evaluation model developed at Ohio State University, Department of Education. *See* Mary Ellen Michael. "Use of the CIPP Model" in *Proceedings of the First CLENE Assembly.* Washington, DC: CLENE, 1976, pp. 39–46.

CIPS/ACI Canadian Information Processing Society/Association Canadienne de L'Informatique. Suite 214, 212 King St, West, Toronto ON M5H 1K5, Canada. Established in 1958. Also known as ACI/CIPS.

CIR Committee on International Relations. National Education Association, 1201 16th St, NW, Washington, DC 20036.

CIR Consortium for Information Resources. 260 Bear Hill Rd, Waltham, MA 02154. Ten hospital libraries cooperate through ILL, reference referral, cooperative selection cataloging, access to MEDLINE and CE program development.

CIRBCA Circolari Ministero Beni Culturali e Ambientali. Centro Elettronico di Documentazion-Italgiure, Corte Suprema di Cassaziono, Palazzo di Giustizia, Via Ulpiano 8, Rome 00193, Italy. Coverage from 1976. Full-text data base covering drafts of the Italian Office for Environment and Cultural Estates.

CIRC Circulation Input Recording. Colorado Instruments, Library Systems Division, One Park St, Broomfield, CO 80020. *See* C. McAllister. "On-Line Library Housekeeping Systems." *Special Libraries* 62 (Nov. 1971): 457–468.

CIRC Circulation Module. A module in the BALLOTS system.

CIRC Collection, Inquiry, Reporting & Communication. University of Toronto, Toronto ON M5S 1A1, Canada. A distributed minicomputer system of UTLAS described as "an on-line catalog & circulation control system in a network environment."

CIRCAL Circuit Analysis. Programs available on the MAC project at MIT (Massachusetts Institute of Technology).

CIRCLE Combined and Integrated Resources for Community Learning Experiment. Florissant Valley

Community College, 3400 Pershall, Saint Louis, MO 63135. Objective is to create a model for integrating information and learning resources for the information and educational needs of the people of the community.

CIRF Centre International d'Information et de la Recherche sur la Formation Professionnelle. International Labour Office, 154 Route de Lausanne, CH-1220 Geneva, Switzerland. Established in 1960.

CIRIA Construction Industry Research and Information Association. Six Storey's Gate, London SW1, England.

CIRK CTC's Information Retrieval from Keywords. Computing Technology Center, Union Carbide Corp, Oak Ridge, TN 37830.

CIS Cable Information Services. Connecticut State Library, 231 Capitol Ave, Hartford, CT 06115. A CATV and telecommunications resources activity to provide service to Connecticut's librarians.

CIS Career Information System. c/o University of Oregon, 247 Hendricks Hall, Eugene, OR 97403. Established in 1971. Both a library and headquarters consortia of Oregon schools and agencies involved in occupational counseling and education.

CIS Cataloging in Source. A project initiated by LC in 1959. Name changed to CIP (Cataloging in Publication) when revived in 1970.

CIS Congressional Information Service. 7101 Wisconsin Ave, Washington, DC 20014. Publishes *CIS Abstracts* and *CIS Highlights*.

CIS Coordinate Indexing System. A technique of indexing individual units of information by the joint use of two or more terms, usually of equal weight, with retrieval obtained through logical associations among the terms.

CIS Current Information Selection. IBM Technical Information Retrieval Center, White Plains, NY. An internal IBM service.

CISAC Confédération Internationale des Sociétés d'Auteurs et Compositeurs (International Confederation of Societies of Authors and Composers). 11 rue Keppler, Paris 16, France.

CISCO Committee on Inter-Society Cooperation. Contact ASIS.

CISE Centro Informazioni Studi Esperienze–Servizio Documentazione. Milan, Italy.

CISI Center for Inventions and Scientific Information. Prague, Czechoslovakia. A part of the Czechoslovak Academy of Sciences.

CISIR Ceylon Institute of Scientific and Industrial Research. 363 Banddhaloka Mawata, Colombo 7, Sri Lanka. Technical library established in 1955.

CISOR Centro de Investigaciones en Ciencias Sociales. Censo Eclesiastico, Apartado 12863, Caracas 101, Venezuela. Produces a data base on religion.

CISTI/ICIST Canadian Institute for Scientific and Technical Information (Institut Canadien de l'Information Scientifique et Technique). Montreal Rd, Ottawa ON K1A 0S2, Canada. Formed in 1974 by the merger of NSL (National Science Library) and TIS of NRC (National Research Council).

CISTIP Committee on International Scientific and Technical Information Programs. Contact National Academy of Science. A committee of the Commission on International Relations of the National Academy of Science/National Research Council.

CIT California Institute of Technology. Pasadena, CA 91109.

CITA Consejo Interamericano de Archiveros. c/o Archivo Nacional de México, México, DF, Mexico.

CITE *Consolidated Index of Translations into English.* New York: National Translation Center, Special Libraries Association, 1969.

CITE Current Information Tapes for Engineers. An experimental tape service in plastics technology and electrical/electronics engineering developed by Engineering Index, Inc. Introduced in 1968 and discontinued in 1969, it provided experience for COMPENDEX.

CITIS Construction Industry Translation and Information Services. 130 Foxrock Park, Foxrock, Dublin, Ireland. Publishes *European Civil Engineering Abstracts*.

CIU Computer Interface Unit. A device which interfaces with the central processing unit and peripheral hardware such as disks or printers.

CIVILE Giurisprudenza Civile. Centro Elettronico di Documentazione-Italgiure, Corte Suprema di Cassaziono, Palazzo di Giustizia, Via Ulpiano 8, Rome 00193, Italy. Coverage from 1961. Full-text data base covering digests of civil decisions of the Supreme Court of Italy.

CIZA Centro de Información de Zonas Aridas (Center for Arid Zone Information). Universidad Autonoma Agroria, "Antonio Marro," Buenavista Saltillo, Coahuila, Mexico.

CJCLS Community and Junior College Libraries Section. *See* ACRL/CJCLS.

CJPI *Criminal Justice Periodical Index.* (Journal). V. 1, 1975. Published by University Microfilms International.

CL *Chemical Literature.* (Journal). V. 1, 1949. News bulletin of the Division of Chemical Literature, American Chemical Society. Continued by *Chemical Information Bulletin* after 1975.

CL Control Leader. The record containing data pertaining to and heading a group of records.

CLA Canadian Library Association. 151 Sparks St, Ottawa ON K1P 5E3, Canada. Established in 1947. Also known as ACB (Association Canadienne des Bibliothèques).

CLA Catholic Library Association. 461 West Lancaster Ave, Haverford, PA 19041. Established in 1921.

CLA Chinese Librarians Association. Box 2688, Stanford, CA 94305. Established in 1974.

CLA Church Literature Association. 199 Uxbridge Rd, London W12, England.

CLA Colorado Library Association. Contact president or ALA (American Library Association).

CLA Comisión Latinoamericana. *See* FID/CLA.

CLA Computer Law Association. 1776 K St, NW, Washington, DC 20006. Established in 1973. Formerly Computer Lawyers Group.

CLA Connecticut Library Association. Contact president or ALA (American Library Association).

CLA/AS CLA Archives Section. Contact CLA (Catholic Library Association).

CLABC Congressional Libraries Association of British Columbia. Contact president. A Canadian association.

CLA/CCRT CLA Cataloging and Classification Roundtable. Contact CLA (Catholic Library Association).

CLA/CLS CLA Children's Libraries Section. Contact CLA (Catholic Library Association).

CLA/CULS CLA College and University Library Section. Contact CLA (Catholic Library Association).

CLA/CUSLS CLA College, University and Seminary Libraries Section. Contact CLA (Catholic Library Association).

CLAE Council of Library Associations Executives. 40 South Third St, Columbus, OH 43215. Established in 1970. Publishes a newsletter.

CLA/HSLS CLA High School Libraries Section. Contact CLA (Catholic Library Association).

CLA/HSRT CLA Health Sciences Roundtable. Contact CLA (Catholic Library Association).

CLA/LES CLA Library Education Section. Contact CLA (Catholic Library Association).

CLAM Consortium for Library Automation in Mississippi. Contact MLA (Mississippi Library Association). Achieved round table status within MLA in 1978.

CLAN California Library Automation Network. c/o Director's Office, Stanford University Libraries, Stanford, CA 94305. Consortium established in 1970. Engaged in sharing bibliographic data through BALLOTS, later RLIN.

CLANN College Libraries Activities Network in New South Wales. ADC House, 13th Fl, 189-193 Kent St, Sydney, New South Wales, 2000 Australia. Publishes a newsletter.

CLA/PCLS CLA Parish and Community Libraries Section. Contact CLA (Catholic Library Association).

CLA/PLS CLA Public Libraries Section. Contact CLA (Catholic Library Association).

CLARUS Case Law Report Updating Service. Infolex Services Ltd, 20 Grange Rd, Wickham Bishops, Witham, Essex CM8 3LT, England. Data base covering UK law report citations. Started in 1977.

CLA/SLS CLA Seminary Libraries Section. Contact CLA (Catholic Library Association).

CLASP Central Massachusetts Library Administration Project. A CMRLS project to develop a library training packet and a workshop method of teaching librarians modern administrative skills.

CLASS California Library Authority for Systems and Services. 1415 Koll Circle, Suite 101, San Jose, CA 95112. One hundred fifty academic, school and special libraries share access to California Data Base of Monographs and Serials, on-line reference services and CE program development.

CLASS Computer–based Laboratory for Automated School Systems. An SDC (System Development Corporation) project.

CLASS Current Literature Alerting Search Service. BioSciences Information Service, 2100 Arch St, Philadelphia, PA 19103. Current awareness service based on *BA (Biological Abstracts)* and *BioI (BioResearch Index)*. Printouts of citations are sent to patrons every two weeks.

CLASSIC Classroom Interactive Computer.

CLCD Clearinghouse and Laboratory for Census Data. Suite 900, 1601 North Kent St, Rosslyn, VA 22209. Founded by CRL under an NSF grant.

CLD Central Library and Documentation. CH 1211 Geneva 20, Switzerland. A branch of the International Labour Office of ILO (International Labor Organisation).

CLD Chemical Literature Division. *See* ACS/CLD.

CLEA Canadian Library Exhibitors Association. 120 Beverly Glen Blvd, No. 59, Scarborough ON M1W 1W6, Canada. Established in 1963.

CLEAR Center for Labor Education and Research. Macky 119, University of Colorado, Boulder, CO 80302.

CLEN Continuing Library Education Network. A program of AALS from 1972 to 1975.

CLENE Continuing Library Education Network and Exchange. 620 Michigan Ave, NE, Washington, DC 20064. Established in 1975. Fosters and provides access to CE opportunities. Members include 50 institutions, state agencies and associations as well as individuals.

CLEOPATRA Comprehensive Language for Elegant Operating System and Translator Design. A programming language.

CLEP College-Level Examination Program. Established by the College Entrance Examination Board to assist students in preparing for examinations for college credit. Administered through various public libraries.

CLEWS Classified Library Employees of Washington State. c/o Mary C. Allsopp, University of Washington, Seattle, WA 98195. Formerly (1973) WNPLA.

CLIC Committee on Library Cooperation. San Diego, CA. A library consortium of the San Diego area.

CLIC Company and Literature Information Center. Exxon Research and Engineering Co, Box 121, Linden, NJ 07036. The acronym applied by Exxon to its libraries and information centers.

CLIC Cooperative Libraries in Consortium. Hill Reference Library, Fourth & Market Sts, Saint Paul, MN 55102.

CLICC Cooperative Libraries in Central Connecticut. c/o Council of Governments of Central Naugatuck Valley, 20 East Main St, Waterbury, CT 06410. Twenty-two academic, public and school libraries cooperate with equipment, staff training, union lists and grant applications.

CLICS Computer-Linked Information for Container Shipping. Computer-derived information supplied to shipping companies for the control of containers.

CLIMBS Countway Library Medical Bibliographic Services. Established in 1978. Harvard University's Countway Library's experiment in providing in-depth services, including preparation of proposals for research grants, preparation of curricula, etc, for a fee.

CLINPROT Clinical Protocol. Data base describing clinical protocol for cancer drug therapy. Coverage from 1976. A subset of CANCERLINE. Available on-line through MEDLINE. Produced by CCRESPAC for ICRDB.

CLIP Compiler Language for Information Processing. SDC (System Development Corporation) programming language.

CLIP Computer Layout Installation Planner.

CLIS Computer Library Service, Inc. Wellesley Hills, MA 02181.

CLISP Conversational LISP.

CLJ *Canadian Library Journal.* V. 1, 1944. Published by CLA (Canadian Library Association).

CLODS Computerized Logic-Oriented Design System.

CLOG Computer Logic Graphics. Diagram used to demonstrate computer logic, which generally consists of five operations: add, subtract, multiply, divide and compare.

CLOUT Concerned Librarians Opposing Unprofessional Trends. Contact president. Established in 1976. A group centered in Orange County, CA, to counteract the use of paraprofessionals for professional library work.

CLP Club der Luftfahrtpublizisten. Postfach 277, 1011 Vienna, Austria. Established in 1959. Association of journalists.

CLR Council on Library Resources, Inc. One Dupont Circle, Suite 620, Washington, DC 20036. Established in 1956.

CLS Children's Libraries Section. *See* CLA/CLS.

CLS College Libraries Section. *See* ACRL/CLS.

CLS Coordinated Library System of New Mexico. New Mexico State Library, Santa Fe, NM 87501.

CLS Cumann Leabharlannaithe Scoile (Irish Association of School Librarians). The Library, University College, Dublin 4, Ireland. Established in 1962.

CLSD Culham (Laboratory) Language for System Development. A programming language.

CLT Communications Line Terminal. There are three basic kinds of CLTs: low speed (up to 300 bps), medium speed (up to 1,600 bps) and high speed (2,000–4,800 bps). Each is easily adjusted to the speed and other characteristics of the line with which it is to operate.

CLTA Canadian Library Trustees Association. c/o Canadian Library Association, 151 Sparks St, Ottawa ON K1P 5E3, Canada. A division of CLA (Canadian Library Association).

CLUE Computer Learning Under Evaluation. Project CLUE, University of Michigan, 1315 Hill St, Ann Arbor, MI 48104.

CM Communication Multiplexor. A device used to interweave two or more signals for retransmission at higher speed.

CM Control Marks. While a central mark supplies special control features to be used in programming, specified CM configurations are reserved for particular features on data tapes.

CMA Colleges of Mid-America. Sioux Falls College, Sioux Falls, SD 57105. Ten colleges in southeastern South Dakota and northwestern Iowa cooperate through ILL and union list of serials.

CMA Computerized Management Account.

CMAA Comics Magazine Association of America, Inc. 41 East 42 St, New York, NY 10017. Established in 1954. Publishes a newsletter.

CMAC Columbus Museum of Arts and Crafts. 1251 Wynnton Rd, Columbus, GA 31906. Maintains a library.

CMC Catholic Microfilm Center. This association has been terminated.

CMC Code for Magnetic Characters.

CMDP Cooperative Media Development Program. An NMAC program. Purpose is to aid in the development of instructional materials for students of the health science profession.

CMES Center for Marine and Environmental Studies. Lehigh University, Mart Library, 15 East Packer Ave, Bethlehem, PA 18015.

CMH Company of Military Historians. 287 Thayer St, Providence, RI 02906.

CMI Commission Mixte Internationale pour la Protection des Lignes de Télécommunications et des Canolisations Souterraines (Joint International Committee for the Protection of Telecommunications Lines and Underground Ducts). 2 Rue de Varembé, Geneva 20, Switzerland.

CMI Computer-Managed Instructions. Computer aids for which the main function of the computer is to assist in planning instructional sequences. For instance, the computer's role may be to handle performance records and curriculum files.

CMIQ Centro Méxicano de Información Química (Mexican Center for Chemical Information). Avenue Industria Militar 261, México, DF, Mexico.

CMIZPAC Centro Méxicano de Información del Zinc y del Plomo (Mexican Center of Information for Zinc and Lead). Avenue Sonora 166, 1 piso México, DF, Mexico.

CMLS Confederate Memorial Literary Society. The Museum of the Confederacy, 1201 East Clay St, Richmond, VA 23219. Established in 1890. Publishes documents. Membership includes authors in Civil War history. Presents awards for writings on the Confederacy.

CMM Computerized Modular Monitoring.

CMOD Customer Must Order Direct. Specified by publishers who do not wish to deal through booksellers.

CMP COBOL Macro Processor.

CMP *Current Mathematical Publications*. V. 1, 1969. Published by the American Mathematical Society.

CMRA Chemical Marketing Research Association. 100 Church St, New York, NY 10007.

CMRLS Central Massachusetts Regional Library System. Worcester Public Library, Salem Sq, Worcester, MA 01608.

CN Canadian National Railways. Library, 935 Lagauchetiere St. West, Montreal PQ H3C 3N4, Canada. Maintains eight libraries, one of which is devoted to telecommunications.

CNBH Conseil National des Bibliothèques d'Hôpitaux (National Council of Hospital Libraries). 98 Chaussée de Vleurgat, B-1050 Brussels, Belgium. Established in 1937.

CNC Canadian National Committee. *See* FID/CNC.

CND National Committee of Documentation. Replaced by BNIST in early 1973.

CNDST Centre National de Documentation Scientifique et Technique (National Center for Scientific and Technical Documentation). 4 boulevard de l'Empereur, Brussels 1, Belgium.

CNEEMA Centre National d'Étude et d'Experimentation de Machinisme Agricole (National Center for Agricultural Machinery Research and Experimentation). Parc de Tourvoie, 92 Antony, Hauts-de-Seine, France.

CNET Centre National d'Études des Télécommunications (National Center of Telecommunication Studies). Lannion 22300, France. Produces data bases covering the reliability of electronic components.

CNET/DI Centre National d'Étude des Télécommunications/Département Documentation Interministérielle. 38-40, rue du General-Leclerc, F-92130 Issy-les-Moulineaux, France. Established in 1945.

CNEXO Centre National pour l'Exploitation des Océans. BP 337, 29273 Brest, Cedex, France. Produces a data base on ocean exploitation.

CNHS Center for Neo-Hellenic Studies. 1010 West 22 St, Austin, TX 78705. Established in 1965. Publishes documents. Members include scholars and authors of modern Greek history and culture.

CNIB Canadian National Institute for the Blind. 1929 Bayview Ave, Toronto ON M4G 3E8, Canada. Established in 1906. Hosted a CLA (Canadian Library Association) sponsored workshop in Nov. 1977 where a resolution was passed which established the Committee on Library Services for the Print Handicapped. Maintains a national library.

CNIES Centro Nacional de Información Económica y Social (National Center for Economic and Social Information). Doctor Mora 15, 8 piso México, DF, Mexico.

CNIPA Committee of National Institutes of Patent Agents. Contact general secretary. Publishes documents.

CNIPE Centre National d'Information pour le Productivité des Entreprises. 92 Courbevoie, Haute de Seine, France. Has a computerized information retrieval system.

CNLA Council of National Library Associations. Name changed to CNLIA in 1978.

CNLIA Council of National Library and Information Associations. Contact secretary. Formerly (1978) CNLA.

CNLIA/JCCC CNLIA Joint Committee on Cataloging and Classification Codes. Contact CNLIA.

CNLIA/JCCPI CNLIA Joint Committee on Copyright Practice and Implementation. Contact CNLIA.

CNMR Carbon-13 Nuclear Magnetic Resonance. Netherlands Information Combine, Box 36, Delft 2600 AA, the Netherlands. Coverage from 1976. Nonbibliographic data base covering properties of carbon-13.

CNR Consiglio Nazionale delle Ricerche. Piazzale delle Scienza 7, I-00185, Rome, Italy. Established in 1928.

CNRS Centre National de la Recherche Scientifique. 15 quai Anatole-France, 75 Paris 7, France. Publishes *Bulletin*

Signaletique and is a foreign affiliate of NFAIS; developed PASCAL.

CNS Chinese National Standards. National Bureau of Standards, Ministry of Economic Affairs, One First St, Cheng Kung Rd, Tainan, Taiwan. Affiliated with ISO (International Standards Organization).

COA Committee on Accreditation. Contact ALA (American Library Association). The group charged with accreditation of library schools in the US and Canada.

COAM Customer Owned and Maintained. Refers to equipment that is customer owned and maintained but connected to the line of a communications common carrier.

CO-ASIS Central Ohio Chapter of ASIS. Contact ASIS.

COBIGO Comité de Coordination des Bibliothèques Gouvernement du Québec. Contact president.

COBOL Common Business-Oriented Language. A programming language utilizing business terminology in describing data processing problems.

COBSA Computer Service Bureaux Association. Berkeley Square House, Berkeley Sq, London W1, England.

COBSI Council on Biological Sciences Information. 3900 Wisconsin Ave, NW, Washington, DC 20016. Affiliated with AIBS.

COCOSEER Coordinating Committee for Slavic–East European Library Services. Contact chairperson.

COCS Container Operating Control System.

CODAP Client-Oriented Data Acquisition Program.

CODAP Comprehensive Occupational Data Analysis Program.

CODAP Control Data Assembly Program.

CODASYL Conference on Data System Languages. A committee composed of representatives from several large COBOL users.

CODATA Committee on Data for Science and Technology. Contact ICSU. Established in 1966. Coordinates worldwide data collection activities in science and technology. Establishes task groups of specialists to study specific problems. Sponsored by ICSU.

CODOC Cooperative Documents. Office of Library Coordination, Council of Ontario Universities, Suite 8039, 130 Saint George St, Toronto ON M5S 2T4, Canada. *See* Carolynne Presser. "CODOC: A Computer-Based Processing and Retrieval System for Government Documents." *C&RL* 39 (March 1978): 94-98.

COED Computers in Education Division. American Society for Engineering Education, One Dupont Circle, Suite 400, Washington, DC 20036. A division of ASEE.

COFAD Computerized Facilities Design.

COGENT Compiler and Generalized Translator. Argonne National Laboratory List Processor.

COGEODATA Committee on Storage, Automatic Processing and Retrieval of Geological Data. Goal is to compile an international index to geological data. Its work is being carried on semiautonomously by CODATA.

COGO Coordinated Geometry. A computer language for civil engineering applications.

COGS Consumer Goods System.

COI Central Office of Information. Hercules Rd, Westminster Bridge Rd, London SE1, England.

COIN Central Ohio Interlibrary Network. 114 Park Ave. West, Mansfield, OH 44902. Sixteen public libraries cooperate through ILL, reference centers and AV program.

COINS Computer and Information Sciences.

COL Computer-Oriented Language. Any programming language having terms that are applicable to a particular computer or a particular set of computers.

COLA Cooperation in Library Automation. London and South Eastern Library Region (LASER), 9/10 Alfred Pl, London WC1E 7EB, England. A project of LASER to investigate use of automation by library networks.

COLASL Compiler Los Alamos Scientific Laboratories. A computer language.

COLBAV Colegio de Bibliotecónomos y Archivistas de Venezuela (Association of Venezuelan Librarians and Archivists). Apartado 6283, Caracas, Venezuela. Established in 1963.

COLEPAC Continuing Library Education Planning and Coordination Project. University of Wisconsin Extension's continuing education clearinghouse for Wisconsin library media personnel. Project ended September 1977.

COLIDAR Coherent Light Detection and Ranging. A sensing system developed by Hughes Aircraft Co.

COLT Council on Library/Media Technical Assistants. Contact chairperson. Formerly COLT (Council on Library Technology).

COLT Council on Library Technical Assistants. Established in 1965. Affiliated with ALA (American Library Association).

COLT Council on Library Technology. Name changed to COLT (Council on Library/Media Technical Assistants).

COM Computer Output Microfilm. Microfilm output, as opposed to line printer or tape output, produced by a microfilm printer that will take output directly from the computer.

COM Computer Output Microfilmer. A camera used to produce COM (Computer Output Microfilm).

COM Computer Output Microfilming. A process which occurs when a microfilm printer takes output directly from the computer, thus substituting for line printer or tape output. Also known as COM (Computer Output to Microfilm).

COM Computer Output to Microfilm. *See* COM (Computer Output Microfilming).

COMAC Continuous Multiple Access Collator. Proposed in 1957 by Mortimer Taube for machine handling of large files.

COMARC Cooperative Machine-Readable Cataloging. An LC project terminated May 30, 1978.

COMIT Computer Language of Massachusetts Institute of Technology. A machine-oriented language for manipulation and pattern matching.

Used by MIT with several IBM computers.

COMLA Commonwealth Library Association. Box 534, Kingston 10, Jamaica, West Indies. Established in 1972.

COMLIP Community Media Library Program. An experimental program at Columbia University. *See* Miriam Braverman and Evelyn Geller. "The COMLIP Experiment: Training Street Librarians in the Groves of Academia." *American Libraries* 6 (July/Aug. 1975): 429–430.

COMLOGNET Combat Logistics Network. A communications network for logistics data set up by the US Department of Defense.

COMPAC Computer Output Microfilm Package. *See* COM (Computer Output Microfilm), COM (Computer Output Microfilmer), COM (Computer Output Microfilming).

COMPAC Computer Program for Automatic Control.

COMPACS Computer Output Microforms Program and Concept Study. A project of the US Army.

COMPAS Committee on Physics and Society. Contact AIP.

COMPASS Computerized Movement Planning and Status System.

COMPENDEX Computerized *Engineering Index*. Engineering Index, Inc, 345 East 47 St, New York, NY 10017. An Engineering Index, Inc, service for engineers consisting of a machine-readable monthly computer tape of the entire *EI* data base beginning with Jan. 1969, the *Engineering Index Annual* and the *Engineering Index Monthly*.

COMPOSE Computerized Production Operation System Extension. Field project of Engineering Index, Inc, second in a series called Transdisciplinary Engineering Information Program. Grant initiated Nov. 1, 1972, and continued for 18 months.

COMPUSTAT Computerized Statistics. Standard and Poor's, Box 239, Denver, CO 80201. A group of nonbibliographic data bases covering banking, industrial and utilities data.

COMRADE Computer-Aided Design Environment. A software system developed by the US Navy to facilitate the design and construction of naval vessels. Now used as a general design tool. *See* Michael Wallace. "COMRADE: Absolute Subroutine Utility Users' Manual." Report 76-0004, Jan. 1976.

COMSAT Communications Satellite Corporation. 950 L'Enfant Plaza, SW, Washington, DC 22304. Involved in satellite telecommunications and in computer science. Maintains a library.

COMSTAC Commission on Standards and Accreditation of Services for the Blind. American Foundation for the Blind, 15 West 16 St, New York, NY 10011.

COMTEC Computer Micrographics and Technology. Contact president. A West Coast based group of users and manufacturers of COM (Computer Output Microfilming) equipment.

CONACS Contractors Accounting System.

CONACYT Consejo Nacional de Ciencia y Tecnologia (National Council of Science and Technology). Insurgentes Sur 1677, México 20, DF, Mexico. Has a school for library technicians and operates on-line searching.

CONCAP Conversational Circuit Analysis Program.

CONDUIT Box 388, Iowa City, IA 52240. A commercial firm that locates, researches, tests and sells computer-assisted teaching software to academic institutions.

CONICET Consejo Nacional de Investigaciones Científicas y Técnicas (National Council for Scientific and Technical Research). Centro de Documentacion Científica, Rivadavia 1917, Buenos Aires, Argentina. National council that guides library education. Library established in 1958.

CONICIT Centro Nacional de Información Científica y Técnica (National Center for Scientific and Technical Information). Caracas, Venezuela.

CONICIT Consejo Nacional de Investigaciones Científicas y Tecnológicas (National Council for Scientific and Technological Research). Apartado 10518, San José, Costa Rica.

Produced a guide to libraries, archives and documentation centers in Costa Rica in 1975.

CONICYT Comisión Nacional de Investigación Científica y Technológica (National Commission on Scientific and Technological Research). Established in 1968. A part of the Ministry of Education of Chile.

CONICYT Consejo Nacional de Investigaciones Científicas y Tecnológicas (National Council for Scientific and Technological Research). Caracas, Venezuela.

CONSAL Conference of South-East Asian Libraries. c/o Singapore Library Association, National Library, Stamford Rd, Singapore 6, Republic of Singapore. First conference held in 1970. Third conference held in Jakarta Dec. 1-5, 1975, with assistance of UNESCO.

CONSER Conversion of Serials Project. Contact NSDP. An ongoing effort to create an authoritative automated bibliography of 300,000 serials held by national, academic and research libraries in the US and Canada. Begun in 1976, the project employs OCLC facilities and is based at LC's NSDP. *See* Paul Vassallo. "The CONSER Project: An Analysis." *Drexel Library Quarterly* 11 (July 1975): 49-59.

CONTRAN Control Translator. A compiler language developed by Honeywell that uses features of FORTRAN IV and ALGOL 60 programming languages.

CONTRON A FORTRAN process control language developed by CDC (Control Data Corporation).

CONTU National Commission on New Technological Uses of Copyrighted Works. Developed the guidelines on library photocopying for the copyright revision bill which took effect Jan. 1, 1978, in the US.

CONVAL Connecticut Valley Libraries. Trinity College, Hartford, CT 06106. A consortium of seven New England liberal arts college libraries.

CONVERSE CONVERSE System. A system for the on-line description and retrieval of structured data using natural language. Constructed at SDC (System Development Corporation) using the IBM Q-32 computer time-sharing

system. *See* C. H. Kellog. "CONVERSE" in *Mechanized Information Storage*, ed. by K. Samuelson. Amsterdam, the Netherlands: North Holland Publishing, 1968, pp. 608-621.

CONZUPLAN Consijo Zuliano de Planificación y Promoción de Universidad Central de Venezuela. Universidad Central de Venezuela, Ciudad Universitaria, Caracas, Venezuela.

COO Committee on Organization. Contact ALA (American Library Association). Makes recommendations to the ALA Council on the establishment or discontinuance of divisions, round tables and committees.

COP Committee on Planning. Contact ALA (American Library Association). Provides ALA members with information and recommendations to assist in the selection of goals.

COP Computer Optimization Package. A group of routines developed by GE for automating program testing, operation and maintenance.

COPE Console Operator Proficiency Examination. An examination for computer operators developed by Computer Usage, Inc, for the IBM 705 II computer.

COPEP Committee on Public Engineering Policy. Contact NAE (National Academy of Engineering).

COPES Committee on Program Evaluation and Support. Contact ALA (American Library Association). Evaluates ALA programs and submits recommended budgets to the Executive Board.

COPI Committee on Policy Implementation. Contact ALA (American Library Association). Determines that the intent of the Program of Action for Mediation, Arbitration, and Inquiry is fulfilled.

COPICS Copyright Office Publication and Interactive Cataloging System. A system of LC.

COPUL Council of Prairie University Libraries. Contact chairperson. A Canadian association.

CORAL Computer On-Line Real-Time Applications Language. A graphical communications and control language.

CORAL Council of Research and Academic Libraries. c/o The University of Texas at San Antonio, John Peace Library, San Antonio, TX 78285. Established in 1966. Incorporated as a nonprofit institution in 1977. Purpose is to develop and strengthen informational resources and services in the San Antonio area. Has 21 members representing public, private and military institutions.

CORMOSEA Committee on Research Materials on Southeast Asia. Dept. of Political Science, Rutgers University, New Brunswick, NJ 08903. Established in 1969. A committee of the Southeast Asia Council of AAS (Association for Asian Studies). Formerly CALROSA and CALROSEA.

CORTEC Giurisprudenza della Corte del Conti. Centro Elettronico di Documentazione-Italgiure, Corte Suprema di Cassazione, Palazzo di Giustizia, Via Ulpiano 8, Rome 00193, Italy. Coverage from 1907. Full-text data base covering digests of decisions of the Court of Audit of Italy.

CORTEZ COBOL-Oriented Real-Time Environment.

COS Compatible Operating System. A series of programs that allow IBM 1401 programs to be operational along with IBM 360 programs, BOS (Basic Operating System) and DOS (Disk Operating System).

COSAP Cooperative Serials Acquisitions Program. National Library of Medicine, 8600 Rockville Pike, Bethesda, MD 20014. A serials resource-sharing plan for NLM.

COSATI Committee on Scientific and Technical Information. Washington, DC. A government interagency group. Formerly (1962) COSI.

COSBA Computer Services and Bureaux Association. Merged into Computer Services Association in 1975.

COSD Council of Organizations Serving the Deaf. This association has been terminated.

COSI Committee on Scientific Information. Established in May 1962 by the Federal Council for Science and Technology. Name changed to COSATI in 1963.

COSINE Committee on Computer Science in Electrical Engineering. National Academy of Engineering, 2101 Constitution Ave, NW, Washington, DC 20037.

COSLA Chief Officers of State Library Agencies. Contact ALA (American Library Association).

COSMEP Committee of Small Magazine Editors and Publishers. Box 703, San Francisco, CA 94101. Established in 1969. Publishes a newsletter.

COSMIC Computer Software and Management Information Center. Computer Center, University of Georgia, Athens, GA 30601. Library consists of taped and card computer programs developed by the US government. Makes these programs available to business, industry, education and government agencies.

COSPAR Committee on Space Research. 55bd Malesherbes, 75 Paris 8, France.

COSPUP Committee on Science and Public Policy. Contact NAS (National Academy of Sciences).

COSTED Committee on Science and Technology in Developing Countries. 7 Via Cornelio Celso, 00161 Rome, Italy.

COSTI Center of Scientific and Technological Information. National Council for Research and Development, 84 Hachashmonaim St, Box 20125, Tel Aviv 61200, Israel. Developed CRI. Also known as CSTI.

COSTIT Giurisprudenza Costituzionale. Centro Elettronico di Documentazione-Italgiure, Corte Suprema di Cassaziono, Palazzo di Giustizia, Via Ulpiano 8, Rome 00193, Italy. Coverage from 1956. Full-text data base covering decisions of the Italian constitutional court.

COU Council of Ontario Universities. 130 Saint George St, Suite 8039, Toronto ON M5S 2T4, Canada.

COWL Council of Wisconsin Librarians. c/o Memorial Library, 728 State St, Madison, WI 53706. Twenty-seven libraries sponsor WILS and coordinate other activities.

CP Command Processor. A request from a terminal for the execution of a particular program.

CPARS Compact Programmed Airline Reservation System.

CPC Card Programmed Calculator. Often associated with a tabulator to read punched cards.

CPC Carolina Population Center. University of North Carolina, University Sq, Chapel Hill, NC 27514. Library established in 1967. Produces a data base and provides computerized searches and document delivery in the field of population.

CPC Carolina Population Center Library Data Base. Contact CPC (Carolina Population Center). Bibliographic data base on population dynamics, fertility and family planning.

CPC Central Pennsylvania Consortium. c/o Dickinson College, Carlisle, PA 17013. Four academic libraries cooperate through ILL, journal analysis and audiotape sharing.

CPC Clock Pulsed Control. The control for a pulse-counting device within a computer system.

CPC Computerized Production Control.

CPC Cycle Program Control. A control program for a self-contained series of instructions in which the last instruction loops until a final result is reached.

CPC Cycle Program Counter. A device that counts and records the number of times repeating events, or cycles, occur.

CPDA Council for Periodical Distributors Associations. 488 Madison Ave, New York, NY 10022. Established in 1955. The national association of independent paperback book and periodical distributors. Publishes a newsletter.

CPDS Computerized Preliminary Design System.

CPI Characters Per Inch.

CPI Conference Papers Index. Courier-Journal and Louisville Times, 620 South Fifth St, Louisville, KY 40202. Coverage from 1973. Bibliographic data base covering papers delivered at conferences.

CPI Consolidated Papers, Inc. Box 50, Wisconsin Rapids, WI 54494. Maintains an R&D library, established in 1966,

which covers pulp paper technology, graphics and management.

CPIA Chemical Propulsion Information Agency. Applied Physics Laboratory, Johns Hopkins University, 8621 Georgia Ave, Silver Spring, MD 20910. A DOD information analysis center. Administered by DSA (Defense Supply Agency) and the Naval Air Systems Command. Sponsored by DSA, NASA, other government agencies, private industry and educational institutions.

CPIP *Current Papers in Physics*. (Journal). V. 1, 1966. Published by the Institution of Electrical Engineers. Also known as *CPP*.

CPL Council of Planning Librarians. Contact president. Established in 1957. Publishes documents.

CPLI *Catholic Periodical and Literature Index*. V. 1, 1930. Published by CLA (Catholic Library Association).

CPLQ/CBPQ Corporation of Professional Librarians of Quebec/Corporation des Bibliothécaires Professionnels du Québec. 360 rue Le Moyne, Montreal PQ H2Y 1Y3, Canada.

CPM Cards Per Minute.

CPM Critical Path Method. A method for measurement and control of the management process of libraries.

CPOMR Computerized Problem-Oriented Medical Record. University of Vermont, Dana Medical Library, Burlington, VT 05401. Medical record referred to is an abstracted and classified bibliographic record of journal articles. Part of MRIS (Medical Record Information Service) of the library.

CPP Card-Punching Printer. Used as an output device for the digital computer.

CPP Computer People for Peace. c/o The Dolphin Center, 137A West 14 St, New York, NY 10011. Active at computer meetings from 1968.

CPP *Current Papers in Physics. See* CPIP.

CPPBS Conseil Pédagogique Provincial des Bibliothèques Scolaires Nouveau-Brunswick. BP 712, Fredericton NB E3B 5B4, Canada. A section of the Association des

Enseignants Francophones du Nouveau-Brunswick.

CPRI Children's Psychiatric Research Institute. University of Western Ontario, Box 2460, London ON N64 4GS, Canada. Maintains a library and publishes documents.

CPS Characters Per Second.

CPS College Press Service. 1140 Delaware St, Suite 1, Denver, CO 80204. Established in 1971. Supersedes USSPA. Publishes documents.

cps Cycles Per Second.

CPSC Consumer Product Safety Commission. 5401 Westbard Ave, Washington, DC 20207. Established in 1974. Maintains a library.

CPST *Computer Programs in Science and Technology*. (Index). V. 1, 1971. Published by Science Associates International.

CPT *Current Physics Titles*. (Journal). V. 1, 1972. Published by the American Institute of Physics.

CPU Central Processing Unit. The portion of a computer, including control, arithmetic and memory units, that decodes and executes instructions for the system and peripheral devices.

CPU Commonwealth Press Union. 154 Fleet St, London EC4, England.

CR Carriage Return Character.

CR Committee on Classification Research. *See* FID/CR.

CR Content Retrieval. *See* R. F. Simmons. "Answering English Questions by Computer." *Communications of ACM* 8 (Jan. 1965): 53–69.

CRAFT Computerized Relative Allocation of Facilities Technique. Developed by IBM. Possible applications include labor-saving redesign of offices and hospitals.

CRAM Card Random Access Memory. Device which provides a single practical unit for both random and sequential processing.

CRC Chemical Rubber Company. CRC Press, Inc, 2255 Palm Beach Lakes Blvd, West Palm Beach, FL 33409.

Publishes various scientific reference books. Formerly located in Cleveland, OH.

CRC Cooperative Raleigh Colleges. c/o Meredith College, Box X-120, Raleigh, NC 27611. Six libraries cooperate through ILL, American history union catalog, union list of serials and microfiche collections.

CRCD Canadian Rehabilitation Council for the Disabled. One Yonge St, Suite 2110, Toronto ON M5E 1E8, Canada. Maintains a library.

CRDSD *Current Research and Development in Scientific Documentation*. Washington, DC: National Science Foundation, Office of Scientific Information, 1957.

CREATE Center for Research and Evaluation in Applications of Technology in Education. American Institution for Research in the Behavioral Sciences, 1791 Arastradero Rd, Palo Alto, CA 94302. Objective is to formulate techniques for course and program evaluation at primary and secondary school levels.

CRECORD Congressional Record File. Bibliographic search tool of the *Congressional Record*. Produced by CSI (Capitol Services, Inc.) and available on-line through SDC (System Development Corporation).

CREDO Centre for Curriculum Renewal and Educational Development Overseas. Tavistock House South, Tavistock Sq, London WC1, England.

CREF College Retirement Equities Fund. 711 Third Ave, New York, NY 10017. Library established in 1973.

CREPUQ Conference des Recteurs et des Principaux des Universités du Québec (Conference of Rectors and Principals of Quebec Universities). Contact secretary. Has a subcommittee on libraries.

CRESAL Centre de Recherche Sociologique Appliqués de la Loire. 6 place de l'Hôtel de Ville, 42000 Saint-Étienne, France. Produces data bases on economics, sociology and urban development.

CRESS Clearinghouse on Rural Education and Small Schools. *See* ERIC/RC.

CRI Current Research and Development in Israel. Center of Scientific and Technological Information (COSTI), National Council for Research and Development, 84 Hachashmonaim St, Box 20125, Tel Aviv 61200, Israel. An in-house system, developed by COSTI, which collects, orders, displays and disseminates data on ongoing research and development activities within Israel.

CRIARL Consortium of Rhode Island Academic and Research Libraries. US Naval War College Library, Newport, RI 02840. Thirteen academic, public and special libraries cooperate through ILL, union list of serials, acquisitions and information exchange.

CRICISAM Center for Research in College Instruction of Science and Mathematics. Florida State University, Tallahassee, FL 32306. Presently inactive.

CRID Centre pour la Recherche Interdisciplinaire sur le Développement. 1420 Chausée de Wavre, B-1160 Brussels, Belgium. Produces data bases in the social sciences.

CRIG Cocoa Research Institute. Box 8, Tafo-Akim, Ghana. Maintains a library.

CRIS Current Research Information System. US Dept. of Agriculture, Research Program Development and Evaluation Staff, Rm. 6816, South Bldg, Washington, DC 20250. Established in 1969. Connected with ASIN. An in-house system designed to improve communication among agricultural research scientists with regard to ongoing research projects and to provide research managers with current information on USDA research programs.

CRISP Catalogued Resources and Information Survey Programs. College of Librarianship, Aberystwyth, Cardiganshire, Wales, England. This system provides programmed materials for teaching library information retrieval procedures.

CRIU Centre de Recherches et d'Innovation Urbaines. Université de Montreal, CP 6128, 3288 avenue Lacombe, Montreal PQ H3C 3J7, Canada. Maintains an urban affairs library.

CRL Center for Research Libraries. 5721 Cottage Grove Ave, Chicago, IL 60637.

Established in 1949 as the Midwest Inter-Library Center by a group of ten universities with grants from foundations. Renamed in 1966. Maintains research collection available to members.

CRLLB Center for Research on Language and Language Behavior. University of Michigan, Ann Arbor, MI 48109. In collaboration with BELC (Bureau pour l'Enseignement de la Langue et de la Civilisation Françaises à l'Étranger), issued *Language and Language Behavior Abstracts* in 1967.

CRLT Center for Research on Learning and Teaching. School of Education, University of Michigan, Ann Arbor, MI 48109.

CRML Connecticut Regional Medical Library. University of Connecticut Health Center Library, Farmington, CT 06032.

CRO Cathode-Ray Oscilloscope. Used for storage and display in analog and digital computers.

CRR Commercial Reference Room. Guildhall Library, Basinghall St, London EC2, England.

CRS Congressional Research Service. Library of Congress, 10 First St, SE, Washington, DC 20540. Provides research services to Congress. See Charles A. Goodrum. "Congress and the Congressional Research Service." *Special Libraries* 65 (July 1974): 253–258.

CRT Cathode-Ray Tube. Electronic tube in which a beam of electrons is made to impinge on various parts of a phosphor-coated screen to form a visual display.

CRYSIS Correctional Records Information Systems. Office of Criminal Justice Plans and Analysis, 1329 E St, NW, Washington, DC 20005. Data base of the DC Department of Corrections. Part of project TRACE (now OBTS).

CS Computer Science.

CS Computer Simulation.

CS Computer Software. The internal programs or routines prepared to simplify programming and computer operations. Various programming aids supplied by the computer manufacturer to facilitate the efficient operation of the computer.

CSA Cambridge Scientific Abstracts, Inc. 6611 Kenilworth Ave, Suite 437, Riverdale, MD 20840. Publishes *Computer and Information Systems*.

CSA Canadian Standards Association. 178 Rexdale Blvd, Rexdale ON M9W 1R3, Canada. Affiliated with ISO (International Standards Organization).

CSA Crystallographic Society of America. Merged with ASXED to form ACA (American Crystallographic Association).

CSC Computer Sciences Corporation. 650 North Sepulveda Blvd, El Segundo, CA 90245. Incorporated in 1959. Provides computer hardware and software. Also maintains a library and publishes documents.

CSC Computer Search Center. Illinois Institute of Technology Research Center, 10 West 35 St, Chicago, IL 60616. Conducts research and does bibliographic computer searches on various data bases.

CSD Children's Services Division. A division of ALA (American Library Association). Name changed to ALSC (Association for Library Service to Children) in 1977.

CSDA Central States Distributors Association. Contact president. A regional association of independent book distributors.

CSEB Computer Science and Engineering Board. Contact NAS (National Academy of Sciences).

CSG Capital Systems Group. CSG Publications Dept, Suite 250, 6110 Executive Blvd, Rockville, MD 20852. Publishes *Directory of On-Line Information Resources*.

CSI Capitol Services, Inc. 511 Second St, NE, Washington, DC 20002. Incorporated in 1972. Produces data bases, including CRECORD and FEDREG, and provides abstracting services for government documents.

CSI *Chemical Substructure Index*. V. 1, 1968. Published by ISI (Institute for Scientific Information).

CSIR Council for Scientific and Industrial Research. Box 395, Pretoria, Republic of South Africa 0001. Maintains a library that attempted, in 1975, to develop machine-readable catalog records.

CSIRO Commonwealth Scientific and Industrial Research Organization. 314 Albert St, East Melbourne, Victoria 3002, Australia. Publishes *CSIRO Abstracts*. Maintains documentation centers throughout Australia.

CSL Comparative Systems Laboratory. Project conducted between 1963 and 1968. *See* Tefko Saracevic. "Selected Results from an Inquiry into Testing of Information Retrieval Systems." *JASIS* 22 (Mar.–Apr. 1971): 126–139.

CSL Computer-Sensitive Language. Programming language dependent upon the machine used to execute the program.

CSL Connecticut State Library. 231 Capitol Ave, Hartford, CT 06115.

CSLA Canadian School Library Association. c/o Canadian Library Association, 151 Sparks St, Ottawa ON K1P 5E3, Canada. Established in 1974.

CSLA Church and Synagogue Library Association. Box 1130, Bryn Mawr, PA 19010. Established in 1967.

CSLA Connecticut School Library Association. Wallingford, CT 06492. Publishes a newsletter.

CSMP Continuous System Modeling Program. A digital simulated analog system.

CSP Control Switching Point. Any of the regional, sectional or primary centers used for national dialing.

CSPA Catholic School Press Association. c/o College of Journalism, Marquette University, Milwaukee, WI 53233. Established in 1931. Presently inactive.

CSPEFF Chambre Syndicale des Producteurs et Exportateurs de Films Français. 5 rue du Cirque, 75008 Paris, France. Established in 1944. Publishes documents.

CSRUIDR Chemical Society Research Unit in Information Dissemination and Retrieval. University of Nottingham, Nottingham NG7 2RD, England.

CSS Circulation Services Section. *See* LAMA/CSS.

CSSA Canadian Social Science Abstracts. Institute for Behavioral Research, York University, 4700 Keele St, Downsview ON M3J 2R6, Canada. Coverage from 1976. Bibliographic data base covering Canadian periodical literature. Available only at York University.

CSSDA Council on Social Science Data Archives. Brings together consortia, scholars and institutes in a broad social sciences data scheme. *See* William A. Glaser and Ralph L. Bisco. "Plans of the Council of Social Science Data Archives." *Social Sciences Information (Information sur les Sciences Social)* 5 (Dec. 1966): 71-96.

CST Channel Status Table. Used by input/output drivers to wait until a specific channel is available prior to using it. Composed of separate entries for each channel available to the system.

C-STAR *Classified Scientific and Technical Aerospace Reports* V 1, 1963. A classified version of *STAR*, published by the Scientific and Technical Information Division of NASA.

CSTB Centre Scientifique et Technique du Bâtiment. 4 avenue du Recteur Poincaré, 75 Paris 16, France.

CSTI Center of Scientific and Technological Information. *See* COSTI.

CSULB California State University at Long Beach. Long Beach, CA 90840. In 1978 was recipient of a major federal grant used for projects which will increase library services to users.

CSW Channel Status Word. The individual element of CST that refers to a particular channel.

CT *Chemical Titles*. (Journal). V. 1, 1961. Published by CAS (Chemical Abstracts Service).

CTAVI Centre Technique Audiovisual International (International Audiovisual Technical Center). 128a Frankrijklei, Antwerp 1, Belgium.

CTB Centre de Techniques Bibliographiques. 44 rue Charles-de-Gaulle, Tunis, Tunisia.

CTB Commonwealth Telecommunications Board. 28 Pall Mall, London SW1, England.

CTC Computing Technology Center, Union Carbide Corporation. Oak Ridge, TN 37830. Maintains a library.

CTC Conditional Transfer of Control. An instruction in a computer code that allows the computer to modify actions according to predetermined variable conditions by transferring from one sequence of instructions to another.

CTCL Community and Technical College Libraries. Contact CLA (Canadian Library Association).

CTDC Chemical Thermodynamics Data Center. National Bureau of Standards, Washington, DC 20234.

CTHB Chalmers Tekniska Högskolas Bibliotek (Library of Chalmers University of Technology). Fack S-402 20, Gothenburg 5, Sweden.

CTIAC Concrete Technology Information Analysis Center. Army Engineers Waterway Experimental Station, Box 631, Vicksburg, MS 39180. Maintains a library.

CTIF Centre Technique des Industries de la Fonderie. Département des Informations Techniques–Bureau de Documentation, 12 avenue Raphael, 75 Paris 16, France.

CTL Compass Test Language. A programming language.

CTNSS Center for Thai National Standard Specifications. Applied Scientific Research Corp. of Thailand, 196 Phahonyothin Rd, Bankhen, Bangkok, Thailand. Issues English-language standards. Affiliated with ISO (International Standards Organization).

CTU Central Terminal Unit. In a banking application this unit supervises communication between the teller consoles and the processing center. Receives incoming messages at random intervals, stores them until the central processor is ready to process them and returns the processed replies to the teller consoles which originated the transactions.

CTUW Project c/o Yale University Library, Interlibrary Loan Office, New Haven,

CT 06520. Consortium of Connecticut academic libraries established in 1966.

CU Career Update. State University of New York, Buffalo, School of Information and Library Studies, Buffalo, NY 14214. An organization to provide professional people with the services necessary to keep them aware of developments in their fields.

CUBE Cooperating Users of Burroughs Equipment. Contact Burroughs Corp.

CUBI Centro Nazionale per il Catalogo Unico delle Biblioteche Italiane per le Informazion Bibliografiche. Biblioteca, via del Collegio Romana 27, 1-00186 Rome, Italy. Established in 1951.

CUDOS Comprehensive University of Dayton On-Line Information Services. University of Dayton Research Institute, KL445, 300 College Park Ave, Dayton, OH 45469. Provides on-line searching of a number of data bases on a contract, deposit account or individual service basis.

CUE Cooperating Users Exchange. A consortium of Burroughs 220 computer users. Shares programs, systems and problem analyses.

CUFC Consortium of University Film Centers. 1325 South Oak St, Champaign, IL 61820.

CUL Cornell University Libraries. Cornell University, Ithaca, NY 14850.

CULP California Union List of Periodicals. Data base of periodical titles with holdings statement of libraries in California. Produced in hard copy and microfiche. Project of the State Library of California.

CULS Coalition in the Use of Learning Skills. Undergraduate Library, University of Michigan, Ann Arbor, MI 48104. A program of the undergraduate library of the University of Michigan which seeks to upgrade the library information-seeking ability of disadvantaged students. *See* M. J. Lynch and G. W. Whitbeck. "Work Experience and Observation in a General Reference Course: More on 'Theory vs. Practice.' " *Journal of Education for Librarianship* 15 (Spring 1975): 271-280.

CULS College and University Library Section. *See* CLA/CULS.

CULS College and University Library Section. A section of NYLA.

CULSA Cornell University Libraries Staff Association. Cornell University Libraries, Cornell University, Ithaca, NY 14850.

CUMBIN City University Mutual Benefit Instructional Network. A closed-circuit television series aired from the CUNY Graduate Center. Programs were received on the campuses of Brooklyn, City, Hunter and Queens colleges from Feb. to May 1972.

CUMWA Consortium of Universities of the Washington Metropolitan Area. 1717 Massachusetts Ave, NW, Washington, DC 20036. Eight universities and colleges administer CAPCON and cooperate through ILL, union list of serials, CE and teletype network.

CUNY City University of New York. Composed of many units located throughout the five boroughs of New York City. Several units publish documents and produce data bases, including CHUM and CUMBIN.

CUPE Canadian Union of Public Employees. Suite 800, 233 Gilmore St, Ottawa, ON, Canada. The bargaining agent for library staff members at Queen's University, Kingston, ON.

CUR Complex Utility Routines. Perform various checks on the validity of output. Messages inform the programmer of the nature of problems.

CURE Computer Users Replacement Equipment. c/o Charles Keene College of Further Education, Leicester, England. A nonprofit organization.

CUSLS College, University and Seminary Libraries Section. *See* CLA/CUSLS.

CUSS Cooperative Union Serials System. 130 Saint George St, Suite 8039, Toronto ON M5S 2T4, Canada. Consortium established in 1972.

CUTA Chama Cha Ukutubi, Tanzania (Tanzania Library Association). Box 2645, Dar-es-Salaam, United Republic of Tanzania. Established in 1971.

CVA Committee for the Visual Arts. 105 Hudson St, New York, NY 10013. Established in 1972. Maintains audio-works archives and a registry of artists in New York State. Publishes exhibition catalogs.

CVT Committee on Vacuum Techniques. Name changed to AVS (American Vacuum Society).

CW Call Waiting. Signal that another message is awaiting entry.

CWA Canada Water. Waste Resources Document Reference Centre, Canadian Dept. of Fisheries and the Environment, Inland Waters Directorate, Ottawa ON K1A E7, Canada. Coverage from 1969. Bibliographic data base covering all aspects of Canadian water resources.

CWA Crime Writers Association. 8 Garden Close, Givons Grove, Leatherhead, Surrey, England.

CWB Commonwealth Writers of Britain. c/o The Status, 2 Fore St, London EC2, England.

CWILS Connecticut Women in Libraries. Contact president.

CWPC Civil War Press Corps. 24 Zollinger Rd, Columbus, OH 43221. Authors, artists, journalists, broadcasters and others interested in the American Civil War. Presently inactive.

CWRU Case Western Reserve University. Cleveland, OH 44106. Has graduate library program and is involved in various library and information science studies.

CWSS Center for Women's Studies and Services. 908 F St, San Diego, CA 92101. Established in 1972. Maintains a library and publishes a bulletin.

CyLA Ceylon Library Association. Name changed to SLLA (Sri Lanka Library Association).

DA Data Acquisition. Process by which data are obtained and converted into digital information and printed to provide records.

DA Differential Analyzer. A computer, usually analog, designed and used primarily for solving differential equations.

DA *Documentation Abstracts.* V. 1-3, 1966-1968. Name changed to *ISA (Information Science Abstracts).*

DAA *Dictionary of Architectural Abbreviations, Signs and Symbols.* David D. Polon, ed. New York: Odyssey Press, 1965.

DAAS Drilling Activity Analysis. A. C. Nielson Co, Box 2612, 1375 Delaware St, Denver, CO 80201. Coverage from 1974. Nonbibliographic data base covering wells and oil drilling.

DAB *Dictionary of American Biography.* New York: Scribner's, 1928– Prepared under the auspices of ACLS.

DAB Display Assignment Bits.

DAB Display Attention Bits.

DAC Data Acquisition and Control System. A system designed to handle a wide variety of real-time applications, process control and high-speed data acquisition.

DAC Design Augmented by Computers. System of General Motors.

DAC Digital-to-Analog Converter. A device to translate digital to analog form.

DACC Data and Computation Center. 4452 Social Science Bldg, University of Wisconsin, Madison, WI 53706.

DACOM Datascope Computer Output Microfilmer. A device developed by Eastman Kodak Co. for microfilming computer output data.

DAEDAC Drug Abuse Epidemiology Data Center. Institute of Behavioral Research, Texas Christian University, Fort Worth, TX 76129. Established in 1973. Produces two computerized data bases, providing analyses of original data on drug abuse and bibliographic access to topical literature.

DAFT Digital Analog Function Table. A function table developed by Packard Bell Computer Corp.

DAI *Dissertation Abstracts International.* V. 1, 1938. Published by University Microfilms International. Full-text dissertations have been available on microfilm, microfiche and in print form (xerographic copies) since 1976.

DAIRS Dial Access Information Retrieval System. Shippensburg State College,

Ezra Lehman Memorial Library, Shippensburg, PA 17257. A system providing audio programs giving instructions on the use of library facilities.

DAIS Direct Access Intelligence Systems. An automated information retrieval system which organizes the intelligence stored in a machine in "such a way that the desired knowledge is directly accessible to the user through a man-machine dialog in the user's natural language." *See* Heinz Von Foerster. *Toward Direct Access Intelligence Systems.* Report AFOSR-70-2991TR, NTIS AD-718 062, 1970.

DAISY Decision-Aiding Information System.

DAISY 201 Double-precision Automatic Interpretive System 201. An interpretive program developed by Bendix Aviation Corp. for use on the Bendix G15 computer.

DAM Data Association Message.

DAM Descriptor Attribute Matrix.

DAMIT Data Analysis Massachusetts Institute of Technology. A computer program for data analysis developed by MIT and by the Kansas City Air Defense Sector and Experimental SAGE Sector to provide the possibility of repeated tests with a controlled environment and regulated input.

DAMOS Data Moving System.

DAMP Database of Atomic and Molecular Physics. Queen's University of Belfast, Computer Centre, University Rd, Belfast BT 9, Northern Ireland. Coverage from 1930. Nonbibliographic data base describing potential energies between pairs of atoms.

DANANET GE model that can be used for production control, and in which a message exchange receives and transmits automatically. Another use is a data collection system for the purpose of transmitting data for a remote station to a central unit. Still another use permits an operator to dial and send perforated tape data over a phone line.

DANBIF Danske Boghandleres Importørforening (Danish Booksellers Import Association). Postboks 70,

Krondalvej 8, 2610 Rodovre, Denmark. Established in 1947.

DAPAL Daystrom Powerplant Automation Language.

DAPIS Danish Agricultural Producers Information Service. 2-3 Conduit St, London W1, England.

DARA Deutsche Arbeitsgemeinschaft für Rechen-Anlagen (German Working Committee for Computing Machines). Contact chairperson.

DARC Description, Acquisition, Retrieval, Correlation. A computerized chemical data processing system used by Centre National d'Information Chimique in France. *See* J. E. DuBois. "French National Policy for Chemical Information and the DARC System as a Potential Tool of This Policy." *Journal of Chemical Documentation* 13 (Nov. 1973): 8–13.

DARE Dictionary of American Regional English. Dept. of English and of Computer Sciences, University of Wisconsin, Madison, WI 53715. *See* R. L. Venezky. "Storage, Retrieval, and Editing of Information for a Dictionary." *American Documentation* 71 (Jan. 1968).

DARE Documentation Automated Retrieval Equipment.

DART Data and Research Technology Corporation. 1102 McNeilly Ave, Pittsburgh, PA 15216. A research and consulting firm, publisher and member of IIA (Information Industry Association).

DAS Data Analysis System.

DAS Datatron Assembly System. Automatic assembly program system used on the Burroughs 205 computer.

DASD Direct Access Storage Device. Access to information is not dependent upon the position of previous information.

DASIAC DOD Nuclear Information and Analysis Center. General Electric TEMPO, 816 State St, Santa Barbara, CA 93102. Sponsored by DNA (Defense Nuclear Agency) of DOD and operated by General Electric TEMPO. Serves as a central collection point and reference center for all technical information pertinent to the effects of nuclear explosions.

DATACOM Data Communications. A global network that is considered one of the largest and most advanced. Used by USAF units in 300 locations to requisition and receive supplies.

DATAPHONE A trademark for the data sets manufactured and supplied by the Bell System.

DATASPEED Marketing term used by AT&T for a product line of medium-speed paper tape transmitting and receiving units.

DATE Dial Access Technical Education. A telephone information service of prerecorded tapes offered by IEEE.

DATOR Digital Data, Auxiliary Storage, Track Display, Outputs, and Radar Display.

DATRIX Dissertations Data Base Search Service. University Microfilms International, 300 North Zeeb Rd, Ann Arbor, MI 48106. A comprehensive computer-produced index to doctoral dissertations. Formerly Direct Access to Reference Information–Xerox.

DATUM Annaberge Strasse 148, 532 Bad Godesberg, Federal Republic of Germany. Produces a social science data base. DATUM is a member of the Inter-University Consortium for Political Research in the US.

DAVI Department of Audiovisual Instruction. Name changed to AECT in 1970.

DAWID II Institute of Phonetics and Communication Research, Bonn University, Adenauerallee 98a, 53 Bonn, Federal Republic of Germany. An attempt to construct a model, also called DAWID II, using acoustical analysis and ADIS (Automatic Diffemic Identification of Speakers).

DB Danmarks Biblioteksforening (Danish Library Association). Trekronergade 15, DK-2500 Valby-Copenhagen, Denmark. Established in 1906. Affiliated with IFLA. Publishes documents. *See* P. Birkelund. ''Denmark, Library Association of'' in *Encyclopedia of Library and Information Science*, ed. by A. Kent et al. New York: Marcel Dekker, 1971, V. 6, pp. 582–584.

DB Deutsche Bibliothek (National Library). D-6000 Frankfurt am Main, 1 Zeppelinalle 8, Federal Republic of Germany. Established in 1946. Became an independent federal institution in 1969.

DBA Data Base Administrator.

DBAM Data Base Access Method.

DB Bih Društvo Bibliotekara Bosne i Hercegovine (Library Association of Bosnia and Herzegovina). Obala 42, 7100 Sarajevo, Yugoslavia. Established in 1949. Affiliated with the Union of Librarians' Associations of Yugoslavia. Publishes documents.

DBDA Data Base Design Aid.

DBMS Data Base Management System.

DBOMP Data Base Organization and Management Processor.

DBPH Division for the Blind and Physically Handicapped. Name changed in 1978 to NLS of LC.

DBRO/DORLS Directeurs des Bibliothèques Régionales de l'Ontario/Directors of Ontario Regional Library Systems. *See* DORLS/DBRO.

DBS Društvo Bibliotekarjev Slovenije (Society of Librarians in Slovenia). Turjaška 1, 61000 Ljubljana, Yugoslavia. Established in 1947. Affiliated with the Union of Librarians' Associations of Yugoslavia. Publishes documents.

DBTC Data Base Task Force (CODASYL). Contact CODASYL.

DBV Deutscher Bibliotheksverband (German Library Association). Fehrbelliner Platz 3, D-1000 Berlin 31, Federal Republic of Germany. Established in 1949. Affiliated with ALA (American Library Association), CLA (Canadian Library Association) and IFLA. Publishes documents. *See* J. D. Young. ''A Short History of Library Associations in Germany.'' *Library Association Record* 69 (1967): 422–426.

DC Committee on Developing Countries. *See* FID/DC.

DC Data Courier, Inc. 620 South Fifth St, Louisville, KY 40202. Publishes abstracting journals and produces data bases.

DC Decimal Classification.

DCA Defense Communications Agency. Eighth St. & South Courthouse Rd, Arlington, VA 22204. A separate agency of DOD established in 1960 to perform system engineering for the department and other governmental agencies.

DCA Digital Computers Association. Contact secretary.

DCA Direction Center Active.

DCABC Dance Collection Automated Book Catalog. Part of SADPO; in operation at NYPL.

DCCCD Dallas County Community College District. Dallas, TX. Formed a committee with the Dallas Public Library to foster greater cooperative efforts.

DCCSA *Dictionary of Computer and Control Systems Abbreviations, Signs and Symbols*. New York: Odyssey Press, 1965.

DCCU Data Communications Control Unit. This unit scans the CTU buffers for transaction messages, transfers the next message to the central processor when requested and returns the processed relay to the same CTU buffer.

DCDS Digital Control Design System.

DCEA *Dictionary of Civil Engineering Abbreviations, Signs and Symbols*. New York: Odyssey Press, 1967.

DCEPC Decimal Classification Editorial Policy Committee. Contact RTSD of ALA (American Library Association).

DCIC Defense Ceramic Information Center. Battelle Memorial Institute, Columbus Laboratories, 505 King Ave, Columbus, OH 43201.

DCIST *Directory of Computerized Information in Science and Technology*. Leonard Cohen, ed. New York: Science Associates International, 1968.

DCL Division of Chemical Literature. *See* ACS/DCL.

DCLA District of Columbia Library Association. Contact president or ALA (American Library Association).

DCPL District of Columbia Public Library. Washington, DC 20001.

DCR Data Conversion Receiver.

DCR Design Change Recommendation.

DCR Detail Condition Register.

DCRT Division of Computer Research and Technology. A division of NIH (National Institutes of Health) that conducts programs in computer-related physical and life sciences in support of NIH biomedical research.

DCS Data Control System.

DCTL Direct Coupled Transistor Logic.

DD Data Definition. A control card for description of a data set to be used in the IBM OS/360 and some other systems.

DD Data Demand.

DD Decimal Display.

DD Delay Drive.

DD Digital Data.

DD Digital Display.

DDA Digital Difference Analyzer.

DDA Digital Display Alarm.

DDB *Directory of Data Bases in the Social and Behavioral Sciences*. Vivian S. Sessions, ed. New York: Science Associates International, 1974.

DDC Defense Documentation Center. Cameron Station, Alexandria, VA 22314. Established in 1963 to replace ASTIA. Operates the RDT&E on-line system.

DDC Dewey Decimal Classification.

DDCE Digital Data Conversion Equipment.

DDCMP Digital Data Communications Message Protocol.

DDD Digital Differential Analyzer. Device in which digital representation and data handling techniques are applied to the solution of differential equations.

DDD Direct Distance Dialing. Telephone service system developed by AT&T enabling subscriber to dial long distance without the intervention of a human operator.

DDD Diretoria de Documentação de Divulgação (Direction of Documentation and Publication). Fundação IBGE,

Instituto Nacional de Estatistica, Diretoria de Documentação e Divulgação, Avenida Franklin Roosevelt, 166-ZC-39, Rio de Janeiro, GB, Brazil. Established in 1934.

DDG Digital Display Generator.

DDGE Digital Display Generator Element.

DDI Data Dynamics, Inc. A system consulting firm specializing in law enforcement applications.

DDM Digital Display Makeup.

DDOCE Digital Data Output Conversion Equipment.

DDP Digital Data Processor.

DDS Digital Display Scope.

DDSI Data Dissemination Systems, Inc. 11161 West Pico Blvd, Los Angeles, CA 90064.

DDT Digital Data Transmitter.

DDT Document Delivery Tests. *See* Richard H. Orr et al. "Development of Methodologic Tools for Planning and Managing Library Services. Part II: Measuring a Library's Capability for Providing Documents." *BMLA* 56 (July 1968): 241–267.

DDT Dynamic Debugging Technique. A debugging package permitting extensive interaction between user and computer program.

DE Decision Element. Device that performs a logic function in a computing or data processing system.

DE Digital Element.

DE Display Element.

DE Display Equipment.

DE Division Entry.

DEA *Dictionary of Electronics Abbreviations, Signs and Symbols.* New York: Odyssey Press, 1965.

DEACON Direct English Access and Control. Developed by GE.

DEC Digital Equipment Corporation. Maynard, MA 01754.

DECADE Digital Equipment Corporation's Automatic Design System. Contact DEC.

DECUS Digital Equipment Computer Users Society. One Iron Way, Marlboro, MA 01752. Established in 1961. Publishes a library catalog.

DEL Delete. Refers to a character in a string of machine-readable data.

DEM Demodulator. Separates a modulating signal and makes it available for use.

DES Department of Education and Science. Curzon St, London W1, England.

DET Division of Educational Technology. A division of OLLR.

DETAB/X Decision Tables/Experimental. A programming language.

DEU Data Exchange Unit. A multiformat input/output device which provides an interface capability to place the computing system at the center of communications networks.

DEU Duplicates Exchange Union. Established in 1942. Voluntary, nonprofit network of libraries for the exchange of periodicals, books and documents and other library materials. Sponsor: RTSD/SS of ALA (American Library Association).

DEVSIS Development of Sciences Information System. A project of UNESCO.

DF Decimal Fraction.

DF Direction Finder.

DF Direction Finding.

DF Dual Facility.

DFG Diode Function Generator. A device capable of generating an arbitrarily specified function using an amplifier whose input and/or feedback impedance consists of networks of resistors and diodes.

DfS Dataflow Systems Inc. 7758 Wisconsin Ave, Bethesda, MD 20014. Produces microform products.

DFT Diagnostic Function Test. A program designed to test the overall reliability of a system.

DGD Deutsche Gesellschaft für Dokumentation (German Association for Documentation). Westendplatz 29, D-6000 Frankfurt am Main 1, Federal

Republic of Germany. Established in 1941. Affiliated with FID, ICR (International Council for Reprography) and IFLA. Publishes documents. *See* Helmut Arntz. "German Society for Documentation (DGD)" in *Encyclopedia of Library and Information Science*, ed. by A. Kent et al. New York: Marcel Dekker, 1974, V. 9, pp. 493–499.

DGIRP Dirección General de Información y Relaciones Publicas (Board of Information and Public Relations). Insurgentes Sur 476, 5 piso, México, DF, Mexico.

DGRST Délégation Générale à la Recherche Scientifique et Technique. Service Inventaire, 35 rue Saint Dominique, 75700 Paris, France. Produces a data base covering laboratories in France and the research undertaken in them.

DHEW Department of Health, Education and Welfare. 200 Independence Ave, SW, Washington, DC 20201. Also known as HEW. Name changed to the Department of Health and Human Services following reorganization in April 1980.

DHLLP Direct-High-Level-Language Processor.

DHUD Department of Housing and Urban Development. 451 Seventh St, SW, Washington, DC 20410. A department of the US government. Also known as HUD.

DIA Drug Information Association. Contact president. Established in 1965. Publishes a journal.

DIAL Dial Interrogation and Loading. A Honeywell system that enables the user to locate information, print, load and unload disks.

DIALOG A conversational programming system with graphical orientation. Used by Lockheed.

DICA Division de la Coopération et de l'Automasation. A division of BN established in 1975.

DID *Datamation Industrial Directory.* Barrington, IL: Technical Publishing Co, 1971.

DID Digital Information Display.

DIDS DLSC Integrated Data System. Defense Logistics Services Center, Battle Creek, MI 49016.

DIEA *Dictionary of Industrial Engineering Abbreviations, Signs and Symbols.* New York: Odyssey Press, 1967.

DIFO Zentraler Datenpool der Kooperativen Agrardokumentation. Zentralstelle für Agrardokumentation und Information, Bundesministerium für Ernährung, Landwirtschaft und Forsten, Konstantinstrasse 110, D-5300 Bonn 2, Federal Republic of Germany. Coverage from 1969. Bibliographic data base on agricultural sciences.

DIMATE A language for automatic equipment testing.

DIMDI Deutsches Institut für Medizinische Dokumentation und Information (German Institute for Medical Documentation and Information). Federal Ministry of Youth, Health and Family Affairs, Weisshausstrasse 27, Postfach 42 05 80, D-5000 Cologne 41, Federal Republic of Germany. Established in 1969. Member of EUSIDIC. Provides computerized searches and acts as a vendor for data base suppliers.

DIMECO Dual Independent Map Encoding File of the Counties of the US. Laboratory for Computer Graphics and Spatial Analysis, Harvard University, 520 Gund Hall, 48 Quincy St, Cambridge, MA 02138. Coverage from 1973. Data base expressing county boundaries as geographic coordinates.

DIMS Data Information and Manufacturing System.

DIN Prefix to publications issued by the Deutsche Normenausschuss.

DIODE Digital Input/Output Display Equipment.

DIS *Drug Information Sources.* Special Libraries Association, Science Technology Division, Pharmaceutical Section. Philadelphia, PA: The Association, 1967. A world list reprinted from the *American Journal of Pharmacy.*

DISC Divisional Interests Special Committee. Contact ALA (American Library Association).

DISC Drug Information Service Center. University of Minnesota, Appleby Hall, Rm. 48, Minneapolis, MN 55455. Maintains a library on drug abuse and drug education. Also produces a data base known as Drug Info.

DISCUS Institute of Library Research, University of California, Berkeley, CA 94720. *See* Steven S. Silver and Joseph C. Meredith. *DISCUS Interactive System User's Manual.* Final report. Berkeley, CA: University of California, Institute of Library Research, Sept. 1971. EDRS: 060 919.

DISISS Design of Information in the Social Sciences. Project at the University of Bath in England on bibliometric analysis of social sciences literature.

DISTRIPRESS International Association of Wholesale Newspaper, Periodical and Book Distributors. Theodor Heuss Ring 32, 5 Cologne, Federal Republic of Germany.

DKI Deutsches Kunststoff-Institut. Bibliothek, Schloßgartenstrasse 6 R, D-6100 Darmstadt, Federal Republic of Germany. Established in 1955.

DLA Delaware Library Association. Contact president or ALA (American Library Association).

DLD Division of Library Development. Used by state governments for a division frequently located in the state library. *See also* DLS.

DLE Data Link Escape. A character in a string of machine-readable data that provides additional communication control operations by means of one or more succeeding characters, thus providing an escape sequence.

DLIMP Descriptive Language for Implementing Macro-Processors. A programming language.

DLO Division Liaison Officer. A designation commonly used by professional associations having divisions.

DLP Division of Library Programs. A division of OLLR. Formerly (1974) BLLR and (1971) BLET.

DLR Dominion Law Reports. QL Systems Limited, 220-90 Sparks St, Ottawa ON K2G-0B8, Canada. Coverage from 1955. Data base headnotes for over 12,000 items.

DLS Division for Library Services. Used by state governments for a division frequently located in the state library. *See also* DLD.

DLSC Defense Logistics Services Center. Battle Creek, MI 49016. Maintains a library.

DLT Data Loop Transceiver. The station arrangement for certain leased channels provided by Western Union.

DM Data Management. A term referring collectively to all OS/360 routines that give access to data, enforce storage and conventions and regulate the use of each individual I/O device.

DMA Data Management Association. 505 Busse Highway, Park Ridge, IL 60068.

DMEA *Dictionary of Mechanical Engineering Abbreviations, Signs and Symbols.* New York: Odyssey Press, 1967.

DMHDD/LISN Illinois Department of Mental Health and Developmental Disabilities Library Services Network. Illinois State Psychiatric Institute, 1601 West Taylor St, Chicago, IL 60612. Fifty-three libraries cooperate to provide workshops, projects and other services. Formerly IDMH.

DMIC Defense Metals Information Center. 505 King Ave, Columbus, OH 43201. A library operated for the Office of the Director of Defense Research and Engineering, under the direction of USAF Materials Laboratory.

DML Data Manipulation Language.

DMPA Direct Mail Producers Association. 129 Chevening Rd, London NW6, England.

DMR Data Management Routines.

DM² Defense Market Measures System. Frost and Sullivan, Inc, 106 Fulton St, New York, NY 10038. Coverage from 1961. Nonbibliographic data base covering announcements of government contract awards.

DNA Defense Nuclear Agency. Washington, DC 20305. An agency of DOD responsible for the direction of nuclear weapons research.

DNA Deutscher Normenausschuss (German Standards Association). Burggrafenstr.

4-7, D-1000 Berlin 30, Federal Republic of Germany. Issues English translations of standards. Affiliated with ISO (International Standards Organization).

DNB *Dictionary of National Biography.* London: Oxford University Press, 1917. With supplements.

DNFF Den Norske Fagpresses Forening. Grensen 12, Oslo 1, Norway. Established in 1898. Members of the International Federation of the Periodical Press.

DOAE Defence Operational Analysis Establishment. Broadoaks, West Blyfleet, Surrey, England.

DOCHSIN District of Columbia Health Science Information Network. c/o Dahlgren Memorial Library, Georgetown University Medical Center, 3900 Reservoir Rd, NW, Washington, DC 20007. Ten medical libraries cooperate through ILL, acquisitions and processing.

DOCTOR Dictionary Operation and Control for Thesaurus Organization. Contact JICST. Project for thesaurus building at JICST (Japan Information Center for Science and Technology).

DOCUS Display-Oriented Computer Usage System. *See Display-Oriented Computer Usage System. Interim Technical Report, Oct. 1964–Apr. 1966.* Bethesda, MD: Informatics, 1966.

DOD Department of Defense. The Pentagon, Washington, DC 20301.

DOE Department of Energy. Washington, DC 20545. Supports many information processing projects.

DOE/TIC Franklin Institute Research Laboratories, The Franklin Institute, 20 & Race Sts, Philadelphia, PA 19103. Coverage from 1977. Bibliographic data base covering geothermal and solar energy.

DoI Department of Industry. A British government agency. Formerly DTI. Maintains OTIU.

DOLARS Disk On-Line Accounts Receivable System.

DOMA Dokumentation Maschinenbau. Lyonerstrasse 16, 6000 Frankfurt-on-Main 71, Federal Republic of Germany. Coverage from 1972. Data base covering mechanical engineering, transportation and utilities.

DOPS Digital Optical Projection System. Radar data plotting system technique.

DORIS Direct Order Recording and Invoicing System. An automatic programming system.

DORLS/DBRO Directors of Ontario Regional Library Systems/Directeurs des Bibliothèques Régionales de l'Ontario. Contact secretary.

DOS Disk Operating System. A versatile operating system for IBM 360 computers having direct access storage devices. Supports every peripheral device for the IBM 360.

DOT Department of Transportation. 400 Seventh St, SW, Washington, DC 20590.

DOTTR Dottrina. Centro Elettronico di Documentazione-Italgiure, Corte Suprema di Cassaziono, Palazzo di Giustizia, Via Ulpiano 8, Rome 00193, Italy. Coverage from 1970. Bibliographic data base covering legal articles relative to positive law.

DOZI-CIINTE Dzialowy Ośrodek Zagadnién Informacyjnych Centralnego Instytutu Informacji Naukowo-Technicznej i Ekonomicznej (Branch Center on Information Problems at the Central Institute for Scientific, Technical and Economic Information). Al. Niepodleglósci 188, Warsaw, Poland. Established in 1956. Became an independent unit in 1965, having started as a unit of the Department of Planning and later the Laboratory of Theory, Methodology and Technics in Information.

DP Data Processing.

DP Dynamic Programming. In this form of programming, an optimum decision must be made at every stage of a multistage problem because the cumulative result may be altered by a previous decision.

DPA Diary Publishers Association. 69 Cannon St, London EC4, England.

DPD Digit Plane Driver. Amplifier for a magnetic core storage unit.

DPED *Data Processing for Education.* (Newsletter). V. 1, 1962. Published by North American Publishing Co.

DPIR Data Processing and Information Retrieval.

DPL/DMA Data Processing Librarians and Documentation Managers Association. Box 572, Bowling Green Sta, New York, NY 10004. Established in 1976.

DPM Data Processing Machine.

DPM Documents Per Minute.

DPMA Data Processing Management Association. 505 Busse Hwy, Park Ridge, IL 60068. Established in 1951. A constituent society of AFIPS. Publishes a journal, reference series and books. Formerly (1962) NMAA.

DPMA *Dictionary of Physics and Mathematics Abbreviations, Signs and Symbols.* New York: Odyssey Press, 1965.

DPRS *Distributed Processing Reporting Service.* Published by IDC (International Data Corporation).

DPS Distributed Processing Support.

DPS Document Processing System. An IBM program package featuring the extracting, indexing, storing of keywords from text, and the storing of bibliographic data, abstracts or full text.

DPSA Display Producers and Screen Printers Association. 243 Gray's Inn Rd, London WC2, England.

DR Document Retrieval.

DRA Direction de la Recherche Agronomique. 99 avenue Temara, BP 415, Rabat, Morocco.

DRACON Drug Abuse Communications Network. c/o NYS Office of Substance Abuse Service, Bureau of Training and Resource Development, 95 Madison Ave, New York, NY 10016.

D-REF Data Reference. Water Resources Document Reference Centre, Canadian Dept. of Fisheries and the Environment, Inland Waters Directorate, Ottawa ON K1A 0E7, Canada. Coverage from 1975. Bibliographic data base covering Canadian wildlife, lands, water and forestry.

DRI Data Resources, Inc. 29 Harwell Ave, Lexington, MA 02173. Incorporated in 1969. Produces a data base on business and industry and prepares analytical reports.

DRL Data Retrieval Language. A high-level programming language. *See* Elizabeth Fong. "A Preliminary Design of a Data Retrieval Language to Handle a Generalized Data Base: DRL" in *NBS Tech Note 590*, 1971.

DRO Destructive Read-Out. A technique used to read directly from a storage device that causes the data being read to be destroyed in the process.

DRTC Documentation Research and Training Centre. 112 Cross Rd. 11, Malleswaram, Bangalore 3, India. Conducts classification research. *See* G. Srihari Raju. "Library Automation Developments in India." *Network* 1 (May 1974): 13–15.

DS Data Set. Collection of data in a prescribed format constituting the principal unit of data storage and retrieval.

DS Dokumentation Schweisstechnik. Deutscher Verband für Schweisstechnik, Bundesanstalt für Materialprüfung, Unter den Eichen, Berlin 1000, Federal Republic of Germany. Established in 1956. Provides computerized searches and document delivery in welding, soldering and allied processes.

DSA Defense Supply Agency. An agency of DOD.

DSB Deutsche Staatsbibliothek (German State Library). Unter den Linden 8, Postfach 1312, 108 Berlin, German Democratic Republic.

DSCB Data Set Control Block. A standard format control block specifying the parameter, for one data set, needed to describe and manipulate the data set in a direct access device.

DSH Deafness, Speech and Hearing Publications, Inc. American Speech and Hearing Association and Gallaudet College, Kendall Green, Washington, DC 20002. Publishes *DSH Abstracts*.

DSH *DSH Abstracts*. V. 1, 1960. Published by Deafness, Speech and Hearing Publications, Inc.

DSI Diffusion Sélective de l'Information. French for SDI (Selective Dissemination of Information).

DSI Diseminación Selectiva de la Información. Spanish for SDI (Selective Dissemination of Information).

DSIR Department of Scientific and Industrial Research. Information Service, 16-17 Kent Terrace, Private Bag, Wellington, New Zealand.

DSIS Directorate of Scientific Information Services. Contact Canadian Defense Research Board.

DSNA Dictionary Society of North America. Dept. of English and Journalism, Indiana State University, Terre Haute, IN 47809. Established in 1975. Purpose is to foster scholarly and professional activities relating to dictionaries. Formerly (1977) SSDL.

DT Committee on the Terminology of Information and Documentation. *See* FID/DT.

DTB Danmarks Tekniske Bibliotek med Dansk Central for Dokumentation (Danish Center for Documentation of the Technological Library of Denmark). Oster Voldgade 10, DK 1350 Copenhagen K, Denmark.

DTI Department of Trade and Industry. Name changed to DoI.

DTIE Division of Technical Information Extension. Formerly a division of AEC. Now TIC (Technical Information Center) of ERDA.

DTO Dansk Teknisk Oplysningstjeneste (Danish Technical Information Service). 30 Ørnevej, Copenhagen DK-2400, Denmark.

DTOL Digital Test-Oriented Language. A programming language.

DTR Distribution Tape Reel.

DTSS Dartmouth Time Sharing System. *See* T. E. Kurtz. "The Many Roles of Computing on the Campus" in *Proceedings of AFIPS 1969 Joint Computer Conference*. Montvale, NJ: AFIPS Press, 1969.

DttP *Documents to the People*. (Journal). V. 1, 1972. Published by the Government Documents Round Table of ALA (American Library Association).

DUALabs National Data Use and Access Laboratories, Inc. 1600 North Kent St, Suite 900, Rosslyn, VA 22209. Makes available US census data on tape.

DYANA Dynamics Analyzer-Programmer. A computer program for use on the IBM 704 computer.

DYNAMO A digital simulation program developed at MIT (Massachusetts Institute of Technology).

DYSTAL Dynamic Storage Allocation Language. *See* James M. Sakoda. *DYSTAL: Dynamic Storage Allocation Language Manual*. Providence, RI: Brown University, 1965.

EAA Experimental Aircraft Association. Box 229, 11311 West Forest Home Ave, Hales Corners, WI 53130. Established in 1972. Maintains a library on aeronautical history.

EAAFRO East African Agriculture and Forestry Research Organization. Box 1587, Nairobi, Kenya.

EAB Education Advice Bureau. Royal Agricultural Society of England, 35 Belgrave Sq, London SW1, England.

EAES European Atomic Energy Society. Kernforschungszentrum, Karlsruhe, Institut für Neutronenphysik, Postfach 3640, 75 Karlsruhe, Federal Republic of Germany.

EALA East African Library Association. This association has been terminated.

EAM Electrical Accounting Machinery. Jargon for punched card handling equipment or data processing machinery that is electromechanical rather than electronic in form.

EAM Electronic Accounting Machine. Used for processing punched cards.

EAMTC European Association of Management Training Centers. 58 rue de la Concorde, Brussels 5, Belgium.

EAN European Article Number. The European equivalent of UPC.

EANDC European-American Nuclear Data Committee. 38 boulevard Suchet, Paris 16, France.

EARS Epilepsy Abstracts Retrieval System. Sponsored by the National Institute of Neurological Diseases and Stroke. *See* Roger J. Porter, J. Kiffin Penry and Joseph E. Caponio. "Epilepsy Abstracts Retrieval System (EARS): A New Concept for Medical Literature Storage and Retrieval." *BMLA* (July 1971): 430–432.

EASE Engineering Automatic System for Solving Equations. An automatic program compiler used on the IBM 650 computer.

EASI Electrical Accounting for the Security Industry. An IBM program for stockbroker accounts.

EASY Efficient Assembly System. An assembler developed for the Honeywell 400 computer.

EAX Electronic Automatic Exchange. Electronic telephone exchange equipment. Term used by General Telephone Company.

EB *Encyclopaedia Britannica*. Chicago, IL: Encyclopaedia Britannica, Inc, 1974.

EB Encyclopaedia Britannica, Inc. 425 North Michigan Ave, Chicago, IL 60611. Publishes *EB* (*Encyclopaedia Britannica*). *See also* AASL/EB.

EBAD École de Bibliothécaires, Archivistes et Documentalistes (School of Librarians, Archivists and Documentalists). EBAD de Dakar, Box 3252, Dakar, Senegal.

EBCDIC Extended Binary Coded Decimal Interchange Code. An eight-bit code that was widely used in computers of the first and second generations, it can represent up to 256 distinct characters.

EBE Encyclopaedia Britannica Educational Corporation. 425 North Michigan Ave, Chicago, IL 60611. An affiliate of Encyclopaedia Britannica, Inc.

EBI *Energy Bibliography and Index.* Houston, TX: Gulf Publishing Co, 1979– . 5 vols.

EBNA *Ethnographic Bibliography of North America*. George Peter Murdock and Timothy J. O'Leary. 4th ed. New Haven, CT: Human Relations Area Files, 1975.

EBR Electron Beam Recording. A method of obtaining microfilm output from a computer by directing a beam of electrons onto an energy-sensitive film.

EBSS Education and Behavioral Sciences Section. *See* ACRL/EBSS.

EBU European Broadcasting Union. One rue de Varembé 1211, Geneva, Switzerland.

EC Error Correcting.

ECA Educational Centres Association. Greenleaf Rd, London E17 6PQ, England. Established in 1921. Publishes documents.

ECAFE Economic Commission for Asia and the Far East. Participated in Seminar on Industrial Information held in Vienna, 1970. *See* proceedings, *Seminar on Industrial Information, 1970*. Vienna, Austria: United Nations Industrial Development Organization, 1970. Name changed to ESCAP in 1977.

ECAP Electric Circuit Analysis Program.

ECARBICA East and Central Africa Regional Branch of the International Council on Archives. c/o Kenya National Archives, Jogoo House "A," Box 30520, Nairobi, Kenya. Established in 1972. Official journal, *ECARBICA Journal*, is published semiannually.

ECARS Electronic Coordinatograph and Readout System. A computer program developed by Burroughs Corp. to yield information for land use control.

ECC European Cultural Center. 122 rue de Lausanne 1211, Geneva, Switzerland.

ECCLA European Committee for Cooperation with Latin America. c/o Union Internationale des Associations Patronates Catholiques, 49 avenue d'Auderghem, Brussels 4, Belgium.

ECDB Electronic Components Data Bank. Space Documentation Service, European Space Agency, Via Galileo Galilei, Franscati, Rome 00044, Italy. Coverage from 1975. Nonbibliographic data base which describes electronic components.

ECER Exceptional Child Education Resources. The Council for Exceptional Children, Reston, VA 22091. On-line bibliographic data base covering the education of handicapped and gifted children.

ECFRPC East Central Florida Regional Planning Council. 807 West Morse Blvd, Winter Park, FL 32789. Produces demographic and statistical data bases on the region.

ECMA European Computer Manufacturers Association. Geneva, Switzerland.

ECOL Environmental Conservation Library. Minneapolis Public Library and

Information Center, 300 Nicollet Mall, Minneapolis, MN 55401. Lends packets of information to elementary and junior high school students and teachers.

ECSLA East Central State School Libraries Association (Nigeria). Contact secretary-treasurer. Established in 1963. Affiliated with IFLA and NLA (Nigerian Library Association). Official journal, *ECS School Libraries Bulletin*, is published three times a year.

ED Error Detecting. Finding errors in a program or in the execution of a program.

ED Expanded Display. The process of requesting greater detail concerning the record identified on the monitor.

ED External Device.

EDA Educational Development Association. 8 Windmill Gardens, Enfield, Middlesex, England.

EDC Education Development Center, Inc. 55 Chapel St, Newton, MA 02160. Established in 1958. Maintains an education library.

EDC European Documentation Centers. A term to encompass the documentation centers of the European countries.

EDCPF Environmental Data Collection and Processing Facility. Bell Aerospace Company, Tucson, AZ. *See* T. J. Flahie et al. *Report on the Operations of the Environmental Data Collection and Processing Facility (EDCPF). Formal Progress Report no. 2, 1 October–31 December 1970.* Tucson, AZ: Bell Aerospace Co, March 1971.

EDCW External Device Control Word. The last operand of the EXD instruction in some systems.

EDF Electricité de France. Direction des Études et Recherches, Electricité de France, One avenue du General de Gaulle 9, Clarmart 92141, France. Coverage from 1972. Bibliographic data base covering the production and use of electricity.

EDGE Electronic Data Gathering Equipment. System for gathering data for computer processing.

EDICT Engineering Departmental Interface Control Technique. Used by Space and

Information Systems Division of North American Aviation to provide the company's engineers with design data in the Saturn rocket and Apollo spacecraft.

EDITS Educators Information Technology System. InTech Corporation, Wilkes-Barre, PA 18701. A project funded by USOE in 1968-1970 to make educators more aware of the impact of computers as teaching tools and as administrative devices.

EDP Electronic Data Processing. Processing of data automatically through the use of electronic machinery such as an electronic digital computer.

EDPAC A package of five related utility computer programs: BLOCKSEARCH, JUSTIFY, SCRAMBLE, SEARCH and SUBSTITUTE made available from NBS.

EDPE Electronic Data Processing Equipment.

EDPM Electronic Data Processing Machine.

EDPS Electronic Data Processing System.

EDRS ERIC Document Reproduction Service. Box 190, Arlington, VA 22210. The microfiche reproduction center for the ERIC system.

EDSAC Electronic Discrete Sequential Automatic Computer. The first internal-stored program computer, built in 1949 at the University of Manchester, England.

EDUCOM Interuniversity Communications Council. Box 364, Rosedale Rd, Princeton, NJ 08540. Established in 1964. Started as a nonprofit corporation to further biomedical communications, EDUCOM later expanded to educational networking to share computational resources. Has been funded by NSF and USOE. Publishes *EDUCOM: Bulletin of the Interuniversity Communications Council.*

EDVAC Electronic Discrete Variable Automatic Computer. Computer developed in 1952 using binary numbers and the internal storage of instructions written in digital form.

EEA Educational Exhibitors Association. One Devonshire Pl, London W1, England.

EEA *Electrical and Electronic Abstracts.* V. 1, 1898. Published by IEE (Institution of Electrical Engineers). Alternative title: *Science Abstracts, Section B.*

EEB Enosis Ellenon Bibliothekarion (Greek Library Association). 11 Amerikis St, Athens 134, Greece. Established in 1969. Affiliated with IFLA. Official journal, *Greek Library Association Bulletin*, is published irregularly.

EEC European Economic Community. 170 rue de la Loi, Brussels 4, Belgium. Also known as CEE (Comunità Economica Europea). Decisions of the EEC Court of Justice are computerized in Rome, Italy. *See* CEE (Giurisprudenza Corte 2. Giurstizia delle CEE).

EECS *European Executive Compensation Survey.* Published annually by Business International Corp.

EEOC Equal Employment Opportunity Commission. 2401 E St, NW, Washington, DC 20506. Established in 1964. Maintains a library on employment discrimination.

EESS *Encyclopedia of Engineering Signs and Symbols.* David D. Polon, ed. New York: Odyssey Press, 1965.

EEUA Engineering Equipment Users Association. 20 Grosvenor Gardens, London SW1, England.

EFCC European Federation of Conference Cities. c/o The Dome, Brighton, Sussex, England.

EFCE European Federation of Chemical Engineering. Institution of Chemical Engineers, 16 Belgrave Sq, London SW1, England.

EFLA Educational Film Library Association. 43 West 61 St, New York, NY 10023.

EFP European Federation of Purchasing. c/o Institute of Purchasing and Supply, York House, Westminster Bridge Rd, London SE1, England.

EFVA European Foundation for Visual Aids. 33 Queen Anne St, London W1M 0A1, England.

EGIS *Executives Guide to Information Sources.* Chicago, IL: Gale Research Co, 1968. 3 volumes.

EGLI *Essay and General Literature Index.* V. 1, 1900. Published by H. W. Wilson Co.

EGMIA Education Group of the Music Industries Association. 25 Oxford St, London W1, England.

EHF Extremely High Frequency. Thirty thousand to 300,000 megahertz.

EI *Engineering Index.* (Journal). V. 1, 1906. Published annually from 1906 to 1961. From 1962– , published monthly by Engineering Index, Inc.

EIA Engineering Industries Association. 3-7 Portman Sq, London W1, England.

EIC Energy Information Center. Name changed to EIC (Environment Information Center, Inc.).

EIC Environment Information Center, Inc. 292 Madison Ave, New York, NY 10017. Incorporated in 1970. Independent clearinghouse for information on energy and the environment. Maintains a library and publishes various indexes and abstracts. Member of IIA (Information Industry Association). Formerly EIC (Energy Information Center).

EID Environmental Information Division. Air Training Command, Maxwell Air Force Base, AL 36112. Provides information services in the fields of environmental extremes and human survival.

EIRMA European Industrial Management Association. 38 Cours Albert 1, Paris 8, France.

EIS Economic Information Systems. 9 East 47 St, New York, NY 10017. A data base of current information on US industrial firms with 2,000 or more employees. Added to Lockheed's DIALOG in 1975.

EIS Educational Institute of Scotland. 46 Moray Pl, Edinburgh EH3 6BH, Scotland. Established in 1847. Publishes documents.

EIT *Engineering Index Thesaurus.* New York: CCM Information Corp, 1972.

EJC Engineers Joint Council. 345 East 47 St, New York, NY 10017. Established in 1945. Publishes a biennial directory and a bulletin.

ELA Edmonton Library Association. Contact president. A Canadian association.

ELA Ethiopian Library Association. Box 30530, Addis Ababa, Ethiopia. Established in 1969. Affiliated with AIDBA (Association Internationale pour le Développement de la Documentation, des Bibliothèques et des Archives en Afrique). Official journal, *Ethiopian Library Association Bulletin*, is published semiannually.

ELI Equitable Life Interpreter. A routine developed by Equitable Life Assurance Society for use on the IBM 650 and IBM 705 computers.

ELMS Exploratory Library Management Systems. IBM, Los Gatos, CA 95030. An on-line, real-time system to handle record-keeping functions in a conversational mode for library users.

ELNA Esperanto League for North America, Inc. Box 1129, El Cerrito, CA 94530. Publishes a bibliography of titles in Esperanto and several dictionaries.

EM End of Medium. A character in a string of machine-readable data that indicates either the physical end or end portion of the data medium on which the desired data is recorded.

EM Excerpta Medica Foundation. Box 211, Amsterdam, the Netherlands. An international system for monitoring, abstracting, translating, classifying and indexing 60 percent of the world's biomedical literature. Started publishing indexes in 1947. Presently issuing 48 indexes.

EMAP European Marketing and Advertising Press. 9-10 Old Bailey, London EC4, England.

EMC Educational Media Council. Association for Educational Communications and Technology, 1126 16th St, NW, Washington, DC 20036. A council of AECT established in 1960. Connected with ALA (American Library Association) and CLENE.

EMCOM *Educational Media Catalogs on Microfiche*. Walter J. Carroll, ed. New York: Olympia Media Information, 1979.

EMEU East Midland Educational Union. One Clinton Terr, Derby Rd, Nottingham, England.

EMIE Educational Media Institute Evaluation Project. Dept. of Audio-Visual Instruction, National Education Association, 1201 16th St, NW, Washington, DC 20036.

EMIETF Ethnic Materials Information Exchange Task Force. 68-71 Bell Blvd, Bayside, NY 11364. Established in 1971. Publishes documents.

EMIS Engineering Maintenance Information System.

EMRLS East Midlands Regional Library System. Central Reference Library, Bishop St, Leicester L11 6AA, England.

EMS Early MARC Search. A project of LC.

EMSC *Educational Media Selection Centers*. John Rowell and M. Ann Heidbreder. Chicago, IL: American Library Association, 1971 (American Library Association Studies in Librarianship, No. 1).

ENDEX Environmental Data Index. Environmental Science Services Administration, National Weather Records Center, Federal Bldg, Asheville, NC 28801. Data base of environmental data collected from 1969.

ENDS European Nuclear Documentation System. Center for Information and Documentation, 29 rue Aldringer, Luxembourg City, Luxembourg. Provides member countries with information services and attempts to improve information flow. Cooperates with INIS.

ENEA European Nuclear Energy Agency. 38 boulevard Suchet, Paris 16, France.

ENERGYLINE [Energy Online]. Environment Information Center, Inc, 292 Madison Ave, New York, NY 10017. Coverage from 1971. Bibliographic data base covering all aspects of energy.

ENIAC Electronic Numerical Integrator and Calculator. Computer developed in 1946 by Eckert and Mauchly. Used electronic components instead of mechanical relays.

ENQ Enquiry Character. A transmission control character used to request a response from a station with which a connection has been made.

ENSPM École Nationale du Pétrole et des Moteurs. ENSPM's courses are deposited in the Documentation Management Section of IFP.

ENVIROBIB Environmental Periodicals Bibliography. *See* EPB.

ENVIROLINE [Environment Information On-Line]. Environment Information Center, Inc, 292 Madison Ave, New York, NY 10017. Coverage from 1971. Bibliographic data base covering land use, transportation, pollution and other environmental areas.

ENVPSYCH [Environmental Psychology]. Center for Human Environments, City University of New York, 33 West 42 St, New York, NY 10036. Coverage from 1970. Data base containing citations and abstracts of books and articles relating to the interaction of people and environments.

EOF End of File. Termination of a quantity of data on a computer tape.

EOJ End of Job. This card returns control to the monitor. The monitor then automatically processes any jobs remaining in the card reader.

EOM End of Message. A character in a string of machine-readable data that indicates the end of the message or record.

EOS Egyptian Organization for Standardization. 2 Latin America St, Garden City, Cairo, Egypt, United Arab Republic. Issues English-language standards. Affiliated with ISO (International Standards Organization).

EOT End of Transmission. A character in a string of machine-readable data that indicates that the sending of data from one location to another is complete.

EPA Environmental Protection Agency. 401 M St, SW, Washington, DC 20460. Established in 1971. Maintains a library and publishes documents. Administers federal environmental policies. Provides information on many environmental problems such as water and land pollution, solid waste disposal, air and noise pollution and pesticides and other hazardous materials.

EPAM Elementary Perceiver and Memorizer. A reading and storing device.

EPB Environmental Periodicals Bibliography. Environmental Studies Institute, 2074 Alameda Padre Serra, Santa Barbara, CA 93103. Coverage from 1973. Bibliographic data base covering ecology, energy, resources, nutrition and health. Also known as ENVIROBIB.

EPDA Education Professions Development Act. Awards fellowships aimed at improving library services to the disadvantaged. Some fellowships are awarded to minority students.

EPIC East Central Pennsylvania Council on Interlibrary Cooperation. c/o Franklin and Marshall College, Fackenthal Library, Lancaster, PA 17604. Consortium established in 1972. Preparing union list of serials.

EPIC Electronic Properties Information Center. Hughes Aircraft Co, Culver City, CA 90230. Provides answers and numerous publications to authorized users. Sponsor: USAF Materials Laboratory.

EPIC Estimation de Propriétés Physiques pour l'Ingenieur Chimiste. Université de l'État a Liège, Laboratoire d'Analyse et Synthèse des Systems Chimiques, Liège, Belgium. Data base covering thermodynamic and physical properties of chemical components.

EPIE Educational Products and Information Exchange. c/o Idaho State University, AV Service Center–Film Library, Box 8064, Pocatello, ID 83209. Established in 1967. Publishes documents. Now known as EPIE Institute.

EPILEPSYLINE [Epilepsy On-Line]. National Institute of Neurological and Communicative Disorders and Stroke, 8600 Rockville Pike, Bethesda, MD 20014. Coverage from 1947. Bibliographic data base on epilepsy and related disorders. Available on-line through NLM.

EPIS Extramural Programs Information System. National Library of Medicine, 8600 Rockville Pike, Bethesda, MD 20014. Nonbibliographic data base covering grants and contract programs authorized by MLAA.

EPNS English Place-Name Society. University College, Gower St, London WC1, England.

EPU Economic Planning Unit of Barbados. Government Headquarters, Bay St, Barbados, West Indies. Issues English-language standards; affiliated with ISO (International Standards Organization).

ERA Engineering Research Associates. Manufactures computers. A division of Remington-Rand UNIVAC.

ERA European Research Associates. Library, rue Gatti de Gamond 95, B-1180 Brussels, Belgium.

ERB Engineering Reference Branch. US Department of the Interior.

ERC Electronics Research Center. Now TSC (Transportation Systems Center).

ERDA Energy Research and Development Administration. Superseded AEC in 1974 and consolidated into DOE in 1977.

ERIC Educational Resources Information Center. National Institute of Education, Washington, DC 20208. Established in 1964 by USOE as a national information system, disseminating educational research results, research-related material and other resource information. Maintains a network of specialized centers or clearinghouses throughout the country, each responsible for a particular educational area.

ERIC/CAPS ERIC Clearinghouse on Counseling and Personnel Services. *See* ERIC/CG.

ERIC/CE ERIC Clearinghouse on Adult, Career, and Vocational Education. Ohio State University, 1960 Kenny Rd, Columbus, OH 43210. One of 16 ERIC clearinghouses responsible for a major area in the field of education.

ERIC/CEC ERIC Clearinghouse on Handicapped and Gifted Children. *See* ERIC/EC.

ERIC/CEM ERIC Clearinghouse on Educational Management. *See* ERIC/EA.

ERIC/CG ERIC Clearinghouse on Counseling and Personnel Services. University of Michigan, School of Education Bldg, Rm. 2108, East University & South University Sts, Ann Arbor, MI 48109. One of 16 ERIC clearinghouses responsible for a major area in the field of education. Also known as ERIC/CAPS.

ERIC/ChESS ERIC Clearinghouse for Social Studies/Social Science Education. *See* ERIC/SO.

ERIC/CLL ERIC Clearinghouse on Languages and Linguistics. *See* ERIC/FL.

ERIC/CRESS ERIC Clearinghouse on Rural Education and Small Schools. *See* ERIC/RC.

ERIC/CS ERIC Clearinghouse on Reading and Communication Skills. National Council of Teachers of English, 1111 Kenyon Rd, Urbana, IL 61801. One of 16 ERIC clearinghouses responsible for a major area in the field of education. Also known as ERIC/RCS.

ERIC/CUE ERIC Clearinghouse on Urban Education. *See* ERIC/UD.

ERIC/EA ERIC Clearinghouse on Educational Management. University of Oregon, Eugene, OR 97403. One of 16 ERIC clearinghouses responsible for a major area in the field of education. Also known as ERIC/CEM.

ERIC/EC ERIC Clearinghouse on Handicapped and Gifted Children. Council for Exceptional Children, 1920 Association Dr, Reston, VA 22091. One of 16 ERIC clearinghouses responsible for a major area in the field of education. Also known as ERIC/CEC.

ERIC/ECE ERIC Clearinghouse on Elementary and Early Childhood Education. *See* ERIC/PS.

ERIC/FL ERIC Clearinghouse on Languages and Linguistics. Center for Applied Linguistics, 1611 North Kent St, Arlington, VA 22209. One of 16 ERIC clearinghouses responsible for a major area in the field of education. Also known as ERIC/CLL.

ERIC/HE ERIC Clearinghouse on Higher Education. George Washington University, One Dupont Circle, NW, Suite 630, Washington, DC 20036. One of 16 ERIC clearinghouses responsible for a major area in the field of education.

ERIC/IR ERIC Clearinghouse on Information Resources. School of Education, 30 Huntington Hall, Syracuse University, Syracuse, NY 13210. One of 16 ERIC clearinghouses responsible for a major area in the field of education.

ERIC/JC ERIC Clearinghouse on Junior Colleges. University of California, Los Angeles, Powell Library, Rm. 96, 405 Hilgard Ave, Los Angeles, CA 90024. One of 16 ERIC clearinghouses responsible for a major area in the field of education.

ERIC/PS ERIC Clearinghouse on Elementary and Early Childhood Education. University of Illinois, College of Education, 805 West Pennsylvania Ave, Urbana, IL 61801. One of 16 ERIC clearinghouses responsible for a major area in the field of education. Also known as ERIC/ECE.

ERIC/RC ERIC Clearinghouse on Rural Education and Small Schools. New Mexico State University, Box 3AP, Las Cruces, NM 88003. One of 16 ERIC clearinghouses responsible for a major area in the field of education. Also known as ERIC/CRESS.

ERIC/RCS ERIC Clearinghouse on Reading and Communication Skills. *See* ERIC/CS.

ERIC/SE ERIC Clearinghouse for Science, Mathematics and Environmental Education. 1200 Chambers Rd, Rm. 310, Columbus, OH 43212. One of 16 ERIC clearinghouses responsible for a major area in the field of education. Also known as ERIC/SMEAC.

ERIC/SMEAC ERIC Clearinghouse for Science, Mathematics and Environmental Education. *See* ERIC/SE.

ERIC/SO ERIC Clearinghouse for Social Studies/Social Science Education. Social Science Education Consortium, Inc, 855 Broadway, Boulder, CO 80302. One of 16 ERIC clearinghouses responsible for a major area in the field of education. Also known as ERIC/ChESS.

ERIC/SP ERIC Clearinghouse on Teacher Education. American Association of Colleges for Teacher Education, One Dupont Circle, NW, Suite 616, Washington, DC 20036. One of 16 ERIC clearinghouses responsible for a major area in the field of education.

ERIC/TM ERIC Clearinghouse on Tests, Measurement, and Evaluation. Educational Testing Service, Rosedale Rd, Princeton, NJ 08541. One of 16 ERIC clearinghouses responsible for a major area in the field of education.

ERIC/UD ERIC Clearinghouse on Urban Education. Teachers College, Columbia University, 525 West 120 St, New York, NY 10027. One of 16 ERIC clearinghouses responsible for a major area in the field of education. Also known as ERIC/CUE.

EROS Earth Resources Observation System. EROS Data Center, US Geological Survey, Sioux Falls, SD 57198. Data center provides information on satellite photography and imagery.

ERR Error. The deviation of an observed or computed result from a correct or true result.

ERS Educational Research Service. 1800 North Kent St, Arlington, VA 22209. Established in 1924. Publishes documents.

ERT Exhibits Round Table. Contact ALA (American Library Association).

ERTS Earth Resources Technology Satellite Program. Now known as the LANDSAT program.

ESA Ecological Society of America. Library 3131, Evergreen State College, Olympia, WA 98505. Established in 1915. Publishes documents. Conducted a joint study with PMM & Co. on the need for an ecological information clearinghouse and referral service.

ESANET European Space Agency Network. European Space Agency, Via Galileo Galilei, Frascati, Rome 00044, Italy. Data base vendor. Member of EUSIDIC.

ESC Escape Character. Refers to a character in a string of machine-readable data that indicates that one or more succeeding characters is in a different code than the one being used.

ESCAP Economic and Social Commission for Asia and the Pacific. United Nations

Bldg, Rajadamnern Ave, Bangkok 2, Thailand. A commission of the UN. Known as ECAFE until 1977.

ESCAPE Expansion Symbolic Compiling Assembly Program for Engineering.

ESD Electrostatic Storage Deflection.

ESD External Symbol Dictionary. Compilation of control information associated with an object or load module so as to identify the external symbols in the module.

ESDAC European Space Data Center. Darmstadt, Federal Republic of Germany.

ESEA Elementary and Secondary Education Act.

ESI Externally Specified Index. Allows a number of communications networks to operate concurrently on a pair of I/O channels.

ESIC Environmental Science and Information Center. Rockville, MD 20852.

ESL Electromagnetic Systems Laboratories. 495 Java Dr, Sunnyvale, CA 94086. Maintains a computer science library.

ESL Engineering Societies Library. United Engineering Center, 345 East 47 St, New York, NY 10017.

ESLA Egyptian School Library Association. 35 Algalaa St, Cairo, Egypt. Established in 1967. Official journal, *Sahifat al Maktaba*, is published three times a year. *See* M. M. Aman. "Egypt, Libraries in" in *Encyclopedia of Library and Information Science*, ed. by A. Kent et al. New York: Marcel Dekker, 1972, V. 7, pp. 574–588.

ESLAB European Space Research Laboratory. European Space Research and Technology Center, Domeinweg, Noordwijk, the Netherlands.

ESLD Engineering School Libraries Division. American Society for Engineering Education, One Dupont Circle, Suite 400, Washington, DC 20036. A division of ASEE.

ESOMAR European Society for Opinion Surveys and Market Research. 30 Magpie Hall Lane, Bickley, Kent, England.

ESRIN European Space Research Institute. Frascati, Rome, Italy.

ESRO European Space Research Organization. 114 Avenue de Neuilly, 92 Neuilly-sur-Seine, France. Members are: Belgium, Denmark, France, Germany, Italy, the Netherlands, Spain, Sweden, Switzerland and the United Kingdom. Promotes cooperation in space research and technology. *See* A. Mauperon. "Où Va l'Information Scientifique?" *Euratom Bulletin* 6 (Mar. 1967): 17–21.

ESS Electronic Security Systems. A system used in library theft control.

ESS Electronic Switching System. Developed by the Bell System to handle central office functions. Has a data switching center which senses the contents of messages and relays such information without the intervention of an operator. Also called automatic switching.

ESTEC European Space Research and Technology Center. Domeinweg, Noordwijk, the Netherlands.

ET Committee on Education and Training. *See* FID/ET.

ETB End of Transmission-Block. A character in a string of machine-readable data that indicates the end of a set of words, characters or records considered as one unit for transmission purposes.

ETC European Translation Center. *See* CET (Centre Européene de Traduction).

ETIC English Teaching Information Centre. State House, High Holborn, London WC1, England.

ETP Electrical Tough Pitch. A grade of copper used in electrical conductors.

ETS Educational Television Stations. National Association of Educational Broadcasters, 1346 Connecticut Ave, NW, Washington, DC 20006. A division of NAEB.

ETS Educational Testing Service. Princeton, NJ 08541.

ETV Educational Television.

ETVO Educational Television Branch of Ontario. Dept. of Education, 1670 Bayview Ave, Toronto 17, ON, Canada.

ETX End of Text. A character in a string of machine-readable data that indicates the end of the part of a message containing information to be communicated.

EUA Electrical Utilities Applications. This program is utilized by various electrical utilities to analyze load flow, short circuit, and transient stability in operations and future systems planning.

EUFTG End User Facility Task Group. A CODASYL task group which is charged with describing and defining an end-user facility for a "complex structured data base."

EULER An extension of ALGOL 60, including list processing capabilities.

EURATOM European Atomic Energy Community. Rue de la Loi 200, 1040 Brussels, Belgium. Has a nuclear documentation system for which a thesaurus of indexing terms has been compiled. *See* CID (Center for Information and Documentation). *See also* CETIS.

EURIM 3 European Conference on the Application of Research in Information Services and Libraries. Conference sponsored by ASLIB, Association National de la Recherche Technique, Bibliothèque Royale de Belgique, Consiglio Nazionale delle Ricerche, Deutsche Gesellschaft für Dokumentation and others. Third conference held in Munich in 1978.

EUROBOIS European Group of Woodworking Journals. 40 rue du Colisée, Paris 7, France.

EUROCOMP European Computing Congress. Contact secretary.

EURODIDAC Association Européenne de Fabricants et des Revendeurs de Matériel Didactique/Verband Europäischer Lehrmittelfirmen. Kartäuserstrasse 160, D-7806 Freiburg-Ebnet, Federal Republic of Germany.

EUROSPACE European Industrial Space Study Group. 10 rue Cognacq-Jay, Paris 7, France.

EUSEC Conference of Engineering Societies of Western Europe and the United States of America. Beethovenstrasse 1, Zurich 8022, Switzerland.

EUSIDIC European Association of Information Services. Box 1766, The Hague, the Netherlands. Established in 1970. Promotes technology of computerized information storage and retrieval. Produces data bases and publishes documents. Formerly CHEOPS.

EUSIREF European Referral Service. Commission of the European Communities, Directorate General, Scientific and Technical Information and Information Management, Jean Monnet B/4, Kinchberg, Luxembourg. European network of referral centers, promoted by EUSIDIC.

EVIMEC Eastern Virginia MEDLINE Consortium. Eastern Virginia Medical School, 700 Olney Rd, Norfolk, VA 23501. A consortium to provide MEDLINE service to member libraries.

EVOP Evolutionary Operations. A statistical technique useful for improving plant operations by slight perturbation of operating conditions repeatedly over a long period of time.

EVR Electronic Videorecording.

EWA Education Writers Association. Box 281, Woodstown, NJ 08098. Established in 1947. Publishes documents.

EXD External Device Control. This action occurs only as a result of a computer external device instruction. Response may be a busy status or an interrupt request status.

EXEC Execute Statement. To carry out an instruction or to perform a routine.

EZPERT Easy PERT.

F Fiction. Designation applied to books of fiction in a collection.

FAA Federal Aviation Administration. 800 Independence Ave, SW, Washington, DC 20591. Part of DOT established in 1967. Regulates aviation commerce to improve air safety.

FAA Film Artists Association. 61 Marloes Rd, London W8, England.

FACES FORTRAN Automatic Code Evaluation System.

FACOM 230-50 Name of the computer used by JICST. *See* K. Sasamori. "Software

Design for Vocabulary Control (DOCTOR) System." *ASIS Proceedings* 7 (1970): 195–197.

FACS Floating-decimal Abstract Coding System. A compiler developed for the IBM 650 computer.

FACS Fluorescence-Activated Cell Sorter.

FACSEA French American Cultural Services and Educational Aid. 972 Fifth Ave, New York, NY 10021. Established in 1955. Maintains a library and publishes documents.

FACT Facility of Automation, Control and Test.

FACT Factual Compiler. Developed by Ramo-Woolridge Corp.

FACT Fast Access Current Text Bank. An experimental electronic library established in 1967. Text bank produces current medical information in facsimile copy from microfiche through telephone linkup. Located at the University of Missouri–Columbia, FACT was based on the Mosler 410 Information System.

FACT *Fuel Abstracts and Current Titles.* V. 1, 1960. Published by the Institute of Fuel, London.

FACT Fully Automatic Cataloging Technique. Used by Library Micrographic Services, Inc., a subsidiary of Opticom Data Management Corp. Combines computer technology, source document microfilming and COM (Computer Output Microfilming).

FACT Fully Automatic Compiler-Translator.

FACT Fully Automatic Compiling Technique.

FACTS Facsimile Transmission System. An experimental project carried out in 1967–1968 under contract between the New York State Library and the New York Public Library. *See* J. M. Cory. "The Network in a Major Metropolitan Center." *Library Quarterly* 39 (Jan. 1969): 90–98.

FAD Flexible Automatic Depot.

FAHSLN Flint Area Health Science Library Network. c/o Saint Joseph Hospital Health Sciences Library, 302 Kensington Ave, Flint, MI 48502.

FAIB Fédération des Associations Internationales Establiés en Belgique (Federation of International Associations Established in Belgium). One rue aux Laines, Brussels 1, Belgium.

FAIME Foreign Affairs Information Management Effort. A project of the US Department of State.

FAIR Failure Analysis Information Retrieval.

FAIR Fast Access Information Retrieval. Clinical Research Centre, Bioengineering Division, Watford Rd, Harrow, Middlesex HA1 3UJ, England. A desk-top document retrieval system in the field of biomedical engineering. Produces a publication, *BEACAN. See* "Project FAIR: A Specialized Information Centre for Biomedical Engineering." *Biomedical Engineering* 7 (1972): 181–182.

FAIRS Federal Aviation Information Retrieval System.

FAIRS Fully Automatic Information System.

FAL Finite Automation Language. A programming language.

FALA Federation of Asian Library Associations. *See* AFLA.

FAMA Free Association of Management Analysis.

FAME Financial Analysis of Management Effectiveness. A project of the US Department of Agriculture.

FAME Florida Association for Media and Education. Contact president. Formerly Florida School Libraries under FLA.

FAME Forecasts, Appraisals, and Management Evaluation.

FAMIS Financial Accounting and Management Information System. *See* E. Reece Harrill, Thomas E. Richards, and Jonathan M. Wallman. "FAMIS: A Financial Accounting and Management Information System for Local Government." *Management Controls* 21 (May 1974): 85–94.

FAMIS Financial and Management Information System. Naval Oceanographic Office, US Dept. of the Navy, Washington, DC 20350.

FAMULUS Named for the title given to the private secretary to a medieval scholar. A computer-based system that provides flexible editing, sorting and indexing features. *See* H. D. Burton and T. B. Yerke. "FAMULUS: A Computer-Based System for Augmenting Personal Documentation Efforts." *ASIS Proceedings* 6 (1969): 53–56.

F&S Frost & Sullivan, Inc. 106 Fulton St, New York, NY 10038. Produces data bases and provides computerized searches and analytical reports.

FAO Food and Agriculture Organization. Viale delle Terme de Caracalla, Rome, Italy. Sponsor of AGRIS.

FAO Foreign and Commonwealth Office. Downing St, London SW1, England.

FAP Failure Analysis Program.

FAP Financial Analysis Program.

FAP Floating-point Arithmetic Package. Automatic coding system for the UNIVAC 1103A computer.

FAP FORTRAN Assembly Procedure. *See* FAP (FORTRAN Assembly Program).

FAP FORTRAN Assembly Program. Assembler for the IBM 704 and IBM 709 computers. Also known as FAP (FORTRAN Assembly Procedure).

FARADA Failure Rate Data Program. US Naval Fleet Missile Systems Analysis and Evaluation Group, Code 862, Corona, CA 91720. Data exchange program sponsored by the US Army, Navy and Air Force and NASA to collect, compile, analyze and disseminate failure rate and failure mode data about parts, components, modules and assemblies.

FARET Fast Reactor Test Facility. An atomic energy reactor test facility at the Argonne National Laboratory.

FARMODEX Geert Grooteplein Zuid 10, Nijmegen 6525 GA, the Netherlands. On-line index of pharmaceutical products and constituent materials available in the Netherlands.

FAS Federation of American Scientists. 307 Massachusetts Ave, NE, Washington, DC 20002. Established in 1946. Publishes a journal.

FASE Fundamentally Analyzable Simplified English.

FASEB Federation of American Societies for Experimental Biology. 9650 Rockville Pike, Bethesda, MD 20014. Established in 1913. Publishes documents.

FAST Facility for Automatic Sorting and Testing.

FAST Flexible Algebraic Scientific Translator. Algebraic translator for scientific problems run by NCR 315 computer users.

FASTI Fast Access to Systems Technical Information.

FATAR Fast Analysis of Tape and Recovery.

FAUL Five Associated University Libraries. 757 Ostrom Ave, Syracuse, NY 13210. Members are Binghamton, Buffalo, Cornell, Rochester and Syracuse. A member of OCLC.

FAX Facsimile. The transmission of pictures, maps, diagrams or text by radio, wire or telephone lines. The image is scanned and duplicated on special paper at the receiving end.

FBI Federal Bureau of Investigation. 117 D St, NW, Washington, DC 20534. Maintains criminology library and extensive computer systems.

FBR Forskningsbiblioteksrådet (Swedish Council of Research Libraries). Box 6404, S113 82 Stockholm 6, Sweden. Established in 1965. Affiliated with IFLA. Official journal, *FBR Aktuellt*, is published quarterly.

FC Feature Count.

FC File Copy.

FC Font Change. A character in a string of machine-readable data that causes a change of font to be executed.

FC Functional Code.

FCBG Federation of Children's Book Groups. 31 Oakhill, Surbiton, Surrey, England. Established in 1968.

FCC Federal Communications Commission. 1919 M St, NW, Washington, DC 20554. Under the Communications Act of 1934, the FCC Board of Commissioners is empowered to regulate all interstate communication and foreign communication originating in the US. Regulates cable television operation.

FCS Facsimile Communications System.

FD Full Duplex. A communication system in which messages proceed in two directions at once, as opposed to HD (Half Duplex), in which messages travel in only one direction. Also called FDX.

FDA Food and Drug Administration. 5600 Fishers La, Rockville, MD 20852.

FDA Freier Deutscher Autoren-Verband. c/o S. K. Menters, Pacellistrasse 8/111, 8 Munich 2, Federal Republic of Germany. Society of authors.

FDFU Federation of Documentary Film Units. 21 Soho Sq, London W1, England.

FDLS Future Directions for a Learning Society. College Board, Box 2815, Princeton, NJ 08541. A project begun in fall 1977 with funding from the Exxon Foundation, to provide assistance for agencies and institutions involved in adult learning. Resulting publications are available from the board.

FDM Frequency Division Multiplex. A technique whereby the total bandwidth of a communications channel is divided into two or more smaller bands, each of which can be used for transmitting messages.

FDTF Federal Documents Task Force. *See* GODORT/FDTF.

FDX Full Duplex. *See* FD (Full Duplex).

FE Format Effector. Any of various characters in a string of machine-readable data that are designed to lay out or position information that is being transferred to a printing or display device.

FEAMIS Foreign Exchange Accounting and Management Information System.

FEAO Federation of European-American Organizations. 13 Hagedoornlaan, Antwerp, Belgium.

FEAT Frequency of Every Allowable Term. An inventory computer program.

FEB Fédération des Éditeurs Belges. Avenue du Parc 111, 1060 Brussels, Belgium. Established in 1921. Publishes documents.

FEBAB Federação Brasileira de Associações de Bibliotecários (Brazilian Federation of Librarian Associations). Rue Avanhandava 40, Conj. 110, São Paulo ZP3, Brazil. Established in 1959. Affiliated with IFLA. Publishes documents. *See* "Brazilian Federation of Associations of Librarians." *Journal of Library History* 7 (Oct. 1972): 313–315.

FEBAB/CBDJ Federação Brasileira de Associações de Bibliotecários–Comissão Brasileira de Documentação Jurídica (Brazilian Federation of Librarian Associations–Brazilian Committee of Legal Documentation). Rue Avanhandava 40, Conj. 110, São Paulo ZP3, Brazil. Established in 1971. Affiliated with IFLA. Publishes documents.

FEBS Federation of European Biological Societies. King's College, Strand, London WC2, England.

FEDLINET Federal Library and Information Network. *See* FEDLINK.

FEDLINK Federal Library and Information Network. c/o Federal Library Committee, Library of Congress, Washington, DC 20540. Primary functions are ILL, acquisitions and the production of card catalog and tape output for publication. Formerly FLECC. Also known as FEDLINET or FEDNET.

FEDNET Federal Library and Information Network. *See* FEDLINK.

FEDREG *Federal Register* File. Coverage from 1977. Nonbibliographic data base covering the *Federal Register*. Produced by CSI (Capitol Services, Inc.). Available on-line through SDC (System Development Corporation).

FEDSIM Federal Computer Performance Evaluation and Simulation Center. Contact US General Services Administration.

FEIEA Federation of European Industrial Editors Associations. c/o Unilever NV, Museumpark 1, Rotterdam, the Netherlands.

FEP Financial Evaluation Program. Program for the IBM 1620 computer.

FF Flip-Flop. Circuit or device, usually containing elements capable of assuming either one of two stable states. Often used to refer to circuits in a computer.

FF Form Feed. A character in a string of machine-readable data that determines the point at which a printing or display device moves to the next page or form.

FFSL Fédération Française des Syndicats de Libraires. 117 boulevard Saint Germain, 75006 Paris, France. Established in 1892.

FHKI Federation of Hong Kong Industries. 31-37 Des Voeux Road C, Hong Kong. Issues English-language standards. Affiliated with ISO (International Standards Organization).

FIAB Fédération Internationale des Associations de Bibliothécaires et des Bibliothèques). *See* IFLA (International Federation of Library Associations and Institutions).

FIABGRAL Federação Internacional de Associações de Bibliotecários–Grupo Regional América Latina. Rua Santo Antônio 733, Saõ Paulo, Brazil.

FIAF Fédération Internationale des Archives du Film (International Federation of Film Archives). FIAF Secretariat, 74 Galerie Ravenstein, 1000 Brussels, Belgium. Established in 1938. Affiliated with UNESCO through IFTC. Publishes documents.

FIAT Field Information Agencies, Technical. An acronym used by the British, French and German governments.

FIBP Federazione Italiana delle Biblioteche Popolari (Federation of Italian Public Libraries). c/o la "Società Umanitaria," Via Daverio 7, Milan 20122, Italy. Established in 1908. Affiliated with the International Federation of Work Associations. Publishes documents.

FIC Flight Information Center.

FICS Factory Information Control System.

FICS Forecasting for Inventory Control System.

FID Fédération Internationale de Documentation (International Federation for Documentation). 7 Hofweg, The Hague, the Netherlands.

Established in 1895. Consists of representatives of 36 countries and two special members. Sponsoring organization of promotion of UDC.

FIDAC Film Input to Digital Automatic Computer. National Biomedical Research Foundation Library, 5900 Reservoir Rd, Georgetown University, Washington, DC 20007.

FIDACSYS Fidac System. National Biomedical Research Foundation, Inc, 11200 Lockwood Dr, Silver Spring, MD 20901. Fidac is a scanning instrument to analyze chromosome karyograms with attention to pattern recognition.

FID/CLA Federación Internacional de Documentación/Comisión Latinoamericana (International Federation for Documentation/Latin American Commission). c/o Consejo Nacional de Ciencia y Technología (CONACYT), Insurgentes Sur 1677, 4 piso, Apartado Postal 20-033, México, DF, Mexico. Established in 1960.

FID/CNC FID Canadian National Committee. Contact FID.

FID/CR FID Committee on Classification Research. Contact FID.

FID/DC FID Committee on Developing Countries. Contact FID.

FID/DT FID Committee on the Terminology of Information and Documentation. Contact FID.

FID/ET FID Committee on Education and Training. Contact FID.

FIDIC Fédération Internationale des Industries du Cinéma de Film Étroit. 17 Via Vincenzo Vela, Turin, Italy.

FID/II FID Committee on Information and Industry. Contact FID.

FIDJC Fédération Internationale des Directeurs de Journaux Catholiques (International Federation of Directors of Catholic Publications). 22 Cours Albert 1, Paris 8, France.

FID/LD FID Committee on Linguistics in Documentation. Contact FID.

FID/MSR FID Working Committee on Mechanical Storage and Retrieval. Contact FID.

FID/OM FID Committee on Operational Machine Technique and Systems. Contact FID.

FID/RI FID Committee on Research on the Theoretical Basis of Information. Contact FID.

FID/TM FID Committee on Theory of Machine Techniques and Systems. Contact FID.

FID/TMO FID Committee on Theory, Methods, and Operations of Information Systems and Networks. Contact FID.

FIEG Federazione Italiana Editori Giornali. Via Piemonte 64, 00187 Rome, Italy. Established in 1945. Member of the International Federation of Newspaper Publishers and the International Federation of the Periodical Press.

FIFO First-In-First-Out. An accounting and data base system term.

FIGs Figures Shift. A physical movement in a teletype printer that allows numbers, symbols and uppercase characters to be printed.

FIJ Fédération Internationale des Journalistes (International Federation of Journalists). 14 rue Dequesnoy, Brussels 1, Belgium. Also known as IFJ.

FIJL Fédération Internationale des Journalistes Libres de l'Europe Central et des Pays Baltes et Balkaniques. *See* IFFJ (International Federation of Free Journalists of Central and Eastern Europe and Baltic and Balkan Countries).

FILA Federation of Indian Library Associations. Misri Bazar, Patiala, Punjab, India. Established in 1966. *See* V. Venkatappaiah. "Festschrift to Professor Kaula." *Herald of Library Science* 13 (Jan. 1974): 44–57.

FINAC Fast Interline Nonactive Automatic Control. A leased automatic teletypewriter service provided by AT&T.

FIND/SVP 500 Fifth Ave, New York, NY 10036. Incorporated in 1970. An information brokering firm. A division of Information Clearinghouse, Inc. Member of IIA (Information Industry Association).

FIP Fédération Internationale des Phonothèques (International Federation of Record Libraries). Contact president. Established in 1963. Publishes documents.

FIPP Fédération Internationale de la Presse Periodique (International Federation of the Periodical Press). 45 rue de Lisbonne, Paris 8, France.

FIPRESCI Fédération Internationale de la Presse Cinématographique (International Federation of the Cinematographic Press). 6 Via Somaini, Lugano, Switzerland.

FIPS Federal Information Processing Standards. National Bureau of Standards, Office of Technical Information and Publications, Washington, DC 20234.

FIPSCAC Federal Information Processing Standards Coordinating and Advisory Committee. Contact FIPS.

FIPSE Fund for the Improvement of Post Secondary Education. 400 Maryland Ave, SW, Rm. 3123, Washington, DC 20202. A federal grant-making organization which can "help educators and librarians get information about funding and other resources." Connected to the Post Secondary Convening Authority of DHEW.

FIT Fédération Internationale des Traducteurs. 5 Square Thiers, 75116 Paris, France. An international association of translators.

FIU Federation of Information Users. 135 North Bellefield Ave, Seventh Fl, Pittsburgh, PA 15260. Established in 1973. Supports unencumbered access to information. Publishes a newsletter.

FJCC Fall Joint Computer Conference. Sponsored by AFIPS from 1962 through 1972. Spring and fall conferences replaced by annual conferences only from 1973.

FJF Finlands Journalistförbund. *See* SSL/FJF.

FLA Federal Librarians Association. 1629 K St, NW, Suite 520, Washington, DC 20006. Established in 1972. Publishes *FLA Newsletter*, irregularly. *See* F. K. Cylke. "Federal Libraries" in *Encyclopedia of Library and*

Information Science, ed. by A. Kent et al. New York: Marcel Dekker, 1972, V. 8, pp. 371-387.

FLA Fiji Library Association. Contact secretary. Established in Nov. 1972. Affiliated with ALA (American Library Association), IFLA and NZLA (New Zealand Library Association). *See* E. T. Coman. "Fiji, Libraries in" in *Encyclopedia of Library and Information Science*, ed. by A. Kent et al. New York: Marcel Dekker, 1971, V. 8, pp. 397-404.

FLA Film Laboratory Association, Ltd. Queen's House, Leicester Pl, London WC2, England.

FLA Florida Library Association. Contact president or ALA (American Library Association).

FLA Foothills Library Association. Contact president. An association of libraries in the Calgary area, Alberta, Canada.

FLANG Flowchart Language. A programming language.

FLAP Program for symbolic mathematics developed by the US Navy Weapons Laboratory.

FLECC Federal Libraries Experiment in Cooperative Cataloging. Name changed to FEDLINK.

FLIC Film Library Information Council. Box 348, Radio City Sta, New York, NY 10019. Established in 1967. A nonprofit educational association. Publishes a journal.

FLIC Film Library Intercollege Cooperative of Pennsylvania. c/o Bucks County Community College, Swamp Rd, Newtown, PA 18940. Eight community colleges purchase and share films and videotapes.

FLIN Florida Library Information Network. c/o Loans Section, State Library of Florida, Tallahassee, FL 32201. Fourteen public and university libraries receive and fulfill title and photocopy requests from 450 libraries.

FLINT Floating Interpretative Language. A programming language.

FLIP Floating Indexed Point Arithmetic. Routine developed by Argonne National Laboratory.

FLIP Floating Point Interpretive Program. Routine for the Bendix G-15 computer.

FLIP Free-form Language for Image Processing. A programming language.

FLIRT Federal Librarians Round Table. Contact ALA (American Library Association). Established in 1972.

FLOP Floating Octal Point. Subroutine for the IBM 701 computer.

FLPL FORTRAN List Processing Language. Developed for use in a program for proving theorems in geometry. FLPL is much like LISP, but has no provision for recursion.

FLSAA Faculty of Library Science Alumni Association. Alumni House, 47 Willcocks St, Toronto ON M5S 1A1, Canada. Established in 1929. Alumni of the University of Toronto.

FLUIDEX Fluid Engineering. Contact BHRA. Data base covering fluid engineering technology and hydraulics.

FMI Food Marketing Institute, 1750 K St, NW, Suite 700, Washington, DC 20006. Established in 1977. Formed by the merger of the National Association of Food Chains and SMI (Super Market Institute). Publishes several periodicals on the supermarket industry.

FNBC Fédération Nationale des Bibliothèques Catholiques. 21 rue du Marais, B-1000 Brussels, Belgium. Established in 1960.

FNDF Fédération Nationale des Distributeurs de Films. 43 boulevard Malesherbes, 75008 Paris, France. Established in 1945.

FNL Friends of the National Libraries. c/o British Museum, Great Russell St, London WC1, England.

FNSI Federazione Nazionale della Stampa Italiana. Corso Vittorio Emanuele 349, 00186 Rome, Italy. Established in 1878. Association of journalists.

FOBID Federatie van Organisaties op het Gebied van Bibliotheek, Informatie en Dokumentatiewezen (Federation of Organizations in Library, Information and Documentation Science). Based in the Netherlands. Official journal, *Open*, is published 11 times per year.

FOCUS An automated accounting system that provides reports and controls for credit union management. Developed by IBM.

FORAST Formula Assembler and Translator. A programming language.

FORC Formula Coder. Automatic coding and programming language for the IBM 704 computer.

FORE Foundation of Record Education. American Medical Record Association, FORE Library, 875 North Chicago Ave, Suite 1850, Chicago, IL 60611. Maintains a library.

FORMAC Formula Manipulation Compiler. Developed by IBM.

FORTOCOM FORTRAN I Compiler.

FORTRAN Formula Translator. A formula translating language developed by IBM. Designed to instruct computers to solve algebraic problems by permitting mathematical language to be converted automatically to machine language.

FORTRAN II Formula Translator II. Added to the power of the original FORTRAN by giving it the ability to define and use almost unlimited hierarchies of subroutines, all capable of sharing a common storage region.

FORTRAN IV Formula Translator IV. A USASI programming language. Added the ability to use Boolean expressions and insert symbolic machine language sequences to the original FORTRAN.

FORTSIM FORTRAN Simulation.

FOSDIC Film Optical Sensing Device for Input to Computers. Developed in 1954 by NBS for the US Bureau of the Census. Senses the position of marks made on census forms. Subsequent FOSDICs accept microfilm as input.

FOSE Federal Office Systems Expo. Sponsor: National Trade Productions, Inc, Lanham, MD. Expositions incorporate all aspects of information handling. Formerly known as Federal Office Equipment Expo.

FPA Film Production Association of Great Britain. 25 Green St, London W1Y 3FD, England.

FPA Foreign Press Association. 11 Carlton House Terr, London SW1, England.

FPG Film Producers Guild, Ltd. Guild House, Upper Saint Martin's La, London WC2, England.

FRC Family Reading Center. A newsstand-type installation offering a mix of books, magazines and related items in food and drug stores.

FRF Freedom to Read Foundation. *See* FTRF.

FRI Fuel Research Institute. Bihar, India. Maintains a library.

FRINGE Film and Report Information Processing Generator. A computer program generator.

FROLIC File Room Online Information Control. An automated file retrieval system based on color coding and machine readability. Introduced in the US in 1979 after successful application in Canada.

FS File Separator. A control character designed to establish a logical boundary between files.

FSFA Federation of Specialised Film Associations. 2 Bourchier St, London W1, England.

FSFF Finlands Svenska Författareföreningen (Society of Swedish Authors in Finland). Runebergsgatan 32 C 27, 00100 Helsingfors 10, Finland. Established in 1919. Publishes documents.

FSK Frequency-Shift Keying. Form of frequency modulation in which the information function is a digital signal.

FSL Formal Semantics Language. Computer program.

FSTA *Food Science and Technology Abstracts.* V. 1, 1969. Published by the International Food Information Service, Bucks, England.

FTC Federal Trade Commission. Pennsylvania Ave. & Sixth St, NW, Washington, DC 20580. Oversees trade practices to prevent monopoly, deceptive practices or unfair restraints.

FTE Full-Time Equivalent. Used to calculate staff time when part-time personnel are used.

FTRF Freedom to Read Foundation. Contact ALA (American Library

Association). Established in 1969. Defends and supports librarians challenging violations of intellectual freedom. Also known as FRF.

FTS Federal Telecommunications System. Telephone system used by federal installations.

FUSE Federation for Unified Science Education. 1460 West Lane Ave, Columbus, OH 43321.

FY Fiscal Year. May differ from calendar year.

GAASP Getting and Abetting Small Press. Project begun in 1978. Purpose is to introduce publications of small presses to college libraries. Sponsor: ALA (American Library Association).

GAC Government Advisory Committee on International Book and Library Programs. Secretariat, Office of US Advisory Commission on International Education and Cultural Affairs, Dept. of State, Washington, DC 20520. Established in 1962. Reviews policies and operations of government overseas library programs.

GAF General Aniline and Film Corporation. 140 West 51 St, New York, NY 10020.

GAJ Guild of Agricultural Journalists. 2 Howard St, London WC2, England.

GAM Globe and Mail. QL Systems Limited, 220-90 Sparks St, Ottawa ON K2G 0B8, Canada. Coverage from 1977. Full text data base of the newspaper *Globe and Mail* from Nov. 14, 1977.

GAMM Gesellschaft für Angewandte Mathematik und Mechanik (German Association for Applied Mathematics and Mechanics). *See* ACM/GAMM.

GAO General Accounting Office. 441 G St, NW, Washington, DC 20001. Established in 1949. Maintains a library and publishes documents.

GAP General Assembly Program. Allows the programmer to write his or her own program in symbolic code rather than in the absolute code of the computer.

GARP Global Atmospheric Research Program. GARP Joint Planning Staff, Case Postale, Numéro 1, 1211 Geneva 20, Switzerland. An international research effort to increase

understanding of the physical processes of the atmosphere.

GASP General Activity Simulation Program. A class of FORTRAN-based languages.

GAT Generalized Algebraic Translator.

GBC Ground-Based Computer.

GBDL Gesellschaft für Bibliothekswesen und Dokumentation des Landbaues (Association for Librarianship and Documentation in Agriculture). Contact executive secretary (Federal Republic of Germany). Established in 1958. Affiliated with IAALD (International Association of Agricultural Librarians and Documentalists). Publishes documents.

GBIL Gosudarstvennaya Biblioteka SSSR Imeni V. I. Lenina. *See* GBL.

GBL Gosudarstvennaya ordena Lenina Biblioteka SSSR Imeni V. I. Lenina (Lenin State Library of the USSR). Prospect Kalinina 3, Moscow 101000, USSR. Also known as GBIL.

GBNE Guild of British Newspapers Editors. Whitefriars' House, 6 Carmelite St, London EC4, England.

GCHQ Government Communications Headquarters (Great Britain). Oakley, Priors Rd, Cheltenham, Gloucestershire, England.

GCL General Control Language. Computer programming language.

GCLC Greater Cincinnati Library Consortium. c/o University of Cincinnati, Central Library, Cincinnati, OH 45221. Twenty-six academic, public and special libraries cooperate through ILL, delivery, film acquisition and staff development.

GDB Gesellschaft für Dokumentation und Bibliographie. Österreichische National Bibliothek, Josefsplatz 1, A1014 Vienna, Austria.

GDBMS Generalized Data Base Management Systems.

GDG Generation Data Group. A group, family or unit of similar data sets which are related to each other because each is a modification of the next most recent data set. Therefore they all have the same name and are distinguished from each other by their generation numbers and their successive dates of development.

GDMB Gesellschaft Deutscher Metallhuttens und Bergleute (Association of German Metallurgical and Mining Engineers). 10 Paul-Ernst Strasse, D 3392 Claisthal-Zellerfield, Federal Republic of Germany. Established in 1912.

GE General Electric Company. 3135 Eastern Tpke, Fairfield, CT 06431. Manufactures electrical equipment, including computer terminals.

GEA Gravure Engravers Association. Merged with APA (American Photoengravers Association) to form APA (American Photoplatemakers Association) in 1969.

GECAP General Electric Computer Analysis Program.

GECOM General Compiler.

GECOS General Comprehensive Operating Supervisor. Software package developed by GE.

GEMAP General Electric Macro Assembly Program.

GEMS General Electric Manufacturing Simulator.

GENDA General Data Analysis and Simulation.

GENISYS Generalized Information System. A master computer program which allows for the variations between different computers. Used in structural engineering.

GEOREF World Geographic Reference System. American Geological Institute, Geo-Ref Retrospective Search Service, 5205 Leesburg Pike, Falls Church, VA 22041.

GERTS General Electric Remote Terminal System.

GESCAN General Electric Scanner. *See* RSM.

GID Gesellschaft für Information und Dokumentation. Herriostrasse 5, Postfach 71 03 70, Frankfurt 71, Federal Republic of Germany. Established in 1975. Member of EUSIDIC.

GIDEP Government-Industry Data Exchange Program. c/o Technical Information Dept, Lockheed-Georgia Co, 86 South Cobb Dr, Marietta, GA 30063. Members include the Engineering Data Bank, the Failure Rate Data Bank and the Metrology Data Bank.

GIFI General Information File Interrogation.

GIGO Garbage In/Garbage Out. Refers to nonsensical data in a computer, implying invalid input.

GIM Generalized Information Management System.

GINA Graphical Input for Network Analysis.

GIPRONTII Vsesojuznyj Gosudarstvennyj Institut po Proektirovaniju Naučno-Issledovatel'skich Institutov i Laboratorij Akademii nauk SSSR. Maronovskij per 26, Moscow V-49, USSR. A government agency for the planning of scientific research institutes and laboratories of the USSR Academy of Science. Library established in 1935.

GIPSY Generalized Information Processing System. The system used in the selection and retrieval of records and documents or of selected entries from them. Patented on October 19, 1971, it is used by NODC and Water Resources Scientific Information Center. *See* D. W. Moody and Alaf Kays. "Development of the US Geological Survey Bibliographic System Using GIPSY." *JASIS* 23 (Jan.-Feb. 1972): 39-49.

GIRL Generalized Information Retrieval Language.

GIRLS Generalized Information Retrieval and Listing System.

GIS Generalized Information System. An IBM executive system with data base/data communications capability.

GIS Geoscience Information Society. c/o American Geological Institute, 2201 M St, NW, Washington, DC 20037.

GLA Georgia Library Association. Contact president or ALA (American Library Association).

GLA Greek Library Association. *See* EEB.

GLA Guam Library Association. Contact president or ALA (American Library Association).

GLA Guyana Library Association. 76/77 Main St, Box 110, Georgetown, Guyana. Established in 1968. Affiliated with IFLA. Publishes documents. *See* T. Kabdebo. "Guyana, Libraries in" in *Encyclopedia of Library and Information Science*, ed. by A. Kent et al. New York: Marcel Dekker, 1973, V. 10, pp. 246–249.

GLASS Greater London Audio Specialization Scheme.

GLEIS Great Lakes Environmental Information Sharing. Formerly IPAHGEIS. Present name adopted in 1978.

GLIN Georgia Library Information Network. c/o Division of Public Library Services, Georgia State Dept. of Education, 156 Trinity Ave, SW, Atlanta, GA 30303. An agency of the Georgia State Department of Education's Public Library Service. Coordinates with SERMLP. One hundred thirty-eight academic, hospital, county, regional, seminary and special libraries cooperate through ILL and bibliographic assistance services.

GLOTRAC Global Tracking.

GLS Graduate Library School. University of Chicago, 1100 East 57 St, Chicago, IL 60637.

GM General Motors Corporation.

GM Group Mark. Character that indicates beginning or end of a set of data.

GMP *Guide to Microforms in Print*. Weston, CT: Microform Review, 1961– . An annual publication.

GOCI General Operator Computer Interaction.

GODORT Government Documents Round Table. c/o ALA, 50 East Huron St, Chicago, IL 60611. An ALA (American Library Association) round table established in 1972. *See American Libraries* 3 (Mar. 1972): 251.

GODORT/FDTF GODORT Federal Documents Task Force. Contact GODORT.

GODORT/IDTF GODORT International Documents Task Force. Contact GODORT.

GODORT/LDTF GODORT Local Documents Task Force. Contact GODORT.

GODORT/SDTF GODORT State Documents Task Force. Contact GODORT.

GP General Processing. May include computing, assembling, compiling, interpreting, generating, storing, retrieving, extracting or any other related steps.

GP General Purpose. *See* GPC (General Purpose Computer).

GP Generalized Programming. Programming expressed in computer code designed to solve problems when appropriate parametric values are supplied.

GPC General Purpose Computer. A computer intended to solve a broad class of problems. Used when the exact nature of the problems to be solved are not known in advance and the programs can be changed rapidly.

GPC Gulf Publishing Company. Box 2608, Houston, TX 77001. Publisher of *EBI*.

GPL General Purpose Programming Language. *See* GPL (Generalized Programming Language).

GPL Generalized Programming Language. Used in business and science. Examples include ALGOL, COBOL and FORTRAN.

GPL Graphic Programming Language. A programming language for pictorial representation.

GPNITL Great Plains National Instructional Television Library. University of Nebraska, Lincoln, NE 68508.

GPO Government Printing Office. Washington, DC 20402. The US government office which provides printing and binding services for Congress and other federal departments and agencies. Supervised by JCP.

GPS General Problem Solver. Programming procedure used on the IBM 704 computer. Developed by Rand Corp.

GPSDIC General Purpose Scientific Document Image Code. Developed by NBS's Office of Standard Reference Data.

GPSDW General Purpose Scientific Document Writer. Capable of producing documents at the same level of symbolic complexity as found in manuscripts produced by scientific typists. Includes a line printer and a typewriter, X-Y plotter, cathode ray display or other suitable equipment. *See also* GPSDIC.

GPSS General Purpose Simulation Program. An IBM discrete system simulation language.

GPSS General Purpose Systems Simulator. Programming language used for simulation.

GPSS Generic Problem Statement Simulator. Class of computer languages based on the use of block diagrams to express problem statements.

GPX Generalized Programming Extended.

GRA *Government Reports Announcements*. V. 71, 1971. Formerly *USGRDR*. Name changed to *GRA&I* in 1975.

GRA&I *Government Reports Announcements and Index*. V. 75, 1975. Published by NTIS. Available on-line, on magnetic tape, on microfiche, and in print form. Issued under various titles since original publication in 1938.

GRACE Graphic Arts Composing Equipment. One of the earliest photocomposing machines was the Photon. GRACE, also known as ZIP, was a Photon 900 developed for NLM to produce *IM* (*Index Medicus*). Capable of 250 characters per second. Now on display at the Smithsonian Institution.

GRAI *Government Reports Annual Index*. V. 74, 1974. Formerly *GRI*. Incorporated into *GRA&I* in 1975.

GRAIL Graphic Input Language. A programming language.

GRASP General Risk Analysis Simulation Program. Data processing program.

GRASP Graduate Regional Accelerated Study Program. Texas Women's University, Denton, TX 76204. Started in 1978. School of Library Science is involved.

GRE Graduate Record Examination. Administered by ETS (Educational Testing Service). Used for admission to graduate schools of library, computer and information science.

GREMAS Genealogische Recherche mit Magnetband-Speicherung. Badishe Anilin- und Soda-Fabrik, A.G., 67 Ludwigshafen am Rhein, Federal Republic of Germany. A code for searching, based on matrices, used for input of chemical structural formulae and reactions.

GRI *Government Reports Index*. V. 71, 1971–V. 73, 1973. Formerly *USGRDRI*. Continued by *GRAI* and now incorporated in *GRA&I*.

GRIPHOS General Retrieval and Information Processor for Humanities-Oriented Studies. New York University computerized bibliographic services for all humanistic disciplines.

GRS German Research Society. Has a library committee, one of whose goals is the development of an effective cooperative acquisitions program in Germany. *See Überregionale Literaturversorgung von Wissenschaft und Forschung in der Bundesrepublik Deutschland: Denkschrift*. Bibliotheksausschuss der Deutschen Forschungsgemeinschaft. Boppard: Harold Boldt Verlag KG, 1975.

GS Group Separator. Character designed to indicate boundaries between different groups of characters.

GSA General Services Administration. GSA Library, General Services Bldg, Rm. 1033, 18 St & F St, NW, Washington, DC 20405. Maintains an engineering and data processing library established in 1961.

GSA Geological Society of America. 3300 Penrose Pl, Boulder, CO 80301. Established in 1888. Publishes *GSA Bulletin* and is involved with the *Bibliography and Index of Geology*.

GSLIS Graduate School of Library and Information Science. Designation commonly used by universities.

GTE General Telephone and Electronics Corporation. 77 A St, Needham

Heights, MA 02194. Maintains a computer and data processing library established in 1952. Involved in communications equipment.

GTIS Gloucestershire Technical Information Service. 205 Gloucester Rd, Cheltenham, Gloucestershire, England.

GULP General Utility Library Programs.

GWL Geowissenschaftliche Literaturinformation. Bundesanstalt für Geowissenschaften und Rohstoffe, Documentation Center, Stilleweg 2, D-3000 Hanover 51, Federal Republic of Germany. Coverage from 1970. Bibliographic data base covering geographical literature.

HADIS Huddersfield and District Information Service. Huddersfield Public Library, Ramsden St, Huddersfield, Yorkshire H91 25U, England. A regional organization.

HAIC Hetero-Atom-in-Context. Indexing system used for heterocyclic chemical compounds in *CA* (*Chemical Abstracts*).

HALDIS Halifax and District Information Service. College Library, Percival Whitley College of Further Education, Francis St, Halifax, Yorkshire, England. A regional organization.

HAPI *Hispanic American Periodicals Index.* Barbara G. Cox, ed. Los Angeles: UCLA Latin American Center, 1975. An annual index of 250 scholarly journals.

HARLIC Houston Area Research Libraries Consortium. Southwest Center for Urban Research, Houston, TX 77001. Consortium established in 1979. Seven university, public and medical libraries cooperate in collection, staff, systems and automation development, resource sharing, preservation and technical services.

HASL Hertfordshire Association of Special Libraries. A regional organization of special libraries in England.

HATRICS Hampshire Technical Research Industrial and Commercial Service. Central Library, Civic Centre, Southampton S09 4XP, England. A regional information service established in 1964 to provide a directory of resources.

HAYSTAQ Have You Stored Answers to Questions? Term used by NBS in reference to a computer program step.

HBD Hrvatsko Bibliotekarsko Društvo (Croatian Library Association). Marculícev trg 21, 41000 Zagreb, Yugoslavia. Established in 1948. Affiliated with IFLA and the Union of Librarians' Associations of Yugoslavia. Publishes documents.

HBR *Harvard Business Review.* V. 1, 1922. Published by the Graduate School of Business Administration, Harvard University.

HC Hard Copy. Refers to a paper copy as opposed to a microform copy.

HCTLDC Hungarian Central Technical Library and Documentation Center. Box 12, Reviczky u. 6, H-1428 Budapest, Hungary. Library started in 1883. Supported by the Hungarian Office of Technical Development. Coordinates science and technology information and is the largest technical library open to the public in the country.

HCUA Honeywell Computer Users Association. Contact Honeywell.

HD Half Duplex. A communication system in which messages travel in only one direction at one time, as opposed to FD or FDX (Full Duplex), in which messages proceed in two directions at once. Also called HDX.

HD High Density. Intense storage on drum, tape or disk.

HDF Hauptverband Deutscher Filmtheater. Langenbeckstrasse 9, 62 Wiesbaden, Federal Republic of Germany. Established in 1950. Association of film exhibitors. Publishes documents.

HDI United States Historical Documents Institute. 1911 Fort Myer Dr, Arlington, VA 22209. A publishing company.

HDL Hardware Description Language. Computer programming language.

HDX Half Duplex. *See* HD (Half Duplex).

HEA Higher Education Act of 1965. A US law that made provisions for NPAC and funds many library projects.

HECC Higher Education Coordinating Council of Metropolitan Saint Louis. Contact chairperson. Established in

1969. Librarians' Steering Committee is involved in producing union catalogs.

HECUS Higher Education Center for Urban Studies. 328 Park Ave, Bridgeport, CT 06604. Ten academic libraries cooperate through ILL, acquisitions, collections and periodical index.

HEEP *Health Effects of Environmental Pollutants*. V. 1, 1972. An abstract journal published by BioSciences Information Service with support from NLM.

HEEP Highway Engineering Exchange Program. An exchange plan for civil engineering computer programs used in the design and construction of highways. All programs are designed to run on the IBM 650 computer.

HEGIS Higher Education General Information Survey. A statistical survey of college and university libraries conducted by USOE.

HEIAC Hydraulic Engineering Information Analysis Center. Army Engineers Waterways Experimental Station, Box 631, Vicksburg, MS 39180.

HEIAS Human Engineering Information and Analysis Service. Tufts University, Medford, MA 02155.

HELP Heckman's Electronic Library Program. The Heckman Bindery, Inc, North Manchester, IN 46962. A computerized record of library clients' binding policies.

HELPIS *Higher Education Learning Programmes Information Service: A Catalogue of Materials Available for Exchange*. London: National Council for Educational Technology, 1971.

HEPI *High Energy Physics Index (Hochenergiephysik-Index)*. V. 1, 1962. Published by Zentralstelle für Atomkernenergie-Dokumentation, Kernforschungszentrum, 7514 Eggenstein-Leopoldshafen, Federal Republic of Germany.

HERB Huxley Environmental Reference Bureau. Huxley College of Environmental Studies, ESC 70, Huxley College, Bellingham, WA 98225. Information center and library established in 1970.

HERMAN Hierarchical Environmental Retrieval for Management Access and Networking. Biological Information Service, 8505 Brunswick Ave, Riverside, CA 92504. Coverage from 1934. Bibliographic data base covering fish, wildlife and marine mammals.

HERMES Heuristic Mechanized Document Information System. A system used in Rumania.

HERO Historical Evaluation and Research Organization. 1403 Dolley Madison Blvd, McLean, VA 22101. Established in 1962. Program includes library and information system research.

HERTIS Hertfordshire County Council Technical Library and Information Service. Hatfield College of Technology, Hatfield, England.

HeSCA Health Sciences Communications Association. Box 79, Millbrae, CA 94030. Established in 1959 as the Council on Medical Television. Became HeSCA in 1971. A nonprofit international organization for application of instructional technology to health education. Has a library section.

HEW Department of Health, Education and Welfare. *See* DHEW.

HGAC Houston–Galveston Area Council. 3311 Richmond Ave, Houston, TX 77006. Produces data bases on the demography, economics and development of the region.

HIAS Human Intellect Augmentation System.

HICLASS Hierarchical Classification. A classification scheme that uses a specified ranking of items.

HICSS Hawaii International Conference on System Sciences. Jan. 1973, sixth conference, Honolulu, HI.

HIE Hibernation Information Exchange. c/o Office of Naval Research, 219 South Dearborn St, Chicago, IL 60604.

HILC Hampshire Interlibrary Center. Hampshire College, Amherst, MA 01002. Jointly owned library of research materials, supplementing the resources of individual participating libraries.

HILOW Health and Information Libraries of Westchester. Pforzheimer Bldg, Purchase, NY 10577.

HINOP Health Information Network of the Pacific. 1221 Punchbowl St, Honolulu, HI 96813. This network has been terminated.

HIRA Health Instructional Resources Association. Shiffman Medical Library, 4325 Brush St, Detroit, MI 48201.

HIS Holt Information Systems. 383 Madison Ave, New York, NY 10017. The reference publishing division of Holt, Rinehart and Winston.

HISAM Hierarchical Indexed Sequential Access Method. Type of organization of data bases. For disk storage only.

HISARS Hydrological Information Storage and Retrieval System. Biological and Agricultural Engineering, North Carolina State University, Box 5906, Raleigh, NC 27607. Nonbibliographic data base covering daily and hourly weather data from 1850.

HISP Health Information Sharing Project. School of Information Studies, Syracuse University, Syracuse, NY 13210. Funded by NLM for 1978–1979 to examine and test ways of improving health information flow.

HISTLINE History of Medicine Online. Project begun on October 1, 1978, as part of NLM's on-line network.

HLA Halifax Library Association. Contact president. A Canadian association.

HLA Hawaii Library Association. Contact president or ALA (American Library Association). Newsletter published from Box 3941, Honolulu, HI 96812.

HLL High Level Language. Type of computer programming language.

HMC Historical Manuscripts Commission. *See* HMC (Royal Commission on Historical Manuscripts).

HMC Royal Commission on Historical Manuscripts. Quality House, Quality Court, Chancery La, London WC2, England. Commission established in 1869. Reconstituted in 1959 to locate manuscripts in Great Britain and Ireland and to assist those wishing to use such for study or research. Reports are published by HMSO. Also known as HMC (Historical Manuscripts Commission).

HMSO Her/His Majesty's Stationery Office. Box 569, London SE1, England. In USA: Pendragon House, Inc, 899 Broadway, Redwood City, CA 94063. The government publishing office of the UK.

HMSS Hospital Management Systems Society. 840 North Lake Shore Dr, Chicago, IL 60611. Established in 1961. Members are professionally qualified to engage in the analysis and design of hospital management systems. Publishes books and a newsletter.

HOLSA Health Oriented Libraries of San Antonio. c/o Santa Rosa Medical Center Health Sciences Library, 519 West Houston St, San Antonio, TX 78285. An informal network.

HOQ Hansard Oral Questions. QL Systems Limited, 220-90 Sparks St, Ottawa ON K2G-0B8, Canada. Coverage from 1973. Full text data base of oral questions and responses in the House of Commons. Updated biweekly. *See also* HQO.

HPB Hand Printed Books Project. School of Library and Information Science, University of Western Ontario, London ON N6A 5B9, Canada.

HPCI Himpunan Pustakawan Chusus Indonesia (Indonesian Association of Special Librarians). Established in 1969. Merged with APADI to form IPI (Ikatan Postakawan Indonesia) in 1973.

HQE Hansard Questions Écrites. QL Systems Limited, 220-90 Sparks St, Ottawa ON K2G 0B8, Canada. French-language equivalent of HWQ.

HQO Hansard Questions Orale. QL Systems Limited, 220-90 Sparks St, Ottawa ON K2G 0B8, Canada. French-language equivalent of HOQ.

HRA Health Resources Administration. 3700 East-West Hwy, Hyattsville, MD 20782. An agency of USPHS.

HRAF Human Relations Area Files. Yale University, Box 2054, Yale Sta, New Haven, CT 06520. Sponsored and controlled by 24 major universities and research institutes in US and abroad. Provides publications, microforms and data bases.

HRIS Highway Research Information Service. Transportation Research

Board, 2101 Constitution Ave, NW, Washington, DC 20418. Library and information service established in 1967. Provides bibliographies, copies of technical literature and resumes of ongoing research projects.

HRLSD Health and Rehabilitative Library Services Division. Formerly AHIL (Association of Hospital and Institution Libraries). Merged into ASCLA in 1978.

HRLSD/LSBPHS HRLSD Library Services to the Blind and Physically Handicapped Section. *See* ASCLA/LSBPHS.

HRLSD/LSPS HRLSD Library Service to Prisoners Section. *See* ASCLA/LSPS.

HRMR Human Readable/Machine Readable.

HRN Human Resources Network. 2010 Chancellor St, Philadelphia, PA 19103. A research and consulting firm that serves as a clearinghouse of information on corporate social responsibility. Maintains a library and issues publications.

HS Hierarchically Structural. Index language arrangement in which a specified rank or ordering of terms is employed.

HS History Section. *See* RASD/HS.

HSA Health Services Administration. An agency of USPHS. Administers federal programs and conducts and funds studies related to the delivery of health services.

HSAM Hierarchical Sequential Access Method. A type of organization of data bases.

HSDA High-Speed Data Acquisition. A monitoring and controlling facility that is used to acquire, evaluate and record data developed during the testing of a system.

HSLS High School Libraries Section. *See* CLA/HSLS.

HSM High-Speed Memory. Capable of producing information at relatively higher speeds. Also an indication of the lower average access time.

HSP High-Speed Printer. A printer that can operate sufficiently fast to be compatible with on-line printing.

HSR High-Speed Reader. A reader capable of obtaining data from a record, medium, document, storage or other form rapidly. HIgh-speed card readers read at least 1,000 cards per minute; high-speed punched paper tape readers read at least 500 characters per second.

HSRT Health Sciences Roundtable. *See* CLA/HSRT.

HT Horizontal Tabulation. Refers to a control character in a string of machine-readable data that causes a printing or display unit to skip forward to the next of a set of predetermined positions on the same line.

HTFS Heat Transfer and Fluid Flow Service. Atomic Energy Research Establishment, Hartwell, England. An information center within the research establishment.

HUD Department of Housing and Urban Development. *See* DHUD.

HULTIS Humberside Libraries Technical Interloan Scheme. Library of Science, Technology and Commerce, Hull Central Library, Albion St, Hull, Yorkshire, England. A consortium of industrial, academic and other specialized libraries. Formerly (1974) Hull Technical Interloan Scheme.

HUMRRO Human Resources Research Organization. Van Evera Library, 300 North Washington St, Alexandria, VA 22314. Maintains a library established in 1951, and publishes documents. Produced report for NLM's Extramural Program.

HURI Harvard Ukrainian Research Institute. 1581-83 Massachusetts Ave, Cambridge, MA 02138. Maintains a reference library established in 1973.

HWQ Hansard Written Questions. QL Systems Limited, 220-90 Sparks St, Ottawa ON K2G 0B8, Canada. Coverage from 1973. Full text data base of written questions and responses in the House of Commons. Updated biweekly. *See also* HQE.

HYK Helsingin Yliopiston Kirjasto (Helsinki University Library). Unioninkatu 36, Helsinki 17, Finland.

IAA *International Aerospace Abstracts.* V. 1, 1961. Published by the Institute of the

Aerospace Sciences. Supersedes International Aeronautical Abstracts Section, included in *Aerospace Engineering*, 1956–1960.

IAALD International Association of Agricultural Librarians and Documentalists. 59 Row Town, Addlestone, Weybridge, Surrey KTI5 1HJ, England. Established in 1955. Affiliated with IFLA and FID. *See* G. Lilley. "The Fifth Congress of the IAALD." *UNESCO Bulletin for Libraries* 29 (1975): 336–340.

IAARC International Administrative Aeronautical Radio Conference. *See* WARC.

IAB International Council of Scientific Unions–Abstracting Board. *See* ICSU-AB.

IABLA Inter-American Bibliographical and Library Association. Box 583, North Miami Beach, FL 33160. Established in 1930. Publishes documents. Also known as IBLA.

IAC Information Analysis Center. A term with the same meaning as "data center" and "data evaluation center." *See* David Garvin. "Information Analysis Center and the Library." *Special Libraries* 62 (Jan. 1971): 17–23.

IACB International Advisory Committee on Bibliography. Name changed to IACBDT.

IACBDT International Advisory Committee on Bibliography, Documentation and Terminology. A committee of UNESCO. Formerly IACB. Publishes *Bibliographical Services Throughout the World*.

IACDT International Advisory Committee for Documentation and Terminology. Contact UNESCO. A committee of UNESCO.

IACP International Association of Chiefs of Police. 11 Firstfield Rd, Gaithersburg, MD 20760. Developed a reporting service and dissemination program about bomb incidents that resulted in a monthly publication, *Bomb Incident Bulletin*. Maintains the Center for Law Enforcement Research.

IAD Initiation Area Discriminator. Picks up data for processing by computer. A CRT combined with a photoelectric cell to identify unmapped or uncorrelated long-range radar data.

IAD International Association of Documentalists and Information Officers. *See* AID (Association Internationale des Documentalistes et Techniciens de l'Information).

IADA Internationale Arbeitsgemeinschaft der Archiv-, Bibliotheks- und Grafikrestauratoren (International Working Group of Restorers of Archives, Libraries and Graphic Reproductions). Friedrichsplatz 15, Postfach 540, D-3550 Marburg, Federal Republic of Germany. Established in 1957. Affiliated with IFLA. Publishes documents.

IADC Inter-American Defense College. Fort McNair, Washington, DC 20319. Maintains a political science library established in 1962.

IADIS Irish Association for Documentation and Information Services. National Library of Ireland, Dublin 2, Ireland.

IADLA International Association for the Development of Documentation, Libraries and Archives in Africa. *See* AIDBA (Association Internationale pour le Développement de la Documentation, des Bibliothèques et des Archives en Afrique).

IAEA International Atomic Energy Agency. 11 Kärntnerring, A-1010 Vienna 1, Austria. Sponsor of INIS.

IAESTE International Association for the Exchange of Students for Technical Experience. American City Bldg, Suite 217, Columbia, MD. Established in 1959. Arranges reciprocal exchange among 48 member countries for students of engineering, architecture, mathematics, agriculture and the sciences.

IAG IFIP Administrative Data Processing Group. Stadhouserkade 6, Amsterdam 13, the Netherlands.

IAIAS Interamerican Institute of Agricultural Sciences of OAS/OEA. *See* IICA (Instituto Interamericano de Ciencias Agrícolas de la OEA).

IAIS Industrial Aerodynamics Information Service. BHRA–Fluid Engineering,

Cranfield, Bedford, England. Service provided to institutions needing information on airflow and the effects of wind. Originally provided for the (British) National Physical Laboratory which financed it. A low-cost package was made available commercially beginning in 1972.

IAL International Algebraic Language. A programming language designed primarily for solving mathematical problems on digital computers. Replaced by ALGOL.

IALINE Documentation en Ligne pour l'Industrie Agro-Alimentaire. Association pour la Promotion Industrie-Agriculture, Centre de Documentation International des Industries Utilisatrices de Produits-Agricoles, avenue des Olympiades, 91305 Massy, France. Bibliographic data base covering industrial use of agricultural products.

IALL International Association of Law Libraries. c/o Vanderbilt Law Library, Nashville, TN 37203.

IAMC Institute for the Advancement of Medical Communication. Established in 1958. A nonprofit organization to attack problems of biomedical communication. Developed the Council on Medical Television in 1960. Produced a number of studies. Became affiliated with the College of Physicians of Philadelphia in 1972. *See* Claire K. Schultz. "Richard H. Orr: Personality Profile." *Information: News, Resources, Profiles* 4 (Jan.–Feb. 1972): 56–60.

IAMCR International Association for Mass Communication Research. Petit-Chêne, 18B, 1003 Lausanne, Switzerland.

IAML International Association of Music Libraries. *See* AIBM/IAML/IVMB.

IAMLANZ International Association of Music Librarians, Australia/New Zealand Branch. Contact president or AIMB/IAML/IVMB.

I&A Indexing and Abstracting. *See* A&I.

I&PS Information & Publishing Systems, Inc. 7101 Wisconsin Ave, Bethesda, MD 20014. Produces computer software.

IAOL International Association of Orientalist Librarians. 2250 The Mall,

University of Hawaii, Honolulu, HI 96822. Established in 1967. Publishes a quarterly newsletter. See *International Cooperation in Orientalist Librarianship: Papers from the Library Seminars of the 28th International Congress of Orientalists, Canberra, 1971*, ed. by E. Bishop and J. M. Waller. Canberra: National Library of Australia, 1972.

IAPG Interagency Advanced Power Group. University City Science Center, 3401 Market St, Philadelphia, PA 19104. Federal agency that maintains a science library established in 1960.

IAPTA International Allied Printing Trades Association. 102 Marquette Bldg, 2710 Hampton Ave, Saint Louis, MO 63139. Established in 1911. Promotes use of union-made school texts.

IAR Instruction Address Register. Contains the address of the next instruction to be executed.

IARD Information Analysis and Retrieval Division. Contact AIP (American Institute of Physics). A division of AIP.

IAS Immediate Access Storage. Fast access time in comparison with operating time; has real-time capabilities.

IASA International Association of Sound Archives. Contact executive secretary. Established in 1969. Affiliated with IAML and ARSC. Official journal, *Phonographic Bulletin*, is published quarterly.

IASC/SCAD Indexing and Abstracting Society of Canada/Société Canadienne pour l'Analyse de Documents. c/o Committee on Bibliographical Services for Canada, National Library of Canada, 395 Wellington St, Ottawa ON K1A 0N4, Canada.

IASL International Association of School Librarianship. c/o School of Librarianship, Western Michigan University, Kalamazoo, MI 49001. Established in 1971 to encourage development of school libraries and library programs throughout the world.

IASLIC Indian Association of Special Libraries and Information Centers. 15 Bankin Chatterjee St, Calcutta 12, India. Established in 1963.

IASP International Association of Scholarly Publishers. c/o University of Toronto Press, Toronto, ON, Canada. Established in 1972. Publishes a bulletin and directory.

IASSA Institute of Archival Science for Southeast Asia. University of Malaya, Kuala Lumpur, Malasia. Had UNESCO funding for 1973–1979.

IAT Institute for Advanced Technology. Corporation for Economics and Industrial Research, 5272 River Rd, Washington, DC 20016.

IATLIS Indian Association of Teachers of Library Science. Contact general secretary. Established in 1970. Publishes documents.

IATUL International Association of Technological University Libraries. University of Technology Library, Loughborough, Leicester, England.

IAVA Industrial Audio-Visual Association. Box 656, Downtown Sta, Chicago, IL 60690.

IBA Independent Broadcasting Authority. 70 Brompton Rd, London SW3, England. Formerly ITA (Independent Television Authority).

IBBD Instituto Brasileiro de Bibliografia e Documentação (Brazilian Institute of Bibliography and Documentation). Avenida General Justo 171, 1, 3, 4 andar, Rio de Janeiro, GB, Brazil. Established in 1954 with the help of UNESCO. Publishes recurring national bibliography.

IBBRIS *International Biodeterioration Bulletin*. Biodeterioration Information Centre, University of Aston in Birmingham, 80 Coleshill St, Birmingham B4 7PF, England. V. 1, 1965. Sponsored by the university and OSTI.

IBBY International Board on Books for Young People. CH-4051 Basel, Leonhardsgraben 38a, Switzerland. Publishes *Bookbird*.

IBFI International Business Forms Industries. Printing Industries of America, Inc, Graphic Communications Center, 1730 North Lynn St, Arlington, VA 22209. Established in 1953 to promote the manufacture of business forms. Theme of third international

forum (1970) was "Data Communication and Business Systems." Publishes surveys, books and pamphlets.

IBID *International Bibliography, Information, Documentation.* V. 1, 1973. Published by UNIPUB. An annotated bibliographic record of United Nations publications.

IBI/ICC Intergovernmental Bureau for Informatics/International Computation Center. Viale Civiltà del Lavoro 23, CP10253, I-00144 Rome, Italy. Established in 1961. Promotes research, education and use of informatics in government.

IBLA Inter-American Bibliographical and Library Association. *See* IABLA.

IBM International Business Machines Corporation. 360 Hamilton Ave, White Plains, NY 10601. Computer manufacturer.

IBR Institute for Behavioral Research. York University, 4700 Keele St, Downsview ON M3J 2R6, Canada. Established in 1973. Member of ASIDIC. Produces data bases CSSA and SSIS (Social Science Information Systems).

IBRA Institute Belge de Régulation et d'Automisme (Belgian Institute for Control and Automation). Rue Ravenstein 3, 1000 Brussels, Belgium. Established in 1955. Member of IFAC. Maintains a library and publishes documents.

IBS International Broadcasters Society. Zwaluwlaan 78, Box 128, Bossum, the Netherlands.

IBSAT Indexing by Statistical Analysis Techniques. *See* CAIC.

IBY International Book Year. Proclaimed by the General Conference of UNESCO for 1972. Under the slogan, "Books for All," IBY had as goals the promotion of authorship and translations; the stimulation of the production and distribution of books, including librarianship; the promotion of reading habits and the use of books in the service of education, international understanding and peaceful cooperation.

IC *Index Chemicus.* V. 1, 1960. Published by ISI (Institute for Scientific Information). Name changed to *CAC&IC (Current Abstracts of Chemistry and Index*

Chemicus) in 1970. *See* G. S. Revesz and A. Warner. ''Retrieving Chemical Information with Index Chemicus.'' *Journal of Chemical Documentation* 9 (1969): 106–109.

IC Instruction Counter. A register indicating to the computer the location of successive instructions.

IC Integrated Circuit. An electronic circuit in which passive and active elements are assembled as a single unit and cannot be disassembled.

ICA International Cartographic Association. Bachlaan 39, Hilversum, the Netherlands.

ICA International Communication Agency. 1750 Pennsylvania Ave, NW, Washington, DC 20547. Replaced USIA in 1978. Administers programs for international exchange of students, teachers and scholars.

ICA International Communication Association. Balcones Research Center, 10100 Burnet Rd, Austin, TX 78758. Established in 1950. Members are professionals interested in studying the nature of communication and its function in society. Publishes documents. Formerly (1969) NSSC.

ICA International Communications Association. Box 836, Bellaire, TX 77401. Established in 1948. Members are representatives of telecommunications services not predominantly engaged in the production, sale or rental of communications services or equipment.

ICA International Cooperation Administration. Name changed to AID (Agency for International Development).

ICA International Council on Archives. *See* CIA/ICA.

ICAI Institute for Computer-Assisted Information. 42 Court St, Doylestown, PA 18901.

ICAI International Commission for Agricultural and Food Industries. 18 avenue de Villars, 75-Paris 7, France.

ICAITI Instituto Centro Americano de Investigacion y Technologia Industrial (Central American Institute of Research and Industrial Technology). Avenida Reforma 4-47, Zona 10, Guatemala City, Guatemala.

ICAO International Civil Aviation Organization. Box 400, Place de l'Aviation Internationale, 1000 Sherbrooke St. West, Montreal PQ H3A 2R2, Canada. Also known as Organisation de l'Aviation Civile Internationale. Maintains a library.

ICBA International Community of Booksellers Association. Lindelaan 12, Delft 2, the Netherlands.

ICBS Interconnected Business System. Any system composed of a combination of smaller business systems.

ICBY International Council on Books for Young People. Fuhrmannsgasse 18a, Vienna 8, Austria.

ICC International Computation Center. *See* IBI/ICC.

ICCC Inter-Council Coordination Committee UNESCO. 6 rue Franklin, Paris 16, France.

ICCC International Conference on Computer Communication. Meeting held in Washington, DC, October 24–26, 1972.

ICCJ International Committee for Cooperation of Journalists. 35 Via Colonna Antonina, Rome, Italy.

ICCP International Conference on Cataloging Principles. Held in 1961 in Paris, France.

ICD Institute for the Crippled and Disabled. ICD Rehabilitation and Research Center, 340 East 24 St, New York, NY 10010. Maintains a library established in 1917.

ICDB Integrated Corporate Data Base.

ICE Institution of Civil Engineers. 26-34 Old St, London EC1V 9AD, England. Publishes *ICE Abstracts*.

ICEF International Children's Emergency Fund. *See* UNICEF.

ICEF International Council for Educational Films. *See* CIFE (Conseil International pour les Films d'Éducation).

ICES International Council for the Exploration of the Sea. Charlottenlund Slot, 2920 Charlottenlund, Denmark. Established in 1902. Coordinates oceanographic research activities of 15 European countries, Canada and the USSR.

ICFC International Center of Films for Children. 241 rue Royale, Brussels 3, Belgium.

ICIA International Center of Information on Antibiotics. 32 boulevard de la Constitution, Liège, Belgium.

ICIP International Conference on Information Processing. Held in Paris, UNESCO House, June 15–20, 1959, with 2,000 participants from 37 countries. See *Information Processing: Proceedings of ICIP Congress.* Amsterdam, the Netherlands: North Holland Publishing (for UNESCO), 1960.

ICIREPAT International Cooperation in Information Retrieval among Examining Patent Offices. 32 Chemin des Colombettes, 1211 Geneva 20, Switzerland. Objective is to promote international cooperation in national patent office documentation of novel applications. Also known as CICIREPATO.

IC/ISDS International Center for the ISDS. *See* ISDS.

ICIST Institut Canadien de l'Information Scientifique et Technique. *See* CISTI/ICIST.

ICL Irish Central Library for Students. 53 Upper Mount St, Dublin 61167, Ireland.

ICLA International Comparative Literature Association. Institut de Litératures Modernes Comparées, 17 rue de la Sorbonne, Paris 5, France.

ICLEBC Institute of Continuing Library Education of British Columbia. Contact secretary. A Canadian association.

ICLTN Interagency Council on Library Tools for Nursing. An advisory body composed of representatives of agencies and organizations having an active interest in library resources for nursing. Among the active members are ALA (American Library Association), MLA (Medical Library Association) and SLA (Special Libraries Association).

ICO Intergovernmental Commission on Oceanography. National Institute of Oceanography, Wormley near Godalming, Surrey, England.

ICOSAL Idaho Council of State Academic Libraries. Contact secretary.

Established in 1968. Members share budget and statistical data.

ICPDATA Industrial Commodity Production Statistics. Statistical Office, United Nations, New York, NY 10017. Coverage from 1958. Nonbibliographic data base of statistics on international industrial output.

ICPI Intersociety Committee on Pathology Information. Information Services, Inc. 9650 Rockville Pike, Bethesda, MD 20014. Established in 1957. Conducts projects to educate the public and individual groups in the practice of pathology. Publishes a directory of training programs and a career brochure.

ICPP Interactive Computer Presentation Panel. An international research and development program administered by the US and the Federal Republic of Germany.

ICPP International Comparative Political Parties Project. Dept. of Political Science, Northwestern University, Evanston, Il 60201. Essentially a library operation that uses a variety of modern microfilm and computer information-processing techniques to control the literature related to the project.

ICPSR Inter-University Consortium for Political and Social Research. Box 1248, University of Michigan, Ann Arbor, MI 48109. Constitutes a library network.

ICPU International Catholic Press Union. 43 rue Saint-Augustin, Paris 2, France.

ICR International Council for Reprography. 9 Argyle St, London W1, England.

ICRD Index of Codes for Research Drugs. A special index contained in the publication *Unlisted Drugs*, published by Pharmaco-Medical Documentation.

ICRDB International Cancer Research Data Bank Program. National Cancer Institute, 8600 Rockville Pike, Bethesda, MD 20014. Established in 1974. Produces data bases, including CANCERLINE.

ICRS *Index Chemicus* Registry System. Institute for Scientific Information, 325 Chestnut Ave, Philadelphia, PA 19106. *See* Eugene Garfield et al. "*Index Chemicus* Registry System: Pragmatic

Approach to Substructure Chemical Retrieval." *Journal of Chemical Documentation* 10 (Feb. 1970): 54–58.

ICS Institute for the Comparative Study of History, Philosophy and the Sciences, Ltd. 23 Brunswick Rd, Kingston-upon-Thames, Surrey, England.

ICSSD International Committee for Social Sciences Documentation. 27 rue Saint-Guillaume, Paris 7, France.

ICST Institute for Computer Sciences and Technology. Part of NBS established in 1965 to develop and recommend federal information-processing standards.

ICSU International Council of Scientific Unions. 51 boulevard de Montmorency, 75016 Paris, France. Established in 1919 as the International Research Council. Maintains CSU-AB. Sponsors CODATA.

ICSU-AB ICSU Abstracting Board. 17 rue Mirabeau, 75016 Paris, France. The board was established in 1952 to promote information exchange through coordination of abstracting and indexing services. Assisted financially by UNESCO. Also known as IAB.

ICTP International Center for Theoretical Physics. Trieste, Italy. Established in 1964. *See* John Ziman. "The 'Winter College' Format." *Science* 171 (Jan. 29, 1971): 352–354.

IDC International Data Corporation. 214 Third Ave, Waltham, MA 02154. Provides market research and data gathering services.

IDC International Development Center. 3514 Plyers Mill Rd, Kensington, MD 20795. A vendor of computer terminals and related equipment.

IDC Internationale Dokumentation-gesellschaft für Chemie. Analin-und Soda-Fabrik A. G, 67 Ludwigshafen am Rhein, Federal Republic of Germany. Established in 1967. A joint venture of 12 chemical firms in West Germany, Austria and the Netherlands to develop and operate a computerized storage and retrieval system for chemical information. *See* "CAS-GDCh Agreement." *Journal of Chemical Documentation* 9 (Nov. 1969): 262.

IDC-KTHB Royal Institute of Technology Library. Vallhallavagen 81, Stockholm 100 44, Sweden. Established in 1967. Provides computerized searches, conducts seminars, and publishes documents.

IDC/VN Industrial Development Center/Viet-Nam (Trung-Tam Khuech-Truong Ky-Ngha). 40-42 Blvd. Nguygen-Hue, Saigon, Vietnam.

IDDC International Demographic Data Center. US Bureau of the Census, Dept. of Commerce, Population Division, Washington, DC 20233. Established in 1968. Maintains a population data base for all countries.

IDEAS Integrated Design and Analysis System.

IDEEA Information and Data Exchange Experimental Activities. A project of the US Army.

IDICT Instituto de Documentación e Información Científica y Tecnica (Institute of Scientific and Technical Documentation and Information). Calle C. n. 301, Vedado, Apartado Postal 4017, Havana 4, Cuba. Established in 1963 with the help of UNESCO. Publishes documents.

IDL&RS International Data Library and Reference Service. Established in 1961. Became SRCDL in 1978.

IDMH Illinois Department of Mental Health and Developmental Disabilities Professional Libraries Consortium. Name changed to DMHDD/LISN.

IDOE International Decade of Ocean Exploration. Contact NODC. A project of the 1970s whose data management support was provided by NODC.

IDP Institute of Data Processing. 418-422 Strand, London WC2, England.

IDP Integrated Data Processing. The processing of data on an organized, systematic and correlated basis.

IDR&DS *International Directory of Research and Development Scientists*. An annual published by ISI (Institute for Scientific Information). Superseded by *WIPIS* in 1971.

IDRS Inter-Departmental Reference Service. College of Public

Administration, University of the Philippines, Padre Faura, Manila 10501, Philippines.

IDS Integrated Data Store. A technique for organizing business data.

IDS Interlibrary Delivery Service of Pennsylvania. c/o Dauphin County Library System, 101 Walnut St, Harrisburg, PA 17101. One hundred twenty-nine academic, public and special libraries cooperate through delivery services, ILL and film services.

IDT Institutul Central de Documentare Technica (Central Institute for Technical Documentation). Str. Cosmonautilor 27-29, Sector I, Bucharest, Rumania. Established in 1949.

IDTF International Documents Task Force. *See* GODORT/IDTF.

IE *Industrial Engineering.* (Journal). V. 1, 1969. Published by the American Institute of Industrial Engineers. Supersedes *Journal of Industrial Engineering.*

IEALC Inland Empire Academic Libraries Cooperative. c/o University of California Library, Riverside, CA 92507. Twenty-one member libraries cooperate through ILL and common cooperative borrowing cards.

IEC International Electrotechnical Commission. One rue de Varembé, 1211 Geneva 20, Switzerland. Carries out international standardization work.

IEE Institution of Electrical Engineers. Savoy Place, London WC2R 0BL, England. Maintains INSPEC data base.

IEEE Institute of Electrical and Electronics Engineers. 345 East 47 St, New York, NY 10017. A constituent society of AFIPS. Established in 1963 through the merger of AIEE and IRE. Publishes documents.

IEEE REFLECS IEEE Retrieval from the Literature on Electronics and Computer Sciences. Information Services, Institute of Electrical and Electronics Engineers, 345 East 47 St, New York, NY 10017. A service in the form of machine-readable magnetic tapes containing indexes and abstracts of papers in the fields of electronics, computers and control and applied physics.

IEETE Institution of Electrical and Electronics Technicians Engineers, Ltd. 2 Savoy Hill, London WC2, England.

IEI Industrial Education Institute. 221 Columbus Ave, Boston, MA 02116.

IEN Xerox Information Exchange Network. 800 Phillips Rd, Webster, NY 14580. Established in 1974. A corporate-wide network of Xerox libraries and information centers.

IERE Institution of Electronic and Radio Engineers. 8-9 Bedford Sq, London WC1, England.

IF Intellectual Freedom. Contact CLA (Canadian Library Association). A committee of CLA.

IFABC International Federation of Audit Bureaus of Circulations. Kölnerstrasse 107b, 532 Bad Godesberg, Federal Republic of Germany. Audits circulation of magazines for the purpose of guaranteeing advertisers' circulation counts.

IFAC International Federation of Automatic Control. Graf-Recke Strasse 84, POB 1139, 4 Düsseldorf 1, Federal Republic of Germany. Covers the field of open and closed loop or feedback control of physical systems, including servomechanics, instrumentation, data processing and computers, in both theoretical and applied aspects.

IFAN Institut Fondamental d'Afrique Noire. Bibliothèque, Université de Dakar, BP 206, Dakar-Fann, Senegal.

IFB Information for Business. 25 West 39 St, New York, NY 10018. An information broker.

IFC Intellectual Freedom Committee. Contact ALA (American Library Association).

IFCJ International Federation of Catholic Journalists. 43 rue Saint-Augustin, Paris 2, France.

IFD International Federation for Documentation. *See* FID (Fédération Internationale de Documentation).

IFFA International Federation of Film Archives. *See* FIAF (Fédération Internationale des Archives du Film).

IFFJ International Federation of Free Journalists of Central and Eastern

Europe and Baltic and Balkan Countries. 54 Regent St, London W1, England. Also known as FIJL (Fédération Internationale des Journalistes Libres de l'Europe Central et des Pays Baltes et Balkaniques).

IFFPA International Federation of Film Producers Associations. 114 Champs Elysées, Paris 8, France.

IFFS International Federation of Film Societies. 81 Dean St, London W1, England.

IFIP International Federation for Information Processing. 25 Dorset Sq, London NW1, England. Established in 1960. Formerly IFIPS.

IFIPS International Federation of Information Processing Societies. Name changed to IFIP.

IFIS International Food Information Service. Commonwealth Bureau of Dairy Science and Technology, Lane End House, Shinfield, Reading RG2 9AT, Berkshire, England.

IFJ International Federation of Journalists. *See* FIJ (Fédération Internationale des Journalistes).

IFLA International Federation of Library Associations and Institutions. Netherlands Congress Building Tower, Postbus 9128, The Hague, the Netherlands. Libraries and library schools may be associate members. Also known as FIAB (Fédération Internationale de Associations de Bibliothécaires et des Bibliothèques).

IFO Institut für Wirtschaftsforschung. Poschingerstrasse 5, D-8000 Munich, Federal Republic of Germany. Produces data bases on economics.

IFOP Institut Français d'Opinion Publique. 20 rue d'Aumale, Paris 9, France. Produces a data base on public opinion.

IFP Institute Française du Petrole. Division Geologie BP 311, 92506 Rueil-Malmaison, Cedex, France. Produces a data base on petroleum. *See also* AID-IFP.

IFRT Intellectual Freedom Round Table. Contact ALA (American Library Association).

IFTC International Film and Television Council. Via Santa Susanna, 17, 00187 Rome, Italy.

IGAEA International Graphic Arts Education Association. 4615 Forbes Ave, Pittsburgh, PA 15213. Established in 1923. Publishes documents. Formerly National Graphic Arts Guild and National Graphic Arts Education Association.

IGC Institute for Graphic Communication, Inc. 375 Commonwealth Ave, Boston, MA 02115. Incorporated in 1969. IGC is a Gorham International Co. that is an R&D contractor. Specializes in visual communication and does consulting, R&D and special reports and offers conferences in North America and Europe.

IGI Information General, Inc. 214 Garden St, Needham, MA 02192.

IGOSS Integrated Global Ocean Stations System. c/o National Institute of Oceanography, Wormley near Godalming, Surrey, England. Project of IOC (Intergovernmental Oceanographic Commission) and WMO.

IGY International Geophysical Year. 1958–1959. *See* WDC (World Data Center).

IHETS Indiana Higher Education Television System. Bloomington, IN. Project to provide an interactive closed-circuit television system to be used in CE.

IHS Information Handling Services. Englewood, CO 80110. Provides software for a joint micropublishing service with 3-M.

II Committee on Information and Industry. *See* FID/II.

IIA Information Industry Association. 316 Pennsylvania Ave, SE, Suite 502, Washington, DC 20003. Established in 1968.

IIA Institute of Internal Auditors, Inc. 249 Maitland Ave, Altamonte Springs, FL 32701. Established in 1941. Constituent society of AFIPS. Maintains a library and publishes several periodicals, a directory, research reports, bibliographies and textbooks.

IIB Instituto de Investigaciones Bibliograficas. Apartado Postal 29-124,

México 1, DF, Mexico. A unit of UNAM which publishes a "Bolétin," the *Anuario Bibliografico Mexicano* and the *Bibliografia Mexicana.*

IIC International Institute for Conservation of Historic and Artistic Works. 6 Buckingham St, London WC2N 6BA, England. Established in 1950. Publishes journals and the proceedings of its triennial conferences.

IIC International Institute of Communications. Viale Brigate Partigiane 18, Genoa, Italy.

IICA Instituto Interamericano de Ciencias Agrícolas de la OEA (Interamerican Institute of Agricultural Sciences of OAS/OEA). Apartado 74, Turrialba, Costa Rica. Connected with OAS/OEA. Conducts conferences and workshops for agricultural librarians. Has many subgroups. Also known as IAIAS.

IIE Institute of International Education. 809 United Nations Pl, New York, NY 10017. Established in 1919. Publishes documents.

IIEP International Institute for Educational Planning. *See* IIPE/IIEP.

IIF Information Item File. An encyclopedic store in which the basic records are information items. *See* Harry Schwarzlander. "Encyclopedic Storage of Scientific and Technical Knowledge." *IEEE Transactions on Engineering Writing and Speech* EWS-13 (Sept. 1970): 48–57.

IIF Institut International du Froid. 177 boulevard Malesherbes, Paris 17, France. Maintains a library.

IIFA International Institute of Films on Art. Piazza Vittorio Veneto 4, Florence, Italy.

IIMP *Information Industry Market Place.* New York: R. R. Bowker Co, 1978. An annual directory of information products and services.

IIOE International Indian Ocean Expedition. Contact NODC. A program for which NODC has provided data forms and/or data processing support.

IIPE/IIEP Institut International de la Planification de l'Éducation/International Institute for Educational Planning. UNESCO, Place de Fontenoy, Paris 7, France.

IIR International Institute of Refrigeration. 177 boulevard Malesherbes, 75 Paris 17, France. Established in 1920 in Paris by intergovernmental agreement. Succeeded the Association Internationale du Froid, established in 1908. Aims to further the development of scientific research and promote technical and economic studies.

IIRS Institute for Industrial Research and Standards. Industrial Research Center, Ballymun Rd, Dublin 9, Ireland. Affiliated with ISO (International Standards Organization).

IIRS International Information Retrieval Service. Box 688, 3800 AR Amersfoort, the Netherlands. Incorporated in 1976. Provides computerized searches and other services. Member of EUSIDIC and IIA (Information Industry Association).

IIS Institut International de la Soudure (International Institute of Welding). General Secretariat, 54 Princes Gate, Exhibition Rd, London SW7, England; Scientific & Technical Secretariat, 32 boulevard de la Chapelle, 75 Paris 18, France. Aims to provide for exchange of scientific and technical information relating to welding research and education.

IIS Institute of Information Scientists. 5-7 Russia Row, London EC2V 8BL, England. Established in 1958. *See* J. E. L. Farradane. "The Institute: The First Twelve Years." *The Information Scientist* 4 (Dec. 1970): 143–151.

IIT Illinois Institute of Technology. 3300 South Federal, Chicago, IL 60616. Maintains a computer research facility, IITRI.

IITRI Illinois Institute of Technology Research Institute. 10 West 35 St, Chicago, IL 60616. Established in 1968. Has a computerized research facility and provides retrospective literature searches in the fields of chemistry, engineering, physics, biology and education.

IIW International Institute of Welding. *See* IIS (Institut International de la Soudure).

ILA Idaho Library Association. Contact president or ALA (American Library Association).

ILA Illinois Library Association. Contact president or ALA (American Library Association).

ILA India Library Association. Delhi Public Library, SP Mukerji Marg, Delhi 6, India.

ILA Indiana Library Association. Contact president or ALA (American Library Association).

ILA Iowa Library Association. Contact president or ALA (American Library Association).

ILA Iranian Library Association. Box 11-1391, Tehran, Iran.

ILA Israel Library Association. Box 7067, Jerusalem, Israel. Established in 1952. Affiliated with IFLA and ASLIB. Publishes documents. *See* J. Rothschild. "Israel, Libraries and Information Services in" in *Encyclopedia of Library and Information Science*, ed. by A. Kent et al. New York: Marcel Dekker, 1975, V. 13, pp. 111–121.

ILAB International League of Antiquarian Booksellers. 95 Wimpole St, London W1, England.

IL&T *Investing, Licensing & Trading Conditions Abroad* (Journal). V. 1, 1955. Published by Business International Corp.

ILAS Interrelated Logic Accumulating Scanner.

ILCE Instituto Latinoamericano de Cinematographía Educativa. Name changed to ILCE (Instituto Latinoamericano de la Communicación Educativa).

ILCE Instituto Latinoamericano de la Communicación Educativa. Auditorio Nacional, México 10, DF, Mexico. Formerly ILCE (Instituto Latinoamericano de Cinematographía Educativa).

ILEA Inner London Educational Authority. Post office cable land line for closed-circuit television to schools, colleges and universities in London.

ILIC International Library Information Center. Graduate School of Library and Information Science, University of Pittsburgh, Pittsburgh, PA 15160. Established in 1964. Collects primary source material for comparative studies in librarianship on an international level.

I-LITE Iowa Library Information Teletype Exchange. Historical Bldg, East 12 & Grand Sts, Des Moines, IA 50319. Nineteen academic and public libraries cooperate through ILL and delivery services.

ILL Interlibrary Loan.

ILLACORS Interlibrary Lending and Cooperative Reference Services. Cornell University Library, Ithaca, NY 14850. Formed in 1972 by the merger of two separate interlibrary loan units within the reference department of the Cornell Libraries.

ILLC International Library to Library Project. A project of MLA (Medical Library Association) in which member libraries exchange services and resources with a "buddy" library.

ILLINET Illinois Library and Information Network. c/o Illinois State Library, Springfield, IL 62756. Illinois libraries, library systems and research and resource centers cooperate through diverse programs including the ILLINET Bibliographic Data Service.

ILMP *International Literary Market Place.* Thirteenth edition. New York: R. R. Bowker Co, 1979.

ILO International Labour Organisation. CH 1211 Geneva 20, Switzerland. Sponsor of ISIS. Foreign affiliate of NFAIS. Also known as OIT (Organisation Internationale du Travail).

ILP *Index to Legal Periodicals.* (Journal). V. 1, 1908. Published by H. W. Wilson Co.

ILR Institute of Library Research. South Hall, University of California, Berkeley, CA 94720.

ILS Integrated Library System. EURATOM Ispra Library, Varese, Italy. An in-house system in use at the EURATOM Ispra Library.

IM *Index Medicus.* V. 1, 1960. Published by the National Library of Medicine.

IM International Microfilm. 3M Center, Saint Paul, MN 55101. Publishes microfiche and microfilm.

IMAC Illinois Microfilm Automated Catalog. Illinois State Library, Springfield, IL 62706. Project initiated by the Illinois State Library and deposited in 17 cooperative public libraries in the state.

IMACS International Association for Mathematics and Computer Simulation. *See* AICA (Association Internationale pour le Calcul Analogique).

IMDS International Microform Distribution Service. c/o Clearwater Publishing Co, 75 Rockefeller Pl, New York, NY 10020. A central clearinghouse for foreign microforms.

IMF International Monetary Fund. 19 St & H St, NW, Washington, DC 20431. Established in 1946. Maintains an economics library and publishes documents.

IMI Iowa-Missouri-Illinois Library Consortium. c/o William Penn College, Wilcox Library, Oskaloosa, IA 52577. Twelve academic libraries cooperate through ILL and union list of serials.

IMIA Instituto Méxicano de Información Avícola. San Juan de Letrán, 21-613 y 614, México 1, DF, Mexico.

IMM Institution of Mining and Metallurgy. 44 Portland Pl, London WIN 4BR, England. Publishes documents.

IMMS International Material Management Society. 3310 Bardaville Dr, Lansing, MI 48906. Established in 1949. Formerly (1969) AMHS. Nine regional groups and 46 local chapters. Publishes journals and other documents.

IMP *Index of Mathematical Papers.* (Journal). V. 1, 1971. Published by the American Mathematical Society.

IMP *Information Market Place. See* IIMP.

IMPRESS Interdisciplinary Machine Processing for Research and Education in the Social Sciences. Dartmouth College, 118 Silsby Hall, Hanover, NH 03755. A project that uses computerization to produce social science data bases.

IMPRINT Imbricated Program for Information Transfer. The Galton Institute, 319 South Robertson Blvd, Beverly Hills, CA 90211. A program using computers, magnetic tape,

recording devices, composition and graphic arts automated devices and published materials for a study concerned with the understanding of higher mental processes.

IMSL International Mathematical and Statistical Library. FORTRAN-callable subroutines to be used only with FORTRAN programs.

IMULS Intermountain Union List of Serials. Hayden Library, Arizona State University, Tempe, AZ 85281. Consortium established in 1968.

INBAD Information System on Research and Development in Building Industry and Construction. Research and Design Center for Industrial Building (BISTYP), Parkingowa 1, 00-518 Warsaw, Poland. Purpose is to design and implement effective tools for research programming in the building industry and to create scientific and technical information systems for the field.

INCAP Instituto de Nutricion de Centro America y Panama. Carretera Roosevelt, Zona 11, Apartado Postal 11-88, Guatemala, C. A. T. 43765. Promotes and encourages the development of nutritional science and its application in member countries.

INCINC International Copyrights Information Center. c/o Association of American Publishers, 1707 L St, NW, Suite 480, Washington, DC 20036. Established in 1970.

INCOLSA Indiana Cooperative Library Services Authority. 1100 West 42 St, Indianapolis, IN 46208. One hundred thirty academic, public, school and special libraries cooperate in cost-reducing services on a statewide basis.

INCRA International Copper Research Association. 708 Third Ave, New York, NY 10017. Established in 1960. Conducts research and development on copper and publishes the series The Metallurgy of Copper.

INDEX Inter NASA Data Exchange. Contact NASA.

INDIRS Indiana Information Retrieval System. 140 North Senate Ave, Indianapolis, IN 46204. Eighteen state, public and academic libraries use common data bases covering socioeconomic statistical information on Indiana.

INEL Idaho National Engineering Laboratory. 550 Second St, Idaho Falls, ID 83401. Operated by ERDA. Maintains a library established in 1952.

INEL International Network of Emerging Libraries. F. D. Buford Library, North Carolina Agricultural & Technical State University, Greensboro, NC 27411. Organized in 1976 with six southern colleges. Eleven members in May 1979 sponsored a second "Conference on Multicultural Academic Library Services in Predominantly Black Institutions of Higher Learning."

INFO Information Center for Southern California Libraries. c/o Los Angeles Public Library, 630 West Fifth St, Los Angeles, CA 90017. Consortium established in 1970. Maintains a referral center for information sources and services.

INFO International Fortean Organization. Box 367, Arlington, VA 22210. Maintains a zoological library established in 1965.

INFORFILM International Association of Information Film Distributors. 147 avenue de l'Hippodrome, Brussels, Belgium.

INFORM Information for Minnesota. Wilson Library, University of Minnesota, Minneapolis, MN 55455. Research service for Minnesota industry.

INFORM Information Needs. *See* ABI/INFORM.

INFORM International Reference Organization in Forensic Medicine and Sciences. c/o Dr. William G. Eckert Laboratory, Saint Francis Hospital, Wichita, KS 67214. Established in 1966.

INFRAL Information Retrieval Automatic Language. A special programming language that provides the ability to construct bibliographies from indexed information.

INFROSS Information Requirements of the Social Sciences. Bath University of Technology, Claverton Down, Bath BA

2 7 AY, England. An OSTI-supported study. *See* J. M. Brittain. *Information and Its Users: A Review with Special Reference to the Social Sciences*. New York: John Wiley, 1971. *See also* M. B. Line. "Information Requirements in the Social Sciences: Some Preliminary Considerations." *Journal of Librarianship* 1 (Jan. 1969): 1–19.

INI Institute Nazionale de l'Informazione (National Institute of Information). Via Culamatta 16, Rome 00193, Italy.

INIBON Institut Nacnoj Informacii i Fundamental'naja Biblioteka po Obscestvennym Naukam (Institute of Scientific Information and Main Library of the Social Sciences). USSR.

INIS International Nuclear Information System. Box 590, A-10011, Vienna, Austria. Established in 1970 by IAEA. The computer-based system covers the world literature in nuclear science and its allied fields. INIS centers in member countries provide input.

INLE Instituto Nacional del Libro Español. Ferraz 11, Madrid, Spain. Established in 1939.

INP In Process. Indicates that materials have arrived in a library and are going through technical services.

INPACON Input Audit and Control. Lockheed-Georgia Co, Sci-Tech Information Center, Marietta, GA 30060.

INPADOC International Patent Documentation Center. Mollwaldplatz 4, Vienna A-1040, Austria. Established in 1972. Produces machine-readable data bases. Division of WIPO and a member of EUSIDIC.

INRA Institut National de la Recherche Agronomique. Centre National de Recherche Agronomique, Route de Saint-Cyr, 78000 Versailles, France. Produces a data base on agronomic research.

INRDG Institut National de Recherches et de Documentation. BP 561, Conakry, Guinea.

INSDOC Indian National Scientific Documentation Centre. Hillside Rd, New Delhi 110012, India. Publishes *ISA* (*Indian Science Abstracts*).

INSEE Institut National de la Statistique et des Études Économique. 18 boulevard Adolph Pinard, 75014 Paris, France. Produces data bases on statistics and economic studies.

INSERM Institut National de la Santé et de la Recherche Medicale. Hôpital de Bicetre, 78 rue du General-Leclerc, Kremlin-Bicetre 94270, Paris, France. Produces a data base on toxic substances.

INSPEC Information Service in Physics, Electrotechnology and Control. Institution of Electrical Engineers, Savoy Pl, London WC2R 0BL, England. Range of products and services includes current-awareness journals, SDI, abstracts and indexes.

INTAMEL International Association of Metropolitan City Libraries. Contact secretary. Established in 1967 as a subsection of IFLA.

INTELSAT International Telecommunications Satellite Consortium. 950 L'Enfant Pl, SW, Washington, DC 20024.

INTERFILM International Inter-Church Film Center. Postbus 515, Borneolaan 27, Hilversum, the Netherlands.

INTIPS Integrated Information Processing System. Air Development Center, Rome, NY 13440.

INTRAFAX Closed-circuit facsimile systems leased to government, military and industrial users by Western Union.

INTRAN Input Translator. Developed for the IBM 709 and 7090 systems.

INTREX Information Transfer Experiments. A research program undertaken at MIT (Massachusetts Institute of Technology) from 1965 to 1973, aimed at developing new methods of information handling for university libraries.

INWATS Inward Wide Area Telephone Service. WATS line for incoming calls only.

I/O Input/Output. Refers to the transfer of information to and from a computer.

IOC Input/Output Control Module. A program-controlled macroprocessor for servicing peripheral equipment. It provides control signals, parity check, time interface and data transformation.

IOC Intergovernmental Oceanographic Commission. UNESCO, 7 Place de Fontenoy, Paris 75700, France. Produces data bases and provides computerized searches.

IOCC Input/Output Control Center. Connected to the central processor; performs control functions for one card reader-punch, one high-speed printer and up to four magnetic tape units.

IOCS Input/Output Control System. Refers to the hardware used in communication to a computer, the data thus communicated or the media in which such data are expressed.

IOJ Institute of Journalists. 2 Tudor St, London EC4, England.

IOJ International Organization of Journalists. Parizska 9-11, Prague 1, Czechoslovakia. Also known as OIJ (Organisation International des Journalistes).

IOP Input/Output Processor. A unit that handles normal data input/output control and sequencing.

IOP Institute of Printing, Ltd. 11 Bedford Row, London WC1, England.

IOPKG Input/Output Package. Developed for the IBM 705 III computer.

IOR Input/Output Register. Contains a mechanism to permit automatic modification of an instruction address without permanently altering the instructions in memory.

IOS International Organization for Standardization. *See* ISO (International Standards Organization).

IOS Iraqi Organization for Standards. Ministry of Industry, Box 11185, Baghdad, Iraq. Issues English-language standards. Affiliated with ISO (International Standards Organization).

IOT Input/Output and Transfer. Enables the computer to communicate with external devices, send control information and transfer data.

IPA Information Processing Association of Israel. Box 13009, Jerusalem, Israel. Established in 1956. Affiliated with IFLA. Publishes documents.

IPA Institute of Public Administration. Box 205, Ridyah, Saudi Arabia. Maintains an information center.

IPA *International Pharmaceutical Abstracts*. V. 1, 1964. Published by American Society of Hospital Pharmacists.

IPA International Publishers Association. Secretariat, avenue Miremont 3, 1206 Geneva, Switzerland.

IPAHGEIS Inter-Professional Ad Hoc Group for Environmental Information Sharing. Name changed to GLEIS in 1978.

IPARA International Publishers Advertising Representatives Association. 525/527 Fulham Rd, London SW6, England.

IPC Industrial Process Control.

IPC Information Processing Code.

IPC International Press Center. Maison de la Presse, boulevard Charlemagne 1, 1040 Brussels, Belgium. Home of various national and international publishing, journalism and press associations.

IPDA International Periodical Distributors Association. 350 Madison Ave, New York, NY 10017. Established in 1972. Ten wholesalers who serve 155,000 retail outlets in the US and Canada.

IPF Irish Printing Federation. 14 Lansdowne Rd, Ballsbridge, Dublin 4, Ireland.

IPG Independent Publishers Guild. 52 Manchester St, London W1, England.

IPI Ikatan Pustakawan Indonesia (Indonesian Library Association). Jalan Merdeka Selatan 11, Belakang, Jakarta, Indonesia. Formed in 1973 by the merger of APADI and HPCI. *See* Ilse Dammerboer. "Indonesian Library Associations: From APSI to IPI." *Australian Library Journal* 24 (Sept. 1975): 355–358.

IPI International Press Institute. 9 Münstergasse, 8001 Zurich, Switzerland.

IPI/MIS IPI Management and Information System. Contact IPI (International Press Institute).

IPL Information Processing Language. A computer programming language dealing in symbols rather than numbers.

IPL Initial Program Loading. A process which brings a program or operating system into a computer with the data records which participate in the process. This routine is then established in the memory, making it possible to load and execute any other desired program.

IPL-5 Information Processing Language-5. A list processing language developed principally to manipulate tree structures.

IPLO Institute of Professional Librarians of Ontario. This association was terminated in 1976.

IPPEC Inventaire Permanent des Périodiques Étrangers en Cours. Union list of periodicals for the libraries which are part of the French BU.

IPS Inches Per Second. Refers to the speed of magnetic tape in a computer.

IPS Incorporated Phonographic Society. 15 Lower Coombe St, Croydon, Surrey, England.

IPTC International Press Telecommunications Committee. Bouverie House, 154 Fleet St, London EC4, England.

IQRP Interactive Query and Report Processor.

IR Information Retrieval. The recovery and interpretation of stored data.

IRA International Reading Association. Box 8139, 800 Barksdale Rd, Newark, DE 19711.

IRANDOC Iranian Documentation Center. Box 11-1387, Tehran, Iran.

IRBEL *Indexed References to Biomedical Engineering Literature*. Ceased publication in 1976. Published by Medical Research Council, Bioengineering Division, Clinical Research Center, Watford Rd, Harrow, Middlesex HA1 3UJ, England.

IRC International Relations Committee. Contact ALA (American Library Association).

IRE Institute of Radio Engineers. Merged with AIEE to form IEEE in 1963. Sponsored annual Joint Computing Conferences with AIEE from 1952 to 1961.

IRF International Road Federation. 1023 Washington Bldg, Washington, DC 20005. A joint office of IRRD, which is a part of OECD.

IRFA Institut de Recherches sur les Fruits et Agrumes. 6 rue du General Clergie, 75016 Paris, France. Produces a data base.

IRG Inter-Record Gap. Blank portion of computer magnetic tape between records.

IRGMA Information Retrieval Group of the Museums Association. Museums Association, 34 Bloomsbury Way, London WC1A 2SF, England. *See* M. F. Porter, R. B. Light and D. A. Roberts. *A Unified Approach to the Computerization of Museum Catalogues.* London: British Library Board, 1977.

IRI Institute de Recherche Industrielle. Beirut, Lebanon.

IRIA Infrared Information and Analysis Center. Environment Research Institute of Michigan, Box 618, Ann Arbor, MI 48107. Sponsored by the Physics Branch of the Office of Naval Research. Provides information on all aspects of infrared technology and especially military infrared technology. Proprietary material available only to authorized government personnel and agencies.

IRIA Institute de Recherche d'Informatique et d'Automatique (French Research Institute of Information and Automatic Processing). Toulouse, France.

IRIS Information Resources Information System. Used to support NRC's (National Referral Center's) information resource register and directory activities.

IRIS Infrared Information System. Sadtler Research Laboratories, Inc, 3316 Spring Garden St, Philadelphia, PA 19104. Coverage from 1960. Data base containing infrared spectra data and chemical descriptions.

IRIS Institute's Retrieval-of-Information Study. Ontario Institute for Studies in Education, 102 Bloor St, West, Toronto, Canada.

IRIS International Rights Information Service. c/o Frieda Johnson, R. R.

Bowker Co, 1180 Ave. of the Americas, New York, NY 10036. Listings appear in the second issue each month of *Publishers Weekly*.

IRL Information Retrieval Language.

IRLA Independent Research Library Association. Contact chairperson. Established in 1972. *See* O. B. Hardison, Jr. "Independent Research Libraries Association (IRLA)" in *Encyclopedia of Library and Information Science*, ed. by A. Kent et al. New York: Marcel Dekker, 1974, V. 11, pp. 285–286.

IRLC Illinois Regional Library Council. 425 North Michigan Ave, Chicago, IL 60611. Three hundred thirteen academic, public, school and special libraries cooperate through ILL, delivery services, coordinated acquisitions, CE program and other resource sharing.

IRO International Relations Office. Contact ALA (American Library Association).

IRP Information Resources Press. 2100 M St, NW, Washington, DC 20037. The publishing division of Herner & Co.

IRPL *Index to Religious Periodical Literature*. V. 1, 1949. Published by the American Theological Library Association.

IRRD International Road Research Documentation. 19 rue de Franqueville 75, Paris 16, France. Part of OECD. Participates in IRF.

IRRT International Relations Round Table. Contact ALA (American Library Association).

IRS Internal Revenue Service. Internal Revenue Service Bldg, 1111 Constitution Ave, NW, Washington, DC 20224. Maintains a tax law library.

IRS International Referral System for Sources of Environmental Information. United Nations Environment Program, Box 30552, Nairobi, Kenya. Established in 1976. Provides computerized searches, conducts seminars and publishes documents.

IRT Institute of Reprographic Technology. 13 Gillingham St, London SW1, England.

IRUC Information and Research Utilization Center. Physical Education and Recreation for the Handicapped, 1201 16th St, NW, Washington, DC 20036. Prepares special packets of resource materials on topics of current interest in the field of physical education and recreation for the handicapped.

IS Information Science.

IS Information Separator. A control character used to indicate boundaries of information.

ISA *Indian Science Abstracts*. V. 1, 1965. Published by the Indian National Scientific Documentation Center.

ISA *Information Science Abstracts*. V. 1, 1966. Published by Documentation Abstracts. Formerly *DA* (*Documentation Abstracts*).

ISA Instrument Society of America. 400 Stanwix St, Pittsburgh, PA 15222. Established in 1945. Constituent society of AFIPS. Publishes several journals, a product directory and books.

ISA *Irregular Serials and Annuals*. 5th ed. New York: R. R. Bowker Co, 1978.

ISAARE Information System for Adaptive, Assistive and Recreational Equipment. United Cerebral Palsy Association of Oregon, 7117 Southeast Harold St, Portland, OR 97206. This system was established in 1969 to provide information flow between equipment manufacturers and programs serving the handicapped.

ISAD Information Science and Automation Division. A division of ALA (American Library Association) that changed its name to LITA in 1978.

ISAD/AVS ISAD Audio Visual Section. *See* LITA/AVS.

ISAD/VCCS ISAD Video and Cable Communications Section. *See* LITA/VCCS.

ISAM Indexed Sequential Access Method. Method of direct access developed by IBM.

ISAR Information Storage and Retrieval.

ISAS Information Science and Automation Section. *See* LITA/ISAS.

ISAW International Society of Aviation Writers. 15 Liszt Gate, No. 407, Willowdale, ON, Canada.

ISBD International Standard Bibliographic Description. A group of standards specifying requirements for the bibliographic description of publications such as monographs, serials, cartographic and audiovisual material and other nonbook material. Assigns an order to the descriptive elements and specifies a punctuation system for the description. *See* Committee on Cataloging, IFLA. *International Standard Bibliographic Description Recommended . . . Copenhagen, 1969*. London: The Committee, 1971.

ISBD (A/V) International Standard Bibliographic Description for Audiovisual Materials. *See* ISBD.

ISBD (CM) International Standard Bibliographic Description for Cartographic Materials. *See* ISBD.

ISBD (M) International Standard Bibliographic Description for Monographic Publications. *See* ISBD.

ISBD (NBM) International Standard Bibliographic Description for Non-Book Materials. *See* ISBD.

ISBD (S) International Standard Bibliographic Description for Serials. *See* ISBD.

ISBN International Standard Book Number. A number that is assigned to every book before publication to identify publisher, title, edition and volume number. Assigned by national standard book numbering agencies, such as the R. R. Bowker Co. in the US and the jointly sponsored Standard Book Numbering Agency Ltd. in the UK.

ISD Information Services Division. Honeywell, 2701 Fourth Ave. South, Minneapolis, MN 55408.

ISDS International Serials Data System. International Center for the ISDS, 20 rue Bachaumont, F-75002 Paris, France. Established in 1973. A cooperative international register (computerized data base) created to provide identification and control of serial publications throughout the world. Coordinates the assignment of ISSNs through national and regional centers, such as NSDP in the US, who report serial records to the IC/ISDS. Supported by UNISIST.

ISFA International Scientific Film Association. 38 avenue des Ternes, Paris 17, France.

ISFL International Scientific Film Library. 31 rue Vautier, Brussels 4, Belgium.

ISI Indian Standards Institution. Nanak Bhavan, 9 Bahadur Shak Zafar Marg, New Delhi 1, India. Issues English-language standards. Affiliated with ISO (International Standards Organization).

ISI Institute for Scientific Information. 325 Chestnut St, Philadelphia, PA 19106. Publisher of *ANSA, SCI, SSCI* and other indexes. Also provides direct information services to researchers.

ISI Iron and Steel Industry. 4 Little Essex St, London WC2, England. Sponsors BISITS.

ISIC International Standard Industrial Classification. Used by UN Statistical Office for ICPDATA.

ISIRI Institute of Standards and Industrial Research of Iran. Ministry of Economy, Box 2937, Tehran, Iran. Issues English-language standards. Affiliated with ISO (International Standards Organization).

ISIS Integrated Set of Information Systems. An ILO computer program package permitting entry of data via visual display terminals into computer storage and instantaneous access to various files.

ISI TB Iron and Steel Industry Training Board. 4 Little Essex St, London WC2, England.

ISL Information Systems Laboratory. An interactive language for information retrieval and string manipulation used at the University of Pennsylvania.

ISLIC Israel Society for Special Libraries and Information Centers. Box 16271, Tel Aviv, Israel.

ISMEC Information Service in Mechanical Engineering. Data Courier Inc, 620 South Fifth St, Louisville, KY 40202. Coverage from 1973. Bibliographic data base covering mechanical and production engineering and engineering management.

ISO Information Systems Office. Contact LC.

ISO International Standards Organization. One rue de Varembé, 1211 Geneva 20, Switzerland. Aim is to develop standards facilitating international exchange of goods and services and cooperation in intellectual, scientific, technological and economic activity. Has liaison with more than 200 organizations. Also referred to as IOS (International Organization for Standardization).

ISORID International Information System on Research in Documentation. UNESCO, 7 Place de Fontenoy, F-75700 Paris, France. Established in 1972. A UNESCO project that collects and disseminates information on research projects in documentation. See *UNESCO Bulletin for Libraries* 27 (Sept.–Oct. 1973): 293.

ISR *Index to Scientific Reviews*. V. 1, 1974. Published by ISI (Institute for Scientific Information).

ISR Information Storage and Retrieval. Also known as ISAR.

ISR *Interdisciplinary Science Reviews*. V. 1, 1976. Published by Heyden & Son, Ltd.

ISRD International Society for Rehabilitation of the Disabled/ Rehabilitation International. 122 East 23 St, New York, NY 10010. Maintains a library.

ISRU International Scientific Radio Union. *See* URSI (Union Radio–Scientifique Internationale).

ISSC International Social Science Council. 6 rue Franklin, Paris 16, France.

ISSHP *Index to Social Sciences and Humanities Proceedings*. V. 1, 1979. Published by ISI (Institute for Scientific Information). ISSHP is trademarked.

ISSN International Standard Serial Number. An internationally accepted code number for the identification of serial publications. ISSNs are assigned by regional and national centers of the ISDS network.

ISTIM Inter-change of Scientific and Technical Information in Machine Language. Task group appointed in 1967 by OST (US Office of Science and

Technology). Objectives related to standardization of data elements and tape formats. *See* Stella Keenan. "Abstracting and Indexing Services in Science and Technology." *ARIST* 4 (1969): 271-298.

ISTP *Index to Scientific and Technical Proceedings*. V. 1, 1978. Published by ISI (Institute for Scientific Information). Annual covering proceedings in all major disciplines of science and engineering.

IT Internal Translator. Programming language translator for use on the IBM 650 computer.

ITA Independent Television Authority. Name changed to IBA (Independent Broadcasting Authority).

ITA Institute du Transport Aerien. 4 rue de Solferino, 75007 Paris, France. Produces a data base on air transportation.

ITCA Independent Television Companies Association, Ltd. Knighton House, 52-66 Mortimer St, London W1, England.

ITIRC IBM Technical Information Retrieval Center. The acronym applied by IBM to its libraries and information retrieval centers. Also known as TIRC (Technical Information Retrieval Center).

ITI/US International Theatre Institute of the United States. 1860 Broadway, New York, NY 10023. Established in 1948. US branch of the International Theatre Institute. Maintains a library and publishes documents.

ITN Independent Television News, Ltd. Television House, Kingsway, London WC2, England.

ITPP Institute of Technical Publicity and Publications. c/o College of Art, Hillcrest, Radford Rd, Conventry, Warwickshire, England.

ITS Invitation to Send. Western Union terminology. A character transmitted to a remote teletypewriter terminal that polls its tape transmitter.

ITT International Telephone and Telegraph Corporation. 320 Park Ave, New York, NY 10022. Maintains a telecommunications library established in 1947.

ITU International Telecommunications Union. Place des Nations 1211, Geneva 20, Switzerland. An intergovernmental organization and an agency of the UN established to provide standards of communications procedures and practices on a worldwide basis, including the allocation of radio frequencies. *See also* WARC.

ITVA International Industrial Television Association. 29 South St, New Providence, NJ 07974. Established in 1973. Seeks to advance the use of television in business training.

IU Information Unlimited. 2510 Channing Way #3, Box 4185, Berkeley, CA 94704. Provides information gathering and indexing services.

IUC Interuniversity Council of the North Texas Area. Box 688, Richardson, TX 75080. Thirteen libraries cooperate through ILL, duplicate exchange center, private line teletype and exchange privileges.

IUG Intercomm User Group. c/o R. D. Stone, Box 1452, Canoga, CA 91304. Established in 1971. Serves as a clearinghouse on technical information.

IUHPS International Union of the History and Philosophy of Science. 12 rue Colbert, Paris 2, France.

IULC Inter-University Library Council. Ohio State University Library, Columbus, OH 43210. Consortium of 12 state-assisted university libraries of Ohio.

IULC-RAILS IULC Reference and Interlibrary Loan Service. Established by IULC in 1969. *See* James C. Schmidt and Kay Shaffer. "A Cooperative Interlibrary Loan Service for the State-Assisted University Libraries in Ohio." *C&RL* 32 (May 1971): 197-204.

IUPAB International Union of Pure and Applied Biophysics. Refer to latest issue of their publication *Quarterly Review of Biophysics*. Established in 1961.

IUPAP International Union of Pure and Applied Physics. Contact secretary. Sponsors international physics meetings.

IUR International University of Radiophonics and Television. 116

avenue du President Kennedy, Paris 16, France.

IVMB Internationale Vereinigung der Musikbibliotheken. *See* AIBM/IAML/IVMB.

IWG International Writers Guild. 7 Harley St, London W1, England.

IWIM Institut für Wissenschaftsinformation in der Medizin. Schumannstrasse 20-21, Postfach 140, 104 Berlin, Federal Republic of Germany. Established in 1973.

IWPA International Word Processing Association. AMS Bldg, Willow Grove, PA 19090. Established in 1972.

IWWG International Women's Writing Guild. Box 810, Gracie Sta, New York, NY 10028. Holds annual women's writing conference/retreat.

JAALD Japanese Association of Agricultural Librarians and Documentalists. 29-31 Sakuragaoka, Shibuya, Tokyo 150, Japan. Established in 1956. Publishes an index and cooperates with AGRIS and AGLINET.

JAAMI *Journal of the Association for the Advancement of Medical Instrumentation.* V. 1, 1967. Published by the Association for the Advancement of Medical Instrumentation. Also known as *Medical Instrumentation Journal.*

JAB *Journal of Applied Bacteriology.* V. 1, 1938. Published by Academic Press for the Society of Applied Bacteriology.

JACM *Journal of the Association for Computing Machinery.* V. 1, 1954. Published by the Association for Computing Machinery.

JACS Journal Article Copy Service. A program begun in 1978 as a means for businesses and other NTIS customers to acquire copies of journal articles listed with government agencies. Canceled in 1979 due to insufficient demand.

JACS *Journal of the American Chemical Society.* V. 1, 1879. Published by the American Chemical Society.

JAICI Japan Association for International Chemical Information. The Chemical Society of Japan Building, 1-5 Kanda, Surugadai, Chiyoda-ku, Tokyo 101, Japan.

JAKIS Japanese Keyword Indexing Simulator.

JAMASS Japanese Medical Abstract Scanning System. System of the International Medical Information Center in Japan.

JAPIC Japan Pharmaceutical Information Center. Fujimoto, Rihei, Japan. Has maintained an abstracting card system since 1972.

JASIS *Journal of the American Society for Information Science.* V. 21, 1970. Published by John Wiley. Formerly *AD* (*American Documentation*).

JBC *Journal of Biological Chemistry.* V. 1, 1905. Published by the American Society of Biological Chemists.

JBI Jugoslovenski Bibliografiski Institut (Yugoslav Bibliographic Institute). Terazija 26, YU-11000, Belgrade, Yugoslavia.

JBIA Jewish Braille Institute of America. 110 East 30 St, New York, NY 10016. Established in 1931. Maintains a free circulating Jewish Braille library and publishes a Hebrew Braille Bible.

JCCC Joint Committee on Cataloging and Classification Codes. *See* CNLIA/JCCC.

JCCPI Joint Committee on Copyright Practice and Implementation. *See* CNLIA/JCCPI.

JCD *Journal of Chemical Documentation.* V. 1, 1961. Published by the American Chemical Society. Title changed to *Journal of Chemical Information and Computer Sciences* in 1975.

JCEB Joint Council on Educational Broadcasting. Name changed to JCET.

JCET Joint Council on Educational Telecommunications. 1126 16th St, NW, Washington, DC 20036. Established in 1950. Publishes documents. Formerly JCEB.

JCIT Jerusalem Conference on Information Technology. Box 7170, Jerusalem, Israel. Met August 16-20, 1971. Produced *Proceedings of the JCIT.* Jerusalem: ILTAM Corp. for Planning and Research, 1971, 2 vols.

JCL Job-Control Language. A high-level programming language to code job-control statements identifying a job to an operating system.

JCLS Junior College Libraries Section. *See* ACRL/JCLS.

JCNAAF Joint Canadian Navy-Army-Air Force Specification. Name changed to CAMESA.

JCP Joint Committee on Printing. A congressional committee which acts as the supervising body over the GPO.

JCPI Joint Committee on Paleontologic Information. Established by AGI (American Geological Institute) in 1968 to standardize paleontological data storage.

JCR *Journal Citation Reports*. Philadelphia, PA: Institute for Scientific Information, 1979. Statistical tables that make it possible to examine characteristics of individual journals.

JCTND Jugoslovenski Centar za Techničku i Naučno Dokumentacijua (Yugoslav Center for Technical and Scientific Documentation). S. Penezica-Krena 29, Postanski fah 724, Belgrade, Yugoslavia. Established in 1949.

JEIPAC JICST Electronic Information Processing Automatic Computer. Located at JICST.

JEL *Journal of Education for Librarianship*. V. 1, 1960. Official journal of the Association of American Library Schools.

JETS Junior Engineering Technical Society. United Engineering Center, 345 East 47 St, New York, NY 10017. Established in 1950. Formerly Junior Engineering Training for Schools.

JGC *Journal of General Chemistry*. V. 1, 1931. The English translation of the USSR publication *Zhurnal Obshchei Khimii*.

JGR *Journal of Geophysical Research*. V. 1, 1896. Official publication of the American Geophysical Union.

JIBF Jerusalem International Book Fair. A biennial book fair held in Jerusalem in April.

JIC Joint Industrial Council of Printing and Allied Trades. 11 Bedford Row, London WC1, England.

JICNARS Joint Industrial Committee for National Readership Surveys. 44 Belgrave Sq, London SW1, England. Established in 1968 as successor to the National Readership Surveys Controlling Committee. Set up under the authority of four organizations, among them NPA (Newspapers Publishers' Association) and PPA.

JICST Japan Information Center for Science and Technology. 5-2-2-chome, Nagatoya, Tiyoda-ku KIA 052, Tokyo, Japan.

JICTAR Joint Industry Committee for Television Advertising Research. 44 Belgrave Sq, London SW1, England.

JIRC *Journal of International Research Communications*. V. 1, 1973. Published by International Research Communications System, Lancaster, England.

JISC Japanese Industrial Standards Committee. Agency of Industrial Science and Technology, Ministry of International Trade and Industry, 3-1 Kasumigaseki, 1 Chiyodaku, Tokyo, Japan. Issues English-language standards. Affiliated with ISO (International Standards Organization).

JLA Jamaica Library Association. Contact president. Established in 1950. Members represent Jamaica and England. *See* Joyce L. Robinson. "Jamaica, Libraries in" in *Encyclopedia of Library and Information Science*, ed. by Allen Kent et al. New York: Marcel Dekker, 1975, V. 13, pp. 169–205.

JLA Japan Library Association (Nippon Toshokan Kyokai). 1-10, 1-chome, Taishido, Setagaya-ku, Tokyo, Japan. Established in 1892. Founded as Nippon Bunko Kyokai. *See* Hatsuo Nakamura. "Japan Library Association" in *Encyclopedia of Library and Information Science*, ed. by Allen Kent et al. New York: Marcel Dekker, 1975, V. 13, pp. 238–247.

JLA Jordan Library Association. Box 6289, Amman, Jordan. Established in 1963. Has published the national bibliography from 1900. *See* Karnel Asali. "The Jordanian Library Scene, 1973: Libraries in Jordan." *International Library Review* 6 (1974): 171–183.

JLH *Journal of Library History.* V. 1, 1966. Published by the School of Library Science, Florida State University, Tallahassee. Name changed to *Journal of Library History, Philosophy, and Comparative Librarianship* in 1972.

JMRT Junior Members Round Table. Contact ALA (American Library Association).

JNUL Jewish National and University Library. Hebrew University Campus, Box 503, Jerusalem, Israel.

JOLA *Journal of Library Automation.* V. 1, 1968. Official journal of LITA.

JOSS Johnniac Open-Shop System. A time-sharing language developed by the Rand Corp. to make calculations too complicated for a calculator.

JPRS Joint Publications Research Service. 5285 Port Royal Rd, Springfield, VA 22161. A division of NTIS that translates and abstracts foreign-language political and technical publications for federal agencies. Most JPRS reports are concerned with publications of Communist countries. Also known as USJPRS.

JRC Majlis al-Bahth al-'Ilmi (Jordan Research Council). Box 6070, Amman, Jordan.

JSA Japanese Standards Association. 1-24 Akasaka 4 Minato-Ku, Tokyo, Japan. Member of ISO (International Standards Organization).

JSC Joint Steering Committee. *See* JSCAACR.

JSCAACR Joint Steering Committee for the Revision of the Anglo-American Cataloging Rules. A five-member committee with representatives from ALA (American Library Association), BL (British Library), CLA (Canadian Library Association), LA and LC.

JSCLCBS Joint Standing Committee on Library Cooperation and Bibliographic Services. Committee of the library associations of Malaysia and Singapore.

JSLS Japan Society of Library Science (Nippon Toshokan Gakkai). Contact president or JLA (Japan Library Association). Established in 1953. Publishes documents.

JUG Joint Users Group. Any group of computer users sharing common interests, software and computers.

JUL Joint University Libraries. An association of university libraries in Nashville, TN. Disbanded in 1979.

JUSTIFY A utility computer program available from NBS. *See* EDPAC.

JWB Jewish Welfare Board. 15 East 26 St, New York, NY 10010. Sponsors the Jewish Book Council.

K Kilo.

K Thousand. Used in speaking of computer capacity, e.g., 32 K words of memory means 32,000 words of computer memory. Sometimes K means 1,024, or 2 to the tenth power, since computer memory is often arranged in powers of 2. Also means 1,000 dollars.

KANEDCO Kansas–Nebraska Educational Consortium. c/o Colby Community College, Colby, KS 67701. Eighteen junior colleges cooperate with ILL.

KASC Knowledge Availability Systems Center. University of Pittsburgh, Pittsburgh, PA 15261.

KB Keyboard Button.

KBF Kommunale Bibliotekarers Forening (Association of Municipal Librarians). Contact president (Norway). Established in 1957. Publishes documents.

KBS Korean Bureau of Standards. Ministry of Commerce and Industry, 1-19 Chong-Ro, Seoul, Republic of Korea. Issues English-language standards. Affiliated with ISO (International Standards Organization).

KCRCHE Kansas City Regional Council for Higher Education. 4343 Oak St, Kansas City, MO 64111. Twenty member libraries maintain a Periodicals Microfilm Bank of periodicals indexed in *Reader's Guide, Social Science and Humanities Index* and *Education Index* from 1955 to date.

KCS One Thousand Characters per Second. Generally accepted measurement of data transmission speed.

KENCLIP Kentucky Cooperative Library Information Project. c/o Western

Kentucky University, Cravens Graduate Center, Office 502, Bowling Green, KY 42101. Nine college libraries cooperate through ILL.

KETAL Kalamazoo (Et Al) Library Consortium. c/o Waldo Library, Western Michigan University, Kalamazoo, MI 49008. Twenty-eight public, academic and special libraries cooperate through ILL and union list of serials.

KIAC Kerr Industrial Applications Center. Southeastern Oklahoma State University, Station A, Durant, OK 74701. Library established in 1964. Part of NASA Technology Transfer Network. Formerly TUSC.

KIC Kansas Information Circuit. Kansas State Library, State Capitol Bldg, Topeka, KS 66612. Consortium established in 1965. Uses teletype equipment to facilitate ILL.

KIP Knowledge Industry Publications, Inc. 2 Corporate Park Dr, White Plains, NY 10604.

KISS Keep It Simple Sir. A computer-related term used with programming.

KKL Kirjastonhoitajien Keskusliitto-Bibliothekariers Centralförbund (Central Federation of Librarians). Museokatu 18 A, SF 00100, Helsinki 10, Finland. Established in 1967. Publishes documents. *See* R. Sievanen-Allen. "Finland, Libraries in" in *Encyclopedia of Library and Information Science*, ed. by A. Kent et al. New York: Marcel Dekker, 1971, V. 8, pp. 477-487.

KKL Kommunale Kinematografers Landsforbund (National Association of Municipal Cinemas in Norway). Nedre Vollgt 9, Oslo 1, Norway. Established in 1917. Association of film exhibitors. Publishes documents.

KLA Kansas Library Association. Contact president or ALA (American Library Association).

KLA Kentucky Library Association. Contact president or ALA (American Library Association).

KLA Korean Library Association (Hanguk Tosogwan Hyophoe). 100 1-Ka,

Hoenyun-Dong, Chung-Ku, Box 2041, Seoul, Korea. Established in 1945. Affiliated with IFLA. Publishes documents. Korean acronym is TOHYOP. *See* G. Koh. "Korea, Libraries in the Republic of" in *Encyclopedia of Library and Information Science*, ed. by A. Kent et al. New York: Marcel Dekker, 1975, V. 13, pp. 455-496.

KLIC Key Letter in Context.

KLSS Korean Library Science Society. c/o Ewha Woman's University Library, Seoul 120, Korea. Established in 1970. Publishes documents. *See* "Korean Library Science Society." *Bibliography, Documentation, Terminology* 12 (July 1972): 178.

KMA Kinematograph Manufacturers Association. 3 Soho Sq, London W1, England.

KNMP Royal Dutch Pharmaceutical Society. Alexanderstraat 11, The Hague, the Netherlands. Established in 1971. Produces a data base (Royal Dutch Pharmaceutical Society Databank) and publishes documents.

KNUB Koninklijke Nederlandse Uitgeversbond. Herengracht 209, Amsterdam, the Netherlands. Established in 1880. Association of publishers. Publishes documents.

KOMRL Kentucky, Ohio, Michigan Regional Medical Library. *See* KOMRML.

KOMRML Kentucky, Ohio, Michigan Regional Medical Library. c/o Shiffman Medical Library, 4325 Brush St, Detroit, MI 48201. One of NLM's Regional Medical Libraries (Region V). Also known as KOMRL. *See* Faith Van Toll. "Kentucky–Ohio–Michigan Regional Medical Library Program." *NLM News* 33 (Oct.–Nov. 1978): 7.

KORSTIC Korean Scientific and Technological Information Center. Box 1229, 2, Waryong-dong, Chongo-ku, Seoul, Korea.

KP Key Punch.

KPIC Key Phrase in Context. A method of indexing.

KPO Key Punch Operator.

KSR Keyboard Send/Receive. Teletypewriter transceiver having transmission capability only from a keyboard.

KWIC Key Word in Context. Method of indexing by listing titles in permuted form and then alphabetizing.

KWIC, Double Double Key Word in Context. *See* A. E. Petrarca and W. M. Lay. "The Double KWIC Coordinate Index." *Journal of Chemical Documentation* 9 (Nov. 1969): 256-261.

KWIT Key Word in Title. A method of indexing.

KWOC Key Word Out of Context. A method of indexing.

LA The Library Association. 7 Ridgmount St, London WC1E 7AE, England. Established in 1877 as The Library Association of the United Kingdom. Publishes numerous journals, indexes and reports.

LAA Library Association of Alberta. Box 5739, Stn. L, Edmonton AB T6C 4G2, Canada.

LAA Library Association of Australia. 32 Belvoir St, Surry Hills, New South Wales 2010, Australia. Formerly (1949) the Australian Institute of Librarians.

LAB Library Association of Barbados. Box 827E, Bridgetown, Barbados. Established in 1968.

LAC Library Advisory Council for England. c/o Dept. of Education and Science, Elizabeth House, 39 York Rd, London SE1, England. Established in 1965 under the Public Libraries and Museums Act of 1964 to advise the Secretary of State for Education and Science.

LAC Library Advisory Council for Wales and Monmouthshire. c/o Dept. of Education and Science, Education Office for Wales, 31 Cathedral Rd, Cardiff CF1 9UJ, Wales. Established in 1965 under the Public Libraries and Museums Act of 1964 to advise the Secretary of State for Education and Science.

LACASIS Los Angeles Chapter of ASIS. Contact president or ASIS.

LACOIN Lowell Area Council on Interlibrary Networks. Northeastern University, Suburban Campus–Library, South Bedford Rd, Burlington, MA 01803. Sixteen academic, special and public libraries operate a radio station (WLTI- FM) and maintain a union list of serials.

LACUNY Library Association of the City University of New York. Contact chairperson.

LAD Library Administration Division. A division of ALA (American Library Association) that changed its name to LAMA in 1978.

LADB Laboratory Animal Data Bank. Developed for NLM by Battelle Columbus Laboratories, Columbus, OH. Projected as a three-year effort and begun in late 1975 to develop a computerized data bank to make the management of information on research using animals more effective.

LAD/BES LAD Buildings and Equipment Section. *See* LAMA/BES.

LAD/CSS LAD Circulation Services System. *See* LAMA/CSS.

LAD/LOMS LAD Library Organization and Management Section. *See* LAMA/LOMS.

LAD/PAS LAD Personnel Administration Section. *See* LAMA/PAS.

LAD/PRS LAD Public Relations Section. *See* LAMA/PRS.

LADSIRLAC Liverpool and District Scientific, Industrial and Research Library Advisory Council. Central Libraries, William Brown St, Liverpool L3 8EW, England.

LAECS *Latin American Executive Compensation Survey.* Published annually by Business International Corp.

LAI Library Association of Ireland. 46 Grafton St, Dublin 2, Ireland. Established in 1928. Affiliated with IFLA. Publishes documents. *See* E. Power. "Ireland, Libraries in" in *Encyclopedia of Library and Information Science*, ed. by A. Kent et al. New York: Marcel Dekker, 1975, V. 13, pp. 67-81.

LAL Latin American Library. Oakland Public Library, 1900 Fruitvale Ave,

Oakland, CA 94601. Library established in 1966.

LAMA Library Administration and Management Association. 50 East Huron St, Chicago, IL 60611. A division of ALA (American Library Association). Formerly (1978) LAD.

LAMA/BES LAMA Buildings and Equipment Section. Contact LAMA. A section of LAMA, which is a division of ALA (American Library Association).

LAMA/CSS LAMA Circulation Services Section. Contact LAMA. A section of LAMA, which is a division of ALA (American Library Association).

LAMA/LOMS LAMA Library Organization and Management Section. Contact LAMA. A section of LAMA, which is a division of ALA (American Library Association).

LAMA/PAS LAMA Personnel Administration Section. Contact LAMA. A section of LAMA, which is a division of ALA (American Library Association).

LAMA/PRS LAMA Public Relations Section. Contact LAMA. A section of LAMA, which is a division of ALA (American Library Association).

LAMA/SS LAMA Statistics Section. Contact LAMA. A section of LAMA, which is a division of ALA (American Library Association).

LAMP Library Additions and Maintenance Program. Honeywell programs that maintain the library of subroutines and microroutines available through the ARGUS and EASY assembly systems.

LAMSAC Local Authorities Management Services and Computer Committee. Eaton House, 66a Eaton Sq, London Sw1, England. Established in 1967 by agreement between local authorities' associations in England, Wales and Scotland to replace the Local Government Computer Committee formed in 1965. Goals are to guide future research, to stimulate and coordinate cooperative enterprises and research and to collect and disseminate information among constituent members.

LANDSAT A system of aerial photography and imagery collection centers that is

part of the US Geological Survey. Information from LANDSAT satellites is distributed through the EROS Data Center. Formerly ERTS.

LAO/ABO Library Association of Ottawa/Association des Bibliothèques d'Ottawa. Contact president.

LAOSA Librarianship and Archives Old Students Association. University College London, 14 Devereux Dr, Watford, Hertfordshire, England.

LAPL Los Angeles Public Library. 630 West Fifth St, Los Angeles, CA 90071.

LARC Library Automation Research and Consulting. (The LARC Association.) Absorbed by WISE in 1975.

LARITA Lewis Audiovisual Research Institute and Teaching Archive. University of Arizona, 1325 East Speedway, Tucson, AZ 85721. Largest single collection of taped oral history materials.

LARS Laboratory for Applications of Remote Sensing. Purdue University, 1220 Potter Dr, West Lafayette, IN 47906. Maintains a photographic library.

LARTS Los Angeles Regional Transportation Study. Division of Highways, Terminal Annex, Los Angeles, CA 90045. Data from the study were used in the production of a transportation data base.

LAS Library Association of Singapore. c/o National Library, Stamford Rd, Singapore 6, Singapore. Established in 1972. English title was adopted as the official name.

LASER Light Amplification by Stimulated Emission of Radiation.

LASER London and South Eastern Library Region. 9/10 Alfred Pl, London WC1E 7EB, England. Consortium established in 1969. Member libraries cooperate through ILL and other resource-sharing measures. *See also* COLA.

LASIE Library Automated Systems Information Exchange. Executive Officer, Box 581, New South Wales 2100, Australia.

LATT Library Association of Trinidad and Tobago. Box 1177, Port of Spain, Established in 1960.

LAUC Librarians Association of the University of California. Includes as members all librarians of the University of California.

LB Library Bureau. 801 Park Ave, Herkimer, NY 13350. Supplies library furniture, equipment and supplies.

LBI Library Binding Institute. 50 Congress St, Boston, MA 02109. Members are bookbinders and suppliers to the bookbinding industry interested in maintaining standards in binding technique.

LC Library of Congress. 10 First St, SE, Washington, DC 20540.

LCA Library Club of America. This association has been terminated.

LCC Library of Congress Classification.

LCCN Library of Congress Card Number. The serially assigned number applied to cataloging copy by LC. In some retrieval systems, searching can be done by LCCN. Also known as LCN.

LCER *Library Computer Equipment Review.* (Journal). V. 1, 1979. Published by Microform Review, Inc.

LCGC Library Council of Greater Cleveland. Cuyahoga County Public Library Headquarters, 4510 Memphis Ave, Cleveland, OH 44144. Consortium established in 1969.

LCLA Lutheran Church Library Association. 122 West Franklin Ave, Minneapolis, MN 55404.

LCN Library of Congress Card Number. *See* LCCN.

LCOMM Library Council of Metropolitan Milwaukee. 814 West Wisconsin Ave, Milwaukee, WI 53233. One hundred twenty-five academic, public, school and special libraries cooperate through coordinated acquisitions, ILL and other services.

LCSH *Library of Congress Subject Headings.* 8th ed. Washington, DC: Library of Congress, Subject Cataloging Div, Processing Dept, 1975. 2 vols. Incorporates material through 1973; kept up-to-date by quarterly supplements.

LD Committee on Linguistics in Documentation. *See* FID/LD.

LDA Lead Development Association. 34 Berkeley Sq, London W1X 6AJ, England. Maintains a library.

LDRI Low Data-Rate Input.

LDTF Local Documents Task Force. *See* GODORT/LDTF.

LDX Long Distance Xerography. Name used by Xerox Corp. to identify its high-speed facsimile system. The system uses Xerox terminal equipment and a wide-band data communication channel.

LEAA Law Enforcement Assistance Administration. 633 Indiana Ave, NW, Washington, DC 20531. Finances computer applications in law enforcement. Library established in 1970.

LEADER Lehigh Automatic Device for Efficient Retrieval. Center for the Information Sciences, Lehigh University, Bethlehem, PA 18105.

LEADS Library Employment and Development for Staff. Section of *American Libraries* providing information useful to both job seekers and employers. Features brief articles, announcements on library employment, staff development, educational opportunities, career outlooks and other related topics.

LEADS Library Experimental Automated Demonstration System. Oregon Total Information System, 354 East 40 St, Eugene, OR 97405. Experiment (1968–1971) in an education district to automate acquisitions, cataloging and processing of all materials; and, ultimately, to produce a printed catalog. Beginning of a statewide information bank.

LEAP Library Exchange Aids Patrons Project. North Haven Memorial Libraries, North Haven, CT 06473. A computerized circulation and resource-sharing control system begun by several Connecticut libraries in 1978.

LEARN Librarians in Education and Research in the Northeast. Established in 1974. A group of education librarians in the Boston area.

LED Library Education Division. A division of ALA (American Library Association) that was dissolved in 1978 and replaced by SCOLE.

LED Light-Emitting Diode.

LEEDS Library Exemplary Elementary
Demonstration of Springfield. Oregon
Total Information System, 354 East 40
St, Eugene, OR 97405. *See* John R. Blair
and Ruby Snyder. "An Automated
Library System Project: LEEDS."
American Libraries 1 (Feb. 1970):
172–173.

LEER Libros Elementales Educativos
Recreativos (Elementary Books for
Education and Recreation). Contact
OLDP. Sponsored by Books for the
People Fund, Inc, in collaboration with
OAS under a grant from NEH.

LEPU Library Education and Personnel
Utilization. A policy adopted by ALA
(American Library Association) in 1970.
Number 54.1 of the Sept. 1978 *Policy
Manual.*

LES Library Education Section. *See*
CLA/LES.

LESS Least-cost Estimating and Scheduling
System. A management procedure
developed by IBM.

LETIS Leicestershire Technical Information
Service. c/o Loughborough University
of Technology, Loughborough,
Leicestershire, England.

LETS Law Enforcement Teletype System.
A national switching station in Phoenix,
AZ, relays messages to all mainland
states in the US.

LEXIS Mead Technology Laboratories,
DATA/CENTRAL, Mead Corp, 200
Park Ave, New York, NY 10017.
Established in 1973. An on-line, full-text
legal information storage and retrieval
system.

LEXR Legislazione Regionale. Centro
Elettronico di Documentazione—
Italgiure, Corte Suprema di Cassaziono,
Palazzo di Giustizia, Via Ulpiano 8,
Rome 00193, Italy. Coverage from 1971.
Full-text data base covering regional laws
of Italy.

LF Line Feed. Control character that causes
print or display position to be advanced
to the next line.

LF Low Frequency. Frequencies between
30 and 300 kilohertz.

LGIO Local Government Information
Office. 36 Old Queen St, London SW1,
England.

LIB Lard Information Bureau. 51
Beauchamp Pl, London SW3, England.

LIBCON System Development Corp, 2500
Colorado Ave, Santa Monica, CA 90406.
Coverage from 1968. Bibliographic data
base containing citations to
monographic and nonprint material
cataloged by LC in Roman alphabet
languages. Includes MARC records.

LIBER Ligue des Bibliothèques
Européennes de Recherche (Association
of European Research Libraries).
Contact president. Established in 1971.
Affiliated with IFLA.

LIBGIS Library General Information
Survey. Federal system of collecting
basic library statistics on a state-by-state
basis.

LIBNAT Library Network Analysis Theory.
A project for network design undertaken
by the Reference Round Table of the
Texas Library Association and the
Texas State Advisory Council. *See* M.
Duggan. *Journal of Library Automation*
2 (Sept. 1969): 157.

LIBRIS Library Information Service. A
service of Baker & Taylor which
provides COM service to convert
catalog cards to microform for
computerized microfilm catalogs.

LIBRIS Library Information System. Kungl
Biblioteket, Box 5039, Stockholm
S-10241, Sweden. Consortium
established in 1972. Fourteen libraries
share on-line cataloging.

L'ICIST L'Institut Canadien de
l'Information Scientifique et Technique.
See CISTI/ICIST.

LID Literaturdienst Medizin. Austrian
Federal Institute for Public Health,
Stubenring 6, A-1010 Vienna, Austria.
Established in 1973. Provides
retrospective data base searches in the
fields of biology, medicine and
psychology.

LIDOK Zentraler Datenpool der
Kooperativen Agrardokumentation.
Zentralstelle für Agrardokumentation
und Information, Bundesministerium für
Ernahrung, Landswirtschaft und

Forsten, Konstantinstrasse 110, D-5300 Bonn 2, Federal Republic of Germany. Coverage from 1950. Bibliographic data base of agricultural sciences, horticulture and plant diseases.

LIFO Last In First Out. Refers to establishing priorities in the order of data handling. An accounting term.

LIFT Logically Integrated FORTRAN Translator. A source-language translator that accepts a FORTRAN II source-language program as input, performs a translation and outputs a source-language program acceptable to any FORTRAN IV compiler.

LILIBU Lista de Libros para Bibliotecos Universitarias. A multinational project started in 1973 and funded by several foundations and by CRL, OAS and UNESCO. Based at the University of Antioguia, Colombia. Purpose is to develop a basic acquisitions list for university libraries.

LILO Last In Last Out. *See* LIFO.

LILRC Long Island Library Resources Council. Box 31, Bellport, NY 11713. One hundred twenty-two academic, public, medical and special libraries cooperate through ILL, direct access, data base searches and union list of serials.

LINC Laboratory Instrument Computer.

LINC Libraries for Nursing Consortium. c/o Peter Bent Brigham Hospital, School of Nursing Library, 300 Brookline Ave, Boston, MA 02115.

LINC Lincoln Laboratory Instrument Center. Massachusetts Institute of Technology, Lincoln Laboratory, Lexington, MA 02173.

LINCS Language Information Network and Clearinghouse System. Center for Applied Linguistics, 1717 Massachusetts Ave, NE, Washington, DC 20036. Purpose is to provide a framework for improving the basic communications patterns of language scientists.

LINOSCO Libraries of North Staffordshire in Cooperation. Central Library, Pall Mall, Hanley, Stoke-on-Trent, Staffordshire ST1 1HW, England.

LIP London International Press, Ltd. 3-4 Ludgate Circus Bldg, London EC4, England.

LIPL Linear Information Processing Language. A version of IPL, a high-order programming language.

LIRES Literature Retrieval System for the Pulp and Paper Industry. Institute of Paper Chemistry, 1043 East South St, Appleton, WI 54911; and Pulp and Paper Research Institute of Canada, Pointe Claire, Montreal, PQ, Canada. Full text, machine-readable tapes of *ABIPC*.

LIRT Library Instruction Round Table. Contact ALA (American Library Association). Begun in 1977.

LIS Library and Information Science.

LIS List and Index Society. Public Records Office, Chancery La, London WC2A 1LR, England. Established in 1965. Distributes, to members only, unpublished public records.

LISA *Library and Information Science Abstracts.* V. 1, 1969. Published jointly by the (British) Library Association and ASLIB. Superseded *LSA*.

LISA Library Information Systems Analysis.

LISE Libraries of the Institutes and Schools of Education. School of Education Library, University of Birmingham, Box 363, Birmingham 15, England.

LIS/MEX Library and Information Science Meetings Exchange, Massachusetts Bureau of Library Extension. A project that attempts to compile a meeting information file containing dates, locations and topics of meetings concerned with librarianship, information processing and nonprint media.

LISP List Processor. A standard programming language intended for list processing.

LISSA Librarians Serving San Antonio. Latin-American Librarian, Trinity University Library, San Antonio, TX 78207. Established in 1971. Group of librarians serving the inmates of Bexar County Jail on a volunteer basis.

LIST *Library and Information Science Today.* New York: Science Associates International, 1971–1973. Annual publication. Subtitle, 1975– : *Library and Information Services Today.*

LIST Library Information Service for Teeside. Central Library, Victoria Sq, Middlesbrough, Teeside, Yorkshire, England. Operated by the Cleveland Central Library, Middlesbrough, to provide access to information for libraries, firms and other organizations in the area.

LISTS Library Information System Time Sharing. Product of SDC (System Development Corporation), it is used by both school and special libraries. *See* C. McAllister. "On-line Library Housekeeping Systems." *Special Libraries* 62 (Nov. 1971): 457–468.

LITA Library and Information Technology Association. 50 East Huron St, Chicago, IL 60611. A division of ALA (American Library Association). Formerly (1978) ISAD.

LITA/AVS LITA Audio Visual Section. Contact LITA. A section of LITA, which is a division of ALA (American Library Association).

LITA/ISAS LITA Information Science and Automation Section. Contact LITA. A section of LITA, which is a division of ALA (American Library Association).

LITA/VCCS LITA Video and Cable Communications Section. Contact LITA. A section of LITA, which is a division of ALA (American Library Association). Formerly ISAD/VCCS.

LITE Legal Information Through Electronics. Training course sponsored by NAL (National Agricultural Library). The program was devised by USAF to disseminate information about retrieval of legal information through computers.

LJ *Library Journal.* V. 1, 1876. Published by R. R. Bowker Co.

LL *Library Literature.* (Index). V. 1, 1936. Published by H. W. Wilson Co.

LLA Lebanese Library Association. c/o National Library, Place de l'Étoile, Beirut, Lebanon. Established in 1960.

LLA Louisiana Library Association. Contact president or ALA (American Library Association).

LLBA *Language and Language Behavior Abstracts.* V. 1, 1967. Published by Sociological Abstracts, Inc. Originally published by CRLLB in collaboration with BELC (Bureau pour l'Enseignement de la Langue et de la Civilisation Françaises à l'Étranger).

LLE Leadership in Library Education. c/o School of Library Science, Florida State University, 625 North Adams St, Tallahassee, FL 32306. Formerly the Leadership Training Institute.

LLRC Library Learning Resource Center. Term sometimes applied to a library that has added audiovisual, microform and/or computer terminals to its traditional collections.

LMFBR Liquid Metal Fast Breeder Reactor. Cladding Information Center, Westinghouse Hanford Co, Hanford Engineering Development Laboratory, Box 1970, Richland, WA 99352. Sponsored by the Division of Reactor Development and Technology of the US Atomic Energy Commission to provide a central computerized data service for users of LMFBR data. The system traces materials and provides a broad base of engineering data for evaluation of cladding and fuel pin performance.

LMIC Liquid Metals Information Center. Box 1449, Canoga Park, CA 91304.

LMP *Literary Market Place.* New York: R. R. Bowker Co, 1940. An annual publication.

LMS Library Micrographic Services, Inc. 225 Park Ave South, Suite 614, New York, NY 10003.

LMTA Library Media Technical Assistant.

LNR Louisiana Numerical Register. A catalog that contains complete retrospective and current holdings for 11 libraries and current holdings for another 10 libraries in Louisiana, including the State Library, one public and 19 academic libraries.

LOB Line of Balance. A method for the measurement and control of management processes of libraries.

LOCAL Load on Call. Data placed in a storage unit which is available for inquiry.

LOCI Logarithmic Computing Instrument.

LOCNET Libraries of Orange County Network. 26 Civic Center Pl, Santa Ana, CA 92701. Eighty-one academic, school, public and special libraries cooperate through ILL, higher-level reference services, union lists and bibliography program.

LOEX Library Orientation Exchange. University Library, Eastern Michigan University, Ypsilanti, MI 48197. Developed to collect and organize information pertaining to orientation or library instruction in academic libraries.

LOGIC Local Government Information Control. 70 West Hidding St, San Jose, CA 95110. A body established by Santa Clara County to produce data bases on criminal justice, social welfare and urban development.

LOLA Library On-Line Acquisitions. *See* T. Burgess and L. Amer. *Washington State University: LOLA, Library On-Line Sub-system.* Pullman, WA: Washington State University Systems Office, July 1968.

LOLITA Library On-Line Information and Text Access. Oregon State University Library, Corvallis, OR 97330.

LOMS Library Organization and Management Section. *See* LAMA/LOMS.

LOPAC Liaison of Provincial Associations Committee. Contact chairperson. A committee of CLA. Each provincial school library association has one representative on the committee.

LP Linear Programming. Mathematical calculating technique concerned with the maximization or minimization of a linear function, some or all of whose variables are subject to a set of linear constraints.

LPD Language Processing and Debugging.

LPM Lines Per Minute.

LPRC Library Public Relations Council. 60 East 42 St, Suite 1242, New York, NY 10017.

LPRT Library Periodicals Round Table. Contact ALA (American Library Association).

LPSS Law and Political Science Section. *See* ACRL/LPSS.

LRACCC Learning Resources Association of California Community Colleges. Fullerton College, Fullerton, CA 92634.

Purpose is to be the state-level spokesperson for community college instruction resources personnel.

LR&TS *Library Resources and Technical Services. See* LRTS.

LRC Learning Resource Centers. A term sometimes used for libraries that incorporate audiovisual, computing and nontraditional resources in addition to print materials.

LRC Longitudinal Redundancy Check Character. On magnetic tape using non-return-to-zero indication, and on which a character is represented by a lateral row of bits, the LRC is a character placed at the end of each block for purposes of checking the parity of each tract in the block longitudinally.

LREP Learning Resources Exchange Program. *See* UICA/LREP.

LRI Library Resources, Inc. A micropublisher which is a subsidiary of Encyclopaedia Britannica. Produces book collections on high-reduction microfiche.

LRRS Library Reports and Research Service, Inc. 1660 South Albion St, Suite 400, Denver, CO 80222. Incorporated in 1972. Provides computerized searches and document delivery in all subjects.

LRRT Library Research Round Table. Contact ALA (American Library Association).

LRS Legislative Reference Service. A section of LC.

LRTS *Library Resources and Technical Services.* (Journal). V. 1, 1957. Published by the Resources and Technical Services Division of ALA (American Library Association). Also known as *LR&TS.*

LS Library Science.

LSA *Library Science Abstracts.* Became *LISA (Library and Information Science Abstracts)* in 1969.

LSBPHS Library Services to the Blind and Physically Handicapped Section. *See* ASCLA/LSBPHS.

LSC Least Significant Character. The least significant character in a word, field or record is farthest to the right.

LSCA Library Services and Construction Act. Passed in 1967, it provided for federal grants to areas in the US with inadequate library services.

LSCU Library Statistics of Colleges and Universities. *See* Bronson Price. *Library Statistics of Colleges and Universities: Data for Individual Institutions, Fall 1967.* Washington, DC: Government Printing Office, June 1969.

LSD Least Significant Digit. The least significant digit in a number is farthest to the right.

LSD Library Service to the Disadvantaged. Contact ALA (American Library Association). Standing advisory committee.

LSEP Library Service Enhancement Program. Council on Library Resources, Inc, One Dupont Circle, Washington, DC 20036.

LSIC Large-Scale Integrated Circuits. *See* IC (Integrated Circuit).

LSIES Library Services to the Impaired Elderly Section. *See* ASCLA/LSIES.

LSPS Library Services to Prisoners Section. *See* ASCLA/LSPS.

LTA Library Technical Assistant.

LTP Library Technology Program. A project of ALA (American Library Association) that tests various supplies and equipment, furniture and related items and publishes reports of the results.

LTR *Library Technology Reports.* (Journal). V. 1, 1965. Published by ALA (American Library Association).

LTRS Letters Shift. Change of position of teletypewriter carriage that allows alphabetic characters to be printed in proper sequence. Acronym also refers to the control character that causes this change of position to occur.

LUCID Language for Utility Checkout and Instrumentation Development. A query language of a data management system. *See* C. H. Kellogg. "CONVERSE: A System for the On-line Description . . . Using Natural Language" in *Mechanized Information Storage*, ed. by K. Samuelson. Amsterdam, the Netherlands: North Holland Publishing, 1968.

LUTFCSUSTC Librarians United to Fight Costly, Silly, Unnecessary Serial Title Changes. c/o Michigan State University, Library–Serials, East Lansing, MI 48824.

LVAHEC Lehigh Valley Area Health Education Center Library Consortium. Allentown Hospital Association Library, 1627 Chew St, Rm. 2422 EP, Allentown, PA 18102.

LVAIC Lehigh Valley Association of Independent Colleges. Moravian College, Bethlehem, PA 18018. Six member libraries cooperate through notification of purchases, delivery and photocopying services, reciprocal borrowing and ILL.

MAA Mathematical Association of America. 1529 18th St, NW, Washington, DC 20036. Established in 1915. Publishes documents.

MAC An autocoding program for the Norwegian Defense Research Establishment on the Ferranti Mercury Computer.

MAC Machine-Aided Cognition. Related to the government-supported, large computing research and technique implementation project carried out at MIT (Massachusetts Institute of Technology). To develop ways in which computers can help in doing creative work. Also known as MAC (Memory-Assisted Cognition).

MAC Memory-Assisted Cognition. *See* MAC (Machine-Aided Cognition).

MAC Multiaction Computer.

MAC Multiple Access Computer.

MACE Machine-Aided Composing and Editing.

MAD Michigan Algorithmic Decoder. A FORTRAN-like language developed at the University of Michigan.

MADAM Moderately Advanced Data Management.

MADAR Malfunction Analysis Detection and Recording.

MADAR Malfunction and Data Recorder.

MADCAP A language for mathematical problems and set operations. An algebraic translator and compiler programming language developed by Los Alamos Scientific Laboratories, UCLA, for use on the MANIAC II computer.

MADE Microalloy Diffused Electrode. A technique of transistor manufacture.

MADRE Magnetic Drum Receiving Equipment.

MADREC Malfunction Detection and Recording.

MADS Machine-Aided Drafting System.

MADS Missile Attitude Determination System.

MADT Microalloy Diffused Base Transistor.

MAESTRO Machine-Assisted Educational System for Teaching by Remote Operation.

MAGB Microfilm Association of Great Britain. 52 High St, Buntingford, Hertfordshire, England.

MAGIC MIDAC Automatic General Integrated Computation. A programming language and compiler.

MAGIS Marine Air-Ground Intelligence System.

MAGLOC Magnetic Logic Computer.

MAHSL Maryland Association of Health Sciences Librarians. Baltimore, MD.

MAID Monrobot Automatic Internal Diagnosis. Computer diagnostic malfunction detection and location program, developed by Monroe Calculating Machine Co, for the Monrobot Computers.

MALC Madison Area Library Council. Suite 215B, Beltline Office Center, 6414 Copps Ave, Madison, WI 53716. One hundred seventy academic, public, school, special and state libraries.

MALC Midwestern Academic Librarians Conference. University of Northern Iowa Library, Cedar Falls, IA 50613. Annual meeting.

MALCAP Maryland Academic Library Center for Automated Processing. c/o McKeldin Library, University of Maryland, College Park, MD 20740. Nineteen libraries currently in the process of establishing a computerized network of Maryland libraries.

MALIMET Master List of Medical Indexing Terms. The computerized thesaurus for Exerpta Medica data base.

MALT Manitoba Association of Library Technicians. Box 1872, Winnipeg MB R3C 3R1, Canada.

MANOVA Multivariate Analysis of Variance.

MANTIS Manchester Technical Information Service. c/o Central Library, St. Peter's Sq, Manchester, England.

MAP Macro Assembly Program. Program to translate a symbolic language program to machine language.

MAP Model and Program. A term to identify the preinstallation techniques and procedures recommended to users of some electronic data processing systems.

MAPDA Mid-America Periodical Distributors Association. Address unknown.

MARC Machine Readable Cataloging. A system, initially developed by LC, to organize and disseminate in machine-readable form bibliographic data structured according to international cataloging standards.

MARC II Machine Readable Cataloging II. MARC on magnetic tapes.

MARCIA Mathematical Analysis of Requirements for Career Information Appraisal.

MARGEN Management Report Generator. A computer report generation and file maintenance system with its own language and compiler, sold as a software package by Randolph Data Services, Inc.

MARLIN Mid-Atlantic Research Libraries Information Network. c/o Pennsylvania State University, Patee Library, University Park, PA 16802. Nine academic libraries cooperate through ILL and acquisitions lists.

MARLIS Multi-Aspect Relevance Linkage Information System. Information storage and retrieval system.

MARML Mid-Atlantic Regional Medical Library. Box 30260, Bethesda, MD 20209. Housed within NLM, this RML

(Region IV) serves DC, MD, NC, VA and WV.

MARN Manitoba Association of Registered Nurses. 647 Broadway, Winnipeg MB R3C 0X2, Canada. Maintains a library for its members.

MARS Machine-Assisted Reference Section. *See* RASD/MARS.

MARS Multi-Aperture Reluctance Switch. Data storage unit.

MASCOT Motorola Automatic Sequential Computer-Operated Tester.

MASS Multiple Access Sequential Selection. Method of data storage and retrieval.

MATHLAB A formal algebraic manipulation on-line system.

MATH-PAC Mathematical Program. Mathematical and statistical programs for simplifying such scientific and engineering applications as the solution of simultaneous linear equations, matrix algebra, multiple linear regression, roots of a polynomial and least squares polynomial fit. Developed by GE.

MATPS Machine-Aided Technical Processing System. Yale University Library, New Haven, CT Designed in 1965 for computer-aided acquisitions.

MAVI Medical Audio-Visual Institute. Association of American Medical Colleges, 2530 Ridge Ave, Evanston, IL 60201. Publishes documents.

MAVIS Maize Virus Information Service. Ohio State Agricultural Research and Development Center Library, Wooster, OH 44691. A special collection of literature on virus diseases of corn.

MB *Microelectronics Bibliography*. A limited current awareness publication of the Hughes Aircraft Co.

MBIP *Medical Books in Print*. New York: R. R. Bowker Co, 1972– . Annual.

MBO Management by Objectives. A management philosophy. *See also* MBO/R.

MBO/R Management by Objectives and Results. A management philosophy that involves a series of concepts including objectives and performance appraisals. It requires meaningful employee participation in the process of goal setting. Used and studied by library managers.

MC Department of Mass Communication. UNESCO, Place de Fontenoy, Paris 7, France.

MCA Microfilming Corporation of America. 1977 South Los Angeles St, Los Angeles, CA 90011.

MCCLPHEI Massachusetts Conference of Chief Librarians in Public Higher Educational Institutions. Fitchburg State College, Pearl St, Fitchburg, MA 01420.

MCIC Metals and Ceramics Information Center. Battelle Columbus Laboratories, 505 King Ave, Columbus, OH 43201. Established in 1958.

MCLP Massachusetts Centralized Library Processing Center. c/o University of Massachusetts at Amherst, University Library, Amherst, MA 01002. Thirty-one academic libraries cooperate through automatic purchasing, processing and shipping.

MCLS Metropolitan Cooperative Library System. Pasadena Public Library, 285 East Walnut St, Pasadena, CA 91101. Twenty-four public libraries cooperate through ILL, union list of periodicals, access to RLIN, SCAN and SCILL, workshops and demonstration program to provide library service to the deaf.

MCP Master Control Program.

MCPS Mechanical Copyright Protection Society. 380 Streatham High Rd, London SW16, England.

MCRMLP Midcontinental Regional Medical Library Program. University of Nebraska Medical Center, 42 St. and Dewey Ave, Omaha, NE 68105. One of NLM's RMLs (Region VIII), serving CO, KS, NE, SD, UT and WY. *See* Elizabeth Petgen. "The Regional Medical Libraries: Region VIII." *NLM News*, 30 (June 1975): 5–6.

MCRS Micrographic Catalog Retrieval System. Provided by 3M Co, 3M Library Systems, Reading, MA 01867. *See* Dilys E. Madison and John E. Galejs. "Application of the Micrographic Catalog Retrieval System in the Iowa State University Library." *LRTS* 15 (Fall 1971): 492–498.

MCUG Military Computer Users Group.

MDC Machinability Data Center. US Dept. of Defense, Defense Logistics Agency, 3980 Rosslyn Dr, Cincinnati, OH 45209. Established in 1964. Provides computerized searches, document delivery and analytical reports on applications of machine principles.

MDE Magnetic Decision Element. A circuit that performs a logical operation on one or more binary digits of input information (represented by "yes" or "no") and expresses the result in its output.

MDF Main Distributing Frame. A distributing frame that serves to associate any outside line entering a central office with any terminal of any subscriber multiple line or with any other outside line.

MDIC Multilateral Disarmament Information Centre. 10 Clarges St, London W1, England.

MDMLG Metropolitan Detroit Medical Library Group. Shiffman Medical Library, Wayne State University, Detroit, MI 48201.

MDO MARC Development Office. Library of Congress, Washington, DC 20540.

MDR Market Data Retrieval–Educational Data Base. Market Data Retrieval, Inc, Ketchum St, Westport, CT 06880. Coverage from 1974. Nonbibliographic data base covering demographic and financial information on schools and school districts.

MEC Media Exchange Cooperative. c/o British Columbia Teachers' Federation Resources Centre, 105-2235 Burrard St, Vancouver BC V6J 3H9, Canada.

MECCA Mechanized Catalog.

MEDCORE Medical Resources Consortium of Central New Jersey. c/o John F. Kennedy Medical Center, Edison, NJ 08817. Twenty-six libraries cooperate through ILL and media and periodical union lists.

MEDI Marine Environmental Data Information Referral System. Intergovernmental Oceanographic Commission, UNESCO, 7 Place de Fontenoy, Paris 75700, France. Data base that describes available data bases covering marine data.

MEDI *Mössbauer Effect Data Index*. Ed. by John G. Stevens and Virginia Stevens. New York: Plenum Publishing Corp, 1972.

MEDISTAT Centre International des Hautes Études Agronomiques Mediterraniennes, BP 1239-34011, Montepellier, Cedex, France. Coverage from 1961. Bibliographic data base covering the social sciences of the Mediterranean countries.

MEDLARS Medical Literature Analysis and Retrieval System. Bibliographic Services Division, National Library of Medicine, 8600 Rockville Pike, Bethesda, MD 20209. Provides bibliographies, computer searches, and indexes of interest to the medical profession. MEDLARS was one of the first successful computerized bibliographic retrieval systems.

MEDLINE MEDLARS-On-Line. Service provided by NLM. Provides on-line bibliographic searching capability for medical schools, medical libraries, hospitals and research institutes. *See also* MEDLARS.

MEDSOC *Medical Socioeconomic Research Sources*. (Journal). V. 1, 1963. Published by Aspen Systems Corp. Formerly the *Index to the Literature of Medical Socioeconomics*.

MEET McGill Elementary Education Teaching Teams. McGill University, 3700 McTavish St, Quebec PQ H3A 1Y2, Canada.

MEIS Military Entomology Information Service. Armed Forces Pest Control Board, Forest Glen Section, Walter Reed Army Medical Center, Washington, DC 20012. Provides information and documents.

MELA Middle East Librarians Association. Rm. 560, University of Chicago Library, Chicago, IL 60637. Established in 1972.

MELSA Metropolitan Library Services Agency. Griggs-Midway Bldg, 1821 University Ave, St. Paul, MN 55104. Of the Minneapolis–St. Paul Public Libraries.

MEP Mechanical Engineering Publications. Box 361, Birmingham, AL 35201. Publisher of *Proceedings of the Institution of Mechanical Engineers*.

MER *Micrographics Equipment Review.* (Journal). V. 1, 1976. Published by Micrographics Review.

MERC Media Equipment Resource Center. c/o Young Filmmakers Foundation, 4 Rivington St, New York, NY 10002. Funded by the State Council on the Arts to publish a directory of New York State-funded videotapes and films.

MERC Middle Atlantic Educational and Research Center. Franklin and Marshall College, College Ave, Lancaster, PA 17604. A nonprofit corporation devoted to sophisticated computer cooperation for education and research.

MERITO Giurisprudenza di Merito. Centro Elettronico di Documentazione-Italgiure, Corte Suprema di Cassaziono, Palazzo di Giustizia, Via Ulpiano 8, Rome 00193, Italy. Coverage from 1965. Full-text data base covering digests of decisions of ordinary magistrates of the Italian courts.

MERLIN Machine-Readable Library Information. A system of BL (British Library).

MERMLS Mid-Eastern Regional Medical Library Service. c/o College of Physicians of Philadelphia, 19 South 22 St, Philadelphia, PA 19103. One of NLM's RMLs (Region III). Serves DE and PA. *See* June H. Fulton. "The Mid-Eastern Regional Medical Library Service." *NLM News* 33 (July–Aug. 1978): 4–5.

MESA Middle East Studies Association of North America. MESA Headquarters and Secretariat, 50 Washington Sq. South, New York, NY 10003.

MESDA Museum of Early Southern Decorative Arts. Old Salem, Inc., Winston-Salem, NC 27108. Established in 1965. Maintains a library.

MeSH Medical Subject Headings. List used by NLM for *Index Medicus* and book cataloging.

META Methods of Extracting Text Automatically. A program of GE.

METADEX Metals Abstracts Index. American Metals Society, Metals Park, OH 44073. Coverage from 1968. Bibliographic data base, including *Metals Abstracts Index* and *Alloys Index*, available on-line and on magnetic tape for current and retrospective searching.

METALERT Metal Alert. American Society for Metals, Metals Park, OH 44073. A monthly computer-selected search of the world's metal-working literature.

METAPLAN Methods of Extracting Text Automatically Programming Language. *See* META.

METRO New York Metropolitan Reference and Research Library Agency. 33 West 42 St, New York, NY 10036. Consortium established in 1964. One hundred libraries sponsor studies, cooperative projects and publishing activities.

MF Medium Frequency. Frequencies between 300 and 3,000 kilohertz.

MF Microfiche. A photographic negative film usually containing 72 frames, each of which represents a page on a single sheet. Other standards call for varying numbers of pages per sheet depending on the reduction ratio.

MFS Magnetic-tape Field Search.

MFSS Manchester Federation of Scientific Societies. 15 The Beecher, Manchester 20, England.

MGA *Meteorological and Geoastrophysical Abstracts.* American Meteorological Society, 45 Beacon St, Boston, MA 02180. V. 1, 1972. Print publication available from the society; machine-readable file available from ESIC.

MGM Metro-Goldwyn-Mayer, Inc. Research Dept. Library, 10202 West Washington Blvd, Culver City, CA 90232. Maintains a library, established in 1925.

MHRA Modern Humanities Research Association. George Washington University, Columbian College, Washington, DC 20052. Publishes bibliographies in English literature.

MHRST *Medical and Health Related Sciences Thesaurus.* Bethesda, MD: National Institutes of Health, 1977. Annual.

MHSLN Midwest Health Science Library Network. 1750 West Polk St, Chicago,

IL 60612. Mailing address: Box 7509, Chicago, IL 60680. One of NLM's RMLs (Region VII), covering IA, IL, IN, ND and WI. Started in 1969; located at John Crerar Library (Chicago) until Dec. 31, 1979. *See* Patricia Jones and William S. Budington. "Midwest Health Science Library Network." *NLM News* 34 (Jan. 1979): 5–6.

MIC Management Information Corporation. 140 Barclay Center, Cherry Hill, NJ 08034. Assists management in automation. A commercial firm.

MICA Macroinstruction Compiler Assembler. A computer program assembler-compiler.

MICR Magnetic Ink Character Recognition. Form of OCR (Optical Character Recognition) widely used by banks and standardized by USASI.

MICRO Multiple Indexing and Console Retrieval Options. An on-line system for retrieving, ranking and qualifying document references.

MICUA Maryland Independent College and University Association, Inc. 33 West St, Annapolis, MD 21401. Seventeen libraries promote the cooperative efforts of Maryland's academic institutions.

MIDA Mid-West Independent Distributors Association. A regional association of independent book distributors located in the Midwest.

MIDAS Medical Information Dissemination Using ASSASSIN. A system developed by Imperial Chemical Industries, Ltd.

MIDAS Micro-Imaged Data Addition System. Developed by CAPS Equipment, Ltd.

MIDAS Modified Integration Digital Analog Simulator. A digital-simulated analog computing program.

MIDLNET Midwest Region Library Network. c/o University of Wisconsin–Green Bay, 2420 Nicolet Dr, Green Bay, WI 54302. Twenty-four libraries promote access to bibliographic resources by Midwest libraries.

MIDONAS Military Documentation System. Of Switzerland's Department of Defense.

MIDORI Modern Information & Documentation Organizing &

Rearrangement, Inc. Box 269, Osaka Central, Osaka, Japan. A commercial firm. Provides information and documentation services. Member of IIA (Information Industry Association).

MILC Manchester Interlibrary Cooperative. c/o Manchester City Library, 405 Pine St, Manchester, NH 03103. Ten academic, public, special, hospital and all city school libraries in Manchester share union list of serials and a multimedia center.

MILO Miami Valley Library Organization. 215 East Third St, Dayton, OH 45402. Twenty public libraries cooperate through ILL, back-up reference services and collection development.

MILTRAN A digital simulation language designed for military applications by Gulton Systems Research Group.

MIMA Montana Instructional Media Association. Contact president or AECT.

MIMP *Magazine Industry Market Place.* New York: R. R. Bowker Co, 1979.

MIMS Medical Information Management System. A project of NASA.

MINE Montana Information Network and Exchange. c/o Montana State Library, 930 East Lyndale, Helena, MT 59601. Established in 1974. Eight academic and public libraries cooperate through ILL.

MINITEX Minnesota Interlibrary Telecommunications Exchange. c/o University of Minnesota, 30 Wilson Library, 309 19th Ave, South, Minneapolis, MN 55455. One hundred fifty academic, public, government and special libraries cooperate with resource-sharing services.

MINPRT Miniature Processing Time.

MINSOP Minimum Slack Time per Operation.

MIRACODE Microfilm Retrieval Access Code. A Kodak project.

MIRFAC A compiler based on standard mathematical notation and plain English.

MIS Management Information System.

MIS-IRPAT Patent Information Retrieval System. Abstracts are created from keywords to describe the content of the patent. *See* Michiji Nakamura and Terukuni Iko. ("An Outline of the Patent Information Retrieval System [MIS-IRPAT] of the Nippon Electric Co., Ltd.") *Dokumentesyon Kenkyu* 22 (Aug. 1972): 257–263.

MISTRAM Missile Trajectory Measurement. Computer system developed by GE.

MIT Massachusetts Institute of Technology. Cambridge, MA 02139.

MIT Master Instruction Tape.

MKE Magyar Könyvtarosok Egyesülete (Association of Hungarian Librarians). Box 452, H-1372 Budapest, Hungary. Established in 1935.

ML Machine Language.

MLA Maine Library Association. Contact president or ALA (American Library Association).

MLA Malta Library Association. c/o Capuchin Friary, Floriana, Malta. Established in 1969.

MLA Manitoba Library Association. c/o Saint Vital Public Library, 6 Fermor Ave. West, Saint Vital MB R2M 0Y2, Canada.

MLA Maryland Library Association. Contact president or ALA (American Library Association).

MLA Massachusetts Library Association. Contact president or ALA (American Library Association).

MLA Medical Library Association. 919 North Michigan Ave, Chicago, IL 60611.

MLA Michigan Library Association. Contact president or ALA (American Library Association).

MLA Minnesota Library Association. Contact president or ALA (American Library Association).

MLA Mississippi Library Association. Contact president or ALA (American Library Association).

MLA Missouri Library Association. Contact president or ALA (American Library Association).

MLA Modern Language Association of America. 62 Fifth Ave, New York, NY

10011. Established in 1883. Publishes a quarterly journal, *PMLA*.

MLA Montana Library Association. Contact president or ALA (American Library Association).

MLA Music Library Association. 343 South Main St, Rm. 205, Ann Arbor, MI 48108. Published *TIRMMS*.

MLAA Medical Library Assistance Act of 1965. PL (Public Law) 89-291 provided funds for improvement of individual medical libraries throughout the country.

MLA/JMRT MLA Junior Members Round Table. Contact MLA (Missouri Library Association).

MLC Medical Library Center. *See* MLCNY.

MLC Michigan Library Consortium. c/o G. Flint Purdy Library, Wayne State University, Detroit, MI 48202. Fifty-five academic and public libraries share resources and link up with national and regional electronic bibliographic communication systems.

MLCNY Medical Library Center of New York. 17 East 102 St, New York, NY 10029. Consortium established in 1959. Provides cooperative housing and acquisition of less-used materials in medicine and its allied sciences for medical libraries in the New York metropolitan area. Also provides delivery service between members and maintains a computerized union list of serials.

MLCS Multitype Library Cooperation Section. *See* ASCLA/MLCS.

MLL Maynard Listener Library. 171 Washington St, Taunton, MA 02780. Formerly (1965) Catholic Listener Library.

MLN *Mississippi Library News*. (Newsletter). V. 1, 1936. Published by MLA (Mississippi Library Association).

MLP Machine Language Programs.

MLS Machine Literature Searching.

MLS Metropolitan Libraries Section. *See* PLA/MLS.

MLTA Manitoba Library Trustees Association. Contact

secretary-treasurer. A Canadian association.

MM Main Memory.

MMA Multiple Module Access. In a multiprocessor system, the MMA unit is positioned between each storage module and the various processors which may access it and provides priority for storage access conflicts.

MMAC Mid-Missouri Associated Colleges. University of Missouri at Columbia, 121 Arts and Science Bldg, Columbia, MO 65201. Consortium established in 1964. Interlibrary Services Section fosters library cooperation.

MMML Monastic Manuscript Microfilm Library. Saint John's University, Collegeville, MN 56321.

MMN Maps, Microtexts, and Newspapers.

MMP Multiplex Message Processor.

MMPT Man-Machine Partnership Translation.

MO Machine Operation.

MO Manual Output.

MOBAC Monterey Bay Area Cooperative. 344 Salinas St, Suite 107, Salinas, CA 93901.

MOBIDIC Mobile Digital Computer. A mobile computer that operates by using numbers to express all the quantities and variables of a problem. Developed by Sylvania Electric Products Co.

MOBILE A universal, machine-independent, computer language translator.

MOBL Macro-Oriented Business Language.

MOBULA Model Building Language. Data processing language.

MOC Memory Operating Characteristic.

MOD/DEM Modulating and Demodulating Unit. A device performing modulation/demodulation and the control functions needed to provide compatibility between computer equipment and communications facilities.

MOL Machine-Oriented Language. Data processing language.

MOLDS Managerial On-Line Data System. *See* J. M. Allderidge and P. J. Knoke. *Design Considerations for an On-Line Management System.* Syracuse, NY: Syracuse University Research Corp, July 1966.

MOLO Mideastern Ohio Library Organization. c/o Louisville Public Library, 700 Lincoln Ave, Louisville, OH 44641. Twelve public libraries cooperate through ILL and reference services.

MONOCLE Mise en Ordinateur d'une Notice Catalographique de Livre. University of Grenoble, 46 avenue Felix-Viallet, F-3800 Grenoble, France. Project based on MARC II and French cataloging practices. *See* Marc Chauveinc. "Automation of the Catalog at the University of Grenoble." *Libri* 21 (1971): 188–192. *See also* Marc Chauveinc. "MONOCLE." *Journal of Library Automation* 4 (Sept. 1971): 113–128.

MONY Mutual of New York Library/Information Service. 1740 Broadway, New York, NY 10019. Provides insurance and management materials through ILL.

MOP Multiple On-Line Programming.

MOSAIC 636 Macro-Operation Symbolic Assembler and Information Compiler.

MOVRI Manually Operated Visual Response Indicator. Levers labeled alphabetically and numerically in large type and braille. Used for people with speech- as well as sight-disabling conditions.

MPA Modern Poetry Association. 1228 North Dearborn Pkwy, Chicago, IL 60610. Established in 1941.

MPA Music Publishers Association. 73 Mortimer St, London W1, England.

MPLA Mountain Plains Library Association. Contact president or ALA (American Library Association).

MPMI Magazine and Paperback Marketing Institute. 5425 Marleton Pike, Pennsauken, NJ 08109. Established in 1946. Formerly BIPAD.

MPS System of Material Product Balances. *See* SNA/MPS.

MQ Multiplier-Quotient Register. A device used to store multipliers and quotients.

MQEM Michigan Quarterly Economic Model. Research Seminar in Quantitative Economics, Dept. of Economics, University of Michigan, 506 East University, Ann Arbor, MI 48109. Coverage from 1954. Full text data base covering econometric models developed in the US.

MR *Microform Review*. (Journal). V. 1, 1972. Published by Microform Review, Inc.

MRAP Management Review and Analysis Program. A self-study program intended for library members of ARL. See *Library Management and Review Program: A Handbook for Guiding Change and Improvement in Research Library Management*. Washington, DC: Office of Management Studies–Association of Research Libraries, 1973.

MRC Medical Research Council. 20 Park Crescent, London W1N 4AL, England. Incorporated by Royal Charter in 1920 and granted a new charter in 1966, it succeeds the Medical Research Committee of 1913. May publish under its own imprint or under HMSO.

MRDF Machine-Readable Data Files.

MRDS MARC Records Distribution Service. 395 Wellington St, Ottawa ON K1A 0N4, Canada. Established to provide Canadian libraries with domestic and foreign machine-readable cataloging information in magnetic tape form.

MRIS Maritime Research Information Service. Maritime Transportation Research Board, National Academy of Sciences, National Research Council, 2101 Constitution Ave, Washington, DC 20418. Provides a computer-based service sponsored by the Maritime Administration. See D. G. Mellor. "An Information Service for the Maritime Industry." *Special Libraries* 70 (Apr. 1979): 170–172.

MRIS Medical Record Information Service. University of Vermont, Dana Medical Library, Burlington, VT 05401. Service and support for CPOMR.

MRT Master Relocatable Tape. A Honeywell routine that contains

checked-out programs to be scheduled for production operation.

MS Machine Selection.

MS The Metallurgical Society. *See* TMS.

MSA Multivariate Statistical Analyzer. Originated at Dartmouth College. *See* K. J. Jones. "The Multivariate Statistical Analyzer." *Behavioral Science* 10 (1965): 326–327.

MSC Management Studies Centre, Ltd. Fenwick House, 292 High Holborn, London WC1, England.

MSC Most Significant Character. The character farthest to the left in a word or number in computer storage.

MSCE Main Storage Control Element.

MSD Most Significant Digit. The digit farthest to the left of a number in computer storage.

MSFC Marshall Space Flight Center Library. Marshall Space Flight Center, AL 35812.

MSI Medium Scale Integrated Circuits. Up to 50 integrated circuits on a single semiconductor chip. Used in modern computers.

MSLAVA Manitoba School Library Audio-Visual Association. 191 Harcourt St, Winnipeg MB R3J 3H2, Canada.

MSR Working Committee on Mechanical Storage and Retrieval. *See* FID/MSR.

MT Machine Translation.

MT Mechanical Translation.

MTAK Magyar Tudományos Akadémía Könyotára (Library of the Hungarian Academy of Sciences). Akademia U.2, Budapest V, Hungary. Established in 1826.

MTBF Mean Time Between Failure.

MTBM Mean Time Between Maintenance.

MTC Memory Test Computer.

MTDATA Inorganic and Metallurgical Thermodynamics Data. National Physical Laboratory, Chemical Standards Division, Dept. of Industry, Teddington, Middlesex TW11 OLW, England. Coverage from 1974. Nonbibliographic data base.

MTM Methods-Time Measurement. Management term, applicable to library services.

MTS Marine Technology Society. 1730 M St, NW, Washington, DC 20005.

MTST Magnetic Tape/Selectric Typewriter. Used to simultaneously type catalog cards and produce computer-stored data acquisition information. *See* Erica Love et al. "Reclassification and Documentation in a Medium-sized Medical Center Library." *BMLA* 59 (Jan. 1976): 41–49.

MTTF Mean Time to Failure.

MTTR Maximum Time to Repair.

MTTR Mean Time to Repair.

MTTR Mean Time to Restore.

MUC Makerere University College. Rue aux Laines 1, Box 16002, Kampala, Uganda; Rue Belliard 51, Box 7072, Kampala, Uganda. The university has two campuses.

MUCIA Midwest Universities Consortium for International Activities, Inc. Office of the Executive Director, 200 Center for International Programs, Michigan State University, East Lansing, MI 48824. Consortium established in 1964. Assists academic exchanges between members and universities abroad.

MUDPIE Museum and University Data, Program and Information Exchange. Smithsonian Institution, Division of Reptiles and Amphibians, Washington, DC 20560. Established in 1967. Publishes a newsletter on the use of time-shared computing for research in museums and libraries.

MULS Minnesota Union List of Serials. Sponsored by MINITEX.

MUMS Multiple Use MARC System. Library of Congress, Washington, DC 20540. A software system designed to support bibliographic applications in both on-line and batch modes, employing MARC tapes.

MWA Mystery Writers of America. 151 West 48 St, New York, NY 10036.

MZTA Zavod Teplovoj Avtomafiki. Mironovskaja 33, Moscow E-58, USSR. Thermal product factory library established in 1933.

NA Not Available.

NABER National Association of Business and Educational Radio. 1330 New Hampshire Ave, Washington, DC 20036. Established in 1965. Informs members on legislative and regulatory action regarding business radio.

NABIN North Alabama Biomedical Information Network. c/o University of Alabama in Huntsville Library, Box 2600, Huntsville, AL 35807. Seventeen member libraries cooperate through ILL and coordinated acquisitions.

NACA National Advisory Committee for Aeronautics. Led to formation of NASA in 1958. Sponsored development of methods for data reduction reported in a 1952 AGARD Conference.

NACE National Association of Corrosion Engineers. Box 986, Katy, TX 77450. Established in 1943. Conducts research on corrosion. Publishes serials.

NACE National Association of County Engineers. c/o W. G. Harrington, Linn County Courthouse, Cedar Rapids, IA 52401. Established in 1956. Publishes serials and monographs.

NACEIC National Advisory Council for Education for Industry and Commerce. Dept. of Education and Science, Curzon St, London W1, England.

NACILA National Council of Indian Library Associations. Became FILA (Federation of Indian Library Associations) in 1975.

NACIS National Credit Information Service. TRW Business Credit Services Division, 100 Oceangate, Long Beach, CA 90802. Coverage from 1976. Nonbibliographic data base covering credit reports on businesses in the US and its territories.

NACO National Association of Counties. 1735 New York Ave, NW, Washington, DC 20006. Established in 1935. Forty-three state groups. Publishes documents. Formerly the National Association of County Officials.

NAE National Academy of Engineering. Office of Information, 2101 Constitution Ave, NW, Washington, DC 20418. Established in 1964.

NAEB National Association of Educational Broadcasters. 1346 Connecticut Ave,

NW, Washington, DC 20036. Established in 1925. Maintains a library of materials relating to educational broadcasting. Publishes serials. Formerly (1934) the Association of College and University Broadcasting Stations.

NAHRO National Association of Housing and Redevelopment Officials Library. 2600 Virginia Ave, NW, Suite 404, Washington, DC 20037. Perhaps the largest private library of material on housing, urban renewal and code enforcements.

NAK Negative Acknowledge Character. A communication control character transmitted by a receiver as a negative response to a sender.

NAL National Agricultural Library. 10301 Baltimore Blvd, Beltsville, MD 20705. Established in 1862. A component of USDA.

NAL Norske Aviers Landsforbund. Pressens Hus, Rosenkrantz Gate 3, Oslo 1, Norway. Established in 1910. Member of the International Federation of Newspaper Publishers. Publishes documents.

NALA North Alabama Library Alliance. Office of the Director of the Library, University of Alabama in Huntsville, Box 1247, Huntsville, AL 35807. Consortium established in 1969. Members pursue complementary acquisitions programs.

NALNET NASA Library Network. NASA Headquarters, Code NST, Washington, DC 20546. Includes 12 NASA flight research center libraries.

NAMDI National Marine Data Inventory. National Oceanographic Data Center, National Oceanic and Atmospheric Administration, 2001 Wisconsin Ave, NW, Washington, DC 20235. A service of NODC, NAMDI contains information on quantities and types of data, area of operations and personnel of oceanographic data collection efforts.

NAND Not AND. Logic operator equivalent to "not and."

NANTIS Nottingham and Nottinghamshire Technical Information Service. Commercial and Technical Dept, Nottingham Public Library, South

Sherwood St, Nottingham NG1 4DA, England.

NANWEP Navy Numerical Weather Prediction. Utilizes digital computers.

NAOGE National Association of Government Engineers. Established in 1964. This association has been terminated.

NAPAC NCR's Applied COBOL Packages. Makes use of a series of COBOL statements required to perform many data processing functions. Provides NCR computer users with a series of generalized source programs that can be tailored to meet their program needs.

NAPCA National Air Pollution Control Administration. Has issued *NAPCA Abstract Bulletin* since 1970.

NAPCU Northwest Association of Private Colleges and Universities. Box 196, Lewis and Clark College, Portland, OR 97219. Has a microform collection housed at Lewis and Clark College Library. Members from Northwestern states cooperate to share infrequently used materials.

NAPE National Association of Power Engineers. 176 West Adams St, Suite 1914, Chicago, IL 60603. Established in 1882. Publishes serials and pamphlets and produces films.

NAPS National Auxiliary Publications Service. Microfiche Publications, Box 3513, Grand Central Sta, New York, NY 10017. Operated for ASIS. Established in 1937, NAPS holds and reproduces copies of adjunct materials for papers published in scholarly or technical journals.

NAPTIC National Air Pollution Technical Information System. A pilot project was conducted in 1965. *See* Herbert Menzel. "Information Needs and Uses in Science and Technology." *ARIST* 1 (1965): 41–69.

NARA North American Radio Archives Library. 1231 Grove St, San Francisco, CA 94117. Holds 15,000 radio programs on tape.

NARDIS Navy Automated Research and Development Information System. *See* J. H. Williams, Jr. "Functions of a Man-Machine Interactive Concept

Retrieval System." *JASIS* 22 (May 1971): 311-317.

NARF Native American Rights Fund. Established in 1970. With a three-year grant (1972-1975), the fund developed its National Indian Law Library in Boulder, CO. Collects, catalogs, and provides copies of documents.

NARS National Archives and Records Service. Eighth & Pennsylvania Aves, NW, Washington, DC 20408.

NARST National Association for Research in Science Teaching. Memorial Hall, Drake University, Des Moines, IA 50311. Established in 1928. Publishes documents.

NAS National Academy of Sciences. 2101 Constitution Ave, NW, Washington, DC 20418. Maintains several research libraries.

NASA National Aeronautics and Space Administration. 400 Maryland Ave, SW, Washington, DC 20546.

NASA/RECON NASA Remote Control.

NASDAQ National Association of Securities Dealers Automated Quotations System. A system which gives price information for "over-the-counter" stocks using computers operated by Bunker Ramo Corp. in Trumbell, CT.

NASIC Northeast Academic Science Information Center. 40 Grove St, Wellesley, MA 02181. Supported by NSF for the purpose of developing a central access point to information resources in computer-readable form by aggregating data bases and existing information services.

NASIS National Association for State Information Systems. Box 11910, Iron Works Pike, Lexington, KY 40578. Publishes documents.

NASL Nevada Association of School Librarians. Contact president or ALA (American Library Association). One of three sections of NLA (Nevada Library Association) established in 1972 at the association's annual conference.

NASM National Association for School Magazines. 68a Hammersmith Grove, London W6, England.

NAS-NAE-NRC National Academy of Sciences-National Academy of Engineering-National Research Council. Office of Information, 2101 Constitution Ave, NW, Washington, DC 20418.

NASORD A programming reference to a file not in sequential order.

NASSL National Association of Spanish Speaking Librarians. Contact president. Established in 1971. Affiliated with ALA (American Library Association).

NASSP National Association of Secondary School Principals. 1904 Association Dr, Reston, VA 22091. Established in 1916. Has a committee on computers in education.

NASTA National Association of State Text Book Administrators. State Dept. of Public Education, Education Bldg, Rm. 381, Raleigh, NC 27611. Formerly NASTBD.

NASTBD National Association of State Text Book Directors. Name changed to NASTA.

NAT Natural Unit of Information.

NATA North American Telephone Association. 1030 15th St, NW, Suite 360, Washington, DC 20005. Established in 1970. Provides legal, legislative and public relations services.

NAUCA National Association of Users of Computer Applications to Learning. c/o John Grate, Associate Director, Program Research and Design, Cincinnati Public Schools, 320 East Ninth St, Cincinnati, OH 45202. An association of large school systems with CAI (Computer-Assisted Instruction) projects.

NAVA National Audio-Visual Association. 3150 Spring St, Fairfax, VA 22031. Publishes documents.

NAVDAC Navigation Data Assimilation Computer.

NBA National Book Awards. Established in 1950 and discontinued in 1979. Administered from 1977 to 1979 by AAP (Association of American Publishers), which now administers TABA.

NBA National Braille Association. 654A Godwin Ave, Midland Park, NJ 07432. Established in 1945.

NBB Nederlandse Boekverkopersbond (Association of Dutch Booksellers). Waalsdorperweg 119, The Hague, the Netherlands. Established in 1907. Publishes documents.

NBBFP Nationale Bond der Belgische Filmproducenten. *See* UNPBF (Union Nationale des Producteurs Belge de Films).

NBC National Bibliographical Center. National Central Library, 43 Nanhai Rd, Taipei, Taiwan.

NBC National Book Council. Name changed to NBL (National Book League).

NBC National Broadcasting Company, Inc. 30 Rockefeller Pl, New York, NY 10020. Maintains a reference library.

NBER National Bureau of Economic Research. 1050 Massachusetts Ave, Cambridge, MA 02138. Established in 1920. Publishes books and manuscripts.

NBF Norsk Bibliotekforening (Norwegian Library Association). Malerhaugverien 20, Oslo 6, Norway. Established in 1913.

NBKM Narodna Biblioteka Kiril i Metodij (National Library of Cyril and Methodius). Boul. Tolbuhin 11, Sofia, Bulgaria. Established in 1878.

NBL National Book League. 7 Albemarle St, London W1X 4BB, England. Formerly NBC (National Book Council).

NBL Norsk Bibliotekarlag (Association of Norwegian Public Librarians). Notodden Bibliotek, N-3670 Notodden, Norway. Established in 1946.

NBLC Netherlands Bibliotheek en Lektuur Centrum (Dutch Center for Public Libraries and Literature). Postbus 2054, The Hague, the Netherlands. Established in 1972.

NBO National Buildings Organization. 11-A Janpath, New Delhi, India. Has a library, established in 1954.

NBP National Braille Press. 88 Saint Stephen St, Boston, MA 02115. Established in 1927.

NBS National Bureau of Standards. E01 Administration Bldg, Washington, DC 20234.

NC Newspaper Conference. Whitefriars' House, 6 Carmelite St, London EC4, England.

NCA National Communications Association. 485 Fifth Ave, Suite 311, New York, NY 10017. Established in 1955. Provides information on electrical communications facilities and systems.

NCA Northwest Computing Association.

NCALI National Clearinghouse for Alcohol Information. 9119 Gaither Rd, Box 2345, Rockville, MD 20852.

NCATE National Council for Accreditation of Teacher Education. 1750 Pennsylvania Ave, NW, Rm. 411, Washington, DC 20006. Established in 1952. Also accredits school librarians. Publishes *Annual List of Accredited Institutions*.

NCAVAE National Committee for Audiovisual Aids in Education. 33 Queen Anne St, London W1M 0AL, England. Established in 1946 as the National Committee for Visual Aids in Education. An independent body, it coordinates work done in the field, publishes the monthly *Visual Education* and arranges conferences, exhibitions and courses.

NCC National Climatic Center. Federal Bldg, Asheville, NC 28801. Provides information on climatology, meteorology, satellites and hydrology. Holdings include all records routinely collected by the US government, as well as large quantities of data acquired from foreign sources. Numerous publications are issued which are global, national or local in focus. User services are provided at cost.

NCC National Computing Centre. Quay House, Quay St, Manchester M3 3HU, England.

NCCAN National Center for Child Abuse and Neglect. Administration for Children, Youth, and Families, 200 Independence Ave, SW, Washington, DC 20201. Produces a data base.

NCCD National Council on Crime and Delinquency. Continental Pl, 411 Hackensack Ave, Hackensack, NJ 07601. Established in 1907. Maintains a library and information files.

NCCLS Nevada Center for Cooperative Library Services. 2351 Arrowhead Dr, Carson City, NV 89701. Established in 1967. Division of the Nevada State

Library. Coordinates the cooperative use of funds, personnel, equipment and facilities.

NCEC National Center for Educational Communication. Office of Education, 400 Maryland Ave, SW, Washington, DC 20202.

NCEE National Council of Engineering Examiners. Box 5000, Seneca, SC 29678. Established in 1920. Publishes several serials and monographs. Formerly (1967) NCSBEE.

NCES National Center for Educational Statistics. US Office of Education, 400 Maryland Ave, SW, Washington, DC 20202. Gathers, stores, analyzes and disseminates statistical data and analytical studies.

NCET National Council for Educational Technology. Established in 1967. Became CET (Council for Educational Technology for the United Kingdom) in 1973.

NCH National Council on the Humanities. 1800 G St, NW, Washington, DC 20006.

NCHS National Center for Health Statistics. Health Services and Mental Health Administration, 5600 Fishers Lane, Rockville, MD 20857. Maintained by USPHS. Provides reference and consultative assistance to foreign, state and local health officials in the field of health statistics. Publishes documents.

NCIC National Cartographic Information Center. US Geological Survey, 507 National Center, 12201 Sunrise Valley Dr, Reston, VA 22092.

NCIC National Crime Information Center. US Dept. of Justice, Federal Bureau of Investigation, Washington, DC 20535.

NCL National Central Library. Formerly the Central Library for Students. In 1974 incorporated as part of BLLD of BL (British Library).

NCLA North Carolina Library Association. Contact president or ALA (American Library Association).

NCLIS National Commission on Libraries and Information Science. 1717 K St, NW, Suite 601, Washington, DC 20036. A permanent, independent agency of the Executive Branch created in 1970 by PL (Public Law) 910345. Advises the President and Congress on implementation of national information policy.

NCME Network for Continuing Medical Education. 15 Columbus Circle, New York, NY 10023. A service linking medical schools and hospitals by closed-circuit television. Supported by Roche Laboratories.

NCMHI National Clearinghouse for Mental Health Information. 5600 Fishers Lane, Rockville, MD 20857. A branch of NIMH.

NCMLG Northern California Medical Library Group. Contact president or PSRMLS.

NCR National Cash Register Company. Producer of the Photochromic Micro-Image System, which can reduce as many as 3,200 pages to a single standard 4 x 6 inch microfiche at the rate of 1,000 pages an hour.

NCRD National Council for Research and Development. 84 Hachashmonaim St, Box 20125, Tel Aviv, Israel.

NCRRRC North Country Reference and Research Resources Council. 73 Park St, Canton, NY 13617. Forty academic, hospital, public, research and special libraries cooperate through ILL, reciprocal borrowing, union lists, personnel training or upgrading and many other functions.

NCS Numerical Control Society. 1800 Pickwick Ave, Glenview, IL 60025. Established in 1962. Publishes serials and monographs.

NCSBEE National Council of State Boards of Engineering Examiners. Established in 1920. Name changed in 1967 to NCEE.

NCSM National Congress on Surveying and Mapping. Name changed to ACSM.

NCTE National Council of Teachers of English. 1111 Kenyon Rd, Urbana, IL 61801. Established in 1911. Publishes several periodicals dealing with English education, including *Abstracts of English Studies*.

NCTJ National Council for the Training of Journalists. 8 Bonverie St, London EC4, England. Established in 1952. Consists of representatives of the principal press organizations. Administers the official training scheme for journalists in the British Isles. Publishes documents, including the journal *Training in Journalism*.

NCTM National Council of Teachers of Mathematics. 1906 Association Dr, Reston, VA 22091. Established in 1920. Publishes several serials and monographs.

NCWTD National Centrum voor Wetenschappelyke en Technische Documentation. *See* CNDST.

NDC Noyes Data Corporation. Noyes Bldg, Park Ridge, NJ 07656.

NDL National Diet Library. 10-1, 1-chome, Nagata-cho, Chiyoda-ku, Tokyo, Japan.

NDLA North Dakota Library Association. Contact president or ALA (American Library Association).

NDP Vereniging de Nederlandse Dagbladpers. Johannes Vermeerstraat 14, Amsterdam 2, the Netherlands. Established in 1908. Member of the International Federation of Newspaper Publishers. Publishes documents.

NDR Nondestructive Read. *See* NDRO.

NDRO Nondestructive Read-Out. A process in which data is read without alteration of that data, as opposed to "destructive read-out," in which data read directly from storage is destroyed in the process. Also known as NDR.

NEA National Education Association. 1201 16th St, NW, Washington, DC 20036. Established in 1857.

NEA National Endowment for the Arts. 2401 East St, NW, Washington, DC 20506. Art-related library projects are eligible for grants.

NEAT National's Electronic Autocoding Technique. An automatic system for programming that is used in creating an object (fully compiled or assembled) program in machine language from a source program written by a programmer. Developed by NCR.

NEBHE New England Board of Higher Education. 40 Grove St, Wellesley, MA 02181. Publishes *Higher Education in New England*, a newsletter. Sponsors NELINET.

NEC National Electronics Conference. 1211 West 22 St, Oak Brook, IL 60521. Established in 1944. Publishes documents.

NECHI Northeast Consortium for Health Information. c/o Beverly Hospital, Herrick & Heather Sts, Beverly, MA 01915. Twenty hospital libraries cooperate through ILL and periodical union lists.

NEDCC New England Document Conservation Center. Abbot Hall, School St, Andover, MA 01810.

NEDL New England Deposit Library, Inc. 135 Western Ave, Allston, MA 02134. Established in 1942.

NEEDS New England Educational Data System. Cambridge, MA 02101.

NEH National Endowment for the Humanities. 806 15th St, NW, Washington, DC 20506. Has a grant program available to libraries with humanities programs.

NEIAL Northeast Iowa Academic Libraries Association. c/o Homuth Memorial Library, Wartburg College, Waverly, IA 50677. Seven libraries cooperate through ILL, union list of serials and depository.

NEICA National Energy Information Center Affiliate. 2500 Central Ave, SE, Albuquerque, NM 87104.

NEIRC New England Interinstitutional Research Council. c/o Dr. Glenda Lee, Associate Dean for Interinstitutional Research, Middlesex Community College, Bedford, MA 01730. Goal is to promote institutional and interinstitutional research in two-year colleges.

NEISS National Electronic Injury Surveillance System. National Injury Information Clearinghouse, 5401 Westbard Ave, Westwood Towers Bldg, Washington, DC 20207. On-line report of accidents and accident investigations.

NELA New England Library Association. Contact president or *NELA Newsletter*, 3 Rita Rd, West Peabody, MA 01960.

NELB New England Library Board. 231 Capitol Ave, Hartford, CT 06115. Six state library agencies coordinate a variety of services.

NELIAC Naval Electronics Laboratory International Algebraic Compiler.

NELINET New England Library Information Network. 40 Grove St, Wellesley, MA 02181. Library program connecting 92 academic and public libraries to a computer system developed by OCLC. Sponsored by NEBHE.

NELL North East Lancashire Libraries. This consortium was disbanded in 1974.

NEMIS Network Management Information System.

NEMISYS New Mexico Information System. c/o New Mexico State Library, Box 1629, Santa Fe, NM 87503. Over 100 public, school, academic and special libraries cooperate through ILL.

NEMSINET National Emergency Medical Services Information Network. c/o American College of Emergency Physicians, Emergency Medical Information Center, 241 East Saginaw, East Lansing, MI 48823.

NERAC New England Research Application Center. Mansfield Professional Pk, Storrs, CT 06268. Specializes in multiple data base searching. Connected with the University of Connecticut at Storrs.

NERCOMP New England Regional Computing Program, Inc. One Broadway, Boston, MA 02174. Begun by MIT (Massachusetts Institute of Technology) in 1936, it became a network of 42 colleges and universities by 1971.

NERIS National Energy Referral and Information System. Environmental Information Center, Inc, 292 Madison Ave, New York, NY 10017. Coverage from 1974. On-line directory of key US energy agencies and personnel.

NERM Northeast Regional Meeting. A meeting of ACS (American Chemical Society). The third NERM was held in Buffalo, NY, in 1971.

NERMLS New England Regional Medical Library Service. Francis A. Countway Library of Medicine, Harvard University, 10 Shattuck St, Boston, MA 02115. One of NLM's RMLs (Region I). NERMLS services the six New England states: CT, MA, ME, NH, RI and VT.

NESCL Northern Engineering Services Company, Ltd. 6511 54th St, NW, Calgary AB T3A 1R5, Canada. Maintains a library employing computerized cataloging.

NESLA New England School Library Association. Publishes a newsletter from the Jamaica Plain High School Library, Jamaica Plain, MA 02130.

NESS National Environmental Satellite Service. National Oceanic and Atmospheric Agency, Federal Office Bldg. 4, Suitland, MD 20233. Provides information on meteorological satellites and atmospheric data. Publishes documents.

NET National Educational Television. 10 Columbus Circle, New York, NY 10019.

NETAC Nuclear Energy Trade Association Conference. 25 Victoria St, London SW1, England.

NETRC National Educational Television and Radio Center. 1619 Massachusetts Ave, NW, Washington, DC 20036.

NEWIL Northeast Wisconsin Intertype Libraries, Inc. c/o Saint Norbert College, Grant St, De Pere, WI 54115. Thirty libraries cooperate through ILL and resource sharing.

NFAIS National Federation of Abstracting and Indexing Services. 112 South 16 St, Philadelphia, PA 19102. Established in 1958. Formerly (1972) NFSAIS.

NFER National Foundation for Educational Research in England and Wales. The Mcre, Upton Park, Slough, Buckinghamshire, England.

NFF Norske Forskningebibliotekarers Forening (Association of Norwegian Research Librarians). Malerhaugveien 20, Oslo 6, Norway.

NFPA National Fire Protection Association. 470 Atlantic Ave, Boston, MA 02210. Established in 1896. Publishes serials, monographs and reports and produces films.

NFRN National Federation of Retail Newsagents, Booksellers and Stationers. 2 Bridewell Pl, London EC4, England.

NFSAIS National Federation of Science Abstracting and Indexing Services. Name changed to NFAIS in 1972.

NGDC National Geophysical Data Center. *See* NGSD.

NGSD National Geophysical and Solar Terrestrial Data Center. Environmental Research Laboratories, National Oceanic and Atmospheric Administration, Boulder, CO 80302. *See* L. Christopher Wright and Elizabeth W. Stone. "Data and Information Services of the National Oceanic and Atmospheric Administration." *Special Libraries* 65 (Aug. 1974): 311–318. Also known as NGDC and NGSTDC. Sponsored by NOAA.

NGSTDC National Geophysical and Solar Terrestrial Data Center. *See* NGSD.

NHCUC New Hampshire College and University Council. Library Policy Committee, 2321 Elm St, Manchester, NH 03104. Twelve member libraries cooperate through ILL, reciprocal borrowing, acquisitions, union list of serials and resource sharing and participate in NELINET.

NHIR Natural History Information Retrieval System. Smithsonian Institution, Washington, DC 20560.

NHLA New Hampshire Library Association. Contact president or ALA (American Library Association). Publishes a newsletter from NHLA, Bedford, NH 03102. V. 1, 1940.

NHLC New Hampshire Library Council. Made up of the Academic Librarians of NH, the Friends of NH Libraries, NH Aides in Instructional Media, the NH Hospital Librarians Association, the NH Library Association and the NH Library Trustees Association.

NHPIC National Health Planning Information Center. Box 1600, Prince George's Plaza Branch, Hyattsville, MD 20788. Part of DHEW's Health Resources Administration. A source for documents in NLM's Health Planning and Administration data base.

NHS National Health Service. Alexander Fleming House, Newington Causeway, London SE1, England.

NIALSA Northwest Indiana Area Library Services Authority. 200 West Indiana Ave, Box 948, Chesterton, IN 46304. Forty-nine academic, public and special libraries cooperate through ILL, resource sharing, CE and other programs.

NIAM Nederlands Instituut voor Audio Visuele Middlelen (Netherlands Institute for Audiovisual Media). The Hague, the Netherlands.

NIB National Information Bureau. 419 Park Ave. South, New York, NY 10016. Established in 1918.

NIC Neighborhood Information Centers Project. National Project Office, Cleveland Public Library, 325 Superior Ave, Cleveland, OH 44114. Originally funded for 1972–1973 to establish neighborhood information centers in Atlanta, Cleveland, Detroit, Houston and New York.

NICA Non-Interactive Computer Applications.

NICB National Industrial Conference Board. Name changed to CB in 1970.

NICE National Information Conference and Exposition. The third annual meeting of AIM (Associated Information Managers), an affiliate of IIA (Information Industry Association), was held in Washington, DC, in 1979.

NICE National Institute of Ceramic Engineers. 65 Ceramic Dr, Columbus, OH 43214. Established in 1938. Publishes a monthly newsletter.

NICEM National Information Center for Educational Media. University of Southern California, University Park, Los Angeles, CA 90007. Established in 1967.

NICS Northern Inter-Library Cooperation Scheme. Regional resource-sharing initiative in the Northern Rivers area of New South Wales, Australia.

NICSEM National Information Center in Special Education Materials. University of Southern California, University Park, Los Angeles, CA 90007. Formerly NIMIS. Provides computer searches, bibliographies and other services to the handicapped.

NIDER Nederlands Instituut voor Informatie, Documentatie en Registratuur (Netherlands Institute for

Information, Documentation and
Filing). Burgemeester van
Karnebeeklaan 19, The Hague, the
Netherlands.

NIE National Institute of Education.
Educational Resources Information
Center, 1700 19th St, NW, Washington,
DC 20208. Provided for as part of the
Education Amendments of 1972.

NIER National Institute for Educational
Research (Kokuritsu Kyoiku
Kenkyusho Fuzoku Kyoiku Toshokan).
Library of Education, 6-5-22,
Shimomeguro, Meguro-ku, Tokyo 153,
Japan.

NIFKI Vsesojuznyj Naučno-
Issledovatel'skij Kinofotoinstitut
Gosudarstvennogo Komiteta po
Kinematografi pre Sovete Ministrov
SSSR. Leningraskij Prospekt 47,
Moscow A-57, USSR. A research
institute of the USSR state committee on
cinematography. Library established in
1932.

NIH National Institutes of Health. 9000
Rockville Pike, Bethesda, MD 20014.
Composed of 11 research institutes.
Library established in 1903. Conducts
and supports biomedical research into
the causes, prevention and cure of
diseases. Supports research training and
the development of research resources
and makes uses of modern methods to
communicate biomedical information.
See also BHME.

NIIRP Naučno-Issledovatel'skij Institut
Rezinovoj Promyšlennosti Ministerstva
Neftpererabatyvajuščej i
Neftechimičeskoj, Promyšlennosti
SSSR. M Trubeckaja 28, Moscow
G-480, USSR. A rubber research
institute of the USSR ministry of the oil
refining and oil chemistry industry.
Library established in 1946.

NIKIMP Naučno-Issledovatel'skij i
Konstruktorskij Institut Ispytatel'nych
Mašin, Priborov i Sredstv Avtomatizacii
i Sistem Upravlenija SSSR. Cholodil'nyj
per 1, Moscow M-26, USSR. A USSR
institute for the research and design of
machines, instruments and automated
systems. Library established in 1947.

NIL Not in Library. Response to a user's
request or to an interlibrary loan
request.

NIMH National Institute of Mental Health.
5600 Fishers La, Rockville, MD 20857.
Library established in 1962.

NIMIS National Instructional Materials
Information System. Name changed to
NICSEM in 1977.

NIMR National Institute for Medical
Research. The Ridgeway, Mill Hill,
London NW7, England.

NINDS National Institute of Neurological
Diseases and Stroke. National Institutes
of Health, 9000 Rockville Pike,
Bethesda, MD 20014.

NINDS Neurological Science Information
Network. Clinical Neurology
Information Center, University of
Nebraska Medical Center, 42 St. &
Dewey, Omaha, NE 68105.

NIOSH National Institute for Occupational
Safety and Health. 5600 Fishers La,
Rockville, MD 20857. Reports to the
Center for Disease Control. Develops
and implements safety standards.
Compiles RTECS.

NIPD Not in the Public Domain. Refers to
copyright status.

NIPDOK Nippon Documentesyon Kyokai
(Japan Documentation Society). c/o
Sasaki Bldg, 5-7 Koisikawa 2,
Bunkyo-ku, Tokyo 112, Japan.
Established in 1950.

NIPHLE National Institute of Packaging,
Handling and Logistics Engineers. Box
2765, Arlington, VA 22202. Established
in 1956. Publishes serials.

NIRC National Information Retrieval
Colloquium. *See* ANIRC.

NIRNS National Institute for Research in
Nuclear Science. Rutherford High
Energy Laboratory, Chilton, Didcot,
Berkshire, England.

NISARC National Information Storage and
Retrieval Centers.

NISP National Information System for
Psychology. American Psychological
Association, 1200 17th St, NW,
Washington, DC 20036.

NISPA National Information System for
Physics and Astronomy. American
Institute of Physics, 335 East 45 St, New
York, NY 10017. A plan for a national

information system for physics and astronomy proposed by AIP and AAPT in Feb. 1971. For descriptive information *see* "AIP Releases Study of Information Patterns of Physicists . . ." *Information* 3 (Jan.-Feb. 1971): 3-11.

NISS National Institute of Social Sciences. Established in 1912. Address unknown since 1972. Published documents.

NITHO Nederlands Instituut voor Toegepast Huishoudkundig Onderzoek. 32a Postbus 60, Wageningen, the Netherlands. Established in 1955.

NJ Norsk Journalistlag (Norwegian Union of Journalists). Rosenkrantz Gate 3, Oslo 1, Norway. Established in 1946. Member of the International Federation of Journalists. Publishes documents.

NJLA New Jersey Library Association. Contact president or ALA (American Library Association).

NL New-Line. A character in a string of machine-readable data that indicates the start of a line.

NLA National Librarians Association. Contact president or refer to the latest *ALA Directory* (American Library Association) of members. Established in 1977. Addresses the concerns of the professional librarian.

NLA National Library of Australia. Canberra 2600, Australia. Established in 1902.

NLA Nebraska Library Association. Contact president or ALA (American Library Association).

NLA Nevada Library Association. Contact president or ALA (American Library Association).

NLA Newfoundland Library Association. Box 4372, Harvey Rd. Post Office, Saint John.'s, NF A1C 2G1, Canada.

NLA Nigerian Library Association. PMB 12655, Lagos, Nigeria. Founded in 1962.

NLB National Library for the Blind. 35 Great Smith St, London SW1, England. Established in 1882. Produces books in braille.

NLC National Libraries Committee. Published the Dainton Report in 1969, which comprises recommendations concerning the management and continued development of BL (British Library).

NLC National Library of Canada. 395 Wellington St, Ottawa ON KIA ON4, Canada. Established in 1953.

NLL National Lending Library for Science and Technology. Established in 1962. In 1973 incorporated as a major part of BLLD of BL (British Library). Also known as NLLST.

NLLST National Lending Library for Science and Technology. *See* NLL.

NLM National Library of Medicine. 8600 Rockville Pike, Bethesda, MD 20014. Established in 1836. Publishes *IM* (*Index Medicus*) and other journals. Maintains 12 RMLs.

NLN National Library of Nigeria. 4 Wesley St, PMB 12626, Lagos, Nigeria. Established in 1974.

NLS National Library of Scotland. Established in 1682 as The Advocates' Library. Present name adopted in 1925.

NLS National Library Services for the Blind and Physically Handicapped. 1291 Taylor St, NW, Washington, DC 20542. A division of LC.

NLTF National Libraries Task Force. Concerned with automation and other cooperative services. Members from LC, NAL (National Agricultural Library) and NLM.

NLW National Library Week. Held each spring in the US since 1958.

NMA National Micrographics Association. 8728 Colesville Rd, Silver Spring, MD 20910. Formerly the National Microfilm Association.

NMAA National Machine Accountants Association. Name changed to DPMA in 1962.

NMAC National Medical Audiovisual Center. 1600 Clifton Rd, NE, Atlanta, GA 30333. A division of NLM.

NMC National Meteorological Center. National Weather Service, National Oceanic and Atmospheric Agency, Camp Springs, MD 20233. Established in 1958. Collects and analyzes data on a worldwide basis and produces weather predictions.

NMHC National Materials Handling Center. Cranefield Institute of Technology, Cranefield, Bedford, England. Publishes *International Handling Review*.

NMLA New Mexico Library Association. Contact president or ALA (American Library Association).

NMTA National Metal Trades Association. Name changed to AAIM in 1965.

NOAA National Oceanic and Atmospheric Administration. 6010 Executive Blvd, Rockville, MD 20852. An agency of the US Dept. of Commerce. Sponsors NSGD.

NOBIN Netherlands Orgaan voor de Bevordering van de Informatieverzorging (Netherlands Organization for Information Policy). Burgemeester van Karnebeeklaan 19, The Hague, the Netherlands. Established in 1971. Member of FID. Publishes documents.

NODC National Oceanographic Data Center. National Oceanic and Atmospheric Administration, 2001 Wisconsin Ave, NW, Washington, DC 20235. Established as an interagency organization in 1961. Sponsored by AEC, the US Departments of Commerce, Interior and Navy, and NSF.

NOLA Northeastern Ohio Library Association. Reference and Information Services, 118 East Wood St, Youngstown, OH 44503.

NOLAG Northwestern Ontario Library Action Group. Reported inactive in 1978.

NOLTN Northeast Ohio Library Teletype Network.

NOM *Newspapers on Microfilm*. Published by the Catalog Publication Division of LC. Records US holdings of domestic and foreign newspapers.

NOMAD An algebraic compiler adapted from the MAD (Michigan Algorithmic Decoder) language to meet the special needs of the installation. It is a high-speed compiler which permits a wide latitude of generality in expressions.

NOR Not Or. Logical operator equivalent to "not or."

NORASIS Northern Ohio Chapter of ASIS. Contact chairperson or ASIS.

NORC National Opinion Research Center. University of Chicago, 6030 South Ellis Ave, Chicago, IL 60637. Established in 1941.

NORIA Normes et Reglementation-Information Automatisée. Association Française de Normalisation, Tour Europe, Cedex 7, Paris la Defense 92080, France. Bibliographic data base covering standards and regulations in science, technology and industry.

NORMARC Norwegian MARC.

NORMATERM Banque de Terminologie Normalisée. Association Française de Normalisation, Tour Europe, Cedex 7, Paris la Defense 92080, France. Full text data base covering standards and regulations in science, technology and industry.

NORWELD Northwest Library District. Box 828, Bowling Green, OH 43402. Thirty-four public libraries cooperate through ILL, reference services, grants, film collection and public relations.

NOTIS Northwestern On-Line Totally Integrated System. Northwestern University, Evanston, IL 60201. An automated system for library acquisitions, cataloging and serials control. *See* Robert C. Emmett. "Automation and Its Impact on a Transportation Library." *Special Libraries* 70 (Nov. 1979): 479-486.

NOTS Naval Ordnance Test Station. The location of the first reported library computerization. Report was presented at a conference in 1954 and published in 1957 (*JACM* 4 [Apr. 1957]: 131-136). *See* Frederick G. Kilgour. "History of Library Computerization." *JOLA* 3 (Sept. 1970): 218-229.

NOTU Nederlandse Organisatie van Tijdschrift Uitgevers. Herengracht 257, Postbus 10568, Amsterdam, the Netherlands. Established in 1946. Member of the International Federation of the Periodical Press.

NP Nonprint Code. An impulse that inhibits line printing under machine control.

NP Norsk Presseforbund (Norwegian Press Association). Rosenkrantz gate 3, Oslo 1, Norway. Established in 1910.

NPA National Paperboard Association. Established in 1932. Superseded by API (American Paper Institute) in 1964.

NPA Newspaper Publishers Association Ltd. 6 Bouverie St, London EC4, England.

NPAC National Program for Acquisition and Cataloging. US program for acquiring and cataloging foreign materials. Funded by the US Higher Education Act of 1965.

NPC National Periodicals Center. Plan being debated. The original NCLIS proposal to house NPC at LC was rejected by LC. CLR proposed a "plan for consideration."

NPIS National Physics Information System. American Institute of Physics, 335 East 45 St, New York, NY 10017.

NPL New South Wales Public Library. Macquarie St, Sydney, New South Wales 2000, Australia. Official name is Public Library of New South Wales.

NRC National Referral Center. Science and Technology Division, Library of Congress, 10 First St, SE, Washington, DC 20540. A telephone reference service.

NRC National Research Council. 100 Sussex Drive, Ottawa, ON, Canada. Maintains CISTI/ICIST.

NRCd National Reprographic Centre for Documentation. The Hatfield Polytechnic Institute, Hatfield, Hertfordshire, England.

NRCST National Referral Center for Science and Technology. *See* NRC.

NRL National Reference Library. *See* NRLSI.

NRL National Registry for Librarians. Illinois State Employment Office, 208 South LaSalle St, Chicago, IL 60604. Arranges for placement service at ALA (American Library Association) conferences.

NRLB Northern Regional Library Bureau. Central Library, New Bridge St, Box IMC, Newcastle upon Tyne NE99 IMC, England.

NRLSI National Reference Library of Science and Invention. Formed in 1966 by the amalgamation of POL (Patent Office Library) with certain science collections of BM. Also known as NRL. Name changed in 1974 to SRL, part of the Reference Division of BL (British Library).

NRMM National Register of Microform Masters. Located in LC. *See* Robert C. Sullivan. "Microform Developments Related to Acquisitions." *C&RL* 34 (Jan. 1973): 16–28.

NRZ Non-Return-to-Zero. Pertains to a method of binary digital data representation.

NRZC Non-Return-to-Zero Change Recording. Method of recording in which 0's and 1's are represented by two specified different conditions of magnetization.

NRZM Non-Return-to-Zero Mark Recording. A recording technique in which a change in the condition of magnetization represents a 1, the absence of such a change representing a 0.

NSA *Nuclear Science Abstracts*. Published from 1948 to 1976 by the US Energy Research and Development Administration. Superseded in part by *Energy Research Abstracts*, published by the US Department of Energy, and *INIS AtomIndex*, published by INIS and distributed in the US by UNIPUB.

NSCCA National Society for Crippled Children and Adults. 2023 West Ogden Ave, Chicago, IL 60612. Publishes indexes, bibliographies and other documents.

NSDP National Serials Data Program. Serial Record Division, Library of Congress, Washington, DC 20540. Established in 1972 and supported by LC, NAL (National Agricultural Library) and NLM. NSDP is the US national center for participation in ISDS, the international cooperative effort to provide worldwide control of serial publications. Contributes records on US serials to the ISDS register in Paris. Also serves as center for the CONSER Project.

NSF National Science Foundation. 1800 G St, NW, Washington, DC 20550. Established in 1950.

NSIC Nuclear Safety Information Center. Oak Ridge National Laboratory, Box Y, Oak Ridge, TN 37830. Sponsored by ERDA. Provides information on all aspects of nuclear safety. Publishes documents.

NSL National Science Library. A Canadian library established in 1953 as the National Research Council Library. In 1974, merged with TIS of NRC (National Research Council) to form CISTI/ICIST.

NSLA Nova Scotia Library Association. Contact secretary. A Canadian association.

NSMR National Society for Medical Research. NSMR Data Bank, 1330 Massachusetts Ave, NW, Suite 103, Washington, DC 20005. Maintains a library.

NSPI National Society for Performance and Instruction. 1126 16th St, NW, Suite 315, Washington, DC 20036. Established in 1962. Publishes documents. Formerly NSPI (National Society for Programmed Instruction).

NSPI National Society for Programmed Instruction. Name changed to NSPI (National Society for Performance and Instruction).

NSRDS National Standard Reference Data System. A system of NBS.

NSSC National Society for the Study of Communication. Name changed to ICA (International Communication Association).

NSSDC National Space Science Data Center. Goddard Space Flight Center, Greenbelt, MD 20771. Provides information on space science, including astronomy, solar physics, particles and fields, ionospheres and radio physics, planetary atmospheres and planetology. Also known as SSDC.

NSSLA Nova Scotia School Library Association. c/o Nova Scotia Teachers Union, Box 1060, Armdale PO, Halifax NS B3L 4L7, Canada.

NST *New Serial Titles*. V. 1, 1950. Published by LC. Lists serials received by LC and other reporting libraries. Supersedes ULS.

NSTA National Science Teachers Association. 1742 Connecticut Ave, NW, Washington, DC 20009. Established in 1895. Publishes documents.

NSTIC Naval Scientific and Technical Information Centre. An agency of the UK. Formerly ACSIL.

NT Narrower Term. Refers to a cross-reference in a thesaurus.

NTC National Translations Center. John Crerar Library, 35 West 33 St, Chicago, IL 61616.

NTCA National Telephone Cooperative Association. 2626 Pennsylvania Ave, NW, Washington, DC 20037. Established in 1954. Aids members in industry and personnel relations.

NTH Norges Tekniske Høgskole (Library of the Norwegian Institute of Technology). N-7034 Trondheim, Norway. Established in 1922. Affiliated with the University of Trondheim.

NTIA National Telecommunications and Information Agency. An agency of the US Department of Commerce.

NTIAC Non-Destructive Testing Information Analysis Center. US Army Materials and Mechanics Center, Arsenal St, Watertown, MA 02172. Library covers radiography ultrasonics, electromagnetics and other nondestructive methods.

NTIS National Technical Information Service. US Dept. of Commerce, 5285 Port Royal Rd, Springfield, VA 22161. Maintains an on-line bibliographic data base covering government-sponsored research reports. Publishes *GRA&I*. Formerly (1970) CFSTI.

NUC Nashville University Center. Library Resources Committee, Box 8, Fisk University, Nashville, TN 37203. Consortium established in 1969. Library Resources Committee operates a cooperative work-study program between the Peabody Library School and JUL.

NUC *National Union Catalog*. Vol. 1, 1956. Published by the Library of Congress. A cumulative author list representing LC printed cards and titles reported by other American libraries. Monthly with various cumulations.

NUCMC *National Union Catalog of Manuscript Collections.* 1962 and Index 1959-1962. 2 Vols. Hamden, CT: Shoe String Press, 1964. Presents uniform descriptions of American repositories of manuscripts. Subsequent biennial and annual volumes published by LC.

NUCOM National Union Catalogue of Monographics. National Library of Australia's file of current and retrospective cataloging information, called NUCOM when the two files were merged in 1968.

NUEA National University Extension Association. A member of the Joint Committee on University Extension Library Services with ACRL/ULS.

NUJ National Union of Journalists. Acorn House, 314 Gray's Inn Rd, London WC1, England.

NUL Null Character. A control character used to fill unused time in a data transmission system or space in a storage medium.

NVB Nederlandse Vereniging van Bibliothecarissen (Netherlands Association of Librarians). c/o Mr. F. H. J. Buijs, c/o Bibliotheck KNAW, Klovenrersburgwal 29, Amsterdam, the Netherlands. Affiliated with IFLA.

NVBA Nederlandse Vereniging van Bedrijfsarchivarissen (Netherlands Association of Business Archivists). c/o T. van de Graaf, Zuidlarenstraat 119, 's-Gravenhage, the Netherlands.

NVBF Nordiska Vetenskapliga Bibliotekarieförbundet (Scandinavian Association of Research Librarians). Jyväskylä University Library, SF-40100 Jyväskylä 10, Finland. Established in 1947.

NVJ Nederlandse Vereniging van Journalisten. Johan Vermeerstraat 55, Amsterdam, the Netherlands. Established in 1946. Association of journalists. Member of the International Federation of Journalists. Publishes documents.

NVLP Nederlandse Vereniging van Lucht-en Ruimtevaarte-Publicisten

(Netherlands Aerospace Writers Association). Jan van Nassaustraat 125, The Hague, the Netherlands. Established in 1960.

NWRLS North Western Regional Library System. Central Library, Saint Peter's Sq, Manchester M2 5PD, England.

NYAC New York Astronomical Corporation. 100 Fuller Rd, Albany, NY 12205. Founded in 1968 by private and public institutions to gather astronomical information and to build and operate a major optical observing facility for New York State astronomers. Funds are sought from private and government sources.

NYAP New York Assembly Program. Assembly program written for the IBM 704 computer.

NYAS New York Academy of Sciences. 2 East 63 St, New York, NY 10021. Established in 1817 and incorporated in 1818. Formerly (1876) the Lyceum of National History of the City of New York. Has a specialty division in Computer and Information Sciences. Publishes documents. Some foreign members.

NYLA New York Library Association. 60 East 42 St, New York, NY 10017.

NYLIC New York Library Instruction Clearinghouse. F. Franklin Moon Library, SUNY College of Environmental Science and Forestry, Syracuse, NY 13210. Acts as a clearinghouse for academic library orientation and instruction information and materials.

NYMS New York Mathematical Society. Name changed to AMS.

NYPL New York Public Library. Astor, Lenox, & Tilden Foundations Library, Fifth Ave. & 42 St, New York, NY 10018. Also serves as the headquarters for all Manhattan, Bronx and Staten Island branch public libraries.

NYSILL New York State Interlibrary Loan Network. c/o New York State Library, Albany, NY 12234. Thirty-one public and research library systems cooperate through ILL.

NYSL New York State Library. Cultural Education Center, Albany, NY 12230.

Established in 1818. Started an automated serials acquisition project as a first step in computerization of library functions in 1966. Has an on-line book and serial catalog.

NZLA New Zealand Library Association. 10 Park St, Box 12-212, Wellington 1, New Zealand. Established in 1910. Affiliated with IFLA and UNESCO. Official journal, *New Zealand Libraries*, is published bimonthly. *See* "Forty-first Conference, New Zealand Library Association, Wellington, Feb. 1974." *New Zealand Libraries* 37 (Aug. 1974): 146-219.

OA Operations Analysis.

OACUL Ontario Association of College and University Libraries. Contact OLA (Ontario Library Association). Also known as l'Association des Bibliothèques des Collèges et des Universités d'Ontario.

OAED Office of Audiovisual Educational Development. 1600 Clifton Rd, NE, Atlanta, GA 30333. Established by BHME and NLM.

OAIDE Operational Assistance and Instructive Data Equipment.

OALT/ABO Ontario Association of Library Technicians/Association des Bibliotechniciens de l'Ontario. Box 682, Oakville ON L6J 5C1, Canada.

OAS Organization of American States. 17 St. & Constitution Ave, NW, Washington, DC 20006. Has an office of Library Development and an Inter-American Program of Library and Bibliographic Development. Publishes documents and catalogs of books. Also known as OEA and OAS/OEA.

OASES Open Access Satellite Education Services. Cooperative venture of the Oklahoma County Libraries System and South Oklahoma City Junior College, started July 1, 1976. *See* Paul L. Little and J. Richard Guilliland. "OASES in Oklahoma." *Library Journal* 102 (July 1977): 1458-1461.

OASIS Oceanic and Atmospheric Scientific Information System. National Oceanic and Atmospheric Administration, Environmental Data Service, 11400 Rockville Pike, Rockville, MD 20852. A computerized information retrieval service.

OASIS Ohio Chapter of ASIS. Contact president or ASIS.

OAS/OEA Organization of American States/Organizacion de los Estados Americanos. *See* OAS.

OATS Original Article Tearsheet. A service of ISI (Institute for Scientific Information). Articles from journals can be secured either in the original tearsheets, or in photocopied form by the individuals purchasing the service. The publisher is paid royalties by ISI.

OBCE Office Belge du Commerce Exterieur. Ministry du Commerce Exterieur, Trade Center Bldg, E. Jacqmain 162, Brussels 1000, Belgium. Established in 1975. Member of ADP. Publishes documents.

OBCH Overseas Booksellers Clearing House. Book Center, Ltd, North Circular Rd, London NW10, England.

OBTS Offender Base Transaction Statistical System. Office of Criminal Justice Plans and Analysis, 1329 E St, NW, Washington, DC 20005. Data base produced for the DC Department of Corrections since 1969. Formerly TRACE.

OCCS Office of Computer and Communications Systems. National Library of Medicine, 8600 Rockville Pike, Bethesda, MD 20014. An office of NLM.

OCDDLS Ontario Committee of Deans and Directors of Library Schools. c/o Council of Ontario Universities, 130 Saint George St, Suite 8039, Toronto ON M5S 2T4, Canada.

OCI Office of Computer Information. An office of the US Department of Commerce.

OCJPA Office of Criminal Justice Plans and Analysis. 1329 E St, NW, Rm. 516, Washington, DC 20005. Produces criminal justice data bases for the DC government.

OCLC Ohio College Library Center, Inc. 1125 Kinnear Rd, Columbus, OH 43212. Maintains a sophisticated data base using MARC tapes and other on-line input data from users. Permits retrieval of cataloging copy, cards, holdings information, etc. Members take part in governance of the system.

OCR Optical Character Reader. Unit which scans printed material and converts it to machine-readable data.

OCR Optical Character Recognition. Machine identification of printed characters through use of light-sensitive devices.

OCT Office of Critical Tables. Established in 1957 to replace the Committee on Tables of Constants. Replaced in 1969 by the Numerical Data Advisory Board of the National Research Council.

OCUL Ontario Council of University Libraries. Also known as Le Conseil des Bibliothèques d'Université de l'Ontario.

ODB Output to Display Buffer. An auxiliary storage area in a computer that holds data in the process of being transmitted from output to display.

ODF Original Data File. Drug Abuse Epidemiology Data Center, Texas Christian University, Fort Worth, TX 76129. Nonbibliographic data base describing schools, hospitals and treatment agencies that are sources of drug abuse data. Coverage from 1935.

ODI Office Document Index.

OE Office of Education. *See* USOE.

OEA Organizacion de los Estados Americanos (Organization of American States). *See* OAS.

OECA Ontario Educational Communications Authority. 2180 Yonge St, Toronto ON M4S 2C1, Canada. Maintains a library and operates an educational television network. Library was started in 1970.

OECD Organization for Economic Cooperation and Development. 2 rue André Pascal, Paris 16, France. Member countries include Australia, Austria, Belgium, Canada, Denmark, Finland, France, Federal Republic of Germany, Greece, Iceland, Ireland, Italy, Japan, Luxembourg, the Netherlands, Norway, Portugal, Spain, Sweden, Switzerland, Turkey, the UK and the US. Sponsors many activities in information exchange and networks and bibliographic projects. Also known as OEEC.

OED *Oxford English Dictionary*. Oxford, England: Clarendon Press, 1933.

OEEC Organization for European Economic Cooperation. *See* OECD.

OEIMC Oklahoma Environmental Information and Media Center. East Central State College, Ado, OK 74820. Provides computerized searches and analytical reports to Oklahoma residents.

OELMA Ohio Educational Library Media Association. Contact president.

OEMI Office Equipment Manufacturers Institute. Name changed in 1961 to BEMA; and in 1972, to CBEMA.

OFMI Office Furniture Manufacturers Institute. Name changed to CBEMA.

OFR Office for Research. Contact ALA (American Library Association). Focuses on the research needs of the profession, surveys existing activity and, in cooperation with units of ALA, universities and other agencies engaged in library research, translates unmet needs into active programs.

OG *Official Gazette*. (Journal). V. 1, 1871. Published by the US Patent Office.

ÖGDI Österreichische Gesellschaft für Dokumentation und Information (Austrian Society for Documentation and Information). c/o Ö.P.Z. Renngasse 5, A-1010 Vienna, Austria. Established in 1951.

OIF Office for Intellectual Freedom. Contact ALA (American Library Association). Charged with implementing ALA policies concerning the concept of intellectual freedom as embodied in the *Library Bill of Rights*.

OIJ Organisation Internationale des Journalistes. *See* IOJ (International Organization of Journalists).

OIRSA Organismo Internacional Regional de Sanid Agroprecuaria. Established in 1953. Covers Mexico, Central America and Panama. Information Session in October 1976 in Guatemala.

OIT Organisation Internationale du Travail. *See* ILO (International Labour Organisation).

OLA Ohio Library Association. Contact president or ALA (American Library Association).

OLA Oklahoma Library Association. Contact president or ALA (American Library Association).

OLA Ontario Library Association. 2397A Bloor St. West, Toronto ON M6S 1P6, Canada.

OLA Oregon Library Association. Contact president or ALA (American Library Association).

OLDP Office of Library Development Program. Organization of American States, 17 St. & Constitution Ave, NW, Washington, DC 20006. Cosponsor of project LEER.

OLLR Office of Libraries and Learning Resources. US Office of Education, 400 Maryland Ave, SW, Washington, DC 20202. An office of the Bureau of Elementary and Secondary Education of USOE. Divisions include DET and DLP.

OLM Office du Livre Malagasy (Malagasy Book Office). Bibliothèque Nationale, BP 257, Malagasy. Established in 1971.

OLO On-Line Operation. Any computer operation directed by CPU (Central Processing Unit) rather than human intervention.

OLPR Office of Library Personnel Resources. Contact ALA (American Library Association).

OLRT On-Line Real Time. Computer operation allowing results to be obtained during the progress of an event.

OLSD Office for Library Service to the Disadvantaged. Contact ALA (American Library Association). Seeks to ensure that all rural and urban poor have convenient access to library service.

OLTA Ontario Library Trustees Association. A division of OLA (Ontario Library Association).

OM Committee on Operational Machine Technique and Systems. See FID/OM.

OMA Ontario Medical Association. 240 Saint George St, Toronto ON M5R 2P4, Canada. Maintains a library started in

1972. Prepares suggested lists of basic books and journals and a *Health Science Library Basic Manual*. Under a grant, it provides consulting service for Ontario hospital libraries.

OMB Office of Management and Budget. Old Executive Office Bldg, Washington, DC 20503. Formerly (1970) BoB. Plans and develops information systems to provide the President with program performance data.

OMKDK Orszagos Muszaki Konyvtar es Dokumentacias Kozpont. *See* HCTLDC (Hungarian Central Technical Library and Documentation Center).

OMM Organisation Météorologique Mondiale. *See* WMO (World Meteorological Organization).

OMNITAB II A general-purpose program which permits direct use of a computer without prior knowledge of computing languages. Tape and documentation package available from NTIS.

OMS Office of Management Studies. Association of Research Libraries, 1527 New Hampshire Ave, NW, Washington, DC 20036. Maintains SPEC.

OMS Organisation Mondiale de la Santé. *See* WHO (World Health Organization).

ONQ Order of Nurses of Quebec. Hersey-Upton Memorial Library, 4200 Dorchester West, Montreal PQ H3Z 1O4, Canada. Maintains a library and publishes documents. Formerly the Association of Nurses of the Province of Quebec.

ONU Organisation des Nations Unies. *See* UN (United Nations).

OOKDK Országos Orvostudományi Könyvtár és Dokumentációs Központ (National Medical Library and Center for Documentation). Szentkirályi u.21, Budapest VIII, Hungary. Established in 1960.

OOPS Off-Line Operating Simulator.

op Out of Print. Refers to published works no longer available from the publisher.

OPAL Ontario Puppetry Association, Ltd. 10 Skyview Cresent, Willowdale ON M2J 1B8, Canada. Maintains a library.

OPBU Operating Budget.

OPC Overseas Press Club of America, Inc. 55 East 43 St, New York, NY 10017.

OPI Office of Public Information. An office maintained in many governmental agencies, departments and bureaus. Its chief is frequently referred to as the PIO.

OPKM Országo Pedagógiai Konyvtár és Múzeum. Honvéd u.19, Budapest V, Hungary. Established in 1958.

OPLA Ontario Public Library Association. Contact OLA (Ontario Library Association). A division of OLA. Formerly the Regional and Public Libraries Division.

OPLAC Ontario Public Librarians Advisory Committee. Contact chairperson. Established in 1975.

OPLC Ontario Provincial Library Council. Contact secretary. A Canadian association.

OPLIC Office of Public Libraries and Interlibrary Cooperation. Minnesota State Dept. of Education, 301 Hanover Bldg, 480 Cedar St, Saint Paul, MN 55101. Established in 1901.

OPM Operations per Minute. Equivalent to ''Characters per Minute'' when control functions are included.

OPMA Overseas Press and Media Association, Ltd. Room 404, Daily Mirror Bldg, Holborn Circus, London EC1, England.

OPRIS Ohio Project for Research in Information Services. Set up by the Battelle Institute, this project's goal is to encourage the use of libraries by government personnel.

OPUS Octal Program Updating System. A Honeywell system used to update EASY 1 program tapes.

OR Operational Research. *See* OR (Operations Research).

OR Operations Research. The use of analytical methods to solve operational problems.

ORACLE A kind of computer.

ORAU Oak Ridge Associated Universities. Box 117, Oak Ridge, TN 37830. Consortium established in 1949.

ORBIT On-Line, Real-Time, Branch Information. An IBM programming language used by SDC (System Development Corporation) for its on-line data bases.

ORBIT ORACLE Binary Internal Translator. An algebraic programming system used on the ORACLE computer.

ORCHIS Oak Ridge Chemical Information System. Oak Ridge National Laboratory, Oak Ridge, TN 37830. A computerized hierarchical information system for chemistry.

ORI Operations Research, Inc. 1400 Spring St, Silver Spring, MD 20910. Provides consulting and information systems services. Member of IIA (Information Industry Association). Operates ERIC's Processing and Reference Facility in Bethesda, MD.

ORION On-Line Retrieval of Information over a Network.

ORNL Oak Ridge National Laboratory. Oak Ridge, TN 37830. The Technical Information Division of ORNL is the locale of ORCHIS. The laboratory, a large interdisciplinary institution, maintains libraries and an information analysis center.

ORS Operation Research Society. 62 Cannon St, London EC4, England.

ORSA Operations Research Society of America. 428 East Preston St, Baltimore, MD 21202. Publishes documents.

OR/SA Operations Research/Systems Analysis.

ORSTOM Office de la Recherche Scientifique et Technique d'Outre-Mer (Office of Overseas Scientific and Technical Research). 70 route d'Aulnay, Bondy F-93140, France. ORSTOM has issued *Bulletin Analytique d'Entomologie Medicale et Veterinaire* (formerly *Bulletin Signalétique d'Entomologie Medicale et Veterinaire*) since 1953. Produces POSEIDON data base.

OS Operating System. Complex computer routine that controls the execution of problem routines, often providing such services as scheduling, input/output control, debugging, compilation and data storage management.

OS Optical Scanning. The scanning of printed or written data with a device that generates digital representations for processing by computer.

os Out of Stock. Term referring to books that are temporarily out of print.

OSA Optical Society of America, Inc. 2000 L St, NW, Washington, DC 20036. Established in 1916 and incorporated in 1932. Has a division on Information Processing. Publishes standards and other documents.

OSD Optical Scanning Device.

OSGAE Osterreichische Studiengesellschaft für Atomenergie, GmbH. Austrian INIS Center, Lenaugasse 10, Vienna A-1082, Austria. Established in 1974. Provides machine searching, SDI and indexing.

OSHA Occupational Safety and Health Administration. US Dept. of Labor, 200 Constitution Ave, NW, Washington, DC 20210.

osi Out of Stock Indefinitely. Term referring to books that publishers have not declared out of print but have not scheduled for reprinting.

OSLA Ontario School Library Association. Contact OLA (Ontario Library Association). A division of OLA. Formerly (1976) the School Libraries Division.

OSR Offender Status Register. Project TRACE, 1329 E St, NW, Washington, DC 20005. Coverage from 1970. Nonbibliographic data base covering parolees in DC.

OSRD Office of Standard Reference Data. Established in 1963 by NBS. Compiles data for materials information centers.

OSSHE-OSL Oregon State System of Higher Education–Oregon State Library. Portland State University Library, Box 1151, Portland, OR 97207. Established in 1967. Developing a serials data base for all major Oregon libraries.

OST Office of Science and Technology. US government office established in 1962 to advise and assist the President and insure that science and technology are used in interest of national security and general welfare. Office abolished and functions transferred to the National Science Foundation in 1973.

OSTI Office for Scientific and Technical Information. Now incorporated as part of the Research and Development Department of BL (British Library).

OTIS Oklahoma Teletype Interlibrary System. 200 Northeast 18 St, Oklahoma City, OK 73105. Sixteen academic, public and special libraries cooperate through ILL and reference services.

OTIS Oregon Total Information System. 354 East 40 St, Eugene, OR 97405. *See* C. McAllister. "On-Line Library Housekeeping Systems." *Special Libraries* 62 (Nov. 1971): 457–468. *See also* LEADS (Library Experimental Automated Demonstration System).

OTIU Overseas Technical Information Unit. An agency of DTI (Department of Trade and Industry), now known as DoI (Department of Industry) of the UK.

OTRAC Oscillogram Trace Reader.

OTS Office of Technical Services. Name changed to CFSTI and, in 1971, to NTIS.

OUBCP Ontario Universities Bibliographic Centre Project. 4 Davonshire Pl, Toronto 18, ON, Canada. A computerized bibliographic project.

OULCS Ontario Universities Library Cooperative System. Office of Library Coordination, Council of Ontario Universities, 130 Saint George St, Suite 8039, Toronto ON M5S 2T4, Canada. A division of COU established in 1973. Twenty-seven academic, public and government libraries share resources, collection development, reciprocal borrowing and other cooperative activities. Operates CODOC.

OUP Oxford University Press. Walton St, Oxford OX2 6DP, England; 200 Madison Ave, New York, NY 10016. Publishes scholarly works in all fields.

OUTRAN Output Translator. An IBM product.

OVAC Overseas Visual Aids Centre. 31 Tavistock Sq, London WC1, England.

OVAL Ohio Valley Area Libraries. 107 West Broadway, Wellston, OH 45692. Twelve public and two academic libraries cooperate through ILL, reference service, acquisitions and processing, grants, bookmobiles and advisory services.

PA *Physics Abstracts.* V. 1, 1898. Published by the Institution of Electrical Engineers.

PA Press Association, Ltd. 85 Fleet St, London EC4, England.

PA *Psychological Abstracts.* V. 1, 1927. Published by the American Psychological Association.

PA Publishers Association. 19 Bedford Sq, London WC1, England.

PABEA Philadelphia's Adult Basic Education Academy. Established in 1968 to offer free tutoring to adults. Expanded into the Center for Literacy, Inc, in 1978.

PABX Private Automatic Branch Exchange. A private automatic telephone exchange that implements the transfer of calls to and from the public telephone system.

PAC Personal Analog Computer.

PACC Product Administration and Contract Control. A concept for business data management.

PACFORNET Pacific Coast Forest Research Information Network. Name changed to WESTFORNET.

PACH Permanent Agricultural Committee. International Labor Office, CH 1211 Geneva 20, Switzerland. A committee of ILO.

PACIMWA Pacific Coast Independent Magazine Wholesalers Association. A regional association of independent book wholesalers.

PACT Project Accounting by Cost and Time. Used by Imperial Chemical Industries in Great Britain.

PACT I Project for the Advancement of Coding Techniques. A project supported by Douglas Aircraft Corp, Lockheed Aircraft Corp, North American Aviation, NOTS and Rand Corp. for use on the IBM 701 computer.

PAD Pontiac–Allen Park–Detroit Consortium. c/o Hutzel Hospital Medical Library, 4707 Saint Antoine, Detroit, MI 48201. Four hospital libraries cooperate as a MEDLINE consortium.

PADAT *Psychological Abstracts* Direct Access Terminal. American Psychological Association, 1200 17th St, NW, Washington, DC 20036. A byproduct of PATELL, PADAT allows the researcher to conduct a search at his or her own facility. Output may be obtained on-line if a printing terminal is used. Became operational in 1972.

PADTIG Paisley and District Technical Information Group. A British association, now terminated.

PAHO Pan American Health Organization. 525 23rd St, NW, Washington, DC 20037. A regional office of WHO (World Health Organization). Also has a library and sponsors library education in Latin America. Supporter of BIREME.

PAIS Public Affairs Information Service. 11 West 40 St, New York, NY 10018. Established in 1914. Publishes an index.

PALA Polish American Librarians Association. Victoria Gale, 757 West Golden Gate, Detroit, MI 48203. Established in 1976 to improve the ability of teachers, authors and publishers to respond to special interests of the large Polish-American segment of the US population.

PALINET Pennsylvania Area Library Network. 3420 Walnut St, Philadelphia, PA 19174. One hundred seventy academic, public and special libraries in DL, MD, NJ and eastern PA share bibliographic services.

PAMAI Program of Action for Mediation, Arbitration, and Inquiry. Contact ALA (American Library Association). A program of ALA in which disputes between library employers and librarians are brought for resolution.

PANS *Pest Articles and News Summaries.* (Journal). Published by the Centre for Overseas Pest Research, Foreign and Commonwealth Office, Overseas Development Association, College House, Wrights Lane, London W8 5SJ, England.

PANSDOC Pakistan National Scientific and Technical Documentation Center. Name changed to PASTIC in 1974.

PAPADI Perhimpunan Ahli Perpustakaan, Arsipdan Dokumentasi Indonesia (Indonesian Association of Librarians, Archives and Documentation). Established in 1956. Became APDI in

1962 and in 1973 joined HPCI to become IPI (Ikatan Pustakawan Indonesia).

PAPRICAN/IRS Pulp and Paper Research Institute of Canada/Information Retrieval Services. 570 Saint John's Blvd, Pointe-Claire PQ H9R 3J9, Canada. Computerized service for retrospective searches of pulp and paper literature.

PAPSI Perkumpulan Ahli Perpustakaan Seluruh Indonesia (Association of Librarians throughout Indonesia). Established in 1954. Name changed to PAPADI in 1956.

PARRS *Psychological Abstracts* Reference Retrieval System. An experimental reference retrieval project begun in 1970 and located at Syracuse University. Funded by the US Air Defense Center's Information Transfer Sciences Section to put three years of abstracts in machine-readable form. On-campus typewriter consoles were to have access to the data base.

PAS Personnel Administration Section. *See* LAMA/PAS.

PAS Publisher's Alert Service. US Office of Education, Washington, DC 20202. Plan announced in 1972 by USOE to establish a communication mechanism between publishers and developers of educational materials.

PASAR *Psychological Abstracts* Search and Retrieval. American Psychological Association, 1200 17th St, NW, Washington, DC 20036. A byproduct of PATELL. Provides for outside purchase of on-line *PA* (*Psychological Abstracts*) service by mail or telephone. The search is done on an individual basis.

PASCAL Programme Appliqué à la Sélection et à la Compilation Automatique de la Littérature. Centre National de la Recherche Scientifique, 15 quai Anatole-France, 75 Paris 7, France. The computer program language used to store and retrieve information in the Bulletin Signalétique series.

PASLIB Pakistan Association of Special Libraries. Box 534, Karachi, Pakistan. Established in 1968.

PASTIC Pakistan Scientific and Technological Information Center. Established in 1957 as PANSDOC.

Became part of the Pakistan Science Foundation in 1974 and renamed PASTIC. *See* M. A. Haleem. "Scientific Research, Science Libraries and Documentation Centers" in *Regional Documentation Centres Conference 1974*. Tehran, Iran: IRANDOC, 1974, pp. 51-56.

PAT Programmer Aptitude Tests.

PATELL *Psychological Abstracts* Tape Edition Lease or Licensing. American Psychological Association, 1200 17th St, NW, Washington, DC 20036. Lease allows use of the tapes for the institution's own personnel. Licensing permits service to others.

PATRICIA Practical Algorithm to Retrieve Information Coded in Alphanumeric.

PAU Pattern Articulation Unit. A parallel processor whose basic mission is the rapid dissection and separation, or articulation, of image data into recognizable parts. *See* S. R. Ray. "Design of an Image-Oriented Information Retrieval System" in *Mechanized Information Storage*, ed. by K. Samuelson. Amsterdam, the Netherlands: North Holland Publishing, 1968, pp. 692-711.

PAULMS *Pacific Area Union List of Medical Serials*. A computer printout of journal titles held by most health science libraries of the Pacific Southwest area. Available from PSRMLS.

PAVE Position and Velocity Extraction. Program used in Semi-Automatic Ground Environment Defense System computers.

PAX Private Automatic Exchange. A dial telephone exchange that provides private service but lacks the capability of transmitting calls to and from the public telephone system.

PB Publication Board. Acronym is the prefix to a numbered series of US research reports available from NTIS.

PBAA Periodical and Book Association of America. 208 East 43 St, New York, NY 10017. An association of publishers oriented toward newsstand sales.

PBI Projected Books, Inc. Commercial firm, now defunct.

PBP *Paperbound Books in Print*. New York: R. R. Bowker Co, 1955– . A semiannual publication.

PBS Public Broadcasting Service. 475 L'Enfant Pl, SW, Washington, DC 20024. A national nonprofit organization responsible for the selection and distribution of programs to public television stations. Started in 1971 as a result of the Public Broadcasting Act of 1967 which changed "educational" television to "public" television.

PBX Private Branch Exchange. A manually operated telephone exchange connected to the public system on the customer's premises and operated by customer-supplied personnel.

PCA Print Council of America. National Gallery of Art, Washington, DC 20565. Established in 1956. Publishes documents.

PCGN Permanent Committee on Geographical Names (for British Official Use). One Kensington Gore, London SW7, England.

PCHE Pittsburgh Council on Higher Education. 222 Craft Ave, Pittsburgh, PA 15213. Ten libraries cooperate to facilitate communications with school administration committees.

PCLA Polish Canadian Librarians Association. Contact secretary. Established in 1977. A Canadian association.

PCLS Parish and Community Libraries Section. *See* CLA/PCLS.

PCM Pulse Code Modulation. Form of pulse modulation in which the information to be transmitted is represented by characters, each character being represented in turn by some combination of pulses.

PCM Punchcard Machine.

PCMI Photochromic Micro-Image. NCR trademark for a film miniature.

PCS Punched Card System.

PCT Patent Cooperation Treaty. Proposed by ICIREPAT in 1970 and reported at the joint ACS (American Chemical Society)/Chemical Institute of Canada meeting May 25–27, 1970.

PDC Publications and Distribution Center. Air Force Logistics Command, Baltimore, MD 21220.

PDIN Pusat Documentasi Ilmiah Nasional (Indonesian Scientific and Technical Documentation Center). Djl. Raden Saleh 43, Dakarta, Indonesia.

PDP Programmed Data Processor. A DEC processor.

PDPS Parts Data Processing System.

PEA Public Education Association. 20 West 40 St, New York, NY 10018.

PEACESAT Pan-Pacific Education and Communication Experiments by Satellite. Project at the University of Hawaii.

PEARL Periodicals Automation Rand Library. Operational since 1969, this batch system manages over 2,000 annual serials subscriptions at Rand Corp. Library.

PEBCO Program Evaluation and Budget Committee. A former committee of ALA (American Library Association).

PEBUL Project for the Evaluation of Benefits from University Libraries. This OSTI-supported study, conducted in 1969 at Durham University in Durham, England, showed the popularity of the current awareness service.

PECBI Professional Engineers Conference Board for Industry. 2029 K St, NW, Washington, DC 20006. Established in 1953. Presently inactive.

PEISLA Prince Edward Island School Library Association. Prince Edward Island Teachers' Federation House, Box 6000, Charlottetown PE C1A 7N9, Canada.

PELB-IF Project Every Library Board Kit on Intellectual Freedom. Available from ALTA (American Library Trustee Association).

PEN Poets, Playwrights, Editors, Essayists and Novelists International English Centre. 62 Glebe Pl, London SW3, England.

PENALE Giurisprudenza Penale. Centro Elettronico di Documentazione-Italgiure, Corte Suprema di Cassaziono, Palazzo di Giustizia, Via Ulpiano 8, Rome 00193, Italy. Coverage from 1966. Full-text data base covering criminal case decisions of the supreme court of Italy.

PENCIL Pictorial Encoding Language. Data processing system for storing and retrieving line drawings.

PENNTAP Pennsylvania Technical Assistance Program. 501 J. Orvis Keller Bldg, University Park, PA 16802. Disseminates scientific and engineering information to business and industries.

PEP Program Evaluation Procedure. A management term.

PEP-402 Princeton Electronic Products–Model 402. Princeton Electronic Products, Inc, Box 101, New Brunswick, NJ 08902. A video scan conversion and image storage terminal produced by Princeton Electronic Products.

PERT Program Evaluation and Review Technique. Method for monitoring the progress of a project.

PERT/COST PERT/Cost. A PERT program for providing management with cost control for all phases of a project.

PERT/TIME PERT/Timing. A PERT program which allows management to plan, schedule and direct programs and projects and to evaluate progress during the project execution.

PESTDOC Pesticidal Literature Documentation. Derwent Publications, Ltd, Rochdale House, 128 Theobalds Rd, London WC1X 8RP, England. Bibliographic data base covering pest control and plant protection.

PET Packets of Educational Topics. Information Retrieval Center, Northern Colorado Educational Board of Cooperative Services, 1750 30th St, Suite 48, Boulder, CO 80301. Intended for independent learning.

PEVA Imam Sokak 1, Beyoglu, Istanbul, Turkey. Produces data bases in communications and economics.

PFB Petroleum Films Bureau. 4 Brook St, London W1, England.

PFL Public Free Library. 76/77 Main St, Box 110, Georgetown, Guyana.

PGEC Professional Group on Electronic Computers. c/o Institute of Electrical

and Electronics Engineers, 345 East 47 St, New York, NY 10017. A technical group devoted to the advancement of computer-related sciences, programming, engineering, storage devices and combinational logic. Formerly within IRE, which merged with AIEE to form IEEE in 1963.

PGIS Project Grant Information System. An education information retrieval system which provides information to USOE about its discretionary grant programs and projects.

PHILSOM Periodical Holdings in the Library of the School of Medicine. Washington University School of Medicine Library, Saint Louis, MO 63110. Originally used exclusively for the collection of the host library, the computer program for PHILSOM is now used by other organizations as well.

PHLAG Phillips Load and Go. Programming system for the IBM 709 computer.

PHRA *Poverty and Human Resources Abstracts.* V. 1–9, 1966–1969. Issued by the Institute of Labor and Industrial Relations, University of Michigan–Wayne State University. Retitled *Poverty and Human Relations: Abstracts and Survey of Current Literature* in 1970.

PHS Printing Historical Society. Saint Bride Institute, Bride Lane, London EC4, England.

PHS Public Health Service. *See* USPHS.

PI Programmed Instruction.

PI Proportional-plus-Integral. An algorithm used in digital control systems by engineers. *See* Cecil L. Smith Shendrikar and Paul W. Murrill. *Report on Project Themis: Studies in Digital Automata.* Baton Rouge, LA: Louisiana State University, College of Engineering, 1969.

PIADIC Programa de Información Agropecuaria del Istmo Centroamericana. Contact IICA-CIDIA. Proposed at the first meeting of Comité Coordinador del Sistema Regional de Información Agropecuaria, San José, Costa Rica, May 25–26, 1976, sponsored by Instituto Interamericano de Ciencias Agrícolas of OAS/OEA.

PIB Petroleum Information Bureau. 4 Brook St, London W1, England.

PIB Publishers Information Bureau. 575 Lexington Ave, New York, NY 10022. Established in 1945.

PIC Primate Information Center. Regional Primate Research Center, University of Washington, Seattle, WA 98195. Supported by NIH and administered by the University of Washington, PIC is a division of the Regional Primate Research Center that is open to any primatologist or any scientist using primates in laboratory research. Scientific literature of nonhuman primates.

PICA Project for Integrated Catalogue Automation. Lange Voorhout 34, The Hague, the Netherlands. A project started in 1968 by the Royal Library and six Dutch university libraries to establish on-line cataloging.

PID Proportional-plus-Integral-plus-Derivative. derivative. An algorithm used in digital control systems by engineers. *See* Cecil L. Smith Shendrikar and Paul W. Murrill. *Report on Project Themis: Studies in Digital Automata*. Baton Rouge, LA: Louisiana State University, College of Engineering, 1969.

PIE *Publications Indexed for Engineering*. Annual publication of Engineering Index, Inc. A listing of journals and other materials included in *EI*.

PIL Processing Information List. Program used in IBM's Yorktown Heights Library. *See* G. E. Randall and Roger P. Bristol. "PIL (Processing Information List) or a Computer-Controlled Processing Record." *Special Libraries* 55 (Feb. 1964): 82–91.

PIMNY Printing Industries of Metropolitan New York. 461 Eighth Ave, New York, NY 10001. Provides instruction in all aspects of the graphic arts industries.

PIN Piece Identification Number. A machine-coded book label.

PIO Public Information Officer. The official who heads the OPI (Office of Public Information) in many governmental agencies, departments or bureaus and is generally charged with releasing news of that agency.

PIP Pollution Information Project. National Research Council, Ottawa, ON, Canada. A data base offered to Canadians by CAN/SDI from 1971. Created by the merging of portions of various data bases.

PIRA Printing Industry Research Association. Randalls Rd, Surrey, Leatherhead 76161, England. Provides technical testing and consultative services. Maintains a data bank and publishes several abstracting journals.

PIRC Public Interest Research Centre. British government agency, now called the Social Audit.

PIRP Prison Information Reform Project. Group of librarians and citizens based in the Maryland–DC area calling for programs of library and information service to prisoners.

PIRS Philosophers Information Retrieval Service. Philosophy Documentation Center, Bowling Green State University, Bowling Green, OH 43403. Bibliographic data base on philosophy. Coverage from 1948.

PKTF Printing and Kindred Trades Federation. 60 Doughty St, London WC1, England.

PL Price List.

PL Public Law.

PL Public Library. Acronym often preceded by initial(s) of the city or town.

PLA Pakistan Library Association. Box 3412, Karachi, Pakistan. Established in 1958.

PLA Pennsylvania Library Association. Contact president or ALA (American Library Association).

PLA Philippine Library Association. c/o The National Library, Teodoro M. Kalaw St, Manila, Philippines. Established in 1923.

PLA Private Libraries Association. Ravelston, South View Rd, Pinner, Middlesex, England.

PLA Public Library Association. 50 East Huron St, Chicago, IL 60611. A division of ALA (American Library Association) formed by the merger of the Division of Public Libraries, the Library Extension Division and the Trustees Division.

PLA/AEPS PLA Alternative Education Programs Section. Contact PLA (Public Library Association). A section of PLA, which is a division of ALA (American Library Association).

PLA/AFLS PLA Armed Forces Librarians Section. Contact PLA (Public Library Association). A section of PLA, which is a division of ALA (American Library Association).

PLA/MLS PLA Metropolitan Libraries Section. Contact PLA (Public Library Association). A section of PLA, which is a division of ALA (American Library Association).

PLAN Public Library Automation Network. c/o Library Development Services, California State Library, Library-Courts Bldg, Box 2037, Sacramento, CA 95809. A public library consortium.

PLANIT Programming Language for Interactive Teaching. *See* J. Rosenbaum et al. *Computer-based Instruction in Statistical Inference: Final Report*. Technical memorandum M-2914/100/00. System Development Corp, Oct. 30, 1967.

PLAN-NALT Public Library Association of Nevada–Nevada Association of Library Trustees. One of the three sections of NLA (Nevada Library Association) established at the association's annual conference in 1972.

PLA/PLSS PLA Public Library Systems Section. Contact PLA (Public Libraries Association). A section of PLA, which is a division of ALA (American Library Association).

PLASDOC *Plastics Documentation*. (Journal). V. 1, 1965. Published by Derwent Publications, Ltd.

PLA/SMLS PLA Small and Medium-sized Libraries Section. Contact PLA (Public Libraries Association). A section of PLA, which is a division of ALA (American Library Association).

PLASTEC Plastics Technical Evaluation Center. Picatinny Arsenal, Bldg. 176, Dover, NJ 07801. Established in 1929. Publishes documents.

PLATO Programmed Logic for Automatic Teaching Operations. A form of computer-aided instruction. *See* Joan

Tomay Hicks. "Computer-Assisted Instruction in Library Orientation and Services." *BMLA* 64 (Apr. 1976): 238-241.

PLMS Preservation of Library Materials Section. *See* RTSD/PLMS.

PL/1 Programming Language, Version 1. Common computer programming language, similar to FORTRAN. Features include string manipulation, data structures and extensive editing capabilities. Useful for information retrieval and command and control applications. A flexible problem-oriented language.

PLR Public Lending Right. Special payment to author in recognition of the fact that one book bought by a UK library may be read by many readers.

PLS Public Libraries Section. *See* CLA/PLS.

PLSS Public Library Systems Section. *See* PLA/PLSS.

PMD Pharmaco-Medical Documentation. Biomedical Information Sciences, Box 401, 205 Main St, Chatham, NJ 07928. Provides computer searches, analytical reports and translations in the life sciences and pharmaceuticals fields. Member of IIA (Information Industry Association).

PMEST Personality, Matter, Energy, Space and Time. Ranganathan's facets.

PML Pierpont Morgan Library. 29 East 36 St, New York, NY 10016.

PMLA *Publications of the Modern Language Association*. (Journal). V. 1, 1884. Published by MLA (Modern Language Association of America).

PMM & Co. Peat, Marwick, Mitchell & Co. 345 Park Ave, New York, NY 10017. Conducted a joint study with ESA on the need for an ecological information clearinghouse and referral service. See *Scientific Information Notes* (NY), 2 (July-Aug. 1970): 149-151.

PMS Public Message Service. Public telegraph system operated by Western Union.

PNBC Pacific Northwest Bibliographic Center. Suzzallo Library, University of Washington, Seattle, WA 98195.

Resource sharing among libraries of AK, ID, MT, OR, WA and British Columbia.

PNI Pharmaceutical News Index. Data Courier Inc, 620 South Fifth St, Louisville, KY 40202. Data base covering current news about pharmaceuticals, cosmetics and medical devices.

PNLA Pacific Northwest Library Association. Contact president or ALA (American Library Association).

PNRHSL Pacific Northwest Regional Health Science Library. University of Washington Health Science Library, Seattle, WA 98185. One of NLM's RMLs (Region X), serving AK, ID, MT, OR and WA. *See* Gerald J. Oppenheimer. "The Regional Medical Libraries: Region X." *NLM News* 30 (Dec. 1975): 3-4.

POCS Patent Office Classification System.

POGO Programmer-Oriented Graphics Operation. Term used in electronics, electrical engineering and computer science.

POISE Personnel Operations Information System. General system used for maintaining personnel records.

POKE Panellinios Organosis Kinimatographikon Epicheirision. Grapheion Gravias 10-12, Athens, Greece. Association of film exhibitors.

POL Patent Office Library. Established in 1855. Incorporated as part of NRLSI in 1966 and, in 1973, as the Holburn Branch of SRL, a part of the Reference Division of BL (British Library).

POL Problem-Oriented Languages. There are hundreds, but the best known are ALGOL and BASIC.

POPINFORM Population Information. George Washington University Medical Center, 1343 H St, NW, Washington, DC 20005. Coverage from 1972. Bibliographic data base covering contraceptive technology, family planning and population policy.

POS Point of Sale. Used to describe electronic retail terminals as opposed to mechanical cash registers. *See also* SKU.

POSEIDON ORSTOM Pedology Data Bank. Office de la Recherche Scientifique et Technique Outre-Mer, 70 route d'Aulnay, Bondy F 93140, France. Coverage from 1970. Full-text data base covering research in the soil sciences.

POSH Permuted on Subject Headings.

POST Polymer Science and Technology. Experiment conducted by CAS (Chemical Abstracts Service) in 1966 to produce a customized subject publication of computer-searchable abstracts.

POST-J Polymer Science and Technology for Journals. Experiment conducted by CAS (Chemical Abstracts Service) in 1968 to cover journal abstracts in a customized computer-searchable mode.

POST-P Polymer Science and Technology for Patents. Experiment conducted by CAS (Chemical Abstracts Service) in 1968 to cover abstracts of patents in a customized computer-searchable mode.

PPA Periodical Publishers Association, Ltd. Imperial House, Kingsway, London WC2, England.

PPBS Planning-Programming-Budgeting System. A business administration concept adopted by libraries. *See* Sul H. Lee, ed. *Planning-Programming-Budgeting System (PPBS): Implications for Library Management*, Library Management Series, no. 1. Ann Arbor, MI: Pierian Press, 1973.

PPDS Physical Property Data Service. Institution of Chemical Engineers, 165-171 Railway Terr, Rugby, Warwickshire CU21 3HQ, England. Nonbibliographic data base covering properties of over 400 mostly organic chemical compounds.

PPITB Printing and Publishing Industry Training Board. Merit House, Edgware Rd, London NW9, England.

PPM Persatuan Perpustakaan Malaysia (Library Association of Malaysia). Box 2072, Kuala Lumpur, Malaysia. Established in 1966.

PPPI Pulp, Paper and Paperboard Institute. Established in 1964. Became API (American Paper Institute) in 1966.

PPS Pulses per Second.

PPUA Precision Plotter Users Association. Name changed to APG (Association for Precision Graphics).

PR Public Relations. PR departments are maintained in many libraries, companies and associations.

PRECIS Preserved Context Index System. System for subject indexing which combines human and computer-aided construction of indexes. Developed initially in the British National Bibliography to produce *BNB*. See *PRECIS: A Rotated Subject Index System*. London: British National Bibliography, 1969.

PRF *Publications Reference File*. V. 1, 1978. A catalog of publications currently offered for sale by the Superintendent of Documents. Published in microfiche by the Government Printing Office.

PRIM Program for Information Managers. Formed in 1978 as an affiliate of IIA (Information Industry Association). Name changed to AIM (Associated Information Managers) in 1979.

PRISM Personnel Records Information System for Management. Used by the British Civil Service Department.

PRLC Pittsburgh Regional Library Center. c/o Chatham College, Beatty Hall, 100 Woodland Rd, Pittsburgh, PA 15232. Fifty academic, public and special libraries cooperate through ILL, OCLC network, resources directory, union lists, borrowing privileges and CE programs.

PRO Public Record Office. Chancery Lane, London WC2, England.

PROCOMP Program Compiler.

PROF Pupil Registering and Operational Filing. Honeywell series of computer programs for educational support, including grade recording, testing and instruction in computer usage and financial accountability.

PROMCOM Project Monitoring and Control Method. A project monitoring and control program that employs the GE critical path method and allows reporting of projected progress and project status for efficient management control.

PROMIS Prosecutors Management Information System. Project TRACE, 1329 E St, NW, Washington, 20005. Coverage from 1971. Nonbibliographic data base produced for the US Attorney's Office in DC.

PROMT (Predicasts Overview of Markets and Technology). (Journal). Published by Predicasts Inc. Domestic and foreign marketing and technical information.

PRONTO A GE program for point-to-point work only. Simple and easy to use, it is a good alternative for smaller operations.

PROSPERO A fill-in-the-blanks process control system developed by IBM and Humble Oil Co.

PROXI Projection by Reflection Optics of Xerographic Images.

PRR Pulse Repetition Rate. The number of electric pulses per unit of time received by a point in a computer.

PRS Public Relations Section. *See* LAMA/PRS.

PRT Production Run Tape. A tape containing checked-out and scheduled production running on various computers.

PRT Program Reference Table. The listing of locations reserved for program variables, data descriptions of data arrays and other program information.

PS Poetry Society. 21 Earls Court Sq, London SW5, England.

PSAC President's Science Advisory Committee. Existed during the Eisenhower Administration.

PSCP Public Service Careers Program. Funded and operated by BLET.

PSI Pakistan Standards Institute. 39 Garden Rd, Saddar, Karachi 3, Pakistan. Issues English-language standards. Affiliated with ISO (International Standards Organization).

PSI Permuterm Subject Index. A permuted keyword index used in *SCI* (*Science Citation Index*) and *SSCI* (*Social Science Citation Index*).

PSI Proto Synthex Indexing. Program for the IBM 7090 computer to index each word in a running English text by a tape address scheme.

PSIP Project on Scientific Information in Psychology. *See* APA-PSIP.

PSRMLS Pacific Southwest Regional Medical Library Service. UCLA Biomedical Library, Los Angeles, CA 90024. One of NLM's RMLs (Region XI). Serves HI, CA and NV. *See* Phyllis S. Mersky. "The Regional Medical Libraries: Region XI." *NLM News* 31 (Jan. 1976): 3-4.

PSSLA Peel Secondary School Librarians Association. Contact CSLA (Canadian School Library Association). Established in 1971. Covers Peel County in Ontario.

PSTIAC Pavements and Soil Trafficability Information Analysis Center. Army Engineers Waterways Sta, Box 631, Vicksburg, MS 39180. A source of documents.

PSW Program Status Word. Stored at a fixed location, the PSW controls the order in which program instructions are executed and indicates the status of a program within the computing system.

PTL Public Television Library. 475 L'Enfant Pl, Washington, DC 20004. National center for exchange of programs between public television stations.

PTLA *Publishers Trade List Annual.* New York: R. R. Bowker Co, 1873-

PTS Predicasts Terminal System. Predicasts Inc, 200 University Circle Research Center, 11001 Cedar Ave, Cleveland, OH 44106. A group of bibliographic and statistical data bases covering investments, industry and commodities.

PTS Program Test System. A specific system that automatically checks out programs, producing diagnostic information where necessary, to aid in production run organization.

PTST Prime Time School Television. Three Prong Television Productions, Inc, 100 North La Salle St, Suite 1208, Chicago, IL 60602. Provides free guides and bibliographies of educational programs appearing on major networks.

PTT Program Test Tape. A specific tape that contains programs and data to be tested during a checkout run.

PTT/8 Paper Tape Transmission 8. An eight-level channel paper tape transmission code.

PTTI Postal, Telegraph and Telephone International. 105 rue Marché aux Herbes, Brussels 1, Belgium.

PTV Public Television. Educational television became "public" as a result of the Public Broadcasting Act of 1967.

PUDOC Centrum voor Landbouwpiblikaties en Landbouwdocumentatie (Center for Agricultural Publishing and Documentation). Duivendaal 62, Box 4, Wageningen, the Netherlands.

PW *Publishers Weekly.* (Journal). V. 1, 1872. Published by R. R. Bowker Co.

QACLD Quebec Association for Children with Learning Disabilities. 4820 Van Horne, Montreal PQ H3W 1J3, Canada. Library established in 1969. Library publishes a newsletter.

QAM Queued Access Method. Automatic synchronization of the transfer of data among devices to eliminate delays.

QASL Quebec Association of School Librarians. c/o Provincial Association of Protestant Teachers of Quebec, 84J Brunswick Blvd, Dollard des Ormeaux PQ H9B 2C5, Canada. A division of the Provincial Association of Protestant Teachers of Quebec.

QCB Queue Control Block. Queue block used in regulation of the sequential use of some programmer-defined facility by a set of competing tasks.

QCIM *Quarterly Cumulative Index Medicus.* V. 1, 1927-v. 60, 1956. Published by the American Medical Association.

QDRI Army Qualitative Development Requirements Information Program. The Los Angeles Chapter of SLA (Special Libraries Association) established a committee in June 1969 to study this program. Also known as QRI.

QED Quick Text Editor. A generalized text editor that allows on-line users to create and modify text for any purpose, by addition, deletion or change.

QISAM Queued Indexed Sequential Access Method.

QLA/ABQ Quebec Library Association/Association des Bibliothécaires de Québec. c/o Dawson College Library, 1001 Sherbrooke St. East, Montreal PQ H2L 1L3, Canada.

QPL Queensland Public Library. William St, Brisbane, Queensland, Australia. Official and correct name is the Public Library of Queensland.

QRI Army Qualitative Development Requirements Information Program. *See* QDRI.

QTAM Queued Telecommunications Access Method. An access method in which data transfer between a program and I/O facilities is automatically synchronized through telecommunications.

QUEASY An automatic coding system developed by NOTS at China Lake, CA, for use on the IBM 701 computer.

QUIC Queen's University Information Centre. QUIC/Law Project, 140 Beverly St, Kingston, ON, Canada. Produces data bases on political science, law and international studies.

QUIKTRAN A programming language, essentially a subset of FORTRAN, employed when a number of terminals use a single control processor on a time-sharing basis. The response time at any one terminal is sufficiently short that each user is unaware that others are using the same processor. Especially useful for conversational mode.

QUIP Questionnaire Interpreter Program. A computer program.

R Revised.

RA Research Assistant. Also applies to Research Associate.

RAC Reliability Analysis Center. Rome Air Development Center, Griffiss Air Force Base, NY 13441. An information analysis center for data on the reliability of microelectronic devices. Also known as RADC and RBRAC.

RACE Random Access Computer Equipment. Computer equipment in which access time is independent of data location.

RACEP Random Access Correlation for Extended Performance.

RACIC Remote Areas Conflict Information Center. Battelle Memorial Institute, Columbus Laboratories, 505 King Ave, Columbus, OH 43201.

RACS Remote Access Computing System.

RAD Rapid Access Disk. Method of computer storage.

RADA Random Access Discrete Address. Location in a computer.

RADAC Rapid Digital Automatic Computing.

RADAS Random Access Discrete Address System.

RADC Reliability Analysis Data Center. *See* RAC.

RADCOL Rome Air Development Center On-Line. *See* RAC.

RADIAC Radioactivity Detection Indication and Computation.

RADIICAL Retrieval and Automatic Dissemination of Information from *Index Chemicus* and Line Notations. Institute for Scientific Information, 325 Chestnut St, Philadelphia, PA 19106. *See* Eugene Garfield et al. *"Index Chemicus* Registry System: Pragmatic Approach to Substructure Chemical Retrieval." *Journal of Chemical Documentation* 10 (Feb. 1970): 54–58.

RADIR Random Access Document Indexing and Retrieval.

RAFES Royal Air Force Education Service. Adastral House, Theobalds Rd, London WC1, England.

RAI Random Access and Inquiry.

RAILS Reference and Interlibrary Loan Service. *See* IULC-RAILS.

RALF Rapid Access to Literature via Fragmentation Codes. *See* K. Loch and W. Neubling. "RALF: A New Software Package for the Whole Complex of Punched Card Oriented Documentation." *Journal of Chemical Documentation* 13 (Nov. 1973): 219–224.

RALI Resource and Land Information. Program of the US Geological Survey.

RAM Random Access Mass Memory. A file that is best used in a system conceived for single query processing as opposed to batch searching. *See* R. T. Chien and F. P. Preparata. "Search Strategy and File Organization in Computerized

Information Retrieval Systems with Mass Memory" in *Mechanized Information Storage*, ed. by K. Samuelson. Amsterdam, the Netherlands: North Holland Publishing Co, 1968, pp. 108-121.

RAM Random Access Memory. A storage technique in which time required to obtain information is independent of the location of that information. Also called Random Access Storage.

RAM Royal Academy of Music. Marylebone Rd, London NW1 5HT, England. Established in 1822.

RAMAC Random Access Method of Accounting and Control.

RAMIS Rapid Access Management Information System.

R&D Research and Development. Also known as RD.

R&EEC Register and Examinations Committee. The Library Association, 7 Ridgmount St, London WC1E 7AE, England. Also known as REEC.

RANDID Rapid Alphanumeric Digital Indicating Device.

RAPCOE Random Access Programming and Checkout Equipment.

RAPID Random Access Personnel Information Dissemination.

RAPID Random Access Photographic Index and Display.

RAPID Relative Access Programming Implementation Device.

RAPID Remote Access Planning for Institutional Development.

RAPID Research in Automatic Photocomposition and Information Dissemination.

RAPID Retrieval through Automated Publication and Information Digest. System Development Corp, 2500 Colorado Ave, Santa Monica, CA 90406. An SDC system.

RAPID Rotating Associative Processor for Information Dissemination.

RAPIDS Random Access Personnel Information Dissemination System.

RAPIDS Result from Action, Prediction, Informative, Diagnostic Sensing. A logical decision sequence which some computer systems follow. *See* K. Samuelson. "Information Structure and Decision Sequence" in *Mechanized Information Storage*, ed. by K. Samuelson. Amsterdam, the Netherlands: North Holland Publishing Co, 1968, pp. 622-636.

RAPRA Rubber and Plastics Research Association. Shawbury, Shrewsbury, Salop SY4 4NR, England. Issues *RAPRA Abstracts*.

RARE Rochester Area Resources Exchange. Consortium established in 1979.

RAS Readers Advisory Service. c/o Science Associates International, Inc, 1841 Broadway, New York, NY 10023. Established in 1973 by Science Associates International, Inc, with the support of libraries and information centers in the US and Canada. Collects and distributes subject bibliographies.

RAS Royal Agricultural Society. *See* RASE.

RASD Reference and Adult Services Division. 50 East Huron St, Chicago, IL 60611. A division of ALA (American Library Association) formed by the merger of ASD and RSD in 1972.

RASD/HS RASD History Section. Contact RASD. A section of RASD, which is a division of ALA (American Library Association).

RASD/MARS RASD Machine-Assisted Reference Section. Contact RASD. A section of RASD, which is a division of ALA (American Library Association).

RASE Royal Agricultural Society of England. 35 Belgrave Sq, London SW1, England. Also known as RAS.

RASP Retrieval and Statistical Processing. An acronym used by The Atomic Energy Authority of Great Britain.

RASTAC Random Access Storage and Control.

RASTAD Random Access Storage and Display.

RAX Remote Access. Term pertaining to communication with data processing facilities by distant stations, usually accomplished with telephone service.

RBA Retail Book, Stationery and Allied Trades Employees Association. Temple Chambers, Temple Ave, London EC4, England.

RBA Royal Society of British Artists. 6 1/2 Suffolk St, London SW1, England.

RBMS Rare Books and Manuscripts Section. *See* ACRL/RBMS.

RBRAC Rome Base Reliability Analysis Center. *See* RAC.

RCA Radio Corporation of America. Princeton, NJ 08540. Incorporated in 1941. Maintains a research library. Involved in communications systems development.

RCA Royal College of Art. Kensington Gore, London SW7, England. Library established in 1953.

RCAS Royal Central Asian Society. 42 Devonshire St, London W1N 1LN, England. Library established in 1901.

RCC Real-time Computer Complex.

RCLS Ramapo Catskill Library System. 619 North St, Middletown, NY 10940.

RCM Royal College of Music. Prince Consort Rd, London SW7, England. Library established in 1882.

RCMP Royal Canadian Mounted Police. 1200 Alta Vista Dr, Ottawa ON K14 OR2, Canada. Maintains a library started in 1946. Also known as Gendarmerie Royale du Canada.

RCN Royal College of Nursing and National Council of Nursing. La Henrietta Pl, Cavendish Sq, London W1M 0AB, England. Library established in 1921.

RCOG Royal College of Obstetricians and Gynaecologists. 27 Sussex Pl, Regent's Pk, London NW1 4R9, England. Library established in 1929.

RCP Royal College of Physicians of London. Saint Andrew's Pl, Regent's Pk, London NW1 4LE, England. Library established in 1518.

RCPE Royal College of Physicians of Edinburgh. 9 Queen St, Edinburgh EH2 1JQ, Scotland. Library established in 1681.

RCSC Radio Components Standardization Committee. Castlewood House, 77-91, New Oxford St, London W1, England.

RCSEd Royal College of Surgeons of Edinburgh. Nicholson St, Edinburgh EH8 9DW, Scotland. Library established in 1807.

RCSEng Royal College of Surgeons of England. Lincoln's Inn Fields, London WC2A 3PN, England. Library established in 1835.

RCSI Royal College of Surgeons in Ireland. Saint Stephen's Green, Dublin 2, Irish Republic. Library established in 1784.

RCTL Resistor-Capacitor Transistor Logic.

RCU Remote Control Unit.

RCVS Royal College of Veterinary Surgeons. 32 Belgrave Sq, London SW1, England. Library established in 1844.

RD Research and Development. Also known as R&D.

RDA Research and Development, Army.

RDC Regional Dissemination Centers. National network of university-based centers established by NASA beginning in 1962 to help regional industry's need for technological information.

RDPE RADAR Data Processing Equipment.

RDR Research and Development Report.

RDTR Research Division Technical Report.

RE Royal Society of Painter-Etchers and Engravers. 26 Conduit St, London W1, England.

REAC Reeves Electronic Analog Computer.

READ Real-Time Electronic Access and Display.

READ Remote Electrical Alphanumeric Display.

REALCOM Real-Time Communications. An RCA system.

REBIS Repertorio Bibliografico Italiano. Centro Elettronico di Documentazione-Italgiure, Corte Suprema di Cassaziono, Palazzo di Giustizia, Via Ulpiano 8, Rome 00193, Italy. Coverage from 1975. On-line catalog of new Italian books.

REBIS Repertorio Bibliografico Straniero. Centro Elettronico di Documentazione-Italgiure, Corte

Suprema di Cassaziono, Palazzo di Giustizia, Via Ulpiano 8, Rome 00193, Italy. Coverage from 1975. On-line catalog of new foreign books in Italian libraries.

RECBIR Regional Coordination of Biomedical Information Resources Program. New York and New Jersey Regional Medical Library, New York Academy of Medicine, 2 East 103 St, New York, NY 10029. Established by MLCNY to coordinate shared cataloging. *See* C. Lee Jones. "A Cooperative Serials Acquisition Program: Thoughts on a Response to Mounting Fiscal Pressures." *BMLA* 62 (Apr. 1974): 120–123.

RECMF Radio and Electric Component Manufacturers Federation. 222 Regent St, London W1R 5EE, England.

RECODEX Report Collection Index. Studsvik Energiteknit AB, Library, S-611 82 Nykoping, Sweden. Coverage from 1975. Bibliographic data base covering energy, physics, mining and metallurgy.

RECOL Retrieval Command Language. An interrogation scheme for the retrieval and manipulation of data records. *See* W. D. Climenson. "RECOL: A Retrieval Command Language." *Communications of the ACM* 6 (Mar. 1963): 117–122.

RECON Remote Console. One of many terminals connected to the main computers at NASA and at ESRO.

RECON Retrospective Conversion. Library of Congress, Washington, DC 20540. Project of LC for converting retrospective cataloging records to machine-readable form. *See* Richard DeGennaro. "A National Bibliographic Data Base in Machine-Readable Form: Progress and Prospects." *Library Trends* 18 (Apr. 1970): 537–550.

REDI Real Estate Data, Inc. 2398 Northwest 119 St, Miami, FL 33167. Provides information services to the real estate industry. Member of IIA (Information Industry Association).

REDINSE Red de Información Socio-Económica (Network for Socio-Economic Information). Coordinated at CONICIT (Venezuela).

REEC Register and Examinations Committee. The Library Association, 7 Ridgmount St, London WC1E 7AE, England. Also known as R&EEC.

REGENT Report Program Generator. A problem-oriented programming system and report program generator designed to substantially reduce the time and effort needed to translate general data processing and reporting requirements into detailed computer instructions.

REIC Radiation Effects Information Center. Battelle Memorial Institute, Columbus Laboratories, 505 King Ave, Columbus, OH 43201.

REL A symbol and list structure adaptive system developed by CIT (California Institute of Technology).

REL Rapidly Extensible Language. A programming language.

RELCODE Relative Coding. Procedure used on the UNIVAC I and UNIVAC II computers.

REMC Joint Departmental Radio and Electronics Measurements Committee. Castlewood House, 77/91, New Oxford St, London WC1, England.

RESPONSA Retrieval of Special Portions from *Nuclear Science Abstracts*. A project of AEC (Atomic Energy Commission).

RETA Refrigerating Engineers and Technicians Association. 435 North Michigan Ave, Rm. 2112, Chicago, IL 60611. Established in 1910. Offers technical information service to members. Formerly the National Association of Practical Refrigerating Engineers.

RETA Retrieval of Enriched Textual Abstracts. A set of computer programs.

RETROSPEC Retrospective Search System on the INSPEC Data Base. Institution of Electrical Engineers, Savoy Pl, London WC2R OBL, England. For computer and control engineering searching.

REX Real-Time Executive Routine.

RFB Recordings for the Blind, Inc. 215 East 58 St, New York, NY 10022. Provides loan services for taped educational books to the visually and physically handicapped.

RFI Radio Frequency Interference. Can prevent operation of a digital computer.

RFP Request for Proposals. Issued by a government department when the department wishes to have vendors bid on a system. *See* R. H. Gregory and R. L. Van Horn. *Automatic Data Processing Systems: Principles and Procedures*. Belmont, CA: Wadsworth, 1963.

RGPL *Readers Guide to Periodical Literature*. (Index). V. 1, 1900. Published by H. W. Wilson Co.

RI Committee on Research on the Theoretical Basis of Information. *See* FID/RI.

RIA Research Institute of America, Inc. 589 Fifth Ave, New York, NY 10017.

RIAA Recording Industry Association of America. One East 57 St, New York, NY 10022. Established in 1952. Maintains a reference library of books, magazines, clippings and other material on the phonograph record industry. Formerly (1970) Record Industry Association of America.

RIACT Retrieval of Information about Census Tapes. A computer system available to libraries. Reported at the 1970 ASIS Conference.

RIBA Royal Institute of British Architects. 66 Portland Pl, London W1N 4AD, England.

RIBDA Reunion Interamericana de Bibliotecarios y Documentalistas Agrícolas. Fifth meeting April 1978, San José, Costa Rica.

RIC Rare-Earth Information Center. Energy and Mineral Resources Research Institute, Iowa State University, Ames, IA 50011. Established in 1966.

RICASIP Research Information Center and Advisory Service on Information Processing. Jointly sponsored by NSF and NBS.

RICC Regional Information Coordinating Center. 3151 Third Ave, North, Suite 540, Saint Petersburg, FL 33713. Part of the Tampa Bay Regional Planning Council. Produces data bases on development of the region.

RICE Regional Information and Communication Exchange. c/o Rice University, Fondren Library, Box 1892, Houston, TX 77001. Serves the scientific and technical information needs of business and industry along the Gulf Coast from Louisiana to Mexico by providing ILL, literature searches and other services.

RIDC Research Industry Document Center. US Army Library, Fort Belvoir, VA 22060.

RIE *Resources in Education*. (Journal). V. 1, 1966. Published by ERIC. Formerly *Research in Education*.

RIF Reading Is Fundamental. An organization started by Mrs. Robert S. McNamara in 1966 with national headquarters in the Smithsonian Institution. Distributes free paperbacks to ghetto children. Now based at LC.

RILA *Répertoire International de la Littérature de l'Art*. (Journal). V. 1, 1975. Published by Clark Art Museum, Williamstown, MA 01267.

RILA Rhode Island Library Association. Contact president or ALA (American Library Association).

RILM Répertoire International de Littérature Musicale. *RILM Abstracts of Music Literature* is published by the City University of New York for the International Association of Music Librarians and the International Musicological Society. V. 1, 1967.

RIMS Regional Information Management System. Houston–Galveston Area Council, 3701 West Alabama St, Box 22777, Houston, TX 77027. Maintains an urban planning library started in 1967.

RIMS Remote Information Management System. Northwestern University, Evanston, IL 60201. Operates from either a teletype or cathode ray tube inquiry/display station. *See* G. Krulee and B. Mittman. "Computer-Based Information Systems for University Research and Teaching" in *Sixth Annual Colloquium on Information Retrieval*. Philadelphia: Medical Documentation Service, 1969.

RINGDOC Derwent Publications, Ltd, Rochdale House, 128 Theobalds Rd, London WC1X 8RP, England. A data base of pharmaceutical literature.

RIR Redgrave Information Resources. 67 Milton Rd, Westport, CT 06880. A publishing firm.

RIS Research Information Services. Rutgers University Libraries, College Ave & Hunting St, New Brunswick, NJ 08901. Provides computerized searches to the public, institutions and businesses of New Jersey.

RISE Research Information Services for Education. 443 South Gulph Rd, King of Prussia, PA 19406.

RISM Research Institute for the Study of Man. Maintains a library, established in 1955, on the social sciences of the Caribbean and the non-Hispanic West Indies.

RIU Riuiste. Centro Elettronico di Documentazione-Italgiure, Corte Suprema di Cassaziono, Palazzo di Giustizia, Via Ulpiano 8, Rome 00193, Italy. Coverage from 1966. Bibliographic data base covering judicial periodicals in which sentences are noted.

RIVE *Resources in Vocational Education.* (Journal). V. 1, 1977. An outgrowth of AIM/ARM, *RIVE* provides abstracts of materials on vocational and technical education. Published by National Center for Research in Vocational Education at Ohio State University.

RJE Remote Job Entry. The inputting of the job information to the main computing system from a remote device.

RKD Rijksbureau voor Kunsthistorische Documentatie (Netherlands Institute for Art History Documentation). Korte Vijverberg 7, 's Gravenhage, the Netherlands.

RKNFSYS Rock Information System. Geophysical Laboratory, 2801 Upton St, NW, Washington, DC 20008. Established in 1971. Supported by NSF, provides retrieval and reduction of data concerning the composition of Cenozoic volcanic rocks.

RLA Rhodesia Library Association. Box 1087, Salisbury, Rhodesia. Established in 1967.

RLB Regional Library Bureau. A British term. Acronym is used for singular and plural (bureaux).

RLD Relocation Dictionary. That part of a computer program that identifies all of the addresses of the program that must be changed when the program is to be relocated.

RLG Research Libraries Group. Encina Commons, Rm. 100, Stanford University, Stanford, CA 94035. Established in 1974. A consortium of university and research libraries united to improve access to materials. Maintains RLIN network.

RLIN Research Libraries Information Network. Contact RLG. Established in 1972. Formerly (1978) BALLOTS. One hundred fifty libraries make use of this computerized bibliographic service. Maintained by RLG.

RLMS Reproduction of Library Materials Section. See RTSD/RLMS.

RML Regional Medical Library. Any one of eleven libraries designated by NLM to serve the libraries within its designated geographic area. For the names of designated libraries, *see* Martin M. Cummings and Mary E. Corning. "The Medical Library Assistance Act: An Analysis of the NLM Extramural Programs, 1965–1970." *BMLA* 59 (July 1971): 375–391.

RNA Romantic Novelists Association. 30 Langham House Close, Ham Common, Richmond, Surrey TW10 7JE, England.

RO Receive Only. Indicating or relating to a device that can receive signals but lacks transmission capability.

ROAR Royal Optimizing Assembly Routing. Assembly program for the Royal McBee RPC 4000 computer.

ROBINS Roberts Information Services. 8305-G Merrifield Ave, Fairfax, VA 22031. Provides computerized searches and document delivery. Member of IIA (Information Industry Association).

ROCAPPI Research on Computer Applications in the Printing and Publishing Industries. Division of Lehigh Press, Inc, 7000 North Park Dr, Pennsauken, NJ 08109. See *LARC Reports* 1 (July 1968): 1–28.

ROD Regional Operational Data.

ROM Read Only Memory. Computer memory that is not intended to be transformed by normal user operation.

ROPP Receive Only Page Printer.

ROSE Remotely Operated Special Equipment.

ROSE Retrieval by On-Line Search.

ROTR Receive Only Typing Reperforator. A TWX receiver whose output consists of perforated tape with characters printed along its edge.

RP Research Publications, Inc. 12 Lunar Dr, Woodbridge, CT 06525. Microform publisher. Member of IIA (Information Industry Association).

RPG Report Program Generator. A language for communicating with third-generation computers. Designed to simplify program writing. *See* Harice Seeds. *Programming RPG: RPG II.* New York: John Wiley, 1970.

RPI Rensselaer Polytechnic Institute. Troy, NY 12181. Established in 1824. Engineering and computer science and communication.

RPL Richmond Public Library. 101 East Franklin St, Richmond, VA 23219. Has issued *RPL News* since 1958.

RPQ Request Price Quotation. Term used by vendors to indicate that price information is supplied on request.

RRF Reading Reform Foundation. 7054 East Indian School Rd, Scottsdale, AZ 85251. Established in 1961. Emphasizes phonetics as the basis of reading instruction. Publishes documents.

RRIS Railroad Research Information Service. 2100 Pennsylvania Ave, NW, Rm. 513, Washington, DC 20004. Provides transportation administrators, engineers and researchers with rapid access to information about ongoing and completed railroad-related research.

RRP Reader and Reader-Printer. Microfilm viewing equipment that can both read and print.

RRRLC Rochester Regional Research Library Council. 339 East Ave, Rm. 300, Rochester, NY 14604. Fifty-two academic, hospital, public, research and special libraries cooperate through ILL, union lists of serials, a map and film collection, regional borrowers card, search service and CE programs.

RS Record Separator. Character intended for the demarcation of the logical boundary between records.

RS Resources Section. *See* RTSD/RS.

RSAMD Royal Scottish Academy of Music and Drama. 58 Saint George's Pl, Glasgow C2, Scotland.

RSBRC Reference and Subscription Book Reviews Committee. Contact ALA (American Library Association).

RSD Reference Services Division. A division of ALA (American Library Association) that merged with ASD in 1972 to form RASD.

RSE Request Select Entry.

RSIC Radiation Shielding Information Center. Oak Ridge National Laboratory, Oak Ridge, TN 37830.

RSIC Redstone Scientific Information Center. Redstone Arsenal, AL 35809. Base for various information projects.

RSM Rapid Search Machine. An information search and retrieval system which uses a word-and-phrase scanning technique to search magnetic tape files. Developed by GE. Also known as GESCAN.

RSNA Radiological Society of North America. 1415 West 22 St, Oak Brook, IL 60521. Established in 1915. Maintains a library. Publishes the monthly *Radiology.*

RSQE Research Seminar in Quantitative Economics. Dept. of Economics, University of Michigan, 506 East University, Ann Arbor, MI 48109. Established in 1954. Produces a data base and publishes documents on econometrics, including *RSQE Forecasting Services.*

RSS Research Community of Slovenia. Vojkova 69, Ljubljana 61000, Yugoslavia. Established in 1976. Produces patent data base available through INPADOC. Member of EUSIDIC.

RSSDA Regional Social Science Data Archive. University of Iowa, Iowa City, IA 52240.

RSVP Research Society for Victorian Periodicals. Dept. of English, University

College, University of Toronto, Toronto ON M5S 1A1, Canada. Established in 1968. A clearinghouse for research projects in the field. Serves as consultant to reprint and microform publishers and advises librarians. Publishes *Victorian Periodicals Review*.

RT Real Time. Pertaining to the operation of a data processing system that proceeds at the same speed as the events being simulated.

RT Related Term. Cross-reference in a thesaurus.

RT Remote Terminals. Terminals located at a distance from the main computing facility.

RTC Real-Time Command.

RTCA Radio Technical Commission for Aeronautics. 1717 H St, NW, Washington, DC 20006. Established in 1935. Publishes annual proceedings, an irregular digest and documents upon completion of studies.

RTECS Registry of Toxic Effects of Chemical Substances. An on-line data retrieval file of NLM. Formerly the *Toxic Substances List*. An annual compilation prepared by NIOSH (National Institute for Occupational Safety and Health). A printed version is available through GPO.

RTL Register Transfer Language. A programming language.

RTSD Resources and Technical Services Division. 50 East Huron St, Chicago, IL 60611. A division of ALA (American Library Association).

RTSD/AS RTSD Acquisitions Section. Contact RTSD. A section of RTSD, which is a division of ALA (American Library Association).

RTSD/CCS RTSD Cataloging and Classification Section. Contact RTSD. A section of RTSD, which is a division of ALA (American Library Association).

RTSD/PLMS RTSD Preservation of Library Materials Section. Contact RTSD. A section of RTSD, which is a division of ALA (American Library Association).

RTSD/RLMS RTSD Reproduction of Library Materials Section. Contact

RTSD. A section of RTSD, which is a division of ALA (American Library Association).

RTSD/RS RTSD Resources Section. Contact RTSD. A section of RTSD, which is a division of ALA (American Library Association).

RTSD/SS RTSD Serials Section. Contact RTSD. A section of RTSD, which is a division of ALA (American Library Association).

RTT Radio Teletypewriter.

RTTY Radio Teletypewriter Communications.

RTU Remote Terminal Unit.

RUIN Regional and Urban Information Network. The Urban Institute, 2100 M St, NW, Washington, DC 20037. A network of small-to-medium-sized libraries in the Washington, DC, area with an interest in urban problems.

RUSH Remote User of Shared Hardware.

R/W Read/Write Head. A small electromagnet used for reading, recording or erasing polarized spots on a magnetic surface. Also called "magnetic head," "read head" and "write head."

RZ Return-to-Zero.

RZh *Referativny Zhurnal*. V. 1, 1909. Russian abstracting journal with various sections. Published by VINITI (Vsesojuznyi Institut Naučnotehniceskoi Informacii).

RZ(NP) Return-to-Zero (Nonpolarized). Said of a recording.

RZ(P) Return-to-Zero (Polarized). Said of a recording.

SA Society of Archivists. County Records Office, County Hall, Hertford, Hertfordshire, England. Established in 1947.

SA *Sociological Abstracts*. V. 1, 1952. Published by Leo P. Chall, San Diego, CA.

SAA Society of American Archivists. The Library, Box 8198, University of Illinois, Chicago Circle, Chicago, IL 60680. Established in 1936. Supersedes the Public Archives Commission of the American Historical Association.

SAA Standards Association of Australia. Box 458, North Sydney, New South Wales 2060, Australia. Affiliated with ISO (International Standards Organization).

SAALCK State Assisted Academic Library Council of Kentucky. Western Kentucky University, Bowling Green, KY 42101. Eight college libraries cooperate through ILL.

SAALIC Swindon Area Association of Libraries for Industry and Commerce. Central Library, Regent Circus, Swindon, Wiltshire, England.

SAB Sveriges Allmänna Biblioteksförening (Swedish Library Association). Fack 22101, Lund, Sweden. Established in 1915.

SABCA Societé Anonyme Belge de Constructions Aeronautiques. Département de Construction Électronique, Centre de Documentation, Chausée de Haecht 1470, B-1130 Brussels, Belgium.

SABE Society for Automation in Business Education. Absorbed in 1975 by SDE.

SABS South African Bureau of Standards. 191 Private Bay, Pretoria, Republic of South Africa. Affiliated with ISO (International Standards Organization).

SABV/SALA Suid-Afrikaanse Biblioteekvereniging/South African Library Association. Ferdinand Postma Library, P.U. for C.H.E, Potchefstroom 2520, South Africa. Established in 1930.

SACA Standards Association of Central Africa. Box 2259, Salisbury, Rhodesia. Issues English-language standards; affiliated with ISO (International Standards Organization).

SACCS Strategic Air Command Control System.

SACHEM Southeastern Association for Cooperation in Higher Education in Massachusetts. 174 Point Rd, Marion, MA 02738.

SADC Southwest Asia Documentation Centers. Iranian Documentation Center, Box 11-1387, Tehran, Iran. Secretariat located at IRANDOC. First conference in Tehran, April 1970.

SADPO Systems Analysis and Data Processing Office of NYPL. 20 West 53

St, New York, NY 10019. See *LARC Reports* 3 (Fall 1970). Special issue on SADPO, ed. by H. Parr.

SAE Society of Automotive Engineers. 400 Commonwealth Ave, Warrendale, PA 15096. Established in 1905. Publishes documents. Formerly (1917) Society of Automobile Engineers.

SAEH Society for Automation in English and the Humanities. Absorbed in 1975 by SDE.

SAEMS Saskatchewan Association of Educational Media Specialists. Saskatchewan Teachers' Federation, 2317 Arlington Ave, Box 1108, Saskatoon SK S7J 2H8, Canada. Established in 1960.

SAERIS South Australia Education Resource Information System. Project to provide on-line cataloging and information retrieval system for both book and nonbook material, through the use of computers and microforms.

SAFA Society for Automation in Fine Arts. Absorbed in 1975 by SDE.

SAFARI Mitre Corp, Bedford, MA 01730. A computer program based on transformational grammar allowing syntactic relations to be represented in the computer-stored information.

SAGE Semi-Automatic Ground Environment. A computerized means of detecting enemy aircraft and missiles.

SAHLC Seattle Area Hospital Library Consortium. Group Health Cooperative-Library, 200 15th Ave, Seattle, WA 98112.

SAHR Society of Army Historical Research. The Library, War Office, Whitehall, London SW1, England.

SAID System Analysis Index for Diagnosis. A multimedia program for teaching psychiatry to medical students, stressing student participation and rapid faculty feedback. *See* P. R. Miller. *SAID Handbook*. Davis, CA: University of California at Davis, 1972.

SAIDC Sistem za Avtomatizacilo Informacijsko Dokumentacijskih Centrov-Elektrotehnika. ISKRA-INDOK Service, Trzaska C 2, Ljubljana 61000, Yugoslavia. Coverage from 1970. Bibliographic data base on communications and electronics.

SAILA Sault Area International Library Association. c/o Lake Superior College Library, Sault Sainte Marie, MI 49783. Established in 1969. Fosters resource-sharing for 17 member libraries in the cities of Sault Sainte Marie, MI, and Sault Sainte Marie, Ontario, Canada.

SAILA South African Indian Library Association. 7 Ascot St, Durban, South Africa. Established in 1968.

SAINT Semi-Automatic Index of National Language. Experimental method for book indexing by computer. *See* Harold Borko. "Experiments in Book Indexing by Computer." *Information Storage and Retrieval* 6 (1970): 5–16. Written as three modules labeled COMBIN, COUNT and EDIT.

SAL Subject Authority List.

SALA South African Library Association. *See* SABV/SALA.

SALALM Seminar on the Acquisition of Latin American Library Materials. Established in 1956. *See* Louella Vine Wetherbee and Anne H. Jordan. *Twenty Years of Latin American Librarianship.* Austin, TX: National Educational Laboratory Publishers, 1979.

SALE Simple Algebraic Language for Engineers. A programming language.

SALINET Satellite Library Information Network. c/o University of Denver, Graduate School of Librarianship, University Park, Denver, CO 80210. A consortium of libraries, a library school and regional agencies with headquarters at Denver Graduate School of Librarianship. Purpose is to expand library services to sparsely populated areas of the 12 Rocky Mountain and Great Plains states via a satellite launched by NASA in 1975.

SALT Saskatchewan Association of Library Technicians. 2233 McKinnon Ave, Saskatoon SK S7J 1N5, Canada. Established in 1973.

SAM Society for the Advancement of Management. 135 West 50 St, New York, NY 10020. Formed in 1936 by the merger of the Taylor Society and the

Society of Industrial Engineers. Maintains a consulting and information service and a reference library. Publishes documents. Absorbed the Industrial Methods Society in 1946.

SAM System Activity Monitor.

SAMANTHA System for the Automated Management of Text from a Hierarchical Arrangement. Information and Publishing Systems, Inc, 7101 Wisconsin Ave, Bethesda, MD 20014. Two major components are data base maintenance and data manipulation, consisting of two languages, DM1 and DM2.

SAMI Selling Areas-Marketing Inc. Time & Life Bldg, New York, NY 10020. Incorporated in 1966. Produces a data base on supermarkets. Provides computerized searches and document delivery in the fields of business and commerce.

SAMP South Asia Microform Project. Center for Research Libraries, 5721 Cottage Grove Ave, Chicago, IL 60637. Cooperative project to acquire, in microform, copies of publications and archives published in South Asia or dealing with South Asia, predating those acquired under PL (Public Law) 480 programs.

SAMPE Society of Aerospace Material and Process Engineers. Box 613, Azusa, CA 91702. Established in 1943. Publishes documents. Formerly (1960) the Society of Aircraft Material and Process Engineers.

SAMS Satellite Auto-Monitor System. A programming language, procedure and control system for the CDC 1604 system.

SANZ Standards Association of New Zealand. Private Bay, Wellington, New Zealand. Affiliated with ISO (International Standards Organization).

SAOLM Subject Analysis and Organization of Library Materials Committee. Contact RTSD. A committee of RTSD/CCS.

SAP Systems Assurance Program. A computer program.

SAPE Society for Automation in Professional Education. Absorbed in 1975 by SDE.

SARBICA Southwest Asian Regional Branch of the International Council on Archives. c/o National Archives and Library of Malaysia, Jalan Sultan, Petaling Jala, Malaysia. Established in 1968.

SARDI *SAMI Retail Distribution Index.* (Journal). Published by Selling Areas-Marketing.

SASM Society for Automation in Science and Mathematics. Address unknown since 1974.

SASS Society for Automation in the Social Sciences. Absorbed in 1975 by SDE.

SATCOM (Committee on) Scientific and Technical Communication. A key report on scientific communication, resulting from a study funded by NAS. *See* Committee on Scientific and Technical Communication (SATCOM). *Scientific and Technical Communication: A Pressing National Problem and Recommendations for Its Solution.* Publication 1707. Washington, DC: NAS, 1969.

SATIN SAGE Air Traffic Integration. An air traffic control system coordinated with air defense, developed by MITRE Corp.

SBCUK School Broadcasting Council for the United Kingdom. The Langham, Portland Pl, London W1A 1AA, England. Established in 1929 to guide BBC (British Broadcasting Corporation) in programs for schools. Publishes documents.

SBF Sveriges Biografägureförbund (Swedish Motion Picture Exhibitors Association). Stureplan 13, 111 45 Stockholm, Sweden. Established in 1915.

SBP Stowarzyszenie Bibliotekarzy Polskich (Polish Library Association). Ul. Konopczyńskiego 5/7, 00953 Warsaw, Poland. Established in 1917 as the Union of Polish Librarians and Archivists. Present name adopted in 1953.

SBPR Sociedad de Bibliotecarios de Puerto Rico (Puerto Rico Library Association). 8 San Valentin, El Pilas, Rio Piedras, PR 00926. Established in 1961.

SBS Svenska Bibliotekariesamfundet (Swedish Association of University and Research Librarians). c/o H. Peter Hallberg, Secretary, Head, Linköpings

Hogskdas Bibliotek, S-58183 Linköping, Sweden. Established in 1921.

SCAD/IASC Société Canadienne pour l'Analyse de Documents/Indexing and Abstracting Society of Canada. c/o Committee on Bibliographic Services for Canada, National Library of Canada, 395 Wellington St, Ottawa ON K1A 0N4, Canada.

SCAG Southern California Association of Governments. Development Guide Program, 1111 West Sixth St, Suite 400, Los Angeles, CA 90017. Produces data bases on regional development, human and national resources, and transportation.

SCALS Standing Conference of African Library Schools. c/o School of Librarians, Archivists and Documentalists, University of Dakar, Dakar, Senegal. Established in 1973.

SCAN Southern California Answering Network. c/o Los Angeles Public Library, 630 West Fifth St, Los Angeles, CA 90071. Regional reference and referral service established in 1969 for cooperating public library systems in southern California.

SCANDOC Scandinavian Documentation Center. Scandinavian Council for Applied Research, 1225 19th St, NW, Washington, DC 20036. Serves as a scientific information exchange center for the US, Canada and Scandinavian countries.

SCANS Scheduling and Control by Automated Network System.

SCAT SHARE Compiler, Assembler and Translator. A programming package for the IBM 709 computer.

SCATS Sequentially Controlled Automatic Transmitter Start. A single service multipoint teletypewriter arrangement that provides for transmission between all stations connected to a network without contention between stations.

SCATT (National) Scientific Communication and Technology Transfer. An idealized design for a national system. *See* Russell L. Ackoff et al. *Designing a National Scientific and Technological Communication System: The SCATT Report.* Philadelphia: University of Pennsylvania, 1976.

SCAUL Standing Conference of African University Librarians. c/o Harold Holdsworth, Librarian, University College of Dar-es-Salaam, Dar-es-Salaam, Tanzania. Established in 1964.

SCAULEA Standing Conference of African University Libraries, Eastern Area. c/o Library, University, Box 1176, Addis Ababa, Ethiopia. Established in 1971.

SCAULWA Standing Conference of African University Libraries, Western Area. Contact president. Established in 1972.

SCFC Southern California Film Circuit. 4819 Regalo Rd, Woodland Hills, CA 91364.

SCHOLAR Schering-Oriented Literature Analysis and Retrieval System. A computer-based reference retrieval system using an indexing vocabulary based on MeSH, employed by Schering Corp. *See* M. J. Mislavitz. "Control and Dissemination of Drug Related Literature." *ASIS Proceedings* 10 (1973): 157–158.

SCI *Science Citation Index*. V. 1, 1961. Published by ISI (Institute for Scientific Information).

SCI Simulation Councils, Inc. *See* SCS.

SCI Society of Scribes and Illuminators. 270 Trinity Rd, London SW18, England. Established in 1921.

SCILL Southern California Interlibrary Loan Network. c/o Los Angeles Public Library, Central Library, 630 West Fifth St, Los Angeles, CA 90071. One hundred thirty-five public, academic and special libraries cooperate through ILL and resource sharing.

SCIM Selected Categories in Microfiche. NTIS standard profile service for the supply of documents.

SCIP Students Chemical Information Project. Project of OSTI.

SCISEARCH *Science Citation Index* Search. Institute for Scientific Information, 325 Chestnut St, Philadelphia, PA 19106. Coverage from 1974. Data base covering the records published in *SCI* (*Science Citation Index*) and *CC* (*Current Contents*).

SCITEL Institute for Scientific Information. 132 High St, Uxbridge, Middlesex UB8

1DP, England. Produces data bases, publishes documents and sponsors meetings.

SCL Scottish Central Library. Lawnmarket, Edinburgh 1, Scotland. Now part of the National Library of Scotland Lending Service.

SCL Society of County Librarians. c/o County Library Headquarters, Mortimer St, Trowbridge, Wiltshire, England. Established in 1954.

SCLA South Carolina Library Association. Contact president or ALA (American Library Association).

SCLA Suffolk County Library Association. Contact president or NYLA.

SCLL State and Court Law Libraries of the United States and Canada. Box 1841, Raleigh, NC 27602. Association established in 1973.

SCLS Southwestern Connecticut Library System, Inc. Bridgeport Public Library, 925 Broad St, Bridgeport, CT 06604. Consortium of 25 libraries in Fairfield County.

SCMAI Staff Committee on Mediation, Arbitration and Inquiry. Contact ALA (American Library Association). Acts as a clearinghouse for requests for ALA action for an individual library employee seeking redress for grievances arising out of library employment.

SCOLCAP Scottish Libraries Cataloging Automation Project. Cooperating libraries include the National Library of Scotland, Edinburgh and Glasgow Public Libraries and Dundee, Glasgow and Stirling universities.

SCOLE Standing Committee on Library Education. Contact ALA (American Library Association). Replaced LED in 1978.

SCOLMA Standing Conference on Library Materials on Africa. c/o Institute of Commonwealth Studies, 27 Russell Sq, London WC1B 5DS, England. Established in 1962.

SConMeL Standing Conference for Mediterranean Librarians. Malta Library Association, 220 Saint Paul St, Valletta, Malta.

SCONUL Standing Conference of National and University Libraries. SCONUL

Secretariat, c/o The Library School of Oriental and African Studies, Malet St, London WC1E 7HP, England. Established in 1950.

SCOP Single-Copy Ordering Plan. Of ABA (American Booksellers Association).

SCOPE Scientific Committee on Problems of the Environment. A committee of ICSU.

SCOPE System to Coordinate the Operation of Peripheral Equipment. A group of Honeywell routines that optimize the use of peripheral devices on Honeywell computers during parallel operation.

SCOPT Subcommittee on Programming Terminology. Contact ACM (Association for Computing Machinery). A subcommittee of the Standards Committee of ACM.

SCORPIO Subject Content-Oriented Retriever for Processing Information Online. Library of Congress, Washington, DC 20540. Information base developed by LC. Available for use only on Capitol Hill.

SCOTS South Coast Transportation Study. c/o County Road Commission, Courthouse, Santa Barbara, CA 93104. Produces data bases on transportation.

SCP Symbolic Conversion Program. A one-to-one compiler for symbolic address and operation codes for ITT systems.

SCPI Scientists Committee for Public Information. 355 Lexington Ave, New York, NY 10017. Established in 1958. Publishes documents.

SCRAMBLE A utility computer program available from NBS. See EDPAC.

SCRLC South Central Research Library Council. DeWitt Bldg, 215 North Cayuga St, Ithaca, NY 14850. Forty member libraries cooperate through ILL, bibliographic and reference services, preservation, conservation and many other services.

SCRTD Southern California Rapid Transit District. Los Angeles Regional Transportation Study, Division of Highways, Terminal Annex, Los Angeles, CA 90045. Produces a data base on transportation in the region. See also LARTS.

SCS Society for Computer Simulation. Box 2228, La Jolla, CA 92038. Established in 1952. Constituent society of AFIPS. Also known as SCI (Simulation Councils, Inc.). Publishes periodicals.

SCTPG Southern California Technical Processes Group. Sponsor of URIS I.

SCUR Southwest Center for Urban Research. 1200 Southmore, Houston, TX 77004. Produces data bases on education and urban development.

SCUU Southern College University Union. Nashville, TN 37203. Consortium established in 1969. Committee on Libraries implements a program of resource sharing.

SDA Secção de Documentação Adontólogica (Department of Dental Documentation). Rua Tres Rios 363, Caixa Postal 8216, São Paulo, Brazil.

SDA Source Data Automation. The methods of recording information in coded forms on paper tapes, punched cards or tags that can be used repeatedly to produce other records without rewriting.

SDC Scientific Documentation Centre, Ltd. Halbeath House, Dunfermline, Fife, Scotland.

SDC Superintendent of Documents Classification.

SDC System Development Corporation. 2500 Colorado Ave, Santa Monica, CA 90406.

SDD Systems Development Division. A division of IBM.

SDE Society of Data Educators. 983 Fairmeadow Rd, Memphis, TN 38117. Established in 1960. Seeks to promote the knowledge, use and teaching of automation, computers and data processing among educators. In 1975, absorbed SABE, SAEH, SAFA, SAPE, SASS, SEDS, SEPSA and SIPSDE.

SDI Selective Dissemination of Information. An information retrieval system utilizing key word methods to alert users to documents of potential interest. Also known as "current awareness."

SDM Selective Dissemination of Microfiche. Distribution system of CFSTI (now NTIS). See also SCIM.

SDNS Scottish Daily Newspaper Society. 90 Mitchell St, Glasgow C1, Scotland.

SDS Space Documentation Service. European Space Agency, Via Galileo Galilei, Franscati, Rome 00044, Italy. Established in 1964. Member of EUSIDIC. Produces data bases, conducts seminars and publishes documents.

SDTF State Documents Task Force. *See* GODORT/SDTF.

SE Systems Engineering. A systematic method of applying engineering knowledge to all the elements of a system down to the smallest unit.

SEAC Standards Electronic Automatic Computer. Of NBS.

SEADAG Southeast Asia Development Advisory Group. Funded by AID (Agency for International Development) and administered by the Asia Society. SEADAG Vietnam Data Archive located at Massachusetts Institute of Technology, Center for International Studies, Cambridge, MA 02139.

SEALLINC Southeast Louisiana Library Network Cooperative. c/o New Orleans Public Library, 219 Loyola Ave, New Orleans, LA 70140. An 18-member consortium that maintains a daily delivery service.

SEAM South East Asia Microforms. Operated with a committee of AAS (Association for Asian Studies), SEAM is an international consortium established in 1970 to finance the microfilming of useful but inaccessible materials related to Southeast Asia.

SEAMEC Southeast Asian Ministers of Education Council. In 1968 established a Regional English Language Center with a library of over 3,000 volumes.

SEAMIC Southeast Asian Medical Information Center. An organization of medical librarians throughout the area who held four workshops on health documentation. See *Medical and Health Libraries in Southeast Asia*, ed. by Takeo Urata. Tokyo: SEAMIC, 1977.

SEARCH A utility computer program, available from NBS, which scans for the occurrence of certain strings of characters and lists the lines in which they occur. *See* EDPAC.

SEARCH System for Electronic Analysis and Retrieval of Criminal Histories. California Crime Technology Research Foundation, 1927 13th St, Sacramento, CA 95814. Project begun in 1970. Uses magnetic tapes, disks, video displays and hard copy and conforms to the computerized criminal history system of NCIC. *See* P. K. Normeli. "The SEARCH for Automated Justice." *Datamation*, June 15, 1971, p. 32.

SEATO Southeast Asia Treaty Organization. Box 517, Bangkok, Thailand. Involved in organizing meetings on libraries and networking.

SEBC Southeastern Bibliographic Center. SUNY College at New Paltz, New Paltz, NY 12562. Center for SENYLRC's reference and resource-sharing services.

SED South East Division. Of AAL (Association of Assistant Librarians). *See* AALSED.

SEDIX Selected Dissemination of Indexes.

SEDS Society for Educational Data Systems. Absorbed, in 1975 by SDE.

SEE Super Eight Experiment. A project at the Pocono District Library Center in Pennsylvania to test the feasibility of home loan of Super-8 projectors and cartridges.

SEEJ *Slavic and East European Journal.* V. 1, 1957. Published by the American Association of Teachers of Slavic and East European Languages.

SEES Slavic and East European Section. *See* ARCL/SEES.

SEFA Scottish Educational Film Association. 16 Woodside Terr, Glasgow C2, Scotland.

SEFT Society for Education in Film and Television. 81 Dean St, London WIV 6AA, England.

SEIMC New York State Special Education Instructional Materials Center. Education Bdlg. Annex, 10th Fl, Albany, NY 12234. Produces data bases on the education of the handicapped. Also provides help in obtaining braille, large-print and recorded books for the handicapped.

SEIS Service d'Échange d'Informations Scientifiques. 131 boulevard Saint-Michel, 75 Paris 5, France.

SELA Southeastern Library Association. Box 987, Tucker, GA 30084. Sponsors VNLW-SELA.

SELCO Southeastern Libraries Cooperating. 304 Marquette Bank Bldg, Rochester, MN 55901. A consortium of public libraries.

SELDOM Selective Dissemination of MARC. Saskatchewan University, Saskatoon SK 57N 0W0, Canada. A service of the university library.

SEMBCS South East Metropolitan Board of Cooperative Services. 2450 South Wabash, Denver, CO 80231.

SEMCOR Semantic Correlation. Machine-aided indexing.

SENTOKYO Senmon Toshokan Kyogikai (Special Libraries Association of Japan). c/o National Diet Library, 1-10-1 Nagata-cho, Chiyoda-ku, Tokyo, Japan. Established in 1952.

SENYLRC Southeastern New York Library Resources Council. Lady Washington House 3, 20 Academy St, Poughkeepsie, NY 12601. Library consortium maintains SEBC, which is housed at SUNY–New Paltz.

SEO Survey of Economic Opportunity. Data and Computation Center, University of Wisconsin, Madison, WI 53706. To provide researchers with a user-oriented processing capability for data files for the Institute for Research on Poverty. Uses the UNIVAC 1108 computer.

SEOL Suomen Elokuvateatterinomistajain Litto. Kaisaniemenkatu 3 B, 00100 Helsinki 10, Finland. Established in 1938. Association of film exhibitors.

SEPOL Soil Engineering Problem-Oriented Language.

SEPSA Society of Educational Programmers and Systems Analysts. Absorbed in 1975 by SDE.

SERETES 72 rue Regnault, 75073 Paris, France. Produces data bases on transportation and urban development.

SERLINE Serials On-Line. National Library of Medicine, 8600 Rockville Pike, Bethesda, MD 20014. On-line catalog of journal titles, with publisher's name, received by NLM.

SERMLP Southeastern Regional Medical Library Program. A. W. Calhoun Medical Library, Emory University, Atlanta, GA 30322. One of NLM's RMLs (Region VI). Serves AL, FL, GA, MS, SC, TN, the Commonwealth of Puerto Rico and the Virgin Islands. *See* Michael J. Torrente. "Southeastern Regional Medical Program." *NLM News* 33 (Dec. 1978): 5–6.

SESAM Systeme Electronique de Selection Automatique de Microfilms. Described in "L'Informatique Documentaire: Une Solution Photo-Electronique: Le Systeme SESAM." Ghent, Belgium: ASTRID, 1972.

SETLIST A FORTRAN program available from NBS. Used with phototypesetting devices.

SEWHSL Southeastern Wisconsin Health Science Libraries Consortium. c/o St. Francis Hospital, Health Science Learning Center, 3237 South 16 St, Milwaukee, WI 53215. Thirty-two health sciences libraries cooperate through ILL, acquisitions and CE programs.

SFC Scottish Film Council. 16-17 Woodside Terr, Glasgow C3, Scotland. Established in 1934. Administers the Scottish Central Film Library and acts as a clearinghouse for information on all matters affecting the production, exhibition and distribution of films in Scotland and abroad.

SFCSI Special Foreign Currency Science Information Program. National Technical Information Service, 5285 Port Royal Rd, Springfield, VA 22161. Program of NSF.

SFF Svenska Folkbibliotekarie Förbundet (Union of Swedish Public Libraries). Becksjudarvägen 45 47, S 13100 Nacka, Sweden. Established in 1938.

SFHR Society for Film History Research. 8 Minerva Rd, Kingston-upon-Thames, Surrey, England.

SFPL San Francisco Public Library. San Francisco, CA 94102.

SFTA Society of Film and Television Arts, Ltd. 80 Great Portland St, London W1N 6JJ, England.

SGA/ASSPA Schweizerische Gesellschaft für Automatik/Association Suisse pour l'Automatique (Swiss Association for Automation). Postfach 8034, Zurich, Switzerland. Established in 1956. Member of IFAC and IFIP. Publishes documents.

SGDBMS Study Group on Data Base Management Systems. *See* ANSI/X3/SPARC/SGDBMS.

SGLA Saskatchewan Government Libraries Association. Contact chairperson. A Canadian association.

SGPIS [Biblíoteka] Szkoly Glównej Planowania i Statystykí (Library of the Central School of Planning and Statistics). Ul. Rakowiecka 22B, Warsaw 12, Poland. Established in 1906.

SGSR Society for General Systems Research. Lisner Hall, Rm. 601, 2023 G St, NW, Washington, DC 20052. Established in 1954. Mathematicians, physical scientists, engineers, psychologists, social scientists, psychiatrists, medical researchers and others interested in general systems research. Formerly (1955) the Society for the Advancement of General Systems Theory.

SHADRAC Shelter-Housed Automatic Digital Random Access.

SHAL Subject Heading Authority List.

SHARES Shared Acquisitions and Retention System. 11 West 40 St, New York, NY 10018. Project of METRO begun in 1968 to improve access to little-used or difficult-to-handle materials and to free shelf space of member libraries.

SHARP Ships Analysis and Retrieval Program. National Center No. 3, 2531 Jefferson Davis Hwy, Arlington, VA 22202. A computerized system for document storage and retrieval operated by the US Navy.

SHAS Shared Hospital Accounting System.

SHE *Subject Headings for Engineering.* 2nd ed. New York: Engineering Index, Inc, 1979. Authority list used in compiling *EI*.

SHF Superhigh Frequencies. Between 3,000 and 30,000 megahertz.

SHIEF Shared Information Elicitation Facility.

SHIRTDIF Storage, Handling and Retrieval of Technical Data in Image Formation.

SI Shift-In Character. A code extension character that can be used alone or to reverse the effect of an SO (Shift-Out Character).

SI [Standards Institute]. Prefix to standards issued by the Standards Institute of Israel.

SI Smithsonian Institution. Washington, DC 20560.

SI Source Index. Author index to current literature included in *SCI* (*Science Citation Index*).

SI Superimpose. Moves data from one location to another, superimposing bits or characters on the contents of specified locations.

SI Système Internationale d'Unités. Contact NBS. Abbreviation for the International System of Units.

SI/ABCD Seminario Interamericano sobre la Integración de los Servicios de Información de Archivos, Bibliotecas y Centros de Documentación en America Central y el Caribe. Meeting held Nov. 6–17, 1972, Washington, DC.

SIAD Società Italiana Autori Drammatici. Via del Sudario 44, 00186 Rome, Italy. Established in 1944. Society of dramatists. Publishes documents.

SIALSA Southeastern Indiana Area Library Services Authority. 520 Sixth St, Columbus, IN 47265. Sixty-five public, school, hospital and special libraries cooperate through ILL and other services.

SIAM Society for Industrial and Applied Mathematics. 33 South 17 St, Philadelphia, PA 19103. Established in 1952. Constituent society of AFIPS. Publishes several journals, the Conference Board of the Mathematical Sciences Series and SIAM Studies in Applied Mathematics.

SIAR Swedish Institute for Administrative Research. Stenkullavagen 43, 11265 Stockholm, Sweden. Produces data bases on economics.

SIBE Sequential In-Basket Exercise. A library teaching technique using computer-assisted instruction. *See* Martha Jane K. Zachert and Veronica

Pantelides. *SIBE: A Sequential In-Basket Technique: The Pilot Study.* Tallahassee, FL: Computer-Assisted Instruction Center, Florida State University, 1971.

SIBIL Système Intégré pour les Bibliothèques Universitaires de Lausanne. Automated system of acquisitions, cataloging and circulation functions. See *SIBIL: Système Intégré pour les Bibliothèques Universitaires de Lausanne.* Lausanne, Switzerland: Bibliothèque Cantonale et Universitaire, Lausanne, 1976.

SIBMAS Société Internationale des Bibliothèques-Musées des Arts du Spectacle (International Society of Libraries and Museums of the Theatre Arts). One rue de Sully, 75004 Paris, France. Present name adopted in 1972. Formerly a section of IFLA.

SICOLDIC Sistema Colombiano de Información Cientifica y Technica. *See* book review in *JOLA* 4 (Dec. 1971): 227–228. Book review gives highlights of the 59-page report of the system.

SICOM A general-purpose interpretive system using floating point arithmetic. The computer can operate as a floating point machine with 10 decimal digit word length.

SID Searches in Depth. Information Retrieval Center, Northern Colorado Educational BOCS, 1750 30th St, Suite 48, Boulder, CO 80301.

SID Society for Information Display. 654 North Sepulveda Blvd, Los Angeles, CA 90049. Established in 1962. Constituent society of AFIPS. Publishes a journal.

SIDAR Selective Information Dissemination and Retrieval.

SIE Science Information Exchange. Name changed to SSIE.

SIE Smithsonian Information Exchange. Name changed to SSIE.

SIECOP Scientific Information and Educational Council of Physicians. Postal Lock Drawer Number 249, Melbourne, FL 32901.

SIG Special Interest Group.

SIGACT Special Interest Group on Automata and Computability Theory. *See* ACM/SIGACT.

SIG/AH Special Interest Group on Arts and Humanities. *See* ASIS/SIG/AH.

SIG/ALP Special Interest Group on Automated Language Processing. *See* ASIS/SIG/ALP.

SIGARCH Special Interest Group on Architecture of Computer Systems. *See* ACM/SIGARCH.

SIGART Special Interest Group on Artificial Intelligence. *See* ACM/SIGART.

SIG/BC Special Interest Group on Biological and Chemical Information Systems. *See* ASIS/SIG/BC.

SIGBDP Special Interest Group on Business Data Processing. *See* ACM/SIGBDP.

SIGBIO Special Interest Group on Biomedical Computing. *See* ACM/SIGBIO.

SIG/BSS Special Interest Group on the Behavioral and Social Sciences. *See* ASIS/SIG/BSS.

SIGCAI Special Interest Group on Computer-Assisted Instruction. *See* ACM/SIGCAI.

SIGCAPH Special Interest Group on Computers and the Physically Handicapped. *See* ACM/SIGCAPH.

SIGCAS Special Interest Group on Computers and Society. *See* ACM/SIGCAS.

SIG/CBE Special Interest Group on Costs Budgeting and Economics. *See* ASIS/SIG/CBE.

SIG/CIS Special Interest Group on Community Information Services. *See* ASIS/SIG/CIS.

SIGCOMM Special Interest Group on Data Communication. *See* ACM/SIGCOMM.

SIGCOSIM Special Interest Group on Computer Systems Installation Management. *See* ACM/SIGCOSIM.

SIGCPR Special Interest Group on Computer Personnel Research. *See* ACM/SIGCPR.

SIG/CR Special Interest Group on Classification Research. *See* ASIS/SIG/CR.

SIG/CRS Special Interest Group on Computerized Retrieval Services. *See* ASIS/SIG/CRS.

SIGCSE Special Interest Group on Computer Science Education. *See* ACM/SIGCSE.

SIGCUE Special Interest Group on Computer Uses in Education. *See* ACM/SIGCUE.

SIGDA Special Interest Group on Design Automation. *See* ACM/SIGDA.

SIG/ED Special Interest Group on Education for Information Science. *See* ASIS/SIG/ED.

SIG/FIS Special Interest Group on Foundations of Information Science. *See* ASIS/SIG/FIS.

SIGGRAPH Special Interest Group on Computer Graphics. *See* ACM/SIGGRAPH.

SIG/IAC Special Interest Group on Information Analysis Centers. *See* ASIS/SIG/IAC.

SIG/IP Special Interest Group on Information Publishing. *See* ASIS/SIG/IP.

SIGIR Special Interest Group on Information Retrieval. *See* ACM/SIGIR.

SIG/ISE Special Interest Group on Information Services to Education. *See* ASIS/SIG/ISE.

SIG/LAN Special Interest Group on Library Automation and Networks. *See* ASIS/SIG/LAN.

SIGLASH Special Interest Group on Language Analysis and Studies in the Humanities. *See* ACM/SIGLASH.

SIG/LAW Special Interest Group on Law and Information Technology. *See* ASIS/SIG/LAW.

SIGMAP Special Interest Group on Mathematical Programming. *See* ACM/SIGMAP.

SIGMETRICS Special Interest Group on Measurement Evaluation. *See* ACM/SIGMETRICS.

SIG/MGT Special Interest Group on Management Information Activities. *See* ASIS/SIG/MGT.

SIGMICRO Special Interest Group on Microprogramming. *See* ACM/SIGMICRO.

SIGMINI Special Interest Group on Minicomputers. *See* ACM/SIGMINI.

SIGMOD Special Interest Group on Management of Data. *See* ACM/SIGMOD.

SIG/MR Special Interest Group on Medical Records. *See* ASIS/SIG/MR.

SIG/NDB Special Interest Group on Numerical Data Bases. *See* ASIS/SIG/NDB.

SIG/NPM Special Interest Group on Non-Print Material. *See* ASIS/SIG/NPM.

SIGNUM Special Interest Group on Numerical Mathematics. *See* ACM/SIGNUM.

SIGOPS Special Interest Group on Operating Systems. *See* ACM/SIGOPS.

SIGPLAN Special Interest Group on Programming Languages. *See* ACM/SIGPLAN.

SIG/PPI Special Interest Group on Public–Private Interface. *See* ASIS/SIG/PPI.

SIGSIM Special Interest Group on Simulation. *See* ACM/SIGSIM.

SIGSOC Special Interest Group on Social and Behavioral Science Computing. *See* ACM/SIGSOC.

SIG/TIS Special Interest Group on Technology, Information, and Society. *See* ASIS/SIG/TIS.

SIGUCC Special Interest Group on University Computing Centers. *See* ACM/SIGUCC.

SIG/UOI Special Interest Group on User On-Line Interaction. *See* ASIS/SIG/UOI.

SII Standard Identifier for Individuals. ANSI Subcommittee X3.8 proposed this standard for identification of individuals for computerized information exchange. Composed of number (SSAN) and name.

SII Standards Institute of Israel. 42 University St, Tel Aviv, Israel. Issues

English-language standards. Affiliated with ISO (International Standards Organization).

SILC System for Interlibrary Communication. Model for enhancing ILL by using a computer-based communication network.

SIM Standards Institute of Malaysia. 117 Jalan Ampang, Box 544, Kuala Lumpur, Malaysia. Issues English-language standards. Affiliated with ISO (International Standards Organization).

SIMALU Self-Instructional Media-Assisted Learning Unit.

SIMILE Simulator of Immediate Memory in Learning Experiments.

SIMS Socioeconomic Information Management System. Data and Computation Center, University of Wisconsin, Madison, WI 53706. Intended to develop a machine-readable document system utilizing a UNIVAC 1108 remote batch system but convertible to other large computer systems and to an on-line teletype system.

SIMSCRIPT Simulation Programming Language. *See* H. M. Markowitz, B. Hausner and H. W. Karr. *SIMSCRIPT: A Simulation Programming Language.* Englewood Cliffs, NJ: Prentice-Hall, 1963.

SINTO Sheffield Interchange Organization. Science and Commerce Library, Surrey St, Sheffield S1 1XZ, England.

SIPI Scientists Institute for Public Information. 30 East 68 St, New York, NY 10021. A national clearinghouse for science information established in 1963.

SIPRI Stockholm International Peace Research Institute. Sveavägen 166, Stockholm S-113 46, Sweden. Publishes books distributed in the US and Canada by Crane, Russak and Co, and elsewhere by their own Information Department.

SIPROS Simultaneous Processing Operating System. Manages all parts and programs of a data processing system.

SIPSDE Society of Independent and Private School Data Education. Absorbed in 1975 by SDE.

SIR Semantic Information Retrieval. Part of the MAC (Machine-Aided Cognition) project at MIT (Massachusetts Institute of Technology).

SIR Statistical Information Retrieval. Phillips Research Center, 185A Research Bldg. 1, Bartlesville, OK 74004. Provides computer literature searching of reports from Phillips Petroleum Company's Research and Development Department from 1962.

SIRA Scientific Instrument Research Association. SIRA Institute, South Hill, Chislehurst, Kent BR7 5EH, England. Issues *Instrument Abstracts*. Also known as BSIRA.

SIRCULS San Bernadino, Inyo, Riverside Counties United Library Services. 216 Brookside Ave, Redlands, CA 92373. Seventy academic, public and special libraries cooperate through ILL and reference services.

SIRSA Special Industrial Radio Service Association. 1901 North Moore St, Suite 602, Rosslyn, VA 22209. Established in 1953. Serves industrial users of two-way mobile radio equipment.

SIS School of Information Studies. Syracuse University, Syracuse, NY 13210.

SIS Specialized Information Services. National Library of Medicine, 8600 Rockville Pike, Bethesda, MD 20014. One of NLM's six service areas.

SISIR Singapore Institute of Standards and Industrial Research. Box 2611, Singapore. Affiliated with ISO (International Standards Organization).

SITA Société Internationale des Télécommunications Aéronautiques (International Society of Aeronautical Telecommunications). Dorland House, Lower Regent St, London SW1, England.

SITCE Servicio de Información sobre Traducciones Científicas en Español. 1917 Avenida Revadavia, Buenos Aires, Argentina.

SITE CACI, 1815 North Fort Myer Dr, Arlington, VA 22044. Coverage from 1970. Nonbibliographic data base covering market research data and consumer expenditures.

SITES Smithsonian Institution Traveling Exhibition Service. Smithsonian

Institution, Dept. PS, Washington, DC 20560. Provides temporary exhibits for local libraries, schools and other institutions.

SITT Syndicat des Industries Téléphoniques et Télégraphiques. 64 rue de Monceau, 75008 Paris, France. Established in 1925. Publishes documents.

SJCC Spring Joint Computer Conference. Sponsored by AFIPS from 1962 through 1972. Spring and fall conferences were replaced by annual conferences in 1973.

SJF Svenska Journalistförbundet (Swedish Association of Journalists). Pressens Hus, Vegagatan 4, 113 29 Stockholm, Sweden. Established in 1901. Member of the International Federation of Journalists. Publishes documents.

SJU/USJ Schweizerische Journalisten-Union/Union Suisse des Journalistes. Postfach 176, 8024 Zurich, Switzerland. Association of journalists.

SK&F Smith, Kline & French Laboratories. Research and Development Library, 1500 Spring Garden St, Philadelphia, PA 19101. Library established in 1947. Maintains information systems for scientists and R&D managers in medicine, chemistry, pharmacology, pharmacy and biological sciences.

SKCSR Státni Knihovna Československe Socialisticke Republiky (State Library of the Czechoslovak Socialist Republic). Klementinum 190, CS-110 00 Prague 1, Czechoslovakia. Established in 1958.

SKED Sort-Key Edit. A computer program for creating sort keys for MARC II records at the user's option.

SKU Stockkeeping Unit. A level of description which defines an article uniquely for purposes of ordering and inventory control. *See* William Power. "Retail Terminals . . . A POS Survey." *Datamation* 17 (July 15, 1971): 22-31.

SL Shelf List. Catalog records, arranged by call number, of the books in a library's collection.

SL *Special Libraries*. (Journal). V. 1, 1910. Published by SLA (Special Libraries Association).

SLA Saskatchewan Library Association. Box 3388, Regina SK S4P 3H1. Canada.

SLA School Library Association. Victoria House, 29-31 George St, Oxford 0X1 2AY, England. Established in 1937. *See* Richard Henwood. "School Libraries: The Prospect Before Us." *The Bookseller*, Oct. 11, 1975, pp. 2026-2029.

SLA Scottish Library Association. Dept. of Librarianship, University of Strathclyde, Livingstone Tower, Richmond St, Glasgow G1 1X4, Scotland. Established in 1908. A branch of LA.

SLA Southeastern Library Association. Contact president or ALA (American Library Association).

SLA Southwestern Library Association. Contact president or ALA (American Library Association). Also known as SWLA.

SLA Special Libraries Association. 235 Park Avenue South, New York, NY 10003. Established in 1909.

SLACES Syndicat de la Libraire Ancienne et du Commerce de l'Estampe en Suisse. *See* VEBUKU/SLACES.

SLAD State Libraries Agencies Division. Merged with AASL (American Association of State Libraries) of ALA (American Library Association) in 1957 to become ASLA (Association of Specialized Library Agencies).

SLAPNG School Library Association of Papua, New Guinea. c/o School Libraries Office, Dept. of Education, Konedabu, New Guinea. Established in 1971. *See* K. E. Avafia. "Library Development in Papua, New Guinea." *Libri* 25 (Dec. 1975): 271-297.

SLAS State Library Agency Section. *See* ASCLA/SLAS.

SLC Simulated Linguistic Computer. *See* S. Perschke. "The Use of the 'SLC' System in Automatic Indexing" in *Mechanized Information Storage*, ed. by K. Samuelson. Amsterdam, the Netherlands: IFIP, 1968, pp. 300-311.

SLESR Société des Libraires et Éditeurs de la Suisse Romande (Booksellers and Publishers Association of French-Speaking Switzerland). Avenue Agassiz, 1001 Lausanne, Switzerland. Established in 1866. Publishes documents. Membership composed of booksellers and publishers.

SLIC Selective Letters in Combination. Computer-programmed system generating an index from keywords chosen by the indexer, not by words in title. Similar to KWIC but not as popular. *See* Helen M. Townley. "Computers and Indexes." *The Indexer* 6 (Spring 1969): 102–107.

SLICE Southwestern Library Interstate Cooperative Endeavor. 11300 North Central Expressway, Suite 321, Dallas, TX 75243. Six member libraries serve as project arm of SLA (Southwestern Library Association) and cooperate with CE and adult public library programs. Member libraries are located in AR, AZ, LA, NM, OK and TX.

SLIS School of Library and Information Science.

SLJ *School Library Journal*. V. 1, 1954. Published by R. R. Bowker Co.

SLLA Sierra Leone Library Association. c/o Sierra Leone Library Board, Rokell St, Freetown, Sierra Leone. Established in 1970.

SLLA Sri Lanka Library Association. c/o University of Sri Lanka, Colombo Campus, Box 1698, Colombo, Ceylon. Established in 1960. *See* Manil Silva. "Trends in Librarianship and Documentation in Sri Lanka." *UNESCO Bulletin for Libraries* 29 (1975): 80–86.

SLMP School Library Manpower Project. *See* Robert N. Case. "Experimental Models for School Library Media Education." *LJ* 96 (Dec. 15, 1971): 4151–4156.

SLP Small Libraries Publications. A committee of LAD, a division of ALA (American Library Association), which was terminated in 1978 due to divisional reorganization; SLP was not continued.

SLR Storage Limits Register. A UNIVAC system to prevent inadvertent program references to out-of-range storage addresses.

SLS Seminary Libraries Section. *See* CLA/SLS.

SLS Suburban Library System. 125 Tower Dr, Hinsdale, IL 60521.

SLT Solid Logic Technology. The use of miniaturized solid-state modules in computers which provide faster circuitry with reduced size and greater reliability.

SLTA Saskatchewan Library Trustees Association. Contact secretary or CLA (Canadian Library Association). Established in 1969.

SLUNT Spoken Language Universal Numeric Translation. A system designed for writers wanting their work translated into several foreign languages. *See* W. Goshawke. "SLUNT: Spoken Language Universal Numeric Translation" in *3rd European Congress on Information Systems and Networks: Overcoming the Language Barrier; Luxembourg, 3–6 May, 1977; Organised by the Commission of the European Communities*. Munich: Verlag Dokumentation, 1977, Vol. 1, pp. 661–675.

SLV Schweizerischer Lichtspieltheater-Verband. Postfach 2674, 3001 Bern, Switzerland. Established in 1915. Association of film exhibitors. Publishes documents.

SLV State Library of Victoria. 328 Swanston St, Melbourne, Victoria 3000, Australia.

SMART Salton's Magical Automatic Retrieval of Texts. Cornell University, Dept. of Computer Science, Ithaca, NY 14850. *See* Gerard Salton and M. E. Lesk. "The SMART Automatic Document Retrieval System: An Illustration." *Communications of the ACM* 8 (June 1965): 391–398.

SMBJ *Style Manual for Biological Journals*. Washington, DC: American Institute of Biological Sciences, 1960.

SMC Scientific Manpower Commission. 1776 Massachusetts Ave, NW, Washington, DC 20036. Established in 1953. Maintains a library on scientific and engineering manpower. Publishes several periodicals.

SMCCL Society of Municipal and County Chief Librarians. County Library Headquarters, Goldlay Gardens, Chelmsford, Essex, England.

SMCCL Southeastern Massachusetts Cooperating College Libraries. *See* SMCL.

SMCL Southeastern Massachusetts Cooperating Libraries. c/o Bridgewater State College Library, Bridgewater, MA 02324. Four academic libraries and three affiliate members cooperate through ILL, notification of purchases, staff development and other resource-sharing services.

SMCSLA Special Libraries Association, Section de Montréal Chapter. Box 727, Station B, Montreal PQ H3B 3K3, Canada. Established in 1932.

SMD System Manufacturing Division. Of IBM.

SME Society of Mining Engineers. Caller Number D, Littleton, CO 80123. Established in 1871. A constituent society of AIME. Publishes several periodicals.

SMI Simulated Machine Indexing. Hughes Aircraft Co, Culver City, CA 90230. *See* Masse Bloomfield. "Evaluation of Indexing. 2. The Simulated Machine Indexing Experiment." *Special Libraries* 6 (Nov. 1970): 501–507. In evaluating information retrieval, the system was not consistent, although it measured the breadth of vocabulary both objectively and consistently.

SMI Super Market Institute. Established in 1937. Merged in 1977 with the National Association of Food Chains to form FMI.

SMIAC Sail Mechanics Information Analysis Center. Army Engineer Waterways Experimental Station, Box 631, Vicksburg, MS 39180. A source of documents.

SMILE South Central Minnesota Inter-Library Exchange. c/o Mankato State University, Mankato, MN 56001. Thirteen academic, public and special libraries cooperate through ILL and other services.

SMIRS School Management Information Retrieval System. c/o ERIC Clearinghouse on Education Management, University of Oregon, Eugene, OR 97403.

SMIS Society for Management Information Systems. One Illinois Center, 111 East Wacker Dr, Chicago, IL 60601. Established in 1968. Members are concerned with all aspects of management information systems in the electronic data processing industry.

SMLS Small and Medium-Sized Libraries Section. *See* PLA/SMLS.

SMMART Society for Mass Media and Resource Technology. 46 Kintore Ave, Adelaide SA 5000, Australia.

SMPTE Society of Motion Picture and Television Engineers. 862 Scarsdale Ave, Scarsdale, NY 10583. Established in 1916. Publishes several periodicals. Formerly (1950) the Society of Motion Picture Engineers.

SMQ *School Media Quarterly*. (Journal). V. 1, 1951. Published by the American Association of School Librarians.

SMS Standard Modular System. A computer component and subassembly packaging system.

SMSA Standard Metropolitan Statistical Area. An integrated economic and social unit with a recognized large population nucleus. Used in census work and, in some instances, to define network areas.

SMX Semi-Micro Xerography. A method of reproduction which produces copies that can be processed by a computer. Developed by Xerox.

S/N Signal-to-Noise Ratio. In a communications channel, the ratio of signal power to noise power, generally expressed in decibels. Also known as SNR.

SNAD Sindacato Nazionale Autori Drammatici. Via dei Baullari 4, 00186 Rome, Italy. Established in 1948. Society of dramatists.

SNAME Society of Naval Architects and Marine Engineers. One World Trade Center, Suite 1369, New York, NY 10048. Established in 1893. Maintains a library and publishes documents.

SNA/MPS System of National Accounts/System of Material Product Balances. Statistical Office, United Nations, New York, NY 10017. Coverage from 1960. Statistical data base. National accounts data by country organized according to SNA for market economics and MPS for centrally planned economics.

SNCF Société Nationale des Chemins de Fer Français. Subdivision de la Documentation, 27 rue de Londres, F-75009 Paris, France. Established in 1940.

SNDA Sunday Newspapers Distributing Association. 89 Kingsway, London WC2, England.

SNICT National Systems of Scientific and Technological Information of Brazil. Instituto Brasileiro de Bibliografia e Documentação, Avenida General Justo 171, 20,000 Rio de Janeiro, GB, Brazil.

SNIG Sistema Nacional de Información de Guatemala. Proposed in 1976.

SNJ Syndicate National des Journalistes. 33 rue du Louvre, 75002 Paris, France. Established in 1918. Association of journalists. Member of the International Federation of Journalists. Publishes documents.

SNOBOL String-Oriented Symbolic Language. A string manipulation and pattern recognition language, developed by Bell Laboratories. *See* R. E. Griswold, J. F. Poage and I. P. Polansky. *The SNOBOL 4 Programming Language*. Englewood Cliffs, NJ: Prentice-Hall, 1965.

SNOP *Systematized Nomenclature of Pathology*. Chicago, IL: College of American Pathologists, 1965.

SNPA Scottish Newspaper Proprietors Association. 10 York Pl, Edinburgh 1, Scotland.

SNR Signal-to-Noise Ratio. *See* S/N.

SNS Syndacato Nazionale Scrittori. Via dei Sansovino 6, 00196 Rome, Italy. Established in 1948. Society of authors.

SNT Society for Nondestructive Testing. Became ASNT (American Society for Nondestructive Testing) in 1969.

SO Shift-Out Character. A code extension character used alone to cause another character set to be substituted for the standard one, generally to allow the use of additional graphics.

SOAP Symbolic Optimum Assembly Programming. A programming language for the IBM 650 computer.

SOASIS Southern Ohio Chapter of ASIS. Contact president or ASIS.

SOCMA Synthetic Organic Chemical Manufacturers Association. 1075 Central Park Ave, Scarsdale, NY 10583. Established in 1921. Maintains a library including congressional hearings, patents, import and export statistics and directories. Publishes a monthly newsletter.

SOCRATES System for Organizing Current Reports to Aid Technology and Science. Defense Research Board, Elgin St, Ottawa, ON, Canada. Processes documents, using computer techniques, to serve Canada's defense community.

SOH Start of Heading Character. A communication control character used to initiate a message heading.

SOKRATUS Státni Knihovna ČSSR, Klementinum 190, SC-11000 Prague 1, Czechoslovakia. Project for centralized cataloging and preparation of bibliographic information for scientific and special libraries at the CSSR State Library (Czechoslovakia).

SOL Simulation-Oriented Language. A programming language.

SOLAPIC Solar Applications Information Center. Franklin Institute Research Laboratories, Science Information Services, 20 St. & Benjamin Franklin Pkwy, Philadelphia, PA 19103. Established in 1974.

SOLID Self-Organizing Large Information Dissemination. *See* R. A. D. De Maine and B. A. Murron. "The SOLID System: A Method for Organizing and Searching Files" in *Information Retrieval: A Critical Review*, ed. by G. Schecter. Washington, DC: Thompson Book Co, 1967.

SOLINET Southeastern Library Network. 615 Peachtree St, NE, Suite 410, Atlanta, GA 30308. Two hundred eight academic, public, state and special libraries share electronic data processing and telecommunications network for access to bibliographic information and resources.

SOLO SAMI On-Line Operations. Selling Areas–Marketing Inc, Time and Life Bldg, New York, NY 10020. Coverage from 1977. Data base consisting of warehouse withdrawal tapes relating to movement of products to supermarkets.

SOLO Southeastern Ohio Library Organization. Rte. 1, Caldwell, OH 43724. Sixteen public, academic and institutional libraries cooperate through ILL, a film circuit and staff development.

SOLO System Ordinary Life Operations. A dynamic, modular total system, tailored to the needs of life insurance companies. Developed by Honeywell.

SOM Start of Message. A character or group of characters transmitted by a polled terminal, indicating to other stations on the line that the data following indicates the addresses of stations on the line which are to receive the answering message.

SOMD Specialized Office for Materials Distribution. Indiana University, Bloomington, IN 47401. Contractor with the USOE Media Services and Captioned Films to authorize accounts and prepare informational catalogs on captioned films for the deaf available through 64 depositories located across the US.

SONDEC Société Nationale de Diffusion Éducative et Culturelle. 4935 Est rue Jarry, Montreal PQ H1R 1Y2, Canada. Maintains a library.

SOP Standard Operating Procedure.

SOQUIP Société Québeçoise d'Initiatives Pétrolières. 3340 de la Perade, Sainte-Foy PQ G1X 2N7, Canada. Maintains a library, started in 1970.

SORT Staff Organization Round Table. Contact ALA (American Library Association).

SOS Share Operating System. An operating system for the IBM 709 computer.

SOSS Sudanese Organization for Standard Specifications. Ministry of Industry and Mining, Box 2184, Khartoum, Sudan. Issues English-language standards. Affiliated with ISO (International Standards Organization).

SOTA State of the Art.

SOTUS Sequentially Operated Teletypewriter Universal Selector. In 81D1 Automatic Teletypewriter Systems, the selecting device at each station.

SOWP Society of Wireless Pioneers. Box 530, Santa Rosa, CA 95402. Established in 1967. Preserves and records early history of wireless telegraphy.

SP Space Character. A character, not normally printed, that is used to separate words.

SPA Sociedade Portuguesa de Autores. Avenida Duque de Loulé 31, Lisbon 1, Portugal. Established in 1925. Society of authors. Publishes documents.

SPA Systems and Procedures Association. Became ASM (Association for Systems Management) in 1968.

SPAR Selection Program for ADMIRAL Runs. Honeywell's three-phase utility system that updates ADMIRAL and object program areas of ART (ADMIRAL Run Type) by selecting or deleting programs from an SPT (Symbolic Program Tape).

SPARC Standards Planning and Requirements Committee. *See* ANSI/SPARC.

SPE Society of Petroleum Engineers. 6200 North Central Expressway, Dallas, TX 75206. A constituent society of AIME.

SPEC Systems and Procedures Exchange Center. Office of Management Studies, Association of Research Libraries, 1527 New Hampshire Ave, NW, Washington, DC 20036. Established in 1973 by ARL. Collects, organizes, analyzes, stores and disseminates information on research library management.

SPECOL Special Customer-Oriented Language. A computer language that can be used interchangeably with many data files. *See* B. Smith. "SPECOL: A Computer Enquiry Language for the Non-Programmer." *Computer Journal* 11 (Aug. 1968): 121–127.

SPEED Self-Programmed Electronic Equation Delineator. A computer program for the solution of equations.

SPEEDI System for the Publication and Efficient, Effective Dissemination of Information. A proposed system for chemical literature. *See* Ajiit Singh, Michael O. Luke and Irving Jenks. "SPEEDI: A Better Information System." *Journal of Chemical Documentation* 14 (Feb. 1974): 36–38.

SPEL *Selected Publications in European Languages.* V. 1, Feb. 1973. Published by the College of Librarianship Wales, Llanbadarn Fawr, Aberystwyth SY 23 3AS, Wales.

SPEX Small and Specialist Publishers Exhibition. Held in London, England, in 1973.

SPIE Society of Photo-Optical Instrumentation Engineers. Box 10, 405 Fieldston Rd, Bellingham, WA 98225. Established in 1954. Maintains a library. Publishes *Optical Engineering* and proceedings of approximately 30 seminars annually.

SPIEL Spokane Inland Empire Libraries. Contact president. Consortium established in Spokane, WA, in 1967. Maintains a union list of serials.

SPIL Society for the Promotion and Improvement of Libraries. 54 M. A. Jinah Rd, Hameed Manzil, Karachi 5, Pakistan. Established in 1960. *See* S. J. Haider. "Library Associations in Pakistan." *UNESCO Bulletin for Libraries* 23 (May June 1969): 148–150.

SPILS Society for the Promotion of the Interests of Librarianship Students. Newcastle upon Tyne College of Commercial Students' Union, Benton Park Centre, Corchester Walk, Newcastle upon Tyne NE7 7SS, England.

SPIN Searchable Physics Information Notices. American Institute of Physics, 335 East 45 St, New York, NY 10017. Coverage from 1970. Monthly machine-readable magnetic tape copies of the current bibliographic input to NISPA (National Information Service in Physics and Astronomy).

SPINES Science and Technology Policies Information Exchange System. Division of Science and Technology Policies, UNESCO, 7 Place de Fontenoy, F-75700 Paris, France. Projected computerized bibliographic data system on international science and technology policies. See *Science and Technology Policies Information Exchange System (SPINES): Feasibility Study* (Science Policy Studies and Documents, No. 33). UNESCO, 1974.

SPIO Spitzenorganisation der Filmwirtschaft eV. Langenbeckstrasse 9, Wiesbaden 62, Federal Republic of Germany. Established in 1950. Publishes documents. Membership composed of film producers, renters and exhibitors.

SPIRES Stanford Physics Information Retrieval System. Stanford University Libraries, Stanford, CA 94305. Goals of this system are to provide computer-based bibliographic retrieval for Stanford users and to develop software that can be used in library automation. See *SPIRES (Stanford Physics Information Retrieval System) 1969–70 Annual Report.* Stanford, CA: Institute for Communication Research, Stanford University, June 1970.

SPL Simple Programming Language. An IBM language. *See* E. J. Neuhold. "The Formal Description of Programming Languages." *IBM Systems Journal* 2 (1971): 86.

SPLC Standard Point Location Code. Adopted by NBS's Transportation Data Coordinating Committee in 1970, SPLC identifies and codes geographic locations in all of North America including Mexico.

SPLQ *Scandinavian Public Library Quarterly.* (Journal). V. 1, 1968. Published by Bibliotekstilsyne, Munkedamsveien 62, Oslo, Norway. Formerly *Reol.*

SPP Society of Private Printers. c/o Private Libraries Association, 41 Cuckoo Hill Rd, Pinner, Middlesex, England.

SPS Symbolic Programming System. A programming system for the IBM 1620 computer or a programming language in which terms may represent quantities and locations.

SPSE Society of Photographic Scientists and Engineers. 1411 K St, NW, Washington, DC 20005. Established in 1948. Maintains a library and publishes documents.

SPSS Statistical Package for the Social Sciences. A computer program language designed for mathematical analysis of social science information.

SPT Symbolic Program Tape. A Honeywell tape that contains a file of programs, each of which is in the original assembly language and also the machine language. From this tape, programs can be selected for either checkout or production runs. *See* SPAR.

SPUR Single Precision Unpacked Rounded Floating-Point Package. A programming system used on the UNIVAC 1103 computer.

SPX Simplex Circuit. A circuit superimposed on an existing two-wire circuit by means of center-tapped repeating coils, the superimposed circuit requiring an additional conductor to complete it.

SR Scientific Report.

SRA Science Research Associates. 259 East Erie St, Chicago, IL 60611. A subsidiary of IBM. Publishes documents.

SRA Sociological Research Association. Contact president. Established in 1928.

SRC Science Research Council. State House, High Holburn, London WC1, England.

SRCDL Survey Research Center Data Library. Survey Research Center, University of California, 2538 Channing Way, Berkeley, CA 94720. Formerly IDL&RS. Became SRCDL in 1978.

SREB Southern Regional Education Board. 130 Sixth St, NW, Atlanta, GA 30313. Sponsor of the 1972 Conference on Computers in the Undergraduate Curricula.

SRI Stanford Research Institute. Stanford, CA 94305. Works in information science research.

SRIM Standing Order Microfiche Service. A service of NTIS which automatically provides subscribers with the full texts of research reports selected to satisfy individual requirements.

SRIS Safety Research Information Service. National Safety Council, 444 North Michigan Ave, Chicago, IL 60611.

SRL Science Reference Library. 25 Southampton Bldgs, Chancery La, London WC2A 1AW, England. Formerly NRLSI. Incorporated in 1973 as part of the Reference Division of BL (British Library). Comprised of the Holburn Branch (the former POL) and the Bayswater Branch.

SRRT Social Responsibilities Round Table. Contact ALA (American Library Association).

SRSA Scientific Research Society of America. Established in 1886. Was absorbed by Sigma XI in 1974.

SS Serials Section. *See* RTSD/SS.

SS Statistics Section. Refers to a section of various organizations which studies statistical data.

SS Supervisors Section. *See* AASL/SS.

SSAN Social Security Account Number. *See* SII (Standard Identifier for Individuals).

SSC Station Selection Code. A Western Union term to indicate a signal which can be directed to an outlying telegraph receiver to activate its printer automatically.

SSCI *Social Science Citation Index*. V. 1, 1973. Published by ISI (Institute for Scientific Information).

SSDC Space Science Data Center. *See* NSSDC.

SSDL Society for the Study of Dictionaries and Lexicography. Became DSNA in 1977.

SSE Société Suisse des Écrivains. *See* SSV/SSE.

SSEC Selective Sequence Electronic Calculator. Built in 1948. Capable of storing instructions or programs in a memory section, making it the first so-called stored program computer.

SSIE Smithsonian Science Information Exchange. 1730 M St, NW, Rm. 300, Washington, DC 20036. Maintains a computerized inventory of unclassified ongoing research projects in the life and physical sciences. Operates CCRESPAC for the ICRDB program. Formerly SIE (Smithsonian Information Exchange) and SIE (Science Information Exchange).

SSIPP Social Sciences Instructional Programming Project. Beloit College, Beloit, WI 53511. Using FORTRAN IV, the project offers listings, card decks and magnetic tapes to noncommercial users.

SSIS Social Science Information System. Institute for Behavioral Research, York University, 4700 Keele St, Downsview ON M3J 2R6, Canada. Coverage from 1969. Bibliographic data base that merges *CIJE*, *CSSA*, and *PA* (*Psychological Abstracts*). Produced by

IBR and available at York University only.

SSL/FJF Suomen Sanomalehtimiesten Litto/Finlands Journalist Förbund (Union of Journalists in Finland). Yrjönkatu 11 A 2, 00120 Helsinki 12, Finland. Established in 1921. Member of FIJ. Publishes documents.

SSN Standard Serial Number. Developed by ANSI's Z-39 Committee. An eight-digit, all numeric, unique serial title identifier. *See* B. H. Weil. "Document Access." *Journal of Chemical Documentation* 11 (Aug. 1971): 178–185.

SSP Society for Scholarly Publishing. 1909 K St, NW, Suite LL, Washington, DC 20006. Established for individuals working in scholarly publishing. First annual meeting June 1979 in Boston, MA.

SSRC Social Sciences Research Council. State House, High Holborn, London WC1R 4TH, England. Established in 1965. Encourages and supports research in the social sciences and makes grants to students for postgraduate instruction.

SSS Suomen Säätöteknillinen Seura (Finnish Society of Automatic Control). Box 13039, 00131 Helsinki 13, Finland. Member of IFAC (International Federation of Automatic Control). Publishes documents.

SSS Symbolic Shorthand System. Developed by Hans Selye at the University of Montreal for classification of physiology and medical literature.

SSSA Soil Science Society of America. 677 South Segoe Rd, Madison, WI 53711. Established in 1936. Publishes journals and indexes.

SSSR *See* USSR.

SSU Semiconductor Storage Unit. An I/O storage unit introduced in 1971 by Advanced Memory System Inc. to bridge the gap between core systems and high-speed disks.

SSV/SSE Schweizerischer Schriftsteller-Verband/Société Suisse des Écrivains. Kirchgasse 25, 8001 Zurich, Switzerland. Established in 1912. Society of authors. Publishes documents.

STA Scottish Typographical Association. 136 West Regent St, Glasgow C2, Scotland.

STACO Standing Committee for the Study of Principles of Standardization. Contact ISO (International Standards Organization).

STAIRS Storage and Information Retrieval System.

STAIS Student Advisory Information Service. University of Dayton, Dayton, OH 45409. Primary purpose is the operation of an in-house advisory service to undergraduates. Also serves as an investigative tool for the Department of Information Science Graduate Studies.

STAMP Systems Tape Addition and Maintenance Program. A Honeywell program that simplifies making up the file of systems programs on the symbolic program tape or master relocatable tape. Significantly reduces the time and effort in updating, correcting and maintaining the systems programs on these tapes.

STAPRC Scientific and Technical Association of the People's Republic of China. A federation of approximately 64 scientific societies which began, in 1979, to hold annual meetings, publish scientific journals and work toward the "popularization" of science. *See* "AAAS Board Visit to China: A Brief Report." *Science* 203 (Feb. 9, 1979): 533–535.

STAR *Scientific and Technical Aerospace Reports.* (Journal). V. 1, 1963. Published by Scientific and Technical Information Division of NASA.

STAT PACK Statistical Routines. A UNIVAC product that goes beyond UNIVAC's MATH PACK. It includes routines for parameters such as chi-square tests, analysis of variance and regression and correlation analysis.

STC *Short Title Catalogue.* London: The Bibliographical Society, 1926. Books printed in England, Scotland and Ireland and English books printed abroad from 1475 to 1640.

STC Society for Technical Communication. 1010 Vermont Ave, NW, Suite 421, Washington, DC 20005. Established in 1960. Persons engaged or interested in some phase of the field of technical communications. Formerly (1971) STWP.

STD Society of Typographical Designers. 6 Ludgate Sq, London EC4, England.

STECC Scottish Technical Education Consultative Council. Room 215, York Bldgs, Queen St, Edinburgh 2, Scotland.

STEP Simple Transition to Electronic Processing. A programming technique.

STEP Standard Tape Executive Program. A program for the NCR 304 computer.

STET Specialized Technique for Efficient Typesetting. A package of precoded subroutines and systems charts for justification and hyphenation of copy. Developed by Honeywell.

STI Scientific and Technical Information. National Research Council, 100 Sussex Dr, Ottawa 7, ON, Canada.

STINFO Science and Technology Information Officer. A government term for the scientific and technical information officer in various departments and agencies.

STISEC Scientific and Technological Information Services Enquiry Committee. National Library of Australia, Canberra 2600, Australia. Produced a report on which Australia's science information system is based.

STM Scientific, Technical and Medical Publishers. Secretariat, Keizersgracht 426, 1016 GE Amsterdam, the Netherlands. An association of publishers.

STR Synchronous Transmitter Receiver. In IBM data terminals that use synchronous transmission, the unit that transmits and receives data and control information and maintains line synchronization.

STRAM Synchronous Transmit Receive Access Method. One of three major levels of access methods in the telecommunications area.

STRESS Structural Engineering System Solver. A language for engineering problems which is problem-oriented instead of machine-oriented.

STRN Standard Technical Report Number. Although assigned by individual agencies, the report codes are monitored by NTIS to avoid duplication of numbers.

STS Science and Technology Section. *See* ACRL/STS.

STW Society of Technical Writers. Established in 1953. Merged with ATWE to become STWE.

STWE Society of Technical Writers and Editors. Formed by merger of STW and ATWE. In 1960, merged with TPS to become STWP, now called STC (Society for Technical Communication).

STWP Society of Technical Writers and Publishers. Became STC (Society for Technical Communication) in 1971.

STX Start of Text Character. A communication control character that terminates a heading and marks the beginning of actual text.

SUB Substitute Character. An accuracy control character used as a replacement for an invalid character or for nonrepresentable characters on a particular device.

SUBSTITUTE A utility computer program available from NBS. *See* EDPAC.

SuDocs Superintendent of Documents. US Government Printing Office, Washington, DC 20402.

SUL Small University Libraries. Contact CLA (Canadian Library Association).

SUN Symbols, Units, Nomenclature. One of the most important commissions of IUPAP regarding information.

SUNKLO Suomen Näytelmäkirjailijaliitto (Finnish Dramatists Society). Vironkatu 12 B, Helsinki 17, Finland. Established in 1921. Publishes documents.

SUNY State University of New York. Albany, NY 12222. A statewide system of publicly supported colleges and universities. Individual units are involved in various computer retrieval and control projects.

SUNY-BCN SUNY Biomedical Communication Network. Provided on-line searching of biomedical literature until April 1977. Now serves only as an access node for NLM MEDLINE service. Sponsored by SUNY.

SUNYLA State University of New York Librarians Association. Contact secretary.

SUPARS Syracuse University *Psychological Abstracts* Retrieval System. Syracuse

University, Syracuse, NY 13210. A project sponsored by the US Air Force to develop an on-line search program for *Psychological Abstracts. See* K. H. Cook. "An Experimental On-Line System for *Psychological Abstracts.*" *Proceedings of ASIS* 7 (1970): 111-114.

SURF Support of User Records and Files.

SURGE Sorting, Updating, Report, Generating, Etc. A data processing compiler for the IBM 704 computer.

SUZDKS Státni Ústav pro Zdravotnickou Dokumentačm a Knihovnickou Sluzbu (State Institute for Medical Documentation and National Medical Library). Sokolska-St. 31, Nove Mesto, Prague 2, Czechoslovakia.

SVAJ/ASJA Schweizerische Vereinigung der Agrarjournalistes/Association Suisse des Journalistes Agricoles (Swiss Association of Agricultural Journalists). Avenue Jordils 1, 1000 Lausanne 6, Switzerland.

SVAL Sangamon Valley Academic Library Consortium. c/o Illinois College Library, Jacksonville, IL 62650. Eleven member libraries have cooperative programs, referral service, directory and workshops.

SVD/ASD Schweizerische Vereinigung für Dokumentation/Association Suisse de Documentation (Swiss Association of Documentation). Postfach A 158, 8032 Zurich, Switzerland. Established in 1939.

SVFBJ/ASJLP Schweizerische Vereinigung Freier Berufsjournalisten/Association Suisse des Journalistes Libres Professionnels (Swiss Association of Independent Professional Journalists). Postfach 262, 8033 Zurich, Switzerland.

SVSF Sveriges Vetenskapliga Specialibiblioteks Förening (Association of Special Research Libraries.). c/o Statens Psykdogisk-Pedagogiska Bibliothek, Box 23099, 10435 Stockholm 23, Sweden. Established in 1945.

SWA Schweizerisches Wirtschaftsarchiv (Swiss Economic Archives). Kollegiengebäude der Universität, Petersgraben, CH-4000 Basel, Switzerland.

SWALO Southern Wisconsin Academic Librarians Organization. University of Wisconsin, 800 West Main St, Whitewater, WI 53190.

SWAMI Software-Aided Multifont Input. A software program designed to read characters directly from source documents. Developed by SCAN-Data Corp.

SWE Society of Women Engineers. 345 East 47 St, New York, NY 10017. Established in 1950. Publishes a newsletter, student survey and pamphlets.

SWEDIS Swedish Drug Information System. National Board of Health and Welfare, Dept. of Drugs, Box 607, Uppsala S-75125, Sweden. Coverage from 1932. Nonbibliographic data base covering pharmaceuticals used in Sweden.

SWELP South Western Educational Library Project. Western Michigan University, Dwight B. Waldo Library, Kalamazoo, MI 49001. Established in 1969. Consortium of smaller libraries in southwestern Michigan.

SWG Songwriters Guild, Ltd. 32 Shaftesbury Ave, London W1, England.

SWIRS Solid Waste Information Retrieval System. 5600 Fishers La, Rm. 15B22, Rockville, MD 20852. Opened in late 1971. System is open to qualified outside users for literature searches and technical information on solid waste management.

SWLA Southwestern Library Association. *See* SLA.

SWORCC Southwestern Ohio Regional Computer Center. Administrative Data Processing Dept, Miami University, Oxford, OH 45056. Operated by the University of Cincinnati and Miami University at Oxford as a consortium to provide computer services support to the academic and administrative functions of both universities and a number of other nonprofit organizations.

SWORL Southwestern Ohio Rural Libraries. 22 1/2 West Locust St, Box 832, Wilmington, OH 45177. Nineteen-member library consortium cooperating through telephone reference service, traveling collections, staff training, ILL and technical processing.

SWRL Southwest Regional Laboratory for Educational Research and

Development. 4665 Lampson Ave, Los Alamitos, CA 90720. Established in 1967. Maintains a library on education, psychology and computer sciences.

SWRLS South Western Regional Library System. Regional Library Office, Central Public Library, College Green, Bristol BS1 5TL, England.

SWRSIC Southern Water Resources Scientific Information Center. 2111 D. H. Hill Library, North Carolina State University, Box 5007, Raleigh, NC 27607. Provides customized searches with citations and abstracts for a fee.

SWWJ Society of Women Writers and Journalists. Royal Scottish Corporation Hall, Fleur-de-Lis Court, London EC4, England.

SYN Synchronous Idle Character. A control character in a synchronous transmission system that is transmitted in the absence of other traffic to maintain synchrony between the various terminals.

SYP Society of Young Publishers. c/o Publishers' Association, 19 Bedford Sq, London WC1, England.

SYSPOP System Programmed Operators. A function which makes monitor mode service routine available to user mode programs without loss of system control or use of user memory space.

SZV/ASEJ/ASEG Schweizerischer Zeitungsverleger-Verband/Association Suisse des Éditeurs de Journaux/Associazione Svizzera degli Editori di Giornale (Swiss Newspaper Publishers Association). Lerchenstrasse 18, Postfach 687, 8027 Zurich, Switzerland. Established in 1899. Member of the International Federation of Newspaper Publishers. Publishes documents.

TA Teaching Assistant.

TAALS The American Association of Language Specialists. 1000 Connecticut Ave, NW, Suite 9, Washington, DC 20036. Established in 1957. Professional association of interpreters, editors, revisers, précis writers and translators.

TAB *Technical Abstract Bulletin*. V. 1, 1944. Published by Defense Documentation Center for Scientific and Technical Information.

TABA The American Book Awards. First TABA awards were presented in 1980. Administered by AAP (Association of American Publishers). Supersedes NBA (National Book Awards).

TABAMLN Tampa Bay Medical Library Network. c/o Medical Center Library, University of South Florida, Tampa, FL 33620. Thirteen libraries cooperate through ILL, CE, centralized cataloging and reference.

TABS Tailored Abstracts. INSPEC, Institution of Electrical Engineers, Savoy Pl, London WC2R 0BL, England. A service of INSPEC which provides users with a monthly set of abstracts in their fields of interest.

TABS Technical and Business Services. 2400 Olentangy River Rd, Columbus, OH 43210. Commercial firm providing referral services and specialized continuing education.

TABSIM Tabulator Simulator. A simulator program that speeds the conversion of tabulating equipment tasks to computer processing. Developed by Honeywell.

TABSOL Tabular Systems-Oriented Language. A programming system for the GE 225 computer.

TAC Transac Assembler Compiler. A system for the Transac 2000 computer.

TACOL Tasmanian Advisory Committee on Libraries. Tasmania, Australia.

TACTEC Tactical Technology Center. Battelle Memorial Institute, Columbus Laboratories, 505 King Ave, Columbus, OH 43201. The center, under contract with several agencies of DOD, collects, analyzes, stores and disseminates information concerning tactical warfare technology. Publishes documents.

TAFEC Technical and Further Education Commission. An Australian government commission.

TAICH Technical Assistance Information Clearinghouse. American Council of Voluntary Agencies for Foreign Service, 200 Park Ave. South, New York, NY 10003. Publishes a directory of technical assistance activities of volunteer agencies in areas such as agriculture, community development, education and health.

TALENT [TALENT Project]. American Institutes for Research, Box 1113, Palo Alto, CA 94302. A data base on magnetic tape of statistics on American students and schools.

TALIC Tyneside Association of Libraries for Industry and Commerce. Commercial and Technical Dept, Central Library, New Bridge St, Box 1MC, Newcastle upon Tyne NE99 1MC, England.

TALINET Telecommunications Library Information Network. c/o University of Denver Graduate School of Librarianship, University Park, Denver, CO 80210. Project started in 1978 to interconnect remote sites with the school and 10 federal libraries, using telefax, rapifax and television.

TALON Texas, Arkansas, Louisiana, Oklahoma and New Mexico. c/o the University of Texas Health Sciences Center at Dallas Library, 5323 Harry Hines Blvd, Dallas, TX 75235. One of NLM's RMLs (Region IX). Established in 1970 to serve the states named. *See* Donald D. Hendricks. "The Regional Medical Libraries: Region IX." *NLM News* 30 (Sept. 1975): 3–4.

TAP Training, Appraisal and Promotion. An affirmative action program at LC to comply with equal employment opportunity rules of the Civil Rights Act. See *Library of Congress Information Bulletin* 33 (June 21, 1974): 104.

TAPPI Technical Association of the Pulp and Paper Industry. One Dunwoody Park, Atlanta, GA 30338. Established in 1915. Publishes several periodicals and monographs.

TASCON Television Automatic Sequence Control. A television control technique developed by Bunker-Ramo.

TAS-PAC Total Analysis System for Production, Accounting, and Control.

TBRI *Technical Book Review Index.* V. 1, 1935. Published by JAAD Publishing Co, Pittsburgh, PA.

TC Tripartite Committee. Founded by EI, EJC and UET in 1965. Dissolved in 1970.

TCA Tele-Communications Association. 6311 Yucca St, Los Angeles, CA 90028. Established in 1961. Serves as an information exchange and supports training programs.

TCBC Twin Cities Biomedical Consortium. c/o Hennepin County Medical Center, Thomas Lowry Library, 701 Park Ave, Minneapolis, MN 55415. Thirty Minnesota health science libraries cooperate through resource sharing to improve efficiency of access to biomedical information, including MEDLINE service.

TCD Tentative Classification of Documents.

TCLC Tri-State College Library Cooperative. Twenty-nine Pennsylvania libraries cooperate through ILL, union lists, reciprocal borrowing privileges, educational programs, literature search service and film library.

TCM Terminal-to-Computer Multiplexer.

TD Transmitter-Distributor. The device in a teletypewriter that makes and breaks the teletype line in timed sequence.

TDB Toxicology Data Bank. US Dept. of Energy, Oak Ridge National Laboratory, Box X, Oak Ridge, TN 37830. On-line chemical handbook providing numeric and bibliographic information on chemical compounds. Maintained with the support of NLM.

TDCC Transportation Data Coordinating Committee. 1101 17th St, NW, Washington, DC 20036. Established in 1970. Aim is to standardize information systems in the field of transportation.

TEACHTRAN Teaching Logic Translator. A language for effective multipurpose CAI (Computer-Assisted Instruction) systems. See *Proceedings of First IFIP World Conference on Computer Education.* Amsterdam, the Netherlands: North Holland Publishing, 1971.

TEAM-A Theological Education Association of Mid-America. c/o Lexington Theological Seminary, 631 South Limestone St, Lexington, KY 40508. Five Kentucky libraries cooperate through ILL, union list of serials, coordinated acquisitions and mutual library privileges.

TEBROC Tehran Book Processing Center. Box 11-1126, Tehran, Iran. Located in IRANDOC. Publishes and processes books for academic libraries of Iran.

TECH MEMO Technical Memorandum.

TECH REPT Technical Report.

TEIP Transdisciplinary Engineering Information Program. Engineering Index, Inc, 345 East 47 St, New York, NY 10017. Development plan for an integrated and flexible high-speed information processing system for computerized publishing.

TELECAT Telecommunication Catalogue. *See* UNICAT/TELECAT.

TELESPEED Marketing term used by Western Union for a product line of medium-speed paper tape transmitting and receiving units.

TELEX Automatic Teletypewriter Exchange Service. A service of Western Union, similar to TWX of AT&T.

TELI Technisch-Literarische Gesellschaft. Graf-Recke-Strasse 84, 4 Düsseldorf, Federal Republic of Germany. Association of journalists. Publishes documents.

TEMP Texas Educational Microwave Project. University of Texas, Austin, TX 78712. Established in 1961. TEMP was developed to improve college education through use of television and other telecommunication techniques and to merge the project into a larger telecommunication network.

TEMPO Technical Environmental and Management Planning Operations. 816 State St, Drawer QQ, Santa Barbara, CA 93101. Part of the Aerospace Business Group of GE.

TERP Terrain Elevation Retrieval Program. A computer program.

TESAT Teaching Sample Tables. *See* CAIC.

TESLA Technical Standards for Library Automation. Formed in 1973 as a committee of ISAD, now LITA, a division of ALA (American Library Association).

TEST *Thesaurus of Engineering and Scientific Terms.* New York: Engineers' Joint Council, 1967.

TEX Teleprinter Exchange. A worldwide service provided by Western Union. Similar to TWX of AT&T.

TGT Transformational Grammar Tester. University of California, 405 Hilgard Ave, Los Angeles, CA 90024. Objective is the integration of transformational analysis of English. *See* "TGT: Transformational Grammar Tester." *AFIDS Conference Proceedings* 32 (Spring 1968): 385–393.

THOMIS Total Hospital Operating and Medical Information System. In use since 1966; employs terminals at nursing stations and outpatient clinics. *See* Robert Geisler. "The THOMIS Medical Information System." *Datamation* 16 (June 1970): 133–136.

THOR Tape Handling Optional Routines. Controls magnetic tape operations.

3M Minnesota Mining and Manufacturing Company. 3M Center St, Saint Paul, MN 55101. Produces printing, photographic, computing and recording materials.

3 Rs Reference and Research Library Resources. New York State Library, Cultural Education Center, Albany, NY 12230. Nine regional consortia of public, academic and special libraries authorized by the NY State Education Department to improve reference materials and resources in the state. *See* J. M. Cory. "The Network in a Major Metropolitan Center." *Library Quarterly* 39 (Jan. 1969): 90–98.

TIB Technische Informationsbibliothek. Technischen Universität, Welfengarten, D-3000 Hannover, Federal Republic of Germany.

TIC Technical Information Center.

TIC Technical Institute Council. Dupont Circle Bldg, 1346 Connecticut Ave, NW, Washington, DC 20036. Established in 1962.

TICA Technical Information Center Administration. Three meetings held on this subject were sponsored by Drexel Institute of Technology, Information Science Department. Proceedings of all three published by Spartan Books, Washington, DC, 1964; 1965; and New York, 1966.

TICCIT Time-Shared Interactive Computer-Controlled Information Television. Developed in 1968 by Mitre Corp. *See* Keith Melville. "Two-Way TV." *The Sciences* 13 (Sept. 1973): 18–23.

TIE Texas Information Exchange. c/o Rice University, Fondren Library, 6100 Main St, Houston, TX 77001. A network of 45 academic and public libraries, including the Texas State Library, cooperate through ILL.

TIE Total Interlibrary Exchange. Box 1369, Goleta, CA 93017. Sixty-eight California libraries cooperate through information service, exchange of materials and access to data banks.

TIES Total Information for Educational Systems. Munn School Districts Data Processing Joint Board, 1925 West County Rd, B2, Saint Paul, MN 55113. Successor to CAM (Comprehensive Achievement Monitoring). Individualized instructional effort utilizes a computer data base covering information on fiscal and administrative matters. Provided to school districts in Minnesota and suburban Chicago.

TIMT Toronto Institute of Medical Technology. 222 Saint Patrick St, Toronto ON M5T 1V4, Canada. Maintains a library.

TIO Television Information Office. National Association of Broadcasters, 745 Fifth Ave, New York, NY 10019.

TIP Technical Information Project. Massachusetts Institute of Technology, Cambridge, MA 02139. Project for research on the utilization of multiaccess computers for storage, retrieval and dissemination of scientific information.

TIP Toxicology Information Program. National Library of Medicine, 8600 Rockville Pike, Bethesda, MD 20014. A program of NLM's Specialized Information Services, TIP produces data bases and printed publications.

TIPL Teach Information Processing Language. A programming language.

TIPS Technical Information Processing System. Rockwell International– Rocketdyne Division, Technical Information Center, 6633 Canoga Ave, Canoga Park, CA 91304.

TIPTOP Tape Input/Tape Output. Relieves the programmer of writing detailed coding for common magnetic tape input and output routines. The programmer writes a few simple macrostatements, causing the necessary coding to be generated automatically. Developed by Honeywell.

TIRC Technical Information Retrieval Center. See ITIRC.

TIRC Toxicology Information Response Center. Oak Ridge National Laboratory, Oak Ridge, TN 37803. Operated by NLM's TIP (Toxicology Information Program). Provides computerized searches and produces bibliographies that are sold through NTIS.

TIRMMS *Technical Information Reports for Music-Media Specialists.* Published by MLA (Music Library Association).

TIS Technical Information Service. National Research Council, 100 Sussex Dr, Ottawa 2, ON, Canada. In 1974 merged with NSL (National Science Library) to form CISTI/ICIST.

TISA Technical Information Systems Activities. Project of the US Army, Office of the Chief of Engineers. Makes grants to Army and other federal librarians to report on technological devices.

TISAP Technical Information Support Activities Project. Formerly (1968) ATLIS, this project was terminated in 1974.

TISCO Technical Information Systems Committee. College Park, MD. A firm jointly owned by Information Dynamics of Reading, MA, and Informatics of Sherman Oaks, CA. Received a contract to upgrade NASA's Scientific and Technical Information Facility in 1969.

TITLEX Legislazione dello Stato. Centro Elettronico di Documentazione-Italgiure, Corte Suprema di Cassaziono, Palazzo di Giustizia, Via Ulpiano 8, Rome 00193, Italy. Coverage from 1940. Full-text data base covering Italian state laws.

TITUS [Textile Industry]. Institute Textile de France, 35 rue des Abondances, 92100 Boulogne sur Seine, France. Coverage from 1968. Bibliographic data base covering the textile industry.

TKD Türk Kütüphaneciler Dernegi (Turkish Librarians Association). Necatibey Caddesi, 19/22, PK 175 Yenisehir, Ankara, Turkey. Established in 1949.

TKV-VBT R.Y. Tieteellisten Kirjastojen Virkailijat–Vetenskapliga Bibliotekens Tjänstemannaförening r. y. (Association of Research and University Librarians). c/o Library of the Scientific Societies,

Snellmaninkatu 9-11, SF-00170 Helsinki 17, Finland. Established in 1965 to improve economic status and salaries.

TLA Tennessee Library Association. Contact president or ALA (American Library Association).

TLA Texas Library Association. Contact secretary or ALA (American Library Association).

TLA Thai Library Association. 241 Phrasumaine Rd, Bangkok 2, Thailand. Established in 1954. *See* S. Ambhanwong. "Thai Library Association." *UNESCO Bulletin for Libraries* 25 (July–Aug. 1971): 217–220.

TLA Theater Library Association. 111 Amsterdam Ave, Rm. 513, New York, NY 10023. Established in 1937.

TLC Tri-County Library Council. University of Wisconsin, Parkside Library, Kenosha, WI 53104.

TLS Tekniska Litteratursällskapet (Swedish Society for Technical Documentation). Contact president. Established in 1936. Swedish affiliate of FID. Sponsored the indexing of *Proceedings of the FID/IFID Joint Conference on Mechanized Information Storage, Retrieval and Dissemination*. Amsterdam, the Netherlands: North Holland Publishing, 1968.

TLU Table Look Up. A procedure in which the value of a function, for various values of its independent variable, is obtained from a table.

TM Committee on Theory of Machine Techniques and Systems. *See* FID/TM.

TMO Committee on Theory, Methods and Operations of Information Systems and Networks. *See* FID/TMO.

TMR Triple Modular Redundancy.

TMS The Metallurgical Society. Box 430, Warrendale, PA 15086. Established in 1957. A constituent society of AIME. Publishes documents. Also known as MS (The Metallurgical Society).

TNR Texas Numeric Register. Texas State Library, 1200 Brazos St, Capital Sta, Box 12927, Austin, TX 78711.

TOHYOP Hanguk Tosogwan Hyophoe. *See* KLA (Korean Library Association).

TOOL Test-Oriented Operated Language. A programming language.

TOS Tape Operating System. An operating system which, except for the segment always in main storage, is stored on magnetic tape.

TOSAR Topological Representation of Synthetic and Analytical Relations of Concepts. Developed to provide capability of formulating concepts as a search condition. *See* Robert Fugmann et al. "TOSAR: A Topical Method for the Representation of Synthetic and Analytical Relations of Concepts." *Angewandte Chemie, International Edition* 9 (Aug. 1970): 589–595.

TOXBACK [Toxicology Backfile]. National Library of Medicine, 8600 Rockville Pike, Bethesda, MD 20014. Coverage from 1950 to 1973. Bibliographic data base covering human and animal toxicity studies. Material since 1973 found in related data base, TOXLINE.

TOXICON Toxicology Information Conversational On-Line Network. Name changed to TOXLINE in 1973.

TOXLINE Toxicology Information On-Line. National Library of Medicine, 8600 Rockville Pike, Bethesda, MD 20014. Coverage from 1974. Bibliographic data base covering human and animal toxicity studies. Older material in related data base, TOXBACK.

TOX-TIPS *Toxicology Testing in Progress.* (Journal). V. 1, 1977. Published by NLM's Toxicology Information Program.

TPR Technical Processes Research Office. Library of Congress, 10 First St, SE, Washington, DC 20540.

TPS Technical Publishing Society. Established in 1954. Merged with STWE in 1960 to become STWP, now called STC (Society for Technical Communication).

TPSIS Transportation Planning Support Information System. California Dept. of Transportation Library, Sacramento, CA 95814.

TRAC Text Reckoner and Compiler. A text-handling language. *See* C. N. Mooers and L. P. Deutsch. "TRAC: A Text Handling Language" in

Proceedings of the 20th National Conference of ACM. New York: ACM, 1965, pp. 229-246.

TRACE Tape-Controlled Recording Automatic Checkout Equipment. A component of automatic pilots in planes.

TRACE Time-Shared Routines for Analysis, Classification, and Evaluation.

TRACE Tracking Retrieval and Analysis of Criminal Events. Name changed to OBTS.

TRAN Transmit. To send information from one location to another, generally by electrical means.

TRANSDEX [Translations Index]. Bell and Howell Micro Photo Division, Old Mansfield Rd, Wooster, OH 44691. Coverage from 1974. Bibliographic data base containing references to JPRS translations.

TRANSDOC [Transportation Documentation]. European Conference of Ministers of Transport, Organization for Economic Cooperation and Development, 19 rue de Franqueville, 75775 Paris, Cedex 16, France. Bibliographic data base covering transportation.

TRC Thermodynamics Research Center. Texas A&M University, College Station, TX 77843. Sponsored by the Office of Standard Reference Data of NBS, API (American Petroleum Institute), the Gulf Oil Foundation, the Texas A&M Research Foundation, and by subscriptions to its publications.

TRI *Translations Register-Index*. V. 1, June 15, 1967. Published by Special Libraries Association Translation Center.

TRIAL Technique for Retrieving Information from Abstracts of Literature. Computing Center, Northwestern University, Evanston, IL 60602. A system developed at the Northwestern University Computing Center for manipulation of bibliographic data. *See* Allen Wynne. "A Computer-Based Index to Book Reviews in the Physics Literature." *Special Libraries* 70 (Mar. 1979): 135-139.

TRIC Therapeutic Recreation Information Center. Dept. of Physical Education & Recreation, Box 354, University of

Colorado, Boulder, CO 80309. Provides bibliographic services and computer searches in the field of therapeutic recreation. Located at the University of Oregon until 1978.

TRIM Test Rules for Inventory Management. A program for simulating a real inventory control system to permit lower investments in inventory.

TRIPS TALON Reporting and Information Processing System. TALON, c/o The University of Texas Health Sciences Center at Dallas Library, 5323 Harry Hines Blvd, Dallas, TX 75235. *See* R. E. Nance, W. K. Wickham and M. Guddan. "A Computer System for Effective Management of a Medical Library Network." *JOLA* (Dec. 1971): 213-220.

TRIS Transportation Research Information System. Battele-Columbus Laboratories, 505 King Ave, Columbus, OH 43201. Maintains library, established in 1972, on transportation research and contacts. Member of TRISNET.

TRISNET Transportation Research Information Services Network. National Research Council-Transportation Research Board Library, 2101 Constitution Ave, NW, Washington, DC 20418. A national network which strives to provide optimum access to transportation research information. Provides on-line services and document delivery.

TRIUL Tri-University Libraries of British Columbia. Contact chairperson. Established in 1970. A Canadian association.

TROLL/I Time-Shared Reactive On-Line Lab. New England Regional Computing Program, One Broadway, Cambridge, MA 02142. An MIT (Massachusetts Institute of Technology) program.

TRPD *Toxicology Research Projects Directory*. (Journal). V. 1, 1976. Published by NLM's Toxicology Information Program. Abstracts are obtained from SSIE.

TRTL Transistor-Resistor-Transistor Logic.

TS Time Sharing. A method of using a computer system to allow concurrent use of programs by multiple users.

TSC Transmitter Start Code. A Bell System term which refers to a sequence of characters that automatically polls its tape transmitter or keyboard when transmitting to a remote teletypewriter.

TSC Transportation Systems Center. Cambridge, MA 02114. Formerly ERC (Electronics Research Center) under NASA.

TSL Tasmania State Library. 91 Murray St, Hobart, Tasmania 7000, Australia. Official name is the State Library of Tasmania.

TSO Time-Sharing Option.

TSS Time-Shared System. A computer system that is used simultaneously by multiple users. Although the system serves each user in sequence, this is not apparent due to the system's high speed.

TSS Time-Sharing System. *See* TSS (Time-Shared System).

TT Teletype.

TT Teletypewriter.

TT Top Term. Top term of the hierarchy in the construction of a thesaurus.

TTD Textile Technology Data Base Keyterm Index. Institute of Textile Technology, Box 391, Charlottesville, VA 22902. Data base covering journal titles and key terms assigned to abstracts in *Textile Technology Digest*. Coverage from 1966.

TTY Teletypewriter Equipment.

TU Svenska Tidningsutgivareföreningen. Norrtullsgatan 5, Box 45136, 104 30 Stockholm 45, Sweden. Established in 1898. Member of the International Federation of Newspaper Publishers and the International Federation of the Periodical Press. Publishes documents.

TUCC Triangle Universities Computation Center. Duke University, Research Triangle Pk, Box 8815, Durham, NC 27707.

TÜRDOK Türkiye Bilimsel ve Teknik Dokümantasyon Merkezi (Turkish Scientific and Technical Documentation Center). Bayindir Sokak 33, Yenisehir, Ankara, Turkey.

TUSC Technology Use Studies Center. Name changed to KIAC.

TV Television.

TVA Tennessee Valley Authority. 500 Union Ave, Knoxville, TN 37902. Library established in 1933. Separate libraries also maintained in Chattanooga, TN, and Muscle Shoals, AL.

TWA Trans World Airlines, Inc. 605 Third Ave, New York, NY 10016. Maintains air transportation library, established in 1965, and computerized reservations system.

TWX Teletypewriter Exchange Service. A public switched teletypewriter service offered by AT&T in which suitably equipped stations are connected to other such stations in the US and Canada.

TWXILL TWX Interlibrary Loan Network. Ohio State Library, 65 South Front St, Columbus, OH 43215.

UA User Area. The area on a disk where semipermanent data may be stored. This area is also used to store programs, subprograms and subroutines.

UACS Union des Associations Cinématographiques Suisses. *See* USLV/UACS.

UB Universitetsbiblioteket i Oslo (National and University Library in Oslo). Drammensveien 42, Oslo 2, Norway.

UBARI Union of Burma Applied Research Institute. Dept. of Standards, One Kanbe Rd, Yankin Post Office, Rangoon, Burma. Issues English-language standards. Affiliated with ISO (International Standards Organization).

UBC Universal Bibliographic Control. Office for Universal Bibliographic Control was supported by a CLR grant to IFLA from July 1975 to June 1977. Basic goal is to make available, in an internationally accepted and standardized form, basic bibliographic data on all publications issued in all countries. Housed at BL (British Library).

UCAE Universities Council for Adult Education. c/o Professor T. Kelly, The University, 9 Abercromby Sq, Liverpool 7, England. Established in 1945. Acts as a clearinghouse for the exchange of ideas and the establishment of common policy on adult education.

UCB Union Chimique-Chemische Bedrijven. Département Documentation Technique et Brevets, Bibliotheek, rue d'Anderlecht 33, B-1620 Drogenbos, Belgium.

UCCA Universities Central Council on Admissions. Rodney House, Rodney Rd, Box 28, Cheltenham, Gloustershire GL50 1HY, England. Produces a machine-readable data base called UCCA Prestel File.

UCIS University Center for International Studies. Publications and Information Services, 230 South Bouquet St, Pittsburgh, PA 15260. Established in 1974. Produces a machine-readable data base, USPSD, and its print equivalent.

UCLA University of California–Los Angeles. 405 Hilgard Ave, Los Angeles, CA 90024.

UCLC Utah College Library Council. c/o Brigham Young University, Law Library, Provo, UT 84602. A consortium of 13 college and university libraries cooperate in the areas of network reference services, acquisitions, use of materials and system applications.

UCMP *Union Catalog of Medical Periodicals.* V. 1, 1966. Published by the Medical Library Center of New York. Computer-produced periodical catalog, available on microfiche.

UCS Universal Classification System.

UCSC University City Science Center. Philadelphia, PA 19104. Sponsored a survey on document delivery services of medical libraries. *See* Richard H. Orr and Arthur P. Schless. "Document Delivery Capabilities of Major Biomedical Libraries in 1968: Results of a National Survey Employing Standardized Tests." *BMLA* 60 (July 1972): 382–422.

UD *Unlisted Drugs.* (Journal). V. 1, 1949. Published by the Pharmaceutical Division, Special Libraries Association. Available as a journal and on cards.

UDC Universal Decimal Classification. Classification scheme characteristic of the prefacet era. *See* A. C. Foskett. *The Universal Decimal Classification.* Sherman, CT: Linnet Books, 1973.

UDUAL Unión de Universidades de América Latina (Union of Universities of Latin America). Apardo Postal 70-232, México, DF, Mexico. Publishes a quarterly, *Universidades*.

UERPIC Undergraduate Excavation and Rock Properties Information Center. Thermophysical Properties Research Center, Purdue University, Purdue Industrial Research Pk, 2595 Yeager Rd, West Lafayette, IN 47906. Established in 1972.

UET United Engineering Trustees, Inc. The United Engineering Center, 345 East 47 St, New York, NY 10017.

UGC University Grants Committee. 14 Park Crescent, London W1N 4DH, England. Established in 1919. Allocates government funds to individual universities. Publishes documents.

UHF Ultrahigh Frequency. Frequencies between 300 and 3,000 megahertz.

UICA Union of Independent Colleges of Art. 4340 Oak, Kansas City, MO 64111. Ten Missouri libraries share resources, problems and solutions unique to art colleges.

UICA/LREP UICA Learning Resources Exchange Program. UICA Film Center, California College of Arts and Crafts, Broadway at College Ave, Oakland, CA 94618. Program established in 1967. Provides interlibrary loan of audiovisual materials to member colleges in six states.

UK United Kingdom.

UKAEA United Kingdom Atomic Energy Authority. 11 Charles II St, London SW1, England. Established in 1954. Functions were extended in 1965. Maintains the Atomic Energy Research Establishment at Harwell, which includes a library. Publishes documents sold by HMSO.

UKCIS United Kingdom Chemical Information Service. The University of Nottingham, Nottingham NGF 2RD, England. A foreign affiliate of NFAIS. Provides SDI service from tapes.

UKSAV Ústredná Kniznica Slovenskej Akademie Vied (Central Library of the Slovak Academy of Sciences). Klemensova 27, Bratislava, Czechoslovakia.

ULA Uganda Library Association. Box 5894, Kampala, Uganda. Established in 1957. Official journal, *Uganda Library Association Bulletin*, is published semiannually. *See* T. K. Lwanga. "Trends of Library Development in Uganda Since 1962" in *International Librarianship*, ed. by George Chandler. London: The Library Association, 1972, pp. 37–44.

ULA Utah Library Association. Contact president or ALA (American Library Association).

ULAA Ukrainian Library Association of America. Box 455, New City, NY 10956.

ULAP University of California–University-Wide Automation Program. c/o Institute of Library Research, South Hall, University of California, Berkeley, CA 94720. Consortium established in 1971. Seeks to improve access to a common pool of bibliographic resources at the nine University of California campuses.

ULC Urban Libraries Council. 78 East Washington St, Chicago, IL 60602. Concerned with state and federal funding for urban programs.

ULS *Union List of Serials*. Third edition. New York: H. W. Wilson Co, 1965. Union list of serials in the libraries of the US and Canada covering titles that began publication before 1950. Superseded (for post-1950 serials) by *NST*.

ULS University Libraries Section. *See* ACRL/ULS.

ULTC Urban Libraries Trustees Council. Contact Chicago Public Library. Established in 1971.

UMCC University of Miami Computing Center. Coral Gables, FL 33124. Publishes *UMCC Newsletter* to promote interchange of ideas.

UMF Ultra Microfiche.

UMI University Microfilms International. 300 North Zeeb Rd, Ann Arbor, MI 48106.

UMPLIS Informations und Dokumentationssystem zum Umweltplanung. Umweltbundesamt, Bismarckplatz 1, D1000 Berlin 33, Federal Republic of Germany. Provides information and documentation service in the field of environmental protection.

UMREL Upper Midwest Regional Educational Laboratory. 160 East 78 St, Minneapolis, MN 55423. *See* Judith P. Fitch, William M. Ammentorp and Marvin F. Daley. "Behaviorally Engineered Educational Environments: An Information System." *Special Libraries* 61 (Oct. 1970): 445–452.

UN United Nations. Has various headquarters in Geneva, Rome, New York and other cities. Sponsors numerous information-related projects.

UNAM Universidad Nacional Autónoma de México. México 20, DF, Mexico. University has a College of Library Science and over 200 libraries.

UNBIS United Nations Bibliographic Information System. Dag Hammarskjold Library, United Nations, New York, NY 10017.

UNCOL Universal Computer-Oriented Language. A programming language.

UNEEPF Union Nationale des Éditeurs-Exportateurs de Publications Françaises. 55 avenue des Champs-Elysées, 75008 Paris, France. Established in 1948. Organization of book exporters. Publishes documents.

UNEP United Nations Environment Program. Nairobi, Kenya. Developing an international referral system for environmental information services.

UNESCO United Nations Educational, Scientific and Cultural Organization. 7 Place de Fontenoy, F-75700 Paris, France. Sponsor of numerous international information systems and services, including UNISIST and other networking projects.

UNICAT/TELECAT Union Catalogue/Telecommunication Catalogue. The union cataloging project of the Ontario Universities Library Cooperative System, which includes libraries in Ontario and Quebec.

UNICEF United Nations Children's Fund. 20 rue Pauline Borghèse, 92 Neiully-sur-Seine, France. Formerly the United Nations International Children's Emergency Fund.

UNICODE UNIVAC Code. Automatic coding system used for the UNIVAC 1103-A computer.

UNICOMP Universal Compiler. Compatible with FORTRAN.

UNIDO United Nations Industrial Development Organization. Felderhaus 2, Rathausplatz, Box 707, Vienna 1010, Austria. Encourages library development.

UNINDUST General Industrial Statistics. Statistical Office, United Nations, New York, NY 10017. Data base covering statistical series in utilities production and distribution. Coverage from 1953.

UNIPUB 345 Park Ave. South, New York, NY 10010. US distributor of publications for international organizations, including the UN.

UNISIST Universal System for Information in Science and Technology. Division of Scientific and Technical Information and Documentation, UNESCO, 7 Place de Fontenoy, F-75700 Paris, France. Sponsor of the World Science Information System, a cooperative international information-exchange program begun in 1971 and supported by ICSU and UNESCO. *See* A. Wysocki and J. Tocatlian. "A World Science Information System: Necessary and Feasible." *UNESCO Bulletin for Libraries* 25 (Mar.-Apr. 1971): 62-66.

UNITAR United Nations Institute for Training and Research. 801 United Nations Pl, New York, NY 10017. Produces a data base on communications and the news media on punched cards and magnetic tape.

UNITEL University Information Technology Corporation. A joint Harvard-MIT (Massachusetts Institute of Technology) venture to investigate areas of cooperation.

UNITRAN UNIVAC FORTRAN. The programming language used on the UNIVAC Solid State 80 computer.

UNIVAC Universal Automatic Computer. The trade name for a series of computers manufactured by the Sperry Rand Corp.

UNPBF Union Nationale des Producteurs Belge de Films (National Union of Belgian Film Producers). Rue Eugène Hubert, 1090 Brussels, Belgium. Established in 1960.

UPAA University Photographers Association of America. c/o Warren Gravois, Executive Manager, University of New Orleans, New Orleans, LA 70122. Established in 1961. Publishes documents.

UPC Universal Product Code. A bar code for optical scanning. Used to identify grocery items and books. *See also* EAN.

UPCC Uniform Product Code Council. 401 Wythe St, Alexandria, VA 22314. Established in 1972. Administers UPC.

UPDBF Union Professionnelle des Distributeurs Belges de Films. Rue Dupont 102, 1030 Brussels, Belgium. Established in 1948. Association of film exhibitors.

UPE Union de la Presse Étrangère en Belgique. International Press Center, Maison de la Presse, blvd. Charlemagne 1, 1040 Brussels, Belgium. Established in 1921. Association of journalists. Publishes documents.

UPGRADE User-Prompted Graphic Data Evaluation. An English-language-prompted system for analyzing computerized data and generating graphic displays. Used primarily for environmental analysis, it can analyze numeric data.

UPI United Press International. An international news-gathering service subscribed to by many newspapers.

UPPB Union de la Presse Périodique Belge. c/o International Press Center, Maison de la Presse, blvd. Charlemagne 1, 1040 Brussels, Belgium. Established in 1891. Association of journalists. Member of International Federation of the Periodical Press.

UQAM Université du Quebec à Montreal. CP 8888, Montreal PQ H3C 3PB, Canada. Maintains several libraries on the Montreal campus although the main campus is in Quebec City.

URBANDOC Urban Documentation Project. A demonstration program of the Office of Urban Technology and Research, US Department of Housing and Urban Development.

URI Université Radiophonique et Télévisuelle Internationale (International Radio-Television University). 116 Avenue du Président Kennedy, Paris 16, France.

URISA Urban and Regional Information Systems Association. c/o Municipal Finance Officers Assn, 180 North Michigan Ave, Chicago, IL 60601. Established in 1964. An international organization with annual conferences in New Orleans, LA, or Toronto.

URIS I Universal Resource Information Symposium. Held February 23, 1972. Sponsored by the Southern California Consortium of Library Associations and Information Societies.

URJ Union Romande de Journaux. Petit-Chêne 18b, 1003 Lausanne, Switzerland. Established in 1920. Association of newspaper publishers.

URL User Requirements Language. A programming language.

URSI Union Radio-Scientifique Internationale (International Scientific Radio Union). 7 place Emil Danco, Brussels 18, Belgium. Also known as ISRU.

US In USASCII, the information separator used at the lowest level of hierarchy.

US United States.

USA United States of America.

USACO US-Asiatic Company, Ltd. 13-12 Shimbashi 1-chome, Minato-ku, Tokyo 105, Japan. Book and subscription agent specializing in science, engineering, business and medicine. Member of IIA.

USACSSEC United States Army Computer Systems Support and Evaluation Command. Technical Reference Library, Washington, DC. *See* P. M. Malley. "Development of a Technical Library to Support Computer Systems Evaluation." *JOLA* 4 (Dec. 1971): 173–184.

USAEC United States Atomic Energy Commission. Also known as AEC. Became ERDA in 1974, incorporated into DOE in 1977.

USAF United States Air Force. The Pentagon, Washington, DC 20330. Sponsors many information centers and funds and supports many computer-applied projects.

USASCII United States of America Standard Code for Information Interchange. The standard code, using a set of seven-bit coded characters and a parity check, that is used for the exchange of information among data processing and communications systems.

USASI United States of America Standards Institute. Became ANSI in 1969.

USBE United States Book Exchange. Formerly ABC (American Book Center for War Devastated Libraries). Name changed to USBE (Universal Serials and Book Exchange) in 1975. *See* "Brief History of USBE." *LR&TS* 14 (Fall 1970): 607–609.

USBE Universal Serials and Book Exchange. 3335 V St, NE, Washington, DC 20018. Established in 1948. Formerly ABC (American Book Center for War Devastated Libraries) and USBE (United States Book Exchange).

USCL United Society for Christian Literature. 6 Bourverie St, London EC4, England.

USC-WHO United States Committee for the World Health Organization. 777 United Nations Pl, New York, NY 10017. Established in 1951. Interested in spreading information about world health. Publishes documents. Also known as the American Association for World Health. Formerly the National Citizens' Committee for the WHO.

USDA United States Department of Agriculture. 14 St. & Independence Ave, SW, Washington, DC 20250. Maintains NAL (National Agricultural Library).

USGI *US Government Reports Index.* Also known as *GRI.*

USGR *US Government Research Reports.* V. 23, 1955–v. 39, 1964. Formerly *World-Wide Index to Federal Research and Development Reports.* Continued by *USGRDR, GRA* and *GRA&I.*

USGRA *US Government Reports Announcements. See GRA.*

USGRDR *US Government Research and Development Reports.* V. 68, 1968–v. 70, 1970. Formerly *USGR.* Continued by *GRA* and later by *GRA&I.*

USGRDRI *US Government Research and Development Reports Index.* V. 68, 1968–v. 70, 1970. Continued by *GRI, GRAI,* and now incorporated in *GRA&I.*

USGRI *US Government Reports Index.* See *GRI.*

USGS United States Geological Survey. USGS Library, National Center, 12201 Sunrise Valley Dr, Mail Stop 950, Reston, VA 22092. Library devised and uses three-level indexing term sets followed by ACI and GSA in their *Bibliography and Index of Geology.*

USIA United States Information Agency. Terminated in 1978. Replaced by ICA (International Communication Agency).

USITA United States Independent Telephone Association. 1801 K St, NW, Suite 1201, Washington, DC 20006. Established in 1897. Serves non-Bell operating telephone companies and publishes documents.

USJ Union Suisse des Journalistes. *See* SJU/USJ.

USJPRS United States Joint Publications Research Service. *See* JPRS.

USLA Uganda School Library Association. Box 7014, Kampala, Uganda. Established in 1968. Affiliated with the Uganda Libraries Board. Publishes a quarterly newsletter in English and other documents.

USLV/UACS Union der Schweizerischen Lichtspieltheater-Verbänd/Union des Associations Cinématographiques Suisses. Effingerstrasse 11, Postfach 2674, 3001 Bern, Switzerland. Association of film exhibitors.

USNCFID US National Committee for the International Federation for Documentation. National Academy of Sciences, 2101 Constitution Ave, Washington, DC 20418.

USOE United States Office of Education. 400 Maryland Ave, SW, Washington, DC 20202. An office of DHEW. Funds library research and demonstrations. Became the largest part of the new US Department of Education, established in April 1980.

USP *United States Pharmacopoeia.* Nineteenth edition. Easton, PA: Mack Publishing Co, 1975.

USPHS United States Public Health Service. 5600 Fishers La, Rockville, MD 20852. This federal agency is charged by law to promote health services to all US citizens. Also conducts and supports medical and related sciences and disseminates scientific information. Reports to DHEW. Parent organization to CDC, FDA, HRA, HSA and NIH and its divisions.

USPI Unione della Stampa Periodica Italiana. Via Po 102, 00198 Rome, Italy. Established in 1953. Publishes documents.

USPSD United States Political Science Documents. University Center for International Studies, Publications and Information Services, 230 South Bouquet St, Pittsburgh, PA 15260. Coverage from 1975. Bibliographic data base available in machine-readable or journal form.

USR United States Reshippers. A publishing trade term for firms that service geographic areas not serviced by independent book wholesalers.

USSPA United States Student Press Association. Superseded by CPS (College Press Service).

USSR Union of Soviet Socialist Republics.

UTHSCSA University of Texas Health Science Center at San Antonio. 7705 Floyd Curl Dr, San Antonio, TX 78284. This center's library was assigned in 1976 to film cards of TALON's *Union Catalog* and to make them available on microfiche. Also charged with converting catalog cards for other TALON libraries into machine-readable form.

UTLAS University of Toronto Library Automation System. University of Toronto, Toronto ON M5S 1A1, Canada. On-line network including Ontario and Quebec university libraries and public and government libraries.

UTTC Universal Tape-to-Tape Converter.

UUA UNIVAC Users Association. Name changed to AUUA in 1976.

UUC Union de la Critique du Cinéma. Chemin de la Source 1, 1180 Brussels, Belgium. Established in 1954. Association of film critics.

UVP Universal Availability of Publications. An IFLA program, begun in 1977.

UVTEI Ústředí Vědeckých Technických a Ekonomických Informací (Central

Office of Scientific, Technical and Economic Information). Konviktska 5, Stare Mesto, Prague 1, Czechoslovakia.

UVTI Ústav Vĕdeckotechnických Informací (Institute of Scientific Technical Information). Slezka 7, Vinohrady, Prague 2, Czechoslovakia.

V Volume.

VAAP Vsesoyuznoe Agentstvo Avortskikh Prav-USSR. Copyright agency of the USSR.

VAB Voice Answer Back. An arrangement in which a computer can provide voice responses to inquiries made from telephone-type terminals, the response being selected from a vocabulary of prerecorded or coded voice signals.

VABB Vereniging van Archivarissen en Bibliothecarissen van België. See AABB/VABB.

VAC Vector Analogue Computer.

VALNET Veterans Administration Library Network. VA Central Office, 810 Vermont Ave, NW, Washington, DC 20420. Three hundred forty hospital and general libraries cooperate through centralized cataloging and union lists.

VAMIS Virginia Medical Information Services. University of Virginia Medical Center Library, Box 234, Charlottesville, VA 22904.

VAÖ Verband de Agrarjournalisten in Österreich. Seilergasse 16, 1010 Vienna, Austria. Established in 1962. Association of agricultural journalists.

VASLA (Virginia Chapter of the Special Libraries Association). Name of the journal is the acronym, *VASLA*. V. 1, 1966. Published by the Virginia Chapter of the Special Libraries Association.

VATE Versatile Automatic Test Equipment. Represents a new concept for computer-controlled checkout of complex instrumentation systems. Used by USAF to test inertial guidance systems.

VBB Verein der Bibliothekare an Öffentlichen Büchereien (Association of Librarians in Public Libraries). Roonstrasse 57, D28 Bremen 1, Federal Republic of Germany. Established in 1922 as Verein Deutscher

Volksbibliothekare. Present name adopted in 1968. Publishes documents.

VBT De Vetenskapliga Bibliotekens Tjänstemannaförening (Union of University and Research Libraries). DIK-SACO/SR, Box 50, S-13101 Nacka 1, Sweden. Established in 1958.

VBT R.Y. Vetenskapliga Bibliotekens Tjänstemannaförening r. y. *See* TKV-VBT R.Y.

VBVB Vereniging ter Bevordering van het Vlaamse Boekwezen. Frankrijklei 93, 2000 Antwerp, Belgium. Established in 1929. Professional association of publishers and booksellers. Publishes documents.

VCCS Video and Cable Communications Section. *See* LITA/VCCS.

VDA Verband Deutscher Agrarjournalisten. Kirchenallee 57/VI, 2 Hamburg 1, Federal Republic of Germany. Established in 1951. Association of agricultural journalists. Publishes documents.

VDA Verein Deutscher Archivare (Association of German Archivists). Voelklinger Strasse 49, D-4000 Düsseldorf, Federal Republic of Germany.

VDB Verein Deutscher Bibliothekare (Association of German Librarians). Contact president. Established in 1948. Professional concerns including continuing education. Developed new cataloging rules. Affiliated with IFLA. *See* Gisela von Busse and Horst Ernestus. *Libraries in the Federal Republic of Germany*. Weisbaden: Otto Harrassowitz, 1972, pp. 162–164.

VDC Voltage to Digital Converter.

VDD Verein Deutscher Dokumentare (Society of German Documentalists). Elsa-Brandströmstrasse 62, Bonn-Beuel, Federal Republic of Germany. Established in 1961. Promotes professional interests.

VdDB Verein der Diplom-Bibliothekare an Wissenschaftlichen Bibliotheken (Association of Certified Librarians at Research Libraries). Contact president (Federal Republic of Germany). Established in 1948. Publishes journal jointly with VDB. Affiliated with IFLA.

VDI Verein Deutscher Ingenieurs. Graf-Recke-Strasse 84, D-4000 Düsseldorf, Federal Republic of Germany. Provides information documentation and abstracting services.

VDJ Verband der Journalisten der Deutsche Democratische Republik. Freidrichstrasse 101, 108 Berlin, German Democratic Republic. Established in 1946. Association of journalists. Publishes documents.

VDU Visual Display Unit. An operator at this unit can see the progress of the program or the solution and can modify or intervene as necessary.

VDZ Verband Deutscher Zeitschriftenverleger. Buchstrasse 85, 53 Bonn 1, Federal Republic of Germany. Member of the International Federation of the Periodical Press.

VEB Vereinigung Evangelischer Buchhändler. Fichtestrasse 2, 7 Stuttgart 1, Federal Republic of Germany. Established in 1925. Publishes documents.

VEBUKU/SLACES Vereinigung der Buchantiquare und Kupferstichhändler in der Schweiz/Syndicat de la Libraire Ancienne et du Commerce de l'Estampe en Suisse. Trittlegasse 19, 8001 Zurich, Switzerland. Established in 1939. Rare-book dealers' association.

VEL Verband Europäischer Lehrmittelfirmen. See EURODIDAC.

VEMA Vermont Educational Media Association. Contact president or AECT.

VEMA Virginia Educational Media Association. Contact president or AECT.

VENISS Visual Education National Information Service for Schools. 33 Queen Anne St, London W1M OAL, England. A service of the National Committee for Audio-Visual Aids in Education of Great Britain.

VEPIS Vocational Education Program Information System.

VEWS Very Early Warning System. A system developed at SK&F for the early recognition and transfer of new technology affecting both present and future R&D activities in the pharmaceutical industry. See Marc Julius et al. "A Very Early Warning System for the Rapid Identification and Transfer of New Technology." *JASIS* 28 (May 1977): 170–174.

VHF Very High Frequency. Frequencies from 30 to 300 megahertz.

VIC Vision Information Center. See VSIC.

VIEMS Vsesojuznyj Naučno-Issledovatel'skij Institut Economiki Mineral'nogo Syr'ja i Geologorazvedocnych Rabot Ministerstva Geologii SSSR i Akademii nauk SSSR. B Vatin per, 8 Moscow Z-240, USSR. A USSR Academy of Science institute for research on the economics of minerals and geological prospecting. Library established in 1964.

VIFS Vsesoyuznogo Informatsionnogo Fonda Standartovi i Technicheskikh Uslovii (All-Union Reference Bank of Standards and Specifications, USSR).

VINE *A Very Informal Newsletter on Library Automation.* Published by OSTI Information Officer for Library Automation, The Library, University of Southhampton, SO9 5NH, England.

VINITI Vsesojuznyi Institut Naučnotehničeskoi Informacii (All-Union Institute of Scientific and Technical Information, USSR). May be the largest information-gathering source in the world. Publishes *RZh* (*Referativny Zhurnal*), not universally available in the Western world.

VIP Variable Information Processing. A generalized information storage and retrieval system for small nonformalized files, providing for retrieval without programming effort.

VIP Vereinigung der Industriefilmproduzenten. Tonndorfer Hauptstrasse 90, 2 Hamburg 70, Federal Republic of Germany. Established in 1950. Publishes documents.

VIP Vermont Information Process. 97 Court St, Middlebury, VT 05753. Incorporated in 1975. Commercial firm which provides computerized searches, translating and indexing in the fields of energy, business and transportation.

VITA Volunteers for International Technical Assistance, Inc. 230 State St,

Schenectady, NY 12305. Association established in 1960.

VITAL Variably Initialized Translator for Algorithmic Languages.

VLA Vermont Library Association. Contact president or ALA (American Library Association).

VLA Virginia Library Association. Contact president or ALA (American Library Association).

VLE BANK Vapour Liquid Equilibria Databank. National Physical Laboratory, Chemical Standards Division, Dept. of Industry, Teddington, Middlesex TW11 0LW, England. Nonbibliographic data base.

VLF Very Low Frequency. Frequencies below 30,000 hertz.

VNIGNI Vsesojuznyj Naučno-Isseldovatel'skij Geologorazvedočnyj Neftjanoj Institut Ministerstra Geologii SSSR. Šosse Entuziatov, 135a Moscow E-275, USSR. An oil-prospecting research institute of the USSR ministry of geology. Library established in 1942.

VNIIKI Vesesojuznii Naučno-Issle-Dovatel'skii Institut Techniceskoi Informaccii, Klassifikaccii i Kodirovaniia (All-Union Scientific Research Institute for Technical Information, Classification and Codification of USSR). Ul Sčuseva 4, Moscow K-1, USSR. Library established in 1928.

VNIIKOP Vsesojuznyj Naučno-Issledovatel'skij Institut Konservnoj i Ovoščesušil'noj Promyšlennosti Ministerstva Pisščevoj Promyšlennosti SSSR. Dmitrovskoe Šosse 5, Moscow, I-434, USSR. A research institute of the canning and dry vegetable industry of the USSR food industry ministry. Library established in 1940.

VNIIMI Vsesoiuznyĭ Nauchno Issle-dovatel'skii Institut Meditsinskoĭ i Medikotekhnicheskoĭ Informatsii Ministerstva Zdravookhraneniia USSR (All-Union Scientific Research Institute of Medical and Medico-Technical Information of the USSR Ministry of Public Health). Ust'inskii Proezd, 2/14, Moscow Z-240, USSR.

VNIIMP Vsesojuznyj Naučno-Issledovatel'skij Institut Mechovoj Promyšlennosti Ministerstva Legleoj Promyšlennosti SSSR. Ul Osipenko 71, Moscow Z-127, USSR. A fur research institute of the USSR ministry of light industry. Library established in 1932.

VNIIMP Vsesojuznyj Naučno-Issledovatel'skij Institut Mjasnoj Promyšlennosti Ministerstva Mjasnoj i Moločnoj promyslennosti SSSR. Ul Talalichina 26, Moscow 2-29, USSR. A meat industry research institute of the USSR ministry of the meat and dairy industry. Library established in 1930.

VNIINP Vsesojuznyj Naučno-Issledovatel'skij Institut po Pererabotke Nefti Ministerstva Nefteprerabatyvajuščej i Neftechimičeskoj Promyšlennosti SSSR. Aviamotornaja 6, Moscow E-116, USSR. A research institute of the USSR ministry of the oil refining and oil chemistry industry. Library established in 1930.

VNIIPCHV Vsesojuznyj Naučno-Issledovatel'skij Institut po Pererabotke Chimičeskich Volokon Ministerstva Legkoj Promyšlennosti SSSR. Ul Timura Frunze 11, Moscow G-21, USSR. A chemical fiber research institute of the USSR ministry of light industry. Library established in 1936.

VNIISSV Vsesojuznyj Naučno-Issledovatel'skij Institut Stekloplastikov i Stekljannogo Volokna Ministerstva Chimičeskoj Promyšlennosti SSSR. Stancija Krjukovo der. Andreevka, Moscow, USSR. A research institute on plastic and glass fibers of the USSR ministry of the chemical industry. Library established in 1946.

VNIIV Vsesojuznyj Naučno-Issledovatel'skij Institut Iskusstvennogo Volokna Ministerstva Chimičeskoj Promyšlennosti SSSR. Ul Koloncova 5, Moscow, g. Mytyšči, USSR. A synthetic fiber research institute of the USSR ministry of the chemical industry. Library established in 1935.

VNIMI Vsesojuznyĭ Naučhno-Issledovatel'skii Institut Molochnoi Promyshiennosti

Ministerstva Miasnoi i Molochnoi Promyshlennosti SSSR. Ul Rustaveli 14/10, Moscow I-322, USSR. A dairy industry research institute of the USSR ministry of the meat and dairy industry. Library established in 1944.

VNIVIKI Vsesojuznyj Naučno-Issledovatel'skij Institut Naučno-Techničeskoj Informacii Klassifikaccii i Kondirovanija Gosudarstvennogo Komiteta Standartov, Mer i Izmeritel'nych Priborov SSSR. *See* VNIIKI.

VNLW Virginia National Library Week Company. Sells low-cost posters and library promotional materials.

VNLW-SELA Virginia National Library Week–Southeastern Library Association. Campaign sponsored by VLA (Virginia Library Association) and SELA to provide materials for NLW.

VÖB Vereinigung Österreichischer Bibliothekare (Association of Austrian Librarians). c/o Österreichische Nationalbibliothek, A-1014 Vienna, Austria. Established in 1896 as Österreichischer Verein für Bibliothekswegen. Reorganized in 1945 under present name. Exchanges publications and maintains liaison with the ministry responsible for library education.

VOGAD Voice Operated Gain-Adjustment Device. In telephone communication, a device that is essentially a compressor, used to reduce the fluctuations in level that are common in speech and therefore to improve the average S/N ratio. It does reduce the natural quality of transmitted speech.

VOLS Voluntary Overseas Library Service. The Ranfurly Library, 37 Charles St, London W1, England.

VÖZ Verband Österreichischer Zeitungsherausgeber und Zeitungsverleger. Schreyvogelgasse 3, 1010 Vienna, Austria. Established in 1945. Member of the International Federation of Newspaper Publishers. Publishes documents.

VRB Vereniging van Religieus-Wetenschappelijke Bibliothecarissen (Association of Theological Librarians). Minderbroedersstraat 5, B-3800

Sint-Truiden, Belgium. Established in 1965. Publishes quarterly *VRB Informatie*.

VS Verband Deutscher Schriftsteller. Clemensstrasse 58/1, 8 Munich 40, Federal Republic of Germany. Society of authors.

VSA Vereinigung Schweizerischer Archivare (Association of Swiss Archivists). c/o Staatsarchiv, Predigerplaz 33, CH 8001 Zurich, Switzerland.

VSB/ABS/ABS Vereinigung Schweizerischer Bibliothekare/Association des Bibliothécaires Suisses/Associazione dei Bibliotecari Svizzeri (Association of Swiss Librarians). Schweizerische Landesbibliothek, 3003 Bern, Switzerland. Established in 1897. Works toward the cooperation among, and professional development of, librarians. Publishes a bimonthly journal with SVD/ASD.

VSCHIZO Vsesojuznyj Sel'skochozjajstvennyj Institut Zaučnogo Obzovanija Ministerstva Sel'skogo Chozjajstva SSSR. Balašicha 8, Moscow, USSR. An agricultural research institute of USSR ministry of rural farming. Library established in 1947.

VSF/ASC/ASC Vereinigung Schweizerischer Filmkritiker/Association Suisse des Critiques de Cinéma/Associazione Svizzera dei Critici Cinematografici (Swiss Association of Film Critics). Töpferstrasse 10, 6004 Luzerne, Switzerland. Established in 1946. Association of film critics. Publishes documents and confers awards for new Swiss filmmakers.

VSFAV/APFAV Verband Schweizerischer Film und AV-Produzenten/Association des Producteurs Suisses de Films et de Production Audio-Visuelle (Association of Swiss Film and Audio-Visual Producers). Contact president. Established in 1934. Publishes documents.

VSIC Visual Science Information Center. University of California, Berkeley, CA 94720. Also known as VIC.

VSKB Vereniging voor het Godsdienstig-Wetenschappelijk Bibliothecariaat. Name changed to VTB

(Vereniging voor het Theologisch Bibliothecariaat).

VSS Variable Stability System.

VT Vertical Tabulation Character.

VTB Vereniging voor het Theologisch Bibliothecariaat (Association of Theological Librarians). Contact president (the Netherlands). Founded in 1947 as VSKB. New name adopted in 1973. Publications are in Dutch. Affiliated with IFLA.

VTOC Volume Table of Contents. A table associated with and describing every data set in a direct access volume.

VTR Videotape Recorder.

VTR Videotape Recording.

VU Voice Unit. A measure of the average amplitude of an electrical signal that represents speech or other similar program material. Also called volume unit.

VU Volume Unit. *See* VU (Voice Unit).

VULBS Virginia Union List of Biomedical Serials. University of Virginia Medical Center Library, Box 234, Charlottesville, VA 22908.

VUMS Vyzkumny Ustav pro Matematickych Stroju (Research Institute for Mathematical Machines). Czechoslovakia.

VVBADP Vlaamse Vereniging van Bibliotheek-Archief en Documentatie-Personeel, Vereniging zonder Winstoogmerken (Flemish Association of Librarians, Archivists and Documentalists). Contact president (Belgium). Established in 1921 as VVBAP. New name adopted in 1974. Publishes documents and has joint conferences with NVB.

VVBAP Vlaamse Vereniging van Bibliotheek- en Archiefpersoneel. Name changed to VVBADP in 1973.

VWOA Veteran Wireless Operators Association. 145 Main Ave, Clifton, NJ 07014. Established in 1925.

WAA World Aluminum Abstracts. American Society for Metals, Metals Park, OH 44073. Coverage from 1968. Bibliographic data base covering all aspects of aluminum processing.

Available in print, on-line and on magnetic tape.

WAC Women's Advisory Committee of the British Standards Institution. 2 Park St, London W1, England.

WAC Wyoming Academic Consortium. c/o Laramie County Community College Library, 1401 College Dr, Cheyenne, WY 82001. Consortium established in 1971. Planned to centralize purchasing and processing of book materials in 1974.

WACL Worcester Area Cooperating Libraries. c/o Worcester State College Learning Resources Center, 486 Chandler St, Worcester, MA 01602. Fourteen academic, public and special libraries cooperate through ILL, acquisitions, participation in NELINET and search service.

WADEX Word and Author Index. *See* A. Merta. "A Mechanized System of Information Retrieval in the Field of Information Science" in *Mechanized Information Storage*, ed. by K. Samuelson. Amsterdam, the Netherlands: North Holland Publishing, 1968, pp. 437–443.

WADS Wide Area Data Service. Similar to WATS. AT&T is asking the FCC for approval to lease teletype-grade circuits on an unlimited dial-up basis from any point in the country.

WAERSA *World Agricultural Economics and Rural Sociology Abstracts.* V. 1, 1959. Published by Commonwealth Agricultural Bureaux, Slough, England.

WAIS Wisconsin Assets and Income Studies. University of Wisconsin, Social Science Bldg, Rm. 7324, Madison, WI 53706. Produces a data base on income of Wisconsin residents on magnetic tape. *See* David H. Martin and Roger F. Miller. "A Naive History of Individual Incomes in Wisconsin, 1947-1959." *Journal of Income and Wealth*, Mar. 1970.

WALA West African Library Association. c/o Ghana Library Association, Box 4105, Accra, Ghana. Established in 1972. *See* "Editorial." *Ghana Library Journal* 5 (June 1973): 1–2; 46–47.

WALL Western Association of Law Libraries. Contact chairperson.

Established in 1972. A Canadian association.

WALU Waukesha Academic Library Union. University of Wisconsin Center, 1500 University Dr, Waukesha, WI 53186. Consortium established in 1968. Publishes union list of serials.

WAMI Washington, Alaska, Montana, and Idaho. Organization based at the University of Washington's Health Sciences Library in Seattle which participates in resource sharing and an outreach program in the states named.

WANDPETLS Wandsworth Public, Educational and Technical Library Services. Established in 1966. Members are attached to educational institutions in Wandsworth, England, and comprise a network for cooperation and exchange.

WARC World Administrative Radio Conference. Held in 1979 in Geneva, Switzerland. Meets every 20 years so that nations who are members of ITU can decide how to allocate different parts of the radio-frequency spectrum. Also known as IAARC.

WASL Wyoming Association of School Libraries. Contact president or ALA (American Library Association).

WATDOC Water Resources Document Reference Centre. Canadian Dept. of Fisheries and the Environment, Inland Waters Directorate, Ottawa ON K1A 0E7, Canada. Established in 1971. Produces data bases.

WATS Wide Area Telephone Service. A service provided by telephone companies which allows a customer to place unlimited calls in a specified zone on a direct dialing basis for a flat monthly charge. Sometimes coupled with INWATS. Often used by consortia or networks.

WBS Welsh Bibliographical Society. c/o National Library of Wales, Aberystwyth, Wales.

WCHE Worcester Consortium for Higher Education. 55 Lake Ave, Worcester, MA 01605.

WDB Werkstoffdatenbank. Betriebsforschungsinstitut, VDEh-Institut für Angewandte Forschung GmbH, Verein Deutscher Eisenhuttenleute, Sohnstrasse 65, Düsseldorf D-4000, Federal Republic of Germany. Coverage from 1969. Data base covering technological and physical properties of steel products.

WDC World Data Center. The WDC system represents an international effort to collect and exchange scientific data in various disciplines. There are three WDCs, each composed of several subcenters: WDC-A units are located in the US; WDC-B in the USSR; and WDC-C in several countries in Western Europe, Australia and Japan. ICSU encouraged the establishment of WDC-A during IGY. *See also* WDC-A, WDC-B and WDC-C.

WDC-A World Data Center-A. Coordination Office, National Academy of Sciences, 2101 Constitution Ave, NW, Washington, DC 20418. The US component of the WDC system. There are eight units in the US coordinated by NAS: Glaciology at US Geological Survey, Tacoma, WA 98402, Longitude and Latitude at US Naval Observatory, Washington, DC 20390; Meteorology at National Climatic Center, Asheville, NC 28801; Oceanography at NOAA, Rockville, MD 20852; Rockets and Satellites at Goddard Space Flight Center, Greenbelt, MD 20771; Solar Terrestrial Physics and Solid Earth Sciences both at Environmental Data Service, NOAA, Boulder, CO 80303; and Tsunamis at NOAA, Honolulu, HI 96822. *See also* WDC.

WDC-B World Data Center-B. The Soviet Union component of the WDC system. *See also* WDC.

WDC-C World Data Center-C. The third component of the WDC system located in various countries of Western Europe and in Australia and Japan. *See also* WDC.

WDG-1 World Data Bank-1 (Modified). Laboratory for Computer Graphics and Digital Analysis, Harvard University, 520 Gund Hall, 48 Quincy St, Cambridge, MA 02138. Coverage from 1973. Data base expressing boundaries of countries of the world as expressed geographic coordinates.

WDPC Western Data Processing Center. University of California, 405 Hilgard Ave, Los Angeles, CA 90024. Established in 1956, it is the first, and one of the largest, university computing centers specifically oriented to business applications.

WEECN Women's Educational Equity Communications Network. Far West Laboratory, 1855 Folsom St, San Francisco, CA 94103. Collects, screens, classifies, stores and provides information and publishes materials.

WELDASEARCH The Welding Institute, Abington Hall, Abington, Cambridge CB1 6AL, England. Bibliographic data base covering welding technology.

WESRAC Western Research Application Center. University of Southern California, 950 West Jefferson Blvd, Rm. 102, Los Angeles, CA 90007. Library established in 1967. Disseminates technological information to US industry using a variety of government-sponsored and commercial data banks.

WESS Western European Specialists Section. *See* ACRL/WESS.

WESTFORNET Western Forest Information Network. US Forest Service, Pacific Southwest Forest & Range Experiment Station, 1960 Addison St, Box 245, Berkeley, CA 94701. Twelve government, state and university libraries produce a monthly bulletin of technical literature and cooperate through ILL and information services. Formerly PACFORNET.

WFEO World Federation of Engineering Organizations. 19 rue Blanche, F-75009 Paris, France. Established in 1968. Encourages information exchange.

WGGB Writers Guild of Great Britain. 430 Edgware Rd, London W2, England.

WHCLIS White House Conference on Library and Information Services. *See* WHCOLIS.

WHCOLIS White House Conference on Library and Information Services. 1717 K St, NW, Washington, DC 20036. Provided for in PL (Public Law) 93-568 and announced in 1976. Purpose is to encourage and support the advancement of the quality of America's informational services. Preceded by state and territorial conferences at which delegates were selected. Held Nov. 15-19, 1979, in Washington, DC. Also known as WHCLIS.

WHCS Well History Control System. A. C. Nielsen Co, Box 2612, 1375 Delaware St, Denver, CO 80201. Nonbibliographic data base covering wells and oil drilling. Coverage from 1859.

WHO World Health Organization. Library and Documentation Services, 20 Avenue Appia, 1211 Geneva, Switzerland. Library established in 1948. Provides comprehensive medical literature and information services to members of WHO, a specialized agency related to the UN. Also known as OMS (Organisation Mondiale de la Santé).

WICHE Western Interstate Commission for Higher Education. Drawer P, Boulder, CO 80302. Established in 1952. Maintains a research library. Involved in library education.

WILCO Western Interstate Library Coordinating Organization. Name changed to Western Council of State Libraries in 1978. Housed at WICHE.

WILS Wisconsin Interlibrary Loan Service. c/o University of Wisconsin–Madison, 464 Memorial Library, 728 State St, Madison, WI 53706. Seventy academic and all public libraries in the state cooperate through CE programs, MHSLN, MINITEX and OCLC access.

WIMA Wyoming Instructional Media Association. Contact president or AECT.

WIN Western Information Network Association. Box 4200, Lubbock, TX 79409. Consortium established in 1967. Links members, academic libraries in Texas, through closed-circuit television.

WIPIS *Who Is Publishing in Science.* Philadelphia, PA: Institute for Scientific Information, 1972– . Published annually until 1978; superseded by *CBD.* Formerly (1971) *IDR&DS.*

WIPO World Intellectual Property Organization. 32 Chemin des Colombettes, 1211 Geneva 20, Switzerland. Seeks international agreement on copyright and related laws. Became affiliated with the UN in 1974.

WIRA Wool Industry Research Association. Headingley La, Leeds LS6 1BW, England. Publishes *World Textile Abstracts* and *WIRA Scan.*

WIRL West India Reference Library. 12 East St, Kingston, Jamaica.

WISC Women's Information and Study Centre. 3 Queen's Ride, London SW13, England.

WISE World Information Systems Exchange. Box 2-J, Tempe, AZ 85282. Established in 1975. Four hundred organizations, including libraries, research centers and educational institutions and associations that seek to encourage and provide for collaboration in the exchange of experiences and discoveries pertaining to the use of new technologies and information systems. Absorbed LARC in 1975.

WITI Wisconsin Indianhead Technical Institute. c/o New Richmond Campus Learning Resources Center, 1019 South Knowles Ave, New Richmond, WI 54017. Maintains a media resource collection.

WIZ While most scientific compilers require two or three passes, WIZ requires only one. The language is much easier to learn and is used primarily for engineering, scientific and other complex mathematical problems. A GE product.

WLA Washington Library Association. Contact president or ALA (American Library Association).

WLA Welsh Library Association. Contact executive secretary or LA. Publishes documents. A branch of LA established in 1931 as the Wales and Monmouthshire Branch. Name changed to WLA in 1971.

WLA Wisconsin Library Association. Contact president or ALA (American Library Association). Publishes a newsletter from the Madison Public Library.

WLA Wyoming Library Association. Contact president or ALA (American Library Association).

WLB *Wilson Library Bulletin.* V. 1, 1914. Published by H. W. Wilson Co.

WLN Washington Library Network. Washington State Library, Olympia, WA 98504. Publicly supported libraries in the state cooperate through ILL, computer system, acquisition and cataloging.

WLN Wiswesser Line Notation. A method of writing chemical formulas in a linear mode especially useful for computer retrieval.

WMO World Meteorological Organization. 41 Avenue Giuseppe Motta, Geneva, Switzerland. Established in 1950. A specialized agency related to the UN. Promotes international exchange of weather reports and standardization of observations. Helps developing countries establish weather services. Also known as OMM (Organisation Météorologique Mondiale).

WN [Wellington] National Library of New Zealand. Private Bag, Wellington, New Zealand.

WNAB Weekly Newspaper Advertising Bureau. 92 Fleet St, London EC4, England.

WNLA West Newfoundland Library Association. Currently inactive.

WNPLA Washington Non-Professional Library Association. Name changed to CLEWS.

WNYHSL Western New York Health Sciences Librarians. Contact president. Includes Buffalo area. Publishes *Newsline.*

WNYLRC Western New York Library Resources Council. c/o Buffalo & Erie County Public Library, Lafayette Sq, Buffalo, NY 14203. One of NY state's 11 resource councils.

WON Netherlands Association for Patent Information. Gist-Brocades nv Box 1, Delft 2600 MA, the Netherlands. Established in 1977.

WORLDENERGY World Energy Supplies System. Statistical Office, United Nations, New York, NY 10017. Statistical data base on production, imports, exports and stocks of fuels, gases and electricity. Coverage from 1950.

WORLDS Western Ohio Regional Library Development System. 640 West Market St, Lima, OH 45801. Fifteen libraries cooperate through ILL, staff development, grants, newsletters, periodicals on microfilm and workshops.

WRAP Committee for Writing and Reading Aids for the Paralysed. c/o Action for the Crippled Child, Vincent House, Vincent Sq, London SW1, England.

WRISC Western Regional Information Service Center. Office of Technical Information, Lawrence Berkeley Laboratory, Bldg. 50, Berkeley, CA 94720. Established in 1972. Provides computerized searches and publishes documents.

WRS *Well Record Service.* (Journal). Published by Petroleum Information Corp. of A. C. Nielsen Co. Also available in microform.

WRSIC Water Resources Scientific Information Center. Office of Water Research and Technology, US Dept. of the Interior, 18 & C Sts, NW, Washington, DC 20040. Designated as the national center for water resources and technical information. Publishes an abstract journal and other documents.

WRU Western Reserve University. Has WRU Retrieval System, a method for searching literature using the GE 225 computer.

WRU Who Are You In USASCII, the enquiry character asking "Who are you?"

WTE World Tapes for Education. 19 Wythenshawe Rd, Sale, Cheshire, England.

WTS Word Terminal Synchronous. Complements the communications subsystem by enabling the central processor to be used more efficiently for high-speed data transmission over a single communications line.

WU Western Union Corp. One Lake St, Upper Saddle River, NJ 07458. Involved in telecommunications and information services.

WVLA West Virginia Library Association. Contact president or ALA (American Library Association).

WVLAC West Virginia Library Commission. Science and Cultural Center, Charleston, WV 25305. Publishes *WVLAC Newsletter.*

WWNSS World Wide Network of Standard Seismograph Stations. *See* Jack Oliver and Leonard Murphy. "WWNSS: Seismology's Global Network of Observing Stations." *Science* 174 (Oct.

15, 1971): 254–261. One hundred twenty continuously recording stations. Includes a microfilming service that provides data.

XACT X Automatic Translation Code. X represents any computer.

XPG Xerox Publishing Group. One Pickwick Plaza, Greenwich, CT 06830. Xerox publishing unit composed of six companies, including R. R. Bowker Co. and UMI.

XPM Xerox Planning Model. A computerized representation of Xerox Corp.'s operation.

XS-3 Excess-3. A binary coded decimal notation in which an arbitrary decimal digit N is represented by the binary equivalent of $N + 3$.

YA Young Adult. An age group designated for particular service in public libraries. Generally applied to patrons between 12 and 18 years of age.

YAKUTOKYO Nippon Yakugaku Toshokan Kyogikai (Japan Pharmaceutical Library Association). c/o Library, Faculty of Pharmaceutical Sciences, University of Tokyo, Hongo 7-3-1, Bunkyo-ku, Tokyo, Japan. Established in 1955. Publishes documents.

YAP Young Adult Project. Santa Clara County, California. Began April 1968 as a cooperative effort between two library systems with five units. *See* Regina Minudri and Reed Coats. "Two Years After: Reflections from YAP." *LJ* 98 (Mar. 15, 1973): 967–971.

YASD Young Adult Services Division. 50 East Huron St, Chicago, IL 60611. A division of ALA (American Library Association).

YNA Young Newspapermen's Association. Whitefriars House, 6 Carmelite St, London EC4, England.

YRLS Yorkshire Regional Library System. Central Library, Surrey St, Sheffield S1 1XZ, England.

YUL Yale University Library. New Haven, CT 06520.

ZAED Zentralstelle für Atomkernenergie Dokumentation (Atomic Energy Documentation Center). Gmelin-Institut für Anorganische Chemie und

Grenzgebiete in der Max-
Planck-Gesellschaft, Frankfurt am
Main, Federal Republic of Germany.
Also known as AED (Atomkernenergie
Dokumentation).

ZAS Zero Access Storage. Storage for which
waiting time is short. Term is becoming
less widely used.

ZDE Zentralstelle Dokumentation
Electrotechnique.
Fachinformationszentrum Technisk
Fazde, Merianstrasse 27, 605
Offenbach, Federal Republic of
Germany. Coverage from 1972.
Bibliographic data base on electrical
engineering.

ZDOK Dokumentationszentrum für
Informationswissenschaften. Deutsche
Gesellschaft für Dokumentation eV,
Westendstrasse 19, Frankfurt D-6000,
Federal Republic of Germany.
Established in 1950.

ZIID Zentralinstitut für Information und
Dokumentation. Köpenicker Strasse
325, 117 Berlin, Federal Republic of
Germany. Established in 1963. Member
of FID. Publishes documents.

ZLA Zambia Library Association. Box 2839,
Lusaka, Zambia. Established in 1967.
Affiliated with IFLA. Official journal,
Zambia Library Association Journal, is
published quarterly. *See* "The Zambia
Library Association: Past History,
Present and Future Development."
Journal of Library History 7 (Oct. 1972):
316–328.

ZMMD Zurich, Mainz, Munich, Darmstadt.
A joint effort of ALGOL processors
involving the four European universities
in the acronym.

ZOOM An assembler or compiler routine
that writes macrostatements which can
be translated into more than one
machine instruction. A part of GAP, it
allows shorthand coding by providing
condensed and readable input and near
optimum output. A GE product.

ZSKBI Zväz Slovenských Knihovníkov,
Bibliografov a Informacných
Pracovníkov. *See* ZSKBIP.

ZSKBIP Zväz Slovenských Knihovníkov,
Bibligrafov a Informacných
Pracovníkov (Association of Slovak
Librarians, Bibliographers and
Documentalists). Contact secretary.
Established in 1947. Affiliated with
IFLA. *See* M. Gigánik.
"Czechoslovakia, Libraries in" in
*Encyclopedia of Library and
Information Science*, ed. by A. Kent et
al. New York: Marcel Dekker, 1971, V.
6, pp. 390–403. Also known as ZSKBI.

Index

ADMIRAL
Selection Program for ADMIRAL Runs,
SPAR

ALGOL
British Computer Society ALGOL
Association, BCSAA

APT
Adaptation of APT (Automatically
Programmed Tools), ADAPT

ASIS
Central Ohio Chapter of ASIS, CO-ASIS
Los Angeles Chapter of ASIS, LACASIS
Northern Ohio Chapter of ASIS, NORASIS
Ohio Chapter of ASIS, OASIS
Southern Ohio Chapter of ASIS, SOASIS

ASLIB
ASLIB Economic and Business Information
Group, AEBIG

ASSASSIN
Medical Information Dissemination Using
ASSASSIN, MIDAS

Abbreviations
*Abbreviations and Related Acronyms
Associated with Defense, Astronautics,
Business and Radio-Electronics*,
ABRACADABRA
*Dictionary of Architectural Abbreviations,
Signs and Symbols*, DAA
*Dictionary of Civil Engineering
Abbreviations, Signs and Symbols*,
DCEA
*Dictionary of Computer and Control Systems
Abbreviations, Signs and Symbols*,
DCCSA
*Dictionary of Electronics Abbreviations,
Signs and Symbols*, DEA
*Dictionary of Industrial Engineering
Abbreviations, Signs and Symbols*,
DIEA
*Dictionary of Mechanical Engineering
Abbreviations, Signs and Symbols*,
DMEA

*Dictionary of Physics and Mathematics
Abbreviations, Signs and Symbols*,
DPMA

Aberdeen
Aberdeen and North of Scotland Library and
Information Cooperative Service,
ANSLICS

Abnormal End
Abnormal End, ABEND

Abridged
Abridged Index Medicus (Journal), AIM
Abridged *Index Medicus*-Teletypewriter
Exchange Service, AIM-TWX
Cumulated Abridged Index Medicus, CAIM

Abstract
Abstract and Book Title Index Card Service,
ABTICS
*Abstract Bulletin of the Institute of Paper
Chemistry*, ABIPC
Floating-decimal Abstract Coding System,
FACS
Japanese Medical Abstract Scanning
System, JAMASS
Technical Abstract Bulletin, TAB

Abstracted
Abstracted Business Information, ABI
Abstracted Business Information/
Information Needs, ABI/INFORM

Abstracting
Abstracting and Indexing, A&I
Central Abstracting and Indexing Services,
CAIS
ICSU Abstracting Board, ICSU-AB
Indexing and Abstracting, I&A
National Federation of Abstracting and
Indexing Services, NFAIS
National Federation of Science Abstracting
and Indexing Services, NFSAIS
Société Canadienne pour l'Analyse de
Documents/Indexing and Abstracting
Society of Canada, SCAD/IASC

Abstracting Service
Cooperative Educational Abstracting
    Service, CEAS

Abstracts
Abstracts in Anthropology, AIA
Abstracts of Instructional and Research
    Materials in Vocational and Technical
    Education, AIM/ARM
Abstracts of Instructional Materials in
    Vocational and Technical Education,
    AIM
Abstracts of Mycology, AM
*Abstracts of Photographic Science and
    Engineering Literature*, APSE
Abstracts of Research and Related Materials
    in Vocational and Technical Education,
    ARM
API Abstracts/Literature, APILIT
API Abstracts/Patents, APIPAT
Aquatic Sciences and Fisheries Abstracts,
    ASFA
Basic Journal Abstracts, BJA
Biological Abstracts, BA
Biological Abstracts on Tape, BAT
Cambridge Scientific Abstracts, Inc, CSA
Canadian Social Science Abstracts, CSSA
Chemical Abstracts, CA
Chemical Abstracts Condensates, CAC
Computer and Control Abstracts, CCA
*Computer Information Library Patent
    Abstracts*. (Journal), C/I/L
Current Abstracts of Chemistry, CAC
*Current Abstracts of Chemistry and Index
    Chemicus*, CAC&IC
DSH Abstracts, DSH
Dissertation Abstracts International, DAI
Documentation Abstracts, DA
Electrical and Electronic Abstracts, EEA
Epilepsy Abstracts Retrieval System, EARS
Food Science and Technology Abstracts,
    FSTA
Fuel Abstracts and Current Titles, FACT
Indian Science Abstracts, ISA
Information Science Abstracts, ISA
International Aerospace Abstracts, IAA
International Pharmaceutical Abstracts,
    IPA
*Language and Language Behavior
    Abstracts*, LLBA
Library and Information Science Abstracts,
    LISA
Library Science Abstracts, LSA
Metals Abstracts Index, METADEX
*Meteorological and Geoastrophysical
    Abstracts*, MGA
Nuclear Science Abstracts, NSA
Physics Abstracts, PA
Poverty and Human Resources Abstracts,
    PHRA
Psychological Abstracts, PA

Psychological Abstracts Direct Access
    Terminal, PADAT
Psychological Abstracts Reference Retrieval
    System, PARRS
Psychological Abstracts Search and
    Retrieval, PASAR
Psychological Abstracts Tape Edition Lease
    or Licensing, PATELL
Retrieval of Enriched Textual Abstracts,
    RETA
Retrieval of Special Portions from *Nuclear
    Science Abstracts*, RESPONSA
Sociological Abstracts, SA
Syracuse University *Psychological
    Abstracts* Retrieval System, SUPARS
Tailored Abstracts, TABS
Technique for Retrieving Information from
    Abstracts of Literature, TRIAL
*World Agricultural Economics and Rural
    Sociology Abstracts*, WAERSA
World Aluminum Abstracts, WAA

Academia
Academia Nacional de Ciencias, ANC

Academic
Academic and Special Libraries Section,
    ASLS
Academic Computer Group, ACCOMP
Academic Press, Inc, AP
California Chapter of Academic and
    Research Libraries, CARL
Canadian Academic Research Libraries,
    CARL
Consortium of Rhode Island Academic and
    Research Libraries, CRIARL
Council of Academic Heads of Agriculture,
    CAHA
Northeast Academic Science Information
    Center, NASIC
Northeast Iowa Academic Libraries
    Association, NEIAL
Sangamon Valley Academic Library
    Consortium, SVAL
Southern Wisconsin Academic Librarians
    Organization, SWALO
State Assisted Academic Library Council of
    Kentucky, SAALCK
Wyoming Academic Consortium, WAC

Academic Librarians
Association of Academic Librarians of
    Ontario, AALO
Council of Academic Librarians of
    Manitoba, CALM
Midwestern Academic Librarians
    Conference, MALC

Academic Libraries
Bi-State Academic Libraries, BI-SAL
Colorado Academic Libraries Book
    Processing Center, CALBPC

Cooperative Action by Victorian Academic
  Libraries, CAVAL
Council of Research and Academic
  Libraries, CORAL
Idaho Council of State Academic Libraries,
  ICOSAL
Inland Empire Academic Libraries
  Cooperative, IEALC

Academic Library
Academic Library Program, ALP
Chicago Academic Library Council, CALC
Maryland Academic Library Center for
  Automated Processing, MALCAP
Waukesha Academic Library Union, WALU

Academy
Academy of Television Arts and
  Sciences–University of California, Los
  Angeles–Television Archives,
  ATAS/UCLA
American Academy and Institute of Arts and
  Letters, AAIL
American Academy of Arts and Letters,
  AAAL
American Academy of Arts and Sciences,
  AAAS
Centrul de Documentare Stiitifică al
  Academiei Republicii Socialiste
  România (Scientific Documentation
  Center of the Academy of the Socialist
  Republic of Rumania), CDS
Magyar Tudományos Akadémía Könyotára
  (Library of the Hungarian Academy of
  Sciences), MTAK
National Academy of Engineering, NAE
National Academy of Sciences, NAS
National Academy of Sciences–National
  Academy of Engineering–National
  Research Council, NAS–NAE–NRC
New York Academy of Sciences, NYAS
Philadelphia's Adult Basic Education
  Academy, PABEA
Royal Academy of Music, RAM
Royal Scottish Academy of Music and
  Drama, RSAMD
Ústredná Kniznica Slovenskej Akademie
  Vied (Central Library of the Slovak
  Academy of Sciences), UKSAV

Accelerated
Graduate Regional Accelerated Study
  Program, GRASP

Access
Agricultural On-Line Access, AGRICOLA
Automatic Direct Access to Information with
  On-line UDC System, AUDACIOUS
Banque de Données à Accès Direct de
  l'Université du Québec (Direct Access
  Data Bank of the University of Quebec),
  BADADUQ

Basic Access Method, BAM
Basic Direct Access Method, BDAM
Basic Indexed Sequential Access Method,
  BISAM
Basic Telecommunications Access Method,
  BTAM
Basic Terminal Access Method, BTAM
Block-Oriented Random Access Memories,
  BORAM
Card Random Access Memory, CRAM
Communications Access Manager, CAM
Computerized Access to Periodicals and
  Serials, CAPSUL
Continuous Multiple Access Collator,
  COMAC
Data Base Access Method, DBAM
Dial Access Information Retrieval System,
  DAIRS
Dial Access Technical Education, DATE
Direct Access Intelligence Systems, DAIS
Direct Access Storage Device, DASD
Direct English Access and Control,
  DEACON
Fast Access Current Text Bank, FACT
Fast Access Information Retrieval, FAIR
Fast Access to Systems Technical
  Information, FASTI
Hierarchical Environmental Retrieval for
  Management Access and Networking,
  HERMAN
Hierarchical Indexed Sequential Access
  Method, HISAM
Hierarchical Sequential Access Method,
  HSAM
Immediate Access Storage, IAS
Indexed Sequential Access Method, ISAM
Library On-Line Information and Text
  Access, LOLITA
Microfilm Retrieval Access Code,
  MIRACODE
Multiple Access Computer, MAC
Multiple Access Sequential Selection, MASS
Multiple Module Access, MMA
National Data Use and Access Laboratories,
  Inc, DUALabs
Open Access Satellite Education Services,
  OASES
Psychological Abstracts Direct Access
  Terminal, PADAT
Queued Access Method, QAM
Queued Indexed Sequential Access Method,
  QISAM
Queued Telecommunications Access
  Method, QTAM
Random Access and Inquiry, RAI
Random Access Computer Equipment,
  RACE
Random Access Correlation for Extended
  Performance, RACEP
Random Access Discrete Address, RADA

Access (cont.)

Random Access Discrete Address System,
RADAS
Random Access Document Indexing and
Retrieval, RADIR
Random Access Mass Memory, RAM
Random Access Memory, RAM
Random Access Method of Accounting and
Control, RAMAC
Random Access Personnel Information
Dissemination, RAPID
Random Access Personnel Information
Dissemination System, RAPIDS
Random Access Photographic Index and
Display, RAPID
Random Access Programming and Checkout
Equipment, RAPCOE
Random Access Storage and Control,
RASTAC
Random Access Storage and Display,
RASTAD
Rapid Access Disk, RAD
Rapid Access Management Information
System, RAMIS
Rapid Access to Literature via
Fragmentation Codes, RALF
Real-Time Electronic Access and Display,
READ
Relative Access Programming
Implementation Device, RAPID
Remote Access, RAX
Remote Access Computing System, RACS
Remote Access Planning for Institutional
Development, RAPID
Shelter-Housed Automatic Digital Random
Access, SHADRAC
Synchronous Transmit Receive Access
Method, STRAM
Zero Access Storage, ZAS

Access Service
Access Service for Profitable Information
Resource Exchanges, ASPIRE

Account
Computerized Management Account, CMA
Social Security Account Number, SSAN

Accountants
Accountants Computer Users Technical
Exchange, ACUTE
American Institute of Certified Public
Accountants, AICPA
National Machine Accountants Association,
NMAA

Accounting
American Accounting Association, AAA
Computer Accounting System, CAS
Contractors Accounting System, CONACS
Electrical Accounting for the Security
Industry, EASI

Electrical Accounting Machinery, EAM
Electronic Accounting Machine, EAM
Financial Accounting and Management
Information System, FAMIS
Foreign Exchange Accounting and
Management Information System,
FEAMIS
General Accounting Office, GAO
Project Accounting by Cost and Time, PACT
Random Access Method of Accounting and
Control, RAMAC
Shared Hospital Accounting System, SHAS
Total Analysis System for Production,
Accounting, and Control, TAS-PAC

Accounts
Business/Accounts Reporting Operating
Network, BARON
System of National Accounts/System of
Material Product Balances, SNA/MPS

Accounts Receivable
Disk On-Line Accounts Receivable System,
DOLARS

Accreditation
Commission on Standards and Accreditation
of Services for the Blind, COMSTAC
Committee on Accreditation, COA
National Council for Accreditation of
Teacher Education, NCATE

Accumulating
Interrelated Logic Accumulating Scanner,
ILAS

Accumulator
Accumulator, ACC

Achievement
Comprehensive Achievement Monitoring,
CAM

Acier
Communauté Européenne du Carbon et de
l'Acier, CECA

**Acieries Réunies de
Burbach-Eich-Dudelange**
Acieries Réunies de
Burbach-Eich-Dudelange, ARBED

Acknowledge
Acknowledge Character, ACK
Command Acknowledge, CAK
Negative Acknowledge Character, NAK

Acoustical
Acoustical Society of America, ASA

Acquisition
Client-Oriented Data Acquisition Program,
CODAP
Data Acquisition, DA
Data Acquisition and Control System, DAC

Description, Acquisition, Retrieval,
    Correlation, DARC
High-Speed Data Acquisition, HSDA
National Program for Acquisition and
    Cataloging, NPAC
Seminar on the Acquisition of Latin
    American Library Materials, SALALM

Acquisitions
Acquisitions, Cataloging, Technical
    Systems, ACTS
Cooperative Acquisitions and Storage
    Center, CASC
Cooperative Acquisitions Program, CAP
Cooperative Serials Acquisitions Program,
    COSAP
Library On-Line Acquisitions, LOLA
RTSD Acquisitions Section, RTSD/AS
Shared Acquisitions and Retention System,
    SHARES

Acronym
Acronym Data Base, ACRODABA

Acronyms
*Abbreviations and Related Acronyms
    Associated with Defense, Astronautics,
    Business and Radio-Electronics*,
    ABRACADABRA

Act
Education Professions Development Act,
    EPDA
Elementary and Secondary Education Act,
    ESEA
Higher Education Act of 1965, HEA
Library Services and Construction Act,
    LSCA
Medical Library Assistance Act of 1965,
    MLAA

Action
Action and Referral Center, ARC
Action Data Automation Language, ADAL
Program of Action for Mediation,
    Arbitration, and Inquiry, PAMAI
Result from Action, Prediction, Informative,
    Diagnostic Sensing, RAPIDS

Active
Direction Center Active, DCA

Activities
ASIS Special Interest Group on Management
    Information Activities, ASIS/SIG/MGT
Chemical-Biological Activities, CBAC
Technical Information Support Activities
    Project, TISAP
Technical Information Systems Activities,
    TISA

Activity
General Activity Simulation Program, GASP
System Activity Monitor, SAM

Ad Hoc Group
Inter-Professional Ad Hoc Group for
    Environmental Information Sharing,
    IPAHGEIS

Adaptable
Adaptable Data Base System, ADABAS

Adaptation
Adaptation of APT (Automatically
    Programmed Tools), ADAPT

Adapter
Binary Synchronous Communicator
    Adapter, BSCA

Adaptive
Adaptive Statistical Processor, APROC

Address
Instruction Address Register, IAR
Random Access Discrete Address, RADA
Random Access Discrete Address System,
    RADAS

Address Constant
Address Constant, ADCON

Administration
Administration for Children, Youth, and
    Families, ACYF
Center for the Advanced Study of
    Educational Administration, CASEA
Energy Research and Development
    Administration, ERDA
Federal Aviation Administration, FAA
Food and Drug Administration, FDA
General Services Administration, GSA
Health Resources Administration, HRA
Health Services Administration, HSA
Institute of Public Administration, IPA
International Cooperation Administration,
    ICA
LAMA Personnel Administration Section,
    LAMA/PAS
Law Enforcement Assistance
    Administration, LEAA
National Aeronautics and Space
    Administration, NASA
National Air Pollution Control
    Administration, NAPCA
National Oceanic and Atmospheric
    Administration, NOAA
Occupational Safety and Health
    Administration, OSHA
Product Administration and Contract
    Control, PACC
Technical Information Center
    Administration, TICA

Administrative
Administrative Terminal System, ATS
IFIP Administrative Data Processing Group,
    IAG

Administrative (cont.)

Swedish Institute for Administrative
Research, SIAR
World Administrative Radio Conference,
WARC

Administrative Information
African Integrated Network of
Administrative Information, AINAI

Administrator
Data Base Administrator, DBA

Administrators
Administrators of Medium Public Libraries
of Ontario, AMPLO
American Association of School
Administrators, AASA
Association of Records Executives and
Administrators, AREA
Association of Records Managers and
Administrators, ARMA
Council of Administrators of Large Urban
Public Libraries, CALUPL
National Association of State Text Book
Administrators, NASTA

Admiralty
Admiralty Centre for Scientific Information
and Liaison, ACSIL

Admissions
Universities Central Council on Admissions,
UCCA

Admissions Officers
American Association of Collegiate
Registrars and Admissions Officers,
AACRAO

Adolescents
Assembly on Literature for Adolescents,
ALAN

Adult
Adult Referral and Information Service in
Education, ARISE
ERIC Clearinghouse on Adult, Career, and
Vocational Education, ERIC/CE
Universities Council for Adult Education,
UCAE

Adult Education
Adult Basic Education, ABE

Adult Services
Adult Services Division, ASD
Reference and Adult Services Division,
RASD

Adults
National Society for Crippled Children and
Adults, NSCCA

Advancement
Institute for the Advancement of Medical
Communication, IAMC
Project for the Advancement of Coding
Techniques, PACT I

Advertising
Advertising Federation of America, AFA
Advertising Research Foundation, ARF
Advertising Typographers Association of
America, Inc, ATAA
American Advertising Federation, AAF
American Association of Advertising
Agencies, AAAA
European Marketing and Advertising Press,
EMAP
Joint Industry Committee for Television
Advertising Research, JICTAR
Weekly Newspaper Advertising Bureau,
WNAB

Advertising Representatives
International Publishers Advertising
Representatives Association, IPARA

Advice
Education Advice Bureau, EAB

Advisory
Central Advisory and Referral Service,
CARES
Student Advisory Information Service,
STAIS

Advisory Board
Advisory Board on Scientific and Technical
Information, ABSTI
Building Research Advisory Board, BRAB

Advisory Commission
Advisory Commission on Intergovernment
Relations, ACIR

Advisory Committee
Advisory Committee for Scientific and
Technical Information, ACSTI
Advisory Committee for the Research and
Development Department, ACORDD
Advisory Committee on Library Research
and Training Projects, ACLRTP
Agricultural Research Policy Advisory
Committee, ARPAC
Automatic Language Processing Advisory
Committee, ALPAC
Book Industry Systems Advisory
Committee, BISAC
Federal Information Processing Standards
Coordinating and Advisory Committee,
FIPSCAC
Government Advisory Committee on
International Book and Library
Programs, GAC

International Advisory Committee for
    Documentation and Terminology,
    IACDT
International Advisory Committee on
    Bibliography, IACB
International Advisory Committee on
    Bibliography, Documentation and
    Terminology, IACBDT
International Advisory Committee on
    Documentation and Terminology in Pure
    and Applied Science, AICDT
National Advisory Committee for
    Aeronautics, NACA
Ontario Public Librarians Advisory
    Committee, OPLAC
President's Science Advisory Committee,
    PSAC
Tasmanian Advisory Committee on
    Libraries, TACOL
Women's Advisory Committee of the British
    Standards Institution, WAC

Advisory Council
Advisory Council on Science Policy, ACSP
Australian Advisory Council on
    Bibliographical Services, AACOBS
Liverpool and District Scientific, Industrial
    and Research Library Advisory Council,
    LADSIRLAC
National Advisory Council for Education for
    Industry and Commerce, NACEIC

Advisory Group
Advisory Group for Aerospace Research and
    Development, AGARD
Southeast Asia Development Advisory
    Group, SEADAG

Advisory Service
Readers Advisory Service, RAS
Research Information Center and Advisory
    Service on Information Processing,
    RICASIP

Aerial
Aerial Phenomena Research Organization,
    APRO

Aerodynamics
Industrial Aerodynamics Information
    Service, IAIS

Aeronautical
Société Internationale des
    Télécommunications Aeronautiques
    (International Society of Aeronautical
    Telecommunications), SITA

Aeronautics
American Institute of Aeronautics and
    Astronautics, AIAA

American Institute of Aeronautics and
    Astronautics, Technical Information
    Services, AIAA-TIS
Canadian Aeronautics and Space Institute,
    CASI
Civil Aeronautics Board, CAB
National Advisory Committee for
    Aeronautics, NACA
National Aeronautics and Space
    Administration, NASA
Radio Technical Commission for
    Aeronautics, RTCA

Aéronautique
Association Belge des Journalistes
    Professionnels de l'Aéronautique et de
    l'Astronautique, ABJPAA
Association Suisse Romande des
    Journalistes de l'Aéronautique et de
    l'Astronautique, ARJA

Aeronautiques
Societé Anonyme Belge de Constructions
    Aeronautiques, SABCA

Aerospace
Advisory Group for Aerospace Research and
    Development, AGARD
Aerospace Education Foundation, AEF
Aerospace Electrical Society, AES
Aerospace Ground-Support Equipment,
    AGE
Aerospace Industries Association of
    America, AIA
Aerospace Intelligence Data System, AIDS
Aerospace Materials Information Center,
    AMIC
Aerospace Research Applications Center,
    ARAC
Aerospace Shared Knowledge, ASK
[Aerospace Standards], AS
Aerospace Technology Division, ATD
*Classified Scientific and Technical
    Aerospace Reports*, C-STAR
International Aerospace Abstracts, IAA
Nederlandse Vereniging van Lucht- en
    Ruimtevaarte-Publicisten (Netherlands
    Aerospace Writers Association), NVLP
Scientific and Technical Aerospace Reports.
    (Journal), STAR
Society of Aerospace Material and Process
    Engineers, SAMPE

Affiliate
National Energy Information Center
    Affiliate, NEICA

Affiliates
Albany Area Health Library Affiliates,
    AAHLA

Affirmative Action
Affirmative Action Program, AAP
Affirmative Action Program for Women
    Committee, AAPWC

Afghan
Afghan Library Association, ALA

Africa
Association Internationale pour le
    Développement de la Documentation,
    des Bibliothèques et des Archives en
    Afrique (International Association for
    the Development of Documentation
    Libraries and Archives in Africa),
    AIDBA
East and Central Africa Regional Branch of
    the International Council on Archives,
    ECARBICA
Standards Association of Central Africa,
    SACA
Standing Conference on Library Materials on
    Africa, SCOLMA

Africain
Centre Africain de Formation et de
    Recherches Administratives pour le
    Développement, CAFRAD

African
ACRL Asian and African Section,
    ACRL/AAS
African Integrated Network of
    Administrative Information, AINAI
Centre de Documentation Africaine (African
    Documentation Center), CEDOCA
Standing Conference of African Library
    Schools, SCALS
Standing Conference of African University
    Librarians, SCAUL
Standing Conference of African University
    Libraries, Eastern Area, SCAULEA
Standing Conference of African University
    Libraries, Western Area, SCAULWA

African Studies
Center for African Studies and Institute for
    Social Research, CAS&ISR

Africana
Cooperative Africana Microform Project,
    CAMP

Afrique
Institut Fondamental d'Afrique Noire, IFAN

Afro-American
Afro-American Music Opportunities
    Association, AAMOA

Agencies
American Association of Advertising
    Agencies, AAAA

Chief Officers of State Library Agencies,
    COSLA
State Libraries Agencies Division, SLAD

Agency
Agency for International Development, AID
Armed Services Technical Information
    Agency, ASTIA
Arms Control and Disarmament Agency,
    ACDA
Canadian Military Electronics Standards
    Agency, CAMESA
Central Intelligence Agency, CIA
Defense Communications Agency, DCA
Defense Nuclear Agency, DNA
Defense Supply Agency, DSA
Environmental Protection Agency, EPA
European Nuclear Energy Agency, ENEA
European Space Agency Network, ESANET
International Atomic Energy Agency, IAEA
International Communication Agency, ICA
Metropolitan Library Services Agency,
    MELSA
New York Metropolitan Reference and
    Research Library Agency, METRO

Agents
Committee of National Institutes of Patent
    Agents, CNIPA

Agrardokumentation
Zentraler Datenpool der Kooperativen
    Agrardokumentation, DIFO
Zentraler Datenpool der Kooperativen
    Agrardokumentation, LIDOK

Agrarjournalisten
Verband de Agrarjournalisten in Österreich,
    VAÖ
Verband Deutscher Agrarjournalisten, VDA

Agricolas
Reunion Interamericana de Bibliotecarios y
    Documentalistas Agrícolas, RIBDA
Sistema Interamericano de Informacion para
    las Ciencias Agricolas, AGRINTER

Agricoles
Centre de Documentation International des
    Industries Utilisatrices de Produits
    Agricoles, CDIUPA
Commission Internationale des Industries
    Agricoles et Alimentaires, CIIA

Agricultural
ACRL Agricultural and Biological Sciences
    Section, ACRL/ABSS
Agricultural Biological Literature
    Exploitation, ABLE
Agricultural Communicators in Education,
    ACE
Agricultural Information Bank of Asia,
    AIBA

Agricultural Information System, AGRIS
Agricultural On-Line Access, AGRICOLA
Agricultural Personal Alerting Card Kits,
    AG/PACK
Agricultural Research Institute, ARI
Agricultural Research Management
    Information System, ARMIS
Agricultural Research Policy Advisory
    Committee, ARPAC
Agricultural Research Projects in the
    European Community, AGREP
Agricultural Sciences Information Network,
    ASIN
Agricultural System for Storage and
    Subsequent Selection of Information,
    ASSASSIN
American Agricultural Editors Association,
    AAEA
American Association of Agricultural
    College Editors, AAACE
Asociación Mexicana de Educación Agricola
    Superior (Mexican Association for
    Agricultural Higher Education),
    AMEAS
Association Française des Journalistes
    Agricoles (French Association of
    Agricultural Journalists), AFJA
Association of Official Agricultural
    Chemists, AOAC
Belgische Vereniging van
    Landbouwjournalistes/Association
    Belge des Journalistes Agricoles
    (Belgian Guild of Agricultural
    Journalists), BVLJ/ABJA
Biological and Agricultural Index, BAI
Centre National d'Étude et
    d'Experimentation de Machinisme
    Agricole (National Center for
    Agricultural Machinery Research and
    Experimentation), CNEEMA
Centrul de Documentare Agricolă
    (Agricultural Documentation Center),
    CDA
Centrum voor Landbouwpiblikaties en
    Landbouwdocumentatie (Center for
    Agricultural Publishing and
    Documentation), PUDOC
Comissão Brasileira de Documentação
    Agricola (Brazilian Commission for
    Agricultural Documentation), CBDA
Commonwealth Agricultural Bureaux, CAB
Current Agricultural Research Information
    System, CARIS
Current Contents/Agricultural, Food and
    Veterinary Sciences. (Journal), CC/AFV
Danish Agricultural Producers Information
    Service, DAPIS
An Foras Taluntais (Irish Agricultural
    Institute), AFT
Guild of Agricultural Journalists, GAJ

Instituto Interamericano de Ciencias
    Agrícolas de la OEA (Interamerican
    Institute of Agricultural Sciences of
    OAS/OEA), IICA
International Commission for Agricultural
    and Food Industries, ICAI
Permanent Agricultural Committee, PACH
Royal Agricultural Society of England,
    RASE
Schweizerische Vereinigung der
    Agrarjournalistes/Association Suisse
    des Journalistes Agricoles (Swiss
    Association of Agricultural Journalists),
    SVAJ/ASJA
World Agricultural Economics and Rural
    Sociology Abstracts, WAERSA

Agricultural Information
Agricultural Information, AGROINFORM
Automation of Agricultural Information and
    Documentation, ALADIN
Centro Interamericano de Documentación e
    Información Agrícola (Interamerican
    Center for Agricultural Documentation
    and Information), CIDIA

Agricultural Librarians
Asociación Interamericana de Bibliotecarios
    y Documentalistas Agricolas
    (Inter-American Association of
    Agricultural Librarians and
    Documentalists), AIBDA
International Association of Agricultural
    Librarians and Documentalists, IAALD
Japanese Association of Agricultural
    Librarians and Documentalists, JAALD

Agricultural Libraries
Agricultural Libraries Information Network,
    AGLINET
Agricultural Libraries Information Notes.
    (Journal), ALIN

Agricultural Library
Centralna Biblioteka Rolnicza (Central
    Agricultural Library), CBR
National Agricultural Library, NAL

Agriculture
Council of Academic Heads of Agriculture,
    CAHA
Current Contents/Agriculture, Biology and
    Environmental Sciences. (Journal),
    CC/AB&ES
East African Agriculture and Forestry
    Research Organization, EAAFRO
Food and Agriculture Organization, FAO
Gesellschaft für Bibliothekswesen und
    Dokumentation des Landbaues
    (Association for Librarianship and
    Documentation in Agriculture), GBDL
United States Department of Agriculture,
    USDA

Agro-Alimentaire
Documentation en Ligne pour l'Industrie
Agro-Alimentaire, IALINE

Agronomique
Direction de la Recherche Agronomique,
DRA
Institut National de la Recherche
Agronomique, INRA

Agroprecuaria
Organismo Internacional Regional de Sanid
Agroprecuaria, OIRSA

Agrumes
Institut de Recherches sur les Fruits et
Agrumes, IRFA

Aid
Cardboard Illustrated Aid to Computation,
CARDIAC
Data Base Design Aid, DBDA
French American Cultural Services and
Educational Aid, FACSEA

Aids
Committee for Writing and Reading Aids for
the Paralysed, WRAP
National Committee for Audiovisual Aids in
Education, NCAVAE

Air
Air World Publications, AWP
Central Air Documents Office, CADO
City Air Defense Evaluation Tool, CADET
Rome Air Development Center On-Line,
RADCOL
SAGE Air Traffic Integration, SATIN

Air Command
Strategic Air Command Control System,
SACCS

Air Force
Air Force English Syntax Project, AFESP
Air Force Office of Scientific Research,
AFOSR
Air Force Publications and Distribution
Center, AF-PDC
Air Force Technical Objectives Documents
Release Program, AFTOD
Air Materiel Command (US Air Force),
AIMACO
Joint Canadian Navy-Army-Air Force
Specification, JCNAAF
Royal Air Force Education Service, RAFES
United States Air Force, USAF

Air Materiel Command
Air Materiel Command (US Air Force),
AIMACO

Air Movement
Air Movement Data, AMD

Air Pollution
Air Pollution Control Association, APCA
Air Pollution Technical Information Center,
APTIC
National Air Pollution Control
Administration, NAPCA
National Air Pollution Technical Information
System, NAPTIC

Air Traffic
Air Traffic Control Association, ATCA

Air Transport
Air Transport Association of America, ATA

Aircraft
Experimental Aircraft Association, EAA

Airline
Airline Tariff Publishers, Inc, ATP

Airline Reservation
Compact Programmed Airline Reservation
System, CPARS

Airlines
Trans World Airlines, Inc, TWA

Airways
British Overseas Airways Digital
Information Computer for Electronic
Automation, BOADICEA

Akademii
Vsesojuznyj Gosudarstvennyj Institut po
Proektirovaniju Naučno-
Issledovatel'skich Institutov i Laboratorij
Akademii nauk SSSR, GIPRONTII

Alabama
Alabama Center for Higher Education,
ACHE
Alabama Consortium for the Development of
Higher Education, ACDHE
Alabama Library Association, ALA
North Alabama Biomedical Information
Network, NABIN
North Alabama Library Alliance, NALA

Alarm
Digital Display Alarm, DDA

Alaska
Alaska Library Association, ALA
Washington, Alaska, Montana, and Idaho,
WAMI

Alaskan
Alaskan Health Sciences Information
Center, AHSIC

Albany
Albany Area Health Library Affiliates,
AAHLA

Alberta
Alberta Alcoholism and Drug Abuse
Commission, AADAC
Alberta Association of Library Technicians,
AALT
Alberta Council of College Librarians,
ACCL
Alberta Government Libraries Council,
AGLC
Alberta Information Retrieval Association,
AIRA
Alberta Information Retrieval for Health,
Physical Education, and Recreation,
AIRHPER
Alberta Library Trustees Association,
ALTA
Library Association of Alberta, LAA

Alcohol Information
National Clearinghouse for Alcohol
Information, NCALI

Alcoholism
Alberta Alcoholism and Drug Abuse
Commission, AADAC

Alcoologie
Centre International
d'Alcoologie/Toxicomanies, CIATO

Aldermaston
Aldermaston Mechanized Cataloging and
Ordering System, AMCOS

Alert
Automatic New Structure Alert (Journal),
ANSA
Automatic Subject Citation Alert, ASCA
Metal Alert, METALERT

Alert Service
Publisher's Alert Service, PAS

Alerting
Current Literature Alerting Search Service,
CLASS

Alerting Service
Automatic Literature Alerting Service,
ALAS

Algebraic
Algebraic and Differential Equations
Processor and Translator, ADEPT
Algebraic Compiler, ALCOM
Algebraic Compiler and Translator I, ACT-I
Algebraic Compiler and Translator III,
ACT-III
Algebraic Translator and Compiler, ALTAC
Boeing Airplane Company Algebraic
Interpretive Computing System,
BACAIC
Conversational Algebraic Language, CAL

Flexible Algebraic Scientific Translator,
FAST
Generalized Algebraic Translator, GAT
International Algebraic Language, IAL
Naval Electronics Laboratory International
Algebraic Compiler, NELIAC
Simple Algebraic Language for Engineers,
SALE

Algorithm
Practical Algorithm to Retrieve Information
Coded in Alphanumeric, PATRICIA

Algorithmic
Algorithmic Language (Algorithmic Oriented
Language), ALGOL
Algorithmic Processor Description
Language, APDL
Michigan Algorithmic Decoder, MAD
Variably Initialized Translator for
Algorithmic Languages, VITAL

Alimentaires
Commission Internationale des Industries
Agricoles et Alimentaires, CIIA

Aliquippa
Aliquippa District Center Library, ADC

Allen Park
Pontiac–Allen Park–Detroit Consortium,
PAD

Alliance
Alliance of Associations for the
Advancement of Education, AAAE
American Alliance for Health, Physical
Education and Recreation, AAHPER
American Composers Alliance, ACA

Allocation
Automatic and Dynamic Monitor with
Immediate Relocation, Allocation and
Loading, ADMIRAL
Automatic Scheduling and Time-dependent
Resource Allocation, ASTRA
Computerized Relative Allocation of
Facilities Technique, CRAFT
Dynamic Storage Allocation Language,
DYSTAL

All-purpose
Beginners All-purpose Symbolic Instruction
Code, BASIC

All-Union
Vesesojuznii Naučno-Issle-Dovatel'skii
Institut Techniceskoi Informaccii,
Klassifikaccii i Kodirovaniia (All-Union
Scientific Research Institute for
Technical Information, Classification
and Codification of USSR), VNIIKI

All-Union (cont.)

Vsesoiuznyĭ Nauchno Issle-dovatel'skii
Institut Meditsinskoĭ i
Medikotekhnicheskoĭ Informatsii
Ministerstva Zdravookhraneniia USSR
(All-Union Scientific Research Institute
of Medical and Medico-Technical
Information of the USSR Ministry of
Public Health), VNIIMI
Vsesojuznyi Institut Naučnotehničeskoi
Informacii (All-Union Institute of
Scientific and Technical Information,
USSR), VINITI
Vsesoyuznogo Informatsionnogo Fonda
Standartovi i Technicheskikh Uslovii
(All-Union Reference Bank of Standards
and Specifications, USSR), VIFS

Alphanumeric

Practical Algorithm to Retrieve Information
Coded in Alphanumeric, PATRICIA
Rapid Alphanumeric Digital Indicating
Device, RANDID
Remote Electrical Alphanumeric Display,
READ

Alpha-Numerical

Alpha-Numerical System for Classification
of Recordings, ANSCR

Alternative

PLA Alternative Education Programs
Section, PLA/AEPS

Alternatives

Alternatives for Learning through
Educational Research and Technology,
ALERT

Aluminum

Aluminum Association, AA
World Aluminum Abstracts, WAA

Alumni

Faculty of Library Science Alumni
Association, FLSAA

Amateur

Amateur Computer Club, ACC
Association Française des Amateurs
Constructeurs d'Ordinateurs (French
Association of Amateur Computer
Builders), AFACO
British Amateur Press Association, BAPA

Ambulance

Ambulance and Medical Services
Association of America, AMSAA

America

America: History and Life, AHL
Bibliographical Society of America, BSA
Center for Information on America, CIOA
College Art Association of America, CAAA
United States of America, USA

America Central

Seminario Interamericano sobre la
Integración de los Servicios de
Información de Archivos, Bibliotecas y
Centros de Documentation en America
Central y el Caribe, SI/ABCD

América Latina

Federação Internacional de Associações de
Bibliotecários–Grupo Regional América
Latina, FIABGRAL

American

American Association of Teachers of Slavic
and East European Languages,
ATSEEL
American Bibliographical Center, ABC
The American Book Awards, TABA
Dictionary of American Regional English,
DARE

American Folklore

American Folklore Society, AFLS

American Libraries

American Libraries. (Journal), AL

American Library

American Library Directory, ALD
American Library in Paris, ALP

American States

Organization of American States, OAS

Americans

Americans for a Music Library in Israel,
AMLI

Amigos

Amigos Bibliographic Council, ABC

Amplitude

Amplitude Modulation, AM

Analog

Analog Data Recording Transcriber, ADRT
Analog Line Driver, ALD
Analog to Digital Converter, ADC
Basic Analog Simulation System, BASS
Boeing Electronic Analog Computer, BEAC
Combined Analog–Digital Systems
Simulator, CADSS
Digital Analog Function Table, DAFT
Modified Integration Digital Analog
Simulator, MIDAS
Personal Analog Computer, PAC
Reeves Electronic Analog Computer, REAC

Analogue

Vector Analogue Computer, VAC

Analysis

Advanced Statistical Analysis Program,
ASTAP
Automated Literature Processing, Handling,
and Analysis System, ALPHA

Basic Analysis and Mapping Program,
    BAMP
Cancer Information Dissemination and
    Analysis, CIDA
Center for Information and Numerical Data
    Analysis and Synthesis, CINDAS
Center of Experiment Design and Data
    Analysis, CEDDA
Circuit Analysis, CIRCAL
Comprehensive Occupational Data Analysis
    Program, CODAP
Computer Analysis of Networks with Design
    Orientation, CANDO
Computer Analysis of Thermo-Chemical
    Data Tables, CATCH
Computer-Assisted Language Analysis
    System, CALAS
Configuration Analysis Program, CAP
Conversational Circuit Analysis Program,
    CONCAP
Cost Analysis Information Report, CAIR
Cost-Effectiveness Analysis, CEA
Data Analysis Massachusetts Institute of
    Technology, DAMIT
Data Analysis System, DAS
Defence Operational Analysis
    Establishment, DOAE
Drilling Activity Analysis, DAAS
Electric Circuit Analysis Program, ECAP
Failure Analysis Information Retrieval,
    FAIR
Failure Analysis Program, FAP
Fast Analysis of Tape and Recovery,
    FATAR
Financial Analysis of Management
    Effectiveness, FAME
Financial Analysis Program, FAP
Free Association of Management Analysis,
    FAMA
General Data Analysis and Simulation,
    GENDA
General Electric Computer Analysis
    Program, GECAP
Graphical Input for Network Analysis,
    GINA
Indexing by Statistical Analysis Techniques,
    IBSAT
Integrated Design and Analysis System,
    IDEAS
Library Information Systems Analysis,
    LISA
Library Network Analysis Theory, LIBNAT
Malfunction Analysis Detection and
    Recording, MADAR
Management Review and Analysis Program,
    MRAP
Mathematical Analysis of Requirements for
    Career Information Appraisal, MARCIA
Medical Literature Analysis and Retrieval
    System, MEDLARS

Multivariate Analysis of Variance,
    MANOVA
Office of Criminal Justice Plans and
    Analysis, OCJPA
Operations Analysis, OA
Operations Research/Systems Analysis,
    OR/SA
Schering-Oriented Literature Analysis and
    Retrieval System, SCHOLAR
Ships Analysis and Retrieval Program,
    SHARP
Subject Analysis and Organization of Library
    Materials Committee, SAOLM
System Analysis Index for Diagnosis, SAID
System for Electronic Analysis and Retrieval
    of Criminal Histories, SEARCH
Systems Analysis and Data Processing Office
    of NYPL, SADPO
Time-Shared Routines for Analysis,
    Classification, and Evaluation, TRACE
Total Analysis System for Production,
    Accounting, and Control, TAS-PAC
Tracking Retrieval and Analysis of Criminal
    Events, TRACE

Analysis Center
Ballistic Missile Radiation Analysis Center,
    BAMIRAC
Current Cancer Research Project Analysis
    Center, CCRESPAC
Infrared Information and Analysis Center,
    IRIA
Reliability Analysis Center, RAC

Analysts
Association of Computer Programmers and
    Analysts, ACPA
Society of Educational Programmers and
    Systems Analysts, SEPSA

Analytic
Analytic Geometry Interpretive Language,
    AGILE

Analytical
An Analytical Information Management
    System, AAIMS
Association of Official Analytical Chemists,
    AOAC

Analytico-Synthetic
Analytico-Synthetic Classification of
    Medicine, ASCOM

Analytico-Synthetica
Classification Analytico-Synthetica Cubana
    de Medicas, CASCUM

Analyzer
Differential Analyzer, DA
Digital Difference Analyzer, DDA
Digital Differential Analyzer, DDD
Multivariate Statistical Analyzer, MSA

Analyzer-Programmer
Dynamics Analyzer-Programmer, DYANA

Anglo-American
Anglo-American Cataloging Rules, AACR
Anglo-American Cataloguing Rules, AACR 2
Joint Steering Committee for the Revision of the Anglo-American Cataloging Rules, JSCAACR

Aniline
General Aniline and Film Corporation, GAF

Animal
Comparative Animal Research Laboratory, CARL
Laboratory Animal Data Bank, LADB

Animation
Association Internationale du Film d'Animation (International Animated Film Association), ASIFA

Anlagendatenbank
Anlagendatenbank, ADB

Annotated
Computerized Annotated Bibliography System, CABS

Announcements
Clearinghouse Announcements in Science and Technology, CAST
Government Reports Announcements, GRA
Government Reports Announcements and Index, GRA&I

Annual
Annual Medical Library Association Conference Committee, AMLAC
Annual National Information Retrieval Colloquium, ANIRC
Government Reports Annual Index, GRAI
Publishers Trade List Annual, PTLA

Annual Review
Annual Review of Information Science and Technology, ARIST

Annuals
Irregular Serials and Annuals, ISA

Answer Back
Voice Answer Back, VAB

Answering
Southern California Answering Network, SCAN

Answering Exchanges
Associated Telephone Answering Exchanges, ATAE

Answering Services
Association of Telephone Answering Services, ATAS

Answers
Have You Stored Answers to Questions, HAYSTAQ

Antenna
Community Antenna Television, CATV

Anthracite
Anthracite Information Bureau, AIB

Anthropological
American Anthropological Association, AAA

Anthropology
ACRL Anthropology Section, ACRL/ANTS
Abstracts in Anthropology, AIA

Antibiotics
International Center of Information on ·Antibiotics, ICIA

Antiquarian
American Antiquarian Society, AAS
Antiquarian Booksellers Association of America, ABAA
International League of Antiquarian Booksellers, ILAB

Anuario
Anuario de Bibliotecologia, Archivologia e Informatica, ANBAI

Aperture Card
Automated Microfilm Aperture Card Update System, AMACUS

Apollo
Apollo Lunar Surface Experimental Package, ALSEP

Appalachia
Appalachia Improved Reference Service, AIRS

Applicant
Applicant Information Service, AIS
College Applicant Status Report, CASTOR

Application
Application Program Evaluator Tool, APET
Application Technology Satellite, ATS
Application Technology Satellite, ATS-F
Application Technology Satellite 1, ATS-1
Application Technology Satellite 6, ATS-6

Applications
Aerospace Research Applications Center, ARAC
Applied Science and Research Applications, ASRA

Center for Research and Evaluation in
  Applications of Technology in
  Education, CREATE
Computer On-Line Real-Time Applications
  Language, CORAL
Electrical Utilities Applications, EUA
National Association of Users of Computer
  Applications to Learning, NAUCA
Non-Interactive Computer Applications,
  NICA
Research on Computer Applications in the
  Printing and Publishing Industries,
  ROCAPPI
Solar Applications Information Center,
  SOLAPIC

Appraisal
Training, Appraisal and Promotion, TAP

Appraisals
Forecasts, Appraisals, and Management
  Evaluation, FAME

Approach
Approach by Concept, ABC
Approach to Distributed Processing
  Transactions, ADOPT

Aptitude
Programmer Aptitude Tests, PAT

Aquatic Sciences
Aquatic Sciences and Fisheries Abstracts,
  ASFA
Aquatic Sciences Information Retrieval
  Center, ASIRC

Arab
Arab Regional Branch of the International
  Council on Archives, ARBICA
Arab University Library Association, AULA

Arbeitsgemeinschaft
Arbeitsgemeinschaft für Datenverarbeitung,
  ADV

Arbitration
Program of Action for Mediation,
  Arbitration, and Inquiry, PAMAI
Staff Committee on Mediation, Arbitration
  and Inquiry, SCMAI

Archéologie
Bibliothèque d'Art et d'Archéologie, BAA

Archeologists
Asociación Nacional de Bibliotecarios,
  Archiveros y Arqueólogos (National
  Association of Librarians, Archivists
  and Archeologists), ANABA

Archer Daniels Midland
Archer Daniels Midland Company, ADM

Architects
American Institute of Architects, AIA
Royal Institute of British Architects, RIBA
Society of Naval Architects and Marine
  Engineers, SNAME

Architectural
American Association of Architectural
  Bibliographers, AAAB
*Dictionary of Architectural Abbreviations,
  Signs and Symbols*, DAA

Architectural Librarians
Association of Architectural Librarians,
  AAL

Architecture
ACM Special Interest Group on Architecture
  of Computer Systems, ACM/SIGARCH
Automated Naval Architecture, ANA

Archival
Archival Association of Atlantic Canada,
  AAAC
Archival Records Management System,
  ARM
Archival Security Program, ASP

Archival Science
Institute of Archival Science for Southeast
  Asia, IASSA

Archive
Asosiasi Perpustakaan Arsip dan
  Dokumentasi Indonesia (Indonesian
  Library, Archive and Documentation
  Association), APADI
Lewis Audiovisual Research Institute and
  Teaching Archive, LARITA
Regional Social Science Data Archive,
  RSSDA

Archiveros
Consejo Interamericano de Archiveros,
  CITA

Archives
Academy of Television Arts and
  Sciences–University of California, Los
  Angeles–Television Archives,
  ATAS/UCLA
Arab Regional Branch of the International
  Council on Archives, ARBICA
Arbeitsgemeinschaft für das Archiv und
  Bibliothekswesen in der Evangelischen
  Kirche, Sektion Bibliothekswesen
  (Working Group for Archives and
  Libraries in the Lutheran Church,
  Library Section), AABevK
Archives On-line, ARCHON
Archivos General de la Nación (National
  Archives), AGN
Asociation di Biblioteka i Archivo di Korsow
  (Association of Libraries and Archives),
  ABAK

Archives (cont.)

Association Internationale pour le
Développement de la Documentation,
des Bibliothèques et des Archives en
Afrique (International Association for
the Development of Documentation
Libraries and Archives in Africa),
AIDBA

Association pour le Développement de la
Documentation, des Bibliothèques et
Archives de la Côte d'Ivoire
(Association for the Development of
Documentation, Libraries and Archives
of the Ivory Coast), ADBACI

Association Sénégalaise pour le
Développement de la Documentation,
des Bibliothèques, des Archives et des
Musées (Senegal Association for the
Development of Documentation,
Libraries, Archives and Museums),
ASDBAM

Association Voltaique pour le
Développement des Bibliothèques, des
Archives et de la Documentation
(Voltan Association for the
Development of Libraries, Archives and
Documentation), AVDBAD

Belgian Archives for the Social Sciences,
BASS

CLA Archives Section, CLA/AS

Commission on Archives and History of the
United Methodist Church, CAHUMC

Committee on Archives and Documents of
Southeast Asia, CARDOSEA

Conseil International des
Archives/International Council on
Archives, CIA/ICA

Council on Social Science Data Archives,
CSSDA

East and Central Africa Regional Branch of
the International Council on Archives,
ECARBICA

Fédération Internationale des Archives du
Film (International Federation of Film
Archives), FIAF

International Association of Sound Archives,
IASA

Librarianship and Archives Old Students
Association, LAOSA

National Archives and Records Service,
NARS

North American Radio Archives Library,
NARA

Perhimpunan Ahli Perpustakaan, Arsipdan
Dokumentasi Indonesia (Indonesian
Association of Librarians, Archives and
Documentation), PAPADI

Schweizerisches Wirtschaftsarchiv (Swiss
Economic Archives), SWA

Southwest Asian Regional Branch of the
International Council on Archives,
SARBICA

Archivists

Asociación de Bibliotecarios y Archiveros de
Honduras (Association of Librarians
and Archivists of Honduras), ABAH

Asociación Nacional de Bibliotecarios,
Archiveros y Arqueólogos (National
Association of Librarians, Archivists
and Archeologists), ANABA

Associação Portuguesa de Bibliotecários,
Arquivistas e Documentalistes
(Portuguese Association of Librarians,
Archivists and Documentalists), BAD

Association des Archivistes du Québec
(Association of Quebec Archivists),
AAQ

Association des Archivistes et
Bibliothécaires de Belgique/Vereniging
van Archivarissen en Bibliothecarissen
van België (Belgian Association of
Archivists and Librarians),
AABB/VABB

Association des Archivistes, Archivistes,
Documentalistes et Muséographes du
Cameroun (Association of Librarians,
Archivists, Documentalists and Museum
Curators of Cameroon), ABADCAM

Association Nationale des Bibliothécaires,
Archivistes et Documentalistes
Sénégalais (National Association of
Librarians, Archivists and
Documentalists of Senegal), ANBADS

Association of British Columbia Archivists,
ABCA

Association of Canadian Archivists, ACA

Association Tunisienne des
Documentalistes, Bibliothécaires et
Archivistes (Tunisian Association of
Documentalists, Librarians and
Archivists), ATD

Association Zairoise des Archivistes,
Bibliothécaires et Documentalistes
(Zairian Association of Archivists,
Librarians and Documentalists),
AZABDO

Associazione Nazionale Archivistica Italiana
(National Association of Italian
Archivists), ANAI

Colegio de Bibliotecónomos y Archivistas de
Venezuela (Association of Venezuelan
Librarians and Archivists), COLBAV

École de Bibliothécaires, Archivistes et
Documentalistes (School of Librarians,
Archivists and Documentalists), EBAD

Nederlandse Vereniging van
Bedrijfsarchivarissen (Netherlands
Association of Business Archivists),
NVBA
Society of American Archivists, SAA
Society of Archivists, SA
Verein Deutscher Archivare (Association of
German Archivists), VDA
Vereinigung Schweizerischer Archivare
(Association of Swiss Archivists), VSA
Vlaamse Vereniging van Bibliotheek-Archief
en Documentatie-Personeel, Vereniging
zonder Winstoogmerken (Flemish
Association of Librarians, Archivists
and Documentalists), VVBADP

Archivologia
*Anuario de Bibliotecologia, Archivologia e
Informatica*, ANBAI

Archivos
Seminario Interamericano sobre la
Integración de los Servicios de
Información de Archivos, Bibliotecas y
Centros de Documentación en America
Central y el Caribe, SI/ABCD

Arctic
Arctic, Desert, Tropic Information Center,
ADTIC
Arctic Institute of North America, AINA

Areas
Remote Areas Conflict Information Center,
RACIC

Argentina
Asociación de Bibliotecarios Graduados de
la República Argentina (Association of
Graduate Librarians of Argentina),
ABGRA

Argentinos
Asociación de Bibliotecarios y
Documentalistas Sislenaticos
Argentinos, ABYDSA

Arid Lands
Arid Lands Information System, ALIS

Arid Zone Information
Centro de Información de Zonas Aridas
(Center for Arid Zone Information),
CIZA

Arithmetic
Arithmetic and Logical Unit, ALU
Arithmetic Register, AR
Floating Indexed Point Arithmetic, FLIP
Floating-point Arithmetic Package, FAP

Arizona
Arizona Library Association, ALA
Arizona Medical Library Network, AMLN
Arizona Water Information System, AWIS
Channeled Arizona Information Network,
CHAIN

Arkansas
Arkansas Foundation of Associated
Colleges, AFAC
Arkansas Library Association, ALA
Texas, Arkansas, Louisiana, Oklahoma and
New Mexico, TALON

Armament
Centre de Documentation de l'Armament,
CEDOCAR

Armed Forces
Armed Forces Communications and
Electronics Association, AFCEA
Armed Forces Information and Education
Division, AFIED

Armed Forces Librarians
PLA Armed Forces Librarians Section,
PLA/AFLS

Armed Services
Armed Services Technical Information
Agency, ASTIA

Arms Control
Arms Control and Disarmament Agency,
ACDA

Army
Army Logistics Management Integrated Data
System, ALMIDS
Army Qualitative Development
Requirements Information Program,
QDRI
Army Research and Development
Information System, ARDIS
Army Technical Library Improvement
Studies, ATLIS
Joint Canadian Navy-Army-Air Force
Specification, JCNAAF
Research and Development, Army, RDA
Society of Army Historical Research, SAHR
United States Army Computer Systems
Support and Evaluation Command,
USACSSEC

Army Library
Army Library Automated System, ALAS

Arrowhead
Arrowhead Professional Libraries
Association, APLA

Art
ACRL Art Section, ACRL/ARTS
Art Gallery of Ontario, AGO
Art Research Libraries of Ohio, ARLO
Bibliothèque d'Art et d'Archéologie, BAA
College Art Association of America, CAAA
Confédération Internationale des Cinémas d'Art et d'Essai (International Experimental and Art Film Theatres Confederation), CICAE
International Institute of Films on Art, IIFA
Répertoire International de la Littérature de l'Art. (Journal), RILA
Rijksbureau voor Kunsthistorische Documentatie (Netherlands Institute for Art History Documentation), RKD
Royal College of Art, RCA
State of the Art, SOTA
Union of Independent Colleges of Art, UICA

Art Libraries
Arbeitsgemeinschaft der Kunstbibliotheken (Working Group of Art Libraries), AKB
Art Libraries Society, ARLIS

Article
European Article Number, EAN
Journal Article Copy Service, JACS
Original Article Tearsheet, OATS

Articles
Pest Articles and News Summaries. (Journal), PANS

Articulation
Pattern Articulation Unit, PAU

Artificial Intelligence
ACM Special Interest Group on Artificial Intelligence, ACM/SIGART

Artistic
Committee for Artistic and Intellectual Freedom in Iran, CAIFI

Artistic Works
American Institute for Conservation of Historic and Artistic Works, AIC
International Institute for Conservation of Historic and Artistic Works, IIC

Artistique
Association Litteraire et Artistique Internationale, ALAI

Artists
American Federation of Television and Radio Artists, AFTRA
American Society of Professional Draftsmen and Artists, ASPDA
Film Artists Association, FAA
Royal Society of British Artists, RBA

Arts
ASIS Special Interest Group on Arts and Humanities, ASIS/SIG/AH
Academy of Television Arts and Sciences-University of California, Los Angeles-Television Archives, ATAS/UCLA
American Academy of Arts and Sciences, AAAS
Arts and Humanities Citation Index, A&HCI
Columbus Museum of Arts and Crafts, CMAC
Current Bibliographic Directory of the Arts and Sciences, CBD
Current Contents/Arts and Humanities. (Journal), CC/A&H
National Endowment for the Arts, NEA
Society for Automation in Fine Arts, SAFA
Society of Film and Television Arts, Ltd, SFTA

Arts and Letters
American Academy and Institute of Arts and Letters, AAIL
American Academy of Arts and Letters, AAAL

Asia
Agricultural Information Bank of Asia, AIBA
Asia/Pacific Forecasting Study, APFS
Business Asia. (Journal), BA
Economic and Social Commission for Asia and the Pacific, ESCAP
Economic Commission for Asia and the Far East, ECAFE

Asian
ACRL Asian and African Section, ACRL/AAS
Asian Federation of Library Associations, AFLA
Asian Information Center for Geotechnical Engineering, AGE
Royal Central Asian Society, RCAS

Asian American
Asian American Librarians Caucus, AALC

Asian Studies
Association for Asian Studies, AAS
Committee on East Asian Libraries of the Association for Asian Studies, CEAL

Assembler
Basic Assembler Program, BAP
Formula Assembler and Translator, FORAST
Macroinstruction Compiler Assembler, MICA
SHARE Compiler, Assembler and Translator, SCAT
Transac Assembler Compiler, TAC

Assembly
Assembly on Literature for Adolescents, ALAN
Assembly System for the Peripheral Processors, ASPER
Basic Assembly Language, BAL
Control Data Assembly Program, CODAP
Datatron Assembly System, DAS
Efficient Assembly System, EASY
Expansion Symbolic Compiling Assembly Program for Engineering, ESCAPE
FORTRAN Assembly Program, FAP
General Assembly Program, GAP
General Electric Macro Assembly Program, GEMAP
Macro Assembly Program, MAP
New York Assembly Program, NYAP
Royal Optimizing Assembly Routing, ROAR
Symbolic Optimum Assembly Programming, SOAP

Assets
Wisconsin Assets and Income Studies, WAIS

Assignment
Automatic Frequency Assignment Model, AFAM
Display Assignment Bits, DAB

Assimilation
Navigation Data Assimilation Computer, NAVDAC

Assistance
Operational Assistance and Instructive Data Equipment, OAIDE
Technical Assistance Information Clearinghouse, TAICH
Volunteers for International Technical Assistance, Inc, VITA

Assistant
Library Media Technical Assistant, LMTA
Library Technical Assistant, LTA
Research Assistant, RA
Teaching Assistant, TA

Assistant Librarians
Association of Assistant Librarians, AAL
Association of Assistant Librarians, South East Division, AALSED

Associações
Federação Internacional de Associações de Bibliotecários-Grupo Regional América Latina, FIABGRAL

Associated
Associated Press, AP

Association Européenne
Association Européenne de Fabricants et des Revendeurs de Matérial Didactique/Verband Europäischer Lehrmittelfirmen, EURODIDAC

Associative
Associative Processor, AP
Associative Processor Computer System, APCS
Associative Processor Programming Language, APPLE
Rotating Associative Processor for Information Dissemination, RAPID

Assurance
Systems Assurance Program, SAP

Astronautical
American Astronautical Society, AAS

Astronautics
Abbreviations and Related Acronyms Associated with Defense, Astronautics, Business and Radio-Electronics, ABRACADABRA
American Institute of Aeronautics and Astronautics, AIAA
American Institute of Aeronautics and Astronautics, Technical Information Services, AIAA-TIS

Astronautique
Association Belge des Journalistes Professionnels de l'Aéronautique et de l'Astronautique, ABJPAA
Association Suisse Romande des Journalistes de l'Aéronautique et de l'Astronautique, ARJA

Astronomical
American Astronomical Society, AAS
New York Astronomical Corporation, NYAC

Astronomy
National Information System for Physics and Astronomy, NISPA

Asynchronous
Asynchronous Circuit Design Language, ACDL

Atlantic
Atlantic Coast Independent Distributors Association, ACIDA
Atlantic Merchant Vessel Report, AMVER
Atlantic Provinces Library Association, APLA

Atmospheric
Global Atmospheric Research Program, GARP

Atmospheric (cont.)

National Oceanic and Atmospheric
  Administration, NOAA
Oceanic and Atmospheric Scientific
  Information System, OASIS

Atomenergie
Osterreichische Studiengesellschaft für
  Atomenergie, GmbH, OSGAE

Atomic
Atomic Weapons Research Establishment,
  AWRE
Database of Atomic and Molecular Physics,
  DAMP

Atomic Energy
Atomic Energy Commission, AEC
Atomic Energy of Canada Limited, AECL
Atomic Energy Research Establishment,
  AERE
Australian Atomic Energy Commission,
  AAEC
Commissariat à L'Energie Atomique
  (Atomic Energy Commission), CEA
European Atomic Energy Community,
  EURATOM
European Atomic Energy Society, EAES
International Atomic Energy Agency, IAEA
United Kingdom Atomic Energy Authority,
  UKAEA
United States Atomic Energy Commission,
  USAEC
Zentralstelle für Atomkernenergie
  Dokumentation (Atomic Energy
  Documentation Center), ZAED

Attack
Computer-Integrated Command and Attack
  Systems, CICAS

Attention
Display Attention Bits, DAB

Attitude
Missile Attitude Determination System,
  MADS

Attribute
Descriptor Attribute Matrix, DAM

Audio
Audio Engineering Society, Inc, AES
Audio Response Unit, ARU
Greater London Audio Specialization
  Scheme, GLASS

Audiographic
Audiographic Learning Facility, ALF

Audiovisual
Association of Audiovisual Technicians,
  AAVT
Audiovisual, AV

Audio-Visual Language Association, AVLA
Audiovisual Market Place, AVMP
Audiovisual Online, AVLINE
Catholic Audio-Visual Educators
  Association, CAVE
Centre Technique Audiovisual International
  (International Audiovisual Technical
  Center), CTAVI
Centro de Documentación Audiovisual para
  A.L., CEDAL
Department of Audiovisual Instruction,
  DAVI
ISAD Audio Visual Section, ISAD/AVS
Industrial Audio-Visual Association, IAVA
LITA Audio Visual Section, LITA/AVS
Lewis Audiovisual Research Institute and
  Teaching Archive, LARITA
Manitoba School Library Audio-Visual
  Association, MSLAVA
Medical Audio-Visual Institute, MAVI
National Audio-Visual Association, NAVA
National Committee for Audiovisual Aids in
  Education, NCAVAE
Nederlands Instituut voor Audio Visuele
  Middlelen (Netherlands Institute for
  Audiovisual Media), NIAM
Office of Audiovisual Educational
  Development, OAED
Verband Schweizerischer Film und
  AV-Produzenten/Association des
  Producteurs Suisses de Films et de
  Production Audio-Visuelle (Association
  of Swiss Film and Audio-Visual
  Producers), VSFAV/APFAV

Audiovisual Center
National Medical Audiovisual Center,
  NMAC

Audit
Audit Command Language, ACL
Audit Trail, AT
Input Audit and Control, INPACON
International Federation of Audit Bureaus of
  Circulations, IFABC

Audit Bureau
Audit Bureau of Circulations, ABC

Auditors
Institute of Internal Auditors, Inc, IIA

Auerbach
Auerbach Information Management System,
  AIMS

Augmentation
Augmentation of Human Intellect, AHI
Human Intellect Augmentation System,
  HIAS

Augmented
Design Augmented by Computers, DAC

Augusta
Augusta Area Committee for Health
    Information Resources, AACHIR

Australasian
Australasian Drug Information Services Pty.
    Limited, ADIS

Australia
ARLIS Australia New Zealand,
    ARLIS/ANZ
Australia, Britain, Canada, United States,
    ABACUS
Bibliographical Society of Australia and New
    Zealand, BSANZ
International Association of Music
    Librarians, Australia/New Zealand
    Branch, IAMLANZ
Library Association of Australia, LAA
National Library of Australia, NLA
South Australia Education Resource
    Information System, SAERIS
Standards Association of Australia, SAA

Australian
Australian Advisory Council on
    Bibliographical Services, AACOBS
Australian and New Zealand Association for
    the Advancement of Science, ANZAAS
Australian Associated Press Proprietary Ltd,
    AAP
Australian Atomic Energy Commission,
    AAEC
Australian Broadcasting Corporation, ABC
Australian Centre for Research in Library
    and Information Science, ACRiLIS
Australian Computer Society, Inc, ACS
Australian Council for Educational
    Research, ACER
Australian Drug and Medical Information
    Group, ADMIG
Australian Information Network, AUSINET
Australian Library Journal, ALJ
Australian Library Promotion Council,
    ALPC
Australian Library Technicians Association,
    ALTA
Australian National Bibliography, ANB
Australian National Committee on
    Computation and Automatic Control,
    ANCCAC
Australian National Scientific and
    Technological Library, ANSTEL
Australian School Library Association,
    ASLA

Austrian
Österreichische Gesellschaft für
    Dokumentation und Information
    (Austrian Society for Documentation
    and Information), ÖGDI

Austrian Librarians
Vereinigung Österreichischer Bibliothekare
    (Association of Austrian Librarians),
    VÖB

Author
Author and Keyword in Context, AKWIC
Author Index Manufacturing System, AIMS
Bibliographic Author or Subject Interactive
    Search, BA•SIS
Word and Author Index, WADEX

Authorities
Area Library Service Authorities, ALSAs

Authority
Independent Broadcasting Authority, IBA
Independent Television Authority, ITA
Indiana Cooperative Library Services
    Authority, INCOLSA
Inner London Educational Authority, ILEA
Northwest Indiana Area Library Services
    Authority, NIALSA
Ontario Educational Communications
    Authority, OECA
Southeastern Indiana Area Library Services
    Authority, SIALSA
Subject Authority List, SAL
Subject Heading Authority List, SHAL
Tennessee Valley Authority, TVA
United Kingdom Atomic Energy Authority,
    UKAEA

Authors
American Guild of Authors and Composers,
    AGAC
American Society of Composers, Authors,
    and Publishers, ASCAP
Bibliographic Guide for Editors and Authors,
    BGEA
Confédération Internationale des Sociétés
    d'Auteurs et Compositeurs
    (International Confederation of
    Societies of Authors and Composers),
    CISAC
Finlands Svenska Författareföreningen
    (Society of Swedish Authors in Finland),
    FSFF

Autocoder
Autocoder to COBOL Translator, ACT

Autocoding
National's Electronic Autocoding
    Technique, NEAT

Auto-Instructional
Auto-Instructional Media for Library
    Orientation, AIMLO

Automasation
Division de la Coopération et de
    l'Automasation, DICA

Automata
ACM Special Interest Group on Automata
and Computability Theory,
ACM/SIGACT

Automated
ASIS Special Interest Group on Automated
Language Processing, ASIS/SIG/ALP
Army Library Automated System, ALAS
Automated Bibliography, AB
Automated Catalog of Computer Equipment
and Software Systems, ACCESS
Automated Combustor Design Code,
AUTOCOM
Automated Computer Science Education
System, ACSES
Automated Data Processing, ADP
Automated Engineering Design System,
AED
Automated Health Multi-Phase Screening,
AHMS
Automated Imagery Processing, AIP
Automated Information Directory Update
System, AIDUS
Automated Information Dissemination
System, AIDS
Automated Input and Document Update
System, AIDUS
Automated Instructional Materials Handling
System of SDC (System Development
Corporation), AIMS
Automated Inventory Management, AIM
Automated Law Enforcement
Communication System, ALECS
Automated Linguistic Extraction and
Retrieval Technique, ALERT
Automated Literature Processing, Handling,
and Analysis System, ALPHA
Automated Microfilm Aperture Card Update
System, AMACUS
Automated Mortgage Management
Information Network, AMMINET
Automated Naval Architecture, ANA
Automated News Clipping, Indexing, and
Retrieval System, ANCIRS
Automated Processing of Medical English,
APME
Automated Retrieval System, ARS
Automated Route Manager, ARM
Bacterial Automated Identification
Technique, BAIT
Baker and Taylor Automated Buying,
BATAB
Battelle Automated Search Information
System for the Seventies, BASIS-70
British Library Automated Information
System, BLAISE
Bucknell Automated Retrieval and Display
System, BARDS

Computer–based Laboratory for Automated
School Systems, CLASS
Dance Collection Automated Book Catalog,
DCABC
Documentation Automated Retrieval
Equipment, DARE
Illinois Microfilm Automated Catalog, IMAC
Library Automated Systems Information
Exchange, LASIE
Library Experimental Automated
Demonstration System, LEADS
Maryland Academic Library Center for
Automated Processing, MALCAP
National Association of Securities Dealers
Automated Quotations System,
NASDAQ
Navy Automated Research and
Development Information System,
NARDIS
Retrieval through Automated Publication
and Information Digest, RAPID
Scheduling and Control by Automated
Network System, SCANS
System for the Automated Management of
Text from a Hierarchical Arrangement,
SAMANTHA

Automated Library
Automated Library Processing System,
ALPS

Automatic
American Automatic Control Council,
AACC
Association Nationale d'Études pour la
Documentation Automatique (National
Association of Automatic
Documentation Studies), ANEDA
Associazione Italiana per il Calco
Automatico (Italian Association for
Automatic Data Processing), AICA
Australian National Committee on
Computation and Automatic Control,
ANCCAC
Automatic and Dynamic Monitor with
Immediate Relocation, Allocation and
Loading, ADMIRAL
Automatic Calling Unit, ACU
Automatic Checkout and Readiness
Equipment, ACRE
Automatic Claiming and Canceling, ACC
Automatic Classification, AUTOCLASS
Automatic Code Translator, ACT
Automatic Computer-Controlled Electronics
Scanning System, ACCESS
Automatic Data Entry, ADE
Automatic Data Exchange, ADX
Automatic Data Processing, ADP
Automatic Data Processing Equipment,
ADPE

Automatic Data Processing Equipment and Software, ADPE/S

Automatic Data Processing Equipment Selection Office, ADPESO

Automatic Data Processing Service Center, ADPSC

Automatic Data Processing System, ADPS

Automatic Data Systems Uniform Practices, ADSUP

Automatic Dialing Unit, ADU

Automatic Diffemic Identification of Speakers, ADIS

Automatic Digital Encoding System, ADES

Automatic Digital Encoding System, ADES-II

Automatic Digital On-line Instrumentation System, ADONIS

Automatic Document Storage and Retrieval, ADSTAR

Automatic Documentation in Action, ADIA

Automatic Fact Information Retrieval and Storage Systems, AFIRSS

Automatic Frequency Assignment Model, AFAM

Automatic Indexing of Documentation of IFP, AID-IFP

Automatic Information Retrieval System, AIRs

Automatic Information System, AIST

Automatic Language Processing Advisory Committee, ALPAC

Automatic List Classification and Profile Production, ALCAPP

Automatic Literature Alerting Service, ALAS

Automatic Mathematical Translation, AMTRAN

Automatic Microfiche Editor, AME

Automatic Microfilm Information System, AMFIS

Automatic New Structure Alert (Journal), ANSA

Automatic Operating and Scheduling Program, AOSP

Automatic Operating System, AUTOPSY

Automatic Personal Identification Code, AUTOPIC

Automatic Picture Transmission, APT

Automatic Programmed Tool, APT

Automatic Programmed Tool III, APT III

Automatic Programming and Recording, APAR

Automatic Programming of Machine Tools, AUTOPROMPT

Automatic Request (for Correction), ARQ

Automatic Routine Generating and Updating System, ARGUS

Automatic Scheduling and Time-dependent Resource Allocation, ASTRA

Automatic Send-Receive Set, ASR

Automatic Subject Citation Alert, ASCA

Automatic Teletypewriter Exchange Service, TELEX

Automatic Traffic Engineering and Management Information System, ATEMIS

Automatic Translation, AUTRAN

Automatic Volume Control, AVC

Bell Laboratories Automatic Design System, BLADES

Bell Laboratories Automatic Device, BLADE

Binary Automatic Computer, BINAC

Committee on Storage, Automatic Processing and Retrieval of Geological Data, COGEODATA

Community Automatic Exchange, CAX

Compact Automatic Retrieval Display, CARD

Computer Program for Automatic Control, COMPAC

Computerized Automatic Rating Technique, CART

Computerized Automatic Reporting Service, CARS

Digital Equipment Corporation's Automatic Design System, DECADE

Double-precision Automatic Interpretive System 201, DAISY 201

Electronic Automatic Exchange, EAX

Electronic Discrete Sequential Automatic Computer, EDSAC

Electronic Discrete Variable Automatic Computer, EDVAC

Engineering Automatic System for Solving Equations, EASE

FORTRAN Automatic Code Evaluation System, FACES

Facility for Automatic Sorting and Testing, FAST

Fast Interline Nonactive Automatic Control, FINAC

Film Input to Digital Automatic Computer, FIDAC

Flexible Automatic Depot, FAD

Fully Automatic Cataloging Technique, FACT

Fully Automatic Compiler-Translator, FACT

Fully Automatic Compiling Technique, FACT

Fully Automatic Information System, FAIRS

Information Retrieval Automatic Language, INFRAL

Institute de Recherche d'Informatique et d'Automatique (French Research Institute of Information and Automatic Processing), IRIA

Automatic (cont.)

International Federation of Automatic Control, IFAC

JICST Electronic Information Processing Automatic Computer, JEIPAC

Lehigh Automatic Device for Efficient Retrieval, LEADER

MIDAC Automatic General Integrated Computation, MAGIC

Monrobot Automatic Internal Diagnosis, MAID

Motorola Automatic Sequential Computer-Operated Tester, MASCOT

Private Automatic Branch Exchange, PABX

Private Automatic Exchange, PAX

Programmed Logic for Automatic Teaching Operations, PLATO

Rapid Digital Automatic Computing, RADAC

Research in Automatic Photocomposition and Information Dissemination, RAPID

Retrieval and Automatic Dissemination of Information from *Index Chemicus* and Line Notations, RADIICAL

Salton's Magical Automatic Retrieval of Texts, SMART

Sequentially Controlled Automatic Transmitter Start, SCATS

Shelter-Housed Automatic Digital Random Access, SHADRAC

Standards Electronic Automatic Computer, SEAC

Suomen Säätöteknillinen Seura (Finnish Society of Automatic Control), SSS

Tape-Controlled Recording Automatic Checkout Equipment, TRACE

Television Automatic Sequence Control, TASCON

Universal Automatic Computer, UNIVAC

Versatile Automatic Test Equipment, VATE

X Automatic Translation Code, XACT

Automatically

Adaptation of APT (Automatically Programmed Tools), ADAPT

Automatically Programmed Tools, APT

Methods of Extracting Text Automatically, META

Methods of Extracting Text Automatically Programming Language, METAPLAN

Automation

ACM Special Interest Group on Design Automation, ACM/SIGDA

Action Data Automation Language, ADAL

Advanced Automation Research Laboratory, AARL

Automation for Storage and Retrieval of Information, AFSARI

Automation of Agricultural Information and Documentation, ALADIN

Automation of Bibliography through Computerization, ABC

Automation of Field Operations and Services, AFOS

Bibliographic Automation of Large Library Operations Using a Time-Sharing System, BALLOTS

British Overseas Airways Digital Information Computer for Electronic Automation, BOADICEA

Daystrom Powerplant Automation Language, DAPAL

Facility of Automation, Control and Test, FACT

Finite Automation Language, FAL

Information Science and Automation Division, ISAD

Institute Belge de Régulation et d'Automisme (Belgian Institute for Control and Automation), IBRA

LITA Information Science and Automation Section, LITA/ISAS

Periodicals Automation Rand Library, PEARL

Project for Integrated Catalogue Automation, PICA

Public Library Automation Network, PLAN

Schweizerische Gesellschaft für Automatik/Association Suisse pour l'Automatique (Swiss Association for Automation), SGA/ASSPA

Scottish Libraries Cataloging Automation Project, SCOLCAP

Society for Automation in Business Education, SABE

Society for Automation in English and the Humanities, SAEH

Society for Automation in Fine Arts, SAFA

Society for Automation in Professional Education, SAPE

Society for Automation in Science and Mathematics, SASM

Society for Automation in the Social Sciences, SASS

Source Data Automation, SDA

Technical Standards for Library Automation, TESLA

University of California-University-Wide Automation Program, ULAP

Automatique

Programme Appliqué à la Sélection et à la Compilation Automatique de la Littérature, PASCAL

Systeme Electronique de Selection Automatique de Microfilms, SESAM

Automatisée
Banque d'Information Automatisée sur les
Médicaments, BIAM

Automatyzacja
Automatyzacja Przetwarzania Informacji
Naukowej, APIN

Automazione
Associazione Nazionale Italiana per
l'Automazione, ANIPLA
Automazione nella Nazionale di Firenze,
ANNA

Auto-Monitor
Satellite Auto-Monitor System, SAMS

Automotive
Society of Automotive Engineers, SAE

Autónoma
Universidad Nacional Autónoma de México,
UNAM

Autoren-Verband
Freier Deutscher Autoren-Verband, FDA

Autores
Sociedade Portuguesa de Autores, SPA

Autorl
Sindacato Nazionale Autori Drammatici,
SNAD
Società Italiana Autori Drammatici, SIAD

Auxiliary
Digital Data, Auxiliary Storage, Track
Display, Outputs, and Radar Display,
DATOR
National Auxiliary Publications Service,
NAPS

Availability
Universal Availability of Publications, UVP

Aviation
Federal Aviation Administration, FAA
Federal Aviation Information Retrieval
System, FAIRS
International Civil Aviation Organization,
ICAO
International Society of Aviation Writers,
ISAW

Avtomatizacilo
Sistem za Avtomatizacilo Informacijsko
Dokumentacijskih
Centrov-Elektrotehnika, SAIDC

Avvocati
Albo Dept Avvocati i Procuratori, ALBO

Awards
The American Book Awards, TABA
National Book Awards, NBA

Awareness
Canadian Technical Awareness Program,
CAN/TAP

BANK
BANK Programming, BANKPAC

BIBLIO
Program BIBLIO, BIBLIO

BIOSIS
BIOSIS Previews Memo, BPM

Backspace
Backspace Character, BS

Back-Up
Back-Up Interceptor Control, BUIC

Backus Normal Form
Backus Normal Form, BNF

Bacterial
Bacterial Automated Identification
Technique, BAIT

Bacteriology
Journal of Applied Bacteriology, JAB

Badische Anilin-und-Soda-Fabrik
Badische Anilin-und-Soda-Fabrik AG,
BASF

Baker and Taylor
Baker and Taylor Automated Buying,
BATAB

Balance
Line of Balance, LOB

Balances
System of National Accounts/System of
Material Product Balances, SNA/MPS

Balancing
Computer-Aided Line Balancing, CALB

Ballistic Missile
Ballistic Missile Radiation Analysis Center,
BAMIRAC

Baltic
International Federation of Free Journalists
of Central and Eastern Europe and
Baltic and Balkan Countries, IFFJ

Baltimore
Baltimore County Public Library, BCPL

Bangladesh
Bangladesh Granthagar Samity (Library
Association of Bangladesh), BGS
Bangladesh National Scientific and
Technical Documentation Center,
BANSDOC

Bank
Barclays (Bank) Advanced Staff Information
Language, BASIL

Bank (cont.)

Customer Bank Communication Terminal,
CBCT
Fast Access Current Text Bank, FACT
Vsesoyuznogo Informatsionnogo Fonda
Standartovi i Technicheskikh Uslovii
(All-Union Reference Bank of Standards
and Specifications, USSR), VIFS

Bankers
American Bankers Association, ABA

Banking
American Institute of Banking, AIB

Banque
Banque de Terminologie Normalisée,
NORMATERM

Banque d'Information
Banque d'Information Automatisée sur les
Médicaments, BIAM

Banques de Données
Banques de Données Toxicologique, BDT

Bantu
Bantu Library Association of South Africa,
BLASA

Baptist
Baptist Information Retrieval System, BIRS

Barbados
Economic Planning Unit of Barbados, EPU
Library Association of Barbados, LAB

Barclays
Barclays (Bank) Advanced Staff Information
Language, BASIL

Base
Microalloy Diffused Base Transistor, MADT
Offender Base Transaction Statistical
System, OBTS

Basic
Basic Access Method, BAM
Basic Analog Simulation System, BASS
Basic Analysis and Mapping Program,
BAMP
Basic Assembler Program, BAP
Basic Assembly Language, BAL
Basic Bibliographic Citation, BBC
Basic Computer Programming Language,
BCPL
Basic Direct Access Method, BDAM
Basic Indexed Sequential Access Method,
BISAM
Basic Journal Abstracts, BJA
Basic Operating System, BOS
Basic Programming Knowledge Test, BPKT
Basic Programming Support, BPS
Basic Telecommunications Access Method,
BTAM
Basic Terminal Access Method, BTAM

Batch
Computer-Aided Batch Scheduling, CABS

Bâtiment
Centre d'Information et de Documentation
du Bâtiment, CIDB
Centre Scientifique et Technique du
Bâtiment, CSTB

Battelle
Battelle Automated Search Information
System for the Seventies, BASIS-70

Battery
Battery, BAT

Battle Area
Battle Area Surveillance and Integrated
Communications, BASIC

Bay
Bay Electric Company, BEC

Bay Area
Bay Area Rapid Transit System, BARTS
Bay Area Reference Center, BARC
Bay Area Transportation Study Commission,
BATSC

Beginners
Beginners All-purpose Symbolic Instruction
Code, BASIC

Beginning-of-Information
Beginning-of-Information Marker, BIM

Behavior
Center for Research on Language and
Language Behavior, CRLLB
*Language and Language Behavior
Abstracts*, LLBA

Behavioral
ASIS Special Interest Group on the
Behavioral and Social Sciences,
ASIS/SIG/BSS
*Current Contents/Behavioral, Social and
Educational Sciences.* (Journal),
CC/BSE
*Directory of Data Bases in the Social and
Behavioral Sciences*, DDB
Institute for Behavioral Research, IBR

Behavioral Science
ACM Special Interest Group on Social and
Behavioral Science Computing,
ACM/SIGSOC

Behavioral Sciences
ACRL Education and Behavioral Sciences
Section, ACRL/EBSS
*Current Contents/Social and Behavioral
Sciences.* (Journal), CC/S&BS

Belge
Association Belge des Journalistes
  Professionnels de l'Aéronautique et de
  l'Astronautique, ABJPAA
Association Professionnelle de la Presse
  Cinématographique Belge, APPCB
Office Belge du Commerce Exterieur, OBCE
Societé Anonyme Belge de Constructions
  Aeronautiques, SABCA
Union de la Presse Périodique Belge, UPPB

Belges
Fédération des Éditeurs Belges, FEB
Union Professionnelle des Distributeurs
  Belges de Films, UPDBF

Belgian
Association Belge de
  Documentation/Belgische Vereniging
  voor Documentatie (Belgian
  Documentation Association),
  ABD/BVD
Association Belge des Editeurs de Langue
  Française (Belgian Association of
  Publishers of French Language Books),
  ABELF
Association des Archivistes et
  Bibliothécaires de Belgique/Vereniging
  van Archivarissen en Bibliothecarissen
  van België (Belgian Association of
  Archivists and Librarians),
  AABB/VABB
Belgian Archives for the Social Sciences,
  BASS
Belgische Vereniging van
  Landbouwjournalistes/Association
  Belge des Journalistes Agricoles
  (Belgian Guild of Agricultural
  Journalists), BVLJ/ABJA
Institute Belge de Régulation et
  d'Automisme (Belgian Institute for
  Control and Automation), IBRA
Union Nationale des Producteurs Belge de
  Films (National Union of Belgian Film
  Producers), UNPBF

Belgique
Association des Directeurs de Théâtres
  Cinématographiques de Belgique,
  ADTCB
Union de la Presse Étrangère en Belgique,
  UPE

Belgium
Cercle Belge de la Libraire (Belgium
  Booksellers Association), CBL
Fédération des Associations Internationales
  Establiés en Belgique (Federation of
  International Associations Established
  in Belgium), FAIB

Bell
Bell Character, BEL

Bell Laboratories
Bell Laboratories Automatic Design System,
  BLADES
Bell Laboratories Automatic Device,
  BLADE
Bell Laboratories Interpretive System, BLIS
Bell Laboratories Library Real-Time Loan
  System, BELLREL

Bell Little
Bell Little Electrodata Symbolic System for
  the Electrodata, BLESSED

Bell Telephone
Bell Telephone Laboratories, BTL

Benefits
Project for the Evaluation of Benefits from
  University Libraries, PEBUL

Beranek
Bolt, Beranek and Newman, Inc, BBN

Betriebsforschungsinstitut
Betriebsforschungsinstitut, VDEh-Institut
  für Angewandte Forschung GmbH, BFI

Bibliografia
Bibliografia, BIBL
Bibliografia di Informatica e Diritto, BID

Bibliograficas
Instituto de Investigaciones Bibliograficas,
  IIB

Bibliografico
Repertorio Bibliografico Italiano, REBIS
Repertorio Bibliografico Straniero, REBIS

Bibliographers
American Association of Architectural
  Bibliographers, AAAB
Zväz Slovenských Knihovníkov, Bibligrafov
  a Informacných Pracovníkov
  (Association of Slovak Librarians,
  Bibliographers and Documentalists),
  ZSKBIP

Bibliographic
ACRL Bibliographic Section, ACRL/BIS
Amigos Bibliographic Council, ABC
Basic Bibliographic Citation, BBC
Bibliographic Author or Subject Interactive
  Search, BA•SIS
Bibliographic Automation of Large Library
  Operations Using a Time-Sharing
  System, BALLOTS
Bibliographic Exchange and
  Communications Network, BEACON
Bibliographic Guide for Editors and Authors,
  BGEA
Bibliographic Network, BIBNET
Bibliographic On-Line Display, BOLD
Bibliographic Records Control, BIBCON

Bibliographic (cont.)

Bibliographic Retrieval Services, Inc, BRS
Central Bibliographic System, CBS
*Current Bibliographic Directory of the Arts
    and Sciences*, CBD
International Standard Bibliographic
    Description, ISBD
Jugoslovenski Bibliografiski Institut
    (Yugoslav Bibliographic Institute), JBI
Universal Bibliographic Control, UBC

Bibliographic Center
Pacific Northwest Bibliographic Center,
    PNBC
Southeastern Bibliographic Center, SEBC
University of California Bibliographic
    Center, BIBCENTER

Bibliographic Centre
Ontario Universities Bibliographic Centre
    Project, OUBCP

Bibliographic Data
Chalk River Bibliographic Data Information
    System, CHARIBIDIS

Bibliographic Information
United Nations Bibliographic Information
    System, UNBIS

Bibliographic Services
Countway Library Medical Bibliographic
    Services, CLIMBS
Joint Standing Committee on Library
    Cooperation and Bibliographic Services,
    JSCLCBS

Bibliographical
American Bibliographical Center, ABC
American Bibliographical Center–Clio Press,
    ABC–Clio
Bibliografiska Institutet (Bibliographical
    Institute), BI
Bibliographical Society of America, BSA
Bibliographical Society of Australia and New
    Zealand, BSANZ
Bibliographical Society of the Philippines,
    BSP
Bibliotechno-Bibliograficheskaya
    Klassificatsiya (Library Bibliographical
    Classification), BBK
Inter-American Bibliographical and Library
    Association, IABLA
Welsh Bibliographical Society, WBS

Bibliographical Center
Bibliografické Středisko pro Techickou
    Literaturu (Bibliographical Center for
    Technical Literature), BSTL
Bibliographical Center for Research, BCR
National Bibliographical Center, NBC

Bibliographical Services
Australian Advisory Council on
    Bibliographical Services, AACOBS

Bibliographie
Gesellschaft für Dokumentation und
    Bibliographie, GDB

Bibliographique
Centre Bibliographique National, CBN

Bibliographiques
Centre de Techniques Bibliographiques,
    CTB

Bibliography
Australian National Bibliography, ANB
Automated Bibliography, AB
Automation of Bibliography through
    Computerization, ABC
*Bibliography of Scientific and Industrial
    Research*, BSIR
Bibliography Production, BIBPRO IV
British National Bibliography, BNB
*Cambridge Bibliography of English
    Literature*, CBEL
Computerized Annotated Bibliography
    System, CABS
*Current Bibliography on Science and
    Technology*, CBST
Energy Bibliography and Index, EBI
Environmental Periodicals Bibliography,
    EPB
*Ethnographic Bibliography of North
    America*, EBNA
Instituto Brasileiro de Bibliografia e
    Documentação (Brazilian Institute of
    Bibliography and Documentation),
    IBBD
International Advisory Committee on
    Bibliography, IACB
International Advisory Committee on
    Bibliography, Documentation and
    Terminology, IACBDT
*International Bibliography, Information,
    Documentation*, IBID
Microelectronics Bibliography, MB

Biblioteca
Biblioteca Regional de Medicina, BIREME

Bibliotecarios
Asociación de Bibliotecarios y
    Documentalistas Sislenaticos
    Argentinos, ABYDSA
Federação International de Associações de
    Bibliotecários–Grupo Regional América
    Latina, FIABGRAL
Reunion Interamericana de Bibliotecarios y
    Documentalistas Agrícolas, RIBDA

Bibliotecas
Seminario Interamericano sobre la
    Integración de los Servicios de
    Información de Archivos, Bibliotecas y
    Centros de Documentación en America
    Central y el Caribe, SI/ABCD

Biblioteche Italiane
Centro Nazionale per il Catalogo Unico delle
Biblioteche Italiane per le Informazion
Bibliografiche, CUBI

Bibliotecologia
*Anuario de Bibliotecologia, Archivologia e
Informatica*, ANBAI

Bibliotecos Universitarias
Lista de Libros para Bibliotecos
Universitarias, LILIBU

Bibliothécaire
Certificat d'Aptitude, Fonctions de
Bibliothécaire, CAFB

Bibliothecariaat
Vereniging voor het
Godsdienstig-Wetenschappelijk
Bibliothecariaat, VSKB

Bibliotheek- en Archiefpersoneel
Vlaamse Vereniging van Bibliotheek- en
Archiefpersoneel, VVBAP

Bibliothèque
Bibliothèque d'Art et d'Archéologie, BAA

Bibliothèque Nationale
Bibliothèque Nationale, BN

Bibliothèques
Bibliothèques Universitaires, BU
Centre de Traitement Informatique des
Bibliothèques, CETIB
Fédération Nationale des Bibliothèques
Catholiques, FNBC

Bibliothèques Centrals de Prêt
Bibliothèques Centrals de Prêt, BCP

Bibliothèques Gouvernement
Comité de Coordination des Bibliothèques
Gouvernement du Québec, COBIGO

Bibliothèques Scolaires
Association des Préposés aux Bibliothèques
Scolaires de Montréal, APBSM
Conseil Pédagogique Provincial des
Bibliothèques Scolaires
Nouveau-Brunswick, CPPBS

Bibliothèques Universitaires
Système Intégré pour les Bibliothèques
Universitaires de Lausanne, SIBIL

Bicentennial Information
Bicentennial Information Network, BINET

Binary
Binary Automatic Computer, BINAC
Binary Coded Decimal, BCD
Binary Coded Octal, BCO
Binary Decimal Counter, BDC
Binary Error-Erasure Channel, BEEC

Binary Synchronous Communicator
Adapter, BSCA
ORACLE Binary Internal Translator,
ORBIT

Binary Coded
Extended Binary Coded Decimal
Interchange Code, EBCDIC

Biochemical
Biochemical Society, BS

Biodeterioration
International Biodeterioration Bulletin,
IBBRIS

Bioengineering
Bioengineering Current Awareness Bulletin,
BECAN

Bioethics
Bioethics Online, BIOETHICSLINE

Biography
Dictionary of American Biography, DAB
Dictionary of National Biography, DNB

Biological
Agricultural Biological Literature
Exploitation, ABLE
Biological and Agricultural Index, BAI
Biological Science Communications Project,
BSCP
Chemical-Biological Activities, CBAC
Federation of European Biological Societies,
FEBS
Journal of Biological Chemistry, JBC
Style Manual for Biological Journals, SMBJ

Biological Abstracts
Biological Abstracts, BA
Biological Abstracts on Tape, BAT
Biological Abstracts. Subjects in Context,
BASIC

Biological and Chemical
ASIS Special Interest Group on Biological
and Chemical Information Systems,
ASIS/SIG/BC

Biological Sciences
ACRL Agricultural and Biological Sciences
Section, ACRL/ABSS
American Institute of Biological Sciences,
AIBS
Council on Biological Sciences Information,
COBSI

Biology
Council of Biology Editors, CBE
*Current Contents/Agriculture, Biology and
Environmental Sciences*. (Journal),
CC/AB&ES
Federation of American Societies for
Experimental Biology, FASEB

Biomedical
ACM Special Interest Group on Biomedical
    Computing, ACM/SIGBIO
Biomedical Computer Programs, BMD
Biomedical Computing Technology
    Information Center, BCTIC
Biomedical Engineering Society, BMES
*Indexed References to Biomedical
    Engineering Literature*, IRBEL
North Alabama Biomedical Information
    Network, NABIN
SUNY Biomedical Communication
    Network, SUNY-BCN
Twin Cities Biomedical Consortium, TCBC
Virginia Union List of Biomedical Serials,
    VULBS

Biomedical Information
Regional Coordination of Biomedical
    Information Resources Program,
    RECBIR

Biophysics
International Union of Pure and Applied
    Biophysics, IUPAB

BioResearch
BioResearch Index, BioI
BioResearch Today, BRT

BioSciences
BioSciences Information Service, BIOSIS
BioSciences Information Service Previews,
    BIOSIS Previews

Bistable
Bistable Magnetic Core, BIMAG

Bi-State
Bi-State Academic Libraries, BI-SAL

Bits
Bits Per Inch, BPI
Bits Per Second, BPS
Display Assignment Bits, DAB
Display Attention Bits, DAB

Bituminous
Bituminous Coal Research, Inc, BCR

Black
Black Employees of the Library of Congress,
    BELC
Black Resources Information Coordinating
    Services, Inc, BRICS

Black Americans
Collection and Evaluation of Materials on
    Black Americans, CEMBA

Blackwell
Blackwell/North America, Inc, BNA

Blind
ASCLA Library Service to the Blind and
    Physically Handicapped Section,
    ASCLA/LSBPHS
American Printing House for the Blind, APH
British Computer Association for the Blind,
    BCAB
Canadian National Institute for the Blind,
    CNIB
Commission on Standards and Accreditation
    of Services for the Blind, COMSTAC
Division for the Blind and Physically
    Handicapped, DBPH
National Library for the Blind, NLB
National Library Services for the Blind and
    Physically Handicapped, NLS
Recordings for the Blind, Inc, RFB

Blip-Scan
Blip-Scan Ratio, BSR

Bliss
Bliss Classification, BC
Bliss Classification Association, BCA

Block
Block Diagram-Graphics, BLODI-G
Block-Oriented Random Access Memories,
    BORAM
Computer-Augmented Block System, CABS
Data Set Control Block, DSCB
Queue Control Block, QCB

Board
Board of Cooperative Educational Services,
    BOCES
Board of Cooperative Services, BOCS
British Board of Film Censors, BBFC
Bureau National d'Information Scientifique
    et Technique (National Board for
    Scientific and Technical Information),
    BNIST
Civil Aeronautics Board, CAB
Commonwealth Telecommunications Board,
    CTB
Computer Science and Engineering Board,
    CSEB
Conference Board, CB
Conference Board of the Mathematical
    Sciences, CBMS
Dirección General de Información y
    Relaciones Publicas (Board of
    Information and Public Relations),
    DGIRP
ICSU Abstracting Board, ICSU-AB
International Board on Books for Young
    People, IBBY
Iron and Steel Industry Training Board, ISI
    TB
Jewish Welfare Board, JWB
National Industrial Conference Board, NICB

New England Board of Higher Education,
NEBHE
Professional Engineers Conference Board for
Industry, PECBI
Publication Board, PB
South East Metropolitan Board of
Cooperative Services, SEMBCS
Southern Regional Education Board, SREB

Boeing
Boeing Electronic Analog Computer, BEAC
Boeing Operational Supervisory System,
BOSS

Boeing Airplane
Boeing Airplane Company Algebraic
Interpretive Computing System,
BACAIC

Bolivian Librarians
Asociación Boliviana de Bibliotecarios
(Association of Bolivian Librarians),
ABB

Bolt
Bolt, Beranek and Newman, Inc, BBN

Book
The American Book Awards, TABA
American Book Publishers Council, ABPC
American Book Publishing Record, ABPR
Book Development Council, BDC
Book Industry Study Groups, Inc, BISG
Book Industry Systems Advisory
Committee, BISAC
Book Inventory Building and Library
Information Oriented System, BIBLIOS
Book Manufacturers Institute, BMI
Book Order and Selection, BOS
Book Publishers Representatives
Association, BPRA
Canadian Book Publishers Council, CBPC
Centro Regional para el Fomento del Libro
en América Latina y el Caribe (Regional
Center for the Encouragement of the
Book in Latin America and the
Caribbean), CERLAL
Children's Book Council, CBC
Colorado Academic Libraries Book
Processing Center, CALBPC
Cumulative Book Index, CBI
Dance Collection Automated Book Catalog,
DCABC
Federation of Children's Book Groups,
FCBG
International Association of Wholesale
Newspaper, Periodical and Book
Distributors, DISTRIPRESS
International Book Year, IBY
Jerusalem International Book Fair, JIBF
National Book Awards, NBA
National Book Council, NBC

National Book League, NBL
Office du Livre Malagasy (Malagasy Book
Office), OLM
Periodical and Book Association of America,
PBAA
Reference and Subscription Book Reviews
Committee, RSBRC
Retail Book, Stationery and Allied Trades
Employees Association, RBA
Tehran Book Processing Center, TEBROC
United States Book Exchange, USBE
Universal Serials and Book Exchange,
USBE

Book Center
American Book Center for War Devastated
Libraries, ABC
Centro Interamericano de Libros
Académicos (Inter-American Scholarly
Book Center), CILA

Book Centre
British National Book Centre, BNBC

Book Number
International Standard Book Number, ISBN

Book Review
Technical Book Review Index, TBRI

Book Title
Abstract and Book Title Index Card Service,
ABTICS

Book Trade
American Book Trade Directory, ABTD

Bookbinding
Bookbinding and Allied Trades Management
Association, BATMA

Bookman's
Bookman's Price Index, BPI

Books
Association Belge des Editeurs de Langue
Française (Belgian Association of
Publishers of French Language Books),
ABELF
Books for College Libraries, BCL
Books for Equal Education, BEE
Children's Books for Schools and Libraries,
CBSL
Council on Interracial Books for Children,
CIBC
Hand Printed Books Project, HPB
International Board on Books for Young
People, IBBY
International Council on Books for Young
People, ICBY
Libros Elementales Educativos Recreativos
(Elementary Books for Education and
Recreation), LEER
Projected Books, Inc, PBI

Books in Print
Books in Print, BIP
British Books in Print, BBIP
Children's Books in Print, CBIP
Medical Books in Print, MBIP
Paperbound Books in Print, PBP

Booksellers
American Booksellers Association, ABA
Antiquarian Booksellers Association of
America, ABAA
Associação Portuguesa dos Editores e
Liveiros (Portuguese Association of
Publishers and Booksellers), APEL
Associazione Librai Italiani (Italian
Booksellers Association), ALI
Booksellers Association of Great Britain and
Ireland, BA
Cercle Belge de la Libraire (Belgium
Booksellers Association), CBL
Danske Boghandleres Importørforening
(Danish Booksellers Import
Association), DANBIF
International Community of Booksellers
Association, ICBA
International League of Antiquarian
Booksellers, ILAB
National Federation of Retail Newsagents,
Booksellers and Stationers, NFRN
Nederlandse Boekverkopersbond
(Association of Dutch Booksellers),
NBB
Overseas Booksellers Clearing House,
OBCH
Société des Libraires et Éditeurs de la Suisse
Romande (Booksellers and Publishers
Association of French-Speaking
Switzerland), SLESR

Booth Library
Booth Library On-Line Circulation, BLOC

Bosnia
Društvo Bibliotekara Bosne i Hercegovine
(Library Association of Bosnia and
Herzegovina), DB Bih

Boston
Boston Public Library, BPL

Botanical
Council on Botanical and Horticultural
Libraries, CBHL

Bradford
Bradford Scientific, Technical and
Commercial Service, BRASTACS

Braille
Braille Institute of America, Inc, BIA
Jewish Braille Institute of America, JBIA

National Braille Association, NBA
National Braille Press, NBP

Brain
Brain Information Service, BIS

Branch
Branch Conditional, BRC
Private Automatic Branch Exchange, PABX
Private Branch Exchange, PBX

Branch Information
On-Line, Real-Time, Branch Information,
ORBIT

Brass
Copper and Brass Research Association,
CBRA

Brazil
National Systems of Scientific and
Technological Information of Brazil,
SNICT

Brazilian
Associação Brasileira de Escolas de
Biblioteconomia e Documentação
(Brazilian Association of Library
Science and Documentation Schools),
ABEBD
(Brazilian) Directory of Researchers,
CADAP
Centro Brasileiro de Pesquisas
Educacionais-Divisão de Documentacão
e Informacão Pedagógica (Brazilian
Center of Educational
Research-Department of Educational
Documentation and Information),
CBPE-DDIP
Comissão Brasileira de Documentação
Agricola (Brazilian Commission for
Agricultural Documentation), CBDA
Federação Brasileira de Associações de
Bibliotecários (Brazilian Federation of
Librarian Associations), FEBAB
Federação Brasileira de Associações de
Bibliotecários-Comissão Brasileira de
Documentação Jurídica (Brazilian
Federation of Librarian
Associations-Brazilian Committee of
Legal Documentation), FEBAB/CBDJ
Instituto Brasileiro de Bibliografia e
Documentação (Brazilian Institute of
Bibliography and Documentation),
IBBD

Brewing
Brewing Industry Research Foundation,
BIRF
Brewing Research Foundation, BRF

Brighton/MARC
Brighton/MARC, BRIMARC

Britain
Australia, Britain, Canada, United States,
ABACUS
Commonwealth Writers of Britain, CWB

Britannica
AASL Encyclopaedia Britannica, AASL/EB
Encyclopaedia Britannica, EB
Encyclopaedia Britannica Educational
Corporation, EBE
Encyclopaedia Britannica, Inc, EB

British
Association of British Library and
Information Studies Schools, ABLISS
Association of British Library Schools,
ABLS
Association of British Science Writers,
ABSW
Association of British Theological and
Philosophical Libraries, ABTAPL
British Amateur Press Association, BAPA
British and Irish Association of Law
Librarians, BIALL
British Association of Industrial Editors,
BAIE
British Board of Film Censors, BBFC
British Books in Print, BBIP
British Broadcasting Corporation, BBC
British Carbonization Research Association,
BCRA
British Cartographic Society, BCS
British Cast Iron Research Association,
BCIRA
British Catalogue of Music, BCM
British Ceramic Research Association,
BCRA
British Ceramic Society, BCS
British Coke Research Association, BCRA
British Commonwealth Scientific Office,
BCSO
British Computer Association for the Blind,
BCAB
British Computer Society, BCS
British Computer Society ALGOL
Association, BCSAA
British Copyright Council, BCC
British Copyright Protection Association,
Ltd, BCPA
British Film Institute, BFI
British Hydromechanics Research
Association, BHRA
British Industrial and Scientific Film
Association Ltd, BISFA
British Information Service, BIS
British Institute of Management, BIM
British Institute of Recording Sounds, BIRS
British Integrated Programme Suite, BIPS
British Iron and Steel Industry Translation
Service, BISITS

British Kinematograph, Sound, and
Television Society, BKSTS
British Lending Library, BLL
British Medical Association, BMA
British Ministry of Technology, BrMTL
British Museum, BM
British National Bibliography, BNB
British National Book Centre, BNBC
British National Discography, BND
British National Film Catalogue, BNFC
British Overseas Airways Digital
Information Computer for Electronic
Automation, BOADICEA
British Pharmacopoeia, BP
British Photographic Manufacturers
Association, BPMA
British Printing Machinery Association,
BPMA
British Records Association, BRA
British Regional Television Association,
BRTA
British Science Fiction Association, BSFA
British Sound Recording Association, BSRA
British Standard Institution, BSI
British Technology Index, BTI
British Union Catalog of Periodicals,
BUCOP
British United Press, BUP
Confederation of British Industries, CBI
Guild of British Newspapers Editors, GBNE
Permanent Committee on Geographical
Names (for British Official Use), PCGN
Royal Institute of British Architects, RIBA
Royal Society of British Artists, RBA
Women's Advisory Committee of the British
Standards Institution, WAC

British Columbia
Association of British Columbia Archivists,
ABCA
British Columbia Institute of Technology
Information Resource Centre, BCIT
British Columbia Library Association,
BCLA
British Columbia Library Trustees
Association, BCLTA
British Columbia Organization of Library
Technicians, BOLT
British Columbia School Librarians
Association, BCSLA
Congressional Libraries Association of
British Columbia, CLABC
Institute of Continuing Library Education of
British Columbia, ICLEBC
Tri-University Libraries of British Columbia,
TRIUL

British Columbia Librarians
Association of British Columbia Librarians,
ABCL

British Library
British Library, BL
British Library Automated Information
    System, BLAISE
British Library Lending Division, BLLD
British Library of Wild Life Sounds,
    BLOWS
British Museum Library, BML

Broadband
Broadband Exchange, BEX

Broadcast
Association for Broadcast Engineering
    Standards, Inc, ABES

Broadcasters
International Broadcasters Society, IBS
National Association of Educational
    Broadcasters, NAEB

Broadcasting
American Broadcasting Companies, Inc,
    ABC
Association on Broadcasting Standards,
    ABS
Australian Broadcasting Corporation, ABC
British Broadcasting Corporation, BBC
Canadian Broadcasting Corporation, CBC
Columbia Broadcasting System, Inc, CBS
European Broadcasting Union, EBU
Independent Broadcasting Authority, IBA
Joint Council on Educational Broadcasting,
    JCEB
National Broadcasting Company, Inc, NBC
Public Broadcasting Service, PBS
School Broadcasting Council for the United
    Kingdom, SBCUK

Broader
Broader Term, BT

Brooklyn
Brooklyn–Queens–Staten Island Health
    Sciences Group, BQSI

Browsing
Browsing On-Line with Selective Retrieval,
    BROWSER

Buchhändler
Vereinigung Evangelischer Buchhändler,
    VEB

Buchhändler–Abrechnungs–Gesellschaft
Buchhändler–Abrechnungs–Gesellschaft
    mbH, BAG

Bucknell
Bucknell Automated Retrieval and Display
    System, BARDS

Budget
Bureau of the Budget, BoB
Office of Management and Budget, OMB

Operating Budget, OPBU
Program Evaluation and Budget Committee,
    PEBCO

Budgeting
ASIS Special Interest Group on Costs
    Budgeting and Economics,
    ASIS/SIG/CBE

Buffer
Output to Display Buffer, ODB

Building
Book Inventory Building and Library
    Information Oriented System, BIBLIOS
[Building Documentation], BYGGDOK
[Building References] (Journal),
    BYGGREFERAT
Building Research Advisory Board, BRAB
Building Research Institute, BRI
Computer-Aided Rationalized Building
    System, CARBS
Information System on Research and
    Development in Building Industry and
    Construction, INBAD

Buildings
LAMA Buildings and Equipment Section,
    LAMA/BES
National Buildings Organization, NBO

Buildings Services
Buildings Services Research and Information
    Association, BSRIA

Built-In
Built-In Test Equipment, BITE

Built-in-Place
Built-in-Place Components, BIPCO

Bulletin
*Abstract Bulletin of the Institute of Paper
    Chemistry*, ABIPC
Bioengineering Current Awareness Bulletin,
    BECAN
*Bulletin of the American Society for
    Information Science*, BASIS
*Bulletin of the Library Association of
    Trinidad and Tobago*, BLATT
Bulletin of the Medical Library Association,
    BMLA
International Biodeterioration Bulletin,
    IBBRIS
Technical Abstract Bulletin, TAB
Wilson Library Bulletin, WLB

Bundesverband
Bundesverband Deutscher Zeitungsverleger,
    BDZV

Bureau
American Bureau of Shipping, ABS
Bureau de Recherche pour l'Innovation et la
    Convergence, BRIC

Business Information
ASLIB Economic and Business Information Group, AEBIG
Abstracted Business Information/ Information Needs, ABI/INFORM

Business International
Business International. (Journal), BI
Business International Money Report. (Journal), BIMR

Business Services
Technical and Business Services, TABS

Buying
Baker and Taylor Automated Buying, BATAB

CADAP
CADAP and CAIN, CAPESQ

CAIN
CADAP and CAIN, CAPESQ

COBOL
Autocoder to COBOL Translator, ACT
COBOL Macro Processor, CMP
COBOL-Oriented Real-Time Environment, CORTEZ

CODASYL
Data Base Task Force (CODASYL), DBTC

CONVERSE
CONVERSE System, CONVERSE

Cable
Cable Information Services, CIS
Cable Television, CATV
ISAD Video and Cable Communications Section, ISAD/VCCS
LITA Video and Cable Communications Section, LITA/VCCS

Calcul Analogique
Association Internationale pour le Calcul Analogique, ASICA

Calculator
Calculator Help in Processing Signals, CHIPS
Card Programmed Calculator, CPC
Electronic Numerical Integrator and Calculator, ENIAC
Selective Sequence Electronic Calculator, SSEC

California
Academy of Television Arts and Sciences-University of California, Los Angeles-Television Archives, ATAS/UCLA
California Chapter of Academic and Research Libraries, CARL

California Education Information System, CEIS
California Educational Data Processing Association, CEDPA
California Institute of Technology, CIT
California Library Authority for Systems and Services, CLASS
California Library Automation Network, CLAN
California Library Network, CALINET
California State University at Long Beach, CSULB
California Union List of Periodicals, CULP
Learning Resources Association of California Community Colleges, LRACCC
Librarians Association of the University of California, LAUC
Northern California Medical Library Group, NCMLG
Southern California Answering Network, SCAN
Southern California Association of Governments, SCAG
Southern California Film Circuit, SCFC
Southern California Interlibrary Loan Network, SCILL
Southern California Rapid Transit District, SCRTD
Southern California Technical Processes Group, SCTPG
University of California Bibliographic Center, BIBCENTER
University of California-Los Angeles, UCLA
University of California-University-Wide Automation Program, ULAP

California Libraries
Information Center for Southern California Libraries, INFO

Call
Call Waiting, CW
Load on Call, LOCAL

Call-Directing
Call-Directing Code, CDC

Calling Unit
Automatic Calling Unit, ACU

Cambridge
Cambridge Bibliography of English Literature, CBEL
Cambridge Scientific Abstracts, Inc, CSA

Cameroon
Association des Bibliothécaires, Archivistes, Documentalistes et Muséographes du Cameroun (Association of Librarians, Archivists, Documentalists and Museum Curators of Cameroon), ABADCAM

Canada
ASIS Western Canada Chapter,
    ASIS/Wes-Can
Archival Association of Atlantic Canada,
    AAAC
Association of Parliamentary Librarians in
    Canada, APLIC
Association of Universities and Colleges of
    Canada/Association des Universités et
    Collèges du Canada, AUCC
Atomic Energy of Canada Limited, AECL
Australia, Britain, Canada, United States,
    ABACUS
Canada Water, CWA
Chemical Institute of Canada, CIC
National Library of Canada, NLC
Pulp and Paper Research Institute of
    Canada/Information Retrieval Services,
    PAPRICAN/IRS
Société Canadienne pour l'Analyse de
    Documents/Indexing and Abstracting
    Society of Canada, SCAD/IASC
State and Court Law Libraries of the United
    States and Canada, SCLL

Canada Centre
Canada Centre for Mineral and Energy
    Technology, CANMET

Canadian
Association of Canadian Archivists, ACA
Association of Canadian Map
    Libraries/Association des Cartothèques
    Canadiennes, ACML/ACC
Association of Canadian Medical
    Colleges/Association des Facultés de
    Médecine du Canada, ACMC/AFMC
Canadian Academic Research Libraries,
    CARL
Canadian Aeronautics and Space Institute,
    CASI
Canadian Association for Applied
    Spectroscopy, CAAS
Canadian Association for Information
    Science/Association Canadienne des
    Sciences de l'Information, CAIS/ACSI
Canadian Association of Children's
    Librarians, CACL
Canadian Association of College and
    University Libraries/Association
    Canadienne des Bibliothèques de
    Collège et d'Université,
    CACUL/ACBCU
Canadian Association of Law
    Libraries/Association Canadienne des
    Bibliothèques de Droit, CALL/ACBD
Canadian Association of Library
    Schools/Association Canadienne des
    Écoles de Bibliothécaires, CALS/ACEB
Canadian Association of Music
    Libraries/Association Canadienne des

Bibliothèques Musicales,
    CAML/ACBM
Canadian Association of Public Libraries,
    CAPL
Canadian Association of Research
    Libraries/Association des Bibliothèques
    de Recherche du Canada, CARL/ABRC
Canadian Association of Special Libraries
    and Information Services, CASLIS
Canadian Association of University
    Teachers/Association Canadienne des
    Professeurs d'Université, CAUT/ACPU
Canadian Book Publishers Council, CBPC
Canadian Broadcasting Corporation, CBC
Canadian Ceramic Society, CCS
Canadian Classification Research
    Group/Groupe Canadien pour la
    Recherche en Classification, CCRG
Canadian Committee on Cataloguing/Comité
    Canadien de Catalogage, CCC
Canadian Committee on MARC/Comité
    Canadien du MARC, CCM
Canadian Council of Library Schools/Conseil
    Canadien des Écoles de Bibliothécaires,
    CCLS/CCEB
Canadian Council of Professional
    Engineers/Conseil Canadien des
    Ingénieurs Professionels, CCPE/CCIP
Canadian Education Association, CEA
Canadian Educational Researchers
    Association/Association Canadienne des
    Chercheurs en Éducation, CERA/ACCE
Canadian Farm Management Data System,
    CANFARM
Canadian Forces Publications, CFP
Canadian General Electric Company, Ltd,
    CGE
Canadian Health Libraries
    Association/Association des
    Bibliothèques de la Santé du Canada,
    CHLA/ABSC
Canadian Hunger Foundation, CHF
Canadian Information Processing
    Society/Association Canadienne de
    L'Informatique, CIPS/ACI
Canadian Institute for Scientific and
    Technical Information (Institut
    Canadien de l'Information Scientifique
    et Technique), CISTI/ICIST
Canadian International Paper Company, CIP
Canadian Library Association, CLA
Canadian Library Exhibitors Association,
    CLEA
Canadian Library Journal, CLJ
Canadian Library Trustees Association,
    CLTA
Canadian MARC, CAN/MARC
Canadian Military Electronics Standards
    Agency, CAMESA
Canadian National Institute for the Blind,
    CNIB

Canadian (cont.)

Canadian National Railways, CN
Canadian On-Line Enquiry, CAN/OLE
Canadian Rehabilitation Council for the
    Disabled, CRCD
Canadian School Library Association, CSLA
Canadian Selective Dissemination of
    Information, CAN/SDI
Canadian Social Science Abstracts, CSSA
Canadian Standards Association, CSA
Canadian Technical Awareness Program,
    CAN/TAP
Canadian Union of Public Employees, CUPE
FID Canadian National Committee,
    FID/CNC
Joint Canadian Navy-Army-Air Force
    Specification, JCNAAF
Polish Canadian Librarians Association,
    PCLA
Royal Canadian Mounted Police, RCMP

Canadian Librarians
Association Canadienne des Bibliothécaires
    de Langue Française (Association of
    French Speaking Canadian Librarians),
    ACBLF

Canadien
Canadian Committee on MARC/Comité
    Canadien du MARC, CCM
Consortium Canadien de Recherches
    Urbaines et Régionales, CCRUR

Canadienne
Association Canadienne d'Éducation de
    Langue Française, ACELF

Canadienne Française
Association Canadienne Française pour
    l'Avancement des Sciences, ACFAS

Cancel
Cancel Transmission, CANTRAN

Canceling
Automatic Claiming and Canceling, ACC

Cancer
Cancer Literature, CANCERLIT
Cancer Network, CANCERNET
Cancer Online, CANCERLINE
Cancer Projects, CANCERPROJ
Current Cancer Research Project Analysis
    Center, CCRESPAC
International Cancer Research Data Bank
    Program, ICRDB

Cancer Information
Cancer Information Dissemination and
    Analysis, CIDA

Capital
Capital Consortium Network, CAPCON
Capital Systems Group, CSG

Capitol Services
Capitol Services, Inc, CSI

Carbon
Communauté Européenne du Carbon et de
    l'Acier, CECA

Carbon-13
Carbon-13 Nuclear Magnetic Resonance,
    CNMR

Carbonization
British Carbonization Research Association,
    BCRA

Card
Card Programmed Calculator, CPC
Card Random Access Memory, CRAM
Punched Card System, PCS

Card Kits
Agricultural Personal Alerting Card Kits,
    AG/PACK

Card Number
Library of Congress Card Number, LCCN

Card-Automated
Card-Automated Reproduction and
    Distribution System, CARDS

Cardboard
Cardboard Illustrated Aid to Computation,
    CARDIAC

Card-Punching
Card-Punching Printer, CPP

Cards
Cards Per Minute, CPM

Career
Career Information System, CIS
Career Retrieval Search System, CARESS
Career Update, CU
ERIC Clearinghouse on Adult, Career, and
    Vocational Education, ERIC/CE

Career Information
Mathematical Analysis of Requirements for
    Career Information Appraisal, MARCIA

Careers
Public Service Careers Program, PSCP

Caribbean
Association of Caribbean University and
    Research Institute Libraries, ACURIL
Association of Caribbean University and
    Research Libraries, ACURL
Centro Regional para el Fomento del Libro
    en América Latina y el Caribe (Regional
    Center for the Encouragement of the
    Book in Latin America and the
    Caribbean), CERLAL

Cooperative Investigations of the Caribbean and Adjacent Regions, CICAR

Caribe
Seminario Interamericano sobre la Integración de los Servicios de Información de Archivos, Bibliotecas y Centros de Documentación en America Central y el Caribe, SI/ABCD

Carolina
Carolina Population Center, CPC
Carolina Population Center Library Data Base, CPC

Carriage Return
Carriage Return Character, CR

Cartographers
American Society of Cartographers, ASC

Cartographic
British Cartographic Society, BCS
International Cartographic Association, ICA
National Cartographic Information Center, NCIC

Cartography
Computer-Assisted Cartography, CASC

Case Western
Case Western Reserve University, CWRU

Cash Register
National Cash Register Company, NCR

Cassette
Cassette Programming System, CAPS

Cast Iron
British Cast Iron Research Association, BCIRA

Catalog
Automated Catalog of Computer Equipment and Software Systems, ACCESS
Catalog Data File, CDF
Catalog of Computerized Subject Searches, CAT
Dance Collection Automated Book Catalog, DCABC
Illinois Microfilm Automated Catalog, IMAC
Mechanized Catalog, MECCA
Micrographic Catalog Retrieval System, MCRS

Catalog Card
Catalog Card Corporation of America, CCC

Catalogage
Catalogage National Centralisé, CANAC

Cataloging
Acquisitions, Cataloging, Technical Systems, ACTS

Aldermaston Mechanized Cataloging and Ordering System, AMCOS
Anglo-American Cataloging Rules, AACR
CLA Cataloging and Classification Roundtable, CLA/CCRT
CNLIA Joint Committee on Cataloging and Classification Codes, CNLIA/JCCC
Cataloging and Indexing System of NAL, CAIN
Cataloging in Publication, CIP
Cataloging in Source, CIS
Cataloging On-Line, CATLINE
Cooperative Machine-Readable Cataloging, COMARC
Copyright Office Publication and Interactive Cataloging System, COPICS
Federal Libraries Experiment in Cooperative Cataloging, FLECC
Fully Automatic Cataloging Technique, FACT
International Conference on Cataloging Principles, ICCP
Joint Steering Committee for the Revision of the Anglo-American Cataloging Rules, JSCAACR
Machine Readable Cataloging, MARC
Machine Readable Cataloging II, MARC II
National Program for Acquisition and Cataloging, NPAC
RTSD Cataloging and Classification Section, RTSD/CCS
Scottish Libraries Cataloging Automation Project, SCOLCAP

Catalogo Unico
Centro Nazionale per il Catalogo Unico delle Biblioteche Italiane per le Informazion Bibliografiche, CUBI

Catalogoción
Catalogoción Centralizada, CATACEN

Catalographique
Mise en Ordinateur d'une Notice Catalographique de Livre, MONOCLE

Catalogs
Educational Media Catalogs on Microfiche, EMCOM

Catalogue
British Catalogue of Music, BCM
British National Film Catalogue, BNFC
Project for Integrated Catalogue Automation, PICA
Short Title Catalogue, STC
Union Catalogue/Telecommunication Catalogue, UNICAT/TELECAT

Catalogue Collectif
Catalogue Collectif des Ouvrages Étrangers, CCOE

Catalogued
Catalogued Resources and Information
 Survey Programs, CRISP

Cataloguing
Anglo-American Cataloguing Rules, AACR
 2
Canadian Committee on Cataloguing/Comité
 Canadien de Catalogage, CCC
Cataloguing Support System, CATSS

Categories
Selected Categories in Microfiche, SCIM

Categorizing
Computer-Assisted Indexing and
 Categorizing, CAIC

Cathode-Ray
Cathode-Ray Oscilloscope, CRO
Cathode-Ray Tube, CRT

Catholic
Arbeitsgemeinschaft
 Katholisch-Theologischer Bibliotheken
 (Working Group of Catholic Theological
 Libraries), AKTHB
Catholic Audio-Visual Educators
 Association, CAVE
Catholic Hospital Association, CHA
Catholic Library Association, CLA
Catholic Microfilm Center, CMC
Catholic Periodical and Literature Index,
 CPLI
Catholic School Press Association, CSPA
Fédération Internationale des Directeurs de
 Journaux Catholiques (International
 Federation of Directors of Catholic
 Publications), FIDJC
International Catholic Press Union, ICPU
International Federation of Catholic
 Journalists, IFCJ

Catholiques
Fédération Nationale des Bibliothèques
 Catholiques, FNBC

Catskill
Ramapo Catskill Library System, RCLS

Cement
Cement and Concrete Association, C&CA

Censors
British Board of Film Censors, BBFC

Census
Clearinghouse and Laboratory for Census
 Data, CLCD
Retrieval of Information about Census
 Tapes, RIACT

Center
Aerospace Research Applications Center,
 ARAC

Alabama Center for Higher Education,
 ACHE
American Bibliographical Center, ABC
American Bibliographical Center–Clio Press,
 ABC–Clio
Aquatic Sciences Information Retrieval
 Center, ASIRC
Center for African Studies and Institute for
 Social Research, CAS&ISR
Center for Applied Linguistics, CAL
Center for Disease Control, CDC
Center for Documentation and
 Communication Research, CDCR
Center for Educational Development
 Overseas, CEDO
Center for Educational Research and
 Innovation, CERI
Center for Environmental Research and
 Development, CERD
Center for Information and Documentation,
 CID
Center for Information and Numerical Data
 Analysis and Synthesis, CINDAS
Center for Information on America, CIOA
Center for Inventions and Scientific
 Information, CISI
Center for Labor Education and Research,
 CLEAR
Center for Marine and Environmental
 Studies, CMES
Center for Neo-Hellenic Studies, CNHS
Center for Research and Evaluation in
 Applications of Technology in
 Education, CREATE
Center for Research in College Instruction of
 Science and Mathematics, CRICISAM
Center for Research Libraries, CRL
Center for Research on Language and
 Language Behavior, CRLLB
Center for Research on Learning and
 Teaching, CRLT
Center for Studies in Economic
 Development, CEDE
Center for Thai National Standard
 Specifications, CTNSS
Center for the Advanced Study of
 Educational Administration, CASEA
Center for the Coordination of Foreign
 Manuscript Copying, CCFMC
Center for Women's Studies and Services,
 CWSS
Center of Experiment Design and Data
 Analysis, CEDDA
Center of Scientific and Technological
 Information, COSTI
Centre National d'Étude et
 d'Experimentation de Machinisme
 Agricole (National Center for
 Agricultural Machinery Research and
 Experimentation), CNEEMA

Centre National d'Études des
Télécommunications (National Center
of Telecommunication Studies), CNET
Centre National de Documentation
Scientifique et Technique (National
Center for Scientific and Technical
Documentation), CNDST
Centro de Desarrollo Industrial (Center for
Industrial Development), CENDES
Centro de Información Cientifica y
Humanistica (Center for Scientific and
Humanistic Information), CICH
Centro de Información de Zonas Aridas
(Center for Arid Zone Information),
CIZA
Centro de Información Metalíurgica (Center
for Metallurgic Information), CIM
Centro Interamericano de Documentación
Económia y Social (Interamerican
Center for Economic and Social
Documentation), CIADES
Centro Nacional de Información Científica y
Técnica (National Center for Scientific
and Technical Information), CONICIT
Centro Nacional de Información Económica
y Social (National Center for Economic
and Social Information), CNIES
Centro Nacional de Información y
Documentación (National Center for
Information and Documentation),
CENID
Centro Regional para el Fomento del Libro
en América Latina y el Caribe (Regional
Center for the Encouragement of the
Book in Latin America and the
Caribbean), CERLAL
Centrum voor Landbouwpiblikaties en
Landbouwdocumentatie (Center for
Agricultural Publishing and
Documentation), PUDOC
Counterinsurgency Information Analysis
Center, CINFAC
Education Development Center, Inc, EDC
Electronics Research Center, ERC
European Center for the Coordination of
Research and Documentation in the
Social Sciences, CEUCORS
European Cultural Center, ECC
European Space Data Center, ESDAC
European Space Research and Technology
Center, ESTEC
Family Reading Center, FRC
Hampshire Interlibrary Center, HILC
Hydraulic Engineering Information Analysis
Center, HEIAC
Industrial Development Center/Viet-Nam
(Trung-Tam Khuech-Truong Ky-Ngha),
IDC/VN
Information Analysis Center, IAC
International Center for Theoretical Physics,
ICTP

International Center of Films for Children,
ICFC
International Center of Information on
Antibiotics, ICIA
International Development Center, IDC
International Inter-Church Film Center,
INTERFILM
Jugoslovenski Centar za Techničku i Naučno
Dokumentacijua (Yugoslav Center for
Technical and Scientific
Documentation), JCTND
Kerr Industrial Applications Center, KIAC
National Geophysical Data Center, NGDC
Országos Orvostudományi Könyvtár és
Dokumentácioś Központ (National
Medical Library and Center for
Documentation), OOKDK
Southwest Center for Urban Research,
SCUR
Thermodynamics Research Center, TRC

Center for Information
Centro de Información de Politica Cientifica
y Tecnológica (Center for Information in
Political Science and Technology), CIPC

Centers
ASIS Special Interest Group on Information
Analysis Centers, ASIS/SIG/IAC
European Documentation Centers, EDC

Central
Central Terminal Unit, CTU
Centralny Instytut Informasui Noukowo
Techniceneu I Economicznej (Central
Institute for Scientific, Technical and
Economic Information), CLINTE

Central American
Instituto Centro Americano de Investigacion
y Technologia Industrial (Central
American Institute of Research and
Industrial Technology), ICAITI

Central Library
Biblioteca Nazionale Centrale—Firenze
(National Central Library of Florence),
BNCF
Bibliotheca Borgoriensis (Central Library for
Natural Science), BB
Central Library and Documentation, CLD
National Central Library, NCL
Ústredná Kniznica Slovenskej Akademie
Vied (Central Library of the Slovak
Academy of Sciences), UKSAV

Central States
Central States Distributors Association,
CSDA

Centrale de Livraison
Centrale de Livraison de Valeurs Mobilieres,
CEDEL

Centralny
Centralny Instytut Informasui Noukowo
Techniceneu I Economicznej (Central
Institute for Scientific, Technical and
Economic Information), CLINTE

Centre
Admiralty Centre for Scientific Information
and Liaison, ACSIL
Australian Centre for Research in Library
and Information Science, ACRiLIS
Centre Bibliographique National, CBN
Centre de Techniques Bibliographiques,
CTB
Centre de Traitement Informatique des
Bibliothèques, CETIB
Centre for Curriculum Renewal and
Educational Development Overseas,
CREDO
Centre for Educational Television Overseas,
CETO
Centre National de la Recherche
Scientifique, CNRS
Centre National pour l'Exploitation des
Océans, CNEXO
Centre pour la Recherche Interdisciplinaire
sur le Développement, CRID
Centre Technique des Industries de la
Fonderie, CTIF
Documentation Research and Training
Centre, DRTC
Overseas Visual Aids Centre, OVAC
Poets, Playwrights, Editors, Essayists and
Novelists International English Centre,
PEN

Centre d'Animation
Centre d'Animation, de Développement et
de Recherche en Education, CADRE

Centre d'Assistance
Centre d'Assistance Technique et de
Documentation, CATED

Centre d'Étude
Centre National d'Étude des
Télécommunications/Département
Documentation Interministérielle,
CNET/DI

Centre d'Études
Centre d'Études et de Recherches de
l'Industrie des Liants Hydrauliques,
CERILH
Centre d'Études et Recherches des
Charbonnages de France, CERCHAR

Centre de Documentation
Centre de Documentation de l'Armament,
CEDOCAR
Centre de Documentation Économique et
Sociale, CIDES

Centre de Documentation et de Recherche
Sociales, CEDORES
Centre de Documentation International des
Industries Utilisatrices de Produits
Agricoles, CDIUPA

Centre de Recherche
Centre de Recherche Sociologique Appliqués
de la Loire, CRESAL

Centre de Recherches
Centre de Recherches et d'Innovation
Urbaines, CRIU

Centre d'Information
Centre d'Information et de Documentation
du Bâtiment, CIDB
Centre International d'Information et de la
Recherche sur la Formation
Professionnelle, CIRF
Centre National d'Information pour le
Productivité des Entreprises, CNIPE

Centre d'Informatique
Centre d'Informatique Juridique, CEDIJ

Centre International
Centre International
d'Alcoologie/Taxicomanies, CIATO

Centre Scientifique
Centre Scientifique et Technique du
Batiment, CSTB

Centres
Educational Centres Association, ECA

Centro
Centro Interamericano de Documentación
Económica y Social (Interamerican
Center for Economic and Social
Documentation), CIADES
Centro Nazionale per il Catalogo Unico delle
Biblioteche Italiane per le Informazion
Bibliografiche, CUBI

Centro America
Instituto de Nutricion de Centro America y
Panama, INCAP

Centro de Documentación
Centro de Documentación, CD
Centro de Documentación Audiovisual para
A.L., CEDAL
Centro de Documentación y Divulgación
Pedagógicas, CDDP

Centro de Información
Centro de Información, CI
Centro de Información Pecuaria, CIP

Centro de Investigaciones
Centro de Investigaciones en Ciencias
Sociales, CISOR

Centro d'Estudios
Centro d'Estudios Sociales y de Población,
CESPO

Centro Europeo
Centro Europeo Informazioni Scientifiche e
Tecniche, CEIST

Centro Informazioni
Centro Informazioni Studi Esperienze–
Servizio Documentazione, CISE

Centro Interamericano
Centro Interamericano de Documentación,
CIDOC

Centroamericana
Programa de Información Agropecuaria del
Istmo Centroamericana, PIADIC

Centros de Documentation
Seminario Interamericano sobre la
Integración de los Servicios de
Información de Archivos, Bibliotecas y
Centros de Documentation en America
Central y el Caribe, SI/ABCD

Centrov-Elektrotehnika
Sistem za Avtomatizacilo Informacijsko
Dokumcntacijskih Ccntrov–
Elektrotehnika, SAIDC

Ceramic
British Ceramic Research Association,
BCRA
British Ceramic Society, BCS
Canadian Ceramic Society, CCS
Defense Ceramic Information Center, DCIC
National Institute of Ceramic Engineers,
NICE

Ceramics
Metals and Ceramics Information Center,
MCIC

Céramique
Céramique Index, CERINDEX

Cereal
American Association of Cereal Chemists,
AACC

Certificat d'Aptitude
Certificat d'Aptitude, Fonctions de
Bibliothécaire, CAFB

Certified Librarians
Verein der Diplom-Bibliothekare an
Wissenschaftlichen Bibliotheken
(Association of Certified Librarians at
Research Libraries), VdDB

Certified Public Accountants
American Institute of Certified Public
Accountants, AICPA

Ceylon
Bureau of Ceylon Standards, BCS
Ceylon Institute of Scientific and Industrial
Research, CISIR
Ceylon Library Association, CyLA

Chalk River
Chalk River Bibliographic Data Information
System, CHARIBIDIS

Chalmers
Chalmers Tekniska Högskolas Bibliotek
(Library of Chalmers University of
Technology), CTHB

Chambre Syndicale
Chambre Syndicale des Producteurs et
Exportateurs de Films Français,
CSPEFF

Change
Design Change Recommendation, DCR
Font Change, FC

Change Recording
Non-Return-to-Zero Change Recording,
NRZC

Channel
Binary Error-Erasure Channel, BEEC
Channel Status Table, CST
Channel Status Word, CSW

Character
Acknowledge Character, ACK
Backspace Character, BS
Bell Character, BEL
Carriage Return Character, CR
Computer-Aided Design Optical Character
Recognition, CADOCR
Enquiry Character, ENQ
Escape Character, ESC
Least Significant Character, LSC
Longitudinal Redundancy Check Character,
LRC
Most Significant Character, MSC
Negative Acknowledge Character, NAK
Null Character, NUL
Optical Character Reader, OCR
Shift-In Character, SI
Shift-Out Character, SO
Space Character, SP
Start of Heading Character, SOH
Start of Text Character, STX
Substitute Character, SUB
Synchronous Idle Character, SYN
Vertical Tabulation Character, VT

Character Recognition
Magnetic Ink Character Recognition, MICR
Optical Character Recognition, OCR

Characteristic
Memory Operating Characteristic, MOC

Characters
Characters Per Inch, CPI
Characters Per Second, CPS
Code for Magnetic Characters, CMC
One Thousand Characters per Second, KCS

Charbonnages
Centre d'Études et Recherches des
    Charbonnages de France, CERCHAR

Charlotte
Charlotte Area Union List of Periodicals and
    Serials, CAULPS

Checkout
Automatic Checkout and Readiness
    Equipment, ACRE
Random Access Programming and Checkout
    Equipment, RAPCOE
Tape-Controlled Recording Automatic
    Checkout Equipment, TRACE

Chemical
ACS Chemical Literature Division,
    ACS/CLD
ACS Division of Chemical Literature,
    ACS/DCL
American Chemical Society, ACS
American Institute of Chemical Engineers,
    AIChE
*Applied Chemistry and Chemical
    Engineering Sections of Chemical
    Abstracts*, ACCESS
Centrul de Documentare al Industriei
    Chimice si Petroliere (Documentation
    Center of the Chemical and Oil
    Industry), CDICIP
Chemical Abstracts Chemical Name
    Dictionary, CHEMNAME
Chemical-Biological Activities, CBAC
Chemical Construction Corporation,
    Chemico
Chemical Dictionary On-Line, CHEMLINE
Chemical Information Systems Operators,
    CHEOPS
Chemical Institute of Canada, CIC
Chemical Literature. (Journal), CL
Chemical Marketing Research Association,
    CMRA
Chemical Propulsion Information Agency,
    CPIA
Chemical Rubber Company, CRC
Chemical Society Research Unit in
    Information Dissemination and
    Retrieval, CSRUIDR
Chemical Substructure Index, CSI
Chemical Thermodynamics Data Center,
    CTDC
Chemical Titles. (Journal), CT

Commercial Chemical Development
    Association, CCDA
Current Chemical Reactions. (Journal), CCR
*Current Contents/Chemical,
    Pharmaco-Medical and Life Sciences*.
    (Journal), CC/CPML
*Current Contents/Physical and Chemical
    Sciences*. (Journal), CC/PC
*Current Contents/Physical, Chemical and
    Earth Sciences*. (Journal), CC/PC&ES
European Federation of Chemical
    Engineering, EFCE
Journal of Chemical Documentation, JCD
Journal of the American Chemical Society,
    JACS
Oak Ridge Chemical Information System,
    ORCHIS
Registry of Toxic Effects of Chemical
    Substances, RTECS
Synthetic Organic Chemical Manufacturers
    Association, SOCMA
United Kingdom Chemical Information
    Service, UKCIS

Chemical Abstracts
*Applied Chemistry and Chemical
    Engineering Sections of Chemical
    Abstracts*, ACCESS
Chemical Abstracts, CA
Chemical Abstracts Chemical Name
    Dictionary, CHEMNAME
Chemical Abstracts Condensates, CAC
Chemical Abstracts Service, CAS
Chemical Abstracts Service Source Index,
    CASSI
Chemical Abstracts Subject Index Alert,
    CASIA

Chemical Information
ACS Division of Chemical Information,
    ACS/DCI
Centro Méxicano de Información Química
    (Mexican Center for Chemical
    Information), CMIQ
Chemical Information and Data System,
    CIDS
Students Chemical Information Project,
    SCIP

Chemicus
Index Chemicus, IC

Chemie
Internationale Dokumentation-gesellschaft
    für Chemie, IDC

Chemins de Fer
Association Internationale du Congres des
    Chemins de Fer, AICCF
Bureau International de Documentation des
    Chemins de Fer, BDC
Société Nationale des Chemins de Fer
    Français, SNCF

Chemistry
Abstract Bulletin of the Institute of Paper Chemistry, ABIPC
Applied Chemistry and Chemical Engineering Sections of Chemical Abstracts, ACCESS
Current Abstracts of Chemistry, CAC
Current Abstracts of Chemistry and Index Chemicus, CAC&IC
Journal of Biological Chemistry, JBC
Journal of General Chemistry, JGC

Chemists
American Association of Cereal Chemists, AACC
American Association of Clinical Chemists, AACC
American Association of Textile Chemists and Colorists, AATCC
American Institute of Chemists, Inc, AIC
American Oil Chemists Society, AOCS
Association of Consulting Chemists and Chemical Engineers, ACC&CE
Association of Official Agricultural Chemists, AOAC
Association of Official Analytical Chemists, AOAC

Chicago
Chicago Academic Library Council, CALC
Chicago Area Theological Library Association, CATLA
Chicago Cluster of Theological Schools, CCTS

Chief Librarians
Association of London Chief Librarians, ALCL
Massachusetts Conference of Chief Librarians in Public Higher Educational Institutions, MCCLPHEI
Society of Municipal and County Chief Librarians, SMCCL

Chiefs
International Association of Chiefs of Police, IACP

Child
Exceptional Child Education Resources, ECER

Child Abuse
National Center for Child Abuse and Neglect, NCCAN

Childhood
Association for Childhood Education International, ACEI
ERIC Clearinghouse on Elementary and Early Childhood Education, ERIC/PS

Children
Administration for Children, Youth, and Families, ACYF
Association for Library Service to Children, ALSC
Council for Exceptional Children Information Services, CEC
Council on Interracial Books for Children, CIBC
ERIC Clearinghouse on Handicapped and Gifted Children, ERIC/EC
International Center of Films for Children, ICFC
National Society for Crippled Children and Adults, NSCCA
Quebec Association for Children with Learning Disabilities, QACLD

Children's
Action for Children's Television, ACT
Children's Book Council, CBC
Children's Books for Schools and Libraries, CBSL
Children's Books in Print, CBIP
Children's Film Foundation Ltd, CFF
Children's Psychiatric Research Institute, CPRI
Clearinghouse for Options in Children's Education, CHOICE
Federation of Children's Book Groups, FCBG
International Children's Emergency Fund, ICEF
United Nations Children's Fund, UNICEF

Children's Librarians
Canadian Association of Children's Librarians, CACL

Children's Libraries
CLA Children's Libraries Section, CLA/CLS
Children's Libraries Section, CLS

Children's Services
Children's Services Division, CSD

Chimique
Union Chimique-Chemische Bedrijven, UCB

Chimiste
Estimation de Proprietés Physiques pour l'Ingenieur Chimiste, EPIC

China
Business China. (Journal), BC
Scientific and Technical Association of the People's Republic of China, STAPRC

Chinese
Chinese Librarians Association, CLA
Chinese National Standards, CNS

Christian
Associated Christian Colleges of Oregon,
    ACCO
United Society for Christian Literature,
    USCL

Church
Church and Synagogue Library Association,
    CSLA
Church Literature Association, CLA
Commission on Archives and History of the
    United Methodist Church, CAHUMC
International Inter-Church Film Center,
    INTERFILM
Lutheran Church Library Association,
    LCLA

Ciencias
Academia Nacional de Ciencias, ANC
Sistema Interamericano de Informacion para
    las Ciencias Agricolas, AGRINTER

Ciencias Sociales
Centro de Investigaciones en Ciencias
    Sociales, CISOR

Cientificas
Servicio de Información sobre Traducciones
    Cientificas en Español, SITCE

Cincinnati
Greater Cincinnati Library Consortium,
    GCLC

Cinema
Association Cattolica Esercenti Cinema,
    ACEC
Association des Exploitants de Cinéma et
    des Distributeurs de Films du
    Grand-Duché de Luxembourg, AECDF
Associazione Nazionale Esercenti Cinema,
    ANEC
Confédération Internationale des Industries
    Techniques du Cinéma (International
    Confederation of the Cinema Industry),
    CIITC
Fédération Internationale des Industries du
    Cinéma de Film Étroit, FIDIC
Union de la Critique du Cinéma, UUC

Cinemas
Kommunale Kinematografers Landsforbund
    (National Association of Municipal
    Cinemas in Norway), KKL

Cinematografia
Associazione Tecnica Italiana per la
    Cinematografia, ATIC

Cinematografiche
Associazione Nazionale Industrie
    Cinematografiche ed Affini, ANICA

Cinematograph
Association of Cinematograph, Television
    and Allied Technicians, ACTT
Cinematograph Exhibitors Association of
    Great Britain and Ireland, CEA

Cinematographers
American Society of Cinematographers,
    ASC

Cinematographía
Instituto Latinoamericano de
    Cinematographía Educativa, ILCE

Cinematographic
Cinematographic Films Council, CFC
Fédération Internationale de la Presse
    Cinématographique (International
    Federation of the Cinematographic
    Press), FIPRESCI

Cinématographique
Association Cinématographique Suisse
    Romande, ACSR
Association Professionnelle de la Presse
    Cinématographique Belge, APPCB

Cinématographiques
Union der Schweizerischen
    Lichtspieltheater-Verbänd/Union des
    Associations Cinématographiques
    Suisses, USLV/UACS

Circolari Ministero
Circolari Ministero Beni Culturali e
    Ambientali, CIRBCA

Circuit
Asynchronous Circuit Design Language,
    ACDL
Circuit Analysis, CIRCAL
Conversational Circuit Analysis Program,
    CONCAP
Electric Circuit Analysis Program, ECAP
Integrated Circuit, IC
Simplex Circuit, SPX
Southern California Film Circuit, SCFC

Circuits
Large-Scale Integrated Circuits, LSIC
Medium Scale Integrated Circuits, MSI

Circulation
Booth Library On-Line Circulation, BLOC
Circulation Input Recording, CIRC
Circulation Module, CIRC

Circulation Services
LAMA Circulation Services Section,
    LAMA/CSS

Circulations
Audit Bureau of Circulations, ABC
International Federation of Audit Bureaus of
    Circulations, IFABC

Citation
Arts and Humanities Citation Index, A&HCI
Automatic Subject Citation Alert, ASCA
Basic Bibliographic Citation, BBC
Journal Citation Reports, JCR
Science Citation Index, SCI
Science Citation Index Search,
    SCISEARCH
Social Science Citation Index, SSCI

Cities
European Federation of Conference Cities,
    EFCC

Citizens
Citizens for Decency through Law, CDL

City
City Air Defense Evaluation Tool, CADET
City University of New York, CUNY

City Libraries
International Association of Metropolitan
    City Libraries, INTAMEL

City University
City University Mutual Benefit Instructional
    Network, CUMBIN
Library Association of the City University of
    New York, LACUNY

Civil
American Society of Civil Engineers, ASCE
Civil Aeronautics Board, CAB
Civil Engineering Problems, CEPS
*Dictionary of Civil Engineering
    Abbreviations, Signs and Symbols*,
    DCEA
Institution of Civil Engineers, ICE
International Civil Aviation Organization,
    ICAO

Civil War
Civil War Press Corps, CWPC

Civile
Giurisprudenza Civile, CIVILE

Claiming
Automatic Claiming and Canceling, ACC

Classification
ASIS Special Interest Group on
    Classification Research, ASIS/SIG/CR
Alpha-Numerical System for Classification
    of Recordings, ANSCR
Analytico-Synthetic Classification of
    Medicine, ASCOM
Automatic Classification, AUTOCLASS
Automatic List Classification and Profile
    Production, ALCAPP
Bibliotechno-Bibliograficheskaya
    Klassificatsiya (Library Bibliographical
    Classification), BBK

Bliss Classification, BC
Bliss Classification Association, BCA
CLA Cataloging and Classification
    Roundtable, CLA/CCRT
CNLIA Joint Committee on Cataloging and
    Classification Codes, CNLIA/JCCC
Canadian Classification Research
    Group/Groupe Canadien pour la
    Recherche en Classification, CCRG
Classification Analytico-Synthetica Cubana
    de Medicas, CASCUM
Colon Classification, CC
Decimal Classification, DC
Decimal Classification Editorial Policy
    Committee, DCEPC
Dewey Decimal Classification, DDC
FID Committee on Classification Research,
    FID/CR
Hierarchical Classification, HICLASS
International Standard Industrial
    Classification, ISIC
Library of Congress Classification, LCC
Patent Office Classification System, POCS
RTSD Cataloging and Classification Section,
    RTSD/CCS
Superintendent of Documents Classification,
    SDC
Tentative Classification of Documents, TCD
Time-Shared Routines for Analysis,
    Classification, and Evaluation, TRACE
Universal Classification System, UCS
Universal Decimal Classification, UDC
Vesesojuznii Naučno-Issle-Dovatel'skii
    Institut Techniceskoi Informaccii,
    Klassifikaccii i Kodirovaniia (All-Union
    Scientific Research Institute for
    Technical Information, Classification
    and Codification of USSR), VNIIKI

Classified
Classified Entries in Lateral Transposition,
    CELT
Classified Library Employees of Washington
    State, CLEWS
*Classified Scientific and Technical
    Aerospace Reports*, C-STAR

Classroom
Classroom Interactive Computer, CLASSIC

Clearance Center
Copyright Clearance Center, CCC

Clearing House
Commerce Clearing House, Inc, CCH
Overseas Booksellers Clearing House,
    OBCH

Clearinghouse
Clearinghouse and Laboratory for Census
    Data, CLCD

Clearinghouse (cont.)

Clearinghouse Announcements in Science and Technology, CAST
Clearinghouse for Federal Scientific and Technical Information, CFSTI
Clearinghouse for Options in Children's Education, CHOICE
ERIC Clearinghouse for Science, Mathematics and Environmental Education, ERIC/SE
ERIC Clearinghouse for Social Studies/Social Science Education, ERIC/SO
ERIC Clearinghouse on Adult, Career, and Vocational Education, ERIC/CE
ERIC Clearinghouse on Counseling and Personnel Services, ERIC/CG
ERIC Clearinghouse on Educational Management, ERIC/EA
ERIC Clearinghouse on Elementary and Early Childhood Education, ERIC/PS
ERIC Clearinghouse on Handicapped and Gifted Children, ERIC/EC
ERIC Clearinghouse on Higher Education, ERIC/HE
ERIC Clearinghouse on Information Resources, ERIC/IR
ERIC Clearinghouse on Junior Colleges, ERIC/JC
ERIC Clearinghouse on Languages and Linguistics, ERIC/FL
ERIC Clearinghouse on Reading and Communication Skills, ERIC/CS
ERIC Clearinghouse on Rural Education and Small Schools, ERIC/RC
ERIC Clearinghouse on Teacher Education, ERIC/SP
ERIC Clearinghouse on Tests, Measurement, and Evaluation, ERIC/TM
ERIC Clearinghouse on Urban Education, ERIC/UD
Language Information Network and Clearinghouse System, LINCS
National Clearinghouse for Alcohol Information, NCALI
National Clearinghouse for Mental Health Information, NCMHI
New York Library Instruction Clearinghouse, NYLIC

Cleveland

Cleveland Area Interloan Network, CAIN
Cleveland Area Metropolitan Library System, CAMLS
Cleveland Health Sciences Library, CHSL
Library Council of Greater Cleveland, LCGC

Client

Client-Oriented Data Acquisition Program, CODAP

Climatic Center

National Climatic Center, NCC

Clinical

American Association of Clinical Chemists, AACC
Clinical Protocol, CLINPROT
Current Contents/Clinical Practice. (Journal), CC/CP

Clio Press

American Bibliographical Center–Clio Press, ABC–Clio

Clock

Clock Pulsed Control, CPC

Closed-Circuit

Closed-Circuit Television, CCTV

Club

Amateur Computer Club, ACC
Club der Luftfahrtpublizisten, CLP
Overseas Press Club of America, Inc, OPC

Cluster

Chicago Cluster of Theological Schools, CCTS

Coal

Bituminous Coal Research, Inc, BCR

Coalition

Coalition in the Use of Learning Skills, CULS

Cocoa

Cocoa Research Institute, CRIG

Code

Automated Combustor Design Code, AUTOCOM
Automatic Code Translator, ACT
Automatic Personal Identification Code, AUTOPIC
Beginners All-purpose Symbolic Instruction Code, BASIC
Call-Directing Code, CDC
Code for Magnetic Characters, CMC
Extended Binary Coded Decimal Interchange Code, EBCDIC
FORTRAN Automatic Code Evaluation System, FACES
Functional Code, FC
General Purpose Scientific Document Image Code, GPSDIC
Information Processing Code, IPC
Microfilm Retrieval Access Code, MIRACODE

Nonprint Code, NP
Pulse Code Modulation, PCM
Standard Point Location Code, SPLC
Station Selection Code, SSC
UNIVAC Code, UNICODE
Uniform Product Code Council, UPCC
Universal Product Code, UPC
X Automatic Translation Code, XACT

Coded
Binary Coded Decimal, BCD
Binary Coded Octal, BCO

Coder
Formula Coder, FORC

Codes
CNLIA Joint Committee on Cataloging and
    Classification Codes, CNLIA/JCCC
Index of Codes for Research Drugs, ICRD
Rapid Access to Literature via
    Fragmentation Codes, RALF

Codification
Vesesojuznii Naučno-Issle-Dovatel'skii
    Institut Techniceskoi Informaccii,
    Klassifikaccii i Kodirovaniia (All-Union
    Scientific Research Institute for
    Technical Information, Classification
    and Codification of USSR), VNIIKI

Coding
Floating-decimal Abstract Coding System,
    FACS
Project for the Advancement of Coding
    Techniques, PACT I
Relative Coding, RELCODE

Cognition
Machine-Aided Cognition, MAC
Memory-Assisted Cognition, MAC

Coherent
Coherent Light Detection and Ranging,
    COLIDAR

Coke
British Coke Research Association, BCRA

Colección
Colección de Consulta, CC

Collator
Continuous Multiple Access Collator,
    COMAC

Collection
Collection and Evaluation of Materials on
    Black Americans, CEMBA
Collection, Inquiry, Reporting &
    Communication, CIRC
Dance Collection Automated Book Catalog,
    DCABC

Environmental Data Collection and
    Processing Facility, EDCPF
Report Collection Index, RECODEX

Collections
Association for Recorded Sound Collections,
    ARSC
*National Union Catalog of Manuscript
    Collections*, NUCMC

College
American Association of Agricultural
    College Editors, AAACE
American College of Surgeons, ACS
American College Personnel Association,
    ACPA
Association of College and Research
    Libraries, ACRL
CLA College and University Library
    Section, CLA/CULS
CLA College, University and Seminary
    Libraries Section, CLA/CUSLS
Canadian Association of College and
    University Libraries/Association
    Canadienne des Bibliothèques de
    Collège et d'Université,
    CACUL/ACBCU
Center for Research in College Instruction of
    Science and Mathematics, CRICISAM
College and Research Libraries. (Journal),
    C&RL
College Applicant Status Report, CASTOR
College Art Association of America, CAAA
College-Level Examination Program, CLEP
College Press Service, CPS
College Retirement Equities Fund, CREF
Inter-American Defense College, IADC
Makerere University College, MUC
Maryland Independent College and
    University Association, Inc, MICUA
New Hampshire College and University
    Council, NHCUC
Ohio College Library Center, Inc, OCLC
Ontario Association of College and
    University Libraries, OACUL
Royal College of Art, RCA
Royal College of Music, RCM
Royal College of Nursing and National
    Council of Nursing, RCN
Royal College of Obstetricians and
    Gynaecologists, RCOG
Royal College of Physicians of Edinburgh,
    RCPE
Royal College of Physicians of London, RCP
Royal College of Surgeons in Ireland, RCSI
Royal College of Surgeons of Edinburgh,
    RCSEd
Royal College of Surgeons of England,
    RCSEng
Royal College of Veterinary Surgeons,
    RCVS

College (cont.)

Southern College University Union, SCUU
Utah College Library Council, UCLC

College Librarians

Alberta Council of College Librarians,
ACCL

College Libraries

ACRL College Libraries Section,
ACRL/CLS
ACRL Community and Junior College
Libraries Section, ACRL/CJCLS
ACRL Junior College Libraries Section,
ACRL/JCLS
Books for College Libraries, BCL
College Libraries Activities Network in New
South Wales, CLANN
Community and Technical College Libraries,
CTCL

College Library

Area College Library Cooperative Program
of Central Pennsylvania, ACLCP
Community College Library Consortium,
CCLIC
Cooperative College Library Center, CCLC
Tri-State College Library Cooperative,
TCLC

Colleges

American Association of Colleges for
Teacher Education, AACTE
American Association of Community and
Junior Colleges, AACJC
American Association of Junior Colleges,
AAJC
Arkansas Foundation of Associated
Colleges, AFAC
Associated Christian Colleges of Oregon,
ACCO
Associated Colleges of Central Kansas,
ACCK
Associated Colleges of the Midwest, ACM
Associated Colleges of the Saint Lawrence
Valley, ACSLV
Associated Mid-Florida Colleges, AMFC
Association of American Colleges, AAC
Association of Canadian Medical
Colleges/Association des Facultés de
Médecine du Canada, ACMC/AFMC
Association of State Colleges and
Universities Forestry Research
Organizations, ASCUFRO
Association of Universities and Colleges of
Canada/Association des Universités et
Collèges du Canada, AUCC
Colleges of Mid-America, CMA
Cooperative Raleigh Colleges, CRC

ERIC Clearinghouse on Junior Colleges,
ERIC/JC
Lehigh Valley Association of Independent
Colleges, LVAIC
Library Statistics of Colleges and
Universities, LSCU
Mid-Missouri Associated Colleges, MMAC
Union of Independent Colleges of Art, UICA

Collegiate

American Association of Collegiate
Registrars and Admissions Officers,
AACRAO
Associated Collegiate Press, ACP
Collegiate Consortium of Western Indiana,
CCWI

Colloquium

Annual National Information Retrieval
Colloquium, ANIRC

Colombian

Asociación Colombiana de Bibliotecarios
(Colombian Library Association),
ASCOLBI
Colegio Colombiano de Bibliotecarios
(Colombian Association of Librarians),
CCB
Colombian Association for the Advancement
of Science, ACAC

Colombian Librarians

Colegio de Bibliotecarios Colombianos
(Association of Colombian Librarians),
CBC

Colombiano

Sistema Colombiano de Información
Cientifica y Technica, SICOLDIC

Colon

Colon Classification, CC

Colorado

Colorado Academic Libraries Book
Processing Center, CALBPC
Colorado Committee for Environmental
Information, CCEI
Colorado Library Association, CLA

Colorists

American Association of Textile Chemists
and Colorists, AATCC

Columbia

Columbia Broadcasting System, Inc, CBS

Columbus

Columbus Area Library and Information
Council of Ohio, CALICO
Columbus Museum of Arts and Crafts,
CMAC

Combat
Combat Logistics Network, COMLOGNET

Combination
Selective Letters in Combination, SLIC

Combined
Combined Analog–Digital Systems
Simulator, CADSS

Combined File
Combined File Search, CFS
Combined File Search System, CFSS

Combustor
Automated Combustor Design Code,
AUTOCOM

Comics
Comics Magazine Association of America,
Inc, CMAA

Comité
Comité de Coordination des Bibliothèques
Gouvernement du Québec, COBIGO

Command
Audit Command Language, ACL
Command Acknowledge, CAK
Command Processor, CP
Computer-Integrated Command and Attack
Systems, CICAS
Real-Time Command, RTC
Retrieval Command Language, RECOL
United States Army Computer Systems
Support and Evaluation Command,
USACSSEC

Commerce
Commerce Clearing House, Inc, CCH
National Advisory Council for Education for
Industry and Commerce, NACEIC
Swindon Area Association of Libraries for
Industry and Commerce, SAALIC
Tyneside Association of Libraries for
Industry and Commerce, TALIC
Vereinigung der Buchantiquare und
Kupferstichhändler in der
Schweiz/Syndicat de la Libraire
Ancienne et du Commerce de l'Estampe
en Suisse, VEBUKU/SLACES

Commerce Exterieur
Office Belge du Commerce Exterieur, OBCE

Commercial
Commercial Chemical Development
Association, CCDA
Commercial Development Association, CDA
Commercial Reference Room, CRR
Cooperative Industrial and Commercial
Reference and Information Service,
CICRIS

Hampshire Technical Research Industrial
and Commercial Service, HATRICS

Commercial Service
Bradford Scientific, Technical and
Commercial Service, BRASTACS

Commission
Alberta Alcoholism and Drug Abuse
Commission, AADAC
Atomic Energy Commission, AEC
Australian Atomic Energy Commission,
AAEC
Bay Area Transportation Study Commission,
BATSC
Comisión Nacional de Investigación
Científica y Technológica (National
Commission on Scientific and
Technological Research), CONICYT
Comissão Brasileira de Documentação
Agricola (Brazilian Commission for
Agricultural Documentation), CBDA
Commissariat à L'Energie Atomique
(Atomic Energy Commission), CEA
Commission Consultative des Études
Postales (Consultative Commission for
the Study of Postal Services), CCEP
Commission Internationale des Industries
Agricoles et Alimentaires, CIIA
Commission on Archives and History of the
United Methodist Church, CAHUMC
Commission on Standards and Accreditation
of Services for the Blind, COMSTAC
Consumer Product Safety Commission,
CPSC
Economic and Social Commission for Asia
and the Pacific, ESCAP
Economic Commission for Asia and the Far
East, ECAFE
Equal Employment Opportunity
Commission, EEOC
Federación Internacional de
Documentación/Comisión
Latinoamericana (International
Federation for Documentation/Latin
American Commission), FID/CLA
Federal Communications Commission, FCC
Federal Trade Commission, FTC
Intergovernmental Commission on
Oceanography, ICO
Intergovernmental Oceanographic
Commission, IOC
International Commission for Agricultural
and Food Industries, ICAI
International Electrotechnical Commission,
IEC
National Commission on Libraries and
Information Science, NCLIS
National Commission on New Technological
Uses of Copyrighted Works, CONTU

Commission (cont.)

Radio Technical Commission for
  Aeronautics, RTCA
Royal Commission on Historical
  Manuscripts, HMC
Scientific Manpower Commission, SMC
Technical and Further Education
  Commission, TAFEC
United States Atomic Energy Commission,
  USAEC
Western Interstate Commission for Higher
  Education, WICHE

Committee
American National Standards
  Institute–Standards Committee Z39,
  ANSI-Z39
Annual Medical Library Association
  Conference Committee, AMLAC
Australian National Committee on
  Computation and Automatic Control,
  ANCCAC
Canadian Committee on MARC/Comité
  Canadien du MARC, CCM
Comité Consultatif International des
  Radiocommunications (International
  Radio Consultative Committee), CCIR
Commission Mixte Internationale pour la
  Protection des Lignes de
  Télécommunications et des
  Canolisations Souterraines (Joint
  International Committee for the
  Protection of Telecommunications Lines
  and Underground Ducts), CMI
Committee for Artistic and Intellectual
  Freedom in Iran, CAIFI
Committee for Environmental Information,
  CEI
Committee for Information and
  Documentation on Science and
  Technology, CIDST
Committee for International Cooperation in
  Information Retrieval among Examining
  Patent Officers, CICIREPATO
Committee for the Visual Arts, CVA
Committee for Writing and Reading Aids for
  the Paralysed, WRAP
Committee of National Institutes of Patent
  Agents, CNIPA
Committee of Small Magazine Editors and
  Publishers, COSMEP
Committee on Accreditation, COA
Committee on American Library Resources
  on South Asia, CALROSA
Committee on American Library Resources
  on Southeast Asia, CALROSEA
Committee on Archives and Documents of
  Southeast Asia, CARDOSEA
Committee on Computer Science in
  Electrical Engineering, COSINE

Committee on Data for Science and
  Technology, CODATA
Committee on East Asian Libraries of the
  Association for Asian Studies, CEAL
Committee on Institutional Cooperation,
  CIC
Committee on International Relations, CIR
Committee on International Scientific and
  Technical Information Programs,
  CISTIP
Committee on Intersociety Cooperation, CIC
Committee on Inter-Society Cooperation,
  CISCO
Committee on Library Cooperation, CLIC
Committee on Organization, COO
Committee on Physics and Society,
  COMPAS
Committee on Planning, COP
Committee on Policy Implementation, COPI
Committee on Program Evaluation and
  Support, COPES
Committee on Public Engineering Policy,
  COPEP
Committee on Research Materials on
  Southeast Asia, CORMOSEA
Committee on Science and Public Policy,
  COSPUP
Committee on Science and Technology in
  Developing Countries, COSTED
Committee on Scientific and Technical
  Information, COSATI
Committee on Scientific Information, COSI
Committee on Space Research, COSPAR
Committee on Storage, Automatic
  Processing and Retrieval of Geological
  Data, COGEODATA
Committee on the Application of Computers
  in the Construction Industry, CAC
Committee on Vacuum Techniques, CVT
Consultative Committee on International
  Telegraph and Telephone (Comité
  Consultatif International Telegraphie et
  Telephonie), CCITT
Coordinating Committee for Slavic–East
  European Library Services,
  COCOSEER
European Committee for Cooperation with
  Latin America, ECCLA
International Committee for Cooperation of
  Journalists, ICCJ
International Committee for Social Sciences
  Documentation, ICSSD
International Press Telecommunications
  Committee, IPTC
International Relations Committee, IRC
Intersociety Committee on Pathology
  Information, ICPI
Japanese Industrial Standards Committee,
  JISC
Joint Industrial Committee for National
  Readership Surveys, JICNARS

Joint Industry Committee for Television
   Advertising Research, JICTAR
Liaison of Provincial Associations
   Committee, LOPAC
National Committee for Audiovisual Aids in
   Education, NCAVAE
National Committee of Documentation,
   CND
National Libraries Committee, NLC
Ontario Committee of Deans and Directors
   of Library Schools, OCDDLS
Permanent Committee on Geographical
   Names (for British Official Use), PCGN
Scientific and Technological Information
   Services Enquiry Committee, STISEC
Staff Committee on Mediation, Arbitration
   and Inquiry, SCMAI
Standing Committee for the Study of
   Principles of Standardization, STACO
Standing Committee on Library Education,
   SCOLE
Transportation Data Coordinating
   Committee, TDCC
Tripartite Committee, TC
United States Committee for the World
   Health Organization, USC-WHO
US National Committee for the International
   Federation for Documentation,
   USNCFID
University Grants Committee, UGC

Commodity
Industrial Commodity Production Statistics,
   ICPDATA

Common
Burroughs Common Language, BCL
Common Data Base, CDB

Commonwealth
Association of Commonwealth Universities,
   ACU
British Commonwealth Scientific Office,
   BCSO
Commonwealth Agricultural Bureaux, CAB
Commonwealth Information Centre, CIC
Commonwealth Library Association,
   COMLA
Commonwealth Press Union, CPU
Commonwealth Scientific and Industrial
   Research Organization, CSIRO
Commonwealth Telecommunications Board,
   CTB
Commonwealth Writers of Britain, CWB
Foreign and Commonwealth Office, FAO

Communauté
Communauté Européenne du Carbon et de
   l'Acier, CECA

Communicación
Instituto Latinoamericano de la
   Communicación Educativa, ILCE

Communication
American Business Communication
   Association, ABCA
Association of Communication Workers,
   ACW
Automated Law Enforcement
   Communication System, ALECS
Center for Communication and Information
   Research, CCIR
Center for Documentation and
   Communication Research, CDCR
Collection, Inquiry, Reporting &
   Communication, CIRC
(Committee on) Scientific and Technical
   Communication, SATCOM
Communication and Data Processing
   Operation, CADPO
Communication and Data Processing
   Operation System, CADPOS
Communication Multiplexor, CM
Council of Communication Societies, CCS
Customer Bank Communication Terminal,
   CBCT
Department of Mass Communication, MC
ERIC Clearinghouse on Reading and
   Communication Skills, ERIC/CS
Institute for Graphic Communication, Inc,
   IGC
Institute for the Advancement of Medical
   Communication, IAMC
International Association for Mass
   Communication Research, IAMCR
International Communication Agency, ICA
International Communication Association,
   ICA
International Conference on Computer
   Communication, ICCC
National Center for Educational
   Communication, NCEC
(National) Scientific Communication and
   Technology Transfer, SCATT
National Society for the Study of
   Communication, NSSC
Pan-Pacific Education and Communication
   Experiments by Satellite, PEACESAT
SUNY Biomedical Communication
   Network, SUNY-BCN
Society for Technical Communication, STC
System for Interlibrary Communication,
   SILC

Communications
ACM Special Interest Group on Data
   Communications, ACM/SIGCOMM
American Communications Association,
   ACA
Armed Forces Communications and
   Electronics Association, AFCEA
Association for Educational
   Communications and Technology,
   AECT

Communications (cont.)

Association of Federal Communications
Consulting Engineers, AFCCE
Battle Area Surveillance and Integrated
Communications, BASIC
Bibliographic Exchange and
Communications Network, BEACON
Biological Science Communications Project,
BSCP
Communications Access Manager, CAM
Communications Input/Output Control
System, CIOCS
Communications Line Terminal, CLT
*Communications of the Association for
Computing Machinery*, CACM
Communications Satellite Corporation,
COMSAT
Conference on Interlibrary Communications
and Information Networks, CICIN
Data Communications, DATACOM
Data Communications Control Unit, DCCU
Defense Communications Agency, DCA
Digital Data Communications Message
Protocol, DDCMP
Drug Abuse Communications Network,
DRACON
Facsimile Communications System, FCS
Federal Communications Commission, FCC
Government Communications Headquarters
(Great Britain), GCHQ
Health Sciences Communications
Association, HeSCA
ISAD Video and Cable Communications
Section, ISAD/VCCS
International Communications Association,
ICA
International Institute of Communications,
IIC
Interuniversity Communications Council,
EDUCOM
*Journal of International Research
Communications*, JIRC
LITA Video and Cable Communications
Section, LITA/VCCS
National Communications Association, NCA
Office of Computer and Communications
Systems, OCCS
Ontario Educational Communications
Authority, OECA
Radio Teletypewriter Communications,
RTTY
Real-Time Communications, REALCOM
Women's Educational Equity
Communications Network, WEECN

Communicator

Binary Synchronous Communicator
Adapter, BSCA

Communicators

Agricultural Communicators in Education,
ACE

Community

ACRL Community and Junior College
Libraries Section, ACRL/CJCLS
ASIS Special Interest Group on Community
Information Services, ASIS/SIG/CIS
Agricultural Research Projects in the
European Community, AGREP
American Association of Community and
Junior Colleges, AACJC
Combined and Integrated Resources for
Community Learning Experiment,
CIRCLE
Community and Technical College Libraries,
CTCL
Community Antenna Television, CATV
Community Automatic Exchange, CAX
Community College Library Consortium,
CCLIC
Community Health Information Network,
CHIN
Community Input/Output Control System,
CIOS
Community Media Library Program,
COMLIP
Computerized Information Network for
Community Health, CINCH
European Atomic Energy Community,
EURATOM
European Economic Community, EEC
International Community of Booksellers
Association, ICBA
Research Community of Slovenia, RSS

Community College

Dallas County Community College District,
DCCCD

Community Colleges

Learning Resources Association of
California Community Colleges,
LRACCC

Community Libraries

CLA Parish and Community Libraries
Section, CLA/PCLS

Compact

Compact Automatic Retrieval Display,
CARD

Compagnie

Compagnie Internationale pour
l'Informatique, CII

Companies

Association of Independent Software
Companies, AISC

Company
American Telephone and Telegraph
Company, AT&T
Bay Electric Company, BEC
Boeing Airplane Company Algebraic
Interpretive Computing System,
BACAIC
Canadian General Electric Company, Ltd,
CGE
Canadian International Paper Company, CIP
Chemical Rubber Company, CRC
Company and Literature Information Center,
CLIC
Company of Military Historians, CMH
General Electric Company, GE
Gulf Publishing Company, GPC
Minnesota Mining and Manufacturing
Company, 3M
National Broadcasting Company, Inc, NBC
National Cash Register Company, NCR
Northern Engineering Services Company,
Ltd, NESCL
US-Asiatic Company, Ltd, USACO
Virginia National Library Week Company,
VNLW

Comparative
Comparative Animal Research Laboratory,
CARL
Comparative Systems Laboratory, CSL
Institute for the Comparative Study of
History, Philosophy and the Sciences,
Ltd, ICS
International Comparative Literature
Association, ICLA
International Comparative Political Parties
Project, ICPP

Compass
Compass Test Language, CTL

Compatible
Compatible Duplex System, CDS
Compatible Operating System, COS

Compensation
European Executive Compensation Survey,
EECS
*Latin American Executive Compensation
Survey*, LAECS

Compilation
Programme Appliqué à la Sélection et à la
Compilation Automatique de la
Littérature, PASCAL

Compiler
Algebraic Compiler, ALCOM
Algebraic Compiler and Translator I, ACT-I
Algebraic Compiler and Translator III,
ACT-III
Algebraic Translator and Compiler, ALTAC

Compiler and Generalized Translator,
COGENT
Compiler Language for Information
Processing, CLIP
Compiler Los Alamos Scientific
Laboratories, COLASL
FORTRAN I Compiler, FORTOCOM
Factual Compiler, FACT
Formula Manipulation Compiler, FORMAC
General Compiler, GECOM
Macroinstruction Compiler Assembler,
MICA
Naval Electronics Laboratory International
Algebraic Compiler, NELIAC
Program Compiler, PROCOMP
SHARE Compiler, Assembler and
Translator, SCAT
Text Reckoner and Compiler, TRAC
Transac Assembler Compiler, TAC
Universal Compiler, UNICOMP

Compiler-Translator
Fully Automatic Compiler-Translator, FACT

Compiling
Expansion Symbolic Compiling Assembly
Program for Engineering, ESCAPE
Fully Automatic Compiling Technique,
FACT

Completely
Completely Automatic Operational System,
CAOS

Complex
Complex Utility Routines, CUR
Real-time Computer Complex, RCC

Component
Radio and Electric Component
Manufacturers Federation, RECMF

Components
Built-in-Place Components, BIPCO
Electronic Components Data Bank, ECDB
Radio Components Standardization
Committee, RCSC

Composers
American Composers Alliance, ACA
American Guild of Authors and Composers,
AGAC
American Society of Composers, Authors,
and Publishers, ASCAP
Confédération Internationale des Sociétés
d'Auteurs et Compositeurs
(International Confederation of
Societies of Authors and Composers),
CISAC

Composing
Graphic Arts Composing Equipment,
GRACE

Composing (cont.)

Machine-Aided Composing and Editing,
 MACE

Compositeurs
Conseil International des Compositeurs, CIC

Composition Automatic
Composition Automatic de Repertoires
 Analytiques, CARA

Comprehensive
Comprehensive Achievement Monitoring,
 CAM
Comprehensive Display System, CDS
Comprehensive Dissertation Index, CDI
Comprehensive Language for Elegant
 Operating System and Translator
 Design, CLEOPATRA
Comprehensive Occupational Data Analysis
 Program, CODAP
Comprehensive University of Dayton
 On-Line Information Services, CUDOS
General Comprehensive Operating
 Supervisor, GECOS

Computability Theory
ACM Special Interest Group on Automata
 and Computability Theory,
 ACM/SIGACT

Computation
Australian National Committee on
 Computation and Automatic Control,
 ANCCAC
Cardboard Illustrated Aid to Computation,
 CARDIAC
Computation and Data Flow Integrated
 Subsystems, CADFISS
MIDAC Automatic General Integrated
 Computation, MAGIC
Radioactivity Detection Indication and
 Computation, RADIAC

Computation Center
Data and Computation Center, DACC
Intergovernmental Bureau for
 Informatics/International Computation
 Center, IBI/ICC
Triangle Universities Computation Center,
 TUCC

Computational
Association for Computational Linguistics,
 ACL
Association for Machine Translation and
 Computational Linguistics, AMTCL

Computer
ACM Special Interest Group on Architecture
 of Computer Systems, ACM/SIGARCH

ACM Special Interest Group on Computer
 Graphics, ACM/SIGGRAPH
ACM Special Interest Group on Computer
 Personnel Research, ACM/SIGCPR
ACM Special Interest Group on Computer
 Uses in Education, ACM/SIGCUE
Academic Computer Group, ACCOMP
Accountants Computer Users Technical
 Exchange, ACUTE
Advanced Science Computer, ASC
Amateur Computer Club, ACC
Association Internationale pour le Calcul
 Analogique (International Association
 for Mathematics and Computer
 Simulation), AICA
Association of Computer Programmers and
 Analysts, ACPA
Association of Computer Time-Sharing
 Users (USA), ACTSU
Association of Computer User Groups,
 ACUG
Associative Processor Computer System,
 APCS
Australian Computer Society, Inc, ACS
Automated Catalog of Computer Equipment
 and Software Systems, ACCESS
Basic Computer Programming Language,
 BCPL
Binary Automatic Computer, BINAC
Biomedical Computer Programs, BMD
Boeing Electronic Analog Computer, BEAC
British Computer Association for the Blind,
 BCAB
British Computer Society, BCS
British Computer Society ALGOL
 Association, BCSAA
British Overseas Airways Digital
 Information Computer for Electronic
 Automation, BOADICEA
Business Computer Users Association,
 BCUA
Classroom Interactive Computer, CLASSIC
Computer Accounting System, CAS
Computer Analysis of Networks with Design
 Orientation, CANDO
Computer Analysis of Thermo-Chemical
 Data Tables, CATCH
Computer and Business Equipment
 Manufacturers Association, CBEMA
Computer and Control Abstracts, CCA
Computer and Information Sciences, COINS
Computer Corporation of America, CCA
Computer Education Group, CEG
Computer-Extended Instruction, CEI
Computer Handling of Reactor
 Data—Safety, CHORD—S
Computer Hardware Description Language,
 CHDL
Computer Input Microfilm, CIM

Computer-Integrated Command and Attack Systems, CICAS

Computer-Integrated Manufacturing System, CIMS

Computer Interface Unit, CIU

Computer Language of Massachusetts Institute of Technology, COMIT

Computer Law Association, CLA

Computer Layout Installation Planner, CLIP

Computer Learning Under Evaluation, CLUE

Computer Library Service, Inc, CLIS

Computer Logic Graphics, CLOG

Computer-Managed Instructions, CMI

Computer Micrographics and Technology, COMTEC

Computer On-Line Real-Time Applications Language, CORAL

Computer Optimization Package, COP

Computer Output Microfilm, COM

Computer Output Microfilm Package, COMPAC

Computer Output Microfilmer, COM

Computer Output Microfilming, COM

Computer Output Microforms Program and Concept Study, COMPACS

Computer People for Peace, CPP

Computer Program for Automatic Control, COMPAC

Computer Programs in Science and Technology (Index), CPST

Computer Science, CS

Computer Search Center, CSC

Computer Simulation, CS

Computer Software, CS

Computer Software and Management Information Center, COSMIC

Computer Users Replacement Equipment, CURE

Datascope Computer Output Microfilmer, DACOM

Dictionary of Computer and Control Systems Abbreviations, Signs and Symbols, DCCSA

Digital Equipment Computer Users Society, DECUS

Display-Oriented Computer Usage System, DOCUS

Division of Computer Research and Technology, DCRT

Electronic Discrete Sequential Automatic Computer, EDSAC

Electronic Discrete Variable Automatic Computer, EDVAC

European Computer Manufacturers Association, ECMA

Fall Joint Computer Conference, FJCC

Federal Computer Performance Evaluation and Simulation Center, FEDSIM

Film Input to Digital Automatic Computer, FIDAC

General Electric Computer Analysis Program, GECAP

General Operator Computer Interaction, GOCI

General Purpose Computer, GPC

Ground-Based Computer, GBC

Honeywell Computer Users Association, HCUA

Interactive Computer Presentation Panel, ICPP

International Association for Mathematics and Computer Simulation, IMACS

International Conference on Computer Communication, ICCC

JICST Electronic Information Processing Automatic Computer, JEIPAC

Laboratory Instrument Computer, LINC

Library Computer Equipment Review. (Journal), LCER

Local Authorities Management Services and Computer Committee, LAMSAC

Magnetic Logic Computer, MAGLOC

Memory Test Computer, MTC

Military Computer Users Group, MCUG

Mobile Digital Computer, MOBIDIC

Multiaction Computer, MAC

Multiple Access Computer, MAC

National Association of Users of Computer Applications to Learning, NAUCA

Navigation Data Assimilation Computer, NAVDAC

Non-Interactive Computer Applications, NICA

Office of Computer and Communications Systems, OCCS

Personal Analog Computer, PAC

Random Access Computer Equipment, RACE

Real-time Computer Complex, RCC

Reeves Electronic Analog Computer, REAC

Research on Computer Applications in the Printing and Publishing Industries, ROCAPPI

Simulated Linguistic Computer, SLC

Society for Computer Simulation, SCS

Spring Joint Computer Conference, SJCC

Standards Electronic Automatic Computer, SEAC

United States Army Computer Systems Support and Evaluation Command, USACSSEC

Universal Automatic Computer, UNIVAC

Vector Analogue Computer, VAC

Computer Builders

Association Française des Amateurs Constructeurs l'Ordinateurs (French Association of Amateur Computer Builders), AFACO

Computer Center
Southwestern Ohio Regional Computer
    Center, SWORCC

Computer Information
*Computer Information Library Patent
    Abstracts.* (Journal), C/I/L
Office of Computer Information, OCI

Computer Language
Computer-Oriented Language, COL
Computer-Sensitive Language, CSL
Universal Computer-Oriented Language,
    UNCOL

Computer Science
ACM Special Interest Group on Computer
    Science Education, ACM/SIGCSE
Automated Computer Science Education
    System, ACSES
Committee on Computer Science in
    Electrical Engineering, COSINE
Computer Science and Engineering Board,
    CSEB

Computer Sciences
Computer Sciences Corporation, CSC
IEEE Retrieval from the Literature on
    Electronics and Computer Sciences,
    IEEE REFLECS
Institute for Computer Sciences and
    Technology, ICST

Computer Service
Computer Service Bureaux Association,
    COBSA

Computer Services
Computer Services and Bureaux
    Association, COSBA

Computer Systems
ACM Special Interest Group on Computer
    Systems Installation Management,
    ACM/SIGCOSIM

Computer Users
Association of Burroughs Computer Users,
    ABCU

Computer-Aided
Computer-Aided Batch Scheduling, CABS
Computer-Aided Design, CAD
Computer-Aided Design Drafting, CADD
Computer-Aided Design Engineering, CADE
Computer-Aided Design Environment,
    COMRADE
Computer-Aided Design Evaluation, CADE
Computer-Aided Design Optical Character
    Recognition, CADOCR
Computer-Aided Design System, CADSYS
Computer-Aided Detection, CAD
Computer-Aided Diagnosis System, CADS

Computer-Aided Instruction, CAI
Computer-Aided Line Balancing, CALB
Computer-Aided Machine Loading, CAMEL
Computer-Aided Manufacturing
    International, CAM-I
Computer-Aided Patient Management,
    CAPM
Computer-Aided Perspective, CAPER
Computer-Aided Problem Solving, CAPS
Computer-Aided Processing and Terminal
    Access Information Network,
    CAPTAIN
Computer-Aided Project Planning System,
    CAPPS
Computer-Aided Project Study, CAPS
Computer-Aided Rationalized Building
    System, CARBS
Computer-Aided Recording of Distribution
    Systems, CARDS
Computer-Aided Stock Holdings, CASH
Computer-Aided Subject Index, CASIN

Computer-Assisted
ACM Special Interest Group on
    Computer-Assisted Instruction,
    ACM/SIGCAI
Computer-Assisted Cartography, CASC
Computer-Assisted Electrocardiography,
    CAE
Computer-Assisted Indexing and
    Categorizing, CAIC
Computer-Assisted Industrial Simulation,
    CAISM
Computer-Assisted Information Retrieval
    System, CAIRS
Computer-Assisted Instruction, CAI
Computer-Assisted Instruction, Inc, CAI
Computer-Assisted Instruction
    Management, CAIM
Computer-Assisted Instruction Regional
    Education Network, CAI
Computer-Assisted Interrogation, CAINT
Computer-Assisted Language Analysis
    System, CALAS
Computer-Assisted Learning, CAL
Computer-Assisted Library Mechanization,
    CALM
Computer-Assisted Logistics Simulation,
    CALOGSM
Computer-Assisted Maintenance Planning
    and Control System, CAMCOS
Computer-Assisted Management of
    Learning, CAMOL
Computer-Assisted Mathematics Program,
    CAMP
Computer-Assisted Movie Production,
    CAMP
Computer-Assisted Program Evaluation
    Review Technique Simulation,
    CAPERTSIM

Computer-Assisted Reliability Statistics,
   CARS
Computer-Assisted Renewal Education,
   CARE
Computer-Assisted Scanning Techniques,
   CAST
Institute for Computer-Assisted Information,
   ICAI

Computer-Augmented
Computer-Augmented Block System, CABS
Computer-Augmented Instruction, CAI

Computer-Based
Association for Development of
   Computer-based Instructional Systems,
   ADCIS
Computer-Based Educational Materials,
   CBEM
Computer-based Laboratory for Automated
   School Systems, CLASS

Computer-Controlled
Automatic Computer-Controlled Electronics
   Scanning System, ACCESS
Computer-Controlled Scanning Electron
   Microscope, CCSEM
Time-Shared Interactive
   Computer-Controlled Information
   Television, TICCIT

Computerization
Automation of Bibliography through
   Computerization, ABC

Computerized
ASIS Special Interest Group on
   Computerized Retrieval Services,
   ASIS/SIG/CRS
Catalog of Computerized Subject Searches,
   CAT
Computerized Access to Periodicals and
   Serials, CAPSUL
Computerized Annotated Bibliography
   System, CABS
Computerized Automatic Rating Technique,
   CART
Computerized Automatic Reporting Service,
   CARS
Computerized *Engineering Index*,
   COMPENDEX
Computerized Facilities Design, COFAD
Computerized Information Network for
   Community Health, CINCH
Computerized Logic-Oriented Design
   System, CLODS
A Computerized London Information
   Service, ACOMPLIS
Computerized Management Account, CMA
Computerized Modular Monitoring, CMM
Computerized Movement Planning and
   Status System, COMPASS

Computerized Preliminary Design System,
   CPDS
Computerized Problem-Oriented Medical
   Record, CPOMR
Computerized Production Control, CPC
Computerized Production Operation System
   Extension, COMPOSE
Computerized Relative Allocation of
   Facilities Technique, CRAFT
Computerized Statistics, COMPUSTAT
Council for Computerized Library
   Networks, CCLN

Computerized Information
*Directory of Computerized Information in
   Science and Technology*, DCIST

Computer-Linked Information
Computer-Linked Information for Container
   Shipping, CLICS

Computer-Operated
Motorola Automatic Sequential
   Computer-Operated Tester, MASCOT

Computers
ACM Special Interest Group on Computers
   and Society, ACM/SIGCAS
ACM Special Interest Group on Computers
   and the Physically Handicapped,
   ACM/SIGCAPH
Committee on the Application of Computers
   in the Construction Industry, CAC
Computers and the Humanities, CHUM
Computers in Education Division, COED
Design Augmented by Computers, DAC
Digital Computers Association, DCA
Film Optical Sensing Device for Input to
   Computers, FOSDIC
Professional Group on Electronic
   Computers, PGEC

Computing
ACM Special Interest Group on Biomedical
   Computing, ACM/SIGBIO
ACM Special Interest Group on Social and
   Behavioral Science Computing,
   ACM/SIGSOC
Association for Computing Machinery, Inc,
   ACM
Association Française de Calcul (French
   Computing Association), AFCAL
Association of Literary and Linguistic
   Computing, ALLC
Biomedical Computing Technology
   Information Center, BCTIC
Boeing Airplane Company Algebraic
   Interpretive Computing System,
   BACAIC
*Communications of the Association for
   Computing Machinery*, CACM

Computing (cont.)

Computing and Data Processing Society,
    CDPS
Computing Technology Center, Union
    Carbide Corporation, CTC
Deutsche Arbeitsgemeinschaft für
    Rechen-Anlagen (German Working
    Committee for Computing Machines),
    DARA
European Computing Congress,
    EUROCOMP
*Journal of the Association for Computing
    Machinery*, JACM
Logarithmic Computing Instrument, LOCI
New England Regional Computing Program,
    Inc, NERCOMP
Northwest Computing Association, NCA
Rapid Digital Automatic Computing,
    RADAC
Remote Access Computing System, RACS

Computing Center
University of Miami Computing Center,
    UMCC

Computing Centers
ACM Special Interest Group on University
    Computing Centers, ACM/SIGUCC

Computing Centre
National Computing Centre, NCC

Concept
Approach by Concept, ABC

Concerned Librarians
Concerned Librarians Opposing
    Unprofessional Trends, CLOUT

Concrete
American Concrete Institute, ACI
Cement and Concrete Association, C&CA
Concrete Technology Information Analysis
    Center, CTIAC

Condensates
Chemical Abstracts Condensates, CAC

Condition
Detail Condition Register, DCR

Conditional
Branch Conditional, BRC

Confederate
Confederate Memorial Literary Society,
    CMLS

Confederation
Confédération Internationale des Cinémas
    d'Art et d'Essai (International
    Experimental and Art Film Theatres
    Confederation), CICAE

Confédération Internationale des Industries
    Techniques du Cinéma (International
    Confederation of the Cinema Industry),
    CIITC
Confédération Internationale des Sociétés
    d'Auteurs et Compositeurs
    (International Confederation of
    Societies of Authors and Composers),
    CISAC
Confederation of British Industries, CBI

Conference
Annual Medical Library Association
    Conference Committee, AMLAC
Conference Board, CB
Conference des Recteurs et des Principaux
    des Universités du Québec (Conference
    of Rectors and Principals of Quebec
    Universities), CREPUQ
Conférence Européene des Administrations
    des Postes et des Télécommunications
    (European Conference of Postal and
    Telecommunication Administrations),
    CEPT
Conference of Engineering Societies of
    Western Europe and the United States
    of America, EUSEC
Conference of South-East Asian Libraries,
    CONSAL
Conference on Data System Languages,
    CODASYL
Conference on Interlibrary Communications
    and Information Networks, CICIN
Conference Papers Index, CPI
European Conference on the Application of
    Research in Information Services and
    Libraries, EURIM 3
European Federation of Conference Cities,
    EFCC
Fall Joint Computer Conference, FJCC
Hawaii International Conference on System
    Sciences, HICSS
International Conference on Cataloging
    Principles, ICCP
International Conference on Computer
    Communication, ICCC
International Conference on Information
    Processing, ICIP
Jerusalem Conference on Information
    Technology, JCIT
Massachusetts Conference of Chief
    Librarians in Public Higher Educational
    Institutions, MCCLPHEI
Midwestern Academic Librarians
    Conference, MALC
National Electronics Conference, NEC
National Industrial Conference Board, NICB
Newspaper Conference, NC
Nuclear Energy Trade Association
    Conference, NETAC

Professional Engineers Conference Board for
  Industry, PECBI
Spring Joint Computer Conference, SJCC
Standing Conference for Mediterranean
  Librarians, SConMeL
Standing Conference of African Library
  Schools, SCALS
Standing Conference of African University
  Librarians, SCAUL
Standing Conference of African University
  Libraries, Eastern Area, SCAULEA
Standing Conference of African University
  Libraries, Western Area, SCAULWA
Standing Conference of National and
  University Libraries, SCONUL
Standing Conference on Library Materials on
  Africa, SCOLMA
White House Conference on Library and
  Information Services, WHCOLIS
World Administrative Radio Conference,
  WARC

Configuration
Configuration Analysis Program, CAP

Congress
American Congress on Surveying and
  Mapping, ACSM
American Federation of Labor and Congress
  of Industrial Organizations, AFL-CIO
European Computing Congress,
  EUROCOMP
National Congress on Surveying and
  Mapping, NCSM

Congressional
Congressional Information Service, CIS
Congressional Research Service, CRS

Congressional Libraries
Congressional Libraries Association of
  British Columbia, CLABC

Congressional Record
Congressional Record File, CRECORD

Connecticut
Connecticut Association of Health Sciences
  Libraries, CAHSL
Connecticut Library Association, CLA
Connecticut Regional Medical Library,
  CRML
Connecticut School Library Association,
  CSLA
Connecticut State Library, CSL
Connecticut Women in Libraries, CWILS
Cooperative Libraries in Central
  Connecticut, CLICC
Southwestern Connecticut Library System,
  Inc, SCLS

Connecticut Libraries
Connecticut Valley Libraries, CONVAL

Conseil
Conseil des Enseignants—Bibliothécaires
  Franco-Ontariens, CEBFO
Conseil International des Compositeurs, CIC

Conseil Pédagogique
Conseil Pédagogique Provincial des
  Bibliothèques Scolaires
  Nouveau-Brunswick, CPPBS

Consejo
Consejo Interamericano de Archiveros,
  CITA

Conservation
American Institute for Conservation of
  Historic and Artistic Works, AIC
Association pour la Conservation et la
  Reproduction Photographique de la
  Presse, ACRPP
Environmental Conservation Library, ECOL
International Institute for Conservation of
  Historic and Artistic Works, IIC

Conservation Center
New England Document Conservation
  Center, NEDCC

Conservation Information
American Association for Conservation
  Information, AACI

Consiglio
Consiglio Nazionale delle Ricerche, CNR

Consijo Zuliano
Consijo Zuliano de Planificación y
  Promoción de Universidad Central de
  Venezuela, CONZUPLAN

Console
Console Operator Proficiency Examination,
  COPE
Multiple Indexing and Console Retrieval
  Options, MICRO
Remote Console, RECON

Consolidated
*Consolidated Index of Translations into
  English*, CITE
Consolidated Papers, Inc, CPI

Consommation
Association des Journalistes de la
  Consommation, AJC

Consortium
Alabama Consortium for the Development of
  Higher Education, ACDHE
Areawide Hospital Library Consortium of
  Southwestern Illinois, AHLC
Capital Consortium Network, CAPCON
Central Pennsylvania Consortium, CPC

Consortium (cont.)

Collegiate Consortium of Western Indiana, CCWI

Community College Library Consortium, CCLIC

Consortium Canadien de Recherches Urbaines et Régionales, CCRUR

Consortium for Higher Education Religion Studies, CHERS

Consortium for Information Resources, CIR

Consortium for International Development Information Network, CIDNET

Consortium for Library Automation in Mississippi, CLAM

Consortium of Hospital and Rehabilitative Geriatric Enterprises, CHARGE

Consortium of Rhode Island Academic and Research Libraries, CRIARL

Consortium of University Film Centers, CUFC

Cooperative Libraries in Consortium, CLIC

Eastern Virginia MEDLINE Consortium, EVIMEC

Houston Area Research Libraries Consortium, HARLIC

Illinois Department of Mental Health and Developmental Disabilities Professional Libraries Consortium, IDMH

International Telecommunications Satellite Consortium, INTELSAT

Inter-University Consortium for Political and Social Research, ICPSR

Kansas–Nebraska Educational Consortium, KANEDCO

Libraries for Nursing Consortium, LINC

Medical Resources Consortium of Central New Jersey, MEDCORE

Midwest Universities Consortium for International Activities, Inc, MUCIA

Northeast Consortium for Health Information, NECHI

Pontiac–Allen Park–Detroit Consortium, PAD

Southeastern Wisconsin Health Science Libraries Consortium, SEWHSL

Twin Cities Biomedical Consortium, TCBC

Worcester Consortium for Higher Education, WCHE

Wyoming Academic Consortium, WAC

Construction

American Institute of Steel Construction, AISC

American Institute of Timber Construction, AITC

Chemical Construction Corporation, Chemico

Committee on the Application of Computers in the Construction Industry, CAC

Construction Industry Research and Information Association, CIRIA

Construction Industry Translation and Information Services, CITIS

Information System on Research and Development in Building Industry and Construction, INBAD

Library Services and Construction Act, LSCA

Consulta

Colecciône de Consulta, CC

Consultative

Comité Consultatif International des Radiocommunications (International Radio Consultative Committee), CCIR

Commission Consultative des Études Postales (Consultative Commission for the Study of Postal Services), CCEP

Consultative Committee on International Telegraph and Telephone (Comité Consultatif International Telegraphie et Telephonie), CCITT

Scottish Technical Education Consultative Council, STECC

Consulting

American Consulting Engineers Council, ACEC

American Institute of Consulting Engineers, AICE

Association of Consulting Chemists and Chemical Engineers, ACC&CE

Association of Consulting Management Engineers, ACME

Association of Federal Communications Consulting Engineers, AFCCE

Consulting Engineers Council, CEC

Library Automation Research and Consulting, LARC

Consumer

American Council on Consumer Interests, ACCI

Consumer Goods System, COGS

Consumer Health Information Program and Service, CHIPS

Consumer Product Safety Commission, CPSC

Consumer Information

Council on Consumer Information, CCI

Container

Computer-Linked Information for Container Shipping, CLICS

Container Operating Control System, COCS

Content

Associative Content Retrieval Network, ACORN

Content Retrieval, CR

Content-Addressed
Content-Addressed Memory, CAM

Contents
Volume Table of Contents, VTOC

Context
Author and Keyword in Context, AKWIC
Biological Abstracts Subjects in Context,
    BASIC
Context, Input, Process Product Model,
    CIPP
Double Key Word in Context, KWIC,
    Double
Hetero-Atom-in-Context, HAIC
Key Letter in Context, KLIC
Key Phrase in Context, KPIC
Key Word in Context, KWIC
Key Word Out of Context, KWOC
Preserved Context Index System, PRECIS

Continuing
Network for Continuing Medical Education,
    NCME

Continuing Education
Augmented Individualized Courses in
    Continuing Education, AICCE
Continuing Education, CE
Continuing Education for Library Staffs in
    the Southwest, CELS
Continuing Education Unit, CEU
Institute of Continuing Library Education of
    British Columbia, ICLEBC

Continuous
Continuous Image Microfilm (or
    Microfilming), CIM
Continuous Multiple Access Collator,
    COMAC
Continuous System Modeling Program,
    CSMP

Contract
Product Administration and Contract
    Control, PACC

Contractors
Contractors Accounting System, CONACS

Control
Air Pollution Control Association, APCA
Air Traffic Control Association, ATCA
American Automatic Control Council,
    AACC
American Production and Inventory Control
    Society, APICS
Australian National Committee on
    Computation and Automatic Control,
    ANCCAC
Automatic Volume Control, AVC
Back-Up Interceptor Control, BUIC
Bibliographic Records Control, BIBCON

Center for Disease Control, CDC
Clock Pulsed Control, CPC
Communications Input/Output Control
    System, CIOCS
Community Input/Output Control System,
    CIOS
Computer and Control Abstracts, CCA
Computer Program for Automatic Control,
    COMPAC
Computer-Assisted Maintenance Planning
    and Control System, CAMCOS
Computerized Production Control, CPC
Conditional Transfer of Control, CTC
Container Operating Control System, COCS
Control Data Assembly Program, CODAP
Control Data Corporation, CDC
Control Footing, CF
Control Heading, CH
Control Leader, CL
Control Marks, CM
Control Switching Point, CSP
Control Translator, CONTRAN
Cursor Control, CC
Cycle Program Control, CPC
Data Acquisition and Control System, DAC
Data Communications Control Unit, DCCU
Data Control System, DCS
Data Set Control Block, DSCB
*Dictionary of Computer and Control Systems
    Abbreviations, Signs and Symbols*,
    DCCSA
Dictionary Operation and Control for
    Thesaurus Organization, DOCTOR
Digital Control Design System, DCDS
Direct English Access and Control,
    DEACON
Engineering Departmental Interface Control
    Technique, EDICT
External Device Control, EXD
External Device Control Word, EDCW
Facility of Automation, Control and Test,
    FACT
Factory Information Control System, FICS
Fast Interline Nonactive Automatic Control,
    FINAC
Forecasting for Inventory Control System,
    FICS
General Control Language, GCL
Industrial Process Control, IPC
Information Service in Physics,
    Electrotechnology and Control,
    INSPEC
Input Audit and Control, INPACON
Input/Output Control Module, IOC
Institute Belge de Régulation et
    d'Automisme (Belgian Institute for
    Control and Automation), IBRA
International Federation of Automatic
    Control, IFAC
Main Storage Control Element, MSCE

Control (cont.)

Master Control Program, MCP
Numerical Control Society, NCS
Product Administration and Contract
    Control, PACC
Project Monitoring and Control Method,
    PROMCOM
Queue Control Block, QCB
Random Access Method of Accounting and
    Control, RAMAC
Random Access Storage and Control,
    RASTAC
Remote Control Unit, RCU
Scheduling and Control by Automated
    Network System, SCANS
Strategic Air Command Control System,
    SACCS
Suomen Säätöteknillinen Seura (Finnish
    Society of Automatic Control), SSS
Television Automatic Sequence Control,
    TASCON
Total Analysis System for Production,
    Accounting, and Control, TAS-PAC
Universal Bibliographic Control, UBC
Well History Control System, WHCS

Control Center
Input/Output Control Center, IOCC

Control System
Input/Output Control System, IOCS

Controlled
Controlled Handling of Internal Executive
    Functions, CHIEF

Convergence
Bureau de Recherche pour l'Innovation et la
    Convergence, CERI

Conversational
Conversational Algebraic Language, CAL
Conversational Circuit Analysis Program,
    CONCAP
Conversational LISP, CLISP
Toxicology Information Conversational
    On-Line Network, TOXICON

Conversion
Central Data Conversion Equipment, CDCE
Conversion of Serials Project, CONSER
Data Conversion Receiver, DCR
Digital Data Conversion Equipment, DDCE
Digital Data Output Conversion Equipment,
    DDOCE
Retrospective Conversion, RECON
Symbolic Conversion Program, SCP

Converter
Analog to Digital Converter, ADC
Digital-to-Analog Converter, DAC

Universal Tape-to-Tape Converter, UTTC
Voltage to Digital Converter, VDC

Cooperating
Cooperating Users Exchange, CUE
Cooperating Users of Burroughs Equipment,
    CUBE
Southeastern Libraries Cooperating, SELCO

Cooperating Libraries
Worcester Area Cooperating Libraries,
    WACL

Cooperation
Committee for International Cooperation in
    Information Retrieval among Examining
    Patent Officers, CICIREPATO
Committee on Institutional Cooperation,
    CIC
Committee on Intersociety Cooperation, CIC
Committee on Inter-Society Cooperation,
    CISCO
Cooperation in Library Automation, COLA
Division de la Coopération et de
    l'Automasation, DICA
East Central Pennsylvania Council on
    Interlibrary Cooperation, EPIC
European Committee for Cooperation with
    Latin America, ECCLA
International Committee for Cooperation of
    Journalists, ICCJ
International Cooperation Administration,
    ICA
International Cooperation in Information
    Retrieval among Examining Patent
    Offices, ICIREPAT
Libraries of North Staffordshire in
    Cooperation, LINOSCO
Northern Inter-Library Cooperation
    Scheme, NICS
Office of Public Libraries and Interlibrary
    Cooperation, OPLIC
Organization for Economic Cooperation and
    Development, OECD
Organization for European Economic
    Cooperation, OEEC
Patent Cooperation Treaty, PCT
Southeastern Association for Cooperation in
    Higher Education in Massachusetts,
    SACHEM

Cooperative
Association of Cooperative Library
    Organizations, ACLO
Association of Specialized and Cooperative
    Library Agencies, ASCLA
Board of Cooperative Educational Services,
    BOCES
Cooperative Acquisitions and Storage
    Center, CASC
Cooperative Acquisitions Program, CAP

Cooperative Action by Victorian Academic
Libraries, CAVAL
Cooperative Africana Microform Project,
CAMP
Cooperative College Library Center, CCLC
Cooperative Documents, CODOC
Cooperative Educational Abstracting
Service, CEAS
Cooperative High School Independent Press
Syndicate, CHIPS
Cooperative Industrial and Commercial
Reference and Information Service,
CICRIS
Cooperative Information Network, CIN
Cooperative Investigations of the Caribbean
and Adjacent Regions, CICAR
Cooperative Machine-Readable Cataloging,
COMARC
Cooperative Media Development Program,
CMDP
Cooperative Raleigh Colleges, CRC
Cooperative Serials Acquisitions Program,
COSAP
Cooperative Union Serials System, CUSS
Federal Libraries Experiment in Cooperative
Cataloging, FLECC
Film Library Intercollege Cooperative of
Pennsylvania, FLIC
Indiana Cooperative Library Services
Authority, INCOLSA
Inland Empire Academic Libraries
Cooperative, IEALC
Interlibrary Lending and Cooperative
Reference Services, ILLACORS
Kentucky Cooperative Library Information
Project, KENCLIP
Manchester Interlibrary Cooperative, MILC
Media Exchange Cooperative, MEC
Metropolitan Cooperative Library System,
MCLS
Monterey Bay Area Cooperative, MOBAC
National Telephone Cooperative
Association, NTCA
Nevada Center for Cooperative Library
Services, NCCLS
Southeast Louisiana Library Network
Cooperative, SEALLINC
Southwestern Library Interstate Cooperative
Endeavor, SLICE
Tri-State College Library Cooperative,
TCLC

Cooperative Libraries
Cooperative Libraries in Central
Connecticut, CLICC
Cooperative Libraries in Consortium, CLIC

Cooperative Program
Area College Library Cooperative Program
of Central Pennsylvania, ACLCP

Cooperative Services
Board of Cooperative Services, BOCS
South East Metropolitan Board of
Cooperative Services, SEMBCS

Coordinate
Coordinate Indexing System, CIS
System to Coordinate the Operation of
Peripheral Equipment, SCOPE

Coordinated
Coordinated Geometry, COGO
Coordinated Library System of New
Mexico, CLS

Coordinating
Coordinating Committee for Slavic-East
European Library Services,
COCOSEER
Coordinating Council of Library
Organizations, CCLO
Coordinating Council of Literary Magazines,
CCLM
Higher Education Coordinating Council of
Metropolitan Saint Louis, HECC
Transportation Data Coordinating
Committee, TDCC
Western Interstate Library Coordinating
Organization, WILCO

Coordination
Center for the Coordination of Foreign
Manuscript Copying, CCFMC
Comité de Coordination des Bibliothèques
Gouvernement du Québec, COBIGO
Continuing Library Education Planning and
Coordination Project, COLEPAC
European Center for the Coordination of
Research and Documentation in the
Social Sciences, CEUCORS
Inter-Council Coordination Committee
UNESCO, ICCC
Regional Coordination of Biomedical
Information Resources Program,
RECBIR

Coordinatograph
Electronic Coordinatograph and Readout
System, ECARS

Copper
Copper and Brass Research Association,
CBRA
Copper Development Association, Inc, CDA
International Copper Research Association,
INCRA

Copy
File Copy, FC
Hard Copy, HC

Copy Service
Journal Article Copy Service, JACS

Copying
Center for the Coordination of Foreign
   Manuscript Copying, CCFMC

Copyright
British Copyright Council, BCC
British Copyright Protection Association,
   Ltd, BCPA
CNLIA Joint Committee on Copyright
   Practice and Implementation,
   CNLIA/JCCPI
Copyright Clearance Center, CCC

Copyright Office
Copyright Office Publication and Interactive
   Cataloging System, COPICS

Copyright Protection
Mechanical Copyright Protection Society,
   MCPS

Copyrighted Works
National Commission on New Technological
   Uses of Copyrighted Works, CONTU

Copyrights
International Copyrights Information Center,
   INCINC

Cornell
Cornell University Libraries, CUL
Cornell University Libraries Staff
   Association, CULSA

Corporate
Integrated Corporate Data Base, ICDB

Corporation
Australian Broadcasting Corporation, ABC
British Broadcasting Corporation, BBC
Canadian Broadcasting Corporation, CBC
Catalog Card Corporation of America, CCC
Chemical Construction Corporation,
   Chemico
Communications Satellite Corporation,
   COMSAT
Computer Corporation of America, CCA
Computer Sciences Corporation, CSC
Computing Technology Center, Union
   Carbide Corporation, CTC
Control Data Corporation, CDC
Corporation for Economics and Industrial
   Research, CEIR
Corporation of Professional Librarians of
   Quebec/Corporation des Bibliothécaires
   Professionnels du Québec, CPLQ/CBPQ
Data and Research Technology Corporation,
   DART
Digital Equipment Corporation, DEC
Encyclopaedia Britannica Educational
   Corporation, EBE
General Aniline and Film Corporation, GAF
General Motors Corporation, GM

General Telephone and Electronics
   Corporation, GTE
International Business Machines
   Corporation, IBM
International Data Corporation, IDC
International Telephone and Telegraph
   Corporation, ITT
Management Information Corporation, MIC
Microfilming Corporation of America, MCA
New York Astronomical Corporation,
   NYAC
Noyes Data Corporation, NDC
Radio Corporation of America, RCA
System Development Corporation, SDC
University Information Technology
   Corporation, UNITEL

Correcting
Error Correcting, EC

Correction
Automatic Request (for Correction), ARQ

Correctional
American Correctional Association, ACA
Correctional Records Information Systems,
   CRYSIS

Correlation
Description, Acquisition, Retrieval,
   Correlation, DARC
Random Access Correlation for Extended
   Performance, RACEP
Semantic Correlation, SEMCOR

Corrosion
National Association of Corrosion
   Engineers, NACE

Corte del Conti
Giurisprudenza della Corte del Conti,
   CORTEC

Cost
Cost Analysis Information Report, CAIR
Project Accounting by Cost and Time, PACT

Cost Estimating
Least-cost Estimating and Scheduling
   System, LESS

Costa Rican Librarians
Asociación Costarricense de Bibliotecarios
   (Association of Costa Rican Librarians),
   ACB

Cost-Benefit
Cost-Benefit, C/B

Cost-Effectiveness
Cost-Effectiveness, C/E
Cost-Effectiveness Analysis, CEA

Costituzionale
Giurisprudenza Costituzionale, COSTIT

Costs
ASIS Special Interest Group on Costs
 Budgeting and Economics,
 ASIS/SIG/CBE

Council
Alberta Council of College Librarians,
 ACCL
American Automatic Control Council,
 AACC
American Book Publishers Council, ABPC
American Consulting Engineers Council,
 ACEC
American Council of Learned Societies,
 ACLS
American Council of Pharmaceutical
 Education, ACPE
American Council on Consumer Interests,
 ACCI
American Council on Education, ACE
American Council on Education for
 Journalism, ACEJ
Amigos Bibliographic Council, ABC
Australian Council for Educational
 Research, ACER
Australian Library Promotion Council,
 ALPC
Book Development Council, BDC
British Copyright Council, BCC
Canadian Book'Publishers Council, CBPC
Canadian Council of Library Schools/Conseil
 Canadien des Écoles de Bibliothécaires,
 CCLS/CCEB
Canadian Council of Professional
 Engineers/Conseil Canadien des
 Ingénieurs Professionels, CCPE/CCIP
Canadian Rehabilitation Council for the
 Disabled, CRCD
Central New York Library Resources
 Council, CENTRO
Chicago Academic Library Council, CALC
Children's Book Council, CBC
Cinematographic Films Council, CFC
Conseil International des
 Archives/International Council on
 Archives, CIA/ICA
Conseil International pour les Films
 d'Éducation (International Council for
 Educational Films), CIFE
Conseil National des Bibliothèques
 d'Hôpitaux (National Council of
 Hospital Libraries), CNBH
Consejo Interamericano de Musica
 (Inter-American Music Council),
 CIDEM
Consejo Nacional de Ciencia y Tecnologia
 (National Council of Science and
 Technology), CONACYT
Consejo Nacional de Investigaciones
 Científicas y Técnicas (National Council
 for Scientific and Technical Research),
 CONICET

Consejo Nacional de Investigaciones
 Científicas y Tecnológicas (National
 Council for Scientific and Technological
 Research), CONICIT
Consejo Nacional de Investigaciones
 Científicas y Tecnológicas (National
 Council for Scientific and Technological
 Research), CONICYT
Conselho Federal de Biblioteconomia
 (National Council of Librarianship),
 CFB
Consulting Engineers Council, CEC
Coordinating Council of Library
 Organizations, CCLO
Coordinating Council of Literary Magazines,
 CCLM
Council for Computerized Library
 Networks, CCLN
Council for Educational Technology, CET
Council for Exceptional Children
 Information Services, CEC
Council for Higher Education in Newark,
 CHEN
Council for International Exchange of
 Scholars, CIES
Council for International Organizations on
 Medical Sciences, CIOMS
Council for Periodical Distributors
 Associations, CPDA
Council for Scientific and Industrial
 Research, CSIR
Council of Academic Heads of Agriculture,
 CAHA
Council of Academic Librarians of
 Manitoba, CALM
Council of Administrators of Large Urban
 Public Libraries, CALUPL
Council of Biology Editors, CBE
Council of Communication Societies, CCS
Council of Engineering and Scientific Society
 Executives, CESSE
Council of Engineering and Scientific Society
 Secretaries, CESS
Council of Library Associations Executives,
 CLAE
Council of National Library and Information
 Associations, CNLIA
Council of National Library Associations,
 CNLA
Council of Ontario Universities, COU
Council of Organizations Serving the Deaf,
 COSD
Council of Planning Librarians, CPL
Council of Prairie University Libraries,
 COPUL
Council of Research and Academic
 Libraries, CORAL
Council of Wisconsin Librarians, COWL
Council on Biological Sciences Information,
 COBSI
Council on Botanical and Horticultural
 Libraries, CBHL

Council (cont.)

Council on Consumer Information, CCI
Council on Economic Priorities, CEP
Council on Interracial Books for Children, CIBC
Council on Library Resources, Inc, CLR
Council on Library Technical Assistants, COLT
Council on Library Technology, COLT
Council on Library/Media Technical Assistants, COLT
Council on Social Science Data Archives, CSSDA
East and Central Africa Regional Branch of the International Council on Archives, ECARBICA
East Central Florida Regional Planning Council, ECFRPC
East Central Pennsylvania Council on Interlibrary Cooperation, EPIC
Educational Media Council, EMC
Engineers Joint Council, EJC
Forskningsbiblioteksrådet (Swedish Council of Research Libraries), FBR
Higher Education Coordinating Council of Metropolitan Saint Louis, HECC
Houston–Galveston Area Council, HGAC
Idaho Council of State Academic Libraries, ICOSAL
International Council for Reprography, ICR
International Council for the Exploration of the Sea, ICES
International Council of Scientific Unions, ICSU
International Council on Books for Young People, ICBY
International Film and Television Council, IFTC
International Social Science Council, ISSC
Interuniversity Communications Council, EDUCOM
Interuniversity Council of the North Texas Area, IUC
Joint Industrial Council of Printing and Allied Trades, JIC
Kansas City Regional Council for Higher Education, KCRCHE
Library Public Relations Council, LPRC
Long Island Library Resources Council, LILRC
Lowell Area Council on Interlibrary Networks, LACOIN
Majlis al-Bahth al-'Ilmi (Jordan Research Council), JRC
Medical Research Council, MRC
National Academy of Sciences-National Academy of Engineering-National Research Council, NAS–NAE–NRC

National Book Council, NBC
National Council for Accreditation of Teacher Education, NCATE
National Council for Educational Technology, NCET
National Council for Research and Development, NCRD
National Council for the Training of Journalists, NCTJ
National Council of Engineering Examiners, NCEE
National Council of Indian Library Associations, NACILA
National Council of State Boards of Engineering Examiners, NCSBEE
National Council of Teachers of English, NCTE
National Council of Teachers of Mathematics, NCTM
National Council on Crime and Delinquency, NCCD
National Council on the Humanities, NCH
National Research Council, NRC
New England Interinstitutional Research Council, NEIRC
New Hampshire College and University Council, NHCUC
North Country Reference and Research Resources Council, NCRRRC
Ontario Council of University Libraries, OCUL
Pittsburgh Council on Higher Education, PCHE
Print Council of America, PCA
Royal College of Nursing and National Council of Nursing, RCN
School Broadcasting Council for the United Kingdom, SBCUK
Science Research Council, SRC
Scientific Information and Educational Council of Physicians, SIECOP
Scottish Film Council, SFC
Scottish Technical Education Consultative Council, STECC
Social Sciences Research Council, SSRC
Southeast Asian Ministers of Education Council, SEAMEC
Southeastern New York Library Resources Council, SENYLRC
Southwest Asian Regional Branch of the International Council on Archives, SARBICA
Technical Institute Council, TIC
Uniform Product Code Council, UPCC
Universities Central Council on Admissions, UCCA
Universities Council for Adult Education, UCAE
Urban Libraries Council, ULC
Urban Libraries Trustees Council, ULTC

Western New York Library Resources
Council, WNYLRC

Councils
Simulation Councils, Inc, SCI

Counseling
ERIC Clearinghouse on Counseling and
Personnel Services, ERIC/CG

Counselors
American School Counselors Association,
ASCA

Count
Feature Count, FC

Counter
Binary Decimal Counter, BDC
Cycle Program Counter, CPC
Instruction Counter, IC

Counterinsurgency
Counterinsurgency Information Analysis
Center, CINFAC

Counties
Dual Independent Map Encoding File of the
Counties of the US, DIMECO
National Association of Counties, NACO

Countries
Committee on Science and Technology in
Developing Countries, COSTED

Countway Library
Countway Library Medical Bibliographic
Services, CLIMBS

County
American Federation of State, County, and
Municipal Employees, AFSCME
County and Regional Municipality
Librarians, CARML
National Association of County Engineers,
NACE
Society of Municipal and County Chief
Librarians, SMCCL

County Librarians
Society of County Librarians, SCL

Coupled
Direct Coupled Transistor Logic, DCTL

Courier
Data Courier, Inc, DC

Courses
Augmented Individualized Courses in
Continuing Education, AICCE

Court
State and Court Law Libraries of the United
States and Canada, SCLL

Coventry
Coventry and District Information Group,
CADIG

Crafts
Columbus Museum of Arts and Crafts,
CMAC

Credit
National Credit Information Service, NACIS

Crime
Crime Writers Association, CWA
National Council on Crime and Delinquency,
NCCD
National Crime Information Center, NCIC

Criminal
Criminal Justice Periodical Index. (Journal),
CJPI
Office of Criminal Justice Plans and
Analysis, OCJPA
System for Electronic Analysis and Retrieval
of Criminal Histories, SEARCH
Tracking Retrieval and Analysis of Criminal
Events, TRACE

Crippled
Institute for the Crippled and Disabled, ICD
National Society for Crippled Children and
Adults, NSCCA

Critical Path
Critical Path Method, CPM

Critical Tables
Office of Critical Tables, OCT

Critics
Vereinigung Schweizerischer
Filmkritiker/Association Suisse des
Critiques de Cinéma/Associazione
Svizzera dei Critici Cinematografici
(Swiss Association of Film Critics),
VSF/ASC/ASC

Critique
Union de la Critique du Cinéma, UUC

Croatian
Hrvatsko Bibliotekarsko Društvo (Croatian
Library Association), HBD

Cryogenic
Cryogenic Data Center, CDC

Crystallographic
American Crystallographic Association,
ACA
Crystallographic Society of America, CSA

Cuadra
Cuadra Associates, Inc, CA

Cubana
Classification Analytico-Synthetica Cubana
de Medicas, CASCUM

Cubic Feet
Cubic Feet per Minute, CFM

Culham
Culham (Laboratory) Language for System Development, CLSD

Cultural
European Cultural Center, ECC
United Nations Educational, Scientific and Cultural Organization, UNESCO

Cultural Services
French American Cultural Services and Educational Aid, FACSEA

Culturali e Ambientali
Circolari Ministero Beni Culturali e Ambientali, CIRBCA

Culturelle
Société Nationale de Diffusion Éducative et Culturelle, SONDEC

Cumulated
Cumulated Abridged Index Medicus, CAIM

Cumulative
Cumulative Book Index, CBI
Cumulative Index to Nursing Literature, CINL
Quarterly Cumulative Index Medicus, QCIM

Curators
Association des Bibliothécaires, Archivistes, Documentalistes et Muséographes du Cameroun (Association of Librarians, Archivists, Documentalists and Museum Curators of Cameroon), ABADCAM

Currency
Special Foreign Currency Science Information Program, SFCSI

Current
Current Abstracts of Chemistry, CAC
Current Abstracts of Chemistry and Index Chemicus, CAC&IC
Current Bibliography on Science and Technology, CBST
Current Cancer Research Project Analysis Center, CCRESPAC
Current Chemical Reactions. (Journal), CCR
Current Index to Journals in Education, CIJE
Current Information Selection, CIS
Current Information Tapes for Engineers, CITE
Current Literature Alerting Search Service, CLASS
Current Mathematical Publications, CMP
Current Papers in Physics. (Journal), CPIP
Current Physics Titles (Journal), CPT

Current Research and Development in Israel, CRI
Current Research and Development in Scientific Documentation, CRDSD
Current Research Information System, CRIS
Fast Access Current Text Bank, FACT
Fuel Abstracts and Current Titles, FACT
System for Organizing Current Reports to Aid Technology and Science, SOCRATES

Current Awareness
Current Awareness and Document Retrieval for Engineers, CADRE
Current Awareness Service, CAS
Current Awareness—Library Literature, CALL

Current Contents
Current Contents, CC
Current Contents/Agricultural, Food and Veterinary Sciences. (Journal), CC/AFV
Current Contents/Agriculture, Biology and Environmental Sciences. (Journal), CC/AB&ES
Current Contents/Arts and Humanities. (Journal), CC/A&H
Current Contents/Behavioral, Social and Educational Sciences. (Journal), CC/BSE
Current Contents/Chemical, Pharmaco-Medical and Life Sciences. (Journal), CC/CPML
Current Contents/Clinical Practice. (Journal), CC/CP
Current Contents/Engineering, Technology and Applied Sciences. (Journal), CC/ET&AS
Current Contents/Life Sciences. (Journal), CC/LS
Current Contents/Physical and Chemical Sciences. (Journal), CC/PC
Current Contents/Physical, Chemical and Earth Sciences. (Journal), CC/PC&ES
Current Contents/Social and Behavioral Sciences. (Journal), CC/S&BS

Curricula
Curricula for Ethnic Education Directory, CEED

Curriculum
Association for Supervision and Curriculum Development, ASCD
Centre for Curriculum Renewal and Educational Development Overseas, CREDO

Cursor
Cursor Control, CC

Customer
Customer Bank Communication Terminal, CBCT
Customer Information Control System, CICS
Customer Must Order Direct, CMOD
Customer Owned and Maintained, COAM
Special Customer-Oriented Language, SPECOL

Cybernetics
American Society for Cybernetics, ASC

Cybernétique
Association Française pour la Cybernétique Économique et Technique, AFCET

Cycle
Cycle Program Control, CPC
Cycle Program Counter, CPC

Cycles
Cycles Per Second, cps

Czechoslovak
Státni Knihovna Československe Socialisticke Republiky (State Library of the Czechoslovak Socialist Republic), SKCSR

DLSC
DLSC Integrated Data System, DIDS

DOD
DOD Nuclear Information and Analysis Center, DASIAC

Dagbladpers
Vereniging de Nederlandse Dagbladpers, NDP

Dallas
Dallas County Community College District, DCCCD

Dance
Dance Collection Automated Book Catalog, DCABC

Danish
Danish Agricultural Producers Information Service, DAPIS
Danmarks Biblioteksforening (Danish Library Association), DB
Dansk Teknisk Oplysningstjeneste (Danish Technical Information Service), DTO
Danske Boghandleres Importørforening (Danish Booksellers Import Association), DANBIF

Darmstadt
Zurich, Mainz, Munich, Darmstadt, ZMMD

Dartmouth
Dartmouth Time Sharing System, DTSS

Data
ACM Special Interest Group on Data Communications, ACM/SIGCOMM
ACM Special Interest Group on Management of Data, ACM/SIGMOD
Action Data Automation Language, ADAL
Advanced Data Management, ADAM
Air Movement Data, AMD
Analog Data Recording Transcriber, ADRT
Association of Data Producers, ADP
Automatic Data Entry, ADE
Automatic Data Exchange, ADX
Catalog Data File, CDF
Center of Experiment Design and Data Analysis, CEDDA
Central Data Conversion Equipment, CDCE
Clearinghouse and Laboratory for Census Data, CLCD
Client-Oriented Data Acquisition Program, CODAP
Committee on Data for Science and Technology, CODATA
Committee on Storage, Automatic Processing and Retrieval of Geological Data, COGEODATA
Comprehensive Occupational Data Analysis Program, CODAP
Computer Analysis of Thermo-Chemical Data Tables, CATCH
Control Data Assembly Program, CODAP
Control Data Corporation, CDC
Council on Social Science Data Archives, CSSDA
DLSC Integrated Data System, DIDS
Data Acquisition, DA
Data Acquisition and Control System, DAC
Data Analysis Massachusetts Institute of Technology, DAMIT
Data Analysis System, DAS
Data and Computation Center, DACC
Data and Research Technology Corporation, DART
Data Association Message, DAM
Data Communications, DATACOM
Data Communications Control Unit, DCCU
Data Control System, DCS
Data Conversion Receiver, DCR
Data Courier, Inc, DC
Data Definition, DD
Data Demand, DD
Data Dissemination Systems, Inc, DDSI
Data Dynamics, Inc, DDI
Data Exchange Unit, DEU
A Data Interchange System, ADIS
Data Link Escape, DLE
Data Loop Transceiver, DLT
Data Management, DM
Data Management Association, DMA
Data Management Routines, DMR
Data Manipulation Language, DML

Data (cont.)

Data Moving System, DAMOS
Data Reference, D-REF
Data Resources, Inc, DRI
Data Retrieval Language, DRL
Data Set, DS
Data Set Control Block, DSCB
Digital Data, DD
Digital Data, Auxiliary Storage, Track
    Display, Outputs, and Radar Display,
    DATOR
Digital Data Communications Message
    Protocol, DDCMP
Digital Data Conversion Equipment, DDCE
Digital Data Output Conversion Equipment,
    DDOCE
Digital Data Processor, DDP
Digital Data Transmitter, DDT
Electronic Data Gathering Equipment,
    EDGE
Environmental Data Collection and
    Processing Facility, EDCPF
Environmental Data Index, ENDEX
European Space Data Center, ESDAC
European-American Nuclear Data
    Committee, EANDC
Failure Rate Data Program, FARADA
General Data Analysis and Simulation,
    GENDA
Generation Data Group, GDG
Government-Industry Data Exchange
    Program, GIDEP
High-Speed Data Acquisition, HSDA
Information and Data Exchange
    Experimental Activities, IDEEA
Inorganic and Metallurgical
    Thermodynamics Data, MTDATA
Inter NASA Data Exchange, INDEX
International Data Corporation, IDC
International Serials Data System, ISDS
Low Data-Rate Input, LDRI
Machine-Readable Data Files, MRDF
Malfunction and Data Recorder, MADAR
Marine Environmental Data Information
    Referral System, MEDI
Moderately Advanced Data Management,
    MADAM
Mössbauer Effect Data Index, MEDI
Museum and University Data, Program and
    Information Exchange, MUDPIE
National Data Use and Access Laboratories,
    Inc, DUALabs
National Geophysical Data Center, NGDC
National Marine Data Inventory, NAMDI
National Serials Data Program, NSDP
Navigation Data Assimilation Computer,
    NAVDAC
Noyes Data Corporation, NDC
Office of Standard Reference Data, OSRD

Operational Assistance and Instructive Data
    Equipment, OAIDE
Original Data File, ODF
Real Estate Data, Inc, REDI
Regional Operational Data, ROD
Regional Social Science Data Archive,
    RSSDA
Society of Data Educators, SDE
Society of Independent and Private School
    Data Education, SIPSDE
Source Data Automation, SDA
Storage, Handling and Retrieval of Technical
    Data in Image Formation, SHIRTDIF
Transportation Data Coordinating
    Committee, TDCC
User-Prompted Graphic Data Evaluation,
    UPGRADE

Data Bank

Banque de Données à Accès Direct de
    l'Université du Québec (Direct Access
    Data Bank of the University of Quebec),
    BADADUQ
Electronic Components Data Bank, ECDB
International Cancer Research Data Bank
    Program, ICRDB
Laboratory Animal Data Bank, LADB
ORSTOM Pedology Data Bank, POSEIDON
Toxicology Data Bank, TDB

Data Base

ANSI/SPARC Study Group on Data Base
    Management Systems,
    ANSI/X3/SPARC/SGDBMS
Acronym Data Base, ACRODABA
Adaptable Data Base System, ADABAS
Carolina Population Center Library Data
    Base, CPC
Common Data Base, CDB
Data Base Access Method, DBAM
Data Base Administrator, DBA
Data Base Design Aid, DBDA
Data Base Management System, DBMS
Data Base Organization and Management
    Processor, DBOMP
Data Base Task Force (CODASYL), DBTC
Dissertations Data Base Search Service,
    DATRIX
Generalized Data Base Management
    Systems, GDBMS
Integrated Corporate Data Base, ICDB
Market Data Retrieval–Educational Data
    Base, MDR
Retrospective Search System on the
    INSPEC Data Base, RETROSPEC
Textile Technology Data Base Keyterm
    Index, TTD

Data Bases

ASIS Special Interest Group on Numerical
    Data Bases, ASIS/SIG/NDB

Directory of Data Bases in the Social and Behavioral Sciences, DDB

Data Center
Chemical Thermodynamics Data Center, CTDC
Cryogenic Data Center, CDC
Drug Abuse Epidemiology Data Center, DAEDAC
International Demographic Data Center, IDDC
Machinability Data Center, MDC
National Geophysical and Solar Terrestrial Data Center, NGSD
National Oceanographic Data Center, NODC
National Space Science Data Center, NSSDC
Neutron Data Compilation Center, CCDN
World Data Center, WDC

Data Flow
Computation and Data Flow Integrated Subsystems, CADFISS

Data Information
Data Information and Manufacturing System, DIMS

Data Library
International Data Library and Reference Service, IDL&RS
Survey Research Center Data Library, SRCDL

Data Processing
ACM Special Interest Group on Business Data Processing, ACM/SIGBDP
Association of Data Processing Service Organizations, ADPSO
Association of Data Processing Service Organizations, Inc, ADAPSO
Associazione Italiana per il Calco Automatico (Italian Association for Automatic Data Processing), AICA
Automated Data Processing, ADP
Automatic Data Processing, ADP
Automatic Data Processing Equipment, ADPE
Automatic Data Processing Equipment and Software, ADPE/S
Automatic Data Processing Equipment Selection Office, ADPESO
Automatic Data Processing Service Center, ADPSC
Automatic Data Processing System, ADPS
California Educational Data Processing Association, CEDPA
Communication and Data Processing Operation, CADPO
Communication and Data Processing Operation System, CADPOS

Computing and Data Processing Society, CDPS
Data Processing, DP
Data Processing and Information Retrieval, DPIR
Data Processing for Education. (Newsletter), DPED
Data Processing Machine, DPM
Data Processing Management Association, DPMA
Electronic Data Processing, EDP
Electronic Data Processing Equipment, EDPE
Electronic Data Processing Machine, EDPM
Electronic Data Processing System, EDPS
IFIP Administrative Data Processing Group, IAG
Institute of Data Processing, IDP
Integrated Data Processing, IDP
Parts Data Processing System, PDPS
RADAR Data Processing Equipment, RDPE
Systems Analysis and Data Processing Office of NYPL, SADPO
Western Data Processing Center, WDPC

Data Processing Librarians
Data Processing Librarians and Documentation Managers Association, DPL/DMA

Data Processor
Programmed Data Processor, PDP

Data Service
Physical Property Data Service, PPDS
Wide Area Data Service, WADS

Data Store
Integrated Data Store, IDS

Data System
Aerospace Intelligence Data System, AIDS
Army Logistics Management Integrated Data System, ALMIDS
Canadian Farm Management Data System, CANFARM
Chemical Information and Data System, CIDS
Conference on Data System Languages, CODASYL
Managerial On-Line Data System, MOLDS
Micro-Imaged Data Addition System, MIDAS
National Standard Reference Data System, NSRDS
New England Educational Data System, NEEDS

Data Systems
Association for Educational Data Systems, AEDS
Automatic Data Systems Uniform Practices, ADSUP

Data Systems (cont.)

Society for Educational Data Systems,
SEDS

Databank
Vapour Liquid Equilibria Databank, VLE
BANK

Database
Database of Atomic and Molecular Physics,
DAMP

Dataflow
Dataflow Systems Inc, DfS

Datamation
Datamation Industrial Directory, DID

Data—Safety
Computer Handling of Reactor
Data—Safety, CHORD—S

Datascope
Datascope Computer Output Microfilmer,
DACOM

Datatron
Datatron Assembly System, DAS

Datenpool
Zentraler Datenpool der Kooperativen
Agrardokumentation, DIFO

Datenverarbeitung
Arbeitsgemeinschaft für Datenverarbeitung,
ADV

Daystrom
Daystrom Powerplant Automation
Language, DAPAL

Dayton
Comprehensive University of Dayton
On-Line Information Services, CUDOS

Deaf
ASCLA Library Service to the Deaf Section,
ASCLA/LSDS
Council of Organizations Serving the Deaf,
COSD

Deafness
Deafness, Speech and Hearing Publications,
Inc, DSH

Dealers
National Association of Securities Dealers
Automated Quotations System,
NASDAQ

Deans
Ontario Committee of Deans and Directors
of Library Schools, OCDDLS

Debugging
Dynamic Debugging Technique, DDT
Language Processing and Debugging, LPD

Decade
International Decade of Ocean Exploration,
IDOE

Decency
Citizens for Decency through Law, CDL

Decimal
Binary Coded Decimal, BCD
Binary Decimal Counter, BDC
Decimal Classification, DC
Decimal Classification Editorial Policy
Committee, DCEPC
Decimal Display, DD
Decimal Fraction, DF
Dewey Decimal Classification, DDC
Extended Binary Coded Decimal
Interchange Code, EBCDIC
Universal Decimal Classification, UDC

Decision
Decision Element, DE
Decision Tables/Experimental, DETAB/X
Decision-Aiding Information System,
DAISY
Magnetic Decision Element, MDE

Decoder
Michigan Algorithmic Decoder, MAD

Decorative Arts
Museum of Early Southern Decorative Arts,
MESDA

Defence
Defence Operational Analysis
Establishment, DOAE

Defense
*Abbreviations and Related Acronyms
Associated with Defense, Astronautics,
Business and Radio-Electronics*,
ABRACADABRA
City Air Defense Evaluation Tool, CADET
Defense Ceramic Information Center, DCIC
Defense Communications Agency, DCA
Defense Documentation Center, DDC
Defense Logistics Services Center, DLSC
Defense Market Measures System, DM^2
Defense Metals Information Center, DMIC
Defense Nuclear Agency, DNA
Defense Supply Agency, DSA
Department of Defense, DOD
Inter-American Defense College, IADC

Definition
Data Definition, DD

Deflection
Electrostatic Storage Deflection, ESD

Delaware
Delaware Library Association, DLA

Delay
Delay Drive, DD

Délégation Générale
Délégation Générale à la Recherche
Scientifique et Technique, DGRST

Delete
Delete, DEL

Delineator
Self-Programmed Electronic Equation
Delineator, SPEED

Delinquency
National Council on Crime and Delinquency,
NCCD

Delivery
Document Delivery Tests, DDT

Delivery Service
Interlibrary Delivery Service of
Pennsylvania, IDS

Demand
Data Demand, DD

Demodulating
Modulating and Demodulating Unit,
MOD/DEM

Demodulator
Demodulator, DEM

Demographic
International Demographic Data Center,
IDDC

Demonstration
Library Experimental Automated
Demonstration System, LEADS

Denmark
Danmarks Tekniske Bibliotek med Dansk
Central for Dokumentation (Danish
Center for Documentation of the
Technological Library of Denmark),
DTB

Density
High Density, HD

Dental
American Dental Association, ADA
Secção de Documentação Adontólogica
(Department of Dental Documentation),
SDA

Department
Department of Audiovisual Instruction,
DAVI

United States Department of Agriculture,
USDA

Deposit Library
New England Deposit Library, Inc, NEDL

Depot
Flexible Automatic Depot, FAD

Description
Algorithmic Processor Description
Language, APDL
Computer Hardware Description Language,
CHDL
Description, Acquisition, Retrieval,
Correlation, DARC
Hardware Description Language, HDL
International Standard Bibliographic
Description, ISBD

Descriptive
Descriptive Language for Implementing
Macro-Processors, DLIMP

Descriptor
Descriptor Attribute Matrix, DAM

Desert
Arctic, Desert, Tropic Information Center,
ADTIC

Design
ACM Special Interest Group on Design
Automation, ACM/SIGDA
Asynchronous Circuit Design Language,
ACDL
Automated Combustor Design Code,
AUTOCOM
Automated Engineering Design System,
AED
Bell Laboratories Automatic Design System,
BLADES
Center of Experiment Design and Data
Analysis, CEDDA
Comprehensive Language for Elegant
Operating System and Translator
Design, CLEOPATRA
Computer Analysis of Networks with Design
Orientation, CANDO
Computer-Aided Design, CAD
Computer-Aided Design Drafting, CADD
Computer-Aided Design Engineering, CADE
Computer-Aided Design Environment,
COMRADE
Computer-Aided Design Evaluation, CADE
Computer-Aided Design Optical Character
Recognition, CADOCR
Computer-Aided Design System, CADSYS
Computerized Facilities Design, COFAD
Computerized Preliminary Design System,
CPDS
Data Base Design Aid, DBDA

Design (cont.)

Design Augmented by Computers, DAC
Design Change Recommendation, DCR
Design of Information in the Social Sciences,
  DISISS
Digital Control Design System, DCDS
Digital Equipment Corporation's Automatic
  Design System, DECADE
Integrated Design and Analysis System,
  IDEAS

Designers
Society of Typographical Designers, STD

Destructive
Destructive Read-Out, DRO

Detail
Detail Condition Register, DCR

Detecting
Error Detecting, ED

Detection
Coherent Light Detection and Ranging,
  COLIDAR
Computer-Aided Detection, CAD
Malfunction Analysis Detection and
  Recording, MADAR
Malfunction Detection and Recording,
  MADREC
Radioactivity Detection Indication and
  Computation, RADIAC

Determination
Missile Attitude Determination System,
  MADS

Detroit
Metropolitan Detroit Medical Library
  Group, MDMLG
Pontiac–Allen Park–Detroit Consortium,
  PAD

Deutsche
Verband der Journalisten der Deutsche
  Democratische Republik, VDJ

Deutscher
Bundesverband Deutscher Zeitungsverleger,
  BDZV
Freier Deutscher Autoren-Verband, FDA
Hauptverband Deutscher Filmtheater, HDF
Verband Deutscher Agrarjournalisten, VDA
Verband Deutscher Schriftsteller, VS
Verband Deutscher Zeitschriftenverleger,
  VDZ
Verein Deutscher Ingenieure, VDI

Deutsches
Deutsches Kunststoff-Institut, DKI

Developing Countries
FID Committee on Developing Countries,
  FID/DC

Development
Advanced Systems Development Division,
  ASDD
Alabama Consortium for the Development of
  Higher Education, ACDHE
American Society for Training and
  Development, ASTD
Area Manpower Institutes for the
  Development of Staffs, AMIDS
Association for the Development of
  Instructional Systems, ADIS
Book Development Council, BDC
Center for Educational Development
  Overseas, CEDO
Center for Studies in Economic
  Development, CEDE
Centre for Curriculum Renewal and
  Educational Development Overseas,
  CREDO
Centro de Desarrollo Industrial (Center for
  Industrial Development), CENDES
Commercial Development Association, CDA
Consortium for International Development
  Information Network, CIDNET
Cooperative Media Development Program,
  CMDP
Copper Development Association, Inc, CDA
Culham (Laboratory) Language for System
  Development, CLSD
Current Research and Development in Israel,
  CRI
Department of Housing and Urban
  Development, DHUD
Development of Sciences Information
  System, DEVSIS
Education Development Center, Inc, EDC
Education Professions Development Act,
  EPDA
Educational Development Association, EDA
Energy Research and Development
  Administration, ERDA
Industrial Development Center/Viet-Nam
  (Trung-Tam Khuech-Truong Ky-Ngha),
  IDC/VN
International Development Center, IDC
Language for Utility Checkout and
  Instrumentation Development, LUCID
Lead Development Association, LDA
Library Employment and Development for
  Staff, LEADS
MARC Development Office, MDO
Office of Audiovisual Educational
  Development, OAED
Organization for Economic Cooperation and
  Development, OECD

Remote Access Planning for Institutional
  Development, RAPID
Research and Development, R&D
Research and Development, RD
Research and Development, Army, RDA
Research and Development Report, RDR
Southeast Asia Development Advisory
  Group, SEADAG
System Development Corporation, SDC
Systems Development Division, SDD
United Nations Industrial Development
  Organization, UNIDO

Development Center
Rome Air Development Center On-Line,
  RADCOL

Developmental Disabilities
Illinois Department of Mental Health and
  Developmental Disabilities Library
  Services Network, DMHDD/LISN
Illinois Department of Mental Health and
  Developmental Disabilities Professional
  Libraries Consortium, IDMH

Développement
Centre Africain de Formation et de
  Recherches Administratives pour le
  Développement, CAFRAD
Centre d'Animation, de Développement et
  de Recherche en Education, CADRE
Centre pour la Recherche Interdisciplinaire
  sur le Développement, CRID

Device
Bell Laboratories Automatic Device,
  BLADE
Direct Access Storage Device, DASD
External Device, ED
External Device Control, EXD
External Device Control Word, EDCW
Optical Scanning Device, OSD
Rapid Alphanumeric Digital Indicating
  Device, RANDID
Relative Access Programming
  Implementation Device, RAPID
Voice Operated Gain-Adjustment Device,
  VOGAD

Dewey
Dewey Decimal Classification, DDC

Diagnosis
Computer-Aided Diagnosis System, CADS
Monrobot Automatic Internal Diagnosis,
  MAID
System Analysis Index for Diagnosis, SAID

Diagnostic
Diagnostic Function Test, DFT
Result from Action, Prediction, Informative,
  Diagnostic Sensing, RAPIDS

Diagram-Graphics
Block Diagram-Graphics, BLODI-G

Dial
Dial Access Information Retrieval System,
  DAIRS
Dial Access Technical Education, DATE
Dial Interrogation and Loading, DIAL

Dialing
Direct Distance Dialing, DDD

Dialing Unit
Automatic Dialing Unit, ADU

Diary
Diary Publishers Association, DPA

Dictionaries
Society for the Study of Dictionaries and
  Lexicography, SSDL

Dictionary
Chemical Abstracts Chemical Name
  Dictionary, CHEMNAME
Chemical Dictionary On-Line, CHEMLINE
Dictionary of American Biography, DAB
Dictionary of American Regional English,
  DARE
*Dictionary of Architectural Abbreviations,
  Signs and Symbols*, DAA
*Dictionary of Civil Engineering
  Abbreviations, Signs and Symbols*,
  DCEA
*Dictionary of Computer and Control Systems
  Abbreviations, Signs and Symbols*,
  DCCSA
*Dictionary of Electronics Abbreviations,
  Signs and Symbols*, DEA
*Dictionary of Industrial Engineering
  Abbreviations, Signs and Symbols*,
  DIEA
*Dictionary of Mechanical Engineering
  Abbreviations, Signs and Symbols*,
  DMEA
Dictionary of National Biography, DNB
*Dictionary of Physics and Mathematics
  Abbreviations, Signs and Symbols*,
  DPMA
Dictionary Operation and Control for
  Thesaurus Organization, DOCTOR
Dictionary Society of North America, DSNA
External Symbol Dictionary, ESD
Oxford English Dictionary, OED
Relocation Dictionary, RLD

Diet
National Diet Library, NDL

Diffemic
Automatic Diffemic Identification of
  Speakers, ADIS

Differential
Differential Analyzer, DA
Digital Differential Analyzer, DDD

Differential Equations
Algebraic and Differential Equations
    Processor and Translator, ADEPT

Diffraction
American Society for X-Ray and Electron
    Diffraction, ASXED

Diffused
Microalloy Diffused Base Transistor, MADT
Microalloy Diffused Electrode, MADE

Diffusion
Diffusion Sélective de l'Information, DSI
Société Nationale de Diffusion Éducative et
    Culturelle, SONDEC

Digit
Digit Plane Driver, DPD
Least Significant Digit, LSD
Most Significant Digit, MSD

Digital
Analog to Digital Converter, ADC
Automatic Digital Encoding System, ADES
Automatic Digital Encoding System,
    ADES-II
Automatic Digital On-line Instrumentation
    System, ADONIS
British Overseas Airways Digital
    Information Computer for Electronic
    Automation, BOADICEA
Digital Analog Function Table, DAFT
Digital Computers Association, DCA
Digital Control Design System, DCDS
Digital Data, DD
Digital Data, Auxiliary Storage, Track
    Display, Outputs, and Radar Display,
    DATOR
Digital Data Communications Message
    Protocol, DDCMP
Digital Data Conversion Equipment, DDCE
Digital Data Output Conversion Equipment,
    DDOCE
Digital Data Processor, DDP
Digital Data Transmitter, DDT
Digital Difference Analyzer, DDA
Digital Differential Analyzer, DDD
Digital Display, DD
Digital Display Alarm, DDA
Digital Display Generator, DDG
Digital Display Generator Element, DDGE
Digital Display Makeup, DDM
Digital Display Scope, DDS
Digital Element, DE
Digital Equipment Computer Users Society,
    DECUS
Digital Equipment Corporation, DEC

Digital Equipment Corporation's Automatic
    Design System, DECADE
Digital Information Display, DID
Digital Input/Output Display Equipment,
    DIODE
Digital Optical Projection System, DOPS
Digital Test-Oriented Language, DTOL
Film Input to Digital Automatic Computer,
    FIDAC
Mobile Digital Computer, MOBIDIC
Modified Integration Digital Analog
    Simulator, MIDAS
Rapid Alphanumeric Digital Indicating
    Device, RANDID
Rapid Digital Automatic Computing,
    RADAC
Shelter-Housed Automatic Digital Random
    Access, SHADRAC
Voltage to Digital Converter, VDC

Digital-to-Analog
Digital-to-Analog Converter, DAC

Diode
Diode Function Generator, DFG
Light-Emitting Diode, LED

Direct
Banque de Données à Accès Direct de
    l'Université du Québec (Direct Access
    Data Bank of the University of Quebec),
    BADADUQ
Basic Direct Access Method, BDAM
Customer Must Order Direct, CMOD
Direct Access Intelligence Systems, DAIS
Direct Access Storage Device, DASD
Direct Coupled Transistor Logic, DCTL
Direct Distance Dialing, DDD
Direct English Access and Control,
    DEACON
Direct Mail Producers Association, DMPA
Direct Order Recording and Invoicing
    System, DORIS
Direct-High-Level-Language Processor,
    DHLLP
Psychological Abstracts Direct Access
    Terminal, PADAT

**Directeurs de Théâtres
    Cinématographiques**
Association des Directeurs de Théâtres
    Cinématographiques de Belgique,
    ADTCB

Direction
Direction Center Active, DCA
Direction de la Recherche Agronomique,
    DRA
Direction Finder, DF
Direction Finding, DF

Directions
Future Directions for a Learning Society,
FDLS

Directorate
Directorate of Scientific Information
Services, DSIS

Directors
Association of Directors of Education in
Scotland, ADES
Association of Library and Learning Center
Directors, ALLCeD
Directors of Ontario Regional Library
Systems/Directeurs des Bibliothèques
Régionales de l'Ontario, DORLS/DBRO
Fédération Internationale des Directeurs de
Journaux Catholiques (International
Federation of Directors of Catholic
Publications), FIDJC
National Association of State Text Book
Directors, NASTBD
Ontario Committee of Deans and Directors
of Library Schools, OCDDLS

Directory
American Book Trade Directory, ABTD
American Library Directory, ALD
Automated Information Directory Update
System, AIDUS
(Brazilian) Directory of Researchers,
CADAP
*Current Bibliographic Directory of the Arts
and Sciences*, CBD
Curricula for Ethnic Education Directory,
CEED
Datamation Industrial Directory, DID
*Directory of Computerized Information in
Science and Technology*, DCIST
*Directory of Data Bases in the Social and
Behavioral Sciences*, DDB
*International Directory of Research and
Development Scientists*, IDR&DS
Toxicology Research Projects Directory.
(Journal), TRPD

Disabilities
Quebec Association for Children with
Learning Disabilities, QACLD

Disabled
Canadian Rehabilitation Council for the
Disabled, CRCD
Institute for the Crippled and Disabled, ICD
International Society for Rehabilitation of
the Disabled/Rehabilitation
International, ISRD

Disadvantaged
Library Service to the Disadvantaged, LSD
Office for Library Service to the
Disadvantaged, OLSD

Disarmament
Arms Control and Disarmament Agency,
ACDA
Multilateral Disarmament Information
Centre, MDIC

Discography
British National Discography, BND

Discrete
Random Access Discrete Address, RADA
Random Access Discrete Address System,
RADAS

Discriminator
Initiation Area Discriminator, IAD

Disease
Center for Disease Control, CDC

Diseases
National Institute of Neurological Diseases
and Stroke, NINDS

Diseminación
Diseminación Selectiva de la Información,
DSI

Disk
Disk On-Line Accounts Receivable System,
DOLARS
Disk Operating System, DOS
Rapid Access Disk, RAD

Display
Bibliographic On-Line Display, BOLD
Bucknell Automated Retrieval and Display
System, BARDS
Compact Automatic Retrieval Display,
CARD
Comprehensive Display System, CDS
Decimal Display, DD
Digital Data, Auxiliary Storage, Track
Display, Outputs, and Radar Display,
DATOR
Digital Display, DD
Digital Display Alarm, DDA
Digital Display Generator, DDG
Digital Display Generator Element, DDGE
Digital Display Makeup, DDM
Digital Display Scope, DDS
Digital Information Display, DID
Digital Input/Output Display Equipment,
DIODE
Display Assignment Bits, DAB
Display Attention Bits, DAB
Display Element, DE
Display Equipment, DE
Display-Oriented Computer Usage System,
DOCUS
Display Producers and Screen Printers
Association, DPSA
Expanded Display, ED

Display (cont.)

Output to Display Buffer, ODB
Random Access Photographic Index and
    Display, RAPID
Random Access Storage and Display,
    RASTAD
Real-Time Electronic Access and Display,
    READ
Remote Electrical Alphanumeric Display,
    READ
Visual Display Unit, VDU

Dissemination

Canadian Selective Dissemination of
    Information, CAN/SDI
Cancer Information Dissemination and
    Analysis, CIDA
Data Dissemination Systems, Inc, DDSI
Retrieval and Automatic Dissemination of
    Information from *Index Chemicus* and
    Line Notations, RADIICAL
Selected Dissemination of Indexes, SEDIX
Selective Dissemination of Information, SDI
Selective Dissemination of MARC,
    SELDOM
Selective Dissemination of Microfiche, SDM
System for the Publication and Efficient,
    Effective Dissemination of Information,
    SPEEDI

Dissemination Centers

Association of Scientific Information
    Dissemination Centers, ASIDIC
Regional Dissemination Centers, RDC

Dissertation

Comprehensive Dissertation Index, CDI
Dissertation Abstracts International, DAI

Dissertations

American Doctoral Dissertations, ADD
Dissertations Data Base Search Service,
    DATRIX

Distance

Direct Distance Dialing, DDD

Distributed

Distributed Processing Reporting Service,
    DPRS
Distributed Processing Support, DPS

Distributeurs

Fédération Nationale des Distributeurs de
    Films, FNDF
Union Professionnelle des Distributeurs
    Belges de Films, UPDBF

Distributeurs de Films

Association des Exploitants de Cinéma et
    des Distributeurs de Films du
    Grand-Duché de Luxembourg, AECDF

Distributing

Sunday Newspapers Distributing
    Association, SNDA

Distributing Frame

Main Distributing Frame, MDF

Distribution

Card-Automated Reproduction and
    Distribution System, CARDS
Computer-Aided Recording of Distribution
    Systems, CARDS
Distribution Tape Reel, DTR
SAMI Retail Distribution Index. (Journal),
    SARDI
Specialized Office for Materials Distribution,
    SOMD

Distribution Center

Publications and Distribution Center, PDC

Distribution Service

International Microform Distribution
    Service, IMDS
MARC Records Distribution Service, MRDS

Distributors

Atlantic Coast Independent Distributors
    Association, ACIDA
Bureau of Independent Publishers and
    Distributors, BIPAD
Central States Distributors Association,
    CSDA
Council for Periodical Distributors
    Associations, CPDA
International Association of Information
    Film Distributors, INFORFILM
International Association of Wholesale
    Newspaper, Periodical and Book
    Distributors, DISTRIPRESS
International Periodical Distributors
    Association, IPDA
Mid-America Periodical Distributors
    Association, MAPDA
Mid-West Independent Distributors
    Association, MIDA

District

Northwest Library District, NORWELD
Southern California Rapid Transit District,
    SCRTD

District Library

Aliquippa District Center Library, ADC

District of Columbia

District of Columbia Health Science
    Information Network, DOCHSIN
District of Columbia Library Association,
    DCLA
District of Columbia Public Library, DCPL

Division
Advanced Systems Development Division, ASDD
Division Entry, DE
Frequency Division Multiplex, FDM
Information Services Division, ISD
Library Administration Division, LAD
Reference and Adult Services Division, RASD
Resources and Technical Services Division, RTSD
Young Adult Services Division, YASD

Divisional Interests
Divisional Interests Special Committee, DISC

Divulgación Pedagógicas
Centro de Documentación y Divulgación Pedagógicas, CDDP

Doctoral Dissertations
American·Doctoral Dissertations, ADD

Document
Automated Input and Document Update System, AIDUS
Automatic Document Storage and Retrieval, ADSTAR
Current Awareness and Document Retrieval for Engineers, CADRE
Document Delivery Tests, DDT
Document Processing System, DPS
Document Retrieval, DR
ERIC Document Reproduction Service, EDRS
General Purpose Scientific Document Image Code, GPSDIC
General Purpose Scientific Document Writer, GPSDW
Heuristic Mechanized Document Information System, HERMES
New England Document Conservation Center, NEDCC
Office Document Index, ODI
Random Access Document Indexing and Retrieval, RADIR
Water Resources Document Reference Centre, WATDOC

Document Center
Research Industry Document Center, RIDC

Documentación
Centro Interamericano de Documentación, CIDOC
Centro Interamericano de Documentación Económica y Social (Interamerican Center for Economic and Social Documentation), CIADES

Documentalistas
Asociación de Bibliotecarios y Documentalistas Sislenaticos Argentinos, ABYDSA
Reunion Interamericana de Bibliotecarios y Documentalistas Agrícolas, RIBDA

Documentalists
Asociación Interamericana de Bibliotecarios y Documentalistas Agricolas (Inter-American Association of Agricultural Librarians and Documentalists), AIBDA
Associação Portuguesa de Bibliotecários, Arquivistas e Documentalistes (Portuguese Association of Librarians, Archivists and Documentalists), BAD
Association des Bibliothécaires, Archivistes, Documentalistes et Muséographes du Cameroun (Association of Librarians, Archivists, Documentalists and Museum Curators of Cameroon), ABADCAM
Association des Bibliothécaires-Documentalistes de l'Institut d'Études Sociales de l'État (Association of Librarians and Documentalists of the State Institute of Social Studies), ABD
Association Internationale des Documentalistes et Techniciens de l'Information (International Association of Documentalists and Information Officers), AID
Association Nationale des Bibliothécaires, Archivistes et Documentalistes Sénégalais (National Association of Librarians, Archivists and Documentalists of Senegal), ANBADS
Association Tunisienne des Documentalistes, Bibliothécaires et Archivistes (Tunisian Association of Documentalists, Librarians and Archivists), ATD
Association Zairoise des Archivistes, Bibliothécaires et Documentalistes (Zairian Association of Archivists, Librarians and Documentalists), AZABDO
École de Bibliothécaires, Archivistes et Documentalistes (School of Librarians, Archivists and Documentalists), EBAD
International Association of Agricultural Librarians and Documentalists, IAALD
Japanese Association of Agricultural Librarians and Documentalists, JAALD
Verein Deutscher Dokumentare (Society of German Documentalists), VDD
Vlaamse Vereniging van Bibliotheek-Archief en Documentatie-Personeel, Vereniging zonder Winstoogmerken (Flemish

Documentalists (cont.)

Association of Librarians, Archivists
and Documentalists), VVBADP
Zväz Slovenských Knihovníkov, Bibligrafov
a Informacných Pracovníkov
(Association of Slovak Librarians,
Bibliographers and Documentalists),
ZSKBIP

Documentary
Federation of Documentary Film Units,
FDFU

Documentation
American Documentation Institute, ADI
American Documentation. (Journal), AD
Arbeitsgemeinschaft für Juristisches
Bibliotheks-und Dokumentationswesen
(Association of Libraries for Law and
Documentation), AJBD
Asosiasi Perpustakaan Arsip dan
Dokumentasi Indonesia (Indonesian
Library, Archive and Documentation
Association), APADI
Association Belge de Documentation/
Belgische Vereniging voor
Documentatie (Belgian Documentation
Association), ABD/BVD
Association pour l'Avancement des Sciences
et des Techniques de la Documentation
(Association for the Advancement of the
Science and Technology of
Documentation), ASTED
Association pour le Développement de la
Documentation, des Bibliothèques et
Archives de la Côte d'Ivoire
(Association for the Development of
Documentation, Libraries and Archives
of the Ivory Coast), ADBACI
Association Sénégalaise pour le
Développement de la Documentation,
des Bibliothèques, des Archives et des
Musées (Senegal Association for the
Development of Documentation,
Libraries, Archives and Museums),
ASDBAM
Association Voltaique pour le
Développement des Bibliothèques, des
Archives et de la Documentation
(Voltan Association for the
Development of Libraries, Archives and
Documentation), AVDBAD
Associazione Italiana per la Documentazione
e l'Informazione (Italian Association for
Documentation and Information), AIDI
Automatic Documentation in Action, ADIA
Automatic Indexing of Documentation of
IFP, AID-IFP
Automation of Agricultural Information and
Documentation, ALADIN

[Building Documentation], BYGGDOK
Bureau International de Documentation des
Chemins de Fer, BDC
Center for Documentation and
Communication Research, CDCR
Center for Information and Documentation,
CID
Central Library and Documentation, CLD
Centre d'Assistance Technique et de
Documentation, CATED
Centre de Documención e Información
Educativa (Educational Documentation
and Information Center), CDIF
Centre d'Information et de Documentation
du Bâtiment, CIDB
Centre National de Documentation
Scientifique et Technique (National
Center for Scientific and Technical
Documentation), CNDST
Centro Interamericano de Documentación
Económia y Social (Interamerican
Center for Economic and Social
Documentation), CIADES
Centro Nacional de Información y
Documentación (National Center for
Information and Documentation),
CENID
Centrul de Documentare si Publicatü
Tehnice al Ministerulue Cailór Ferate
(Technical Documentation and
Publications Center of the Railway
Ministry), CDPT-MCF
Centrum voor Landbouwpiblikaties en
Landbouwdocumentatie (Center for
Agricultural Publishing and
Documentation), PUDOC
Comissão Brasileira de Documentação
Agricola (Brazilian Commission for
Agricultural Documentation), CBDA
Committee for Information and
Documentation on Science and
Technology, CIDST
*Current Research and Development in
Scientific Documentation*, CRDSD
Danmarks Tekniske Bibliotek med Dansk
Central for Dokumentation (Danish
Center for Documentation of the
Technological Library of Denmark),
DTB
Data Processing Librarians and
Documentation Managers Association,
DPL/DMA
Deutsche Gesellschaft für Dokumentation
(German Association for
Documentation), DGD
Deutsches Institut für Medizinische
Dokumentation und Information
(German Institute for Medical
Documentation and Information),
DIMDI

Diretoria de Documentação de Divulgação (Direction of Documentation and Publication), DDD
Documentation Abstracts, DA
Documentation Automated Retrieval Equipment, DARE
Documentation en Ligne pour l'Industrie Agro-Alimentaire, IALINE
Documentation Research and Training Centre, DRTC
European Center for the Coordination of Research and Documentation in the Social Sciences, CEUCORS
European Documentation Centers, EDC
European Nuclear Documentation System, ENDS
FID Committee on Linguistics in Documentation, FID/LD
FID Committee on the Terminology of Information and Documentation, FID/DT
Federação Brasileira de Associações de Bibliotecários–Comissão Brasileira de Documentação Jurídica (Brazilian Federation of Librarian Associations–Brazilian Committee of Legal Documentation), FEBAB/CBDJ
Federación Internacional de Documentación/Comisión Latinoamericana (International Federation for Documentation/Latin American Commission), FID/CLA
Fédération Internationale de Documentation (International Federation of Documentation), FID
Gesellschaft für Bibliothekswesen und Dokumentation des Landbaues (Association for Librarianship and Documentation in Agriculture), GBDL
Institut National de Recherches et de Documentation, INRDG
Instituto Brasileiro de Bibliografia e Documentação (Brazilian Institute of Bibliography and Documentation), IBBD
Instituto de Documentación e Información Científica y Tecnica (Institute of Scientific and Technical Documentation and Information), IDICT
Institutul Central de Documentare Technica (Central Institute for Technical Documentation), IDT
International Advisory Committee for Documentation and Terminology, IACDT
International Advisory Committee on Bibliography, Documentation and Terminology, IACBDT
International Advisory Committee on Documentation and Terminology in Pure and Applied Science, AICDT

International Bibliography, Information, Documentation, IBID
International Committee for Social Sciences Documentation, ICSSD
International Information System on Research in Documentation, ISORID
International Road Research Documentation, IRRD
Irish Association for Documentation and Information Services, IADIS
Journal of Chemical Documentation, JCD
Jugoslovenski Centar za Techničku i Naučno Dokumentacijua (Yugoslav Center for Technical and Scientific Documentation), JCTND
Military Documentation System, MIDONAS
Modern Information & Documentation Organizing & Rearrangement, Inc, MIDORI
National Committee of Documentation, CND
National Reprographic Centre for Documentation, NRCd
Nederlands Instituut voor Informatie, Documentatie en Registratuur (Netherlands Institute for Information, Documentation and Filing), NIDER
Nippon Documentesyon Kyokai (Japan Documentation Society), NIPDOK
Országos Orvostudományi Könyvtár és Dokumentáció Központ (National Medical Library and Center for Documentation), OOKDK
Österreichische Gesellschaft für Dokumentation und Information (Austrian Society for Documentation and Information), ÖGDI
Perhimpunan Ahli Perpustakaan, Arsipdan Dokumentasi Indonesia (IndonesianAssociation of Librarians, Archives and Documentation), PAPADI
Pesticidal Literature Documentation, PESTDOC
Pharmaco-Medical Documentation, PMD
Plastics Documentation. (Journal), PLASDOC
Rijksbureau voor Kunsthistorische Documentatie (Netherlands Institute for Art History Documentation), RKD
Schweizerische Vereinigung für Dokumentation/Association Suisse de Documentation (Swiss Association of Documentation), SVD/ASD
Secção de Documentação Adontólogica (Department of Dental Documentation), SDA
Státni Ústav pro Zdravotnickou Dokumentačm a Knihovnickou Sluzbu (State Institute for Medical Documentation and National Medical Library), SUZDKS

Documentation (cont.)

Tekniska Litteratursällskapet (Swedish
　Society for Technical Documentation),
　TLS
[Transportation Documentation],
　TRANSDOC
US National Committee for the International
　Federation for Documentation,
　USNCFID
Urban Documentation Project,
　URBANDOC

Documentation Center

Bangladesh National Scientific and
　Technical Documentation Center,
　BANSDOC
Centre de Documentation Africaine (African
　Documentation Center), CEDOCA
Centre de Documentation de la Biblothèque
　de l'Université Laval (Documentation
　Center of the Library of l'Université
　Laval), CEDOBUL
Centre de Documentation Nationale
　(National Documentation Center), CDN
Centro de Documentação Cientifica
　(Scientific Documentation Center), CDC
Centro de Esploroj Kaj Documentado
　(Research and Documentation Center),
　CED
Centrul de Documentare Agricolă
　(Agricultural Documentation Center),
　CDA
Centrul de Documentare al Industriei
　Chimice si Petroliere (Documentation
　Center of the Chemical and Oil
　Industry), CDICIP
Centrul de Documentare Medicală (Medical
　Documentation Center), CDM
Centrul de Documentare Stiitifică al
　Academiei Republicii Socialiste
　România (Scientific Documentation
　Center of the Academy of the Socialist
　Republic of Rumania), CDS
Centrul de Documentare Technică Pentru
　Economia Forestieră (Documentation
　Center on Forestry), CDF
Comisión de Documentación Científica
　(Scientific Documentation Center),
　CDDC
Defense Documentation Center, DDC
Hungarian Central Technical Library and
　Documentation Center, HCTLDC
International Patent Documentation Center,
　INPADOC
Iranian Documentation Center, IRANDOC
Pakistan National Scientific and Technical
　Documentation Center, PANSDOC
Pusat Documentasi Ilmiah Nasional
　(Indonesian Scientific and Technical
　Documentation Center), PDIN

Scandinavian Documentation Center,
　SCANDOC
Türkiye Bilimsel ve Teknik Dokümantasyon
　Merkezi (Turkish Scientific and
　Technical Documentation Center),
　TÜRDOK
Zentralstelle für Atomkernenergie
　Dokumentation (Atomic Energy
　Documentation Center), ZAED

Documentation Centers

Southwest Asia Documentation Centers,
　SADC

Documentation Centre

Indian National Scientific Documentation
　Centre, INSDOC
Scientific Documentation Centre, Ltd, SDC

Documentation Libraries

Association Internationale pour le
　Développement de la Documentation,
　des Bibliothèques et des Archives en
　Afrique (International Association for
　the Development of Documentation
　Libraries and Archives in Africa),
　AIDBA

Documentation Service

Space Documentation Service, SDS

Documentation Studies

Association Nationale d'Études pour la
　Documentation Automatique (National
　Association of Automatic
　Documentation Studies), ANEDA

Documents

Central Air Documents Office, CADO
Committee on Archives and Documents of
　Southeast Asia, CARDOSEA
Cooperative Documents, CODOC
Documents Per Minute, DPM
Documents to the People. (Journal), DttP
GODORT Federal Documents Task Force,
　GODORT/FDTF
GODORT International Documents Task
　Force, GODORT/IDTF
GODORT Local Documents Task Force,
　GODORT/LDTF
GODORT State Documents Task Force,
　GODORT/SDTF
Government Documents Round Table,
　GODORT
Superintendent of Documents, SuDocs
Superintendent of Documents Classification,
　SDC
Tentative Classification of Documents, TCD
United States Historical Documents
　Institute, HDI
United States Political Science Documents,
　USPSD

Documents Release
Air Force Technical Objectives Documents
Release Program, AFTOD

Dokumentacijskih
Sistem za Avtomatizacilo Informacijsko
Dokumentacijskih Centrov-
Elektrotehnika, SAIDC

Dokumentation
Dokumentation Maschinenbau, DOMA
Dokumentation Schweisstechnik, DS
Gesellschaft für Dokumentation und
Bibliographie, GDB
Gesellschaft für Information und
Dokumentation, GID
Zentralinstitut für Information und
Dokumentation, ZIID
Zentralstelle Dokumentation
Electrotechnique, ZDE

Dokumentation-gesellschaft
Internationale Dokumentation-gesellschaft
für Chemie, IDC

Dokumentationssystem
Informations und Dokumentationssystem
zum Umweltplanung, UMPLIS

Dokumentationszentrum
Dokumentationszentrum für
Informationswissenschaften, ZDOK

Dominican Librarians
Asociación Dominicana de Bibliotecarios
(Dominican Association of Librarians),
ASODOBI

Dominion
Dominion Law Reports, DLR

Dottrina
Dottrina, DOTTR

Double-precision
Double-precision Automatic Interpretive
System 201, DAISY 201

Drafting
Computer-Aided Design Drafting, CADD
Machine-Aided Drafting System, MADS

Draftsmen
American Society of Professional Draftsmen
and Artists, ASPDA

Drama
Royal Scottish Academy of Music and
Drama, RSAMD

Dramatists
Suomen Näytelmäkirjailijaliitto (Finnish
Dramatists Society), SUNKLO

Drammatici
Sindacato Nazionale Autori Drammatici,
SNAD
Società Italiana Autori Drammatici, SIAD

Drilling
Drilling Activity Analysis, DAAS

Drive
Delay Drive, DD

Driver
Digit Plane Driver, DPD

Drug
Australasian Drug Information Services Pty.
Limited, ADIS
Australian Drug and Medical Information
Group, ADMIG
Drug Information Service Center, DISC
Drug Information Sources, DIS
Food and Drug Administration, FDA

Drug Abuse
Alberta Alcoholism and Drug Abuse
Commission, AADAC
Drug Abuse Communications Network,
DRACON
Drug Abuse Epidemiology Data Center,
DAEDAC

Drug Information
Drug Information Association, DIA
Swedish Drug Information System, SWEDIS

Drugs
Index of Codes for Research Drugs, ICRD
Unlisted Drugs. (Journal), UD

Drum
Magnetic Drum Receiving Equipment,
MADRE

Dual
Dual Facility, DF

Duplex
Compatible Duplex System, CDS
Full Duplex, FD
Half Duplex, HD

Duplicates
Duplicates Exchange Union, DEU

Dutch
Nederlandse Boekverkopersbond
(Association of Dutch Booksellers),
NBB
Royal Dutch Pharmaceutical Society,
KNMP

Dutch Center
Netherlands Bibliotheek en Lektuur
Centrum (Dutch Center for Public
Libraries and Literature), NBLC

Dynamic
Automatic and Dynamic Monitor with
  Immediate Relocation, Allocation and
  Loading, ADMIRAL
Dynamic Debugging Technique, DDT
Dynamic Programming, DP
Dynamic Storage Allocation Language,
  DYSTAL

Dynamics
Data Dynamics, Inc, DDI
Dynamics Analyzer-Programmer, DYANA

Earth
Earth Resources Observation System, EROS
Earth Resources Technology Satellite
  Program, ERTS

Earth Science
Association of Earth Science Editors, AESE

Earth Sciences
*Current Contents/Physical, Chemical and
  Earth Sciences.* (Journal), CC/PC&ES

East
American Association of Teachers of Slavic
  and East European Languages,
  ATSEEL

East African
East African Agriculture and Forestry
  Research Organization, EAAFRO
East African Library Association, EALA

East Asian Libraries
Committee on East Asian Libraries of the
  Association for Asian Studies, CEAL

East European
ACRL Slavic and East European Section,
  ACRL/SEES
American Association of Teachers of Slavic
  and East European Languages,
  AATSEEL
Coordinating Committee for Slavic–East
  European Library Services,
  COCOSEER
Slavic and East European Journal, SEEJ

Eastern Europe
Business Eastern Europe. (Journal), BEE

École
École Nationale du Petrole et des Moteurs,
  ENSPM

Ecological
Ecological Society of America, ESA

Economic
ASLIB Economic and Business Information
  Group, AEBIG
Center for Studies in Economic
  Development, CEDE

Centro Interamericano de Documentación
  Económia y Social (Interamerican
  Center for Economic and Social
  Documentation), CIADES
Centro Nacional de Información Económica
  y Social (National Center for Economic
  and Social Information), CNIES
Council on Economic Priorities, CEP
Economic and Social Commission for Asia
  and the Pacific, ESCAP
Economic Commission for Asia and the Far
  East, ECAFE
Economic Planning Unit of Barbados, EPU
European Economic Community, EEC
Michigan Quarterly Economic Model,
  MQEM
National Bureau of Economic Research,
  NBER
Organization for Economic Cooperation and
  Development, OECD
Organization for European Economic
  Cooperation, OEEC
Schweizerisches Wirtschaftsarchiv (Swiss
  Economic Archives), SWA
Survey of Economic Opportunity, SEO

Economic Information
Centralny Instytut Informacji Naukowo
  Technicznej i Ekonomicznej (Central
  Institute for Scientific, Technical and
  Economic Information), CIINTE
Economic Information Systems, EIS
Ústředí Vědeckých Technických a
  Ekonomických Informací (Central
  Office of Scientific, Technical and
  Economic Information), UVTEI

Economics
ASIS Special Interest Group on Costs
  Budgeting and Economics,
  ASIS/SIG/CBE
Bibliothekarisch-Analytisches System zur
  Informations-Speicherung-Erschliessung
  (Library Analytical System for
  Information Storage/
  Retrieval-Economics), BASIS-E
Corporation for Economics and Industrial
  Research, CEIR
Research Seminar in Quantitative
  Economics, RSQE
*World Agricultural Economics and Rural
  Sociology Abstracts*, WAERSA

Economicznej
Centralny Instytut Informasui Noukowo
  Techniceneu I Economicznej (Central
  Institute for Scientific, Technical and
  Economic Information), CLINTE

Économique
Association Française pour la Cybernétique
  Économique et Technique, AFCET

Centre de Documentation Économique et
Sociale, CIDES
Institut National de la Statistique et des
Études Économique, INSEE

Économiques
Association des Journalistes Économiques et
Financiers, AJEF

Écrites
Hansard Questions Écrites, HQE

Écrivains
Schweizerischer Schriftsteller-
Verband/Société Suisse des Écrivains,
SSV/SSE

Ecuadorian
Asociación Ecuatoriana de Bibliotecarios
(Ecuadorian Library Association), AEB

Edinburgh
Royal College of Physicians of Edinburgh,
RCPE
Royal College of Surgeons of Edinburgh,
RCSEd

Edit
Sort-Key Edit, SKED

Éditeurs
Fédération des Éditeurs Belges, FEB
Union Nationale des Éditeurs-Exportateurs
de Publications Françaises, UNEEPF

Éditeurs de Journaux
Association Luxembourgeoise des Éditeurs
de Journaux, ALEJ

Editing
Machine-Aided Composing and Editing,
MACE

Editor
Automatic Microfiche Editor, AME
Quick Text Editor, QED

Editori
Federazione Italiana Editori Giornali, FIEG

Editorial
Decimal Classification Editorial Policy
Committee, DCEPC

Editors
American Agricultural Editors Association,
AAEA
American Association of Agricultural
College Editors, AAACE
American Association of Industrial Editors,
AAIE
Association of Earth Science Editors, AESE
Association of Technical Writers and
Editors, ATWE

Bibliographic Guide for Editors and Authors,
BGEA
British Association of Industrial Editors,
BAIE
Committee of Small Magazine Editors and
Publishers, COSMEP
Council of Biology Editors, CBE
Federation of European Industrial Editors
Associations, FEIEA
Guild of British Newspapers Editors, GBNE
Poets, Playwrights, Editors, Essayists and
Novelists International English Centre,
PEN
Society of Technical Writers and Editors,
STWE

Edmonton
Edmonton Library Association, ELA

Education
ACM Special Interest Group on Computer
Science Education, ACM/SIGCSE
ACM Special Interest Group on Computer
Uses in Education, ACM/SIGCUE
ACRL Education and Behavioral Sciences
Section, ACRL/EBSS
ASIS Special Interest Group on Education
for Information Science, ASIS/SIG/ED
ASIS Special Interest Group on Information
Services to Education, ASIS/SIG/ISE
Abstracts of Instructional and Research
Materials in Vocational and Technical
Education, AIM/ARM
Abstracts of Instructional Materials in
Vocational and Technical Education,
AIM
Abstracts of Research and Related Materials
in Vocational and Technical Education,
ARM
Adult Referral and Information Service in
Education, ARISE
Acrospace Education Foundation, AEF
Agricultural Communicators in Education,
ACE
Alabama Center for Higher Education,
ACHE
Alabama Consortium for the Development of
Higher Education, ACDHE
Alliance of Associations for the
Advancement of Education, AAAE
American Association for Higher Education,
AAHE
American Association for Public
Information, Education and Research,
AAPIER
American Association of Colleges for
Teacher Education, AACTE
American Council of Pharmaceutical
Education, ACPE
American Council on Education, ACE
American Council on Education for
Journalism, ACEJ

Education (cont.)

American Education Association, AEA
American Society for Engineering
    Education, ASEE
Armed Forces Information and Education
    Division, AFIED
Asociación de Bibliotecarios de Instituciones
    de Enseñanza Superior y de
    Investigación (Association of Librarians
    of Institutions of Higher Education and
    Research), ABIESI
Asociación Mexicana de Educación Agricola
    Superior (Mexican Association for
    Agricultural Higher Education),
    AMEAS
Association Canadienne d'Éducation de
    Langue Française, ACELF
Association for Childhood Education
    International, ACEI
Association for Education by
    Radio-Television, AERT
Association for Education in Journalism,
    AEJ
Association for Higher Education, AHE
Association Internationale d'Information
    Scolaire Universitaire et Professionelle
    (International Association for Education
    and Vocational Information), AIISUP
Association of Directors of Education in
    Scotland, ADES
Augmented Individualized Courses in
    Continuing Education, AICCE
Automated Computer Science Education
    System, ACSES
Books for Equal Education, BEE
Bureau of Health Manpower Education,
    BHME
California Education Information System,
    CEIS
Canadian Education Association, CEA
Center for Labor Education and Research,
    CLEAR
Center for Research and Evaluation in
    Applications of Technology in
    Education, CREATE
Centre d'Animation, de Développement et
    de Recherche en Education, CADRE
Clearinghouse for Options in Children's
    Education, CHOICE
Computer Education Group, CEG
Computer-Assisted Instruction Regional
    Education Network, CAI
Computer-Assisted Renewal Education,
    CARE
Computers in Education Division, COED
Consortium for Higher Education Religion
    Studies, CHERS
Continuing Education, CE
Council for Higher Education in Newark,
    CHEN

Current Index to Journals in Education,
    CIJE
Curricula for Ethnic Education Directory,
    CEED
Data Processing for Education.
    (Newsletter), DPED
Department of Education and Science, DES
Department of Health, Education and
    Welfare, DHEW
Department of Health, Education and
    Welfare, HEW
Dial Access Technical Education, DATE
ERIC Clearinghouse for Science,
    Mathematics and Environmental
    Education, ERIC/SE
ERIC Clearinghouse for Social
    Studies/Social Science Education,
    ERIC/SO
ERIC Clearinghouse on Adult, Career, and
    Vocational Education, ERIC/CE
ERIC Clearinghouse on Elementary and
    Early Childhood Education, ERIC/PS
ERIC Clearinghouse on Higher Education,
    ERIC/HE
ERIC Clearinghouse on Rural Education and
    Small Schools, ERIC/RC
ERIC Clearinghouse on Teacher Education,
    ERIC/SP
ERIC Clearinghouse on Urban Education,
    ERIC/UD
Education Advice Bureau, EAB
Education Development Center, Inc, EDC
Education Group of the Music Industries
    Association, EGMIA
Education Professions Development Act,
    EPDA
Education Writers Association, EWA
Elementary and Secondary Education Act,
    ESEA
Exceptional Child Education Resources,
    ECER
FID Committee on Education and Training,
    FID/ET
Federation for Unified Science Education,
    FUSE
Florida Association for Media and
    Education, FAME
Foundation of Record Education, FORE
Fund for the Improvement of Post Secondary
    Education, FIPSE
Higher Education Act of 1965, HEA
Higher Education Coordinating Council of
    Metropolitan Saint Louis, HECC
Higher Education General Information
    Survey, HEGIS
Higher Education Learning Programmes
    Information Service: A Catalogue of
    Materials Available for Exchange,
    HELPIS
Indiana Higher Education Television
    System, IHETS

Industrial Education Institute, IEI
Institute of International Education, IIE
Interdisciplinary Machine Processing for Research and Education in the Social Sciences, IMPRESS
International Graphic Arts Education Association, IGAEA
Journal of Education for Librarianship, JEL
Kansas City Regional Council for Higher Education, KCRCHE
Librarians in Education and Research in the Northeast, LEARN
Libraries of the Institutes and Schools of Education, LISE
Libros Elementales Educativos Recreativos (Elementary Books for Education and Recreation), LEER
McGill Elementary Education Teaching Teams, MEET
National Advisory Council for Education for Industry and Commerce, NACEIC
National Committee for Audiovisual Aids in Education, NCAVAE
National Council for Accreditation of Teacher Education, NCATE
National Education Association, NEA
National Institute of Education, NIE
Network for Continuing Medical Education, NCME
New England Board of Higher Education, NEBHE
Oregon State System of Higher Education–Oregon State Library, OSSHE-OSL
PLA Alternative Education Programs Section, PLA/AEPS
Pan-Pacific Education and Communication Experiments by Satellite, PEACESAT
Philadelphia's Adult Basic Education Academy, PABEA
Pittsburgh Council on Higher Education, PCHE
Public Education Association, PEA
Research Information Services for Education, RISE
Resources in Education. (Journal), RIE
Resources in Vocational Education. (Journal), RIVE
Scottish Technical Education Consultative Council, STECC
Society for Automation in Business Education, SABE
Society for Automation in Professional Education, SAPE
Society for Education in Film and Television, SEFT
Society of Independent and Private School Data Education, SIPSDE
South Australia Education Resource Information System, SAERIS
Southeast Asian Ministers of Education Council, SEAMEC
Southeastern Association for Cooperation in Higher Education in Massachusetts, SACHEM
Southern Regional Education Board, SREB
Technical and Further Education Commission, TAFEC
Theological Education Association of Mid-America, TEAM-A
United States Office of Education, USOE
Universities Council for Adult Education, UCAE
Visual Education National Information Service for Schools, VENISS
Vocational Education Program Information System, VEPIS
Western Interstate Commission for Higher Education, WICHE
Worcester Consortium for Higher Education, WCHE
World Tapes for Education, WTE

Education Center
Higher Education Center for Urban Studies, HECUS
Lehigh Valley Area Health Education Center Library Consortium, LVAHEC

Education Service
Royal Air Force Education Service, RAFES

Education Services
Open Access Satellite Education Services, OASES

Educational
Alternatives for Learning through Educational Research and Technology, ALERT
American Educational Publishers Institute, AEPI
American Educational Research Association, AERA
Associated Library and Educational Research Team for Survival, ALERTS
Association for Educational Communications and Technology, AECT
Association for Educational Data Systems, AEDS
Association of Publishers Educational Representatives, APER
Australian Council for Educational Research, ACER
Board of Cooperative Educational Services, BOCES
Bureau of Libraries and Educational Technology, BLET
California Educational Data Processing Association, CEDPA

Educational (cont.)

Canadian Educational Researchers Association/Association Canadienne des Chercheurs en Éducation, CERA/ACCE

Center for Educational Development Overseas, CEDO

Center for Educational Research and Innovation, CERI

Center for the Advanced Study of Educational Administration, CASEA

Centre de Documención e Información Educativa (Educational Documentation and Information Center), CDIF

Centre for Curriculum Renewal and Educational Development Overseas, CREDO

Centre for Educational Television Overseas, CETO

Centro Brasileiro de Pesquisas Educacionais–Divisão de Documentacão e Informacão Pedagógica (Brazilian Center of Educational Research–Department of Educational Documentation and Information), CBPE-DDIP

Computer-Based Educational Materials, CBEM

Conseil International pour les Films d'Éducation (International Council for Educational Films), CIFE

Cooperative Educational Abstracting Service, CEAS

Council for Educational Technology, CET

Current Contents/Behavioral, Social and Educational Sciences. (Journal), CC/BSE

Division of Educational Technology, DET

ERIC Clearinghouse on Educational Management, ERIC/EA

East Midland Educational Union, EMEU

Educational Centres Association, ECA

Educational Development Association, EDA

Educational Exhibitors Association, EEA

Educational Film Library Association, EFLA

Educational Institute of Scotland, EIS

Educational Media Catalogs on Microfiche, EMCOM

Educational Media Council, EMC

Educational Media Institute Evaluation Project, EMIE

Educational Media Selection Centers, EMSC

Educational Products and Information Exchange, EPIE

Educational Research Service, ERS

Educational Resources Information Center, ERIC

Educational Television, ETV

Educational Television Branch of Ontario, ETVO

Educational Television Stations, ETS

Educational Testing Service, ETS

Encyclopaedia Britannica Educational Corporation, EBE

French American Cultural Services and Educational Aid, FACSEA

Inner London Educational Authority, ILEA

Institut International de la Planification de l'Éducation/International Institute for Educational Planning, IIPE/IIEP

Joint Council on Educational Broadcasting, JCEB

Joint Council on Educational Telecommunications, JCET

Kansas–Nebraska Educational Consortium, KANEDCO

Machine-Assisted Educational System for Teaching by Remote Operation, MAESTRO

Massachusetts Conference of Chief Librarians in Public Higher Educational Institutions, MCCLPHEI

Middle Atlantic Educational and Research Center, MERC

National Association of Business and Educational Radio, NABER

National Association of Educational Broadcasters, NAEB

National Center for Educational Communication, NCEC

National Center for Educational Statistics, NCES

National Council for Educational Technology, NCET

National Educational Television, NET

National Educational Television and Radio Center, NETRC

National Foundation for Educational Research in England and Wales, NFER

National Information Center for Educational Media, NICEM

National Institute for Educational Research (Kokuritsu Kyoiku Kenkyusho Fuzoku Kyoiku Toshokan), NIER

New England Educational Data System, NEEDS

Office of Audiovisual Educational Development, OAED

Ohio Educational Library Media Association, OELMA

Ontario Educational Communications Authority, OECA

Packets of Educational Topics, PET

Saskatchewan Association of Educational Media Specialists, SAEMS

Scientific Information and Educational Council of Physicians, SIECOP

Scottish Educational Film Association,
SEFA
Society for Educational Data Systems,
SEDS
Society of Educational Programmers and
Systems Analysts, SEPSA
South Western Educational Library Project,
SWELP
Southwest Regional Laboratory for
Educational Research and
Development, SWRL
Texas Educational Microwave Project,
TEMP
Total Information for Educational Systems,
TIES
United Nations Educational, Scientific and
Cultural Organization, UNESCO
Upper Midwest Regional Educational
Laboratory, UMREL
Vermont Educational Media Association,
VEMA
Virginia Educational Media Association,
VEMA
Wandsworth Public, Educational and
Technical Library Services,
WANDPETLS
Women's Educational Equity
Communications Network, WEECN

Educational Libraries
Arbeitsgemeinschaft Pädagogischer
Bibliotheken und Medienzentren
(Working Group of Educational
Libraries and Media Centers), APB

Educativa
Instituto Latinoamericano de
Cinematographía Educativa, ILCE
Instituto Latinoamericano de la
Communicación Educativa, ILCE

Éducative
Société Nationale de Diffusion Éducative et
Culturelle, SONDEC

Educators
Catholic Audio-Visual Educators
Association, CAVE
Educators Information Technology System,
EDITS
Society of Data Educators, SDE

Effectiveness
Financial Analysis of Management
Effectiveness, FAME

Effector
Format Effector, FE

Efficient
Efficient Assembly System, EASY

Egyptian
Egyptian Organization for Standardization,
EOS
Egyptian School Library Association, ESLA

Elderly
ASCLA Library Services to the Impaired
Elderly Section, ASCLA/LSIES

Electric
Bay Electric Company, BEC
Electric Circuit Analysis Program, ECAP
Radio and Electric Component
Manufacturers Federation, RECMF

Electrical
Aerospace Electrical Society, AES
American Institute of Electrical Engineers,
AIEE
Committee on Computer Science in
Electrical Engineering, COSINE
Electrical Accounting for the Security
Industry, EASI
Electrical Accounting Machinery, EAM
Electrical and Electronic Abstracts, EEA
Electrical Tough Pitch, ETP
Electrical Utilities Applications, EUA
Institute of Electrical and Electronics
Engineers, IEEE
Institution of Electrical and Electronics
Technicians Engineers, Ltd, IEETE
Institution of Electrical Engineers, IEE
Remote Electrical Alphanumeric Display,
READ

Electricité
Electricité de France, EDF

Electrocardiography
Computer-Assisted Electrocardiography,
CAE

Electrodata
Bell Little Electrodata Symbolic System for
the Electrodata, BLESSED

Electrode
Microalloy Diffused Electrode, MADE

Electromagnetic
Electromagnetic Systems Laboratories, ESL

Electron
American Society for X-Ray and Electron
Diffraction, ASXED
Computer-ControlledScanning Electron
Microscope, CCSEM
Electron Beam Recording, EBR

Electronic

Boeing Electronic Analog Computer, BEAC
British Overseas Airways Digital
    Information Computer for Electronic
    Automation, BOADICEA
Electrical and Electronic Abstracts, EEA
Electronic Accounting Machine, EAM
Electronic Automatic Exchange, EAX
Electronic Components Data Bank, ECDB
Electronic Coordinatograph and Readout
    System, ECARS
Electronic Data Gathering Equipment,
    EDGE
Electronic Data Processing, EDP
Electronic Data Processing Equipment,
    EDPE
Electronic Data Processing Machine, EDPM
Electronic Data Processing System, EDPS
Electronic Discrete Sequential Automatic
    Computer, EDSAC
Electronic Discrete Variable Automatic
    Computer, EDVAC
Electronic Numerical Integrator and
    Calculator, ENIAC
Electronic Properties Information Center,
    EPIC
Electronic Security Systems, ESS
Electronic Switching System, ESS
Electronic Videorecording, EVR
Heckman's Electronic Library Program,
    HELP
Institution of Electronic and Radio
    Engineers, IERE
JICST Electronic Information Processing
    Automatic Computer, JEIPAC
National Electronic Injury Surveillance
    System, NEISS
National's Electronic Autocoding
    Technique, NEAT
Princeton Electronic Products–Model 402,
    PEP-402
Professional Group on Electronic
    Computers, PGEC
Real-Time Electronic Access and Display,
    READ
Reeves Electronic Analog Computer, REAC
Selective Sequence Electronic Calculator,
    SSEC
Self-Programmed Electronic Equation
    Delineator, SPEED
Simple Transition to Electronic Processing,
    STEP
Standards Electronic Automatic Computer,
    SEAC
System for Electronic Analysis and Retrieval
    of Criminal Histories, SEARCH

Electronics

Armed Forces Communications and
    Electronics Association, AFCEA

Automatic Computer-Controlled Electronics
    Scanning System, ACCESS
Canadian Military Electronics Standards
    Agency, CAMESA
*Dictionary of Electronics Abbreviations,
    Signs and Symbols*, DEA
Electronics Research Center, ERC
General Telephone and Electronics
    Corporation, GTE
IEEE Retrieval from the Literature on
    Electronics and Computer Sciences,
    IEEE REFLECS
Institute of Electrical and Electronics
    Engineers, IEEE
Institution of Electrical and Electronics
    Technicians Engineers, Ltd, IEETE
Joint Departmental Radio and Electronics
    Measurements Committee, REMC
Legal Information Through Electronics,
    LITE
National Electronics Conference, NEC
Naval Electronics Laboratory International
    Algebraic Compiler, NELIAC

Electronique

Systeme Electronique de Selection
    Automatique de Microfilms, SESAM

Electrostatic

Electrostatic Storage Deflection, ESD

Electrotechnical

International Electrotechnical Commission,
    IEC

Electrotechnique

Zentralstelle Dokumentation
    Electrotechnique, ZDE

Electrotechnology

Information Service in Physics,
    Electrotechnology and Control,
    INSPEC

Element

Decision Element, DE
Digital Display Generator Element, DDGE
Digital Element, DE
Display Element, DE
Main Storage Control Element, MSCE

Elementary

ERIC Clearinghouse on Elementary and
    Early Childhood Education, ERIC/PS
Elementary and Secondary Education Act,
    ESEA
Elementary Perceiver and Memorizer,
    EPAM
Libros Elementales Educativos Recreativos
    (Elementary Books for Education and
    Recreation), LEER
McGill Elementary Education Teaching
    Teams, MEET

Elevation
Terrain Elevation Retrieval Program, TERP

Emergency
International Children's Emergency Fund,
    ICEF
National Emergency Medical Services
    Information Network, NEMSINET

Emerging Libraries
International Network of Emerging
    Libraries, INEL

Empire
Inland Empire Academic Libraries
    Cooperative, IEALC

Employees
American Federation of Government
    Employees, AFGE
American Federation of State, County, and
    Municipal Employees, AFSCME
Black Employees of the Library of Congress,
    BELC
Canadian Union of Public Employees, CUPE
Retail Book, Stationery and Allied Trades
    Employees Association, RBA

Employment
Equal Employment Opportunity
    Commission, EEOC

Encoding
Automatic Digital Encoding System, ADES
Automatic Digital Encoding System,
    ADES-II
Dual Independent Map Encoding File of the
    Counties of the US, DIMECO
Pictorial Encoding Language, PENCIL

Encyclopaedia
AASL Encyclopaedia Britannica, AASL/EB
Encyclopaedia Britannica, EB
Encyclopaedia Britannica Educational
    Corporation, EBE
Encyclopaedia Britannica, Inc, EB

Encyclopedia
*Encyclopedia of Engineering Signs and
    Symbols*, EESS

End
End of File, EOF
End of Job, EOJ
End of Medium, EM
End of Message, EOM
End of Text, ETX
End of Transmission, EOT
End of Transmission-Block, ETB

End User
End User Facility Task Group, EUFTG

Endowment
National Endowment for the Arts, NEA
National Endowment for the Humanities,
    NEH

Energy
Canada Centre for Mineral and Energy
    Technology, CANMET
Department of Energy, DOE
Energy Bibliography and Index, EBI
Energy Information Center, EIC
[Energy Online], ENERGYLINE
Energy Research and Development
    Administration, ERDA
*High Energy Physics Index
    (Hochenergiephysik-Index)*, HEPI
National Energy Information Center
    Affiliate, NEICA
National Energy Referral and Information
    System, NERIS
Personality, Matter, Energy, Space and
    Time, PMEST
World Energy Supplies System,
    WORLDENERGY

Engineering
*Abstracts of Photographic Science and
    Engineering Literature*, APSE
American Society for Engineering
    Education, ASEE
*Applied Chemistry and Chemical
    Engineering Sections of Chemical
    Abstracts*, ACCESS
Asian Information Center for Geotechnical
    Engineering, AGE
Associated Engineering Services, Limited,
    AESL
Association for Broadcast Engineering
    Standards, Inc, ABES
Association of Engineering Geologists, AEG
Association of European Engineering
    Periodicals, AEEP
Association of Scientists and Professional
    Engineering Personnel, ASPEP
Audio Engineering Society, Inc, AES
Automated Engineering Design System,
    AED
Automatic Traffic Engineering and
    Management Information System,
    ATEMIS
Biomedical Engineering Society, BMES
Business and Engineering Enriched
    FORTRAN, BEEF
Civil Engineering Problems, CEPS
Committee on Computer Science in
    Electrical Engineering, COSINE
Committee on Public Engineering Policy,
    COPEP
Computer Science and Engineering Board,
    CSEB
Computer-Aided Design Engineering, CADE

Engineering (cont.)

Computerized *Engineering Index*,
    COMPENDEX
Conference of Engineering Societies of
    Western Europe and the United States
    of America, EUSEC
Council of Engineering and Scientific Society
    Executives, CESSE
Council of Engineering and Scientific Society
    Secretaries, CESS
*Current Contents/Engineering, Technology
    and Applied Sciences*. (Journal),
    CC/ET&AS
*Dictionary of Civil Engineering
    Abbreviations, Signs and Symbols*,
    DCEA
*Dictionary of Industrial Engineering
    Abbreviations, Signs and Symbols*,
    DIEA
*Dictionary of Mechanical Engineering
    Abbreviations, Signs and Symbols*,
    DMEA
*Encyclopedia of Engineering Signs and
    Symbols*, EESS
Engineering Automatic System for Solving
    Equations, EASE
Engineering Departmental Interface Control
    Technique, EDICT
Engineering Equipment Users Association,
    EEUA
Engineering Index. (Journal), EI
Engineering Index Thesaurus, EIT
Engineering Industries Association, EIA
Engineering Maintenance Information
    System, EMIS
Engineering Reference Branch, ERB
Engineering Research Associates, ERA
Engineering School Libraries Division,
    ESLD
Engineering Societies Library, ESL
European Federation of Chemical
    Engineering, EFCE
Expansion Symbolic Compiling Assembly
    Program for Engineering, ESCAPE
Fluid Engineering, FLUIDEX
Highway Engineering Exchange Program,
    HEEP
Hydraulic Engineering Information Analysis
    Center, HEIAC
Idaho National Engineering Laboratory,
    INEL
*Indexed References to Biomedical
    Engineering Literature*, IRBEL
Industrial Engineering. (Journal), IE
Information Service in Mechanical
    Engineering, ISMEC
Junior Engineering Technical Society, JETS
Mechanical Engineering Publications, MEP
National Academy of Engineering, NAE

National Academy of Sciences–National
    Academy of Engineering–National
    Research Council, NAS–NAE–NRC
National Council of Engineering Examiners,
    NCEE
National Council of State Boards of
    Engineering Examiners, NCSBEE
Publications Indexed for Engineering, PIE
Soil Engineering Problem-Oriented
    Language, SEPOL
Structural Engineering System Solver,
    STRESS
Subject Headings for Engineering, SHE
Systems Engineering, SE
*Thesaurus of Engineering and Scientific
    Terms*, TEST
Transdisciplinary Engineering Information
    Program, TEIP
United Engineering Trustees, Inc, UET
World Federation of Engineering
    Organizations, WFEO

Engineering Services
Northern Engineering Services Company,
    Ltd, NESCL

Engineers
American Consulting Engineers Council,
    ACEC
American Institute of Chemical Engineers,
    AIChE
American Institute of Consulting Engineers,
    AICE
American Institute of Electrical Engineers,
    AIEE
American Institute of Industrial Engineers,
    AIIE
American Institute of Mining, Metallurgical
    and Petroleum Engineers, AIME
American Society of Civil Engineers, ASCE
American Society of Mechanical Engineers,
    ASME
American Society of Naval Engineers,
    ASNE
Association of Consulting Chemists and
    Chemical Engineers, ACC&CE
Association of Consulting Management
    Engineers, ACME
Association of Federal Communications
    Consulting Engineers, AFCCE
Association of Iron and Steel Engineers,
    AISE
Canadian Council of Professional
    Engineers/Conseil Canadien des
    Ingénieurs Professionels, CCPE/CCIP
Consulting Engineers Council, CEC
Current Awareness and Document Retrieval
    for Engineers, CADRE
Current Information Tapes for Engineers,
    CITE
Engineers Joint Council, EJC

Gesellschaft Deutscher Metallhuttens und
Bergleute (Association of German
Metallurgical and Mining Engineers),
GDMB
Institute of Electrical and Electronics
Engineers, IEEE
Institute of Radio Engineers, IRE
Institution of Civil Engineers, ICE
Institution of Electrical and Electronics
Technicians Engineers, Ltd, IEETE
Institution of Electrical Engineers, IEE
Institution of Electronic and Radio
Engineers, IERE
National Association of Corrosion
Engineers, NACE
National Association of County Engineers,
NACE
National Association of Government
Engineers, NAOGE
National Association of Power Engineers,
NAPE
National Institute of Ceramic Engineers,
NICE
National Institute of Packaging, Handling
and Logistics Engineers, NIPHLE
Professional Engineers Conference Board for
Industry, PECBI
Refrigerating Engineers and Technicians
Association, RETA
Simple Algebraic Language for Engineers,
SALE
Society of Aerospace Material and Process
Engineers, SAMPE
Society of Automotive Engineers, SAE
Society of Mining Engineers, SME
Society of Motion Picture and Television
Engineers, SMPTE
Society of Naval Architects and Marine
Engineers, SNAME
Society of Petroleum Engineers, SPE
Society of Photographic Scientists and
Engineers, SPSE
Society of Photo-Optical Instrumentation
Engineers, SPIE
Society of Women Engineers, SWE

England
Library Advisory Council for England, LAC
National Foundation for Educational
Research in England and Wales, NFER
Royal Agricultural Society of England,
RASE
Royal College of Surgeons of England,
RCSEng

English
Air Force English Syntax Project, AFESP
Associated Organizations of Teachers of
English, AOTE
Automated Processing of Medical English,
APME

*Cambridge Bibliography of English
Literature*, CBEL
*Consolidated Index of Translations into
English*, CITE
Dictionary of American Regional English,
DARE
Direct English Access and Control,
DEACON
English Place-Name Society, EPNS
English Teaching Information Centre, ETIC
Fundamentally Analyzable Simplified
English, FASE
National Council of Teachers of English,
NCTE
Oxford English Dictionary, OED
Poets, Playwrights, Editors, Essayists and
Novelists International English Centre,
PEN
Society for Automation in English and the
Humanities, SAEH

Engravers
Gravure Engravers Association, GEA
Royal Society of Painter-Etchers and
Engravers, RE

Enhancement
Library Service Enhancement Program,
LSEP

Enlightenment
Association for Research and
Enlightenment, ARE

Enquiry
Canadian On-Line Enquiry, CAN/OLE
Enquiry Character, ENQ
Scientific and Technological Information
Services Enquiry Committee, STISEC

Enseignants Bibliothécaires
Association des Enseignants Bibliothécaires
du Québec, AEBQ

Enseignants—Bibliothécaires
Conseil des Enseignants—Bibliothécaires
Franco-Ontariens, CEBFO

Enseignement
Bureau pour l'Enseignement de la Langue et
de la Civilisation Françaises à
l'Étranger, BELC

Entomology
Military Entomology Information Service,
MEIS

Entries
Classified Entries in Lateral Transposition,
CELT

Entry
Automatic Data Entry, ADE
Division Entry, DE
Request Select Entry, RSE

Environment
COBOL-Oriented Real-Time Environment,
    CORTEZ
Computer-Aided Design Environment,
    COMRADE
Environment Information Center, Inc, EIC
[Environment Information On-Line],
    ENVIROLINE
Scientific Committee on Problems of the
    Environment, SCOPE
United Nations Environment Program,
    UNEP

Environmental
Center for Environmental Research and
    Development, CERD
Center for Marine and Environmental
    Studies, CMES
*Current Contents/Agriculture, Biology and
    Environmental Sciences.* (Journal),
    CC/AB&ES
ERIC Clearinghouse for Science,
    Mathematics and Environmental
    Education, ERIC/SE
Environmental Conservation Library, ECOL
Environmental Data Collection and
    Processing Facility, EDCPF
Environmental Data Index, ENDEX
Environmental Periodicals Bibliography,
    EPB
Environmental Protection Agency, EPA
[Environmental Psychology], ENVPSYCH
Environmental Science and Information
    Center, ESIC
Great Lakes Environmental Information
    Sharing, GLEIS
Health Effects of Environmental Pollutants,
    HEEP
Hierarchical Environmental Retrieval for
    Management Access and Networking,
    HERMAN
Huxley Environmental Reference Bureau,
    HERB
Inter-Professional Ad Hoc Group for
    Environmental Information Sharing,
    IPAHGEIS
Marine Environmental Data Information
    Referral System, MEDI
National Environmental Satellite Service,
    NESS
Technical Environmental and Management
    Planning Operations, TEMPO

Environmental Information
Colorado Committee for Environmental
    Information, CCEI

Committee for Environmental Information,
    CEI
Environmental Information Division, EID
International Referral System for Sources of
    Environmental Information, IRS
Oklahoma Environmental Information and
    Media Center, OEIMC

Epidemiology
Drug Abuse Epidemiology Data Center,
    DAEDAC

Epilepsy
Epilepsy Abstracts Retrieval System, EARS
[Epilepsy On-Line], EPILEPSYLINE

Equal
Equal Employment Opportunity
    Commission, EEOC

Equation
Self-Programmed Electronic Equation
    Delineator, SPEED

Equations
Algebraic and Differential Equations
    Processor and Translator, ADEPT
Engineering Automatic System for Solving
    Equations, EASE

Equilibria
Vapour Liquid Equilibria Databank, VLE
    BANK

Equipment
Aerospace Ground-Support Equipment,
    AGE
Automated Catalog of Computer Equipment
    and Software Systems, ACCESS
Automatic Checkout and Readiness
    Equipment, ACRE
Automatic Data Processing Equipment,
    ADPE
Automatic Data Processing Equipment and
    Software, ADPE/S
Automatic Data Processing Equipment
    Selection Office, ADPESO
Built-In Test Equipment, BITE
Business Equipment Manufacturers
    Association, BEMA
Business Equipment Trade Association,
    BETA
Central Data Conversion Equipment, CDCE
Computer and Business Equipment
    Manufacturers Association, CBEMA
Computer Users Replacement Equipment,
    CURE
Cooperating Users of Burroughs Equipment,
    CUBE
Digital Data Conversion Equipment, DDCE
Digital Data Output Conversion Equipment,
    DDOCE

Digital Equipment Computer Users Society, DECUS

Digital Equipment Corporation, DEC

Digital Equipment Corporation's Automatic Design System, DECADE

Digital Input/Output Display Equipment, DIODE

Display Equipment, DE

Documentation Automated Retrieval Equipment, DARE

Electronic Data Gathering Equipment, EDGE

Electronic Data Processing Equipment, EDPE

Engineering Equipment Users Association, EEUA

Graphic Arts Composing Equipment, GRACE

Information System for Adaptive, Assistive and Recreational Equipment, ISAARE

LAMA Buildings and Equipment Section, LAMA/BES

Library Computer Equipment Review. (Journal), LCER

Magnetic Drum Receiving Equipment, MADRE

Media Equipment Resource Center, MERC

Micrographics Equipment Review. (Journal), MER

Office Equipment Manufacturers Institute, OEMI

Operational Assistance and Instructive Data Equipment, OAIDE

RADAR Data Processing Equipment, RDPE

Random Access Computer Equipment, RACE

Random Access Programming and Checkout Equipment, RAPCOE

Remotely Operated Special Equipment, ROSE

System to Coordinate the Operation of Peripheral Equipment, SCOPE

Tape-Controlled Recording Automatic Checkout Equipment, TRACE

Teletypewriter Equipment, TTY

Versatile Automatic Test Equipment, VATE

Equitable Life
Equitable Life Interpreter, ELI

Equities
College Retirement Equities Fund, CREF

Equity
Women's Educational Equity Communications Network, WEECN

Equivalent
Full-Time Equivalent, FTE

Erasure Channel
Binary Error-Erasure Channel, BEEC

Error
Binary Error-Erasure Channel, BEEC
Error, ERR
Error Correcting, EC
Error Detecting, ED

Escape
Data Link Escape, DLE
Escape Character, ESC

Esercenti
Association Cattolica Esercenti Cinema, ACEC
Associazione Nazionale Esercenti Cinema, ANEC

Español
Instituto Nacional del Libro Español, INLE
Servicio de Información sobre Traducciones Cientificas en Español, SITCE

Española
Asociación Española de Prensa Tecnica, AEPT

Esperanto
Esperanto League for North America, Inc, ELNA

Essay
Essay and General Literature Index, EGLI

Essayists
Poets, Playwrights, Editors, Essayists and Novelists International English Centre, PEN

Establishment
Atomic Energy Research Establishment, AERE
Atomic Weapons Research Establishment, AWRE
Defence Operational Analysis Establishment, DOAE

Estampe
Vereinigung der Buchantiquare und Kupferstichhändler in der Schweiz/Syndicat de la Libraire Ancienne et du Commerce de l'Estampe en Suisse, VEBUKU/SLACES

Estimation
Estimation de Proprietés Physiques pour l'Ingenieur Chimiste, EPIC

Ethiopian
Ethiopian Library Association, ELA

Ethnic
Curricula for Ethnic Education Directory, CEED
Ethnic Materials Information Exchange Task Force, EMIETF

Ethnographic
Ethnographic Bibliography of North America, EBNA

Étrangère
Union de la Presse Étrangère en Belgique, UPE

Étude des Eaux
Association Française pour l'Étude des Eaux, AFEE

Europäischer Lehrmittelfirmen
Association Européenne de Fabricants et des Revendeurs de Matérial Didactique/Verband Europäischer Lehrmittelfirmen, EURODIDAC

Europe
Business Europe, BE
Conference of Engineering Societies of Western Europe and the United States of America, EUSEC
International Federation of Free Journalists of Central and Eastern Europe and Baltic and Balkan Countries, IFFJ

European
Agricultural Research Projects in the European Community, AGREP
American Association of Teachers of Slavic and East European Languages, ATSEEL
Association of European Engineering Periodicals, AEEP
Centre de Traitement de l'Information Scientifique (European Scientific Information Processing Center), CETIS
Centre d'Information et de Publicité des Chemins de Fer Européens (Information and Publicity Center of European Railways), CIPCE
Centre Européene de Traduction (European Translation Center), CET
Conférence Européene des Administrations des Postes et des Télécommunications (European Conference of Postal and Telecommunication Administrations), CEPT
European Article Number, EAN
European Association of Information Services, EUSIDIC
European Association of Management Training Centers, EAMTC
European Atomic Energy Community, EURATOM
European Atomic Energy Society, EAES
European Broadcasting Union, EBU
European Center for the Coordination of Research and Documentation in the Social Sciences, CEUCORS

European Committee for Cooperation with Latin America, ECCLA
European Computer Manufacturers Association, ECMA
European Computing Congress, EUROCOMP
European Conference on the Application of Research in Information Services and Libraries, EURIM 3
European Cultural Center, ECC
European Documentation Centers, EDC
European Economic Community, EEC
European Executive Compensation Survey, EECS
European Federation of Chemical Engineering, EFCE
European Federation of Conference Cities, EFCC
European Federation of Purchasing, EFP
European Foundation for Visual Aids, EFVA
European Group of Woodworking Journals, EUROBOIS
European Industrial Management Association, EIRMA
European Industrial Space Study Group, EUROSPACE
European Marketing and Advertising Press, EMAP
European Nuclear Documentation System, ENDS
European Nuclear Energy Agency, ENEA
European Referral Service, EUSIREF
European Research Associates, ERA
European Society for Opinion Surveys and Market Research, ESOMAR
European Space Agency Network, ESANET
European Space Data Center, ESDAC
European Space Research and Technology Center, ESTEC
European Space Research Institute, ESRIN
European Space Research Laboratory, ESLAB
European Space Research Organization, ESRO
Federation of European Biological Societies, FEBS
Federation of European Industrial Editors Associations, FEIEA
Ligue des Bibliothèques Européennes de Recherche (Association of European Research Libraries), LIBER
Organization for European Economic Cooperation, OEEC
Selected Publications in European Languages, SPEL

European-American
European-American Nuclear Data Committee, EANDC

Federation of European-American
    Organizations, FEAO

European Center
Centre Européene pour la Recherche
    Nucléaire (European Center for Nuclear
    Research), CERN

Européenne
Communauté Européenne du Carbon et de
    l'Acier, CECA

Evaluation
Center for Research and Evaluation in
    Applications of Technology in
    Education, CREATE
City Air Defense Evaluation Tool, CADET
Collection and Evaluation of Materials on
    Black Americans, CEMBA
Committee on Program Evaluation and
    Support, COPES
Computer Learning Under Evaluation,
    CLUE
Computer-Aided Design Evaluation, CADE
Computer-Assisted Program Evaluation
    Review Technique Simulation,
    CAPERTSIM
ERIC Clearinghouse on Tests,
    Measurement, and Evaluation,
    ERIC/TM
Educational Media Institute Evaluation
    Project, EMIE
FORTRAN Automatic Code Evaluation
    System, FACES
Federal Computer Performance Evaluation
    and Simulation Center, FEDSIM
Financial Evaluation Program, FEP
Forecasts, Appraisals, and Management
    Evaluation, FAME
Historical Evaluation and Research
    Organization, HERO
Program Evaluation and Budget Committee,
    PEBCO
Program Evaluation and Review Technique,
    PERT
Program Evaluation Procedure, PEP
Project for the Evaluation of Benefits from
    University Libraries, PEBUL
Time-Shared Routines for Analysis,
    Classification, and Evaluation, TRACE
United States Army Computer Systems
    Support and Evaluation Command,
    USACSSEC
User-Prompted Graphic Data Evaluation,
    UPGRADE

Evaluation Center
Plastics Technical Evaluation Center,
    PLASTEC

Evaluator
Application Program Evaluator Tool, APET

Evangelischer
Vereinigung Evangelischer Buchhändler,
    VEB

Events
Tracking Retrieval and Analysis of Criminal
    Events, TRACE

Evolutionary
Evolutionary Operations, EVOP
An Evolutionary System for On-line
    Processing, AESOP

Examination
College-Level Examination Program, CLEP
Console Operator Proficiency Examination,
    COPE
Graduate Record Examination, GRE

Examinations
Register and Examinations Committee,
    R&EEC
Register and Examinations Committee,
    REEC

Examiners
National Council of Engineering Examiners,
    NCEE
National Council of State Boards of
    Engineering Examiners, NCSBEE

Excavation
Undergraduate Excavation and Rock
    Properties Information Center, UERPIC

Exceptional
Council for Exceptional Children
    Information Services, CEC
Exceptional Child Education Resources,
    ECER

Excerpta Medica
Excerpta Medica Foundation, EM

Excess
Excess-3, XS-3

Exchange
Accountants Computer Users Technical
    Exchange, ACUTE
Automatic Data Exchange, ADX
Bibliographic Exchange and
    Communications Network, BEACON
Broadband Exchange, BEX
Community Automatic Exchange, CAX
Continuing Library Education Network and
    Exchange, CLENE
Cooperating Users Exchange, CUE
Council for International Exchange of
    Scholars, CIES
Data Exchange Unit, DEU
Duplicates Exchange Union, DEU
Electronic Automatic Exchange, EAX

Exchange (cont.)

Foreign Exchange Accounting and
  Management Information System,
  FEAMIS
Government-Industry Data Exchange
  Program, GIDEP
Highway Engineering Exchange Program,
  HEEP
Information and Data Exchange
  Experimental Activities, IDEEA
Inter NASA Data Exchange, INDEX
International Association for the Exchange
  of Students for Technical Experience,
  IAESTE
Library Orientation Exchange, LOEX
Media Exchange Cooperative, MEC
Minnesota Interlibrary Telecommunications
  Exchange, MINITEX
Montana Information Network and
  Exchange, MINE
Private Automatic Branch Exchange, PABX
Private Automatic Exchange, PAX
Private Branch Exchange, PBX
Rochester Area Resources Exchange, RARE
South Central Minnesota Inter-Library
  Exchange, SMILE
Teleprinter Exchange, TEX
Total Interlibrary Exchange, TIE
UICA Learning Resources Exchange
  Program, UICA/LREP
United States Book Exchange, USBE
Universal Serials and Book Exchange,
  USBE
World Information Systems Exchange,
  WISE

Exchange Center

Systems and Procedures Exchange Center,
  SPEC

Exchange Service

Abridged *Index Medicus*-Teletypewriter
  Exchange Service, AIM-TWX
Automatic Teletypewriter Exchange
  Service, TELEX
Teletypewriter Exchange Service, TWX

Execute Statement

Execute Statement, EXEC

Executive

Controlled Handling of Internal Executive
  Functions, CHIEF
European Executive Compensation Survey,
  EECS
*Latin American Executive Compensation
  Survey*, LAECS
Real-Time Executive Routine, REX
Standard Tape Executive Program, STEP

Executives

American Society of Association
  Executives, ASAE
Association of Records Executives and
  Administrators, AREA
Chief Executives of Large Public Libraries,
  CELPLO
Council of Engineering and Scientific Society
  Executives, CESSE
Council of Library Associations Executives,
  CLAE
Executives Guide to Information Sources,
  EGIS

Exercise

Sequential In-Basket Exercise, SIBE

Exhibition

Small and Specialist Publishers Exhibition,
  SPEX

Exhibition Service

Smithsonian Institution Traveling Exhibition
  Service, SITES

Exhibitors

Cinematograph Exhibitors Association of
  Great Britain and Ireland, CEA
Educational Exhibitors Association, EEA
Sveriges Biografägureförbund (Swedish
  Motion Picture Exhibitors Association),
  SBF

Exhibits

Exhibits Round Table, ERT

Expanded

Expanded Display, ED

Expansion

Expansion Symbolic Compiling Assembly
  Program for Engineering, ESCAPE

Expedition

International Indian Ocean Expedition, IIOE

Experience

International Association for the Exchange
  of Students for Technical Experience,
  IAESTE

Experiment

A Better Language Experiment, ABLE
Center of Experiment Design and Data
  Analysis, CEDDA
Combined and Integrated Resources for
  Community Learning Experiment,
  CIRCLE
Federal Libraries Experiment in Cooperative
  Cataloging, FLECC
Super Eight Experiment, SEE

Experimental
Apollo Lunar Surface Experimental
    Package, ALSEP
Confédération Internationale des Cinémas
    d'Art et d'Essai (International
    Experimental and Art Film Theatres
    Confederation), CICAE
Experimental Aircraft Association, EAA
Federation of American Societies for
    Experimental Biology, FASEB
Information and Data Exchange
    Experimental Activities, IDEEA
Library Experimental Automated
    Demonstration System, LEADS

Experimentation
Centre National d'Étude et
    d'Experimentation de Machinisme
    Agricole (National Center for
    Agricultural Machinery Research and
    Experimentation), CNEEMA

Experiments
Information Transfer Experiments, INTREX
Pan-Pacific Education and Communication
    Experiments by Satellite, PEACESAT
Simulator of Immediate Memory in Learning
    Experiments, SIMILE

Exploitants de Cinéma
Association des Exploitants de Cinéma et
    des Distributeurs de Films du
    Grand-Duché de Luxembourg, AECDF

Exploitation
Centre National pour l'Exploitation des
    Océans, CNEXO

Exploration
American Institute for Exploration, AIFE
International Council for the Exploration of
    the Sea, ICES
International Decade of Ocean Exploration,
    IDOE

Exploratory
Exploratory Library Management Systems,
    ELMS

Expo
Federal Office Systems Expo, FOSE

Exportateurs
Chambre Syndicale des Producteurs et
    Exportateurs de Films Français,
    CSPEFF

Exposition
National Information Conference and
    Exposition, NICE

Extended
Extended Binary Coded Decimal
    Interchange Code, EBCDIC
Generalized Programming Extended, GPX
Random Access Correlation for Extended
    Performance, RACEP

Extensible
Rapidly Extensible Language, REL

Extension
Business and Industry Extension Program,
    BIEP
National University Extension Association,
    NUEA

External
External Device, ED
External Device Control, EXD
External Device Control Word, EDCW
External Symbol Dictionary, ESD

Externally
Externally Specified Index, ESI

Extracting Text
Methods of Extracting Text Automatically,
    META
Methods of Extracting Text Automatically
    Programming Language, METAPLAN

Extraction
Automated Linguistic Extraction and
    Retrieval Technique, ALERT
Position and Velocity Extraction, PAVE

Extramural
Extramural Programs Information System,
    EPIS

FORTRAN
Business and Engineering Enriched
    FORTRAN, BEEF
FORTRAN Assembly Program, FAP
FORTRAN Automatic Code Evaluation
    System, FACES
FORTRAN I Compiler, FORTOCOM
FORTRAN List Processing Language,
    FLPL
FORTRAN Simulation, FORTSIM
Logically Integrated FORTRAN Translator,
    LIFT
UNIVAC FORTRAN, UNITRAN

Fabricants
Association Européenne de Fabricants et des
    Revendeurs de Matériel
    Didactique/Verband Europäischer
    Lehrmittelfirmen, EURODIDAC

Facilities
Computerized Facilities Design, COFAD
Computerized Relative Allocation of
    Facilities Technique, CRAFT

Facility
Audiographic Learning Facility, ALF
Dual Facility, DF
End User Facility Task Group, EUFTG
Environmental Data Collection and
    Processing Facility, EDCPF
Facility for Automatic Sorting and Testing,
    FAST
Facility of Automation, Control and Test,
    FACT
Fast Reactor Test Facility, FARET
Shared Information Elicitation Facility,
    SHIEF

Facsimile
Facsimile, FAX
Facsimile Communications System, FCS
Facsimile Transmission System, FACTS

Factory
Factory Information Control System, FICS

Factual
Factual Compiler, FACT

Faculty
Faculty of Library Science Alumni
    Association, FLSAA

Fagpresses
Den Norske Fagpresses Forening, DNFF

Failure
Failure Analysis Information Retrieval,
    FAIR
Failure Analysis Program, FAP
Mean Time Between Failure, MTBF
Mean Time to Failure, MTTF

Failure Rate
Failure Rate Data Program, FARADA

Fair
Jerusalem International Book Fair, JIBF

Families
Administration for Children, Youth, and
    Families, ACYF

Family
Family Reading Center, FRC

Family Planning Libraries
Association for Population/Family Planning
    Libraries and Information Centers,
    APLIC

Far East
Economic Commission for Asia and the Far
    East, ECAFE

Farm
Canadian Farm Management Data System,
    CANFARM

Fast
Fast Access Current Text Bank, FACT
Fast Access Information Retrieval, FAIR
Fast Access to Systems Technical
    Information, FASTI
Fast Analysis of Tape and Recovery,
    FATAR
Fast Interline Nonactive Automatic Control,
    FINAC
Fast Reactor Test Facility, FARET

Fast Breeder Reactor
Liquid Metal Fast Breeder Reactor, LMFBR

Feature
Feature Count, FC

Federação
Federação Internacional de Associações de
    Bibliotecários–Grupo Regional América
    Latina, FIABGRAL

Federal
Association of Federal Communications
    Consulting Engineers, AFCCE
Clearinghouse for Federal Scientific and
    Technical Information, CFSTI
GODORT Federal Documents Task Force,
    GODORT/FDTF

Federal Librarians
Federal Librarians Round Table, FLIRT

Federal Libraries
Federal Libraries Experiment in Cooperative
    Cataloging, FLECC

Federal Library
Federal Library and Information Network,
    FEDLINK

Federal Register
Federal Register File, FEDREG

Federal Republic of Germany
Arbeitsgemeinschaft der Spezialbibliotheken
    (Association of Special Libraries in the
    Federal Republic of Germany), ASpB

Federation
Advertising Federation of America, AFA
American Advertising Federation, AAF
American Federation for Information
    Processing, AFIP
American Federation of Film Societies,
    AFFS
American Federation of Government
    Employees, AFGE
American Federation of Information
    Processing Societies, AFIPS
American Federation of Labor and Congress
    of Industrial Organizations, AFL-CIO

American Federation of State, County, and Municipal Employees, AFSCME
American Federation of Television and Radio Artists, AFTRA
Asian Federation of Library Associations, AFLA
European Federation of Chemical Engineering, EFCE
European Federation of Conference Cities, EFCC
European Federation of Purchasing, EFP
Federação Brasileira de Associações de Bibliotecários (Brazilian Federation of Librarian Associations), FEBAB
Federação Brasileira de Associações de Bibliotecários–Comissão Brasileira de Documentação Jurídica (Brazilian Federation of Librarian Associations–Brazilian Committee of Legal Documentation), FEBAB/CBDJ
Federación Internacional de Documentación/Comisión Latinoamericana (International Federation for Documentation/Latin American Commission), FID/CLA
Federatie van Organisaties op het Gebied van Bibliotheek, Informatie en Dokumentatiewezen (Federation of Organizations in Library, Information and Documentation Science), FOBID
Fédération des Associations Internationales Establiés in Belgique (Federation of International Associations Established in Belgium), FAIB
Fédération des Éditeurs Belges, FEB
Federation for Unified Science Education, FUSE
Fédération Française des Syndicats de Libraires, FFSL
Fédération Internationale de Documentation (International Federation of Documentation), FID
Fédération Internationale de la Presse Cinématographique (International Federation of the Cinematographic Press), FIPRESCI
Fédération Internationale de la Presse Periodique (International Federation of the Periodical Press), FIPP
Fédération Internationale des Archives du Film (International Federation of Film Archives), FIAF
Fédération Internationale des Directeurs de Journaux Catholiques (International Federation of Directors of Catholic Publications), FIDJC
Fédération Internationale des Industries du Cinéma de Film Étroit, FIDIC
Fédération Internationale des Journalistes (International Federation of Journalists), FIJ

Fédération Internationale des Phonothèques (International Federation of Record Libraries), FIP
Fédération Internationale des Traducteurs, FIT
Fédération Nationale des Bibliothèques Catholiques, FNBC
Fédération Nationale des Distributeurs de Films, FNDF
Federation of American Scientists, FAS
Federation of American Societies for Experimental Biology, FASEB
Federation of Children's Book Groups, FCBG
Federation of Documentary Film Units, FDFU
Federation of European Biological Societies, FEBS
Federation of European Industrial Editors Associations, FEIEA
Federation of European-American Organizations, FEAO
Federation of Hong Kong Industries, FHKI
Federation of Indian Library Associations, FILA
Federation of Information Users, FIU
Federation of Specialised Film Associations, FSFA
Federazione Italiana delle Biblioteche Popolari (Federation of Italian Public Libraries), FIBP
International Federation for Information Processing, IFIP
International Federation of Audit Bureaus of Circulations, IFABC
International Federation of Automatic Control, IFAC
International Federation of Catholic Journalists, IFCJ
International Federation of Film Producers Associations, IFFPA
International Federation of Film Societies, IFFS
International Federation of Free Journalists of Central and Eastern Europe and Baltic and Balkan Countries, IFFJ
International Federation of Information Processing Societies, IFIPS
International Federation of Journalists, IFJ
International Federation of Library Associations and Institutions, IFLA
International Road Federation, IRF
Irish Printing Federation, IPF
Manchester Federation of Scientific Societies, MFSS
National Federation of Abstracting and Indexing Services, NFAIS
National Federation of Retail Newsagents, Booksellers and Stationers, NFRN
National Federation of Science Abstracting and Indexing Services, NFSAIS

Federation (cont.)

Printing and Kindred Trades Federation, PKTF

Radio and Electric Component Manufacturers Federation, RECMF

US National Committee for the International Federation for Documentation, USNCFID

World Federation of Engineering Organizations, WFEO

Federazione

Federazione Italiana Editori Giornali, FIEG

Federazione Nazionale della Stampa Italiana, FNSI

Feed

Form Feed, FF

Line Feed, LF

Fiction

Fiction, F

Field

Field Information Agencies, Technical, FIAT

Magnetic-tape Field Search, MFS

Field Operations

Automation of Field Operations and Services, AFOS

Figures

Figures Shift, FIGs

Fiji

Fiji Library Association, FLA

File

Catalog Data File, CDF

Congressional Record File, CRECORD

Dual Independent Map Encoding File of the Counties of the US, DIMECO

End of File, EOF

Federal Register File, FEDREG

File Copy, FC

File Separator, FS

General Information File Interrogation, GIFI

Information Item File, IIF

Original Data File, ODF

Publications Reference File, PRF

File Room

File Room Online Information Control, FROLIC

Files

Human Relations Area Files, HRAF

Machine-Readable Data Files, MRDF

Support of User Records and Files, SURF

Filing

Nederlands Instituut voor Informatie, Documentatie en Registratuur

(Netherlands Institute for Information, Documentation and Filing), NIDER

Pupil Registering and Operational Filing, PROF

Film

Allied Non-theatrical Film Association, ANFA

American Federation of Film Societies, AFFS

American Film Institute, AFI

American Science Film Association, ASFA

Association Internationale du Film d'Animation (International Animated Film Association), ASIFA

Association of Specialised Film Producers, ASFP

British Board of Film Censors, BBFC

British Film Institute, BFI

British Industrial and Scientific Film Association Ltd, BISFA

British National Film Catalogue, BNFC

Children's Film Foundation Ltd, CFF

Confédération Internationale des Cinémas d'Art et d'Essai (International Experimental and Art Film Theatres Confederation), CICAE

Educational Film Library Association, EFLA

Fédération Internationale des Archives du Film (International Federation of Film Archives), FIAF

Fédération Internationale des Industries du Cinéma de Film Étroit, FIDIC

Federation of Documentary Film Units, FDFU

Federation of Specialised Film Associations, FSFA

Film and Report Information Processing Generator, FRINGE

Film Artists Association, FAA

Film Input to Digital Automatic Computer, FIDAC

Film Laboratory Association, Ltd, FLA

Film Optical Sensing Device for Input to Computers, FOSDIC

Film Producers Guild, Ltd, FPG

Film Production Association of Great Britain, FPA

General Aniline and Film Corporation, GAF

International Federation of Film Producers Associations, IFFPA

International Federation of Film Societies, IFFS

International Federation of Information Film Distributors, INFORFILM

International Film and Television Council, IFTC

International Inter-Church Film Center, INTERFILM

International Scientific Film Association, ISFA

International Scientific Film Library, ISFL
Scottish Educational Film Association,
    SEFA
Scottish Film Council, SFC
Society for Education in Film and
    Television, SEFT
Society for Film History Research, SFHR
Society of Film and Television Arts, Ltd,
    SFTA
Southern California Film Circuit, SCFC
Union Nationale des Producteurs Belge de
    Films (National Union of Belgian Film
    Producers), UNPBF
Verband Schweizerischer Film und
    AV-Produzenten/Association des
    Producteurs Suisses de Films et de
    Production Audio-Visuelle (Association
    of Swiss Film and Audio-Visual
    Producers), VSFAV/APFAV
Vereinigung Schweizerischer
    Filmkritiker/Association Suisse des
    Critiques de Cinéma/Associazione
    Svizzera dei Critici Cinematografici
    (Swiss Association of Film Critics),
    VSF/ASC/ASC

Film Centers
Consortium of University Film Centers,
    CUFC

Film Library
Central Film Library, CFL
Film Library Information Council, FLIC
Film Library Intercollege Cooperative of
    Pennsylvania, FLIC

Films
Association des Exploitants de Cinéma et
    des Distributeurs de Films du
    Grand-Duché de Luxembourg, AECDF
Chambre Syndicale des Producteurs et
    Exportateurs de Films Français,
    CSPEFF
Cinematographic Films Council, CFC
Conseil International pour les Films
    d'Éducation (International Council for
    Educational Films), CIFE
Fédération Nationale des Distributeurs de
    Films, FNDF
International Center of Films for Children,
    ICFC
International Institute of Films on Art, IIFA
Petroleum Films Bureau, PFB
Union Professionnelle des Distributeurs
    Belges de Films, UPDBF

Filmtheater
Hauptverband Deutscher Filmtheater, HDF

Filmwirtschaft
Spitzenorganisation der Filmwirtschaft eV,
    SPIO

Financial
Financial Accounting and Management
    Information System, FAMIS
Financial Analysis of Management
    Effectiveness, FAME
Financial Analysis Program, FAP
Financial and Management Information
    System, FAMIS
Financial Evaluation Program, FEP

Financiers
Association des Journalistes Économiques et
    Financiers, AJEF

Finder
Direction Finder, DF

Finding
Direction Finding, DF

Fine Arts
Society for Automation in Fine Arts, SAFA

Finite
Finite Automation Language, FAL

Finland
Finlands Svenska Författareföreningen
    (Society of Swedish Authors in Finland),
    FSFF
Suomen Sanomalehtimiesten Litto/Finlands
    Journalist Förbund (Union of Journalists
    in Finland), SSL/FJF

Finnish
Suomen Näytelmäkirjailijaliitto (Finnish
    Dramatists Society), SUNKLO
Suomen Säätöteknillinen Seura (Finnish
    Society of Automatic Control), SSS

Fire Protection
National Fire Protection Association, NFPA

Firenze
Automazione nella Nazionale di Firenze,
    ANNA

First-In
First-In-First-Out, FIFO

First Out
First-In-First-Out, FIFO
Last In First Out, LIFO

Fiscal
Fiscal Year, FY

Fisheries
Aquatic Sciences and Fisheries Abstracts,
    ASFA

Flemish
Vlaamse Vereniging van Bibliotheek-Archief
    en Documentatie-Personeel, Vereniging
    zonder Winstoogmerken (Flemish
    Association of Librarians, Archivists
    and Documentalists), VVBADP

Flexible
Flexible Algebraic Scientific Translator,
   FAST
Flexible Automatic Depot, FAD

Flight
Flight Information Center, FIC

Flint
Flint Area Health Science Library Network,
   FAHSLN

Flip-Flop
Flip-Flop, FF

Floating
Floating Interpretative Language, FLINT

Floating-decimal
Floating-decimal Abstract Coding System,
   FACS

Floating Point
Floating Indexed Point Arithmetic, FLIP
Floating Octal Point, FLOP
Floating Point Interpretive Program, FLIP

Floating-point
Floating-point Arithmetic Package, FAP
Single Precision Unpacked Rounded
   Floating-Point Package, SPUR

Florence
Biblioteca Nazionale Centrale—Firenze
   (National Central Library of Florence),
   BNCF

Florida
Associated Mid-Florida Colleges, AMFC
East Central Florida Regional Planning
   Council, ECFRPC
Florida Association for Media and
   Education, FAME
Florida Library Association, FLA
Florida Library Information Network, FLIN

Flowchart
Flowchart Language, FLANG

Fluid
Fluid Engineering, FLUIDEX

Fluid Flow
Heat Transfer and Fluid Flow Service,
   HTFS

Fluorescence
Fluorescence-Activated Cell Sorter, FACS

Folklore
American Folklore Society, AFLS

Fonderie
Centre Technique des Industries de la
   Fonderie, CTIF

Font
Font Change, FC

Food
*Current Contents/Agricultural, Food and
   Veterinary Sciences*. (Journal), CC/AFV
Food and Agriculture Organization, FAO
Food and Drug Administration, FDA
Food Marketing Institute, FMI
Food Science and Technology Abstracts,
   FSTA
International Commission for Agricultural
   and Food Industries, ICAI
International Food Information Service,
   IFIS

Footing
Control Footing, CF

Forecasting
Asia/Pacific Forecasting Study, APFS
Forecasting for Inventory Control System,
   FICS

Forecasts
Forecasts, Appraisals, and Management
   Evaluation, FAME

Foreign
Buitenlandse Persvereniging in Nederland
   (Foreign Press Association in the
   Netherlands), BPV
Foreign and Commonwealth Office, FAO
Foreign Exchange Accounting and
   Management Information System,
   FEAMIS
Foreign Press Association, FPA
Special Foreign Currency Science
   Information Program, SFCSI

Foreign Affairs
Foreign Affairs Information Management
   Effort, FAIME

Forening
Den Norske Fagpresses Forening, DNFF

Forensic
International Reference Organization in
   Forensic Medicine and Sciences,
   INFORM

Forest
Western Forest Information Network,
   WESTFORNET
Pacific Coast Forest Research Information
   Network, PACFORNET

Forestry
Association of State Colleges and
   Universities Forestry Research
   Organizations, ASCUFRO

Centrul de Documentare Technică Pentru
    Economia Forestieră (Documentation
    Center on Forestry), CDF
East African Agriculture and Forestry
    Research Organization, EAAFRO

Form
Form Feed, FF

Formal
Formal Semantics Language, FSL

Format
Format Effector, FE

Formation Professionnelle
Centre International d'Information et de la
    Recherche sur la Formation
    Professionnelle, CIRF

Formula
Formula Assembler and Translator,
    FORAST
Formula Coder, FORC
Formula Manipulation Compiler, FORMAC
Formula Translator, FORTRAN
Formula Translator II, FORTRAN II
Formula Translator IV, FORTRAN IV

Fortean
International Fortean Organization, INFO

Foundation
Advertising Research Foundation, ARF
Aerospace Education Foundation, AEF
Arkansas Foundation of Associated
    Colleges, AFAC
Brewing Industry Research Foundation,
    BIRF
Brewing Research Foundation, BRF
Canadian Hunger Foundation, CHF
Children's Film Foundation Ltd, CFF
European Foundation for Visual Aids,
    EFVA
Excerpta Medica Foundation, EM
Foundation of Record Education, FORE
Freedom to Read Foundation, FTRF
National Foundation for Educational
    Research in England and Wales, NFER
National Science Foundation, NSF
Reading Reform Foundation, RRF

Foundations
ASIS Special Interest Group on Foundations
    of Information Science, ASIS/SIG/FIS

Foundry
American Machine and Foundry, Inc, AMF

Fraction
Decimal Fraction, DF

Fragmentation
Rapid Access to Literature via
    Fragmentation Codes, RALF

Français
Chambre Syndicale des Producteurs et
    Exportateurs de Films Français,
    CSPEFF
Institut Français d'Opinion Publique, IFOP
Société Nationale des Chemins de Fer
    Français, SNCF

Française
Association Française de Normalisation,
    AFNOR
Association Française d'Informatique et de
    Recherche Opérationnelle, AFIRO
Association Française pour l'Étude des
    Eaux, AFEE
Association Française pour la Cybernétique
    Économique et Technique, AFCET
Fédération Française des Syndicats de
    Libraires, FFSL
Institute Française du Petrole, IFP

Françaises
Bureau pour l'Enseignement de la Langue et
    de la Civilisation Françaises à
    l'Étranger, BELC
Union Nationale des Éditeurs-Exportateurs
    de Publications Françaises, UNEEPF

France
Centre d'Études et Recherches des
    Charbonnages de France, CERCHAR
Electricité de France, EDF

Franco-Ontariens
Conseil des Enseignants–Bibliothécaires
    Franco-Ontariens, CEBFO

Free Association
Free Association of Management Analysis,
    FAMA

Free Library
Public Free Library, PFL

Freedom
Freedom to Read Foundation, FTRF

Free-form
Free-form Language for Image Processing,
    FLIP

Freier
Freier Deutscher Autoren-Verband, FDA

French
Association des Bibliothèques
    Ecclésiastiques de France (Association
    of French Theological Libraries), ABEF
Association Française de Calcul (French
    Computing Association), AFCAL

French (cont.)

Association Française des Amateurs
   Constructeurs l'Ordinateurs (French
   Association of Amateur Computer
   Builders), AFACO
Association Française des Documentalistes
   et des Bibliothécaires Spécialisés
   (French Association of Information
   Scientists and Special Librarians),
   ADBS
Association Française des Journalistes
   Agricoles (French Association of
   Agricultural Journalists), AFJA
Institute de Recherche d'Informatique et
   d'Automatique (French Research
   Institute of Information and Automatic
   Processing), IRIA

French American
French American Cultural Services and
   Educational Aid, FACSEA

French Language
Association Belge des Editeurs de Langue
   Française (Belgian Association of
   Publishers of French Language Books),
   ABELF
Association des Universités Partiellement ou
   Entierement de Langue Française
   (Association of Wholly or Partially
   French-language Universities),
   AUPELF

French Librarians
Association des Bibliothécaires Français
   (Association of French Librarians),
   ABF

French Speaking
Association Nationale des Bibliothécaires
   d'Expression Française (National
   Association of French-Speaking
   Librarians), ANBEF
Association Canadienne des Bibliothécaires
   de Langue Française (Association of
   French Speaking Canadian Librarians),
   ACBLF
Société des Libraires et Éditeurs de la Suisse
   Romande (Booksellers and Publishers
   Association of French-Speaking
   Switzerland), SLESR

Frequencies
Superhigh Frequencies, SHF

Frequency
Automatic Frequency Assignment Model,
   AFAM
Extremely High Frequency, EHF

Frequency Division Multiplex, FDM
Frequency of Every Allowable Term, FEAT
Low Frequency, LF
Medium Frequency, MF
Radio Frequency Interference, RFI
Ultrahigh Frequency, UHF
Very High Frequency, VHF
Very Low Frequency, VLF

Frequency-Shift
Frequency-Shift Keying, FSK

Friends
Friends of the National Libraries, FNL

Froid
Institut International du Froid, IIF

Frost
Frost & Sullivan, Inc, F&S

Fruits
Institut de Recherches sur les Fruits et
   Agrumes, IRFA

Fuel
Central Fuel Research Institute, CFRI
Fuel Abstracts and Current Titles, FACT
Fuel Research Institute, FRI

Full
Full Duplex, FD

Full-Time
Full-Time Equivalent, FTE

Function
Diagnostic Function Test, DFT
Digital Analog Function Table, DAFT
Diode Function Generator, DFG

Functional
Functional Code, FC

Functions
Controlled Handling of Internal Executive
   Functions, CHIEF

Fund
College Retirement Equities Fund, CREF
Fund for the Improvement of Post Secondary
   Education, FIPSE
International Children's Emergency Fund,
   ICEF
International Monetary Fund, IMF
Native American Rights Fund, NARF
United Nations Children's Fund, UNICEF

Fundamental
Reading Is Fundamental, RIF

Fundamentally Analyzable
Fundamentally Analyzable Simplified
   English, FASE

Furniture
Office Furniture Manufacturers Institute,
OFMI

Gain-Adjustment
Voice Operated Gain-Adjustment Device,
VOGAD

Gallery
Art Gallery of Ontario, AGO

Galveston
Houston-Galveston Area Council, HGAC

Gap
Inter-Record Gap, IRG

Garbage
Garbage In/Garbage Out, GIGO

Gas
American Gas Association, Inc, AGA
American Public Gas Association, APGA

Gazette
Official Gazette. (Journal), OG

Genealogische
Genealogische Recherche mit
Magnetband-Speicherung, GREMAS

General
General Activity Simulation Program, GASP
General Assembly Program, GAP
General Compiler, GECOM
General Comprehensive Operating
Supervisor, GECOS
General Control Language, GCL
General Data Analysis and Simulation,
GENDA
General Industrial Statistics, UNINDUST
General Information File Interrogation, GIFI
General Operator Computer Interaction,
GOCI
General Problem Solver, GPS
General Processing, GP
General Risk Analysis Simulation Program,
GRASP

General Electric
Canadian General Electric Company, Ltd,
CGE
General Electric Company, GE
General Electric Computer Analysis
Program, GECAP
General Electric Macro Assembly Program,
GEMAP
General Electric Manufacturing Simulator,
GEMS
General Electric Remote Terminal System,
GERTS
General Electric Scanner, GESCAN

General Motors
General Motors Corporation, GM

General Purpose
General Purpose Computer, GPC
General Purpose Scientific Document Image
Code, GPSDIC
General Purpose Scientific Document
Writer, GPSDW
General Purpose Simulation Program, GPSS
General Purpose Systems Simulator, GPSS

General Services
General Services Administration, GSA

General Utility
General Utility Library Programs, GULP

Generalized
Generalized Algebraic Translator, GAT
Generalized Data Base Management
Systems, GDBMS
Generalized Information Management
System, GIM
Generalized Information Processing System,
GIPSY
Generalized Information Retrieval and
Listing System, GIRLS
Generalized Information Retrieval
Language, GIRL
Generalized Information System, GENISYS
Generalized Information System, GIS
Generalized Programming, GP
Generalized Programming Extended, GPX
Generalized Programming Language, GPL

Generating
Automatic Routine Generating and Updating
System, ARGUS
Sorting, Updating, Report, Generating, Etc,
SURGE

Generation
Generation Data Group, GDG

Generator
Digital Display Generator, DDG
Digital Display Generator Element, DDGE
Diode Function Generator, DFG
Film and Report Information Processing
Generator, FRINGE
Management Report Generator, MARGEN
Report Program Generator, REGENT
Report Program Generator, RPG

Generic
Generic Problem Statement Simulator, GPSS

Geoastrophysical
*Meteorological and Geoastrophysical
Abstracts*, MGA

Geographers
Association of American Geographers, AAG

Geographic
World Geographic Reference System, GEOREF

Geographical
Permanent Committee on Geographical Names (for British Official Use), PCGN

Geological
American Geological Institute, AGI
Committee on Storage, Automatic Processing and Retrieval of Geological Data, COGEODATA
Geological Society of America, GSA
United States Geological Survey, USGS

Geologii
Vsesojuznyj Naučno-Isseldovatel'skij Geologorazvedočnyj Neftjanoj Institut Ministerstra Geologii SSSR, VNIGNI
Vsesojuznyj Naučno-Issledovatel'skij Institut Economiki Mineral'nogo Syr'ja i Geologorazvedocnych Rabot Ministerstva Geologii SSSR i Akademii nauk SSSR, VIEMS

Geologists
American Association of Petroleum Geologists, AAPG
Association of Engineering Geologists, AEG

Geometry
Analytic Geometry Interpretive Language, AGILE
Coordinated Geometry, COGO

Geophysical
American Geophysical Union, AGU
International Geophysical Year, IGY
Journal of Geophysical Research, JGR
National Geophysical and Solar Terrestrial Data Center, NGSD
National Geophysical Data Center, NGDC

Georgia
Georgia Library Association, GLA

Georgia Library
Georgia Library Information Network, GLIN

Geoscience
Geoscience Information Society, GIS

Geotechnical
Asian Information Center for Geotechnical Engineering, AGE

Geowissenschaftliche
Geowissenschaftliche Literaturinformation, GWL

Geriatric
Consortium of Hospital and Rehabilitative Geriatric Enterprises, CHARGE

German
ACM German Association for Applied Mathematics and Mechanics, ACM/GAMM
Deutsche Arbeitsgemeinschaft für Rechen-Anlagen (German Working Committee for Computing Machines), DARA
Deutsche Gesellschaft für Dokumentation (German Association for Documentation), DGD
Deutsche Staatsbibliothek (German State Library), DSB
Deutscher Bibliotheksverband (German Library Association), DBV
Deutscher Normenausschuss (German Standards Association), DNA
Deutsches Institut für Medizinische Dokumentation und Information (German Institute for Medical Documentation and Information), DIMDI
German Research Society, GRS
Gesellschaft Deutscher Metallhuttens und Bergleute (Association of German Metallurgical and Mining Engineers), GDMB
Verein Deutscher Archivare (Association of German Archivists), VDA
Verein Deutscher Dokumentare (Society of German Documentalists), VDD

German Librarians
Verein Deutscher Bibliothekare (Association of German Librarians), VDB

Gesellschaft
Gesellschaft für Dokumentation und Bibliographie, GDB
Gesellschaft für Information und Dokumentation, GID
Technisch-Literarische Gesellschaft, TELI

Gestion
Application de la Gestion aux Périodiques, AGAPE

Gifted
ERIC Clearinghouse on Handicapped and Gifted Children, ERIC/EC

Giornali
Federazione Italiana Editori Giornali, FIEG

Giurisprudenza
Giurisprudenza Civile, CIVILE
Giurisprudenza Corte 2. Giurstizia delle CEE, CEE

Giurisprudenza Costituzionale, COSTIT
Giurisprudenza della Corte del Conti,
    CORTEC
Giurisprudenza di Merito, MERITO
Giurisprudenza Penale, PENALE

Global
Global Atmospheric Research Program,
    GARP
Global Tracking, GLOTRAC
Integrated Global Ocean Stations System,
    IGOSS

Globe and Mail
Globe and Mail, GAM

Gloucestershire
Gloucestershire Technical Information
    Service, GTIS

Godsdienstig
Vereniging voor het
    Godsdienstig-Wetenschappelijk
    Bibliothecariaat, VSKB

Government
Alberta Government Libraries Council,
    AGLC
American Federation of Government
    Employees, AFGE
Government Advisory Committee on
    International Book and Library
    Programs, GAC
Government Communications Headquarters
    (Great Britain), GCHQ
Government Documents Round Table,
    GODORT
Government-Industry Data Exchange
    Program, GIDEP
Government Printing Office, GPO
Local Government Information Control,
    LOGIC
Local Government Information Office,
    LGIO
National Association of Government
    Engineers, NAOGE
Saskatchewan Government Libraries
    Association, SGLA
US Government Reports Index, USGI
*US Government Research and Development
    Reports*, USGRDR
*US Government Research and Development
    Reports Index*, USGRDRI
US Government Research Reports, USGR

Government Libraries
Association of Saskatchewan Government
    Libraries, ASGL

Government Reports
Government Reports Announcements, GRA
*Government Reports Announcements and
    Index*, GRA&I

Government Reports Annual Index, GRAI
Government Reports Index, GRI

Governments
Southern California Association of
    Governments, SCAG

Graduate
Graduate Library School, GLS
Graduate Record Examination, GRE
Graduate Regional Accelerated Study
    Program, GRASP

Graduate Librarians
Asociación de Bibliotecarios Graduados de
    la República Argentina (Association of
    Graduate Librarians of Argentina),
    ABGRA

Graduate School
Graduate School of Library and Information
    Science, GSLIS

Grammar
Transformational Grammar Tester, TGT

Grant
Project Grant Information System, PGIS

Grants
University Grants Committee, UGC

Graphic
Graphic Input Language, GRAIL
Graphic Programming Language, GPL
Institute for Graphic Communication, Inc,
    IGC

Graphic Arts
American Institute of Graphic Arts, AIGA
Graphic Arts Composing Equipment,
    GRACE
International Graphic Arts Education
    Association, IGAEA

Graphic Reproductions
Internationale Arbeitsgemeinschaft der
    Archiv-, Bibliotheks- und
    Grafikrestauratoren (International
    Working Group of Restorers of
    Archives, Libraries and Graphic
    Reproductions), IADA

Graphical
Graphical Input for Network Analysis,
    GINA

Graphics
ACM Special Interest Group on Computer
    Graphics, ACM/SIGGRAPH
Association for Precision Graphics, APG
Computer Logic Graphics, CLOG
Programmer-Oriented Graphics Operation,
    POGO

Gravure
Gravure Engravers Association, GEA

Great Britain
Booksellers Association of Great Britain and
Ireland, BA
Cinematograph Exhibitors Association of
Great Britain and Ireland, CEA
Film Production Association of Great
Britain, FPA
Government Communications Headquarters
(Great Britain), GCHQ
Microfilm Association of Great Britain,
MAGB
Writers Guild of Great Britain, WGGB

Great Lakes
Great Lakes Environmental Information
Sharing, GLEIS

Great Plains
Great Plains National Instructional
Television Library, GPNITL

Greek
Enosis Ellenon Bibliothekarion (Greek
Library Association), EEB
Greek Library Association, GLA

Ground Environment
Semi-Automatic Ground Environment,
SAGE

Ground-Based
Ground-Based Computer, GBC

Ground-Support
Aerospace Ground-Support Equipment,
AGE

Group
Education Group of the Music Industries
Association, EGMIA
Generation Data Group, GDG
Group Mark, GM
Group Separator, GS
Research Libraries Group, RLG

Guam
Guam Library Association, GLA

Guanabara
Associação Profissional de Bibliotecários do
Estado da Guanabara (Professional
Association of Librarians in
Guanabara), APBEG

Guatemala
Sistema Nacional de Información de
Guatemala, SNIG

Guide
Bibliographic Guide for Editors and Authors,
BGEA

Executives Guide to Information Sources,
EGIS
Guide to Microforms in Print, GMP
Readers Guide to Periodical Literature.
(Index), RGPL

Guild
American Guild of Authors and Composers,
AGAC
Belgische Vereniging van
Landbouwjournalistes/Association
Belge des Journalistes Agricoles
(Belgian Guild of Agricultural
Journalists), BVLJ/ABJA
Film Producers Guild, Ltd, FPG
Guild of Agricultural Journalists, GAJ
Guild of British Newspapers Editors, GBNE
Independent Publishers Guild, IPG
International Women's Writing Guild,
IWWG
International Writers Guild, IWG
Songwriters Guild, Ltd, SWG
Writers Guild of Great Britain, WGGB

Gulf
Gulf Publishing Company, GPC

Guyana
Guyana Library Association, GLA

Gynaecologists
Royal College of Obstetricians and
Gynaecologists, RCOG

Half Duplex
Half Duplex, HD

Halifax
Halifax and District Information Service,
HALDIS
Halifax Library Association, HLA

Hampshire
Hampshire Interlibrary Center, HILC
Hampshire Technical Research Industrial
and Commercial Service, HATRICS

Hand Printed
Hand Printed Books Project, HPB

Handicapped
ACM Special Interest Group on Computers
and the Physically Handicapped,
ACM/SIGCAPH
Division for the Blind and Physically
Handicapped, DBPH
ERIC Clearinghouse on Handicapped and
Gifted Children, ERIC/EC

Handling
Automated Literature Processing, Handling,
and Analysis System, ALPHA
Computer Handling of Reactor
Data—Safety, CHORD—S

Controlled Handling of Internal Executive
  Functions, CHIEF
National Institute of Packaging, Handling
  and Logistics Engineers, NIPHLE
Storage, Handling and Retrieval of Technical
  Data in Image Formation, SHIRTDIF

Hansard
Hansard Oral Questions, HOQ
Hansard Questions Écrites, HQE
Hansard Questions Orale, HQO
Hansard Written Questions, HWQ

Hard Copy
Hard Copy, HC

Hardware
Computer Hardware Description Language,
  CHDL
Hardware Description Language, HDL
Remote User of Shared Hardware, RUSH

Harvard
Harvard Business Review, HBR
Harvard Ukrainian Research Institute,
  HURI

Hauptverband
Hauptverband Deutscher Filmtheater, HDF

Hawaii
Hawaii International Conference on System
  Sciences, HICSS
Hawaii Library Association, HLA

Head
Read/Write Head, R/W

Heading
Control Heading, CH
Start of Heading Character, SOH

Headquarters
Government Communications Headquarters
  (Great Britain), GCHQ

Heads
Council of Academic Heads of Agriculture,
  CAHA

Health
Alberta Information Retrieval for Health,
  Physical Education, and Recreation,
  AIRHPER
American Alliance for Health, Physical
  Education and Recreation, AAHPER
American Association for Health, Physical
  Education and Recreation, AAHPER
American Health Planning Association,
  AHPA
American Public Health Association, APHA
American Social Health Association, ASHA
Automated Health Multi-Phase Screening,
  AHMS

Bureau of Health Manpower Education,
  BHME
Community Health Information Network,
  CHIN
Computerized Information Network for
  Community Health, CINCH
Department of Health, Education and
  Welfare, DHEW
Department of Health, Education and
  Welfare, HEW
Health and Information Libraries of
  Westchester, HILOW
Health and Rehabilitative Library Services
  Division, HRLSD
Health Effects of Environmental Pollutants,
  HEEP
Health Information Network of the Pacific,
  HINOP
Health Information Sharing Project, HISP
Health Instructional Resources Association,
  HIRA
Health Resources Administration, HRA
Lehigh Valley Area Health Education Center
  Library Consortium, LVAHEC
National Center for Health Statistics, NCHS
National Institute for Occupational Safety
  and Health, NIOSH
National Institutes of Health, NIH
Occupational Safety and Health
  Administration, OSHA
Pan American Health Organization, PAHO
United States Committee for the World
  Health Organization, USC-WHO
World Health Organization, WHO

Health Information
Augusta Area Committee for Health
  Information Resources, AACHIR
Consumer Health Information Program and
  Service, CHIPS
Northeast Consortium for Health
  Information, NECHI

Health Libraries
ASCLA Health Care Libraries Section,
  ASCLA/HCLS
Canadian Health Libraries
  Association/Association des
  Bibliothèques de la Santé du Canada,
  CHLA/ABSC
Health Oriented Libraries of San Antonio,
  HOLSA

Health Library
Albany Area Health Library Affiliates,
  AAHLA
Cleveland Health Sciences Library, CHSL

Health Planning
National Health Planning Information
  Center, NHPIC

Health Science
District of Columbia Health Science
   Information Network, DOCHSIN
University of Texas Health Science Center at
   San Antonio, UTHSCSA

Health Science Libraries
Southeastern Wisconsin Health Science
   Libraries Consortium, SEWHSL

Health Science Library
Flint Area Health Science Library Network,
   FAHSLN
Midwest Health Science Library Network,
   MHSLN
Pacific Northwest Regional Health Science
   Library, PNRHSL

Health Sciences
Alaskan Health Sciences Information
   Center, AHSIC
Brooklyn–Queens–Staten Island Health
   Sciences Group, BQSI
CLA Health Sciences Roundtable,
   CLA/HSRT
Health Sciences Communications
   Association, HeSCA
*Medical and Health Related Sciences
   Thesaurus*, MHRST
Western New York Health Sciences
   Librarians, WNYHSL

Health Sciences Librarians
Maryland Association of Health Sciences
   Librarians, MAHSL

Health Sciences Libraries
Connecticut Association of Health Sciences
   Libraries, CAHSL

Health Service
National Health Service, NHS
United States Public Health Service, USPHS

Health Services
Health Services Administration, HSA

Hearing
Deafness, Speech and Hearing Publications,
   Inc, DSH

Heat Transfer
Heat Transfer and Fluid Flow Service,
   HTFS

Heckman's
Heckman's Electronic Library Program,
   HELP

Helsinki
Helsingin Yliopiston Kirjasto (Helsinki
   University Library), HYK

Hertfordshire
Hertfordshire Association of Special
   Libraries, HASL
Hertfordshire County Council Technical
   Library and Information Service,
   HERTIS

Herzegovina
Društvo Bibliotekara Bosne i Hercegovine
   (Library Association of Bosnia and
   Herzegovina), DB Bih

Hetero-Atom
Hetero-Atom-in-Context, HAIC

Heuristic
Heuristic Mechanized Document
   Information System, HERMES

Hibernation
Hibernation Information Exchange, HIE

Hierarchical
Hierarchical Classification, HICLASS
Hierarchical Environmental Retrieval for
   Management Access and Networking,
   HERMAN
Hierarchical Indexed Sequential Access
   Method, HISAM
Hierarchical Sequential Access Method,
   HSAM
System for the Automated Management of
   Text from a Hierarchical Arrangement,
   SAMANTHA

Hierarchically
Hierarchically Structural, HS

High
Extremely High Frequency, EHF
High Density, HD
Very High Frequency, VHF

High Level
Direct-High-Level-Language Processor,
   DHLLP
High Level Language, HLL

High School
Cooperative High School Independent Press
   Syndicate, CHIPS

High School Libraries
CLA High School Libraries Section,
   CLA/HSLS

High-Speed
High-Speed Data Acquisition, HSDA
High-Speed Memory, HSM
High-Speed Printer, HSP
High-Speed Reader, HSR

Highway
Highway Engineering Exchange Program,
    HEEP
Highway Research Information Service,
    HRIS

Hispanic American
Hispanic American Periodicals Index, HAPI

Historians
Company of Military Historians, CMH

Historic
American Institute for Conservation of
    Historic and Artistic Works, AIC
International Institute for Conservation of
    Historic and Artistic Works, IIC

Historical
American Historical Association, AHA
Historical Evaluation and Research
    Organization, HERO
Printing Historical Society, PHS
Royal Commission on Historical
    Manuscripts, HMC
Society of Army Historical Research, SAHR
United States Historical Documents
    Institute, HDI

History
America: History and Life, AHL
American Printing History Association,
    APHA
Commission on Archives and History of the
    United Methodist Church, CAHUMC
History of Medicine Online, HISTLINE
Institute for the Comparative Study of
    History, Philosophy and the Sciences,
    Ltd, ICS
International Union of the History and
    Philosophy of Science, IUHPS
RASD History Section, RASD/HS
Rijksbureau voor Kunsthistorische
    Documentatie (Netherlands Institute for
    Art History Documentation), RKD
Society for Film History Research, SFHR
Well History Control System, WHCS

Holdings
Periodical Holdings in the Library of the
    School of Medicine, PHILSOM

Holt
Holt Information Systems, HIS

Home Economics
American Home Economics Association,
    AHEA

Honduras
Asociación de Bibliotecarios y Archiveros de
    Honduras (Association of Librarians
    and Archivists of Honduras), ABAH

Honeywell
Honeywell Computer Users Association,
    HCUA

Hong Kong
Federation of Hong Kong Industries, FHKI

Horizontal
Horizontal Tabulation, HT

Horticultural Libraries
Council on Botanical and Horticultural
    Libraries, CBHL

Hospital
American Hospital Association, AHA
American Society of Hospital Pharmacists,
    ASHP
Association of Hospital and Institution
    Libraries, AHIL
Catholic Hospital Association, CHA
Consortium of Hospital and Rehabilitative
    Geriatric Enterprises, CHARGE
Hospital Management Systems Society,
    HMSS
Seattle Area Hospital Library Consortium,
    SAHLC
Shared Hospital Accounting System, SHAS
Total Hospital Operating and Medical
    Information System, THOMIS

Hospital Libraries
Conseil National des Bibliothèques
    d'Hôpitaux (National Council of
    Hospital Libraries), CNBH

Hospital Library
Areawide Hospital Library Consortium of
    Southwestern Illinois, AHLC

Housing
Department of Housing and Urban
    Development, DHUD
National Association of Housing and
    Redevelopment Officials Library,
    NAHRO

Houston
Houston Area Research Libraries
    Consortium, HARLIC
Houston–Galveston Area Council, HGAC

Huddersfield
Huddersfield and District Information
    Service, HADIS

Human Engineering
Human Engineering Information and
    Analysis Service, HEIAS

Human Intellect
Augmentation of Human Intellect, AHI
Human Intellect Augmentation System,
    HIAS

Human Readable
Human Readable/Machine Readable, HRMR

Human Relations
Human Relations Area Files, HRAF

Human Resources
Human Resources Network, HRN
Human Resources Research Organization,
    HUMRRO
Poverty and Human Resources Abstracts,
    PHRA

Humanistic Information
Centro de Información Científica y
    Humanistica (Center for Scientific and
    Humanistic Information), CICH

Humanities
ACM Special Interest Group on Language
    Analysis and Studies in the Humanities,
    ACM/SIGLASH
ASIS Special Interest Group on Arts and
    Humanities, ASIS/SIG/AH
American Association for the Advancement
    of the Humanities, AAAH
Arts and Humanities Citation Index, A&HCI
Computers and the Humanities, CHUM
Current Contents/Arts and Humanities.
    (Journal), CC/A&H
General Retrieval and Information Processor
    for Humanities-Oriented Studies,
    GRIPHOS
*Index to Social Sciences and Humanities
    Proceedings*, ISSHP
Modern Humanities Research Association,
    MHRA
National Council on the Humanities, NCH
National Endowment for the Humanities,
    NEH
Society for Automation in English and the
    Humanities, SAEH

Humberside Libraries
Humberside Libraries Technical Interloan
    Scheme, HULTIS

Hungarian
Hungarian Central Technical Library and
    Documentation Center, HCTLDC
Magyar Tudományos Akadémía Könyotára
    (Library of the Hungarian Academy of
    Sciences), MTAK

Hungarian Librarians
Magyar Könyvtarosok Egyesülete
    (Association of Hungarian Librarians),
    MKE

Hunger
Canadian Hunger Foundation, CHF

Huxley
Huxley Environmental Reference Bureau,
    HERB

Hydraulic
Hydraulic Engineering Information Analysis
    Center, HEIAC

Hydrological
Hydrological Information Storage and
    Retrieval System, HISARS

Hydromechanics
British Hydromechanics Research
    Association, BHRA

IBM
IBM Technical Information Retrieval
    Center, ITIRC

IFIP
IFIP Administrative Data Processing Group,
    IAG

IFP
Automatic Indexing of Documentation of
    IFP, AID-IFP

INSPEC
Retrospective Search System on the
    INSPEC Data Base, RETROSPEC

Idaho
Idaho Council of State Academic Libraries,
    ICOSAL
Idaho Library Association, ILA
Idaho National Engineering Laboratory,
    INEL
Washington, Alaska, Montana, and Idaho,
    WAMI

Identification
Automatic Diffemic Identification of
    Speakers, ADIS
Automatic Personal Identification Code,
    AUTOPIC
Bacterial Automated Identification
    Technique, BAIT
Piece Identification Number, PIN

Identifier
Standard Identifier for Individuals, SII

Idle
Synchronous Idle Character, SYN

Illinois
Areawide Hospital Library Consortium of
    Southwestern Illinois, AHLC
Illinois Department of Mental Health and
    Developmental Disabilities Library
    Services Network, DMHDD/LISN

Automatic Indexing of Documentation of
   IFP, AID-IFP
Cataloging and Indexing System of NAL,
   CAIN
Computer-Assisted Indexing and
   Categorizing, CAIC
Coordinate Indexing System, CIS
Indexing and Abstracting, I&A
Indexing by Statistical Analysis Techniques,
   IBSAT
Japanese Keyword Indexing Simulator,
   JAKIS
Master List of Medical Indexing Terms,
   MALIMET
Multiple Indexing and Console Retrieval
   Options, MICRO
National Federation of Abstracting and
   Indexing Services, NFAIS
National Federation of Science Abstracting
   and Indexing Services, NFSAIS
Proto Synthex Indexing, PSI
Random Access Document Indexing and
   Retrieval, RADIR
Simulated Machine Indexing, SMI
Société Canadienne pour l'Analyse de
   Documents/Indexing and Abstracting
   Society of Canada, SCAD/IASC

Indexing Services
Central Abstracting and Indexing Services,
   CAIS

India
India Library Association, ILA

Indian
Federation of Indian Library Associations,
   FILA
Indian Association of Special Libraries and
   Information Centers, IASLIC
Indian Association of Teachers of Library
   Science, IATLIS
Indian National Scientific Documentation
   Centre, INSDOC
Indian Science Abstracts, ISA
Indian Standards Institution, ISI
National Council of Indian Library
   Associations, NACILA
South African Indian Library Association,
   SAILA

Indian Ocean
International Indian Ocean Expedition, IIOE

Indiana
Collegiate Consortium of Western Indiana,
   CCWI
Indiana Cooperative Library Services
   Authority, INCOLSA
Indiana Higher Education Television
   System, IHETS
Indiana Information Retrieval System,
   INDIRS

Indiana Library Association, ILA
Northwest Indiana Area Library Services
   Authority, NIALSA
Southeastern Indiana Area Library Services
   Authority, SIALSA

Indianhead
Wisconsin Indianhead Technical Institute,
   WITI

Indicating
Rapid Alphanumeric Digital Indicating
   Device, RANDID

Indication
Radioactivity Detection Indication and
   Computation, RADIAC

Indicator
Manually Operated Visual Response
   Indicator, MOVRI

Individuals
Standard Identifier for Individuals, SII

Indonesia
Perkumpulan Ahli Perpustakaan Seluruh
   Indonesia (Association of Librarians
   throughout Indonesia), PAPSI

Indonesian
Himpunan Pustakawan Chusus Indonesia
   (Indonesian Association of Special
   Librarians), HPCI
Ikatan Pustakawan Indonesia (Indonesian
   Library Association), IPI
Perhimpunan Ahli Perpustakaan, Arsipdan
   Dokumentasi Indonesia (Indonesian
   Association of Librarians, Archives and
   Documentation), PAPADI
Pusat Documentasi Ilmiah Nasional
   (Indonesian Scientific and Technical
   Documentation Center), PDIN

Indonesian Library
Asosiasi Perpustakaan Arsip dan
   Dokumentasi Indonesia (Indonesian
   Library, Archive and Documentation
   Association), APADI

Industrial
American Association of Industrial Editors,
   AAIE
American Association of Industrial
   Management, AAIM
American Federation of Labor and Congress
   of Industrial Organizations, AFL-CIO
American Institute of Industrial Engineers,
   AIIE
*Bibliography of Scientific and Industrial
   Research*, BSIR
British Association of Industrial Editors,
   BAIE

Industrial (cont.)

British Industrial and Scientific Film
    Association Ltd, BISFA
Centro de Desarrollo Industrial (Center for
    Industrial Development), CENDES
Centro de Información Industrial (Industrial
    Information Center), CININ
Ceylon Institute of Scientific and Industrial
    Research, CISIR
Commonwealth Scientific and Industrial
    Research Organization, CSIRO
Computer-Assisted Industrial Simulation,
    CAISM
Cooperative Industrial and Commercial
    Reference and Information Service,
    CICRIS
Corporation for Economics and Industrial
    Research, CEIR
Council for Scientific and Industrial
    Research, CSIR
Datamation Industrial Directory, DID
Department of Scientific and Industrial
    Research, DSIR
*Dictionary of Industrial Engineering
    Abbreviations, Signs and Symbols*,
    DIEA
European Industrial Management
    Association, EIRMA
European Industrial Space Study Group,
    EUROSPACE
Federation of European Industrial Editors
    Associations, FEIEA
General Industrial Statistics, UNINDUST
Hampshire Technical Research Industrial
    and Commercial Service, HATRICS
Industrial Aerodynamics Information
    Service, IAIS
Industrial Audio-Visual Association, IAVA
Industrial Commodity Production Statistics,
    ICPDATA
Industrial Development Center/Viet-Nam
    (Trung-Tam Khuech-Truong Ky-Ngha),
    IDC/VN
Industrial Education Institute, IEI
Industrial Engineering. (Journal), IE
Industrial Process Control, IPC
Institute for Industrial Research and
    Standards, IIRS
Institute of Standards and Industrial
    Research of Iran, ISIRI
Instituto Centro Americano de Investigacion
    y Technologia Industrial (Central
    American Institute of Research and
    Industrial Technology), ICAITI
International Industrial Television
    Association, ITVA
International Standard Industrial
    Classification, ISIC
Japanese Industrial Standards Committee,
    JISC

Joint Industrial Committee for National
    Readership Surveys, JICNARS
Joint Industrial Council of Printing and Allied
    Trades, JIC
Kerr Industrial Applications Center, KIAC
Liverpool and District Scientific, Industrial
    and Research Library Advisory Council,
    LADSIRLAC
National Industrial Conference Board, NICB
Singapore Institute of Standards and
    Industrial Research, SISIR
Society for Industrial and Applied
    Mathematics, SIAM
Special Industrial Radio Service Association,
    SIRSA
United Nations Industrial Development
    Organization, UNIDO

Industrie

Associazione Nazionale Industrie
    Cinematografiche ed Affini, ANICA
Documentation en Ligne pour l'Industrie
    Agro-Alimentaire, IALINE

Industriefilmproduzenten

Vereinigung der Industriefilmproduzenten,
    VIP

Industrielle

Institute de Recherche Industrielle, IRI

Industries

Aerospace Industries Association of
    America, AIA
Centre de Documentation International des
    Industries Utilisatrices de Produits
    Agricoles, CDIUPA
Centre Technique des Industries de la
    Fonderie, CTIF
Commission Internationale des Industries
    Agricoles et Alimentaires, CIIA
Confederation of British Industries, CBI
Education Group of the Music Industries
    Association, EGMIA
Engineering Industries Association, EIA
Fédération Internationale des Industries du
    Cinéma de Film Étroit, FIDIC
Federation of Hong Kong Industries, FHKI
International Business Forms Industries,
    IBFI
International Commission for Agricultural
    and Food Industries, ICAI
Printing Industries of Metropolitan New
    York, PIMNY
Research on Computer Applications in the
    Printing and Publishing Industries,
    ROCAPPI
Syndicat des Industries Téléphoniques et
    Télégraphiques, SITT

Industry

Association of Information Officers in the
    Pharmaceutical Industry, AIOPI

Book Industry Study Groups, Inc, BISG
Book Industry Systems Advisory
    Committee, BISAC
Brewing Industry Research Foundation,
    BIRF
British Iron and Steel Industry Translation
    Service, BISITS
Business and Industry Extension Program,
    BIEP
Centrul de Documentare al Industriei
    Chimice si Petroliere (Documentation
    Center of the Chemical and Oil
    Industry), CDICIP
Committee on the Application of Computers
    in the Construction Industry, CAC
Confédération Internationale des Industries
    Techniques du Cinéma (International
    Confederation of the Cinema Industry),
    CIITC
Construction Industry Research and
    Information Association, CIRIA
Construction Industry Translation and
    Information Services, CITIS
Department of Industry, DoI
Department of Trade and Industry, DTI
Electrical Accounting for the Security
    Industry, EASI
FID Committee on Information and
    Industry, FID/II
Government-Industry Data Exchange
    Program, GIDEP
Information System on Research and
    Development in Building Industry and
    Construction, INBAD
Iron and Steel Industry, ISI
Iron and Steel Industry Training Board, ISI
    TB
Joint Industry Committee for Television
    Advertising Research, JICTAR
Literature Retrieval System for the Pulp and
    Paper Industry, LIRES
Magazine Industry Market Place, MIMP
National Advisory Council for Education for
    Industry and Commerce, NACEIC
Printing and Publishing Industry Training
    Board, PPITB
Printing Industry Research Association,
    PIRA
Professional Engineers Conference Board for
    Industry, PECBI
Recording Industry Association of America,
    RIAA
Research Industry Document Center, RIDC
Swindon Area Association of Libraries for
    Industry and Commerce, SAALIC
Technical Association of the Pulp and Paper
    Industry, TAPPI
Tyneside Association of Libraries for
    Industry and Commerce, TALIC
Wool Industry Research Association, WIRA

Informacijsko
Sistem za Avtomatizacilo Informacijsko
    Dokumentacijskih
    Centrov-Elektrotehnika, SAIDC

Información
Diseminación Selectiva de la Información,
    DSI

Información Agropecuaria
Programa de Información Agropecuaria del
    Istmo Centroamericana, PIADIC

Información Avícola
Instituto Méxicano de Información Avícola,
    IMIA

Información Cientifica
Sistema Colombiano de Información
    Cientifica y Technica, SICOLDIC

Informacji
Automatyzacja Przetwarzania Informacji
    Naukowej, APIN

Informasui
Centralny Instytut Informasui Noukowo
    Techniceneu I Economicznej (Central
    Institute for Scientific, Technical and
    Economic Information), CLINTE

Informatica
*Anuario de Bibliotecologia, Archivologia e
    Informatica*, ANBAI
Bibliografia di Informatica e Diritto, BID

Informatics
Intergovernmental Bureau for
    Informatics/International Computation
    Center, IBI/ICC

Information
ASIS Special Interest Group on Technology,
    Information, and Society,
    ASIS/SIG/TIS
Agricultural System for Storage and
    Subsequent Selection of Information,
    ASSASSIN
Armed Forces Information and Education
    Division, AFIED
Automation for Storage and Retrieval of
    Information, AFSARI
BioSciences Information Service, BIOSIS
BioSciences Information Service Previews,
    BIOSIS Previews.
Canadian Selective Dissemination of
    Information, CAN/SDI
Center for Information and Documentation,
    CID
Center for Information on America, CIOA
Central Office of Information, COI
Centralny Instytut Informasui Noukowo
    Techniceneu I Economicznej (Central

Information (cont.)

Institute for Scientific, Technical and Economic Information), CIINTE

Centro Brasileiro de Pesquisas Educacionais–Divisão de Documentacão e Informacão Pedagógica (Brazilian Center of Educational Research–Department of Educational Documentation and Information), CBPE-DDIP

Centro Méxicano de Información del Zinc y del Plomo (Mexican Center of Information for Zinc and Lead), CMIZPAC

Centro Nacional de Información y Documentación (National Center for Information and Documentation), CENID

Committee for Information and Documentation on Science and Technology, CIDST

Construction Industry Research and Information Association, CIRIA

Cost Analysis Information Report, CAIR

Design of Information in the Social Sciences, DISISS

Deutsches Institut für Medizinische Dokumentation und Information (German Institute for Medical Documentation and Information), DIMDI

Diffusion Sélective de l'Information, DSI

Digital Information Display, DID

Dirección General de Información y Relaciones Publicas (Board of Information and Public Relations), DGIRP

FID Committee on Information and Industry, FID/II

FID Committee on Research on the Theoretical Basis of Information, FID/RI

FID Committee on the Terminology of Information and Documentation, FID/DT

General Information File Interrogation, GIFI

Generalized Information Management System, GIM

Gesellschaft für Information und Dokumentation, GID

Information & Publishing Systems, Inc, I&PS

Information and Data Exchange Experimental Activities, IDEEA

Information for Business, IFB

Information for Minnesota, INFORM

Information Unlimited, IU

Institute de Recherche d'Informatique et d'Automatique (French Research

Institute of Information and Automatic Processing), IRIA

Institute for Computer-Assisted Information, ICAI

Institute Nazionale de l'Informazione (National Institute of Information), INI

Instituto de Documentación e Información Científica y Tecnica (Institute of Scientific and Technical Documentation and Information), IDICT

International Bibliography, Information, Documentation, IBID

International Center of Information on Antibiotics, ICIA

Modern Information & Documentation Organizing & Rearrangement, Inc, MIDORI

Natural Unit of Information, NAT

Nederlands Instituut voor Informatie, Documentatie en Registratuur (Netherlands Institute for Information, Documentation and Filing), NIDER

Österreichische Gesellschaft für Dokumentation und Information (Austrian Society for Documentation and Information), ÖGDI

Retrieval and Automatic Dissemination of Information from *Index Chemicus* and Line Notations, RADIICAL

Selective Dissemination of Information, SDI

Storage and Information Retrieval System, STAIRS

Subject Content-Oriented Retriever for Processing Information Online, SCORPIO

System for the Publication and Efficient, Effective Dissemination of Information, SPEEDI

Total Information for Educational Systems, TIES

Universal System for Information in Science and Technology, UNISIST

Vsesoiuznyĭ Nauchno Issle-dovatel'skii Institut Meditsinskoĭ i Medikotekhnicheskoĭ Informatsii Ministerstva Zdravookhraneniia USSR (All-Union Scientific Research Institute of Medical and Medico-Technical Information, VNIIMI

Women's Information and Study Centre, WISC

Zentralinstitut für Information und Dokumentation, ZIID

Information Agencies
Field Information Agencies, Technical, FIAT

Information Agency
Chemical Propulsion Information Agency, CPIA

National Telecommunications and
   Information Agency, NTIA
United States Information Agency, USIA

Information Analysis
ASIS Special Interest Group on Information
   Analysis Centers, ASIS/SIG/IAC
Counterinsurgency Information Analysis
   Center, CINFAC
Hydraulic Engineering Information Analysis
   Center, HEIAC
Information Analysis and Retrieval Division,
   IARD
Information Analysis Center, IAC
Non-Destructive Testing Information
   Analysis Center, NTIAC
Pavements and Soil Trafficability
   Information Analysis Center, PSTIAC
Sail Mechanics Information Analysis Center,
   SMIAC

Information Association
Buildings Services Research and Information
   Association, BSRIA

Information Automatisée
Normes et Reglementation–Information
   Automatisée, NORIA

Information Bank
Agricultural Information Bank of Asia,
   AIBA

Information Bureau
Anthracite Information Bureau, AIB
Lard Information Bureau, LIB
National Information Bureau, NIB
Petroleum Information Bureau, PIB
Publishers Information Bureau, PIB

Information Bureaux
Association of Special Libraries and
   Information Bureaux, ASLIB

Information Center
Aerospace Materials Information Center,
   AMIC
Air Pollution Technical Information Center,
   APTIC
Alaskan Health Sciences Information
   Center, AHSIC
Arctic, Desert, Tropic Information Center,
   ADTIC
Asian Information Center for Geotechnical
   Engineering, AGE
Biomedical Computing Technology
   Information Center, BCTIC
Centre de Documención e Información
   Educativa (Educational Documentation
   and Information Center), CDIF
Centre d'Information et de Publicité des
   Chemins de Fer Européens (Information

and Publicity Center of European
   Railways), CIPCE
Centre pour le Traitement de l'Information
   (Information Processing Center),
   CENTI
Centro de Información Industrial (Industrial
   Information Center), CININ
Centro de Información y Documentación del
   Patronato de Investigación Cientifica y
   Técnica Juan de la Cierva (Information
   and Documentation Center of the Juan
   de la Cierva Patronage), CID
Company and Literature Information Center,
   CLIC
Computer Software and Management
   Information Center, COSMIC
Concrete Technology Information Analysis
   Center, CTIAC
DOD Nuclear Information and Analysis
   Center, DASIAC
Defense Ceramic Information Center, DCIC
Defense Metals Information Center, DMIC
Drug Information Service Center, DISC
Educational Resources Information Center,
   ERIC
Electronic Properties Information Center,
   EPIC
Energy Information Center, EIC
Environment Information Center, Inc, EIC
Environmental Science and Information
   Center, ESIC
Flight Information Center, FIC
IBM Technical Information Retrieval
   Center, ITIRC
Information and Research Utilization
   Center, IRUC
Information Center for Southern California
   Libraries, INFO
International Copyrights Information Center,
   INCINC
International Library Information Center,
   ILIC
Japan Information Center for Science and
   Technology, JICST
Japan Pharmaceutical Information Center,
   JAPIC
Korean Scientific and Technological
   Information Center, KORSTIC
Liquid Metals Information Center, LMIC
Metals and Ceramics Information Center,
   MCIC
National Cartographic Information Center,
   NCIC
National Crime Information Center, NCIC
National Energy Information Center
   Affiliate, NEICA
National Health Planning Information
   Center, NHPIC
National Information Center for Educational
   Media, NICEM

Information Center (cont.)

National Information Center in Special
Education Materials, NICSEM
Northeast Academic Science Information
Center, NASIC
Nuclear Safety Information Center, NSIC
Pakistan Scientific and Technological
Information Center, PASTIC
Primate Information Center, PIC
Radiation Effects Information Center, REIC
Radiation Shielding Information Center,
RSIC
Rare-Earth Information Center, RIC
Redstone Scientific Information Center,
RSIC
Regional Information Coordinating Center,
RICC
Remote Areas Conflict Information Center,
RACIC
Research Information Center and Advisory
Service on Information Processing,
RICASIP
Solar Applications Information Center,
SOLAPIC
Southeast Asian Medical Information
Center, SEAMIC
Southern Water Resources Scientific
Information Center, SWRSIC
Technical Information Center, TIC
Technical Information Center
Administration, TICA
Therapeutic Recreation Information Center,
TRIC
Undergraduate Excavation and Rock
Properties Information Center, UERPIC
Visual Science Information Center, VSIC
Water Resources Scientific Information
Center, WRSIC
Western Regional Information Service
Center, WRISC

Information Centers

Association for Population/Family Planning
Libraries and Information Centers,
APLIC
Association of Information and
Dissemination Centers, AIDC
Indian Association of Special Libraries and
Information Centers, IASLIC
Israel Society for Special Libraries and
Information Centers, ISLIC
Neighborhood Information Centers Project,
NIC

Information Centre

British Columbia Institute of Technology
Information Resource Centre, BCIT
Commonwealth Information Centre, CIC
English Teaching Information Centre, ETIC
Multilateral Disarmament Information
Centre, MDIC

Naval Scientific and Technical Information
Centre, NSTIC
Queen's University Information Centre,
QUIC

Information Circuit

Kansas Information Circuit, KIC

Information Clearinghouse

Technical Assistance Information
Clearinghouse, TAICH

Information Compiler

Macro-Operation Symbolic Assembler and
Information Compiler, MOSAIC 636

Information Conference

National Information Conference and
Exposition, NICE

Information Control

Customer Information Control System,
CICS
Factory Information Control System, FICS
File Room Online Information Control,
FROLIC
Local Government Information Control,
LOGIC

Information Council

Film Library Information Council, FLIC

Information Digest

Retrieval through Automated Publication
and Information Digest, RAPID

Information Display

Society for Information Display, SID

Information Dissemination

Automated Information Dissemination
System, AIDS
Chemical Society Research Unit in
Information Dissemination and
Retrieval, CSRUIDR
Medical Information Dissemination Using
ASSASSIN, MIDAS
Random Access Personnel Information
Dissemination, RAPID
Random Access Personnel Information
Dissemination System, RAPIDS
Research in Automatic Photocomposition
and Information Dissemination, RAPID
Rotating Associative Processor for
Information Dissemination, RAPID
Selective Information Dissemination and
Retrieval, SIDAR
Self-Organizing Large Information
Dissemination, SOLID

Information Elicitation

Shared Information Elicitation Facility,
SHIEF

Information Exchange
Educational Products and Information
Exchange, EPIE
Ethnic Materials Information Exchange Task
Force, EMIETF
Hibernation Information Exchange, HIE
Iowa Library Information Teletype
Exchange, I-LITE
Library Automated Systems Information
Exchange, LASIE
Museum and University Data, Program and
Information Exchange, MUDPIE
Regional Information and Communication
Exchange, RICE
Science and Technology Policies Information
Exchange System, SPINES
Science Information Exchange, SIE
Smithsonian Information Exchange, SIE
Smithsonian Science Information Exchange,
SSIE
Texas Information Exchange, TIE
Xerox Information Exchange Network, IEN

Information Exchanges
Access Service for Profitable Information
Resource Exchanges, ASPIRE

Information Film
International Association of Information
Film Distributors, INFORFILM

Information General
Information General, Inc, IGI

Information Group
Coventry and District Information Group,
CADIG

Information Industry
Information Industry Association, IIA
Information Industry Market Place, IIMP

Information Interchange
United States of America Standard Code for
Information Interchange, USASCII

Information Item
Information Item File, IIF

Information Libraries
Health and Information Libraries of
Westchester, HILOW

Information List
Processing Information List, PIL

Information Management
An Analytical Information Management
System, AAIMS
Auerbach Information Management System,
AIMS
Foreign Affairs Information Management
Effort, FAIME
Medical Information Management System,
MIMS

Regional Information Management System,
RIMS
Remote Information Management System,
RIMS
Socioeconomic Information Management
System, SIMS

Information Managers
Associated Information Managers, AIM
Program for Information Managers, PRIM

Information Médicale
Association Nationale des Journalistes
d'Information Médicale, ANJIM

Information Needs
Abstracted Business
Information/Information Needs,
ABI/INFORM

Information Network
Agricultural Libraries Information Network,
AGLINET
Agricultural Sciences Information Network,
ASIN
Australian Information Network, AUSINET
Automated Mortgage Management
Information Network, AMMINET
Channeled Arizona Information Network,
CHAIN
Community Health Information Network,
CHIN
Computer-Aided Processing and Terminal
Access Information Network,
CAPTAIN
Computerized Information Network for
Community Health, CINCH
Consortium for International Development
Information Network, CIDNET
Cooperative Information Network, CIN
District of Columbia Health Science
Information Network, DOCHSIN
Federal Library and Information Network,
FEDLINK
Georgia Library Information Network,
GLIN
Health Information Network of the Pacific,
HINOP
Illinois Library and Information Network,
ILLINET
Mid-Atlantic Research Libraries Information
Network, MARLIN
Montana Information Network and
Exchange, MINE
National Emergency Medical Services
Information Network, NEMSINET
Neurological Science Information Network,
NINDS
North Alabama Biomedical Information
Network, NABIN
Pacific Coast Forest Research Information
Network, PACFORNET

Information Network (cont.)

Regional and Urban Information Network, RUIN
Research Libraries Information Network, RLIN
Western Forest Information Network, WESTFORNET
Western Information Network Association, WIN

Information Networks
Conference on Interlibrary Communications and Information Networks, CICIN

Information Notes
Agricultural Libraries Information Notes. (Journal), ALIN

Information Notices
Searchable Physics Information Notices, SPIN

Information Office
Local Government Information Office, LGIO
Television Information Office, TIO

Information Officer
Public Information Officer, PIO
Science and Technology Information Officer, STINFO

Information Officers
Association Internationale des Documentalistes et Techniciens de l'Information (International Association of Documentalists and Information Officers), AID
Association of Information Officers in the Pharmaceutical Industry, AIOPI

Information Policy
Netherlands Orgaan voor de Bevordering van de Informatieverzorging (Netherlands Organization for Information Policy), NOBIN

Information Problems
Dzialowy Ośrodek Zagadnién Informacyjnych Centralnego Instytutu Informacji Naukowo-Technicznej i Ekonomicznej (Branch Center on Information Problems at the Central Institute for Scientific, Technical and Economic Information), DOZI-CIINTE

Information Process
Vermont Information Process, VIP

Information Processing
American Federation for Information Processing, AFIP

American Federation of Information Processing Societies, AFIPS
Canadian Information Processing Society/Association Canadienne de L'Informatique, CIPS/ACI
Compiler Language for Information Processing, CLIP
Federal Information Processing Standards, FIPS
Federal Information Processing Standards Coordinating and Advisory Committee, FIPSCAC
Film and Report Information Processing Generator, FRINGE
Generalized Information Processing System, GIPSY
Information Processing Association of Israel, IPA
Information Processing Code, IPC
Information Processing Language, IPL
Information Processing Language-5, IPL-5
Integrated Information Processing System, INTIPS
International Conference on Information Processing, ICIP
International Federation for Information Processing, IFIP
International Federation of Information Processing Societies, IFIPS
JICST Electronic Information Processing Automatic Computer, JEIPAC
Linear Information Processing Language, LIPL
Research Information Center and Advisory Service on Information Processing, RICASIP
TALON Reporting and Information Processing System, TRIPS
Teach Information Processing Language, TIPL
Technical Information Processing System, TIPS
Variable Information Processing, VIP

Information Processor
General Retrieval and Information Processor for Humanities-Oriented Studies, GRIPHOS

Information Program
Army Qualitative Development Requirements Information Program, QDRI
Transdisciplinary Engineering Information Program, TEIP

Information Project
Kentucky Cooperative Library Information Project, KENCLIP
Pollution Information Project, PIP

Information Publishing
ASIS Special Interest Group on Information
Publishing, ASIS/SIG/IP

Information Referral
Marine Environmental Data Information
Referral System, MEDI

Information Requirements
Information Requirements of the Social
Sciences, INFROSS

Information Research
Center for Communication and Information
Research, CCIR

Information Resources
Consortium for Information Resources, CIR
ERIC Clearinghouse on Information
Resources, ERIC/IR
Information Resources Information System,
IRIS
Information Resources Press, IRP
Redgrave Information Resources, RIR

Information Retrieval
ACM Special Interest Group on Information
Retrieval, ACM/SIGIR
Alberta Information Retrieval Association,
AIRA
Alberta Information Retrieval for Health,
Physical Education, and Recreation,
AIRHPER
Annual National Information Retrieval
Colloquium, ANIRC
Aquatic Sciences Information Retrieval
Center, ASIRC
Automatic Fact Information Retrieval and
Storage Systems, AFIRSS
Automatic Information Retrieval System,
AIRs
Baptist Information Retrieval System, BIRS
CTC's Information Retrieval from
Keywords, CIRK
Committee for International Cooperation in
Information Retrieval among Examining
Patent Officers, CICIREPATO
Computer Assisted Information Retrieval
System, CAIRS
Data Processing and Information Retrieval,
DPIR
Dial Access Information Retrieval System,
DAIRS
Failure Analysis Information Retrieval,
FAIR
Fast Access Information Retrieval, FAIR
Federal Aviation Information Retrieval
System, FAIRS
Generalized Information Retrieval and
Listing System, GIRLS
Generalized Information Retrieval
Language, GIRL

Indiana Information Retrieval System, INDIRS
Information Retrieval, IR
Information Retrieval Automatic Language,
INFRAL
Information Retrieval Group of the Museums
Association, IRGMA
Information Retrieval Language, IRL
International Cooperation in Information
Retrieval among Examining Patent
Offices, ICIREPAT
International Information Retrieval Service,
IIRS
Natural History Information Retrieval
System, NHIR
Philosophers Information Retrieval Service,
PIRS
Pulp and Paper Research Institute of
Canada/Information Retrieval Services,
PAPRICAN/IRS
School Management Information Retrieval
System, SMIRS
Semantic Information Retrieval, SIR
Solid Waste Information Retrieval System,
SWIRS
Stanford Physics Information Retrieval
System, SPIRES
Statistical Information Retrieval, SIR

Information Science
ASIS Special Interest Group on Education
for Information Science, ASIS/SIG/ED
ASIS Special Interest Group on Foundations
of Information Science, ASIS/SIG/FIS
American Society for Information Science,
ASIS
*Annual Review of Information Science and
Technology*, ARIST
Australian Centre for Research in Library
and Information Science, ACRiLIS
*Bulletin of the American Society for
Information Science*, BASIS
Canadian Association for Information
Science/Association Canadienne des
Sciences de l'Information, CAIS/ACSI
Graduate School of Library and Information
Science, GSLIS
Information Science, IS
Information Science Abstracts, ISA
Information Science and Automation
Division, ISAD
*Journal of the American Society for
Information Science*, JASIS
LITA Information Science and Automation
Section, LITA/ISAS
Library and Information Science, LIS
Library and Information Science Abstracts,
LISA
Library and Information Science Meetings
Exchange, Massachusetts Bureau of
Library Extension, LIS/MEX

Information Science (cont.)

Library and Information Science Today, LIST
National Commission on Libraries and Information Science, NCLIS
School of Library and Information Science, SLIS

Information Sciences

Association de l'Institut National des Techniques de la Documentation (Association of the National Institute for Information Sciences), AINTD
Computer and Information Sciences, COINS

Information Scientists

Association Française des Documentalistes et des Bibliothécaires Spécialisés (French Association of Information Scientists and Special Librarians), ADBS
Institute of Information Scientists, IIS

Information Selection

Current Information Selection, CIS

Information Separator

Information Separator, IS

Information Service

Aberdeen and North of Scotland Library and Information Cooperative Service, ANSLICS
Adult Referral and Information Service in Education, ARISE
Applicant Information Service, AIS
Brain Information Service, BIS
British Information Service, BIS
A Computerized London Information Service, ACOMPLIS
Congressional Information Service, CIS
Cooperative Industrial and Commercial Reference and Information Service, CICRIS
Danish Agricultural Producers Information Service, DAPIS
Dansk Teknisk Oplysningstjeneste (Danish Technical Information Service), DTO
Gloucestershire Technical Information Service, GTIS
Halifax and District Information Service, HALDIS
Hertfordshire County Council Technical Library and Information Service, HERTIS
Higher Education Learning Programmes Information Service: A Catalogue of Materials Available for Exchange, HELPIS
Highway Research Information Service, HRIS

Huddersfield and District Information Service, HADIS
Human Engineering Information and Analysis Service, HEIAS
Industrial Aerodynamics Information Service, IAIS
Information Service in Mechanical Engineering, ISMEC
Information Service in Physics, Electrotechnology and Control, INSPEC
International Food Information Service, IFIS
International Rights Information Service, IRIS
Leicestershire Technical Information Service, LETIS
Library Information Service, LIBRIS
Library Information Service for Teeside, LIST
Maize Virus Information Service, MAVIS
Manchester Technical Information Service, MANTIS
Maritime Research Information Service, MRIS
Medical Record Information Service, MRIS
Military Entomology Information Service, MEIS
National Credit Information Service, NACIS
National Technical Information Service, NTIS
Nottingham and Nottinghamshire Technical Information Service, NANTIS
Public Affairs Information Service, PAIS
Railroad Research Information Service, RRIS
Safety Research Information Service, SRIS
Student Advisory Information Service, STAIS
Technical Information Service, TIS
United Kingdom Chemical Information Service, UKCIS
Visual Education National Information Service for Schools, VENISS

Information Services

ASIS Special Interest Group on Community Information Services, ASIS/SIG/CIS
ASIS Special Interest Group on Information Services to Education, ASIS/SIG/ISE
American Institute of Aeronautics and Astronautics, Technical Information Services, AIAA-TIS
Australasian Drug Information Services Pty. Limited, ADIS
Black Resources Information Coordinating Services, Inc, BRICS
Cable Information Services, CIS
Canadian Association of Special Libraries and Information Services, CASLIS

Comprehensive University of Dayton
On-Line Information Services, CUDOS
Construction Industry Translation and
Information Services, CITIS
Council for Exceptional Children
Information Services, CEC
Directorate of Scientific Information
Services, DSIS
European Association of Information
Services, EUSIDIC
European Conference on the Application of
Research in Information Services and
Libraries, EURIM 3
Information Handling Services, IHS
Information Services Division, ISD
Irish Association for Documentation and
Information Services, IADIS
Ohio Project for Research in Information
Services, OPRIS
Research Information Services, RIS
Research Information Services for
Education, RISE
Roberts Information Services, ROBINS
Scientific and Technological Information
Services Enquiry Committee, STISEC
Specialized Information Services, SIS
Transportation Research Information
Services Network, TRISNET
White House Conference on Library and
Information Services, WHCOLIS

Information Sharing
Great Lakes Environmental Information
Sharing, GLEIS
Health Information Sharing Project, HISP
Inter-Professional Ad Hoc Group for
Environmental Information Sharing,
IPAHGEIS

Information Society
Geoscience Information Society, GIS

Information Sources
Drug Information Sources, DIS
Executives Guide to Information Sources,
EGIS

Information Storage
Hydrological Information Storage and
Retrieval System, HISARS
Information Storage and Retrieval, ISAR
Information Storage and Retrieval, ISR
National Information Storage and Retrieval
Centers, NISARC

Information Storage/Retrieval
Bibliothekarisch-Analytisches System zur
Informations-Speicherung-Erschliessung
(Library Analytical System for
Information Storage/Retrieval-
Economics), BASIS-E

Bibliothekarisch-Analytisches System zur
Informations-Speicherung-Leihverkehr
(Library Analytical System for
Information Storage/Retrieval-Loan),
BASIS-L

Information Studies
School of Information Studies, SIS

Information Study
Institute's Retrieval-of-Information Study,
IRIS

Information sur les Télécommunications
Bureau International d'Information sur les
Télécommunications, BIIT

Information Survey
Catalogued Resources and Information
Survey Programs, CRISP
Higher Education General Information
Survey, HEGIS

Information Symposium
Universal Resource Information
Symposium, URIS I

Information System
Agricultural Information System, AGRIS
Agricultural Research Management
Information System, ARMIS
Arid Lands Information System, ALIS
Arizona Water Information System, AWIS
Army Research and Development
Information System, ARDIS
Automatic Information System, AIST
Automatic Microfilm Information System,
AMFIS
Automatic Traffic Engineering and
Management Information System,
ATEMIS
Battelle Automated Search Information
System for the Seventies, BASIS-70
British Library Automated Information
System, BLAISE
Business Information System, BIS
California Education Information System,
CEIS
Career Information System, CIS
Chalk River Bibliographic Data Information
System, CHARIBIDIS
Current Agricultural Research Information
System, CARIS
Current Research Information System, CRIS
Decision-Aiding Information System,
DAISY
Development of Sciences Information
System, DEVSIS
Engineering Maintenance Information
System, EMIS
Extramural Programs Information System,
EPIS

Information System (cont.)

Financial Accounting and Management
Information System, FAMIS
Financial and Management Information
System, FAMIS
Foreign Exchange Accounting and
Management Information System,
FEAMIS
Fully Automatic Information System,
FAIRS
Generalized Information System, GENISYS
Generalized Information System, GIS
Heuristic Mechanized Document
Information System, HERMES
IPI Management and Information System,
IPI/MIS
Information Resources Information System,
IRIS
Information System for Adaptive, Assistive
and Recreational Equipment, ISAARE
Information System on Research and
Development in Building Industry and
Construction, INBAD
International Information System on
Research in Documentation, ISORID
International Nuclear Information System,
INIS
Library Information System, LIBRIS
Library Information System Time Sharing,
LISTS
Management Information System, MIS
Multi-Aspect Relevance Linkage
Information System, MARLIS
National Air Pollution Technical Information
System, NAPTIC
National Energy Referral and Information
System, NERIS
National Information System for Physics and
Astronomy, NISPA
National Information System for
Psychology, NISP
National Instructional Materials Information
System, NIMIS
National Physics Information System, NPIS
Navy Automated Research and
Development Information System,
NARDIS
Network Management Information System,
NEMIS
New Mexico Information System,
NEMISYS
Oak Ridge Chemical Information System,
ORCHIS
Oceanic and Atmospheric Scientific
Information System, OASIS
Oregon Total Information System, OTIS
Personnel Operations Information System,
POISE
Personnel Records Information System for
Management, PRISM

Project Grant Information System, PGIS
Prosecutors Management Information
System, PROMIS
Social Science Information System, SSIS
South Australia Education Resource
Information System, SAERIS
Total Hospital Operating and Medical
Information System, THOMIS
Transportation Planning Support
Information System, TPSIS
Transportation Research Information
System, TRIS
Vocational Education Program Information
System, VEPIS

Information Systems

ASIS Special Interest Group on Biological
and Chemical Information Systems,
ASIS/SIG/BC
Association for the Development of
Religious Information Systems, ADRIS
Chemical Information Systems Operators,
CHEOPS
Correctional Records Information Systems,
CRYSIS
FID Committee on Theory, Methods, and
Operations of Information Systems and
Networks, FID/TMO
Holt Information Systems, HIS
Information Systems Laboratory, ISL
Information Systems Office, ISO
Integrated Set of Information Systems, ISIS
Library Information Systems Analysis,
LISA
National Association for State Information
Systems, NASIS
Technical Information Systems Activities,
TISA
Technical Information Systems Committee,
TISCO
Urban and Regional Information Systems
Association, URISA
World Information Systems Exchange,
WISE

Information Tapes

Current Information Tapes for Engineers,
CITE

Information Technology

ASIS Special Interest Group on Law and
Information Technology,
ASIS/SIG/LAW
Educators Information Technology System,
EDITS
Jerusalem Conference on Information
Technology, JCIT
Library and Information Technology
Association, LITA
University Information Technology
Corporation, UNITEL

Information Transfer
Imbricated Program for Information
Transfer, IMPRINT
Information Transfer Experiments, INTREX

Information Users
Federation of Information Users, FIU

Informations
Informations und Dokumentationssystem
zum Umweltplanung, UMPLIS

Informations Scientifiques
Service d'Échange d'Informations
Scientifiques, SEIS

Informationsbibliothek
Technische Informationsbibliothek, TIB

Informationswissenschaften
Dokumentationszentrum für
Informationswissenschaften, ZDOK

Informatique
Association Française d'Informatique et de
Recherche Opérationnelle, AFIRO
Compagnie Internationale pour
l'Informatique, CII

Informatique Documentaire
Association Scientifique et Technique pour
la Recherche en Informatique
Documentaire, ASTRID

Informative
Result from Action, Prediction, Informative,
Diagnostic Sensing, RAPIDS

Informazion Bibliografiche
Centro Nazionale per il Catalogo Unico delle
Biblioteche Italiane per le Informazion
Bibliografiche, CUBI

Informazioni Scientifiche
Centro Europeo Informazioni Scientifiche e
Tecniche, CEIST

Infrared Information
Infrared Information and Analysis Center,
IRIA
Infrared Information System, IRIS

Ingenieur
Estimation de Proprietés Physiques pour
l'Ingenieur Chimiste, EPIC

Ingenieurs
Verein Deutscher Ingenieurs, VDI

Initial
Initial Program Loading, IPL

Initiation Area
Initiation Area Discriminator, IAD

Initiatives
Société Québeçoise d'Initiatives Pétrolières,
SOQUIP

Injury
National Electronic Injury Surveillance
System, NEISS

Ink
Magnetic Ink Character Recognition, MICR

Inland
Inland Empire Academic Libraries
Cooperative, IEALC

Innovation
Bureau de Recherche pour l'Innovation et la
Convergence, BRIC
Center for Educational Research and
Innovation, CERI

Innovation Urbaines
Centre de Recherches et d'Innovation
Urbaines, CRIU

Inorganic
Inorganic and Metallurgical
Thermodynamics Data, MTDATA

Input
Automated Input and Document Update
System, AIDUS
Circulation Input Recording, CIRC
Computer Input Microfilm, CIM
Context, Input, Process Product Model,
CIPP
Film Input to Digital Automatic Computer,
FIDAC
Film Optical Sensing Device for Input to
Computers, FOSDIC
Graphic Input Language, GRAIL
Graphical Input for Network Analysis,
GINA
Input Audit and Control, INPACON
Input Translator, INTRAN
Low Data-Rate Input, LDRI
Software-Aided Multifont Input, SWAMI

Input-Output
Business Input-Output Rerun, BIOR
Communications Input/Output Control
System, CIOCS
Community Input/Output Control System,
CIOS
Digital Input/Output Display Equipment,
DIODE
Input/Output, I/O
Input/Output and Transfer, IOT
Input/Output Control Center, IOCC
Input/Output Control Module, IOC
Input/Output Control System, IOCS
Input/Output Package, IOPKG
Input/Output Processor, IOP
Input/Output Register, IOR
Tape Input/Tape Output, TIPTOP

Inquiry
Collection, Inquiry, Reporting &
Communication, CIRC
Program of Action for Mediation,
Arbitration, and Inquiry, PAMAI
Random Access and Inquiry, RAI
Staff Committee on Mediation, Arbitration
and Inquiry, SCMAI

Installation
Computer Layout Installation Planner, CLIP

Installation Management
ACM Special Interest Group on Computer
Systems Installation Management,
ACM/SIGCOSIM

Institut
Institut de Recherches sur les Fruits et
Agrumes, IRFA
Institut Fondamental d'Afrique Noire, IFAN
Institut Français d'Opinion Publique, IFOP
Institut für Wirtschaftsforschung, IFO
Institut für Wissenschaftsinformation in der
Medizin, IWIM
Institut International du Froid, IIF
Institut National de la Santé et de la
Recherche Medicale, INSERM
Institut National de la Statistique et des
Études Économique, INSEE
Institut National de Recherches et de
Documentation, INRDG
Naučno-Issledovatel'skij i Konstruktorskij
Institut Ispytatel'nych Mašin, Priborov i
Sredstv Avtomatizacii i Sistem
Upravlenija SSSR, NIKIMP
Naučno-Issledovatel'skij Institut Rezinovoj
Promyšlennosti Ministerstva
Neftpererabatyvajuščej i
Neftechimičeskoj, Promyšlennosti
SSSR, NIIRP
Vsesojuznyĭ Naučhno-Issledovatel'skii
Institut Molochnoi Promyshiennosti
Ministerstva Miasnoi i Molochnoi
Promyshlennosti SSSR, VNIMI
Vsesojuznyj Naučno-Isseldovatel'skij
Geologorazvedočnyj Neftjanoj Institut
Ministerstra Geologii SSSR, VNIGNI
Vsesojuznyj Naučno-Issledovatel'skij
Institut Economiki Mineral'nogo Syr'ja i
Geologorazvedocnych Rabot
Ministerstva Geologii SSSR i Akademii
nauk SSSR, VIEMS
Vsesojuznyj Naučno-Issledovatel'skij
Institut Iskusstvennogo Volokna
Ministerstva Chimičeskoj
Promyšlennosti SSSR, VNIIV
Vsesojuznyj Naučno-Issledovatel'skij
Institut Konservnoj i Ovoščesušil'noj
Promyšlennosti Ministerstva Pisščevoj
Promyšlennosti SSSR, VNIIKOP

Vsesojuznyj Naučno-Issledovatel'skij
Institut Mechovoj Promyšlennosti
Ministerstva Legleoj Promyšlennosti
SSSR, VNIIMP
Vsesojuznyj Naučno-Issledovatel'skij
Institut Mjasnoj Promyšlennosti
Ministerstva Mjasnoj i Moločnoj
promyslennosti SSSR, VNIIMP
Vsesojuznyj Naučno-Issledovatel'skij
Institut po Pererabotke Chimičeskich
Volokon Ministerstva Legkoj
Promyšlennosti SSSR, VNIIPCHV
Vsesojuznyj Naučno-Issledovatel'skij
Institut po Pererabotke Nefti
Ministerstva Nefteprerabatyvajuščej i
Neftechimičeskoj Promyšlennosti
SSSR, VNIINP
Vsesojuznyj Naučno-Issledovatel'skij
Institut Stekloplastikov i Stekljannogo
Volokna Ministerstva Chimičeskoj
Promyšlennosti SSSR, VNIISSV
Vsesojuznyj Sel'skochozjajstvennyj Institut
Zaučnogo Obzovanija Ministerstva
Sel'skogo Chozjajstva SSSR, VSCHIZO

Institut für Angewandte Forschung
Betriebsforschungsinstitut, VDEh-Institut
für Angewandte Forschung GmbH, BFI

Institute
Abstract Bulletin of the Institute of Paper
Chemistry, ABIPC
Agricultural Research Institute, ARI
American Academy and Institute of Arts and
Letters, AAIL
American Concrete Institute, ACI
American Documentation Institute, ADI
American Educational Publishers Institute,
AEPI
American Film Institute, AFI
American Geological Institute, AGI
American Institute for Conservation of
Historic and Artistic Works, AIC
American Institute for Exploration, AIFE
American Institute for Research, AIR
American Institute of Aeronautics and
Astronautics, AIAA
American Institute of Aeronautics and
Astronautics, Technical Information
Services, AIAA-TIS
American Institute of Architects, AIA
American Institute of Banking, AIB
American Institute of Biological Sciences,
AIBS
American Institute of Certified Public
Accountants, AICPA
American Institute of Chemical Engineers,
AIChE
American Institute of Chemists, Inc, AIC
American Institute of Consulting Engineers,
AICE

American Institute of Electrical Engineers,
    AIEE
American Institute of Graphic Arts, AIGA
American Institute of Industrial Engineers,
    AIIE
American Institute of Management, AIM
American Institute of Marine Underwriters,
    AIMU
American Institute of Mining, Metallurgical
    and Petroleum Engineers, AIME
American Institute of Physics, AIP
American Institute of Steel Construction,
    AISC
American Institute of Timber Construction,
    AITC
American Iron and Steel Institute, AISI
American National Standards Institute,
    ANSI
American Paper Institute, API
American Petroleum Institute, API
American Textbook Publishers Institute,
    ATPI
Arctic Institute of North America, AINA
Association de l'Institut National des
    Techniques de la Documentation
    (Association of the National Institute for
    Information Sciences), AINTD
Association des Bibliothécaires-
    Documentalistes de l'Institut
    d'Études Sociales de l'État (Association
    of Librarians and Documentalists
    of the State Institute of Social
    Studies), ABD
Bibliografiska Institutet (Bibliographical
    Institute), BI
Book Manufacturers Institute, BMI
Braille Institute of America, Inc, BIA
British Columbia Institute of Technology
    Information Resource Centre, BCIT
British Film Institute, BFI
British Institute of Management, BIM
British Institute of Recording Sounds, BIRS
Building Research Institute, BRI
California Institute of Technology, CIT
Canadian Acronautics and Space Institute,
    CASI
Canadian Institute for Scientific and
    Technical Information (Institut
    Canadien de l'Information Scientifique
    et Technique), CISTI/ICIST
Canadian National Institute for the Blind,
    CNIB
Center for African Studies and Institute for
    Social Research, CAS&ISR
Central Fuel Research Institute, CFRI
Centralny Instytut Informacji Naukowo
    Technicznej i Ekonomicznej (Central
    Institute for Scientific, Technical and
    Economic Information), CIINTE
Ceylon Institute of Scientific and Industrial
    Research, CISIR

Chemical Institute of Canada, CIC
Children's Psychiatric Research Institute,
    CPRI
Cocoa Research Institute, CRIG
Computer Language of Massachusetts
    Institute of Technology, COMIT
Data Analysis Massachusetts Institute of
    Technology, DAMIT
Deutsches Institut für Medizinische
    Dokumentation und Information
    (German Institute for Medical
    Documentation and Information),
    DIMDI
Dzialowy Ośrodek Zagadnién
    Informacyjnych Centralnego Instytutu
    Informacji Naukowo-Technicznej i
    Ekonomicznej (Branch Center on
    Information Problems at the Central
    Institute for Scientific, Technical and
    Economic Information), DOZI-CIINTE
Educational Institute of Scotland, EIS
Educational Media Institute Evaluation
    Project, EMIE
European Space Research Institute, ESRIN
Food Marketing Institute, FMI
An Foras Taluntais (Irish Agricultural
    Institute), AFT
Fuel Research Institute, FRI
Harvard Ukrainian Research Institute,
    HURI
Illinois Institute of Technology, IIT
Illinois Institute of Technology Research
    Institute, IITRI
Industrial Education Institute, IEI
Institut International de la Planification de
    l'Éducation/International Institute for
    Educational Planning, IIPE/IIEP
Institut International de la Soudure
    (International Institute of Welding), IIS
Institut Nacnoj Informacii i
    Fundamental'naja Biblioteka po
    Obscestvennym Naukam (Institute of
    Scientific Information and Main Library
    of the Social Sciences), INIBON
Institute Belge de Régulation et
    d'Automisme (Belgian Institute for
    Control and Automation), IBRA
Institute de Recherche d'Informatique et
    d'Automatique (French Research
    Institute of Information and Automatic
    Processing), IRIA
Institute de Recherche Industrielle, IRI
Institute du Transport Aerien, ITA
Institute for Advanced Technology, IAT
Institute for Behavioral Research, IBR
Institute for Computer Sciences and
    Technology, ICST
Institute for Computer-Assisted Information,
    ICAI
Institute for Graphic Communication, Inc,
    IGC

Institute (cont.)

Institute for Industrial Research and
    Standards, IIRS
Institute for Scientific Information, ISI
Institute for Scientific Information, SCITEL
Institute for the Advancement of Medical
    Communication, IAMC
Institute for the Comparative Study of
    History, Philosophy and the Sciences,
    Ltd, ICS
Institute for the Crippled and Disabled, ICD
Institute Française du Petrole, IFP
Institute National de la Recherche
    Agronomique, INRA
Institute Nazionale de l'Informazione
    (National Institute of Information), INI
Institute of Archival Science for Southeast
    Asia, IASSA
Institute of Continuing Library Education of
    British Columbia, ICLEBC
Institute of Data Processing, IDP
Institute of Electrical and Electronics
    Engineers, IEEE
Institute of Information Scientists, IIS
Institute of Internal Auditors, Inc, IIA
Institute of International Education, IIE
Institute of Journalists, IOJ
Institute of Library Research, ILR
Institute of Printing, Ltd, IOP
Institute of Professional Librarians of
    Ontario, IPLO
Institute of Public Administration, IPA
Institute of Radio Engineers, IRE
Institute of Reprographic Technology, IRT
Institute of Standards and Industrial
    Research of Iran, ISIRI
Institute of Technical Publicity and
    Publications, ITPP
Institute's Retrieval-of-Information Study,
    IRIS
Instituto Brasileiro de Bibliografia e
    Documentação (Brazilian Institute of
    Bibliography and Documentation),
    IBBD
Instituto Centro Americano de Investigacion
    y Technologia Industrial (Central
    American Institute of Research and
    Industrial Technology), ICAITI
Instituto de Documentación e Información
    Científica y Tecnica (Institute of
    Scientific and Technical Documentation
    and Information), IDICT
Instituto Interamericano de Ciencias
    Agrícolas de la OEA (Interamerican
    Institute of Agricultural Sciences of
    OAS/OEA), IICA
Institutul Central de Documentare Technica
    (Central Institute for Technical
    Documentation), IDT

International Institute for Conservation of
    Historic and Artistic Works, IIC
International Institute of Communications,
    IIC
International Institute of Films on Art, IIFA
International Institute of Refrigeration, IIR
International Press Institute, IPI
International Theatre Institute of the United
    States, ITI/US
Jewish Braille Institute of America, JBIA
Jugoslovenski Bibliografiski Institut
    (Yugoslav Bibliographic Institute), JBI
Lewis Audiovisual Research Institute and
    Teaching Archive, LARITA
Library Binding Institute, LBI
Magazine and Paperback Marketing
    Institute, MPMI
Massachusetts Institute of Technology, MIT
Medical Audio-Visual Institute, MAVI
National Institute for Educational Research
    (Kokuritsu Kyoiku Kenkyusho Fuzoku
    Kyoiku Toshokan), NIER
National Institute for Medical Research,
    NIMR
National Institute for Occupational Safety
    and Health, NIOSH
National Institute for Research in Nuclear
    Science, NIRNS
National Institute of Ceramic Engineers,
    NICE
National Institute of Education, NIE
National Institute of Mental Health, NIMH
National Institute of Neurological Diseases
    and Stroke, NINDS
National Institute of Packaging, Handling
    and Logistics Engineers, NIPHLE
National Institute of Social Sciences, NISS
Nederlands Instituut voor Audio Visuele
    Middlelen (Netherlands Institute for
    Audiovisual Media), NIAM
Nederlands Instituut voor Informatie,
    Documentatie en Registratuur
    (Netherlands Institute for Information,
    Documentation and Filing), NIDER
Norges Tekniske Høgskole (Library of the
    Norwegian Institute of Technology),
    NTH
Office Equipment Manufacturers Institute,
    OEMI
Office Furniture Manufacturers Institute,
    OFMI
Pakistan Standards Institute, PSI
Pulp and Paper Research Institute of
    Canada/Information Retrieval Services,
    PAPRICAN/IRS
Pulp, Paper and Paperboard Institute, PPPI
Rensselaer Polytechnic Institute, RPI
Research Institute for the Study of Man,
    RISM
Research Institute of America, Inc, RIA

Rijksbureau voor Kunsthistorische Documentatie (Netherlands Institute for Art History Documentation), RKD
Royal Institute of British Architects, RIBA
Royal Institute of Technology Library, IDC-KTHB
Scientists Institute for Public Information, SIPI
Singapore Institute of Standards and Industrial Research, SISIR
[Standards Institute], SI
Standards Institute of Israel, SII
Standards Institute of Malaysia, SIM
Stanford Research Institute, SRI
Státni Ústav pro Zdravotnickou Dokumentačm a Knihovnickou Sluzbu (State Institute for Medical Documentation and National Medical Library), SUZDKS
Stockholm International Peace Research Institute, SIPRI
Super Market Institute, SMI
Swedish Institute for Administrative Research, SIAR
Technical Institute Council, TIC
Toronto Institute of Medical Technology, TIMT
Union of Burma Applied Research Institute, UBARI
United Nations Institute for Training and Research, UNITAR
United States Historical Documents Institute, HDI
United States of America Standards Institute, USASI
Ústav Vědeckotechnických Informací (Institute of Scientific Technical Information), UVTI
Vsesojuznyi Institut Naučnotehničeskoi Informacii (All-Union Institute of Scientific and Technical Information, USSR), VINITI
Vyzkumny Ustav pro Matematickych Stroju (Research Institute for Mathematical Machines), VUMS
Wisconsin Indianhead Technical Institute, WITI

Institute Libraries
Association of Caribbean University and Research Institute Libraries, ACURIL

Institutes
Area Manpower Institutes for the Development of Staffs, AMIDS
Committee of National Institutes of Patent Agents, CNIPA
Libraries of the Institutes and Schools of Education, LISE
National Institutes of Health, NIH

Institution
British Standard Institution, BSI
Indian Standards Institution, ISI
Institution of Civil Engineers, ICE
Institution of Electrical and Electronics Technicians Engineers, Ltd, IEETE
Institution of Electrical Engineers, IEE
Institution of Electronic and Radio Engineers, IERE
Institution of Mining and Metallurgy, IMM
Smithsonian Institution, SI
Smithsonian Institution Traveling Exhibition Service, SITES
Women's Advisory Committee of the British Standards Institution, WAC

Institution Libraries
Association of Hospital and Institution Libraries, AHIL

Institutional
Committee on Institutional Cooperation, CIC
Remote Access Planning for Institutional Development, RAPID

Institutions
Asociación de Bibliotecarios de Instituciones de Enseñanza Superior y de Investigación (Association of Librarians of Institutions of Higher Education and Research), ABIESI
Association of Southeast Asian Institutions of Higher Learning, ASAIHL
International Federation of Library Associations and Institutions, IFLA
Massachusetts Conference of Chief Librarians in Public Higher Educational Institutions, MCCLPHEI

Instituto
Instituto de Investigaciones Bibliograficas, IIB
Instituto de Nutricion de Centro America y Panama, INCAP
Instituto Latinoamericano de Cinematographía Educativa, ILCE
Instituto Latinoamericano de la Communicación Educativa, ILCE
Instituto Méxicano de Información Avícola, IMIA
Instituto Nacional del Libro Español, INLE

Institutov i Laboratorij
Vsesojuznyj Gosudarstvennyj Institut po Proektirovaniju Naučno-Issledovatel'skich Institutov i Laboratorij Akademii nauk SSSR, GIPRONTII

Instituut
Nederlands Instituut voor Toegepast Huishoudkundig Onderzoek, NITHO

Instruction

ACM Special Interest Group on
  Computer-Assisted Instruction,
  ACM/SIGCAI
Beginners All-purpose Symbolic Instruction
  Code, BASIC
Center for Research in College Instruction of
  Science and Mathematics, CRICISAM
Computer-Aided Instruction, CAI
Computer-Assisted Instruction, CAI
Computer-Assisted Instruction, Inc, CAI
Computer-Assisted Instruction
  Management, CAIM
Computer-Assisted Instruction Regional
  Education Network, CAI
Computer-Augmented Instruction, CAI
Computer-Extended Instruction, CEI
Department of Audiovisual Instruction,
  DAVI
Instruction Address Register, IAR
Instruction Counter, IC
Master Instruction Tape, MIT
National Society for Performance and
  Instruction, NSPI
National Society for Programmed
  Instruction, NSPI
Programmed Instruction, PI

Instructions

Computer-Managed Instructions, CMI

Instructional

Abstracts of Instructional and Research
  Materials in Vocational and Technical
  Education, AIM/ARM
Abstracts of Instructional Materials in
  Vocational and Technical Education,
  AIM
Association for Development of
  Computer-based Instructional Systems,
  ADCIS
Association for Instructional Materials, AIM
Association for the Development of
  Instructional Systems, ADIS
Auto-Instructional Media for Library
  Orientation, AIMLO
Automated Instructional Materials Handling
  System of SDC (System Development
  Corporation), AIMS
City University Mutual Benefit Instructional
  Network, CUMBIN
Great Plains National Instructional
  Television Library, GPNITL
Health Instructional Resources Association,
  HIRA
Montana Instructional Media Association,
  MIMA
Social Sciences Instructional Programming
  Project, SSIPP
Wyoming Instructional Media Association,
  WIMA

Instructional Materials

National Instructional Materials Information
  System, NIMIS

Instructional Materials Center

New York State Special Education
  Instructional Materials Center, SEIMC

Instructions

Computer-Managed Instructions, CMI

Instructive

Operational Assistance and Instructive Data
  Equipment, OAIDE

Instrument

Instrument Society of America, ISA
Laboratory Instrument Computer, LINC
Logarithmic Computing Instrument, LOCI

Instrument Center

Lincoln Laboratory Instrument Center,
  LINC

Instrumentation

Automatic Digital On-line Instrumentation
  System, ADONIS
*Journal of the Association for the
  Advancement of Medical
  Instrumentation*, JAAMI
Language for Utility Checkout and
  Instrumentation Development, LUCID
Society of Photo-Optical Instrumentation
  Engineers, SPIE

Instruments

Advanced Scientific Instruments Symbolic
  Translator, ASIST

Instytut

Centralny Instytut Informasui Noukowo
  Techniceneu I Economicznej (Central
  Institute for Scientific, Technical and
  Economic Information), CLINTE

Integrated

Army Logistics Management Integrated Data
  System, ALMIDS
Battle Area Surveillance and Integrated
  Communications, BASIC
British Integrated Programme Suite, BIPS
Computation and Data Flow Integrated
  Subsystems, CADFISS
DLSC Integrated Data System, DIDS
Integrated Circuit, IC
Integrated Corporate Data Base, ICDB
Integrated Data Processing, IDP
Integrated Data Store, IDS
Integrated Design and Analysis System,
  IDEAS
Integrated Global Ocean Stations System,
  IGOSS

Integrated Information Processing System, INTIPS
Integrated Library System, ILS
Integrated Set of Information Systems, ISIS
Large-Scale Integrated Circuits, LSIC
Logically Integrated FORTRAN Translator, LIFT
MIDAC Automatic General Integrated Computation, MAGIC
Medium Scale Integrated Circuits, MSI
Project for Integrated Catalogue Automation, PICA

Integrated System
Northwestern On-Line Totally Integrated System, NOTIS

Integration
Modified Integration Digital Analog Simulator, MIDAS
SAGE Air Traffic Integration, SATIN

Integrator
Electronic Numerical Integrator and Calculator, ENIAC

Intégré
Système Intégré pour les Bibliothèques Universitaires de Lausanne, SIBIL

Intellectual Freedom
Committee for Artistic and Intellectual Freedom in Iran, CAIFI
Intellectual Freedom, IF
Intellectual Freedom Committee, IFC
Intellectual Freedom Round Table, IFRT
Office for Intellectual Freedom, OIF
Project Every Library Board Kit on Intellectual Freedom, PELB-IF

Intellectual Property
Bureaux Internationaux Réunis pour la Protection de la Propriété Intellectuelle (United International Bureaus for the Protection of Intellectual Property), BIRPI
World Intellectual Property Organization, WIPO

Intelligence
Aerospace Intelligence Data System, AIDS
Central Intelligence Agency, CIA
Direct Access Intelligence Systems, DAIS
Marine Air-Ground Intelligence System, MAGIS

Inter NASA
Inter NASA Data Exchange, INDEX

Interaction
ASIS Special Interest Group on User On-line Interaction, ASIS/SIG/UOI

General Operator Computer Interaction, GOCI

Interactive
Bibliographic Author or Subject Interactive Search, BA•SIS
Classroom Interactive Computer, CLASSIC
Copyright Office Publication and Interactive Cataloging System, COPICS
Interactive Computer Presentation Panel, ICPP
Interactive Query and Report Processor, IQRP
Programming Language for Interactive Teaching, PLANIT
Time-Shared Interactive Computer-Controlled Information Television, TICCIT

Interagency
Interagency Advanced Power Group, IAPG
Interagency Council on Library Tools for Nursing, ICLTN

Interamerican
Asociación de Egresados de la Escuela Interamericana de Bibliotecología (Association of Graduates of the Interamerican Library School), ASEIB
Asociación Interamericana de Bibliotecarios y Documentalistas Agrícolas (Inter-American Association of Agricultural Librarians and Documentalists), AIBDA
Centro Interamericano de Documentación e Información Agrícola (Interamerican Center for Agricultural Documentation and Information), CIDIA
Centro Interamericano de Documentación Económia y Social (Interamerican Center for Economic and Social Documentation), CIADES
Centro Interamericano de Libros Académicos (Inter-American Scholarly Book Center), CILA
Consejo Interamericano de Musica (Inter-American Music Council), CIDEM
Instituto Interamericano de Ciencias Agrícolas de la OEA (Interamerican Institute of Agricultural Sciences of OAS/OEA), IICA
Inter-American Bibliographical and Library Association, IABLA
Inter-American Defense College, IADC

Interamericana
Reunion Interamericana de Bibliotecarios y Documentalistas Agrícolas, RIBDA

Interamericano
Centro Interamericano de Documentación
  Económica y Social (Interamerican
  Center for Economic and Social
  Documentation), CLADES
Consejo Interamericano de Archiveros,
  CITA
Seminario Interamericano sobre la
  Integración de los Servicios de
  Información de Archivos, Bibliotecas y
  Centros de Documentation en America
  Central y el Caribe, SI/ABCD
Sistema Interamericano de Informacion para
  las Ciencias Agricolas, AGRINTER

Interceptor
Back-Up Interceptor Control, BUIC

Interchange
A Data Interchange System, ADIS
Extended Binary Coded Decimal
  Interchange Code, EBCDIC
Inter-change of Scientific and Technical
  Information in Machine Language,
  ISTIM
Sheffield Interchange Organization, SINTO

Intercollege
Film Library Intercollege Cooperative of
  Pennsylvania, FLIC

Intercomm
Intercomm User Group, IUG

Interconnected
Interconnected Business System, ICBS

Inter-Council
Inter-Council Coordination Committee
  UNESCO, ICCC

Inter-Departmental
Inter-Departmental Reference Service, IDRS

Interdisciplinaire
Centre pour la Recherche Interdisciplinaire
  sur le Développement, CRID

Interdisciplinary
Interdisciplinary Machine Processing for
  Research and Education in the Social
  Sciences, IMPRESS
Interdisciplinary Science Reviews, ISR

Interface
Computer Interface Unit, CIU
Engineering Departmental Interface Control
  Technique, EDICT

Interference
Radio Frequency Interference, RFI

Intergovernment
Advisory Commission on Intergovernment
  Relations, ACIR

Intergovernmental
Intergovernmental Bureau for
  Informatics/International Computation
  Center, IBI/ICC
Intergovernmental Commission on
  Oceanography, ICO
Intergovernmental Oceanographic
  Commission, IOC

Interinstitutional
New England Interinstitutional Research
  Council, NEIRC

Interlibrary
Central Ohio Interlibrary Network, COIN
Conference on Interlibrary Communications
  and Information Networks, CICIN
East Central Pennsylvania Council on
  Interlibrary Cooperation, EPIC
Hampshire Interlibrary Center, HILC
IULC Reference and Interlibrary Loan
  Service, IULC-RAILS
Interlibrary Delivery Service of
  Pennsylvania, IDS
Interlibrary Lending and Cooperative
  Reference Services, ILLACORS
Interlibrary Loan, ILL
Lowell Area Council on Interlibrary
  Networks, LACOIN
Manchester Interlibrary Cooperative, MILC
Minnesota Interlibrary Telecommunications
  Exchange, MINITEX
New York State Interlibrary Loan Network,
  NYSILL
Northern Inter-Library Cooperation
  Scheme, NICS
Office of Public Libraries and Interlibrary
  Cooperation, OPLIC
Oklahoma Teletype Interlibrary System,
  OTIS
South Central Minnesota Inter-Library
  Exchange, SMILE
Southern California Interlibrary Loan
  Network, SCILL
System for Interlibrary Communication,
  SILC
TWX Interlibrary Loan Network, TWXILL
Total Interlibrary Exchange, TIE
Wisconsin Interlibrary Loan Service, WILS

Interline
Fast Interline Nonactive Automatic Control,
  FINAC

Interloan
Cleveland Area Interloan Network, CAIN
Humberside Libraries Technical Interloan
  Scheme, HULTIS

Interministérielle
Centre National d'Étude des
  Télécommunications/Département

Documentation Interministérielle,
CNET/DI

Intermountain
Intermountain Union List of Serials, IMULS

Internacional
Federação Internacional de Associações de
Bibliotecários–Grupo Regional América
Latina, FIABGRAL
Organismo Internacional Regional de Sanid
Agroprecuaria, OIRSA

Internal
Internal Translator, IT

Internal Revenue
Internal Revenue Service, IRS

International
Agency for International Development, AID
Association for Childhood Education
International, ACEI
Association Internationale des Bibliothèques
Musicales/International Association of
Music Libraries/Internationale
Vereinigung der Musikbibliotheken,
AIBM/IAML/IVMB
Association Internationale des
Documentalistes et Techniciens de
l'Information (International Association
of Documentalists and Information
Officers), AID
Association Internationale d'Information
Scolaire Universitaire et Professionelle
(International Association for Education
and Vocational Information), AIISUP
Association Internationale du Film
d'Animation (International Animated
Film Association), ASIFA
Association Internationale pour le Calcul
Analogique (International Association
for Mathematics and Computer
Simulation), AICA
Association Internationale pour le
Développement de la Documentation,
des Bibliothèques et des Archives en
Afrique (International Association for
the Development of Documentation
Libraries and Archives in Africa),
AIDBA
Association of International Publishers
Representatives, AIPR
Bureau International de Documentation des
Chemins de Fer, BDC
Bureau International d'Information sur les
Télécommunications, BIIT
Bureaux Internationaux Réunis pour la
Protection de la Propriété Intellectuelle
(United International Bureaus for the
Protection of Intellectual Property),
BIRPI
Canadian International Paper Company, CIP

Centre de Documentation International des
Industries Utilisatrices de Produits
Agricoles, CDIUPA
Centre Technique Audiovisual International
(International Audiovisual Technical
Center), CTAVI
Comité Consultatif International des
Radiocommunications (International
Radio Consultative Committee), CCIR
Commission Mixte Internationale pour la
Protection des Lignes de
Télécommunications et des
Canolisations Souterraines (Joint
International Committee for the
Protection of Telecommunications Lines
and Underground Ducts), CMI
Committee for International Cooperation in
Information Retrieval among Examining
Patent Officers, CICIREPATO
Committee on International Relations, CIR
Committee on International Scientific and
Technical Information Programs,
CISTIP
Computer-Aided Manufacturing
International, CAM-I
Confédération Internationale des Cinémas
d'Art et d'Essai (International
Experimental and Art Film Theatres
Confederation), CICAE
Confédération Internationale des Industries
Techniques du Cinéma (International
Confederation of the Cinema Industry),
CIITC
Confédération Internationale des Sociétés
d'Auteurs et Compositeurs
(International Confederation of
Societies of Authors and Composers),
CISAC
Conseil International des
Archives/International Council on
Archives, CIA/ICA
Conseil International des Compositeurs, CIC
Conseil International pour les Films
d'Éducation (International Council for
Educational Films), CIFE
Consortium for International Development
Information Network, CIDNET
Consultative Committee on International
Telegraph and Telephone (Comité
Consultatif International Telegraphie et
Telephonie), CCITT
Council for International Exchange of
Scholars, CIES
Council for International Organizations on
Medical Sciences, CIOMS
Dissertation Abstracts International, DAI
East and Central Africa Regional Branch of
the International Council on Archives,
ECARBICA
Federación internacional de
Documentación/Comisión

International (cont.)

Latinoamericana (International Federation for Documentation/Latin American Commission), FID/CLA

Fédération des Associations Internationales Establiés in Belgique (Federation of International Associations Established in Belgium), FAIB

Fédération Internationale de Documentation (International Federation of Documentation), FID

Fédération Internationale de la Presse Cinématographique (International Federation of the Cinematographic Press), FIPRESCI

Fédération Internationale de la Presse Periodique (International Federation of the Periodical Press), FIPP

Fédération Internationale des Archives du Film (International Federation of Film Archives), FIAF

Fédération Internationale des Directeurs de Journaux Catholiques (International Federation of Directors of Catholic Publications), FIDJC

Fédération Internationale des Journalistes (International Federation of Journalists), FIJ

Fédération Internationale des Phonothèques (International Federation of Record Libraries), FIP

GODORT International Documents Task Force, GODORT/IDTF

Hawaii International Conference on System Sciences, HICSS

Institut International de la Planification de l'Éducation/International Institute for Educational Planning, IIPE/IIEP

Institut International de la Soudure (International Institute of Welding), IIS

Institut International du Froid, IIF

Institute of International Education, IIE

International Advisory Committee for Documentation and Terminology, IACDT

International Advisory Committee on Bibliography, IACB

International Advisory Committee on Bibliography, Documentation and Terminology, IACBDT

International Advisory Committee on Documentation and Terminology in Pure and Applied Science, AICDT

International Aerospace Abstracts, IAA

International Algebraic Language, IAL

International Allied Printing Trades Association, IAPTA

International Association for Mass Communication Research, IAMCR

International Association for Mathematics and Computer Simulation, IMACS

International Association for the Exchange of Students for Technical Experience, IAESTE

International Association of Agricultural Librarians and Documentalists, IAALD

International Association of Chiefs of Police, IACP

International Association of Information Film Distributors, INFORFILM

International Association of Law Libraries, IALL

International Association of Metropolitan City Libraries, INTAMEL

International Association of Music Librarians, Australia/New Zealand Branch, IAMLANZ

International Association of Orientalist Librarians, IAOL

International Association of Scholarly Publishers, IASP

International Association of School Librarianship, IASL

International Association of Sound Archives, IASA

International Association of Technological University Libraries, IATUL

International Association of Wholesale Newspaper, Periodical and Book Distributors, DISTRIPRESS

International Atomic Energy Agency, IAEA

International Bibliography, Information, Documentation, IBID

International Biodeterioration Bulletin, IBBRIS

International Board on Books for Young People, IBBY

International Book Year, IBY

International Broadcasters Society, IBS

Intergovernmental Bureau for Informatics/International Computation Center, IBI/ICC

International Business Forms Industries, IBFI

International Business Machines Corporation, IBM

International Cancer Research Data Bank Program, ICRDB

International Cartographic Association, ICA

International Catholic Press Union, ICPU

International Center for Theoretical Physics, ICTP

International Center of Films for Children, ICFC

International Center of Information on Antibiotics, ICIA

International Children's Emergency Fund, ICEF

International Civil Aviation Organization,
ICAO
International Commission for Agricultural
and Food Industries, ICAI
International Committee for Cooperation of
Journalists, ICCJ
International Committee for Social Sciences
Documentation, ICSSD
International Communication Agency, ICA
International Communication Association,
ICA
International Communications Association,
ICA
International Community of Booksellers
Association, ICBA
International Comparative Literature
Association, ICLA
International Comparative Political Parties
Project, ICPP
International Conference on Cataloging
Principles, ICCP
International Conference on Computer
Communication, ICCC
International Conference on Information
Processing, ICIP
International Cooperation Administration,
ICA
International Cooperation in Information
Retrieval among Examining Patent
Offices, ICIREPAT
International Copper Research Association,
INCRA
International Copyrights Information Center,
INCINC
International Council for Reprography, ICR
International Council for the Exploration of
the Sea, ICES
International Council of Scientific Unions,
ICSU
International Council on Books for Young
People, ICBY
International Data Corporation, IDC
International Data Library and Reference
Service, IDL&RS
International Decade of Ocean Exploration,
IDOE
International Demographic Data Center,
IDDC
International Development Center, IDC
*International Directory of Research and
Development Scientists*, IDR&DS
International Electrotechnical Commission,
IEC
International Federation for Information
Processing, IFIP
International Federation of Audit Bureaus of
Circulations, IFABC
International Federation of Automatic
Control, IFAC

International Federation of Catholic
Journalists, IFCJ
International Federation of Film Producers
Associations, IFFPA
International Federation of Film Societies,
IFFS
International Federation of Free Journalists
of Central and Eastern Europe and
Baltic and Balkan Countries, IFFJ
International Federation of Information
Processing Societies, IFIPS
International Federation of Journalists, IFJ
International Federation of Library
Associations and Institutions, IFLA
International Film and Television Council,
IFTC
International Food Information Service,
IFIS
International Fortean Organization, INFO
International Geophysical Year, IGY
International Graphic Arts Education
Association, IGAEA
International Indian Ocean Expedition, IIOE
International Industrial Television
Association, ITVA
International Information Retrieval Service,
IIRS
International Information System on
Research in Documentation, ISORID
International Institute for Conservation of
Historic and Artistic Works, IIC
International Institute of Communications,
IIC
International Institute of Films on Art, IIFA
International Institute of Refrigeration, IIR
International Inter-Church Film Center,
INTERFILM
International Labour Organisation, ILO
International League of Antiquarian
Booksellers, ILAB
International Library to Library Project,
ILLC
International Literary Market Place, ILMP
International Material Management Society,
IMMS
International Mathematical and Statistical
Library, IMSL
International Microfilm, IM
International Microform Distribution
Service, IMDS
International Monetary Fund, IMF
International Network of Emerging
Libraries, INEL
International Nuclear Information System,
INIS
International Organization for
Standardization, IOS
International Organization of Journalists,
IOJ

International (cont.)

International Patent Documentation Center, INPADOC

International Periodical Distributors Association, IPDA

International Pharmaceutical Abstracts, IPA

International Press Center, IPC

International Press Institute, IPI

International Press Telecommunications Committee, IPTC

International Publishers Advertising Representatives Association, IPARA

International Publishers Association, IPA

International Reading Association, IRA

International Reference Organization in Forensic Medicine and Sciences, INFORM

International Referral System for Sources of Environmental Information, IRS

International Rights Information Service, IRIS

International Road Federation, IRF

International Road Research Documentation, IRRD

International Scientific Film Association, ISFA

International Scientific Film Library, ISFL

International Serials Data System, ISDS

International Social Science Council, ISSC

International Society for Rehabilitation of the Disabled/Rehabilitation International, ISRD

International Society of Aviation Writers, ISAW

International Standard Bibliographic Description, ISBD

International Standard Book Number, ISBN

International Standard Industrial Classification, ISIC

International Standard Serial Number, ISSN

International Standards Organization, ISO

International Telecommunications Satellite Consortium, INTELSAT

International Telecommunications Union, ITU

International Telephone and Telegraph Corporation, ITT

International Theatre Institute of the United States, ITI/US

International Union of Pure and Applied Physics, IUPAP

International Union of the History and Philosophy of Science, IUHPS

International University of Radiophonics and Television, IUR

International Women's Writing Guild, IWWG

International Word Processing Association, IWPA

International Writers Guild, IWG

Internationale Arbeitsgemeinschaft der Archiv-, Bibliotheks- und Grafikrestauratoren (International Working Group of Restorers of Archives, Libraries and Graphic Reproductions), IADA

Japan Association for International Chemical Information, JAICI

Jerusalem International Book Fair, JIBF

Journal of International Research Communications, JIRC

London International Press, Ltd, LIP

Midwest Universities Consortium for International Activities, Inc, MUCIA

Naval Electronics Laboratory International Algebraic Compiler, NELIAC

Poets, Playwrights, Editors, Essayists and Novelists International English Centre, PEN

Postal, Telegraph and Telephone International, PTTI

Répertoire International de la Littérature de l'Art. (Journal), RILA

Répertoire International de Littérature Musicale, RILM

Sault Area International Library Association, SAILA

Société Internationale des Bibliothèques–Musées des Arts du Spectacle (International Society of Libraries and Museums of the Theatre Arts), SIBMAS

Société Internationale des Télécommunications Aeronautiques (International Society of Aeronautical Telecommunications), SITA

Southwest Asian Regional Branch of the International Council on Archives, SARBICA

Stockholm International Peace Research Institute, SIPRI

Union Radio-Scientifique Internationale (International Scientific Radio Union), URSI

United Press International, UPI

US National Committee for the International Federation for Documentation, USNCFID

Université Radiophonique et Télévisuelle Internationale (International Radio-Television University), URI

University Microfilms International, UMI

Volunteers for International Technical Assistance, Inc, VITA

International Book

Government Advisory Committee on International Book and Library Programs, GAC

International Council
Arab Regional Branch of the International
    Council on Archives, ARBICA

International Libraries
Association of International
    Libraries/Association des Bibliothèques
    Internationales, AIL/ABI

International Library
International Library Information Center,
    ILIC

International Relations
International Relations Committee, IRC
International Relations Office, IRO
International Relations Round Table, IRRT

International Studies
University Center for International Studies,
    UCIS

International Union
International Union of Pure and Applied
    Biophysics, IUPAB

Internationale
Association Internationale du Congres des
    Chemins de Fer, AICCF
Association Internationale pour le Calcul
    Analogique, ASICA
Association Litteraire et Artistique
    Internationale, ALAI
Commission Internationale des Industries
    Agricoles et Alimentaires, CIIA
Compagnie Internationale pour
    l'Informatique, CII
Fédération Internationale des Industries du
    Cinéma de Film Étroit, FIDIC
Fédération Internationale des Traducteurs,
    FIT
Internationale Dokumentationgesellschaft
    für Chemie, IDC
Système Internationale d'Unités, SI

Interpretative
Floating Interpretative Language, FLINT

Interpreter
Equitable Life Interpreter, ELI
Questionnaire Interpreter Program, QUIP

Interpretive
Analytic Geometry Interpretive Language,
    AGILE
Bell Laboratories Interpretive System, BLIS
Boeing Airplane Company Algebraic
    Interpretive Computing System,
    BACAIC
Double-precision Automatic Interpretive
    System 201, DAISY 201
Floating Point Interpretive Program, FLIP

Inter-Professional
Inter-Professional Ad Hoc Group for
    Environmental Information Sharing,
    IPAHGEIS

Interracial
Council on Interracial Books for Children,
    CIBC

Inter-Record
Inter-Record Gap, IRG

Interrelated
Interrelated Logic Accumulating Scanner,
    ILAS

Interrogation
Computer-Assisted Interrogation, CAINT
Dial Interrogation and Loading, DIAL
General Information File Interrogation, GIFI

Intersociety
Committee on Intersociety Cooperation, CIC
Committee on Inter-Society Cooperation,
    CISCO
Intersociety Committee on Pathology
    Information, ICPI

Interstate
Southwestern Library Interstate Cooperative
    Endeavor, SLICE
Western Interstate Commission for Higher
    Education, WICHE

Interstate Library
Western Interstate Library Coordinating
    Organization, WILCO

Interuniversity
Interuniversity Communications Council,
    EDUCOM
Inter-University Consortium for Political and
    Social Research, ICPSR
Interuniversity Council of the North Texas
    Area, IUC
Inter-University Library Council, IULC

Inventaire Permanent
Inventaire Permanent des Périodiques
    Étrangers en Cours, IPPEC

Invention
National Reference Library of Science and
    Invention, NRLSI

Inventions
Center for Inventions and Scientific
    Information, CISI

Inventory
American Production and Inventory Control
    Society, APICS
Automated Inventory Management, AIM
Book Inventory Building and Library
    Information Oriented System, BIBLIOS

Inventory (cont.)

Forecasting for Inventory Control System, FICS
National Marine Data Inventory, NAMDI
Test Rules for Inventory Management, TRIM

Investigaciones

Instituto de Investigaciones Bibliograficas, IIB

Investigation

Federal Bureau of Investigation, FBI

Investigations

Cooperative Investigations of the Caribbean and Adjacent Regions, CICAR

Investing

Investing, Licensing & Trading Conditions Abroad (Journal), IL&T

Invitation to Send

Invitation to Send, ITS

Invoicing

Direct Order Recording and Invoicing System, DORIS

Inyo

San Bernadino, Inyo, Riverside Counties United Library Services, SIRCULS

Iowa

Iowa Library Association, ILA
Iowa Library Information Teletype Exchange, I-LITE
Iowa–Missouri–Illinois Library Consortium, IMI
Northeast Iowa Academic Libraries Association, NEIAL

Iran

Committee for Artistic and Intellectual Freedom in Iran, CAIFI
Institute of Standards and Industrial Research of Iran, ISIRI

Iranian

Iranian Documentation Center, IRANDOC
Iranian Library Association, ILA

Iraqi

Iraqi Organization for Standards, IOS

Ireland

Booksellers Association of Great Britain and Ireland, BA
Cinematograph Exhibitors Association of Great Britain and Ireland, CEA
Library Association of Ireland, LAI
Royal College of Surgeons in Ireland, RCSI

Irish

British and Irish Association of Law Librarians, BIALL
Cumann Leabharlannaithe Scoile (Irish Association of School Librarians), CLS
An Foras Taluntais (Irish Agricultural Institute), AFT
Irish Association for Documentation and Information Services, IADIS
Irish Printing Federation, IPF

Irish Library

Irish Central Library for Students, ICL

Iron

American Iron and Steel Institute, AISI
Association of Iron and Steel Engineers, AISE
British Iron and Steel Industry Translation Service, BISITS
Iron and Steel Industry, ISI
Iron and Steel Industry Training Board, ISITB

Irregular

Irregular Serials and Annuals, ISA

Israel

Americans for a Music Library in Israel, AMLI
Current Research and Development in Israel, CRI
Information Processing Association of Israel, IPA
Israel Library Association, ILA
Israel Society for Special Libraries and Information Centers, ISLIC
Standards Institute of Israel, SII

Italian

Associazione Italiana Editori (Italian Publishers Association), AIE
Associazione Italiana per il Calco Automatico (Italian Association for Automatic Data Processing), AICA
Associazione Italiana per la Documentazione e l'Informazione (Italian Association for Documentation and Information), AIDI
Associazione Librai Italiani (Italian Booksellers Association), ALI
Associazione Nazionale Archivistica Italiana (National Association of Italian Archivists), ANAI
Federazione Italiana delle Biblioteche Popolari (Federation of Italian Public Libraries), FIBP

Italian Libraries

Associazione Italiana Biblioteche (Italian Libraries Association), AIB

Italiana
Associazione Nazionale Italiana per
l'Automazione, ANIPLA
Associazione Stampa Medica Italiana, ASMI
Associazione Tecnica Italiana per la
Cinematografia, ATIC
Federazione Italiana Editori Giornali, FIEG
Federazione Nazionale della Stampa
Italiana, FNSI
Società Italiana Autori Drammatici, SIAD
Unione della Stampa Periodica Italiana,
USPI

Italiano
Repertorio Bibliografico Italiano, REBIS

Ivory Coast
Association pour le Développement de la
Documentation, des Bibliothèques et
Archives de la Côte d'Ivoire
(Association for the Development of
Documentation, Libraries and Archives
of the Ivory Coast), ADBACI

Jamaica
Jamaica Library Association, JLA

Japan
Japan Association for International Chemical
Information, JAICI
Japan Information Center for Science and
Technology, JICST
Japan Library Association (Nippon
Toshokan Kyokai), JLA
Japan Pharmaceutical Information Center,
JAPIC
Japan Society of Library Science (Nippon
Toshokan Gakkai), JSLS
Nippon Documentesyon Kyokai (Japan
Documentation Society), NIPDOK
Nippon Yakugaku Toshokan Kyogikai
(Japan Pharmaceutical Library
Association), YAKUTOKYO
Senmon Toshokan Kyogikai (Special
Libraries Association of Japan),
SENTOKYO

Japanese
Japanese Association of Agricultural
Librarians and Documentalists, JAALD
Japanese Industrial Standards Committee,
JISC
Japanese Keyword Indexing Simulator,
JAKIS
Japanese Medical Abstract Scanning
System, JAMASS
Japanese Standards Association, JSA

Jerusalem
Jerusalem Conference on Information
Technology, JCIT
Jerusalem International Book Fair, JIBF

Jewish
Jewish Braille Institute of America, JBIA
Jewish National and University Library,
JNUL
Jewish Welfare Board, JWB

Jewish Libraries
Association of Jewish Libraries, AJL

Job
End of Job, EOJ

Job Entry
Remote Job Entry, RJE

Job-Control
Job-Control Language, JCL

Johnniac
Johnniac Open-Shop System, JOSS

Joint
Joint Publications Research Service, JPRS

Joint Committee
CNLIA Joint Committee on Cataloging and
Classification Codes, CNLIA/JCCC
CNLIA Joint Committee on Copyright
Practice and Implementation,
CNLIA/JCCPI
Joint Committee on Paleontologic
Information, JCPI
Joint Committee on Printing, JCP
Joint Standing Committee on Library
Cooperation and Bibliographic Services,
JSCLCBS
Joint Steering Committee for the Revision of
the Anglo-American Cataloging Rules,
JSCAACR

Joint Council
Joint Council on Educational Broadcasting,
JCEB
Joint Council on Educational
Telecommunications, JCET

Jordan
Jordan Library Association, JLA
Majlis al-Bahth al-'Ilmi (Jordan Research
Council), JRC

Journal
Basic Journal Abstracts, BJA
Journal Article Copy Service, JACS
Journal Citation Reports, JCR
Journal of Applied Bacteriology, JAB
Journal of Biological Chemistry, JBC
Journal of Chemical Documentation, JCD
Journal of Education for Librarianship, JEL
Journal of General Chemistry, JGC
Journal of Geophysical Research, JGR
*Journal of International Research
Communications*, JIRC
Journal of Library Automation, JOLA

Journal (cont.)

Journal of Library History, JLH
Journal of the American Chemical Society, JACS
Journal of the American Society for Information Science, JASIS
Journal of the Association for Computing Machinery, JACM
Journal of the Association for the Advancement of Medical Instrumentation, JAAMI
Library Journal, LJ
School Library Journal, SLJ
Slavic and East European Journal, SEEJ

Journalism

American Association of Schools and Departments of Journalism, AASDJ
American Council on Education for Journalism, ACEJ
Association for Education in Journalism, AEJ

Journalisten

Nederlandse Vereniging van Journalisten, NVJ
Verband der Journalisten der Deutsche Democratische Republik, VDJ

Journalisten-Union

Schweizerische Journalisten-Union/Union Suisse des Journalistes, SJU/USJ

Journalistes

Association Belge des Journalistes Professionnels de l'Aéronautique et de l'Astronautique, ABJPAA
Association des Journalistes de la Consommation, AJC
Association des Journalistes Économiques et Financiers, AJEF
Association Nationale des Journalistes d'Information Médicale, ANJIM
Association Suisse Romande des Journalistes de l'Aéronautique et de l'Astronautique, ARJA
Schweizerische Journalisten-Union/Union Suisse des Journalistes, SJU/USJ
Syndicate National des Journalistes, SNJ

Journalists

Association Française des Journalistes Agricoles (French Association of Agricultural Journalists), AFJA
Belgische Vereniging van Landbouwjournalistes/Association Belge des Journalistes Agricoles (Belgian Guild of Agricultural Journalists), BVLJ/ABJA
Fédération Internationale des Journalistes (International Federation of Journalists), FIJ
Guild of Agricultural Journalists, GAJ
Institute of Journalists, IOJ
International Committee for Cooperation of Journalists, ICCJ
International Federation of Catholic Journalists, IFCJ
International Federation of Free Journalists of Central and Eastern Europe and Baltic and Balkan Countries, IFFJ
International Federation of Journalists, IFJ
International Organization of Journalists, IOJ
National Council for the Training of Journalists, NCTJ
National Union of Journalists, NUJ
Norsk Journalistlag (Norwegian Union of Journalists), NJ
Schweizerische Vereinigung der Agrarjournalistes/Association Suisse des Journalistes Agricoles (Swiss Association of Agricultural Journalists), SVAJ/ASJA
Schweizerische Vereinigung Freier Berufsjournalisten/Association Suisse des Journalistes Libres Professionnels (Swiss Association of Independent Professional Journalists), SVFBJ/ASJLP
Society of Women Writers and Journalists, SWWJ
Suomen Sanomalehtimiesten Litto/Finlands Journalist Förbund (Union of Journalists in Finland), SSL/FJF
Svenska Journalistförbundet (Swedish Association of Journalists), SJF

Journals

Current Index to Journals in Education, CIJE
European Group of Woodworking Journals, EUROBOIS
Polymer Science and Technology for Journals, POST-J
Style Manual for Biological Journals, SMBJ

Journaux

Union Romande de Journaux, URJ

Juan de la Cierva Patronage

Centro de Información y Documentación del Patronato de Investigación Científica y Técnica Juan de la Cierva (Information and Documentation Center of the Juan de la Cierva Patronage), CID

Junior

Junior Engineering Technical Society, JETS

Junior College Libraries

ACRL Community and Junior College Libraries Section, ACRL/CJCLS

ACRL Junior College Libraries Section,
ACRL/JCLS
Junior College Libraries Section, JCLS

Junior Colleges
American Association of Community and
Junior Colleges, AACJC
American Association of Junior Colleges,
AAJC
ERIC Clearinghouse on Junior Colleges,
ERIC/JC

Junior Members
Junior Members Round Table, JMRT
MLA Junior Members Round Table,
MLA/JMRT

Juridique
Centre d'Informatique Juridique, CEDIJ

Justice
Criminal Justice Periodical Index. (Journal),
CJPI
Office of Criminal Justice Plans and
Analysis, OCJPA

Kalamazoo
Kalamazoo (Et Al) Library Consortium,
KETAL

Kansas
Associated Colleges of Central Kansas,
ACCK
Kansas Information Circuit, KIC
Kansas Library Association, KLA
Kansas–Nebraska Educational Consortium,
KANEDCO

Kansas City
Kansas City Regional Council for Higher
Education, KCRCHE

Keep It Simple Sir
Keep It Simple Sir, KISS

Kentucky
Kentucky Cooperative Library Information
Project, KENCLIP
Kentucky Library Association, KLA
Kentucky, Ohio, Michigan Regional Medical
Library, KOMRML
State Assisted Academic Library Council of
Kentucky, SAALCK

Kerr
Kerr Industrial Applications Center, KIAC

Keskusliitto
Kirjastonhoitajien
Keskusliitto-Bibliothekariers
Centralförbund (Central Federation of
Librarians), KKL

Key Letter
Key Letter in Context, KLIC

Key Phrase
Key Phrase in Context, KPIC

Key Punch
Key Punch, KP
Key Punch Operator, KPO

Key Word
Double Key Word in Context, KWIC,
Double
Key Word in Context, KWIC
Key Word in Title, KWIT
Key Word Out of Context, KWOC

Keyboard
Keyboard Button, KB
Keyboard Send/Receive, KSR

Keying
Frequency-Shift Keying, FSK

Keyterm
Textile Technology Data Base Keyterm
Index, TTD

Keyword
Author and Keyword in Context, AKWIC
Japanese Keyword Indexing Simulator,
JAKIS

Keywords
CTC's Information Retrieval from
Keywords, CIRK

Kilo
Kilo, K

Kinematografi
Vsesojuznyj Naučno-Issledovatel'skij
Kinofotoinstitut Gosudarstvennogo
Komiteta po Kinematografi pre Sovete
Ministrov SSSR, NIFKI

Kinematograph
British Kinematograph, Sound, and
Television Society, BKSTS
Kinematograph Manufacturers Association,
KMA

Kinimatographikon Epicheirision
Panellinios Organosis Kinimatographikon
Epicheirision, POKE

Kirjastonhoitajien
Kirjastonhoitajien
Keskusliitto-Bibliothekariers
Centralförbund (Central Federation of
Librarians), KKL

Kit
Project Every Library Board Kit on
Intellectual Freedom, PELB-IF

Knowledge
Aerospace Shared Knowledge, ASK
Basic Programming Knowledge Test, BPKT

Knowledge Availability
Knowledge Availability Systems Center,
    KASC

Knowledge Industry
Knowledge Industry Publications, Inc, KIP

Koninklijke
Koninklijke Nederlandse Uitgeversbond,
    KNUB

Kooperativen
Zentraler Datenpool der Kooperativen
    Agrardokumentation, DIFO

Korean
Korean Bureau of Standards, KBS
Korean Library Association (Hanguk
    Tosogwan Hyophoe), KLA
Korean Library Science Society, KLSS
Korean Scientific and Technological
    Information Center, KORSTIC

Kunststoff-Institut
Deutsches Kunststoff-Institut, DKI

Kupferstichhändler
Vereinigung der Buchantiquare und
    Kupferstichhändler in der
    Schweiz/Syndicat de la Libraire
    Ancienne et du Commerce de l'Estampe
    en Suisse, VEBUKU/SLACES

Lab
Time-Shared Reactive On-Line Lab,
    TROLL/I

Labor
American Federation of Labor and Congress
    of Industrial Organizations, AFL-CIO
Bureau of Labor Statistics, BLS
Center for Labor Education and Research,
    CLEAR

Laboratories
Bell Telephone Laboratories, BTL
Compiler Los Alamos Scientific
    Laboratories, COLASL
Electromagnetic Systems Laboratories, ESL
National Data Use and Access Laboratories,
    Inc, DUALabs
Smith, Kline & French Laboratories, SK&F

Laboratory
Advanced Automation Research
    Laboratory, AARL
Clearinghouse and Laboratory for Census
    Data, CLCD
Comparative Animal Research Laboratory,
    CARL
Comparative Systems Laboratory, CSL
Computer-based Laboratory for Automated
    School Systems, CLASS

Culham (Laboratory) Language for System
    Development, CLSD
European Space Research Laboratory,
    ESLAB
Film Laboratory Association, Ltd, FLA
Idaho National Engineering Laboratory,
    INEL
Information Systems Laboratory, ISL
Laboratory Animal Data Bank, LADB
Laboratory for Applications of Remote
    Sensing, LARS
Laboratory Instrument Computer, LINC
Lincoln Laboratory Instrument Center,
    LINC
Naval Electronics Laboratory International
    Algebraic Compiler, NELIAC
Oak Ridge National Laboratory, ORNL
Southwest Regional Laboratory for
    Educational Research and
    Development, SWRL
Upper Midwest Regional Educational
    Laboratory, UMREL

Labour
International Labour Organisation, ILO

Lancashire Libraries
North East Lancashire Libraries, NELL

Land Information
Resource and Land Information, RALI

Language
ASIS Special Interest Group on Automated
    Language Processing, ASIS/SIG/ALP
Action Data Automation Language, ADAL
Algorithmic Language (Algorithmic Oriented
    Language), ALGOL
Algorithmic Processor Description
    Language, APDL
The American Association of Language
    Specialists, TAALS
Analytic Geometry Interpretive Language,
    AGILE
Associative Processor Programming
    Language, APPLE
Asynchronous Circuit Design Language,
    ACDL
Audio-Visual Language Association, AVLA
Audit Command Language, ACL
Automatic Language Processing Advisory
    Committee, ALPAC
Barclays (Bank) Advanced Staff Information
    Language, BASIL
Basic Assembly Language, BAL
Basic Computer Programming Language,
    BCPL
A Better Language Experiment, ABLE
Burroughs Common Language, BCL
Center for Research on Language and
    Language Behavior, CRLLB

Language Analysis

Language Information

Languages

Languages (cont.)

Conference on Data System Languages,
CODASYL
ERIC Clearinghouse on Languages and
Linguistics, ERIC/FL
Problem-Oriented Languages, POL
*Selected Publications in European
Languages*, SPEL
Variably Initialized Translator for
Algorithmic Languages, VITAL

Langue
Bureau pour l'Enseignement de la Langue et
de la Civilisation Françaises à
l'Étranger, BELC

Langue Française
Association Canadienne d'Éducation de
Langue Française, ACELF

Lard
Lard Information Bureau, LIB

Large
Self-Organizing Large Information
Dissemination, SOLID

Large-Scale
Large-Scale Integrated Circuits, LSIC

Last
Last In First Out, LIFO
Last In Last Out, LILO

Lateral
Classified Entries in Lateral Transposition,
CELT

Latin America
Business Latin America. (Journal), BL
Centro Regional para el Fomento del Libro
en América Latina y el Caribe (Regional
Center for the Encouragement of the
Book in Latin America and the
Caribbean), CERLAL
European Committee for Cooperation with
Latin America, ECCLA
Unión de Universidades de América Latina
(Union of Universities of Latin
America), UDUAL

Latin American
Asociación Latinoamericana de Escuelas de
Bibliotecología y Ciencias de la
Información (Latin American Library
Schools Association), ALEBCI
Federación Internacional de
Documentación/Comisión
Latinoamericana (International

Federation for Documentation/Latin
American Commission), FID/CLA
*Latin American Executive Compensation
Survey*, LAECS
Latin American Library, LAL
Seminar on the Acquisition of Latin
American Library Materials, SALALM

Latinoamericano
Instituto Latinoamericano de
Cinematographía Educativa, ILCE
Instituto Latinoamericano de la
Communicación Educativa, ILCE

Lausanne
Système Intégré pour les Bibliothèques
Universitaires de Lausanne, SIBIL

Laval
Centre de Documentation de la Biblothèque
de l'Université Laval (Documentation
Center of the Library of l'Université
Laval), CEDOBUL

Law
ACRL Law and Political Science Section,
ACRL/LPSS
ASIS Special Interest Group on Law and
Information Technology,
ASIS/SIG/LAW
American Patent Law Association, APLA
Arbeitsgemeinschaft für Juristisches
Bibliotheks-und Dokumentationswesen
(Association of Libraries for Law and
Documentation), AJBD
Case Law Report Updating Service,
CLARUS
Citizens for Decency through Law, CDL
Computer Law Association, CLA
Dominion Law Reports, DLR
Public Law, PL

Law Enforcement
Automated Law Enforcement
Communication System, ALECS
Law Enforcement Assistance
Administration, LEAA
Law Enforcement Teletype System, LETS

Law Librarians
British and Irish Association of Law
Librarians, BIALL

Law Libraries
American Association of Law Libraries,
AALL
Canadian Association of Law
Libraries/Association Canadienne des
Bibliothèques de Droit, CALL/ACBD
International Association of Law Libraries,
IALL

State and Court Law Libraries of the United
States and Canada, SCLL
Western Association of Law Libraries,
WALL

Layout
Computer Layout Installation Planner, CLIP

Lead
Centro Méxicano de Información del Zinc y
del Plomo (Mexican Center of
Information for Zinc and Lead),
CMIZPAC
Lead Development Association, LDA

Leader
Control Leader, CL

Leadership
Leadership in Library Education, LLE

League
American Radio Relay League, ARRL
Esperanto League for North America, Inc,
ELNA
International League of Antiquarian
Booksellers, ILAB
National Book League, NBL

Learned Societies
American Council of Learned Societies,
ACLS

Learning
Alternatives for Learning through
Educational Research and Technology,
ALERT
Association for Programmed Learning, APL
Association of Southeast Asian Institutions
of Higher Learning, ASAIHL
Audiographic Learning Facility, ALF
Bureau of Libraries and Learning Resources,
BLLR
Center for Research on Learning and
Teaching, CRLT
Coalition in the Use of Learning Skills,
CULS
Combined and Integrated Resources for
Community Learning Experiment,
CIRCLE
Computer Learning Under Evaluation,
CLUE
Computer-Assisted Learning, CAL
Computer-Assisted Management of
Learning, CAMOL
Future Directions for a Learning Society,
FDLS
*Higher Education Learning Programmes
Information Service: A Catalogue of
Materials Available for Exchange*,
HELPIS

Learning Resources Association of
California Community Colleges,
LRACCC
National Association of Users of Computer
Applications to Learning, NAUCA
Office of Libraries and Learning Resources,
OLLR
Quebec Association for Children with
Learning Disabilities, QACLD
Simulator of Immediate Memory in Learning
Experiments, SIMILE
UICA Learning Resources Exchange
Program, UICA/LREP

Learning Center
Association of Library and Learning Center
Directors, ALLCeD

Learning Centers
Learning Resource Centers, LRC

Learning Unit
Self-Instructional Media-Assisted Learning
Unit, SIMALU

Lease
Psychological Abstracts Tape Edition Lease
or Licensing, PATELL

Least Significant
Least Significant Character, LSC
Least Significant Digit, LSD

Lebanese
Lebanese Library Association, LLA

Legal
Federação Brasileira de Associações de
Bibliotecários–Comissão Brasileira de
Documentação Jurídica (Brazilian
Federation of Librarian
Associations–Brazilian Committee of
Legal Documentation), FEBAB/CBDJ
Index to Legal Periodicals. (Journal), ILP

Legal Information
Legal Information Through Electronics,
LITE

Legislative
Legislative Reference Service, LRS

Legislazione
Legislazione dello Stato, TITLEX
Legislazione Regionale, LEXR

Lehigh
Lehigh Automatic Device for Efficient
Retrieval, LEADER

Lehigh Valley
Lehigh Valley Area Health Education Center
Library Consortium, LVAHEC

Lehigh Valley (cont.)

Lehigh Valley Association of Independent
Colleges, LVAIC

Leicestershire
Leicestershire Technical Information
Service, LETIS

Lending
British Library Lending Division, BLLD
Interlibrary Lending and Cooperative
Reference Services, ILLACORS

Lending Library
British Lending Library, BLL
National Lending Library for Science and
Technology, NLL

Lending Right
Public Lending Right, PLR

Lenin
Gosudarstvennaya ordena Lenina Biblioteka
SSSR Imeni V. I. Lenina (Lenin State
Library of the USSR), GBL

Letters
Selective Letters in Combination, SLIC

Letters Shift
Letters Shift, LTRS

Lewis
Lewis Audiovisual Research Institute and
Teaching Archive, LARITA

Lexicography
Society for the Study of Dictionaries and
Lexicography, SSDL

Liaison
Division Liaison Officer, DLO
Liaison of Provincial Associations
Committee, LOPAC

Liants Hydrauliques
Centre d'Études et de Recherches de
l'Industrie des Liants Hydrauliques,
CERILH

Libraire Ancienne
Vereinigung der Buchantiquare und
Kupferstichhändler in der
Schweiz/Syndicat de la Libraire
Ancienne et du Commerce de l'Estampe
en Suisse, VEBUKU/SLACES

Librarian Associations
Federação Brasileira de Associações de
Bibliotecários (Brazilian Federation of
Librarian Associations), FEBAB
Federação Brasileira de Associações de
Bibliotecários-Comissão Brasileira de
Documentação Jurídica (Brazilian
Federation of Librarian
Associations-Brazilian Committee of
Legal Documentation), FEBAB/CBDJ

Librarians
Asociación de Bibliotecarios de Instituciones
de Enseñanza Superior y de
Investigación (Association of Librarians
of Institutions of Higher Education and
Research), ABIESI
Asociación de Bibliotecarios y Archiveros de
Honduras (Association of Librarians
and Archivists of Honduras), ABAH
Asociación Nacional de Bibliotecarios,
Archiveros y Arqueólogos (National
Association of Librarians, Archivists
and Archeologists), ANABA
Associação Portuguesa de Bibliotecários,
Arquivistas e Documentalistes
(Portuguese Association of Librarians,
Archivists and Documentalists), BAD
Association des Archivistes et
Bibliothécaires de Belgique/Vereniging
van Archivarissen en Bibliothecarissen
van België (Belgian Association of
Archivists and Librarians),
AABB/VABB
Association des Bibliothécaires, Archivistes,
Documentalistes et Muséographes du
Cameroun (Association of Librarians,
Archivists, Documentalists and Museum
Curators of Cameroon), ABADCAM
Association des Bibliothécaires-
Documentalistes de l'Institut
d'Études Sociales de l'État
(Association of Librarians and
Documentalists of the State Institute of
Social Studies), ABD
Association Nationale des Bibliothécaires,
Archivistes et Documentalistes
Sénégalais (National Association of
Librarians, Archivists and
Documentalists of Senegal), ANBADS
Association Tunisienne des
Documentalistes, Bibliothécaires et
Archivistes (Tunisian Association of
Documentalists, Librarians and
Archivists), ATD
Association Zairoise des Archivistes,
Bibliothécaires et Documentalistes
(Zairian Association of Archivists,
Librarians and Documentalists),
AZABDO
Bibliotekarforeningen (Association of
Librarians), BF
Colegio Colombiano de Bibliotecarios
(Colombian Association of Librarians),
CCB
Council of Wisconsin Librarians, COWL

Društvo Bibliotekarjev Slovenije (Society of
Librarians in Slovenia), DBS
École de Bibliothécaires, Archivistes et
Documentalistes (School of Librarians,
Archivists and Documentalists), EBAD
Kirjastonhoitajien
Keskusliitto-Bibliothekariers
Centralförbund (Central Federation of
Librarians), KKL
Librarians in Education and Research in the
Northeast, LEARN
Librarians Serving San Antonio, LISSA
Librarians United to Fight Costly, Silly,
Unnecessary Serial Title Changes,
LUTFCSUSTC
National Registry for Librarians, NRL
Nederlandse Vereniging van
Bibliothecarissen (Netherlands
Association of Librarians), NVB
Perhimpunan Ahli Perpustakaan, Arsipdan
Dokumentasi Indonesia (Indonesian
Association of Librarians, Archives and
Documentation), PAPADI
Perkumpulan Ahli Perpustakaan Seluruh
Indonesia (Association of Librarians
throughout Indonesia), PAPSI
Verein der Bibliothekare an Öffentlichen
Büchereien (Association of Librarians in
Public Libraries), VBB
Vlaamse Vereniging van Bibliotheek-Archief
en Documentatie-Personeel, Vereniging
zonder Winstoogmerken (Flemish
Association of Librarians, Archivists
and Documentalists), VVBADP
Western New York Health Sciences
Librarians, WNYHSL

Librarians Association
British Columbia School Librarians
Association, BCSLA
Chinese Librarians Association, CLA
Federal Librarians Association, FLA
Librarians Association of the University of
California, LAUC
Middle East Librarians Association, MELA
National Librarians Association, NLA
Peel Secondary School Librarians
Association, PSSLA
Polish American Librarians Association,
PALA
Polish Canadian Librarians Association,
PCLA
State University of New York Librarians
Association, SUNYLA
Türk Kütüphaneciler Dernegi (Turkish
Librarians Association), TKD

Librarians Caucus
Asian American Librarians Caucus, AALC

Librarians Council
Association of Atlantic Universities
Librarians Council, AAULC

Librarians Organization
Southern Wisconsin Academic Librarians
Organization, SWALO

Librarianship
Association de l'École Nationale Supérieure
de Bibliothécaires (Association of the
National School of Librarianship),
AENSB
Conselho Federal de Biblioteconomia
(National Council of Librarianship),
CFB
Gesellschaft für Bibliothekswesen und
Dokumentation des Landbaues
(Association for Librarianship and
Documentation in Agriculture), GBDL
International Association of School
Librarianship, IASL
Journal of Education for Librarianship, JEL
Librarianship and Archives Old Students
Association, LAOSA
Society for the Promotion of the Interests of
Librarianship Students, SPILS

Libraries
Arbeitsgemeinschaft für das Archiv und
Bibliothekswesen in der Evangelischen
Kirche, Sektion Bibliothekswesen
(Working Group for Archives and
Libraries in the Lutheran Church,
Library Section), AABevK
Arbeitsgemeinschaft für Juristisches
Bibliotheks-und Dokumentationswesen
(Association of Libraries for Law and
Documentation), AJBD
Asociation di Biblioteka i Archivo di Korsow
(Association of Libraries and Archives),
ABAK
Association pour le Développement de la
Documentation, des Bibliothèques et
Archives de la Côte d'Ivoire
(Association for the Development of
Documentation, Libraries and Archives
of the Ivory Coast), ADBACI
Association Sénégalaise pour le
Développement de la Documentation,
des Bibliothèques, des Archives et des
Musées (Senegal Association for the
Development of Documentation,
Libraries, Archives and Museums),
ASDBAM
Association Voltaique pour le
Développement des Bibliothèques, des
Archives et de la Documentation
(Voltan Association for the
Development of Libraries, Archives and
Documentation), AVDBAD

Libraries (cont.)

Bureau of Libraries and Educational
Technology, BLET
Bureau of Libraries and Learning Resources,
BLLR
Central Association of Libraries, CAL
Children's Books for Schools and Libraries,
CBSL
Connecticut Women in Libraries, CWILS
European Conference on the Application of
Research in Information Services and
Libraries, EURIM 3
Libraries for Nursing Consortium, LINC
Libraries of North Staffordshire in
Cooperation, LINOSCO
Libraries of Orange County Network,
LOCNET
Libraries of the Institutes and Schools of
Education, LISE
National Commission on Libraries and
Information Science, NCLIS
Office of Libraries and Learning Resources,
OLLR
Société Internationale des
Bibliothèques–Musées des Arts du
Spectacle (International Society of
Libraries and Museums of the Theatre
Arts), SIBMAS
Society for the Promotion and Improvement
of Libraries, SPIL
Swindon Area Association of Libraries for
Industry and Commerce, SAALIC
Tasmanian Advisory Committee on
Libraries, TACOL
Tri-University Libraries of British Columbia,
TRIUL
Tyneside Association of Libraries for
Industry and Commerce, TALIC

Libraries Association

East Central State School Libraries
Association (Nigeria), ECSLA
Northeast Iowa Academic Libraries
Association, NEIAL
Private Libraries Association, PLA
Saskatchewan Government Libraries
Association, SGLA
Special Libraries Association, SLA
(Virginia Chapter of the Special Libraries
Association), VASLA

Libraries Council

Alberta Government Libraries Council,
AGLC

Library

Associated Library and Educational
Research Team for Survival, ALERTS

Association of Library and Learning Center
Directors, ALLCeD
Bell Laboratories Library Real-Time Loan
System, BELLREL
[Biblíoteka] Szkoly Glównej Planowania i
Statystykí (Library of the Central
School of Planning and Statistics),
SGPIS
Centre de Documentation de la Biblothèque
de l'Université Laval (Documentation
Center of the Library of l'Université
Laval), CEDOBUL
Committee on American Library Resources
on South Asia, CALROSA
Computer-Assisted Library Mechanization,
CALM
Coordinating Council of Library
Organizations, CCLO
Engineering Societies Library, ESL
Environmental Conservation Library, ECOL
Great Plains National Instructional
Television Library, GPNITL
Institut Nacnoj Informacii i
Fundamental'naja Biblioteka po
Obscestvennym Naukam (Institute of
Scientific Information and Main Library
of the Social Sciences), INIBON
International Scientific Film Library, ISFL
Library and Information Technology
Association, LITA
Library Automated Systems Information
Exchange, LASIE
Library Bureau, LB
Library Computer Equipment Review.
(Journal), LCER
Library Experimental Automated
Demonstration System, LEADS
Library Information Service, LIBRIS
Library Information Service for Teeside,
LIST
Library Information System, LIBRIS
Library Information System Time Sharing,
LISTS
Library Information Systems Analysis,
LISA
Library Literature. (Index), LL
Library Micrographic Services, Inc, LMS
Library Network Analysis Theory, LIBNAT
Library On-Line Acquisitions, LOLA
Library On-Line Information and Text
Access, LOLITA
Library Public Relations Council, LPRC
Library Technical Assistant, LTA
National Diet Library, NDL
Not in Library, NIL
Periodical Holdings in the Library of the
School of Medicine, PHILSOM
Pierpont Morgan Library, PML
Public Library, PL
Science Reference Library, SRL

Virginia National Library
Week–Southeastern Library
Association, VNLW-SELA

Library Action
Northwestern Ontario Library Action
Group, NOLAG

Library Additions
Library Additions and Maintenance
Program, LAMP

Library Administration
Central Massachusetts Library
Administration Project, CLASP
Library Administration and Management
Association, LAMA
Library Administration Division, LAD

Library Advisory Council
Library Advisory Council for England, LAC
Library Advisory Council for Wales and
Monmouthshire, LAC

Library Agencies
Association of Specialized and Cooperative
Library Agencies, ASCLA
Association of State Library Agencies,
ASLA

Library Agency
ASCLA State Library Agency Section,
ASCLA/SLAS

Library Alliance
North Alabama Library Alliance, NALA

Library Analytical System
Bibliothekarisch-Analytisches System zur
Informations-Speicherung-Erschliessung
(Library Analytical System for
Information Storage/Retrieval-
Economics), BASIS-E
Bibliothekarisch-Analytisches System zur
Informations-Speicherung-Leihverkehr
(Library Analytical System for
Information Storage/Retrieval-Loan),
BASIS-L

Library and Information Science
Australian Centre for Research in Library
and Information Science, ACRiLIS
Graduate School of Library and Information
Science, GSLIS
Library and Information Science, LIS
Library and Information Science Abstracts,
LISA
Library and Information Science Meetings
Exchange, Massachusetts Bureau of
Library Extension, LIS/MEX
Library and Information Science Today,
LIST

School of Library and Information Science,
SLIS

Library and Information Service
Aberdeen and North of Scotland Library and
Information Cooperative Service,
ANSLICS

Library and Information Services
White House Conference on Library and
Information Services, WHCOLIS

Library Assistance
Medical Library Assistance Act of 1965,
MLAA

Library Association
Afghan Library Association, ALA
Alabama Library Association, ALA
Alaska Library Association, ALA
American Library Association, ALA
Arab University Library Association, AULA
Arizona Library Association, ALA
Arkansas Library Association, ALA
Asociación Colombiana de Bibliotecarios
(Colombian Library Association),
ASCOLBI
Asociación Ecuatoriana de Bibliotecarios
(Ecuadorian Library Association), AEB
Asociación Nicaragüense de Bibliotecarios
(Nicaraguan Library Association),
ASNIBI
Associação Paulista de Bibliotecários (São
Paulo Library Association), APB
Atlantic Provinces Library Association,
APLA
Australian School Library Association,
ASLA
Bangladesh Granthagar Samity (Library
Association of Bangladesh), BGS
Bantu Library Association of South Africa,
BLASA
British Columbia Library Association,
BCLA
*Bulletin of the Library Association of
Trinidad and Tobago*, BLATT
Bulletin of the Medical Library Association,
BMLA
Canadian Library Association, CLA
Canadian School Library Association, CSLA
Catholic Library Association, CLA
Ceylon Library Association, CyLA
Chama Cha Ukutubi, Tanzania (Tanzania
Library Association), CUTA
Chicago Area Theological Library
Association, CATLA
Church and Synagogue Library Association,
CSLA
Colorado Library Association, CLA
Commonwealth Library Association,
COMLA

Library Association (cont.)

Connecticut Library Association, CLA
Connecticut School Library Association,
    CSLA
Danmarks Biblioteksforening (Danish
    Library Association), DB
Delaware Library Association, DLA
Deutscher Bibliotheksverband (German
    Library Association), DBV
District of Columbia Library Association,
    DCLA
Društvo Bibliotekara Bosne i Hercegovine
    (Library Association of Bosnia and
    Herzegovina), DB Bih
East African Library Association, EALA
Edmonton Library Association, ELA
Educational Film Library Association,
    EFLA
Egyptian School Library Association, ESLA
Enosis Ellenon Bibliothekarion (Greek
    Library Association), EEB
Ethiopian Library Association, ELA
Fiji Library Association, FLA
Florida Library Association, FLA
Foothills Library Association, FLA
Georgia Library Association, GLA
Greek Library Association, GLA
Guam Library Association, GLA
Guyana Library Association, GLA
Halifax Library Association, HLA
Hawaii Library Association, HLA
Hrvatsko Bibliotekarsko Društvo (Croatian
    Library Association), HBD
Idaho Library Association, ILA
Ikatan Pustakawan Indonesia (Indonesian
    Library Association), IPI
Illinois Library Association, ILA
India Library Association, ILA
Indiana Library Association, ILA
Inter-American Bibliographical and Library
    Association, IABLA
Iowa Library Association, ILA
Iranian Library Association, ILA
Israel Library Association, ILA
Jamaica Library Association, JLA
Japan Library Association (Nippon
    Toshokan Kyokai), JLA
Jordan Library Association, JLA
Kansas Library Association, KLA
Kentucky Library Association, KLA
Korean Library Association (Hanguk
    Tosogwan Hyophoe), KLA
Lebanese Library Association, LLA
The Library Association, LA
Library Association of Alberta, LAA
Library Association of Australia, LAA
Library Association of Barbados, LAB
Library Association of Ireland, LAI
Library Association of Ottawa/Association
    des Bibliothèques d'Ottawa, LAO/ABO

Library Association of Singapore, LAS
Library Association of the City University of
    New York, LACUNY
Library Association of Trinidad and Tobago,
    LATT
Louisiana Library Association, LLA
Lutheran Church Library Association,
    LCLA
Maine Library Association, MLA
Malta Library Association, MLA
Manitoba Library Association, MLA
Maryland Library Association, MLA
Massachusetts Library Association, MLA
Medical Library Association, MLA
Michigan Library Association, MLA
Minnesota Library Association, MLA
Mississippi Library Association, MLA
Missouri Library Association, MLA
Montana Library Association, MLA
Mountain Plains Library Association, MPLA
Music Library Association, MLA
Nebraska Library Association, NLA
Nevada Library Association, NLA
New England Library Association, NELA
New England School Library Association,
    NESLA
New Hampshire Library Association,
    NHLA
New Jersey Library Association, NJLA
New Mexico Library Association, NMLA
New York Library Association, NYLA
New Zealand Library Association, NZLA
Newfoundland Library Association, NLA
Nigerian Library Association, NLA
Nippon Yakugaku Toshokan Kyogikai
    (Japan Pharmaceutical Library
    Association), YAKUTOKYO
Norsk Bibliotekforening (Norwegian Library
    Association), NBF
North Carolina Library Association, NCLA
North Dakota Library Association, NDLA
Northeastern Ohio Library Association,
    NOLA
Nova Scotia Library Association, NSLA
Nova Scotia School Library Association,
    NSSLA
Ohio Library Association, OLA
Oklahoma Library Association, OLA
Ontario Library Association, OLA
Ontario Public Library Association, OPLA
Ontario School Library Association, OSLA
Oregon Library Association, OLA
Pacific Northwest Library Association,
    PNLA
Pakistan Library Association, PLA
Pennsylvania Library Association, PLA
Persatuan Perpustakaan Malaysia (Library
    Association of Malaysia), PPM
Philippine Library Association, PLA
Prince Edward Island School Library
    Association, PEISLA

Public Library Association, PLA
Quebec Library Association/Association des
  Bibliothécaires de Québec, QLA/ABQ
Rhode Island Library Association, RILA
Rhodesia Library Association, RLA
Saskatchewan Library Association, SLA
Sault Area International Library
  Association, SAILA
School Library Association, SLA
School Library Association of Papua, New
  Guinea, SLAPNG
Scottish Library Association, SLA
Sierra Leone Library Association, SLLA
Sociedad de Bibliotecarios de Puerto Rico
  (Puerto Rico Library Association),
  SBPR
South African Indian Library Association,
  SAILA
South Carolina Library Association, SCLA
Southeastern Library Association, SELA
Southeastern Library Association, SLA
Southwestern Library Association, SLA
Sri Lanka Library Association, SLLA
Stowarzyszenie Bibliotekarzy Polskich
  (Polish Library Association), SBP
Suffolk County Library Association, SCLA
Suid-Afrikaanse Biblioteekvereniging/South
  African Library Association,
  SABV/SALA
Sveriges Allmänna Biblioteksförening
  (Swedish Library Association), SAB
Tennessee Library Association, TLA
Texas Library Association, TLA
Thai Library Association, TLA
Theater Library Association, TLA
Uganda Library Association, ULA
Uganda School Library Association, USLA
Ukrainian Library Association of America,
  ULAA
Utah Library Association, ULA
Vermont Library Association, VLA
Virginia Library Association, VLA
Virginia National Library
  Week–Southeastern Library
  Association, VNLW-SELA
Washington Library Association, WLA
Washington Non-Professional Library
  Association, WNPLA
Welsh Library Association, WLA
West African Library Association, WALA
West Newfoundland Library Association,
  WNLA
West Virginia Library Association, WVLA
Wisconsin Library Association, WLA
Wyoming Library Association, WLA
Zambia Library Association, ZLA

Library Associations
Asian Federation of Library Associations,
  AFLA

Council of Library Associations Executives,
  CLAE
Council of National Library and Information
  Associations, CNLIA
Council of National Library Associations,
  CNLA
Federation of Indian Library Associations,
  FILA
International Federation of Library
  Associations and Institutions, IFLA
National Council of Indian Library
  Associations, NACILA

Library Authority
California Library Authority for Systems and
  Services, CLASS

Library Automation
ASIS Special Interest Group on Library
  Automation and Networks,
  ASIS/SIG/LAN
Consortium for Library Automation in
  Mississippi, CLAM
Cooperation in Library Automation, COLA
Journal of Library Automation, JOLA
Library Automation Research and
  Consulting, LARC
Technical Standards for Library
  Automation, TESLA
University of Toronto Library Automation
  System, UTLAS
*A Very Informal Newsletter on Library
  Automation*, VINE

Library Binding
Library Binding Institute, LBI

Library Board
New England Library Board, NELB
Project Every Library Board Kit on
  Intellectual Freedom, PELB-IF

Library Bulletin
Wilson Library Bulletin, WLB

Library Bureau
Northern Regional Library Bureau, NRLB
Regional Library Bureau, RLB

Library Center
Medical Library Center, MLC
Medical Library Center of New York,
  MLCNY
Ohio College Library Center, Inc, OCLC
Pittsburgh Regional Library Center, PRLC

Library Club
Library Club of America, LCA

Library Commission
West Virginia Library Commission,
  WVLAC

Library Consortium
Greater Cincinnati Library Consortium, GCLC
Iowa–Missouri–Illinois Library Consortium, IMI
Kalamazoo (Et Al) Library Consortium, KETAL
Lehigh Valley Area Health Education Center Library Consortium, LVAHEC
Michigan Library Consortium, MLC
Sangamon Valley Academic Library Consortium, SVAL
Seattle Area Hospital Library Consortium, SAHLC

Library Cooperation
ASCLA Multitype Library Cooperation Section, ASCLA/MLCS
Committee on Library Cooperation, CLIC
Joint Standing Committee on Library Cooperation and Bibliographic Services, JSCLCBS

Library Cooperative
Ontario Universities Library Cooperative System, OULCS

Library Council
Columbus Area Library and Information Council of Ohio, CALICO
Illinois Regional Library Council, IRLC
Inter-University Library Council, IULC
Library Council of Greater Cleveland, LCGC
Library Council of Metropolitan Milwaukee, LCOMM
Madison Area Library Council, MALC
New Hampshire Library Council, NHLC
Ontario Provincial Library Council, OPLC
Rochester Regional Research Library Council, RRRLC
South Central Research Library Council, SCRLC
State Assisted Academic Library Council of Kentucky, SAALCK
Tri-County Library Council, TLC
Utah College Library Council, UCLC

Library Demonstration
Library Exemplary Elementary Demonstration of Springfield, LEEDS

Library Development
Division of Library Development, DLD
Office of Library Development Program, OLDP
Western Ohio Regional Library Development System, WORLDS

Library Education
CLA Library Education Section, CLA/LES
Continuing Library Education Network, CLEN

Continuing Library Education Network and Exchange, CLENE
Continuing Library Education Planning and Coordination Project, COLEPAC
Leadership in Library Education, LLE
Library Education and Personnel Utilization, LEPU
Library Education Division, LED
Standing Committee on Library Education, SCOLE

Library Employees
Classified Library Employees of Washington State, CLEWS

Library Employment
Library Employment and Development for Staff, LEADS

Library Exchange
Library Exchange Aids Patrons Project, LEAP

Library Exhibitors
Canadian Library Exhibitors Association, CLEA

Library Extension
Library and Information Science Meetings Exchange, Massachusetts Bureau of Library Extension, LIS/MEX

Library History
American Library History Round Table, ALHRT
Journal of Library History, JLH

Library Information
Book Inventory Building and Library Information Oriented System, BIBLIOS
Library General Information Survey, LIBGIS
Machine-Readable Library Information, MERLIN
Telecommunications Library Information Network, TALINET

Library/Information Service
Mutual of New York Library/Information Service, MONY

Library Instruction
Library Instruction Round Table, LIRT
New York Library Instruction Clearinghouse, NYLIC

Library Journal
Australian Library Journal, ALJ
Canadian Library Journal, CLJ
Library Journal, LJ
School Library Journal, SLJ

Library Learning Center
Library Learning Resource Center, LLRC

Library Literature
Current Awareness—Library Literature,
CALL

Library Management
Exploratory Library Management Systems,
ELMS

Library Materials
RTSD Preservation of Library Materials
Section, RTSD/PLMS
RTSD Reproduction of Library Materials
Section, RTSD/RLMS
Seminar on the Acquisition of Latin
American Library Materials, SALALM
Standing Conference on Library Materials on
Africa, SCOLMA
Subject Analysis and Organization of Library
Materials Committee, SAOLM

Library Media
Library Media Technical Assistant, LMTA
Ohio Educational Library Media
Association, OELMA

Library Network
Area Wide Library Network, AWLNET
California Library Automation Network,
CLAN
California Library Network, CALINET
Florida Library Information Network, FLIN
Midwest Region Library Network,
MIDLNET
NASA Library Network, NALNET
New England Library Information Network,
NELINET
Pennsylvania Area Library Network,
PALINET
Satellite Library Information Network,
SALINET
Southeast Louisiana Library Network
Cooperative, SEALLINC
Southeastern Library Network, SOLINET
Tampa Bay Medical Library Network,
TABAMLN
Veterans Administration Library Network,
VALNET
Washington Library Network, WLN

Library Networks
Council for Computerized Library
Networks, CCLN

Library News
Mississippi Library News. (Newsletter),
MLN

Library of Congress
Black Employees of the Library of Congress,
BELC
Library of Congress, LC
Library of Congress Card Number, LCCN
Library of Congress Classification, LCC

Library of Congress Subject Headings,
LCSH

Library Operations
Bibliographic Automation of Large Library
Operations Using a Time-Sharing
System, BALLOTS

Library Organization
LAMA Library Organization and
Management Section, LAMA/LOMS
Miami Valley Library Organization, MILO
Mideastern Ohio Library Organization,
MOLO
Southeastern Ohio Library Organization,
SOLO

Library Organizations
Association of Cooperative Library
Organizations, ACLO

Library Orientation
Auto-Instructional Media for Library
Orientation, AIMLO
Library Orientation Exchange, LOEX

Library Periodicals
Library Periodicals Round Table, LPRT

Library Personnel
Office of Library Personnel Resources,
OLPR

Library Program
Community Media Library Program,
COMLIP
Heckman's Electronic Library Program,
HELP

Library Programs
Division of Library Programs, DLP
General Utility Library Programs, GULP
Government Advisory Committee on
International Book and Library
Programs, GAC

Library Project
South Western Educational Library Project,
SWELP

Library Promotion
Australian Library Promotion Council,
ALPC

Library Region
London and South Eastern Library Region,
LASER

Library Reports
Library Reports and Research Service, Inc,
LRRS

Library Research
Advisory Committee on Library Research
and Training Projects, ACLRTP

Library Research (cont.)

Institute of Library Research, ILR
Library Research Round Table, LRRT

Library Resources
Central New York Library Resources
  Council, CENTRO
Committee on American Library Resources
  on Southeast Asia, CALROSEA
Council on Library Resources, Inc, CLR
Library Resources and Technical Services.
  (Journal), LRTS
Library Resources, Inc, LRI
Long Island Library Resources Council,
  LILRC
Reference and Research Library Resources,
  3 Rs
Southeastern New York Library Resources
  Council, SENYLRC
Western New York Library Resources
  Council, WNYLRC

Library School
Asociación de Egresados de la Escuela
  Interamericana de Bibliotecología
  (Association of Graduates of the
  Interamerican Library School), ASEIB
Graduate Library School, GLS

Library Schools
Asociación Latinoamericana de Escuelas de
  Bibliotecología y Ciencias de la
  Información (Latin American Library
  Schools Association), ALEBCI
Associação Brasileira de Escolas de
  Biblioteconomia e Documentação
  (Brazilian Association of Library
  Science and Documentation Schools),
  ABEBD
Association of American Library Schools,
  AALS
Association of British Library Schools,
  ABLS
Canadian Association of Library
  Schools/Association Canadienne des
  Écoles de Bibliothécaires, CALS/ACEB
Canadian Council of Library Schools/Conseil
  Canadien des Écoles de Bibliothécaires,
  CCLS/CCEB
Ontario Committee of Deans and Directors
  of Library Schools, OCDDLS
Standing Conference of African Library
  Schools, SCALS

Library Science
Agrupación Bibliotecologica del Uruguay
  (Library Science Association of
  Uruguay), ABU
Faculty of Library Science Alumni
  Association, FLSAA

Federatie van Organisaties op het Gebied
  van Bibliotheek, Informatie en
  Dokumentatiewezen (Federation of
  Organizations in Library, Information
  and Documentation Science), FOBID
Indian Association of Teachers of Library
  Science, IATLIS
Japan Society of Library Science (Nippon
  Toshokan Gakkai), JSLS
Korean Library Science Society, KLSS
Library Science, LS
Library Science Abstracts, LSA

Library Service
ASCLA Library Service to the Blind and
  Physically Handicapped Section,
  ASCLA/LSBPHS
ASCLA Library Service to the Deaf Section,
  ASCLA/LSDS
Area Library Service Authorities, ALSAs
Area Library Service Organizations of Ohio,
  ALSO
Association for Library Service to Children,
  ALSC
Computer Library Service, Inc, CLIS
Library Service Enhancement Program,
  LSEP
Library Service to the Disadvantaged, LSD
Mid-Eastern Regional Medical Library
  Service, MERMLS
New England Regional Medical Library
  Service, NERMLS
Office for Library Service to the
  Disadvantaged, OLSD
Voluntary Overseas Library Service, VOLS

Library Services
ASCLA Library Services to Prisoners
  Section, ASCLA/LSPS
ASCLA Library Services to the Impaired
  Elderly Section, ASCLA/LSIES
Coordinating Committee for Slavic–East
  European Library Services,
  COCOSEER
Division for Library Services, DLS
Health and Rehabilitative Library Services
  Division, HRLSD
Illinois Department of Mental Health and
  Developmental Disabilities Library
  Services Network, DMHDD/LISN
Indiana Cooperative Library Services
  Authority, INCOLSA
Library Services and Construction Act,
  LSCA
Metropolitan Library Services Agency,
  MELSA
National Library Services for the Blind and
  Physically Handicapped, NLS
Nevada Center for Cooperative Library
  Services, NCCLS

Northwest Indiana Area Library Services
    Authority, NIALSA
San Bernadino, Inyo, Riverside Counties
    United Library Services, SIRCULS
Southeastern Indiana Area Library Services
    Authority, SIALSA
Wandsworth Public, Educational and
    Technical Library Services,
    WANDPETLS

Library Society
American Library Society, ALS

Library Staffs
Continuing Education for Library Staffs in
    the Southwest, CELS

Library Statistics
Library Statistics of Colleges and
    Universities, LSCU

Library System
Central Massachusetts Regional Library
    System, CMRLS
Cleveland Area Metropolitan Library
    System, CAMLS
Coordinated Library System of New
    Mexico, CLS
East Midlands Regional Library System,
    EMRLS
Integrated Library System, ILS
Metropolitan Cooperative Library System,
    MCLS
North Western Regional Library System,
    NWRLS
Ramapo Catskill Library System, RCLS
South Western Regional Library System,
    SWRLS
Southwestern Connecticut Library System,
    Inc, SCLS
Suburban Library System, SLS
Yorkshire Regional Library System, YRLS

Library Systems
Directors of Ontario Regional Library
    Systems/Directeurs des Bibliothèques
    Régionales de l'Ontario, DORLS/DBRO

Library Technical Assistants
Council on Library Technical Assistants,
    COLT

Library Technicians
Alberta Association of Library Technicians,
    AALT
Australian Library Technicians Association,
    ALTA
British Columbia Organization of Library
    Technicians, BOLT
Manitoba Association of Library
    Technicians, MALT

Ontario Association of Library
    Technicians/Association des
    Bibliotechniciens de l'Ontario,
    OALT/ABO
Saskatchewan Association of Library
    Technicians, SALT

Library Technology
Council on Library Technology, COLT
Library Technology Program, LTP
Library Technology Reports. (Journal), LTR

Library to Library
International Library to Library Project,
    ILLC

Library Tools
Interagency Council on Library Tools for
    Nursing, ICLTN

Library Trustee
American Library Trustee Association,
    ALTA

Library Trustees
Alberta Library Trustees Association,
    ALTA
British Columbia Library Trustees
    Association, BCLTA
Canadian Library Trustees Association,
    CLTA
Manitoba Library Trustees Association,
    MLTA
Ontario Library Trustees Association,
    OLTA
Public Library Association of
    Nevada–Nevada Association of Library
    Trustees, PLAN-NALT
Saskatchewan Library Trustees Association,
    SLTA

Library Week
National Library Week, NLW
Virginia National Library Week Company,
    VNLW

Libro
Instituto Nacional del Libro Español, INLE

Libros
Lista de Libros para Bibliotecos
    Universitarias, LILIBU

Licensing
*Investing, Licensing & Trading Conditions
    Abroad* (Journal), IL&T
Psychological Abstracts Tape Edition Lease
    or Licensing, PATELL

Lichtspieltheater-Verband
Schweizerischer Lichtspieltheater-Verband,
    SLV

Lichtspieltheater-Verband (cont.)

Union der Schweizerischen
    Lichtspieltheater-Verbänd/Union des
    Associations Cinématographiques
    Suisses, USLV/UACS

Life Sciences
Current Contents/Chemical,
    Pharmaco-Medical and Life Sciences.
    (Journal), CC/CPML
Current Contents/Life Sciences. (Journal),
    CC/LS

Light
Coherent Light Detection and Ranging,
    COLIDAR

Light Amplification
Light Amplification by Stimulated Emission
    of Radiation, LASER

Light-Emitting
Light-Emitting Diode, LED

Ligne
Documentation en Ligne pour l'Industrie
    Agro-Alimentaire, IALINE

Limits
Storage Limits Register, SLR

Lincoln
Lincoln Laboratory Instrument Center,
    LINC

Line
Communications Line Terminal, CLT
Computer-Aided Line Balancing, CALB
Line Feed, LF
Line of Balance, LOB
Wiswesser Line Notation, WLN

Line Driver
Analog Line Driver, ALD

Line Notations
Retrieval and Automatic Dissemination of
    Information from *Index Chemicus* and
    Line Notations, RADIICAL

Linear
Advanced Linear Programming System,
    ALPS
Linear Information Processing Language,
    LIPL
Linear Programming, LP

Lines
Lines Per Minute, LPM

Linguistic
Association of Literary and Linguistic
    Computing, ALLC

Automated Linguistic Extraction and
    Retrieval Technique, ALERT
Simulated Linguistic Computer, SLC

Linguistics
Association for Computational Linguistics,
    ACL
Association for Machine Translation and
    Computational Linguistics, AMTCL
Center for Applied Linguistics, CAL
ERIC Clearinghouse on Languages and
    Linguistics, ERIC/FL
FID Committee on Linguistics in
    Documentation, FID/LD

Link
Data Link Escape, DLE

Liquid
Vapour Liquid Equilibria Databank, VLE
    BANK

Liquid Metal
Liquid Metal Fast Breeder Reactor, LMFBR

Liquid Metals
Liquid Metals Information Center, LMIC

List
Automatic List Classification and Profile
    Production, ALCAPP
FORTRAN List Processing Language,
    FLPL
List and Index Society, LIS
List Processor, LISP
Price List, PL
Shelf List, SL
Subject Authority List, SAL
Subject Heading Authority List, SHAL

Lista
Lista de Libros para Bibliotecos
    Universitarias, LILIBU

Listener Library
Maynard Listener Library, MLL

Listing
Generalized Information Retrieval and
    Listing System, GIRLS

Literary
Association of Literary and Linguistic
    Computing, ALLC
Association of Literary Magazines of
    America, ALMA
Confederate Memorial Literary Society,
    CMLS
Coordinating Council of Literary Magazines,
    CCLM
International Literary Market Place, ILMP
Literary Market Place, LMP

Literaturdienst
Literaturdienst Medizin, LID

Literature
ACS Chemical Literature Division,
    ACS/CLD
ACS Division of Chemical Literature,
    ACS/DCL
API Abstracts/Literature, APILIT
*Abstracts of Photographic Science and
    Engineering Literature*, APSE
Agricultural Biological Literature
    Exploitation, ABLE
Assembly on Literature for Adolescents,
    ALAN
Automated Literature Processing, Handling,
    and Analysis System, ALPHA
Automatic Literature Alerting Service,
    ALAS
Bibliografické Středisko pro Techickou
    Literaturu (Bibliographical Center for
    Technical Literature), BSTL
*Cambridge Bibliography of English
    Literature*, CBEL
Cancer Literature, CANCERLIT
Catholic Periodical and Literature Index,
    CPLI
Chemical Literature. (Journal), CL
Church Literature Association, CLA
Company and Literature Information Center,
    CLIC
Cumulative Index to Nursing Literature,
    CINL
Current Literature Alerting Search Service,
    CLASS
Essay and General Literature Index, EGLI
IEEE Retrieval from the Literature on
    Electronics and Computer Sciences,
    IEEE REFLECS
Index to Religious Periodical Literature,
    IRPL
*Indexed References to Biomedical
    Engineering Literature*, IRBEL
International Comparative Literature
    Association, ICLA
Library Literature. (Index), LL
Literature Retrieval System for the Pulp and
    Paper Industry, LIRES
Machine Literature Searching, MLS
Medical Literature Analysis and Retrieval
    System, MEDLARS
Netherlands Bibliotheek en Lektuur
    Centrum (Dutch Center for Public
    Libraries and Literature), NBLC
Pesticidal Literature Documentation,
    PESTDOC
Rapid Access to Literature via
    Fragmentation Codes, RALF
Readers Guide to Periodical Literature.
    (Index), RGPL

Technique for Retrieving Information from
    Abstracts of Literature, TRIAL
United Society for Christian Literature,
    USCL

Literaturinformation
Geowissenschaftliche Literaturinformation,
    GWL

Litteraire
Association Litteraire et Artistique
    Internationale, ALAI

Littérature
Programme Appliqué à la Sélection et à la
    Compilation Automatique de la
    Littérature, PASCAL
*Répertoire International de la Littérature de
    l'Art*. (Journal), RILA
Répertoire International de Littérature
    Musicale, RILM

Liverpool
Liverpool and District Scientific, Industrial
    and Research Library Advisory Council,
    LADSIRLAC

Livre
Mise en Ordinateur d'une Notice
    Catalographique de Livre, MONOCLE

Load
Load on Call, LOCAL
Phillips Load and Go, PHLAG

Loading
Automatic and Dynamic Monitor with
    Immediate Relocation, Allocation and
    Loading, ADMIRAL
Computer-Aided Machine Loading, CAMEL
Dial Interrogation and Loading, DIAL

Loan
Bell Laboratories Library Real-Time Loan
    System, BELLREL
Bibliothekarisch-Analytisches System zur
    Informations-Speicherung-Leihverkehr
    (Library Analytical System for
    Information Storage/Retrieval-Loan),
    BASIS-L
IULC Reference and Interlibrary Loan
    Service, IULC-RAILS
Interlibrary Loan, ILL
New York State Interlibrary Loan Network,
    NYSILL
Southern California Interlibrary Loan
    Network, SCILL
TWX Interlibrary Loan Network, TWXILL

Loan Service
Wisconsin Interlibrary Loan Service, WILS

Local
GODORT Local Documents Task Force, GODORT/LDTF
Local Government Information Control, LOGIC
Local Government Information Office, LGIO

Local Authorities
Local Authorities Management Services and Computer Committee, LAMSAC

Local History
American Association for State and Local History, AASLH

Location
Standard Point Location Code, SPLC

Logarithmic
Logarithmic Computing Instrument, LOCI

Logic
Association for Symbolic Logic, ASL
Computer Logic Graphics, CLOG
Direct Coupled Transistor Logic, DCTL
Interrelated Logic Accumulating Scanner, ILAS
Magnetic Logic Computer, MAGLOC
Programmed Logic for Automatic Teaching Operations, PLATO
Resistor-Capacitor Transistor Logic, RCTL
Teaching Logic Translator, TEACHTRAN
Transistor-Resistor-Transistor Logic, TRTL

Logical
Arithmetic and Logical Unit, ALU

Logically
Logically Integrated FORTRAN Translator, LIFT

Logic-Oriented
Computerized Logic-Oriented Design System, CLODS

Logistics
Army Logistics Management Integrated Data System, ALMIDS
Combat Logistics Network, COMLOGNET
Computer-Assisted Logistics Simulation, CALOGSM
Defense Logistics Services Center, DLSC
National Institute of Packaging, Handling and Logistics Engineers, NIPHLE

Loire
Centre de Recherche Sociologique Appliqués de la Loire, CRESAL

London
Association of London Chief Librarians, ALCL

A Computerized London Information Service, ACOMPLIS
Greater London Audio Specialization Scheme, GLASS
Inner London Educational Authority, ILEA
London and South Eastern Library Region, LASER
London International Press, Ltd, LIP
Royal College of Physicians of London, RCP

Long Beach
California State University at Long Beach, CSULB

Long Distance
Long Distance Xerography, LDX

Long Island
Long Island Library Resources Council, LILRC

Longitudinal
Longitudinal Redundancy Check Character, LRC

Look Up
Table Look Up, TLU

Loop
Data Loop Transceiver, DLT

Los Alamos
Compiler Los Alamos Scientific Laboratories, COLASL

Los Angeles
Academy of Television Arts and Sciences–University of California, Los Angeles–Television Archives, ATAS/UCLA
Los Angeles Chapter of ASIS, LACASIS
Los Angeles Public Library, LAPL
Los Angeles Regional Transportation Study, LARTS
University of California–Los Angeles, UCLA

Louisiana
Louisiana Library Association, LLA
Louisiana Numerical Register, LNR
Southeast Louisiana Library Network Cooperative, SEALLINC
Texas, Arkansas, Louisiana, Oklahoma and New Mexico, TALON

Low
Low Data-Rate Input, LDRI
Low Frequency, LF
Very Low Frequency, VLF

Lowell
Lowell Area Council on Interlibrary Networks, LACOIN

Luftfahrtpublizisten
Club der Luftfahrtpublizisten, CLP

Lunar Surface
Apollo Lunar Surface Experimental
Package, ALSEP

Lutheran
Arbeitsgemeinschaft für das Archiv und
Bibliothekswesen in der Evangelischen
Kirche, Sektion Bibliothekswesen
(Working Group for Archives and
Libraries in the Lutheran Church,
Library Section), AABevK
Lutheran Church Library Association,
LCLA

Luxembourg
Association des Exploitants de Cinéma et
des Distributeurs de Films du
Grand-Duché de Luxembourg, AECDF

Luxembourgeoise
Association Luxembourgeoise des Éditeurs
de Journaux, ALEJ

MARC
Canadian Committee on MARC/Comité
Canadien du MARC, CCM
Canadian MARC, CAN/MARC
Early MARC Search, EMS
MARC Development Office, MDO
MARC Records Distribution Service, MRDS
Multiple Use MARC System, MUMS
Norwegian MARC, NORMARC
Selective Dissemination of MARC,
SELDOM

MEDLARS-On-Line
MEDLARS-On-Line, MEDLINE

MEDLINE
Eastern Virginia MEDLINE Consortium,
EVIMEC

MIDAC
MIDAC Automatic General Integrated
Computation, MAGIC

Machinability
Machinability Data Center, MDC

Machine
American Machine and Foundry, Inc, AMF
Association for Machine Translation and
Computational Linguistics, AMTCL
Automatic Programming of Machine Tools,
AUTOPROMPT
Computer-Aided Machine Loading, CAMEL
Data Processing Machine, DPM
Electronic Accounting Machine, EAM
Electronic Data Processing Machine, EDPM

FID Committee on Operational Machine
Technique and Systems, FID/OM
FID Committee on Theory of Machine
Techniques and Systems, FID/TM
Inter-change of Scientific and Technical
Information in Machine Language,
ISTIM
Interdisciplinary Machine Processing for
Research and Education in the Social
Sciences, IMPRESS
Machine Language, ML
Machine Language Programs, MLP
Machine Literature Searching, MLS
Machine Operation, MO
Machine Selection, MS
Machine Translation, MT
National Machine Accountants Association,
NMAA
Punchcard Machine, PCM
Rapid Search Machine, RSM
Simulated Machine Indexing, SMI

Machine-Aided
Machine-Aided Cognition, MAC
Machine-Aided Composing and Editing,
MACE
Machine-Aided Drafting System, MADS
Machine-Aided Technical Processing
System, MATPS

Machine-Assisted
Machine-Assisted Educational System for
Teaching by Remote Operation,
MAESTRO
RASD Machine-Assisted Reference Section,
RASD/MARS

Machine-Oriented
Machine-Oriented Language, MOL

Machine Readable
Cooperative Machine-Readable Cataloging,
COMARC
Human Readable/Machine Readable, HRMR
Machine Readable Cataloging, MARC
Machine Readable Cataloging II, MARC II
Machine-Readable Data Files, MRDF
Machine-Readable Library Information,
MERLIN

Machinery
Association for Computing Machinery, Inc,
ACM
British Printing Machinery Association,
BPMA
Centre National d'Étude et
d'Experimentation de Machinisme
Agricole (National Center for

Machinery (cont.)

Agricultural Machinery Research and Experimentation), CNEEMA
Communications of the Association for Computing Machinery, CACM
Electrical Accounting Machinery, EAM
Journal of the Association for Computing Machinery, JACM

Machines
Deutsche Arbeitsgemeinschaft für Rechen-Anlagen (German Working Committee for Computing Machines), DARA
International Business Machines Corporation, IBM
Vyzkumny Ustav pro Matematickych Stroju (Research Institute for Mathematical Machines), VUMS

Macro
COBOL Macro Processor, CMP
General Electric Macro Assembly Program, GEMAP
Macro Assembly Program, MAP
Macro-Oriented Business Language, MOBL
A Macro Programming Language, AMPL

Macroinstruction
Macroinstruction Compiler Assembler, MICA

Macro-Operation
Macro-Operation Symbolic Assembler and Information Compiler, MOSAIC 636

Macro-Processors
Descriptive Language for Implementing Macro-Processors, DLIMP

Madison
Madison Area Library Council, MALC

Magazine
Comics Magazine Association of America, Inc, CMAA
Committee of Small Magazine Editors and Publishers, COSMEP
Magazine and Paperback Marketing Institute, MPMI
Magazine Industry Market Place, MIMP
Pacific Coast Independent Magazine Wholesalers Association, PACIMWA

Magazines
Association of Literary Magazines of America, ALMA
Coordinating Council of Literary Magazines, CCLM
National Association for School Magazines, NASM

Magical
Salton's Magical Automatic Retrieval of Texts, SMART

Magnetband-Speicherung
Genealogische Recherche mit Magnetband-Speicherung, GREMAS

Magnetic
Bistable Magnetic Core, BIMAG
Carbon-13 Nuclear Magnetic Resonance, CNMR
Code for Magnetic Characters, CMC
Magnetic Decision Element, MDE
Magnetic Drum Receiving Equipment, MADRE
Magnetic Ink Character Recognition, MICR
Magnetic Logic Computer, MAGLOC
Magnetic Tape/Selectric Typewriter, MTST

Magnetic-tape
Magnetic-tape Field Search, MFS

Mail
Direct Mail Producers Association, DMPA

Main
Main Distributing Frame, MDF
Main Memory, MM
Main Storage Control Element, MSCE

Maine
Maine Library Association, MLA

Maintenance
Computer-Assisted Maintenance Planning and Control System, CAMCOS
Engineering Maintenance Information System, EMIS
Library Additions and Maintenance Program, LAMP
Mean Time Between Maintenance, MTBM
Systems Tape Addition and Maintenance Program, STAMP

Mainz
Zurich, Mainz, Munich, Darmstadt, ZMMD

Maize Virus
Maize Virus Information Service, MAVIS

Makerere
Makerere University College, MUC

Makeup
Digital Display Makeup, DDM

Malagasy
Office du Livre Malagasy (Malagasy Book Office), OLM

Malaysia
Persatuan Perpustakaan Malaysia (Library Association of Malaysia), PPM

Standards Institute of Malaysia, SIM

Malfunction

Malfunction Analysis Detection and
  Recording, MADAR
Malfunction and Data Recorder, MADAR
Malfunction Detection and Recording,
  MADREC

Malta

Malta Library Association, MLA

Man

Research Institute for the Study of Man,
  RISM

Management

ACM Special Interest Group on Management
  of Data, ACM/SIGMOD
ANSI/SPARC Study Group on Data Base
  Management Systems,
  ANSI/X3/SPARC/SGDBMS.
Advanced Data Management, ADAM
Advanced Management Research, AMR
Agricultural Research Management
  Information System, ARMIS
American Association of Industrial
  Management, AAIM
American Institute of Management, AIM
American Management Associations, AMA
American Records Management
  Association, ARMA
Archival Records Management System,
  ARM
Army Logistics Management Integrated Data
  System, ALMIDS
Association for Systems Management, ASM
Association of Consulting Management
  Engineers, ACME
Automated Inventory Management, AIM
Automated Mortgage Management
  Information Network, AMMINET
Automatic Traffic Engineering and
  Management Information System,
  ATEMIS
Bookbinding and Allied Trades Management
  Association, BATMA
British Institute of Management, BIM
Canadian Farm Management Data System,
  CANFARM
Computer Software and Management
  Information Center, COSMIC
Computer-Aided Patient Management,
  CAPM
Computer-Assisted Instruction
  Management, CAIM
Computer-Assisted Management of
  Learning, CAMOL
Computerized Management Account, CMA
Data Base Management System, DBMS

Data Base Organization and Management
  Processor, DBOMP
Data Management, DM
Data Management Association, DMA
Data Management Routines, DMR
Data Processing Management Association,
  DPMA
ERIC Clearinghouse on Educational
  Management, ERIC/EA
European Association of Management
  Training Centers, EAMTC
European Industrial Management
  Association, EIRMA
Financial Accounting and Management
  Information System, FAMIS
Financial Analysis of Management
  Effectiveness, FAME
Financial and Management Information
  System, FAMIS
Forecasts, Appraisals, and Management
  Evaluation, FAME
Foreign Exchange Accounting and
  Management Information System,
  FEAMIS
Free Association of Management Analysis,
  FAMA
Generalized Data Base Management
  Systems, GDBMS
Generalized Information Management
  System, GIM
Hierarchical Environmental Retrieval for
  Management Access and Networking,
  HERMAN
Hospital Management Systems Society,
  HMSS
IPI Management and Information System,
  IPI/MIS
International Material Management Society,
  IMMS
LAMA Library Organization and
  Management Section, LAMA/LOMS
Library Administration and Management
  Association, LAMA
Management by Objectives, MBO
Management by Objectives and Results,
  MBO/R
Management Information System, MIS
Management Report Generator, MARGEN
Management Review and Analysis Program,
  MRAP
Moderately Advanced Data Management,
  MADAM
Network Management Information System,
  NEMIS
Office of Management and Budget, OMB
Personnel Records Information System for
  Management, PRISM
Prosecutors Management Information
  System, PROMIS

Management (cont.)

School Management Information Retrieval
  System, SMIRS
Society for the Advancement of
  Management, SAM
System for the Automated Management of
  Text from a Hierarchical Arrangement,
  SAMANTHA
Technical Environmental and Management
  Planning Operations, TEMPO
Test Rules for Inventory Management,
  TRIM

Management Information
ASIS Special Interest Group on Management
  Information Activities, ASIS/SIG/MGT
Management Information Corporation, MIC
Rapid Access Management Information
  System, RAMIS
Society for Management Information
  Systems, SMIS

Management Services
Local Authorities Management Services and
  Computer Committee, LAMSAC

Management Studies
Management Studies Centre, Ltd, MSC
Office of Management Studies, OMS

Manager
Automated Route Manager, ARM
Communications Access Manager, CAM

Managerial
Managerial On-Line Data System, MOLDS

Managers
Association of Records Managers and
  Administrators, ARMA
Data Processing Librarians and
  Documentation Managers Association,
  DPL/DMA

Manchester
Manchester Federation of Scientific
  Societies, MFSS
Manchester Interlibrary Cooperative, MILC
Manchester Technical Information Service,
  MANTIS

Manipulation
Data Manipulation Language, DML
Formula Manipulation Compiler, FORMAC

Manitoba
Council of Academic Librarians of
  Manitoba, CALM
Manitoba Association of Library
  Technicians, MALT
Manitoba Association of Registered Nurses,
  MARN

Manitoba Library Association, MLA
Manitoba Library Trustees Association,
  MLTA
Manitoba School Library Audio-Visual
  Association, MSLAVA

Man-Machine
Man-Machine Partnership Translation,
  MMPT

Manpower
Area Manpower Institutes for the
  Development of Staffs, AMIDS
Bureau of Health Manpower Education,
  BHME
School Library Manpower Project, SLMP
Scientific Manpower Commission, SMC

Manual
Manual Output, MO

Manually Operated
Manually Operated Visual Response
  Indicator, MOVRI

Manufacturers
Book Manufacturers Institute, BMI
British Photographic Manufacturers
  Association, BPMA
Business Equipment Manufacturers
  Association, BEMA
Computer and Business Equipment
  Manufacturers Association, CBEMA
European Computer Manufacturers
  Association, ECMA
Kinematograph Manufacturers Association,
  KMA
Office Equipment Manufacturers Institute,
  OEMI
Office Furniture Manufacturers Institute,
  OFMI
Radio and Electric Component
  Manufacturers Federation, RECMF
Synthetic Organic Chemical Manufacturers
  Association, SOCMA

Manufacturing
Author Index Manufacturing System, AIMS
Computer-Aided Manufacturing
  International, CAM-I
Computer-Integrated Manufacturing System,
  CIMS
Data Information and Manufacturing
  System, DIMS
General Electric Manufacturing Simulator,
  GEMS
Minnesota Mining and Manufacturing
  Company, 3M
System Manufacturing Division, SMD

Manuscript
Center for the Coordination of Foreign
  Manuscript Copying, CCFMC

Monastic Manuscript Microfilm Library,
MMML
*National Union Catalog of Manuscript
Collections*, NUCMC

Manuscripts
ACRL Rare Books and Manuscripts Section,
ACRL/RBMS
Royal Commission on Historical
Manuscripts, HMC

Map
Dual Independent Map Encoding File of the
Counties of the US, DIMECO

Map Libraries
Association of Canadian Map
Libraries/Association des Cartothèques
Canadiennes, ACML/ACC

Mapping
American Congress on Surveying and
Mapping, ACSM
Basic Analysis and Mapping Program,
BAMP
National Congress on Surveying and
Mapping, NCSM

Maps
Maps, Microtexts, and Newspapers, MMN

Marine
American Institute of Marine Underwriters,
AIMU
Association for Marine Research and
Technology Information, AIM
Center for Marine and Environmental
Studies, CMES
Marine Air-Ground Intelligence System,
MAGIS
Marine Environmental Data Information
Referral System, MEDI
Marine Technology Society, MTS
National Marine Data Inventory, NAMDI
Society of Naval Architects and Marine
Engineers, SNAME

Maritime
Maritime Research Information Service,
MRIS

Mark
Group Mark, GM

Mark Recording
Non-Return-to-Zero Mark Recording,
NRZM

Marker
Beginning-of-Information Marker, BIM

Market
Defense Market Measures System, DM^2
European Society for Opinion Surveys and
Market Research, ESOMAR

Market Data Retrieval–Educational Data
Base, MDR

Market Place
Audiovisual Market Place, AVMP
Information Industry Market Place, IIMP
International Literary Market Place, ILMP
Literary Market Place, LMP
Magazine Industry Market Place, MIMP

Marketing
Chemical Marketing Research Association,
CMRA
European Marketing and Advertising Press,
EMAP
Food Marketing Institute, FMI
Magazine and Paperback Marketing
Institute, MPMI
Selling Areas-Marketing Inc, SAMI

Markets
(Predicasts Overview of Markets and
Technology) (Journal), PROMT

Marks
Control Marks, CM

Marshall
Marshall Space Flight Center Library,
MSFC

Maryland
Maryland Academic Library Center for
Automated Processing, MALCAP
Maryland Association of Health Sciences
Librarians, MAHSL
Maryland Independent College and
University Association, Inc, MICUA
Maryland Library Association, MLA

Maschinenbau
Dokumentation Maschinenbau, DOMA

Mass
Department of Mass Communication, MC
International Association for Mass
Communication Research, IAMCR
Random Access Mass Memory, RAM
Society for Mass Media and Resource
Technology, SMMART

Massachusetts
Central Massachusetts Library
Administration Project, CLASP
Central Massachusetts Regional Library
System, CMRLS
Computer Language of Massachusetts
Institute of Technology, COMIT
Data Analysis Massachusetts Institute of
Technology, DAMIT
Library and Information Science Meetings
Exchange, Massachusetts Bureau of
Library Extension, LIS/MEX

Massachusetts (cont.)

Massachusetts Conference of Chief
    Librarians in Public Higher Educational
    Institutions, MCCLPHEI
Massachusetts Institute of Technology, MIT
Massachusetts Library Association, MLA
Southeastern Association for Cooperation in
    Higher Education in Massachusetts,
    SACHEM

Massachusetts Libraries

Southeastern Massachusetts Cooperating
    Libraries, SMCL

Massachusetts Library

Massachusetts Centralized Library
    Processing Center, MCLP

Master

Master Control Program, MCP
Master Instruction Tape, MIT
Master Relocatable Tape, MRT

Master List

Master List of Medical Indexing Terms,
    MALIMET

Masters

National Register of Microform Masters,
    NRMM

Material

International Material Management Society,
    IMMS
Society of Aerospace Material and Process
    Engineers, SAMPE

Matériel Didactique

Association Européenne de Fabricants et des
    Revendeurs de Matériel
    Didactique/Verband Europäischer
    Lehrmittelfirmen, EURODIDAC

Material Handling

American Material Handling Society, AMHS

Material Product

System of National Accounts/System of
    Material Product Balances, SNA/MPS

Materials

American Society for Testing and Materials,
    ASTM
Committee on Research Materials on
    Southeast Asia, CORMOSEA
Computer-Based Educational Materials,
    CBEM
National Information Center in Special
    Education Materials, NICSEM
Specialized Office for Materials Distribution,
    SOMD

Materials Handling

Automated Instructional Materials Handling
    System of SDC (System Development
    Corporation), AIMS
National Materials Handling Center, NMHC

Mathematical

ACM Special Interest Group on
    Mathematical Programming,
    ACM/SIGMAP
American Mathematical Society, AMS
Automatic Mathematical Translation,
    AMTRAN
Conference Board of the Mathematical
    Sciences, CBMS
Current Mathematical Publications, CMP
Index of Mathematical Papers. (Journal),
    IMP
International Mathematical and Statistical
    Library, IMSL
Mathematical Analysis of Requirements for
    Career Information Appraisal, MARCIA
Mathematical Association of America, MAA
Mathematical Program, MATH-PAC
New York Mathematical Society, NYMS
Vyzkumny Ustav pro Matematickych Stroju
    (Research Institute for Mathematical
    Machines), VUMS

Mathematics

ACM German Association for Applied
    Mathematics and Mechanics,
    ACM/GAMM
ACM Special Interest Group on Numerical
    Mathematics, ACM/SIGNUM
Association Internationale pour le Calcul
    Analogique (International Association
    for Mathematics and Computer
    Simulation), AICA
Center for Research in College Instruction of
    Science and Mathematics, CRICISAM
Computer-Assisted Mathematics Program,
    CAMP
*Dictionary of Physics and Mathematics
    Abbreviations, Signs and Symbols*,
    DPMA
ERIC Clearinghouse for Science,
    Mathematics and Environmental
    Education, ERIC/SE
International Association for Mathematics
    and Computer Simulation, IMACS
National Council of Teachers of
    Mathematics, NCTM
Society for Automation in Science and
    Mathematics, SASM
Society for Industrial and Applied
    Mathematics, SIAM

Matrix

Descriptor Attribute Matrix, DAM

Matter
Personality, Matter, Energy, Space and
Time, PMEST

Mauritanian
AIDBA–Section Mauritanienne
(AIDBA–Mauritanian Branch),
AIDBA–Section Mauritanienne

Maximum Time
Maximum Time to Repair, MTTR

McGill
McGill Elementary Education Teaching
Teams, MEET

Mean Time
Mean Time Between Failure, MTBF
Mean Time Between Maintenance, MTBM
Mean Time to Failure, MTTF
Mean Time to Repair, MTTR
Mean Time to Restore, MTTR

Measurement
ERIC Clearinghouse on Tests,
Measurement, and Evaluation,
ERIC/TM
Methods-Time Measurement, MTM
Missile Trajectory Measurement,
MISTRAM

Measurement Evaluation
ACM Special Interest Group on
Measurement Evaluation,
ACM/SIGMETRICS

Measurements
Joint Departmental Radio and Electronics
Measurements Committee, REMC

Measures
Defense Market Measures System, DM²

Mechanical
American Society of Mechanical Engineers,
ASME
*Dictionary of Mechanical Engineering
Abbreviations, Signs and Symbols*,
DMEA
FID Working Committee on Mechanical
Storage and Retrieval, FID/MSR
Information Service in Mechanical
Engineering, ISMEC
Mechanical Copyright Protection Society,
MCPS
Mechanical Engineering Publications, MEP
Mechanical Translation, MT

Mechanics
ACM German Association for Applied
Mathematics and Mechanics,
ACM/GAMM

Matter
Sail Mechanics Information Analysis Center,
SMIAC

Mechanization
Computer-Assisted Library Mechanization,
CALM

Mechanized
Aldermaston Mechanized Cataloging and
Ordering System, AMCOS
Heuristic Mechanized Document
Information System, HERMES
Mechanized Catalog, MECCA

Media
Auto-Instructional Media for Library
Orientation, AIMLO
Community Media Library Program,
COMLIP
Cooperative Media Development Program,
CMDP
Educational Media Catalogs on Microfiche,
EMCOM
Educational Media Council, EMC
Educational Media Institute Evaluation
Project, EMIE
Educational Media Selection Centers,
EMSC
Florida Association for Media and
Education, FAME
Media Equipment Resource Center, MERC
Media Exchange Cooperative, MEC
Montana Instructional Media Association,
MIMA
National Information Center for Educational
Media, NICEM
Nederlands Instituut voor Audio Visuele
Middlelen (Netherlands Institute for
Audiovisual Media), NIAM
Overseas Press and Media Association, Ltd,
OPMA
School Media Quarterly. (Journal), SMQ
Society for Mass Media and Resource
Technology, SMMART
Vermont Educational Media Association,
VEMA
Virginia Educational Media Association,
VEMA
Wyoming Instructional Media Association,
WIMA

Media-Assisted
Self-Instructional Media-Assisted Learning
Unit, SIMALU

Media Center
Oklahoma Environmental Information and
Media Center, OEIMC

Media Centers
Arbeitsgemeinschaft Pädagogischer
    Bibliotheken und Medienzentren
    (Working Group of Educational
    Libraries and Media Centers), APB

Media Specialists
Saskatchewan Association of Educational
    Media Specialists, SAEMS

Mediation
Program of Action for Mediation,
    Arbitration, and Inquiry, PAMAI
Staff Committee on Mediation, Arbitration
    and Inquiry, SCMAI

Medica
Associazione Stampa Medica Italiana, ASMI

Medical
ASIS Special Interest Group on Medical
    Records, ASIS/SIG/MR
American Association of Medical Records
    Librarians, AAMRL
American Medical Association, AMA
American Medical Publishers Association,
    AMPA
American Medical Record Association,
    AMRA
American Medical Writers Association,
    AMWA
Association of Canadian Medical
    Colleges/Association des Facultés de
    Médecine du Canada, ACMC/AFMC
Automated Processing of Medical English,
    APME
British Medical Association, BMA
Bulletin of the Medical Library Association,
    BMLA
Centrul de Documentare Medicală (Medical
    Documentation Center), CDM
Council for International Organizations on
    Medical Sciences, CIOMS
Countway Library Medical Bibliographic
    Services, CLIMBS
Deutsches Institut für Medizinische
    Dokumentation und Information
    (German Institute for Medical
    Documentation and Information),
    DIMDI
Institute for the Advancement of Medical
    Communication, IAMC
Japanese Medical Abstract Scanning
    System, JAMASS
*Journal of the Association for the
    Advancement of Medical
    Instrumentation*, JAAMI
Master List of Medical Indexing Terms,
    MALIMET
*Medical and Health Related Sciences
    Thesaurus*, MHRST

Medical Audio-Visual Institute, MAVI
Medical Books in Print, MBIP
Medical Information Dissemination Using
    ASSASSIN, MIDAS
Medical Information Management System,
    MIMS
Medical Library Assistance Act of 1965,
    MLAA
Medical Library Association, MLA
Medical Library Center, MLC
Medical Library Center of New York,
    MLCNY
Medical Literature Analysis and Retrieval
    System, MEDLARS
Medical Record Information Service, MRIS
Medical Research Council, MRC
Medical Resources Consortium of Central
    New Jersey, MEDCORE
Medical Socioeconomic Research Sources.
    (Journal), MEDSOC
Medical Subject Headings, MeSH
Mid-Eastern Regional Medical Library
    Service, MERMLS
National Institute for Medical Research,
    NIMR
National Medical Audiovisual Center,
    NMAC
National Society for Medical Research,
    NSMR
Network for Continuing Medical Education,
    NCME
New England Regional Medical Library
    Service, NERMLS
Ontario Medical Association, OMA
Pacific Area Union List of Medical Serials,
    PAULMS
Scientific, Technical and Medical Publishers,
    STM
Southeast Asian Medical Information
    Center, SEAMIC
Státni Ústav pro Zdravotnickou
    Dokumentačm a Knihovnickou Sluzbu
    (State Institute for Medical
    Documentation and National Medical
    Library), SUZDKS
Tampa Bay Medical Library Network,
    TABAMLN
Toronto Institute of Medical Technology,
    TIMT
Total Hospital Operating and Medical
    Information System, THOMIS
Union Catalog of Medical Periodicals,
    UCMP
Vsesoiuznyĭ Nauchno Issle-dovatel'skii
    Institut Meditsinskoĭ i
    Medikotekhnicheskoĭ Informatsii
    Ministerstva Zdravookhraneniia USSR
    (All-Union Scientific Research Institute
    of Medical and Medico-Technical
    Information, VNIIMI

Medical Information
Australian Drug and Medical Information
Group, ADMIG
Virginia Medical Information Services,
VAMIS

Medical Library
Annual Medical Library Association
Conference Committee, AMLAC
Arizona Medical Library Network, AMLN
Connecticut Regional Medical Library,
CRML
Kentucky, Ohio, Michigan Regional Medical
Library, KOMRML
Metropolitan Detroit Medical Library
Group, MDMLG
Mid-Atlantic Regional Medical Library,
MARML
Midcontinental Regional Medical Library
Program, MCRMLP
Northern California Medical Library Group,
NCMLG
Országos Orvostudományi Könyvtár és
Dokumentációś Központ (National
Medical Library and Center for
Documentation), OOKDK
Pacific Southwest Regional Medical Library
Service, PSRMLS
Regional Medical Library, RML
Southeastern Regional Medical Library
Program, SERMLP

Medical Services
Ambulance and Medical Services
Association of America, AMSAA
National Emergency Medical Services
Information Network, NEMSINET

Medicale
Institut National de la Santé et de la
Recherche Medicale, INSERM

Médicaments
Banque d'Information Automatisée sur les
Médicaments, BIAM

Medicas
Classification Analytico-Synthetica Cubana
de Medicas, CASCUM

Medicina
Biblioteca Regional de Medicina, BIREME

Medicine
Analytico-Synthetic Classification of
Medicine, ASCOM
History of Medicine Online, HISTLINE
International Reference Organization in
Forensic Medicine and Sciences,
INFORM
National Library of Medicine, NLM

Periodical Holdings in the Library of the
School of Medicine, PHILSOM

Mediterranean Librarians
Standing Conference for Mediterranean
Librarians, SConMeL

Medium
End of Medium, EM
Medium Frequency, MF

Medium Scale
Medium Scale Integrated Circuits, MSI

Medium-sized Libraries
PLA Small and Medium-sized Libraries
Section, PLA/SMLS

Medizin
Institut für Wissenschaftsinformation in der
Medizin, IWIM
Literaturdienst Medizin, LID

Meeting
Annual General Meeting, AGM
Northeast Regional Meeting, NERM

Meetings Exchange
Library and Information Science Meetings
Exchange, Massachusetts Bureau of
Library Extension, LIS/MEX

Memorandum
Technical Memorandum, TECH MEMO

Memorial
Confederate Memorial Literary Society,
CMLS

Memories
Block-Oriented Random Access Memories,
BORAM

Memorizer
Elementary Perceiver and Memorizer,
EPAM

Memory
Card Random Access Memory, CRAM
Content-Addressed Memory, CAM
High-Speed Memory, HSM
Main Memory, MM
Memory Operating Characteristic, MOC
Memory Test Computer, MTC
Random Access Mass Memory, RAM
Random Access Memory, RAM
Read Only Memory, ROM
Simulator of Immediate Memory in Learning
Experiments, SIMILE

Memory-Assisted
Memory-Assisted Cognition, MAC

Mental Health
Illinois Department of Mental Health and
    Developmental Disabilities Library
    Services Network, DMHDD/LISN
Illinois Department of Mental Health and
    Developmental Disabilities Professional
    Libraries Consortium, IDMH
National Institute of Mental Health, NIMH

Mental Health Information
National Clearinghouse for Mental Health
    Information, NCMHI

Merchant
Atlantic Merchant Vessel Report, AMVER

Merchant Marine Library
American Merchant Marine Library
    Association, AMMLA

Merito
Giurisprudenza di Merito, MERITO

Message
Data Association Message, DAM
Digital Data Communications Message
    Protocol, DDCMP
End of Message, EOM
Multiplex Message Processor, MMP
Start of Message, SOM

Message Routing
Automatic Message Routing, AMR

Message Service
Public Message Service, PMS

Metal
Metal Alert, METALERT
National Metal Trades Association, NMTA

Metallurgic Information
Centro de Información Metalíurgica (Center
    for Metallurgic Information), CIM

Metallurgical
American Institute of Mining, Metallurgical
    and Petroleum Engineers, AIME
Gesellschaft Deutscher Metallhuttens und
    Bergleute (Association of German
    Metallurgical and Mining Engineers),
    GDMB
Inorganic and Metallurgical
    Thermodynamics Data, MTDATA
The Metallurgical Society, TMS

Metallurgy
Institution of Mining and Metallurgy, IMM

Metals
American Society for Metals, ASM
Defense Metals Information Center, DMIC
Metals Abstracts Index, METADEX
Metals and Ceramics Information Center,
    MCIC

Meteorological
American Meteorological Society, AMETS
*Meteorological and Geoastrophysical
    Abstracts*, MGA
World Meteorological Organization, WMO

Meteorological Center
National Meteorological Center, NMC

Method
Basic Access Method, BAM
Basic Direct Access Method, BDAM
Basic Indexed Sequential Access Method,
    BISAM
Basic Telecommunications Access Method,
    BTAM
Basic Terminal Access Method, BTAM
Critical Path Method, CPM
Data Base Access Method, DBAM
Hierarchical Indexed Sequential Access
    Method, HISAM
Hierarchical Sequential Access Method,
    HSAM
Indexed Sequential Access Method, ISAM
Project Monitoring and Control Method,
    PROMCOM
Queued Access Method, QAM
Queued Indexed Sequential Access Method,
    QISAM
Queued Telecommunications Access
    Method, QTAM
Random Access Method of Accounting and
    Control, RAMAC
Synchronous Transmit Receive Access
    Method, STRAM

Methodist
Commission on Archives and History of the
    United Methodist Church, CAHUMC

Methods
FID Committee on Theory, Methods, and
    Operations of Information Systems and
    Networks, FID/TMO
Methods of Extracting Text Automatically,
    META
Methods of Extracting Text Automatically
    Programming Language, METAPLAN
Methods-Time Measurement, MTM

Metro-Goldwyn-Mayer
Metro-Goldwyn-Mayer, Inc, MGM

Metropolitan
Cleveland Area Metropolitan Library
    System, CAMLS
Higher Education Coordinating Council of
    Metropolitan Saint Louis, HECC
International Association of Metropolitan
    City Libraries, INTAMEL
Metropolitan Cooperative Library System,
    MCLS

Metropolitan Detroit Medical Library
  Group, MDMLG
Metropolitan Library Services Agency,
  MELSA
New York Metropolitan Reference and
  Research Library Agency, METRO
Printing Industries of Metropolitan New
  York, PIMNY
South East Metropolitan Board of
  Cooperative Services, SEMBCS
Standard Metropolitan Statistical Area,
  SMSA

Metropolitan Libraries
PLA Metropolitan Libraries Section,
  PLA/MLS

Mexican
Asociación Mexicana de Educación Agricola
  Superior (Mexican Association for
  Agricultural Higher Education),
  AMEAS

Mexican Center
Centro Méxicano de Información del Zinc y
  del Plomo (Mexican Center of
  Information for Zinc and Lead),
  CMIZPAC
Centro Méxicano de Información Química
  (Mexican Center for Chemical
  Information), CMIQ

Mexican Librarians
Asociación Mexicana de Bibliotecarios, A.
  C. (Mexican Association of Librarians),
  AMBAC

Méxicano
Instituto Méxicano de Información Avícola,
  IMIA

México
Universidad Nacional Autónoma de México,
  UNAM

Miami
Miami Valley Library Organization, MILO
University of Miami Computing Center,
  UMCC

Michigan
Kentucky, Ohio, Michigan Regional Medical
  Library, KOMRML
Michigan Algorithmic Decoder, MAD
Michigan Library Association, MLA
Michigan Library Consortium, MLC
Michigan Quarterly Economic Model,
  MQEM

Microalloy
Microalloy Diffused Base Transistor, MADT
Microalloy Diffused Electrode, MADE

Microelectronics
Microelectronics Bibliography, MB

Microfiche
Automatic Microfiche Editor, AME
Educational Media Catalogs on Microfiche,
  EMCOM
Microfiche, MF
Selected Categories in Microfiche, SCIM
Selective Dissemination of Microfiche, SDM
Ultra Microfiche, UMF

Microfiche Service
Standing Order Microfiche Service, SRIM

Microfilm
Automated Microfilm Aperture Card Update
  System, AMACUS
Automatic Microfilm Information System,
  AMFIS
Computer Input Microfilm, CIM
Computer Output Microfilm, COM
Computer Output Microfilm Package,
  COMPAC
Continuous Image Microfilm (or
  Microfilming), CIM
Illinois Microfilm Automated Catalog, IMAC
International Microfilm, IM
Microfilm Association of Great Britain,
  MAGB
Microfilm Retrieval Access Code,
  MIRACODE
Newspapers on Microfilm, NOM

Microfilm Center
Catholic Microfilm Center, CMC

Microfilm Library
Monastic Manuscript Microfilm Library,
  MMML

Microfilmer
Computer Output Microfilmer, COM
Datascope Computer Output Microfilmer,
  DACOM

Microfilming
Computer Output Microfilming, COM
Microfilming Corporation of America, MCA

Microfilms
Systeme Electronique de Selection
  Automatique de Microfilms, SESAM
University Microfilms International, UMI

Microform
Cooperative Africana Microform Project,
  CAMP
International Microform Distribution
  Service, IMDS
Microform Review. (Journal), MR
National Register of Microform Masters,
  NRMM
South Asia Microform Project, SAMP

Microforms
Computer Output Microforms Program and
Concept Study, COMPACS
Guide to Microforms in Print, GMP
South East Asia Microforms, SEAM

Micrographic
Micrographic Catalog Retrieval System,
MCRS

Micrographic Services
Library Micrographic Services, Inc, LMS

Micrographics
Computer Micrographics and Technology,
COMTEC
Micrographics Equipment Review. (Journal),
MER
National Micrographics Association, NMA

Micro-Image
Photochromic Micro-Image, PCMI

Micro-Imaged
Micro-Imaged Data Addition System,
MIDAS

Microprogrammable
Advanced Microprogrammable Processor,
AMPP

Microprogramming
ACM Special Interest Group on
Microprogramming, ACM/SIGMICRO

Microscope
Computer-Controlled Scanning Electron
Microscope, CCSEM

Microtexts
Maps, Microtexts, and Newspapers, MMN

Microwave
Texas Educational Microwave Project,
TEMP

Mid-America
Colleges of Mid-America, CMA
Mid-America Periodical Distributors
Association, MAPDA
Theological Education Association of
Mid-America, TEAM-A

Mid-Atlantic
Mid-Atlantic Regional Medical Library,
MARML
Mid-Atlantic Research Libraries Information
Network, MARLIN

Midcontinental
Midcontinental Regional Medical Library
Program, MCRMLP

Middle Atlantic
Middle Atlantic Educational and Research
Center, MERC

Middle East
Middle East Librarians Association, MELA

Middle East Studies
Middle East Studies Association of North
America, MESA

Mid-Eastern
Mid-Eastern Regional Medical Library
Service, MERMLS

Midland
East Midland Educational Union, EMEU

Midlands
East Midlands Regional Library System,
EMRLS

Midwest
Associated Colleges of the Midwest, ACM
Midwest Health Science Library Network,
MHSLN
Mid-West Independent Distributors
Association, MIDA
Midwest Region Library Network,
MIDLNET
Midwest Universities Consortium for
International Activities, Inc, MUCIA
Upper Midwest Regional Educational
Laboratory, UMREL

Midwestern
Midwestern Academic Librarians
Conference, MALC

Military
Canadian Military Electronics Standards
Agency, CAMESA
Company of Military Historians, CMH
Military Computer Users Group, MCUG
Military Documentation System, MIDONAS
Military Entomology Information Service,
MEIS

Milwaukee
Library Council of Metropolitan Milwaukee,
LCOMM

Mineral
Canada Centre for Mineral and Energy
Technology, CANMET

Miniature
Miniature Processing Time, MINPRT

Minicomputers
ACM Special Interest Group on
Minicomputers, ACM/SIGMINI

Minimum
Minimum Slack Time per Operation,
MINSOP

Mining
American Institute of Mining, Metallurgical
    and Petroleum Engineers, AIME
Gesellschaft Deutscher Metallhuttens und
    Bergleute (Association of German
    Metallurgical and Mining Engineers),
    GDMB
Institution of Mining and Metallurgy, IMM
Minnesota Mining and Manufacturing
    Company, 3M
Society of Mining Engineers, SME

Ministers
Southeast Asian Ministers of Education
    Council, SEAMEC

Ministry
British Ministry of Technology, BrMTL
Centrul de Documentare si Publicatü
    Tehnice al Ministerulue Cailór Ferate
    (Technical Documentation and
    Publications Center of the Railway
    Ministry), CDPT-MCF

Minnesota
Information for Minnesota, INFORM
Minnesota Interlibrary Telecommunications
    Exchange, MINITEX
Minnesota Library Association, MLA
Minnesota Mining and Manufacturing
    Company, 3M
Minnesota Union List of Serials, MULS
South Central Minnesota Inter-Library
    Exchange, SMILE

Minute
Cards Per Minute, CPM
Cubic Feet per Minute, CFM
Documents Per Minute, DPM
Lines Per Minute, LPM
Operations per Minute, OPM

Missile
Missile Attitude Determination System,
    MADS
Missile Trajectory Measurement,
    MISTRAM

Mississippi
Consortium for Library Automation in
    Mississippi, CLAM
Mississippi Library Association, MLA
Mississippi Library News. (Newsletter),
    MLN

Missouri
Iowa–Missouri–Illinois Library Consortium,
    IMI
Mid-Missouri Associated Colleges, MMAC
Missouri Library Association, MLA

Mobile
Mobile Digital Computer, MOBIDIC

Model
Automatic Frequency Assignment Model,
    AFAM
Context, Input, Process Product Model,
    CIPP
Michigan Quarterly Economic Model,
    MQEM
Model and Program, MAP
Xerox Planning Model, XPM

Model Building
Model Building Language, MOBULA

Modeling
Continuous System Modeling Program,
    CSMP

Moderately
Moderately Advanced Data Management,
    MADAM

Modern
Modern Humanities Research Association,
    MHRA
Modern Information & Documentation
    Organizing & Rearrangement, Inc,
    MIDORI
Modern Language Association of America,
    MLA
Modern Poetry Association, MPA
*Publications of the Modern Language
    Association.* (Journal), PMLA

Modular
Computerized Modular Monitoring, CMM
Standard Modular System, SMS
Triple Modular Redundancy, TMR

Modulating
Modulating and Demodulating Unit,
    MOD/DEM

Modulation
Amplitude Modulation, AM
Pulse Code Modulation, PCM

Module
Circulation Module, CIRC
Input/Output Control Module, IOC
Multiple Module Access, MMA

Molecular
Database of Atomic and Molecular Physics,
    DAMP

Monastic
Monastic Manuscript Microfilm Library,
    MMML

Monetary
International Monetary Fund, IMF

Money
Business International Money Report.
    (Journal), BIMR

Monitor
Automatic and Dynamic Monitor with
    Immediate Relocation, Allocation and
    Loading, ADMIRAL
System Activity Monitor, SAM

Monitoring
Comprehensive Achievement Monitoring,
    CAM
Computerized Modular Monitoring, CMM
Project Monitoring and Control Method,
    PROMCOM

Monmouthshire
Library Advisory Council for Wales and
    Monmouthshire, LAC

Monographics
National Union Catalogue of Monographics,
    NUCOM

Monrobot
Monrobot Automatic Internal Diagnosis,
    MAID

Montana
Montana Information Network and
    Exchange, MINE
Montana Instructional Media Association,
    MIMA
Montana Library Association, MLA
Washington, Alaska, Montana, and Idaho,
    WAMI

Monterey
Monterey Bay Area Cooperative, MOBAC

Montréal
Association des Préposés aux Bibliothèques
    Scolaires de Montréal, APBSM
Special Libraries Association, Section de
    Montréal Chapter, SMCSLA
Université du Quebec à Montreal, UQAM

Mortgage
Automated Mortgage Management
    Information Network, AMMINET

Mössbauer Effect
Mössbauer Effect Data Index, MEDI

Most Significant
Most Significant Character, MSC
Most Significant Digit, MSD

Moteurs
École Nationale du Pêtrole et des Moteurs,
    ENSPM

Motion Picture
Society of Motion Picture and Television
    Engineers, SMPTE
Sveriges Biografägureförbund (Swedish
    Motion Picture Exhibitors Association),
    SBF

Motorola
Motorola Automatic Sequential
    Computer-Operated Tester, MASCOT

Mountain Plains
Mountain Plains Library Association, MPLA

Mounted Police
Royal Canadian Mounted Police, RCMP

Movement
Computerized Movement Planning and
    Status System, COMPASS

Movie
Computer-Assisted Movie Production,
    CAMP

Multiaction
Multiaction Computer, MAC

Multi-Aperture
Multi-Aperture Reluctance Switch, MARS

Multi-Aspect
Multi-Aspect Relevance Linkage
    Information System, MARLIS

Multilateral
Multilateral Disarmament Information
    Centre, MDIC

Multi-Phase
Automated Health Multi-Phase Screening,
    AHMS

Multiple
Continuous Multiple Access Collator,
    COMAC
Multiple Access Computer, MAC
Multiple Access Sequential Selection, MASS
Multiple Indexing and Console Retrieval
    Options, MICRO
Multiple Module Access, MMA
Multiple On-Line Programming, MOP

Multiple Use
Multiple Use MARC System, MUMS

Multiplex
Frequency Division Multiplex, FDM
Multiplex Message Processor, MMP

Multiplexer
Terminal-to-Computer Multiplexer, TCM

Multiplexor
Communication Multiplexor, CM

Multiplier-Quotient
Multiplier-Quotient Register, MQ

Multitype
ASCLA Multitype Library Cooperation
    Section, ASCLA/MLCS

Multivariate
Multivariate Analysis of Variance,
    MANOVA
Multivariate Statistical Analyzer, MSA

Munich
Zurich, Mainz, Munich, Darmstadt, ZMMD

Municipal
American Federation of State, County, and
    Municipal Employees, AFSCME
Kommunale Kinematografers Landsforbund
    (National Association of Municipal
    Cinemas in Norway), KKL
Society of Municipal and County Chief
    Librarians, SMCCL

Municipal Librarians
Kommunale Bibliotekarers Forening
    (Association of Municipal Librarians),
    KBF

Municipality Librarians
County and Regional Municipality
    Librarians, CARML

Museum
Association des Bibliothécaires, Archivistes,
    Documentalistes et Muséographes du
    Cameroun (Association of Librarians,
    Archivists, Documentalists and Museum
    Curators of Cameroon), ABADCAM
British Museum, BM
Columbus Museum of Arts and Crafts,
    CMAC
Museum and University Data, Program and
    Information Exchange, MUDPIE
Museum of Early Southern Decorative Arts,
    MESDA

Museums
Association Sénégalaise pour le
    Développement de la Documentation,
    des Bibliothèques, des Archives et des
    Musées (Senegal Association for the
    Development of Documentation,
    Libraries, Archives and Museums),
    ASDBAM
Information Retrieval Group of the Museums
    Association, IRGMA
Société Internationale des
    Bibliothèques–Musées des Arts du
    Spectacle (International Society of
    Libraries and Museums of the Theatre
    Arts), SIBMAS

Music
Afro-American Music Opportunities
    Association, AAMOA
British Catalogue of Music, BCM
Consejo Interamericano de Musica
    (Inter-American Music Council),
    CIDEM

Education Group of the Music Industries
    Association, EGMIA
Music Library Association, MLA
Music Publishers Association, MPA
Royal Academy of Music, RAM
Royal College of Music, RCM
Royal Scottish Academy of Music and
    Drama, RSAMD

Music Librarians
International Association of Music
    Librarians, Australia/New Zealand
    Branch, IAMLANZ

Music Libraries
Association Internationale des Bibliothèques
    Musicales/International Association of
    Music Libraries/Internationale
    Vereinigung der Musikbibliotheken,
    AIBM/IAML/IVMB
Canadian Association of Music
    Libraries/Association Canadienne des
    Bibliothèques Musicales,
    CAML/ACBM

Music Library
Americans for a Music Library in Israel,
    AMLI

Musicale
Répertoire International de Littérature
    Musicale, RILM

Mutual Benefit
City University Mutual Benefit Instructional
    Network, CUMBIN

Mutual of New York
Mutual of New York Library/Information
    Service, MONY

Múzeum
Ország Pedagógiai Konyvtár és Múzeum,
    OPKM

Mycology
Abstracts of Mycology, AM

Mystery
Mystery Writers of America, MWA

NAL
Cataloging and Indexing System of NAL,
    CAIN

NASA
Inter NASA Data Exchange, INDEX
NASA Library Network, NALNET
NASA Remote Control, NASA/RECON

NCR
NCR's Applied COBOL Packages, NAPAC

NYPL
Systems Analysis and Data Processing Office
of NYPL, SADPO

Nacional
Academia Nacional de Ciencias, ANC

Name
American Name Society, ANS
Chemical Abstracts Chemical Name
Dictionary, CHEMNAME

Names
Permanent Committee on Geographical
Names (for British Official Use), PCGN

Narrower Term
Narrower Term, NT

Nashville
Nashville University Center, NUC

National
Catalogage National Centralisé, CANAC
National Air Pollution Technical Information
System, NAPTIC
National Book Awards, NBA
National Geophysical Data Center, NGDC
National Oceanic and Atmospheric
Administration, NOAA
National Reprographic Centre for
Documentation, NRCd
Semi-Automatic Index of National
Language, SAINT
Standing Conference of National and
University Libraries, SCONUL
System of National Accounts/System of
Material Product Balances, SNA/MPS

National Affairs
Bureau of National Affairs, BNA

National Archives
Archivos General de la Nación (National
Archives), AGN

National Center
National Center for Child Abuse and
Neglect, NCCAN
National Center for Educational
Communication, NCEC
National Center for Educational Statistics,
NCES
National Center for Health Statistics, NCHS

National Libraries
Friends of the National Libraries, FNL
National Libraries Committee, NLC
National Libraries Task Force, NLTF

National Library
Biblioteca Nacional do Rio de Janeiro
(National Library of Rio de Janeiro),
BNRJ

Deutsche Bibliothek (National Library), DB
Narodna Biblioteka Kiril i Metodij (National
Library of Cyril and Methodius),
NBKM
National Agricultural Library, NAL
National Library for the Blind, NLB
National Library of Australia, NLA
National Library of Canada, NLC
National Library of Medicine, NLM
National Library of Nigeria, NLN
National Library of Scotland, NLS
Státni Ústav pro Zdravotnickou
Dokumentačm a Knihovnickou Sluzbu
(State Institute for Medical
Documentation and National Medical
Library), SUZDKS
Universitetsbiblioteket i Oslo (National and
University Library in Oslo), UB
[Wellington] National Library of New
Zealand, WN

National Opinion
National Opinion Research Center, NORC

National Union Catalog
National Union Catalog, NUC
*National Union Catalog of Manuscript
Collections*, NUCMC

National Union Catalogue
National Union Catalogue of Monographics,
NUCOM

Native American
Native American Rights Fund, NARF

Natural
Natural Unit of Information, NAT

Natural History
Natural History Information Retrieval
System, NHIR

Natural Science
Bibliotheca Borgoriensis (Central Library for
Natural Science), BB

Naval
American Society of Naval Engineers,
ASNE
Automated Naval Architecture, ANA
Naval Electronics Laboratory International
Algebraic Compiler, NELIAC
Naval Ordnance Test Station, NOTS
Naval Scientific and Technical Information
Centre, NSTIC
Society of Naval Architects and Marine
Engineers, SNAME

Navigation
Navigation Data Assimilation Computer,
NAVDAC

Navy
Joint Canadian Navy-Army-Air Force
    Specification, JCNAAF
Navy Automated Research and
    Development Information System,
    NARDIS
Navy Numerical Weather Prediction,
    NANWEP

Nebraska
Kansas–Nebraska Educational Consortium,
    KANEDCO
Nebraska Library Association, NLA

Nederlands
Nederlands Instituut voor Toegepast
    Huishoudkundig Onderzoek, NITHO

Nederlandse
Koninklijke Nederlandse Uitgeversbond,
    KNUB
Nederlandse Organisatie van Tijdschrift
    Uitgevers, NOTU
Nederlandse Vereniging van Journalisten,
    NVJ
Vereniging de Nederlandse Dagbladpers,
    NDP

Negative
Negative Acknowledge Character, NAK

Neglect
National Center for Child Abuse and
    Neglect, NCCAN

Neighborhood
Neighborhood Information Centers Project,
    NIC

Neo-Hellenic
Center for Neo-Hellenic Studies, CNHS

Netherlands
Buitenlandse Persvereniging in Nederland
    (Foreign Press Association in the
    Netherlands), BPV
Nederlands Instituut voor Audio Visuele
    Middlelen (Netherlands Institute for
    Audiovisual Media), NIAM
Nederlands Instituut voor Informatie,
    Documentatie en Registratuur
    (Netherlands Institute for Information,
    Documentatie and Filing), NIDER
Nederlandse Vereniging van
    Bedrijfsarchivarissen (Netherlands
    Association of Business Archivists),
    NVBA
Nederlandse Vereniging van
    Bibliothecarissen (Netherlands
    Association of Librarians), NVB
Nederlandse Vereniging van Lucht- en
    Ruimtevaarte-Publicisten (Netherlands
    Aerospace Writers Association), NVLP

Netherlands Association for Patent
    Information, WON
Netherlands Orgaan voor de Bevordering
    van de Informatieverzorging
    (Netherlands Organization for
    Information Policy), NOBIN
Rijksbureau voor Kunsthistorische
    Documentatie (Netherlands Institute for
    Art History Documentation), RKD

Network
African Integrated Network of
    Administrative Information, AINAI
Agricultural Libraries Information Network,
    AGLINET
Area Wide Library Network, AWLNET
Arizona Medical Library Network, AMLN
Associative Content Retrieval Network,
    ACORN
Australian Information Network, AUSINET
Bibliographic Exchange and
    Communications Network, BEACON
Bibliographic Network, BIBNET
Bicentennial Information Network, BINET
Business/Accounts Reporting Operating
    Network, BARON
Cancer Network, CANCERNET
Capital Consortium Network, CAPCON
Central Ohio Interlibrary Network, COIN
City University Mutual Benefit Instructional
    Network, CUMBIN
Cleveland Area Interloan Network, CAIN
College Libraries Activities Network in New
    South Wales, CLANN
Combat Logistics Network, COMLOGNET
Computer-Assisted Instruction Regional
    Education Network, CAI
Continuing Library Education Network,
    CLEN
Continuing Library Education Network and
    Exchange, CLENE
Drug Abuse Communications Network,
    DRACON
European Space Agency Network, ESANET
Flint Area Health Science Library Network,
    FAHSLN
Georgia Library Information Network,
    GLIN
Graphical Input for Network Analysis,
    GINA
Human Resources Network, HRN
Illinois Department of Mental Health and
    Developmental Disabilities Library
    Services Network, DMHDD/LISN
International Network of Emerging
    Libraries, INEL
Language Information Network and
    Clearinghouse System, LINCS
Libraries of Orange County Network,
    LOCNET
Library Network Analysis Theory, LIBNAT

Network (cont.)

Midwest Health Science Library Network,
MHSLN
Network for Continuing Medical Education,
NCME
Network Management Information System,
NEMIS
New York State Interlibrary Loan Network,
NYSILL
On-Line Retrieval of Information over a
Network, ORION
Public Library Automation Network, PLAN
Red de Información Socio-Económica
(Network for Socio-Economic
Information), REDINSE
SUNY Biomedical Communication
Network, SUNY-BCN
Scheduling and Control by Automated
Network System, SCANS
Southern California Answering Network,
SCAN
Southern California Interlibrary Loan
Network, SCILL
TWX Interlibrary Loan Network, TWXILL
Telecommunications Library Information
Network, TALINET
Toxicology Information Conversational
On-Line Network, TOXICON
Transportation Research Information
Services Network, TRISNET
Women's Educational Equity
Communications Network, WEECN
World Wide Network of Standard
Seismograph Stations, WWNSS
Xerox Information Exchange Network, IEN

Networking

Hierarchical Environmental Retrieval for
Management Access and Networking,
HERMAN

Networks

ASIS Special Interest Group on Library
Automation and Networks,
ASIS/SIG/LAN
Computer Analysis of Networks with Design
Orientation, CANDO
FID Committee on Theory, Methods, and
Operations of Information Systems and
Networks, FID/TMO
Lowell Area Council on Interlibrary
Networks, LACOIN

Neurological

National Institute of Neurological Diseases
and Stroke, NINDS
Neurological Science Information Network,
NINDS

Neutron

Neutron Data Compilation Center, CCDN

Nevada

Nevada Association of School Librarians,
NASL
Nevada Library Association, NLA
Public Library Association of
Nevada–Nevada Association of Library
Trustees, PLAN-NALT

Nevada Center

Nevada Center for Cooperative Library
Services, NCCLS

New England

New England Board of Higher Education,
NEBHE
New England Deposit Library, Inc, NEDL
New England Document Conservation
Center, NEDCC
New England Educational Data System,
NEEDS
New England Interinstitutional Research
Council, NEIRC
New England Library Association, NELA
New England Library Board, NELB
New England Library Information Network,
NELINET
New England Regional Computing Program,
Inc, NERCOMP
New England Regional Medical Library
Service, NERMLS
New England Research Application Center,
NERAC
New England School Library Association,
NESLA

New Guinea

School Library Association of Papua, New
Guinea, SLAPNG

New Hampshire

New Hampshire College and University
Council, NHCUC
New Hampshire Library Association,
NHLA
New Hampshire Library Council, NHLC

New Jersey

Medical Resources Consortium of Central
New Jersey, MEDCORE
New Jersey Library Association, NJLA

New Mexico

Coordinated Library System of New
Mexico, CLS
New Mexico Information System,
NEMISYS
New Mexico Library Association, NMLA
Texas, Arkansas, Louisiana, Oklahoma and
New Mexico, TALON

New South Wales
College Libraries Activities Network in New South Wales, CLANN
New South Wales Public Library, NPL

New York
Central New York Library Resources Council, CENTRO
City University of New York, CUNY
Library Association of the City University of New York, LACUNY
Medical Library Center of New York, MLCNY
New York Academy of Sciences, NYAS
New York Assembly Program, NYAP
New York Astronomical Corporation, NYAC
New York Library Association, NYLA
New York Library Instruction Clearinghouse, NYLIC
New York Mathematical Society, NYMS
New York Metropolitan Reference and Research Library Agency, METRO
New York Public Library, NYPL
New York State Interlibrary Loan Network, NYSILL
New York State Library, NYSL
New York State Special Education Instructional Materials Center, SEIMC
Printing Industries of Metropolitan New York, PIMNY
Southeastern New York Library Resources Council, SENYLRC
State University of New York, SUNY
State University of New York Librarians Association, SUNYLA
Western New York Health Sciences Librarians, WNYHSL
Western New York Library Resources Council, WNYLRC

New York Libraries
Association of New York Libraries for Technical Services, ANYLTS

New Zealand
ARLIS Australia New Zealand, ARLIS/ANZ
Australian and New Zealand Association for the Advancement of Science, ANZAAS
Bibliographical Society of Australia and New Zealand, BSANZ
International Association of Music Librarians, Australia/New Zealand Branch, IAMLANZ
New Zealand Library Association, NZLA
Standards Association of New Zealand, SANZ
[Wellington] National Library of New Zealand, WN

Newark
Council for Higher Education in Newark, CHEN

Newfoundland
Newfoundland Library Association, NLA
West Newfoundland Library Association, WNLA

New-Line
New-Line, NL

Newman
Bolt, Beranek and Newman, Inc, BBN

News
Independent Television News, Ltd, ITN
Pest Articles and News Summaries. (Journal), PANS
Pharmaceutical News Index, PNI

News Clipping
Automated News Clipping, Indexing, and Retrieval System, ANCIRS

Newsagents
National Federation of Retail Newsagents, Booksellers and Stationers, NFRN

Newsletter
A Very Informal Newsletter on Library Automation, VINE

Newspaper
American Newspaper Publishers Association, ANPA
International Association of Wholesale Newspaper, Periodical and Book Distributors, DISTRIPRESS
Newspaper Conference, NC
Newspaper Publishers Association Ltd, NPA
Schweizerischer Zeitungsverleger-Verband/Association Suisse des Éditeurs de Journaux/Associazione Svizzera degli Editori di Giornale (Swiss Newspaper Publishers Association), SZV/ASEJ/ASEG
Scottish Daily Newspaper Society, SDNS
Scottish Newspaper Proprietors Association, SNPA
Weekly Newspaper Advertising Bureau, WNAB

Newspapermen
Young Newspapermen's Association, YNA

Newspapers
Guild of British Newspapers Editors, GBNE
Maps, Microtexts, and Newspapers, MMN
Newspapers on Microfilm, NOM
Sunday Newspapers Distributing Association, SNDA

Nicaragua
Asociación de Bibliotecas Universitarias y
    Especializadas de Nicaragua
    (Association of University and Special
    Libraries of Nicaragua), ABUEN

Nicaraguan
Asociación Nicaragüense de Bibliotecarios
    (Nicaraguan Library Association),
    ASNIBI

Nigeria
East Central State School Libraries
    Association (Nigeria), ECSLA
National Library of Nigeria, NLN

Nigerian
Nigerian Library Association, NLA

Nomenclature
Symbols, Units, Nomenclature, SUN
Systematized Nomenclature of Pathology,
    SNOP

Nondestructive
American Society for Nondestructive
    Testing, ASNT
Nondestructive Read, NDR
Nondestructive Read-Out, NDRO
Non-Destructive Testing Information
    Analysis Center, NTIAC
Society for Nondestructive Testing, SNT

Non-Interactive
Non-Interactive Computer Applications,
    NICA

Nonpolarized
Return-to-Zero (Nonpolarized), RZ(NP)

Nonprint
Nonprint Code, NP

Non-Print Material
ASIS Special Interest Group on Non-Print
    Material, ASIS/SIG/NPM

Non-Professional
Washington Non-Professional Library
    Association, WNPLA

Non-Return-to-Zero
Non-Return-to-Zero, NRZ
Non-Return-to-Zero Change Recording,
    NRZC
Non-Return-to-Zero Mark Recording,
    NRZM

Non-theatrical
Allied Non-theatrical Film Association,
    ANFA

Normalisation
Association Française de Normalisation,
    AFNOR

Normes et Reglementation
Normes et Reglementation–Information
    Automatisée, NORIA

Norske
Den Norske Fagpresses Forening, DNFF

Norske Aviers Landsforbund
Norske Aviers Landsforbund, NAL

North America
ARLIS North America, ARLIS/NA
Arctic Institute of North America, AINA
Blackwell/North America, Inc, BNA
Dictionary Society of North America, DSNA
Esperanto League for North America, Inc,
    ELNA
*Ethnographic Bibliography of North
    America*, EBNA
Middle East Studies Association of North
    America, MESA
Radiological Society of North America,
    RSNA

North American
North American Radio Archives Library,
    NARA
North American Telephone Association,
    NATA

North Carolina
North Carolina Library Association, NCLA

North Dakota
North Dakota Library Association, NDLA

Northwest Library
Northwest Library District, NORWELD

Northwestern
Northwestern On-Line Totally Integrated
    System, NOTIS

Norway
Kommunale Kinematografers Landsforbund
    (National Association of Municipal
    Cinemas in Norway), KKL

Norwegian
Norges Tekniske Høgskole (Library of the
    Norwegian Institute of Technology),
    NTH
Norsk Bibliotekarlag (Association of
    Norwegian Public Librarians), NBL
Norsk Bibliotekforening (Norwegian Library
    Association), NBF
Norsk Journalistlag (Norwegian Union of
    Journalists), NJ
Norsk Presseforbund (Norwegian Press
    Association), NP
Norske Forskningebibliotekarers Forening
    (Association of Norwegian Research
    Librarians), NFF
Norwegian MARC, NORMARC

Not AND
Not AND, NAND

Not Available
Not Available, NA

Not Or
Not Or, NOR

Notation
Wiswesser Line Notation, WLN

Nottingham
Nottingham and Nottinghamshire Technical Information Service, NANTIS

Noukowo
Centralny Instytut Informasui Noukowo Techniceneu I Economicznej (Central Institute for Scientific, Technical and Economic Information), CLINTE

Nouveau-Brunswick
Conseil Pédagogique Provincial des Bibliothèques Scolaires Nouveau-Brunswick, CPPBS

Nova Scotia
Nova Scotia Library Association, NSLA
Nova Scotia School Library Association, NSSLA

Novelists
Poets, Playwrights, Editors, Essayists and Novelists International English Centre, PEN
Romantic Novelists Association, RNA

Noyes
Noyes Data Corporation, NDC

Nuclear
American Nuclear Society, ANS
Carbon-13 Nuclear Magnetic Resonance, CNMR
Centre Européene pour la Recherche Nucléaire (European Center for Nuclear Research), CERN
DOD Nuclear Information and Analysis Center, DASIAC
Defense Nuclear Agency, DNA
European Nuclear Documentation System, ENDS
European-American Nuclear Data Committee, EANDC
International Nuclear Information System, INIS
National Institute for Research in Nuclear Science, NIRNS
Nuclear Science Abstracts, NSA

Nuclear Energy
European Nuclear Energy Agency, ENEA

Nuclear Energy Trade Association Conference, NETAC

Nuclear Safety
Nuclear Safety Information Center, NSIC

Nuclear Science
Retrieval of Special Portions from *Nuclear Science Abstracts*, RESPONSA

Null
Null Character, NUL

Number
European Article Number, EAN
Piece Identification Number, PIN
Social Security Account Number, SSAN
Standard Serial Number, SSN
Standard Technical Report Number, STRN

Numeric
Spoken Language Universal Numeric Translation, SLUNT
Texas Numeric Register, TNR

Numerical
ACM Special Interest Group on Numerical Mathematics, ACM/SIGNUM
ASIS Special Interest Group on Numerical Data Bases, ASIS/SIG/NDB
Electronic Numerical Integrator and Calculator, ENIAC
Louisiana Numerical Register, LNR
Navy Numerical Weather Prediction, NANWEP
Numerical Control Society, NCS

Numerical Data
Center for Information and Numerical Data Analysis and Synthesis, CINDAS

Nurses
Manitoba Association of Registered Nurses, MARN
Order of Nurses of Quebec, ONQ

Nursing
Cumulative Index to Nursing Literature, CINL
Interagency Council on Library Tools for Nursing, ICLTN
Libraries for Nursing Consortium, LINC
Royal College of Nursing and National Council of Nursing, RCN

Nutricion
Instituto de Nutricion de Centro America y Panama, INCAP

OAS/OEA
Instituto Interamericano de Ciencias Agrícolas de la OEA (Interamerican Institute of Agricultural Sciences of OAS/OEA), IICA

ORACLE
ORACLE Binary Internal Translator,
ORBIT

ORSTOM
ORSTOM Pedology Data Bank, POSEIDON

Oak Ridge
Oak Ridge Associated Universities, ORAU
Oak Ridge Chemical Information System,
ORCHIS
Oak Ridge National Laboratory, ORNL

Objectives
Management by Objectives, MBO
Management by Objectives and Results,
MBO/R

Observation
Earth Resources Observation System, EROS

Obstetricians
Royal College of Obstetricians and
Gynaecologists, RCOG

Occupational
Comprehensive Occupational Data Analysis
Program, CODAP
National Institute for Occupational Safety
and Health, NIOSH
Occupational Safety and Health
Administration, OSHA

Ocean
Integrated Global Ocean Stations System,
IGOSS
International Decade of Ocean Exploration,
IDOE

Oceanic
National Oceanic and Atmospheric
Administration, NOAA
Oceanic and Atmospheric Scientific
Information System, OASIS

Oceanographic
Intergovernmental Oceanographic
Commission, IOC
National Oceanographic Data Center,
NODC

Oceanography
Intergovernmental Commission on
Oceanography, ICO

Océans
Centre National pour l'Exploitation des
Océans, CNEXO

Octal
Binary Coded Octal, BCO
Octal Program Updating System, OPUS

Offender
Offender Base Transaction Statistical
System, OBTS
Offender Status Register, OSR

Office
Air Force Office of Scientific Research,
AFOSR
Automatic Data Processing Equipment
Selection Office, ADPESO
British Commonwealth Scientific Office,
BCSO
Central Air Documents Office, CADO
Central Office of Information, COI
Federal Office Systems Expo, FOSE
Foreign and Commonwealth Office, FAO
General Accounting Office, GAO
Government Printing Office, GPO
Her/His Majesty's Stationery Office, HMSO
Information Systems Office, ISO
International Relations Office, IRO
MARC Development Office, MDO
Office Belge du Commerce Exterieur, OBCE
Office de la Recherche Scientifique et
Technique d'Outre-Mer (Office of
Overseas Scientific and Technical
Research), ORSTOM
Office Document Index, ODI
Office du Livre Malagasy (Malagasy Book
Office), OLM
Office Equipment Manufacturers Institute,
OEMI
Office for Intellectual Freedom, OIF
Office for Library Service to the
Disadvantaged, OLSD
Office for Research, OFR
Office for Scientific and Technical
Information, OSTI
Office Furniture Manufacturers Institute,
OFMI
Office of Audiovisual Educational
Development, OAED
Office of Computer and Communications
Systems, OCCS
Office of Computer Information, OCI
Office of Criminal Justice Plans and
Analysis, OCJPA
Office of Critical Tables, OCT
Office of Libraries and Learning Resources,
OLLR
Office of Library Development Program,
OLDP
Office of Library Personnel Resources,
OLPR
Office of Management and Budget, OMB
Office of Management Studies, OMS
Office of Public Information, OPI
Office of Public Libraries and Interlibrary
Cooperation, OPLIC
Office of Science and Technology, OST

Office of Standard Reference Data, OSRD
Office of Technical Services, OTS
Public Record Office, PRO
Specialized Office for Materials Distribution, SOMD
Systems Analysis and Data Processing Office of NYPL, SADPO
Technical Processes Research Office, TPR
United States Office of Education, USOE
Ústředí Vědeckých Technických a Ekonomických Informací (Central Office of Scientific, Technical and Economic Information), UVTEI

Officer
Division Liaison Officer, DLO

Officers
Chief Officers of State Library Agencies, COSLA
Committee for International Cooperation in Information Retrieval among Examining Patent Officers, CICIREPATO

Offices
International Cooperation in Information Retrieval among Examining Patent Offices, ICIREPAT

Official
Official Gazette. (Journal), OG

Officials
American Society of Planning Officials, ASPO

Officials Library
National Association of Housing and Redevelopment Officials Library, NAHRO

Off-Line
Off-Line Operating Simulator, OOPS

Ohio
Area Library Service Organizations of Ohio, ALSO
Art Research Libraries of Ohio, ARLO
Central Ohio Chapter of ASIS, CO-ASIS
Central Ohio Interlibrary Network, COIN
Columbus Area Library and Information Council of Ohio, CALICO
Kentucky, Ohio, Michigan Regional Medical Library, KOMRML
Mideastern Ohio Library Organization, MOLO
Northeast Ohio Library Teletype Network, NOLTN
Northeastern Ohio Library Association, NOLA
Northern Ohio Chapter of ASIS, NORASIS
Ohio Chapter of ASIS, OASIS
Ohio College Library Center, Inc, OCLC

Ohio Educational Library Media Association, OELMA
Ohio Library Association, OLA
Ohio Project for Research in Information Services, OPRIS
Ohio Valley Area Libraries, OVAL
Southeastern Ohio Library Organization, SOLO
Southern Ohio Chapter of ASIS, SOASIS
Southwestern Ohio Regional Computer Center, SWORCC
Southwestern Ohio Rural Libraries, SWORL
Western Ohio Regional Library Development System, WORLDS

Oil
American Oil Chemists Society, AOCS
Centrul de Documentare al Industriei Chimice si Petroliere (Documentation Center of the Chemical and Oil Industry), CDICIP

Oklahoma
Oklahoma Environmental Information and Media Center, OEIMC
Oklahoma Library Association, OLA
Oklahoma Teletype Interlibrary System, OTIS
Texas, Arkansas, Louisiana, Oklahoma and New Mexico, TALON

Old Students
Librarianship and Archives Old Students Association, LAOSA

On-line
ASIS Special Interest Group on User On-line Interaction, ASIS/SIG/UOI
Agricultural On-Line Access, AGRICOLA
Archives On-line, ARCHON
Audiovisual Online, AVLINE
Automatic Digital On-line Instrumentation System, ADONIS
Automatic Direct Access to Information with On-line UDC System, AUDACIOUS
Bibliographic On-Line Display, BOLD
Bioethics Online, BIOETHICSLINE
Booth Library On-Line Circulation, BLOC
Browsing On-Line with Selective Retrieval, BROWSER
Canadian On-Line Enquiry, CAN/OLE
Cancer Online, CANCERLINE
Cataloging On-Line, CATLINE
Chemical Dictionary On-Line, CHEMLINE
Comprehensive University of Dayton On-Line Information Services, CUDOS
Computer On-Line Real-Time Applications Language, CORAL
Disk On-Line Accounts Receivable System, DOLARS
[Energy Online], ENERGYLINE

On-line (cont.)

[Environment Information On-Line], ENVIROLINE
[Epilepsy On-Line], EPILEPSYLINE
An Evolutionary System for On-line Processing, AESOP
File Room Online Information Control, FROLIC
History of Medicine Online, HISTLINE
Library On-Line Acquisitions, LOLA
Library On-Line Information and Text Access, LOLITA
Managerial On-Line Data System, MOLDS
Multiple On-Line Programming, MOP
Northwestern On-Line Totally Integrated System, NOTIS
On-Line Operation, OLO
On-Line Real Time, OLRT
On-Line, Real-Time, Branch Information, ORBIT
On-Line Retrieval of Information over a Network, ORION
Retrieval by On-Line Search, ROSE
Rome Air Development Center On-Line, RADCOL
SAMI On-Line Operations, SOLO
Serials On-Line, SERLINE
Subject Content-Oriented Retriever for Processing Information Online, SCORPIO
Time-Shared Reactive On-Line Lab, TROLL/I
Toxicology Information Conversational On-Line Network, TOXICON
Toxicology Information On-Line, TOXLINE

Ontario

Administrators of Medium Public Libraries of Ontario, AMPLO
Art Gallery of Ontario, AGO
Association of Academic Librarians of Ontario, AALO
Council of Ontario Universities, COU
Directors of Ontario Regional Library Systems/Directeurs des Bibliothèques Régionales de l'Ontario, DORLS/DBRO
Educational Television Branch of Ontario, ETVO
Institute of Professional Librarians of Ontario, IPLO
Northwestern Ontario Library Action Group, NOLAG
Ontario Association of College and University Libraries, OACUL
Ontario Association of Library Technicians/Association des Bibliotechniciens de l'Ontario, OALT/ABO
Ontario Committee of Deans and Directors of Library Schools, OCDDLS

Ontario Council of University Libraries, OCUL
Ontario Educational Communications Authority, OECA
Ontario Library Association, OLA
Ontario Library Trustees Association, OLTA
Ontario Medical Association, OMA
Ontario Provincial Library Council, OPLC
Ontario Public Librarians Advisory Committee, OPLAC
Ontario Public Library Association, OPLA
Ontario Puppetry Association, Ltd, OPAL
Ontario School Library Association, OSLA
Ontario Universities Bibliographic Centre Project, OUBCP
Ontario Universities Library Cooperative System, OULCS

Open

Open Access Satellite Education Services, OASES

Open-Shop

Johnniac Open-Shop System, JOSS

Operating

ACM Special Interest Group on Operating Systems, ACM/SIGOPS
Automatic Operating and Scheduling Program, AOSP
Automatic Operating System, AUTOPSY
Basic Operating System, BOS
Business/Accounts Reporting Operating Network, BARON
Disk Operating System, DOS
General Comprehensive Operating Supervisor, GECOS
Off-Line Operating Simulator, OOPS
Operating Budget, OPBU
Operating System, OS
Share Operating System, SOS
Simultaneous Processing Operating System, SIPROS
Standard Operating Procedure, SOP
Tape Operating System, TOS
Total Hospital Operating and Medical Information System, THOMIS

Operating System

Comprehensive Language for Elegant Operating System and Translator Design, CLEOPATRA

Operation

Communication and Data Processing Operation, CADPO
Communication and Data Processing Operation System, CADPOS
Dictionary Operation and Control for Thesaurus Organization, DOCTOR
Machine Operation, MO

Minimum Slack Time per Operation,
    MINSOP
On-Line Operation, OLO
Operation Research Society, ORS
System to Coordinate the Operation of
    Peripheral Equipment, SCOPE

Operational
Boeing Operational Supervisory System,
    BOSS
Completely Automatic Operational System,
    CAOS
Operational Assistance and Instructive Data
    Equipment, OAIDE
Pupil Registering and Operational Filing,
    PROF
Regional Operational Data, ROD

Operations
Evolutionary Operations, EVOP
FID Committee on Theory, Methods, and
    Operations of Information Systems and
    Networks, FID/TMO
Operations Analysis, OA
Operations per Minute, OPM
Operations Research, OR
Operations Research, Inc, ORI
Operations Research Society of America,
    ORSA
Operations Research/Systems Analysis,
    OR/SA
Programmed Logic for Automatic Teaching
    Operations, PLATO
SAMI On-Line Operations, SOLO
System Ordinary Life Operations, SOLO
Technical Environmental and Management
    Planning Operations, TEMPO

Operator
Console Operator Proficiency Examination,
    COPE
General Operator Computer Interaction,
    GOCI
Key Punch Operator, KPO

Operators
Chemical Information Systems Operators,
    CHEOPS
System Programmed Operators, SYSPOP
Veteran Wireless Operators Association,
    VWOA

Opinion
European Society for Opinion Surveys and
    Market Research, ESOMAR

Opinion Publique
Institut Français d'Opinion Publique, IFOP

Opportunity
Survey of Economic Opportunity, SEO

Optical
Computer-Aided Design Optical Character
    Recognition, CADOCR
Digital Optical Projection System, DOPS
Film Optical Sensing Device for Input to
    Computers, FOSDIC
Optical Character Reader, OCR
Optical Character Recognition, OCR
Optical Scanning, OS
Optical Scanning Device, OSD
Optical Society of America, Inc, OSA

Optics
Projection by Reflection Optics of
    Xerographic Images, PROXI

Optimization
Computer Optimization Package, COP

Optimizing
Royal Optimizing Assembly Routing, ROAR

Optimum
Symbolic Optimum Assembly Programming,
    SOAP

Option
Time-Sharing Option, TSO

Optional
Tape Handling Optional Routines, THOR

Options
Clearinghouse for Options in Children's
    Education, CHOICE

Optometric
American Optometric Association, AOA

Oral
Hansard Oral Questions, HOQ

Orale
Hansard Questions Orale, HQO

Orange County
Libraries of Orange County Network,
    LOCNET

Order
Book Order and Selection, BOS
Customer Must Order Direct, CMOD
Direct Order Recording and Invoicing
    System, DORIS
Order of Nurses of Quebec, ONQ

Ordering
Aldermaston Mechanized Cataloging and
    Ordering System, AMCOS

Ordering Plan
Single-Copy Ordering Plan, SCOP

Ordinary Life
System Ordinary Life Operations, SOLO

Ordnance
American Ordnance Association, AOA
Naval Ordnance Test Station, NOTS

Oregon
Associated Christian Colleges of Oregon,
ACCO
Oregon Library Association, OLA
Oregon Total Information System, OTIS

Organisatie
Nederlandse Organisatie van Tijdschrift
Uitgevers, NOTU

Organisation
International Labour Organisation, ILO

Organismo
Organismo Internacional Regional de Sanid
Agroprecuaria, OIRSA

Organization
Aerial Phenomena Research Organization,
APRO
British Columbia Organization of Library
Technicians, BOLT
Committee on Organization, COO
Commonwealth Scientific and Industrial
Research Organization, CSIRO
Data Base Organization and Management
Processor, DBOMP
Dictionary Operation and Control for
Thesaurus Organization, DOCTOR
East African Agriculture and Forestry
Research Organization, EAAFRO
Egyptian Organization for Standardization,
EOS
European Space Research Organization,
ESRO
Food and Agriculture Organization, FAO
Historical Evaluation and Research
Organization, HERO
Human Resources Research Organization,
HUMRRO
International Civil Aviation Organization,
ICAO
International Fortean Organization, INFO
International Organization for
Standardization, IOS
International Organization of Journalists,
IOJ
International Reference Organization in
Forensic Medicine and Sciences,
INFORM
International Standards Organization, ISO
Iraqi Organization for Standards, IOS
National Buildings Organization, NBO
Netherlands Orgaan voor de Bevordering
van de Informatieverzorging
(Netherlands Organization for
Information Policy), NOBIN

Organization for Economic Cooperation and
Development, OECD
Organization for European Economic
Cooperation, OEEC
Organization of American States, OAS
Pan American Health Organization, PAHO
Sheffield Interchange Organization, SINTO
Southeast Asia Treaty Organization, SEATO
Staff Organization Round Table, SORT
Subject Analysis and Organization of Library
Materials Committee, SAOLM
Sudanese Organization for Standard
Specifications, SOSS
United Nations Educational, Scientific and
Cultural Organization, UNESCO
United Nations Industrial Development
Organization, UNIDO
United States Committee for the World
Health Organization, USC-WHO
Western Interstate Library Coordinating
Organization, WILCO
World Health Organization, WHO
World Intellectual Property Organization,
WIPO
World Meteorological Organization, WMO

Organizations
American Federation of Labor and Congress
of Industrial Organizations, AFL-CIO
Area Library Service Organizations of Ohio,
ALSO
Associated Organizations of Teachers of
English, AOTE
Association of State Colleges and
Universities Forestry Research
Organizations, ASCUFRO
Coordinating Council of Library
Organizations, CCLO
Council for International Organizations on
Medical Sciences, CIOMS
Council of Organizations Serving the Deaf,
COSD
Federatie van Organisaties op het Gebied
van Bibliotheek, Informatie en
Dokumentatiewezen (Federation of
Organizations in Library, Information
and Documentation Science), FOBID
Federation of European-American
Organizations, FEAO
World Federation of Engineering
Organizations, WFEO

Orientalist Librarians
International Association of Orientalist
Librarians, IAOL

Orientation
Computer Analysis of Networks with Design
Orientation, CANDO

Original
Original Data File, ODF

Országo Pedagógiai Konyvtár
Országo Pedagógiai Konyvtár és Múzeum,
OPKM

Oscillogram
Oscillogram Trace Reader, OTRAC

Oscilloscope
Cathode-Ray Oscilloscope, CRO

Oslo
Universitetsbiblioteket i Oslo (National and
University Library in Oslo), UB

Österreich
Verband de Agrarjournalisten in Österreich,
VAÖ

Osterreichische
Osterreichische Studiengesellschaft für
Atomenergie, GmbH, OSGAE

Österreichischer
Verband Österreichischer
Zeitungsherausgeber und
Zeitungsverleger, VÖZ

Ottawa
Library Association of Ottawa/Association
des Bibliothèques d'Ottawa, LAO/ABO

Out of Print
Out of Print, op

Out of Stock
Out of Stock, os
Out of Stock Indefinitely, osi

Output
Computer Output Microfilm, COM
Computer Output Microfilm Package,
COMPAC
Computer Output Microfilmer, COM
Computer Output Microfilming, COM
Computer Output Microforms Program and
Concept Study, COMPACS
Datascope Computer Output Microfilmer,
DACOM
Digital Data Output Conversion Equipment,
DDOCE
Manual Output, MO
Output to Display Buffer, ODB
Output Translator, OUTRAN

Outputs
Digital Data, Auxiliary Storage, Track
Display, Outputs, and Radar Display,
DATOR

Ouvrages Étrangers
Catalogue Collectif des Ouvrages Étrangers,
CCOE

Overseas
Center for Educational Development
Overseas, CEDO
Centre for Curriculum Renewal and
Educational Development Overseas,
CREDO
Centre for Educational Television Overseas,
CETO
Overseas Booksellers Clearing House,
OBCH
Overseas Press and Media Association, Ltd,
OPMA
Overseas Press Club of America, Inc, OPC
Overseas Technical Information Unit, OTIU
Overseas Visual Aids Centre, OVAC
Voluntary Overseas Library Service, VOLS

Overview
(Predicasts Overview of Markets and
Technology) (Journal), PROMT

Oxford
Oxford English Dictionary, OED
Oxford University Press, OUP

PERT
Easy PERT, EZPERT
PERT/Cost, PERT/COST
PERT/Timing, PERT/TIME

Pacific
Asia/Pacific Forecasting Study, APFS
Economic and Social Commission for Asia
and the Pacific, ESCAP
Health Information Network of the Pacific,
HINOP
Pacific Area Union List of Medical Serials,
PAULMS
Pacific Northwest Bibliographic Center,
PNBC
Pacific Northwest Library Association,
PNLA
Pacific Northwest Regional Health Science
Library, PNRHSL

Pacific Coast
Pacific Coast Forest Research Information
Network, PACFORNET
Pacific Coast Independent Magazine
Wholesalers Association, PACIMWA

Pacific Southwest
Pacific Southwest Regional Medical Library
Service, PSRMLS

Package
Apollo Lunar Surface Experimental
Package, ALSEP
Computer Optimization Package, COP
Computer Output Microfilm Package,
COMPAC
Floating-point Arithmetic Package, FAP

Package (cont.)

Input/Output Package, IOPKG
Single Precision Unpacked Rounded
Floating-Point Package, SPUR
Statistical Package for the Social Sciences,
SPSS

Packaging
National Institute of Packaging, Handling
and Logistics Engineers, NIPHLE

Packets
Packets of Educational Topics, PET

Page
Receive Only Page Printer, ROPP

Painter-Etchers
Royal Society of Painter-Etchers and
Engravers, RE

Paisley
Paisley and District Technical Information
Group, PADTIG

Pakistan
Pakistan Association of Special Libraries,
PASLIB
Pakistan Library Association, PLA
Pakistan National Scientific and Technical
Documentation Center, PANSDOC
Pakistan Scientific and Technological
Information Center, PASTIC
Pakistan Standards Institute, PSI

Paleontologic Information
Joint Committee on Paleontologic
Information, JCPI

Pan American
Pan American Health Organization, PAHO

Panama
Instituto de Nutricion de Centro America y
Panama, INCAP

Panellinios Organosis
Panellinios Organosis Kinimatographikon
Epicheirision, POKE

Pan-Pacific
Pan-Pacific Education and Communication
Experiments by Satellite, PEACESAT

Paper
*Abstract Bulletin of the Institute of Paper
Chemistry*, ABIPC
American Paper Institute, API
American Pulp and Paper Association,
APPA
Canadian International Paper Company, CIP
Literature Retrieval System for the Pulp and
Paper Industry, LIRES

Pulp and Paper Research Institute of
Canada/Information Retrieval Services,
PAPRICAN/IRS
Pulp, Paper and Paperboard Institute, PPPI
Technical Association of the Pulp and Paper
Industry, TAPPI

Paper Tape
Paper Tape Transmission 8, PTT/8

Paperback
Magazine and Paperback Marketing
Institute, MPMI

Paperboard
National Paperboard Association, NPA
Pulp, Paper and Paperboard Institute, PPPI

Paperbound
Paperbound Books in Print, PBP

Papers
Conference Papers Index, CPI
Consolidated Papers, Inc, CPI
Current Papers in Physics. (Journal), CPIP
Index of Mathematical Papers. (Journal),
IMP

Paraguayan Librarians
Asociación de Bibliotecarios de Paraguay
(Paraguayan Librarians Association),
ABIPAR

Paralysed
Committee for Writing and Reading Aids for
the Paralysed, WRAP

Paris
American Library in Paris, ALP

Parish
CLA Parish and Community Libraries
Section, CLA/PCLS

Parliamentary Librarians
Association of Parliamentary Librarians in
Canada, APLIC

Partnership
Man-Machine Partnership Translation,
MMPT

Parts
Parts Data Processing System, PDPS

Patent
American Patent Law Association, APLA
Committee for International Cooperation in
Information Retrieval among Examining
Patent Officers, CICIREPATO
Committee of National Institutes of Patent
Agents, CNIPA
*Computer Information Library Patent
Abstracts*. (Journal), C/I/L

International Cooperation in Information
    Retrieval among Examining Patent
    Offices, ICIREPAT
International Patent Documentation Center,
    INPADOC
Patent Cooperation Treaty, PCT

Patent Information
Netherlands Association for Patent
    Information, WON
Patent Information Retrieval System,
    MIS-IRPAT

Patent Library
Patent Office Library, POL

Patent Office
Patent Office Classification System, POCS

Patents
API Abstracts/Patents, APIPAT
Polymer Science and Technology for
    Patents, POST-P

Pathology
Intersociety Committee on Pathology
    Information, ICPI
Systematized Nomenclature of Pathology,
    SNOP

Patient
Computer-Aided Patient Management,
    CAPM

Patrons
Library Exchange Aids Patrons Project,
    LEAP

Pattern
Pattern Articulation Unit, PAU

Pavements
Pavements and Soil Trafficability
    Information Analysis Center, PSTIAC

Peace
Computer People for Peace, CPP
Stockholm International Peace Research
    Institute, SIPRI

Peat, Marwick
Peat, Marwick, Mitchell & Co, PMM & Co.

Pecuaria
Centro de Información Pecuaria, CIP

Pedology
ORSTOM Pedology Data Bank, POSEIDON

Peel
Peel Secondary School Librarians
    Association, PSSLA

Penale
Giurisprudenza Penale, PENALE

Pennsylvania
Area College Library Cooperative Program
    of Central Pennsylvania, ACLCP
Central Pennsylvania Consortium, CPC
East Central Pennsylvania Council on
    Interlibrary Cooperation, EPIC
Film Library Intercollege Cooperative of
    Pennsylvania, FLIC
Interlibrary Delivery Service of
    Pennsylvania, IDS
Pennsylvania Area Library Network,
    PALINET
Pennsylvania Library Association, PLA
Pennsylvania Technical Assistance Program,
    PENNTAP

People
Computer People for Peace, CPP
Documents to the People. (Journal), DttP

Perceiver
Elementary Perceiver and Memorizer,
    EPAM

Performance
Federal Computer Performance Evaluation
    and Simulation Center, FEDSIM
National Society for Performance and
    Instruction, NSPI
Random Access Correlation for Extended
    Performance, RACEP

Periodica
Unione della Stampa Periodica Italiana,
    USPI

Periodical
Catholic Periodical and Literature Index,
    CPLI
Council for Periodical Distributors
    Associations, CPDA
Criminal Justice Periodical Index. (Journal),
    CJPI
Fédération Internationale de la Presse
    Periodique (International Federation of
    the Periodical Press), FIPP
Index to Religious Periodical Literature,
    IRPL
International Association of Wholesale
    Newspaper, Periodical and Book
    Distributors, DISTRIPRESS
International Periodical Distributors
    Association, IPDA
Mid-America Periodical Distributors
    Association, MAPDA
Periodical and Book Association of America,
    PBAA
Periodical Holdings in the Library of the
    School of Medicine, PHILSOM
Periodical Publishers Association, Ltd, PPA
Readers Guide to Periodical Literature.
    (Index), RGPL

Royal Dutch Pharmaceutical Society,
KNMP

Pharmacists
American Society of Hospital Pharmacists,
ASHP

Pharmaco-Medical
*Current Contents/Chemical,
Pharmaco-Medical and Life Sciences.*
(Journal), CC/CPML
Pharmaco-Medical Documentation, PMD

Pharmacopoeia
British Pharmacopoeia, BP
United States Pharmacopoeia, USP

Phenomena
Aerial Phenomena Research Organization,
APRO

Philadelphia
Philadelphia's Adult Basic Education
Academy, PABEA

Philippine
Philippine Library Association, PLA

Philippines
Association of Special Libraries of the
Philippines, ASLP
Bibliographical Society of the Philippines,
BSP
Bureau of Standards of the Philippines, BSP

Phillips
Phillips Load and Go, PHLAG

Philosophers
Philosophers Information Retrieval Service,
PIRS

Philosophy
Institute for the Comparative Study of
History, Philosophy and the Sciences,
Ltd, ICS
International Union of the History and
Philosophy of Science, IUHPS

Phonographic
Incorporated Phonographic Society, IPS

Photochromic
Photochromic Micro-Image, PCMI

Photocomposition
Research in Automatic Photocomposition
and Information Dissemination, RAPID

Photoengravers
American Photoengravers Association, APA

Photogrammetry
American Society for Photogrammetry, ASP

Photographers
University Photographers Association of
America, UPAA

Photographic
*Abstracts of Photographic Science and
Engineering Literature*, APSE
British Photographic Manufacturers
Association, BPMA
Random Access Photographic Index and
Display, RAPID
Society of Photographic Scientists and
Engineers, SPSE

Photo-Optical
Society of Photo-Optical Instrumentation
Engineers, SPIE

Photoplatemakers
American Photoplatemakers Association,
APA

Physical
American Physical Society, APS
*Current Contents/Physical and Chemical
Sciences.* (Journal), CC/PC
*Current Contents/Physical, Chemical and
Earth Sciences.* (Journal), CC/PC&ES

Physical Education
Alberta Information Retrieval for Health,
Physical Education, and Recreation,
AIRHPER
American Alliance for Health, Physical
Education and Recreation, AAHPER
American Association for Health, Physical
Education and Recreation, AAHPER

Physical Property
Physical Property Data Service, PPDS

Physically Handicapped
ACM Special Interest Group on Computers
and the Physically Handicapped,
ACM/SIGCAPH
ASCLA Library Service to the Blind and
Physically Handicapped Section,
ASCLA/LSBPHS
Division for the Blind and Physically
Handicapped, DBPH
National Library Services for the Blind and
Physically Handicapped, NLS

Physicians
Royal College of Physicians of Edinburgh,
RCPE
Royal College of Physicians of London, RCP
Scientific Information and Educational
Council of Physicians, SIECOP

Physics
American Association of Physics Teachers,
AAPT

Physics (cont.)

American Institute of Physics, AIP
Committee on Physics and Society,
COMPAS
Current Papers in Physics. (Journal), CPIP
Current Physics Titles (Journal), CPT
Database of Atomic and Molecular Physics,
DAMP
*Dictionary of Physics and Mathematics
Abbreviations, Signs and Symbols,*
DPMA
*High Energy Physics Index
(Hochenergiephysik-Index),* HEPI
Information Service in Physics,
Electrotechnology and Control,
INSPEC
International Center for Theoretical Physics,
ICTP
International Union of Pure and Applied
Physics, IUPAP
National Information System for Physics and
Astronomy, NISPA
National Physics Information System, NPIS
Physics Abstracts, PA
Searchable Physics Information Notices,
SPIN
Stanford Physics Information Retrieval
System, SPIRES

Pictorial
Pictorial Encoding Language, PENCIL

Picture
Automatic Picture Transmission, APT

Piece
Piece Identification Number, PIN

Pierpont Morgan
Pierpont Morgan Library, PML

Pioneers
Society of Wireless Pioneers, SOWP

Pitch
Electrical Tough Pitch, ETP

Pittsburgh
Pittsburgh Council on Higher Education,
PCHE
Pittsburgh Regional Library Center, PRLC

Placement
Advanced Placement Program, APP

Place-Name
English Place-Name Society, EPNS

Plane
Digit Plane Driver, DPD

Planificación
Consijo Zuliano de Planificación y
Promoción de Universidad Central de
Venezuela, CONZUPLAN

Planner
Computer Layout Installation Planner, CLIP

Planning
ANSI Standards Planning and Requirements
Committee, ANSI/SPARC
American Health Planning Association,
AHPA
American Planning Association, APA
American Society of Planning Officials,
ASPO
[Biblíoteka] Szkoly Glównej Planowania i
Statystykí (Library of the Central
School of Planning and Statistics),
SGPIS
Committee on Planning, COP
Computer-Aided Project Planning System,
CAPPS
Computer-Assisted Maintenance Planning
and Control System, CAMCOS
Computerizcd Movement Planning and
Status System, COMPASS
Continuing Library Education Planning and
Coordination Project, COLEPAC
East Central Florida Regional Planning
Council, ECFRPC
Economic Planning Unit of Barbados, EPU
Institut International de la Planification de
l'Éducation/International Institute for
Educational Planning, IIPE/IIEP
Planning-Programming-Budgeting System,
PPBS
Remote Access Planning for Institutional
Development, RAPID
Technical Environmental and Management
Planning Operations, TEMPO
Transportation Planning Support
Information System, TPSIS
Xerox Planning Model, XPM

Planning Librarians
Council of Planning Librarians, CPL

Plans
Office of Criminal Justice Plans and
Analysis, OCJPA

Plastics
Centre d'Étude des Matières Plastiques
(Plastics Research Center), CEMP
Plastics Documentation. (Journal),
PLASDOC
Plastics Technical Evaluation Center,
PLASTEC
Rubber and Plastics Research Associaticn,
RAPRA

Playwrights
Poets, Playwrights, Editors, Essayists and
Novelists International English Centre,
PEN

Plotter
Precision Plotter Users Association, PPUA

Población
Centro d'Estudios Sociales y de Población,
CESPO

Poetry
Modern Poetry Association, MPA
Poetry Society, PS

Poets
Poets, Playwrights, Editors, Essayists and
Novelists International English Centre,
PEN

Point
Point of Sale, POS

Polarized
Return-to-Zero (Polarized), RZ(P)

Police
International Association of Chiefs of Police,
IACP
Royal Canadian Mounted Police, RCMP

Policies
Science and Technology Policies Information
Exchange System, SPINES

Policy
Advisory Council on Science Policy, ACSP
Agricultural Research Policy Advisory
Committee, ARPAC
Committee on Public Engineering Policy,
COPEP
Decimal Classification Editorial Policy
Committee, DCEPC

Policy Implementation
Committee on Policy Implementation, COPI

Polish
Polish Canadian Librarians Association,
PCLA
Stowarzyszenie Bibliotekarzy Polskich
(Polish Library Association), SBP

Polish American
Polish American Librarians Association,
PALA

Political
Inter-University Consortium for Political and
Social Research, ICPSR

Political Parties
International Comparative Political Parties
Project, ICPP

Political Science
ACRL Law and Political Science Section,
ACRL/LPSS
Centro de Información de Política Cientifica
y Tecnológica (Center for Information in
Political Science and Technology), CIPC
United States Political Science Documents,
USPSD

Pollutants
Health Effects of Environmental Pollutants,
HEEP

Pollution
Air Pollution Control Association, APCA
Air Pollution Technical Information Center,
APTIC
Pollution Information Project, PIP

Polymer
Polymer Science and Technology, POST
Polymer Science and Technology for
Journals, POST-J
Polymer Science and Technology for
Patents, POST-P

Polytechnic
Rensselaer Polytechnic Institute, RPI

Pontiac
Pontiac–Allen Park–Detroit Consortium,
PAD

Population
Association for Population/Family Planning
Libraries and Information Centers,
APLIC

Population Center
Carolina Population Center, CPC
Carolina Population Center Library Data
Base, CPC

Population Information
Population Information, POPINFORM

Portuguesa
Sociedade Portuguesa de Autores, SPA

Portuguese
Associação Portuguesa de Bibliotecários,
Arquivistas e Documentalistes
(Portuguese Association of Librarians,
Archivists and Documentalists), BAD
Associação Portuguesa dos Editores e
Liveiros (Portuguese Association of
Publishers and Booksellers), APEL

Position
Position and Velocity Extraction, PAVE

Post Secondary
Fund for the Improvement of Post Secondary
Education, FIPSE

Postal

Conférence Européene des Administrations
    des Postes et des Télécommunications
    (European Conference of Postal and
    Telecommunication Administrations),
    CEPT
Postal, Telegraph and Telephone
    International, PTTI

Postal Services

Commission Consultative des Études
    Postales (Consultative Commission for
    the Study of Postal Services), CCEP

Poverty

Poverty and Human Resources Abstracts,
    PHRA

Power

American Public Power Association, APPA
Interagency Advanced Power Group, IAPG
National Association of Power Engineers,
    NAPE

Powerplant

Daystrom Powerplant Automation
    Language, DAPAL

Practice

Current Contents/Clinical Practice.
    (Journal), CC/CP

Practices

Automatic Data Systems Uniform Practices,
    ADSUP

Prairie

Council of Prairie University Libraries,
    COPUL

Precision

Association for Precision Graphics, APG
Precision Plotter Users Association, PPUA
Single Precision Unpacked Rounded
    Floating-Point Package, SPUR

Predicasts

(Predicasts Overview of Markets and
    Technology) (Journal), PROMT
Predicasts Terminal System, PTS

Prediction

Navy Numerical Weather Prediction,
    NANWEP
Result from Action, Prediction, Informative,
    Diagnostic Sensing, RAPIDS

Prensa Tecnica

Asociación Española de Prensa Tecnica,
    AEPT

Presentation Panel

Interactive Computer Presentation Panel,
    ICPP

Preservation

RTSD Preservation of Library Materials
    Section, RTSD/PLMS

Preserved

Preserved Context Index System, PRECIS

Press

Academic Press, Inc, AP
Associated Collegiate Press, ACP
Associated Press, AP
Australian Associated Press Proprietary Ltd,
    AAP
British Amateur Press Association, BAPA
British United Press, BUP
Buitenlandse Persvereniging in Nederland
    (Foreign Press Association in the
    Netherlands), BPV
Catholic School Press Association, CSPA
Civil War Press Corps, CWPC
Commonwealth Press Union, CPU
Cooperative High School Independent Press
    Syndicate, CHIPS
European Marketing and Advertising Press,
    EMAP
Fédération Internationale de la Presse
    Cinématographique (International
    Federation of the Cinematographic
    Press), FIPRESCI
Fédération Internationale de la Presse
    Periodique (International Federation of
    the Periodical Press), FIPP
Foreign Press Association, FPA
Getting and Abetting Small Press, GAASP
Information Resources Press, IRP
International Catholic Press Union, ICPU
International Press Institute, IPI
International Press Telecommunications
    Committee, IPTC
London International Press, Ltd, LIP
National Braille Press, NBP
Norsk Presseforbund (Norwegian Press
    Association), NP
Overseas Press and Media Association, Ltd,
    OPMA
Overseas Press Club of America, Inc, OPC
Oxford University Press, OUP
Press Association, Ltd, PA
United States Student Press Association,
    USSPA

Press Center

International Press Center, IPC

Press Service

College Press Service, CPS

Presse

Association pour la Conservation et la
    Reproduction Photographique de la
    Presse, ACRPP

Association Professionnelle de la Presse
    Cinématographique Belge, APPCB
Union de la Presse Étrangère en Belgique,
    UPE
Union de la Presse Périodique Belge, UPPB

Presses
Association of American University Presses,
    AAUP

Previews
BIOSIS Previews Memo, BPM
BioSciences Information Service Previews,
    BIOSIS Previews.

Price
Bookman's Price Index, BPI
Price List, PL

Price Quotation
Request Price Quotation, RPQ

Primate
Primate Information Center, PIC

Prime Time
Prime Time School Television, PTST

Prince Edward Island
Prince Edward Island School Library
    Association, PEISLA

Princeton
Princeton Electronic Products–Model 402,
    PEP-402

Principals
Conference des Recteurs et des Principaux
    des Universités du Québec (Conference
    of Rectors and Principals of Quebec
    Universities), CREPUQ
National Association of Secondary School
    Principals, NASSP

Print
Guide to Microforms in Print, GMP
Print Council of America, PCA

Printer
Card-Punching Printer, CPP
High-Speed Printer, HSP
Reader and Reader-Printer, RRP
Receive Only Page Printer, ROPP

Printers
Display Producers and Screen Printers
    Association, DPSA
Society of Private Printers, SPP

Printing
American Printing History Association,
    APHA
American Printing House for the Blind, APH
British Printing Machinery Association,
    BPMA

Government Printing Office, GPO
Institute of Printing, Ltd, IOP
International Allied Printing Trades
    Association, IAPTA
Irish Printing Federation, IPF
Joint Committee on Printing, JCP
Joint Industrial Council of Printing and Allied
    Trades, JIC
Printing and Kindred Trades Federation,
    PKTF
Printing and Publishing Industry Training
    Board, PPITB
Printing Historical Society, PHS
Printing Industries of Metropolitan New
    York, PIMNY
Printing Industry Research Association,
    PIRA
Research on Computer Applications in the
    Printing and Publishing Industries,
    ROCAPPI

Priorities
Council on Economic Priorities, CEP

Prison Information
Prison Information Reform Project, PIRP

Prisoners
ASCLA Library Services to Prisoners
    Section, ASCLA/LSPS

Private
Private Automatic Branch Exchange, PABX
Private Automatic Exchange, PAX
Private Branch Exchange, PBX
Private Libraries Association, PLA
Society of Independent and Private School
    Data Education, SIPSDE
Society of Private Printers, SPP

Private Colleges
Northwest Association of Private Colleges
    and Universities, NAPCU

Problem-Oriented
Computerized Problem-Oriented Medical
    Record, CPOMR
Problem-Oriented Languages, POL
Soil Engineering Problem-Oriented
    Language, SEPOL

Problem Solver
General Problem Solver, GPS

Problem Solving
Computer-Aided Problem Solving, CAPS

Problem Statement
Generic Problem Statement Simulator, GPSS

Problems
Civil Engineering Problems, CEPS

Procedure
Program Evaluation Procedure, PEP
Standard Operating Procedure, SOP

Procedures
Systems and Procedures Association, SPA
Systems and Procedures Exchange Center,
   SPEC

Proceedings
*Index to Scientific and Technical
   Proceedings*, ISTP
*Index to Social Sciences and Humanities
   Proceedings*, ISSHP

Process
Context, Input, Process Product Model,
   CIPP
In Process, INP
Industrial Process Control, IPC
A Retrieval Process Language, ARPL
Society of Aerospace Material and Process
   Engineers, SAMPE

Processes
Southern California Technical Processes
   Group, SCTPG
Technical Processes Research Office, TPR

Processing
ASIS Special Interest Group on Automated
   Language Processing, ASIS/SIG/ALP
Approach to Distributed Processing
   Transactions, ADOPT
Automated Imagery Processing, AIP
Automated Library Processing System,
   ALPS
Automated Literature Processing, Handling,
   and Analysis System, ALPHA
Automated Processing of Medical English,
   APME
Automatic Language Processing Advisory
   Committee, ALPAC
Calculator Help in Processing Signals,
   CHIPS
Central Processing Unit, CPU
Committee on Storage, Automatic
   Processing and Retrieval of Geological
   Data, COGEODATA
Distributed Processing Reporting Service,
   DPRS
Distributed Processing Support, DPS
Document Processing System, DPS
Environmental Data Collection and
   Processing Facility, EDCPF
An Evolutionary System for On-line
   Processing, AESOP
FORTRAN List Processing Language,
   FLPL
Free-form Language for Image Processing,
   FLIP
General Processing, GP

Institute de Recherche d'Informatique et
   d'Automatique (French Research
   Institute of Information and Automatic
   Processing), IRIA
Interdisciplinary Machine Processing for
   Research and Education in the Social
   Sciences, IMPRESS
Language Processing and Debugging, LPD
Machine-Aided Technical Processing
   System, MATPS
Maryland Academic Library Center for
   Automated Processing, MALCAP
Miniature Processing Time, MINPRT
Processing Information List, PIL
Retrieval and Statistical Processing, RASP
Simple Transition to Electronic Processing,
   STEP
Simultaneous Processing Operating System,
   SIPROS
Subject Content-Oriented Retriever for
   Processing Information Online,
   SCORPIO

Processing and Access
Computer-Aided Processing and Terminal
   Access Information Network,
   CAPTAIN

Processing Center
Centre de Traitement de l'Information
   Scientifique (European Scientific
   Information Processing Center), CETIS
Colorado Academic Libraries Book
   Processing Center, CALBPC
Massachusetts Centralized Library
   Processing Center, MCLP
Tehran Book Processing Center, TEBROC

Processor
Adaptive Statistical Processor, APROC
Advanced Microprogrammable Processor,
   AMPP
Algebraic and Differential Equations
   Processor and Translator, ADEPT
Algorithmic Processor Description
   Language, APDL
Associative Processor, AP
Associative Processor Computer System,
   APCS
Associative Processor Programming
   Language, APPLE
Attached Support Processor, ASP
COBOL Macro Processor, CMP
Command Processor, CP
Data Base Organization and Management
   Processor, DBOMP
Digital Data Processor, DDP
Direct-High-Level-Language Processor,
   DHLLP
Input/Output Processor, IOP

Interactive Query and Report Processor,
    IQRP
List Processor, LISP
Multiplex Message Processor, MMP
Rotating Associative Processor for
    Information Dissemination, RAPID

Processors
Assembly System for the Peripheral
    Processors, ASPER

Procuratori
Albo Dept Avvocati i Procuratori, ALBO

Producers
Association of Data Producers, ADP
Association of Specialised Film Producers,
    ASFP
Danish Agricultural Producers Information
    Service, DAPIS
Direct Mail Producers Association, DMPA
Display Producers and Screen Printers
    Association, DPSA
Film Producers Guild, Ltd, FPG
International Federation of Film Producers
    Associations, IFFPA
Union Nationale des Producteurs Belge de
    Films (National Union of Belgian Film
    Producers), UNPBF
Verband Schweizerischer Film und
    AV-Produzenten/Association des
    Producteurs Suisses de Films et de
    Production Audio-Visuelle (Association
    of Swiss Film and Audio-Visual
    Producers), VSFAV/APFAV

Product
Consumer Product Safety Commission,
    CPSC
Context, Input, Process Product Model,
    CIPP
Product Administration and Contract
    Control, PACC
Uniform Product Code Council, UPCC
Universal Product Code, UPC

Producteurs
Chambre Syndicale des Producteurs et
    Exportateurs de Films Français,
    CSPEFF

Production
American Production and Inventory Control
    Society, APICS
Automatic List Classification and Profile
    Production, ALCAPP
Bibliography Production, BIBPRO IV
Computer-Assisted Movie Production,
    CAMP
Computerized Production Control, CPC
Film Production Association of Great
    Britain, FPA

Industrial Commodity Production Statistics,
    ICPDATA
Total Analysis System for Production,
    Accounting, and Control, TAS-PAC

Production Run
Production Run Tape, PRT

Production System
Computerized Production Operation System
    Extension, COMPOSE

Productivité des Entreprises
Centre National d'Information pour le
    Productivité des Entreprises, CNIPE

Products
Educational Products and Information
    Exchange, EPIE
Princeton Electronic Products–Model 402,
    PEP-402

Professional
Professional Engineers Conference Board for
    Industry, PECBI
Professional Group on Electronic
    Computers, PGEC

Professional Librarians
Associação Profissional de Bibliotecários do
    Estado da Guanabara (Professional
    Association of Librarians in
    Guanabara), APBEG
Corporation of Professional Librarians of
    Quebec/Corporation des Bibliothécaires
    Professionnels du Québec, CPLQ/CBPQ
Institute of Professional Librarians of
    Ontario, IPLO

Professional Libraries
Arrowhead Professional Libraries
    Association, APLA

Professions
Education Professions Development Act,
    EPDA

Professors
American Association of University
    Professors, AAUP

Proficiency
Console Operator Proficiency Examination,
    COPE

Profile
Automatic List Classification and Profile
    Production, ALCAPP

Program
Academic Library Program, ALP
Advanced Placement Program, APP
Advanced Statistical Analysis Program,
    ASTAP

Program (cont.)

Affirmative Action Program, AAP
Affirmative Action Program for Women
  Committee, AAPWC
Air Force Technical Objectives Documents
  Release Program, AFTOD
Application Program Evaluator Tool, APET
Archival Security Program, ASP
Automatic Operating and Scheduling
  Program, AOSP
Basic Analysis and Mapping Program,
  BAMP
Basic Assembler Program, BAP
Business and Industry Extension Program,
  BIEP
Canadian Technical Awareness Program,
  CAN/TAP
Client-Oriented Data Acquisition Program,
  CODAP
College-Level Examination Program, CLEP
Committee on Program Evaluation and
  Support, COPES
Comprehensive Occupational Data Analysis
  Program, CODAP
Computer Output Microforms Program and
  Concept Study, COMPACS
Computer Program for Automatic Control,
  COMPAC
Computer-Assisted Mathematics Program,
  CAMP
Computer-Assisted Program Evaluation
  Review Technique Simulation,
  CAPERTSIM
Configuration Analysis Program, CAP
Consumer Health Information Program and
  Service, CHIPS
Continuous System Modeling Program,
  CSMP
Control Data Assembly Program, CODAP
Conversational Circuit Analysis Program,
  CONCAP
Cooperative Acquisitions Program, CAP
Cooperative Media Development Program,
  CMDP
Cooperative Serials Acquisitions Program,
  COSAP
Cycle Program Control, CPC
Cycle Program Counter, CPC
Earth Resources Technology Satellite
  Program, ERTS
Electric Circuit Analysis Program, ECAP
Expansion Symbolic Compiling Assembly
  Program for Engineering, ESCAPE
FORTRAN Assembly Program, FAP
Failure Analysis Program, FAP
Failure Rate Data Program, FARADA
Financial Analysis Program, FAP
Financial Evaluation Program, FEP
Floating Point Interpretive Program, FLIP
General Activity Simulation Program, GASP

General Assembly Program, GAP
General Electric Computer Analysis
  Program, GECAP
General Electric Macro Assembly Program,
  GEMAP
General Purpose Simulation Program, GPSS
General Risk Analysis Simulation Program,
  GRASP
Global Atmospheric Research Program,
  GARP
Government-Industry Data Exchange
  Program, GIDEP
Graduate Regional Accelerated Study
  Program, GRASP
Highway Engineering Exchange Program,
  HEEP
Imbricated Program for Information
  Transfer, IMPRINT
International Cancer Research Data Bank
  Program, ICRDB
Library Additions and Maintenance
  Program, LAMP
Library Service Enhancement Program,
  LSEP
Library Technology Program, LTP
Macro Assembly Program, MAP
Management Review and Analysis Program,
  MRAP
Master Control Program, MCP
Mathematical Program, MATH-PAC
Midcontinental Regional Medical Library
  Program, MCRMLP
Model and Program, MAP
Museum and University Data, Program and
  Information Exchange, MUDPIE
National Program for Acquisition and
  Cataloging, NPAC
National Serials Data Program, NSDP
New England Regional Computing Program,
  Inc, NERCOMP
New York Assembly Program, NYAP
Octal Program Updating System, OPUS
Office of Library Development Program,
  OLDP
Pennsylvania Technical Assistance Program,
  PENNTAP
Program BIBLIO, BIBLIO
Program Compiler, PROCOMP
Program Evaluation and Budget Committee,
  PEBCO
Program Evaluation and Review Technique,
  PERT
Program Evaluation Procedure, PEP
Program for Information Managers, PRIM
Program of Action for Mediation,
  Arbitration, and Inquiry, PAMAI
Program Reference Table, PRT
Program Status Word, PSW
Program Test System, PTS
Program Test Tape, PTT
Public Service Careers Program, PSCP

Programming (cont.)

Subcommittee on Programming
    Terminology, SCOPT
Symbolic Optimum Assembly Programming,
    SOAP
Symbolic Programming System, SPS

Programs
Biomedical Computer Programs, BMD
Catalogued Resources and Information
    Survey Programs, CRISP
Committee on International Scientific and
    Technical Information Programs,
    CISTIP
*Computer Programs in Science and
    Technology* (Index), CPST
Extramural Programs Information System,
    EPIS
Machine Language Programs, MLP
PLA Alternative Education Programs
    Section, PLA/AEPS

Progress
Toxicology Testing in Progress. (Journal),
    TOX-TIPS

Project
APA Project on Scientific Information in
    Psychology, APA-PSIP
Air Force English Syntax Project, AFESP
Biological Science Communications Project,
    BSCP
Central Massachusetts Library
    Administration Project, CLASP
Computer-Aided Project Planning System,
    CAPPS
Computer-Aided Project Study, CAPS
Continuing Library Education Planning and
    Coordination Project, COLEPAC
Conversion of Serials Project, CONSER
Cooperative Africana Microform Project,
    CAMP
Current Cancer Research Project Analysis
    Center, CCRESPAC
Educational Media Institute Evaluation
    Project, EMIE
Hand Printed Books Project, HPB
Health Information Sharing Project, HISP
International Comparative Political Parties
    Project, ICPP
International Library to Library Project,
    ILLC
Library Exchange Aids Patrons Project,
    LEAP
Neighborhood Information Centers Project,
    NIC
Ohio Project for Research in Information
    Services, OPRIS
Ontario Universities Bibliographic Centre
    Project, OUBCP

Prison Information Reform Project, PIRP
Project Accounting by Cost and Time, PACT
Project Every Library Board Kit on
    Intellectual Freedom, PELB-IF
Project for Integrated Catalogue
    Automation, PICA
Project for the Advancement of Coding
    Techniques, PACT I
Project for the Evaluation of Benefits from
    University Libraries, PEBUL
Project Grant Information System, PGIS
Project Monitoring and Control Method,
    PROMCOM
School Library Manpower Project, SLMP
Scottish Libraries Cataloging Automation
    Project, SCOLCAP
Social Sciences Instructional Programming
    Project, SSIPP
South Asia Microform Project, SAMP
Students Chemical Information Project,
    SCIP
Technical Information Project, TIP
Technical Information Support Activities
    Project, TISAP
Texas Educational Microwave Project,
    TEMP
Urban Documentation Project,
    URBANDOC
Young Adult Project, YAP

Projected
Projected Books, Inc, PBI

Projection
Digital Optical Projection System, DOPS
Projection by Reflection Optics of
    Xerographic Images, PROXI

Projects
Agricultural Research Projects in the
    European Community, AGREP
Cancer Projects, CANCERPROJ
Toxicology Research Projects Directory.
    (Journal), TRPD

Promoción
Consijo Zuliano de Planificación y
    Promoción de Universidad Central de
    Venezuela, CONZUPLAN

Promotion
Society for the Promotion and Improvement
    of Libraries, SPIL
Training, Appraisal and Promotion, TAP

Properties
Electronic Properties Information Center,
    EPIC

Property
World Intellectual Property Organization,
    WIPO

Proportional
Proportional-plus-Integral, PI
Proportional-plus-Integral-plus-Derivative,
    PID

Proposals
Request for Proposals, RFP

Proprietés Physiques
Estimation de Proprietés Physiques pour
    l'Ingenieur Chimiste, EPIC

Proprietors
Scottish Newspaper Proprietors Association,
    SNPA

Propulsion
Chemical Propulsion Information Agency,
    CPIA

Prosecutors
Prosecutors Management Information
    System, PROMIS

Protection
British Copyright Protection Association,
    Ltd, BCPA
Bureaux Internationaux Réunis pour la
    Protection de la Propriété Intellectuelle
    (United International Bureaus for the
    Protection of Intellectual Property),
    BIRPI
Environmental Protection Agency, EPA

Proto Synthex
Proto Synthex Indexing, PSI

Protocol
Clinical Protocol, CLINPROT
Digital Data Communications Message
    Protocol, DDCMP

Provincial
Ontario Provincial Library Council, OPLC

Provincial Associations
Liaison of Provincial Associations
    Committee, LOPAC

Psychiatric
Children's Psychiatric Research Institute,
    CPRI

Psychological
American Psychological Association, APA

Psychological Abstracts
Psychological Abstracts, PA
Psychological Abstracts Direct Access
    Terminal, PADAT
Psychological Abstracts Reference Retrieval
    System, PARRS
Psychological Abstracts Search and
    Retrieval, PASAR

Psychological Abstracts Tape Edition Lease
    or Licensing, PATELL
Syracuse University *Psychological
    Abstracts* Retrieval System, SUPARS

Psychology
APA Project on Scientific Information in
    Psychology, APA-PSIP
[Environmental Psychology], ENVPSYCH
National Information System for
    Psychology, NISP

Public
American Public Health Association, APHA
American Public Power Association, APPA
American Public Transit Association, APTA
Canadian Union of Public Employees, CUPE
Committee on Public Engineering Policy,
    COPEP
Institute of Public Administration, IPA
Ontario Public Library Association, OPLA
Public Broadcasting Service, PBS
Public Education Association, PEA
Public Free Library, PFL
Public Information Officer, PIO
Public Law, PL
Public Lending Right, PLR
Public Library, PL
Public Message Service, PMS
Public Record Office, PRO
Public Relations, PR
Public Television, PTV
Public Television Library, PTL
United States Public Health Service, USPHS
Wandsworth Public, Educational and
    Technical Library Services,
    WANDPETLS

Public Affairs
Public Affairs Information Service, PAIS

Public Domain
Not in the Public Domain, NIPD

Public Health
American Association for Vital Records and
    Public Health Statistics, AAVRPHS

Public Information
American Association for Public
    Information, Education and Research,
    AAPIER
Office of Public Information, OPI
Scientists Committee for Public Information,
    SCPI
Scientists Institute for Public Information,
    SIPI

Public Interest
Public Interest Research Centre, PIRC

Public Librarians
Norsk Bibliotekarlag (Association of
    Norwegian Public Librarians), NBL
Ontario Public Librarians Advisory
    Committee, OPLAC

Public Libraries
Administrators of Medium Public Libraries
    of Ontario, AMPLO
Association Nationale pour le
    Développement des Bibliothèques
    Publiques (National Association for the
    Development of Public Libraries),
    ANDBP
CLA Public Libraries Section, CLA/PLS
Canadian Association of Public Libraries,
    CAPL
Chief Executives of Large Public Libraries,
    CELPLO
Council of Administrators of Large Urban
    Public Libraries, CALUPL
Federazione Italiana delle Biblioteche
    Popolari (Federation of Italian Public
    Libraries), FIBP
Netherlands Bibliotheek en Lektuur
    Centrum (Dutch Center for Public
    Libraries and Literature), NBLC
Office of Public Libraries and Interlibrary
    Cooperation, OPLIC
Svenska Folkbibliotekarie Förbundet (Union
    of Swedish Public Libraries), SFF
Verein der Bibliothekare an Öffentlichen
    Büchereien (Association of Librarians in
    Public Libraries), VBB

Public Library
Baltimore County Public Library, BCPL
Boston Public Library, BPL
District of Columbia Public Library, DCPL
Los Angeles Public Library, LAPL
New South Wales Public Library, NPL
New York Public Library, NYPL
PLA Public Library Systems Section,
    PLA/PLSS
Public Library Association of
    Nevada-Nevada Association of Library
    Trustees, PLAN-NALT
Public Library Automation Network, PLAN
Queensland Public Library, QPL
Richmond Public Library, RPL
San Francisco Public Library, SFPL
Scandinavian Public Library Quarterly.
    (Journal), SPLQ

Public Library Association
Public Library Association, PLA

Public Policy
Committee on Science and Public Policy,
    COSPUP

Public Relations
Dirección General de Información y
    Relaciones Publicas (Board of
    Information and Public Relations),
    DGIRP
LAMA Public Relations Section,
    LAMA/PRS
Library Public Relations Council, LPRC
Public Relations, PR

Public Service
Public Service Careers Program, PSCP

Publication
Cataloging in Publication, CIP
Copyright Office Publication and Interactive
    Cataloging System, COPICS
Diretoria de Documentação de Divulgação
    (Direction of Documentation and
    Publication), DDD
Publication Board, PB
Retrieval through Automated Publication
    and Information Digest, RAPID
System for the Publication and Efficient,
    Effective Dissemination of Information,
    SPEEDI

Publications
Air World Publications, AWP
Canadian Forces Publications, CFP
Current Mathematical Publications, CMP
Deafness, Speech and Hearing Publications,
    Inc, DSH
Fédération Internationale des Directeurs de
    Journaux Catholiques (International
    Federation of Directors of Catholic
    Publications), FIDJC
Institute of Technical Publicity and
    Publications, ITPP
Joint Publications Research Service, JPRS
Knowledge Industry Publications, Inc, KIP
Mechanical Engineering Publications, MEP
Publications and Distribution Center, PDC
Publications Indexed for Engineering, PIE
*Publications of the Modern Language
    Association.* (Journal), PMLA
Publications Reference File, PRF
Research Publications, Inc, RP
*Selected Publications in European
    Languages*, SPEL
Small Libraries Publications, SLP
Union Nationale des Éditeurs-Exportateurs
    de Publications Françaises, UNEEPF
Universal Availability of Publications, UVP

Publications Center
Centrul de Documentare si Publicatü
    Tehnice al Ministerulue Cailór Ferate
    (Technical Documentation and
    Publications Center of the Railway
    Ministry), CDPT-MCF

Publications Service
National Auxiliary Publications Service,
NAPS

Publicity
Institute of Technical Publicity and
Publications, ITPP

Public-Private Interface
ASIS Special Interest Group on
Public-Private Interface, ASIS/SIG/PPI

Publishers
Airline Tariff Publishers, Inc, ATP
American Book Publishers Council, ABPC
American Educational Publishers Institute,
AEPI
American Medical Publishers Association,
AMPA
American Newspaper Publishers
Association, ANPA
American Society of Composers, Authors,
and Publishers, ASCAP
American Textbook Publishers Institute,
ATPI
Associação Portuguesa dos Editores e
Liveiros (Portuguese Association of
Publishers and Booksellers), APEL
Association Belge des Editeurs de Langue
Française (Belgian Association of
Publishers of French Language Books),
ABELF
Association of American Publishers, AAP
Association of International Publishers
Representatives, AIPR
Association of Publishers Educational
Representatives, APER
Associazione Italiana Editori (Italian
Publishers Association), AIE
Book Publishers Representatives
Association, BPRA
Bureau of Independent Publishers and
Distributors, BIPAD
Canadian Book Publishers Council, CBPC
Committee of Small Magazine Editors and
Publishers, COSMEP
Diary Publishers Association, DPA
Independent Publishers Guild, IPG
International Association of Scholarly
Publishers, IASP
International Publishers Advertising
Representatives Association, IPARA
International Publishers Association, IPA
Music Publishers Association, MPA
Newspaper Publishers Association Ltd,
NPA
Periodical Publishers Association, Ltd, PPA
Publisher's Alert Service, PAS
Publishers Association, PA
Publishers Information Bureau, PIB
Publishers Trade List Annual, PTLA

Publishers Weekly. (Journal), PW
Schweizerischer Zeitungsverleger-
Verband/Association Suisse des
Éditeurs de Journaux/Associazione
Svizzera degli Éditori di Giornale
(Swiss Newspaper Publishers
Association), SZV/ASEJ/ASEG
Scientific, Technical and Medical Publishers,
STM
Small and Specialist Publishers Exhibition,
SPEX
Société des Libraires et Éditeurs de la Suisse
Romande (Booksellers and Publishers
Association of French-Speaking
Switzerland), SLESR
Society of Technical Writers and Publishers,
STWP
Society of Young Publishers, SYP

Publishing
ASIS Special Interest Group on Information
Publishing, ASIS/SIG/IP
American Book Publishing Record, ABPR
Centrum voor Landbouwpiblikaties en
Landbouwdocumentatie (Center for
Agricultural Publishing and
Documentation), PUDOC
Gulf Publishing Company, GPC
Information & Publishing Systems, Inc,
I&PS
Printing and Publishing Industry Training
Board, PPITB
Research on Computer Applications in the
Printing and Publishing Industries,
ROCAPPI
Society for Scholarly Publishing, SSP
Technical Publishing Society, TPS
Xerox Publishing Group, XPG

Puerto Rico
Sociedad de Bibliotecarios de Puerto Rico
(Puerto Rico Library Association),
SBPR

Pulp
American Pulp and Paper Association,
APPA
Literature Retrieval System for the Pulp and
Paper Industry, LIRES
Pulp and Paper Research Institute of
Canada/Information Retrieval Services,
PAPRICAN/IRS
Pulp, Paper and Paperboard Institute, PPPI
Technical Association of the Pulp and Paper
Industry, TAPPI

Pulse
Pulse Code Modulation, PCM
Pulse Repetition Rate, PRR

Pulsed
Clock Pulsed Control, CPC

Pulses
Pulses per Second, PPS

Punchcard
Punchcard Machine, PCM

Punched
Punched Card System, PCS

Pupil
Pupil Registering and Operational Filing,
    PROF

Puppetry
Ontario Puppetry Association, Ltd, OPAL

Purchasing
European Federation of Purchasing, EFP

Qualitative Development
Army Qualitative Development
    Requirements Information Program,
    QDRI

Quality Control
American Society for Quality Control,
    ASQC

Quality Level
Acceptable Quality Level, AQL

Quantitative
Research Seminar in Quantitative
    Economics, RSQE

Quarterly
Michigan Quarterly Economic Model,
    MQEM
Quarterly Cumulative Index Medicus, QCIM
Scandinavian Public Library Quarterly.
    (Journal), SPLQ
School Media Quarterly. (Journal), SMQ

Quebec
Association des Archivistes du Québec
    (Association of Quebec Archivists),
    AAQ
Association des Enseignants Bibliothécaires
    du Québec, AEBQ
Banque de Données à Accès Direct de
    l'Université du Québec (Direct Access
    Data Bank of the University of Quebec),
    BADADUQ
Comité de Coordination des Bibliothèques
    Gouvernement du Québec, COBIGO
Conference des Recteurs et des Principaux
    des Universités du Québec (Conference
    of Rectors and Principals of Quebec
    Universities), CREPUQ
Corporation of Professional Librarians of
    Quebec/Corporation des Bibliothécaires
    Professionnels du Québec, CPLQ/CBPQ

Order of Nurses of Quebec, ONQ
Quebec Association for Children with
    Learning Disabilities, QACLD
Quebec Association of School Librarians,
    QASL
Quebec Library Association/Association des
    Bibliothécaires de Québec, QLA/ABQ
Université du Quebec à Montreal, UQAM

Québeçoise
Société Québeçoise d'Initiatives Pétrolières,
    SOQUIP

Queens
Brooklyn-Queens-Staten Island Health
    Sciences Group, BQSI

Queen's University
Queen's University Information Centre,
    QUIC

Queensland
Queensland Public Library, QPL

Query and Report
Interactive Query and Report Processor,
    IQRP

Questionnaire
Questionnaire Interpreter Program, QUIP

Questions
Hansard Oral Questions, HOQ
Hansard Questions Écrites, HQE
Hansard Questions Orale, HQO
Hansard Written Questions, HWQ
Have You Stored Answers to Questions,
    HAYSTAQ

Queue
Queue Control Block, QCB

Queued
Queued Access Method, QAM
Queued Indexed Sequential Access Method,
    QISAM
Queued Telecommunications Access
    Method, QTAM

Quick
Quick Text Editor, QED

Quotations
National Association of Securities Dealers
    Automated Quotations System,
    NASDAQ

Radar
Digital Data, Auxiliary Storage, Track
    Display, Outputs, and Radar Display,
    DATOR
RADAR Data Processing Equipment, RDPE

Radiation
Ballistic Missile Radiation Analysis Center,
    BAMIRAC
Light Amplification by Stimulated Emission
    of Radiation, LASER
Radiation Effects Information Center, REIC
Radiation Shielding Information Center,
    RSIC

Radio
American Federation of Television and
    Radio Artists, AFTRA
American Radio Relay League, ARRL
Comité Consultatif International des
    Radiocommunications (International
    Radio Consultative Committee), CCIR
Institute of Radio Engineers, IRE
Institution of Electronic and Radio
    Engineers, IERE
Joint Departmental Radio and Electronics
    Measurements Committee, REMC
National Association of Business and
    Educational Radio, NABER
National Educational Television and Radio
    Center, NETRC
North American Radio Archives Library,
    NARA
Radio and Electric Component
    Manufacturers Federation, RECMF
Radio Components Standardization
    Committee, RCSC
Radio Corporation of America, RCA
Radio Frequency Interference, RFI
Radio Technical Commission for
    Aeronautics, RTCA
Radio Teletypewriter, RTT
Radio Teletypewriter Communications,
    RTTY
Union Radio-Scientifique Internationale
    (International Scientific Radio Union),
    URSI
World Administrative Radio Conference,
    WARC

Radio Service
Special Industrial Radio Service Association,
    SIRSA

Radioactivity
Radioactivity Detection Indication and
    Computation, RADIAC

Radio-Electronics
*Abbreviations and Related Acronyms
    Associated with Defense, Astronautics,
    Business and Radio-Electronics*,
    ABRACADABRA

Radiologic
American Society of Radiologic
    Technologists, ASRT

Radiological
Radiological Society of North America,
    RSNA

Radiophonics
International University of Radiophonics and
    Television, IUR

Radio-Television
Association for Education by
    Radio-Television, AERT
Université Radiophonique et Télévisuelle
    Internationale (International
    Radio-Television University), URI

Railroad
Railroad Research Information Service,
    RRIS

Railway
Centrul de Documentare si Publicatü
    Tehnice al Ministerulue Cailór Ferate
    (Technical Documentation and
    Publications Center of the Railway
    Ministry), CDPT-MCF

Railways
Canadian National Railways, CN
Centre d'Information et de Publicité des
    Chemins de Fer Européens (Information
    and Publicity Center of European
    Railways), CIPCE

Raleigh
Cooperative Raleigh Colleges, CRC

Ramapo
Ramapo Catskill Library System, RCLS

Rand Library
Periodicals Automation Rand Library,
    PEARL

Random
Block-Oriented Random Access Memories,
    BORAM
Card Random Access Memory, CRAM
Random Access and Inquiry, RAI
Random Access Computer Equipment,
    RACE
Random Access Correlation for Extended
    Performance, RACEP
Random Access Discrete Address, RADA
Random Access Discrete Address System,
    RADAS
Random Access Document Indexing and
    Retrieval, RADIR
Random Access Mass Memory, RAM
Random Access Memory, RAM
Random Access Method of Accounting and
    Control, RAMAC
Random Access Personnel Information
    Dissemination, RAPID

Random (cont.)

Random Access Personnel Information
    Dissemination System, RAPIDS
Random Access Photographic Index and
    Display, RAPID
Random Access Programming and Checkout
    Equipment, RAPCOE
Random Access Storage and Control,
    RASTAC
Random Access Storage and Display,
    RASTAD
Shelter-Housed Automatic Digital Random
    Access, SHADRAC

Ranging
Coherent Light Detection and Ranging,
    COLIDAR

Rapid
Rapid Access Disk, RAD
Rapid Access Management Information
    System, RAMIS
Rapid Access to Literature via
    Fragmentation Codes, RALF
Rapid Alphanumeric Digital Indicating
    Device, RANDID
Rapid Digital Automatic Computing,
    RADAC
Rapid Search Machine, RSM

Rapid Transit
Southern California Rapid Transit District,
    SCRTD

Rapidly
Rapidly Extensible Language, REL

Rare Books
ACRL Rare Books and Manuscripts Section,
    ACRL/RBMS

Rare-Earth
Rare-Earth Information Center, RIC

Rating
Computerized Automatic Rating Technique,
    CART

Ratio
Blip-Scan Ratio, BSR
Signal-to-Noise Ratio, S/N

Reactions
Current Chemical Reactions. (Journal), CCR

Reactive
Time-Shared Reactive On-Line Lab,
    TROLL/I

Reactor
Computer Handling of Reactor
    Data—Safety, CHORD—S
Fast Reactor Test Facility, FARET
Liquid Metal Fast Breeder Reactor, LMFBR

Read
Freedom to Read Foundation, FTRF
Nondestructive Read, NDR

Read Only
Read Only Memory, ROM

Reader
High-Speed Reader, HSR
Optical Character Reader, OCR
Oscillogram Trace Reader, OTRAC

Reader-Printer
Reader and Reader-Printer, RRP

Readers
Readers Advisory Service, RAS
Readers Guide to Periodical Literature.
    (Index), RGPL

Readership
Joint Industrial Committee for National
    Readership Surveys, JICNARS

Readiness
Automatic Checkout and Readiness
    Equipment, ACRE

Reading
Committee for Writing and Reading Aids for
    the Paralysed, WRAP
ERIC Clearinghouse on Reading and
    Communication Skills, ERIC/CS
Family Reading Center, FRC
International Reading Association, IRA
Reading Is Fundamental, RIF
Reading Reform Foundation, RRF

Read-Out
Destructive Read-Out, DRO
Electronic Coordinatograph and Readout
    System, ECARS
Nondestructive Read-Out, NDRO

Read/Write
Read/Write Head, R/W

Real Estate
Real Estate Data, Inc, REDI

Real Time
Bell Laboratories Library Real-Time Loan
    System, BELLREL
COBOL-Oriented Real-Time Environment,
    CORTEZ
Computer On-Line Real-Time Applications
    Language, CORAL
On-Line Real Time, OLRT
On-Line, Real-Time, Branch Information,
    ORBIT
Real Time, RT
Real-Time Command, RTC
Real-Time Communications, REALCOM

Real-time Computer Complex, RCC
Real-Time Electronic Access and Display,
    READ
Real-Time Executive Routine, REX

Receive
Receive Only, RO
Synchronous Transmit Receive Access
    Method, STRAM

Receive Only
Receive Only Page Printer, ROPP
Receive Only Typing Reperforator, ROTR

Receiver
Data Conversion Receiver, DCR
Synchronous Transmitter Receiver, STR

Receiving
Magnetic Drum Receiving Equipment,
    MADRE

Recherche
Association Française d'Informatique et de
    Recherche Opérationnelle, AFIRO
Association National de la Recherche
    Technique, ANRT
Association Scientifique et Technique pour
    la Recherche en Informatique
    Documentaire, ASTRID
Bureau de Recherche pour l'Innovation et la
    Convergence, BRIC
Centre d'Animation, de Développement et
    de Recherche en Education, CADRE
Centre International d'Information et de la
    Recherche sur la Formation
    Professionnelle, CIRF
Centre National de la Recherche
    Scientifique, CNRS
Centre pour la Recherche Interdisciplinaire
    sur le Développement, CRID
Délégation Générale à la Recherche
    Scientifique et Technique, DGRST
Direction de la Recherche Agronomique,
    DRA
Genealogische Recherche mit
    Magnetband-Speicherung, GREMAS
Institut National de la Santé et de la
    Recherche Medicale, INSERM
Institute de Recherche Industrielle, IRI
Institute National de la Recherche
    Agronomique, INRA

Recherche Sociales
Centre de Documentation et de Recherche
    Sociales, CEDORES

Recherches
Centre d'Études et Recherches des
    Charbonnages de France, CERCHAR
Institut de Recherches sur les Fruits et
    Agrumes, IRFA
Institut National de Recherches et de
    Documentation, INRDG

Recherches Administratives
Centre Africain de Formation et de
    Recherches Administratives pour le
    Développement, CAFRAD

Recherches de l'Industrie
Centre d'Études et de Recherches de
    l'Industrie des Liants Hydrauliques,
    CERILH

Recherches Urbaines
Consortium Canadien de Recherches
    Urbaines et Régionales, CCRUR

Reckoner
Text Reckoner and Compiler, TRAC

Recognition
Computer-Aided Design Optical Character
    Recognition, CADOCR

Recommendation
Design Change Recommendation, DCR

Record
American Book Publishing Record, ABPR
American Medical Record Association,
    AMRA
Computerized Problem-Oriented Medical
    Record, CPOMR
Foundation of Record Education, FORE
Graduate Record Examination, GRE
Medical Record Information Service, MRIS
Public Record Office, PRO
Record Separator, RS

Record Libraries
Fédération Internationale des Phonothèques
    (International Federation of Record
    Libraries), FIP

Record Service
Well Record Service. (Journal), WRS

Recorded Sound
Association for Recorded Sound Collections,
    ARSC

Recorder
American Recorder Society, ARS
Malfunction and Data Recorder, MADAR
Videotape Recorder, VTR

Recording
Analog Data Recording Transcriber, ADRT
Automatic Programming and Recording,
    APAR
British Institute of Recording Sounds, BIRS
British Sound Recording Association, BSRA
Circulation Input Recording, CIRC
Computer-Aided Recording of Distribution
    Systems, CARDS
Direct Order Recording and Invoicing
    System, DORIS

Recording (cont.)

Electron Beam Recording, EBR
Malfunction Analysis Detection and
    Recording, MADAR
Malfunction Detection and Recording,
    MADREC
Recording Industry Association of America,
    RIAA
Videotape Recording, VTR

Recordings
Alpha-Numerical System for Classification
    of Recordings, ANSCR
Recordings for the Blind, Inc, RFB

Records
ASIS Special Interest Group on Medical
    Records, ASIS/SIG/MR
American Records Management
    Association, ARMA
Archival Records Management System,
    ARM
Association of Records Executives and
    Administrators, AREA
Association of Records Managers and
    Administrators, ARMA
Bibliographic Records Control, BIBCON
British Records Association, BRA
Correctional Records Information Systems,
    CRYSIS
MARC Records Distribution Service, MRDS
Personnel Records Information System for
    Management, PRISM
Support of User Records and Files, SURF

Records Librarians
American Association of Medical Records
    Librarians, AAMRL

Records Service
National Archives and Records Service,
    NARS

Recovery
Fast Analysis of Tape and Recovery,
    FATAR

Recreation
Alberta Information Retrieval for Health,
    Physical Education, and Recreation,
    AIRHPER
American Alliance for Health, Physical
    Education and Recreation, AAHPER
American Association for Health, Physical
    Education and Recreation, AAHPER
Libros Elementales Educativos Recreativos
    (Elementary Books for Education and
    Recreation), LEER
Therapeutic Recreation Information Center,
    TRIC

Recreational
Information System for Adaptive, Assistive
    and Recreational Equipment, ISAARE

Rectors
Conference des Recteurs et des Principaux
    des Universités du Québec (Conference
    of Rectors and Principals of Quebec
    Universities), CREPUQ

Redevelopment
National Association of Housing and
    Redevelopment Officials Library,
    NAHRO

Redgrave
Redgrave Information Resources, RIR

Redstone
Redstone Scientific Information Center,
    RSIC

Redundancy
Triple Modular Redundancy, TMR

Redundancy Check
Longitudinal Redundancy Check Character,
    LRC

Reel
Distribution Tape Reel, DTR

Reeves
Reeves Electronic Analog Computer, REAC

Referativny
Referativny Zhurnal, RZh

Reference
Cooperative Industrial and Commercial
    Reference and Information Service,
    CICRIS
Data Reference, D-REF
Engineering Reference Branch, ERB
Huxley Environmental Reference Bureau,
    HERB
IULC Reference and Interlibrary Loan
    Service, IULC-RAILS
International Reference Organization in
    Forensic Medicine and Sciences,
    INFORM
National Standard Reference Data System,
    NSRDS
North Country Reference and Research
    Resources Council, NCRRRC
Office of Standard Reference Data, OSRD
Program Reference Table, PRT
Psychological Abstracts Reference Retrieval
    System, PARRS
Publications Reference File, PRF
RASD Machine-Assisted Reference Section,
    RASD/MARS

Registering
Pupil Registering and Operational Filing, PROF

Registrars
American Association of Collegiate Registrars and Admissions Officers, AACRAO

Registry
Index Chemicus Registry System, ICRS
National Registry for Librarians, NRL
Registry of Toxic Effects of Chemical Substances, RTECS

Rehabilitation
Canadian Rehabilitation Council for the Disabled, CRCD
International Society for Rehabilitation of the Disabled/Rehabilitation International, ISRD

Rehabilitative
Consortium of Hospital and Rehabilitative Geriatric Enterprises, CHARGE
Health and Rehabilitative Library Services Division, HRLSD

Related Term
Related Term, RT

Relations of Concepts
Topological Representation of Synthetic and Analytical Relations of Concepts, TOSAR

Relative
Relative Access Programming Implementation Device, RAPID
Relative Coding, RELCODE

Relevance Linkage
Multi-Aspect Relevance Linkage Information System, MARLIS

Reliability
Computer-Assisted Reliability Statistics, CARS
Reliability Analysis Center, RAC

Religion
Consortium for Higher Education Religion Studies, CHERS

Religious
Association for the Development of Religious Information Systems, ADRIS
Index to Religious Periodical Literature, IRPL

Relocation
Automatic and Dynamic Monitor with Immediate Relocation, Allocation and Loading, ADMIRAL
Relocation Dictionary, RLD

Reluctance
Multi-Aperture Reluctance Switch, MARS

Remote
General Electric Remote Terminal System, GERTS
Machine-Assisted Educational System for Teaching by Remote Operation, MAESTRO
Remote Access, RAX
Remote Access Computing System, RACS
Remote Access Planning for Institutional Development, RAPID
Remote Areas Conflict Information Center, RACIC
Remote Console, RECON
Remote Control Unit, RCU
Remote Electrical Alphanumeric Display, READ
Remote Information Management System, RIMS
Remote Job Entry, RJE
Remote Terminal Unit, RTU
Remote Terminals, RT
Remote User of Shared Hardware, RUSH

Remote Control
NASA Remote Control, NASA/RECON

Remote Sensing
Laboratory for Applications of Remote Sensing, LARS

Remotely Operated
Remotely Operated Special Equipment, ROSE

Rensselaer
Rensselaer Polytechnic Institute, RPI

Repair
Maximum Time to Repair, MTTR
Mean Time to Repair, MTTR

Reperforator
Receive Only Typing Reperforator, ROTR

Répertoire
Répertoire International de la Littérature de l'Art. (Journal), RILA
Répertoire International de Littérature Musicale, RILM

Repertoires Analytiques
Composition Automatic de Repertoires Analytiques, CARA

Repertorio
Repertorio Bibliografico Italiano, REBIS
Repertorio Bibliografico Straniero, REBIS

Repetition Rate
Pulse Repetition Rate, PRR

Replacement
Computer Users Replacement Equipment,
CURE

Report
Atlantic Merchant Vessel Report, AMVER
Business International Money Report.
(Journal), BIMR
Case Law Report Updating Service,
CLARUS
College Applicant Status Report, CASTOR
Cost Analysis Information Report, CAIR
Film and Report Information Processing
Generator, FRINGE
Management Report Generator, MARGEN
Report Collection Index, RECODEX
Report Program Generator, REGENT
Report Program Generator, RPG
Research and Development Report, RDR
Research Division Technical Report, RDTR
Scientific Report, SR
Sorting, Updating, Report, Generating, Etc,
SURGE
Standard Technical Report Number, STRN
Technical Report, TECH REPT

Reporting
Business/Accounts Reporting Operating
Network, BARON
Collection, Inquiry, Reporting &
Communication, CIRC
Computerized Automatic Reporting Service,
CARS
TALON Reporting and Information
Processing System, TRIPS

Reporting Service
Distributed Processing Reporting Service,
DPRS

Reports
*Classified Scientific and Technical
Aerospace Reports*, C-STAR
Dominion Law Reports, DLR
Journal Citation Reports, JCR
Library Technology Reports. (Journal), LTR
Scientific and Technical Aerospace Reports.
(Journal), STAR
System for Organizing Current Reports to
Aid Technology and Science,
SOCRATES
US Government Reports Index, USGI
*US Government Research and Development
Reports*, USGRDR
*US Government Research and Development
Reports Index*, USGRDRI
US Government Research Reports, USGR

Representatives
Association of International Publishers
Representatives, AIPR

Book Publishers Representatives
Association, BPRA

Reproduction
Card-Automated Reproduction and
Distribution System, CARDS
RTSD Reproduction of Library Materials
Section, RTSD/RLMS

Reproduction Photographique
Association pour la Conservation et la
Reproduction Photographique de la
Presse, ACRPP

Reproduction Service
ERIC Document Reproduction Service,
EDRS

Reprographic
Institute of Reprographic Technology, IRT

Reprographic Centre
National Reprographic Centre for
Documentation, NRCd

Reprography
International Council for Reprography, ICR

Republics
Union of Soviet Socialist Republics, USSR

Request
Automatic Request (for Correction), ARQ
Request for Proposals, RFP
Request Price Quotation, RPQ
Request Select Entry, RSE

Requirements
ANSI Standards Planning and Requirements
Committee, ANSI/SPARC
User Requirements Language, URL

Rerun
Business Input-Output Rerun, BIOR

Research
ACM Special Interest Group on Computer
Personnel Research, ACM/SIGCPR
ASIS Special Interest Group on
Classification Research, ASIS/SIG/CR
Abstracts of Instructional and Research
Materials in Vocational and Technical
Education, AIM/ARM
Abstracts of Research and Related Materials
in Vocational and Technical Education,
ARM
Advanced Automation Research
Laboratory, AARL
Advanced Management Research, AMR
Advertising Research Foundation, ARF
Aerial Phenomena Research Organization,
APRO
Aerospace Research Applications Center,
ARAC

Research (cont.)

Agricultural Research Institute, ARI
Agricultural Research Management
  Information System, ARMIS
Agricultural Research Policy Advisory
  Committee, ARPAC
Agricultural Research Projects in the
  European Community, AGREP
Air Force Office of Scientific Research,
  AFOSR
Alternatives for Learning through
  Educational Research and Technology,
  ALERT
American Association for Public
  Information, Education and Research,
  AAPIER
American Educational Research
  Association, AERA
American Institute for Research, AIR
Applied Science and Research Applications,
  ASRA
Asociación de Bibliotecarios de Instituciones
  de Enseñanza Superior y de
  Investigación (Association of Librarians
  of Institutions of Higher Education and
  Research), ABIESI
Associated Library and Educational
  Research Team for Survival, ALERTS
Association for Marine Research and
  Technology Information, AIM
Association for Research and
  Enlightenment, ARE
Association of Caribbean University and
  Research Institute Libraries, ACURIL
Association of State Colleges and
  Universities Forestry Research
  Organizations, ASCUFRO
Atomic Energy Research Establishment,
  AERE
Atomic Weapons Research Establishment,
  AWRE
Australian Centre for Research in Library
  and Information Science, ACRiLIS
Australian Council for Educational
  Research, ACER
Bibliographical Center for Research, BCR
*Bibliography of Scientific and Industrial
  Research*, BSIR
Bituminous Coal Research, Inc, BCR
Brewing Industry Research Foundation,
  BIRF
Brewing Research Foundation, BRF
British Carbonization Research Association,
  BCRA
British Cast Iron Research Association,
  BCIRA
British Ceramic Research Association,
  BCRA
British Coke Research Association, BCRA

British Hydromechanics Research
  Association, BHRA
Building Research Advisory Board, BRAB
Building Research Institute, BRI
Buildings Services Research and Information
  Association, BSRIA
Bureau of Applied Social Research, BASR
Canadian Classification Research
  Group/Groupe Canadien pour la
  Recherche en Classification, CCRG
Center for African Studies and Institute for
  Social Research, CAS&ISR
Center for Documentation and
  Communication Research, CDCR
Center for Educational Research and
  Innovation, CERI
Center for Labor Education and Research,
  CLEAR
Center for Research and Evaluation in
  Applications of Technology in
  Education, CREATE
Center for Research in College Instruction of
  Science and Mathematics, CRICISAM
Center for Research on Language and
  Language Behavior, CRLLB
Center for Research on Learning and
  Teaching, CRLT
Central Fuel Research Institute, CFRI
Centre Européene pour la Recherche
  Nucléaire (European Center for Nuclear
  Research), CERN
Centre National d'Étude et
  d'Experimentation de Machinisme
  Agricole (National Center for
  Agricultural Machinery Research and
  Experimentation), CNEEMA
Centro Brasileiro de Pesquisas
  Educacionais-Divisão de Documentacão
  e Informacão Pedagógica (Brazilian
  Center of Educational
  Research-Department of Educational
  Documentation and Information),
  CBPE-DDIP
Centro de Esploroj Kaj Documentado
  (Research and Documentation Center),
  CED
Ceylon Institute of Scientific and Industrial
  Research, CISIR
Chemical Marketing Research Association,
  CMRA
Chemical Society Research Unit in
  Information Dissemination and
  Retrieval, CSRUIDR
Children's Psychiatric Research Institute,
  CPRI
Cocoa Research Institute, CRIG
Comisión Nacional de Investigación
  Científica y Technológica (National
  Commission on Scientific and
  Technological Research), CONICYT

Committee on Research Materials on
Southeast Asia, CORMOSEA
Committee on Space Research, COSPAR
Commonwealth Scientific and Industrial
Research Organization, CSIRO
Comparative Animal Research Laboratory,
CARL
Consejo Nacional de Investigaciones
Científicas y Técnicas (National Council
for Scientific and Technical Research),
CONICET
Consejo Nacional de Investigaciones
Científicas y Tecnológicas (National
Council for Scientific and Technological
Research), CONICIT
Consejo Nacional de Investigaciones
Científicas y Tecnológicas (National
Council for Scientific and Technological
Research), CONICYT
Construction Industry Research and
Information Association, CIRIA
Copper and Brass Research Association,
CBRA
Corporation for Economics and Industrial
Research, CEIR
Council for Scientific and Industrial
Research, CSIR
Council of Research and Academic
Libraries, CORAL
Current Agricultural Research Information
System, CARIS
Current Cancer Research Project Analysis
Center, CCRESPAC
Current Research and Development in Israel,
CRI
Current Research Information System, CRIS
Data and Research Technology Corporation,
DART
Department of Scientific and Industrial
Research, DSIR
Division of Computer Research and
Technology, DCRT
Documentation Research and Training
Centre, DRTC
East African Agriculture and Forestry
Research Organization, EAAFRO
Educational Research Service, ERS
Electronics Research Center, ERC
Energy Research and Development
Administration, ERDA
Engineering Research Associates, ERA
European Center for the Coordination of
Research and Documentation in the
Social Sciences, CEUCORS
European Conference on the Application of
Research in Information Services and
Libraries, EURIM 3
European Research Associates, ERA
European Society for Opinion Surveys and
Market Research, ESOMAR

European Space Research and Technology
Center, ESTEC
European Space Research Institute, ESRIN
European Space Research Laboratory,
ESLAB
European Space Research Organization,
ESRO
FID Committee on Classification Research,
FID/CR
FID Committee on Research on the
Theoretical Basis of Information,
FID/RI
Fuel Research Institute, FRI
German Research Society, GRS
Global Atmospheric Research Program,
GARP
Hampshire Technical Research Industrial
and Commercial Service, HATRICS
Harvard Ukrainian Research Institute,
HURI
Highway Research Information Service,
HRIS
Historical Evaluation and Research
Organization, HERO
Human Resources Research Organization,
HUMRRO
Illinois Institute of Technology Research
Institute, IITRI
Index of Codes for Research Drugs, ICRD
Institute de Recherche d'Informatique et
d'Automatique (French Research
Institute of Information and Automatic
Processing), IRIA
Institute for Behavioral Research, IBR
Institute for Industrial Research and
Standards, IIRS
Institute of Standards and Industrial
Research of Iran, ISIRI
Instituto Centro Americano de Investigacion
y Technologia Industrial (Central
American Institute of Research and
Industrial Technology), ICAITI
Interdisciplinary Machine Processing for
Research and Education in the Social
Sciences, IMPRESS
International Association for Mass
Communication Research, IAMCR
International Cancer Research Data Bank
Program, ICRDB
International Copper Research Association,
INCRA
International Information System on
Research in Documentation, ISORID
International Road Research
Documentation, IRRD
Inter-University Consortium for Political and
Social Research, ICPSR
Joint Industry Committee for Television
Advertising Research, JICTAR
Journal of Geophysical Research, JGR

Research (cont.)

Journal of International Research Communications, JIRC
Lewis Audiovisual Research Institute and Teaching Archive, LARITA
Librarians in Education and Research in the Northeast, LEARN
Library Automation Research and Consulting, LARC
Majlis al-Bahth al-'Ilmi (Jordan Research Council), JRC
Maritime Research Information Service, MRIS
Medical Research Council, MRC
Medical Socioeconomic Research Sources. (Journal), MEDSOC
Modern Humanities Research Association, MHRA
National Academy of Sciences-National Academy of Engineering-National Research Council, NAS-NAE-NRC
National Association for Research in Science Teaching, NARST
National Bureau of Economic Research, NBER
National Foundation for Educational Research in England and Wales, NFER
National Institute for Educational Research (Kokuritsu Kyoiku Kenkyusho Fuzoku Kyoiku Toshokan), NIER
National Institute for Medical Research, NIMR
National Institute for Research in Nuclear Science, NIRNS
National Research Council, NRC
National Society for Medical Research, NSMR
New England Interinstitutional Research Council, NEIRC
North Country Reference and Research Resources Council, NCRRRC
Office de la Recherche Scientifique et Technique d'Outre-Mer (Office of Overseas Scientific and Technical Research), ORSTOM
Office for Research, OFR
Ohio Project for Research in Information Services, OPRIS
Operation Research Society, ORS
Operations Research, OR
Operations Research, Inc, ORI
Operations Research Society of America, ORSA
Operations Research/Systems Analysis, OR/SA
Pacific Coast Forest Research Information Network, PACFORNET
Printing Industry Research Association, PIRA

Pulp and Paper Research Institute of Canada/Information Retrieval Services, PAPRICAN/IRS
Railroad Research Information Service, RRIS
Reference and Research Library Resources, 3 Rs
Research and Development, R&D
Research and Development, RD
Research and Development, Army, RDA
Research and Development Report, RDR
Research Assistant, RA
Research Community of Slovenia, RSS
Research Division Technical Report, RDTR
Research in Automatic Photocomposition and Information Dissemination, RAPID
Research Industry Document Center, RIDC
Research Information Center and Advisory Service on Information Processing, RICASIP
Research Information Services, RIS
Research Information Services for Education, RISE
Research Institute for the Study of Man, RISM
Research Institute of America, Inc, RIA
Research on Computer Applications in the Printing and Publishing Industries, ROCAPPI
Research Publications, Inc, RP
Research Seminar in Quantitative Economics, RSQE
Research Society for Victorian Periodicals, RSVP
Rochester Regional Research Library Council, RRRLC
Rubber and Plastics Research Association, RAPRA
Safety Research Information Service, SRIS
Science Research Associates, SRA
Science Research Council, SRC
Scientific Instrument Research Association, SIRA
Scientific Research Society of America, SRSA
Singapore Institute of Standards and Industrial Research, SISIR
Social Sciences Research Council, SSRC
Society for Film History Research, SFHR
Society for General Systems Research, SGSR
Society of Army Historical Research, SAHR
Sociological Research Association, SRA
South Central Research Library Council, SCRLC
Southwest Center for Urban Research, SCUR
Stanford Research Institute, SRI
Stockholm International Peace Research Institute, SIPRI

Swedish Institute for Administrative
Research, SIAR
Technical Processes Research Office, TPR
Thermodynamics Research Center, TRC
Tieteellisten Kirjastojen
Virkailijat-Vetenskapliga Bibliotekens
Tjänstemannaförening r. y. (Association
of Research and University Librarians),
TKV-VBT R.Y.
Toxicology Research Projects Directory.
(Journal), TRPD
Transportation Research Information
Services Network, TRISNET
Transportation Research Information
System, TRIS
Union of Burma Applied Research Institute,
UBARI
United Nations Institute for Training and
Research, UNITAR
US Government Research Reports, USGR
Vyzkumny Ustav pro Matematickych Stroju
(Research Institute for Mathematical
Machines), VUMS
Wool Industry Research Association, WIRA

Research and Development
Advisory Committee for the Research and
Development Department, ACORDD
Advisory Group for Aerospace Research and
Development, AGARD
Army Research and Development
Information System, ARDIS
Center for Environmental Research and
Development, CERD
*Current Research and Development in
Scientific Documentation*, CRDSD
Information System on Research and
Development in Building Industry and
Construction, INBAD
*International Directory of Research and
Development Scientists*, IDR&DS
National Council for Research and
Development, NCRD
Navy Automated Research and
Development Information System,
NARDIS
Southwest Regional Laboratory for
Educational Research and
Development, SWRL
*US Government Research and Development
Reports*, USGRDR
*US Government Research and Development
Reports Index*, USGRDRI

Research Center
Centre d'Étude des Matières Plastiques
(Plastics Research Center), CEMP
Middle Atlantic Educational and Research
Center, MERC
National Opinion Research Center, NORC

New England Research Application Center,
NERAC
Survey Research Center Data Library,
SRCDL
Western Research Application Center,
WESRAC

Research Centre
Public Interest Research Centre, PIRC

Research Librarians
Nordiska Vetenskapliga
Bibliotekarieförbundet (Scandinavian
Association of Research Librarians),
NVBF
Norske Forskningebibliotekarers Forening
(Association of Norwegian Research
Librarians), NFF
Svenska Bibliotekariesamfundet (Swedish
Association of University and Research
Librarians), SBS

Research Libraries
Art Research Libraries of Ohio, ARLO
Association of Caribbean University and
Research Libraries, ACURL
Association of College and Research
Libraries, ACRL
Association of Research Libraries, ARL
Association of Southeastern Research
Libraries, ASERL
California Chapter of Academic and
Research Libraries, CARL
Canadian Academic Research Libraries,
CARL
Canadian Association of Research
Libraries/Association des Bibliothèques
de Recherche du Canada, CARL/ABRC
Center for Research Libraries, CRL
College and Research Libraries. (Journal),
C&RL
Consortium of Rhode Island Academic and
Research Libraries, CRIARL
De Vetenskapliga Bibliotekens
Tjänstemannaförening (Union of
University and Research Libraries),
VBT
Forskningsbiblioteksrådet (Swedish Council
of Research Libraries), FBR
Houston Area Research Libraries
Consortium, HARLIC
Ligue des Bibliothèques Européennes de
Recherche (Association of European
Research Libraries), LIBER
Mid-Atlantic Research Libraries Information
Network, MARLIN
Research Libraries Group, RLG
Research Libraries Information Network,
RLIN

Research Libraries (cont.)

Sveriges Vetenskapliga Specialibiblioteks Förening (Association of Special Research Libraries), SVSF

Verein der Diplom-Bibliothekare an Wissenschaftlichen Bibliotheken (Association of Certified Librarians at Research Libraries), VdDB

Research Library

Independent Research Library Association, IRLA

Liverpool and District Scientific, Industrial and Research Library Advisory Council, LADSIRLAC

New York Metropolitan Reference and Research Library Agency, METRO

Research Service

Congressional Research Service, CRS

Joint Publications Research Service, JPRS

Library Reports and Research Service, Inc, LRRS

Researchers

(Brazilian) Directory of Researchers, CADAP

Canadian Educational Researchers Association/Association Canadienne des Chercheurs en Éducation, CERA/ACCE

Operations Research/Systems Analysis, OR/SA

Reshippers

United States Reshippers, USR

Resistor

Resistor-Capacitor Transistor Logic, RCTL

Transistor-Resistor-Transistor Logic, TRTL

Resonance

Carbon-13 Nuclear Magnetic Resonance, CNMR

Resource

Automatic Scheduling and Time-dependent Resource Allocation, ASTRA

Resource and Land Information, RALI

Society for Mass Media and Resource Technology, SMMART

South Australia Education Resource Information System, SAERIS

Universal Resource Information Symposium, URIS I

Resource Center

Media Equipment Resource Center, MERC

Resources

American Water Resources Association, AWRA

Augusta Area Committee for Health Information Resources, AACHIR

Black Resources Information Coordinating Services, Inc, BRICS

Bureau of Libraries and Learning Resources, BLLR

Catalogued Resources and Information Survey Programs, CRISP

Combined and Integrated Resources for Community Learning Experiment, CIRCLE

Committee on American Library Resources on South Asia, CALROSA

Data Resources, Inc, DRI

Earth Resources Observation System, EROS

Earth Resources Technology Satellite Program, ERTS

Educational Resources Information Center, ERIC

Exceptional Child Education Resources, ECER

Health Instructional Resources Association, HIRA

Health Resources Administration, HRA

Learning Resources Association of California Community Colleges, LRACCC

Medical Resources Consortium of Central New Jersey, MEDCORE

North Country Reference and Research Resources Council, NCRRRC

Office of Libraries and Learning Resources, OLLR

Office of Library Personnel Resources, OLPR

RTSD Resources Section, RTSD/RS

Regional Coordination of Biomedical Information Resources Program, RECBIR

Resources and Technical Services Division, RTSD

Resources in Education. (Journal), RIE

Resources in Vocational Education. (Journal), RIVE

Rochester Area Resources Exchange, RARE

Southern Water Resources Scientific Information Center, SWRSIC

UICA Learning Resources Exchange Program, UICA/LREP

Water Resources Document Reference Centre, WATDOC

Water Resources Scientific Information Center, WRSIC

Response

Audio Response Unit, ARU

Response Center

Toxicology Information Response Center, TIRC

Restore
Mean Time to Restore, MTTR

Restorers
Internationale Arbeitsgemeinschaft der Archiv-, Bibliotheks- und Grafikrestauratoren (International Working Group of Restorers of Archives, Libraries and Graphic Reproductions), IADA

Result
Result from Action, Prediction, Informative, Diagnostic Sensing, RAPIDS

Retail
National Federation of Retail Newsagents, Booksellers and Stationers, NFRN
Retail Book, Stationery and Allied Trades Employees Association, RBA
SAMI Retail Distribution Index. (Journal), SARDI

Retention
Shared Acquisitions and Retention System, SHARES

Retirement
College Retirement Equities Fund, CREF

Retrieval
Associative Content Retrieval Network, ACORN
Automated Linguistic Extraction and Retrieval Technique, ALERT
Automated News Clipping, Indexing, and Retrieval System, ANCIRS
Automated Retrieval System, ARS
Automatic Document Storage and Retrieval, ADSTAR
Automatic Fact Information Retrieval and Storage Systems, AFIRSS
Automation for Storage and Retrieval of Information, AFSARI
Bibliographic Retrieval Services, Inc, BRS
Browsing On-Line with Selective Retrieval, BROWSER
Bucknell Automated Retrieval and Display System, BARDS
Career Retrieval Search System, CARESS
Chemical Society Research Unit in Information Dissemination and Retrieval, CSRUIDR
Committee on Storage, Automatic Processing and Retrieval of Geological Data, COGEODATA
Compact Automatic Retrieval Display, CARD
Content Retrieval, CR
Current Awareness and Document Retrieval for Engineers, CADRE
Data Retrieval Language, DRL

Description, Acquisition, Retrieval, Correlation, DARC
Document Retrieval, DR
Documentation Automated Retrieval Equipment, DARE
Epilepsy Abstracts Retrieval System, EARS
FID Working Committee on Mechanical Storage and Retrieval, FID/MSR
General Retrieval and Information Processor for Humanities-Oriented Studies, GRIPHOS
Hierarchical Environmental Retrieval for Management Access and Networking, HERMAN
Hydrological Information Storage and Retrieval System, HISARS
IEEE Retrieval from the Literature on Electronics and Computer Sciences, IEEE REFLECS
Information Analysis and Retrieval Division, IARD
Information Storage and Retrieval, ISAR
Information Storage and Retrieval, ISR
Lehigh Automatic Device for Efficient Retrieval, LEADER
Literature Retrieval System for the Pulp and Paper Industry, LIRES
Market Data Retrieval–Educational Data Base, MDR
Medical Literature Analysis and Retrieval System, MEDLARS
Microfilm Retrieval Access Code, MIRACODE
Multiple Indexing and Console Retrieval Options, MICRO
On-Line Retrieval of Information over a Network, ORION
Psychological Abstracts Search and Retrieval, PASAR
Random Access Document Indexing and Retrieval, RADIR
Retrieval and Automatic Dissemination of Information from *Index Chemicus* and Line Notations, RADIICAL
Retrieval and Statistical Processing, RASP
Retrieval by On-Line Search, ROSE
Retrieval Command Language, RECOL
Retrieval of Enriched Textual Abstracts, RETA
Retrieval of Information about Census Tapes, RIACT
Retrieval of Special Portions from *Nuclear Science Abstracts*, RESPONSA
A Retrieval Process Language, ARPL
Retrieval through Automated Publication and Information Digest, RAPID
Salton's Magical Automatic Retrieval of Texts, SMART
Schering-Oriented Literature Analysis and Retrieval System, SCHOLAR

Retrieval (cont.)

Selective Information Dissemination and
    Retrieval, SIDAR
Ships Analysis and Retrieval Program,
    SHARP
Storage and Information Retrieval System,
    STAIRS
Storage, Handling and Retrieval of Technical
    Data in Image Formation, SHIRTDIF
Syracuse University *Psychological
    Abstracts* Retrieval System, SUPARS
System for Electronic Analysis and Retrieval
    of Criminal Histories, SEARCH
Terrain Elevation Retrieval Program, TERP
Tracking Retrieval and Analysis of Criminal
    Events, TRACE

Retrieval Centers
National Information Storage and Retrieval
    Centers, NISARC

Retrieval Services
ASIS Special Interest Group on
    Computerized Retrieval Services,
    ASIS/SIG/CRS

Retrieval System
Micrographic Catalog Retrieval System,
    MCRS
Patent Information Retrieval System,
    MIS-IRPAT
Psychological Abstracts Reference Retrieval
    System, PARRS

Retrieve
Practical Algorithm to Retrieve Information
    Coded in Alphanumeric, PATRICIA

Retriever
Subject Content-Oriented Retriever for
    Processing Information Online,
    SCORPIO

Retrieving
Technique for Retrieving Information from
    Abstracts of Literature, TRIAL

Retrospective
Retrospective Conversion, RECON
Retrospective Search System on the
    INSPEC Data Base, RETROSPEC

Return-to-Zero
Return-to-Zero, RZ
Return-to-Zero (Nonpolarized), RZ(NP)
Return-to-Zero (Polarized), RZ(P)

Reunion
Reunion Interamericana de Bibliotecarios y
    Documentalistas Agrícolas, RIBDA

Review
Harvard Business Review, HBR
Library Computer Equipment Review.
    (Journal), LCER
Management Review and Analysis Program,
    MRAP
Microform Review. (Journal), MR
Micrographics Equipment Review. (Journal),
    MER
Program Evaluation and Review Technique,
    PERT

Reviews
Index to Scientific Reviews, ISR
Interdisciplinary Science Reviews, ISR
Reference and Subscription Book Reviews
    Committee, RSBRC

Revised
Revised, R

Revision
Joint Steering Committee for the Revision of
    the Anglo-American Cataloging Rules,
    JSCAACR

Rhode Island
Consortium of Rhode Island Academic and
    Research Libraries, CRIARL
Rhode Island Library Association, RILA

Rhodesia
Rhodesia Library Association, RLA

Ricerche
Consiglio Nazionale delle Ricerche, CNR

Richmond
Richmond Public Library, RPL

Rights
International Rights Information Service,
    IRIS
Native American Rights Fund, NARF

Rio de Janeiro
Biblioteca Nacional do Rio de Janeiro
    (National Library of Rio de Janeiro),
    BNRJ

Risk Analysis
General Risk Analysis Simulation Program,
    GRASP

Riuiste
Riuiste, RIU

Riverside
San Bernadino, Inyo, Riverside Counties
    United Library Services, SIRCULS

Road
International Road Federation, IRF
International Road Research
    Documentation, IRRD

Roberts
Roberts Information Services, ROBINS

Rochester
Rochester Area Resources Exchange, RARE
Rochester Regional Research Library
Council, RRRLC

Rock Information
Rock Information System, RKNFSYS

Rock Properties
Undergraduate Excavation and Rock
Properties Information Center, UERPIC

Romande
Union Romande de Journaux, URJ

Romantic
Romantic Novelists Association, RNA

Rome
Rome Air Development Center On-Line,
RADCOL

Rotating
Rotating Associative Processor for
Information Dissemination, RAPID

Round Table
American Library History Round Table,
ALHRT
CLA Cataloging and Classification
Roundtable, CLA/CCRT
CLA Health Sciences Roundtable,
CLA/HSRT
Exhibits Round Table, ERT
Federal Librarians Round Table, FLIRT
Government Documents Round Table,
GODORT
Intellectual Freedom Round Table, IFRT
International Relations Round Table, IRRT
Junior Members Round Table, JMRT
Library Instruction Round Table, LIRT
Library Periodicals Round Table, LPRT
Library Research Round Table, LRRT
MLA Junior Members Round Table,
MLA/JMRT
Social Responsibilities Round Table, SRRT
Staff Organization Round Table, SORT

Route
Automated Route Manager, ARM

Routine
Automatic Routine Generating and Updating
System, ARGUS
Real-Time Executive Routine, REX

Routines
Complex Utility Routines, CUR
Data Management Routines, DMR
Statistical Routines, STAT PACK

Tape Handling Optional Routines, THOR
Time-Shared Routines for Analysis,
Classification, and Evaluation, TRACE

Routing
Royal Optimizing Assembly Routing, ROAR

Royal
Royal Academy of Music, RAM
Royal Agricultural Society of England,
RASE
Royal Air Force Education Service, RAFES
Royal Canadian Mounted Police, RCMP
Royal Central Asian Society, RCAS
Royal College of Art, RCA
Royal College of Music, RCM
Royal College of Nursing and National
Council of Nursing, RCN
Royal College of Obstetricians and
Gynaecologists, RCOG
Royal College of Physicians of Edinburgh,
RCPE
Royal College of Physicians of London, RCP
Royal College of Surgeons in Ireland, RCSI
Royal College of Surgeons of Edinburgh,
RCSEd
Royal College of Surgeons of England,
RCSEng
Royal College of Veterinary Surgeons,
RCVS
Royal Commission on Historical
Manuscripts, HMC
Royal Dutch Pharmaceutical Society,
KNMP
Royal Institute of British Architects, RIBA
Royal Institute of Technology Library,
IDC-KTHB
Royal Optimizing Assembly Routing, ROAR
Royal Scottish Academy of Music and
Drama, RSAMD
Royal Society of British Artists, RBA
Royal Society of Painter-Etchers and
Engravers, RE

Rubber
Chemical Rubber Company, CRC
Rubber and Plastics Research Association,
RAPRA

Rules
Anglo-American Cataloging Rules, AACR
Anglo-American Cataloguing Rules, AACR
2
Joint Steering Committee for the Revision of
the Anglo-American Cataloging Rules,
JSCAACR
Test Rules for Inventory Management,
TRIM

Rumania
Centrul de Documentare Stiitifică al
Academiei Republicii Socialiste

Rumania (cont.)

România (Scientific Documentation
Center of the Academy of the Socialist
Republic of Rumania), CDS

Rural
ERIC Clearinghouse on Rural Education and
Small Schools, ERIC/RC
*World Agricultural Economics and Rural
Sociology Abstracts*, WAERSA

Rural Libraries
Southwestern Ohio Rural Libraries, SWORL

SAGE
SAGE Air Traffic Integration, SATIN

SAMI
SAMI On-Line Operations, SOLO
SAMI Retail Distribution Index. (Journal),
SARDI

SHARE
SHARE Compiler, Assembler and
Translator, SCAT

SSSR
Naučno-Issledovatel'skij i Konstruktorskij
Institut Ispytatel'nych Mašin, Priborov i
Sredstv Avtomatizacii i Sistem
Upravlenija SSSR, NIKIMP
Naučno-Issledovatel'skij Institut Rezinovoj
Promyšlennosti Ministerstva
Neftpererabatyvajuščej i
Neftechimičeskoj, Promyšlennosti
SSSR, NIIRP
Vsesojuznyï Naučhno-Issledovatel'skii
Institut Molochnoi Promyshiennosti
Ministerstva Miasnoi i Molochnoi
Promyshlennosti SSSR, VNIMI
Vsesojuznyj Gosudarstvennyj Institut po
Proektirovaniju Naučno-
Issledovatel'skich Institutov i
Laboratorij Akademii nauk SSSR,
GIPRONTII
Vsesojuznyj Naučno-Isseldovatel'skij
Geologorazvedočnyj Neftjanoj Institut
Ministerstra Geologii SSSR, VNIGNI
Vsesojuznyj Naučno-Issledovatel'skij
Institut Economiki Mineral'nogo Syr'ja i
Geologorazvedocnych Rabot
Ministerstva Geologii SSSR i Akademii
nauk SSSR, VIEMS
Vsesojuznyj Naučno-Issledovatel'skij
Institut Iskusstvennogo Volokna
Ministerstva Chimičeskoj
Promyšlennosti SSSR, VNIIV
Vsesojuznyj Naučno-Issledovatel'skij
Institut Konservnoj i Ovoščesušil'noj
Promyšlennosti Ministerstva Pisščevoj
Promyšlennosti SSSR, VNIIKOP

Vsesojuznyj Naučno-Issledovatel'skij
Institut Mechovoj Promyšlennosti
Ministerstva Legleoj Promyšlennosti
SSSR, VNIIMP
Vsesojuznyj Naučno-Issledovatel'skij
Institut Mjasnoj Promyšlennosti
Ministerstva Mjasnoj i Moločnoj
promyslennosti SSSR, VNIIMP
Vsesojuznyj Naučno-Issledovatel'skij
Institut po Pererabotke Chimičeskich
Volokon Ministerstva Legkoj
Promyšlennosti SSSR, VNIIPCHV
Vsesojuznyj Naučno-Issledovatel'skij
Institut po Pererabotke Nefti
Ministerstva Nefteprerabatyvajuščej i
Neftechimičeskoj Promyšlennosti
SSSR, VNIINP
Vsesojuznyj Naučno-Issledovatel'skij
Institut Stekloplastikov i Stekljannogo
Volokna Ministerstva Chimičeskoj
Promyšlennosti SSSR, VNIISSV
Vsesojuznyj Naučno-Issledovatel'skij
Kinofotoinstitut Gosudarstvennogo
Komiteta po Kinematografi pre Sovete
Ministrov SSSR, NIFKI
Vsesojuznyj Sel'skochozjajstvennyj Institut
Zaučnogo Obzovanija Ministerstva
Sel'skogo Chozjajstva SSSR, VSCHIZO

SUNY
SUNY Biomedical Communication
Network, SUNY-BCN

Safety
Consumer Product Safety Commission,
CPSC
National Institute for Occupational Safety
and Health, NIOSH
Occupational Safety and Health
Administration, OSHA
Safety Research Information Service, SRIS

Saint Lawrence Valley
Associated Colleges of the Saint Lawrence
Valley, ACSLV

Saint Louis
Higher Education Coordinating Council of
Metropolitan Saint Louis, HECC

Sale
Point of Sale, POS

Salton's
Salton's Magical Automatic Retrieval of
Texts, SMART

Salvador Librarians
Asociación de Bibliotecarios de El Salvador
(Association of El Salvador Librarians),
ABES

Sample Tables
Teaching Sample Tables, TESAT

San Antonio
Health Oriented Libraries of San Antonio, HOLSA
Librarians Serving San Antonio, LISSA
University of Texas Health Science Center at San Antonio, UTHSCSA

San Bernadino
San Bernadino, Inyo, Riverside Counties United Library Services, SIRCULS

San Francisco
San Francisco Public Library, SFPL

Sangamon Valley
Sangamon Valley Academic Library Consortium, SVAL

Santé
Institut National de la Santé et de la Recherche Medicale, INSERM

São Paulo
Associação Paulista de Bibliotecários (São Paulo Library Association), APB

Saskatchewan
Association of Saskatchewan Government Libraries, ASGL
Saskatchewan Association of Educational Media Specialists, SAEMS
Saskatchewan Association of Library Technicians, SALT
Saskatchewan Government Libraries Association, SGLA
Saskatchewan Library Association, SLA
Saskatchewan Library Trustees Association, SLTA

Satellite
Application Technology Satellite, ATS
Application Technology Satellite, ATS-F
Application Technology Satellite 1, ATS-1
Application Technology Satellite 6, ATS-6
Communications Satellite Corporation, COMSAT
Earth Resources Technology Satellite Program, ERTS
International Telecommunications Satellite Consortium, INTELSAT
Open Access Satellite Education Services, OASES
Pan-Pacific Education and Communication Experiments by Satellite, PEACESAT
Satellite Auto-Monitor System, SAMS
Satellite Library Information Network, SALINET

Satellite Service
National Environmental Satellite Service, NESS

Sault
Sault Area International Library Association, SAILA

Scandinavian
Nordiska Vetenskapliga Bibliotekarieförbundet (Scandinavian Association of Research Librarians), NVBF
Scandinavian Documentation Center, SCANDOC
Scandinavian Public Library Quarterly. (Journal), SPLQ

Scanner
General Electric Scanner, GESCAN
Interrelated Logic Accumulating Scanner, ILAS

Scanning
Automatic Computer-Controlled Electronics Scanning System, ACCESS
Computer-Assisted Scanning Techniques, CAST
Computer-Controlled Scanning Electron Microscope, CCSEM
Japanese Medical Abstract Scanning System, JAMASS
Optical Scanning, OS
Optical Scanning Device, OSD

Scheduling
Automatic Operating and Scheduling Program, AOSP
Automatic Scheduling and Time-dependent Resource Allocation, ASTRA
Computer-Aided Batch Scheduling, CABS
Least-cost Estimating and Scheduling System, LESS
Scheduling and Control by Automated Network System, SCANS

Scheme
Greater London Audio Specialization Scheme, GLASS
Humberside Libraries Technical Interloan Scheme, HULTIS
Northern Inter-Library Cooperation Scheme, NICS

Schering
Schering-Oriented Literature Analysis and Retrieval System, SCHOLAR

Scholarly
Centro Interamericano de Libros Académicos (Inter-American Scholarly Book Center), CILA

Scholarly (cont.)

International Association of Scholarly
Publishers, IASP
Society for Scholarly Publishing, SSP

Scholars
Council for International Exchange of
Scholars, CIES

School
American Association of School
Administrators, AASA
American School Counselors Association,
ASCA
Association de l'École Nationale Supérieure
de Bibliothécaires (Association of the
National School of Librarianship),
AENSB
Australian School Library Association,
ASLA
[Biblíoteka] Szkoly Glównej Planowania i
Statystykí (Library of the Central
School of Planning and Statistics),
SGPIS
British Columbia School Librarians
Association, BCSLA
Canadian School Library Association, CSLA
Catholic School Press Association, CSPA
Connecticut School Library Association,
CSLA
East Central State School Libraries
Association (Nigeria), ECSLA
École de Bibliothécaires, Archivistes et
Documentalistes (School of Librarians,
Archivists and Documentalists), EBAD
Egyptian School Library Association, ESLA
International Association of School
Librarianship, IASL
National Association for School Magazines,
NASM
National Association of Secondary School
Principals, NASSP
New England School Library Association,
NESLA
Nova Scotia School Library Association,
NSSLA
Ontario School Library Association, OSLA
Peel Secondary School Librarians
Association, PSSLA
Periodical Holdings in the Library of the
School of Medicine, PHILSOM
Prime Time School Television, PTST
Prince Edward Island School Library
Association, PEISLA
School Broadcasting Council for the United
Kingdom, SBCUK
School Library Association, SLA
School Library Association of Papua, New
Guinea, SLAPNG
School Library Journal, SLJ

School Management Information Retrieval
System, SMIRS
School Media Quarterly. (Journal), SMQ
School of Information Studies, SIS
School of Library and Information Science,
SLIS
Society of Independent and Private School
Data Education, SIPSDE
Uganda School Library Association, USLA

School Librarians
American Association of School Librarians,
AASL
Cumann Leabharlannaithe Scoile (Irish
Association of School Librarians), CLS
Nevada Association of School Librarians,
NASL
Quebec Association of School Librarians,
QASL

School Libraries
Engineering School Libraries Division,
ESLD
Wyoming Association of School Libraries,
WASL

School Library
Manitoba School Library Audio-Visual
Association, MSLAVA
School Library Manpower Project, SLMP

School Systems
Computer–based Laboratory for Automated
School Systems, CLASS

Schools
American Association of Schools and
Departments of Journalism, AASDJ
Chicago Cluster of Theological Schools,
CCTS
Children's Books for Schools and Libraries,
CBSL
ERIC Clearinghouse on Rural Education and
Small Schools, ERIC/RC
Libraries of the Institutes and Schools of
Education, LISE
Visual Education National Information
Service for Schools, VENISS

Schriftsteller
Verband Deutscher Schriftsteller, VS

Schriftsteller-Verband
Schweizerischer
Schriftsteller-Verband/Société Suisse
des Écrivains, SSV/SSE

Schweisstechnik
Dokumentation Schweisstechnik, DS

Schweiz
Vereinigung der Buchantiquare und
Kupferstichhändler in der

Schweiz/Syndicat de la Libraire
Ancienne et du Commerce de l'Estampe
en Suisse, VEBUKU/SLACES

Schweizerische
Schweizerische Journalisten-Union/Union
Suisse des Journalistes, SJU/USJ

Schweizerischen
Union der Schweizerischen
Lichtspieltheater-Verbänd/Union des
Associations Cinématographiques
Suisses, USLV/UACS

Schweizerischer
Schweizerischer Lichtspieltheater-Verband,
SLV
Schweizerischer
Schriftsteller-Verband/Société Suisse
des Écrivains, SSV/SSE

Science
ACRL Science and Technology Section,
ACRL/STS
*Abstracts of Photographic Science and
Engineering Literature*, APSE
Academy of Applied Science, AAS
Advanced Science Computer, ASC
Advisory Council on Science Policy, ACSP
American Association for the Advancement
of Science, AAAS
American Men and Women of Science. 14th
Edition, AMWS
American Science Film Association, ASFA
Applied Science and Research Applications,
ASRA
Applied Science and Technology Index,
AS&T
Association of British Science Writers,
ABSW
Association pour l'Avancement des Sciences
et des Techniques de la Documentation
(Association for the Advancement of the
Science and Technology of
Documentation), ASTED
Australian and New Zealand Association for
the Advancement of Science, ANZAAS
Biological Science Communications Project,
BSCP
Center for Research in College Instruction of
Science and Mathematics, CRICISAM
*Clearinghouse Announcements in Science
and Technology*, CAST
Colombian Association for the Advancement
of Science, ACAC
Committee for Information and
Documentation on Science and
Technology, CIDST
Committee on Data for Science and
Technology, CODATA

Committee on Science and Public Policy,
COSPUP
Committee on Science and Technology in
Developing Countries, COSTED
*Computer Programs in Science and
Technology* (Index), CPST
Computer Science, CS
Consejo Nacional de Ciencia y Tecnologia
(National Council of Science and
Technology), CONACYT
*Current Bibliography on Science and
Technology*, CBST
Department of Education and Science, DES
*Directory of Computerized Information in
Science and Technology*, DCIST
ERIC Clearinghouse for Science,
Mathematics and Environmental
Education, ERIC/SE
Environmental Science and Information
Center, ESIC
Federation for Unified Science Education,
FUSE
Food Science and Technology Abstracts,
FSTA
Indian Science Abstracts, ISA
Interdisciplinary Science Reviews, ISR
International Advisory Committee on
Documentation and Terminology in Pure
and Applied Science, AICDT
International Union of the History and
Philosophy of Science, IUHPS
Japan Information Center for Science and
Technology, JICST
National Association for Research in Science
Teaching, NARST
National Federation of Science Abstracting
and Indexing Services, NFSAIS
National Institute for Research in Nuclear
Science, NIRNS
National Lending Library for Science and
Technology, NLL
National Reference Library of Science and
Invention, NRLSI
National Referral Center for Science and
Technology, NRCST
National Science Foundation, NSF
National Science Teachers Association,
NSTA
National Space Science Data Center,
NSSDC
Neurological Science Information Network,
NINDS
Northeast Academic Science Information
Center, NASIC
Nuclear Science Abstracts, NSA
Office of Science and Technology, OST
Polymer Science and Technology, POST
Polymer Science and Technology for
Journals, POST-J

Science (cont.)

Polymer Science and Technology for
    Patents, POST-P
President's Science Advisory Committee,
    PSAC
Science and Technology Information Officer,
    STINFO
Science and Technology Policies Information
    Exchange System, SPINES
Science Citation Index, SCI
Science Citation Index Search,
    SCISEARCH
Science Information Exchange, SIE
Science Reference Library, SRL
Science Research Associates, SRA
Science Research Council, SRC
Smithsonian Science Information Exchange,
    SSIE
Society for Automation in Science and
    Mathematics, SASM
Soil Science Society of America, SSSA
System for Organizing Current Reports to
    Aid Technology and Science,
    SOCRATES
Universal System for Information in Science
    and Technology, UNISIST
Who Is Publishing in Science, WIPIS

Science Center
University City Science Center, UCSC

Science Fiction
British Science Fiction Association, BSFA

Science Information
Special Foreign Currency Science
    Information Program, SFCSI

Science Library
National Science Library, NSL

Sciences
Agricultural Sciences Information Network,
    ASIN
American Academy of Arts and Sciences,
    AAAS
Aquatic Sciences and Fisheries Abstracts,
    ASFA
Association Canadienne Français pour
    l'Avancement des Sciences, ACFAS
Conference Board of the Mathematical
    Sciences, CBMS
Council for International Organizations on
    Medical Sciences, CIOMS
*Current Bibliographic Directory of the Arts
    and Sciences*, CBD
*Current Contents/Agricultural, Food and
    Veterinary Sciences*. (Journal), CC/AFV
*Current Contents/Agriculture, Biology and
    Environmental Sciences*. (Journal),
    CC/AB&ES

*Current Contents/Behavioral, Social and
    Educational Sciences*. (Journal),
    CC/BSE
*Current Contents/Chemical,
    Pharmaco-Medical and Life Sciences*.
    (Journal), CC/CPML
*Current Contents/Engineering, Technology
    and Applied Sciences*. (Journal),
    CC/ET&AS
*Current Contents/Physical and Chemical
    Sciences*. (Journal), CC/PC
Development of Sciences Information
    System, DEVSIS
*Directory of Data Bases in the Social and
    Behavioral Sciences*, DDB
Hawaii International Conference on System
    Sciences, HICSS
Institute for the Comparative Study of
    History, Philosophy and the Sciences,
    Ltd, ICS
Instituto Interamericano de Ciencias
    Agrícolas de la OEA (Interamerican
    Institute of Agricultural Sciences of
    OAS/OEA), IICA
International Reference Organization in
    Forensic Medicine and Sciences,
    INFORM
Magyar Tudományos Akadémía Könyotára
    (Library of the Hungarian Academy of
    Sciences), MTAK
National Academy of Sciences, NAS
National Academy of Sciences–National
    Academy of Engineering–National
    Research Council, NAS–NAE–NRC
New York Academy of Sciences, NYAS
Ústredná Kniznica Slovenskej Akademie
    Vied (Central Library of the Slovak
    Academy of Sciences), UKSAV

Scientific
Advanced Scientific Instruments Symbolic
    Translator, ASIST
Advisory Board on Scientific and Technical
    Information, ABSTI
Advisory Committee for Scientific and
    Technical Information, ACSTI
Air Force Office of Scientific Research,
    AFOSR
Australian National Scientific and
    Technological Library, ANSTEL
Bangladesh National Scientific and
    Technical Documentation Center,
    BANSDOC
*Bibliography of Scientific and Industrial
    Research*, BSIR
Bradford Scientific, Technical and
    Commercial Service, BRASTACS
British Commonwealth Scientific Office,
    BCSO
British Industrial and Scientific Film
    Association Ltd, BISFA

Bureau National d'Information Scientifique et Technique (National Board for Scientific and Technical Information), BNIST

Cambridge Scientific Abstracts, Inc, CSA

Canadian Institute for Scientific and Technical Information (Institut Canadien de l'Information Scientifique et Technique), CISTI/ICIST

Center of Scientific and Technological Information, COSTI

Center of Scientific and Technological Information, CSTI

Centralny Instytut Informacji Naukowo Technicznej i Ekonomicznej (Central Institute for Scientific, Technical and Economic Information), CIINTE

Centre National de Documentation Scientifique et Technique (National Center for Scientific and Technical Documentation), CNDST

Centro de Documentação Cientifica (Scientific Documentation Center), CDC

Centro de Información Cientifica y Humanistica (Center for Scientific and Humanistic Information), CICH

Centro Nacional de Información Científica y Técnica (National Center for Scientific and Technical Information), CONICIT

Centrul de Documentare Stiitifică al Academiei Republicii Socialiste România (Scientific Documentation Center of the Academy of the Socialist Republic of Rumania), CDS

Ceylon Institute of Scientific and Industrial Research, CISIR

Classified Scientific and Technical Aerospace Reports, C-STAR

Clearinghouse for Federal Scientific and Technical Information, CFSTI

Comisión de Documentación Científica (Scientific Documentation Center), CDDC

Comisión Nacional de Investigación Científica y Technológica (National Commission on Scientific and Technological Research), CONICYT

Committee on International Scientific and Technical Information Programs, CISTIP

(Committee on) Scientific and Technical Communication, SATCOM

Committee on Scientific and Technical Information, COSATI

Commonwealth Scientific and Industrial Research Organization, CSIRO

Compiler Los Alamos Scientific Laboratories, COLASL

Consejo Nacional de Investigaciones Científicas y Técnicas (National Council for Scientific and Technical Research), CONICET

Consejo Nacional de Investigaciones Científicas y Tecnológicas (National Council for Scientific and Technological Research), CONICIT

Consejo Nacional de Investigaciones Científicas y Tecnológicas (National Council for Scientific and Technological Research), CONICYT

Council for Scientific and Industrial Research, CSIR

Council of Engineering and Scientific Society Executives, CESSE

Council of Engineering and Scientific Society Secretaries, CESS

Current Research and Development in Scientific Documentation, CRDSD

Department of Scientific and Industrial Research, DSIR

Directorate of Scientific Information Services, DSIS

Flexible Algebraic Scientific Translator, FAST

General Purpose Scientific Document Image Code, GPSDIC

General Purpose Scientific Document Writer, GPSDW

Index to Scientific and Technical Proceedings, ISTP

Index to Scientific Reviews, ISR

Indian National Scientific Documentation Centre, INSDOC

Instituto de Documentación e Información Científica y Tecnica (Institute of Scientific and Technical Documentation and Information), IDICT

Inter-change of Scientific and Technical Information in Machine Language, ISTIM

International Council of Scientific Unions, ICSU

International Scientific Film Association, ISFA

International Scientific Film Library, ISFL

Jugoslovenski Centar za Technicku i Naučno Dokumentaciju (Yugoslav Center for Technical and Scientific Documentation), JCTND

Korean Scientific and Technological Information Center, KORSTIC

Liverpool and District Scientific, Industrial and Research Library Advisory Council, LADSIRLAC

Manchester Federation of Scientific Societies, MFSS

(National) Scientific Communication and Technology Transfer, SCATT

National Systems of Scientific and Technological Information of Brazil, SNICT

Scientific (cont.)

Naval Scientific and Technical Information Centre, NSTIC

Oceanic and Atmospheric Scientific Information System, OASIS

Office de la Recherche Scientifique et Technique d'Outre-Mer (Office of Overseas Scientific and Technical Research), ORSTOM

Office for Scientific and Technical Information, OSTI

Pakistan National Scientific and Technical Documentation Center, PANSDOC

Pakistan Scientific and Technological Information Center, PASTIC

Pusat Documentasi Ilmiah Nasional (Indonesian Scientific and Technical Documentation Center), PDIN

Redstone Scientific Information Center, RSIC

Scientific and Technical Aerospace Reports. (Journal), STAR

Scientific and Technical Association of the People's Republic of China, STAPRC

Scientific and Technical Information, STI

Scientific and Technological Information Services Enquiry Committee, STISEC

Scientific Committee on Problems of the Environment, SCOPE

Scientific Documentation Centre, Ltd, SDC

Scientific Manpower Commission, SMC

Scientific Report, SR

Scientific Research Society of America, SRSA

Scientific, Technical and Medical Publishers, STM

Southern Water Resources Scientific Information Center, SWRSIC

Thesaurus of Engineering and Scientific Terms, TEST

Türkiye Bilimsel ve Teknik Dokümantasyon Merkezi (Turkish Scientific and Technical Documentation Center), TÜRDOK

Union Radio-Scientifique Internationale (International Scientific Radio Union), URSI

United Nations Educational, Scientific and Cultural Organization, UNESCO

Ústav Vědeckotechnických Informací (Institute of Scientific Technical Information), UVTI

Ústředí Vědeckých Technických a Ekonomických Informací (Central Office of Scientific, Technical and Economic Information), UVTEI

Water Resources Scientific Information Center, WRSIC

Scientific Information

APA Project on Scientific Information in Psychology, APA-PSIP

Admiralty Centre for Scientific Information and Liaison, ACSIL

Association of Scientific Information Dissemination Centers, ASIDIC

Center for Inventions and Scientific Information, CISI

Centre de Traitement de l'Information Scientifique (European Scientific Information Processing Center), CETIS

Committee on Scientific Information, COSI

Institut Nacnoj Informacii i Fundamental'naja Biblioteka po Obscestvennym Naukam (Institute of Scientific Information and Main Library of the Social Sciences), INIBON

Institute for Scientific Information, ISI

Institute for Scientific Information, SCITEL

Scientific Information and Educational Council of Physicians, SIECOP

Scientific Instrument

Scientific Instrument Research Association, SIRA

Scientific Research Institute

Vesesojuznii Naučno-Issle-Dovatel'skii Institut Techniceskoi Informaccii, Klassifikaccii i Kodirovaniia (All-Union Scientific Research Institute for Technical Information, Classification and Codification of USSR), VNIIKI

Vsesoiuznyǐ Nauchno Issle-dovatel'skii Institut Meditsinskoǐ i Medikotekhnicheskoǐ Informatsii Ministerstva Zdravookhraneniia USSR (All-Union Scientific Research Institute of Medical and Medico-Technical Information, VNIIMI

Scientifique

Centre National de la Recherche Scientifique, CNRS

Délégation Générale à la Recherche Scientifique et Technique, DGRST

Scientists

Association of Scientists and Professional Engineering Personnel, ASPEP

Federation of American Scientists, FAS

International Directory of Research and Development Scientists, IDR&DS

Scientists Committee for Public Information, SCPI

Scientists Institute for Public Information, SIPI

Society of Photographic Scientists and Engineers, SPSE

Scope
Digital Display Scope, DDS

Scotland
Aberdeen and North of Scotland Library and
    Information Cooperative Service,
    ANSLICS
Association of Directors of Education in
    Scotland, ADES
Educational Institute of Scotland, EIS
National Library of Scotland, NLS

Scottish
Royal Scottish Academy of Music and
    Drama, RSAMD
Scottish Daily Newspaper Society, SDNS
Scottish Educational Film Association,
    SEFA
Scottish Film Council, SFC
Scottish Library Association, SLA
Scottish Newspaper Proprietors Association,
    SNPA
Scottish Technical Education Consultative
    Council, STECC
Scottish Typographical Association, STA

Scottish Libraries
Scottish Libraries Cataloging Automation
    Project, SCOLCAP

Scottish Library
Scottish Central Library, SCL

Screen
Display Producers and Screen Printers
    Association, DPSA

Screening
Automated Health Multi-Phase Screening,
    AHMS

Scribes
Society of Scribes and Illuminators, SCI

Scrittori
Syndacato Nazionale Scrittori, SNS

Sea
International Council for the Exploration of
    the Sea, ICES

Search
Battelle Automated Search Information
    System for the Seventies, BASIS-70
Bibliographic Author or Subject Interactive
    Search, BA•SIS
Career Retrieval Search System, CARESS
Combined File Search, CFS
Combined File Search System, CFSS
Early MARC Search, EMS
Magnetic-tape Field Search, MFS
Psychological Abstracts Search and
    Retrieval, PASAR

Rapid Search Machine, RSM
Retrieval by On-Line Search, ROSE
Retrospective Search System on the
    INSPEC Data Base, RETROSPEC
Science Citation Index Search,
    SCISEARCH

Search Center
Computer Search Center, CSC

Search Service
Current Literature Alerting Search Service,
    CLASS
Dissertations Data Base Search Service,
    DATRIX

Searchable
Searchable Physics Information Notices,
    SPIN

Searches
Catalog of Computerized Subject Searches,
    CAT

Searches in Depth
Searches in Depth, SID

Searching
Machine Literature Searching, MLS

Seattle
Seattle Area Hospital Library Consortium,
    SAHLC

Second
Bits Per Second, BPS
Characters Per Second, CPS
Cycles Per Second, cps
Inches Per Second, IPS
One Thousand Characters per Second, KCS
Pulses per Second, PPS

Secondary
Elementary and Secondary Education Act,
    ESEA
National Association of Secondary School
    Principals, NASSP
Peel Secondary School Librarians
    Association, PSSLA

Secretaries
Council of Engineering and Scientific Society
    Secretaries, CESS

Securities
National Association of Securities Dealers
    Automated Quotations System,
    NASDAQ

Security
Archival Security Program, ASP
Electrical Accounting for the Security
    Industry, EASI
Electronic Security Systems, ESS

Seismograph
World Wide Network of Standard
 Seismograph Stations, WWNSS

Select
Request Select Entry, RSE

Selected
Selected Categories in Microfiche, SCIM
Selected Dissemination of Indexes, SEDIX
*Selected Publications in European
 Languages*, SPEL

Selection
Agricultural System for Storage and
 Subsequent Selection of Information,
 ASSASSIN
Automatic Data Processing Equipment
 Selection Office, ADPESO
Book Order and Selection, BOS
Machine Selection, MS
Multiple Access Sequential Selection, MASS
Programme Appliqué à la Sélection et à la
 Compilation Automatique de la
 Littérature, PASCAL
Selection Program for ADMIRAL Runs,
 SPAR
Station Selection Code, SSC
Systeme Electronique de Selection
 Automatique de Microfilms, SESAM

Selection Centers
Educational Media Selection Centers,
 EMSC

Selectiva
Diseminación Selectiva de la Información,
 DSI

Selective
Browsing On-Line with Selective Retrieval,
 BROWSER
Canadian Selective Dissemination of
 Information, CAN/SDI
Diffusion Sélective de l'Information, DSI
Selective Dissemination of Information, SDI
Selective Dissemination of MARC,
 SELDOM
Selective Dissemination of Microfiche, SDM
Selective Information Dissemination and
 Retrieval, SIDAR
Selective Letters in Combination, SLIC
Selective Sequence Electronic Calculator,
 SSEC

Selector
Sequentially Operated Teletypewriter
 Universal Selector, SOTUS

Self-Instructional
Self-Instructional Media-Assisted Learning
 Unit, SIMALU

Self-Organizing
Self-Organizing Large Information
 Dissemination, SOLID

Self-Programmed
Self-Programmed Electronic Equation
 Delineator, SPEED

Selling Areas
Selling Areas-Marketing Inc, SAMI

Semantic
Semantic Correlation, SEMCOR
Semantic Information Retrieval, SIR

Semantics
Formal Semantics Language, FSL

Semi-Automatic
Semi-Automatic Ground Environment,
 SAGE
Semi-Automatic Index of National
 Language, SAINT

Semiconductor
Semiconductor Storage Unit, SSU

Semi-Micro
Semi-Micro Xerography, SMX

Seminar
Research Seminar in Quantitative
 Economics, RSQE
Seminar on the Acquisition of Latin
 American Library Materials, SALALM

Seminario
Seminario Interamericano sobre la
 Integración de los Servicios de
 Información de Archivos, Bibliotecas y
 Centros de Documentación en America
 Central y el Caribe, SI/ABCD

Seminary Libraries
CLA College, University and Seminary
 Libraries Section, CLA/CUSLS
CLA Seminary Libraries Section, CLA/SLS

Send-Receive
Automatic Send-Receive Set, ASR
Keyboard Send/Receive, KSR

Senegal
Association Nationale des Bibliothécaires,
 Archivistes et Documentalistes
 Sénégalais (National Association of
 Librarians, Archivists and
 Documentalists of Senegal), ANBADS
Association Sénégalaise pour le
 Développement de la Documentation,
 des Bibliothèques, des Archives et des
 Musées (Senegal Association for the
 Development of Documentation,
 Libraries, Archives and Museums),
 ASDBAM

Sensing
Result from Action, Prediction, Informative,
    Diagnostic Sensing, RAPIDS

Sensing Device
Film Optical Sensing Device for Input to
    Computers, FOSDIC

Separator
File Separator, FS
Group Separator, GS
Record Separator, RS

Sequence
Selective Sequence Electronic Calculator,
    SSEC
Television Automatic Sequence Control,
    TASCON

Sequential
Basic Indexed Sequential Access Method,
    BISAM
Electronic Discrete Sequential Automatic
    Computer, EDSAC
Hierarchical Indexed Sequential Access
    Method, HISAM
Hierarchical Sequential Access Method,
    HSAM
Indexed Sequential Access Method, ISAM
Motorola Automatic Sequential
    Computer-Operated Tester, MASCOT
Multiple Access Sequential Selection, MASS
Queued Indexed Sequential Access Method,
    QISAM
Sequential In-Basket Exercise, SIBE

Sequentially
Sequentially Controlled Automatic
    Transmitter Start, SCATS
Sequentially Operated Teletypewriter
    Universal Selector, SOTUS

Serial
Librarians United to Fight Costly, Silly,
    Unnecessary Serial Title Changes,
    LUTFCSUSTC
New Serial Titles, NST
Standard Serial Number, SSN

Serial Number
International Standard Serial Number, ISSN

Serials
Charlotte Area Union List of Periodicals and
    Serials, CAULPS
Computerized Access to Periodicals and
    Serials, CAPSUL
Conversion of Serials Project, CONSER
Cooperative Serials Acquisitions Program,
    COSAP
Cooperative Union Serials System, CUSS
Intermountain Union List of Serials, IMULS
International Serials Data System, ISDS
Irregular Serials and Annuals, ISA

Minnesota Union List of Serials, MULS
National Serials Data Program, NSDP
Pacific Area Union List of Medical Serials,
    PAULMS
RTSD Serials Section, RTSD/SS
Serials On-Line, SERLINE
Union List of Serials, ULS
Universal Serials and Book Exchange,
    USBE
Virginia Union List of Biomedical Serials,
    VULBS

Service
BioSciences Information Service, BIOSIS
BioSciences Information Service Previews,
    BIOSIS Previews.
Chemical Abstracts Service, CAS
Computerized Automatic Reporting Service,
    CARS
Consumer Health Information Program and
    Service, CHIPS
Current Awareness Service, CAS
Educational Research Service, ERS
Educational Testing Service, ETS

Service Center
Automatic Data Processing Service Center,
    ADPSC

Service d'Échange
Service d'Échange d'Informations
    Scientifiques, SEIS

Service Organizations
Association of Data Processing Service
    Organizations, ADPSO
Association of Data Processing Service
    Organizations, Inc, ADAPSO

Services
Bibliographic Retrieval Services, Inc, BRS
Board of Cooperative Educational Services,
    BOCES
California Library Authority for Systems and
    Services, CLASS

Services Center
Defense Logistics Services Center, DLSC

Servicio de Información
Servicio de Información sobre Traducciones
    Científicas en Español, SITCE

Servicios Bibliotecarios
Agencia Metropolitanado Servicios
    Bibliotecarios, AMERSERBI

Servicios de Información
Seminario Interamericano sobre la
    Integración de los Servicios de
    Información de Archivos, Bibliotecas y
    Centros de Documentación en America
    Central y el Caribe, SI/ABCD

Servizio Documentazione
Centro Informazioni Studi
    Esperienze–Servizio Documentazione,
    CISE

Set
Data Set, DS
Data Set Control Block, DSCB
Integrated Set of Information Systems, ISIS

Share
Share Operating System, SOS

Shared
Remote User of Shared Hardware, RUSH
Shared Acquisitions and Retention System,
    SHARES
Shared Hospital Accounting System, SHAS
Shared Information Elicitation Facility,
    SHIEF

Sheffield
Sheffield Interchange Organization, SINTO

Shelf
Shelf List, SL

Shelter-Housed
Shelter-Housed Automatic Digital Random
    Access, SHADRAC

Shielding
Radiation Shielding Information Center,
    RSIC

Shift
Figures Shift, FIGs

Shift-In
Shift-In Character, SI

Shift-Out
Shift-Out Character, SO

Shipping
American Bureau of Shipping, ABS
Computer-Linked Information for Container
    Shipping, CLICS

Ships
Ships Analysis and Retrieval Program,
    SHARP

Short Title
Short Title Catalogue, STC

Shorthand
Symbolic Shorthand System, SSS

Sierra Leone
Sierra Leone Library Association, SLLA

Signal
Signal-to-Noise Ratio, S/N

Signals
Calculator Help in Processing Signals,
    CHIPS

Signs
Dictionary of Architectural Abbreviations,
    Signs and Symbols, DAA
Dictionary of Civil Engineering
    Abbreviations, Signs and Symbols,
    DCEA
Dictionary of Computer and Control Systems
    Abbreviations, Signs and Symbols,
    DCCSA
Dictionary of Electronics Abbreviations,
    Signs and Symbols, DEA
Dictionary of Industrial Engineering
    Abbreviations, Signs and Symbols,
    DIEA
Dictionary of Mechanical Engineering
    Abbreviations, Signs and Symbols,
    DMEA
Dictionary of Physics and Mathematics
    Abbreviations, Signs and Symbols,
    DPMA
Encyclopedia of Engineering Signs and
    Symbols, EESS

Simple
Simple Algebraic Language for Engineers,
    SALE
Simple Programming Language, SPL

Simplex
Simplex Circuit, SPX

Simplified
Fundamentally Analyzable Simplified
    English, FASE

Simulated
Simulated Linguistic Computer, SLC
Simulated Machine Indexing, SMI

Simulation
ACM Special Interest Group on Simulation,
    ACM/SIGSIM
Association Internationale pour le Calcul
    Analogique (International Association
    for Mathematics and Computer
    Simulation), AICA
Basic Analog Simulation System, BASS
Computer Simulation, CS
Computer-Assisted Industrial Simulation,
    CAISM
Computer-Assisted Logistics Simulation,
    CALOGSM
Computer-Assisted Program Evaluation
    Review Technique Simulation,
    CAPERTSIM
FORTRAN Simulation, FORTSIM
General Activity Simulation Program, GASP

General Data Analysis and Simulation,
GENDA
General Purpose Simulation Program, GPSS
General Risk Analysis Simulation Program,
GRASP
International Association for Mathematics
and Computer Simulation, IMACS
Simulation Councils, Inc, SCI
Simulation-Oriented Language, SOL
Simulation Programming Language,
SIMSCRIPT
Society for Computer Simulation, SCS

Simulation Center
Federal Computer Performance Evaluation
and Simulation Center, FEDSIM

Simulator
Combined Analog-Digital Systems
Simulator, CADSS
General Electric Manufacturing Simulator,
GEMS
General Purpose Systems Simulator, GPSS
Generic Problem Statement Simulator, GPSS
Japanese Keyword Indexing Simulator,
JAKIS
Modified Integration Digital Analog
Simulator, MIDAS
Off-Line Operating Simulator, OOPS
Simulator of Immediate Memory in Learning
Experiments, SIMILE
Tabulator Simulator, TABSIM

Simultaneous
Simultaneous Processing Operating System,
SIPROS

Sindacato
Sindacato Nazionale Autori Drammatici,
SNAD

Singapore
Library Association of Singapore, LAS
Singapore Institute of Standards and
Industrial Research, SISIR

Single-Copy
Single-Copy Ordering Plan, SCOP

Sistem
Sistem za Avtomatizacilo Informacijsko
Dokumentacijskih Centrov-
Elektrotehnika, SAIDC

Sistema
Sistema Colombiano de Información
Cientifica y Technica, SICOLDIC
Sistema Interamericano de Informacion para
las Ciencias Agricolas, AGRINTER

Sistema de Información
Sistema Nacional de Información de
Guatemala, SNIG

Skills
Coalition in the Use of Learning Skills,
CULS

Slack Time
Minimum Slack Time per Operation,
MINSOP

Slavic
ACRL Slavic and East European Section,
ACRL/SEES
American Association of Teachers of Slavic
and East European Languages,
AATSEEL
Coordinating Committee for Slavic-East
European Library Services,
COCOSEER
Slavic and East European Journal, SEEJ

Slovak
Ústredná Kniznica Slovenskej Akademie
Vied (Central Library of the Slovak
Academy of Sciences), UKSAV

Slovak Librarians
Zväz Slovenských Knihovníkov, Bibligrafov
a Informacných Pracovníkov
(Association of Slovak Librarians,
Bibliographers and Documentalists),
ZSKBIP

Slovenia
Društvo Bibliotekarjev Slovenije (Society of
Librarians in Slovenia), DBS
Research Community of Slovenia, RSS

Small
PLA Small and Medium-sized Libraries
Section, PLA/SMLS
Small University Libraries, SUL

Small Libraries
Small Libraries Publications, SLP

Small Press
Getting and Abetting Small Press, GAASP

Smith, Kline & French
Smith, Kline & French Laboratories, SK&F

Smithsonian
Smithsonian Information Exchange, SIE
Smithsonian Institution, SI
Smithsonian Institution Traveling Exhibition
Service, SITES
Smithsonian Science Information Exchange,
SSIE

Social
ACM Special Interest Group on Social and
Behavioral Science Computing,
ACM/SIGSOC
American Social Health Association, ASHA

Social (cont.)

Bureau of Applied Social Research, BASR
Center for African Studies and Institute for
Social Research, CAS&ISR
Centro Interamericano de Documentación
Económia y Social (Interamerican
Center for Economic and Social
Documentation), CIADES
*Current Contents/Behavioral, Social and
Educational Sciences.* (Journal),
CC/BSE
*Current Contents/Social and Behavioral
Sciences.* (Journal), CC/S&BS
*Directory of Data Bases in the Social and
Behavioral Sciences*, DDB
Economic and Social Commission for Asia
and the Pacific, ESCAP
Inter-University Consortium for Political and
Social Research, ICPSR

Social Information

Centro Nacional de Información Económica
y Social (National Center for Economic
and Social Information), CNIES

Social Responsibilities

Social Responsibilities Round Table, SRRT

Social Science

Canadian Social Science Abstracts, CSSA
Council on Social Science Data Archives,
CSSDA
ERIC Clearinghouse for Social
Studies/Social Science Education,
ERIC/SO
International Social Science Council, ISSC
Regional Social Science Data Archive,
RSSDA
Social Science Citation Index, SSCI
Social Science Information System, SSIS

Social Sciences

ASIS Special Interest Group on the
Behavioral and Social Sciences,
ASIS/SIG/BSS
Belgian Archives for the Social Sciences,
BASS
Design of Information in the Social Sciences,
DISISS
European Center for the Coordination of
Research and Documentation in the
Social Sciences, CEUCORS
*Index to Social Sciences and Humanities
Proceedings*, ISSHP
Information Requirements of the Social
Sciences, INFROSS
Institut Nacnoj Informacii i
Fundamental'naja Biblioteka po
Obscestvennym Naukam (Institute of
Scientific Information and Main Library
of the Social Sciences), INIBON

Interdisciplinary Machine Processing for
Research and Education in the Social
Sciences, IMPRESS
International Committee for Social Sciences
Documentation, ICSSD
National Institute of Social Sciences, NISS
Social Sciences Instructional Programming
Project, SSIPP
Social Sciences Research Council, SSRC
Society for Automation in the Social
Sciences, SASS
Statistical Package for the Social Sciences,
SPSS

Social Security

Social Security Account Number, SSAN

Social Studies

Association des Bibliothécaires-
Documentalistes de l'Institut
d'Etudes Sociales de l'Etat
(Association of Librarians and
Documentalists of the State Institute of
Social Studies), ABD
ERIC Clearinghouse for Social
Studies/Social Science Education,
ERIC/SO

Sociale

Centre de Documentation Économique et
Sociale, CIDES

Sociales

Centro d'Estudios Sociales y de Población,
CESPO

Socialist

Union of Soviet Socialist Republics, USSR

Sociedade

Sociedade Portuguesa de Autores, SPA

Società

Società Italiana Autori Drammatici, SIAD

Societé

Societé Anonyme Belge de Constructions
Aeronautiques, SABCA
Société Nationale de Diffusion Éducative et
Culturelle, SONDEC
Société Nationale des Chemins de Fer
Français, SNCF
Société Québeçoise d'Initiatives Pétrolières,
SOQUIP

Societies

American Federation of Film Societies,
AFFS
American Federation of Information
Processing Societies, AFIPS
Confédération Internationale des Sociétés
d'Auteurs et Compositeurs
(International Confederation of

Societies of Authors and Composers),
    CISAC
Conference of Engineering Societies of
    Western Europe and the United States
    of America, EUSEC
Council of Communication Societies, CCS
Engineering Societies Library, ESL
Federation of American Societies for
    Experimental Biology, FASEB
Federation of European Biological Societies,
    FEBS
International Federation of Film Societies,
    IFFS
International Federation of Information
    Processing Societies, IFIPS
Manchester Federation of Scientific
    Societies, MFSS

Society
ACM Special Interest Group on Computers
    and Society, ACM/SIGCAS
ASIS Special Interest Group on Technology,
    Information, and Society,
    ASIS/SIG/TIS
Acoustical Society of America, ASA
Aerospace Electrical Society, AES
American Antiquarian Society, AAS
American Astronautical Society, AAS
American Astronomical Society, AAS
American Chemical Society, ACS
American Folklore Society, AFLS
American Material Handling Society, AMHS
American Mathematical Society, AMS
American Meteorological Society, AMETS
American Name Society, ANS
American Nuclear Society, ANS
American Oil Chemists Society, AOCS
American Physical Society, APS
American Production and Inventory Control
    Society, APICS
American Recorder Society, ARS
American Society for Cybernetics, ASC
American Society for Engineering
    Education, ASEE
American Society for Information Science,
    ASIS
American Society for Metals, ASM
American Society for Nondestructive
    Testing, ASNT
American Society for Photogrammetry, ASP
American Society for Quality Control,
    ASQC
American Society for Testing and Materials,
    ASTM
American Society for Training and
    Development, ASTD
American Society for X-Ray and Electron
    Diffraction, ASXED
American Society of Association
    Executives, ASAE

American Society of Cartographers, ASC
American Society of Cinematographers,
    ASC
American Society of Civil Engineers, ASCE
American Society of Composers, Authors,
    and Publishers, ASCAP
American Society of Hospital Pharmacists,
    ASHP
American Society of Indexers, ASI
American Society of Mechanical Engineers,
    ASME
American Society of Naval Engineers,
    ASNE
American Society of Planning Officials,
    ASPO
American Society of Professional Draftsmen
    and Artists, ASPDA
American Society of Radiologic
    Technologists, ASRT
American Technical Society, ATS
American Vacuum Society, AVS
American Welding Society, AWS
Art Libraries Society, ARLIS
Audio Engineering Society, Inc, AES
Australian Computer Society, Inc, ACS
Bibliographical Society of America, BSA
Bibliographical Society of Australia and New
    Zealand, BSANZ
Bibliographical Society of the Philippines,
    BSP
Biochemical Society, BS
Biomedical Engineering Society, BMES
British Cartographic Society, BCS
British Ceramic Society, BCS
British Computer Society, BCS
British Computer Society ALGOL
    Association, BCSAA
British Kinematograph, Sound, and
    Television Society, BKSTS
*Bulletin of the American Society for
    Information Science*, BASIS
Canadian Ceramic Society, CCS
Canadian Information Processing
    Society/Association Canadienne de
    L'Informatique, CIPS/ACI
Chemical Society Research Unit in
    Information Dissemination and
    Retrieval, CSRUIDR
Committee on Physics and Society,
    COMPAS
Computing and Data Processing Society,
    CDPS
Confederate Memorial Literary Society,
    CMLS
Council of Engineering and Scientific Society
    Executives, CESSE
Council of Engineering and Scientific Society
    Secretaries, CESS
Crystallographic Society of America, CSA
Dictionary Society of North America, DSNA

Society (cont.)

Digital Equipment Computer Users Society, DECUS
Društvo Bibliotekarjev Slovenije (Society of Librarians in Slovenia), DBS
Ecological Society of America, ESA
English Place-Name Society, EPNS
European Atomic Energy Society, EAES
European Society for Opinion Surveys and Market Research, ESOMAR
Finlands Svenska Författareföreningen (Society of Swedish Authors in Finland), FSFF
Future Directions for a Learning Society, FDLS
Geological Society of America, GSA
German Research Society, GRS
Hospital Management Systems Society, HMSS
Incorporated Phonographic Society, IPS
Instrument Society of America, ISA
International Broadcasters Society, IBS
International Material Management Society, IMMS
International Society for Rehabilitation of the Disabled/Rehabilitation International, ISRD
International Society of Aviation Writers, ISAW
Israel Society for Special Libraries and Information Centers, ISLIC
Japan Society of Library Science (Nippon Toshokan Gakkai), JSLS
Journal of the American Chemical Society, JACS
Journal of the American Society for Information Science, JASIS
Junior Engineering Technical Society, JETS
Korean Library Science Society, KLSS
List and Index Society, LIS
Marine Technology Society, MTS
Mechanical Copyright Protection Society, MCPS
The Metallurgical Society, TMS
National Society for Crippled Children and Adults, NSCCA
National Society for Medical Research, NSMR
National Society for Performance and Instruction, NSPI
National Society for Programmed Instruction, NSPI
National Society for the Study of Communication, NSSC
New York Mathematical Society, NYMS
Nippon Documentesyon Kyokai (Japan Documentation Society), NIPDOK
Numerical Control Society, NCS
Operation Research Society, ORS

Operations Research Society of America, ORSA
Optical Society of America, Inc, OSA
Österreichische Gesellschaft für Dokumentation und Information (Austrian Society for Documentation and Information), ÖGDI
Poetry Society, PS
Printing Historical Society, PHS
Radiological Society of North America, RSNA
Research Society for Victorian Periodicals, RSVP
Royal Agricultural Society of England, RASE
Royal Central Asian Society, RCAS
Royal Dutch Pharmaceutical Society, KNMP
Royal Society of British Artists, RBA
Royal Society of Painter-Etchers and Engravers, RE
Scientific Research Society of America, SRSA
Scottish Daily Newspaper Society, SDNS
Société Canadienne pour l'Analyse de Documents/Indexing and Abstracting Society of Canada, SCAD/IASC
Société Internationale des Bibliothèques–Musées des Arts du Spectacle (International Society of Libraries and Museums of the Theatre Arts), SIBMAS
Société Internationale des Télécommunications Aeronautiques (International Society of Aeronautical Telecommunications), SITA
Society for Automation in Business Education, SABE
Society for Automation in English and the Humanities, SAEH
Society for Automation in Fine Arts, SAFA
Society for Automation in Professional Education, SAPE
Society for Automation in Science and Mathematics, SASM
Society for Automation in the Social Sciences, SASS
Society for Computer Simulation, SCS
Society for Education in Film and Television, SEFT
Society for Educational Data Systems, SEDS
Society for Film History Research, SFHR
Society for General Systems Research, SGSR
Society for Industrial and Applied Mathematics, SIAM
Society for Information Display, SID
Society for Management Information Systems, SMIS

Society for Mass Media and Resource
Technology, SMMART
Society for Nondestructive Testing, SNT
Society for Scholarly Publishing, SSP
Society for Technical Communication, STC
Society for the Advancement of
Management, SAM
Society for the Promotion and Improvement
of Libraries, SPIL
Society for the Promotion of the Interests of
Librarianship Students, SPILS
Society for the Study of Dictionaries and
Lexicography, SSDL
Society of Aerospace Material and Process
Engineers, SAMPE
Society of American Archivists, SAA
Society of Archivists, SA
Society of Army Historical Research, SAHR
Society of Automotive Engineers, SAE
Society of County Librarians, SCL
Society of Data Educators, SDE
Society of Educational Programmers and
Systems Analysts, SEPSA
Society of Film and Television Arts, Ltd,
SFTA
Society of Independent and Private School
Data Education, SIPSDE
Society of Mining Engineers, SME
Society of Motion Picture and Television
Engineers, SMPTE
Society of Municipal and County Chief
Librarians, SMCCL
Society of Naval Architects and Marine
Engineers, SNAME
Society of Petroleum Engineers, SPE
Society of Photographic Scientists and
Engineers, SPSE
Society of Photo-Optical Instrumentation
Engineers, SPIE
Society of Private Printers, SPP
Society of Scribes and Illuminators, SCI
Society of Technical Writers, STW
Society of Technical Writers and Editors,
STWE
Society of Technical Writers and Publishers,
STWP
Society of Typographical Designers, STD
Society of Wireless Pioneers, SOWP
Society of Women Engineers, SWE
Society of Women Writers and Journalists,
SWWJ
Society of Young Publishers, SYP
Soil Science Society of America, SSSA
Suomen Näytelmäkirjailijaliitto (Finnish
Dramatists Society), SUNKLO
Suomen Säätöteknillinen Seura (Finnish
Society of Automatic Control), SSS
Technical Publishing Society, TPS

Tekniska Litteratursällskapet (Swedish
Society for Technical Documentation),
TLS
United Society for Christian Literature,
USCL
Verein Deutscher Dokumentare (Society of
German Documentalists), VDD
Welsh Bibliographical Society, WBS

Socioeconomic
Medical Socioeconomic Research Sources.
(Journal), MEDSOC
Socioeconomic Information Management
System, SIMS

Socio-Economic Information
Agrupación de Bibliotecas para la
Integración de la Información
Socio-Economica (Group of Special
Libraries for the Integration of
Socio-Economic Information), ABIISE
Red de Información Socio-Económica
(Network for Socio-Economic
Information), REDINSE

Sociological
Sociological Abstracts, SA
Sociological Research Association, SRA

Sociologique
Centre de Recherche Sociologique Appliqués
de la Loire, CRESAL

Sociology
*World Agricultural Economics and Rural
Sociology Abstracts*, WAERSA

Software
Association of Independent Software
Companies, AISC
Automated Catalog of Computer Equipment
and Software Systems, ACCESS
Automatic Data Processing Equipment and
Software, ADPE/S
Business Oriented Software Systems, BOSS
Computer Software, CS
Computer Software and Management
Information Center, COSMIC
Software-Aided Multifont Input, SWAMI

Soil
Soil Engineering Problem-Oriented
Language, SEPOL
Soil Science Society of America, SSSA

Soil Trafficability
Pavements and Soil Trafficability
Information Analysis Center, PSTIAC

Solar
National Geophysical and Solar Terrestrial
Data Center, NGSD

Solar (cont.)

Solar Applications Information Center,
SOLAPIC

Solid Logic
Solid Logic Technology, SLT

Solid Waste
Solid Waste Information Retrieval System,
SWIRS

Solver
Structural Engineering System Solver,
STRESS

Songwriters
Songwriters Guild, Ltd, SWG

Sorter
Fluorescence-Activated Cell Sorter, FACS

Sorting
Facility for Automatic Sorting and Testing,
FAST
Sorting, Updating, Report, Generating, Etc,
SURGE

Sort-Key
Sort-Key Edit, SKED

Sound
British Kinematograph, Sound, and
Television Society, BKSTS
British Sound Recording Association, BSRA
International Association of Sound Archives,
IASA

Sounds
British Institute of Recording Sounds, BIRS
British Library of Wild Life Sounds,
BLOWS

Source
Cataloging in Source, CIS
Chemical Abstracts Service Source Index,
CASSI
Source Data Automation, SDA
Source Index, SI

Sources
Medical Socioeconomic Research Sources.
(Journal), MEDSOC

South Africa
Bantu Library Association of South Africa,
BLASA

South African
South African Bureau of Standards, SABS
South African Indian Library Association,
SAILA
Suid-Afrikaanse Biblioteekvereniging/South
African Library Association,
SABV/SALA

South Asia
Committee on American Library Resources
on South Asia, CALROSA
South Asia Microform Project, SAMP

South Carolina
South Carolina Library Association, SCLA

South Coast
South Coast Transportation Study, SCOTS

Southeast Asia
Committee on American Library Resources
on Southeast Asia, CALROSEA
Committee on Archives and Documents of
Southeast Asia, CARDOSEA
Committee on Research Materials on
Southeast Asia, CORMOSEA
Institute of Archival Science for Southeast
Asia, IASSA
Southeast Asia Development Advisory
Group, SEADAG
South East Asia Microforms, SEAM
Southeast Asia Treaty Organization, SEATO

Southeast Asian
Association of Southeast Asian Institutions
of Higher Learning, ASAIHL
Association of South East Asian Nations,
ASEAN
Southeast Asian Medical Information
Center, SEAMIC
Southeast Asian Ministers of Education
Council, SEAMEC

South-East Asian Libraries
Conference of South-East Asian Libraries,
CONSAL

Southeastern
Southeastern Library Association, SLA
Southeastern Library Network, SOLINET
Southeastern Regional Medical Library
Program, SERMLP

Southeastern Libraries
Southeastern Libraries Cooperating, SELCO

Southern
Southern Water Resources Scientific
Information Center, SWRSIC

Southwest
Continuing Education for Library Staffs in
the Southwest, CELS

Southwest Asia
Southwest Asia Documentation Centers,
SADC

Southwest Asian
Southwest Asian Regional Branch of the
International Council on Archives,
SARBICA

Southwestern
Southwestern Library Association, SLA
Southwestern Library Interstate Cooperative
    Endeavor, SLICE

Soviet
Union of Soviet Socialist Republics, USSR

Space
Canadian Aeronautics and Space Institute,
    CASI
Committee on Space Research, COSPAR
European Industrial Space Study Group,
    EUROSPACE
European Space Agency Network, ESANET
European Space Data Center, ESDAC
European Space Research and Technology
    Center, ESTEC
European Space Research Institute, ESRIN
European Space Research Laboratory,
    ESLAB
European Space Research Organization,
    ESRO
National Aeronautics and Space
    Administration, NASA
National Space Science Data Center,
    NSSDC
Personality, Matter, Energy, Space and
    Time, PMEST
Space Character, SP
Space Documentation Service, SDS

Space Flight Library
Marshall Space Flight Center Library,
    MSFC

Spanish Speaking Librarians
National Association of Spanish Speaking
    Librarians, NASSL

Speakers
Automatic Diffemic Identification of
    Speakers, ADIS

Special
Special Customer-Oriented Language,
    SPECOL
Special Libraries Association, SLA
Sveriges Vetenskapliga Specialibiblioteks
    Förening (Association of Special
    Research Libraries.), SVSF
(Virginia Chapter of the Special Libraries
    Association), VASLA

Special Committee
Divisional Interests Special Committee,
    DISC

Special Education
National Information Center in Special
    Education Materials, NICSEM
New York State Special Education
    Instructional Materials Center, SEIMC

Special Interest Group
ACM Special Interest Group on Architecture
    of Computer Systems, ACM/SIGARCH
ACM Special Interest Group on Artificial
    Intelligence, ACM/SIGART
ACM Special Interest Group on Automata
    and Computability Theory,
    ACM/SIGACT
ACM Special Interest Group on Biomedical
    Computing, ACM/SIGBIO
ACM Special Interest Group on Business
    Data Processing, ACM/SIGBDP
ACM Special Interest Group on Computer
    Graphics, ACM/SIGGRAPH
ACM Special Interest Group on Computer
    Personnel Research, ACM/SIGCPR
ACM Special Interest Group on Computer
    Science Education, ACM/SIGCSE
ACM Special Interest Group on Computer
    Systems Installation Management,
    ACM/SIGCOSIM
ACM Special Interest Group on Computer
    Uses in Education, ACM/SIGCUE
ACM Special Interest Group on
    Computer-Assisted Instruction,
    ACM/SIGCAI
ACM Special Interest Group on Computers
    and Society, ACM/SIGCAS
ACM Special Interest Group on Computers
    and the Physically Handicapped,
    ACM/SIGCAPH
ACM Special Interest Group on Data
    Communications, ACM/SIGCOMM
ACM Special Interest Group on Design
    Automation, ACM/SIGDA
ACM Special Interest Group on Information
    Retrieval, ACM/SIGIR
ACM Special Interest Group on Language
    Analysis and Studies in the Humanities,
    ACM/SIGLASH
ACM Special Interest Group on Management
    of Data, ACM/SIGMOD
ACM Special Interest Group on
    Mathematical Programming,
    ACM/SIGMAP
ACM Special Interest Group on
    Measurement Evaluation,
    ACM/SIGMETRICS
ACM Special Interest Group on
    Microprogramming, ACM/SIGMICRO
ACM Special Interest Group on
    Minicomputers, ACM/SIGMINI
ACM Special Interest Group on Numerical
    Mathematics, ACM/SIGNUM
ACM Special Interest Group on Operating
    Systems, ACM/SIGOPS
ACM Special Interest Group on
    Programming Languages,
    ACM/SIGPLAN

Special Interest Group (cont.)

ACM Special Interest Group on Simulation, ACM/SIGSIM

ACM Special Interest Group on Social and Behavioral Science Computing, ACM/SIGSOC

ACM Special Interest Group on University Computing Centers, ACM/SIGUCC

ASIS Special Interest Group on Arts and Humanities, ASIS/SIG/AH

ASIS Special Interest Group on Automated Language Processing, ASIS/SIG/ALP

ASIS Special Interest Group on Biological and Chemical Information Systems, ASIS/SIG/BC

ASIS Special Interest Group on Classification Research, ASIS/SIG/CR

ASIS Special Interest Group on Community Information Services, ASIS/SIG/CIS

ASIS Special Interest Group on Computerized Retrieval Services, ASIS/SIG/CRS

ASIS Special Interest Group on Costs Budgeting and Economics, ASIS/SIG/CBE

ASIS Special Interest Group on Education for Information Science, ASIS/SIG/ED

ASIS Special Interest Group on Foundations of Information Science, ASIS/SIG/FIS

ASIS Special Interest Group on Information Analysis Centers, ASIS/SIG/IAC

ASIS Special Interest Group on Information Publishing, ASIS/SIG/IP

ASIS Special Interest Group on Information Services to Education, ASIS/SIG/ISE

ASIS Special Interest Group on Law and Information Technology, ASIS/SIG/LAW

ASIS Special Interest Group on Library Automation and Networks, ASIS/SIG/LAN

ASIS Special Interest Group on Management Information Activities, ASIS/SIG/MGT

ASIS Special Interest Group on Medical Records, ASIS/SIG/MR

ASIS Special Interest Group on Non-Print Material, ASIS/SIG/NPM

ASIS Special Interest Group on Numerical Data Bases, ASIS/SIG/NDB

ASIS Special Interest Group on Public-Private Interface, ASIS/SIG/PPI

ASIS Special Interest Group on Technology, Information, and Society, ASIS/SIG/TIS

ASIS Special Interest Group on the Behavioral and Social Sciences, ASIS/SIG/BSS

ASIS Special Interest Group on User On-line Interaction, ASIS/SIG/UOI

Special Interest Group, SIG

Special Librarians

Association Française des Documentalistes et des Bibliothécaires Spécialisés (French Association of Information Scientists and Special Librarians), ADBS

Himpunan Pustakawan Chusus Indonesia (Indonesian Association of Special Librarians), HPCI

Special Libraries

Academic and Special Libraries Section, ASLS

Agrupación de Bibliotecas para la Integración de la Información Socio-Economica (Group of Special Libraries for the Integration of Socio-Economic Information), ABIISE

Arbeitsgemeinschaft der Spezialbibliotheken (Association of Special Libraries in the Federal Republic of Germany), ASpB

Asociación de Bibliotecas Universitarias y Especializadas de Nicaragua (Association of University and Special Libraries of Nicaragua), ABUEN

Association of Special Libraries and Information Bureaux, ASLIB

Association of Special Libraries of the Philippines, ASLP

Canadian Association of Special Libraries and Information Services, CASLIS

Hertfordshire Association of Special Libraries, HASL

Indian Association of Special Libraries and Information Centers, IASLIC

Israel Society for Special Libraries and Information Centers, ISLIC

Pakistan Association of Special Libraries, PASLIB

Senmon Toshokan Kyogikai (Special Libraries Association of Japan), SENTOKYO

Special Libraries Association, Section de Montréal Chapter, SMCSLA

Special Libraries. (Journal), SL

Specialised

Association of Specialised Film Producers, ASFP

Federation of Specialised Film Associations, FSFA

Specialist

Small and Specialist Publishers Exhibition, SPEX

Specialists

ACRL Western European Specialists Section, ACRL/WESS

The American Association of Language Specialists, TAALS

Specialization
Greater London Audio Specialization
Scheme, GLASS

Specialized
Association of Specialized and Cooperative
Library Agencies, ASCLA
Specialized Information Services, SIS
Specialized Office for Materials Distribution,
SOMD
Specialized Technique for Efficient
Typesetting, STET

Specification
Joint Canadian Navy-Army-Air Force
Specification, JCNAAF

Specifications
Center for Thai National Standard
Specifications, CTNSS
Sudanese Organization for Standard
Specifications, SOSS
Vsesoyuznogo Informatsionnogo Fonda
Standartovi i Technicheskikh Uslovii
(All-Union Reference Bank of Standards
and Specifications, USSR), VIFS

Spectroscopy
Canadian Association for Applied
Spectroscopy, CAAS

Speech
Deafness, Speech and Hearing Publications,
Inc, DSH

Spitzenorganisation
Spitzenorganisation der Filmwirtschaft eV,
SPIO

Spokane Libraries
Spokane Inland Empire Libraries, SPIEL

Spoken
Spoken Language Universal Numeric
Translation, SLUNT

Spring
Spring Joint Computer Conference, SJCC

Springfield
Library Exemplary Elementary
Demonstration of Springfield, LEEDS

Sri Lanka
Sri Lanka Library Association, SLLA

Stability
Variable Stability System, VSS

Staff
Cornell University Libraries Staff
Association, CULSA
Library Employment and Development for
Staff, LEADS
Staff Organization Round Table, SORT

Staff Information
Barclays (Bank) Advanced Staff Information
Language, BASIL

Staffordshire
Libraries of North Staffordshire in
Cooperation, LINOSCO

Staffs
Area Manpower Institutes for the
Development of Staffs, AMIDS

Stampa
Federazione Nazionale della Stampa
Italiana, FNSI
Unione della Stampa Periodica Italiana,
USPI

Standard
British Standard Institution, BSI
Center for Thai National Standard
Specifications, CTNSS
International Standard Bibliographic
Description, ISBD
International Standard Book Number, ISBN
International Standard Industrial
Classification, ISIC
International Standard Serial Number, ISSN
National Standard Reference Data System,
NSRDS
Office of Standard Reference Data, OSRD
Standard Identifier for Individuals, SII
Standard Metropolitan Statistical Area,
SMSA
Standard Modular System, SMS
Standard Operating Procedure, SOP
Standard Point Location Code, SPLC
Standard Serial Number, SSN
Standard Tape Executive Program, STEP
Standard Technical Report Number, STRN
Sudanese Organization for Standard
Specifications, SOSS
World Wide Network of Standard
Seismograph Stations, WWNSS

Standard Code
United States of America Standard Code for
Information Interchange, USASCII

Standardization
Egyptian Organization for Standardization,
EOS
International Organization for
Standardization, IOS
Radio Components Standardization
Committee, RCSC
Standing Committee for the Study of
Principles of Standardization, STACO

Standards
ANSI Standards Planning and Requirements
Committee, ANSI/SPARC

Standards (cont.)

[Aerospace Standards], AS
American National Standards, ANS
American National Standards Institute,
    ANSI
American Standards Association, ASA
Association for Broadcast Engineering
    Standards, Inc, ABES
Association on Broadcasting Standards,
    ABS
Bureau of Ceylon Standards, BCS
Bureau of Standards of the Philippines, BSP
Canadian Military Electronics Standards
    Agency, CAMESA
Canadian Standards Association, CSA
Chinese National Standards, CNS
Commission on Standards and Accreditation
    of Services for the Blind, COMSTAC
Deutscher Normenausschuss (German
    Standards Association), DNA
Federal Information Processing Standards,
    FIPS
Indian Standards Institution, ISI
Institute for Industrial Research and
    Standards, IIRS
Institute of Standards and Industrial
    Research of Iran, ISIRI
International Standards Organization, ISO
Iraqi Organization for Standards, IOS
Japanese Industrial Standards Committee,
    JISC
Japanese Standards Association, JSA
Korean Bureau of Standards, KBS
National Bureau of Standards, NBS
Pakistan Standards Institute, PSI
Singapore Institute of Standards and
    Industrial Research, SISIR
South African Bureau of Standards, SABS
Standards Association of Australia, SAA
Standards Association of Central Africa,
    SACA
Standards Association of New Zealand,
    SANZ
Standards Electronic Automatic Computer,
    SEAC
[Standards Institute], SI
Standards Institute of Israel, SII
Standards Institute of Malaysia, SIM
Technical Standards for Library
    Automation, TESLA
United States of America Standards
    Institute, USASI
Vsesoyuznogo Informatsionnogo Fonda
    Standartovi i Technicheskikh Uslovii
    (All-Union Reference Bank of Standards
    and Specifications, USSR), VIFS
Women's Advisory Committee of the British
    Standards Institution, WAC

Standards Coordinating
Federal Information Processing Standards
    Coordinating and Advisory Committee,
    FIPSCAC

Standing Order
Standing Order Microfiche Service, SRIM

Stanford
Stanford Physics Information Retrieval
    System, SPIRES
Stanford Research Institute, SRI

Star Observers
American Association of Variable Star
    Observers, AAVSO

Start
Start of Heading Character, SOH
Start of Message, SOM
Start of Text Character, STX

Start Code
Transmitter Start Code, TSC

State
ASCLA State Library Agency Section,
    ASCLA/SLAS
American Association for State and Local
    History, AASLH
American Federation of State, County, and
    Municipal Employees, AFSCME
GODORT State Documents Task Force,
    GODORT/SDTF
National Association for State Information
    Systems, NASIS
National Association of State Text Book
    Administrators, NASTA
National Association of State Text Book
    Directors, NASTBD
State and Court Law Libraries of the United
    States and Canada, SCLL
State of the Art, SOTA
State University of New York, SUNY
State University of New York Librarians
    Association, SUNYLA
Státni Ústav pro Zdravotnickou
    Dokumentаčm a Knihovnickou Sluzbu
    (State Institute for Medical
    Documentation and National Medical
    Library), SUZDKS

State Boards
National Council of State Boards of
    Engineering Examiners, NCSBEE

State Colleges
American Association of State Colleges and
    Universities, AASCU

State Libraries
American Association of State Libraries,
    AASL
State Libraries Agencies Division, SLAD

State Library
Chief Officers of State Library Agencies,
    COSLA
Connecticut State Library, CSL
Deutsche Staatsbibliothek (German State
    Library), DSB
Gosudarstvennaya ordena Lenina Biblioteka
    SSSR Imeni V. I. Lenina (Lenin State
    Library of the USSR), GBL
New York State Library, NYSL
Oregon State System of Higher
    Education–Oregon State Library,
    OSSHE-OSL
State Library of Victoria, SLV
Státni Knihovna Československe
    Socialisticke Republiky (State Library
    of the Czechoslovak Socialist Republic),
    SKCSR
Tasmania State Library, TSL

Staten Island
Brooklyn–Queens–Staten Island Health
    Sciences Group, BQSI

Station
Station Selection Code, SSC

Stationers
National Federation of Retail Newsagents,
    Booksellers and Stationers, NFRN

Stationery
Her/His Majesty's Stationery Office, HMSO
Retail Book, Stationery and Allied Trades
    Employees Association, RBA

Stations
Educational Television Stations, ETS
World Wide Network of Standard
    Seismograph Stations, WWNSS

Statistical
Adaptive Statistical Processor, APROC
Advanced Statistical Analysis Program,
    ASTAP
American Statistical Association, ASA
Indexing by Statistical Analysis Techniques,
    IBSAT
Multivariate Statistical Analyzer, MSA
Offender Base Transaction Statistical
    System, OBTS
Retrieval and Statistical Processing, RASP
Statistical Information Retrieval, SIR

Statistical Package for the Social Sciences,
    SPSS
Statistical Routines, STAT PACK

Statistical Area
Standard Metropolitan Statistical Area,
    SMSA

Statistical Library
International Mathematical and Statistical
    Library, IMSL

Statistics
American Association for Vital Records and
    Public Health Statistics, AAVRPHS
American Statistics Index, ASI
[Biblíoteka] Szkoly Glównej Planowania i
    Statystykí (Library of the Central
    School of Planning and Statistics),
    SGPIS
Bureau of Labor Statistics, BLS
Computer-Assisted Reliability Statistics,
    CARS
Computerized Statistics, COMPUSTAT
General Industrial Statistics, UNINDUST
Industrial Commodity Production Statistics,
    ICPDATA
LAMA Statistics Section, LAMA/SS
National Center for Educational Statistics,
    NCES
National Center for Health Statistics, NCHS
Statistics Section, SS

Statistique
Institut National de la Statistique et des
    Études Économique, INSEE

Stato
Legislazione dello Stato, TITLEX

Status
Channel Status Table, CST
Channel Status Word, CSW
College Applicant Status Report, CASTOR
Computerized Movement Planning and
    Status System, COMPASS
Offender Status Register, OSR
Program Status Word, PSW

Steel
American Institute of Steel Construction,
    AISC
American Iron and Steel Institute, AISI
Association of Iron and Steel Engineers,
    AISE
British Iron and Steel Industry Translation
    Service, BISITS
Iron and Steel Industry, ISI
Iron and Steel Industry Training
    Board, ISI TB

Stock
Computer-Aided Stock Holdings, CASH

Stockholm
Stockholm International Peace Research
    Institute, SIPRI

Stockkeeping
Stockkeeping Unit, SKU

Storage
Agricultural System for Storage and
    Subsequent Selection of Information,
    ASSASSIN
Automatic Document Storage and Retrieval,
    ADSTAR
Automatic Fact Information Retrieval and
    Storage Systems, AFIRSS
Automation for Storage and Retrieval of
    Information, AFSARI
Committee on Storage, Automatic
    Processing and Retrieval of Geological
    Data, COGEODATA
Digital Data, Auxiliary Storage, Track
    Display, Outputs, and Radar Display,
    DATOR
Direct Access Storage Device, DASD
Dynamic Storage Allocation Language,
    DYSTAL
Electrostatic Storage Deflection, ESD
FID Working Committee on Mechanical
    Storage and Retrieval, FID/MSR
Immediate Access Storage, IAS
Main Storage Control Element, MSCE
Random Access Storage and Control,
    RASTAC
Random Access Storage and Display,
    RASTAD
Semiconductor Storage Unit, SSU
Storage and Information Retrieval System,
    STAIRS
Storage, Handling and Retrieval of Technical
    Data in Image Formation, SHIRTDIF
Storage Limits Register, SLR
Zero Access Storage, ZAS

Storage Center
Cooperative Acquisitions and Storage
    Center, CASC

Straniero
Repertorio Bibliografico Straniero, REBIS

Strategic
Strategic Air Command Control System,
    SACCS

String-Oriented
String-Oriented Symbolic Language,
    SNOBOL

Stroke
National Institute of Neurological Diseases
    and Stroke, NINDS

Structural
Hierarchically Structural, HS
Structural Engineering System Solver,
    STRESS

Structure
Automatic New Structure Alert (Journal),
    ANSA

Student
Student Advisory Information Service,
    STAIS
United States Student Press Association,
    USSPA

Students
International Association for the Exchange
    of Students for Technical Experience,
    IAESTE
Irish Central Library for Students, ICL
Society for the Promotion of the Interests of
    Librarianship Students, SPILS
Students Chemical Information Project,
    SCIP

Studiengesellschaft
Osterreichische Studiengesellschaft für
    Atomenergie, GmbH, OSGAE

Studies
Army Technical Library Improvement
    Studies, ATLIS
Center for Studies in Economic
    Development, CEDE
Wisconsin Assets and Income Studies,
    WAIS

Studies Center
Technology Use Studies Center, TUSC

Study
Asia/Pacific Forecasting Study, APFS
Bay Area Transportation Study Commission,
    BATSC
Center for the Advanced Study of
    Educational Administration, CASEA
Computer-Aided Project Study, CAPS
Graduate Regional Accelerated Study
    Program, GRASP
Los Angeles Regional Transportation Study,
    LARTS
South Coast Transportation Study, SCOTS

Study Centre
Women's Information and Study Centre,
    WISC

Study Group
ANSI/SPARC Study Group on Data Base
    Management Systems,
    ANSI/X3/SPARC/SGDBMS.
European Industrial Space Study Group,
    EUROSPACE

Study Groups
Book Industry Study Groups, Inc, BISG

Style Manual
Style Manual for Biological Journals, SMBJ

Subcommittee
Subcommittee on Programming
    Terminology, SCOPT

Subject
Automatic Subject Citation Alert, ASCA
Bibliographic Author or Subject Interactive
    Search, BA•SIS
Catalog of Computerized Subject Searches,
    CAT
Chemical Abstracts Subject Index Alert,
    CASIA
Computer-Aided Subject Index, CASIN
Permuterm Subject Index, PSI
Subject Analysis and Organization of Library
    Materials Committee, SAOLM
Subject Authority List, SAL

Subject Content
Subject Content-Oriented Retriever for
    Processing Information Online,
    SCORPIO

Subject Heading
Subject Heading Authority List, SHAL

Subject Headings
Library of Congress Subject Headings,
    LCSH
Medical Subject Headings, MeSH
Permuted on Subject Headings, POSH
Subject Headings for Engineering, SHE

Subjects
Biological Abstracts Subjects in Context,
    BASIC

Subscription
Reference and Subscription Book Reviews
    Committee, RSBRC

Substitute
Substitute Character, SUB

Substructure
Chemical Substructure Index, CSI

Subsystems
Computation and Data Flow Integrated
    Subsystems, CADFISS

Suburban
Suburban Library System, SLS

Sudanese
Sudanese Organization for Standard
    Specifications, SOSS

Suffolk County
Suffolk County Library Association, SCLA

Suisse
Schweizerische Journalisten-Union/Union
    Suisse des Journalistes, SJU/USJ
Schweizerischer Schriftsteller-
    Verband/Société Suisse
    des Écrivains, SSV/SSE
Vereinigung der Buchantiquare und
    Kupferstichhändler in der
    Schweiz/Syndicat de la Libraire
    Ancienne et du Commerce de l'Estampe
    en Suisse, VEBUKU/SLACES

Suisse Romande
Association Cinématographique Suisse
    Romande, ACSR
Association Suisse Romande des
    Journalistes de l'Aéronautique et de
    l'Astronautique, ARJA

Suisses
Union der Schweizerischen
    Lichtspieltheater-Verbänd/Union des
    Associations Cinématographiques
    Suisses, USLV/UACS

Suite
British Integrated Programme Suite, BIPS

Sullivan
Frost & Sullivan, Inc, F&S

Summaries
Pest Articles and News Summaries.
    (Journal), PANS

Sunday
Sunday Newspapers Distributing
    Association, SNDA

Suomen Elokuvateatterinomistajain Litto
Suomen Elokuvateatterinomistajain Litto,
    SEOL

Super Eight
Super Eight Experiment, SEE

Super Market
Super Market Institute, SMI

Superhigh
Superhigh Frequencies, SHF

Superimpose
Superimpose, SI

Superintendent
Superintendent of Documents, SuDocs
Superintendent of Documents Classification,
    SDC

Supervision
Association for Supervision and Curriculum
    Development, ASCD

Supervisor
General Comprehensive Operating
   Supervisor, GECOS

Supervisors
AASL Supervisors Section, AASL/SS

Supervisory
Boeing Operational Supervisory System,
   BOSS

Supplies
World Energy Supplies System,
   WORLDENERGY

Supply
Defense Supply Agency, DSA

Support
Attached Support Processor, ASP
Basic Programming Support, BPS
Cataloguing Support System, CATSS
Committee on Program Evaluation and
   Support, COPES
Distributed Processing Support, DPS
Support of User Records and Files, SURF
Transportation Planning Support
   Information System, TPSIS
United States Army Computer Systems
   Support and Evaluation Command,
   USACSSEC

Surgeons
American College of Surgeons, ACS
Royal College of Surgeons in Ireland, RCSI
Royal College of Surgeons of Edinburgh,
   RCSEd
Royal College of Surgeons of England,
   RCSEng
Royal College of Veterinary Surgeons,
   RCVS

Surveillance
Battle Area Surveillance and Integrated
   Communications, BASIC
National Electronic Injury Surveillance
   System, NEISS

Survey
European Executive Compensation Survey,
   EECS
*Latin American Executive Compensation
   Survey*, LAECS
Library General Information Survey,
   LIBGIS
Survey of Economic Opportunity, SEO
Survey Research Center Data Library,
   SRCDL
United States Geological Survey, USGS

Surveying
American Congress on Surveying and
   Mapping, ACSM

National Congress on Surveying and
   Mapping, NCSM

Surveys
European Society for Opinion Surveys and
   Market Research, ESOMAR
Joint Industrial Committee for National
   Readership Surveys, JICNARS

Survival
Associated Library and Educational
   Research Team for Survival, ALERTS

Svenska
Svenska Tidningsutgivareföreningen, TU

Swedish
Finlands Svenska Författareföreningen
   (Society of Swedish Authors in Finland),
   FSFF
Forskningsbiblioteksrådet (Swedish Council
   of Research Libraries), FBR
Svenska Bibliotekariesamfundet (Swedish
   Association of University and Research
   Librarians), SBS
Svenska Folkbibliotekarie Förbundet (Union
   of Swedish Public Libraries), SFF
Svenska Journalistförbundet (Swedish
   Association of Journalists), SJF
Sveriges Allmänna Biblioteksförening
   (Swedish Library Association), SAB
Sveriges Biografägureförbund (Swedish
   Motion Picture Exhibitors Association),
   SBF
Swedish Drug Information System, SWEDIS
Swedish Institute for Administrative
   Research, SIAR
Tekniska Litteratursällskapet (Swedish
   Society for Technical Documentation),
   TLS

Swindon
Swindon Area Association of Libraries for
   Industry and Commerce, SAALIC

Swiss
Schweizerische Gesellschaft für
   Automatik/Association Suisse pour
   l'Automatique (Swiss Association for
   Automation), SGA/ASSPA
Schweizerische Vereinigung der
   Agrarjournalistes/Association Suisse
   des Journalistes Agricoles (Swiss
   Association of Agricultural Journalists),
   SVAJ/ASJA
Schweizerische Vereinigung Freier
   Berufsjournalisten/Association Suisse
   des Journalistes Libres Professionnels
   (Swiss Association of Independent
   Professional Journalists),
   SVFBJ/ASJLP

Schweizerische Vereinigung für
  Dokumentation/Association Suisse de
  Documentation (Swiss Association of
  Documentation), SVD/ASD
Schweizerischer Zeitungsverleger-
  Verband/Association Suisse des
  Éditeurs de Journaux/
  Associazione Svizzera degli Editori
  di Giornale (Swiss Newspaper
  Publishers Association),
  SZV/ASEJ/ASEG
Schweizerisches Wirtschaftsarchiv (Swiss
  Economic Archives), SWA
Verband Schweizerischer Film und
  AV-Produzenten/Association des
  Producteurs Suisses de Films et de
  Production Audio-Visuelle (Association
  of Swiss Film and Audio-Visual
  Producers), VSFAV/APFAV
Vereinigung Schweizerischer Archivare
  (Association of Swiss Archivists), VSA
Vereinigung Schweizerischer
  Filmkritiker/Association Suisse des
  Critiques de Cinéma/Associazione
  Svizzera dei Critici Cinematografici
  (Swiss Association of Film Critics),
  VSF/ASC/ASC

Swiss Librarians
Vereinigung Schweizerischer
  Bibliothekare/Association des
  Bibliothécaires Suisses/Associazione dei
  Bibliotecari Svizzeri (Association of
  Swiss Librarians), VSB/ABS/ABS

Switch
Multi-Aperture Reluctance Switch, MARS

Switching
Electronic Switching System, ESS

Switching Point
Control Switching Point, CSP

Switzerland
Société des Libraires et Éditeurs de la Suisse
  Romande (Booksellers and Publishers
  Association of French-Speaking
  Switzerland), SLESR

Symbol
External Symbol Dictionary, ESD

Symbolic
Advanced Scientific Instruments Symbolic
  Translator, ASIST
Association for Symbolic Logic, ASL
Beginners All-purpose Symbolic Instruction
  Code, BASIC
Bell Little Electrodata Symbolic System for
  the Electrodata, BLESSED

Expansion Symbolic Compiling Assembly
  Program for Engineering, ESCAPE
Macro-Operation Symbolic Assembler and
  Information Compiler, MOSAIC 636
String-Oriented Symbolic Language,
  SNOBOL
Symbolic Conversion Program, SCP
Symbolic Optimum Assembly Programming,
  SOAP
Symbolic Program Tape, SPT
Symbolic Programming System, SPS
Symbolic Shorthand System, SSS

Symbols
*Dictionary of Architectural Abbreviations,
  Signs and Symbols*, DAA
*Dictionary of Civil Engineering
  Abbreviations, Signs and Symbols*,
  DCEA
*Dictionary of Computer and Control Systems
  Abbreviations, Signs and Symbols*,
  DCCSA
*Dictionary of Electronics Abbreviations,
  Signs and Symbols*, DEA
*Dictionary of Industrial Engineering
  Abbreviations, Signs and Symbols*,
  DIEA
*Dictionary of Mechanical Engineering
  Abbreviations, Signs and Symbols*,
  DMEA
*Dictionary of Physics and Mathematics
  Abbreviations, Signs and Symbols*,
  DPMA
*Encyclopedia of Engineering Signs and
  Symbols*, EESS
Symbols, Units, Nomenclature, SUN

Synagogue
Church and Synagogue Library Association,
  CSLA

Synchronous
Binary Synchronous Communicator
  Adapter, BSCA
Synchronous Idle Character, SYN
Synchronous Transmit Receive Access
  Method, STRAM
Synchronous Transmitter Receiver, STR
Word Terminal Synchronous, WTS

Syndacato
Syndacato Nazionale Scrittori, SNS

Syndicat
Syndicat des Industries Téléphoniques et
  Télégraphiques, SITT

Syndicate
Cooperative High School Independent Press
  Syndicate, CHIPS
Syndicate National des Journalistes, SNJ

Syndicats de Libraires
Fédération Française des Syndicats de
Libraires, FFSL

Syntax
Air Force English Syntax Project, AFESP

Synthesis
Center for Information and Numerical Data
Analysis and Synthesis, CINDAS

Synthetic and Analytical
Topological Representation of Synthetic and
Analytical Relations of Concepts,
TOSAR

Synthetic Organic
Synthetic Organic Chemical Manufacturers
Association, SOCMA

Syracuse
Syracuse University *Psychological
Abstracts* Retrieval System, SUPARS

System
AUTOCOMM Business System,
AUTOCOMM
Adaptable Data Base System, ADABAS
Administrative Terminal System, ATS
Advanced Linear Programming System,
ALPS
Agricultural System for Storage and
Subsequent Selection of Information,
ASSASSIN
Aldermaston Mechanized Cataloging and
Ordering System, AMCOS
Alpha-Numerical System for Classification
of Recordings, ANSCR
An Analytical Information Management
System, AAIMS
Archival Records Management System,
ARM
Army Library Automated System, ALAS
Assembly System for the Peripheral
Processors, ASPER
Associative Processor Computer System,
APCS
Auerbach Information Management System,
AIMS
Author Index Manufacturing System, AIMS
Automated Computer Science Education
System, ACSES
Automated Engineering Design System,
AED
Automated Information Directory Update
System, AIDUS
Automated Information Dissemination
System, AIDS
Automated Input and Document Update
System, AIDUS

Automated Instructional Materials Handling
System of SDC (System Development
Corporation), AIMS
Automated Law Enforcement
Communication System, ALECS
Automated Library Processing System,
ALPS
Automated Literature Processing, Handling,
and Analysis System, ALPHA
Automated Microfilm Aperture Card Update
System, AMACUS
Automated News Clipping, Indexing, and
Retrieval System, ANCIRS
Automated Retrieval System, ARS
Automatic Computer-Controlled Electronics
Scanning System, ACCESS
Automatic Data Processing System, ADPS
Automatic Digital Encoding System, ADES
Automatic Digital Encoding System,
ADES-II
Automatic Digital On-line Instrumentation
System, ADONIS
Automatic Direct Access to Information with
On-line UDC System, AUDACIOUS
Automatic Information Retrieval System,
AIRs
Automatic Operating System, AUTOPSY
Automatic Routine Generating and Updating
System, ARGUS
Baptist Information Retrieval System, BIRS
Basic Analog Simulation System, BASS
Basic Operating System, BOS
Bay Area Rapid Transit System, BARTS
Bell Laboratories Automatic Design System,
BLADES
Bell Laboratories Interpretive System, BLIS
Bell Laboratories Library Real-Time Loan
System, BELLREL
Bell Little Electrodata Symbolic System for
the Electrodata, BLESSED
Bibliographic Automation of Large Library
Operations Using a Time-Sharing
System, BALLOTS
Boeing Airplane Company Algebraic
Interpretive Computing System,
BACAIC
Boeing Operational Supervisory System,
BOSS
Book Inventory Building and Library
Information Oriented System, BIBLIOS
Bucknell Automated Retrieval and Display
System, BARDS
CONVERSE System, CONVERSE
Card-Automated Reproduction and
Distribution System, CARDS
Career Retrieval Search System, CARESS
Cassette Programming System, CAPS
Cataloging and Indexing System of NAL,
CAIN

Cataloguing Support System, CATSS
Central Bibliographic System, CBS
Columbia Broadcasting System, Inc, CBS
Combined File Search System, CFSS
Communication and Data Processing
    Operation System, CADPOS
Communications Input/Output Control
    System, CIOCS
Community Input/Output Control System,
    CIOS
Compact Programmed Airline Reservation
    System, CPARS
Compatible Duplex System, CDS
Compatible Operating System, COS
Completely Automatic Operational System,
    CAOS
Comprehensive Display System, CDS
Computer Accounting System, CAS
Computer-Aided Design System, CADSYS
Computer-Aided Diagnosis System, CADS
Computer-Aided Project Planning System,
    CAPPS
Computer-Aided Rationalized Building
    System, CARBS
Computer-Assisted Information Retrieval
    System, CAIRS
Computer-Assisted Language Analysis
    System, CALAS
Computer-Assisted Maintenance Planning
    and Control System, CAMCOS
Computer-Augmented Block System, CABS
Computer-Integrated Manufacturing System,
    CIMS
Computerized Annotated Bibliography
    System, CABS
Computerized Logic-Oriented Design
    System, CLODS
Computerized Movement Planning and
    Status System, COMPASS
Computerized Preliminary Design System,
    CPDS
Consumer Goods System, COGS
Container Operating Control System, COCS
Continuous System Modeling Program,
    CSMP
Contractors Accounting System, CONACS
Cooperative Union Serials System, CUSS
Coordinate Indexing System, CIS
Copyright Office Publication and Interactive
    Cataloging System, COPICS
Culham (Laboratory) Language for System
    Development, CLSD
Customer Information Control System,
    CICS
DLSC Integrated Data System, DIDS
Dartmouth Time Sharing System, DTSS
Data Acquisition and Control System, DAC
Data Analysis System, DAS
Data Base Management System, DBMS

Data Control System, DCS
Data Information and Manufacturing
    System, DIMS
A Data Interchange System, ADIS
Data Moving System, DAMOS
Datatron Assembly System, DAS
Defense Market Measures System, DM^2
Dial Access Information Retrieval System,
    DAIRS
Digital Control Design System, DCDS
Digital Equipment Corporation's Automatic
    Design System, DECADE
Digital Optical Projection System, DOPS
Direct Order Recording and Invoicing
    System, DORIS
Disk On-Line Accounts Receivable System,
    DOLARS
Disk Operating System, DOS
Display-Oriented Computer Usage System,
    DOCUS
Document Processing System, DPS
Double-precision Automatic Interpretive
    System 201, DAISY 201
Earth Resources Observation System, EROS
Educators Information Technology System,
    EDITS
Efficient Assembly System, EASY
Electronic Coordinatograph and Readout
    System, ECARS
Electronic Data Processing System, EDPS
Electronic Switching System, ESS
Engineering Automatic System for Solving
    Equations, EASE
Epilepsy Abstracts Retrieval System, EARS
European Nuclear Documentation System,
    ENDS
An Evolutionary System for On-line
    Processing, AESOP
FORTRAN Automatic Code Evaluation
    System, FACES
Facsimile Communications System, FCS
Facsimile Transmission System, FACTS
Factory Information Control System, FICS
Federal Aviation Information Retrieval
    System, FAIRS
Federal Telecommunications System, FTS
Fidac System, FIDACSYS
Floating-decimal Abstract Coding System,
    FACS
Forecasting for Inventory Control System,
    FICS
General Electric Remote Terminal System,
    GERTS
Generalized Information Management
    System, GIM
Generalized Information Processing System,
    GIPSY
Generalized Information Retrieval and
    Listing System, GIRLS

System (cont.)

Hawaii International Conference on System Sciences, HICSS

Human Intellect Augmentation System, HIAS

Hydrological Information Storage and Retrieval System, HISARS

Index Chemicus Registry System, ICRS

Indiana Higher Education Television System, IHETS

Indiana Information Retrieval System, INDIRS

Infrared Information System, IRIS

Integrated Design and Analysis System, IDEAS

Integrated Global Ocean Stations System, IGOSS

Integrated Information Processing System, INTIPS

Interconnected Business System, ICBS

International Referral System for Sources of Environmental Information, IRS

International Serials Data System, ISDS

Japanese Medical Abstract Scanning System, JAMASS

Johnniac Open-Shop System, JOSS

Language Information Network and Clearinghouse System, LINCS

Law Enforcement Teletype System, LETS

Least-cost Estimating and Scheduling System, LESS

Library Experimental Automated Demonstration System, LEADS

Literature Retrieval System for the Pulp and Paper Industry, LIRES

Machine-Aided Drafting System, MADS

Machine-Aided Technical Processing System, MATPS

Machine-Assisted Educational System for Teaching by Remote Operation, MAESTRO

Marine Air-Ground Intelligence System, MAGIS

Marine Environmental Data Information Referral System, MEDI

Medical Information Management System, MIMS

Medical Literature Analysis and Retrieval System, MEDLARS

Military Documentation System, MIDONAS

Missile Attitude Determination System, MADS

Multiple Use MARC System, MUMS

National Association of Securities Dealers Automated Quotations System, NASDAQ

National Electronic Injury Surveillance System, NEISS

Natural History Information Retrieval System, NHIR

Octal Program Updating System, OPUS

Offender Base Transaction Statistical System, OBTS

Oklahoma Teletype Interlibrary System, OTIS

Ontario Universities Library Cooperative System, OULCS

Operating System, OS

Parts Data Processing System, PDPS

Planning-Programming-Budgeting System, PPBS

Predicasts Terminal System, PTS

Preserved Context Index System, PRECIS

Program Test System, PTS

Punched Card System, PCS

Random Access Discrete Address System, RADAS

Random Access Personnel Information Dissemination System, RAPIDS

Rapid Access Management Information System, RAMIS

Regional Information Management System, RIMS

Remote Access Computing System, RACS

Remote Information Management System, RIMS

Retrospective Search System on the INSPEC Data Base, RETROSPEC

Rock Information System, RKNFSYS

Satellite Auto-Monitor System, SAMS

Scheduling and Control by Automated Network System, SCANS

Schering-Oriented Literature Analysis and Retrieval System, SCHOLAR

School Management Information Retrieval System, SMIRS

Science and Technology Policies Information Exchange System, SPINES

Share Operating System, SOS

Shared Acquisitions and Retention System, SHARES

Shared Hospital Accounting System, SHAS

Simultaneous Processing Operating System, SIPROS

Socioeconomic Information Management System, SIMS

Solid Waste Information Retrieval System, SWIRS

Standard Modular System, SMS

Stanford Physics Information Retrieval System, SPIRES

Storage and Information Retrieval System, STAIRS

Strategic Air Command Control System, SACCS

Structural Engineering System Solver, STRESS

Swedish Drug Information System, SWEDIS

Symbolic Programming System, SPS

Symbolic Shorthand System, SSS

Syracuse University *Psychological
    Abstracts* Retrieval System, SUPARS
System Activity Monitor, SAM
System Analysis Index for Diagnosis, SAID
System Development Corporation, SDC
System for Electronic Analysis and Retrieval
    of Criminal Histories, SEARCH
System for Interlibrary Communication,
    SILC
System for Organizing Current Reports to
    Aid Technology and Science,
    SOCRATES
System for the Automated Management of
    Text from a Hierarchical Arrangement,
    SAMANTHA
System for the Publication and Efficient,
    Effective Dissemination of Information,
    SPEEDI
System Manufacturing Division, SMD
System of National Accounts/System of
    Material Product Balances, SNA/MPS
System Ordinary Life Operations, SOLO
System Programmed Operators, SYSPOP
System to Coordinate the Operation of
    Peripheral Equipment, SCOPE
TALON Reporting and Information
    Processing System, TRIPS
Tape Operating System, TOS
Technical Information Processing System,
    TIPS
Time-Shared System, TSS
Time-Sharing System, TSS
Total Analysis System for Production,
    Accounting, and Control, TAS-PAC
United Nations Bibliographic Information
    System, UNBIS
Universal Classification System, UCS
Universal System for Information in Science
    and Technology, UNISIST
University of Toronto Library Automation
    System, UTLAS
Variable Stability System, VSS
Very Early Warning System, VEWS
Well History Control System, WHCS
Western Ohio Regional Library
    Development System, WORLDS
World Energy Supplies System,
    WORLDENERGY
World Geographic Reference System,
    GEOREF

Systematized
Systematized Nomenclature of Pathology,
    SNOP

Systeme
Systeme Electronique de Selection
    Automatique de Microfilms, SESAM
Système Intégré pour les Bibliothèques
    Universitaires de Lausanne, SIBIL
Système Internationale d'Unités, SI

Systems
ACM Special Interest Group on Architecture
    of Computer Systems, ACM/SIGARCH
ACM Special Interest Group on Operating
    Systems, ACM/SIGOPS
ANSI/SPARC Study Group on Data Base
    Management Systems,
    ANSI/X3/SPARC/SGDBMS.
Acquisitions, Cataloging, Technical
    Systems, ACTS
Advanced Systems Development Division,
    ASDD
Association for Development of
    Computer-based Instructional Systems,
    ADCIS
Association for Systems Management, ASM
Association for the Development of
    Instructional Systems, ADIS
Automated Catalog of Computer Equipment
    and Software Systems, ACCESS
Automatic Fact Information Retrieval and
    Storage Systems, AFIRSS
Book Industry Systems Advisory
    Committee, BISAC
Business EDP Systems Technique, BEST
Business Oriented Software Systems, BOSS
California Library Authority for Systems and
    Services, CLASS
Capital Systems Group, CSG
Combined Analog–Digital Systems
    Simulator, CADSS
Comparative Systems Laboratory, CSL
Computer-Aided Recording of Distribution
    Systems, CARDS
Computer-Integrated Command and Attack
    Systems, CICAS
Data Dissemination Systems, Inc, DDSI
Dataflow Systems Inc, DfS
*Dictionary of Computer and Control Systems
    Abbreviations, Signs and Symbols*,
    DCCSA
Direct Access Intelligence Systems, DAIS
Economic Information Systems, EIS
Electromagnetic Systems Laboratories, ESL
Electronic Security Systems, ESS
Exploratory Library Management Systems,
    ELMS
FID Committee on Operational Machine
    Technique and Systems, FID/OM
FID Committee on Theory of Machine
    Techniques and Systems, FID/TM
Fast Access to Systems Technical
    Information, FASTI
Federal Office Systems Expo, FOSE
General Purpose Systems Simulator, GPSS
Generalized Data Base Management´
    Systems, GDBMS
Hospital Management Systems Society,
    HMSS
Information & Publishing Systems, Inc,
    I&PS

Systems (cont.)

Library Automated Systems Information
    Exchange, LASIE
National Systems of Scientific and
    Technological Information of Brazil,
    SNICT
Office of Computer and Communications
    Systems, OCCS
Operations Research/Systems Analysis,
    OR/SA
PLA Public Library Systems Section,
    PLA/PLSS
Society for General Systems Research,
    SGSR
Society for Management Information
    Systems, SMIS
Society of Educational Programmers and
    Systems Analysts, SEPSA
Systems Analysis and Data Processing Office
    of NYPL, SADPO
Systems and Procedures Association, SPA
Systems and Procedures Exchange Center,
    SPEC
Systems Assurance Program, SAP
Systems Development Division, SDD
Systems Engineering, SE
Systems Tape Addition and Maintenance
    Program, STAMP
Total Information for Educational Systems,
    TIES
United States Army Computer Systems
    Support and Evaluation Command,
    USACSSEC

Systems Center

Knowledge Availability Systems Center,
    KASC
Transportation Systems Center, TSC

Systems-Oriented

Tabular Systems-Oriented Language,
    TABSOL

TALENT Project

[TALENT Project], TALENT

TALON

TALON Reporting and Information
    Processing System, TRIPS

TWX

TWX Interlibrary Loan Network, TWXILL

Table

Channel Status Table, CST
Digital Analog Function Table, DAFT
Program Reference Table, PRT
Table Look Up, TLU
Volume Table of Contents, VTOC

Tables

Computer Analysis of Thermo-Chemical
    Data Tables, CATCH
Decision Tables/Experimental, DETAB/X

Tabular

Tabular Systems-Oriented Language,
    TABSOL

Tabulation

Horizontal Tabulation, HT
Vertical Tabulation Character, VT

Tabulator

Tabulator Simulator, TABSIM

Tactical

Tactical Technology Center, TACTEC

Tailored

Tailored Abstracts, TABS

Tampa Bay

Tampa Bay Medical Library Network,
    TABAMLN

Tanzania

Chama Cha Ukutubi, Tanzania (Tanzania
    Library Association), CUTA

Tape

Biological Abstracts on Tape, BAT
Distribution Tape Reel, DTR
Fast Analysis of Tape and Recovery,
    FATAR
Magnetic Tape/Selectric Typewriter, MTST
Master Instruction Tape, MIT
Master Relocatable Tape, MRT
Production Run Tape, PRT
Program Test Tape, PTT
Standard Tape Executive Program, STEP
Symbolic Program Tape, SPT
Tape-Controlled Recording Automatic
    Checkout Equipment, TRACE
Tape Input/Tape Output, TIPTOP
Tape Operating System, TOS

Tape Addition

Systems Tape Addition and Maintenance
    Program, STAMP

Tape Edition

Psychological Abstracts Tape Edition Lease
    or Licensing, PATELL

Tape Handling

Tape Handling Optional Routines, THOR

Tapes

Retrieval of Information about Census
    Tapes, RIACT
World Tapes for Education, WTE

Tape-to-Tape
Universal Tape-to-Tape Converter, UTTC

Tariff
Airline Tariff Publishers, Inc, ATP

Task Force
Data Base Task Force (CODASYL), DBTC
Ethnic Materials Information Exchange Task
Force, EMIETF
GODORT Federal Documents Task Force,
GODORT/FDTF
GODORT International Documents Task
Force, GODORT/IDTF
GODORT Local Documents Task Force,
GODORT/LDTF
GODORT State Documents Task Force,
GODORT/SDTF
National Libraries Task Force, NLTF

Task Group
End User Facility Task Group, EUFTG

Tasmania
Tasmania State Library, TSL

Tasmanian
Tasmanian Advisory Committee on
Libraries, TACOL

Taxicomanies
Centre International
d'Alcoologie/Taxicomanies, CIATO

Teach
Teach Information Processing Language,
TIPL

Teacher
American Association of Colleges for
Teacher Education, AACTE
ERIC Clearinghouse on Teacher Education,
ERIC/SP
National Council for Accreditation of
Teacher Education, NCATE

Teachers
American Association of Physics Teachers,
AAPT
American Association of Teachers of Slavic
and East European Languages,
AATSEEL
Associated Organizations of Teachers of
English, AOTE
Canadian Association of University
Teachers/Association Canadienne des
Professeurs d'Université, CAUT/ACPU
Indian Association of Teachers of Library
Science, IATLIS
National Council of Teachers of English,
NCTE
National Council of Teachers of
Mathematics, NCTM

National Science Teachers Association,
NSTA

Teaching
Center for Research on Learning and
Teaching, CRLT
English Teaching Information Centre, ETIC
Lewis Audiovisual Research Institute and
Teaching Archive, LARITA
Machine-Assisted Educational System for
Teaching by Remote Operation,
MAESTRO
National Association for Research in Science
Teaching, NARST
Programmed Logic for Automatic Teaching
Operations, PLATO
Programming Language for Interactive
Teaching, PLANIT
Teaching Assistant, TA
Teaching Logic Translator, TEACHTRAN
Teaching Sample Tables, TESAT

Teaching Teams
McGill Elementary Education Teaching
Teams, MEET

Tearsheet
Original Article Tearsheet, OATS

Technica
Sistema Colombiano de Información
Cientifica y Technica, SICOLDIC

Technical
Abstracts of Instructional and Research
Materials in Vocational and Technical
Education, AIM/ARM
Abstracts of Instructional Materials in
Vocational and Technical Education,
AIM
Abstracts of Research and Related Materials
in Vocational and Technical Education,
ARM
Accountants Computer Users Technical
Exchange, ACUTE
Acquisitions, Cataloging, Technical
Systems, ACTS
Air Force Technical Objectives Documents
Release Program, AFTOD
Air Pollution Technical Information Center,
APTIC
American Institute of Aeronautics and
Astronautics, Technical Information
Services, AIAA-TIS
American Technical Society, ATS
Association of Technical Writers and
Editors, ATWE
Bangladesh National Scientific and
Technical Documentation Center,
BANSDOC
Bibliografické Středisko pro Techickou
Literaturu (Bibliographical Center for
Technical Literature), BSTL

Technical (cont.)

Bradford Scientific, Technical and
Commercial Service, BRASTACS
Canadian Technical Awareness Program,
CAN/TAP
Centralny Instytut Informacji Naukowo
Technicznej i Ekonomicznej (Central
Institute for Scientific, Technical and
Economic Information), CIINTE
Centre National de Documentation
Scientifique et Technique (National
Center for Scientific and Technical
Documentation), CNDST
Centrul de Documentare si Publicatü
Tehnice al Ministerulue Cailór Ferate
(Technical Documentation and
Publications Center of the Railway
Ministry), CDPT-MCF
*Classified Scientific and Technical
Aerospace Reports*, C-STAR
(Committee on) Scientific and Technical
Communication, SATCOM
Community and Technical College Libraries,
CTCL
Consejo Nacional de Investigaciones
Científicas y Técnicas (National Council
for Scientific and Technical Research),
CONICET
Dansk Teknisk Oplysningstjeneste (Danish
Technical Information Service), DTO
Dial Access Technical Education, DATE
Field Information Agencies, Technical,
FIAT
Gloucestershire Technical Information
Service, GTIS
Hampshire Technical Research Industrial
and Commercial Service, HATRICS
Humberside Libraries Technical Interloan
Scheme, HULTIS
IBM Technical Information Retrieval
Center, ITIRC
*Index to Scientific and Technical
Proceedings*, ISTP
Institute of Technical Publicity and
Publications, ITPP
Instituto de Documentación e Información
Científica y Tecnica (Institute of
Scientific and Technical Documentation
and Information), IDICT
Institutul Central de Documentare Technica
(Central Institute for Technical
Documentation), IDT
International Association for the Exchange
of Students for Technical Experience,
IAESTE
Jugoslovenski Centar za Techničku i Naučno
Dokumentacijua (Yugoslav Center for
Technical and Scientific
Documentation), JCTND

Junior Engineering Technical Society, JETS
Leicestershire Technical Information
Service, LETIS
Library Media Technical Assistant, LMTA
Library Technical Assistant, LTA
Machine-Aided Technical Processing
System, MATPS
Manchester Technical Information Service,
MANTIS
National Air Pollution Technical Information
System, NAPTIC
National Technical Information Service,
NTIS
Naval Scientific and Technical Information
Centre, NSTIC
Nottingham and Nottinghamshire Technical
Information Service, NANTIS
Office de la Recherche Scientifique et
Technique d'Outre-Mer (Office of
Overseas Scientific and Technical
Research), ORSTOM
Pakistan National Scientific and Technical
Documentation Center, PANSDOC
Plastics Technical Evaluation Center,
PLASTEC
Pusat Documentasi Ilmiah Nasional
(Indonesian Scientific and Technical
Documentation Center), PDIN
Radio Technical Commission for
Aeronautics, RTCA
Research Division Technical Report, RDTR
Scientific and Technical Aerospace Reports.
(Journal), STAR
Scientific and Technical Association of the
People's Republic of China, STAPRC
Scientific, Technical and Medical Publishers,
STM
Scottish Technical Education Consultative
Council, STECC
Society for Technical Communication, STC
Society of Technical Writers, STW
Society of Technical Writers and Editors,
STWE
Society of Technical Writers and Publishers,
STWP
Southern California Technical Processes
Group, SCTPG
Standard Technical Report Number, STRN
Storage, Handling and Retrieval of Technical
Data in Image Formation, SHIRTDIF
Technical Abstract Bulletin, TAB
Technical and Business Services, TABS
Technical and Further Education
Commission, TAFEC
Technical Assistance Information
Clearinghouse, TAICH
Technical Association of the Pulp and Paper
Industry, TAPPI
Technical Book Review Index, TBRI
Technical Environmental and Management
Planning Operations, TEMPO

Technical Information Center, TIC
Technical Information Center
   Administration, TICA
Technical Information Processing System,
   TIPS
Technical Information Service, TIS
Technical Information Systems Activities,
   TISA
Technical Information Systems Committee,
   TISCO
Technical Institute Council, TIC
Technical Memorandum, TECH MEMO
Technical Processes Research Office, TPR
Technical Publishing Society, TPS
Technical Report, TECH REPT
Technical Standards for Library
   Automation, TESLA
Tekniska Litteratursällskapet (Swedish
   Society for Technical Documentation),
   TLS
Türkiye Bilimsel ve Teknik Dokümantasyon
   Merkezi (Turkish Scientific and
   Technical Documentation Center),
   TÜRDOK
Ústředí Vědeckých Technických a
   Ekonomických Informací (Central
   Office of Scientific, Technical and
   Economic Information), UVTEI
Volunteers for International Technical
   Assistance, Inc, VITA
Wandsworth Public, Educational and
   Technical Library Services,
   WANDPETLS
Wisconsin Indianhead Technical Institute,
   WITI

Technical Assistance
Pennsylvania Technical Assistance Program,
   PENNTAP

Technical Center
Centre Technique Audiovisual International
   (International Audiovisual Technical
   Center), CTAVI

Technical Information
Advisory Board on Scientific and Technical
   Information, ABSTI
Advisory Committee for Scientific and
   Technical Information, ACSTI
Armed Services Technical Information
   Agency, ASTIA
Bureau National d'Information Scientifique
   et Technique (National Board for
   Scientific and Technical Information),
   BNIST
Canadian Institute for Scientific and
   Technical Information (Institut
   Canadien de l'Information Scientifique
   et Technique), CISTI/ICIST

Centro Nacional de Información Científica y
   Técnica (National Center for Scientific
   and Technical Information), CONICIT
Clearinghouse for Federal Scientific and
   Technical Information, CFSTI
Committee on International Scientific and
   Technical Information Programs,
   CISTIP
Committee on Scientific and Technical
   Information, COSATI
Division of Technical Information
   Extension, DTIE
Fast Access to Systems Technical
   Information, FASTI
Inter-change of Scientific and Technical
   Information in Machine Language,
   ISTIM
Office for Scientific and Technical
   Information, OSTI
Overseas Technical Information Unit, OTIU
Paisley and District Technical Information
   Group, PADTIG
Scientific and Technical Information, STI
Technical Information Project, TIP
Technical Information Support Activities
   Project, TISAP
Ústav Vědeckotechnických Informací
   (Institute of Scientific Technical
   Information), UVTI
Vesesojuznii Naučno-Issle-Dovatel'skii
   Institut Techniceskoi Informaccii,
   Klassifikaccii i Kodirovaniia (All-Union
   Scientific Research Institute for
   Technical Information, Classification
   and Codification of USSR), VNIIKI
Vsesojuznyi Institut Naučnotehničeskoi
   Informacii (All-Union Institute of
   Scientific and Technical Information,
   USSR), VINITI

Technical Library
Army Technical Library Improvement
   Studies, ATLIS
Hertfordshire County Council Technical
   Library and Information Service,
   HERTIS
Hungarian Central Technical Library and
   Documentation Center, HCTLDC

Technical Services
Association of New York Libraries for
   Technical Services, ANYLTS
Library Resources and Technical Services.
   (Journal), LRTS
Office of Technical Services, OTS
Resources and Technical Services Division,
   RTSD

Techniceneu
Centralny Instytut Informasui Noukowo
    Techniceneu I Economicznej (Central
    Institute for Scientific, Technical and
    Economic Information), CLINTE

Technicians
Association of Audiovisual Technicians,
    AAVT
Association of Cinematograph, Television
    and Allied Technicians, ACTT
Institution of Electrical and Electronics
    Technicians Engineers, Ltd, IEETE
Refrigerating Engineers and Technicians
    Association, RETA

Technique
Association National de la Recherche
    Technique, ANRT
Automated Linguistic Extraction and
    Retrieval Technique, ALERT
Bacterial Automated Identification
    Technique, BAIT
Business EDP Systems Technique, BEST
Centre Technique des Industries de la
    Fonderie, CTIF
Computerized Automatic Rating Technique,
    CART
Computerized Relative Allocation of
    Facilities Technique, CRAFT
Dynamic Debugging Technique, DDT
Engineering Departmental Interface Control
    Technique, EDICT
FID Committee on Operational Machine
    Technique and Systems, FID/OM
Fully Automatic Cataloging Technique,
    FACT
Fully Automatic Compiling Technique,
    FACT
National's Electronic Autocoding
    Technique, NEAT
Program Evaluation and Review Technique,
    PERT
Specialized Technique for Efficient
    Typesetting, STET
Technique for Retrieving Information from
    Abstracts of Literature, TRIAL

Techniques
Committee on Vacuum Techniques, CVT
Computer-Assisted Scanning Techniques,
    CAST
FID Committee on Theory of Machine
    Techniques and Systems, FID/TM
Indexing by Statistical Analysis Techniques,
    IBSAT
Project for the Advancement of Coding
    Techniques, PACT I

Technische
Technische Informationsbibliothek, TIB

Technisch-Literarische
Technisch-Literarische Gesellschaft, TELI

Technological
Comisión Nacional de Investigación
    Científica y Technológica (National
    Commission on Scientific and
    Technological Research), CONICYT
Consejo Nacional de Investigaciones
    Científicas y Tecnológicas (National
    Council for Scientific and Technological
    Research), CONICIT
Consejo Nacional de Investigaciones
    Científicas y Tecnológicas (National
    Council for Scientific and Technological
    Research), CONICYT
International Association of Technological
    University Libraries, IATUL
Korean Scientific and Technological
    Information Center, KORSTIC
National Commission on New Technological
    Uses of Copyrighted Works, CONTU
Pakistan Scientific and Technological
    Information Center, PASTIC
Scientific and Technological Information
    Services Enquiry Committee, STISEC

Technological Information
Center of Scientific and Technological
    Information, COSTI
Center of Scientific and Technological
    Information, CSTI
National Systems of Scientific and
    Technological Information of Brazil,
    SNICT

Technological Library
Australian National Scientific and
    Technological Library, ANSTEL
Danmarks Tekniske Bibliotek med Dansk
    Central for Dokumentation (Danish
    Center for Documentation of the
    Technological Library of Denmark),
    DTB

Technologists
American Society of Radiologic
    Technologists, ASRT

Technology
ACRL Science and Technology Section,
    ACRL/STS
ASIS Special Interest Group on Technology,
    Information, and Society,
    ASIS/SIG/TIS
Advanced Technology/Libraries (Journal),
    AT/L
Aerospace Technology Division, ATD
Alternatives for Learning through
    Educational Research and Technology,
    ALERT

Technology (cont.)

Solid Logic Technology, SLT
System for Organizing Current Reports to
Aid Technology and Science,
SOCRATES
Technology Use Studies Center, TUSC
Textile Technology Data Base Keyterm
Index, TTD
Toronto Institute of Medical Technology,
TIMT
Universal System for Information in Science
and Technology, UNISIST

Technology Center
Computing Technology Center, Union
Carbide Corporation, CTC
Tactical Technology Center, TACTEC

Technology Information
Association for Marine Research and
Technology Information, AIM

Technology Library
Royal Institute of Technology Library,
IDC-KTHB

Teeside
Library Information Service for Teeside,
LIST

Tehran
Tehran Book Processing Center, TEBROC

Telecommunication
Centre National d'Études des
Télécommunications (National Center
of Telecommunication Studies), CNET
Conférence Européene des Administrations
des Postes et des Télécommunications
(European Conference of Postal and
Telecommunication Administrations),
CEPT
Union Catalogue/Telecommunication
Catalogue, UNICAT/TELECAT

Telecommunications
Basic Telecommunications Access Method,
BTAM
Bureau International d'Information sur les
Télécommunications, BIIT
Commonwealth Telecommunications Board,
CTB
Federal Telecommunications System, FTS
International Press Telecommunications
Committee, IPTC
International Telecommunications Satellite
Consortium, INTELSAT
International Telecommunications Union,
ITU
Joint Council on Educational
Telecommunications, JCET

Minnesota Interlibrary Telecommunications
Exchange, MINITEX
National Telecommunications and
Information Agency, NTIA
Queued Telecommunications Access
Method, QTAM
Société Internationale des
Télécommunications Aeronautiques
(International Society of Aeronautical
Telecommunications), SITA
Tele-Communications Association, TCA
Telecommunications Library Information
Network, TALINET

Telecommunications Lines
Commission Mixte Internationale pour la
Protection des Lignes de
Télécommunications et des
Canolisations Souterraines (Joint
International Committee for the
Protection of Telecommunications Lines
and Underground Ducts), CMI

Télécommunications
Centre National d'Étude des
Télécommunications/Département
Documentation Interministérielle,
CNET/DI

Telegraph
American Telephone and Telegraph
Company, AT&T
Consultative Committee on International
Telegraph and Telephone (Comité
Consultatif International Telegraphie et
Telephonie), CCITT
International Telephone and Telegraph
Corporation, ITT
Postal, Telegraph and Telephone
International, PTTI

Télégraphiques
Syndicat des Industries Téléphoniques et
Télégraphiques, SITT

Telephone
American Telephone and Telegraph
Company, AT&T
Associated Telephone Answering
Exchanges, ATAE
Association of Telephone Answering
Services, ATAS
Consultative Committee on International
Telegraph and Telephone (Comité
Consultatif International Telegraphie et
Telephonie), CCITT
General Telephone and Electronics
Corporation, GTE
International Telephone and Telegraph
Corporation, ITT
National Telephone Cooperative
Association, NTCA

Terminal (cont.)

Psychological Abstracts Direct Access
    Terminal, PADAT
Remote Terminal Unit, RTU
Word Terminal Synchronous, WTS

Terminals
Remote Terminals, RT

Terminal-to-Computer
Terminal-to-Computer Multiplexer, TCM

Terminologie Normalisée
Banque de Terminologie Normalisée,
    NORMATERM

Terminology
FID Committee on the Terminology of
    Information and Documentation,
    FID/DT
International Advisory Committee for
    Documentation and Terminology,
    IACDT
International Advisory Committee on
    Bibliography, Documentation and
    Terminology, IACBDT
International Advisory Committee on
    Documentation and Terminology in Pure
    and Applied Science, AICDT
Subcommittee on Programming
    Terminology, SCOPT

Terms
*Thesaurus of Engineering and Scientific
    Terms*, TEST

Terrain
Terrain Elevation Retrieval Program, TERP

Terrestrial
National Geophysical and Solar Terrestrial
    Data Center, NGSD

Test
Basic Programming Knowledge Test, BPKT
Built-In Test Equipment, BITE
Compass Test Language, CTL
Diagnostic Function Test, DFT
Digital Test-Oriented Language, DTOL
Facility of Automation, Control and Test,
    FACT
Fast Reactor Test Facility, FARET
Memory Test Computer, MTC
Program Test System, PTS
Program Test Tape, PTT
Test-Oriented Operated Language, TOOL
Test Rules for Inventory Management,
    TRIM
Versatile Automatic Test Equipment, VATE

Test Station
Naval Ordnance Test Station, NOTS

Tester
Motorola Automatic Sequential
    Computer-Operated Tester, MASCOT
Transformational Grammar Tester, TGT

Testing
American Society for Nondestructive
    Testing, ASNT
American Society for Testing and Materials,
    ASTM
Educational Testing Service, ETS
Facility for Automatic Sorting and Testing,
    FAST
Non-Destructive Testing Information
    Analysis Center, NTIAC
Society for Nondestructive Testing, SNT
Toxicology Testing in Progress. (Journal),
    TOX-TIPS

Tests
Document Delivery Tests, DDT
ERIC Clearinghouse on Tests,
    Measurement, and Evaluation,
    ERIC/TM
Programmer Aptitude Tests, PAT

Texas
Interuniversity Council of the North Texas
    Area, IUC
Texas, Arkansas, Louisiana, Oklahoma and
    New Mexico, TALON
Texas Educational Microwave Project,
    TEMP
Texas Information Exchange, TIE
Texas Library Association, TLA
Texas Numeric Register, TNR
University of Texas Health Science Center at
    San Antonio, UTHSCSA

Text
End of Text, ETX
Fast Access Current Text Bank, FACT
Library On-Line Information and Text
    Access, LOLITA
Quick Text Editor, QED
Start of Text Character, STX
System for the Automated Management of
    Text from a Hierarchical Arrangement,
    SAMANTHA
Text Reckoner and Compiler, TRAC

Text Book
American Textbook Publishers Institute,
    ATPI
National Association of State Text Book
    Administrators, NASTA
National Association of State Text Book
    Directors, NASTBD

Textile
American Association for Textile
    Technology, Inc, AATT

American Association of Textile Chemists
and Colorists, AATCC
[Textile Industry], TITUS
Textile Technology Data Base Keyterm
Index, TTD

Texts
Salton's Magical Automatic Retrieval of
Texts, SMART

Textual
Retrieval of Enriched Textual Abstracts,
RETA

Thai
Center for Thai National Standard
Specifications, CTNSS
Thai Library Association, TLA

Theater
Theater Library Association, TLA

Theatre
International Theatre Institute of the United
States, ITI/US

Theatre Arts
Société Internationale des
Bibliothèques–Musées des Arts du
Spectacle (International Society of
Libraries and Museums of the Theatre
Arts), SIBMAS

Theatres
Confédération Internationale des Cinémas
d'Art et d'Essai (International
Experimental and Art Film Theatres
Confederation), CICAE

Theological
Chicago Area Theological Library
Association, CATLA
Chicago Cluster of Theological Schools,
CCTS
Theological Education Association of
Mid-America, TEAM-A

Theological Librarians
Vereniging van Religieus-Wetenschappelijke
Bibliothecarissen (Association of
Theological Librarians), VRB
Vereniging voor het Theologisch
Bibliothecariaat (Association of
Theological Librarians), VTB

Theological Libraries
Arbeitsgemeinschaft
Katholisch-Theologischer Bibliotheken
(Working Group of Catholic Theological
Libraries), AKTHB
Association des Bibliothèques
Ecclésiastiques de France (Association
of French Theological Libraries), ABEF

Association of British Theological and
Philosophical Libraries, ABTAPL

Theological Library
American Theological Library Association,
Inc, ATLA

Theoretical
FID Committee on Research on the
Theoretical Basis of Information,
FID/RI
International Center for Theoretical Physics,
ICTP

Theory
FID Committee on Theory, Methods, and
Operations of Information Systems and
Networks, FID/TMO
FID Committee on Theory of Machine
Techniques and Systems, FID/TM
Library Network Analysis Theory, LIBNAT

Therapeutic
Therapeutic Recreation Information Center,
TRIC

Thermo-Chemical
Computer Analysis of Thermo-Chemical
Data Tables, CATCH

Thermodynamics
Chemical Thermodynamics Data Center,
CTDC
Inorganic and Metallurgical
Thermodynamics Data, MTDATA
Thermodynamics Research Center, TRC

Thesaurus
Dictionary Operation and Control for
Thesaurus Organization, DOCTOR
Engineering Index Thesaurus, EIT
*Medical and Health Related Sciences
Thesaurus*, MHRST
*Thesaurus of Engineering and Scientific
Terms*, TEST

Thousand
Thousand, K

Tidningsutgivareföreningen
Svenska Tidningsutgivareföreningen, TU

Tijdschrift Uitgevers
Nederlandse Organisatie van Tijdschrift
Uitgevers, NOTU

Timber
American Institute of Timber Construction,
AITC

Time
Methods-Time Measurement, MTM
Miniature Processing Time, MINPRT

Time (cont.)

Personality, Matter, Energy, Space and
Time, PMEST
Project Accounting by Cost and Time, PACT

Time-dependent
Automatic Scheduling and Time-dependent
Resource Allocation, ASTRA

Time-Shared
Time-Shared Interactive
Computer-Controlled Information
Television, TICCIT
Time-Shared Reactive On-Line Lab,
TROLL/I
Time-Shared Routines for Analysis,
Classification, and Evaluation, TRACE
Time-Shared System, TSS

Time Sharing
Dartmouth Time Sharing System, DTSS
Library Information System Time Sharing,
LISTS
Time Sharing, TS

Time-Sharing
Association of Computer Time-Sharing
Users (USA), ACTSU
Association of Time-Sharing Users, ATSU
Bibliographic Automation of Large Library
Operations Using a Time-Sharing
System, BALLOTS
Time-Sharing Option, TSO
Time-Sharing System, TSS

Title
Key Word in Title, KWIT

Title Changes
Librarians United to Fight Costly, Silly,
Unnecessary Serial Title Changes,
LUTFCSUSTC

Titles
Chemical Titles. (Journal), CT
Current Physics Titles (Journal), CPT
Fuel Abstracts and Current Titles, FACT
New Serial Titles, NST

Tobago
*Bulletin of the Library Association of
Trinidad and Tobago*, BLATT
Library Association of Trinidad and Tobago,
LATT

Toegepast Huishoudkundig Onderzoek
Nederlands Instituut voor Toegepast
Huishoudkundig Onderzoek, NITHO

Togo
AIDBA–Section Togolaise (AIDBA–Togo
Branch), AIDBA–Section Togolaise

Tool
Application Program Evaluator Tool, APET
Automatic Programmed Tool, APT
Automatic Programmed Tool III, APT III
City Air Defense Evaluation Tool, CADET

Tools
Adaptation of APT (Automatically
Programmed Tools), ADAPT
Automatic Programming of Machine Tools,
AUTOPROMPT
Automatically Programmed Tools, APT

Top
Top Term, TT

Topics
Packets of Educational Topics, PET

Topological Representation
Topological Representation of Synthetic and
Analytical Relations of Concepts,
TOSAR

Toronto
Toronto Institute of Medical Technology,
TIMT
University of Toronto Library Automation
System, UTLAS

Toxic Effects
Registry of Toxic Effects of Chemical
Substances, RTECS

Toxicologique
Banques de Données Toxicologique, BDT

Toxicology
[Toxicology Backfile], TOXBACK
Toxicology Data Bank, TDB
Toxicology Research Projects Directory.
(Journal), TRPD
Toxicology Testing in Progress. (Journal),
TOX-TIPS

Toxicology Information
Toxicology Information Conversational
On-Line Network, TOXICON
Toxicology Information On-Line, TOXLINE
Toxicology Information Program, TIP
Toxicology Information Response Center,
TIRC

Track
Digital Data, Auxiliary Storage, Track
Display, Outputs, and Radar Display,
DATOR

Tracking
Global Tracking, GLOTRAC
Tracking Retrieval and Analysis of Criminal
Events, TRACE

Trade
Business Equipment Trade Association,
    BETA
Department of Trade and Industry, DTI
Federal Trade Commission, FTC
Nuclear Energy Trade Association
    Conference, NETAC

Trade List
Publishers Trade List Annual, PTLA

Trades
Bookbinding and Allied Trades Management
    Association, BATMA
International Allied Printing Trades
    Association, IAPTA
Joint Industrial Council of Printing and Allied
    Trades, JIC
National Metal Trades Association, NMTA
Printing and Kindred Trades Federation,
    PKTF
Retail Book, Stationery and Allied Trades
    Employees Association, RBA

Trading Conditions
*Investing, Licensing & Trading Conditions
    Abroad* (Journal), IL&T

Traducciones
Servicio de Información sobre Traducciones
    Científicas en Español, SITCE

Traducteurs
Fédération Internationale des Traducteurs,
    FIT

Traffic
Air Traffic Control Association, ATCA
Automatic Traffic Engineering and
    Management Information System,
    ATEMIS
SAGE Air Traffic Integration, SATIN

Trail
Audit Trail, AT

Training
American Society for Training and
    Development, ASTD
Documentation Research and Training
    Centre, DRTC
FID Committee on Education and Training,
    FID/ET
Iron and Steel Industry Training Board, ISI
    TB
National Council for the Training of
    Journalists, NCTJ
Training, Appraisal and Promotion, TAP
United Nations Institute for Training and
    Research, UNITAR

Training Board
Printing and Publishing Industry Training
    Board, PPITB

Training Centers
European Association of Management
    Training Centers, EAMTC

Training Projects
Advisory Committee on Library Research
    and Training Projects, ACLRTP

Traitement Informatique
Centre de Traitement Informatique des
    Bibliothèques, CETIB

Trans World
Trans World Airlines, Inc, TWA

Transac
Transac Assembler Compiler, TAC

Transaction
Offender Base Transaction Statistical
    System, OBTS

Transactions
Approach to Distributed Processing
    Transactions, ADOPT

Transceiver
Data Loop Transceiver, DLT

Transcriber
Analog Data Recording Transcriber, ADRT

Transdisciplinary
Transdisciplinary Engineering Information
    Program, TEIP

Transfer
Conditional Transfer of Control, CTC
Input/Output and Transfer, IOT
(National) Scientific Communication and
    Technology Transfer, SCATT
Register Transfer Language, RTL

Transformational
Transformational Grammar Tester, TGT

Transistor
Direct Coupled Transistor Logic, DCTL
Microalloy Diffused Base Transistor, MADT
Resistor-Capacitor Transistor Logic, RCTL

Transit
American Public Transit Association, APTA
American Transit Association, ATA
Bay Area Rapid Transit System, BARTS

Transition
Simple Transition to Electronic Processing,
    STEP

Translation
Association for Machine Translation and
Computational Linguistics, AMTCL
Automatic Mathematical Translation,
AMTRAN
Automatic Translation, AUTRAN
Construction Industry Translation and
Information Services, CITIS
Machine Translation, MT
Man-Machine Partnership Translation,
MMPT
Mechanical Translation, MT
Spoken Language Universal Numeric
Translation, SLUNT
X Automatic Translation Code, XACT

Translation Center
Centre Européene de Traduction (European
Translation Center), CET

Translation Service
British Iron and Steel Industry Translation
Service, BISITS

Translations
*Consolidated Index of Translations into
English*, CITE
[Translations Index], TRANSDEX
Translations Register–Index, TRI

Translations Center
National Translations Center, NTC

Translator
Advanced Scientific Instruments Symbolic
Translator, ASIST
Algebraic and Differential Equations
Processor and Translator, ADEPT
Algebraic Compiler and Translator I, ACT-I
Algebraic Compiler and Translator III,
ACT-III
Algebraic Translator and Compiler, ALTAC
Autocoder to COBOL Translator, ACT
Automatic Code Translator, ACT
Compiler and Generalized Translator,
COGENT
Comprehensive Language for Elegant
Operating System and Translator
Design, CLEOPATRA
Control Translator, CONTRAN
Flexible Algebraic Scientific Translator,
FAST
Formula Assembler and Translator,
FORAST
Formula Translator, FORTRAN
Formula Translator II, FORTRAN II
Formula Translator IV, FORTRAN IV
Generalized Algebraic Translator, GAT
Input Translator, INTRAN
Internal Translator, IT
Logically Integrated FORTRAN Translator,
LIFT

ORACLE Binary Internal Translator,
ORBIT
Output Translator, OUTRAN
SHARE Compiler, Assembler and
Translator, SCAT
Teaching Logic Translator, TEACHTRAN
Variably Initialized Translator for
Algorithmic Languages, VITAL

Transmission
Automatic Picture Transmission, APT
Cancel Transmission, CANTRAN
End of Transmission, EOT
End of Transmission-Block, ETB
Facsimile Transmission System, FACTS
Paper Tape Transmission 8, PTT/8

Transmit
Synchronous Transmit Receive Access
Method, STRAM
Transmit, TRAN

Transmitter
Digital Data Transmitter, DDT
Sequentially Controlled Automatic
Transmitter Start, SCATS
Synchronous Transmitter Receiver, STR
Transmitter Start Code, TSC

Transmitter-Distributor
Transmitter-Distributor, TD

Transport
Air Transport Association of America, ATA

Transport Aerien
Institute du Transport Aerien, ITA

Transportation
Bay Area Transportation Study Commission,
BATSC
Department of Transportation, DOT
Los Angeles Regional Transportation Study,
LARTS
South Coast Transportation Study, SCOTS
Transportation Data Coordinating
Committee, TDCC
[Transportation Documentation],
TRANSDOC
Transportation Planning Support
Information System, TPSIS
Transportation Research Information
Services Network, TRISNET
Transportation Research Information
System, TRIS
Transportation Systems Center, TSC

Transposition
Classified Entries in Lateral Transposition,
CELT

Traveling
Smithsonian Institution Traveling Exhibition
  Service, SITES

Treaty
Patent Cooperation Treaty, PCT
Southeast Asia Treaty Organization, SEATO

Triangle
Triangle Universities Computation Center,
  TUCC

Tri-County
Tri-County Library Council, TLC

Trinidad
*Bulletin of the Library Association of
  Trinidad and Tobago*, BLATT
Library Association of Trinidad and Tobago,
  LATT

Tripartite
Tripartite Committee, TC

Triple
Triple Modular Redundancy, TMR

Tri-State
Tri-State College Library Cooperative,
  TCLC

Tropic
Arctic, Desert, Tropic Information Center,
  ADTIC

Trustees
United Engineering Trustees, Inc, UET
Urban Libraries Trustees Council, ULTC

Tube
Cathode-Ray Tube, CRT

Tunisian
Association Tunisienne des
  Documentalistes, Bibliothécaires et
  Archivistes (Tunisian Association of
  Documentalists, Librarians and
  Archivists), ATD

Turkish
Türk Kütüphaneciler Dernegi (Turkish
  Librarians Association), TKD
Türkiye Bilimsel ve Teknik Dokümantasyon
  Merkezi (Turkish Scientific and
  Technical Documentation Center),
  TÜRDOK

Twin Cities
Twin Cities Biomedical Consortium, TCBC

Tyneside
Tyneside Association of Libraries for
  Industry and Commerce, TALIC

Typesetting
Specialized Technique for Efficient
  Typesetting, STET

Typewriter
Magnetic Tape/Selectric Typewriter, MTST

Typing
Receive Only Typing Reperforator, ROTR

Typographers
Advertising Typographers Association of
  America, Inc, ATAA

Typographical
Scottish Typographical Association, STA
Society of Typographical Designers, STD

UNESCO
Inter-Council Coordination Committee
  UNESCO, ICCC

UNIVAC
American UNIVAC Users Association,
  AUUA
UNIVAC Code, UNICODE
UNIVAC FORTRAN, UNITRAN
UNIVAC Users Association, UUA

US
Dual Independent Map Encoding File of the
  Counties of the US, DIMECO
US Government Reports Index, USGI
*US Government Research and Development
  Reports*, USGRDR
*US Government Research and Development
  Reports Index*, USGRDRI
US Government Research Reports, USGR
US National Committee for the International
  Federation for Documentation,
  USNCFID

US–Asiatic
US–Asiatic Company, Ltd, USACO

USSR
Gosudarstvennaya ordena Lenina Biblioteka
  SSSR Imeni V. I. Lenina (Lenin State
  Library of the USSR), GBL
Vesesojuznii Naučno-Issle-Dovatel'skii
  Institut Techniceskoi Informaccii,
  Klassifikaccii i Kodirovaniia (All-Union
  Scientific Research Institute for
  Technical Information, Classification
  and Codification of USSR), VNIIKI
Vsesojuznyi Institut Naučnotehničeskoi
  Informacii (All-Union Institute of
  Scientific and Technical Information,
  USSR), VINITI
Vsesoyuznoe Agentstvo Avortskikh
  Prav-USSR, VAAP
Vsesoyuznogo Informatsionnogo Fonda
  Standartovi i Technicheskikh Uslovii

USSR (cont.)

(All-Union Reference Bank of Standards and Specifications, USSR), VIFS

Uganda
Uganda Library Association, ULA
Uganda School Library Association, USLA

Uitgeversbond
Koninklijke Nederlandse Uitgeversbond, KNUB

Ukrainian
Harvard Ukrainian Research Institute, HURI
Ukrainian Library Association of America, ULAA

Ultra
Ultra Microfiche, UMF

Ultrahigh
Ultrahigh Frequency, UHF

Umweltplanung
Informations und Dokumentationssystem zum Umweltplanung, UMPLIS

Undergraduate
Undergraduate Excavation and Rock Properties Information Center, UERPIC

Underground Ducts
Commission Mixte Internationale pour la Protection des Lignes de Télécommunications et des Canolisations Souterraines (Joint International Committee for the Protection of Telecommunications Lines and Underground Ducts), CMI

Underwriters
American Institute of Marine Underwriters, AIMU

Uniform
Uniform Product Code Council, UPCC

Union
American Geophysical Union, AGU
Canadian Union of Public Employees, CUPE
Commonwealth Press Union, CPU
Cooperative Union Serials System, CUSS
De Vetenskapliga Bibliotekens Tjänstemannaförening (Union of University and Research Libraries), VBT
Duplicates Exchange Union, DEU
East Midland Educational Union, EMEU
European Broadcasting Union, EBU
International Catholic Press Union, ICPU
International Telecommunications Union, ITU

International Union of Pure and Applied Physics, IUPAP
International Union of the History and Philosophy of Science, IUHPS
National Union of Journalists, NUJ
Norsk Journalistlag (Norwegian Union of Journalists), NJ
Southern College University Union, SCUU
Suomen Sanomalehtimiesten Litto/Finlands Journalist Förbund (Union of Journalists in Finland), SSL/FJF
Union Chimique-Chemische Bedrijven, UCB
Union de la Critique du Cinéma, UUC
Union de la Presse Étrangère en Belgique, UPE
Union de la Presse Périodique Belge, UPPB
Unión de Universidades de América Latina (Union of Universities of Latin America), UDUAL
Union der Schweizerischen Lichtspieltheater-Verbänd/Union des Associations Cinématographiques Suisses, USLV/UACS
Union Nationale des Éditeurs-Exportateurs de Publications Françaises, UNEEPF
Union Nationale des Producteurs Belge de Films (National Union of Belgian Film Producers), UNPBF
Union of Independent Colleges of Art, UICA
Union of Soviet Socialist Republics, USSR
Union Professionnelle des Distributeurs Belges de Films, UPDBF
Union Radio-Scientifique Internationale (International Scientific Radio Union), URSI
Union Romande de Journaux, URJ
Waukesha Academic Library Union, WALU

Union Carbide
Computing Technology Center, Union Carbide Corporation, CTC

Union Catalog
British Union Catalog of Periodicals, BUCOP
National Union Catalog, NUC
National Union Catalog of Manuscript Collections, NUCMC
Union Catalog of Medical Periodicals, UCMP

Union Catalogue
National Union Catalogue of Monographics, NUCOM
Union Catalogue/Telecommunication Catalogue, UNICAT/TELECAT

Union List
California Union List of Periodicals, CULP
Charlotte Area Union List of Periodicals and Serials, CAULPS

Intermountain Union List of Serials, IMULS
Minnesota Union List of Serials, MULS
Pacific Area Union List of Medical Serials,
  PAULMS
Union List of Serials, ULS
Virginia Union List of Biomedical Serials,
  VULBS

Unione
Unione della Stampa Periodica Italiana,
  USPI

Unions
International Council of Scientific Unions,
  ICSU

Unit
Arithmetic and Logical Unit, ALU
Audio Response Unit, ARU
Central Processing Unit, CPU
Central Terminal Unit, CTU
Data Communications Control Unit, DCCU
Data Exchange Unit, DEU
Economic Planning Unit of Barbados, EPU
Natural Unit of Information, NAT
Overseas Technical Information Unit, OTIU
Pattern Articulation Unit, PAU
Remote Control Unit, RCU
Remote Terminal Unit, RTU
Semiconductor Storage Unit, SSU
Stockkeeping Unit, SKU
Visual Display Unit, VDU
Voice Unit, VU
Volume Unit, VU

United
British United Press, BUP
San Bernadino, Inyo, Riverside Counties
  United Library Services, SIRCULS
United Engineering Trustees, Inc, UET
United Society for Christian Literature,
  USCL
United States Pharmacopoeia, USP

United Kingdom
School Broadcasting Council for the United
  Kingdom, SBCUK
United Kingdom, UK
United Kingdom Atomic Energy Authority,
  UKAEA
United Kingdom Chemical Information
  Service, UKCIS

United Nations
United Nations, UN
United Nations Bibliographic Information
  System, UNBIS
United Nations Children's Fund, UNICEF
United Nations Educational, Scientific and
  Cultural Organization, UNESCO
United Nations Environment Program,
  UNEP

United Nations Industrial Development
  Organization, UNIDO
United Nations Institute for Training and
  Research, UNITAR

United Press
United Press International, UPI

United States
Australia, Britain, Canada, United States,
  ABACUS
Conference of Engineering Societies of
  Western Europe and the United States
  of America, EUSEC
International Theatre Institute of the United
  States, ITI/US
State and Court Law Libraries of the United
  States and Canada, SCLL
United States, US
United States Air Force, USAF
United States Army Computer Systems
  Support and Evaluation Command,
  USACSSEC
United States Atomic Energy Commission,
  USAEC
United States Book Exchange, USBE
United States Committee for the World
  Health Organization, USC-WHO
United States Department of Agriculture,
  USDA
United States Geological Survey, USGS
United States Historical Documents
  Institute, HDI
United States Independent Telephone
  Association, USITA
United States Information Agency, USIA
United States of America, USA
United States of America Standard Code for
  Information Interchange, USASCII
United States of America Standards
  Institute, USASI
United States Office of Education, USOE
United States Pharmacopoeia, USP
United States Political Science Documents,
  USPSD
United States Public Health Service, USPHS
United States Reshippers, USR
United States Student Press Association,
  USSPA

Unités
Système Internationale d'Unités, SI

Units
Federation of Documentary Film Units,
  FDFU
Symbols, Units, Nomenclature, SUN

Universal
Sequentially Operated Teletypewriter
  Universal Selector, SOTUS

Universal (cont.)

Spoken Language Universal Numeric
    Translation, SLUNT
Universal Automatic Computer, UNIVAC
Universal Availability of Publications, UVP
Universal Bibliographic Control, UBC
Universal Classification System, UCS
Universal Compiler, UNICOMP
Universal Computer-Oriented Language,
    UNCOL
Universal Decimal Classification, UDC
Universal Product Code, UPC
Universal Resource Information
    Symposium, URIS I
Universal Serials and Book Exchange,
    USBE
Universal System for Information in Science
    and Technology, UNISIST
Universal Tape-to-Tape Converter, UTTC

Universidad
Consijo Zuliano de Planificación y
    Promoción de Universidad Central de
    Venezuela, CONZUPLAN
Universidad Nacional Autónoma de México,
    UNAM

Universitaires
Bibliothèques Universitaires, BU

Université
Centre de Documentation de la Biblothèque
    de l'Université Laval (Documentation
    Center of the Library of l'Université
    Laval), CEDOBUL
Université du Quebec à Montreal, UQAM

Universities
American Association of State Colleges and
    Universities, AASCU
Association des Universités Partiellement ou
    Entierement de Langue Française
    (Association of Wholly or Partially
    French-language Universities),
    AUPELF
Association of American Universities, AAU
Association of Atlantic Universities
    Librarians Council, AAULC
Association of Commonwealth Universities,
    ACU
Association of State Colleges and
    Universities Forestry Research
    Organizations, ASCUFRO
Association of Universities and Colleges of
    Canada/Association des Universités et
    Collèges du Canada, AUCC
Conference des Recteurs et des Principaux
    des Universités du Québec (Conference
    of Rectors and Principals of Quebec
    Universities), CREPUQ

Council of Ontario Universities, COU
Library Statistics of Colleges and
    Universities, LSCU
Midwest Universities Consortium for
    International Activities, Inc, MUCIA
Northwest Association of Private Colleges
    and Universities, NAPCU
Oak Ridge Associated Universities, ORAU
Ontario Universities Bibliographic Centre
    Project, OUBCP
Ontario Universities Library Cooperative
    System, OULCS
Triangle Universities Computation Center,
    TUCC
Unión de Universidades de América Latina
    (Union of Universities of Latin
    America), UDUAL
Universities Central Council on Admissions,
    UCCA
Universities Council for Adult Education,
    UCAE

University
ACM Special Interest Group on University
    Computing Centers, ACM/SIGUCC
American Association of University
    Professors, AAUP
American Association of University Women,
    AAUW
Arab University Library Association, AULA
Asociación de Bibliotecas Universitarias y
    Especializadas de Nicaragua
    (Association of University and Special
    Libraries of Nicaragua), ABUEN
Association of American University Presses,
    AAUP
Association of Caribbean University and
    Research Institute Libraries, ACURIL
Association of Caribbean University and
    Research Libraries, ACURL
Banque de Données à Accès Direct de
    l'Université du Québec (Direct Access
    Data Bank of the University of Quebec),
    BADADUQ
CLA College, University and Seminary
    Libraries Section, CLA/CUSLS
California State University at Long Beach,
    CSULB
Canadian Association of University
    Teachers/Association Canadienne des
    Professeurs d'Université, CAUT/ACPU
Case Western Reserve University, CWRU
Chalmers Tekniska Högskolas Bibliotek
    (Library of Chalmers University of
    Technology), CTHB
City University of New York, CUNY
Comprehensive University of Dayton
    On-Line Information Services, CUDOS
Consortium of University Film Centers,
    CUFC

De Vetenskapliga Bibliotekens
  Tjänstemannaförening (Union of
  University and Research Libraries),
  VBT
International University of Radiophonics and
  Television, IUR
Librarians Association of the University of
  California, LAUC
Makerere University College, MUC
Maryland Independent College and
  University Association, Inc, MICUA
Museum and University Data, Program and
  Information Exchange, MUDPIE
National University Extension Association,
  NUEA
New Hampshire College and University
  Council, NHCUC
Oxford University Press, OUP
Queen's University Information Centre,
  QUIC
Southern College University Union, SCUU
State University of New York, SUNY
State University of New York Librarians
  Association, SUNYLA
Svenska Bibliotekariesamfundet (Swedish
  Association of University and Research
  Librarians), SBS
Syracuse University *Psychological
  Abstracts* Retrieval System, SUPARS
Tri-University Libraries of British Columbia,
  TRIUL
Université Radiophonique et Télévisuelle
  Internationale (International
  Radio-Television University), URI
University City Science Center, UCSC
University Grants Committee, UGC
University Information Technology
  Corporation, UNITEL
University Microfilms International, UMI
University of California Bibliographic
  Center, BIBCENTER
University of California–Los Angeles,
  UCLA
University of California–University-Wide
  Automation Program, ULAP
University of Miami Computing Center,
  UMCC
University of Texas Health Science Center at
  San Antonio, UTHSCSA
University of Toronto Library Automation
  System, UTLAS
University Photographers Association of
  America, UPAA
Western Reserve University, WRU

University Center
Nashville University Center, NUC
University Center for International Studies,
  UCIS

University Librarians
Standing Conference of African University
  Librarians, SCAUL
Tieteellisten Kirjastojen
  Virkailijat–Vetenskapliga Bibliotekens
  Tjänstemannaförening r. y. (Association
  of Research and University Librarians),
  TKV-VBT R.Y.

University Libraries
ACRL University Libraries Section,
  ACRL/ULS
Canadian Association of College and
  University Libraries/Association
  Canadienne des Bibliothèques de
  Collège et d'Université,
  CACUL/ACBCU
Cornell University Libraries, CUL
Cornell University Libraries Staff
  Association, CULSA
Council of Prairie University Libraries,
  COPUL
Five Associated University Libraries, FAUL
International Association of Technological
  University Libraries, IATUL
Joint University Libraries, JUL
Ontario Association of College and
  University Libraries, OACUL
Ontario Council of University Libraries,
  OCUL
Project for the Evaluation of Benefits from
  University Libraries, PEBUL
Small University Libraries, SUL
Standing Conference of African University
  Libraries, Eastern Area, SCAULEA
Standing Conference of African University
  Libraries, Western Area, SCAULWA
Standing Conference of National and
  University Libraries, SCONUL

University Library
CLA College and University Library
  Section, CLA/CULS
Helsingin Yliopiston Kirjasto (Helsinki
  University Library), HYK
Jewish National and University Library,
  JNUL
Yale University Library, YUL

Unlisted
Unlisted Drugs. (Journal), UD

Unprofessional Trends
Concerned Librarians Opposing
  Unprofessional Trends, CLOUT

Update
Automated Information Directory Update
  System, AIDUS
Automated Input and Document Update
  System, AIDUS

Update (cont.)

Automated Microfilm Aperture Card Update
System, AMACUS
Career Update, CU

Updating
Automatic Routine Generating and Updating
System, ARGUS
Octal Program Updating System, OPUS
Sorting, Updating, Report, Generating, Etc,
SURGE

Updating Service
Case Law Report Updating Service,
CLARUS

Urban
Council of Administrators of Large Urban
Public Libraries, CALUPL
Department of Housing and Urban
Development, DHUD
ERIC Clearinghouse on Urban Education,
ERIC/UD
Regional and Urban Information Network,
RUIN
Southwest Center for Urban Research,
SCUR
Urban and Regional Information Systems
Association, URISA
Urban Documentation Project,
URBANDOC

Urban Libraries
Urban Libraries Council, ULC
Urban Libraries Trustees Council, ULTC

Urban Studies
Higher Education Center for Urban Studies,
HECUS

Uruguay
Agrupación Bibliotecologica del Uruguay
(Library Science Association of
Uruguay), ABU

Usage
Display-Oriented Computer Usage System,
DOCUS

Use
Coalition in the Use of Learning Skills,
CULS
National Data Use and Access Laboratories,
Inc, DUALabs
Technology Use Studies Center, TUSC

User
ASIS Special Interest Group on User On-line
Interaction, ASIS/SIG/UOI
Remote User of Shared Hardware, RUSH
Support of User Records and Files, SURF
User Area, UA

User-Prompted Graphic Data Evaluation,
UPGRADE
User Requirements Language, URL

User Group
Intercomm User Group, IUG

User Groups
Association of Computer User Groups,
ACUG

Users
Accountants Computer Users Technical
Exchange, ACUTE
American UNIVAC Users Association,
AUUA
Association of Computer Time-Sharing
Users (USA), ACTSU
Association of Time-Sharing Users, ATSU
Business Computer Users Association,
BCUA
Computer Users Replacement Equipment,
CURE
Cooperating Users Exchange, CUE
Cooperating Users of Burroughs Equipment,
CUBE
Digital Equipment Computer Users Society,
DECUS
Engineering Equipment Users Association,
EEUA
Honeywell Computer Users Association,
HCUA
Military Computer Users Group, MCUG
National Association of Users of Computer
Applications to Learning, NAUCA
Precision Plotter Users Association, PPUA
UNIVAC Users Association, UUA

Users Group
Joint Users Group, JUG

Uses
National Commission on New Technological
Uses of Copyrighted Works, CONTU

Utah
Utah College Library Council, UCLC
Utah Library Association, ULA

Utilities
Electrical Utilities Applications, EUA

Utility
Complex Utility Routines, CUR

Utility Checkout
Language for Utility Checkout and
Instrumentation Development, LUCID

Vacuum
American Vacuum Society, AVS
Committee on Vacuum Techniques, CVT

Valeurs Mobilieres
Centrale de Livraison de Valeurs Mobilieres, CEDEL

Vapour
Vapour Liquid Equilibria Databank, VLE BANK

Variable
Electronic Discrete Variable Automatic Computer, EDVAC
Variable Information Processing, VIP
Variable Stability System, VSS

Variable Star Observers
American Association of Variable Star Observers, AAVSO

Variance
Multivariate Analysis of Variance, MANOVA

Vector
Vector Analogue Computer, VAC

Velocity
Position and Velocity Extraction, PAVE

Venezuela
Consijo Zuliano de Planificación y Promoción de Universidad Central de Venezuela, CONZUPLAN

Venezuelan Librarians
Colegio de Bibliotecónomos y Archivistas de Venezuela (Association of Venezuelan Librarians and Archivists), COLBAV

Verband
Association Européenne de Fabricants et des Revendeurs de Matériel Didactique/Verband Europäischer Lehrmittelfirmen, EURODIDAC
Verband de Agrarjournalisten in Österreich, VAÖ
Verband der Journalisten der Deutsche Democratische Republik, VDJ
Verband Deutscher Agrarjournalisten, VDA
Verband Deutscher Schriftsteller, VS
Verband Deutscher Zeitschriftenverleger, VDZ
Verband Österreichischer Zeitungsherausgeber und Zeitungsverleger, VÖZ

Verein
Verein Deutscher Ingenieurs, VDI

Vereinigung
Vereinigung der Industriefilmproduzenten, VIP
Vereinigung Evangelischer Buchhändler, VEB

Vereinigung der Buchantiquare
Vereinigung der Buchantiquare und Kupferstichhändler in der Schweiz/Syndicat de la Libraire Ancienne et du Commerce de l'Estampe en Suisse, VEBUKU/SLACES

Vereniging
Nederlandse Vereniging van Journalisten, NVJ
Vereniging de Nederlandse Dagbladpers, NDP
Vereniging voor het Godsdienstig-Wetenschappelijk Bibliothecariaat, VSKB
Vlaamse Vereniging van Bibliotheek- en Archiefpersoneel, VVBAP

Vereniging ter Bevordering
Vereniging ter Bevordering van het Vlaamse Boekwezen, VBVB

Vermont
Vermont Educational Media Association, VEMA
Vermont Information Process, VIP
Vermont Library Association, VLA

Versatile
Versatile Automatic Test Equipment, VATE

Vertical
Vertical Tabulation Character, VT

Very
Very Early Warning System, VEWS
Very High Frequency, VHF
Very Low Frequency, VLF"

Vessel
Atlantic Merchant Vessel Report, AMVER

Veteran
Veteran Wireless Operators Association, VWOA

Veterans
Veterans Administration Library Network, VALNET

Veterinary
Current Contents/Agricultural, Food and Veterinary Sciences. (Journal), CC/AFV
Royal College of Veterinary Surgeons, RCVS

Victoria
State Library of Victoria, SLV

Victorian
Cooperative Action by Victorian Academic Libraries, CAVAL
Research Society for Victorian Periodicals, RSVP

Video
ISAD Video and Cable Communications
    Section, ISAD/VCCS
LITA Video and Cable Communications
    Section, LITA/VCCS

Videorecording
Electronic Videorecording, EVR

Videotape
Videotape Recorder, VTR
Videotape Recording, VTR

Viet-Nam
Industrial Development Center/Viet-Nam
    (Trung-Tam Khuech-Truong Ky-Ngha),
    IDC/VN

Virginia
Eastern Virginia MEDLINE Consortium,
    EVIMEC
(Virginia Chapter of the Special Libraries
    Association), VASLA
Virginia Educational Media Association,
    VEMA
Virginia Library Association, VLA
Virginia Medical Information Services,
    VAMIS
Virginia National Library Week Company,
    VNLW
Virginia National Library
    Week–Southeastern Library
    Association, VNLW-SELA
Virginia Union List of Biomedical Serials,
    VULBS

Visual
Visual Display Unit, VDU
Visual Education National Information
    Service for Schools, VENISS

Visual Aids
European Foundation for Visual Aids,
    EFVA
Overseas Visual Aids Centre, OVAC

Visual Arts
Committee for the Visual Arts, CVA

Visual Response
Manually Operated Visual Response
    Indicator, MOVRI

Visual Science
Visual Science Information Center, VSIC

Visual Science Librarians
Association of Visual Science Librarians,
    AVSL

Vital Records
American Association for Vital Records and
    Public Health Statistics, AAVRPHS

Vlaamse
Vlaamse Vereniging van Bibliotheek- en
    Archiefpersoneel, VVBAP

Vlaamse Boekwezen
Vereniging ter Bevordering van het Vlaamse
    Boekwezen, VBVB

Vocational
Abstracts of Instructional and Research
    Materials in Vocational and Technical
    Education, AIM/ARM
Abstracts of Instructional Materials in
    Vocational and Technical Education,
    AIM
Abstracts of Research and Related Materials
    in Vocational and Technical Education,
    ARM
ERIC Clearinghouse on Adult, Career, and
    Vocational Education, ERIC/CE
Resources in Vocational Education.
    (Journal), RIVE
Vocational Education Program Information
    System, VEPIS

Vocational Information
Association Internationale d'Information
    Scolaire Universitaire et Professionelle
    (International Association for Education
    and Vocational Information), AIISUP

Voice
Voice Answer Back, VAB
Voice Unit, VU

Voice Operated
Voice Operated Gain-Adjustment Device,
    VOGAD

Voltage
Voltage to Digital Converter, VDC

Voltan
Association Voltaique pour le
    Développement des Bibliothèques, des
    Archives et de la Documentation
    (Voltan Association for the
    Development of Libraries, Archives and
    Documentation), AVDBAD

Volume
Automatic Volume Control, AVC
Volume, V
Volume Table of Contents, VTOC
Volume Unit, VU

Voluntary
Voluntary Overseas Library Service, VOLS

Volunteers
Volunteers for International Technical
    Assistance, Inc, VITA

Vsesoyuznoe Agentstvo Avortskikh Prav
Vsesoyuznoe Agentstvo Avortskikh
    Prav-USSR, VAAP

Wales
Library Advisory Council for Wales and
    Monmouthshire, LAC
National Foundation for Educational
    Research in England and Wales, NFER

Wandsworth
Wandsworth Public, Educational and
    Technical Library Services,
    WANDPETLS

War Devastated Libraries
American Book Center for War Devastated
    Libraries, ABC

Warning
Very Early Warning System, VEWS

Washington
Classified Library Employees of Washington
    State, CLEWS
Washington, Alaska, Montana, and Idaho,
    WAMI
Washington Library Association, WLA
Washington Library Network, WLN
Washington Non-Professional Library
    Association, WNPLA

Water
American Water Resources Association,
    AWRA
Arizona Water Information System, AWIS
Canada Water, CWA
Southern Water Resources Scientific
    Information Center, SWRSIC
Water Resources Document Reference
    Centre, WATDOC
Water Resources Scientific Information
    Center, WRSIC

Waukesha
Waukesha Academic Library Union, WALU

Weapons
Atomic Weapons Research Establishment,
    AWRE

Weather
Navy Numerical Weather Prediction,
    NANWEP

Weekly
Publishers Weekly. (Journal), PW
Weekly Newspaper Advertising Bureau,
    WNAB

Welding
American Welding Society, AWS
Institut International de la Soudure
    (International Institute of Welding), IIS

Welfare
Department of Health, Education and
    Welfare, DHEW
Department of Health, Education and
    Welfare, HEW
Jewish Welfare Board, JWB

Well
Well History Control System, WHCS
Well Record Service. (Journal), WRS

Wellington
[Wellington] National Library of New
    Zealand, WN

Welsh
Welsh Bibliographical Society, WBS
Welsh Library Association, WLA

Werkstoffdatenbank
Werkstoffdatenbank, WDB

West African
West African Library Association, WALA

West India
West India Reference Library, WIRL

West Virginia
West Virginia Library Association, WVLA
West Virginia Library Commission,
    WVLAC

Westchester
Health and Information Libraries of
    Westchester, HILOW

Western
Western Association of Law Libraries,
    WALL
Western Data Processing Center, WDPC
Western Forest Information Network,
    WESTFORNET
Western Information Network Association,
    WIN
Western Interstate Commission for Higher
    Education, WICHE
Western Interstate Library Coordinating
    Organization, WILCO
Western Regional Information Service
    Center, WRISC
Western Research Application Center,
    WESRAC

Western European
ACRL Western European Specialists
    Section, ACRL/WESS

Western Reserve
Western Reserve University, WRU

Western Union
Western Union Corp, WU

White House
White House Conference on Library and
Information Services, WHCOLIS

Who Is Publishing
Who Is Publishing in Science, WIPIS

Wholesalers
Pacific Coast Independent Magazine
Wholesalers Association, PACIMWA

Wide Area
Inward Wide Area Telephone Service,
INWATS
Wide Area Data Service, WADS
Wide Area Telephone Service, WATS

Wild Life
British Library of Wild Life Sounds,
BLOWS

Wilson
Wilson Library Bulletin, WLB

Wireless
Society of Wireless Pioneers, SOWP
Veteran Wireless Operators Association,
VWOA

Wirtschaftsforschung
Institut für Wirtschaftsforschung, IFO

Wisconsin
Council of Wisconsin Librarians, COWL
Southeastern Wisconsin Health Science
Libraries Consortium, SEWHSL
Southern Wisconsin Academic Librarians
Organization, SWALO
Wisconsin Assets and Income Studies,
WAIS
Wisconsin Indianhead Technical Institute,
WITI
Wisconsin Interlibrary Loan Service, WILS
Wisconsin Library Association, WLA

Wisconsin Libraries
Northeast Wisconsin Intertype Libraries,
Inc, NEWIL

Wissenschaftsinformation
Institut für Wissenschaftsinformation in der
Medizin, IWIM

Wiswesser
Wiswesser Line Notation, WLN

Women
Affirmative Action Program for Women
Committee, AAPWC
American Association of University Women,
AAUW
Connecticut Women in Libraries, CWILS
Society of Women Engineers, SWE
Society of Women Writers and Journalists,
SWWJ

Women's
International Women's Writing Guild,
IWWG
Women's Advisory Committee of the British
Standards Institution, WAC
Women's Educational Equity
Communications Network, WEECN
Women's Information and Study Centre,
WISC

Women's Studies
Center for Women's Studies and Services,
CWSS

Woodworking
European Group of Woodworking Journals,
EUROBOIS

Wool
Wool Industry Research Association, WIRA

Worcester
Worcester Area Cooperating Libraries,
WACL
Worcester Consortium for Higher
Education, WCHE

Word
Channel Status Word, CSW
External Device Control Word, EDCW
Program Status Word, PSW
Word and Author Index, WADEX
Word Terminal Synchronous, WTS

Word Processing
International Word Processing Association,
IWPA

Workers
Association of Communication Workers,
ACW

Working Committee
Deutsche Arbeitsgemeinschaft für
Rechen-Anlagen (German Working
Committee for Computing Machines),
DARA

Working Group
Arbeitsgemeinschaft der Kunstbibliotheken
(Working Group of Art Libraries), AKB
Arbeitsgemeinschaft für das Archiv und
Bibliothekswesen in der Evangelischen
Kirche, Sektion Bibliothekswesen
(Working Group for Archives and
Libraries in the Lutheran Church,
Library Section), AABevK
Arbeitsgemeinschaft
Katholisch-Theologischer Bibliotheken
(Working Group of Catholic Theological
Libraries), AKTHB
Arbeitsgemeinschaft Pädagogischer
Bibliotheken und Medienzentren

(Working Group of Educational
Libraries and Media Centers), APB
Internationale Arbeitsgemeinschaft der
Archiv-, Bibliotheks- und
Grafikrestauratoren (International
Working Group of Restorers of
Archives, Libraries and Graphic
Reproductions), IADA

World
United States Committee for the World
Health Organization, USC-WHO
World Administrative Radio Conference,
WARC
*World Agricultural Economics and Rural
Sociology Abstracts*, WAERSA
World Aluminum Abstracts, WAA
World Energy Supplies System,
WORLDENERGY
World Federation of Engineering
Organizations, WFEO
World Geographic Reference System,
GEOREF
World Health Organization, WHO
World Information Systems Exchange,
WISE
World Intellectual Property Organization,
WIPO
World Meteorological Organization, WMO
World Tapes for Education, WTE

World Data Center
World Data Center, WDC
World Data Center-A, WDC-A
World Data Center-B, WDC-B
World Data Center-C, WDC-C

World Wide
World Wide Network of Standard
Seismograph Stations, WWNSS

Writer
General Purpose Scientific Document
Writer, GPSDW

Writers
American Medical Writers Association,
AMWA
Association of British Science Writers,
ABSW
Association of Technical Writers and
Editors, ATWE
Commonwealth Writers of Britain, CWB
Crime Writers Association, CWA
Education Writers Association, EWA
International Society of Aviation Writers,
ISAW
International Writers Guild, IWG
Mystery Writers of America, MWA
Nederlandse Vereniging van Lucht- en
Ruimtevaarte-Publicisten (Netherlands
Aerospace Writers Association), NVLP
Society of Technical Writers, STW

Society of Technical Writers and Editors,
STWE
Society of Technical Writers and Publishers,
STWP
Society of Women Writers and Journalists,
SWWJ
Writers Guild of Great Britain, WGGB

Writing
American Business Writing Association,
ABWA
Committee for Writing and Reading Aids for
the Paralysed, WRAP
International Women's Writing Guild,
IWWG

Written
Hansard Written Questions, HWQ

Wyoming
Wyoming Academic Consortium, WAC
Wyoming Association of School Libraries,
WASL
Wyoming Instructional Media Association,
WIMA
Wyoming Library Association, WLA

X-Ray
American Society for X-Ray and Electron
Diffraction, ASXED

Xerographic
Projection by Reflection Optics of
Xerographic Images, PROXI

Xerography
Long Distance Xerography, LDX
Semi-Micro Xerography, SMX

Xerox
Xerox Information Exchange Network, IEN
Xerox Planning Model, XPM
Xerox Publishing Group, XPG

Yale
Yale University Library, YUL

Year
Fiscal Year, FY
International Book Year, IBY
International Geophysical Year, IGY

Yorkshire
Yorkshire Regional Library System, YRLS

Young
Young Newspapermen's Association, YNA

Young Adult
Young Adult, YA
Young Adult Project, YAP
Young Adult Services Division, YASD

Young People
International Board on Books for Young
People, IBBY

Young People (cont.)

International Council on Books for Young
People, ICBY

Youth
Administration for Children, Youth, and
Families, ACYF

Yugoslav
Jugoslovenski Bibliografiski Institut
(Yugoslav Bibliographic Institute), JBI
Jugoslovenski Centar za Tehničku i Naučno
Dokumentacijua (Yugoslav Center for
Technical and Scientific
Documentation), JCTND

Zairian
Association Zairoise des Archivistes,
Bibliothécaires et Documentalistes
(Zairian Association of Archivists,
Librarians and Documentalists),
AZABDO

Zambia
Zambia Library Association, ZLA

Zavod Teplovoj Avtomafiki
Zavod Teplovoj Avtomafiki, MZTA

Zeitschriftenverleger
Verband Deutscher Zeitschriftenverleger,
VDZ

Zeitungsherausgeber
Verband Österreichischer
Zeitungsherausgeber und
Zeitungsverleger, VÖZ

Zeitungsverleger
Bundesverband Deutscher Zeitungsverleger,
BDZV
Verband Österreichischer
Zeitungsherausgeber und
Zeitungsverleger, VÖZ

Zentraler Datenpool
Zentraler Datenpool der Kooperativen
Agrardokumentation, LIDOK

Zentralinstitut
Zentralinstitut für Information und
Dokumentation, ZIID

Zentralstelle
Zentralstelle Dokumentation
Electrotechnique, ZDE

Zero
Zero Access Storage, ZAS

Zhurnal
Referativny Zhurnal, RZh

Zinc
Centro Méxicano de Información del Zinc y
del Plomo (Mexican Center of
Information for Zinc and Lead),
CMIZPAC

Zurich
Zurich, Mainz, Munich, Darmstadt, ZMMD

WITHDRAWAL